CJ
REALITIES AND CHALLENGES
3RD EDITION

Ruth E. Masters   California State University–Fresno

Lori Beth Way   California State University–San Francisco

Phyllis B. Gerstenfeld   California State University–Stanislaus

Bernadette T. Muscat   California State University–Fresno

Michael Hooper   Sonoma State University

John P. J. Dussich   California State University–Fresno

Candice A. Skrapec   California State University–Fresno

CJ: REALITIES AND CHALLENGES, THIRD EDITION

Published by McGraw-Hill Education, 2 Penn Plaza, New York, NY 10121. Copyright © 2017 by McGraw-Hill Education. All rights reserved. Printed in the United States of America. Previous editions © 2013 and 2011. No part of this publication may be reproduced or distributed in any form or by any means, or stored in a database or retrieval system, without the prior written consent of McGraw-Hill Education, including, but not limited to, in any network or other electronic storage or transmission, or broadcast for distance learning.

Some ancillaries, including electronic and print components, may not be available to customers outside the United States.

This book is printed on acid-free paper.

1 2 3 4 5 6 7 8 9 0 DOW 21 20 19 18 17 16

ISBN 978-0-07-814094-5
MHID 0-07-814094-3

Chief Product Officer, SVP Products & Markets: *G. Scott Virkler*
Vice President, General Manager, Products & Markets: *Michael Ryan*
Vice President, Content Design & Delivery: *Kimberly Meriwether David*
Managing Director: *David Patterson*
Brand Manager: *Penina Braffman*
Director, Product Development: *Meghan Campbell*
Product Developer: *Anthony McHugh*
Marketing Manager: *Meredith Leo*
Director, Content Design & Delivery: *Terri Schiesl*
Program Manager: *Marianne Musni*
Content Project Managers: *Jane Mohr, George Theofanopoulos, Sandra Schnee*
Buyer: *Jennifer Pickel*
Design: *Studio Montage, St. Louis, MO*
Content Licensing Specialist: *Lori Slattery*
Cover Image: *moodboard/Getty Images*
Compositor: *Aptara, Inc.*
Printer: *R. R. Donnelley*

All credits appearing on page or at the end of the book are considered to be an extension of the copyright page.

Library of Congress Cataloging-in-Publication Data

Names: Masters, Ruth, author.
Title: CJ : realities and challenges / Ruth E. Masters, California State
    University-Fresno, Lori Beth Way, California State University-San Francisco,
    Phyllis B. Gerstenfeld, California State University-Stanislaus,
    Bernadette T. Muscat, California State University-Fresno, Michael Hooper,
    Sonoma State University, John P. J. Dussich, California State University-Fresno,
    Candice A. Skrapec, California State University-Fresno.
Other titles: Criminal justice
Description: 3rd edition. | New York, NY : McGraw-Hill Education, [2017]
Identifiers: LCCN 2016012258| ISBN 9780078140945 (alk. paper) | ISBN 0078140943 (alk. paper)
Subjects: LCSH: Criminal justice, Administration of--United States. |
    Criminal justice, Administration of--Study and teaching (Higher)--United States.
Classification: LCC HV9950 .C495 2017 | DDC 364.973--dc23 LC record available at
https://lccn.loc.gov/2016012258

mheducation.com

Brief Contents

Contents

PART 5 Special Issues

A Note from the Author Team

As both practitioners and academics, we have endeavored to write a compelling, contemporary, and fact-based account of vital American institutions. We understand that this course is faculty's first chance to engage students in a meaningful exposure to the ideals of the American criminal justice system. *CJ: Realities and Challenges,* Third Edition, translates the passion that we feel in the classroom into a learning program that nourishes students' enthusiasm for the field while dispelling widely held myths.

CJ: Realities and Challenges, Third Edition, encourages students to think critically about how the American criminal justice system operates in practice. Recognizing the myths and interpreting the facts underlying the system lead to an appreciation of its complexities. Students who succeed in this course will emerge with a realistic understanding of the system and of the opportunities that await them if they should choose to pursue a career in criminal justice.

OBSERVE → INVESTIGATE → UNDERSTAND

A Critical Thinking Approach to Criminal Justice

CJ: Realities and Challenges, Third Edition, takes a critical thinking approach to examining traditional and emerging issues and topics in criminal justice. A three-part framework—Observe, Investigate, Understand—asks students to:

OBSERVE the core principles underlying the criminal justice system.

INVESTIGATE how these foundational principles are applied in the real world.

UNDERSTAND how and why these principles and practices are still evolving.

6 Policing Operations

OBSERVE → INVESTIGATE → UNDERSTAND

After reading this chapter, you should be able to:
- Identify the principal policing roles.
- Compare the various policing strategies.
- Describe the different jobs in policing.
- Explain how police departments strive to maximize their resources.
- Identify the factors that shape public opinion about the police.
- Compare the service needs of diverse populations.

Each chapter opens with a series of learning objectives tied to this framework. These goals are explored in the chapter using vivid examples to reinforce student learning. At the end of each chapter, this same framework is used to recap key concepts and conclusions. Students revisit chapter-specific learning objectives in Connect Criminal Justice, where all activities are linked specifically to these learning outcomes.

The **OBSERVE→INVESTIGATE→UNDERSTAND** framework helps students make logical connections between the principles and the practices of criminal justice. As a case in point, in Chapter 6, "Policing Operations," students learn about the varied tactics of community policing, including foot patrol. Reading the opening vignette, students **OBSERVE** how the city of Philadelphia has used foot patrol in high-crime areas. The chapter narrative then guides students to **INVESTIGATE** effective policing strategies, which may include foot patrol. This discussion leads students to **UNDERSTAND** the difficulties law enforcers face in their efforts to prevent crime, as well as the varied consequences of the strategies they choose to employ. In these ways, the **OBSERVE→INVESTIGATE→UNDERSTAND** pedagogy actively involves students in making connections and exploring ideas that support learning.

Probing the Myths and the Realities of Criminal Justice

Another main goal of this text is to erase rampant misconceptions about the criminal justice system. We created the **MYTH/REALITY** feature to reinforce the text's real-world basis. Integrated throughout the chapters, **MYTH/REALITY** selections challenge students to reflect critically on their own beliefs and to develop an understanding of the way the system actually works. Each entry is connected to a broader discussion that uses supporting data to explain a key principle. Among the persistent myths we investigate are:

- Older adults are more likely to be victimized than people in any other age group. (Chapter 2, "Types of Crime")
- Police must always read suspects their *Miranda rights*. (Chapter 7, "Legal and Special Issues in Policing")
- Drug offenders are treated leniently by the criminal justice system. (Chapter 10, "Sentencing")
- Juvenile crime rates are skyrocketing. (Chapter 15, "Juvenile Justice")

OBSERVE → INVESTIGATE → UNDERSTAND

Reality-Relevant Special Features That Reinforce the Text's Framework

CJ: Realities and Challenges, Third Edition, offers an array of special-feature boxes that highlight and reinforce the *Observe, Investigate, Understand* framework:

- **Matters of Ethics** explores moral dilemmas and problems that may arise in various criminal justice scenarios and settings; see, for example, Chapter 8's selection, "Expert Witnesses: The Good, the Bad, and the Criminal," and Chapter 11's example, "Private Prisons."

- **A Case in Point** links key text concepts to actual events and cases.
- **A Global View** compares American justice to international justice.
- **Disconnects** explores the gap between the intent of policies and law and their application in the real world.

Matters of Ethics

Private Prisons

The fact that private prisons are lucrative business has led to charges of corruption in several states. For example, in 2010 the New Mexico corrections secretary refused to penalize a private prison contractor for understaffing prisons it operated—a violation of its contract with the state. New Mexico lost more than $18 million in penalties due to this lack of contract enforcement. The state saved money, but at the expense of adequately staffing the prison. It turns out that the corrections secretary in New Mexico was a former employee of and a warden for the same private prison corporation. Furthermore, the prison corporation had been accused of unfair political activity by contributing to the campaign of a candidate for sheriff while using unregistered lobbyists to secure a lease renewal of a jail it operated.

In another case, a private prison company took advantage of the small town of Hardin, Montana. It convinced the town to sell $27 million in bonds for the construction of a facility that was built but never used. The bonds have since gone into default.

Arizona, too, has seen private prisons entangled with politics. In 2010 the two major nationwide prison corporations helped draft a tough new immigration law in Arizona that would yield hundreds of millions of dollars in revenue by increasing the number of illegal immigrants detained in their private prisons. The prison companies not only lobbied hard for this legislation, they also contributed to the governor's electoral campaign. In addition, two of the governor's top advisers were former lobbyists for private prison companies. The governor signed the immigration bill and has advocated the privatization of the prisons housing these immigrants.

OBSERVE → INVESTIGATE → UNDERSTAND

- What is a compelling argument for barring current or former employees of private prison corporations who assume political office from developing contracts with private prison corporations?
- Should states be allowed to contract with private corporations to incarcerate prisoners? Why or why not?
- Might prisoners be subject to longer incarceration in private prisons than in government-run facilities? Explain.

SOURCES: Trip Jennings, "No Penalties for Understaffed Private Prisons," *New Mexico Independent*, September 2, 2010; Trip Jennings, "Corrections Secretary's Previous Work for Private Prison Operator Highlighted," *New Mexico Independent*, September 7, 2010; Trip Jennings, "NM Could Have Repeatedly Fined Private Prisons for Low Staffing Levels," *New Mexico Independent*, September 10, 2010; Trip Jennings, "Corrections Gave Up $18 Million in Uncollected Penalties," *New Mexico Independent*, September 15, 2010; *East County Magazine*, "Private Prison Group Uses Unregistered Lobbyists while Giving Money to Sheriff Gore." www.eastcountymagazine.org/node/3463 (retrieved December 31, 2010); Matthew Reichback, "Private Prison Developer Behind Montana Fiasco Involved in Construction of NM Private Prisons," *New Mexico Independent*, October 12, 2009; Trip Jennings, "Private Prisons Pushed for AZ Immigration Law," *New Mexico Independent*, October 28, 2010; Casey Newton, Ginger Rough, and J. J. Hensley, "Arizona Inmate Escape Puts Spot'light on State Private Prisons: Questions Arise over Safety Standards, Taxpayer Savings," *Arizona Republic*, August 22, 2010; Michael Birley, "Private Prison Companies Have Significant Ties to Arizona Immigration Law SB 1070," *San Francisco Examiner*, October 29, 2010. www.examiner.com/crime-in-san-francisco/private-prison-companies-have-significant-ties-to-arizona-immigration-law-sb-1070 (retrieved January 5, 2011).

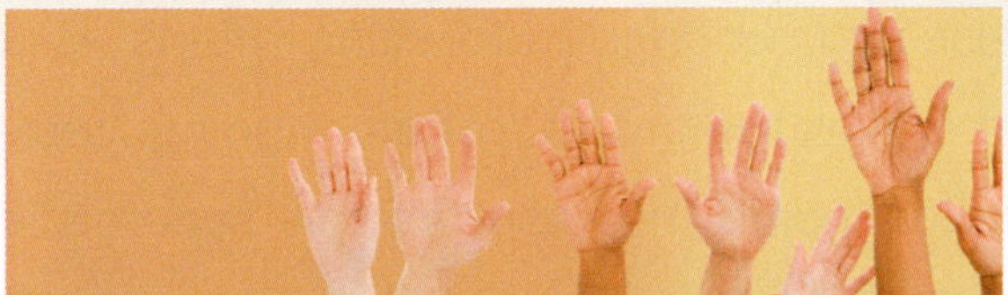

What about the Victim?

Victims of Culture Conflict

In 2010, the TLC Network launched a reality television show offering a glimpse into the daily lives of the Brown family, whose members are living a plural family lifestyle in Lehi, Utah. The show, *Sister Wives*, features the husband, Kody, his 4 wives, and their 13 children and 3 stepchildren. Though legally married only to his first wife for many years, Kody legally divorced her to legally marry his fourth wife. The sister wives claim the legal divorce and marriage was a joint family decision. Kody has had marriage rituals with the other three women and calls them his wives, and they refer to him as their husband. All the wives entered into the polygamist lifestyle voluntarily. In fact, the wedding planning for Brown's fourth ceremony and reception was the focus of one of the series' episodes.

This show is an excellent illustration of culture conflict—in this case, how not only the norms but also the laws of mainstream society clash with fundamentalist Mormon values. The modern Mormon Church has not advocated polygamy since 1890; however, an estimated 38,000 fundamentalist Mormons continue to believe in, and practice, multiple marriage secretly in the United States.

Although rarely prosecuted unless children are being harmed, bigamy is a crime in Utah, punishable by a sentence of up to five years in prison. A person may be found guilty of bigamy in Utah through *cohabitation*—not just by entering into legal marriage contracts. By going public, the Browns exposed themselves to possible criminal prosecution, and the state of Utah launched an investigation. In 2012 Utah's case against the Brown parents under the state's bigamy statute was dismissed. However, the family is continuing its suit against Utah's bigamy law.

The Brown family adults decided to come out of the closet with their lifestyle to help others understand that they are deeply committed to one another, their children, and their family structure and to show that their children are well adjusted. Moreover, the parents do not want their children to have to live in secrecy or shame, denying to others the truth about their family.

OBSERVE → INVESTIGATE → UNDERSTAND

- Are the Browns' 16 children victims of their parents' lifestyle choice? Explain.
- Is it emotionally abusive to raise children in a lifestyle for which the parents might be arrested and go to jail? Why or why not?
- Is it emotionally abusive to raise children in a lifestyle that makes it difficult for them to fit into the dominant society, or that makes it impossible for them to have privacy? Why or why not?
- Do some research into other cases in which culture conflict has resulted in law violation.

SOURCES: Jennifer Dobner, "Police Investigating Family in 'Sister Wives' Show," *KOMOnews.com*, November 30, 2010. www.komonews.com/news/entertainment/103940544.html (retrieved November 30, 2010); "Sister Wives' Lawsuit: Kody Brown and Family Suing Utah over Bigamy Law," *Huffingtonpost.com*, July 25, 2012. http://www.huffingtonpost.com/2012/07/25/sister-wives-lawsuit-kody-brown-utah-bigamy-law_n_1701450.html (retrieved January 5, 2013); Esther Lee, "Sister Wives Stars Say Polygamist Kody Brown's Divorce, New Marriage Will 'Legally Restructure' Family," *US Weekly*, February 4, 2015. http://www.usmagazine.com/celebrity-news/news/sister-wives-divorce-brown-family-to-legally-restructure-201542 (retrieved April 18, 2015).

Race, Class, Gender

Gender and Crime

Females represent a small but increasing percentage of the offending population in the United States for all crimes. In 2010, there were approximately 1.6 million people in state and federal institutions, of whom 113,000 were female offenders. Almost half of incarcerated females are White, whereas 32 percent of incarcerated males are White. Black males (37 percent) make up the largest portion of incarcerated males. Black females (22 percent) were imprisoned at a rate twice that of White females (113 per 100,000 for Black females versus 51 per 100,000 for White females).[a] Since 2000, the growth in the incarceration rate of females in state or federal institutions increased 21 percent in comparison to only 15 percent for males.[b]

Although males represent the largest percentage of prison inmates, female inmates present with more mental health problems than do males. A 2006 study of the mental health of those incarcerated found that 23 percent of females both in state facilities and in local jails were diagnosed with a mental health problem, compared to 8 and 9 percent of male inmates, respectively.[c]

Males offend with significantly greater frequency than do females, and in general male offenders are more likely than are female offenders to be violent. Women are much less likely than men to commit assault or murder, and the rate of murders committed by women has declined since 1980.[d] Yet the data show that women increasingly are engaging in violent crimes. A study that examined the gender of violent felons in the 75 largest counties from 1990 to 2002 found that males were responsible for 91 percent of all violent felonies and females for 9 percent.[e] The most recent data, from 2008, support previous statistics: At year-end 2008, there were 1,267,400 males incarcerated in state facilities as compared to 94,800 women. When comparing males and females in specific crime categories, the statistics from year-end 2008 indicate that 53.8 percent of males and 35.6 percent of women were incarcerated for violent crimes; 17.7 percent of males and 29 percent of females were incarcerated for property crimes; and 17.8 percent of males and 26.9 percent of females were incarcerated for drug crimes. As these data indicate, while males are committing more violent crimes, females are committing more property and drug crimes.[f]

According to National Crime Victimization data of juvenile victims (ages 12–17), despite the increase in female violence, males continue to commit certain violent crimes with greater frequency than do females, including intimate partner violence, stalking, aggravated assault, forcible rape, robbery, and murder. In 2010, juveniles of both genders were equally likely to experience a violent crime such as rape, robbery, or aggravated assault.[g]

OBSERVE → INVESTIGATE → UNDERSTAND

- What might explain why a larger proportion of incarcerated women than men presents with mental health problems?
- Why do you think the rate of murders committed by women has declined since 1980?
- The statistics indicate that females are becoming more violent than ever before, but not for murder. What might explain this finding?

SOURCES: [a]E. Anne Carson, "Prisoners in 2013," Bureau of Justice Statistics Bulletin (Washington, DC: U.S. Department of Justice, September 16, 2014), NCJ 247282. www.bjs.gov/index.cfm?ty=pbdetail&iid=5109 (retrieved May 18, 2015).

[b]Lauren E. Glaze and Danielle Kaeble, "Correctional Populations in the United States, 2013," Bureau of Justice Statistics, December 19, 2014, NCJ 248479. www.bjs.gov/index.cfm?ty=pbdetail&iid=5177 (retrieved May 18, 2015).

[c]Doris J. James and Lauren E. Glaze, "Mental Health Problems of Jail and Prison Inmates," *Bureau of Justice Statistics Special Report*, September 2006, NCJ 213600. www.ojp.usdoj.gov/bjs/pub/pdf/mhppji.pdf (retrieved December 20, 2008).

[d]Lawrence Greenfield and Tracy Snell, "Women Offenders," *Bureau of Justice Statistics Special Report* (Washington, DC: U.S. Department of Justice, December 1999).

[e]Brian A. Reaves, "State Court Processing Statistics, 1990–2002: Violent Felons in Large Urban Counties," *Bureau of Justice Statistics*, July 2006. www.ojp.usdoj.gov/bjs/pub/pdf/vfluc.pdf (retrieved December 28, 2008).

[f]Heather C. West, William J. Sabol, and Sarah J. Greenman, "Prisoners in 2009" (Washington, DC: Bureau of Justice Statistics, December 2010, NCJ 231675). http://bjs.ojp.usdoj.gov/content/pub/pdf/p09.pdf (retrieved July 3, 2011).

[g]Nicole White and Janet L. Lauritsen, "Violent Crime against Youth, 1994–2010," Bureau of Justice Statistics, December 2012, NCJ 240106. www.bjs.gov/content/pub/ascii/vcay9410.txt (retrieved May 19, 2015).

- **Real Careers** profiles recent graduates who have chosen a career in criminal justice.
- **Real Crime Tech** illuminates the ways in which technology is currently used in a range of criminal justice situations and settings.
- **Race, Class, Gender** traces the experiences of people who historically have been left behind in the process of criminal justice.
- **What about the Victim?** reminds us that the criminal justice story is also about the victim.

An Author Team That's Connected to the Real World

CJ: Realities and Challenges, Third Edition, provides a uniquely interdisciplinary view of criminal justice not found in any other text. As both academics and practitioners with diverse backgrounds in law enforcement, the courts, corrections, and victim services, we provide a comprehensive, contemporary, and realistic perspective on these vital institutions.

We wrote this text using a highly collaborative process. To ensure that each branch of the criminal justice system was thoroughly represented, we organized our research, writing, and editing efforts as a peer review circle. Each chapter was the product of an ongoing, iterative review by the entire author team. The result of this synergistic effort is a unified voice providing a balanced, insightful point of view that is informed by the experience of the entire author team and has been affirmed by the feedback of course instructors.

We encourage students to read this text much in the spirit in which it was created: to have an open mind, think critically, engage in discussion, and exploit the wide knowledge and practical experience represented by the author team. Our collective experience demonstrates the need for collaboration in addressing the complexity of the criminal justice system.

The Authors

Ruth E. Masters, Ed.D.

Professor Emerita, Department of Criminology, California State University, Fresno. Expertise: Ruth E. Masters's specialties are corrections, correctional counseling, drug addiction, criminological theory, and cross-cultural administration of justice. She has worked for the California Department of Corrections (now California Department of Corrections and Rehabilitation) as a Parole Agent supervising addicted adult felons. She has been teaching criminology since 1972.

Lori Beth Way, Ph.D.

Associate Dean of Academic Planning and Professor of Criminal Justice, San Francisco State University. Expertise: Lori Beth Way's research and teaching areas include policing, the courts, and issues of race, class, and gender. Her policing research primarily focuses on police behavior and discretion. She published *Hunting for 'Dirtbags': Why Cops Overpolice the Poor and Minorities* with Northeastern University Press in 2013. She was the director of a U.S. Department of Justice Violence Against Women Campus Grant for Chico State, where she was a faculty member for 14 years, and Butte College, where she was a police academy instructor. She also has a master's certificate in Women's Studies from Syracuse University, where she earned her doctorate.

Phyllis B. Gerstenfeld, J.D., Ph.D.

Chair and Professor, Department of Criminal Justice, California State University, Stanislaus. Expertise: Phyllis Gerstenfeld has a law degree as well as a Ph.D. in Social Psychology. Her primary areas of research include hate crimes, juvenile justice, and psychology and law. She has published a monograph and co-edited an anthology on hate crimes. She has worked for a large private law firm as well as a public legal services agency and has been teaching criminal justice since 1993.

Bernadette T. Muscat, Ph.D.

Interim Associate Dean, College of Social Sciences, and Professor, Department of Criminology, California State University, Fresno. Expertise: Bernadette Muscat has worked with victims of domestic violence by serving as a legal advocate and by providing counseling, education, and legal advocacy in shelter and court environments. She has worked with law enforcement agencies, victim service programs, and court programs in program and policy development, evaluation, research, and training to ensure effective administration of victim assistance. She works extensively with local, state, and national level multidisciplinary task force groups to address family violence and violence against women. She has worked with the California Office of Emergency Services (OES) Victim Witness Division on the creation and implementation of the California State Victim Assistance Academy (CVAA) to provide 40-hour training to victim service practitioners throughout California.

Michael Hooper, Ph.D.

Lecturer, Department of Criminology and Criminal Justice Studies, Sonoma State University. Expertise: Michael Hooper began his involvement with the criminal justice system as a member of the Los Angeles Police Department. His 23 years of LAPD experience encompassed positions as a patrol officer, field supervisor, and watch commander. This was followed by five years of service on the Criminal Justice Program faculty at Penn State University's Capitol Campus. He subsequently served 13 years as a bureau chief at the California Commission on Peace Officer Standards and Training.

John P. J. Dussich, Ph.D.

Professor Emeritus, Department of Criminology, California State University, Fresno. Expertise: John P. J. Dussich is one of the world's leading authorities on victimology, victim services, criminology, victimological theory, and criminological and victimological research. He has worked as a criminal justice planner, as a police officer, as a warden of a prison, as a director of a program evaluation unit, and as a director of an international victimology research institute in Japan. He is the founding and immediate past editor-in-chief of the online journal *International Perspectives in Victimology*. He has taught criminology since 1966 and victimology since 1976. The American Society of Victimology has named the John P. J. Dussich Award in his honor, and gives it each year to a person who has made significant lifelong achievements to the field of victimology. The National Organization for Victim Assistance's service award in 1980 was named the "John Dussich Founder's Award," to be given to individuals who perform outstanding service on behalf of NOVA. He was recently awarded the prestigious 2016 Ronald Wilson Reagan Public Policy Award. This award "honors those whose leadership, vision, and innovation have led to significant changes in public policy and practice that benefit crime victims." The award is given by the U.S. Office for Victims of Crime, and the nominee is approved by the U.S. Attorney General.

Candice A. Skrapec, Ph.D.

Professor, Department of Criminology, California State University, Fresno. Expertise: Candice Skrapec is a psychologist and criminologist. For the past 30 years she has maintained her research focus on psychopathy and serial murder (particularly in terms of underlying biological and psychological factors) and continues her interviews of incarcerated serial murderers in different countries. Her professional works and academic research result in regular calls from the media, movie and documentary producers, as well as authors of fact and fiction books in the areas of serial murder and investigative profiling. With over 30 years of experience in the law enforcement field working with officers and agencies in Canada, the United States, and Mexico, she is also frequently consulted by police around the world to assist in the investigation of homicide cases. She has taught a wide range of criminology courses since 1988 and has trained police and correctional officers in different countries in the areas related to her academic research and professional experience.

Required=Results

McGraw-Hill Connect®
Learn Without Limits

Connect is a teaching and learning platform that is proven to deliver better results for students and instructors.

Connect empowers students by continually adapting to deliver precisely what they need, when they need it, and how they need it, so your class time is more engaging and effective.

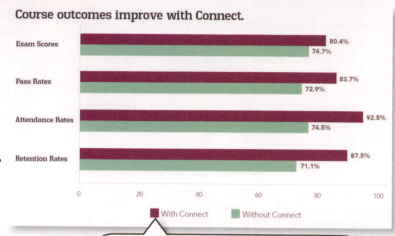

Course outcomes improve with Connect.

	With Connect	Without Connect
Exam Scores	80.4%	74.7%
Pass Rates	83.7%	72.9%
Attendance Rates	92.5%	74.5%
Retention Rates	87.5%	71.1%

Using **Connect** improves passing rates by **10.8%** and retention by **16.4%**.

88% of instructors who use **Connect** require it; instructor satisfaction **increases** by 38% when **Connect** is required.

Analytics

Connect helps students achieve better grades

	A	B	C	D	F
With Connect	36%	29.5%	22%	4.3%	8.2%
Without Connect	22.2%	22.3%	25.6%	9.8%	20%

Based on McGraw-Hill Education Connect Effectiveness Study 2013

Connect Insight®

Connect Insight is Connect's new one-of-a-kind visual analytics dashboard—now available for both instructors and students—that provides at-a-glance information regarding student performance, which is immediately actionable. By presenting assignment, assessment, and topical performance results together with a time metric that is easily visible for aggregate or individual results, Connect Insight gives the user the ability to take a just-in-time approach to teaching and learning, which was never before available. Connect Insight presents data that empowers students and helps instructors improve class performance in a way that is efficient and effective.

Students can view their results for any **Connect** course.

Mobile

Connect's new, intuitive mobile interface gives students and instructors flexible and convenient, anytime–anywhere access to all components of the Connect platform.

Adaptive

THE FIRST AND ONLY ADAPTIVE READING EXPERIENCE DESIGNED TO TRANSFORM THE WAY STUDENTS READ

More students earn **A's** and **B's** when they use McGraw-Hill Education **Adaptive** products.

SmartBook®

Proven to help students improve grades and study more efficiently, SmartBook contains the same content within the print book, but actively tailors that content to the needs of the individual. SmartBook's adaptive technology provides precise, personalized instruction on what the student should do next, guiding the student to master and remember key concepts, targeting gaps in knowledge and offering customized feedback, and driving the student toward comprehension and retention of the subject matter. Available on smartphones and tablets, SmartBook puts learning at the student's fingertips—anywhere, anytime.

Over **4 billion questions** have been answered, making McGraw-Hill Education products more intelligent, reliable, and precise.

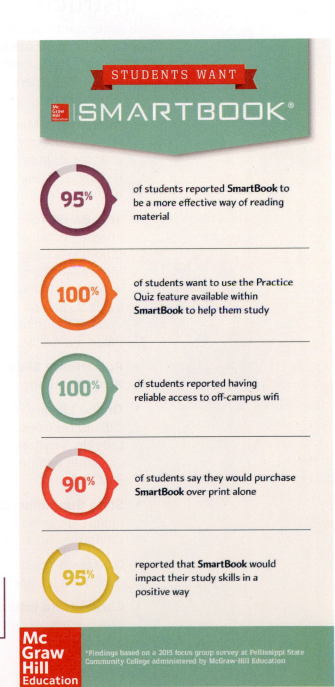

STUDENTS WANT

Mc Graw Hill Education SMARTBOOK®

95% of students reported **SmartBook** to be a more effective way of reading material

100% of students want to use the Practice Quiz feature available within **SmartBook** to help them study

100% of students reported having reliable access to off-campus wifi

90% of students say they would purchase **SmartBook** over print alone

95% reported that **SmartBook** would impact their study skills in a positive way

Mc Graw Hill Education

*Findings based on a 2015 focus group survey at Pellissippi State Community College administered by McGraw-Hill Education

www.learnsmartadvantage.com

The Learning Support System for
CJ: Realities and Challenges

The third edition of *CJ: Realities and Challenges* is available online with Connect, McGraw-Hill Education's integrated assignment and assessment platform. Online tools make managing assignments easier for instructors—and make learning and studying more motivating for students.

Instructor Resources

Supplements provide teaching aids and tools to help instructors leverage the classroom experience and provide students with a wide range of study and assessment tools to reinforce comprehension of the text. These supplements are available on the Instructor Resources sections of Connect.

- **Instructor's Manual.** Provides a comprehensive guide to teaching the introductory course using CJ: Realities and Challenges, including chapter guides that feature learning objectives, chapter previews and reviews, detailed outlines, lecture summaries, additional lecture ideas, and class discussion topics.

- **Test Bank.** The Test Bank contains 70 multiple-choice questions per chapter, of which 20 are scenario-based. Each question is tagged with bloom's Taxonomy learning domains and page references from the text. McGraw-Hill's computerized EZ Test allows you to create customized exams using the publisher's supplied test items or your own questions. EZ Test runs on your computer without a connection to the Internet. A version of the test bank will also be provided in Microsoft Word files for those instructors who prefer this format.

- **PowerPoint Slides.** The PowerPoint slides provide instructors with dynamic lecture support and include chapter outlines and key figures.

- **Online Library of CJ Video Clips.** Instructors frequently request video clips to be used in their CJ classes. Using the Internet as a resource, we provide a dynamically updated annotated index of CJ-related video clips that can be viewed online. The list is organized both by chapter and topic.

- **State Supplements.** A collection of useful background essays on the unique histories and development of laws in key states, including California, Texas, and Florida.

- **Quizzes.** Provides multiple-choice, true-false, and critical thinking questions for each chapter.

- **Careers and Internships.** Offers students additional information about a wide variety of careers in criminal justice and how to prepare for them.

- **Source Connection.** Links to source material for each chapter give the student an opportunity to explore individual cases more deeply.
- **Internet Exercises.** Provides research and interpretive activities associated with Internet sites related to criminal justice.

With McGraw-Hill's **Create** at **www.mcgrawhillcreate.com**, design your own ideal course materials. You can rearrange or omit chapters, combine material from other sources, and/or upload your syllabus or any other content you have written to make the perfect resources for your students. You can search thousands of leading McGraw-Hill textbooks to find the best content for your students, then arrange it to fit your teaching style. You can even personalize your book's appearance by selecting the cover and adding your name, school, and course information. When you order a Create book, you receive a complimentary review copy. Get a printed copy in 3 to 5 business days or an electronic copy (eComp) via e-mail in about an hour. Register today at **www.mcgrawhillcreate.com** and craft your course resources to match the way you teach.

McGraw-Hill Campus is the first-of-its-kind institutional service providing faculty with true, single sign-on access to all of McGraw-Hill's course content, digital tools, and other high-quality learning resources from any learning management system (LMS). This innovative offering allows for secure and deep integration and seamless access to any of our course solutions such as McGraw-Hill Connect, McGraw-Hill Create, McGraw-Hill LearnSmart, or Tegrity. McGraw-Hill Campus includes access to our entire content library, including eBooks, assessment tools, presentation slides, and multimedia content, among other resources, providing faculty open and unlimited access to prepare for class, create tests/quizzes, develop lecture material, integrate interactive content, and much more.

Chapter-by-Chapter Changes

PART 1:
CRIME, LAW, AND THE CRIMINAL JUSTICE SYSTEM

Chapter 1: What Is the Criminal Justice System?

- New Realities and Challenges vignette, "Media Portrayals of Real Crime: Fact or Fiction?"
- New A Global View box, "How U.S. Legal Norms Differ from Those in Singapore: The Case of Michael Fay"
- Updated discussion of changing views on marijuana use and trends toward decriminalization
- Revised Disconnects box, "Evolution of Marijuana Laws"

Chapter 2: Types of Crime

- New Realities and Challenges vignette,
- New A Global View box, "Measuring Crime around the World"
- Updated A Case in Point box, "Michigan's Task Force Approach to Violent Crime Reduction"
- New mass murder example focusing on the Hawke-Petit case
- New Matters of Ethics box, "Ethical Issues When Dealing with Treatment of Offenders or Victims"
- Updated coverage of legalization of marijuana for recreational use
- Updated statistics of state and federal prisoners convicted of drug offenses
- Discussion of drug and alcohol use among veterans of Iraq and Afghanistan
- Updated Real Crime Tech box, "Emerging Drug-Testing Technologies"
- Updated Race, Class, Gender box, "Gender and Crime"
- Updated crime statistics
- Updated material on immigration offenses

Chapter 3: Causes of Crime

- New Realities and Challenges vignette, "Theater 9 at Century 16: 12 Dead, 70 Wounded"
- Updated, expanded Real Crime Tech box, "Lie Detection by Brainwave Analysis"
- Updated Matters of Ethics box, "Revising the *DSM:* A Process on Trial in the Court of Professional Opinion"
- Updated and expanded discussion of mental disorders
- New A Case in Point box, An Awakening in India for Women: A Rape in New Delhi
- New What about the Victim? box, "Victims of Culture Conflict"
- Updated coverage of crime desistance
- New Disconnects box, "Mentally Ill Death Row Inmates"

Chapter 4: Criminal Law and Defenses

- Updated Realities and Challenges vignette, "Is Hazing a Crime?"
- Updated A Global View box, "Intellectual Property Piracy in the Twenty-First Century"
- New A Case in Point box, "Convicted *without* Criminal Intent"
- New extended discussion of "Criminal Defenses"

PART 2:
LAW ENFORCEMENT

Chapter 5: Overview of Policing

- New Realities and Challenges vignette, "The Power of Community Partnerships"
- Reorganized section on the English model
- New A Case in Point box, "Conflict with Occupy Wall Street Protestors"
- Discussion of police departments' growing use of background checks on social media activity by candidates for police positions
- Updated Disconnects box, "Where Are the Women?"
- New What about the Victim? box, "The Police Subculture and a Linkage to Intimate Partner Strife"
- New Matters of Ethics box, "Department of Justice Investigation of the Ferguson, Missouri, Police Department"
- Updated Global View box, "India's Growing Reliance on the Security Industry"

Chapter 6: Policing Operations

- Updated Realities and Challenges vignette, "Foot Patrol in a Big City"
- New A Case in Point box, "Problem-Oriented Policing in Action: The Colorado Springs Police Department's HOT Program—Providing Outreach to the Homeless"
- Updated Disconnects box, "A Literal Disconnect: Agencies' Inabilities to Communicate"
- New text material on robotic workstations to keep up with the accelerated demand for DNA testing by players in the criminal justice system
- Updated discussion of evidence-based policing and its value
- Updated discussion of CompStat
- New A Global View box, "Public Perceptions of the Police in Russia"

Chapter 7: Legal and Special Issues in Policing

- New Realities and Challenges vignette, "An In-Custody Death in Baltimore"
- New text discussion of recent Supreme Court cases

- New text section, "Dynamics of Use of Force"
- New text discussion of video evidence
- Updated Race, Class, Gender box, "Pedestrian Stop-and-Frisk in the Big Apple"
- Updated What about the Victim? box, "Providing Transition Assistance for the Police Officer Returning from Combat Deployment"
- New details in the text on the problem of suicide among police officers

PART 3:
ADJUDICATION

Chapter 8: The Courts
- Updated opening vignette
- Updated statistics on court processes
- Updated Race, Class, Gender box, "Race and Jury Decision Making"
- Updated Real Crime Tech box, "Freeing Wrongfully Convicted Persons"
- Added details on presentence investigation reports and elocution in the text discussion of victim impact statements

Chapter 9: Pretrial and Trial
- New Realities and Challenges vignette, "Tried for the Third Time—Over 30 Years Later"
- Updated What about the Victim? box, "Balancing Victims' and Offenders' Rights to a Speedy Trial"
- Expanded, fine-tuned discussion of the pretrial process, featuring substantially augmented discussions under the headings "Discovery" and "Plea Bargaining"
- New Matters of Ethics box "A Jury of Your Peers? . . . Not Really"

Chapter 10: Sentencing
- New text details updating the discussion of the revised USSC sentencing guidelines
- New A Matter of Ethics box, "When Is a Mandatory Minimum Sentence Unjust?"
- Updated text discussion of controversies and court challenges over lethal injections—and the effect on executions
- Updated and expanded discussion on capital punishment
- Updated Race, Class, Gender box, "Exonerating the Innocent"

PART 4:
CORRECTIONS

Chapter 11: Overview of Corrections
- New Realities and Challenges vignette, "Values are the Driving Force behind Corrections Models"
- Updated Myth/Reality features

- Updated statistics and figures throughout
- In-depth coverage of Public Safety Realignment Policy and mass incarceration
- New What About the Victim? box, "Implications for Victims of California's Realignment Policy"
- New A Case in Point box, "Hawaii's HOPE Program for High-Risk Offenders"
- New Race, Class, Gender box, "Treating Women in Prisons . . . as Second-Class Citizens of the System"
- New coverage of California's Public Safety Realignment Policy and women prisoners
- Updated discussion of inmate race and gender differences
- Updated discussion of private and faith-based prisons
- Updated Critical Thinking Questions
- Updated coverage of correctional populations in the United States
- Updated coverage of, state prison inmates

Chapter 12: Jails and Prisons
- New coverage of jails becoming de facto asylums for the mentally ill and dumping grounds for poor and addicted populations
- Updated jail and prison statistics throughout
- New coverage of the shift away from the policy of mass incarceration and "get tough" sentencing practices
- Coverage of how mass incarceration affects people of color
- Matters of Ethics box replaces second edition What about the Victim? box, "Prisoners as Research Subjects"
- New A Case in Point box, "The National Emotional Literacy Program for Prisoners"
- California Public Safety Realignment policy and female prisoners
- Updated examples of prisoner rights
- Updated prison gang discussion
- New coverage of transgender, lesbian, gay, and bisexual prisoners
- Updated coverage on AIDS and ill inmates
- Updated Critical Thinking Questions
- Expanded discussion of prisoner rights
- New A Global View box, "A Different Kind of Prison: Venezuela's San Antonio Prison"
- New Real Crime Tech box, "Personal Communication Technology and Prisons," that emphasizes tablet technology
- Updated discussion of rapidly rising number of women in U.S. prisons

Chapter 13: Community Corrections
- Updated "Probation" and "Parole" sections
- Coverage of how Public Safety Realignment policy affects probation, parole, and community corrections

- Updated statistics throughout
- New Race, Class, Gender box, "Celebrity Justice?"
- Expanded discussion of the role of the probation officer
- Expanded discussion on factors in the future success of probation
- New A Case in Point box, "Parole and the Jaycee Dugard Case"
- Expanded discussion on the effectiveness of parole in the future
- New coverage on the relationship between doing away with policies of mass incarceration and community-based corrections
- New Disconnects box, "What Is an Appropriate Fine?"
- Updated Matters of Ethics box, "Relationships between Correctional Personnel and Offenders"

PART 5:
SPECIAL ISSUES

Chapter 14: Understanding and Helping Victims
- New Race, Class, Gender box, "Charleston Shooting"
- New text on the U.S. Census of Domestic Violence Services
- New Disconnects box, "When Victims Are Revictimized"
- Updated perspectives on victim assistance for older adults
- New A Case in Point box, "The Killings at Sandy Hook Elementary School"

Chapter 15: Juvenile Justice
- New Realities and Challenges vignette, "Two Years in Solitary"
- Updated discussion and analysis of measuring juvenile crime
- Updated statistics on juvenile crime

- Updated Matters of Ethics box, "Policing the Schools"
- Updated discussion of juvenile court jurisdiction
- New Disconnects box, "Punishing Truancy"
- Updated Juvenile Corrections statistics
- Expanded discussion of sexual abuse of male and female juveniles held in custody
- New discussion of the Juvenile Justice Realignment bill

Chapter 16: Contemporary Challenges in Criminal Justice
- New Realities and Challenges vignette, "Boston Marathon Bombing"
- New resources for victims of identity theft
- New contextual framework for combating identity theft
- Updated information on the extent of cybercrime
- New information on the ever-expanding value of digital evidence
- New information sharing protocols to combat cybercrime
- New text discussion on occurrences of worldwide terrorist attacks, their impact, and law enforcement's responses to them
- New information on the extent and nature of terrorism
- New text on the USA FREEDOM Act
- Updated A Case in Point, "The Fusion Center Approach to Preventing Terrorism"
- New Matters of Ethics box, "Airport Security Technology in the United States"
- Updated hate crime statistics
- New Race, Class, Gender box, "The Killing of Onesimo Marcelino Lopez"
- Consideration of the first National Professional Training Conference on Responding to Crime Victims with Disabilities

Contributors

The author team is very appreciative of all the hard work of the McGraw-Hill professionals who worked on this book. Our work is better for their assistance. We would like to thank Lester Pincu for his important contributions to the first and second editions. In addition, we thank the many contributors for their work in helping shape this text. More than 100 professors helped to influence the development of the first edition of *CJ: Realities and Challenges*. We'd like to thank the following professors for their help in developing this third edition (NB: inclusion in this preface does not equal an endorsement of our materials).

Connect Reviews

VICTORIA BECK, University of Wisconsin–Oshkosh

RANDALL DAVIS, Santa Ana College and Santiago Canyon College

MARTHA EARWOOD, University of Alabama at Birmingham

RICHARD FINN, Western Nevada College

SHANA MAIER, Widener University

PATRICIA MAREK O'NEILL, Hudson Valley Community College

JACQUELINE M. MULLANY, Triton College

MICHAEL PITTARO, East Stroudsburg University

WAYNE D. POSNER, East Los Angeles College

DARREN K. STOCKER, Cape Cod Community College

MICHAEL SUCH, Hudson Valley Community College

"The Masters text is a comprehensive collection of information presented in an easy to read manner. The pictorial display presented in the text highlights and supplements the written material in [a] student-friendly way. And, the text incorporates information about the victim throughout the material, which is a pleasant rarity in a textbook."
—Lisa A. Hoston, Allegany College of Maryland

"This is a thorough and highly relevant textbook that will encourage students to further their pursuit of criminal justice as a field of academic study."
—Martha Earwood, University of Alabama at Birmingham

Content Reviewers

VICTORIA BECK, University of Wisconsin–Oshkosh

RANDALL DAVIS, Santa Ana College and Santiago Canyon College

MARTHA EARWOOD, University of Alabama at Birmingham

RICHARD FINN, Western Nevada College

ANDY GONIS, Santa Ana College

LISA A. HOSTON, Allegany College of Maryland

LI YING LI, Metropolitan State University–Denver

SHANA MAIER, Widener University

PATRICIA MAREK O'NEILL, Hudson Valley Community College

PAMELA MERTENS, University of the District of Columbia

JACQUELINE M. MULLANY, Triton College

MICHAEL PITTARO, East Stroudsburg University

WAYNE D. POSNER, East Los Angeles College

SHANNON SANTANA, University of North Carolina–Wilmington

DAREN K. STOCKER, Cape Cod Community College

MICHAEL SUCH, Hudson Valley Community College

ARNOLD RAY WAGGONER, Rose State College

TRACEY WOODARD, University of North Florida

Dedications

Thanks to an awesome author team and to Elizabeth and Viola, who gave up so much of their time with me so I could work.

—Ruth Masters

I'd like to thank my family for their constant support. I'd also like to thank several colleagues who have provided valuable feedback for this 3rd edition—Matthew O. Thomas, Ryan Patten, Jonathan Caudill, and Kimberlee Candela.

—Lori Beth Way

I'd like to thank Dennis, Allison, and Quinn for their continuing support, and for giving up so much of their time so I could work.

—Phyllis Gerstenfeld

Much appreciation for the understanding of my wife, Jill, and all family members on those occasions when the manuscript "train" required some deferring of time together—and for acceptance of "walk IOUs" by Abbie, canine guardian of manuscripts.

—Mike Hooper

I would like to thank my wife, Edda, for all the time away from her, especially for the late night and weekend calls, both at home and while on vacations. She has been an important source of support throughout the entire process.

—John Dussich

CJ

REALITIES
AND CHALLENGES

3RD EDITION

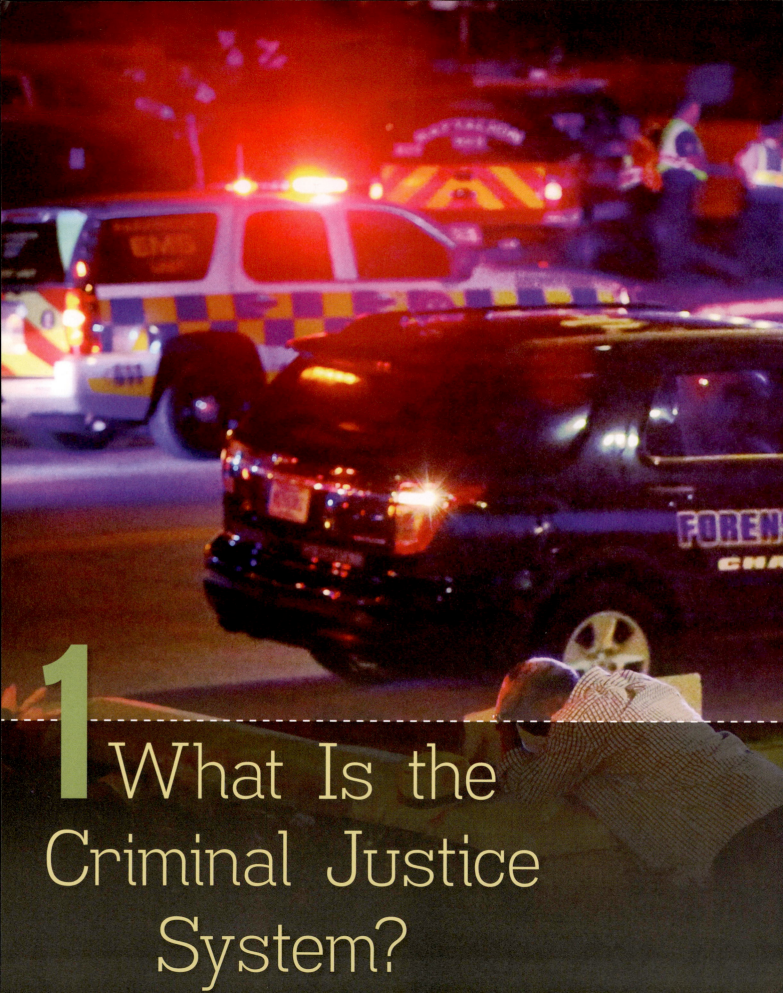

1 What Is the Criminal Justice System?

OBSERVE → INVESTIGATE → UNDERSTAND

After reading this chapter, you should be able to:

- Illustrate how social norms help us define crime.
- Define crime and explain how it is classified.
- Describe the consequences of crime for the offender and the victim.
- Outline the basic structure of the criminal justice system.
- Describe key models of the workings of the criminal justice system.
- Describe how criminal justice is influenced by public opinion, the media, politics, and policy.
- Review the challenges to the criminal justice system today.

Realities and Challenges

Media Portrayals of Real Crime: Fact or Fiction?

Many of us are fascinated by crime and the many questions that surround it. *Who did it, and why did this happen?* Depictions of crime abound in the media, with stories and headlines that both shock and call into question how these crimes can occur in seemingly serene locales like the historic Emanuel African Methodist Episcopal Church in Charleston, South Carolina, where nine people were shot to death during their evening prayer meeting—apparently because they were African American. Stories of the Boston Marathon bombings, Sandy Hook, the Aurora theater shootings, kidnappings, serial murders, and other heinous crimes are depicted on the news, in documentaries, and true crime shows and are dissected by criminologists, lawyers, and other pundits offering varying perspectives on the crimes and the perpetrators. People watch courtroom dramas unfold, and the interest in crime extends to the popularity of television shows such as *The Jinx: The Life and Deaths of Robert Durst, Orange Is the New Black, Law & Order: Special Victims Unit*, and a proliferation of true crime-related shows. There is even an entire network, Investigation Discovery, featuring crime-related shows. People also tuned in in droves to listen to the *Serial* podcasts, and other comparable podcasts are in the works. While we may see and hear so much, often as consumers we cannot separate fact from fiction and are not privy to how the criminal justice system works. This book seeks to help you understand the nature of crime, how crime is measured, the laws that govern criminal behavior, and the practitioners who work within the criminal justice system. The intent of this text is to highlight the myths about criminal justice, but to focus on the realities and the challenges faced by those who interact with and work within the criminal justice system. As you read the text, critically assess the current criminal justice practices described. Consider which practices are working positively and ensuring justice, and which perhaps need to be revisited or abandoned.

Police, detectives, victim advocates, judges, lawyers, prosecutors, jurors, correctional officers, parole officers–these are the people with whom the suspect, the victim, and the victim's family deal when interacting with the criminal justice system. It is a complex and sometimes lumbering machine, as it tackles the job of taking criminals off the street, ensuring a fair trial, supporting victims, protecting society, and punishing and attempting to rehabilitate offenders.

Of course, there are challenges to match the complexity. Have the police followed proper procedures? Has the victim been treated fairly, and does the individual understand his or her rights? Have the prosecutors shared all the relevant evidence with the defending lawyers? Was the jury trial fair? What role did the victim and/or the victim's family play in the criminal justice process? Were due process rights protected? Was the sentencing appropriate for the offense? Has the offender been mistreated in prison? Are there opportunities to rehabilitate? Has parole been granted (or denied) in a fair manner? There are many points at which justice may be either served or derailed.

We hope that this book will help you learn to think critically about the realities and challenges of the world of criminal justice. We want to help you interpret facts and recognize myths about the criminal justice system so you will understand and appreciate its complexities. We hope you come to understand how the roles of offenders, protectors, and victims are interwoven in a system dedicated to detecting those who violate the rules, determining their guilt, and carrying out an appropriate punishment. We begin in this chapter with a brief exploration of the nature of rules whose violations constitute crime and an introduction to how the criminal justice system is structured and works.

THE RULES THAT BIND: NORMS AND LAWS

MYTH/REALITY

MYTH: Some behaviors are so wrong that they are crimes in all societies.

REALITY: It is not the nature of an act that makes that act a crime; it is the nature of society that defines a particular act as a crime in that society.

A **norm** is a rule that makes clear what behavior is appropriate and expected in a particular situation. If, for example, it is the norm to arrive at meetings on time, being late violates the norm. The term *abnormal* connotes **deviance,** the violation of a norm. (The prefix "ab" means "away from," so *abnormal* means "away from the norm.") No behavior is inherently deviant—that is, deviant solely by virtue of its nature. Rather, whether a particular act is considered deviant depends on many factors, including context, place, time, and the individual(s) judging it.

Let's consider how a behavior's deviance depends on the context in which it occurs. For example, if you were to spit on 42nd Street in New York City, people might frown at you, but you would not be arrested. But if you were to spit in the subway, you would be violating a formal regulation of the New York City Transit Authority and could face criminal prosecution in a municipal court. The fact that each week 7 million people pass through the close quarters of the subway system makes hygiene a factor in determining what is deviant in that situation.

Our ideas of deviance also change over time. For example, before the 1970s, being divorced conferred the status of deviant in society. In contrast, today's social norms recognize divorce as acceptable behavior. In other words, there is nothing inherently deviant in getting divorced: Society found it deviant until the 1970s, and then our attitudes changed.

Norms vary from place to place as well. In eastern Europe, men greet other men with kisses on the cheek. In the United States this behavior is considered unusual. The "A Global View" box on page 4 shows how norms about corporal punishment can vary from one country to another. Norms also vary from group to group within a society. While some may consider it deviant to have tattoos covering one's body, it is the norm within many gangs and among many professional athletes.

A **social norm** specifies how people are expected to behave. Social norms are informal rules that are not written but that we nonetheless know and follow. We learn them from parents, peers, and teachers. In North American society, informal social norms include

norm
A rule that makes clear what behavior is appropriate and expected in a particular situation.

deviance
The violation of a norm.

social norm
A rule that specifies how people are expected to behave.

◄ **Tattoos: Sign of Deviance or Body Art?**

Some groups may consider tattoos a sign of deviance; for others, including many professional athletes, tattoos are a normal means of expression.

A Global View

How U.S. Legal Norms Differ from Those in Singapore: The Case of Michael Fay

The focus of this case is not so much on the crime as it is on the punishment. On March 3, 1994, Michael Peter Fay, a St Louis, Missouri, teenager living in Singapore, was sentenced to four months in jail, a fine of 3,500 Singapore dollars (about 2,214 U.S. dollars at the time), and six strokes of a rattan cane for the crimes of theft and vandalism. Norms differ regarding the appropriateness of the type of corporal punishment known as caning between the United States and Singapore. To understand the context of these crimes and their punishment, it is relevant to know that the Singapore government had been trying to cope with a rash of vandalisms leading up to this case. About six months earlier, car vandalism emerged as a noticeable new problem and was reported in one of the local newspapers. Cars parked near apartments were being damaged with hot tar, paint remover, red spray paint, and hatchets; and some taxi drivers reported having their tires slashed. In both countries vandalism and theft are usually considered nonviolent crimes and are considered as misdemeanors. The exception to this rule is when the property damaged or stolen has high value (in the United States if it exceeds $500), in which case it can be considered as a felony. In Singapore it is quite normal for the criminal courts to issue sentences of caning; this punishment is unheard of in the United States. Ironically, 19 U.S. states do permit corporal punishment to be used to "discipline" children and to be administered by parents and/or teachers. In Singapore this form of punishment may only be used on males. President Clinton considered Michael Fay's punishment so inappropriate that he interceded and appealed to the president of Singapore, who, out of deference to the U.S. president, reduced the number of strokes from six to four. The caning was carried out on May 5, 1994, and the rest of the sentence was completed after four months. In the United States, the typical forms of punishment for vandalism can include fines, probation, community service, restitution, and/or jail sentence.

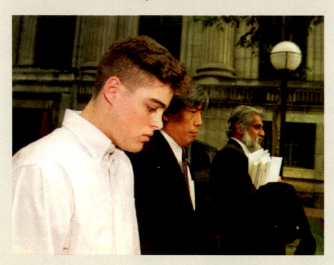

▲ **Michael Fay**

OBSERVE → INVESTIGATE → UNDERSTAND

- Should the Singapore court have taken into account that the offender had been socialized in a different culture? Explain.

- When living in a foreign country, should a guest from the United States be held to a higher standard? What are your reasons?

- Was it appropriate for the president of the United States to intervene? What might have been the consequences either way? What message did his intervention send to other Americans living in foreign countries?

SOURCES: "U.S. Student Tells of Pain of His Caning in Singapore," *New York Times*, June 26, 1994. http://www.nytimes.com/1994/06/26/us/us-student-tells-of-pain-of-his-caning-in-singapore.html (retrieved May 15, 2015); Alejandro Reyes, "Rough Justice: A Caning in Singapore Stirs Up a Fierce Debate about Crime and Punishment," *Asiaweek*, Hong Kong, May 25, 1994. http://www.corpun.com/awfay9405.htm (retrieved May 16, 2015); Valerie Strauss, "19 States Still Allow Corporal Punishment in School," *Washington Post*, September 18, 2014. http://www.washingtonpost.com/blogs/answer-sheet/wp/2014/09/18/19-states-still-allow-corporal-punishment-in-school/ (retrieved May 18, 2015).

NO SPITTING

▲ **Violating a Legal Norm**

Spitting in the subway is a crime that violates a formal regulation of the New York City Transit Authority.

waiting your turn in line to purchase tickets at a movie theater and not eating mashed potatoes with your fingers.

Formal social norms, also called *legal norms*, are formally written. Formal norms forbid theft and assault, for instance. Although not all deviance from norms constitutes a crime, the violation of formal norms, or *laws*, sets the criminal justice system in motion. In fact, informal social norms can evolve into legal norms. Because it is laws that determine what crimes are, we need to take a closer look at how these legal norms come about.

WHAT IS CRIME?

What constitutes crime? The answer is not as obvious as it may seem. Certainly, a crime is an act that breaks a law. But this description, though concise, does not help us understand the complexity of classifying criminal behavior. As we will see in this section, it is common to distinguish between two broad categories of crime: *mala in se* and *mala prohibita* crimes.

Can Crimes Be Inherently Wrong?

A crime is referred to as **mala in se** if it is categorized, as its Latin name suggests, as an "evil unto itself," a behavior that is morally wrong. This definition implies that a given behavior would be wrong in any context, even if there were no law against it. However, just as there is no such thing as an inherently deviant act, there is no such thing as an inherently criminal act. Society creates crime in the same way it creates deviance—by labeling specific behaviors as such.

Because no behavior is criminal until society makes it so, distinguishing a category of crime as *mala in se* can be confusing. We discuss this category of crime here because it is a term often used by researchers and practitioners in the field of criminal justice.

Traditionally, *mala in se* offenses are seen as a violation of a basic universal social value. On the surface, it may seem reasonable to identify an act such as forcible rape as violating some universal code of morality. But no universal social code of justice exists. For example, historically the victim of a sexual assault was not considered the woman herself but rather her husband, father, or brother. The "What about the Victim?" box illustrates that the definition of sexual assault crimes is influenced not only by time period but also by the understanding of the victim and the relationship to the perpetrator.

Crimes Prohibited by Law

Mala prohibita crimes, also known as **statutory crimes,** are acts that are criminal because they are prohibited by law. *Mala prohibita* crimes reflect public opinion at a particular moment in time. As standards of social tolerance change, so do the behaviors included in this category.

Laws against adultery provide a case in point. Historically, when a married person had consensual sexual relations with someone

What about the Victim?

"No Means No" . . . at Least in Some States

Depending upon the legal jurisdiction (that is, the legal authority whose laws are binding), the element of force is no longer necessary to be convicted of forcible rape. Two state jurisdictions have changed their rape laws in this regard. In January 2003, the California Supreme Court decided that 16-year-old John Z. raped 17-year-old Laura T. when, at a party in 2000, he continued to have sexual intercourse with her for 1 to 2 minutes over her objections. In fact, they had engaged in intercourse for approximately 10 minutes, during which time Laura repeatedly told him she had to go home while physically struggling to stop him. John's response was "to give [him] a minute." The court held that even though Laura initially consented to intercourse, John's failure to stop when she withdrew her consent—after penetration—constituted rape. By 2004, courts in eight states, including California, had extended the interpretation of their rape laws. No longer is the use of force, violence, or threat of harm to the victim required to convict for rape.

Illinois went a step further. After the John Z. decision, the state legislature passed the "No Means No" Act later in the same year. This legislation added a section to the Illinois rape statute that recognizes an individual's legal right to withdraw consent to intercourse at any point after giving that consent. This development made Illinois the first state to pass a law explicitly protecting the rights of women in this regard. As Matthew Lyon (2004) notes in his discussion of how definitions of rape are evolving over time, cases like that of John Z., legislative initiatives like that of Illinois, and media coverage of cases like the accusation of rape against basketball phenomenon Kobe Bryant are likely to prompt other state legislatures to consider similar statutes.

Other countries are also adopting various "no means no" laws. In Scotland and Australia, for example, similar legislation was passed in 2007. One illustration is a New South Wales case of an alleged rape where withdrawal of consent was at issue. In ruling for the victim, one of the judges noted, "The rights of modern women include the right to refuse to consent to sexual intercourse, at any time, and for any reason."

OBSERVE → INVESTIGATE → UNDERSTAND

- Although the California court rejected John Z.'s "primal urge" claim—that is, the idea that he just could not stop himself—what do you think about the argument that once a male has begun to have consensual intercourse, it is not reasonable to expect that he can "just stop"? What is a reasonable time for a partner to stop after a woman removes her consent?
- What if a woman is too drunk to give consent?

SOURCES: *People v. John Z.*, 60 P.3d 183, 184 (Cal. 2003); Matthew R. Lyon, "No Means No? Withdrawal of Consent during Intercourse and the Continuing Evolution of the Definition of Rape," *Journal of Criminal Law and Criminology* 95 (2004): 277–314.

mala in se
A behavior categorized as morally wrong ("evil in itself").

mala prohibita
A statutory crime that reflects public opinion at a moment in time.

statutory crime
An act that is criminal because it is prohibited by law.

consensus perspective
A view of crime that sees laws as the product of social agreement or consensus about what criminal behavior is.

conflict perspective
A view of crime as one outcome of a struggle among different groups competing for resources in their society.

outside the marriage, the punishment could be death. Under some laws today, such as strict Islamic law (known as *Shariah*), adulterers can still be executed. Although adultery remains illegal in many countries today, penalties are relatively minor and are rarely enforced. Currently in the United States more than 20 states have laws prohibiting adultery. While prosecutions are rare, legal penalties range from a $10 fine to life in prison.

What motivates a society to criminalize some behaviors and not others? Two predominant points of view about how crimes become defined capture the essence of this divergence: the consensus perspective and the conflict perspective.

Consensus and Conflict Perspectives

The **consensus perspective** of crime views laws as the product of social agreement or consensus about what criminal behavior is. According to this view, criminals are individuals whose behavior expresses values and beliefs at odds with those of mainstream society. For example, they rob banks while most of us work for a living. Laws, as the product of social consensus, promote solidarity: "We're all together on this." In this perspective, murder is a crime because it violates a consensus belief in the sanctity of life. We agree that killing is wrong, so we criminalize this act. Those who subscribe to the consensus perspective believe that defining some behaviors as criminal is necessary (or functional) because it is in everyone's interest to control those who deviate.

The **conflict perspective,** on the other hand, views the definition of crime as one outcome of a struggle among different groups competing for resources in society. The people who own and control society's resources (land, power, money) are able to influence those who determine what laws are passed. Rather than looking at individual wrongdoers to understand crime, the conflict perspective looks at the process that determines who is a criminal and who is not. It asks, for example, why we apply more law enforcement resources to the bank robber than to the stockbroker who steals millions of dollars through insider trading on Wall Street.

The conflict perspective holds that laws are influenced and created by those who control the political and economic power within the society. The unequal distribution of resources in society generates competition, and hence conflict, among the groups vying for power. The "Disconnects" box illustrates how powerful corporate interests may have aided, if not been largely responsible for, passage of laws prohibiting marijuana use. An overview of marijuana's long and complicated history reveals that nothing about the nature of the act itself makes marijuana use a crime. But whether laws against it are consensus or conflict based is a matter of debate. Let's consider both sides.

Is using marijuana illegal because society agrees it should be (consensus model)? The fact is that public views on the use of marijuana have changed over time. A Gallup Poll conducted in 2010 revealed 46 percent of Americans support the legalization of marijuana (and 70 percent support it for medical use). In contrast, only about 20 percent favored its legalization in the early 1970s.[2] Accordingly, and consistent with the position that consensus drives legislation, a number of states are introducing initiatives toward the decriminalization of marijuana use.

Alternatively, is marijuana use illegal because powerful interests are served by making it so (conflict model)? For example, it is conceivable that profits related to particular drugs produced by the pharmaceutical industry could be threatened by the legalization of marijuana use. A third possibility may be that marijuana laws are the result of both consensus and conflict—to varying degrees at different points in time.

DISConnects

Evolution of Marijuana Laws

The evolution of marijuana laws illustrates that laws are mere social constructions that change as we and our social landscape change.

In the United States from the mid-1800s until 1937, marijuana was largely a medicinal drug legally available by prescription. Few knew it as a recreational drug beyond people living in the Mexican American communities close to the Mexican border. But growing anti-Mexican sentiment in various regions of the country spread fears of Mexicans' bringing their "loco weed" into the United States and fueled the call for marijuana prohibition. Legislation proposed to control marijuana use cited its alleged harmful effects and reflected the views of authorities like the commissioner of the Federal Bureau of Narcotics, Harry Anslinger, who testified before Congress that "marijuana is an addictive drug that produces in its users insanity, criminality, and death." Such claims made it appear that marijuana laws would be for the good of the whole society—reflecting a consensus view. Remarkably, however, the American Medical Association went on record in those same 1937 congressional hearings to note that there was no medical evidence to support the contention that the drug was harmful. It is unlikely the medical profession would offer the same testimony today. For example, the National Institute on Drug Abuse links long-term marijuana use to addiction and symptoms of serious mental disorder, and there is research documenting the carcinogenic properties of marijuana smoke. Such research is only likely to increase as more states decriminalize marijuana use for medicinal or recreational purposes.

But back in 1937, a conflict view was at work as well. Powerful corporate interests joined the crusade against marijuana when they recognized that hemp—the source plant for the drug—could be used to make textiles and paper, thereby posing a threat to already established U.S. industries. Fears of the economic potential of the hemp plant—not its psychoactive properties—largely stimulated calls for passage of the Marijuana Tax Act of 1937. Under this law, anyone who imported, distributed, or sold marijuana was required to register with the Internal Revenue Service and to pay a prohibitive tax. Although the act did not outlaw marijuana, it sought to severely curtail its use. Similarly, opposition to the legalization of marijuana for medicinal and/or recreational use today has been alleged to come from, among other sources, the pharmaceutical industry and alcohol companies—both of which stand to lose profit if marijuana is accepted as an alternative to existing products.

Public support for decriminalizing marijuana use has been increasing since the 1990s. A 2012 poll found a majority of U.S. voters (51 percent versus 44 percent) agree with the legalization of marijuana for recreational use, and it is legal for medicinal purposes in at least 20 states. And while its use—recreational or otherwise—continues to be prohibited under federal law, individual states are making moves toward decriminalization. In 2012, Colorado and Washington became the first states to legalize and regulate the possession of an ounce or less of marijuana by adults over 21. Alaska, Oregon, and the District of Columbia have passed similar legislation. It remains to be seen whether the federal government will enforce federal law in these jurisdictions.

"...A MAJOR INFLUENCE IN FORMING THE ATTITUDES THAT LED TO THE PRESENT LEGAL SITUATION REGARDING MARIJUANA... HILARIOUS WHEN VIEWED FROM THE OTHER SIDE OF THE GENERATION GAP, A GAP THIS FILM DID SO MUCH TO CREATE..."

THE NATIONAL ORGANIZATION FOR THE REFORM OF MARIJUANA LAWS presents

MARIJUANA
WEED FROM THE DEVIL'S GARDEN!

One MOMENT of BLISS — A LIFETIME of REGRET!

HUNTING A THRILL, THEY INHALED A DRAG OF CONCENTRATED SIN!

"Reefer" MADNESS

A 1936 CLASSIC

A NORML FILM

WAKE UP AMERICA! HERE'S A ROADSIDE WEED THAT'S FAST BECOMING A NATIONAL HIGH-WAY!

OBSERVE → INVESTIGATE → UNDERSTAND

- In what ways have the laws against marijuana reflected a consensus perspective? In what ways have they represented a conflict perspective?
- What might make the campaign against marijuana different from campaigns against other recreational drugs, such as cocaine?
- Do you think a tax is a better way to control marijuana use than a law against it? State your reasons.

SOURCES: John Galliher, David Keys, and Michael Elsner, "Lindesmith v. Anslinger: An Early Government Victory in the Failed War on Drugs," Journal of Criminal Law and Criminology 88 (Winter 1988): 66; Richard Bonnie and Charles Whitehead, The Marijuana Conviction: A History of Marijuana Prohibition in the United States (New York: Lindesmith Center, 1999); National Institute on Drug Abuse, "NIDA InfoFacts: Marijuana," revised November 2010, National Institute on Drug Abuse, Bethesda, MD. http://drugabuse.gov/PDF/InfoFacts/Marijuana.pdf (retrieved December 18, 2010); Quinnipiac University Poll, "American Voters Back Legalized Marijuana, Quinnipiac University National Poll Finds; Voters Split on Gay Marriage, but Catholics Back It," December 5, 2012. http://www.quinnipiac.edu/institutes-centers/polling-institute/national/release-detail/?ReleaseID=1820.

The conflict perspective is well illustrated in the case of vagrancy laws in England.[3] Vagrancy laws were passed in the fourteenth century to prevent peasants from leaving the employ of wealthy landowners to seek independent work in neighboring towns. Because it took time to develop a trade and become established in the towns, peasants who wandered would, at least initially, lack any apparent means of support. Laws defining unemployed wanderers as vagrants targeted those peasants. Given the choice of being imprisoned for vagrancy or returning to the landowners, many returned to work the land.

Vagrancy laws served the interest of the wealthy by preserving the status quo and their position of power and privilege. Such laws could also, however, be seen as a protection for society because the wandering unemployed would eventually have to commit crimes to support themselves.

Using the evolution of vagrancy laws as a model can help us understand many of today's laws in the United States. Most of our laws and the resources of the criminal justice system focus on "crime in the streets" at the expense of attention to corporate crime and government corruption, the "crime in the suites" that costs society billions of dollars each year. Like the wealthy landowners of feudal England, today's large corporations get their interests translated into laws. Those who come to be identified as criminals are often, like the peasants of medieval society, those who lack power and wealth.

The basis for a particular law also may change over time. For example, we could argue that laws against theft were initially consistent with the conflict model because the will of the more powerful "haves" dictated the passage of laws against theft to protect their own property. The "have-nots" had less in the way of material goods and tended to be the ones identified as criminals. With the passage of time and a decrease in the previously massive disparity in economic well-being, however, most people came to a consensus about laws against theft.

THE CONSEQUENCES OF CRIME

The consequences of crime—for victims and perpetrators alike—are numerous and varied. Some are obvious and can be readily measured. For example, the victim of an assault suffers a broken nose that requires surgery, and she loses two weeks of work as a result. The convicted offender spends five years in prison. Other consequences are indirect and more difficult to assess. How, for instance, do we measure the fear that accompanies the victim every time she walks alone to her car? How do we measure what is lost by spending years in prison? The criminal justice system is society's formal response to criminal behavior. But, of course, not all offenders are caught and convicted, and the effects of victimization can extend far beyond the legal arena.

Sanctions

sanctions
Prescribed consequences intended to reinforce people's conformity to norms.

There is no sense in having rules if there are no consequences for those who break them. **Sanctions** are prescribed consequences intended to reinforce people's conformity to norms; they can be positive (rewarding) or negative (punishing). Although we are well acquainted with the rationale behind punishing bad behavior, we tend not to associate the term *sanction* with rewards for good behavior. In fact, positive sanctions can be just as effective—if not more so—than negative sanctions in shaping people's behavior. Rewarding an ex-convict's efforts to learn to read and write, for example, may prove more effective in changing his criminal ways than sending him to jail a second time.

Sanctions can be formal or informal. For example, someone who behaves badly in public is likely to be met with disapproving glances, an informal response designed to encourage the deviant to cease and desist. Even though informal sanctions generally do not carry the weight of their formal counterparts, they can have a major impact on behavior.

Our criminal justice system delivers a range of formal negative sanctions in response to criminal behavior. If the crime is relatively minor–say, driving 10 miles per hour over the speed limit–the offender may be given a fine. A criminal infraction of a more serious nature–say, vandalizing a park–is likely to be sanctioned by a harsher penalty such as probation, which restricts personal freedom by requiring regular meetings with a probation officer and avoidance of drugs, alcohol, and other people on probation. For more serious crimes, such as robbery and assault, the court may set a term of incarceration. Prison inmates are removed from society and deprived of their liberty. For the most serious crimes, in 35 states the offender can be executed.[4]

We have considered the formal and informal sanctions that offenders face as consequences of their criminal behavior. As would be expected, victims also suffer consequences from criminal behavior; however, often these consequences are not as well understood given our criminal justice system's focus on offenders.

Impact of Crime on Victims

Victims are the targets of illegal actions by others. As a result, victims suffer physical, sexual, or emotional harm, death, or a combination of these injuries.

More often than not, criminals and their victims are of the same race and in the same age range, live in the same neighborhood, belong to the same socioeconomic strata, and–with the important exception of rapists and most of their victims–are the same sex. Victims tend to occupy the same social space as do offenders. Would-be criminals notice the victims' vulnerabilities, seize the opportunity, and commit a crime.[5]

Victims are often neglected and even abused by the criminal justice system, and this reality makes their suffering significantly worse. Some become fearful and less willing to cooperate with the prosecution. It is normal to want to avoid fear and pain. That is why many victims choose not to report their crime, not to cooperate with criminal justice officials, and not to serve as key witnesses.

The plight of victims gave rise to the victim rights' movement (see Chapter 14). This movement began to have an effect on the criminal justice system, initiating reforms in the early 1970s. As a result, victims are now being treated better and can receive compensation for their injuries and losses. Furthermore, most suffer fewer hardships and recover more quickly from monetary losses. However, much remains to be done before all victims are treated with the respect, dignity, and care they deserve.

THE STRUCTURE OF THE CRIMINAL JUSTICE SYSTEM

The **criminal justice system,** our focus in this section, comprises the wide array of actors and agencies at the local, state, and federal levels of government that deal with the problem of crime. The term *criminal justice system* denotes the process by which adult offenders are handled, while *juvenile justice system* (see Chapter 15) refers to the process for those under 18. The major institutional components of the traditional criminal justice system include law enforcement, the judiciary, and corrections. These components are interdependent in that decisions made in one component often affect decisions made in others.

A contemporary view of the system also considers victim services as an emerging element of the system because of the collaborative effort to incorporate victim services into law enforcement agencies, the courts, and corrections

criminal justice system
The interdependent actors and agencies—law enforcement agencies, the courts, the correctional system, and victim services—at the local, state, and federal levels of government that deal with the problem of crime.

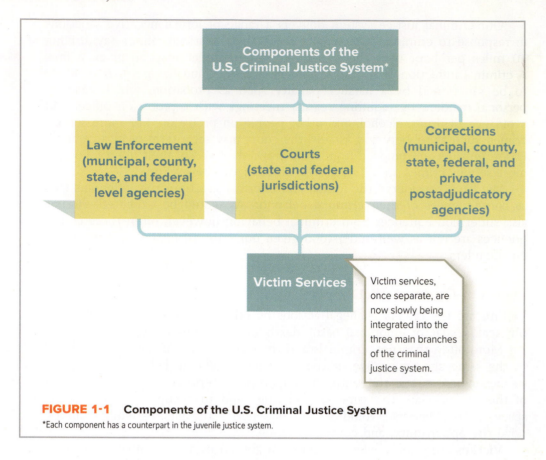

FIGURE 1-1   **Components of the U.S. Criminal Justice System**
*Each component has a counterpart in the juvenile justice system.

(Figure 1-1). Generally, we think of law enforcement as starting the process of the administration of justice, the courts as deciding guilt and punishment, and correctional agencies as carrying out that punishment. Victim services, although not traditionally considered a major branch of the criminal justice system, is an important determinant of whether justice is served.

The U.S. criminal justice system is the sum of all these parts and more. Because of its size and complexity, communication among the parts is not always efficient. In addition, like a chain whose strength is determined by its weakest link, the criminal justice system depends for its success on the effectiveness and integrity of each component. In the "Matters of Ethics" box, we see the extent to which unethical behavior on the part of one individual working in a crime lab ultimately compromised justice in thousands of criminal cases.

▼ **School Resource Officer with Elementary School Students**

School resource officers bring awareness of crime and the law into the classroom.

Law Enforcement

The part of the criminal justice system familiar to most U.S. citizens is law enforcement. From childhood, we can identify a police officer and an officer's car and understand the basic functions of the police–to protect the community and arrest criminals.

But realistically, the police are called upon to do far more than protect and arrest. They are dispatched to deal with a host of matters ranging from the mundane (checking on the security of a home while the owner is traveling; writing a traffic ticket), to the bizarre (finding

Matters *of* Ethics

Lies That Convicted the Innocent

For justice to be served, judges and juries must trust in the integrity of both expert witness testimony and physical evidence in considering whether there is reasonable doubt that a suspect committed the crime. Major doubts about that integrity fell upon the Boston area in the fall of 2012.

In late August 2012, it was revealed that a chemist in the Massachusetts state crime lab, Annie Dookhan, had mishandled drug evidence and failed to follow required procedures. Governor Deval Patrick ordered the lab closed, and the extent of the damage began to be revealed. Dookhan had been considered the lab's "Superwoman," testing drug evidence at much higher rates than her colleagues. But her rates were so high that eventually some colleagues grew suspicious. Dookhan ultimately admitted to investigators that she had been negligent in the processing of evidence in some cases and had outright faked results in others.

Dookhan had worked at the lab for a decade and told investigators she had been compromising evidence "for about the last two or three years." Specifically, she admitted to documenting samples as narcotics based on their appearance rather than actually testing them; she estimated she had tested only about 5 of every 25 samples. The investigation also included a review of Dookhan's e-mail correspondence with prosecutors, in which she revealed an eagerness to cooperate and gratification at being able to help win convictions. To support her qualifications as an expert witness, she also claimed to have a master's degree that she did not have.

In November 2013, Dookhan was found guilty of tampering with evidence and obstructing justice. The final costs of her behavior will be immense. Governor Patrick has asked for $30 million to fund a review of her cases, and several county district attorneys have requested a further $12 million. As many as 60,000 cases may need to be reviewed, more than half of which may be overturned, and untold numbers of convicted drug defendants may have their convictions voided. By January 2013, in fact, 187 defendants had been released (with 15 later rearrested).

Troubling ethical questions have arisen regarding oversight of the lab. Many ask how a chemist could have tampered with so many cases without raising red flags. Colleagues had notified supervisors of their concerns, but those concerns were not acted upon. Ultimate responsibility for the state's crime labs lay with the public health commissioner, who resigned as a result of the scandal. Several supervisors were also disciplined or fired.

Dookhan's ethics are also puzzling. Why did she do it? Why would a biochemist with a seemingly great career taint evidence and lie about her credentials? The only answers appear to center around her desire to be a "helpful" employee and her commitment to convicting people the police had arrested.

OBSERVE → INVESTIGATE → UNDERSTAND

- How can trust in the criminal justice system be restored after a scandal like this?
- What kind of oversight should be employed in crime labs?
- What guidelines should be in place to verify expert witnesses?

SOURCES: Brian Ballou and Andrea Estes, "Chemist Admitted Wrongdoing in Lab Scandal," *Boston Globe*, September 26, 2012; Andrea Estes, "Indicted Drug Analyst Annie Dookhan's E-mails Reveal Close Personal Ties to Prosecutors," *Boston Globe*, December 20, 2012.

---

ghosts in a home), to the most serious (homicide)—and nearly any imaginable incident in between. Law enforcement officers are expected to resolve many of society's problems and are entrusted to use force only when necessary. Ideally, they make decisions quickly, use discretion, show courage and sacrifice in the face of danger, and treat individuals with dignity and respect even when threatened, harassed, abused, or assaulted.[6]

In recent years, police responsibilities have moved into the educational setting as school resource officers and educators raise awareness about crime, drugs, and prevention. Community-based initiatives have tried to foster a more collaborative relationship between police and citizens to address crime control and prevention.[7]

The Courts

The United States has a dual court system made up of **state courts** and **federal courts.** As their names suggest, crimes against state laws are prosecuted in state courts, and crimes violating federal statutes are prosecuted in the federal court. State courts differ from state to state, but all have trial courts and **appellate courts,** where cases can be appealed. The federal system consists of district courts (comparable to the state trial courts), appellate courts or circuit courts where appeals are heard, and the U.S. Supreme Court (see Chapter 9).

Within each of these settings, a prosecutor first decides whether to prosecute a case. If the prosecutor chooses to move forward, he or she presents

state courts
The system in which state crimes are prosecuted; it includes both trial and appellate courts.

federal courts
The system in which federal crimes are prosecuted consisting of district courts, appellate courts or circuit courts, and the U.S. Supreme Court.

appellate courts
Courts that hear appeals from trial courts or other lower courts.

▲ **Demonstration for Victims' Rights**

The victims' rights movement began in the 1970s and pushed for more involvement of the victim in the criminal justice process.

corrections
The systematic, organized effort by society to punish offenders, protect the public, and change an offender's behavior.

alternative sentence
A sentence that is served in a treatment facility or in community service.

probation
An alternative to jail or prison in which the offender remains in the community under court supervision, usually within the caseload of a probation officer.

parole
An early release from prison conditional on complying with certain standards while free.

the case against the defendant on behalf of the state or federal government. A grand jury decides whether a case should go to trial. The prosecutor is then responsible for arguing that case at trial. Defense attorneys, hired by a client or assigned by the court, protect the legal rights of the defendant. If the case goes to trial, the defendant is entitled to fair and proper procedures. Finally, judges are the arbiters in the courtroom and are responsible for ensuring that the rules of evidence and law are not violated. They also provide a jury with instructions for rendering a verdict or decision about the case.

Corrections

Corrections is the systematic, organized effort by society to punish offenders, protect the public, and change an offender's behavior. These efforts are realized through programs, services, and facilities that deal with the offender before and after conviction. The purpose of corrections is to achieve the goals of sentencing, which include retribution, deterrence, incapacitation, rehabilitation, (re)integration, and restitution (see Chapter 11).

Once convicted of a crime, offenders may be imprisoned or serve their sentences under supervision within the community while on probation. An offender also may be given an **alternative sentence** that can be served in a treatment facility or carried out in the form of community service. **Probation** is an alternative to jail or prison in which the offender remains in the community under court supervision, usually within the caseload of a probation officer. Offenders who have been sent to prison can be freed on **parole,** an early release based on their compliance with certain standards while free. A parole officer supervises the offender, who can be sent back to prison if he or she violates the terms or conditions of the parole (see Chapter 13).

When most people think of corrections and the corrections system, they think of the prison system (see Chapter 12). The general practice of using imprisonment as punishment for crime is less than two centuries old. The Bureau of Justice Statistics of the U.S. Department of Justice reported that as of year-end 2014, 2.3 million adults were held in federal or state prisons or in local jails. This figure also includes the number of individuals on probation and parole, making the total number of people under correctional supervision as of year-end 2014 almost 6.9 million.[8]

Victim Services

Until the late twentieth century, the U.S. criminal justice system focused primarily on the criminal rather than the victim. Since the 1970s, under pressure from the law-and-order movement, the civil rights movement, the women's movement, and other victim-oriented coalitions, the pendulum began to swing the other way. The promotion of victims' rights to participate in criminal proceedings and to enjoy personal safety contributed to the formation of an array of **victim services** inside and outside the criminal justice system, including shelters and transitional housing programs, counseling services, and 24-hour hotlines.[9] Victim services were an integral part of the victims' rights movement that began in the mid-1970s; another dimension of these rights was greater involvement of the victim in the criminal justice process.

Other services focus on the victim's legal needs, including the appointment of a **victim advocate** to assist the victim with every aspect of the postvictimization period, from the initial crisis and investigation through case adjudication and ultimately to the offender's release. Two important goals of victim services are to lessen victims' suffering and to facilitate their recovery.

Today, victim advocates work in government and nongovernment organizations and in all sectors of the criminal justice system. Some are employed in victim/witness units within district attorneys' offices, others are in probation departments, and still others are part of special units in police departments or within correctional institutions.[10] When a victim is also a family member of the offender, legal services are available to assist with divorce and custody concerns, supervised visitation requests, orders of protection (such as restraining and/or harassment orders), and mediation. The latter is used to help disputing parties work with a court-appointed mediator to ensure that a mutual agreement is reached on a specific issue such as child custody.[11]

Victim services may also include helping victims apply for victim compensation and write **victim impact statements** about how their victimization affected them. These statements are generally read in open court prior to sentencing (in a process called *elocution*) and at probation and parole hearings. In other cases, victim advocates work with **secondary victims** and/or witnesses to help them cope with the victimization of a loved one. Victim services also include removing a dependent individual from a violent environment and conducting site visits at the new location, assisting victims to obtain a job, and a host of other activities to ensure that victims are able to live a life free of the violence they once experienced.[12]

RealCrimeTech

AMBER ALERT SYSTEM

The U.S. Department of Justice created the Amber Alert program to foster partnerships among law enforcement agencies, transportation agencies, and broadcast and wireless companies. The goal of the program is to return missing children to their caregivers by widely broadcasting information that would help recover the children. Information such as a description of the suspect's car can be scrolled across electronic highway signs and television screens. As of December 2015, the Amber Alert system has contributed to the rescue and return of 794 children.

SOURCE: U.S. Department of Justice, Office of Justice Programs, "Amber Alert." www.amberalert.gov/index.htm (retrieved February 16, 2016).

HOW CRIMINAL JUSTICE WORKS: THE REALITIES

There are various explanations for—and debates about—how the criminal justice system works in reality. These explanations complement debates about how it *should work*—that is, the theoretical ideal. This section surveys some of the explanations and debates regarding how the system works in practice and how it should work in theory.

victim services
A range of resources—such as shelters, transitional housing, counseling, and 24-hour hotlines—aimed at reducing the suffering and facilitating the recovery of victims, especially those who participate in the criminal justice process.

victim advocate
A professional who assists the victim during the postvictimization period.

victim impact statement
A victim's written statement, usually in the Presentence Report, about how the experience with crime affected him or her. Sometimes judges ask victims to read this statement in open court prior to sentencing.

secondary victims
Family and friends of an individual who has been victimized.

The Criminal Justice Funnel and the Wedding Cake Model

The result of decisions by criminal justice professionals, suspects, and others creates what is often referred to as the *criminal justice funnel*. The process begins as a large number of people are arrested, many fewer of whom, through a process of filtering, ultimately go to trial or are sentenced. Think about it: If every case were to go to trial, the criminal justice system would collapse from the overload. There has to be a filtering of cases. All criminal justice professionals have a high level of discretion and can filter out cases along the way.

For example, a police officer can decide not to arrest a particular individual who has committed a crime. A prosecutor can decide not to charge someone whom the police arrested. A judge can dismiss a case. When any of those decisions are made, the suspect drops out of the criminal justice process. A guilty plea by a suspect keeps the offender within the system but also eliminates the need for a trial.

A variety of factors influence criminal justice professionals' decisions regarding whether a defendant should enter and proceed through the system. One significant consideration, of course, is the quality of the evidence. If, for example, an officer gets a statement from a witness who then retracts that statement, the prosecutor might be left with insufficient evidence, so she chooses to drop the charges. Another factor is the resources–both time and money–that are needed to take a case to trial. Frequently those expenses are judged to be too great given that a suspect often will agree to plead guilty in exchange for a reduced sentence. From the perspective of professionals in the system, justice can be obtained without a trial outcome. Of course, the system cannot do its work if crimes are not reported, as occurs 50 percent of the time. These are just a few examples of the many reasons why in 1,000 crimes committed, only 25 people are convicted (Figure 1-2).

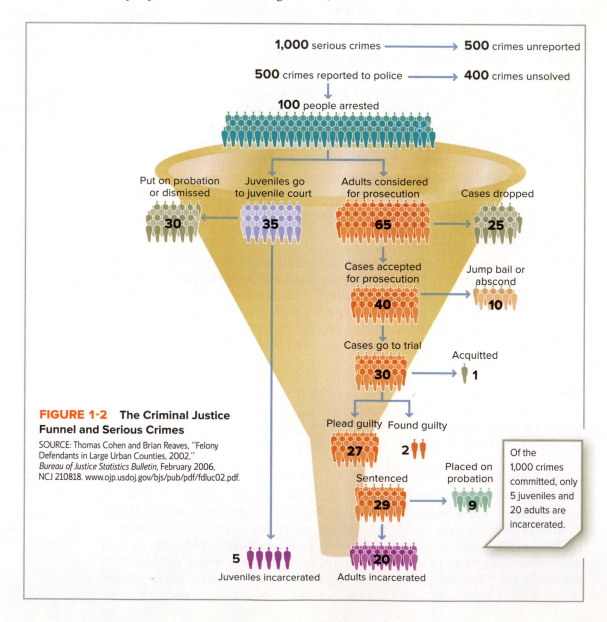

FIGURE 1-2 **The Criminal Justice Funnel and Serious Crimes**

SOURCE: Thomas Cohen and Brian Reaves, "Felony Defendants in Large Urban Counties, 2002," *Bureau of Justice Statistics Bulletin*, February 2006, NCJ 210818. www.ojp.usdoj.gov/bjs/pub/pdf/fdluc02.pdf.

Some scholars and practitioners use the **wedding cake model** to help explain why some cases make it through the funnel and some do not. Figure 1-3 depicts the four different layers of the criminal justice wedding cake. The vast majority of cases, about 90 percent, are contained within the base of the cake, Layer 4. These offenses are largely misdemeanor and infraction cases. *Misdemeanor cases* are those that can result in a sentence of one year of incarceration or less, probation, or other alternative sentences. *Infractions* are even more minor offenses, such as traffic violations. These cases are generally considered not serious or worth much of the system's time. The focus in this layer is to minimize the amount of resources expended on these cases. To that end, there is a very high level of guilty pleas in exchange for lenient treatment.

The next three layers account for the other 10 percent of cases. Layer 3 includes *felony* cases of a less serious nature (such as car theft) or ones in which the defendant has not previously had trouble with the law. These cases are also dispatched rather quickly. The system starts slowing down with Layer 2. This tier includes serious felonies. Here you would find murder cases, defendants with many prior offenses, and cases that include victims who were strangers to their perpetrators. The criminal justice system regards all of these situations as serious, and they are more likely to result in trials than the cases in either Layer 4 or 3.

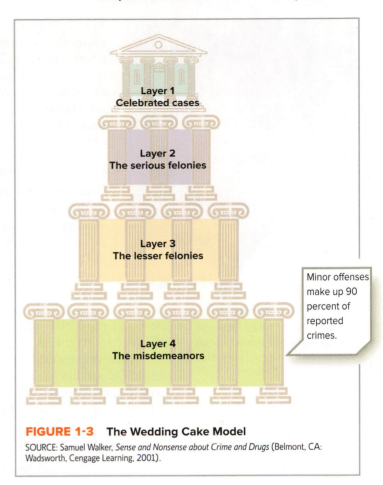

Minor offenses make up 90 percent of reported crimes.

FIGURE 1-3   The Wedding Cake Model

SOURCE: Samuel Walker, *Sense and Nonsense about Crime and Drugs* (Belmont, CA: Wadsworth, Cengage Learning, 2001).

wedding cake model
An explanation of the workings of the criminal justice system that shows how cases get filtered according to the seriousness of the offense.

The top of the cake, Layer 1, includes the very few cases that are considered celebrated cases, such as serial killings. They garner the most media attention. They may or may not involve celebrities, but the defendant in the case generally becomes a household name. These cases almost always involve a long trial, unless the defendant strikes a plea bargain. For example, Gary Ridgway, known as the Green River Killer, spared himself the risk of the death penalty by pleading guilty to killing 48 women in Washington State. Law enforcement believes he killed many more women, and Ridgway himself claims to have killed 90 or more.

The wedding cake model reminds us that most cases do not get the attention or resources spent on them that the high-profile cases do. The system does not work as TV shows like *Law & Order* would have us believe. Justice is usually not swift, and some observers worry that it is not deliberate enough. People who see the criminal justice system that way categorize the process as an assembly line with little consideration for the unique characteristics of a case. Criminal justice professionals defend their actions by arguing that the system cannot handle a thorough deliberation of all the cases.

Now that we have examined how the criminal justice system works in practice, we focus next on a key recurring point in discourse about the system—the idea of preventing crime from occurring altogether. A frequent topic of discussion, many people view crime prevention as the "elephant in the room" because they believe that crime springs from societal conditions and that the criminal justice system is incapable of effectively handling the problem. In the absence of a "vaccination" to address criminality at its

▲ **Serial Killer Gary Ridgway**

Ridgway was convicted and sentenced to life for killing more than 40 women. *Should Ridgway have been allowed to plead guilty to avoid execution?*

crime prevention
Measures taken to reduce the opportunity for crime commission by individuals predisposed to such.

crime control model
A model of the criminal justice system that emphasizes the efficient arrest and processing of alleged criminal offenders.

due process model
A model of the criminal justice system that emphasizes individual rights at all stages of the justice process.

roots, preventive actions have been relegated in large part to the system's vanguard component: law enforcement. Two additional points of discussion–or, rather, debates–ensue after prevention measures have proved ineffective. These are centered on two models of how the system should process individuals who come within its purview. These models–crime control and due process–represent distinct value systems that compete for priority in a democratic society.[14]

Crime Prevention

Crime prevention rests on the notion that it is better to take measures to prevent crime than to respond to crime after its occurrence.[15] Preventing crime has been a central element of modern law enforcement's mission, and these efforts are mostly focused on high-crime activity–for example, hot spots policing (the concentration of policing on crime clusters);[16] target hardening, as through neighborhood crime prevention and environmental design (the elimination of physical conditions conducive to crime);[17] police–public partnerships such as community policing; potential offenders, as with general and specific deterrence; and offender intervention programs.

Crime prevention also has significant applications to victimization. From the results of studies of repeat victimization[18] and victim vulnerabilities,[19] crime prevention resources can be delivered to individuals lacking such protections, especially those whose behaviors, personal conditions, and lifestyles increase their risk for victimization–for example, young children, young adults, marginalized individuals such as the homeless and ex-offenders, and people with a disability.[20]

The Crime Control Model

The **crime control model** emphasizes the efficient arrest and processing of alleged criminal offenders. The value system underlying this model considers the repression of criminal conduct as the most important function of criminal justice. In other words, what matters most is to reduce, quickly respond to, and punish criminal behavior. According to this model, the failure to bring criminal conduct under control leads to the breakdown of public order, a vital condition of human freedom. Because the crime control model emphasizes quick conviction and sentencing, advocates resist strong procedural protections that others would say help society ensure that only the guilty are punished.

As you will see in many parts of this book, the crime control model has dominated the public debate over how the criminal justice system should work since the 1980s. It has led to a tough-on-crime stance that doubts whether perpetrators can be rehabilitated and stresses that offenders have historically been treated too leniently by the criminal justice system. Proponents of the crime control model are satisfied with assembly-line justice because it speeds up the justice system and treats similar offenses and offenders in a consistent way. They worry more about criminal threats to people's safety than about the constitutional protections of suspects.

The Due Process Model

The **due process model** emphasizes individual rights at all stages of the justice process. This model is more concerned with the threat to procedural rights of the offenders than with the general public's right to be free of crime. Advocates of the due process model argue that it is better to let guilty people go free than to convict the innocent.

Due process is the term used in the Constitution to describe procedural protections for the accused. Under the due process model, the police would recognize all the constitutional rights guaranteed to persons suspected of criminal conduct. Prosecutors and judicial authorities would actively support the same constitutional provisions before, during, and after any criminal proceeding. If the crime control model is more akin to an assembly line, then the due process model looks more like a maze with a variety of barriers to ensure that those punished are truly guilty.

The due process model likely reached its height in the 1960s when the U.S. Supreme Court was extending constitutional due process requirements to local and state criminal justice agents as well as federal ones. The law enforcement requirement to notify suspects of their rights, first introduced in 1966 in the famous case of *Miranda v. Arizona*, is consistent with the values of the due process model.

Although these two models seem to work as a dichotomy—one on each end of a value continuum—values of both models are at work in the criminal justice system today. In fact, the continued debate between these two positions helps us to evaluate from day to day how we want our criminal justice system to work.

INFLUENCES ON CRIMINAL JUSTICE

In an ideal society, the criminal justice system protects, defends, and upholds laws in an equitable way for all citizens. In the real world, however, people bring genuine fears and prejudices to the courtroom, the media can stoke those fears and prejudices, and lawmakers hold the purse strings to criminal justice initiatives. Thus, the criminal justice system does not operate in isolation; it is subject to many outside influences that can change the course of justice, either intentionally or unintentionally.

MYTH/REALITY

MYTH: People fear strangers as being very likely to victimize them.

REALITY: Individuals are more likely to be victimized by someone they know.[21]

Fear of Crime

In general, U.S. residents believe there is much more crime than there actually is, and their fears are often misplaced. For example, women are consistently told that they should not walk alone at night and should fear male strangers. Being cautious about one's surroundings is wise, but the truth is that women are much more likely to be harmed by someone they know than by a stranger. It is uncomfortable to think about, but given the statistics on women's victimization, women should fear the men they know more than the men they do not know.[22] Still, 50 percent of women, but only 22 percent of men, say they are afraid to walk alone at night.[23] Fear of crime, specifically of crimes by strangers, influences where and when women are comfortable in public spaces and how they behave in those spaces. In other words, fear of stranger crime works to control women's choices.[24]

One measure of our fear of crime is the Gallup survey's question "Is there any area near where you live—that is, within a mile—where you would be afraid to walk alone at night?" In October 2010, 37 percent responded yes.[25] That response was down from the 1982 high of 48 percent and may reflect a significant reduction in crime during that time period. Specifically, in 1982 there were 50.7 violent crime victims per 1,000 U.S. residents, whereas in 2009 there were only 16.9 violent crime victims per 1,000 people.[26] That reality is clearly not reflected in people's *perception* of crime, however; consider that in October 2010, 66 percent of U.S. residents thought that crime had *increased* since 2009.[27] Sixty percent of Americans said they believed that the nation's crime problem today was either "extremely serious" or "serious."

Various factors can affect the level of fear we experience about crime generally, including our gender, age, past experiences with crime, ethnicity, income, educational attainment, and the area in which we live. Criminologists point out that some of the most fearful groups are those less likely to be victimized.[28] For example, older people and women tend to have higher levels of fear than do young men, yet as a group young men are most likely to be victims of crime.[29] Women may have a greater fear of crime than men because their fear of sexual assault generalizes into an overall fear of crime.[30] Older people may be influenced in their fears by media exaggerations of crime in the streets, attention given to elder fraud and nursing home abuse, and heightened feelings of vulnerabilities that come with advanced age.[31]

Those who have experienced crime typically have elevated fears of crime. Victims of robbery tend to have high levels of fear afterward due to the sudden, unexpected, and personal nature of the crime. Victims of burglary likewise

Real Careers

RACHEL DREIFUS

Work location: Redmond, WA

College(s): Bellevue College

Major(s): Criminal Justice (AA)

Job title: Assistant Investigator, Securitas Security Services USA

Salary range for jobs like this: $40,000–$48,000

Time in job: 5 years

Work Responsibilities

Securitas Security is a vendor company contracted by Microsoft Corporation to provide investigative services. My job consists of reviewing and investigating cases requiring follow-up, such as ones involving theft, threats of violence, and assault. I am assigned between 5 and 25 cases per month, and I manage them by interviewing witnesses, communicating with police departments, and maintaining physical evidence in our secure climate-controlled evidence room. Some of the tools that make my investigations possible are video cameras, audio recorders, phone logs, and covert cameras that are as small as a pin! Every day I make sure all of my case notes are recorded in our database, which can be accessed by other Securitas Security investigators.

Why Criminal Justice?

I returned to college as an adult after having spent five years raising my children. When my youngest daughter became old enough to enter kindergarten, I decided to pursue the career that I always wanted: U.S. marshal. After researching the qualifications to enter the U.S. Marshals Service, I found that an AA in criminal justice along with at least three years in private security was recommended. Although at times it has been a juggling act to balance family, work, and school, my classes were a purely rewarding experience. I am now proficient in all aspects of investigations, including gathering data, collecting evidence, analyzing crime scenes, and interviewing subjects. After five enjoyable years in corporate security, I no longer plan to pursue employment as a U.S. marshal. My current job allows me to practice criminal justice without the dangers associated with police investigations.

Expectations and Realities of the Job

The realities of the job are a little bit different than I originally expected. First, I thought my deadlines would be more long term, but as it turns out, I am challenged on a daily basis to meet business objectives, such as resolving a certain number of cases and following through with a report to our legal department. After five years on the job, I have never gotten tired of what I do. I make my work more interesting and rewarding by striving to go above and beyond my supervisors' expectations.

My Advice to Students

Textbooks provide the knowledge you need for your job, but they cannot prepare you for the emotional aspects of starting a new job, particularly the nervousness. Taking responsibility for managing cases and any mistakes that might happen during the investigation put a lot of pressure on me. By speaking with experienced colleagues, I learned that these feelings are normal. Remind yourself that your employer thinks you are qualified for the job. After a few months of getting settled, your confidence will grow.

tend to become more fearful due to the invasion of their home and the loss of significant money or property.[32]

A moderate level of fear might serve citizens in a positive way by generating caution, a factor that makes them less vulnerable to victimization. Some people might purchase alarms or security systems designed to keep them safe. Some might avoid situations they perceive as dangerous. Locking an automobile or a home is a prudent action. However, when the public's unreasonable or unwarranted fear of crime influences public policy, it results in crime policies that are based on irrational conclusions rather than sound reasons. The fear of crime also can have a major economic and social impact on society. How we spend money, go out to dinner, buy our houses, shop, travel, and spend our leisure time can all be affected by our fear of crime.

▲ **Graffiti-Tagged Shops**
Some people may regard a neighborhood with defaced storefronts as a sign that the area is unsafe.

moral panic
The reaction by a group of people based on exaggerated or false perceptions about crime and criminal behavior.

Media Coverage

Media coverage of crime inflates individuals' levels of fear. It produces a **moral panic,** a group reaction based on exaggerated or false perceptions about crime and criminal behavior. Individuals who watch local television news are more likely to be fearful of crime than those who watch national television news, listen to radio news, or access their news from the Internet.[33] The old adage "If it bleeds, it leads" appears to be especially true for local television news. Sensational media reports fuel fear of crime and result in support for the death penalty and handgun ownership, indicating that media coverage of crime can affect people's policy positions.[34]

Most criminal behaviors are not crimes against persons and are nonconfrontational. However, media reports focus heavily on violent crime. For example, homicides make up more than one-fourth of the crime stories reported on the evening news, but murder is actually a very rare event.[35] Further, in 2008 the incidence of violent crime in the United States was 454 per 100,000 population, as contrasted with an incidence of 3,215.5 property crimes per 100,000 population in the same year.[36] Media focus on these incidents via television, radio, newspapers, magazines, books, billboards, and the Internet leads people to believe that violent crime occurs very frequently.

The media usually report or portray perpetrators of crime as minorities. White people are shown as victims out of proportion to their actual rates of victimization.[37] The image of the African American male, especially, as the victimizer of White people has a long historical legacy. Following the Civil War many African American males were lynched because of often unsubstantiated claims that they had made sexual advances toward–or sexually assaulted–White women.[38] In actuality, most crime today is intraracial–individuals most often victimize people of their own race.[39]

A significant downside to the "if it bleeds, it leads" mentality is the shallowness of reporting that results, as demonstrated by research from the City University of New York. A systematic analysis of 12 school shootings (all but one of which occurred in a high school) that took place between 1997 and 2002 in cities from Alaska to Georgia revealed a high incidence of dating violence and sexual harassment as precursors to the shootings, but those incidents went unreported in the news. In five of the incidents, boys targeted and shot girls who had just rejected them. In three cases, boys' motivation to kill sprang from general unhappiness related to difficulties with girls. In three other cases, boys felt that they had "protected" their girlfriends by shooting other boys who threatened the relationships.[40]

The media have a public responsibility to report the news, but they are also in the business of making money for their shareholders. If the public chose sources that relayed a more accurate view of crime, the media might change the way they cover the news.

As we have discussed, the media can affect people's fear of crime. Such fear can be translated into political positions and policy preferences.

Politics

The criminal justice system works within the larger U.S. political system, and politics influences the administration of justice in many ways. The legal system controls what actions are legitimate for criminal justice professionals. Legislators decide how much money the country will spend on prisons, policing, the court system, and victim services. Federal policies influence the priorities established by local justice agencies. For example, the Violent Crime and Law Enforcement Act of 1994 established the COPS office in the Department of Justice to provide grants for hiring community police officers. At the time, this was a new way to approach policing and required a high level of contact and cooperation between police officers and members of communities.

The U.S. Congress does not always require change by passing new laws. Instead, lawmakers can make access to federal funds dependent on states' compliance with certain standards. For example, in 1984 Congress passed the National Minimum Drinking Age Act. The law did not mandate that states make their drinking age 21, but it specified that states that did not raise their minimum drinking age to 21 would not receive highway transportation funds. Even though some states objected to the higher drinking age, they agreed to it so they could access federal monies. Federal agents (such as the attorney general) can also choose to prosecute individuals under federal laws if they disagree with changes in state laws. For example, after California voters approved a proposition in 1996 allowing the use of marijuana for medicinal purposes, federal prosecutors charged medicinal marijuana growers with federal offenses.

Political positions toward crime and justice have changed over time. Beginning in the 1920s, some political leaders held that criminals could be rehabilitated, and criminal justice policies for the most part reflected that belief. However, by the 1980s, the political mood had shifted to a tough-on-crime approach. At that point, the "war on crime" and the "war on drugs" were in full swing, and politicians of both parties pushed for more punitive criminal justice policies, among them stricter sentencing guidelines. Still, there is much debate about whether tougher sentences have reduced crime in the last few years or whether the decline is due to other factors.

Some individuals who seek to influence the administration of justice band together in *interest groups* composed of people who have common social or political goals that they try to achieve by influencing government decision making. These individuals focus either on the overall administration of justice or on one particular aspect of the system or law to forward their interests. A particularly effective victim interest group is Mothers Against Drunk Driving (MADD), which was instrumental in passing the National Minimum Drinking Age Act. Other organizations focus on broader issues such as reducing sentences for offenders. The Sentencing Project, Families Against Mandatory Minimums, and the Drug Policy Alliance argue that the tough-on-crime approach is not effective in reducing criminal behavior but

Race, Class, Gender

Stings or Entrapment?

Today's criminal justice professionals work in politically sensitive times. For example, following the terrorist acts of September 11, 2001, Muslims in the United States have complained of increased surveillance on Muslim individuals, Muslim groups, and mosques. In December 2010 Attorney General Eric Holder spoke to 300 Muslim community leaders from all over the United States. Holder argued that the use of sting operations and undercover informants is an "essential law enforcement tool in uncovering and preventing terrorist attacks." Holder had been given a standing ovation when he took the stage, and the audience applauded during the speech, but when he began to defend such tactics, the room went silent.

The reality is that many Muslims are suspicious of the use of undercover informants and sting operations. They argue that the use of such tactics by the Federal Bureau of Investigation (FBI) amounts to *entrapment* — that is, inducement for a person to commit a crime that he or she would not normally be inclined to commit. Muslims are specifically concerned about undercover agents who work directly with an individual to plan a terrorist attack and who then arrest the suspect. Less than a month previous to Holder's outreach effort, for instance, FBI activities in Portland, Oregon, had come under fire. In the Portland case, FBI agents admitted to having helped the suspect, a teenager, plan an attack. The key question is, Would the suspect have engaged in criminal activity without the agents' involvement? Some Muslims are also concerned that after media reporting on such attempts, they themselves will be subject to terrorist attacks from an anti-Muslim backlash, and some have specifically pointed to the bombing of a mosque in a Portland suburb following the FBI incident there.

U.S. Muslims have continued to cooperate with law enforcement to identify individuals who they think may become violent. Notably, since September 11, 2001, Muslims have helped foil 4 out of 10 al-Qaeda–related terrorism plots. Muslim residents also have looked to law enforcement to protect them from hate crimes, and Holder noted in his December 2010 speech that hate-crime prosecutions of offenders who targeted Muslims or Arab Americans were at their highest since 2000. The attorney general asserted that hate crimes against their community was a priority to the U.S. government.

These complex considerations illustrate how difficult it is for the criminal justice system to balance the various pressures and priorities it faces. Muslims want to help and be helped by law enforcement, but at the same time they are becoming more cautious about working with law enforcement because of FBI tactics such as stings. Hussam Ayloush, a Muslim community leader and graduate of an FBI Citizens' Academy (a program in which agents explain to civic, business, and religious leaders what the FBI does on a regular basis), seemed to speak for many: "My worry would be that the FBI is pushing to a point where it becomes difficult to trust the FBI. When people start doubting, then they might feel like, 'Well, maybe it might make things worse if I call,' and we don't want this." Both sides need to continue to communicate in sessions like Holder's outreach event if they are to navigate successfully today's politically charged environment.

OBSERVE → INVESTIGATE → UNDERSTAND

- What types of activities or conversations do you think could occur to improve the relationship between Muslims in the United States and the federal government?
- Has the U.S. ideal of protecting all people equally been threatened by actions taken after the crimes of September 11?
- How would you evaluate Holder's speech?

SOURCES: Malia Wollen and Charlie Savage, "Holder Calls Terrorism Sting Operations 'Essential,'" *New York Times*, December 11, 2010; William Yardley and Jesse McKinley, "Terror Stings Strain Ties with Some Who Can Help," *New York Times*, November 30, 2010.

does increase racial disparity. (See the "Race, Class, Gender" box on other racial considerations.) Crime Victims United, on the other hand, advocates more punitive sentences for offenders.

Many interest groups are intent on shifting the criminal justice system away from its sole focus on punishment and back to its emphasis on rehabilitation. The critique of the criminal justice system's almost sole focus on punishment includes concerns about racial disparities in criminal law and punishment, which we review next.

Discrimination

Individuals in jail or prison or on probation are disproportionately people of color.[41] This fact has raised a variety of questions regarding fairness in the administration of justice. The serious disparity can be seen in the imprisonment rates; per 100,000 U.S. residents, 410 White males, 3,188 Black males, and

1,419 Latinos are imprisoned.[42] In fact, nearly one-third of Black males aged 20–29 are under some form of criminal justice supervision on any given day.[43]

The conflict perspective would explain racial disparities in the criminal justice system as an extension of social divisions in U.S. society.[44] Historically, some definitions of what is criminal were clearly discriminatory. For example, in early America when slavery was legal, it was a crime for antislavery activists to harbor African Americans seeking freedom. A patchwork of discriminatory laws against African Americans—generally called *Jim Crow laws*—was enforced from the years following the Civil War until the late 1960s. In the late nineteenth century, at a time when the White population considered Chinese immigrants a threat to their jobs, opium smoking, a fairly common habit in China, was criminalized in the United States.[45]

Today some observers argue that drug laws are discriminatory in their impact. Young Blacks report less alcohol and drug use than White youth,[46] yet Blacks are much more likely to be arrested for the possession of illicit substances. The "war on drugs" has also had a significant disparate impact on women. Women's incarceration rates have increased steeply in the last few decades, most often for drug possession.[47]

CHALLENGES TO CRIMINAL JUSTICE TODAY

Any discussion about the criminal justice system needs to consider how the system must adapt to the changing needs of the twenty-first century. Challenges confronting criminal justice today and into the future place significant strains on its resources. Adaptability on the part of the system and its practitioners is more crucial than ever before. The scope and pace of challenges show no signs of slowing. One is bombarded daily with a succession of images and sounds that reflect a United States and a world that are seriously imperiled. Phrases such as "I can't breathe" and "Black lives matter" have echoed throughout the country as civilian deaths at the hands of the police have become a touchstone for troubled race relations. Video reports of horrific beheadings of individuals caught in the web of Middle East upheaval stream online simultaneously with reports of stateside incidents of extreme violence. Thus, it could be inferred that American society and the world's other inhabitants are incapable of attaining a more peaceful existence. However, while on the surface the array of challenges confronting the criminal justice system may appear incalculably daunting, delving into the underlying realities reveals that for every challenge there can be reasoned, research-based processes brought to bear.

Analysis of the manner in which terrorism has been addressed since the infamous 9/11 attacks, through the Boston Marathon bombing, and into the evolving global jihadist threat reveals a consistent collaborative and data-driven approach that was not nearly as pronounced prior to 9/11. In the aftermath of 9/11, the Department of Homeland Security was created, along with the Transportation Security Administration and a national network of intelligence-gathering fusion centers. The Federal Bureau of Investigation (FBI) was assigned lead agency responsibility for countering terrorist threats within the United States and its interests overseas. The foreign-fighter recruitment phenomenon has emerged as a formidable threat, as has that posed by radicalized, homegrown violent extremists who remain poised for violence in their home countries. Innovative counterterrorism communications have been developed for direct online engagement of propaganda emanating from afar, and community policing has been adapted to address violent extremism at the local level.[48]

As a nation, the United States has become highly digitally dependent. Our economy, national security, educational systems, critical infrastructure, and social lives have become deeply reliant on cyberspace. However, the richness of cyberspace's content is a treasure trove for malicious actors. One international event in 2013, involving thefts from ATMs over a 10-hour period, resulted in losses of $45 million, which is more than the total losses from all "traditional" bank robberies in the United States in one year.[49] The number of reported data breaches has spiked with an increase in state-sponsored cybercrime and organized crime networks.[50] Amid all the data breach stories and gloomy predictions, though, we do know what preventive strategies work and what changes can be made to improve security. In 2014, identity theft declined by three percent, due in part to more aggressive actions from financial institutions, identity theft protection providers, and consumers and a series of extraordinary responses to high-profile data breaches.[51] On the governmental front, the FBI has gained unprecedented visibility into cyber threats and has steadily gained proficiency in coordinating operational responses.[52]

One of the most important issues facing the criminal justice system is how to leverage technology to improve its services. DNA analysis continues to demonstrate its extraordinary value, and it has been recognized by funding authorities accordingly. The FBI Combined DNA Index System's (CODIS) database contains the DNA profiles contributed by federal, state, and local forensic labs. One recurring issue among states, though, is whether or not to include arrestees as is done with all federal offenders. Less than half of states upload offender profiles. Moreover, entities such as the Innocence Project do not have access to the CODIS database without the government's consent, and there is often resistance to requests.[53] "A Case in Point" spotlights a U.S. Supreme Court's decision affecting convicted persons' access to DNA.

Other technologies continue to transform crime and its control. As renowned futurist Gene Stephens observes, "Technology provides the means to commit crimes, to thwart crimes, to cover up crimes, and to detect crimes."[54] Many criminal justice executives are making decisions about whether to procure devices that were not in existence at the start of their careers such as facial recognition systems, predictive analytics systems, and GPS applications. Indeed, incorporation of unmanned aircraft systems ("drones") into local public safety agency operations is well under way.[55] For many decision makers a significant challenge is not deciding to adopt one particular technology but, rather, finding the appropriate mix of technologies for a specific jurisdiction based on its crime problems, funding levels, and community attitudes. Perhaps the overriding challenge is how to balance public safety and civil liberties. Is the dilemma unresolvable? It certainly is not unresolvable if society and criminal justice entities devote attention and resources to the situation.

What makes a person walk into a place of worship, theater, or classroom and open fire? What combination of circumstances compels a human being to commit the most inhuman of crimes? How much can science tell us about a brain at risk for violence? The extraordinarily complex nature of human behavior continually challenges the criminal justice system. While there are no one-size-fits-all answers, as we have come to better understand the causes of criminal behavior we are better positioned to deal with that behavior more effectively, possibly even preventing it from occurring in some cases.

The extent and quality of imprisonment within the United States is a lightning rod for divergence of opinion on crime and punishment along philosophical, sociological, psychological, and economic lines. The United States continues to lead industrialized nations in incarcerating its citizens. Criminologists and policymakers increasingly agree that we have reached a tipping point with incarceration. New offender supervision strategies and technologies, combined with tight state budgets, are prompting shifts toward alternatives to incarceration, especially for lower-level offenders.[56]

Within the field of victims' rights, a current concern is that in spite of the presence of such rights, many are not being upheld in the courts due to the weak "legal standing" of crime victims. Many judges seemingly consider these new victims' rights as illusory. Because there is sparse case law in this area, many violations of rights have not been prosecuted. Victims' rights organizations are aggressively pursuing measures to effectively create intolerance for noncompliance of victims' rights by agents of the criminal justice system.

a case in point

The Right to DNA Testing after Conviction

The due process clauses of the Fifth and Fourteenth Amendments of the U.S. Constitution protect individuals from unfair treatment by federal, state, or local government. If an individual can prove that he or she was unjustly convicted of a crime, fairness seems to dictate that the individual should be exonerated. The right for a review after a conviction, however, is not automatic everywhere in the United States. In some states the prosecutor must grant permission for this review. If a state does not have a law granting prisoner access to DNA testing, the prosecutor can deny the request without even giving a reason.

Such is the case in Alaska, one of three states that do not have a DNA testing law. Alaska has steadfastly refused to turn over DNA evidence to William G. Osborne, who was convicted in 1994 of kidnapping, sexual assault, and assault. Osborne claims that DNA evidence could prove his innocence, and he has offered to pay the costs of a newer sophisticated test of the DNA, a procedure not available at the time of his original trial.

On June 19, 2009, the U.S. Supreme Court ruled in a 5–4 decision that prisoners do not have a constitutional right to DNA testing to challenge their convictions. The Court ruled that the due process clause of the Constitution does not apply in this situation. While acknowledging that DNA can positively identify the guilty while exonerating the wrongly convicted, the justices held that a defendant found guilty after a fair trial does not have the same rights as a free man.

It is important, the Court argued, that the certainty of convictions be final and not undermined. The Court also said that access to DNA evidence for convicted individuals should be left up to the states, most of which have already enacted such laws. As noted, however, Alaska has no such laws, and no prisoner in Alaska has ever been granted permission to obtain DNA evidence after conviction. Until Alaska changes this policy, William Osborne will not be able to introduce DNA evidence in his appeals.

In a Texas case, a hair was the only physical evidence placing a would-be murderer at the scene of the crime. Claude Jones was executed in 2000 for a murder he insisted he did not commit. A hair found at the scene was a critical piece of evidence since Texas law required that there be physical evidence to corroborate other testimony in a capital (death penalty) case. State officials refused Jones's request for DNA testing of the hair, but in 2010, 10 years after his execution, DNA tests were conducted showing that the hair did not belong to Jones. The test did not prove that Jones was not guilty, but without the physical evidence, Texas could not have put him to death—and it is even possible that a jury might not have convicted him. Think about it: Had the tests been done when originally requested, Jones might be alive today.

OBSERVE → INVESTIGATE → UNDERSTAND

- How and why would a defendant's rights be different before trial and after conviction?

- Why would Alaska not want to retest Osborne?

- Do you think the Supreme Court was correct in its 2009 decision? State your reasons.

- Why would Texas not have wanted to DNA-test the hair in the Jones case?

- If a test is not done before a conviction, why might a state consider it too late to test afterward?

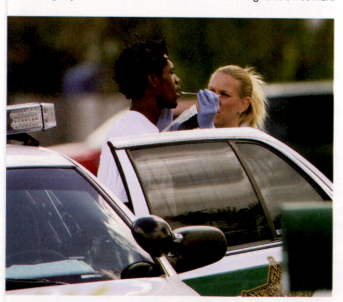

SOURCES: *District Attorney's Office for the Third Judicial District v. Osborne*, 129 S. Ct. 2308 (2009); Adam Liptak, "Justices Reject Inmate Right to DNA Tests," *New York Times*, June 19, 2009; Jess Bravin and Jennifer S. Forsyth, "Court Upholds States in DNA Testing of Convicts," *Wall Street Journal*, June 19, 2009; "The Supreme Court's DNA Ruling: Wrong on Rights," *Los Angeles Times*, Editorial, June 19, 2009; "DNA Testing: Supreme Court's Ruling Put Procedure before Justice," *Star-Ledger*, Editorial. http://blog.nj.com/njv_editorial_page/2009/06/ dna_testing_supreme_courts_rul.html (retrieved July 3, 2009); Dave Mann, "DNA Tests Undermine Evidence in Texas Execution," *Texas Observer*, November 11, 2010; "The DNA Non-Redemption," *Los Angeles Times*, Editorial, November 27, 2010.

Perhaps the most conspicuous challenge confronting the criminal justice system is the lingering rage emanating from the African American community over perceived unequal treatment by components of the justice system, especially law enforcement. A succession of citizens' videos raising concerns about the appropriateness of use of force against African Americans ultimately reached a boiling point in Baltimore in 2015. The most violent civil unrest since the assassination of Martin Luther King Jr. erupted in Baltimore in the wake of the death of a 25-year-old unarmed Black man who suffered a fatal spinal injury while in police custody.[57] Most alarming, despite the years of community engagement ostensibly practiced by police departments nationally, a racial divide, or rather, a police–African American community divide, apparently persists. The severity of this crisis in trust, while greatly concerning, is stimulating what may prove to be an unprecedented level of attention directed toward a markedly improved and enduring relationship.

In the chapters that follow, all these challenges, among many others, will be discussed in the context of their evolution. It is an exciting time as criminal justice practitioners, educators, and students attempt to forge new solutions to long-standing problems, while at the same time develop strategies to contend with nascent challenges such as those driven by technological advancements.

SUMMARY

The criminal justice system is based in law. However, laws only reflect what societies agree should be the norm for behavior. What works or is acceptable or is normal in one society, in one place, or in one time period may be considered deviant in another society, place, or period of time. When a law or formal norm is broken, the criminal justice system is set in motion.

The main parts of the criminal justice system are law enforcement, the courts, corrections, and victim services. The actors in these different sectors interact in various ways with the offender and the victim in the process of protecting society, providing a fair trial, and carrying out punishment and rehabilitation.

The challenge is to administer justice consistently, to balance efficiency with fairness, to keep the system up to date, and to avoid undue influence from outside sources, such as the media and interest groups.

OBSERVE → INVESTIGATE → UNDERSTAND

Review

Illustrate how social norms help us define crime.

- A norm is a rule that makes clear what behavior is appropriate and expected in a particular situation. The term *abnormal* connotes deviance, the violation of a norm.

- Whether we consider a behavior deviant always depends on the context in which it occurs.

- Formal social norms, also called legal norms, are formally written, such as laws that result from a legislative process.

- Violation of formal norms, or laws, sets the criminal justice system in motion.

Define crime and explain how it is classified.

- Society defines crime in the same way it defines deviance—by labeling specific behaviors as such. Thus, behaviors considered criminal in one country (or place or time) may not only be legal in another country (or place or time) but the norm.

- One way of classifying crimes is as *mala in se* (an "evil unto itself," a behavior that is considered morally wrong). But no act or behavior is an inherently criminal act; society only labels it as criminal.

- Crimes can also be classified as *mala prohibita* (acts that are criminal because they are prohibited by law). *Mala prohibita* crimes reflect public opinion at a point in time.

- The consensus perspective of crime views laws defining crime as the product of social agreement or consensus about what criminal behavior is. The conflict perspective of crime views the definition of crime as one outcome of a struggle among different groups competing for resources in their society.

Describe the consequences of crime for the offender and the victim.

- Those who break the law must face sanctions, which are used to reinforce people's conformity to norms. Sanctions can be positive or negative, and they can be formal or informal.

- Victims generally suffer some sort of loss or injury or even death. When victims are neglected or abused by the criminal justice system, their suffering worsens.

Outline the basic structure of the criminal justice system.

- The three major institutions of the criminal justice system are law enforcement, the courts, and corrections, with victim services additionally involved in these major components.

- The police are called upon to do far more than protect and arrest. Law enforcement officers are expected to correct many of society's problems and are entrusted to use force when necessary.

- The U.S. judiciary consists of a dual court system made up of state courts (trial and appellate courts) and federal courts (district courts, appellate courts or circuit courts where appeals are heard, and the U.S. Supreme Court).

- Corrections is the systematic, organized effort by society to punish offenders, protect the public, and change an offender's behavior. Correctional efforts include incarceration, probation, parole, treatment, and community service.

- Victim services offer a broad array of services within and outside government agencies to help the victim, including shelters and transitional housing programs, counseling services, 24-hour hotlines, and the appointment of a victim advocate to assist with legal needs.

Describe key models of the workings of the criminal justice system.

- Criminal justice professionals have discretion, which results in a filtering of cases so that not all of them end up in court.

- The wedding cake model helps explain what cases make it through the criminal justice funnel. The bottom layer (4) represents the vast majority of cases (largely misdemeanor and infraction cases), which are dispatched rather quickly. Each of the three layers on top represent more and more serious cases, with the most celebrated cases in the top layer (1) getting the most attention and resources.

- The crime control model emphasizes the efficient arrest and processing of alleged criminal offenders.

- The due process model values individual rights and procedural protections for the accused at all stages of the justice process.

Describe how criminal justice is influenced by public opinion, the media, politics, and policy.

- Public fears of crime are often inflated and misplaced. The level of fear we experience can be affected by factors such as gender, age, past experiences with crime, ethnicity, income, educational attainment, and the area in which we live.

- Media coverage of crime inflates levels of fear by presenting exaggerated or false perceptions about crime and criminal behavior. Media reports disproportionately focus on violent and sensational crime.

- Politics influences the administration of justice in many ways. Legislators define crimes, determine what actions are legitimate for agents of criminal justice, and decide how much money to allocate to the criminal justice system. Some individuals who seek to influence the administration of justice band together in interest groups.

Review the challenges to the criminal justice system today.

- Crimes such as cybercrime and international terrorism exemplify the globalization of crime.

- The continually increasing prison population has created problems of overpopulation.

- DNA testing has greatly affected the administration of justice, but there is a large backlog of evidence that has not been analyzed, as well as questions about who should have access to DNA evidence and at what stage of the criminal justice process.

Key Terms

alternative sentence 12	due process model 16	secondary victims 13
appellate courts 11	federal courts 11	social norm 3
conflict perspective 6	*mala in se* 5	state courts 11
consensus perspective 6	*mala prohibita* 5	statutory crime 5
corrections 12	moral panic 19	victim advocate 13
crime control model 16	norm 3	victim impact statement 13
crime prevention 16	parole 12	victim services 12
criminal justice system 9	probation 12	wedding cake model 15
deviance 3	sanctions 8	

Study Questions

1. Norms can
   a. inform us as to what behaviors are acceptable.
   b. clarify what behaviors are unacceptable.
   c. vary according to culture.
   d. all of the above

2. All of the following are formal negative sanctions delivered in response to criminal behavior *except*
   a. incarceration.
   b. court requirement of drug treatment.
   c. dirty looks.
   d. probation.

3. A true statement about victims in the U.S. criminal justice system is that
   a. most of the time, victims and criminals are of the same race, class, and age.
   b. historically, victims were neglected and abused by the criminal justice system.
   c. today victims participate more in the criminal justice process and can receive money for their injuries and losses.
   d. all of the above

4. The model illustrating that most criminal cases do not go through the trial process is the
   a. crime control model.
   b. due process model.
   c. wedding cake model.
   d. conflict model.

5. A person who believes that the focus of the criminal justice system should be on protecting individual rights and freedoms is a believer in the
   a. due process model.
   b. crime control model.

   c. United Nations model.
   d. criminology model.

6. All of the following have given substantial support to the victims' rights movement *except*
   a. drug and alcohol movements.
   b. law-and-order movements.
   c. women's movements.
   d. victim-oriented coalitions.

7. Laws are examples of
   a. statistical norms.
   b. informal social norms.
   c. cultural norms.
   d. formal norms.

8. The perspective that sees laws defining crime as the product of social agreement about criminal behavior is the
   a. conflict perspective.
   b. consensus perspective.
   c. wedding cake model.
   d. crime control model.

9. Based on who in reality is most likely to be victimized, the group that should be most fearful of crime is
   a. women.
   b. older individuals.
   c. young men.
   d. children.

10. All of the following are true of media coverage of crime *except*
    a. media reporting is sensational.
    b. media reporting accurately represents criminal behavior.
    c. media reporting affects people's fear of crime.
    d. media reporting focuses on violent crimes.

Critical Thinking Questions

For further review, go to the LearnSmart study module for this chapter.

1. What is considered a crime in one place may not be a crime in another place. How, then, is justice possible?

2. Do you believe the basis of most U.S. criminal laws is consensus or conflict? Explain.

3. How do you think media coverage of crime affects decisions about policies and the workings of the criminal justice system?

2 Types of Crime

OBSERVE → INVESTIGATE → UNDERSTAND

After reading this chapter, you should be able to:

- Understand how crime rates are measured.
- Differentiate the types of crimes against persons.
- Describe the different types of property crimes.
- Identify types of public order crimes.
- Describe some of the political crimes that have occurred in recent years.
- Discuss organized crime and who engages in it today.
- Contrast the types of crimes generally perpetrated by males and by females.

Realities and Challenges

On April 4, 2011, Russlynn Ali, Assistant Secretary for the U.S. Department of Education and its Office of Civil Rights, penned the now famous "Dear Colleague Letter" outlining that sexual harassment and violence against students interferes with a student's right to receive an education free from discrimination. The letter further outlines that Title IX of the Education Amendments of 1972 (Title IX) prohibits discrimination on the basis of sex in education, including all related programs and activities. The letter goes on to discuss the statistics associated with sexual violence: One in five women will experience a completed or attempted sexual attack, whereas approximately 6 percent of males will experience the same. However, when looking at university campus data required to be collected under the Clery Act, there is significant discrepancy, with far fewer cases being reported. The letter also notes that existing practices for assisting victims of sexual assault, domestic violence, and stalking fall far short of the appropriate response and services needed by students. The letter calls upon schools to take immediate and effective steps to eliminate violence, raise awareness to prevent abuse, provide immediate and effective services, and ensure appropriate responses through established procedures and training for students and university employees alike. Failure to take these steps will result in losing crucial federal funding. This letter has contributed to several widespread and long overdue changes to address these crimes against students on campuses nationwide.[1]

Drawing upon our understanding from Chapter 1 of how society determines what behaviors are crimes, this chapter will begin by determining how crime is measured. As you can see from the opening vignette, data on the same types of crime, for the same population, and from the same location can be collected from various sources with wide disparities in final count. This chapter discusses how this is possible and outlines the various sources for crime data collection in the United States. Next, we consider how crimes are categorized in the United States today. Finally, we examine the effects of various kinds of offenses on victims and communities.

MEASURING CRIME

Information about crime and criminals is assembled by government agencies, private groups, and scholars. Four of the most frequently used data sources for estimating crime are the Uniform Crime Reports (UCR), the National Incident-Based Reporting System (NIBRS), the National Crime Victimization Survey (NCVS), and self-report studies. Each has advantages and disadvantages, as we will see in this section. Together, however, they yield a comprehensive picture of the extent and nature of crime.

As you read this chapter, note that, as in Figures 2-1, 2-2, and 2-3, the term *rate* is used. *Rate* is a simple term that allows criminologists to compare geographic units (cities, counties, states, and nations) or certain categories of people (for example, males and females) according to a constant number of persons. The three constants most used are 1,000 (usually for cities and counties), 10,000 (usually for states), and 100,000 (usually for nations).

Uniform Crime Reports

In the 1920s, the International Association of Chiefs of Police saw the need for national crime statistics. They formed the Committee on Uniform Crime Records to create a system for uniformly measuring crime. The most serious of these crimes, defined as *Part I offenses*, constituted the **Crime Index.** This index served as a gauge of the state of crime in the United States. The Part I offenses comprised seven felonies: murder and nonnegligent manslaughter, forcible rape, robbery, aggravated assault, burglary, larceny, and motor vehicle theft.[2] Congress later mandated the addition of arson to the Part I offenses.[3]

Crime Index
An officially compiled statistical measure of the incidence of crime in the United States.

Uniform definitions of crimes were created to provide standardization across jurisdictions. As an example, for reporting purposes, the crime of "rape" required that the act be forcible (rather than *statutory*, which described sexual activities in which one participant was below the age required to legally consent to the behavior). Similarly, the crime of "aggravated assault" required that an attack be for the purpose of inflicting severe bodily harm, usually accompanied by use of a weapon—not, for example, a hand slap.

In 1930, the Federal Bureau of Investigation (FBI) was given the task of annually collecting, publishing, and archiving crime statistics from all the states' law enforcement agencies in the form of the **Uniform Crime Reports (UCR).** Since 1996, the UCR requires authorities to provide additional information when a crime appears to have been motivated by hate. Under a 1990 federal law, other felonies can be designated as hate crimes if they are motivated by the perpetrator's hatred of the victim's "race, color, religion, national origin, ethnicity, gender, or sexual orientation."[4] Racism motivates about half of all hate crime convictions; most of the rest involve hatred for the victim's religion, sexual orientation, or ethnicity.[5] A notorious example of a hate crime is the 1999 murder of James Byrd Jr., a Black man killed by three Whites who chained him to their pickup truck and dragged him for 3 miles; Byrd's head and many other body parts were scattered along the road. Two of the killers, members of a White supremacist gang, were sentenced to death (one was executed in 2011, and the other one is currently on death row awaiting the outcome of an appeal); the third got life imprisonment without parole.[6]

Uniform Crime Reports (UCR)
An annual series of U.S. statistical measures of the incidence of selected crimes reported by police departments and compiled by the FBI.

MYTH/REALITY

MYTH: The UCR (the FBI's annual tally of serious crimes) accurately reflects the nature and level of crime in the United States.

REALITY: The UCR contains only crimes reported by police and thus does not cover all crimes committed. As a result, the greater volume of property crimes overshadows the occurrence of more serious but less frequently committed crimes.

Use of the Crime Index as an indicator of criminality was discontinued in 2004 because it was skewed toward property crimes. The Crime Index had been calculated by adding the total of Part I offenses. Offenses such as larceny, which accounts for a majority of reported crimes, distorted the crime total by overshadowing the incidence of more serious but less frequently committed offenses. Crime statistics are now categorized and published as "violent crimes" and "property crimes."[7]

Effective January 2013, the definition of rape was revised to eliminate the requirement that the crime be perpetrated through the use of force. "Without consent" is the new language.[8] The UCR data can be confusing. For example, UCR definitions of crimes may differ from a state's definitions. In California, breaking into a locked car constitutes a "burglary" (entering with the objective of stealing), but the UCR classifies it as "theft" (defined simply as stealing). Another problem with the UCR system of data collection is that it undercounts offenses. Police have to report only the most serious offense when multiple offenses are committed in one incident. For example, a home invasion robbery that includes a rape and an auto theft would yield only one offense for UCR reporting purposes. Most likely the rape would be the offense counted because rape is considered the most serious offense of these three.

The UCR also includes a schematic presentation of offenses–a "crime clock" designed to convey the relative frequency of crimes, such as one burglary every 16.4 seconds. However, by omitting variables such as time of day, day of week, location, and any relationship between offender and victim, it shows crimes occurring with a regularity (and implied randomness) that is not realistic.

UCR data are not the final word when it comes to assessing the level of crime in a given jurisdiction. Many other variables should be considered. Accurate assessments are possible only with careful study and analysis of the various unique conditions affecting each jurisdiction, such as the strength of law enforcement agencies, stability of the population, family cohesiveness, local highway system, percentage of youth, and economic conditions.[9]

National Incident-Based Reporting System

National Incident-Based Reporting System (NIBRS)
A U.S. crime index (not yet fully national in scope) compiled by the FBI and the Department of Justice that tracks detailed information about 22 categories of crime incidents and arrests.

For more than five decades, the UCR program remained unchanged. Then, in response to the need for more informative data, the Department of Justice's Bureau of Crime Statistics collaborated with the FBI to formulate the **National Incident-Based Reporting System (NIBRS).** This enhancement to the UCR program collects detailed information about criminal incidents and arrests in 22 offense categories made up of 46 specific crimes. NIBRS can provide information about type of premises involved, method of entry, type of property loss, weapon/force used, relationship of victim to offender, alcohol/drug use by offender, and many other details.[10] Data on when and where crime takes place and the characteristics of victims and perpetrators provide leads for follow-up investigations and strategies to prevent crime.

As valuable as NIBRS is, not every law enforcement agency has all the resources necessary for collecting, processing, and reporting the required array of data. As of 2013, 34 percent of the nation's law enforcement agencies participating in the UCR program submitted their data via the NIBRS. This rate of participation covered 29 percent of the nation's population.[11] NIBRS can provide information on nearly every major criminal issue confronting society today, including terrorism, computer crime, drug/narcotics offenses, elder abuse, white-collar crime, organized crime, intimate partner violence, and driving under the influence. When NIBRS is fully implemented, individual states and the nation will have markedly upgraded investigative capabilities.[12]

National Crime Victimization Survey

Some criminologists and, more recently, *victimologists*–those who study victims and victimization–criticize the UCR as an inaccurate barometer of society's well-being. For a variety of reasons, many victims do not report the crimes perpetrated against them. Consequently, a large number of crimes remain unknown to police and never get into a database.

Criminal justice professionals ultimately realized that the only way to measure the true extent of crime accurately was to go directly to citizens and avoid the "filter" of the criminal justice system. The method that emerged was **victim surveys,** a term not entirely accurate because those interviewed are not always victims. However, the idea was well conceived, and in 1966 a presidential commission prompted the carrying out of the first national crime survey, based on a random sample of 10,000 households. The results

victim surveys
Interviews with individuals (including but not limited to actual victims) who have been personally affected by specific crimes.

confirmed that significant numbers of people did not report their victimization to the police.[13]

From 1972 to 1977, the Department of Justice (DOJ) undertook an annual victimization survey of residences and businesses in 26 large cities and published its reports annually. In 1973, the DOJ's Bureau of Crime Statistics and the Bureau of the Census launched the National Crime Surveys (NCS), and these have continued to the present. In 1992, the name was changed to **National Crime Victimization Survey (NCVS)** to reflect more accurately the central focus of this research: the extent of victimization among the general population.

The survey questionnaire for the NCVS has three sections: Personal Characteristics, Household Screen, and Individual Screen. If someone has been victimized, the survey asks a series of further questions about the victimization(s). The current sample size is about 76,000 households and encompasses 135,300 people over the age of 12. These households remain in the sample for 3 years and are interviewed every 6 months.[14]

The NCVS differs substantially from the UCR. It *does not* include homicide, kidnapping, so-called victimless crimes, commercial crimes, or victimizations of children under the age of 12. It *does* include both reported and nonreported crimes, and it counts each crime separately, whereas the UCR counts only the most serious crime in an incident. (The NIBRS remedies that flaw.) The NCVS includes details about the victims as well as about the crime and its consequences. Perhaps most important for victimologists, the NCVS focuses mainly on victims and their victimizations, whereas the UCR is primarily oriented toward criminals and their crimes.

A comparison of data from both the NCVS and the UCR revealed that most crimes in the categories of rape/sexual assault, simple assault, and theft were not recorded by law enforcement. The actual number of people victimized by violent crimes is almost double the reported figure. The actual number of victims of property crimes is almost two-thirds more than reported to the police. In the 2004-2005 time period, only 48.7 percent of all violent victimizations and 39.3 percent of all property crimes were reported. Since 1992 the trend for reporting crimes has been increasing steadily.[15] This group of unreported and unrecorded crimes is called the **dark figure of crime.**

The NCVS has made a major contribution to how we understand the crime problem and how we respond to victims, especially those who choose not to report their victimizations. We now have a much better understanding of victims of crime and the differences between those who report and those who do not. For example, the NCVS results suggest that some victims do not report victimization if the perpetrator is known to them. This finding has major implications for prosecuting sexual crimes and crimes within the family.

The NCVS has also helped to clarify how the criminal justice system, especially the police, influences victim reporting and cooperation with law enforcement. Victimologists are particularly concerned about **secondary victimization,** when the victim who reports the crime is victimized again—this time, by the police, by medical personnel, by the courts, or even by friends who respond inappropriately or judge his or her actions at the time of the offense. NCVS data show that victims take into consideration the way they think police will react to their report of victimization. Today, police know that treating victims with greater respect and taking victims seriously greatly improves individuals' willingness to report and encourages victims to be more cooperative witnesses. Consequently, the efficiency of the criminal justice system significantly improves, and the victims take a more meaningful role in that process. "A Global View" discusses victim surveys on an international scale.

National Crime Victimization Survey (NCVS)
A statistical sampling of households and individuals who have been personally victimized by specific crimes.

dark figure of crime
The group of unreported and unrecorded crimes as revealed by crime victim surveys.

secondary victimization
The suffering of crime victims caused by their subsequent treatment by the police, the courts, or personal acquaintances.

Self-Report Data

In 1946, criminologist Austin Porterfield experimented with a method called *self-disclosure* in a small research project comparing college students to juvenile delinquents.[16] Porterfield's method was simple: He asked respondents to reveal the crimes they had committed. He found that the actual numbers of crimes disclosed were far greater than expected. This surprising result challenged the view, commonly held by criminologists and laypersons alike, that people are either criminal or not. Porterfield's findings suggest a very different and much more likely scenario: that criminality exists on a continuum in which some people commit few crimes, most people commit some crimes, and a very few people commit many crimes.

self-report
Surveys in which individuals (who are guaranteed confidentiality) reveal offenses that they have committed but for which they may or may not have been arrested and held accountable. These surveys uncover another part of the dark figure of crime.

Self-report studies are an important source of information about offenders and their offenses. Academic and clinical researchers can choose from a wide range of methods to collect and analyze the information they get from offenders through the self-report method. They may engage a sample of burglars in personal interviews and learn that they have a human face and do not spend all their time plotting or engaging in crime. Or researchers can give a written questionnaire to a class of college students and learn, as Porterfield did, that more than 90 percent of us commit a crime during our adolescence for which we could have been incarcerated had we been caught and prosecuted. Telephone and mail surveys allow researchers to pose a series of prepared questions to a sample of people representative of a larger population. If we wish to learn more about serial rapists, for example, we could conduct a survey of incarcerated serial rapists and compare their results with responses from a control group of men of the same age and socioeconomic background who lack a criminal background. *Case studies,* a self-report approach in which the experiences of an individual offender are examined at length and in detail, can suggest useful hypotheses to test later with a larger sample of the same kind of offender.

Self-reports tell us about crimes committed by people who were never caught–and even about crimes unknown to the police (because the victims did not report them) but about which the offenders are willing to talk. To maximize their confidence in information from self-reports, researchers can use various methods to ensure valid and reliable results. Since the 1950s when self-report research in criminology began, the quality of the methodology has increased. Although there is room for improvement, the self-report method of data collection has acceptable validity and reliability.[17] Thus we can learn much from the offenders themselves–even when they choose to lie.

The various sources of information from police, victims, and offenders complement one another by offering overlapping data and filling in missing information. When we consider the information as a whole, it paints a more comprehensive picture of crime than any one approach can provide on its own.

CRIMES AGAINST PERSONS

crimes against persons
Attacks or threats of an attack to a person's body, including murder and manslaughter (taking a life), sexual assault, kidnapping, robbery (theft with force or the threat of force), and battery (the intentional unwanted touching of one person by another).

Attacks or threats of an attack on a person's body constitute **crimes against persons.** The most serious of these offenses are murder and manslaughter (both mean wrongfully taking a life), sexual assault, kidnapping, robbery (theft with force or the threat of force), and battery (the intentional unwanted touching of one person by another with intent to injure). Laws defining crimes against persons are probably the oldest rules in human societies. This continuity demonstrates both the enduring nature of human violence and the heavy toll violent acts take on individuals and communities.

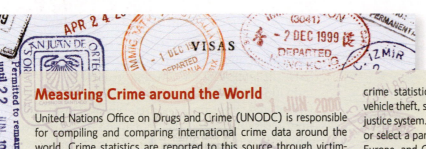

A Global View

Measuring Crime around the World

United Nations Office on Drugs and Crime (UNODC) is responsible for compiling and comparing international crime data around the world. Crime statistics are reported to this source through victim-reported crimes as well as crimes reported to the police. UNODC experiences the same challenges with data collection that we have in the United States, as disparities persist between crimes reported by victims and crimes reported to the police. UNODC website (www.unodc.org) has a searchable database that allows anyone to look at crime statistics for assault, kidnapping, robbery, burglary, motor vehicle theft, sexual violence, and homicide, as well as for the criminal justice system. By searching the database, one can compare all regions or select a particular region (for example, Africa, the Americas, Asia, Europe, and Oceania, as well as subregions and specific countries). Data are available on varying topics from 1970 to the present. UNODC also sponsors the Commission on Narcotic Drugs (CND) and the Commission on Crime Prevention and Criminal Justice (CCPCJ), which are responsible for creating resolutions and decisions that provide guidance to member states. In addition to collecting data, UNODC hosts the UN Crime Congress each year, whereby academics and practitioners meet in a different part of the world to discuss crime issues including the administration of justice, prevention, laws, and interventions in a global context. UNODC also marks June 26 as the International Day against Drug Abuse and Illicit Trafficking and December 9 as International Anti-Corruption Day. A wealth of information about their programs, activities, and publications can be found on the organization's website.

OBSERVE → INVESTIGATE → UNDERSTAND

- What role can UNODC play in improving data collection about crime and victimization throughout the world?
- How reliable a picture of crime do you think UNODC data provide?
- How likely is it that persons contacted by UNODC researchers will give honest answers? Explain.

SOURCE: United Nations Office on Drugs and Crime. www.unodc.org (retrieved May 18, 2015).

Data on Crimes against Persons

In 1973, the UCR cited 715,900 police reports for these violent offenses, but during the same period more than 1.8 million cases of violent crimes were reported in the NCVS about individuals' experiences with crime. This is *more than double* the number of victimizations reported to the police. The UCR and NCVS numbers then rose steadily each year, fluctuating during the 1970s and 1980s. As you can see from Figure 2-1, UCR data peaked in 1992 at just more than 1.6 million cases reported by the police, and the next year, 1993, the NCVS survey of victimizations reported to the police peaked above 2.2 million cases. Both measures began a steady decline after these peaks, continuing their downward trend through the last year for which data are available, 2013, when the UCR reported more than 1.2 million serious violent crimes. Given the dramatic drop in total violent crime from 1993 to 2013, consider what conditions might be responsible for that change.

Fortunately, crimes against persons constitute a relatively small proportion of all crime. For example, in 2013, FBI data show that about 1.2 million violent crimes were reported to the police in the United States compared to 8.7 million property crimes.[18] If we consider that many more property crimes than violent crimes probably go unreported, the disparity becomes even greater. Furthermore, contrary to popular belief, the rate of violent crimes committed in the United States has declined considerably since 1993.[19]

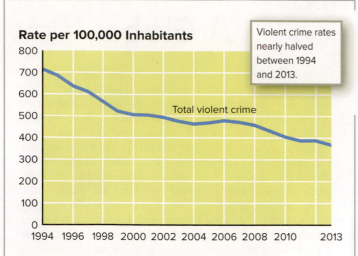

Rate per 100,000 Inhabitants

Violent crime rates nearly halved between 1994 and 2013.

Total violent crime

FIGURE 2-1   Violent Crime Rates, 1994–2013

Given the dramatic drop in total violent crime (rape, robbery, aggravated assault, and homicide) rates from 1994 to 2013, consider what conditions might be responsible for that change.

SOURCE: U.S. Department of Justice, Federal Bureau of Investigation, Criminal Justice Information Services Division, "Crime in the United State 2013," https://www.fbi.gov/about-us/cjis/ucr/crime-in-the-u.s/2013/crime-in-the-u.s.-2013/tables/1tabledatadecoverviewpdf/table_1_crime_in_the_united_states_by_volume_and_rate_per_100000_inhabitants_1994-2013.xls (retrieved November 10, 2015).

The Victims: The Influence of Gender, Age, and Other Factors

More than any other act, crimes against persons have the potential for causing greater damage to individuals, including economic losses, psychological and emotional trauma, physical pain and injury, disability, and death. These crimes generally rank as highest priorities among law enforcement agencies. Increasingly, multijurisdictional law enforcement and prosecutorial entities are combining resources to investigate, apprehend, and prosecute perpetrators of violent crimes. The pooling of resources not only can help to offset the resource losses sustained by any one agency in the wake of budgetary reductions, but also can provide investigative expertise that may be missing within the jurisdiction where a crime has occurred. "A Case in Point" shows how local, state, and federal agencies in Michigan have joined forces to impact the incidence of violent crime statewide.

Who are the "persons" against whom crimes against persons are committed? Anyone, of course, can be a victim. However, gender, health, intelligence, social associations, location, mental state, and age often determine an individual's likelihood of becoming a victim of particular types of crimes. In general, men are more likely than women to become victims of reported violent crimes. For example, the FBI reported that 77 percent of murder victims in 2009 were male.[20]

An earlier study concluded that 60 percent of violent crime victims were male.[21] From 1973 until 2005, the NCVS provided data about violent crime rates by gender for individuals 12 years of age and older. As you can see from 35 years of collected data in Figure 2-2, males are consistently victimized at a higher rate than females. It is also apparent, however, that the overall violent crime rate has been decreasing since 1994, and the rates for male victims have fallen more than rates for females. Thus, the disparity of victimization rates between males and females has narrowed considerably.

Men and women have different patterns of violent crime victimization. Most women are attacked by someone they know, whereas about half of the attacks on men are perpetrated by strangers.[22] Women are more likely to be attacked in the home; men, in public places. Most intimate partner violence and sexual assault victims are female. In fact, 85 percent of violent crimes committed by intimates (people in a romantic relationship) have female victims.[23] The number one cause of assault and murder of women in the United States is intimate partner violence.[24]

Age is also an important factor in victimization. In general, younger people are more likely than older people to be victims of violent crime. Children are vulnerable to abuse by parents and other caregivers.

Adjusted Victimization Rate per 1,000 Persons Age 12 or Older

Males

Females

FIGURE 2-2   Violent Crime Rates by Gender of Victims

Current rates for both males and females are well below rates of previous years.

SOURCE: U.S. Department of Justice, Bureau of Justice Statistics, "Violent Crime Rates by Gender of Victim." http://bjs.ojp.usdoj.gov/content/glance/vsx2.cfm (retrieved July 11, 2011).

a case in point

Michigan's Task Force Approach to Violent Crime Reduction

The state of Michigan has set an exemplary record in combining local, state, and federal resources to combat violent crime. Within the greater Detroit area, the Detroit Violent Crimes Task Force typically focuses on offenses involving homicide, firearm use in the commission of a violent crime, and operation of a criminal enterprise. This violent crimes task force comprises six local, state, and federal agencies: the Detroit Police Department; the Federal Bureau of Investigation; the Bureau of Alcohol, Tobacco, Firearms, and Explosives; the Drug Enforcement Administration; the Wayne County Sheriff's Office; and the Michigan State Police. The task force targets specific incidents of violent crime, as well as zones of violent crime occurrence.[a] The task force has proved to be adept in solving complex cases through developing leads and evidence from cellular phone records, using mapping programs, and mining data from a variety of sources.

A recent case that applied this three-pronged approach involved a kidnapping, an extortion, and a murder. After combing phone records and pinpointing the location of cell towers within the region from which ransom calls were being made, investigators plotted the general location of the kidnapping victim, which they referred to as the "triangle of death." Through additional review of the phone records of the primary suspect (a suspected contract killer), investigators identified an individual who resided within the triangle of death.

A follow-up to this individual's residence led to the recovery of the body of the kidnapping victim—and ultimately to closure of the case through the perpetrator's conviction.[b]

Detroit's task force has also significantly impacted the activities of violent gangs, major players in the region's drug trafficking, which is responsible for an estimated 65–70 percent of Detroit's homicides. The task force has arrested and prosecuted scores of Detroit gang members for charges related to homicide, drug distribution, and illegal weapons possession. Among those apprehended have been members of the "Joy Road," "Thug Lordz," "Almighty Latin King Nation," and "New World Order"—all gangs heavily engaged in drug trafficking, assaults, robberies, and homicides. U.S. Attorney Stephen Murphy of the Eastern Judicial District of Michigan has commended the collaborative effort in bringing down the gang leaders as yielding extraordinary results. Special Agent-in-Charge Valerie Goddard of the Bureau of Alcohol, Firearms, Tobacco, and Explosives echoes Murphy's perspective, commenting in the aftermath of a gang sweep on how "this case highlights the success of the tactical intelligence driven enforcement approach using innovative technology, analytical investigative resources, and integrated law enforcement strategies to identify, disrupt, arrest, and prosecute the most violent criminals in Detroit."[c]

Another of Michigan's multiagency task forces, Operation Violence Reduction, operated in the greater Detroit area for six weeks during early 2015. During the six-week period, 233 people were arrested. Individual charges included 9 for homicide, 14 for weapons, 31 for assault, 29 for sexual assault, 33 for robbery, 48 for narcotics, and 69 for other violent offenses.[d]

OBSERVE → INVESTIGATE → UNDERSTAND

- What are the advantages of the increased use of violent crimes task forces?
- What problems might arise with communication or behavior among task force members? Why? How might these problems be addressed?
- What measures might be taken to prevent the residents of a "target zone" from perceiving that task force members are an "occupying army"?

SOURCES: [a]State of Michigan, "Detroit Violent Crime Task Force Focuses on Offenders Who Commit Violent Crimes." www.michigan.gov/msp/0,1607,7-123-1589_3492-73104–,00.html (accessed December 24, 2010).

[b]Art Wimmer, "Using Technology to Help Solve Crimes," *FBI Law Enforcement Bulletin* 77 no. 12 (2008): 7–10.

[c]PR Newswire, "Operation TIDE Task Force Arrests Members of the Joy Road Drug Gang," July 11, 2010. www.prnewswire.com/news-releases/operation-tide-task-force-arrests-members-of-the-joy-road-drug-gang-52724847.html.

[d]David Jesse, "Task Force Nabs 200 Fugitives in Suburban Detroit," *Detroit Free Press*, April 17, 2015. www.freep.com/story/news/local/michigan/2015/04/17/task-force-warrants-arrests/25926399 (retrieved April 21, 2015).

▲ **Sex Differences in Reporting Violent Crimes**

Women may be less likely than men to report a violent crime.

In 2008, there were 3.3 million reports of child abuse and neglect in the United States, 20.9 percent of which were later substantiated.[25] Very young children are at particular risk of being abused and are especially likely to suffer severe injuries or death as a consequence. Of course, much child abuse goes unreported.

MYTH/REALITY

MYTH: Older adults are more likely to be victimized than people in any other age group.

REALITY: In 2013, individuals aged 12 to 17 had the highest prevalence of being victims of violent crime at 2.2 percent of all persons of that age, or 52.1 per 1,000 persons in that age group. By comparison, elders had the lowest prevalence of violent crime at 0.3 percent of all persons of that age, or only 5.4 per 1,000 persons in that age group.[26]

Elder people are significantly less likely than young people to be victims of violent crime, though like children, some older persons may have a heightened potential for being abused, physically and emotionally. Research on elder abuse is relatively new. The vulnerability of older people is unique, and law enforcement personnel must understand it as a separate phenomenon, whether they are dealing with crime prevention or victim assistance. Elder abuse is likely to increase significantly as the population shifts with the entry of baby boomers into their senior years. It is estimated that half a million elder people in the United States are abused each year.[27] This troubling statistic notwithstanding, of all age groups, it is teenagers who are most likely to be victims of violent crime.[28]

Homicide

homicide
The act of unjustifiably causing the death of another human being.

first-degree murder
The most serious kind of murder. To be convicted of first-degree murder, an offender must have purposely killed the victim and must have planned the killing at least a short time in advance.

second-degree murder
In most states, an intentional killing that is not planned ahead of time.

manslaughter
A killing in which the offender is less blameworthy than for murder; it usually carries a less severe penalty than murder.

voluntary manslaughter
Killing in the heat of passion.

involuntary manslaughter
A killing that results from an offender's careless actions.

vehicular manslaughter
In some states, a classification for a death that results from careless driving.

Homicide occurs when someone unjustifiably causes the death of another human being. The different types of homicide are distinguished primarily by the culpability of the offender.

Most intentional homicides are classified as murders. Different jurisdictions classify murders in different ways, but usually the most serious kind is first-degree murder. To be convicted of **first-degree murder,** an offender must have purposely killed his or her victim and must have planned to do so at least a short time in advance. In some states, people may receive the death penalty for first-degree murder. In most states, **second-degree murder** is an intentional killing not planned ahead of time.

Manslaughter is a killing in which the offender is less blameworthy, and it usually carries a less severe penalty than murder. There is more than one type of manslaughter. **Voluntary manslaughter** occurs when an offender is provoked and loses control, killing his or her victim in the heat of passion; **involuntary manslaughter** refers to a killing that results from an offender's careless actions. For example, 20-year-old Collin Viens was playing with his hunting rifle and shot at a tractor he believed was empty. In fact, Rejean Lussier was sitting in the tractor and was killed. Viens was convicted of involuntary manslaughter and given a sentence of 1 to 5 years.[29] In some states, deaths resulting from careless driving are classified as involuntary manslaughter. Careless driving might include excessive speed or the failure to stop for pedestrians at a crosswalk. Other states, such as California, classify such deaths as **vehicular manslaughter.**

According to the UCR, the U.S. murder and voluntary manslaughter rate is approximately 4.6 per 100,000 inhabitants, but it varies by geographic areas.[30] Homicide rates are highest in the South and lowest in New England and the Rocky Mountain West.[31] Internationally, the United States has some

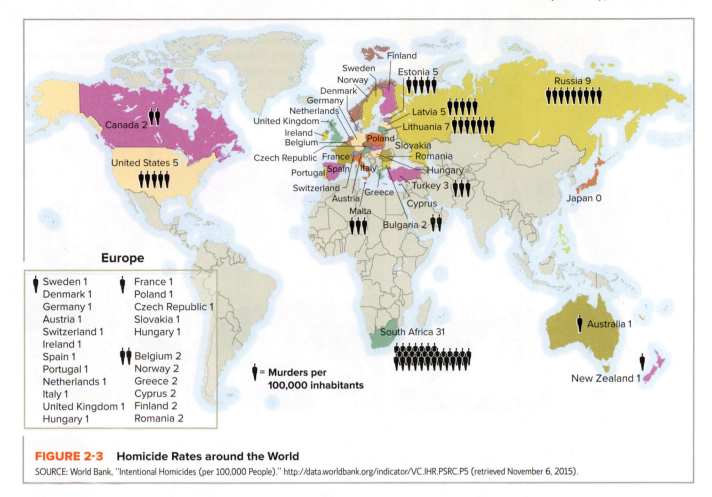

FIGURE 2-3   Homicide Rates around the World

SOURCE: World Bank, "Intentional Homicides (per 100,000 People)." http://data.worldbank.org/indicator/VC.IHR.PSRC.P5 (retrieved November 6, 2015).

of the world's highest homicide rates (Figure 2-3). Some nations with higher murder rates than the United States are Estonia, Lithuania, Russia, and South Africa; among the lowest are Japan, Spain, Greece, and Switzerland.[32]

The most grievous of crimes, homicide takes away a person's most prized possession–life. As the only form of victimization from which the victim cannot recover, it therefore incurs the severest penalties. Depending on the kind of homicide committed, an offender might receive anything from probation or a short time in prison to, in many states, a death sentence. The survivor victims (the deceased person's loved ones) are asked to cooperate with a system that they often perceive as being demanding, at times uncaring, and sometimes even abusive. The impact of the crime and criminal justice proceedings on grieving survivor victims is usually traumatic and long lasting. For victim service providers, this is the most challenging form of victimization.[33]

One of the most intriguing areas in the study of crime is *multiple murder*, in which perpetrators kill many victims. Serial murder, mass murder, and spree murder are each a type of multiple murder, differentiated by time. **Serial murder** is the killing of three or more people over an extended period. **Mass murders** are multiple murders that occur at one place and time. In a **spree murder**, victims are killed within a fairly narrow time span, from several hours to a few days.[34]

People in mainstream society, and certainly students of criminology, are fascinated with serial killers–their lives, motivations, methods or *modus operandi* (MO), and selection of victims. The media fuel this interest through sensational movies, television shows, and stories that are filled with gory details but short on facts. The stereotype of a serial killer is a "ruthless, blood-thirsty sex monster who lives a Jekyll-and-Hyde existence–probably next door to you."[35] In fact, not

serial murder
The killing of three or more people over an extended period of time for personal gratification.

mass murder
Multiple murders that occur at one place and at one time.

spree murder
The killing of several people within a fairly narrow period, such as several hours or days.

◄▼ John Wayne Gacy: The Jekyll-and-Hyde Serial Killer

Gacy was a known and trusted member of his community. He sometimes entertained neighborhood children in full costume as "Pogo the Clown." (The photo below is Gacy's self-portrait as Pogo.) But Gacy also raped and murdered 33 boys and young men between 1972 and 1978, usually burying their corpses in a crawl space under his house.

all serial murders are motivated by sex, and not all serial killers sexually violate their victims. That they live a Jekyll-and-Hyde existence is true to the extent that they present themselves in society as at least minimally acceptable individuals, hiding their darker nature. They are not so much "taken over by strange forces" that change their fundamental identity; rather, they succeed in hiding their criminality from others. Some do this with more success than others.

Stereotypes often have some validity, but serial murderers are not homogeneous. Most exhibit particular patterns or have a specific modus operandi, but some are less consistent in the commission of their crimes, using, for

► Survivor of Connecticut Mass Murder

Although Dr. William Petit (speaking here at a press conference after the conviction of Hayes) escaped his captors, his wife Jennifer and the couple's daughters, Hayley and Michaela, did not survive their brutal attacks. This 2007 home invasion involved crimes of robbery, rape, arson, attempted murder, and murder.

example, a variety of weapons. Some seek a specific type of victim, and others are more opportunistic and kill because a victim is an easy target. Most known serial killers are male and use weapons or other means of physical violence to kill. Other serial killers, usually female, kill by relatively passive methods such as poison or suffocation. For many male serial murderers, motivation includes sexual gratification; for many female offenders, the killings bring them attention or money from victims' insurance policies. Serial killers can murder within a specific location such as a home or known neighborhood, or they can be mobile, murdering across a city, state, or even the country. Some victims know their assailant, perhaps through an intimate or familial relationship, or as a passing acquaintance; others are total strangers.[36]

Mass murders, those that occur when several individuals are killed within minutes in the same location or after being held hostage together, have been committed in workplaces and other public locales, such as post offices and schools. However, in some intimate partner violence or family abuse cases, one person will take an entire family hostage within the home, kill each person, and then commit suicide.[37] A 2007 mass murder case that attracted headlines across the nation involved a 7-hour home invasion, robbery, rape, and arson in Cheshire, Connecticut, that resulted in the deaths of Jennifer Hawke-Petit, who was raped and strangled, and her daughters aged 17 and 11, the youngest of whom was also raped. All three were tied up and died in the fire set by their captors, parolees Steven Hayes and Joshua Komisarjevsky. The husband and father of the murder victims, Dr. William Petit Jr., was beaten and restrained but survived by escaping through a basement door of the home before the fire swept through the house. Both Hayes and Komisarjevsky were given the death penalty for their heinous crimes.[38]

In the third category of multiple murder, spree killing, the offender is usually mobile and often acts erratically and boldly; these crimes frequently involve the use of drugs and alcohol. The spree murderer may kill several victims in a single location before moving on.[39] Andrew Cunanan killed five men over an 80-day period in 1997. Some classify him as a spree killer because his killings began when he left California in April and continued as he traveled across the country until he committed suicide in July—as if he left home to go on an apparently

KEY CONCEPTS Types of Homicide

Type	Definition
First-degree murder	A murder in which the offender must have purposely killed his or her victim and must have planned to do so at least a short time in advance.
Second-degree murder	An intentional killing not planned ahead of time.
Manslaughter	A killing in which the offender is less blameworthy, usually carrying a less severe penalty.
Voluntary manslaughter	A killing in which an offender is provoked and loses control, slaying his or her victim in the heat of passion.
Involuntary manslaughter	A killing resulting from an offender's careless actions.
Vehicular manslaughter	Death resulting from careless driving.
Serial murder	The killing of three or more people over an extended period for personal gratification.
Mass murder	Multiple murders that occur at one place and time.
Spree murder	Killing of several victims within a fairly narrow time span, generally from several hours to a few days.

continuous killing campaign. Others see Cunanan as a serial murderer because his murders took place over an extended time period. Such cases illustrate how even professionals may classify the same multiple murderer differently.

Assault and Battery

assault and battery
A harmful or offensive physical attack by one person upon another.

Another type of crime against persons is **assault and battery,** a harmful or offensive physical attack by one person upon another. The UCR reported that in 2013 there were approximately 234 aggravated assaults in the United States per 100,000 population.[40] (The crime of *aggravated assault* means attacking another person with the intent to commit another felony, or using a deadly weapon.)

Like homicide, assault usually starts with interpersonal conflict and escalates to violence. When a victim and an assaulter are married or partnered and charges are filed, the victim must come to terms with the prosecution of the offender. The criminal justice system offers both parties input in deciding whether to stay in or leave the relationship. Many relationships that include assault victimizations are not easy to leave, and those that include children, intrafamilial relationships, and employment may be complicated, even binding. If the relationship continues and the interpersonal problem cannot be resolved, the same conflict or similar ones are highly likely to erupt again and, over time, to escalate into serious violence. Victims who cooperate with the criminal justice system thus may require special protections.

Sexual Assault

sexual violence
A range of crimes including vaginal, anal, digital, and/or oral penetration that can include the use of weapons and foreign objects to torture and terrorize the victim.

sexual victimization
Forced or coerced sexual intimacy.

Sexual assault is one of the most sensationalized of all victimizations and has characteristics of both physical and sexual violence. **Sexual violence** encompasses a range of crimes, including sexual intercourse by force with vaginal, anal, digital, and/or oral penetration and the use of weapons and foreign objects as sexual devices to torture and terrorize the victim. **Sexual victimization** means "forced or coerced sexual intimacy."[41] Sexual assault is a devastating experience for victims, depriving them of their dignity and traumatizing them for a significant time. Anyone, regardless of age, sex, race, or other characteristics, may be sexually victimized.

The Victims of Sexual Violence Victims are likely to know their assailant; three-fourths of reported rape victims 18 and older named as the rapist their current or former husband or unmarried partner, or someone they had been dating.[42] The most common types of sexual assault perpetrated by a known assailant are *marital rape* and *date rape.* Another example is *acquaintance rape,* in which the victim knows–or has at least seen–the perpetrator prior to the assault, but the two are not dating or in an intimate relationship. In all these cases, the perpetrator can be of the opposite or the same sex as the victim.

The most recent data from the National Crime Victimization Survey (NCVS) show that in 2010, approximately 270,000 women experienced a sexual assault, with completed rapes comprising more than 50 percent of the total of sexually violent victimizations that year. In a five-year period from 2005 to 2010, females who were under 34 years old and who also identified as lower income and living in rural areas had some of the highest rates of sexual violence. During the same five-year period, almost 80 percent of sexual violence was perpetrated by a family member, intimate partner, or acquaintance; 11 percent of rapes involved a gun, knife, or other weapon; and 35 percent of women were treated for their injuries. Of those treated for their injuries, 80 percent went to a hospital, emergency room, or doctor's office, and almost one-quarter of victims contacted a victim services agency. Slightly more than one-third of sexual assaults were reported to police in 2010, a decrease from the all-time high of 56 percent that were reported in 2003.[43]

Victimization research based on individuals and their experiences of crime, however, suggests that only one in four sexual assaults is reported to the police.[44] The remaining victims do not report assaults, for a number of reasons. They may view it as a personal matter (25 percent) or fear retaliation (17 percent). Sometimes the crime was reported to a different official (13 percent), the victim wished to protect the offender (10 percent), or the victim believed the criminal justice system would be biased against her (6 percent).[45] Victimization survey data also show that victims do not report for various reasons, among them: self-blame (especially if the victim was under the influence of alcohol), an expectation of being judged negatively, a fear of retaliation (especially when the victim and offender know each other), a preference for dealing with the assault privately, a desire to avoid shame, and a wish to protect family from embarrassment.[46] Ethnic and cultural background seems to play a role in determining the willingness of women to report sexual attacks.

▲ **People Participating in "Take Back the Night"**

"Take Back the Night" demonstrations increase people's awareness of rape and sexual assault.

The closer the relationship between offender and victim, the less likely it is that the victim will contact police. Some reasons are: fear of retaliation, fear that family or friends will side with the perpetrator, and fear that the crime will be perceived as "no big deal." One-fourth of victims reported the sexual assault when the offender was a current or former intimate partner, compared to 18 percent when it was an acquaintance or a friend. In contrast, 66 percent of victims reported the crime to the police when the assailant was a stranger.[47]

Ultimately, the nonreporting of sexual assault ensures that the offender goes unpunished and keeps the crime a secret. Some observers denounce this situation as a conspiracy of silence that encourages victims (and witnesses) to accept victimization as not serious enough to report. Some victims develop a sense of helplessness that lasts long after the initial victimization.[48]

The Role of Alcohol and Date Rape Drugs   Many rapes occur when the perpetrator and/or the victim use alcohol or other substances. In recent years, any substance used to facilitate a rape has been referred to as a *date rape drug*. Among the most common of these odorless and tasteless drugs are Rohypnol (also known as ruffies), gamma hydroxybutyrate (GHB), ketamine (also known as K or Special K), and ecstasy (or E). The would-be rapist slips the drug into a beverage that a potential victim consumes. Within minutes of drinking it, the victim is likely to feel dizzy and nauseated and very soon will lose consciousness. Depending on the drug or combination of drugs used, the victim may not regain consciousness for several hours, sometimes even for days.

Date rape drugs are also called *mind erasers* because once the victim awakens, she typically has no memory of the preceding 24 to 48 hours. She may not remember being unconscious, what she drank, or even whom she was with. These memory gaps make the prosecution of these cases especially difficult.[49] Despite the availability of date rape drugs, the most commonly used substance in committing a sexual assault is still alcohol, the age-old means of lowering perpetrators' inhibitions and intoxicating or otherwise incapacitating victims.[50]

The Urgency of Medical Attention   Once a rape has been committed, it is very important for the victim to receive medical attention, specifically, a sexual

rape trauma syndrome
The three phases (acute, outward adjustment, and resolution) of symptoms that many victims experience after a sexual assault.

assault forensic exam. This exam allows for the collection of DNA evidence, which is vital when there is an unknown assailant.

Although each victim responds differently to sexual victimization, many experience a number of symptoms collectively known as **rape trauma syndrome,** which has three phases. The *acute phase* occurs immediately after the crisis, and the symptoms usually linger for several weeks. During this phase, some victims' reactions may include fear, anxiety, agitation, and crying. However, other victims may appear in control, calm, and emotionless in the acute phase, sometimes leading service providers to conclude inaccurately that the sexual assault was not serious or did not actually happen. The reality is that some individuals respond in a controlled manner initially, only to experience an emotional breakdown several days or even months after the attack. Some victims first express shock, disbelief, and disorientation. They may have difficulty concentrating, making decisions, or answering questions. Service providers may misinterpret these normal reactions as uncooperativeness.[51]

The second, or *outward adjustment phase*, features a seeming return to normal life but an inward struggle to cope with the assault. Some victims suppress the event and refuse to talk about what happened or what they are currently feeling. They try to live as if the rape never occurred. Others completely alter their lives to begin anew, moving to a new city or home, switching jobs, breaking off relationships, or changing their appearance. Some victims minimize the situation, saying that things could have been worse or that everything is fine. Others in this phase cannot stop talking about the crime; it becomes the focal point of their life. Regardless of the coping technique used, behaviors associated with this phase include fear, helplessness, anxiety, flashbacks, difficulty concentrating, depression, severe mood swings, rage, eating and sleeping difficulties, sexual and relationship problems, and isolation from loved ones and familiar activities. The presence, intensity, and duration of these symptoms differ for each victim and can last from a few months to years.

Finally comes the *resolution phase*, marked by the victim's shifting focus from the crisis and the intensity of the attack to coping or resolution and moving on with life. This shift does not mean the victim has forgotten about the sexual assault; rather, she or he has placed the rape in perspective as a part, but not the totality, of her or his life. The victim does not feel the intensity and range of emotions that followed the assault or were the hallmarks of the outward adjustment phase. Instead, she or he may briefly experience a range of emotions, but the feelings subside and the pain lessens with time. Resolution occurs through a strong support system, counseling, and sometimes the ending of her or his involvement with the criminal justice system.[52]

Robbery

In 1999, the FBI reported that on average, one robbery occurred every minute.[53] According to the UCR, in 2013 approximately 113 robberies were committed in the United States per 100,000 population.[54]

robbery
A crime against a person in which the offender takes personal property from the victim by either using or threatening force.

A **robbery** is always a crime against a person because, while taking personal property from the victim, the robber either uses or threatens to use force. In 41 percent of all robberies, the perpetrator instills fear with a handgun. Some victims were robbed of their cars while stopped at a traffic light; some, while walking the streets; some while at work. Many believe robbery is the victimization most people fear, thinking that they could be killed in a robbery attempt. Despite this fear, the likelihood of murder during a robbery is low; since 1980, 99.8 percent of all robbery victims have survived their victimizations.[55] Primarily because of the intense fear and sense of helplessness it causes, some robbery victims suffer severe and lasting psychological trauma.

Matters *of* Ethics

Ethical Issues When Dealing with Treatment of Offenders or Victims

Many professional organizations that deal with trauma have formal ethical standards for issues concerning treatment. For example, the American Psychological Association has *The Ethical Principles for Psychologists*. These principles are applicable for clinicians and their relationships with all types of patients. It might be surprising that the available case histories about psychologists who fall into these ethical dilemmas more frequently have to do with trauma than one would think. Having to cope with clinical, legal, and moral issues simultaneously significantly exacerbates the challenges of competent therapy, often resulting in maltreatment. Having offenders and victims as trauma clients can increase the likelihood of ethical transgressions. Three essential requirements for those treating offenders and victims are: (1) to be properly credentialed with offenders or victims; (2) to maintain current awareness of innovations and findings in the research literature; and (3) to understand the unique standards that apply to these types of clients. Additionally, one of the common recommendations is to obtain the assistance of a consultant, especially for complicated cases. Getting a second opinion from a trusted, competent, and respected colleague not only can reduce the risks of ethical violations but also can confirm the use of treatment techniques that serve the needs of both clients.

OBSERVE → INVESTIGATE → UNDERSTAND

- What are the differences between clinical, legal, and moral treatment decisions? Explain.
- When dealing with offenders or victims, can you imagine what types of severe outcomes could result when ethical transgressions occur?
- What might be some of the barriers to exercising good ethical judgment in providing therapy with such cases as child abuse, sexual assault, or incest? Discuss the possible complexities.

SOURCE: Constance J. Dalenberg and Lina Brown, "Ethical Issues," in Michele Winterstein and Scott R. Scribner (Eds.), *Mental Health Care for Child Crime Victims: Standards of Care Task Force Guidelines* (California Victim Compensation and Government Claims Board, 2001). http://www.vcgcb.ca.gov/docs/forms/victims/standardsofcare/Chapter_2.pdf (retrieved May 21, 2015).

Crimes against Children

A crime against persons that is particularly difficult for most people to understand occurs when children are the targets of violence. Children are the most vulnerable of all groups, a fact accounting for why child abuse victims are of great concern to society.

Forms of Child Abuse **Child abuse** refers, for the most part, to neglect of or violence against children. Although child abuse has been a major social concern only since the 1950s, adults have victimized children throughout history. From 1998 to 2002, among the 3.5 million victims of family violence, 10.5 percent of them, or 367,600, were children harmed by their parents.[56] The major forms of child abuse are physical abuse, sexual abuse, drug endangerment, emotional maltreatment, and neglect. Each is unique and requires different responses by society and victim services providers.

Physical abuse, which includes corporal punishment (such as spanking), has been in the forefront of child abuse literature and research since the 1960s when the term *battered child syndrome* was coined. This phrase describes the condition whereby a child suffers serious physical injury, usually inflicted by parents.[57] **Physical abuse** includes intentionally beating, biting, burning, strangling, hitting, kicking, shaking, or pushing a child. Indeed, many argue there is a very fine line–if there is one at all–between spanking and abuse. One of the foremost opponents of corporal punishment has researched this topic for

child abuse
Neglect of and/or violence against children.

physical abuse
The condition whereby an individual suffers serious physical injury from the intentional aggressive acts of others, such as slapping, spanking, beating, biting, burning, strangling, hitting, kicking, shaking, or pushing.

more than 30 years and concludes that children who are physically hurt by their parents may suffer significant long-term psychological harm.[58]

With respect to the sexual abuse of children, most people find this offense particularly disturbing, as it serves primarily not to control or correct a child's behavior but to gratify the perpetrator. With the exception of murder, sexual assault is the least commonly reported form of family violence (it constitutes just 0.9 percent of all such cases).[59] For the most part, child sex abusers are family members, friends, and neighbors of the victim. In one large survey, roughly 43 percent of sexual abusers were family members with whom victims had a long-lasting, trusting relationship. The psychological trauma is generally surmountable, although recovery becomes more difficult when the offender used coercive force or the child was older.[60]

MYTH/REALITY

MYTH: All child sexual abuse victims are girls.

REALITY: Recent large studies in the United States indicate that girls are at least twice—and in some studies four times—as frequently abused sexually as are boys.[61]

Drug-endangered children (DEC) form another category of abused children. The offspring of parents who are selling or manufacturing drugs, these children live in deplorable conditions and are in imminent danger. Often exposed to the drugs themselves, DEC are on occasion left behind since they are sometimes not identified as victims by first responders. DEC agencies in many states have developed programs that link law enforcement with child services and have begun programs and practices to rescue these children and place them in safe environments.[62]

A more subtle type of abuse against children is **emotional abuse.** In this form of victimization, sometimes called *psychological abuse*, power or control is used to harm the victim's sense of self. Emotional abuse often includes such acts as "verbal threats, social isolation, intimidation, exploitation, or routinely making unreasonable demands, terrorizing a child, or exposing [him] to family violence."[63] Other examples of emotional abuse are shaming and putting down a child.[64] Such abuse often results in impaired psychological growth, health, and development. Emotional abuse also can occur when a parent does not notice or seek help for a child's emotional problems. Due to vague and conflicting definitions of emotional abuse, and the difficulties in measuring it, the extent of this crime is unknown.

Some forms of child abuse are acts of omission. **Child neglect** is the chronic and repetitive failure to provide children with food, clothing, shelter, cleanliness, medical care, or protection from harm. It constitutes the largest category of child abuse offenses; 52 percent of all child abuse cases in the United States (and roughly 40 percent in Canada) involve neglect.[65] Researchers once assumed the negative outcomes of neglect were relatively minor. Recent research indicates that child neglect, especially at an early age, causes substantial problems. In fact, some forms of early neglect lead to "severe, chronic, and irreversible damage."[66]

Most commonly, adults commit child abuse. However, children may sometimes abuse other children. This type of abuse can also be traumatic and leave long-lasting effects.

emotional abuse
A form of victimization by means of power or control that harms the victim's sense of self and is sometimes referred to as psychological abuse, including verbal threats, social isolation, intimidation, exploitation, or routinely making unreasonable demands, terrorizing, shaming, and putting the victim down.

child neglect
Chronic and repetitive failure to provide children with food, clothing, shelter, cleanliness, medical care, or protection from harm.

MYTH/REALITY

MYTH: Bullying at school is a normal process that teaches children about life and helps them to mature.

REALITY: Bullying is not a necessary rite of passage that all children must endure to mature. It is an unnecessary experience that can and often does cause trauma and severe psychological injury if not properly treated, and it can result in lifelong disability to the victims.[67]

Student Bullying: When Children Abuse Children One of the more disconcerting forms of child abuse, and a serious problem in schools nationwide, is **student bullying.** This form of victimization occurs when, over a span of time, a student repeatedly experiences harmful acts committed by other students.[68]

Examples of student bullying—and its tragic aftermath—are all too common. In April 2009 a woman in Springfield, Massachusetts, found her 11-year-old son Carl Joseph Walker-Hoover hanging by an extension cord at their home after having endured another day of homophobic taunts at his school.[69] In September 2010 Asher Brown, a 13-year-old boy in Houston, Texas, committed suicide by shooting himself in the head in response to harassment and bullying at school.[70] And in November 2010 Brandon Bitner, a 14-year-old boy in Pennsylvania, committed suicide by walking several miles to a highway to step in front of an oncoming tractor-trailer. He had written a suicide note stating that he had endured years of constant bullying at school.[71]

It was previously thought that school bullying peaked in middle school and decreased in high school. However, a national survey of 43,000 students, conducted in 2010, reported that half the high school students said they had bullied another person during the past year, and almost half of the students said that they had been the victim of bullying.[72] Additionally, a study conducted in England found that those students who are engaged in bullying—whether they are victims, bullies, or bystanders—are significantly more likely to have thoughts about ending their own life.[73] Other studies indicate that lesbian, gay, and bisexual students have a higher risk of emotional distress—such as depression, self-harm, and suicidal thoughts—and of suicide attempts than their classmates due to homophobic bullying.[74]

Bullying is especially disturbing for school administrators and teachers, because most of it takes place in and around school grounds and often seriously disrupts learning. Ironically, bullying originates within the bully's home. The act of bullying—throughout the bully's life—seems to be highly correlated with the physical abuse the child suffered at the hands of his parents. For some children, being a bully is an early indication of later criminal behavior. For other children, victimization appears to be an early indicator of further, even lifelong victimization. Fortunately, research indicates that child abuse interventions can have beneficial effects in the homes of both offenders and victims.[75] (For additional information about child abuse, see Chapter 14.)

▲ **The community rallies against bullying children**

student bullying
A form of victimization in which a student is repeatedly exposed to threats and harmful acts from other students over a period of time.

MYTH/REALITY

MYTH: A child kidnapped by one of the child's own parents does not suffer significantly because the kidnapper is usually known to the child.

REALITY: A child who is taken by a parent suffers more than we generally realize. There can be enormous damage to the child's psyche from being trapped between warring parents, sometimes living on the run, using false names, and missing school and appropriate medical attention.[76]

KEY CONCEPTS Types of Child Abuse

Type	Definition
Physical abuse	Intentional slapping, spanking, beating, biting, burning, strangling, hitting, kicking, shaking, or pushing of a child.
Sexual abuse	Nonconsensual, forced, or coerced sexual touching of genitalia, anus, mouth, or breasts. Also can include forced masturbation or use of another person for prostitution, pornography, or voyeurism.
Neglect	Chronic and repetitive failure to provide a child with food, clothing, shelter, cleanliness, medical care, or protection from harm.
Emotional abuse	Subjection of a child to verbal threats, social isolation, intimidation, exploitation, unreasonable demands, terrorizing, or exposure to family violence.
School bullying	A student's repeated experience of harmful acts perpetrated by other schoolchildren.
Missing children	Children not accounted for by their next of kin because they have been kidnapped (and perhaps killed), have wandered away on their own due to a disability, or have intentionally fled from home violence.
Abandonment	The act of intentionally leaving a child in circumstances in which the child might suffer serious harm; or the situation where the parent or guardian's identity or whereabouts are unknown, or the parent or guardian has failed to maintain reasonable contact with the child or to provide reasonable support for a specified period, with the intent of never resuming his or her interest or claim over the child. Sometimes also called *foundling* or *throwaway*.
Homicide	The intentional illegal taking of a child's life, in some cases caused by the use of physical abuse that results in the child's death.

missing children
Children not accounted for by their next of kin because they were kidnapped or killed, wandered away due to a developmental disability, or are intentionally missing in order to escape violence at home.

Missing Children: An Often Overlooked Problem   One of the most ignored child victim types today is **missing children.** This category includes children who are not accounted for by their next of kin because they have been kidnapped (and perhaps killed); those who have wandered away on their own due to a developmental disability or mental illness; and those who have intentionally gone missing to escape violence at home. On December 31, 2006, there were 110,484 active missing person records in the National Crime Information Center's (NCIC) Missing Person File. About half the people in these files were under 18.[77]

The family and friends of a missing child sometimes offer special monetary rewards to help locate their loved one. The parents of a California kidnapping victim established one of the more elaborate efforts. The reward ultimately led to the location of the remains of their daughter, their granddaughter, and her friend, and it contributed to the successful prosecution of the three victims' killer. Subsequently these parents established a foundation that today provides these same services–in many cases successfully–across the United States.[78]

PROPERTY CRIMES

property crimes
The taking of money and/or material goods without the use of force, as well as the intentional destruction of property.

Although society clearly recognizes the seriousness of violent crimes, property offenses also can have a major impact on victims' lives. **Property crimes** include the taking of money or goods *without the use of force,* as well as the intentional destruction of property. Such crimes include any act of *burglary* (entering another's property with the intent to commit a felony such as theft), *theft* or *larceny* (taking another's property without permission), *motor vehicle theft,* and offenses that involve destruction of property, such as *arson.*

Rates of Property Crime

About three-quarters of all crimes committed in the United States in any given year are property crimes. According to the UCR, in 2013 approximately 2,730 property crimes were committed in the United States per 100,000 population.[79] As you can see from Figure 2-4, property crimes peaked in 1975, with a high of 553.6 victimizations per 1,000 households. Burglary peaked in 1974, at 111.8 victimizations per 1,000 households. Crimes of theft peaked in 1975, with 424.1 victimizations. In contrast, motor vehicle thefts did not peak until 1991, with 22.2 victimizations per 1,000 households.

In general, beginning in the mid-1970s, all categories of property crimes have decreased steadily. In 2004, approximately 16 million households, or 12 percent of the U.S. total, experienced one or more property crimes—a 9 percent decrease from a high of 21 percent in 1994.[80] It is unclear why this decrease occurred. One possible explanation may be that people have taken more security measures to protect their homes, decreasing their vulnerability to property crimes.

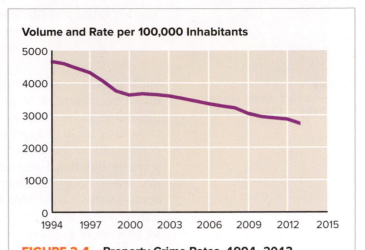

Volume and Rate per 100,000 Inhabitants

FIGURE 2-4   Property Crime Rates, 1994–2013
SOURCE: Federal Bureau of Investigation, "Crime in the United States 2013" (Washington, DC: U.S. Department of Justice). www.fbi.gov/about-us/cjis/ucr/crime-in-the-u.s/2013/crime-in-the-u.s.-2013/tables/1tabledatadecoverviewpdf/table_1_crime_in_the_united_states_by_volume_and_rate_per_100000_inhabitants_1994-2013.xls (retrieved November 19, 2015).

There is mixed evidence on whether difficult economic times result in higher than normal rates of property crimes. It makes sense that crime rates might increase as more people have difficulty finding jobs and as law enforcement budgets are slashed. For example, recent studies in Delaware and Virginia have linked rising property crimes rates with economic recession.[81] However, despite the struggling economy and high unemployment rates across the United States, the FBI reported that property crime rates continued to fall from 2008 through 2013.[82]

The Victims of Property Crime

People over the age of 65 experience more property crimes than other age groups. Between 1993 and 2002, 9 of 10 crimes reported by the elderly were property crimes, compared to 4 of 10 reported by persons between 12 and 24 years old. Latinos were more likely to be victimized by property crimes (204 per 1,000 households) than African Americans (191 per 1,000) or Caucasians (157 per 1,000 households). The same trend holds true for motor vehicle thefts, with Latinos (19 per 1,000 households) victimized more frequently than African Americans (16 per 1,000 households) or Caucasians (8 per 1,000 households). Finally, people with annual incomes under $7,500, including teens and unemployed persons, are victimized at a higher rate than those with higher incomes.[83]

Although property crime can happen anywhere, it is more common in urban than in rural areas and in the western region of the United States. Urban population densities and the resulting anonymity do contribute to the ease of stealing, but it is unclear why there are more property crimes in the West.

The pervasiveness of property crime suggests that many people who would never consider physically attacking others as the sole criminal act are willing to take others' belongings, sometimes even using violence. It may be tempting to let property crime take a distant second to violent crime in our attention, but we should not underrate it. Victims of theft, for example, can be devastated financially and psychologically, and the fear and stress of victimization can contribute to physical ailments.[84] Corporate crimes of theft in particular take an enormous financial toll on the economy as well as on public trust.

Much property crime also occurs in conjunction with violent criminal acts, making it worthy of every effort to understand and control it.

Burglary

burglary
Entering another's property with the intent to commit a felony such as larceny.

With the exception of larceny, **burglary**–entering another's property with the intent to commit a felony such as larceny–is the most common serious victimization perpetrated on people living in the United States. UCR statistics show that in 2013 approximately 610 burglaries per 100,000 population were committed in the United States.[85] Household burglary victimization produces a strong emotional reaction because it invades the victim's privacy and security, even though confrontations between burglars and victims are rare. A U.S. study in the early 1970s found that 92 percent of those who reported being burglarized stated there was no confrontation.[86] However, in a Canadian study, 44 percent of burglary victims reported being at home when the burglary took place.[87] Regardless of the value of the property that is stolen, and even if the victims are not at home, burglary may have a particularly adverse impact on victims because of the psychological trauma involved in having strangers enter one's home and disturb private belongings.

Larceny

larceny
A type of theft that includes both completed and attempted taking of cash or property from a location without attacking or threatening the victim and without obtaining permission.

The most common form of victimization in the United States is **larceny,** a type of theft that includes both completed and attempted taking of cash or property from a location without attacking or threatening the victim and without obtaining permission. (If property is taken with force or the threat of force, the crime is considered robbery.) The larceny rate in the United States is close to 1,915 per 100,000 population.[88] In 2013 there were about 6 million thefts.[89]

Theft victimization usually has the fewest physical and emotional effects. The most significant loss is the value of the object or cash taken. Victims of larceny are among the least likely victims to seek victim services because the crime normally does not result in significant fear or trauma. When they do request help, it is usually for administrative information to facilitate their cooperation with the criminal justice system's prosecution, to learn about applying for restitution or compensation, and to help prevent future victimization.

Motor Vehicle Theft

motor vehicle theft
A property crime that involves the theft of a motorized road vehicle.

Another property crime that usually does not include contact with the offender and accompanying fear or trauma is **motor vehicle theft,** the theft of a

▶ **Motor Vehicle Theft**

Breaking into a car can happen within minutes.

motorized road vehicle. Motor vehicle theft is less common than household burglary or larceny. According to the UCR, in 2013 approximately 221 motor vehicle thefts were committed in the United States per 100,000 population.[90]

The physical impact of motor vehicle theft is relatively minor. However, because the financial loss is high, victims often experience significant anger and a sense of major loss. Like other kinds of theft victims, they rarely see victim service providers. Their primary needs are for information about their role in the prosecution of the offender. Moreover, they want to find out how to obtain either restitution or compensation and how to avoid becoming a victim of future auto thefts.

White-Collar Crime

White-collar crime is an illegal, unethical action by an agent of an organization.[91] Because it is nonconfrontational, white-collar crime is frequently classified as a property crime. Certainly, pain and suffering result from the victim's realization of loss, but violence has not been threatened or inflicted to accomplish the unlawful taking of money or goods. White-collar crime can range in scope from a lowly employee's embezzlement of a few thousand dollars from a Main Street business to the gigantic frauds perpetrated by executives of the energy behemoth Enron Corporation or by financier Bernard Madoff. Defining white-collar crime has proved so problematic that some criminologists avoid it, favoring instead the broader concept of "occupational crime." In 1996, the National White-Collar Crime Center held a conference of researchers on the subject from across the United States and defined **white-collar crime** as "illegal or unethical acts that violate fiduciary responsibility or public trust, committed by an individual or organization, usually during the course of legitimate occupational activity, by persons of high or respectable social status for personal or organizational gain."[92]

white-collar crime
Illegal or unethical acts that violate fiduciary responsibility or public trust, committed by an individual or organization, usually during the course of legitimate occupational activity, by persons of high or respectable social status for personal or organizational gain.

MYTH/REALITY

MYTH: More people in the United States are affected by street crime than by white-collar crime.

REALITY: Although it is difficult to measure precisely the financial losses attributable to white-collar crime, criminologists generally agree that white-collar crime dwarfs street-crime losses.[93]

White-collar crimes include such offenses as corporate fraud, health care fraud, environmental crime, and money laundering. The actual extent and costs of white-collar crime are unknown; although, it is estimated by the FBI to cost the United States more than $300 billion annually.[94] This dwarfs losses from street crime, estimated at $14 billion per year.[95] A survey by the National White-Collar Crime Center revealed that 1 in 4 households surveyed reported experiencing at least one form of white-collar crime victimization within the previous year.[96]

During the 1990s, the exponential growth of the securities and commodities markets, combined with the erosion of government regulations, led to the involvement of great numbers of individuals in intentional corporate fraud. For example, using deceptive accounting practices, officers of Enron misled investors and regulators by falsifying its true financial condition.[97] Enron's collapse cost $60 billion in market value on Wall Street, almost $2.1 billion to pension plans, and 5,600 jobs.[98]

Despite increased public scrutiny, an enormous gap remains between the number of white-collar crimes committed and those actually brought to the attention of law enforcement.[99] Moreover, federal attorneys frequently decline to prosecute cases referred to them by the Securities and Exchange Commission (SEC).

Two principal reasons for their reluctance are the difficulty establishing criminal intent and the extent of harm, as well as complexity of the crimes. These offenses and losses (which often involve conspiracies) can be very hard to prove to juries of ordinary citizens, especially when accused white-collar offenders are wealthy business figures who can afford the best defense attorneys.

Many criminologists have long contended that the greatest damage done by white-collar crime lies not in its financial costs but in the corruption of U.S. society by those who occupy key roles in the economic and political systems.[100] The integrity of the financial markets and the public's resulting willingness to invest in them are crucial components of a capitalist economy. Widespread false reports of a company's robustness or other means of causing its shares to sell at inflated prices could cause people to lose trust in corporate reports altogether. The fallout to the economy could be devastating in terms of actual losses sustained directly by victims and the reluctance of others to invest in corporations.

PUBLIC ORDER CRIMES

Society considers as criminal a number of acts that, unlike property crimes, seemingly do not directly harm other people. Rather, the public believes public order crimes are harmful to society in general or to the person who commits the crime.

public order crimes
A wide variety of offenses considered immoral or public nuisances, including disorderly conduct, disturbing the peace, loitering, public intoxication, panhandling, bigamy, drunk driving, weapons violations, prostitution, obscenity, gambling, and possession of controlled substances.

Public order crimes encompass a wide variety of offenses, including disorderly conduct, disturbing the peace, loitering, public intoxication, panhandling, bigamy, drunk driving, weapons violations, prostitution, obscenity, gambling, and possession of controlled substances. In general, these are considered immoral acts or public nuisances. Crimes against public order often are called **victimless crimes** because, unlike property crimes and crimes against persons, they usually have no identifiable victim. However, the expression *victimless crime* may be misleading in that crimes against public order often do indirectly harm others.

victimless crimes
Often called crimes against public order and considered victimless because they usually have no identifiable victim.

For example, a store owner may lose sales if panhandlers or prostitutes who loiter outside drive away customers. On a larger scale, some argue that rampant obscenity, gambling, and drug use harm society itself. Arguably the most compelling case against such public order crimes as prostitution, money laundering, weapons offenses, and drug offenses is their link to organized crime and even terrorism. Some proponents of laws against public order crimes argue that such laws serve to protect people from themselves. The idea is that if people face potential criminal sanctions, they may be less tempted to harm themselves through substance abuse or excessive gambling.

Data on public order offenses are not collected by the FBI and are not part of the Uniform Crime Reports. A great many public order laws are local ordinances rather than state statutes, and few of them are regularly or systematically enforced. It is therefore difficult to determine accurately who commits public order crimes and how often.

Crimes against Morality

crimes against morality
Particular public order crimes, which include offenses related to sexuality, prostitution, gambling, and pornography.

Loud calls to enact specific laws against particular public order crimes, called *crimes against morality,* frequently dominate legislative agendas. **Crimes against morality** include offenses related to sexuality, prostitution, gambling, and pornography. Some observers see these laws as necessary to a civil and moral society. However, the morals they invoke may be questionable, if not unconstitutional. For example, at one time many states had *antimiscegenation laws,* which made it a crime for people of different races to marry. The Supreme Court declared these laws unconstitutional in 1967 in the case of *Loving v. Virginia.* Likewise, in *Lawrence v. Texas* in 2003, the Court struck down state laws forbidding couples to engage in acts of sodomy (oral or anal sex).[101]

Critics of morality laws have long argued that it is both wrong and impractical for society to legislate morality. What business is it of the state, they ask, to punish acts between consenting adults that harm nobody (except maybe the people willingly engaging in them)? Many public order laws that are still on the books—against gambling, fornication (sex outside marriage), and adultery, for example—are ignored so frequently and universally as to make them virtually meaningless. Proponents of public order laws counter, however, that these acts do harm to others, indirectly if not directly, and that even if the laws are difficult to enforce, they have a symbolic purpose in signifying that certain behaviors are wrong.

Another argument used against public order laws is that they are often vague and broad and can easily lead to abuse of discretion by police and other public officials. Laws against disorderly conduct, for instance, often are used to arrest peaceful protesters. Public nuisance laws serve as a pretext for raids on gay bars and bathhouses. Riot laws are invoked to quash strikes. Under antilewdness laws, women who acted independently of their fathers' or husbands' control have been imprisoned, and laws against panhandling and sleeping in public are used in attempts to rid cities of homeless people. In fact, critics have noted that those in power use public order laws as a way of keeping relatively powerless people—minorities, women, and the poor—"in their place."

In 2004 almost 70 percent of prostitution arrests were of women. Yet not only must there be male customers in order for prostitutes to engage in sex work, but female prostitutes are often controlled by a pimp, a male who monitors their work and takes a percentage of their pay. Pimps, too, are arrested, but much less frequently than are prostitutes. The disparity between female and male arrests for the sale of sex has led to cries of "foul" by those who view the criminalization of sexual behaviors of women as a means of controlling women's sexuality.[102] Female runaways, 73 percent of whom were victims of sexual abuse, often turn to sex work to survive. Drug-addicted women are more likely to use sex to obtain drugs than are male drug users.[103] Other women are forced into prostitution through human trafficking.

Recent examples of problematic public order laws are the antigang laws passed in some locales. These laws allow the police to arrest people for such acts as talking with known gang members, wearing clothing with gang-related colors or symbols, blocking sidewalks, or approaching vehicles. Some argue

Common Types of Abused Drugs

Drug	Examples
Stimulants	Cocaine, crack, and methamphetamines, including trade-name drugs Benzedrine, Dexedrine, and Methedrine
Depressants	Barbiturates, methaqualone, inhalants, meprobamate, and alcohol; trade-name drugs include Seconal, Nembutal, Amytal, Librium, Valium, and Thorazine
Opioids	Heroin, morphine, codeine, and fentanyl
Hallucinogens	LSD, PCP, mescaline, psilocybin, ecstasy or MDMA, and DPT
Marijuana	Cannabis and hashish
Performance-enhancing drugs (anabolic steroids)	Ethylestrenol, methandriol, methenolone, and methandrostenolone

these laws are an effective way to protect communities from gang-related violence, but opponents contend police use them to harass and intimidate youths, especially young people of color.[104]

Drug Offenses

drug offenses
Public order crimes that include the unlawful possession, use, manufacturing, selling, growing, making, or distributing of drugs classified as having potential for abuse.

Public order crimes include such **drug offenses** as the unlawful possession, use, manufacturing, selling, growing, making, or distributing of drugs classified as having potential for abuse. Illicit drugs may include (but are not limited to) *stimulants* such as cocaine and amphetamines; *depressants* such as barbiturates, inhalants, and alcohol; *opioids* such as heroin and cocaine; *hallucinogens* such as LSD and ecstasy; *marijuana*; and *performance-enhancing drugs* such as anabolic steroids. As you can see from the table "Common Types of Abused Drugs," there are many types of illicit drugs. Societal attempts to regulate drugs stretch back to the United States' early history, as we consider here.

U.S. Drug Regulation: A Historical View Drug regulation in the United States began in 1791, when Congress passed a tax on whiskey that led to the so-called Whiskey Rebellion. Refusing to pay the tax, Appalachian farmers tarred and feathered the federal revenue agents sent into the region by the government to collect the fees. In the end, the federal government won the confrontation, an outcome that established the U.S. government's power to enforce federal laws perceived to be in the national interest. Since then, numerous federal laws have imposed and increased punishments for drug offenses.

During the nineteenth and twentieth centuries, the negative effects of drug abuse by U.S. citizens grew into a major issue. Morphine and cocaine dependency became problems after the hypodermic syringe was invented in 1856. Opium smoking by Chinese immigrants and the widespread use of patent medicines containing opiates escalated during the late nineteenth and early twentieth centuries. Among major twentieth-century federal laws regulating narcotics, dangerous drugs, and controlled substances were the Pure Food and Drug Act (1906), the Harrison Act (1914), the Eighteenth (or Prohibition) Amendment (1919–1933), the Jones-Miller Act (1922), the Drug Abuse and Control Amendments (1965), the Comprehensive

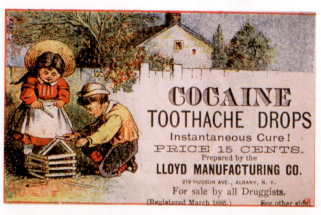

▲ **Ad for "Cocaine Toothache Drops"**

During the late nineteenth and early twentieth centuries, cocaine was a common pain medication.

Drug Abuse and Prevention and Control Act (1970), and the Omnibus Drug Act (1988), which created a U.S. "drug czar" with responsibility to develop a national drug-control strategy and a budget for federal agencies involved in drug enforcement. Each of these acts signifies increasing federal control and involvement in the "war on drugs."

The 1906 Pure Food and Drug Act required manufacturers of products containing drugs to clearly label the type of drug and to state how much of it was in the product. At the turn of the twentieth century, problematic drugs included alcohol, opium, morphine, cocaine, and marijuana. However, as long as the product containing the drug was not mislabeled, citizens could buy, sell, and use it freely, without prescriptions. The 1914 Harrison Act required individuals who sold or dispensed opiates and cocaine to register annually, pay a fee, and file a federal tax form. Users of these drugs could still do so without fear of penalty as long as they received the drugs from a registered physician who prescribed them for medical treatment. The 1922 Jones-Miller Act established the Federal Narcotics Control Board to deal with the illicit drug market. This law imposed a $5,000 fine and 10 years in prison for those convicted of illegally importing narcotics. The Jones-Miller Act also made addicted persons criminals if they had illegally obtained drugs in their possession. Between 1919 and 1933 the Eighteenth Amendment authorized federal legislation (the Volstead Act) making the manufacture, sale, and use of alcohol illegal.

Responding to an increase in the use of illegal drugs and to a change in the type of drugs used by U.S. citizens during the 1960s, the 1965 Drug Abuse Control Amendment classified hallucinogens, barbiturates, and amphetamines as dangerous drugs and established the Bureau of Narcotics and Dangerous Drugs. In 1970 the Comprehensive Drug Abuse Prevention and Control Act (often called the Controlled Substances Act) replaced or updated earlier laws dealing with narcotics and dangerous drugs. This act created five different schedules of controlled substances (see "Controlled Substances Schedules" table). It also funded drug prevention and treatment, moved drug enforcement from the Treasury Department to the Drug Enforcement Administration (DEA), made the attorney general responsible for drug enforcement laws, and empowered the secretary of Health and Human Services to decide—on the basis of medical research—which substances should be controlled. The act also established penalties for drug possession and sales.

Then, the 1988 Omnibus Drug Act toughened approaches that dealt with drug users. For example, under this law those who use illegal marijuana face a civil fine up to $10,000; loss of federal benefits, forfeiture of airplanes, cars, and boats used to transport drugs; and a family's removal from public housing if any member of that family engages in drug-related behavior on or near the housing complex. One part of this act makes it possible for a person who murders someone or orders the killing of someone in conjunction with a drug-related felony to receive the death penalty.[105] Despite these efforts, people in the United States continue to use illegal drugs, and enforcement remains a serious, difficult, and costly problem.

An alarming trend in drug abuse today is the use of **designer drugs,** such as ecstasy (a variation of methamphetamine), that mimic the chemical makeup of particular illicit drugs. Designer drugs get their name from the fact that the drug's manufacturer changes the chemical structure to get around existing drug laws.

Another alarming trend is the use of caffeinated alcohol drinks such as Four Loko. The U.S. Food and Drug Administration is concerned about the danger of these beverages, and so are the states. Michigan's Liquor Control Commission banned alcoholic energy drinks in November 2010, and other states are following suit.[106] As of January 2013, Massachusetts, New York, Washington, Utah, Michigan, Kansas, and California had banned beer drinks laced with caffeine.[107]

designer drugs
Drugs that mimic the chemical makeup of particular illicit drugs, named for the fact that drug manufacturers may change the chemical structure to get around existing drug laws.

Additionally, in March 2015, the U.S. Alcohol and Tobacco Tax and Trade Bureau approved Palcohol, powdered alcohol that can be mixed with water to achieve a drink with the same alcohol content as a standard mixed drink. A number of flavors, such as vodka, rum, cosmopolitan, and margarita, are available, with more on the way. Lawmakers are alarmed about the potential for abuse. South Carolina, Louisiana, and Vermont have banned Palcohol, and other states are taking steps to do likewise.[108]

Illicit Drugs in Global Perspective   Globally, there are cultural differences in attitudes toward drug use, addiction, regulation, and punishment. For example, the Netherlands takes a distinctive approach to regulating the use of certain types of drugs. The Dutch decriminalized marijuana in 1976, for instance, and the drug is now sold, publicly and without penalty, in many of Amsterdam's licensed coffeehouses. In contrast, in the United States, the dominant approach

Controlled Substances Schedules

Type	Use	Examples
Schedule I	The drug or other substance has a high potential for abuse.	Heroin, LSD, marijuana, and methaqualone
	The drug or other substance has no currently accepted medical use in treatment in the United States.	
	There is a lack of accepted safety for use of the drug or other substance under medical supervision.	
Schedule II	The drug or other substance has a high potential for abuse.	Morphine, PCP, cocaine, methadone, and methamphetamine
	The drug or other substance has a currently accepted medical use in treatment in the United States or a currently accepted medical use with severe restrictions.	
	Abuse of the drug or other substance may lead to severe psychological or physical dependence.	
Schedule III	The drug or other substance has less potential for abuse than the drugs or other substances in Schedules I and II.	Anabolic steroids, codeine and hydrocodone with aspirin or Tylenol, and some barbiturates
	The drug or other substance has a currently accepted medical use in treatment in the United States.	
	Abuse of the drug or other substance may lead to moderate or low physical dependence or high psychological dependence.	
Schedule IV	The drug or other substance has a low potential for abuse relative to the drugs or other substances in Schedule III.	Darvon, Talwin, Equanil, Valium, and Xanax
	The drug or other substance has a currently accepted medical use in treatment in the United States.	
	Abuse of the drug or other substance may lead to limited physical dependence or psychological dependence relative to the drugs or other substances in Schedule III.	
Schedule V	The drug or other substance has a low potential for abuse relative to the drugs or other substances in Schedule IV.	Cough medicines with codeine
	The drug or other substance has a currently accepted medical use in treatment in the United States.	
	Abuse of the drug or other substances may lead to limited physical dependence or psychological dependence relative to the drugs or other substances in Schedule IV.	

centers on the idea that strict penalties are the best way to deter use. However, a comprehensive study comparing marijuana use in San Francisco and Amsterdam concluded that there were no differences between the two cities in age at onset of use, age at first regular use, or age at the start of maximum use.[109] And although the Dutch are concerned about illicit drugs and enforcement, they embrace the idea that addiction is a disease and are committed to treatment instead of punishment. These views influence Dutch drug policy.

Great Britain has taken a different approach to regulating heroin than has the United States. Today in the United States, there are no medical applications, under any circumstances, where heroin is considered legal. In contrast, in the 1960s and 1970s, registered British heroin addicts were given legal prescriptions that allowed them to obtain the drug in medical clinics to prevent withdrawal symptoms and to reduce their heroin habits. Then, in the 1980s, the United Kingdom replaced prescription heroin in these clinics with a narcotic antagonist, methadone—another very highly addictive substance. (An *antagonist* is a drug that counteracts the effect of another drug.)

MYTH/REALITY

MYTH: If law enforcement would destroy drugs at the source, we could eliminate the drug problem or reduce the supply of drugs entering the United States.

REALITY: Seizing drugs at the source does not solve the drug problem because many drugs are easy to produce, because demand persists, and because profits are high.[110]

Many illicit drugs are easy to produce. Marijuana, coca (the main ingredient of cocaine), and poppies (the main ingredient of heroin) thrive in many locales and climates. Specialized training is not required to harvest these crops and produce the drugs, and poor people in remote locations make profitable, easily replaced labor forces.[111] As a result, and because demand in rich countries persists and profits are high, the drug trade continues even when major drug busts occur. When production is stopped or interrupted in one place, it continues in another.[112] Latin American countries such as Colombia and Mexico have replaced Asia as the largest suppliers of heroin to the United States.[113]

◀ **Powdered Alcohol**

Lawmakers are concerned about the risks that powdered alcohol pose to public health.

Science Matters

Alcohol powder, yes it exists

Government regulators are studying the safety of the new "powdered alcohol" products, a new use of the starch-like chemicals called **cyclodextrins.** *How they work:*

How powdered alcohol works

U.S. powdered alcohol product called Palcohol is packaged in a foil envelope about 4 x 6 in. (20 x 30 cm)

55% Grain alcohol (ethanol) by weight

Also contains flavoring, sweetener

1 Envelope contains about 1 oz. (29 g) of powder; about 80 calories

2 Add 6 oz. (180 ml) of water or other liquid

3 Mixture is equivalent to a standard glass of liquor, wine or beer

Source: Lipsmark LLC, AP, LiveScience, TNS Photos   Graphic: Helen Lee McComas, Tribune News Service

Addiction and Crime   We usually think of drugs as positive when they are used medically, in appropriately prescribed ways. On the other hand, when they are misused and people become addicted to them, we view drugs negatively. Drug addiction is frequently considered a public order offense because the user has lost control over taking drugs and faces harmful physical, personal, social, and legal consequences as a result. Today addiction to heroin use and opioid use in the United States is epidemic. In 2016 the Obama Administration proposed $1.1 billion to combat it primarily through prevention and treatment programs.[114] The Comprehensive Addiction and Recovery Act (CARA) of 2015 passed the U.S. Senate by an almost unanimous vote in March 2016.[115]

Many experts today view substance abuse as a progressive disease (not a character defect or the result of willful choice) that changes the user for the worse until treatment occurs. It is a common misconception that people will turn to crime as a primary means of supporting their habit once they are addicted. With treatment, however, they can replace drug-using attitudes and behaviors with conventional ones and are often able to resume drug- and crime-free lifestyles. Regular recreational use of drugs, even heroin, does not mean addiction will automatically follow. Many veterans who used heroin during the Vietnam War (when it was pure, cheap, and readily available) stopped using it after returning home.[116] Studies are limited but have shown that veterans of the Afghanistan and Iraq wars suffer from excessive alcohol and drug use, and more than 11 percent have been diagnosed with a substance abuse disorder.[117]

Drug use, however, has several connections to crime. Many criminals are addicted to or abuse alcohol or other drugs and follow a drug-using lifestyle. Although addicted offenders typically have a drug of choice, many will use any available and convenient drug. Criminal and violent behaviors can result from effects of the ingested drug on the user's central nervous system. Certain drugs lower inhibitions, paving the way for behaviors that an individual would normally avoid, like initiating a fight. Moreover, the addict's need for the drug—to prevent agonizing withdrawal symptoms—motivates such crimes as burglary and robbery to obtain money to buy the drug. On a broader scale, manufacturing and trafficking in drugs can be so profitable that they command the power to corrupt and intimidate entire police agencies and high officials.

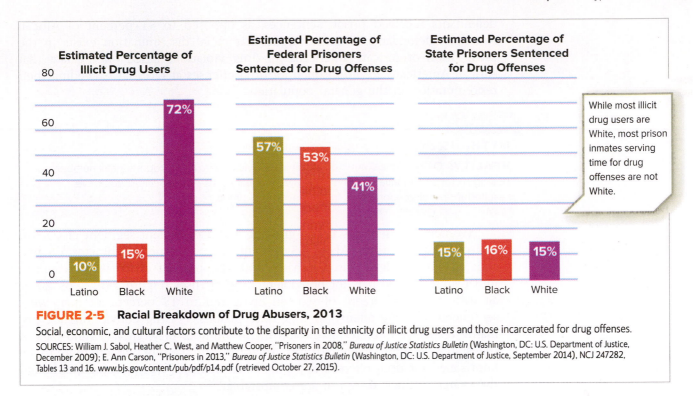

Estimated Percentage of Illicit Drug Users

- Latino 10%
- Black 15%
- White 72%

Estimated Percentage of Federal Prisoners Sentenced for Drug Offenses

- Latino 57%
- Black 53%
- White 41%

Estimated Percentage of State Prisoners Sentenced for Drug Offenses

- Latino 15%
- Black 16%
- White 15%

While most illicit drug users are White, most prison inmates serving time for drug offenses are not White.

FIGURE 2-5   **Racial Breakdown of Drug Abusers, 2013**

Social, economic, and cultural factors contribute to the disparity in the ethnicity of illicit drug users and those incarcerated for drug offenses.

SOURCES: William J. Sabol, Heather C. West, and Matthew Cooper, "Prisoners in 2008," *Bureau of Justice Statistics Bulletin* (Washington, DC: U.S. Department of Justice, December 2009); E. Ann Carson, "Prisoners in 2013," *Bureau of Justice Statistics Bulletin* (Washington, DC: U.S. Department of Justice, September 2014), NCJ 247282, Tables 13 and 16. www.bjs.gov/content/pub/pdf/p14.pdf (retrieved October 27, 2015).

Race, Gender, Income, and Other Factors in Drug Conviction   When we look at the results of U.S. drug laws and their enforcement, we find that although 72 percent of illicit drug users are White, 15 percent Black, and 10 percent Latino, most prison inmates serving time for drug offenses are not White (Figure 2-5). By 2013, among all state inmates, 16 percent were serving time for drug offenses. About 38 percent were Black, 31 percent were White, and 20 percent were Latino or other. Furthermore, by 2013, 16 percent of sentenced state inmates were convicted of drug offenses in comparison to about 51 percent of sentenced federal inmates.[118]

When we look at those convicted of drug felonies in federal courts, Whites are also less likely to be sent to prison. Thirty-three percent of convicted White

◀ **Women in Prison**

Incarcerated women have a great deal of time to think about their freedom.

defendants received prison sentences, as opposed to 51 percent of African American defendants.[119] Critics argue that racial discrimination exists in the prosecution of African Americans for drug violations based on the fact that African Americans are imprisoned for drug offenses at rates far exceeding their representation in the general population.

MYTH/REALITY

MYTH: U.S. drug laws are color and gender blind.

REALITY: Of individuals arrested for drug law violations, a disproportionate number belong to racial minorities. Further, the laws prohibiting use of specific drugs have resulted in the disproportionate incarceration of women of color.[120]

Women represent the fastest-growing and least violent segment of U.S. jail and prison populations. About 85 percent of U.S. female jail inmates, 65 percent of female federal prison inmates, and 31.5 percent of female state prison inmates are behind bars for nonviolent drug offenses (Figure 2-6).[121] By 2013, an estimated 25 percent of women compared to 15 percent of men were sentenced for drug offenses in U.S. state prisons.[122] Drug convictions are primarily responsible for the explosion in the number of women behind bars in the states.[123] Additionally, African American and Latino women tend to be imprisoned for drug offenses at higher rates than do White women, although their rates of illicit drug use are comparable.[124]

Critics contend that drug enforcement does disproportionate harm to women—who are generally minor players in the world of illegal drugs. For example, women who are not drug users may become implicated if they fail to notify authorities of a partner's drug use. They typically have little or no exposure to the criminal justice system and lack knowledge about such strategies as bargaining for reduced sentences. Many female partners of male offenders feel powerless and dependent, do not assume responsibility for their life, and are dominated by their partners. In some cases, nonviolent women with no criminal history are given sentences on a par with those of drug kingpins when in fact they are minimally involved or are low-level users or dealers. In these instances, the disruption of family and the impact on minor children is devastating; 60 to 80 percent of incarcerated women are mothers with dependent children.[125]

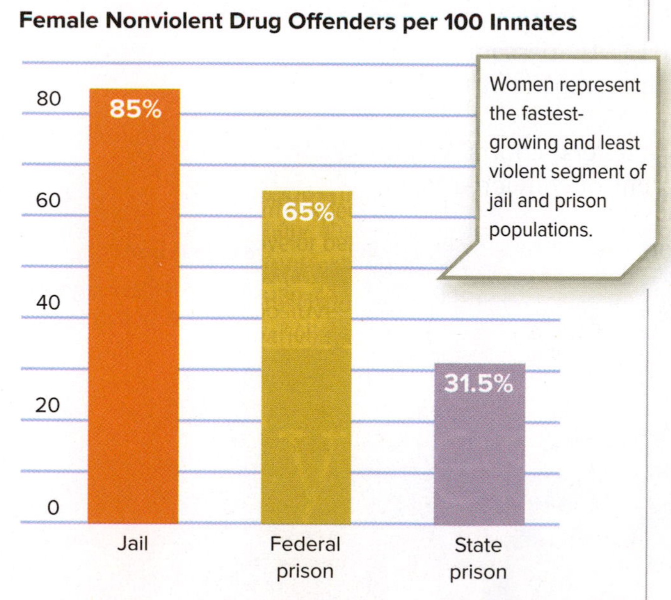

MYTH/REALITY

MYTH: Intensive law enforcement efforts at the street level will lead to the control of illicit drug use and abuse.

REALITY: Law enforcement efforts at the street level generally do not target those most directly engaged in drug trafficking. The main targets of arrest are low-level dealers and users.[126]

Female Nonviolent Drug Offenders per 100 Inmates

> Women represent the fastest-growing and least violent segment of jail and prison populations.

- Jail: 85%
- Federal prison: 65%
- State prison: 31.5%

FIGURE 2-6   **Incarceration of Women for Nonviolent Drug Offenses**

SOURCES: John Irwin, Vincent Schiraldi, and Jason Ziedenberg, "America's One Million Nonviolent Prisoners" (Washington, DC: Justice Policy Institute, March 1999), 6–7; Paige M. Harrison and Allen J. Beck, "Prisoners in 2005," *Bureau of Justice Statistics Bulletin* (Washington, DC: U.S. Department of Justice, November 2007), 5; Natalie Sokoloff, "Women Prisoners at the Dawn of the 21st Century," *Women and Criminal Justice* 16, no. 1–2 (2005): 127–137; Allison T. Chappell and Scott R. Maggard, "Applying Black's Theory of Law to Crack and Cocaine Dispositions," *International Journal of Offender Therapy and Comparative Criminology* 51, no. 3 (2007): 264–278.

It is easy to get the wrong impression about drugs and their relationship to income level. When statisticians compose reports, they combine drug sales with drug use and assume that poor minority neighborhoods are the center of drug use. In fact, drug use in minority neighborhoods is only slightly higher than that in more affluent nonminority areas.[127] Residents of disadvantaged neighborhoods– with high population densities and high concentrations of minorities–have only slightly higher levels of drug use and somewhat higher levels of drug dependency than do residents of more affluent nonminority neighborhoods. On the other hand, residents living in poor minority neighborhoods have much higher levels of visible drug sales. Also in poor minority neighborhoods, a major drug distribution market serves all segments of society (including purchases from those outside the minority community). Drug dealing plays a large role in the economies of poor urban neighborhoods.[128] Those who deal drugs tend to have little formal education and few job skills, and these obstacles make it difficult for them to find well-paying lawful employment.

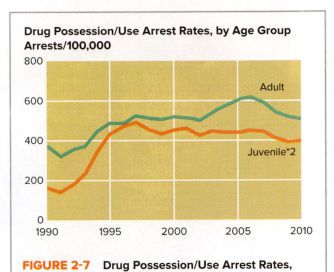

FIGURE 2-7   **Drug Possession/Use Arrest Rates, by Age Group**

SOURCE: Howard N. Snyder, "Arrest in the United States 1990-2010" (Washington, DC: U.S. Department of Justice, Bureau of Justice Statistics, October 2012), 12, figure 39.

Consider Figure 2-7, showing that arrests for drug abuse violations have increased for adults and juveniles between 1990 and 1997. The juvenile rate gradually declined while the adult rate experienced a peak in 2006 before beginning to decline again.[129] By 1997, the number of juvenile arrests had reached an all-time high of 213,200 arrests.[130] Competing explanations for why drug abuse violations have increased vary from weak drug laws to a poor economy.

An Unsolvable Problem?   Cultural attitudes, politics, economics, and perceived harm to individuals drive policy proposals to solve the U.S. drug problem. In November 2012, residents of Colorado and the state of Washington passed ballot initiatives to legalize marijuana for recreational use–a large victory for the legalization movement.[131] Strategies include imposing harsher punishments for drug offenders, decriminalizing drug use and abuse, legalizing certain types of illegal drugs, enhancing law enforcement control efforts, and focusing on medical solutions to drug problems. For example, between 1998 and 2015, approximately 23 states and Washington, DC, enacted laws that legalize medical marijuana for patients with documentation from their doctors stating that they might benefit from the drug's medical use. Some of the conditions for which medical marijuana has been approved are cancer, AIDS, HIV, glaucoma, severe pain and nausea, seizures, and muscle spasms. States are responsible for determining the number of ounces a patient is allowed, and thus the amount permitted varies significantly from place to place. Depending on the state, a patient may possess 1 to 24 ounces. Patients must register and pay a fee to use medical marijuana legally. In contrast, as of 2015 only 4 states and the District of Columbia have legalized recreational use of marijuana, as shown in Figure 2-8. Figure 2-9 illustrates states that have legalized medical marijuana.

All these solutions have been attempted, but none has worked. Certainly, the lack of resources limits law enforcement efforts–but even with unlimited resources, it is impossible for law enforcement to prevent all illicit drugs from entering the country. Asset forfeiture laws, which allow the state to confiscate a person's assets, have been passed to deter drug offenses and are frequently criticized as unfair and overly harsh, but the enormous profits derived from the cultivation of poppies, coca, and marijuana mean that crop control efforts meet resistance. Ultimately, addicts need to be highly motivated to find success in drug treatment, because addiction is a relapsing disease, and victory is often incremental, transient, and temporary.

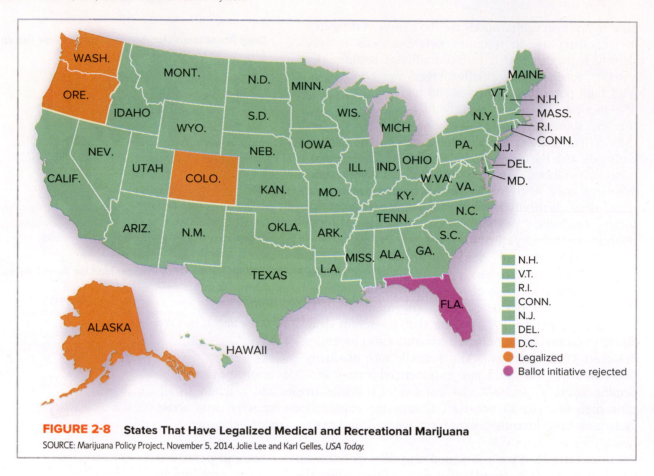

FIGURE 2-8 **States That Have Legalized Medical and Recreational Marijuana**

SOURCE: Marijuana Policy Project, November 5, 2014. Jolie Lee and Karl Gelles, *USA Today*.

Legend:
- N.H.
- V.T.
- R.I.
- CONN.
- N.J.
- DEL.
- D.C.
- Legalized
- Ballot initiative rejected

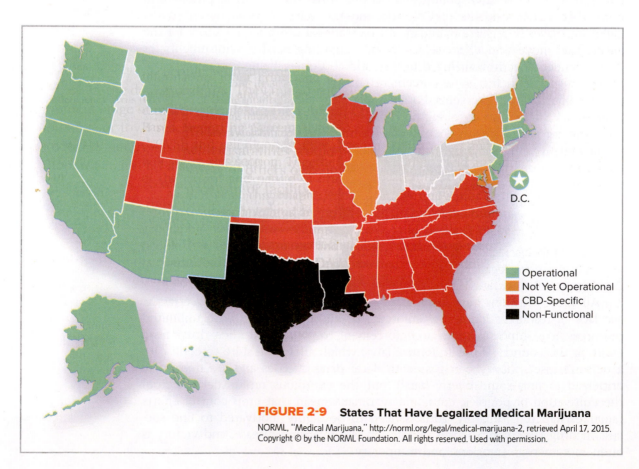

FIGURE 2-9 **States That Have Legalized Medical Marijuana**

NORML, "Medical Marijuana," http://norml.org/legal/medical-marijuana-2, retrieved April 17, 2015. Copyright © by the NORML Foundation. All rights reserved. Used with permission.

Legend:
- Operational
- Not Yet Operational
- CBD-Specific
- Non-Functional

POLITICAL CRIMES

Acts, whether violent or nonviolent, that society perceives as threats to a government's survival constitute **political crimes.** At one extreme are crimes such as terrorism and treason, which directly challenge the state (see Chapter 16). At the other end of the spectrum are the relatively minor offenses of immigration law violations and unlawful demonstrations. These offenses, while not intended as confrontational, may still threaten the established order and the state's political authority. They may also focus government resources on a perceived threat: for example, stationing the National Guard along the United States–Mexico border to counter illegal immigration. Choosing to fund National Guard troops at the border means that there is less money available for other priorities and therefore affects all U.S. residents.

Immigration Offenses

Federal immigration law determines whether a person is an *alien* (not a U.S. citizen) and stipulates all the legal rights, duties, and obligations aliens have in the United States. The law also establishes when aliens can become *naturalized citizens* (that is, citizens through law rather than through birth) with full rights of citizenship, who may enter the United States, and how long they may stay.[132] Individuals who violate these laws commit **immigration offenses.**

According to the most recent data from the Bureau of Justice Statistics, 2010, saw the lowest level of apprehensions for immigration violations since 1972 with almost 520,000 apprehensions. Most immigration suspects were arrested for illegal entry or reentry. The vast majority (90 percent) of arrests in 2010 occurred in four southwest states: California, Arizona, New Mexico, and Texas. Crimes for which individuals saw a U.S. attorney included illegal entry (51 percent), reentry (42 percent), alien smuggling (5 percent), and misusing a visa (2 percent). In the same year, those arrested were largely male (90 percent) and between 25 and 34 years old (41 percent); 81 percent received a median prison term of 15 months. The majority of immigration offenders in a federal prison were there for illegal entry or reentry (90 percent), alien smuggling (10 percent), and visa fraud (less than 1 percent). Of those released from a federal prison in 2007, 14 percent were readmitted to a federal prison by 2010.[133]

U.S. immigration policy has become a divisive political issue over the past four decades. Until the late 1970s, Republicans and Democrats alike expressed concern for families separated by immigration, as well as for people displaced by wars, famine, and political oppression. The focus was humanitarian, emphasizing the need for family unification and assimilation. However, in the 1980s, as concerns mounted nationwide over the costs of health care for the uninsured, bipartisan support evaporated, and many Americans began demanding change.[134] Citing the skyrocketing costs of extending public benefits to illegal immigrants, and reluctant to grant them amnesty, the federal government called for immigration reform, with emphasis on the criminality of immigration offenses. After September 11, 2001, fears of terrorism

RealCrimeTech

EMERGING DRUG-TESTING TECHNOLOGIES

Once, drug tests involved taking urine, blood, or hair samples and required weeks of laboratory analysis. In recent years, newer drug tests, including the following, have been providing results in less invasive ways:

- The *sweat patch* is a gauzelike patch in the middle of adhesive tape. It is placed on a visually accessible part of the body such as the upper arm, which is cleansed with rubbing alcohol before the device is attached. The patch is worn for up to 14 days and then removed and sent to a lab for analysis. This process can take several weeks—not always ideal for the purposes of the criminal justice system.[a]

- The *saliva swab,* a handheld device that tests saliva, provides much faster drug analysis than the sweat patch. Results are available in less than 90 seconds—ideal when criminal justice professionals need instantaneous readings.

- With respect to the *breathalyzer,* the latest version is the iBreath, which plugs into the base of an iPod and acts as a field sobriety test. The suspect exhales into the breath wand, and the sensor automatically measures the results within seconds. A reading over .08 (the legal limit for being under the influence of a substance) sounds an alarm, indicating legal intoxication.[b]

- A new breathalyzer created in Sweden can detect both alcohol and drugs in one's system. The device can detect 12 different drugs including cocaine, heroin, marijuana, methamphetamine, and morphine. The device shows an accuracy of almost 90 percent, comparable to the accuracy of blood and urine tests.[c]

- Another technology includes using fingerprints to test for cocaine use. Previous fingerprint testing only showed if someone handled drugs. This new technology sprays a special solvent called Desorption Electrospray Ionization (DEI) to detect benzoylecgonine and methylecgonine, compounds that can be found in fingerprints once the body metabolizes cocaine. While this method continues to be tested for accuracy, it holds promise because it is efficient and the uniqueness of an individual's fingerprints makes it hard to falsify results.[d]

Continued

Continued from previous page

All drug-testing systems can be tampered with, and all can provide false-positive results. The development of more accurate and more advanced devices will continue to be a real technology need for the criminal justice system well into the future.

SOURCES: [a]Drug Policy Alliance Network, "Drugs, Police, and the Law." www.drugpolicy.org/law/drugtesting/sweatpatch_/ (retrieved January 2, 2009).

[b]"Philips and Concateno Announce Revolutionary Drugs-of-Abuse Testing System," *Marwyn*, November 21, 2008. www.marwyn.com/index.stm?article_id573 (retrieved January 2, 2009); Dawn C. Chmielewski, "Blow into the iBreath and Your iPod Plays a Blood Alcohol Alert," *Los Angeles Times*, December 19, 2008. www.latimes.com/business/la-fi-idrunk19-2008dec19,0,3073178.storyn (retrieved January 1, 2008).

[c]Melissa Stusinski, "New Breathalyzer Test Detects Drugs Too" *Inquisitr*, April 28, 2013.www.inquisitr.com/639275/new-breathalyzer-test-detects-drugs-too/ (retrieved May 18, 2015).

[d]Fox News, "New Test Uses Single Fingerprint to Detect Drug Use." *FoxNews.com*, May 15, 2015. www.foxnews.com/health/2015/05/15/new-test-uses-single-fingerprint-to-detect-drug-use/ (retrieved May 18, 2015).

political crimes
Violent or nonviolent acts that society perceives as threats to a government's survival.

immigration offenses
Violation of federal immigration law, which determines whether a person is an alien and stipulates all the legal rights, duties, and obligations aliens have in the United States.

▶ **Customs Agent on the Lookout**

U.S. Customs and Border Protection is responsible for keeping terrorists and their arms out of the country and for enforcing laws concerning immigration and drugs.

KEY CONCEPTS   Crimes Committed Due to Drugs

Crime Category	Types of Crime
Crimes against persons	First-degree murder, voluntary and involuntary manslaughter, vehicular manslaughter, serial murder, spree murder, assault, battery, sexual assault, robbery, child abuse, child neglect, child abandonment, school bullying, kidnapping
Crimes against property	Burglary; larceny/theft; motor vehicle theft; white-collar crimes such as embezzlement, fraud, and corporate fraud; environmental crime; money laundering; manufacturing, trafficking, and distributing drugs; selling drugs
Crimes against public order and morality	Disorderly conduct, disturbing the peace, panhandling, prostitution, pimping, public intoxication, loitering, drunk driving, weapons violations, gambling, obscenity, fornication, bigamy, adultery

perpetrated by aliens made immigration a topic of great and widespread concern. The federal government focused intensely on illegal immigration, aiming to enforce and strengthen existing laws.[135] In November 2014, President Obama outlined an executive order that provided temporary legal status and protection from deportation for 4 million illegal immigrants. The executive order provided for a reprieve for undocumented parents whose children are U.S. citizens and permanent residents who have lived in the United States for at least five years, thus removing the threat of deportation. The order also expanded the 2012 Deferred Action for Childhood Arrivals (DACA) program, which allows those who arrived as children and who are not yet 30 years old to apply for a deportation deferral. Both groups will have to reapply for a deportation deferral every three years. The executive order will include a program to facilitate visas for those who pursue science, technology, and math (STEM) degrees, as well as strengthening resources for border security and immigrant detention procedures.[136]

Immigrants–legal and illegal–are vital to the U.S. economy. They make up 12 percent of the U.S. population and 14 percent of its workforce. From 1994 to 2004, the number of foreign-born workers grew from 13 million to 21 million, accounting for more than half the growth of the U.S. labor force in that period. According to the American Immigration Lawyers Association, illegal immigrants hold 40 percent of jobs in farming, fishing, and forestry in the United States, 33 percent of jobs in building and grounds maintenance, 22 percent of jobs in food preparation, and 22 percent of jobs in construction. Opinions differ as to what impact immigration reform will have on the United States and its economy, particularly in states like California that earn much of their revenue from immigrant farm workers, agriculture, and tourism.[137]

Real Careers

AMY NYE

Work location: (cannot disclose)

College(s): Wayne State University, Detroit, MI

Major(s): Criminal Justice (BS), Near Eastern Studies (MA)

Job title: Special Agent with Immigration and Customs Enforcement

Salary range for jobs like this: $29,000–$37,000

Time in job: 1 year

Work Responsibilities
I conduct criminal investigations on a wide range of matters, such as visa security, illegal arms trafficking, document and identity fraud, drug trafficking, gang activity, child pornography and sex tourism, immigration and customs fraud, and intellectual property rights violations.

As a special agent, I enjoy a balance between working at the office and working in the field. Some of my more exciting field experiences include conducting surveillance on targets, working undercover operations, and executing search and arrest warrants. But being a special agent is certainly not a 9-to-5 job: very early mornings and late nights are often required.

Why Criminal Justice?
I had been interested in criminal justice since high school. My history teacher, a retired police officer, often told stories about his experience in that profession. Wanting to learn more about law enforcement, I took an independent study course with him and researched the challenges currently facing law enforcement agents, especially females in a traditionally male-dominated career path.

I entered college originally with the intention of obtaining an associate's degree in criminal justice in order to become a city police officer. However, once I began college, I loved my criminal justice classes so much that I decided to pursue a BS and eventually an MA. When I began looking for employment after graduation, I primarily used Wayne State's website to find criminal justice career opportunities. However, before applying for a job, I always did some of my own online research to learn more about the agency's mission and the requisites for the job.

Expectations and Realities of the Job
Working in law enforcement is vastly different from the way it is portrayed in novels and TV shows. Criminals do not always confess, and investigations can carry over for weeks, months, or even years. For example, a lot of intelligence gathering and database mining must be performed before an agent can even begin questioning a subject. Postenforcement procedures can be just as lengthy: Agents are required to report and update databases so that the most current intel is available for future cases.

But regardless of the separation between reality and fiction, I love having a job that makes a difference. I don't just talk about making my country and my community safer—I am actually doing something about it.

My Advice to Students
The entire process of getting hired as a special agent can take a couple of years, so if you are interested in becoming an agent, apply as soon as possible. To increase your chances of finding employment, I suggest you apply to a variety of agencies that specialize in different areas of investigation. Your strengths and abilities might be better suited for one agency over another. But no matter which agency you apply to, federal agents must keep a clean criminal record. Background checks are always a component of the application process.

Try to get involved in extracurricular activities related to the field you want to enter. For example, during college I rode with local police agencies, which gave me a great feel for the career path I was choosing. I also took classes at the local gun range on firearm safety, weapon retention, and carrying a concealed weapon. Beginning my career training with prior firearm knowledge was quite valuable. Finally, keep yourself in great physical condition. Any type of martial arts training will also be beneficial.

▶ **Day Laborers Waiting to Work**

Day laborers, who are frequently in the United States illegally, are eager to find work.

organized crime
An ongoing criminal conspiracy that profits from providing illicit goods and services, using or threatening violence to facilitate its criminal enterprise and to maintain monopolistic control of illicit markets.

ORGANIZED CRIME

Groups can also commit crimes. **Organized crime** is an ongoing criminal conspiracy that profits from providing illicit goods and services. It uses or threatens violence to further its criminal enterprises and to maintain monopolistic control of specific markets.[138]

Organized crime, much like serial murder, fascinates the American public. Mainstream society loves fiction and films about mob bosses, their families, and their associates. Indeed, much of what people believe they know about the underworld comes from mass media, which have focused almost exclusively on the Italian community and which may not be based on reality.

Historically, Italians' involvement in U.S. organized crime was preceded by that of Irish and German Jewish immigrants. Most members of each ethnic group attempted to enter the mainstream of American life and attain financial security in law-abiding ways, but some pursued illicit shortcuts.[139] In the United States, organized crime groups originally drawn from successive waves of immigrants have yielded to a range of diverse criminal associations such as urban street gangs, outlaw motorcycle gangs, and prison gangs. A few large organizations once controlled an illicit market, but now an expanded number of small organizations operate autonomously.[140] Other organized crime groups have gained considerable influence in the United States; some are based on foreign soil, including the Colombian drug cartels and the Russian mafia.[141]

Crimes perpetrated or controlled by criminal enterprises include gambling, prostitution, auto theft, and drug trafficking. Organized crime groups use legitimate business ventures as a cover and as a way to launder illegal profits. They may employ or contract with specialists, such as corrupt governmental officials or individuals in the private sector, who are in a position to ignore violations, conceal or move assets, or otherwise assist illegal activities.[142]

Members of the criminal organization may comprise a crime "family," a gang, a cartel, or a criminal network. Membership is restricted to those who have been formally accepted after demonstrating loyalty to the group's principles and its members. Most crime groups are local in scope and do not have cooperative relationships with other organized crime groups.[143]

By the late twentieth century, organized crime groups were able to exploit the same open borders and technological advances that have enabled multinational corporations to prosper. In fact, transnational crime groups may have profited more from globalization than legitimate business enterprises, which are subject to the laws and regulations of domestic and host countries. Organized criminals are increasingly involved in high-tech operations involving identity theft and counterfeiting of goods.[144] Transnational activities require numerous independent groups operating in source, transit, and destination countries.[145]

CRIMES BY GENDER

Anyone can commit a particular crime, but strong trends differentiate by gender the types of crimes committed and the frequency of offending.[146] Stalking today is a crime dominated by one sex: For the most part, men stalk women.

Stalking has existed since the beginning of human history, and through the ages has been depicted in music, poetry, novels, paintings, and films as part of romantic behavior. In the last decade, stalking has been criminalized throughout the United States.[147] Although definitions vary from state to state, a 1990 California statute defines **stalking** as involving anyone who "willfully, maliciously, and repeatedly follow[s] or willfully and maliciously harass[es] another person and . . . makes a credible threat with the intent to place that person in reasonable fear for his or her safety, or of the safety of his or her family."[148]

A national survey of American women revealed that 1 in 12 survey participants had been stalked. (One man in 45 also had been followed or harassed at some point in his life.)[149] The victim's obvious reaction to stalking is fear, and that fear is justified because stalkers eventually assault 81 percent of targeted individuals. Although the notoriety of stalking results from cases of celebrities who are stalked by strangers but rarely endangered, the overwhelming majority of cases involve intimate partners or former partners stalking women who are not celebrities and whose lives are often at considerable risk. As Figure 2-10 illustrates, stalking occurs in six types of relationships. Note the differences in gender between victims. Males often are stalked by an acquaintance or a stranger, but females are more likely to be stalked by a

stalking
Willfully, maliciously, and repeatedly following or harassing another person and making a credible threat with the intent to place that person in reasonable fear for his or her safety, or for the safety of his or her family.

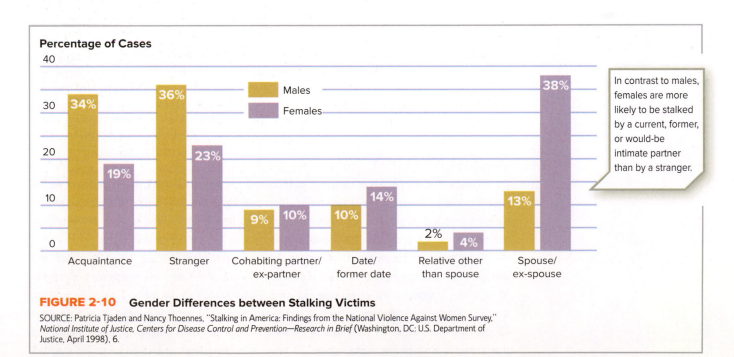

> In contrast to males, females are more likely to be stalked by a current, former, or would-be intimate partner than by a stranger.

FIGURE 2-10   **Gender Differences between Stalking Victims**

SOURCE: Patricia Tjaden and Nancy Thoennes, "Stalking in America: Findings from the National Violence Against Women Survey," *National Institute of Justice, Centers for Disease Control and Prevention—Research in Brief* (Washington, DC: U.S. Department of Justice, April 1998), 6.

Race, Class, Gender

Gender and Crime

Females represent a small but increasing percentage of the offending population in the United States for all crimes. In 2010, there were approximately 1.6 million people in state and federal institutions, of whom 113,000 were female offenders. Almost half of incarcerated females are White, whereas 32 percent of incarcerated males are White. Black males (37 percent) make up the largest portion of incarcerated males. Black females (22 percent) were imprisoned at a rate twice that of White females (113 per 100,000 for Black females versus 51 per 100,000 for White females).[a] Since 2000, the growth in the incarceration rate of females in state or federal institutions increased 21 percent in comparison to only 15 percent for males.[b]

Although males represent the largest percentage of prison inmates, female inmates present with more mental health problems than do males. A 2006 study of the mental health of those incarcerated found that 23 percent of females both in state facilities and in local jails were diagnosed with a mental health problem, compared to 8 and 9 percent of male inmates, respectively.[c]

Males offend with significantly greater frequency than do females, and in general male offenders are more likely than are female offenders to be violent. Women are much less likely than men to commit assault or murder, and the rate of murders committed by women has declined since 1980.[d] Yet the data show that women increasingly are engaging in violent crimes. A study that examined the gender of violent felons in the 75 largest counties from 1990 to 2002 found that males were responsible for 91 percent of all violent felonies and females for 9 percent.[e] The most recent data, from 2008, support previous statistics: At year-end 2008, there were 1,267,400 males incarcerated in state facilities as compared to 94,800 women. When comparing males and females in specific crime categories, the statistics from year-end 2008 indicate that 53.8 percent of males and 35.6 percent of women were incarcerated for violent crimes; 17.7 percent of males and 29 percent of females were incarcerated for property crimes; and 17.8 percent of males and 26.9 percent of females were incarcerated for drug crimes. As these data indicate, while males are committing more violent crimes, females are committing more property and drug crimes.[f]

According to National Crime Victimization data of juvenile victims (ages 12–17), despite the increase in female violence, males continue to commit certain violent crimes with greater frequency than do females, including intimate partner violence, stalking, aggravated assault, forcible rape, robbery, and murder. In 2010, juveniles of both genders were equally likely to experience a violent crime such as rape, robbery, or aggravated assault.[g]

OBSERVE → INVESTIGATE → UNDERSTAND

- What might explain why a larger proportion of incarcerated women than men presents with mental health problems?
- Why do you think the rate of murders committed by women has declined since 1980?
- The statistics indicate that females are becoming more violent than ever before, but not for murder. What might explain this finding?

SOURCES: [a]E. Anne Carson, "Prisoners in 2013," Bureau of Justice Statistics Bulletin (Washington, DC: U.S. Department of Justice, September 16, 2014), NCJ 247282. www.bjs.gov/index.cfm?ty=pbdetail&iid=5109 (retrieved May 18, 2015).

[b]Lauren E. Glaze and Danielle Kaeble, "Correctional Populations in the United States, 2013." Bureau of Justice Statistics, December 19, 2014, NCJ 248479. www.bjs.gov/index.cfm?ty=pbdetail&iid=5177 (retrieved May 18, 2015).

[c]Doris J. James and Lauren E. Glaze, "Mental Health Problems of Jail and Prison Inmates," Bureau of Justice Statistics Special Report, September 2006, NCJ 213600. www.ojp.usdoj.gov/bjs/pub/pdf/mhppji.pdf (retrieved December 20, 2008).

[d]Lawrence Greenfield and Tracy Snell, "Women Offenders," Bureau of Justice Statistics Special Report (Washington, DC: U.S. Department of Justice, December 1999).

[e]Brian A. Reaves, "State Court Processing Statistics, 1990–2002: Violent Felons in Large Urban Counties," Bureau of Justice Statistics, July 2006. www.ojp.usdoj.gov/bjs/pub/pdf/vfluc.pdf (retrieved December 28, 2008).

[f]Heather C. West, William J. Sabol, and Sarah J. Greenman, "Prisoners in 2009" (Washington, DC: Bureau of Justice Statistics, December 2010, NCJ 231675. http://bjs.ojp.usdoj.gov/content/pub/pdf/p09.pdf (retrieved July 3, 2011).

[g]Nicole White and Janet L. Lauritsen, "Violent Crime against Youth, 1994–2010," Bureau of Justice Statistics, December 2012, NCJ 240106. www.bjs.gov/content/pub/ascii/vcay9410.txt (retrieved May 19, 2015).

---

current, former, or would-be intimate partner. In these cases, the stalking is a form of abuse, used to control the victim.[150]

There are other differences in the incarceration rates and types of crimes committed by males and females. The "Race, Class, Gender" box on page 68 highlights these patterns based on gender.

SUMMARY

For 20 years after the FBI began compiling its Uniform Crime Reports in 1973, the incidence of serious violent crimes increased in the United States. After peaking in the early 1990s, the number of both violent crimes and property crimes reported to police has been declining, and rates of victim-reported and police-reported crime have been converging, for reasons not entirely understood.

Other important trends also stand out. On a global scale, the United States has a high murder rate, and within this country, murder rates are highest in the South. Males are more frequently victimized by all categories of violent crime except rape and intimate partner violence. Women are less likely to report a violent attack—especially rape, a crime in which perpetrator and victim very often know each other. Children are more frequently victimized by violent crime than are older people. Despite the great fear that crimes against people evoke, almost 10 times as many crimes against property are reported.

Property crimes account for about three-fourths of all crimes reported in the United States, but as in the case of violent crime, the rate has been falling since the 1990s. Property crimes are usually less traumatizing, although white-collar crime can inflict devastating economic losses.

A common characteristic of public order crimes is that they are offenses against morality. Although they often are called victimless crimes, in fact many of them have negative consequences for the perpetrator as well as for others.

Drug offenses have been a great source of concern in the United States for a century. Although most crime is not drug related, drugs are a factor in both violent crimes (homicide, assault, and robbery) and nonviolent crimes (burglary and theft). Abusers can be physically and psychologically devastated by drug use. Enforcing drug laws and controlling drug-related crime has not been very successful. One significant impact of the U.S. "war on drugs" is an ever-rising proportion of persons incarcerated for drug-related offenses, including disproportionate numbers of women and racial minorities. A second major impact is the corrupting effect on the police and public officials that stems from organized crime's domination of the drug trade.

Political crimes directly challenge government authority. They run the gamut from such relatively minor offenses as immigration law violations to major crimes against the state—espionage, treason, and terrorism.

In the United States, organized crime was once largely associated with immigrant ethnic groups. Organized crime is a serious problem in modern societies. It uses violence to exploit and profit from such public order offenses as prostitution, gambling, and drug trafficking. Organized crime frequently is implicated in the corruption of public authorities.

OBSERVE → INVESTIGATE → UNDERSTAND

Review

Understand how crime rates are measured.

- The Uniform Crime Reports (UCR) are compiled annually by the FBI from data reported by local police departments. Today, the UCR covers murder and nonnegligent manslaughter, rape, robbery, aggravated assault, burglary, larceny, motor vehicle theft, arson, and hate crimes.
- The National Incident-Based Reporting System (NIBRS), compiled by the FBI and the Department of Justice, is an index that tracks detailed information about 22 specific categories of crime incidents and arrests. Data are submitted by state authorities, but not all states are as yet able to take part in the system.
- The National Crime Victimization Survey (NCVS) is an annual national survey of selected households and individuals to discover who has been victimized by crime and whether or not the crime was reported to the police. Through this survey, the so-called dark figure of crime can be estimated—the gap between reported crime and crime that goes unreported and is therefore unrecorded. It can also reveal the extent of secondary victimization: that is, the negative experiences of crime victims based on their treatment by the police, the courts, and personal acquaintances.

Differentiate the types of crimes against persons.

- Crimes against persons involve attacks upon or threats to a person's body. The most serious crimes against persons are murder and manslaughter (both mean taking a life), sexual assault, kidnapping, robbery (theft with force or the threat of force), and battery (the intentional unwanted touching of one person by another).

- Homicide occurs when someone unjustifiably causes the death of another human being. Different types of homicide include first-degree murder (purposely planning to kill the victim), manslaughter (the offender is less blameworthy than for murder; it usually carries a less severe penalty than murder), voluntary manslaughter (the offender is provoked and loses control, killing the victim in the heat of passion), involuntary manslaughter (killing that results from an offender's careless actions), and vehicular manslaughter (the careless use of one's vehicle that results in a victim's death).
- Serial murder means killing three or more people over an extended period; mass murders are multiple killings that occur at one place and at one time; spree murder refers to multiple victims killed within a fairly narrow time span, such as several hours or days.
- Sexual violence encompasses nonconsensual vaginal, anal, digital, and oral penetration and can include the use of weapons and foreign objects to torture and terrorize the victim.

Describe the different types of property crimes.

- Property crimes include taking money or material goods without using force, as well as intentionally destroying property. They include any act of burglary (entering another's property with the intent to commit a felony such as theft), theft (or larceny, both of which mean taking another's property without permission), motor vehicle theft (taking one's motor vehicle or its contents), the intentional destruction of property (as in the case of arson), and white-collar crime (theft or other nonviolent offenses in a business setting).

Identify types of public order crimes.

- Public order crimes encompass a wide variety of offenses, including disorderly conduct, disturbing the peace, loitering, public intoxication, panhandling, bigamy, drunk driving, weapons violations, prostitution, obscenity, gambling, and possession of controlled substances.

- Public order crimes are characterized as immoral or public nuisances.

- Crimes against public order often are called victimless crimes because, unlike property crimes or crimes against persons, they do not have an easily identifiable victim.

Describe some of the political crimes that have occurred in recent years.

- Political crimes include acts, violent and nonviolent, that threaten a government's survival.

- Terrorism and treason are two extreme forms of political crimes; they are extreme because they represent a direct challenge to the government.

- Less extreme examples of political crimes include violations of immigration laws and unlawful demonstrations. These offenses, although not intended to be confrontational, may still represent a threat to the established order and to political authority.

- Political crimes may serve to turn government resources toward a perceived threat, such as when National Guard troops are stationed at the United States–Mexico border as a force to counter illegal immigration. The choice to use money to fund troops at the border reduces the amount of resources available for other priorities and therefore affects all U.S. residents.

Discuss organized crime and who engages in it today.

- Organized crime is an ongoing criminal conspiracy that profits from providing illicit goods and services. By its nature, organized crime uses or threatens violence to facilitate its criminal enterprises and maintain monopolistic control of illicit markets.

- Crimes committed or controlled by criminal enterprises include gambling, prostitution, auto theft, and drug trafficking. Organized crime groups engage in many legitimate business ventures as a cover and as a way to launder monies from their criminal activities. They may employ or contract with specialists such as corrupt government officials or members of the private sector who can ignore violations, conceal or move assets, or otherwise assist the network of illegal activities.

- Members of the criminal organization may form a crime "family," a gang, a cartel, or some other kind of criminal network. Membership is restricted to those who have been formally accepted after demonstrating loyalty to the group's criminal principles and its members.

- By the late twentieth century, organized crime had exploited the same open borders and technological advances that have enabled multinational corporations to prosper. In fact, transnational crime groups may have profited more from globalization than have legitimate business enterprises, which are subject to domestic and host country laws and regulations.

Contrast the types of crimes generally perpetrated by males and by females.

- In general, male offenders are more likely to be violent than female offenders. However, data show that women are increasingly participating in violent crimes.

- Women are committing more property, drug, and public order offenses than are men. Men continue to commit more violent offenses than women, but the gap is narrowing.

- Women are much less likely than men to commit assault or murder.

- Despite the increase in female violence, males continue to commit certain violent crimes with much greater frequency than females, including intimate partner violence, stalking, aggravated assault, sexual assault, robbery, and murder.

Key Terms

assault and battery 42

burglary 50

child abuse 45

child neglect 46

Crime Index 30

crimes against morality 52

crimes against persons 34

dark figure of crime 33

designer drugs 55

drug offenses 54

emotional abuse 46

first-degree murder 38

homicide 38

immigration offenses 63

involuntary manslaughter 38

larceny 50

manslaughter 38

mass murder 39

missing children 48

motor vehicle theft 50

National Crime Victimization Survey (NCVS) 33

National Incident-Based Reporting System (NIBRS) 32

organized crime 66

physical abuse 45

political crimes 63

property crimes 48

public order crimes 52

rape trauma syndrome 44

robbery 44

secondary victimization 33

second-degree murder 38

self-report 34

serial murder 39

sexual victimization 42

sexual violence 42

spree murder 39

stalking 67

student bullying 47

Uniform Crime Reports (UCR) 31

vehicular manslaughter 38

victim surveys 32

victimless crimes 52

voluntary manslaughter 38

white-collar crime 51

Study Questions

1. The Uniform Crime Reports (UCR) are annual surveys that
   a. track the most serious crimes as reported by victims.
   b. track the most serious crimes as reported by police departments.
   c. provide detailed information about criminal incidents and arrests in 22 categories.
   d. are compiled by telephoning individuals in different countries about crimes against household members during the previous 12 months.

2. The number one cause of injuries and death to women in the United States is
   a. traffic collisions.
   b. suicide.
   c. drug abuse.
   d. intimate partner violence.

3. Offenses against another person's belongings are known as
   a. victimless crimes.
   b. property crimes.
   c. attempted crimes.
   d. infractions.

4. Crimes against public order often are referred to as
   a. inchoate offenses.
   b. victimless crimes.
   c. property crimes.
   d. attempted crimes.

5. All of the following are characteristics of organized crime *except*
   a. part-time participation by the perpetrators.
   b. provision of illicit goods and services.
   c. use of violence or the threat of violence.
   d. corruption of public officials.

6. All of the following are examples of a public order crime *except*
   a. disorderly conduct.
   b. disturbing the peace.
   c. loitering.
   d. immigration offenses.

7. All of the following are examples of an immigration offense *except*
   a. entering the United States illegally.
   b. improper entry into the United States.
   c. alien smuggling.
   d. white-collar crimes.

8. The age group that is most vulnerable to crime is
   a. young people.
   b. middle-aged people.
   c. older adults.
   d. All age ranges are equally likely to be victimized.

9. Although property crime can happen everywhere, it is more common in urban than in rural areas, and in the _____ region of the United States.
   a. eastern
   b. northern
   c. southern
   d. western

10. The 1967 Supreme Court decision that declared antimiscegenation laws unconstitutional is
    a. *Loving v. Virginia.*
    b. *Lawrence v. Texas.*
    c. *Brown v. Board of Education.*
    d. *Gideon v. Wainwright.*

11. Which statement based on the NCVS is not true?
    a. It has four sections—community characteristics, personal characteristics, household characteristics, and individual characteristics
    b. It does not include homicide victimizations
    c. It does not include victimizations of children under the age of 12
    d. The actual number of people victimized by violent crimes is almost double the reported figure

Critical Thinking Questions

For further review, go to the LearnSmart study module for this chapter.

1. Can crimes truly be victimless? Explain.

2. If white-collar crime is so costly, why doesn't the criminal justice system do more to prosecute these types of offenses?

3. How should we deal with the drug problem in the United States?

3 Causes of Crime

OBSERVE → INVESTIGATE → UNDERSTAND

After reading this chapter, you should be able to:

- Understand the roles of biological (including genetic) and environmental factors on brain function and criminal behavior.

- Explain the key aspects of mental disorders and understand how they are classified.

- Recognize the cognitive factors of intelligence and moral reasoning as brain functions that influence criminal behavior.

- Understand how economic, class, and social inequalities can be linked to the causes of crime.

- Describe factors that cause some people to become victims of crime.

Realities and Challenges

Theater 9 at Century 16: 12 Dead, 70 Wounded

Although his hair was not green like the Joker, the comic book character he sought to mimic, its blazing orange color could not be ignored. Nor can the role of mental illness in his rampage at the midnight screening of Batman's latest quest to save Gotham City, *The Dark Knight Rises*.[1] Along with some 400 other people, James Earl Holmes bought a ticket for the show at the Aurora, Colorado, theater. He sat in the first row. Less than 20 minutes into the film, Holmes left via an emergency exit and propped the door open for his

planned return. At his car he put on tactical, bullet-resistant clothing, complete with a helmet and gas mask, and retrieved his arsenal of a military-style AR-15 assault rifle, shotgun, and Glock handgun. Immediately upon reentering the theater, Holmes tossed two tear gas grenades into the crowd. Then he began shooting. Had the assault rifle not jammed, there is no telling how many more people would have been killed by the 218 bullets that could not fire.

What started in fall 2011—with Holmes's acceptance into a neuroscience doctoral program that generally admits only half a dozen new students each year—ended in June 2012 with Holmes's withdrawal from university.[2] In the months leading to the July 20, 2012, mass murder, his professors noted his deteriorating academic performance.[3] A university psychiatrist who had been treating him reported her concerns about the 25-year-old's mental state to the university's threat assessment team. Would mental illness explain why James Holmes killed 12 people and wounded 70 others? Would it explain why he booby-trapped his apartment with explosive devices capable of killing many more?[4] Most people are surprised to learn that individuals with serious mental disorders can be capable of sophisticated planning and able to carry out elaborate criminal schemes. Their behavior can be purposeful even if their motivation is irrational. In an interview with a court-appointed psychiatrist, Holmes explained that his self-worth would increase by one "value unit" with each person he killed. Crazy talk. In his journal (which he mailed to the psychiatrist, along with a stack of burnt $20 bills) he wrote the word "Why?" 247 times over eight pages. He noted, "Life has no value whatsoever . . . Untruth is converted to truth by violence times zero, problem equals question mark, zero times problem equals question mark times zero, based on an incorrect theorem, zero equals zero, problem solved."[5] Crazy thinking. Would it suffice to say he shot 90 people because he was mentally ill?

If it weren't for his mental disorder, it is difficult to imagine any of us would ever have heard of James Earl Holmes. At Holmes's trial, defense attorneys argued that his sense of right and wrong was distorted by schizophrenia.[6] Does this mean his schizophrenia "caused" him to commit mass murder? It is evident the schizophrenia distorted his thinking. But the simple fact that schizophrenia is a serious mental disorder and that Holmes has it does not explain his crimes, since the vast majority of schizophrenics are not dangerous people. The role Holmes's mental disorder played would depend on a number of additional factors such as whether his life circumstances were particularly stressful (he had recently failed a major exam and instead of repeating it, dropped out of university) or whether he had an effective support system (apart from a girlfriend who terminated their relationship, he appeared to be a reclusive loner).

It is not having any particular mental illness that makes people commit crimes. (To be sure, most mentally ill people are not criminals.) Rather, it is how specific aspects of the brain dysfunction in mentally disordered people affect their responses to their environment that explains their unconventional or even criminal behaviors.

At the end of the day, however, an understanding of why James Holmes committed mass murder may not be a determining factor in the jury's decision regarding his guilt. At the time of this writing the defense is beginning to present its case for insanity. In spite of the evidence of serious mental disorder, the extreme nature of the crime bodes strongly for a guilty verdict. On the other hand, assuming Holmes is convicted, the matter of his mental illness is likely to carry considerable weight in the final decision regarding his punishment, whether he is sentenced to life without parole or death.

The case of James Holmes illustrates the kinds of challenges that mental illness presents to the criminal justice system. Schizophrenia, the mental disorder from which Holmes apparently suffers, is considered in this chapter. Mass murderers, discussed briefly in Chapter 2, tend to be unlike other types of murderers in that most often they are seriously mentally disordered. But like other people with serious mental disorder, their illness generally has a course of development where symptoms emerge over time. Accordingly, as the illness is untreated and progresses, symptoms become worse. Unlike what many people think, mass murderers do not simply "go crazy;" they do not just "snap." In fact, in the majority of cases there is a long trail of signals that are either not recognized as possible danger signs or are overlooked. There is usually a series of increasingly disturbed behaviors that, on their own, do not portend violence but together signal an individual who is becoming at risk for committing acts of violence. Nonetheless, the vast majority of people who are mentally ill–even seriously mentally ill–are not violent. This makes it very difficult to predict those few whose behavior will make the headlines.

The extraordinarily complex nature of human behavior continually challenges the criminal justice system. How do we predict with accuracy which individuals are most likely to be violent? For example, which accused wife batterer should be freed on his own recognizance before a court appearance is scheduled? Which ones should be kept in jail until that hearing? Which inmates should be selected for early release from prison? Or when is treatment–rather than punishment–the appropriate response for the offender? What role should mental illness play in these decisions? While there are no one-size-fits-all answers, as we come to better understand the causes of criminal behavior we will be better positioned to deal with it more effectively, possibly even preventing it from occurring in some cases.

Much research has been devoted to understanding why people commit crimes. Knowing the causes of crime–its *etiology*–is an important key to preventing criminal acts and changing the behavior of offenders. Being able to explain crime also influences the decisions of the courts. In the Holmes case, the defendant pleaded not guilty by reason of insanity to the crimes, suggesting that what caused him to commit them would lead reasonable people to raise doubts about his criminal responsibility. Certainly he was responsible for the deaths of 12 people and the shooting of 70 more; but whether Holmes was capable of asserting complete control over his behavior at the time of the killings was a difficult matter for the criminal court to decide and continues to be the subject of contentious public debate.

This chapter looks at the causes of crime from different angles–biology, psychology, and sociology–and explores why some people are victimized, even repeatedly, and others are not. As James Holmes's case shows, how factors like mental disorder are understood has important implications for how we conduct the business of criminal justice.

SEEKING THE CAUSES OF CRIME: EARLY SCHOOLS OF THOUGHT

The causes of crime have been the subject of research in the disciplines of biology, psychology, sociology, and victimology for years. Criminologists recognize two major schools of thought or belief systems as among the first attempts to organize a view of crime causation: the classical and the positive schools of criminology.

The Classical School: Choosing to Be a Criminal

The **classical school of criminology** viewed the criminal as having free will, the freedom of individual choice to choose a criminal path deliberately. The Italian economist and jurist Cesare Beccaria (1738-1794) articulated this position in *On Crimes and Punishments* (1764), the cornerstone of the classical school of criminology.[7] Jeremy Bentham (1748-1832), an English philosopher, also contributed to the classical school's view of crime causation with his *Introduction to the Principles of Morals and Legislation* (1789).[8] Both Beccaria and Bentham believed that criminal behavior resulted from a person's rational and conscious choices–that is, criminals were responsible for their behavior–and that appropriate punishments would deter further criminal actions.

According to Beccaria, if punishment is to deter offenders, it must be dictated by law, proportionate to the crime committed (neither too harsh nor too easy), certain, swiftly imposed, and dispensed in public.[9] Bentham proposed that people acted in a way that brought them the greatest pleasure and the least pain and that they would not commit crime if the pain of punishment was greater than what might be gained from carrying out the crime. This idea was known as Bentham's *hedonistic calculus*. Bentham also developed *utilitarianism*, an ethical philosophy of social control that focused on imposing punishments that were believed best for the majority of people in society.[10]

Like the classical school from which it is derived, the **neoclassical school of criminology** is based on the principle of free will, the belief that people are responsible for their actions, and the idea that punishment can prevent crime. However, the neoclassical school incorporates some practical modifications necessary for the equitable administration of criminal law and justice. For example, the neoclassical school recognizes differences in criminal circumstances and assumes that some people–such as children, the insane, and the intellectually deficient–cannot reason. In such cases, the criminal justice system

▶ **Classical School of Criminology**

The classical school of criminology believes that the criminal has a free will and should be punished as dictated by law.

must consider the offender's needs in determining appropriate punishments. Proponents of the classical and neoclassical schools frequently support the crime control model discussed in Chapters 1 and 11.

A present-day derivative of the classical and neoclassical schools of criminology is **rational choice theory.** This theory assumes that criminals choose to commit crime because they believe that the benefits they will derive will overshadow the risks of getting caught.[11] The benefits of crime may be economic, physiological, or both. For example, one offender may commit a crime because she thinks she will obtain a great deal of money; another offender might receive an adrenaline high or a boost in self-esteem from committing the crime. In both cases, the offender considers her crime and victims carefully before proceeding and comes to the conclusion that there is little chance of getting caught or of being punished.

rational choice theory
A theory of crime causation that assumes that criminals choose to commit crime because they believe that the benefits they will derive will outweigh the risks of getting caught.

The Positivist School: Tendency Toward Criminal Behavior Is Predetermined

The **positivist school of criminology,** which emerged after 1850, replaced the classical school concepts of free will and rational choice with the concept of *determinism*—the idea that criminal behavior is a product of biological, psychological, and social forces that are beyond a person's control. Moreover, the positivist school de-emphasized punishment as a deterrent to crime and stressed instead the need to treat the offender. If they were to be treated successfully, offenders had to be scientifically studied to determine what factors caused them to commit crime.

positivist school of criminology
The view that criminal behavior is a product of biological, psychological, and social forces beyond a person's control.

The positivist school is associated with Cesare Lombroso (1835–1909), who is known as the father of modern criminology. Lombroso was one of the first researchers to apply the scientific method to his study of offenders. He spent much of his life measuring the skulls of criminals and recording his findings. As a biological determinist, he believed that biological factors (particularly heredity) were the main determinants of criminal behavior. Lombroso proposed that criminals were born with criminal traits, and he espoused the concept of **atavism**—the idea that, viewed from an evolutionary perspective, criminals were primitive, subhuman, biological throwbacks characterized by certain "inferior" identifiable physical and mental characteristics.[12] For example, Lombroso described criminals as having small glassy eyes, big ears, and excessive amounts of hair. Proponents of the positivist school of criminology are frequently supporters of the rehabilitation model discussed in Chapter 11. The major tenets of the classical and positivist schools of criminology are compared in Key Concepts.

atavism
The belief that criminals are evolutionarily primitive or subhuman people characterized by certain "inferior" identifiable physical and mental characteristics.

The classical and positivist schools of thought are starting points from which to view crime and criminal behavior, but their ability to predict who will engage in criminal behavior and who will be victimized by crime is limited. Although free will and biological determinism continue to be useful explanations of crime, today we recognize that crime is caused by multiple factors. Research focusing on biological, psychological, sociological, and victimological factors contributes further to our understanding of what causes crime and victimization.

KEY CONCEPTS   Principles of the Classical and Positivist Schools of Criminology

Classical School	Positivist School
Criminal behavior is the product of free will.	Criminal behavior is a result of determinism.
The presence of punishment in the general population prevents crime.	Treatment of convicted offenders prevents them from committing crime.

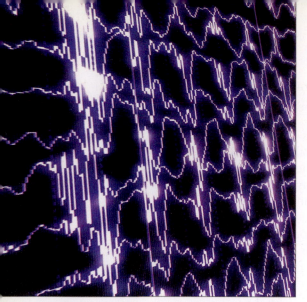

RealCrimeTech

LIE DETECTION BY BRAINWAVE ANALYSIS

The *electroencephalogram (EEG)*, long used to detect abnormal brain function, has been adapted to indicate when a person is lying. Electrodes are placed at specific points on the surface of an individual's head to pick up electrical fields generated by impulses as they are transmitted between systems of neurons. Then the "brain fingerprinting" technique examines the brain's response to crime scene–related images. When the brain recognizes a familiar image, EEG waves are different from those that are observed when the brain is presented with a novel stimulus. Thus, if a criminal suspect lies about committing a burglary, his brain may "say" otherwise when it recognizes images from the burglarized house.

In 2008, an Indian court of law accepted the findings from this technology as evidence against Aditi Sharma for the poisoning murder of her fiancé. The defendant was convicted and sentenced to life

Continued

BIOLOGICAL FACTORS

Social forces can lead people to behave in criminal and violent ways, yet most people who experience social challenges such as poverty and racism do not become criminals. Differences in the biological and psychological makeup of individuals largely account for this fact. The ways each person thinks and feels–and thus behaves–are largely the result of brain structure and function. Understanding the psychology of an offender's mind requires first knowing something about the biology of the brain.

Criminologists have benefited greatly from new technologies that permit the study of brain activity and function. Today's technologies enable researchers to see various structures of the brain as well as to observe the brain in action. Although much of human behavior is largely influenced by the thought processes associated with making choices (individual free will), biological factors are also involved.

Advances in science and medicine, and their respective technologies, are making it possible to identify and measure a variety of biological factors related to the expression and suppression of criminal and violent behaviors. For this reason, much current research on criminal and violent behavior is turning to investigating the structure and function of the brain.

Neurobiological Factors of Brain Function

Teenagers are known to make careless decisions and to engage in high-risk behaviors, but is it their fault? Neurological studies have shown that the teenage brain is still a work in progress. Not all of its structures have matured. In teenagers, the immature prefrontal cortex area of the brain is not yet capable of maintaining control over a teen's impulses. Thus even teenagers known to be "good kids" sometimes behave recklessly: for example, skateboarding down some steps without wearing a helmet or stepping on the gas to speed away from a stoplight.[13] Many delinquent behaviors are the result of poor impulse control that is due, at least in part, to a brain that has not yet completely developed.

But what of adults who act on impulse? In many cases their behavior is the result of a brain that has been injured or has

▶ **Reckless Teen Behavior**

Many delinquent behaviors on the part of youths result from poor impulse control that is due, at least in part, to a brain that has not yet completely developed.

developed in abnormal ways. Brain functioning may be affected by disease or injury or by the effects of chemical agents such as alcohol and drugs. There is no scale for predicting the degree to which any of these factors might induce criminal behavior, but these abnormalities are widely recognized as factors contributing to aberrant and violent behavior.

How a person's behavior may change after a head injury depends largely on the site and extent of the trauma. Forensics expert Gail Anderson examined a variety of studies of violent offenders in which their violent and criminal behaviors (for example, spousal battery, murder) were linked to brain damage.[14] Other studies have linked head injury to violent behavior in juveniles who grow up in a home where there is violence and where the juvenile has a mental disorder (most often depression, and usually undiagnosed at the time).[15] Although it is not clear how these three factors–trauma to the brain, violence in the home, and psychological disorder–specifically relate to one another (that is, whether depressed children are more prone to head injury or whether head injury results in depression), their combined result can be chronic violent behavior.

A simple explanation of brain function shows that behavior results from interactions between the rational prefrontal cortex and the emotional *limbic system*–the part of the brain responsible for the experience of emotions (such as rage) and basic drives (such as sex). When an individual has an urge to act in a particular way (to yell at someone for cutting in line at the movie theater, for example), that person's prefrontal cortex will judge whether that behavior is the best response. If the person cutting in line is a large and imposing stranger, yelling at him may provoke him to become violent. The prefrontal cortex may then decide that no action is the best course of action. For some individuals, however, the urge to yell at the stranger is uninhibited by rational thought. Because their prefrontal cortex is not functioning properly, they yell without thinking about the possible consequences of doing so.

Impulsive behaviors are characteristic of individuals with *attention deficit hyperactivity disorder (ADHD)*, a syndrome with many symptoms, including poor impulse control, restlessness, and an inability to concentrate. Considering the structure of the brain, we can understand how a stimulant medication such as Ritalin works to calm the behavior of someone with ADHD. Normally, such a drug would stimulate a person; however, in those with ADHD, the drug acts to stimulate the underaroused prefrontal cortex, prompting it to do its job of dampening impulses that come from the emotion-generating limbic system.

Using scanning imagery, we can identify the activity in the brain as people under the same experimental conditions are given a task (such as counting backward by multiples of 7) to stimulate the prefrontal cortex. During such an experiment, activated regions of the brain appear as red areas on the scan. The brain scan of a control subject with no psychiatric or criminal history produces an image in which much of the prefrontal cortex is red, indicating its activation as the brain concentrates and performs the task. In contrast, the scan of an impulsive murderer shows shades of blue and green in the prefrontal cortex, reflecting reduced activity in this region. Such a scan is consistent with what we would

Continued from previous page

imprisonment—this was before the scientific community had assessed the validity and reliability of using EEGs to detect lying. Because science and the law are not always in sync with each other, such cases pose serious challenges to the quest for justice.

In the United States, there is considerable resistance to the admissibility of brain fingerprints as evidence in the courtroom. Nonetheless, this technology has been used effectively in criminal cases. For example, after spending 25 years in prison for the 1977 murder of a security guard in Nebraska, Terry Harrington's conviction was reversed and he was released in 2003, largely because of information derived from brain fingerprinting tests. Psychophysiologist Lawrence Farwell applied the technology to Harrington and concluded his brain did not contain any memory of the 1977 crime scene but did recognize details related to the alibi he had provided for the time the crime was committed.

Interestingly, it was not the brain fingerprint results themselves that led to Harrington's release from prison, but rather how those results influenced the key prosecution witness to recant his original testimony that Harrington had committed the murder. Specifically, when Farwell showed Kevin Hughes the results of Harrington's brain fingerprinting test, that witness recanted his testimony and admitted he had lied in the murder trial; he had feared he would be prosecuted for the murder himself.

This case shows that even though courts may be reluctant to allow the results of brain fingerprinting as evidence in criminal trials, the technology holds potential to assist in criminal investigations—to elicit confessions and reveal deception—much like the polygraph. In court, greater allowance tends to be given to brain scans that are presented as mitigating evidence in the penalty phase of capital cases. In these cases the defense offers results of brain imaging tests to show deficits in how the defendant's brain functions. Thus, even if a defendant is found guilty of capital murder, the apparent fact of his brain dysfunction may lead a jury to vote for life imprisonment instead of death.

SOURCE: Anand Giridharadas, "India's Novel Use of Brain Scans in Courts Is Debated," *New York Times*, September 15, 2008.

expect in people who tend to behave on impulse. Indeed, it is the type of image seen in the scan of an impulsive murderer–an individual who kills out of feelings of rage at that moment. Interestingly, the brain scans of individuals who kill in the heat of the moment appear to differ from those of predatory murderers. The scans of those who plan their series of killings reveal higher than normal levels of activity in the prefrontal cortex during such cognitive tasks. The elevated level of activity in this region of the brain could explain, in part, why serial murderers succeed in committing a number of killings. Their behavior may be under better self-control and less susceptible to impulse.

The human brain contains some 100 billion *neurons,* the basic nerve cells that process and respond to incoming signals from the outside world through the five senses: vision, hearing, touch, taste, and smell. **Neurotransmitters** are chemicals secreted by neurons that facilitate the transmission of information from one neuron to another. These chemicals operate much like switches, turning neurons off and on–terminating the impulse or passing along the information. The neurotransmitter serotonin has been linked to impulsive and aggressive behaviors. A person whose serotonin levels in particular regions of the brain are too low will be significantly more likely to act on impulse and behave aggressively.[16] Another neurotransmitter, dopamine, appears to play a major role in the disordered thinking of schizophrenics.[17]

Like neurotransmitters, *hormones* are also chemical messengers, except that they are released into the bloodstream and so circulate throughout the body. The male sex hormone testosterone has long been associated with aggressive behavioral tendencies such as competitiveness and dominance. Increasing the level of testosterone (for example, by injecting it into the bloodstream) can result in higher levels of aggression.[18] Although being aggressive does not necessarily involve violence, the probability of a violent outcome increases when an individual is highly aggressive in interactions with others.

The adrenal gland secretes the stress hormone cortisol in response to a threatening situation. Extremely violent boys tend to have abnormally low levels of cortisol, a finding suggesting that they would be less physiologically responsive to situations most others would experience as threatening.[19] This "no fear" state in the face of potential threat could serve a criminal well. Consider that for most of us, our stress level alone would deter us from committing a serious crime. If we tried to rob a bank, we would probably bail out by the time we got to the front of the teller line, sweating profusely and with our heart beating out of our chest. An individual whose body does not register the situation as threatening is much more likely to execute the crime successfully, in a calm and controlled manner.

Genetic Factors: The Inheritance of Criminal Tendencies

Do criminals inherit their criminality? The basic unit of heredity is the *gene*– a segment of an individual's DNA that contains the information for making specific proteins that, in turn, contribute to particular biological or behavioral traits. The field of behavioral genetics explores the roles of genes in behavior. Of the approximately 25,000 genes that humans have, no single gene codes for any particular behavior. There is no "crime gene" per se. Rather, a variety of genetic and environmental factors interact to produce specific traits. Fetal exposure to toxins and viruses, stress and emotional trauma in childhood, and nutritional status are just a few of the factors that affect the way genes are expressed.

neurotransmitter
A chemical secreted by neurons that facilitates the transmission of information from one neuron to another.

MYTH/REALITY

MYTH: A specific gene, when inherited, results in criminal behavior.

REALITY: More likely, some individuals inherit particular combinations of genes that make them more likely to act on impulse or respond with aggression to certain situations.[20]

Criminal behavior tends to run in families.[21] Some families produce successive generations of criminals largely because of the way those families raise their children. In other cases, genes that predispose individuals to behave in aggressive and impulsive ways are carried along family lines. Dutch geneticist Han Brunner discovered a mutation in a specific gene that affects, among other things, serotonin levels. Every male in the family he studied who had the mutated gene also had a history of violent behavior.[22] This particular mutation is so rare, however, that it cannot explain violent behavior in general. Future researchers will no doubt identify other contributing genes, along with the kinds of environments in which they come to be expressed as criminal behaviors.

What are the respective contributions of genes and the environment? Studies of twin siblings offer substantial evidence of the role genes play in criminal behavior.[23] Identical twins have identical genes, and they tend to behave more similarly than do other brothers and sisters. With regard to criminal behavior, when one identical twin is criminal, the other twin is more likely to be criminal as well–this occurs more frequently than with other siblings. In research on adoptees, the genetic influences of biological parents who themselves were criminal were found to outweigh the influence of the parents who raised the children, whether those parents were criminal or not. Thus, although both the rearing environment and genetic makeup have a role in a child's (and later an adult's) behavior, genes appear to carry more weight.[24]

The recognition that, except for identical twins, individual humans have stretches of DNA that uniquely identify them has broad application in criminal investigations. DNA can be extracted from bone tissue to identify skeletal remains of victims of crime. In addition, offenders leave traces of their DNA (for example, from semen) at the scenes of their crimes. Just as current research strives to link specific genes and combinations of genes to physical and mental illnesses, genetic "profiles" are being sought for behavioral traits such as violence.

Many people, researchers and the general public included, believe that linking criminal behavior to biological factors unjustly frees offenders from criminal responsibility for their crimes. However, the complexity of criminal behavior makes it both difficult to understand and difficult to control. Perhaps the most admirable goal would be to identify what we are capable of changing and recognizing what we are not, at least not with current knowledge.

▲ **Identical Twins**
When one identical twin is criminal, the twin sibling is more likely to be criminal as well. This occurs more frequently in identical twins than in other siblings.

PSYCHOLOGICAL FACTORS

All aspects of our psychological makeup have biological underpinnings. The question is not whether mental illnesses have a genetic component but how combinations of genes work to increase an individual's vulnerability to mental disorder. When an individual's brain does not work properly, the person's psychological responses may lead to deviant behavior and crime. Some people commit crimes because there is something psychologically wrong with them. Some have mental disorders that affect their ability to function in accordance with society's laws. Others may have psychological problems even if they do not suffer from a recognized mental illness.

MYTH/REALITY

MYTH: People with mental disorders are more likely than other people to commit crimes.

REALITY: In general, mentally disordered people are no more likely than others to commit crimes. There is, however, a relationship between some kinds of mental disorder and criminal behavior. The way a particular mental disorder affects an individual's thinking and feeling will affect that person's behavior.[25]

Mental Disorders and Criminal Behavior

A *mental illness* or *mental disorder* is a medical condition that interferes with a person's ability to function on a day-to-day basis. The most serious disorders–**psychoses**–leave individuals out of touch with reality and unable to cope with their surroundings. A person suffering from a psychotic disorder may experience *hallucinations*, which are sensory experiences, such as hearing voices or seeing things that are not there, in the absence of actual stimuli. The individual may also have *delusions*, false and sometimes preposterous beliefs about the world, such as believing that people are out to get him or her.

Criminals depicted on television and in movies are often stereotyped as having mental problems.[26] The truth is that mentally disordered individuals are generally not violent, nor are they criminal.[27] The best predictor of future criminal behavior–for those with and without mental disorders–is a history of past criminal behavior.[28] No particular mental disorder indicates that a person will behave violently or break the law. Some mental disorders do, however, make certain individuals more susceptible to acting in criminal or violent ways. This is especially true when a person's mental state is further altered by the abuse of drugs or alcohol or when a person has gone without prescribed medication for such a disorder.[29]

Classifying Mental Disorders The American Psychiatric Association publishes the ***Diagnostic and Statistical Manual of Mental Disorders (DSM),*** the standard classification reference used by mental health professionals in the United States. The *DSM,* now in its fifth edition (thus *DSM-V*), describes the approximately 400 mental disorders currently recognized by the psychiatric community, along with their identifying symptoms.[30] The criminal justice system regularly calls upon mental health professionals to assist in making a wide range of decisions, and these professionals rely on the *DSM,* which describes mental disorders largely based on their effects on an individual's ability to meet the demands of everyday life. (See "Matters of Ethics" on page 83 for a discussion of the *DSM* and the controversies it prompts.)

The *DSM-V* lists several categories of serious mental disorders that include schizophrenia spectrum disorders, paranoid disorders, and severe mood disorders. A number of criminal cases making the news involve schizophrenic disorders or some form of major mood disorder. We discuss both of these types of disorders in the following sections to illustrate the influence of serious mental disorders on behavior–including criminal behavior.

Schizophrenia Spectrum Disorders The term **schizophrenia** comes from Greek and then New Latin *schizo* (meaning "split") and *phrenia* (meaning "mind"). The word's origins may explain why so many people wrongly believe that schizophrenia means split personality. In fact, schizophrenia refers to the individual's split from reality that is the result of profound aberrations in cognitive processes. Schizophrenics typically suffer from both delusions and hallucinations. Approximately 1 percent of U.S. adults have a form of this debilitating mental disorder.[31] The majority of schizophrenics are not violent, but the odds of their being so increase if they have the paranoid type of the disorder[32] and are not taking medication for it. Substance-abusing schizophrenics also are more likely to be violent.[33]

Andrei Chikatilo, executed for murdering 52 fellow Russian citizens over a 12-year period beginning in 1978, likely suffered from paranoid schizophrenia. He mutilated most of his victims, removing or wounding their eyes because he believed that the image of a killer could be retrieved from his victim's eyes. He also cannibalized some victims. Chikatilo seemed quite normal on the outside; he was married with two children and held down a steady job as a factory clerk. The bizarre nature of his crimes, however, betrayed his serious mental illness.

Matters *of* Ethics

Revising the *DSM:* A Process on Trial in the Court of Professional Opinion

The *Diagnostic and Statistical Manual of Mental Disorders (DSM)*—often referred to as the "shrinks' bible"—is the book that mental health professionals in North America use to diagnose mental disorders. Medical insurance companies require therapists to provide *DSM* diagnoses in order to be paid for their services. Expert witnesses regularly testify as to specific *DSM* disorders in insanity trials. Forensic psychologists and psychiatrists refer to *DSM* diagnoses in their assessments of whether or not a defendant is mentally fit to stand trial or should be granted early release from prison. Diagnoses are important factors in community placement decisions regarding parolees who are mentally ill. Suffice it to say, the diagnoses in this manual carry tremendous weight in the lives of many people—both in and out of the criminal justice system.

The National Institute of Mental Health estimates that in a given year, 26 percent of Americans over the age of 18 have a diagnosable mental disorder.[a] While this figure is sufficiently high to generate concern about the welfare of society, the percentage of jail and prison inmates with mental disorders is considerably higher. A 2006 U.S. Department of Justice study found that 64 percent of jail inmates, 54 percent of inmates in state prisons, and 45 percent of inmates in federal prisons had symptoms consistent with a major mental disorder.[b] Whether we are talking about people in the general community or individuals convicted of crimes, the consequences of being diagnosed with a mental disorder are far-reaching. Whether your medical insurance company will pay for your psychotherapy or a defendant's plea of insanity will prevail in court largely depends upon the application of *DSM* diagnoses.

Since the American Psychiatric Association published the first edition of the *DSM* in 1952, the manual has gone through six revisions (two of which were not substantial enough to warrant new editions). The fact that the *DSM* continues to be revised reflects the arbitrariness of diagnostic categories. So, who decides what mental disorders are included in the *DSM?* For that matter, who decides what combinations of symptoms constitute any particular mental disorder? And what criteria are used to select the behaviors that are cited as symptoms of the various disorders? The process by which diagnoses (and their criteria) become part of the *DSM* involves a number of working groups (known as advisory panels), each of which is responsible for a particular diagnostic category. Their recommendations have significant influence on the choice of which mental disorders are ultimately included in (or excluded from) subsequent *DSM* editions.

In a study in 2006, Lisa Cosgrove and her colleagues examined financial investments that members of advisory panels had with pharmaceutical companies at the time they were making recommendations to revise the *DSM-III*.[c] A wide range of conflicts of interest were uncovered that included such practices as panel members' holding stock in drug companies, serving as expert witnesses for drug companies that were being sued, and receiving gifts (in the form of travel, grants, contracts, and research funding) from drug companies. Cosgrove and her colleagues found that of the 170 panel members, 56 percent had financial ties to pharmaceutical companies. In fact, *100 percent* of the panelists making recommendations about schizophrenia and other psychotic disorders had financial conflicts of interest with the pharmaceutical industry! Since drug companies have such a vested interest in the *DSM,* it would be naive to think that their relationships with *DSM* panelists are born of altruistic motives in support of the psychiatric profession.

In 2013, the American Psychiatric Association again revised the manual. Decisions were made about which disorders should be included in the *DSM-V* and what criteria should be used to diagnose them. Of this most recent *DSM* panel-based revision process, Cosgrove and Krimsky reported that 75 percent of the work groups "continue to have a majority of their members with financial ties to the pharmaceutical industry." Further, as was found with *DSM-IV* revisions, "the most conflicted panels are those for which pharmacological treatment is the first-line intervention." Thus, it would seem that ethical questions about the process remain, conferring dubious validity on the work product—the *DSM-V*.[d]

OBSERVE → INVESTIGATE → UNDERSTAND

- Why is it important to know *how* mental health professionals decide on what should be considered a mental disorder?
- What kind of weight should diagnoses be given as a factor in the outcome of criminal trials?
- Should shareholders in pharmaceutical companies be banned from giving input in the process of revising the *DSM?* Why *and* why not?

SOURCES: [a]The National Institute of Mental Health, "The Numbers Count: Mental Disorders in America." www.nimh.nih.gov/health/publications/the-numbers-count-mental-disorders-in-america/index.shtml#Intro (retrieved December 11, 2010).

[b]Doris J. James and Lauren E. Glaze, "Mental Health of Prison and Jail Inmates." *Bureau of Justice Statistics Special Report* (Washington, DC: DOJ, 2006). www.nami.org/Template.cfm?Section=Press_September_2006&Template=/ContentManagement/ContentDisplay.cfm&ContentID=38175 (retrieved December 20, 2010).

[c]Lisa Cosgrove, Sheldon Krimsky, Manisha Vijayaraghavan, and Lisa Schneider, "Financial ties between *DSM-IV* panel members and the pharmaceutical industry," *Psychotherapy and Psychosomatics* 75 (2006): 154–160.

[d]Lisa Cosgrove and Sheldon Krimsky, "A Comparison of *DSM-IV* and *DSM-5* Panel Members' Financial Associations with Industry: A Pernicious Problem Persists," *PLoS Medicine* 9, no. 3 (2012): e1001190. doi:10.1371/journal.pmed.1001190.

The search for the causes of schizophrenia focuses on a number of factors. Because the disorder tends to run in families, genetic studies are a logical area of research. Multiple genes that affect brain structure and function appear to be involved. A particularly productive line of research is focusing on abnormalities in different neurotransmitter systems. As the biochemistry of schizophrenia becomes better understood, medications to manage its symptoms more effectively will undoubtedly follow.[34]

▲ Aftermath of the James Oliver Huberty Massacre

James Oliver Huberty was killed by a police sharpshooter after murdering 21 people and wounding 19 others in a McDonald's restaurant. The media frequently refer to such murderers as "going postal" since some of the infamous ones were former postal workers who returned to the workplace and killed coworkers. In the Huberty case, the media introduced the term "McRage" to reflect the killer's apparent emotions and the scene of his crime.

bipolar disorder
A major mood disorder manifested by bouts of serious depression alternating with periods of extreme elation and exaggerated self-importance.

postpartum psychosis
A serious mental illness characterized by hallucinations, delusions, and obsessive thoughts about the baby.

Major Mood Disorders   *Major mood disorders* involve extreme and prolonged emotional states that render the individual incapable of coping with the demands of everyday life. Approximately 6 percent of the adult population has a major depressive disorder marked by feelings of guilt and worthlessness, loss of appetite for food and sexual activity, sleep disturbance, and thoughts of suicide.[35] The severity of these symptoms distinguishes the person with major depressive disorder from someone who is only mildly depressed. In the same way that medications can treat the symptoms of schizophrenia, drugs can affect the biochemistry of the brain in ways that alleviate serious depression.

People suffering serious depression may be inclined to harm themselves, and they may also present a risk to others. There are highly publicized cases of individuals with serious depression who murder others before taking their own lives ("angry suicides") or who position themselves to be killed by police after they have murdered others ("suicide-by-cop"). On a July morning in 1984, for example, 41-year-old James Oliver Huberty told his wife "society had its chance." As he was leaving home dressed in military-style camouflage clothes, he told her: "I'm going hunting. Hunting humans." Seventy-seven minutes after Huberty entered the McDonald's restaurant close to his home in San Ysidro, California, 21 people were dead and 19 wounded. A police sharpshooter killed Huberty, making him the 22nd fatality and ending the incident—thus aiding Huberty in his apparent suicidal quest.

The day before, Huberty had called a local mental health center seeking help. Since he did not say it was an emergency situation, his name, incorrectly spelled as Shouberty, was apparently put on a waiting list. Huberty's wife later told the media that her husband appeared to be delusional around this time, a symptom indicating a major depressive disorder. The autopsy revealed extremely high levels of lead and cadmium in his body, perhaps from his years of work as a welder. Both are toxic elements known to significantly affect brain function. Thus, in Huberty's case, brain function may have been compromised by toxic elements. It appears that altered brain function coupled with major depression proved a fatal mix, resulting in a mass murder.

Another form of major mood disorder is **bipolar disorder.** Formerly known as manic depression, bipolar disorder is characterized by periods of severe depression that can alternate with periods of mania, whose symptoms include extreme elation and exaggerated self-importance. Persons suffering from major depression may become suicidal, whereas individuals in the manic phase of bipolar disorder are often irritable and hostile and can turn violent. Hallucinations or delusions may contribute to their aggression.

A woman who has bipolar disorder is at higher risk of experiencing **postpartum psychosis,** a serious mental illness whose symptoms include delusions, hallucinations, and obsessive thoughts about her baby. These symptoms generally start within the first 6 weeks after the baby's birth but may not appear for as long as a year. It is not surprising that some mothers with postpartum depression kill their babies.[36] Postpartum psychosis, combined with a number of other factors, likely led Andrea Yates to a mental state in which, in 1991, she decided that killing her five children was the only way to save them from eternal damnation. As her grip on reality faded, the influence of extremist religious views took hold, and her increasing isolation increased her vulnerability. Andrea's family also had a history of mental illness: One brother had bipolar disorder, and another brother and a sister had long-standing histories of depression, as did their mother.[37] This family history of mood disorder suggests that Yates's psychological problems, as is true of most others with serious mental illness, had genetic roots.[38] In her initial trial, a Texas jury found Andrea Yates guilty and sentenced her to life in prison. Following the discovery that a prosecution expert witness had given false testimony that may have led jurors to believe in her culpability, another trial was conducted. The jury in the second trial decided that Yates was not guilty by reason of insanity.

Mental illness × Social isolation × Fascination with violence × Access to guns = Sandy Hook mass murder.

Most mental disorders are not as debilitating as the psychoses previously described. Yet many of the most serious and brutal crimes are the product of these so-called less serious mental disorders. For example, in 2012, 20-year-old Adam Lanza shot and killed 26 people, 20 of whom were elementary school students. The "Sandy Hook Shooter" reportedly suffered from more than one mental disorder—none of which was a psychosis. A formal review of the case concluded he had autism spectrum disorder, anxiety, and obsessive-compulsive disorder.[39] The report concluded that Lanza's mental disorders, coupled with his fascination with mass murder, social isolation, and access to guns, proved to be a recipe for mass murder. (See Chapter 14 for more on the Lanza case.)

Psychopathy   In the *DSM-IV, antisocial personality disorder* was the diagnosis for the presence of a pattern of behavioral problems before age 15 that include truancy, theft, and compulsive lying, and the continuation of such a pattern into adulthood. In fact, repeated lawbreaking is considered a core symptom of antisocial personality disorder, and most prison inmates would qualify for this diagnosis.[40] Beyond confirming that these individuals have a pattern of antisocial behavior, however, this diagnosis offers little to distinguish among offenders or to explain their behavior.

An alternative approach, particularly in the forensic arena, relies on the concept of psychopathy. **Psychopathy** is a disorder of personality revealed by a lifelong pattern of antisocial behavior about which the individual has no remorse. It differs from antisocial personality disorder in that it involves distinct cognitive and emotional deficits that have been linked to specific brain abnormalities. The current struggle regarding these two terms—antisocial personality disorder and psychopathy—is evidenced by the replacement of antisocial personality disorder in the *DSM-IV* with antisocial/psychopathic types (of personality disorder) in the *DSM-V*. For the time being, it is fair to say that most clinicians are continuing to refer to their clients as having antisocial personality disorder, whereas forensic behavioral professionals are increasingly focusing on the psychopathy of the suspects, defendants, and convicts they evaluate.

Most people have heard of psychopathy but do not fully understand what it is. A common mistake is to confuse the word *psycho*, a slang term for "psychotic," with the term *psychopath*. Whereas psychotics typically experience distorted thoughts and perceptions, psychopaths are in touch with reality and

psychopathy
A personality disorder involving specific cognitive and emotional deficits that is exhibited by a lifelong pattern of antisocial behavior for which the individual has no remorse.

appear to be normal on the surface. Typically, psychopaths are manipulative, superficial, and self-centered. They lack the ability to empathize emotionally with others and do not experience remorse for their antisocial behavior. Psychopaths do experience emotions, but their feelings tend to be shallow. They tend to act on impulse and are, by and large, irresponsible. Their behavior is thus like that of people with antisocial personality disorder; but the nature of their behavior is more complex in that psychopaths have specific neurobiological deficits as well. Taking this definition to its logical conclusion, psychologist Robert Hare noted that "[i]f crime is the job description, the psychopath is the perfect applicant."[41]

Many criminals who commit serial offenses, from burglary to confidence schemes to serial murder, are psychopaths. The kinds of feelings and associations that stop us from engaging in antisocial acts are notably absent in psychopaths. They do not care about others or the harm that their antisocial behaviors—criminal and otherwise—do to them. This is one reason that criminal psychopaths are significantly more likely to reoffend than are nonpsychopathic offenders.[42] Moreover, while most psychopaths are not criminal or violent, criminal psychopaths as a group commit more than half the violent crimes in society.[43]

Other nonpsychotic disorders have been linked to criminal behavior. Individuals suffering from *posttraumatic stress disorder (PTSD),* for example, have been reported to perpetrate serious crimes. The woman who kills her long-abusive husband, and the war veteran who engages in violence following his return from active duty, are two examples. In both cases, prior experience with a situation perceived to be life-threatening has serious and long-term psychological consequences. In fact, virtually any mental disorder can contribute to, if not be the basis for, criminal behavior.

Intelligence and Morality—The Cognitive Brain

The way in which the brain processes information is another factor related to the causes of crime. Two areas of cognitive research that warrant discussion in relation to crime are intelligence and moral reasoning.

intelligence
The capacity to learn or comprehend, manifested by the ability to solve problems and adapt to life's everyday experiences.

Intelligence **Intelligence** is the capacity to learn or comprehend, shown through the ability to solve problems and adapt to life's everyday experiences.[44] *Intelligence tests* such as IQ tests provide a standardized measure of cognitive ability (as demonstrated by, for example, solving problems or engaging in abstract reasoning). The Wechsler Adult Intelligence Scale is commonly used in clinical and forensic settings.[45] In addition to providing measures of capacities such as verbal comprehension and motor coordination, scores on particular subtests can indicate brain damage and other deficits. Incarcerated offenders tend to score lower on average than nonoffenders on such intelligence tests.[46]

The relationship between intelligence and criminal behavior is complex. Complicating this discussion is the fact that there are different kinds of intelligence. People with high *emotional intelligence* accurately perceive others' emotions, understand emotional meanings, and can manage their own emotions.[47] The behavior of serial murderers would indicate, however, that they are low in emotional intelligence, as they appear to lack the ability to understand emotional information or to reason with emotions. Psychopaths, in particular, lack these abilities.

Real Careers

JESSICA DUBNOFF

Work location: New York City

College(s): Northeastern University (2008)

Major(s): Criminal Justice with a minor in Political Science (BS)

Job title: Contracted Area Coordinator in the Department of Probation, Special Offenders Unit

Salary range for jobs like this: $30,000–$35,000

Time in job: 1.5 years

Work Responsibilities

As area coordinator for a mental health treatment program for sex offenders, I act as a liaison among the probation officers, probationers, and mental health clinicians. My responsibilities include gathering information for new referrals, explaining the program to probationers, and scheduling appointments for probationers with one of our mental health clinicians. I also make sure all the relevant monthly paperwork—such as progress reports, monthly updates, sign-in sheets, session notes, and billings—is distributed to the proper probation officer and a copy is filed at our office. My favorite part of this job is when I oversee containment meetings with the sex offender and probation officer and serve as a moderator, an integral part of this multidisciplinary team. Through my current employment, I have found myself becoming much more interested in the social work aspects of supervising and monitoring a case than in the department administration and law enforcement aspects.

Why Criminal Justice?

Since high school I knew I wanted to work in the criminal justice field. However, I was unsure which career was right for me—criminal defense attorney, police officer, forensic psychologist, and prosecutor all seemed like excellent choices. I decided to attend Northeastern University for guidance in making this difficult decision. Northeastern is well known for its co-op program, which allows students to work full-time for 6 months per year for class credit in a hands-on environment. By the time I was a senior, I had participated in three co-ops. In fact, I landed the job I have now because my co-op experience led me to a successful internship with the same company.

Expectations and Realities of the Job

From my co-ops, academics, and employment, I gained a wealth of knowledge about the field, and I knew what to expect in terms of financial compensation and work hours. However, my education did not fully prepare me for the negative effects that my job would have on my personal life. For example, when riding the subway, I found myself questioning whether those everyday unavoidable physical brushes against others were intentional (a crime called *frotteurism*). Similarly, if I passed a car with tinted windows, I would wonder if a sexual crime was being committed within. It took some time before I was able to go about my everyday life without thinking about sexually related crimes.

My Advice to Students

If you want to work in a setting that deals with the rehabilitation of offenders, you need to be able to separate the person from the crime. There are many other facets of a person's character and personality that need to be considered apart from the crime he or she committed. Offenders need solid, unbiased counseling to improve their lives and avoid future arrests. It can be tough to do this at first, but experienced colleagues or supervisors can be supportive and offer advice.

With an IQ in the genius range, serial murderer Edmund Emil Kemper III is unusual both as a person and as a serial killer. Yet there is reason to believe that his high cognitive abilities came with significant emotional deficits. Consider: After he had picked up a young woman hitchhiker, Kemper saw that as he drove her around, she began to get anxious because they did not seem to be going to her destination. "So I pulled out the gun to calm her down."[48] Kemper knew, intellectually, that pulling out his gun would have an effect on the hitchhiker, but it was evident that–even with his superior IQ–he could not identify, emotionally, with the terror she felt when she saw the gun. Brain-imaging studies and other research show that the brains of violent psychopaths work differently from those of people who do not suffer from mental disorders and of individuals who do not commit violent crimes.[49]

moral reasoning
Application of a set of ethical principles based on what society views as good versus bad behavior.

social learning theory
Theory that behavior is learned and is maintained or extinguished based on the rewards or punishments associated with it.

▼ **Edmund Emil Kemper III**

A most unusual serial killer, Kemper has an IQ in the genius range.

Moral Reasoning   **Moral reasoning** involves the application of a set of ethical principles based on what society views as good versus bad behavior. For most people, the ability to discern right from wrong develops and is internalized in childhood. Young children tend to see things as right or wrong, black or white. Children do not begin to identify "shades of gray" until about 7 years of age.[50]

Like children, many criminals appear to have immature moral reasoning. Damage to the prefrontal cortex (the part of the brain responsible for making decisions and judgments, planning, and self-control) from stroke, injury, or infection can result in a pattern of reckless, antisocial, and violent behavior about which the individual has no remorse.[51] This knowledge offers a model with which to understand how some offenders can repeatedly violate the rights of others and not feel guilty about it. The biology that sets the moral compass for their behavior is undeveloped or defective.

Learning Criminal Behavior from Others: Social Learning Theory

Behavioral psychologists argue that we learn behavior, which is then maintained or extinguished by the rewards or punishments we associate with it.[52] This perspective is known as **social learning theory.** How a person behaves is also influenced by experiences with the behavior of others. Thus, social learning can entail watching others and noting the consequences of their behaviors. This type of social learning may explain the boy who grows up to batter his wife. For years he observed his own father gain the compliance of his mother through acts of violence and intimidation. Similarly, children can learn to behave violently by seeing violent behavior rewarded in movies or through the instant rewards of killing the enemy in video games.[53] A major aspect of the socialization of every individual involves internalizing the rules for appropriate behavior. Anticipating punishment for bad behavior facilitates learning these rules.

Psychodynamic Factors

Sigmund Freud, the father of psychoanalysis, believed that humans have primitive urges and drives that exist below the level of conscious awareness.[54] A main principle of Freudian thinking–also known as *psychodynamic psychology*–is that an individual's personality and behavior traits develop early in life.

Freud posited that there are three parts to personality:

- The *id* consists of unconscious drives that demand instant gratification, always seeking pleasure and avoiding pain. Sexual urges and the cry of a baby to be fed are expressions of the *id*. We are born with an *id*; it helps us to survive during a stage in life when we cannot communicate with language.

- The *ego* incorporates conscious thoughts that cope with the demands of reality. The *ego* tries to satisfy the *id* by bringing the individual pleasure within accepted norms of society. The *ego* develops early in childhood and can be adversely affected by abuse and neglect.

- The *superego* constitutes the moral aspect of personality, or *conscience*, and internally judges one's actions based on principles of right and wrong. The *superego* regulates behavior by generating feelings of guilt in response to a person's immoral behavior.

Freud believed that the *id*, the *ego*, and the *superego* work together in a psychologically healthy individual to regulate behavior. Others have used Freud's conception of the three-part personality to explain aspects of criminal behavior. For example, some theorists have proposed that the personality of offenders often suffers from an imbalance in the roles played by *id*, *ego*, and *superego*. A person with a damaged *ego* (say, from child abuse) may be prone to act on impulses because the urges that come from the *id* go unchecked by what otherwise would be the rational judgment offered by a healthy *ego*. A person with a weak *superego* might be less able to control his violent or sexual impulses. Conversely, a person with an overactive *superego* might experience overwhelming feelings of guilt, persecution, and worthlessness, factors that can lead her to commit crimes–so that she will get the punishment she deserves.

KEY CONCEPTS Examples of Biological and Psychological Factors Involved in Criminal and Delinquent Behavior

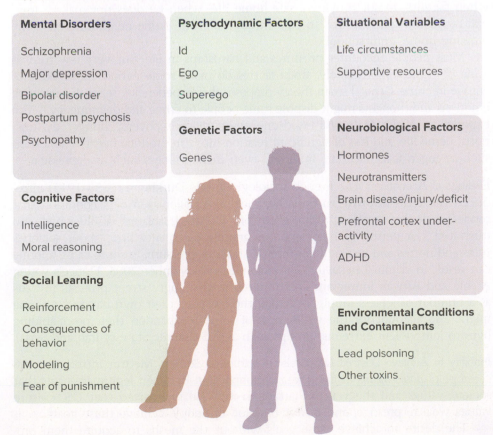

Mental Disorders

Schizophrenia

Major depression

Bipolar disorder

Postpartum psychosis

Psychopathy

Cognitive Factors

Intelligence

Moral reasoning

Social Learning

Reinforcement

Consequences of behavior

Modeling

Fear of punishment

Psychodynamic Factors

Id

Ego

Superego

Genetic Factors

Genes

Situational Variables

Life circumstances

Supportive resources

Neurobiological Factors

Hormones

Neurotransmitters

Brain disease/injury/deficit

Prefrontal cortex under-activity

ADHD

Environmental Conditions and Contaminants

Lead poisoning

Other toxins

Freud based his psychological theories on his clinical observations of patients. He did not have available to him the technologies that we currently utilize. What he described as id, for example, today might be explained as activity in the brain's limbic system; what he called ego might be what we see in brain scans as activity in the prefrontal cortex. The lesson is that different approaches may on the surface appear to lead to different conclusions because they are limited by their own theoretical concepts or by differences in the availability of technological advances.

The Key Concepts table illustrates some of the known biological and psychological factors involved in criminal and delinquent behavior.

SOCIOLOGICAL FACTORS

Sociology is the study of human beings within their social environments and includes looking carefully at how people behave and interact in societies. Sociological factors that relate to the study of crime and its causes include income, racism, sexism, capitalism, education, religion, ethnicity, neighborhood, subculture values, geography, family, occupation, politics, media, gang membership, health status, socialization, and the presence of weapons.

For most of the twentieth century, U.S. criminologists embraced sociological explanations of crime causation more fervently than biological and psychological theories. However, with advances in science, biological and psychological theories are gaining more interest. Nevertheless, many researchers and theorists still look closely at the role of sociological factors in explaining crime and criminal behavior.

When Adversity Leads to Crime: Strain Factors

strain theory
Theory that extraordinary pressures make people more likely to commit crime.

Strain theory proposes that extraordinary pressures make a person more likely to commit crime. Strain factors can come from a variety of sources—individuals, groups, and social institutions. For example, a teenager can experience strain when parents do not provide a safe home life, when he does not make a football team, and when he has to pass through a crime-prone neighborhood while walking home from school.

Most people encounter pressures and hardships in life, but very few turn to a life of crime. Unfortunately, strain factors do make some people more likely to engage in crime. General strain theory proposes that experiencing repetitive negative emotions and thoughts might dispose some people to crime and delinquency.[55] The experiences of the death of a loved one, abuse, divorce, poverty, hunger, dysfunctional home life, and loss of significant relationships can produce negative emotions such as anger, fear, rejection, hurt, and even mental illness such as depression.

anomie
A feeling of alienation or a condition that leaves people feeling hopeless, rootless, cut off, alienated, isolated, disillusioned, and frustrated.

Feelings of Alienation   The French sociologist Émile Durkheim (1858–1917) introduced the term **anomie** to describe a feeling of alienation or a condition that renders a person hopeless, rootless, cut off, alienated, isolated, disillusioned, and frustrated.[56] A person who experiences anomie cares very little about society's rules and norms and instead feels intense strain or pressure. In some cases, anomie can result in criminal behavior. For example, in November 2005, France's young Arabic and African immigrant communities staged angry street protests in Paris as a number of jobless immigrants took the law into their own hands.[57] Anomie might also account for the willingness of some to abandon their norm-abiding lives to join violent extremist groups such as ISIS (Islamic State of Iraq and Syria).

Inability to Achieve Desired Life Goals   Sociologist Robert Merton introduced the concept of *goals–means disjunction*—a disconnection between legitimate goals that society values and the way we attain them.[58] He recognized that U.S. culture values wealth, prestige, and power but not all people achieve these goals.

The desire to achieve these goals without the means to acquire them produces pressure, frustration, and anomie for many. Merton suggested that crime is

more prevalent in the lower classes because those with lower economic status are less likely to succeed, a situation that results in extraordinary stress—or strain—on some individuals. If the pressure is great enough on some individuals, they may feel pressured into breaking the law. People have different kinds of responses when they cannot reach their desired goals (see the table "Merton's Adaptations to the Goals-Means Disjunction"). Not all people choose to commit a crime just because they lack opportunity to achieve society's desired goals. Most people conform, some innovate to achieve success, some retreat or drop out of the race, some basically accept their fate (ritualism), and others rebel, often turning to crime.

Other strain factors that contribute to criminal behavior are lack of available opportunities, coupled with pressure to be part of a gang. One of the major reasons that boys—primarily from working-class neighborhoods—join gangs is their discomfort with unfamiliar middle-class values that are expected of them while attending school. They temporarily resolve their anxiety and discomfort by finding others who feel the same way and hanging out together in a gang.

The gang experience provides members with a heightened sense of social status, respect, fellowship, and relief from strain by opposing middle-class values. Committing delinquent acts is gang members' way of saying middle-class values are unimportant.[59] The "Race, Class, Gender" box examines why so many poor kids become members of a gang and what can be done to combat the problem.

Merton's Adaptations to the Goals–Means Disjunction

Cultural Goals	Institutionalized Means	Modes of Adaptation
+	+	Conformity
+	−	Innovation
−	+	Ritualism
−	−	Retreatism
±	±	Rebellion

Race, Class, Gender

Why Join Gangs?

In the United States today and throughout the nation's history, a variety of groups have formed gangs. In early U.S. history, Irish gangs were common. Today there are Southeast Asian gangs, Russian gangs, and Mexican American gangs, among others. The race or ethnicity of gangs varies, but their class rarely does. The bottom line is that individuals who join gangs are poor. There is very little economic diversity among those—both male and female—who choose to be members of gangs or associates of gang members.

Few professionals have reached out to understand why poor young males often turn to gang life. Jesuit priest Father Gregory Boyle in Los Angeles is an exception. He has worked with thousands of former gang members, many of whose backgrounds include psychological, emotional, and physical abuse, poverty, and neglect. Boyle finds a set of characteristics common to them all—lack of opportunity, social alienation, and economic vulnerability—any of which may lead to criminal behavior.

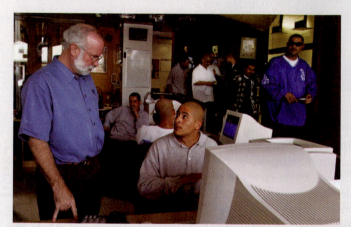

He concludes, quite simply, that people join gangs in order to feel connected to something, to feel included and loved, and to give meaning to their lives.[a]

To combat factors that lead to gang membership, Boyle created a more positive organization for them to join, Homeboy and Homegirl Industries. The organization provides troubled youths a means by which to feel connected to others, and it helps former gang members find jobs so that they are not as economically vulnerable. Homeboy Industries offers tattoo removal, counseling, and job training, among other services. Boyle likes to say, "If you want to get someone out of a gang, offer him a job."

Father Boyle's work is important for many reasons. Not only does he help many leave the life of gangs, but he also teaches the rest of us who do not have firsthand experiences with gang members that they are just like us—people who want to be loved and to be successful.[b] Boyle does not say that their actions should be excused, but rather that they should be given a chance to do right in the world. That is the same opportunity we all want. We need to be mindful, however, that some of us were born into situations that made it easy for us to live a life absent of crime. For others it is much more difficult.

OBSERVE → INVESTIGATE → UNDERSTAND

- Why is it important to understand why people join gangs?
- Why are jobs important for people who want to get out of gangs?
- Can gang membership ever be a positive experience? Explain.

SOURCES: [a]Celeste Fremon, *G-Dog and the Homeboys* (Albuquerque: University of New Mexico Press, 2004).

[b]David De Cremer and Tom Tyler. "Am I Respected or Not? Inclusion and Reputation as Issues in Group Membership," *Social Justice Research* 18, no. 2 (2005): 121–153.

On a Path to Crime: The Life Course Delinquency Perspective

Juvenile delinquency refers to illegal acts committed by minors. According to the *life course delinquency perspective,* delinquency follows identifiable trends from birth to old age. When a person is very young, delinquency is rare, but it becomes more frequent during a person's early adolescence. Delinquency is most common during the late teens and early adulthood and then declines during old age.[60]

Dual taxonomic theory, a contemporary offshoot of strain theory of criminal behavior that combines biological and psychological elements with social factors, asserts that because of brain damage, chemical imbalances, and other neuropsychological deficits, as well as factors such as poverty and dysfunctional families, some individuals get into trouble and engage in delinquency at young ages and continue their criminal behavior throughout the course of their lives.[61] These offenders are referred to as **life course persistent offenders.** By contrast, **adolescence-limited offenders** tend to participate in antisocial behavior during limited periods of time during adolescence, while maintaining school performance and respectful relationships with adults such as parents and teachers. Adolescence-limited offenders frequently give up criminal behaviors when they get older as they begin to realize the problems they will bring on themselves if their offending behavior continues. Offending behavior tends to peak around age 17 to 18 and then declines as offenders mature. Many take up a conventional law-abiding lifestyle by age 35.[62] In 2011 the researchers of an extensive

life course persistent offenders
Those who engage in delinquency at young ages and continue their criminal behavior throughout their lives.

adolescence-limited offenders
Young people who participate in antisocial behavior for a limited period of time during adolescence while maintaining school performance and respectful relationships with parents and teachers.

Pathways to Desistance Study concluded that offenders who commit serious felonies during their youth are not destined for a life of recidivism and adult crime. The term **desistance** means cessation of crime commission. The study's findings were that serious young offenders who have low rates of substance abuse, have stable living arrangements, and work and attend school cease offending as time goes by, regardless of the interventions they receive; longer incarcerations in juvenile facilities do not prevent reoffending and can possibly lead to increased recidivism; community-based supervision after incarceration is important for desistance; and longer-duration substance abuse counseling where family members are involved can contribute to desistance in the short term.[63]

desistance
The cessation of crime commission.

Social Bonds and Crime: Social Control Factors

Social control theory focuses primarily on belief systems–not laws or formal rules–that hold people to society's standards by putting limits on their actions. According to this theory, what keeps people from wrongdoing most of the time is their belief system. Whether on the street, at home, at parties, at school, at church, with friends, or in prison, beliefs regulate behavior. Control factors exist at several different levels in society.

social control theory
Theory that an individual's belief system, the police, and parental supervision are important in preventing the individual from getting into trouble.

Control by the Community Small and large communities control the behavior of their citizens in different ways. Small communities whose inhabitants live closely together frequently have tight bonds to one another. Citizens know what their neighbors do and are able to quickly identify and report anything out of the ordinary. In small communities, most citizens share the same norms and traditions and tend to think similarly, and those who do not follow norms are dealt with swiftly. Deviance tends to be rare in this type of community.

In contrast, people living in larger communities are not as tightly bonded with others in their community. Citizens do not get involved with many of their neighbors or their comings and goings and are less likely to identify and report unusual happenings. In these large and diverse communities, norms and traditions vary across different subcultures. People are accustomed to being among those who are different and tend to tolerate many types of deviance.[64]

Beyond One's Control—Avoiding Responsibility Some criminologists argue that for people to break the law, they must accept rationalizations that allow them to overcome feelings of responsibility. This perspective, known as **neutralization theory,** was developed by Gresham Sykes and David Matza.[65] Sykes and Matza note that when caught and arrested, many offenders point to others, not themselves, as the sources of their problems with the law. The justifications used to avoid taking responsibility are called *techniques of neutralization* because they neutralize the feelings of responsibility that would otherwise prevent a person from committing crime. Neutralization techniques include:

neutralization theory
Theory that if people break the law, they overcome their feelings of responsibility through rationalizations.

- Denial of responsibility: "It wasn't my fault; I was a victim of circumstances."
- Denial of injury: "No one was hurt, and they have insurance, so what's the problem?"
- Denial of victim: "Anyone would have done the same thing in my position; I did what I had to do given the situation."
- Condemnation of the condemners: "I bet the judge and everyone else on the jury has done much worse than what I was arrested for."
- Appeal to higher loyalties: "My friends were depending on me and I see them every day. What was I supposed to do?"[66]

There are other ways to justify or neutralize unlawful behavior. For instance, a person may protest that the law itself is unjust. Or an offender might claim that since everyone else is doing something illegal, such as speeding, he or she should be able to do it too. When people use neutralizations to excuse their actions and overcome their guilt, their beliefs may not prevent them from committing crime.

Personal Bonds to Society   The types of bonds people have to society also are factors that control behavior and keep individuals from committing crime. One type of bond essential in controlling or containing delinquency is the *"good boy" concept*– the perception boys have of themselves as good, law-abiding people. These ideas are the basis of Walter Reckless's **containment theory,** which argues that some factors that keep behavior in check are personal, such as self-concept, self-control, goal-directedness, conscience, tolerance for frustration, sense of responsibility, realistic levels of aspiration, and identification with lawful norms. When these control mechanisms fail to restrain or check behavior, delinquency is likely to occur.[67]

Travis Hirschi's **social bond theory** focuses on four facets of the social bond people have with society:

- Attachment: development of an emotional connection with and affection for people and institutions that make up society
- Commitment: the act of pledging and promising to people and institutions

containment theory
Theory emphasizing that some of the factors that keep behavior in check are personal, such as self-concept, self-control, goal-directedness, conscience, tolerance for frustration, sense of responsibility, realistic levels of aspiration, and identification with lawful norms.

social bond theory
Theory detailing the social bond people have with society, consisting of attachment, commitment, involvement, and belief.

a case in point

An Awakening in India for Women: A Rape in New Delhi

On December 16, 2012, a 23-year-old medical student on a private bus with a male companion in New Delhi was robbed, kidnapped, and brutally raped by six men who left her for dead. Those who assaulted her used a rusted metal bar to penetrate her; in addition to other injuries, she suffered a massive infection. She lived only a few days after being airlifted to a Singapore hospital for treatment.

The accused men were formally charged with robbery, kidnapping, rape, and murder. The authorities sought the death penalty for four of the accused, with many calling for death by hanging. India was so appalled by the crime it was difficult to find lawyers to represent the accused. In March 2014, the Delhi high court affirmed the death penalty awarded by the trial court and dismissed appeals by the convicts.

In a country where sexual harassment is a common problem for women and reported rape cases have increased about 875 percent in the past 30 years, this crime rallied the nation and led to a groundswell of reaction against the subjugation and degradation of women. Massive protests against gender-based violence and widespread debate over the way India handles sexual assaults–and treats women generally–occurred daily in the weeks following the incident. The protesters were male and female and came from all walks of life and political positions. They called for reforms and legislation to deal with the culture of impunity for sexual crimes and the broken public safety system.

Social conflict and critical theorists frequently note that it takes a galvanizing or watershed event to spark the flames of reform in a society. This horrific crime may well become the symbol of change for important reforms for Indian women.

OBSERVE→INVESTIGATE→UNDERSTAND

- What are some of the ways that structural conditions and inequalities might have influenced the men who committed this crime?
- How would critical theorists explain this crime and other crimes against women?
- How important are protests in changing the way a country deals with rape?

SOURCES: Jethro Mullen and Aliza Kassim, "New Delhi Gang-Rape Suspects Charged with Murder, Rape, Kidnapping," *CNN,* January 4, 2013. http://www.cnn.com/2013/01/03/world/asia/india-rape-case/index.html (retrieved January 6, 2013); Harmeet Shah Singh and Mallika Kapur, "New Delhi Rape Exposes the Perils of Being a Woman in India," *CNN,* January 3, 2013. www.cnn.com/2012/12/21/world/asia/india-rape-danger/index.html (retrieved January 6, 2013); "Nirbhaya Gang-Rape Case: Delhi HC Upholds Death Penalty Awarded to 4 Convicts, *The Times of India,* March 13, 2014. http://timesofindia.indiatimes.com/city/delhi/Nirbhaya-gang-rape-case-Delhi-HC-upholds-death-penalty-awarded-to-4-convicts/articleshow/31938726.cms (retrieved April 18, 2015).

- Involvement: the time spent engaged in conventional activities with others
- Belief: holding society's values and beliefs as true for oneself[68]

When all these aspects of the social bond are present, a person is unlikely to commit crime. Social bonds in the form of strong ties to work and family can also move youthful offenders away from crime, and a secure marriage and job can be turning points in a young offender's life course.[69]

Another social bond that keeps people from engaging in crime is *self-control*, or the ability to control one's own impulses, emotions, desires, and behaviors.[70] Michael Gottfredson and Hirschi propose that individuals with low or limited self-control exhibit certain characteristics that make them more likely to engage in crime. People who are impulsive, narcissistic, risk-taking, physical, and active are more likely to commit crime. Those who do not derive pleasure from hard work and mastering tasks and who are insensitive to how others feel are more likely to take the chance of committing crime.[71]

Self-esteem, the feelings of self-worth that stem from positive or negative beliefs about being valuable and capable, is another facet of the social bond with society.[72] In some cases, low self-esteem appears to contribute to delinquency, whereas in others delinquent behavior might serve to enhance low self-esteem.[73] Low self-esteem is frequently cited as a cause of crime and delinquency,[74] and being successful in crime can raise self-esteem.[75] Low self-esteem is related to problems in school achievement, drug and alcohol abuse, hostility, conflicts with others, frustration, attraction to gangs, and engaging in violence.

Inequality and Crime: Power and Social Conflict Theory

Social conflict theory views criminal behavior as the product of the conflict between the wealthy and powerful on the one hand, and the poor and powerless on the other hand. Social conflict theory emerged in the United States following the turbulent 1960s, a period characterized by a range of social movements that sought to improve the civil rights of various subgroups in American society. The economic gains made by corporate America stood in stark contrast to the abject poverty of large numbers of people living in the nation's great industrial centers. The women's movement called for women's greater equality with the economic standing of men. African Americans exposed racial and class discrimination and demanded change, and the gay rights movement gained momentum. These developments demanded new theories to explain the problems threatening social stability.

Critical theory is a branch of social conflict theory concerned with the ways in which structural conditions and social inequalities influence crime. *Structural conditions* refers to factors rooted in corporate, political, and environmental conditions that block and exploit the less powerful in society. In this view, those in power strive to maintain their social status by dictating laws and policies to reinforce their control over people of lesser advantage. Critical theorists attribute criminal activity to the social and economic institutions that adversely affect the lower socioeconomic classes.[76] The social and economic gap between rich and poor who live close together can also influence crime. When impoverished people observe the extravagant lifestyles of the wealthy, they may experience a sense of deprivation that leads to anger, resentment, and jealousy. These negative feelings can bring about behavior that ultimately results in crime.[77]

Social conflict criminologists view crime from a broad perspective and are highly critical of the criminal justice system, lawmakers, corporations, and others in privileged positions who set policy in society. "A Case in Point" on page 94

social conflict theory
The view that crime is the result of conflict between a society's wealthy and powerful people on the one hand, and its poor and powerless people on the other hand.

critical theory
A branch of social conflict theory concerned with the ways in which structural conditions and social inequalities influence crime.

describes the case of a brutal gang rape of a young woman on a bus in New Delhi and the ways in which structural conditions and social inequalities influenced the crime.

feminist criminology
The application of feminist thought and analysis to the study of crime.

Feminist criminology applies feminist thought to the study of crime. Feminist criminologists argue that women's inequality is partly explained by the power differences between men and women and by social expectations of both.[78] Most studies conducted prior to the 1970s assumed that women were like men and therefore concluded that what was learned about men's behavior would also apply to women.[79] Studies of women's criminality relied on gender stereotypes and assumptions about healthy and unhealthy sexuality. Theorists often explained female criminality by pointing to what was said to be women's sexual misbehavior.[80]

By 1975, some theorists believed that the success of the women's movement would result in a corresponding increase in crimes committed by women.[81] They argued that as women gained equality with men, women would also begin to act more like men, even committing crimes with the same frequency as men. Evidence has not supported this hypothesis, however, and today women's criminal patterns are still significantly different from men's (see Chapter 2).[82] After gaining a foothold in the 1970s, feminist criminologists have continued to explain not only women's criminality but also the treatment of female suspects and offenders by criminal justice institutions.

Feminist criminologists also draw attention to a number of criminology's sexist practices and point out that women and men experience the world differently. As a result, it is essential that women researchers and activists be involved in interpreting crime as perpetrated by and against women. As women have entered the field of criminology, they have made a variety of contributions, including a fuller understanding of the complexity of women's offending and victimization.

Feminist criminologists find the roots of crime in economic and political conditions that contribute to the exploitation of women. Most recently, their research has examined the ways in which women's experiences with crime, victimization, and the criminal justice system differ based on race, class, and gender.[83] Not all women are treated the same by the criminal justice system, nor do they experience or commit crimes in exactly the same ways. In other words, female victims and offenders should not be treated as homogenous groups. They have important differences, just as there are differences among men.[84]

peacemaking criminology
A branch of criminology that views crime as a form of violence and urges criminology to advocate a nonviolent, peaceful society.

A contemporary theme stemming from critical criminology is **peacemaking criminology.** This perspective of criminology represents a departure from mainstream criminology and urges us to think of crime causation from a different point of view.[85] Peacemaking criminologists point out that crime is a form of violence and assert that criminology should thus advocate a nonviolent, peaceful society.[86] They argue that widespread social justice would eliminate crime and that new forms of punishment should replace coercive methods.[87] Peacemaking criminology urges a transformation of policies in the criminal justice system to achieve a more just, peaceful, and crime-free world where the needs of offenders, communities, and victims are balanced.[88] Peacemaking criminology is the cornerstone of the humanistic restorative justice approaches discussed in Chapter 13.

A Different Set of Values: Cultural Deviance Factors

cultural deviance theory
The view that the adoption of negative and antisocial values learned in neighborhoods and subcultures produces criminal behavior.

Cultural deviance theory focuses on how the social traditions with which people live and the subcultures with which they identify contribute to the values that guide their behaviors. Criminologists who subscribe to this perspective

◀ **Migration to Chicago in the Early Twentieth Century**

People from the rural South and immigrants began moving into large northern U.S. cities during the early twentieth century, resulting in rapid social disorganization.

believe that adoption of negative and antisocial values learned in neighborhoods and subcultures produces criminal behavior.

Social Disorganization: Factors Related to Where We Live

Social disorganization theory, a particular type of cultural deviance theory, attributes crime to the failure of social institutions and organizations–such as police, churches, and welfare services–to meet the needs of a community or neighborhood. Social disorganization factors are typically found in high crime areas that have been subject to rapid change due to industrialization, immigration, and urbanization. Social disorganization theorists examine neighborhood characteristics to find explanations of high crime rates among urban immigrants from other countries and communities.

social disorganization theory
The theory that explains crime by examining city neighborhood characteristics.

During the early twentieth century, large numbers of immigrants and people from the rural South began moving into large northern U.S. cities. Researchers from the University of Chicago began studying the social disorganization and other problems that resulted from these population shifts, and they became known as the Chicago School of Social Ecology.[89] Chicago School researchers Robert Ezra Park and Ernest Burgess examined Chicago's disorganized neighborhoods by analyzing ecological (geographic) areas. This research led Burgess to develop a model of Chicago that consisted of concentric zones (Figure 3-1).

Each zone in Burgess's model has its own structure, organization, culture, and unique people. According to Clifford Shaw and Henry McKay (sociologists who in later decades expanded the research of Park, Burgess, and McKenzie), the city center and Zone II are the zones of transition–home to the city's poor, unskilled, and disadvantaged, living in dilapidated housing, frequently near factories. Moving away from this region, neighborhoods exhibit signs of greater social organization. For example, in Zone III, more working-class people own

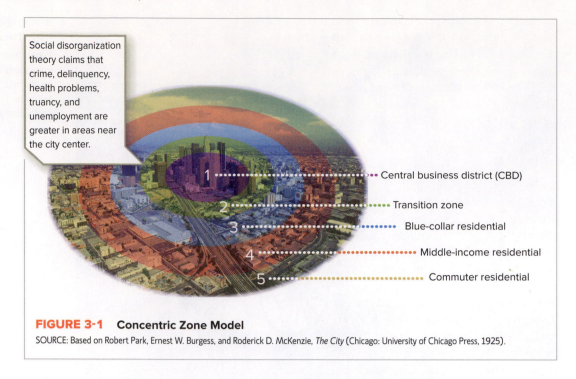

Social disorganization theory claims that crime, delinquency, health problems, truancy, and unemployment are greater in areas near the city center.

1 •• Central business district (CBD)

2 ••••• Transition zone

3 ••••• Blue-collar residential

4 ••••••• Middle-income residential

5 ••••••• Commuter residential

FIGURE 3-1   **Concentric Zone Model**

SOURCE: Based on Robert Park, Ernest W. Burgess, and Roderick D. McKenzie, *The City* (Chicago: University of Chicago Press, 1925).

---

homes than rent, and in Zone IV the affluent purchase homes that reflect their status. Crime, delinquency, health problems, truancy, and unemployment are greater in areas near the city center than in neighborhoods farther away from the center. Social institutions and organizations have a difficult time responding to the needs of residents in areas where people are transient and not invested in the community.[90]

This *concentric circle theory* has been modified over the years to reflect changes in residential patterns in cities. As affluent suburbanites move back into city centers, for example, many poor inner-city residents are forced to relocate in order to find affordable housing and jobs. Future geographic studies of crime and delinquency are likely to yield results different from those found by Shaw and McKay.

Various crimes arise from social disorganization. For example, neighborhoods that do not discourage vandalism of homes and buildings may seem to encourage–or at least tolerate–crime. That is, how society is structured, largely in relation to the distribution of its wealth, affects the behavior of its residents. In response to the social disorganization brought on by economic disparities, people cope with whatever is their lot in life by forming groups of common interests and values, our next topic.

Subcultures and Crime   A **subculture** is a group that has some of the same norms, values, and beliefs as members of the dominant, mainstream culture but also other norms, values, and beliefs not held by society at large. A subculture is not necessarily bad or violent. For example, college students and animal lovers can be considered subcultures. However, a juvenile gang is also an example of a subculture. Its members could be said to value loyalty (as members of the dominant culture do), but they hold other values not consistent with mainstream culture (such as graffiti-tagging buildings). Marvin Wolfgang and Franco Ferracuti formulated the theory that an independent subculture of violence exists in some extremely poor and disorganized areas.[91] In these areas, people are socialized to resolve conflicts by resorting to violence. In fact, violence is the expected and valued response.[92]

subculture
A group that has some of the same norms, values, and beliefs as members of the dominant, mainstream culture but also other norms, values, and beliefs not held by society at large.

culture conflict
Clash between the norms of conduct for one group and the norms of conduct for another group.

social process theory
The view that criminal behavior results from successive interactions with others and with society's institutions.

looking-glass self
The idea that we come to define ourselves the way we perceive that others see us.

labeling theory
Theory that the social process that individuals experience has the potential to define them as "bad" or "good," and that some people become bad because others do not believe them to be good.

When the norms of conduct for one group conflict with conduct norms of another group, the result is **culture conflict.**[93] Crime may occur when there is culture conflict, but not all culture conflict results in law violation. The "What about the Victim?" box illustrates a case of culture conflict.

Acting-Out Expectations: Social Process Factors

Assuming that criminality results from a sequence of successive interactions with others and society's institutions, **social process theory** seeks to explain the developmental stages leading to delinquent or criminal behavior. Proponents of social process theory minimize influences such as poverty, social institutions, and mental disorders, emphasizing instead factors such as interaction with others, socialization, imitation, reinforcement, role-modeling, stereotyping, and reaction of others to one's behavior. Key concepts in social process theory include the looking-glass self, labeling, tagging, and differential association.

Charles H. Cooley developed the idea of the **looking-glass self** in 1902 based on his belief that we come to define ourselves by the way others see us.[94] If we perceive that others see us as good, bad, smart, dumb, responsible, flakey, manipulative, or criminal, we learn to see ourselves in those ways. How we see ourselves, in turn, will affect who we become and what we do in life. A person who sees himself as a crook is more likely to commit criminal acts; a person who sees himself as a law-abiding citizen is less likely to commit criminal acts.

Labeling theory, associated primarily with Howard Becker,[95] is related to the theory of the looking-glass self. Labeling theory attempts to explain the complicated route a person takes in becoming criminal, progressing through gradual stages of criminality, and the role that society plays in defining a person as a criminal. According to this theory, the social process a person experiences has the potential to define him or her as "bad" or "good," and some people become bad because others do not believe them to be good. The label is powerful and defines a person as criminal in his or her own eyes as well as in the eyes of others. Once an individual accepts and internalizes a label, negative behavior can follow. Criminals often act in accordance with these labels, and it is hard for them to reject and change their labels, a reality that makes reformation difficult.[96]

What about the Victim?

Victims of Culture Conflict

In 2010, the TLC Network launched a reality television show offering a glimpse into the daily lives of the Brown family, whose members are living a plural family lifestyle in Lehi, Utah. The show, *Sister Wives,* features the husband, Kody, his 4 wives, and their 13 children and 3 stepchildren. Though legally married only to his first wife for many years, Kody legally divorced her to legally marry his fourth wife. The sister wives claim the legal divorce and marriage was a joint family decision. Kody has had marriage rituals with the other three women and calls them his wives, and they refer to him as their husband. All the wives entered into the polygamist lifestyle voluntarily. In fact, the wedding planning for Brown's fourth ceremony and reception was the focus of one of the series' episodes.

This show is an excellent illustration of culture conflict—in this case, how not only the norms but also the laws of mainstream society clash with fundamentalist

Mormon values. The modern Mormon Church has not advocated polygamy since 1890; however, an estimated 38,000 fundamentalist Mormons continue to believe in, and practice, multiple marriage secretly in the United States.

Although rarely prosecuted unless children are being harmed, bigamy is a crime in Utah, punishable by a sentence of up to five years in prison. A person may be found guilty of bigamy in Utah through *cohabitation*—not just by entering into legal marriage contracts. By going public, the Browns exposed themselves to possible criminal prosecution, and the state of Utah launched an investigation. In 2012 Utah's case against, the Brown parents under the state's bigamy statute was dismissed. However, the family is continuing its suit against Utah's bigamy law.

The Brown family adults decided to come out of the closet with their lifestyle to help others understand that they are deeply committed to one another, their children, and their family structure and to show that their children are well adjusted. Moreover, the parents do not want their children to have to live in secrecy or shame, denying to others the truth about their family.

OBSERVE → INVESTIGATE → UNDERSTAND

- Are the Browns' 16 children victims of their parents' lifestyle choice? Explain.
- Is it emotionally abusive to raise children in a lifestyle for which the parents might be arrested and go to jail? Why or why not?
- Is it emotionally abusive to raise children in a lifestyle that makes it difficult for them to fit into the dominant society, or that makes it impossible for them to have privacy? Why or why not?
- Do some research into other cases in which culture conflict has resulted in law violation.

SOURCES: Jennifer Dobner, "Police Investigating Family in 'Sister Wives' Show," *KOMOnews. com,* November 30, 2010. www.komonews.com/news/entertainment/103940544.html (retrieved November 30, 2010); "Sister Wives' Lawsuit: Kody Brown and Family Suing Utah over Bigamy Law," *Huffingtonpost.com,* July 25, 2012. http://www.huffingtonpost.com/2012/07/25/sister-wives-lawsuit-kody-brown-utah-bigamy-law_n_1701450.html (retrieved January 5, 2013); Esther Lee, "Sister Wives Stars Say Polygamist Kody Brown's Divorce, New Marriage Will 'Legally Restructure' Family," *US Weekly,* February 4, 2015. http://www.usmagazine.com/celebrity-news/news/sister-wives-divorce-brown-family-to-legally-restructure-201542 (retrieved April 18, 2015).

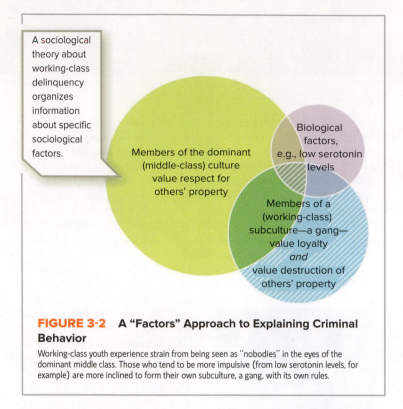

A sociological theory about working-class delinquency organizes information about specific sociological factors.

Members of the dominant (middle-class) culture value respect for others' property

Biological factors, e.g., low serotonin levels

Members of a (working-class) subculture—a gang— value loyalty *and* value destruction of others' property

FIGURE 3-2   **A "Factors" Approach to Explaining Criminal Behavior**
Working-class youth experience strain from being seen as "nobodies" in the eyes of the dominant middle class. Those who tend to be more impulsive (from low serotonin levels, for example) are more inclined to form their own subculture, a gang, with its own rules.

differential association theory
Theory that criminal behavior is learned during normal social interactions, and the same learning principles are involved in reinforcing criminal and law-abiding behavior.

As people progress through the criminal justice system, they are marked each step of the way in a process known as *tagging*. Tagging reinforces offenders' negative traits. During tagging, offenders shift from perceiving their acts as bad to seeing themselves as bad or evil. Opportunities for offenders to change this view decline over time.[97]

Differential association theory, developed by Edwin Sutherland, suggests that criminal behavior is learned during normal social interactions and that the same learning principles are involved in reinforcing criminal and law-abiding behavior. A person who is exposed to and learns a large number of criminal attitudes and values is more likely to commit criminal acts than someone who is exposed to and learns very few criminal attitudes and values. Perhaps most important, differential association theory emphasizes that learning criminal behavior occurs in intimate groups and assumes that anyone can become criminal if placed in a situation that fosters such behavior.[98]

Social process theories attempt to explain how we become who we are and how changing our identity is a monumentally difficult job. Figure 3-2 shows how a sociological theory about working-class delinquency organizes information about specific sociological factors and can also take into consideration individual (for example, biological) factors to explain why, for instance, not all working-class youths become gang members.

It is extremely difficult for the criminal justice system to deal with all the biological, psychological, and sociological factors that affect criminal behavior. The "Disconnects" box highlights the difficulty in connecting the factors that produce crime and criminality with the ability of criminal justice professionals to consider those factors in the administration of justice.

The table "Examples of Internal and External Factors Leading to Criminal Behavior" presents the biological, psychological, and sociological factors that interact with one another to produce criminal behavior. In the next section we consider factors related to victims: their characteristics, their behavior, and their responses to being victimized.

Examples of Internal and External Factors Leading to Criminal Behavior

Internal Factors	External Factors
Genetics	Toxins
Intelligence	Nutrition and diet
Mental disorders	Socioeconomic status
Hormones	Cultural values
Neurotransmitters	Geographic conditions
Brain disease and deficits	Environmental change

DIS Connects

Mentally Ill Death Row Inmates

Under normal circumstances, when people are mentally ill we seek to provide them with the treatment they need to relieve their symptoms. How, then, could withholding treatment be in an individual's best interest? The answer: When that person is a seriously mentally ill inmate on death row and it is approaching time for his or her execution. Because of the U.S. Supreme Court's decision in *Ford v. Wainright* (1986), a condemned inmate must be aware of his or her impending execution and the reasons for it in order for the execution to take place. The inmate must be able to understand that he is about to be killed as the punishment for the crime he committed. As part of its rationale, the Court held that to execute someone who is not capable of knowing what is happening and why serves little or no retributive function, since the inmate is not able to appreciate why he is being put to death. How could the inmate experience it as punishment if he is unaware of what is going on? To execute a person under such circumstances, the Court wrote, offends humanity.[a]

A logical way to resolve the problem would be to give the inmate drugs that would restore the senses to reality and to an understanding that he is going to be put to death because that was the sentence for the crime. But what if the condemned inmate refuses to take the medication? Defense attorneys will encourage him not to take it in order to try to save the life of their client. The inmate may choose not to comply with a medication order—not to evade execution, but more likely because of paranoid fears that medication is poison and that people are trying to kill him (which, ironically, they actually are).

Steven Staley, convicted of shooting a restaurant manager he took hostage during a failed robbery attempt in 1989, was diagnosed with paranoid schizophrenia while on death row. He bangs his head against walls and believes polygraph machines are controlling him.

He has been catatonic, lying immobile on his back for such long periods of time that he has worn a bald spot on the back of his head. Texas courts stopped his first scheduled execution in 2005 and have since stayed it several times due to questions about his mental status.[b] Texas does have the right to forcibly medicate Staley as long as it is in his best medical interest. The dilemma is clear: Medicating him may relieve him of his frightening delusions, but it may also serve to make him mentally fit to be executed. The latter could hardly be seen as being in Staley's best medical interest. It remains to be seen whether the courts will ultimately order that he be forcibly medicated. In the meantime his situation is not unique. It is estimated that 5 to 10 percent of condemned inmates are seriously mentally ill.[c]

OBSERVE → INVESTIGATE → UNDERSTAND

- Do you think condemned inmates should have a right to refuse medication? Why or why not?

- What are some of the moral dilemmas facing medical professionals who forcibly administer drugs in such situations?

- Do you agree with the U.S. Supreme Court's decision that people who are not able to know they are about to be executed for their crimes should not be executed? If you agree, what would you say about justice for the victims of their crimes?

SOURCES: [a]*Ford v. Wainright*, 477 U.S. 399 (1986).

[b]Emily Bazelon, "Texas Wants to Drug a Prisoner So They Can Kill Him," *Slate*, May 11, 2012. www.slate.com/articles/news_and_politics/crime/2012/05/the_execution_of_steven_staley_forcible_medication_on_death_row_in_texas_.html (retrieved on June 26, 2015).

[c]Death Penalty Focus, "Mental Illness on Death Row." www.deathpenalty.org/article.php?id=53 (retrieved on June 20, 2015).

VICTIMIZATION FACTORS

The U.S. population is much more aware of efforts to apprehend criminals and prevent crime than it is of the plight of crime victims. Lack of concern for the victim even extends to criminal justice practitioners.[99] One of the major themes of the victim rights' movement, which began in England in 1957, was recognizing and correcting the way crime victims had been neglected. Providing victims with some form of reparation and compensation was one of the first types of assistance.[100] In the United States, California was the first state to respond to the financial needs of crime victims. In 1965 the state established a victim compensation program that repaid crime victims for damages and injuries resulting from a crime.[101]

Most of the pioneers in **victimology,** the scientific study of victims, were criminologists who were intrigued by the role that victims played in crime causation.[102] To appreciate the role of victims in the study of crime and criminal justice, criminologists and victimologists need to understand victims without judging them. They must know the factors that shaped victims' development, especially any childhood circumstances that might have influenced their behaviors before their adult victimization. For example, some victims of intimate partner violence contribute to the violence that

victimology
The scientific study of victims, which includes their behaviors, injuries, assistance, legal rights, and recovery.

▲ **At Risk of Victimization?**

Consider the characteristics of this individual that might increase her vulnerability to becoming a victim.

ultimately injures them.[103] Some of those factors have to do with the coping behaviors victims have learned for dealing with conflicts, the kinds of victimizing situations they are unable to avoid, and the circumstances that put them at risk.

The Risk of Becoming a Victim

Offenders tend to target individuals who display a variety of attributes that make them easy prey. These attributes can be behavioral, physical, social, or attitudinal and may change over time.[104]

Vulnerability factors are human characteristics that can be exploited by criminals and can result in victimization. Two examples are having been previously victimized[105] and having a disability (for example, blindness, deafness, or muteness).[106] Demographic factors also may increase vulnerability and the likelihood of being victimized. Such factors include being female,[107] working in a high-risk profession,[108] being in a foreign country,[109] or belonging to a discriminated group.[110] The risk of victimization can increase when vulnerabilities are combined. For example, an individual may have multiple conditions such as physical disability, advanced age, diminished intellectual capacity, and mental impairment that, when combined with being in a dangerous environment like a bar where high-risk activities take place, can further increase the risk of victimization.

Obtrusive vulnerabilities are those that are visible, obvious, and recognizable. For example, a person who is very drunk or very old often lacks the mental awareness or ability to think clearly to avoid a criminal attack. *Unobtrusive vulnerabilities* are not easily observed. For example, a child who has been victimized in the past by a classmate might develop a sense of helplessness. Persons in a state of helplessness are convinced that they cannot protect themselves and consequently are more likely to give up when attacked.[111] When threatened again, they are likely to put up little resistance. When offenders know the vulnerabilities of potential victims, and especially when they live in close proximity to them, the probability of harm significantly increases.[112] In general, most crimes against persons occur between acquaintances largely because there are more opportunities for conflict, and the offender has greater awareness of the victim's vulnerabilities.[113]

recidivist victims

Persons who are victimized repeatedly.

Persons with high levels of both obtrusive and unobtrusive vulnerabilities are often victimized repeatedly and are thus known as **recidivist victims.** The children of battered women, for example, often live in situations of high stress, often observe violence in their homes, are usually not properly protected from family abuse, do not receive proper guidance from their parents, and do not experience consistent child rearing and positive disciplinary practices. As a consequence, these children lack many important social skills and do not know how to cope well with conflicts within the family—factors that make them more vulnerable to repeat victimization than children who come from nonviolent families.[114]

MYTH/REALITY

MYTH: People who want to avoid being victimized can—if they put their mind to it.

REALITY: A large part of what causes people to become victims is mostly out of their control. An example of how different settings, different behaviors, and different lifestyles result in different levels of victimization can be seen in the differences between the rates of victimization in public and private schools. In public schools, 71 percent of children in grades 6 to 12 reported knowing about events of bullying, physical attacks, or robberies; in the same grades in private schools, only 45 percent knew about these incidents of violence.[115]

Another type of victim vulnerability theory is **routine activities theory,** which views victimization as the result of an individual's daily routine activities. Examples include leaving and returning home at the same time each day, taking the same route to school or work, and going to the same hangouts on weekends. Offenders learn to recognize the victim's predictable and patterned behaviors. Some lifestyles, such as barhopping and getting drunk with friends every weekend, and some occupations, such as those requiring late-night work shifts, provide greater opportunities for criminals than do others.[116] While these behaviors may make some individuals more vulnerable to potential offenders, it is the actions of the offenders (as determined by the law) that cause the victimizations.

Victim Behavior during the Crime

During the commission of most personal crimes, some level of communication generally occurs between the offender and the victim.[117] During a property crime, the interaction between offender and victim starts when the offender makes contact with an object that belongs to the victim. The outcome of this interaction will determine whether victimization will occur and the degree of injury or damage that will result. For example, in a first encounter with an unknown victim, an offender will start a conversation with someone the offender identifies as vulnerable. The victim's response depends on his or her perception of threat. The offender will then test the victim's vulnerability; either the vulnerability is confirmed as a weakness or the offender realizes he or she made a mistake in judgment.

A male offender may be physically aggressive with a female victim. In such a case, the victim will test defenses she assumes are effective. If she perceives the threat as significant, she may attempt to fight back. If the victim feels that she is too vulnerable, she may attempt to flee the scene as quickly as possible. In one study comparing victims' and nonvictims' responses to hypothetical scenarios, victims tended to be confrontational or abusive to an initial approach by the perpetrator. In contrast, nonvictims were more likely to withdraw quietly and say or do nothing.[118] A confrontational or abusive response in an offensive situation increases a person's chances of becoming a victim. A person who withdraws from an offensive situation will likely not become a victim. Some offenders will commit their crimes regardless of the victim's response to the initial confrontation, but the way a potential victim responds may convince the offender not to continue.

A Typology of Victimology

The man known as the father of victimology is Benjamin Mendelsohn, who was a defense attorney. In preparing for his cases, Mendelsohn interviewed both victims and offenders in an effort to understand who contributed more to the criminal act. Mendelsohn coined the term *victimology* and defined it as the science of victims. He also created a *typology* (that is, a classification of types) of crime victims based on the degree to which they contributed to the criminal act (see the table "Mendelsohn's Typology of Crime Victims").

Mendelsohn's typology focused attention on the notion that victims' actions play a significant role in the outcome of a criminal act. With this typology and his later proposals for victim clinics, victim studies, a victim journal, an international victimology organization, and victim institutes–all of which have been realized–Mendelsohn started a movement that today spans the globe and has had a major impact on the way victims are understood and treated. (See the table on page 104, "Factors Associated with Criminal, Delinquent, and Victim Behavior.")

routine activities theory
Theory suggesting that crime occurs when an opportunity is available, the victim is not adequately protected, and the effort brings reward. Applied to victims, the theory argues that some individuals' daily activities make them more vulnerable than others to being victimized.

Mendelsohn's Early Victim-Blaming Typology of Crime Victims

Victim	Example
Completely innocent victim or ideal victim	Children and individuals who are unconscious during the crime
Ignorant victim with minor culpability	A woman who induces a miscarriage and dies as a result
Victim who is as guilty as the offender and the voluntary victim	Suicides
Victim who is guiltier than the offender	A victim who provokes an attack against which the "offender" defends him or herself
Guiltiest victim	An aggressive "victim" who is alone guilty, or an attacker who is killed by another in self-defense
Simulating an imaginary victim, who tries to mislead justice and have the accused punished	Paranoids, hysterical persons, senile persons, and some children

SOURCES: Beniamin Mendelsohn, "The Victimology," *Etudes Internationale de Psycho-sociologie Criminelle* (July–September, 1956): 23–26; Stephen Schafer, *The Victim and His Criminal: A Study in Functional Responsibility* (New York: Random House, 1968).

Factors Associated with Criminal, Delinquent, and Victim Behavior

Psychological and Biological Factors	Sociological Factors	Victim Factors
Mental Disorders Schizophrenia Major depression Bipolar disorder Postpartum psychosis Psychopathy	*Strain Factors* Life pressures Feelings of alienation Inability to achieve desired life goals Lack of opportunity and gang membership Maturation during the life course	*Previctimization Factors* Behaviors Attitudes Physical attributes Vulnerabilities Prior victimizations
Cognitive Factors Intelligence and IQ Moral reasoning	*Control Factors* Communities Taking responsibility Rationalization Bonds to society Self-control Self-esteem	*Victim Behavior during the Crime* Aggressiveness Passivity Weakness Confrontation Helplessness
Social Learning Factors Reinforcement Consequences of behavior Modeling Fear of punishment	*Critical Factors* Capitalism Racism Sexism Discrimination Poverty Power Inequality	*Victimology Theory* Victim's role in a crime Psycho/social coping
Situational Variables Life circumstances Supportive resources	*Cultural Deviance Factors* Neighborhoods Social disorganization Subcultures Culture conflict	*Patterned Activity Factors* Victim availability Victim unguarded Inadequate resources Limited-time conditions

Continued

Continued from previous page

Psychodynamic Factors	Social Process Factors	Psychological Trauma Factors
Id	Looking-glass self	Increased arousal
Ego	Labeling	Avoidance of objects and people
Superego development	Tagging	Event reexperiencing
	Differential association	Fear and anxiety

Neurobiological Factors		Physical Factors
Hormones		Diminished brain function
Neurotransmitters		Physical disabilities
Brain disease, injury, or deficit		Illness
Prefrontal cortex underactivity		Hormonal imbalance
ADHD		

Environmental Conditions and Contaminants		Coping Space Factors
Lead poisoning		High-risk places
Effects of other toxins		Unfamiliar locations

Genetic Factors		Genetic Factors
Genetic abnormalities		Genetic abnormalities

SUMMARY

Traditional approaches to the study of the causes of criminal and victim behavior tended to focus separately on psychological, biological, or sociological theories. Theories represent different ways of organizing information about factors. In reality, a person's behavior is the product of the interactions among many psychological, biological, and sociological factors. Different factors interact with one another in complex ways.

Most crimes are the product of the interactions between victim and offender, and one area of the focus on victims involves understanding how victim behavior interacts with offender behavior to produce a crime. Victimologists are interested in victims' perception of their victimization, their contributions to their own victimization, the extent of their injuries, and their responses to the experience of victimization. Many of the same biological, psychological, and sociological factors that produce criminal behavior are related to why people become victims.

OBSERVE → INVESTIGATE → UNDERSTAND

Review

Understand the roles of biological (including genetic) and environmental factors on brain function and criminal behavior.

- Biological factors associated with brain function influence behavior and the thought processes associated with making choices.

- Biological factors related to the expression and suppression of criminal and violent behaviors can be identified and measured.

Explain the key aspects of mental disorders and understand how they are classified.

- Mental disorders are psychiatric conditions that interfere with a person's ability to function on a day-to-day basis.

- The *Diagnostic and Statistical Manual of Mental Disorders (DSM)* includes mental disorders (psychotic and nonpsychotic), mood disorders, and personality disorders.

Recognize the cognitive factors of intelligence and moral reasoning as brain functions that influence criminal behavior.

- On average, incarcerated offenders tend to score lower than nonoffenders on standardized intelligence tests. Offenders may have lower emotional intelligence, which can influence criminal behavior.

- Damage to the prefrontal cortex area of the brain can affect moral reasoning and lower impulse control and lead to criminal behavior.

Understand how economic, class, and social inequalities can be linked to the causes of crime.

■ When people need and want to make money and are not able to, they may experience extraordinary strain and feel pressured to break the law to obtain the things they need and want.

■ Social and economic differences among the classes adversely affect the lower socioeconomic classes, resulting in crime.

Describe factors that cause some people to become victims of crime.

■ Many of the same biological, psychological, and social factors that influence why people commit crimes are related to why people become victims.

■ A variety of behavioral, physical, social, and attitudinal factors can cause people to become victims of crime.

Key Terms

adolescence-limited offenders 92
anomie 90
atavism 77
bipolar disorder 84
classical school of criminology 76
containment theory 94
critical theory 95
cultural deviance theory 96
culture conflict 99
Diagnostic and Statistical Manual of Mental Disorders (DSM) 82
differential association theory 100
feminist criminology 96
intelligence 86

labeling theory 99
life course persistent offenders 92
looking-glass self 99
moral reasoning 88
neoclassical school of criminology 76
neurotransmitter 80
neutralization theory 93
peacemaking criminology 96
positivist school of criminology 77
postpartum psychosis 84
psychopathy 85
psychoses 82
rational choice theory 77

recidivist victims 102
routine activities theory 103
schizophrenia 82
social bond theory 94
social conflict theory 95
social control theory 93
social disorganization theory 97
social learning theory 88
social process theory 99
strain theory 90
subculture 98
victimology 101

Study Questions

1. Psychoses are
   a. false beliefs.
   b. false perceptions.
   c. serious mental disorders.
   d. all of the above

2. According to psychoanalysts, criminals are dominated by their _____, which resulted from a damaged _____ during childhood.
   a. ego; id
   b. superego; ego
   c. ego; superego
   d. id; ego

3. The following are all true of psychopaths *except*
   a. they tend to experience hallucinations and delusions.
   b. they exhibit a lifelong pattern of antisocial behavior.
   c. they have no guilt for their antisocial behaviors.
   d. they tend to act on their impulses.

4. All of the following are major categories of thought regarding sociological factors *except*
   a. social conflict.
   b. social process.
   c. techniques of neutralization.
   d. control.

5. An example of a social process factor is
   a. looking-glass self.
   b. anomie.
   c. socioeconomic status.
   d. techniques of neutralization.

6. The attributes of potential victims that are visible, obvious, and recognized are called
   a. obtrusive vulnerabilities.
   b. routine activities.
   c. victim susceptibilities.
   d. precipitating clues.

7. A strain factor that can lead to criminal behavior is
   a. feelings of alienation.
   b. inability to achieve desired life goals.
   c. frustration.
   d. all of the above

8. Offenders who begin their criminal activities when young and continue them throughout their lives are called
   a. adolescence-limited offenders.
   b. delinquent recidivist offenders.
   c. life course persistent offenders.
   d. all of the above

9. All of the following factors are control factors *except*
   a. feelings of alienation.
   b. community responses.
   c. taking responsibility.
   d. bonds to society.

10. A statement that accurately describes feminist criminology is
    a. Feminist criminology is an outgrowth of social conflict theories of crime causation.
    b. Feminist criminology was developed in the 1990s.
    c. Feminist criminology points out that men and women experience the world in similar ways.
    d. all of the above

Critical Thinking Questions

For further review, go to the LearnSmart study module for this chapter.

1. Why are we so quick to embrace the research that has found specific genes associated with breast cancer but so reluctant to accept a genetic basis for criminal behavior?

2. What are some of the factors that contribute to anomie in modern life? What are some of the things that can be done to prevent anomie from occurring?

3. Why is it important to understand that victims are not all 100 percent innocent, and offenders are not all 100 percent guilty?

4 Criminal Law and Defenses

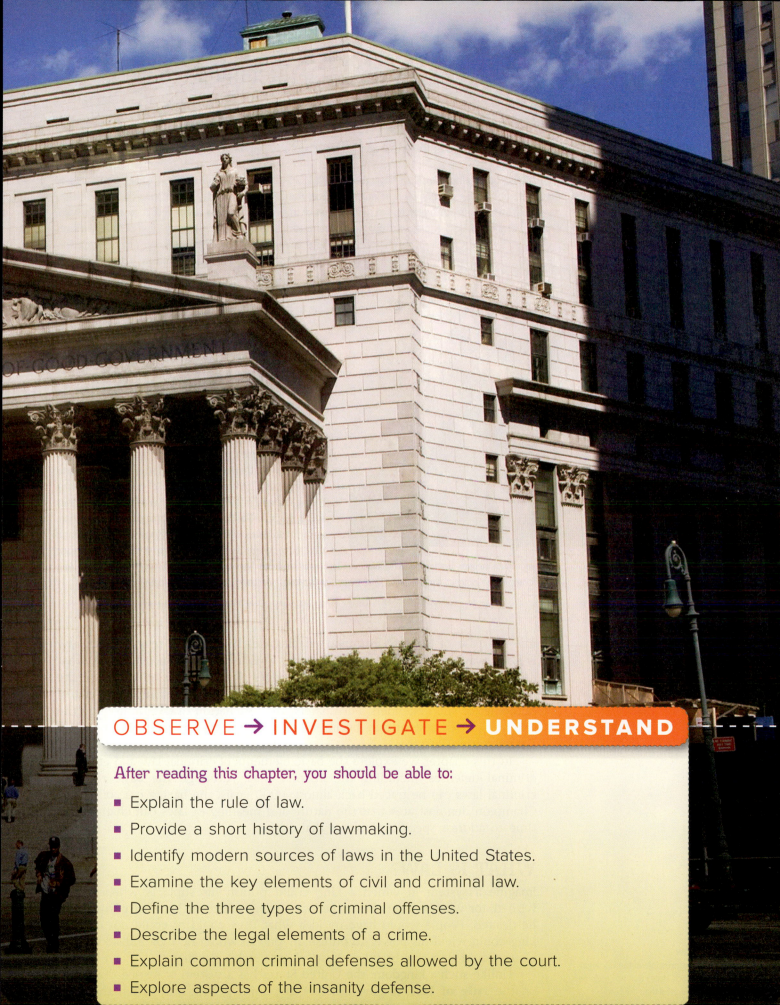

After reading this chapter, you should be able to:

- Explain the rule of law.
- Provide a short history of lawmaking.
- Identify modern sources of laws in the United States.
- Examine the key elements of civil and criminal law.
- Define the three types of criminal offenses.
- Describe the legal elements of a crime.
- Explain common criminal defenses allowed by the court.
- Explore aspects of the insanity defense.

Realities and Challenges

Is Hazing a Crime?

Why did 13 Florida students disregard their school's hazing laws, leading to the death of a fellow student?

After a band performance on November 19, 2011, 26-year-old drum major Robert Champion voluntarily participated in an illegal hazing ritual in which 12 fellow Florida A&M University (FAMU) marching band members beat him to death. Champion had to run the gauntlet from the front of the band's motor coach to the back, exposing himself to kicks and blows from hands, drumsticks, straps, and other objects. One of the individuals who beat him claimed Champion wanted to complete this feat as a sign he could endure the ordeal, which would give him status and respect from his peers. Tragically, according to the medical examiner, "he died from hemorrhagic shock due to internal bleeding from blunt force trauma."

The inspector general of the Florida Board of Governors completed a 32-page report that concluded the university did not have adequate internal controls to prevent this type of hazing and that poor communication existed among senior school officials, the office responsible for disciplining students, and the police. The report also found that university rules specifically designed to prevent hazing were in place and were disregarded.

FAMU denied responsibility for Robert Champion's death, but what the police call hazing, state law calls a felony. On May 2, 2012, the police charged 13 students with felony hazing charges, making this one of the largest hazing cases ever brought in Florida. The band, some of whose members were not students, was suspended for one year, and the band director resigned. The university claims it has instituted many changes, which include limiting band membership to FAMU students. New policies were put in place, to be backed by a "compliance officer" for the band, and a special top-level position was created to focus on hazing.[1]

The sad case of Robert Champion's hazing death illustrates that criminal law is not always easy to interpret. Sometimes it is a challenge to determine what crimes were committed. Attorneys and judges often are pressed to define the meaningful legal elements of a case and to spell out an appropriate judicial outcome for such offenders. Fortunately, the foundation of law underlying the criminal justice system may be interpreted and tailored to meet the needs of a wide variety of cases.

In this chapter we explore the basic elements of criminal law and common criminal defenses, including the insanity plea. Although the basic roots of criminal laws can be traced back almost 4,000 years, the hazing case of Robert Champion demonstrates that the nature and meaning of laws can change over time to address specific problems that arise.

WHAT IS LAW?

Imagine a system in which a king could punish his subjects whenever he wished, for whatever acts he wished, and using whatever kinds of punishment he desired. People would have no idea what they could or could not do. The king could wield his power to punish anyone to whom he took a dislike. Most of us would find this brand of "justice" intolerably unfair.

Unlike such a kingdom, the United States has a system of justice that relies on the **rule of law.** A government can punish people only when there are

rule of law
The guiding principle of the U.S. legal system, which states that no single person is more powerful than the law.

written laws, created by established procedures, prohibiting specific activities. Furthermore, under the rule of law, no government official, no matter how powerful, is above the law.

Purpose and Function of the Law

Laws are formal rules of conduct sanctioned by the state. Laws have governed human conduct for thousands of years, and today the criminal laws of just a single state are complex enough to fill hundreds of pages. Why do we have all these laws?

Criminal laws serve a number of functions. By providing penalties for certain behaviors, they protect people and property from harm. By designating which behaviors are forbidden, they provide clear standards of behavior, warning people about acts that will or will not be punished. They also limit the government's power to penalize people unfairly or arbitrarily. On a broader scale, criminal laws regulate and sometimes maintain social order. Criminal laws also serve a symbolic function, sending a message that a society disapproves of particular acts.

History of Criminal Laws

Long before recorded history, human behavior was governed by unwritten social norms, and these norms continue to shape daily life. Norms evolve slowly through social consensus, but some of them have been imposed by those in power. As people began living in larger communities—in cities and kingdoms—the first formal rules of conduct were devised, and eventually put in writing, by heads of state and their representatives. Not only did these rules require or prohibit certain behaviors, but they also specified sanctions for violations. Sanctions could include fines, enslavement, banishment, physical punishments such as whipping or maiming, and execution. These rules of state became the earliest laws.

The earliest written complete law code still in existence is the Code of King Ur-Nammu from the twenty-first century BCE written in the Sumerian language. It provided a uniform law for the entire reign of King Ur-Nammu and included such capital crimes as murder, rape, and robbery. In spite of its age, it provided for compensation to victims of bodily injury, something not provided in the

laws
Formal rules of conduct sanctioned by the state.

Hammurabi's Code
The second earliest known written law, which was set down by Babylonian king Hammurabi (1792–1750 BCE). The basic principle was that violators should suffer punishment equal to their offense.

◄ **Ur-Nammu's Code**

Sumerian King Ur-Nammu's Code, the earliest complete law text, which is dated 2050 BCE and predated King Hammurabi's Code by roughly three centuries. One of the unique features, especially at this early period, was its use of victim compensation.

ca 2050 BCE
The Code of Ur-Nammu

ca 1792–1750 BCE
Hammurabi's Code

ca 600 BCE
Mosaic Law recorded in
written form in the Bible

529–565 CE
Corpus Iuris Civilis
codified under Justinian

Henry II 12ᵗʰ Century
REIGNED 1154 TO 1189

ca 1170
Development of common
law in England

1610   Jamestown;
first permanent
settlement in America

1788
U.S. Constitution ratified

1791
U.S. Bill of Rights
(the first 10 constitutional
amendments) ratified

more barbaric Code of Hammurabi of ancient Babylonia some three centuries later, which used the principle of an eye for an eye and a tooth for a tooth. The Code of Ur-Nammu is now on display at the Istanbul Archeology Museum in Turkey.[2]

The second earliest known record of written laws dates from the time of Babylonian king Hammurabi (reigned 1792–1750 BCE). The laws known as **Hammurabi's Code** established high standards of behavior, setting forth 252 written rules and designating punishments for violators. The core of Hammurabi's Code was the principle that violators should suffer punishment equal to their offense.

Hammurabi had his code carved in stone and set up for all to see; it still survives and today is displayed at the Louvre in Paris. The entire text of the code has been translated into English and is available online.[3]

Another early system of written laws was *Mosaic Law*, which like Hammurabi's Code rested on the principle of an eye for an eye. Because these laws are included in the books of Exodus, Leviticus, and Deuteronomy in the Bible, they became the basis for Judaism and, to some extent, Christianity. The Ten Commandments are part of Mosaic Law. (Figure 4-1 displays a timeline of the history of law.)

In antiquity, both the Greeks and the Romans relied heavily on written laws. In the sixth century CE, the Roman emperor Justinian created a series of law books that eventually served as the basis of the legal system implemented across most of Europe. Those books were called the *Corpus Iuris Civilis* ("Body of the Civil Law"). *Justinian's Code* was one of the first systematic collections of laws. Countries with systems based upon the *Corpus Iuris Civilis* have civil or Roman law systems; these countries include most of continental Europe and many other countries throughout the world.

Prior to the Norman Conquest of England in 1066, laws in England varied a great deal from place to place. England had previously consisted of several smaller kingdoms, which traced their roots to many different countries and cultures.

FIGURE 4-1   **History of Law Timeline**
What factors impelled societies to begin writing down formal laws?

As late as the twelfth century, England had no uniform system of laws or courts. But King Henry II (reigned 1154-1189) created, under his own control, a single system of laws for the entire kingdom. Henry dispatched royal judges to "ride circuit"–that is, to travel around the country hearing cases, assisted by locally chosen juries. Royal judges carried with them a consistent set of rules that became known as **common law,** so called because it was uniform, or common, throughout England.

Common law relies on judges' interpretations of previous cases. A previous case that guides decisions in later cases is known as **precedent.** In contrast, civil (Roman) law systems do not rely on precedent. The fact that courts rely on precedent to shape their decisions–a concept known as *stare decisis*, or "to stand on the decision"–means that courts themselves become a significant source of laws and law interpretation. The use of precedent also helps ensure uniformity and predictability of legal decisions.

When the first British colonists arrived in North America in the seventeenth century, they brought from their homeland many traditions and practices, including the common law system. But English law was not the only law in colonial America. Other European colonizers–such as the Dutch, Spanish, and French–brought with them civil law–based legal systems, and Native American societies had their own (unwritten) laws. In the end, the English system prevailed. As the colonies grew, however, the settlers encountered a number of conditions and challenges that had not existed in England and that required new laws. Two obvious examples arose from the colonists' desire to subdue the American Indians and to control their slaves. Common law made no provision for slavery. Then, after the Revolutionary War, the new United States faced the opportunity to create a legal system virtually from scratch rather than relying on bits and pieces cobbled together over several hundred years. Still, common law remains the foundation of the legal system of the United States, as well as in England, Canada, Australia, India, and other countries that were once British colonies.

As the government of the United States evolved, common law remained one source of law. Over time, other vital sources were added to the body of laws that govern the country. These include the federal and state constitutions, case law, regulations, and *statutes* (the laws enacted by Congress and the state legislatures). We consider these sources of law in the next section.

common law
The legal system created in England after the Norman Conquest and still used in the United States today.

precedent
Previous court decisions that have binding authority on subsequent cases.

◄ **U.S. Constitution**

The Constitution is the supreme law of the United States; it establishes the powers of the federal government and limits those powers.

Modern Sources of Law in the United States

Today, the average citizen of the United States is governed by a large number of laws from a variety of sources. These laws and regulations emanate from federal, state, and local administrative agencies and affect everything from getting a dog license to serious criminal acts. Some acts are illegal throughout the United States, but wide variation continues to exist from place to place in the way we enforce laws and define and punish crime. The Key Concepts feature on page 114 illustrates the different sources of law that govern our behavior.

A **constitution** specifies the components of a government, the duties of each component, and the limits of their power. The U.S. Constitution is the supreme law of the United States, which means that all laws within all jurisdictions in the United States must conform to its requirements. The U.S. Constitution regulates the federal government, and each state has its own constitution as well.

The U.S. Constitution contains sections specifying the powers and responsibilities of the three branches of the federal government (Congress, the executive, and the courts) and the qualifications for holding various federal offices. It also contains 27 amendments, many of which specify certain rights that are afforded to individuals in the United States, and with which the government cannot interfere without good cause. Freedom of speech, which is guaranteed in the First Amendment, is one of these rights. We examine many of these rights in later chapters of this book.

Statutes are written laws enacted either by legislatures or (in states that allow for this procedure) by the citizens themselves through the voting process. Federal statutes form a multivolume set known as the United States Code. Each state also has its own set of statutes. Thousands of statutes cover everything from business licenses to water use. Both federal and state statutes include laws that specify punishments for certain kinds of acts, but because most crimes are considered primarily to be matters of local concern, there are many more of these criminal laws in state codes than in the federal code. Cities and counties also create their own written laws. These are usually called **ordinances.**

In 1962 the American Law Institute (ALI)–a board of judges, lawyers, and legal scholars–published the first version of its **Model Penal Code (MPC).** It was most recently updated in 1981. The MPC is not a set of laws but a suggested prototype for criminal laws, intended to guide states in bringing their systems of criminal law up to date and making them more uniform. In some places, the MPC offers states several options, among which they are invited to choose. No state uses the entire MPC, but four have adopted it almost whole, and two-thirds have used it extensively in modernizing their criminal laws. Many definitions of crimes and of criminal responsibility used in this book reflect usages suggested in the Model Penal Code.

Another major source of law in the United States is **case law,** which consists of decisions that judges have made in court cases. Federal, state, and

constitution
A document that specifies the components of a government, the duties of each component, and the limits of their power.

statutes
Laws enacted by state legislatures or by Congress.

ordinances
Laws enacted by local governments such as cities and counties.

Model Penal Code
A suggested code of criminal law drafted by the American Law Institute and used to guide the states in modernizing their laws.

case law
Decisions judges have made in previous court cases.

KEY CONCEPTS Sources of Law

International	Federal	State	Local
Compacts and treaties	U.S. Constitution	State constitutions	
	U.S. Code (consists of U.S. statutes)	State statutes	Local ordinances
	Federal case law	State case law	
	Federal administrative regulations	State administrative regulations	Local administrative regulations

local judges cannot actually write or pass laws, but they interpret them in the course of formulating their court decisions. Other judges generally follow these interpretations in later cases.

Administrative agencies provide still another source of law in the United States. The hundreds of such agencies at the federal, state, and local levels include the Environmental Protection Agency, the Department of Motor Vehicles, and the Board of Education. Many of these agencies can create rules that carry the force of law. These rules are usually called *regulations*. The body of law that concerns the content and use of these regulations is known as *administrative law*, and it is quite extensive.

A final source of law in the United States is *international law*, which consists of the rules that operate among nations and among the citizens of different nations. International law generally resides in *treaties* and *compacts* that countries enter into with one another; these are agreements between two or more nations. International law also includes regulations created by organizations such as the United Nations. In the United States, the Constitution grants Congress the power to make and sign international treaties. "A Global View" illustrates that it can be extremely difficult to enforce laws across international borders.

Civil and Criminal Laws

The system of laws in the United States is large, complicated, and diverse. We can understand it more easily when we separate American laws into broad categories. Two of the most important of these are civil law and criminal law. The term *civil law*, as used here, differs from the meaning of civil law in the legal tradition deriving from ancient Roman law.

Civil law governs relationships between individuals. In civil law, a party who is injured financially or physically by another person or organization can bring a lawsuit against that entity. Civil proceedings focus on the injuries of the victim. The party who initiates the lawsuit is the **plaintiff,** and the other party is the **defendant.** For example, if a person is trimming a tree on her own property and a branch falls onto her neighbor's car, damaging it, the owner of the car could bring a civil lawsuit against the person trimming the tree. Lawsuits of this kind are called **torts.** If a pedestrian is struck by a car and wins a lawsuit against the driver, the latter may have to pay for the pedestrian's medical bills, lost wages, pain and suffering, and any other losses experienced as a result of the accident. These payments are known as **damages.** Other kinds of civil law include *contract law* (disputes arising from legal agreements between parties) and *property law* (disputes related to land ownership and use).

Criminal law is distinguished from civil law in a number of important ways:

- Criminal law operates under the assumption that society–rather than an individual–has been injured by the defendant's actions.

- Only the government may bring criminal cases. Although many people believe that the victim must press charges, the prosecutor alone decides whether to pursue criminal cases. Furthermore, prosecutors are not bound by the wishes of the victim. Prosecutors will pursue a criminal case based on the merits of the case, regardless of what the victim may want. In civil proceedings, however, the victim, not the government, brings the case to court.

- Defendants who lose criminal cases may pay fines to the government, but they also may be incarcerated in a jail or prison and, in some jurisdictions, even be put to death. Civil defendants who lose are not incarcerated or executed; instead, they pay damages to the victim.

- Criminal defendants are found guilty; civil defendants are found liable.

civil law
(1) The system of laws, sometimes known as the Roman system, used in many countries that do not use the common law system; or (2) noncriminal law, or law that concerns disputes between individual parties.

plaintiff
The party who initiates the lawsuit in a civil case.

defendant
The person against whom criminal charges or a civil lawsuit are filed.

torts
Civil disputes in which one party sues another for the damages that the defendant's actions have caused.

damages
Payments that a defendant must make to a winning plaintiff in a civil lawsuit to compensate the plaintiff for the injuries or costs that the defendant's actions have caused.

criminal law
A body of laws in which people are punished by the government for specific prohibited actions.

A Global View

Intellectual Property Piracy in the Twenty-First Century

On November 29, 2010—Cyber Monday, the biggest Internet shopping day of the year—the U.S. Immigration and Customs Enforcement agency shut down 82 websites of companies that were selling counterfeit sporting goods, DVDs, and other pirated items. This action was part of an ongoing government effort to combat illegal sales of copyrighted materials.

The piracy of copyrighted works is a serious problem in the twenty-first century. Creative works such as books, music, movies, software, and video games are protected internationally under copyright laws. These laws are meant to ensure that for a specified period of years, nobody profits from protected works without their creators' permission. When someone downloads a copyrighted song or makes a copy of a copyrighted DVD, that person has deprived the creative artist of income and has broken the law. These actions are now commonly known as *piracy.*

Piracy is big business, and it affects many forms of mass media. A 2014 study estimated that piracy cost the United States motion picture industry over $20 billion per year and cost the music industry $12.5 billion. When the book *Harry Potter and the Deathly Hallows* was published in 2007, it was almost immediately accompanied by illegally posted scans of the novel and unauthorized translations into other languages. In China, unauthorized Chinese translations of the Potter book were sold for the equivalent of about $2.50—approximately 10 percent of the novel's retail value if purchased through legitimate booksellers. A 2008 study concluded that if software piracy in the United States were reduced by only 10 percent, more than 30,000 new jobs would be created, and $7 billion in additional tax revenues would be collected. Although individuals making illegal copies for their personal use commit much piracy, organized crime rings also are participating and profiting from such acts.

Content producers make numerous attempts to reduce piracy, many aimed at college students. In 2008, for example, hundreds of students at the University of Texas were sued for illegally downloading music. In 2010, the U.S. Supreme Court refused to allow one young woman to defend herself on the basis that she was very young at the time—16—and did not realize she was committing illegal acts.

Content producers file lawsuits against individuals, lobby for stricter copyright protection laws, and encourage law enforcement agencies to pursue pirates vigorously. Producers also employ high-tech methods of piracy prevention, such as embedding invisible codes in movies that enable them to trace illegal copies to their source.

Despite these ongoing efforts, billions of dollars worth of works are pirated each year. Some countries—including China, Argentina, Pakistan, and Russia—are notoriously lax in policing copyright violations.

Although there are international treaties prohibiting piracy, not all countries have signed these treaties, and those that have do not always enforce them well. Some have pledged to do better; in 2007, for example, Russian authorities promised stricter adherence to copyright protections. In 2015, Russia added additional antipiracy provisions to its laws. The same year, Vietnam announced measures intended to decrease software piracy. But even in countries such as the United States where there is strong enforcement, piracy flourishes because it is difficult to prevent illegal copying. Many individuals who download unauthorized music or make illegal photocopies do not view their own activities as immoral or criminal. As one Lehigh University student put it, "I was just downloading some Bruce Springsteen. What's the big deal?"

OBSERVE → INVESTIGATE → UNDERSTAND

- Evaluate this statement: It is wrong to prosecute people for downloading pirated materials.
- What measures can be taken to reduce the piracy of music, books, and movies?
- Why do you think China and Russia are among the leading offenders in permitting piracy?

SOURCES: Business Software Alliance, "The Economic Benefits of Lowering PC Software Piracy," January 2008. www.bsa.org/sitecore/shell/Controls/Richpercent20Textpercent20Editor/~/media./Files/idc_studies/bsa_idc_us_finalpercent20pdf.ashx (retrieved January 22, 2008); John Healey and Chuck Philips, "Piracy Spins a Global Web," *Los Angeles Times,* October 9, 2005. www.latimes.com/business/lafipiracy90ct09m1m641553.story (retrieved October 24, 2005); BBC News, "Pirate Chinese Potter Book Sold," August 1, 2005. news.bbc.co.uk/2/hi/entertainment/4734161.stm (retrieved October 17, 2005); Kristen Blake, "Download Crackdown: File-Sharing Problems May Cause Computer, Legal Headaches for Students," *The Brown and White,* September 26, 2004. www.bw.lehigh.edu/story.asp?ID=17818 (retrieved October 17, 2005); Jerry Markon and Cecilia Kang, "Customs Agents Seize Web Sites Suspected of Selling Knockoffs," *Washington Post,* November 29, 2010. www.washingtonpost.com/wpdyn/content/article/2010/11/29/AR2010112902410.html?hpid=topnews&sid= ST2010112903845 (retrieved December 8, 2010); MSNBC, "Court Rejects Texas Teen's Web Music Case," November 29, 2010. www.msnbc.msn.com/id/40425691 (retrieved December 8, 2010); The Guardian, "Piracy Study Shows Illegal Downloaders More Likely to Pay for Films than Music," May 6, 2014. http://www.theguardian.com/technology/2014/may/06/piracy-film-music-study-pay-illegal-download-damage (retrieved June 1, 2015).

- A criminal conviction tends to bring greater moral condemnation from society than does losing a civil lawsuit.
- Criminal defendants are entitled to a number of legal protections, such as access to a government-paid attorney if they are unable to afford one, the presumption of innocence, and a speedy trial. Civil defendants do not automatically have such government protections.
- In the U.S. criminal justice system, the state, not the victim, charges the defendant. Therefore, victims have little or no influence on how a criminal

KEY CONCEPTS   Criminal versus Civil Law

	Criminal Law	Civil Law
Harm	To society	To individual
Case brought by	Government	Injured party
Sanctions	Fines, incarceration, death	Damages
Terminology	Guilty	Liable
Brings moral condemnation	Usually yes	Usually no
Special legal protections	Yes	No
Control by victim	Very little	Very much
Standard of proof	Beyond a reasonable doubt	Preponderance of the evidence

case proceeds. Victims have more control in the civil justice system because they, not the government, make the decision to begin the court process. They also hire their own attorneys, and they have the right to be present during the entire proceeding.

■ The standard of proof in criminal cases is high: Guilt must be proved beyond a reasonable doubt. In civil cases, the party that proves its case by a pre-ponderance of the evidence (a lower legal threshold) can win. (Standards of proof are discussed in more detail in Chapter 9.)

The differences between criminal and civil law are summarized in the Key Concepts feature on page 114.

MYTH/REALITY

MYTH: Double jeopardy occurs when someone is sued in civil court and tried in criminal court for the same act.

REALITY: According to the U.S. Constitution, double jeopardy protection does not apply to civil cases.

The Fifth Amendment's protection against **double jeopardy** prohibits a defendant from being tried twice for the same crime. However, many acts can result in both civil and criminal cases, and double jeopardy protection does not prohibit the victim from filing a civil lawsuit. In 1995, former football star O. J. Simpson was tried in a criminal case by the state of California for the murders of his ex-wife Nicole Brown Simpson and her friend Ronald Goldman. Simpson was tried but acquitted (found not guilty) of the criminal charges. After the acquittal, the victims' families brought a civil lawsuit against Simpson for "wrongful death." In the civil case, the jury found Simpson responsible for the deaths, and he was ordered to pay the families $33.5 million. Contrary to what many people believe, the civil trial did not violate Simpson's constitu-tional protection against double jeopardy, because that protection only prohib-its trying someone more than once on criminal charges for the same offense. Similarly, actor Robert Blake was found not guilty in 2005 of murdering his wife, but her children successfully sued him in 2006 for killing their mother.[4] If a man is criminally convicted and then a civil lawsuit is brought, that con-viction can be used against him in the civil trial.

Not only may a single act result in both criminal and civil trials, but those trials will bear many similarities. Both may take place in the same courtroom,

double jeopardy
The Fifth Amendment right that protects anyone from being tried twice for the same offense.

What about the Victim?

Civil Damages in Action: Creating the Jeanne Clery Act

Jeanne Clery was a 19-year-old freshman at Lehigh University, located in a quiet community outside Philadelphia. On the evening of April 5, 1986, another student entered Jeanne's dorm room and brutally raped and killed her. Access to the dormitory was easy because other students had propped open the outside doors.

Jeanne's parents were outraged, not only by the rape and murder of their daughter but also by the fact that the university had provided inadequate protection for its students. As the Clerys wrote on the website for the organization they started, Security On Campus:

> We learned that institutional response to such tragedies could involve callousness, cover-ups and stone-walling. Lehigh officials publicly passed off Jeanne's torture/murder as an "aberration." The college, in an ill-conceived attempt to protect its "image," produced a self-serving "report," written by one of its trustees, K. P. Pendleton, which concluded that there was no negligence on the part of the university and that "our present safety policies were complete"; this, despite the administration's knowledge of prior violent crimes on the campus and that there had been 181 reports of propped-open doors in Jeanne's dormitory in the four months prior to her death.

Source: http://www.saveardmorecoalition.org/

Jeanne's parents also discovered that students had not been informed about 38 violent crimes at Lehigh University in the three years prior to her murder.

As a result, the Clerys filed a civil lawsuit against the university for negligent failure of security and for failure to warn of foreseeable dangers on campus. They received an undisclosed financial settlement. They used the money to create Security On Campus, Inc., a grassroots, nonprofit organization devoted to creating safe campuses for college and university students. The organization also lobbies for state and federal laws for campus security.

In the late 1980s, Pennsylvania enacted a law requiring all postsecondary education institutions receiving federal aid to collect crime statistics. Institutions must publish and disseminate these statistics in a campus security report that is updated each year by October 1. These statistics must cover all campus and noncampus properties, including those controlled by student organizations and recognized by the institution (such as officially sanctioned Greek housing), and all public areas in close geographic proximity to university property that are accessed by students for school-related activities. Each year, all students, faculty, staff, and administrators must be informed that the statistics are available, and the institution must inform the campus community whenever a crime is committed and the alleged offender remains at large, posing a continued threat to those on campus.

The Pennsylvania law and comparable legislation in nine other states gave the Clerys the momentum they needed to persuade Congress to enact the Crime Awareness and Campus Security Act of 1990. The law later was amended twice, and in 1998 it was renamed the Jeanne Clery Act. Collectively, these amendments provide for campus victims' rights, expanded reporting requirements, and the disclosure of results from disciplinary hearings to victims. The Clery Act is just one example of the ways in which victims use the civil justice system not for personal monetary gain but to bring about policy changes in an attempt to prevent future victimizations.

OBSERVE → INVESTIGATE → UNDERSTAND

- In what ways did the Clery Act pave the way for victim awareness?
- What steps has your college taken to ensure your on-campus safety? Are they appropriate? If not, what additional measures do you feel should be taken? If the current steps are appropriate, do you think they stem from the concerns the Clery Act highlighted?
- Could the objectives of the Clery Act have been achieved without the Clery family's resorting to a civil suit? Explain.

SOURCE: Security on Campus. www.securityoncampus.org/index.php?option=com_content&view=article&id=52:jeanne-clearys-victimblog&catid=34:victim-blog-category&Itemid=54 (retrieved July 3, 2009).

---

restitution
In a criminal case, the money or services a defendant must provide as reparations to the victim for the cost and inconvenience suffered.

although not at the same time and not in front of the same judge or jury. The outcomes also may share similarities. Defendants who lose civil cases may be required to pay punitive damages if their behaviors are held to be especially unconscionable or malicious. Similarly, criminal defendants may be required to provide victims **restitution,** which is reparation for their losses.

Many people believe that victims use the civil justice system as a way to obtain huge monetary settlements. In fact, many victims do not go through the civil justice system at all because they cannot afford to hire an attorney. Others use the civil justice system in an attempt to bring about policy changes that can occur when civil juries grant large monetary settlements. Sometimes a multimillion-dollar judgment is granted, but others are for undisclosed amounts, and still others are for only a few hundred dollars. "What about the Victim?" on page 118 describes a case that led to victim-initiated policy changes.

Criminal Laws: Misdemeanors, Felonies, and Infractions

A useful way to categorize criminal laws is according to the seriousness of the offense. In the United States, most crimes are felonies, misdemeanors, or infractions. This classification scheme dates back more than a thousand years, to the Norman Conquest of England in 1066. Prior to the conquest, early medieval English kings punished only a small number of crimes. Usually victims were expected to deal with wrongdoers themselves, either by taking compensation or (more commonly) through private vengeance. However, those who committed serious acts such as murder could be executed by the king's representatives, and their property could be seized by the crown. These serious acts were called **felonies.**

Following the Norman Conquest, and especially after Henry II established his system of royal courts in the late twelfth century, the number of acts defined as felonies increased, and people faced execution or property forfeiture for a variety of acts, many of which we would not consider very serious today. But juries often were hesitant to find defendants guilty of relatively minor offenses if the judge's sentence would be death. Consequently, some less serious crimes came to be classified as **misdemeanors** and carried relatively mild punishments. The procedures for prosecuting misdemeanors were considerably less complex than those for felonies.[5]

Today, the most serious crimes are still classified as felonies; less serious offenses constitute misdemeanors and infractions. Jurisdictions differ in how they classify specific offenses, although very serious crimes such as murder and rape are always felonies. But in Florida, for example, stealing something worth $350 is grand theft, a felony, whereas in California it is petty theft, a misdemeanor. **Infractions** include minor traffic offenses such as speeding, as well as violations of local laws, such as failure to license a dog properly.

People convicted of felonies can be punished by incarceration in state or federal prisons, usually for terms of more than one year. *Capital felonies* are those that in some states might result in a death sentence. In contrast, people who commit misdemeanors usually face sentences of fines, probation, or incarceration in local jails, usually for less than one year. In states that have three-strikes laws (which punish repeat offenders with harsher penalties), felonies may count as "strikes" but misdemeanors usually do not. There are also procedural differences between the two categories of crimes. Felony defendants in some places may be entitled to a grand jury (see Chapter 8), but misdemeanor defendants are not. In some states, misdemeanor cases are heard by different courts than those that try felonies.

In many states, certain crimes are known as *wobblers*, which may be charged either as misdemeanors or as felonies, usually at the discretion of the judge or prosecutor. For example, in Florida certain kinds of vandalism are wobblers.

felony
A serious criminal offense that brings a potential punishment of a year or more in state or federal prison.

misdemeanor
A criminal offense that is punished by fines or a maximum of a year in a county or city jail.

infraction
A minor violation of a local ordinance or state law that brings a potential punishment of fines.

MYTH/REALITY

MYTH: Speeding tickets and other infractions are not criminal offenses.

REALITY: All infractions, even minor ones, are criminal.

Depending on the jurisdiction, some minor offenses are categorized as violations or infractions. For example, common traffic offenses such as illegal parking and speeding are punished only with fines. Although those found guilty of violations or infractions do not incur a criminal record, the U.S. Supreme Court has held that people may be placed under arrest and taken into custody even for relatively minor matters such as speeding and seat belt violations (see "A Case in Point" on page 120).

a case in p♥int

Convicted *without* Criminal Intent?

In the fall of 1948, Joseph Edward Morissette, a 27-year-old honorably discharged soldier, was deer hunting with two friends when he decided to remove three tons of empty, discarded, rusted bomb casings from a small Army air base in the northeastern rural Michigan town of Oscoda. Sometime later, he sold these casings as scrap metal for $84. At his trial, Morissette claimed he believed these casings were abandoned and thus did not know it was illegal to take them. However, dealing with the question of intent, the judge charged the jury with the words:

> And I instruct you that if you believe the testimony of the government in this case, he intended to take it. He had no right to take this property, and it is no defense to claim that it was abandoned, because it was on private property. And I instruct you to this effect: That if this young man took this property (and he says he did), without any permission (he says he did), that was on the property of the United States Government (he says it was), that it was of the value of one cent or more (and evidently it was), that he is guilty of the offense charged here. If you believe the government, he is guilty.

Subsequently, Morissette was found guilty for unlawfully, willfully, and knowingly stealing and converting the metal casings to his own use, violating Title 18 U.S.C.A. § 641.[a] On appeal the conviction was affirmed; however, because the key issue—the requirement of knowledge that the property was abandoned—was removed by the judge's instruction, a principal element of the case was missing; thus, the U.S. Supreme Court reversed the findings of both the trial court and the district appellate court. The key point of this case centered on the admissibility of the evidence that Mr. Morissette was unaware that what he took in fact belonged to the U.S. government. Furthermore, this case illustrates the importance of mens rea as an important element in these types of offenses. This point is embodied in Justice Robert Jackson's now famous statement for the Supreme Court regarding mens rea, which states that crime is "generally constituted only from concurrence of an evil-meaning mind with an evil-doing hand."[b]

OBSERVE→INVESTIGATE→UNDERSTAND

- Does the judge's instruction to the jury seem fair? Explain?
- Do you think the district appellate court made a mistake? What is your opinion?
- Why did the trial and appellate courts ignore what the Supreme Court ruled was an important legal point?

SOURCES: [a]Andrew J. Transue, (2014) Flint, Mich., on brief for appellant, *Morissette v. United States, LEAGLE*, United States Court of Appeals Sixth Circuit. February 5, 1951. www.leagle.com/decision/1951614187F2d427_1485.xml/MORISSETTE%20v.%20UNITED%20STATES (retrieved May 23, 2015).

[b]Invispress, Law School Case Briefs: Criminal Law, *Morissette v. United States,* 342 U.S. 246 (1952). www.invispress.com/law/criminal/morissette.html (retrieved May 23, 2015); *Wikipedia,* "Morissette v. United States," http://en.wikipedia.org/wiki/Morissette_v._United_States#cite_ref-3 (retrieved May 23, 2015).

LEGAL ELEMENTS OF A CRIME

Whether a crime is a felony, a misdemeanor, or an infraction, before an individual can be convicted, the state must prove that a crime has actually occurred. The legal requirements for identifying a criminal action are quite precise, as we now consider.

Corpus Delicti—Proof That a Crime Has Been Committed

corpus delicti
"The body of the crime"; the specific elements that must be proved to convict someone of a specific offense.

criminal intent
The degree to which a defendant must have intended his or her actions or the consequences of those actions.

The **corpus delicti** of a crime (literally "the body of the offense") refers to the particular elements required in order for prosecutors to establish that a crime was indeed committed.[6] To meet the corpus delicti requirement, the prosecutor must show that a defendant's criminal action (*actus reus*) was the product of his or her **criminal intent** (*mens rea*) and that this intended action (or failure to act) resulted in some manner of harm or injury to the victim. Collectively, these three elements—action, intent, and harm—constitute the essence of a crime. Each crime requires a specific actus reus and a specific mens rea. All three are generally required to convict a criminal defendant. In some cases, however, a defendant can be found guilty of a crime even though one or more of the key elements is absent. The Latin terms *corpus delicti, actus reus*, and *mens rea* come from ancient and medieval law.

The term *corpus delicti* is often mistakenly taken to mean the corpse of a victim. But in a homicide case the body of the murdered victim is only one of the elements constituting the corpus delicti. In some cases, if circumstantial evidence is compelling enough, the actual body of an alleged murder victim need not be found for the killer to be convicted. British serial murderer John George Haigh used acid to decompose the bodies of people he had killed for financial gain, under the mistaken belief that without a corpse murder could not be proved because there was no corpus delicti. "No bodies. No crime. No punishment."[7] Haigh made the common error of misunderstanding the word *corpus*. That was his undoing. The evidence against him, albeit circumstantial, was substantial. Haigh was found guilty of nine murders and was executed in 1949.[8]

▲ **John George Haigh**

Haigh was a notorious English serial killer during the 1940s. *How should the U.S. criminal justice system deal with serial killers?*

Actus Reus—The Criminal Act

Each kind of crime has a specific **actus reus,** literally the "evil" or "guilty act." For example, the actus reus for the crime of perjury in Florida is making a false statement under oath during a public proceeding (such as a trial).[9]

To be found guilty of murder, you must cause another person's death. Usually this means that you, the defendant, must have used the murder weapon yourself. There are, however, exceptions to this requirement. If a person hires or compels somebody else to do the actual killing, he or she can still be found guilty of murder by having caused the crime. This would obviously be the case if a person were to hire a hit man to kill his spouse. (Of course, the hit man would also be guilty of murder.)

The murder conviction of cult leader Charles Manson is another example of how a person can be found guilty of a crime without meeting the usual requirement of actus reus.[10] In 1971, Manson was convicted of the murders of seven people in 1969, even though he had not been present during the killings. In fact, it was a small group of his followers who had committed the murders. Manson and four members of his "family" were all sentenced to death, though their punishment was reduced to life sentences when the U.S. Supreme Court temporarily abolished capital punishment in 1972. Except for one of the followers, Susan Atkins, who died in prison in 2009, they are still imprisoned.

actus reus
The specific act required to convict a person for a specific crime.

Mens Rea—The Defendant's Mental State

Actus non facit reum nisi mens sit rea.
(An act does not make a man guilty unless his mind be also guilty.)

–Sir Edward Coke (1644)[11]

To say that a person committed a criminal act is not the same as saying that he is criminally responsible (or criminally liable) for the crime. What makes the difference is the perpetrator's **mens rea,** or state of mind at the time of the crime.

Different crimes represent different levels of mens rea, or criminal intent. To be convicted of first-degree murder, the offender usually must commit the crime with "premeditation and malice aforethought"; that is, with having planned and intended ahead of time to kill the victim. First-degree murder carries the heaviest penalty–usually long-term sentences, life imprisonment, or death. Other levels of mens rea required for different offenses include *purposefully* (intending the offense and its consequences), *knowingly* (being certain in the result of the actions, regardless of whether the offender wants them to happen), *recklessly*

mens rea
The level of criminal intent, or the mental state usually required to convict a person of a criminal act.

▲ **Derrick Robie**

Four-year-old Derrick was beaten to death by a 13-year-old. *Do you think a 13-year-old can understand how his crime will affect others?*

(knowing that there is a substantial risk of the consequences), and *negligently* (behaving differently from the way a reasonable person would have behaved).

For a deed to be criminal, intent and act must concur. In other words, if you intend to do one kind of harm to someone (for example, rob him) and attempt to carry out that actus reus, but accidentally do unrelated, unplanned harm to that person (such as run over and kill him while driving to his house), then the concurrence of act and intent for murder has not been established.

Some offenses do not require that the offender actually intended to commit the actus reus or cause the victim harm. Reckless or very careless behavior may be sufficient. For example, Michael Derderian owned a nightclub in Rhode Island. He knew that the cheap soundproofing material around the stage was highly flammable, and he also frequently allowed the nightclub to become crowded beyond capacity. On one such packed evening in 2003, he permitted the band Great White to use pyrotechnics during their performance. The pyrotechnics set the soundproofing material on fire, and many of the club's patrons were unable to escape. One hundred people died in the inferno. Derderian was convicted of involuntary manslaughter and sentenced to four years in prison.

The general idea behind the mens rea requirement is that people should usually not be held criminally liable if they did not intend to commit certain acts or to cause certain consequences. Furthermore, the law often assumes that people should receive more severe criminal sanctions when they intended to harm others, as opposed to when the harm was careless or accidental.

In some instances, the perpetrator may not understand the consequences of the injurious act. For example, a child might know that an act is wrong but not truly comprehend how the crime affects others. A chilling example is the beating death of 4-year-old Derrick Robie in Savona, New York, in 1993. The murderer was another child, 13-year-old Eric Smith. Smith lured Robie into the woods and there beat him to death with large rocks. Although Smith was aware he had committed a crime, he did not fully comprehend how the murder would affect others. In a televised interview a year after the crime, when Smith was asked how the parents of the murdered child might feel about the killing, Smith replied, "I guess they're mad at me and stuff."[12] He still did not "get it." A jury convicted the juvenile of second-degree murder. He has been in prison ever since.

Generally speaking, when a defendant lacks the required mens rea or intent for a particular crime, he is not held criminally responsible for that crime. To establish mens rea, the judge or jury makes a judgment of the individual's capability of forming it. Assuming that the person is capable of forming mens rea, the judge or jury must then establish whether the person actually did have the requisite mens rea at the time of committing the actus reus. In most states, a defendant with an extraordinarily low IQ is considered incapable of forming mens rea.[13]

Example of Elements of Crime

Offense	Actus Reus	Mens Rea
Silent or abusive calls to 9-1-1 service (Texas Pen. Code §42.061)	A person makes a phone call to 9-1-1 when there is not an emergency and remains silent or makes abusive or harassing statements.	Knowingly or intentionally
Kidnapping (Texas Pen. Code §20.03)	A person abducts another person.	Knowingly or intentionally
Criminally negligent homicide (Texas Pen. Code §19.05)	A person causes the death of an individual.	Criminal negligence

It is often difficult to determine whether a person had the required mens rea. This is particularly true when the person is an adolescent or has a mental disability. Criminal law attaches culpability to criminal intent, yet mens rea cannot be measured in any objective way. (The table "Examples of Elements of Crime" provides instances of offenses, actus reus, and mens rea.)

The same requirements of proving actus reus and mens rea apply when it comes to the accomplices to a crime. The prosecution must establish beyond a reasonable doubt that someone who supplied a weapon, served as a lookout, drove a getaway car, or sheltered a fugitive did so with the conscious intent of aiding and abetting the crime. Sometimes this can be difficult to prove. Suppose, for example, that Mary sells a gun to John, who uses it to commit a holdup or a murder. If it can be proved that Mary had foreknowledge of the use to which John would put the weapon, or if she knowingly accepted from John some of the proceeds of the robbery or murder, then she is liable as an accomplice. She might also face criminal consequences if she supplied the weapon to John in reckless or negligent disregard of the consequences—for example, knowing that he was a violent lawbreaker.

Some specific acts constitute crimes regardless of the presence or absence of criminal intent. These **strict liability offenses** are generally associated with less harsh punishments than if they were accompanied by mens rea. Statutory rape is one controversial example. By law, an adult who has sex with a minor is committing a crime, regardless of whether the sexual activity was consensual or whether the adult had a good-faith belief that the minor was older. In most states, the age of consent is 16, but in some it is 17 or 18. If sexual relations occur, the law dictates that the adult be held criminally responsible. But because mens rea is not an element of the offense, the punishment is typically less severe than for the crime of forcible rape.

strict liability offenses
Crimes that have no mens rea requirement; a person who commits the requisite actus reus may be convicted of the offense regardless of intent.

MYTH/REALITY

MYTH: The law excuses children from criminal responsibility.

REALITY: Even young children may be found criminally responsible for their criminal behaviors and can be tried as adults in some states.

Inchoate Offenses

Sometimes a person has the mens rea to commit a crime and even takes some steps to commit the actus reus, but for various reasons is unable to complete the offense. The individual may still face criminal liability, however. These incomplete criminal acts are called **inchoate crimes.**

One common inchoate crime is *attempt.* For example, suppose that a person decides to rob a liquor store. She obtains a gun, drives to the store, enters, points the gun at the clerk, and demands the money in the till. Before the clerk can respond, however, an off-duty police officer tackles the would-be robber to the ground, disarms her, and places her under arrest. Should she escape criminal liability merely because she was unable to complete the actus reus for robbery, which is taking another person's property through force or threats? That would seem unjust. Because she clearly intended to commit robbery and had taken substantial steps to commit it, she could be charged with attempted robbery. Attempt usually carries the same penalties as the completed offense.

Other inchoate crimes include *conspiracy* (an agreement with other people to commit a criminal act) and *solicitation* (persuading or inducing someone else to commit a crime). In general, the idea behind all inchoate offenses is that someone who tries to commit a crime, but who is unsuccessful, is as dangerous and as culpable as someone who succeeds.

inchoate crimes
Crimes that have been begun but are not completed or are crimes that are completed by someone else.

▲ **What If the Boss Had Died?**

In the film *9 to 5*, a character believed she had accidentally poisoned her awful boss.

Other Elements of Crime

While all crimes require a specific actus reus and a specific mens rea, some crimes have additional elements as well. Some crimes require that a particular result occur. For example, in order for someone to be convicted of homicide, the prosecutor must prove that the defendant's actions resulted in the death of a human being. The legal name for this requirement is *causation*. Sometimes causation is easy to prove, but other times it is quite difficult, especially when there may be several intervening causes or when several people could potentially be blamed for a particular act. In 1972, three members of a motorcycle gang severely beat Danny Centrone. He survived the attack but with severe brain damage. Twenty-one years later, Centrone died from choking on a piece of food he was eating. The medical examiner determined that Centrone's death was due to his impaired chewing and swallowing, which resulted from the attack years earlier. The examiner declared Centrone's death to be a homicide.[14]

Most crimes also require *concurrence;* that is, the mens rea and the actus reus must occur at more or less the same time and in concert. Concurrence is a complex concept, but it generally means that the defendant must have the requisite mens rea at the time she commits the actus reus. In the 1980 movie *9 to 5*, a woman accidentally serves her hateful boss coffee containing rat poison; at the time she prepared the coffee, she thought the powder was sweetener.[15] If the boss had died from the poison, and if the woman had rejoiced afterward over the death, she still would not have been guilty of murder because at the time she served him the poison, she didn't intend to kill him. In this case, there would have been no concurrence between the actus reus and the mens rea.

CRIMINAL DEFENSES

The law views human beings as conscious, rational, and intentional agents of behavior. In the U.S. judicial system, criminal defendants have the opportunity to claim a variety of circumstances and conditions that may serve as defenses if they are accused of committing crimes.

There are certainly instances where the defendant is wrongly accused of committing the crime for which he or she is on trial. These include the case in which an eyewitness has mistakenly identified the accused as the actual offender. The defendant is truly innocent and would present to the court an alibi that explains where he was and what he was doing at the time of the crime—details that, if verified during trial, would be exculpatory (meaning that they would clear the defendant of guilt). An alibi can be proved in a variety of ways. For example, the defense could use testimony from individuals who were present with the defendant at another location during the time the crime was committed, or video surveillance footage that places the defendant across town at the time of the crime. The defense of alibi holds that the defendant is not guilty because the person did not commit the crime. All other defenses concede that the defendant committed the crime, but argue that the person should not be held criminally responsible. Such defenses are known as affirmative defenses because the defendant is admitting she broke the law (affirming she did it) but argues that she had a legal justification for doing so. What all these other defenses have in common is the argument that mens rea was lacking or diminished at the time of the crime.

Although the courts determine criminal responsibility, criminal defenses are set by statute and are heavily influenced by common law. We look next at the criminal defenses allowed in courts in the United States.

Mistake of Fact

We are generally presumed to know the law, but its enormity and its changing nature make it impossible for everyone to know all the laws all the time. Nonetheless, ignorance of the law is not an acceptable defense. If it were, it is easy to imagine how flooded the courts would be with defendants claiming "I didn't know there was a law against that!" The defense of mistake of fact argues that a mistake related to a *fact of the crime* may have affected the state

Real Careers

CHRISTOPHER GOWEN

Work location: Washington, DC

College(s): Villanova University (2000); University of Miami School of Law (2005)

Major(s): Business Administration (BS); Juris Doctorate (JD)

Job title: Senior Staff Attorney, American Bar Association (ABA)

Salary range for job like this: $60,000–$80,000

Time in job: 1 year

Work Responsibilities

As the senior staff attorney for the Criminal Justice Section of the American Bar Association (ABA), I am responsible for overseeing and developing new policy on pertinent criminal justice issues with our attorney members. Once our section has decided on a policy, it goes for a vote by the ABA House of Delegates. If the policy passes, the ABA will then take it to the United States Congress and lobby the legislators to make it law. I am currently developing policy that would not allow schools and employers to deny opportunities to applicants based on their contact with the criminal justice system as juveniles.

My section also follows criminal cases before the Supreme Court and reports on them to our members. When the Court is going to hear a criminal case that has a legal issue on which the

ABA has developed policy, we will write an amicus brief in favor of the side our policy supports.

I also develop programs to train attorneys on different aspects of the law around the country in such areas as evidence, criminal procedure, and public corruption. Last but not least, the ABA allows me to practice law on a pro bono basis. I can represent indigent children in criminal cases for free, and the ABA will allow me to work on the cases during normal work hours.

Why Criminal Justice?

After law school I worked for the Miami Dade Public Defender's Office, where I learned how important the role of a public defender is to society—the only hope to protect people falsely accused by the police or whose rights have been violated by the government.

After my second year as a public defender, I worked in Iowa in a senior position for the Hillary Clinton for President campaign. Following the campaign, I moved to Washington, DC, married, and took a job with the ABA. If I could still afford to be a public defender, I would return in a heartbeat. Unfortunately, public defender offices around the country are facing serious budget problems and can't afford to pay their attorneys reasonable salaries.

Expectations and Realities of the Job

I had expected things to move a little faster in Washington, DC. The reality is it takes a very long time to get new law passed. But the pace at which a new public defender or prosecutor works is incredible—you get thrown right into the fire and are representing clients on day one. In two years I tried over 40 cases as a public defender. Many trial lawyers do not try that many cases in a lifetime.

My Advice to Students

Get some real-life experience (bill paying, working 9–5) before you go to graduate school, especially law school. In law school you learn about cases that shaped and developed law, each of which is based on facts that occurred in someone's life. The more you have experienced in life, the better you will understand the consequences of the law and the cases you are learning about.

of mind of the defendant in such a way as to cause the person to commit the crime, but without mens rea.

Generally, people can use mistake of fact as a defense if they were mistaken about a fact, but not if they were mistaken about a law. For example, imagine a woman whose husband disappears overboard while they are on a cruise ship together. Ten years later, believing him to be dead, she remarries. If her first husband then suddenly reappears, alive and well, is the woman guilty of bigamy? Most likely not, as she reasonably (although mistakenly) believed her husband was dead.

But now imagine a woman who is married, who knows her husband is alive, but who (mistakenly, she says) believes her state permits people to have multiple spouses. If she marries a second time before divorcing her first husband, she will be guilty of bigamy because she is mistaken about the law. Cases involving mistake of fact or law are uncommon.

Intoxication

In most cases, people who become intoxicated by alcohol or other drugs cannot use intoxication as a defense. However, if a person becomes so intoxicated that the individual cannot form the mens rea required for a particular crime, the person may have a successful intoxication defense. For example, if a man were so impaired that he did not realize what he was doing when he killed his friend, he would probably not be convicted of first-degree murder, which requires that the crime be premeditated. He would probably be convicted of a lesser offense, such as involuntary manslaughter. On the other hand, if he wanted to kill the friend but lacked the courage to do so in a sober state and so drank in order to be able to commit the murder, his intoxication would generally not serve to reduce his culpability.

In the United States, states vary as to whether they will accept intoxication as a defense at all, and if so, when. Montana, for example, never allows voluntarily intoxicated people to use the defense, whereas New York accepts voluntary intoxication as a defense in cases not involving extremely reckless behavior.[16]

However, the intoxication defense can be used when someone becomes intoxicated involuntarily. For example, if someone slipped a drug into a woman's soft drink without her being aware of it, and she committed a crime while under the drug's influence, she would be able to claim intoxication as a defense.

The Justification Defenses

In other cases, a defendant admits to having broken the law but presents the court with a justification for his behavior. While he knew that what he was doing was a criminal act, he argues that his actions were justified by the circumstances surrounding the incident. Justification defenses include duress, necessity, self-defense, and entrapment.

duress
A defense in which the defendant claims that he or she was forced or coerced into committing a crime.

Duress: Being Coerced into Committing a Crime
Situations may occur in which a person is literally forced into committing a crime because failure to commit it would result in more serious harm. As long as the crime is not murder (owing to the principle that one person's life is no more valuable than another's), the defendant may make the claim of **duress.**

Consider this example: A man forces his way into a home and holds a handgun to the wife's head. Because he is convinced that mind-controlling waves are emanating from the neighbor's television set, he directs the husband to break into the neighbor's house and destroy the set. The husband is given 10 minutes to complete the deed and return with the remote control for the television, or his wife will be killed. Even though the husband realizes the man has a serious mental illness, he does as he is told and returns (with the remote control) to report the television destroyed. Although the husband indeed committed more than one crime (burglary, destruction of property, and theft), it would be clear to any reasonable person that not to have done so could have resulted in a much more serious outcome: the killing of his wife by this deranged man. Should the husband ultimately be charged with the crimes? Under the circumstances, a plea of duress may be appropriate.

A defense of duress would not be accepted, however, if the husband were directed to murder his neighbor's wife instead of destroying the television. The law would not recognize that the life of his wife was more valuable than that of his neighbor's wife.

Necessity: When Circumstances Require an Illegal Act   Sometimes, under extreme circumstances, a person cannot avoid taking criminal action to resolve a situation. A case such as this might use the defense of **necessity.** Such was thought to be the situation when, in 1884, a ship capsized off the coast of Africa. For a week, four crew members survived in a lifeboat by sharing two cans of turnips and the carcass of a sea turtle. During the second week, the youngest member of the crew, Richard Parker, was approaching death from starvation. At one point the ship's captain Dudley and first mate Stephens decided that if help did not arrive by the following morning, they would kill Parker and consume his remains. (The other crew member refused to participate in the plan.) The help did not come. The two stabbed Parker and ate from his remains over the next four days, until a German ship rescued them. On their return to England, Dudley and Stephens were put on trial for Parker's death.

Courtroom debate examined questions of how to measure and compare the value of lives. The opinion of the court was delivered by Chief Justice Lord Coleridge, who wrote: "Is it to be strength, or intellect, or what? . . . In this case the weakest, the youngest, the most unresisting, was chosen. Was it more necessary to kill him than one of the grown men? The answer must be 'No.'" A panel of five judges found Dudley and Stephens guilty of murder and sentenced them to die. However, public outrage about the trial's outcome prompted Queen Victoria to commute the death sentences to six months in prison.[17]

Subsequent cases have etched out exceptions whereby killing is deemed a necessity. If, for example, the death of the victim was imminent and the continuation of the victim's life threatens the life of others, the defendant can make a case for necessity. This is the kind of determination made in cases where the life of one conjoined twin is taken in order to save the other. Necessity would also have applied as a defense on September 11, 2001, if military jets had managed to shoot down any of the hijacked planes, together with the kidnapped passengers, before the terrorists' mission was accomplished.

To use the necessity defense successfully, the defendant generally must demonstrate that he or she had to commit the crime in order to avoid more severe consequences. For this reason, it is sometimes called the "lesser of two evils" defense. In the nineteenth century, many states prohibited people from doing business on Sundays. Courts permitted the necessity defense in the cases of shipping companies that had set sail on Sundays to avoid storms, and in the case of telegraph companies that had transmitted telegrams concerning emergencies.[18]

In 1976, four inmates of a jail in Washington, DC, escaped by removing a bar from a window and sliding down a knotted bedsheet. When they were eventually caught and charged with escape, they claimed that there were frequent fires in the jail, the guards had beaten them, and one of them was not receiving adequate care for his medical conditions. They said that they had left the jail to protect their health and lives.[19] A majority of the U.S. Supreme Court eventually upheld the convictions for their escape. The "Matters of Ethics" box examines this issue further.

necessity
A defense in which the defendant must demonstrate that he or she had to commit the crime to avoid more severe consequences.

Matters *of* Ethics

When Is It Right to Do the Wrong Thing?

On April 27, 2008, Lisa Marie Leprowse left a bar and drove 14 miles toward her house before being pulled over by a deputy and charged with drunk driving. She admitted that she was intoxicated but claimed that she had been forced to drive under the influence in order to save herself from harm. She asserted that she had been in a fight with another woman at the bar, that the other woman had threatened her life, and that Leprowse had fled in order to escape injury. At trial, she wished to use the necessity defense, but the judge would not permit it. Later, however, the Montana Supreme Court overturned the lower court's decision and remanded the case for a new trial, holding that Leprowse should have been allowed to attempt this defense.

In March 2008, a jury in Amarillo, Texas, took less than 15 minutes to find Tim Stevens not guilty of possession of 3 grams of marijuana. Although Stevens admitted that he had possessed the drug, he employed the necessity defense, claiming that he used marijuana to treat the symptoms of his HIV infection.

On May 31, 2009, Scott Roeder shot and killed George Tiller during a church service. Tiller was a physician who provided abortion services. At his murder trial, Roeder attempted to use the necessity defense, claiming that Tiller's death was necessary in order to save unborn children.

The judge did not permit the defense, and Roeder was convicted and sentenced to life in prison.

In September 2010, John Coughlin was pulled over at 3:30 a.m. for driving over 100 mph in a 50 mph zone. Coughlin's wife, Angela Coughlin, was pregnant, and her water had just broken; John was speeding to get her to the hospital. When the New Hampshire trooper who had stopped the couple understood the situation, he escorted the Coughlins to the hospital. The baby was born just 6 minutes after they arrived—but the officer still wrote Coughlin a speeding ticket. The ticket carried a potential fine of $1,000. A legal analyst suggested that Coughlin use the necessity defense.

These four cases illustrate one of the problems associated with justification defenses. When defendants use these defenses, they admit that they have done something illegal, and yet claim that under the circumstances, their illegal behavior was the right thing to do. Judges and juries must then face the often difficult task of weighing alternatives that were available to the defendants and deciding whether it is just to punish them for their acts.

OBSERVE → INVESTIGATE → UNDERSTAND

- How would you have decided these cases if you had been on the juries?
- Under what circumstances do you think illegal acts are justified? Can killing another person ever be justified? Explain.
- In cases such as these, should jurors put themselves in the defendants' shoes in order to reach a decision, or should they rely on their own morals and values? Defend your answer.

SOURCES: *Montana v. Leprowse*, 353 Mont. 312 (2009); "Marijuana User Found Not Guilty," *NewsChannel10*, March 27, 2008. www.newschannel10.com/global/story.asp?s=8080908 (retrieved December 31, 2010); MSNBC, " 'Necessity Defense' in Abortion Case Ruled Out," December 22, 2009. www.msnbc.msn.com/id/34525160/ns/us_news-crime_and_courts/ (retrieved December 21, 2010); Ron Sylvester, "Scott Roeder Gets Hard 50 in Murder of Abortion Provider George Tiller," *Wichita Eagle*, April 1, 2010. www.kansas.com/2010/04/01/1249310/roeder-to-be-sentenced-thursday.html (retrieved December 31, 2010); "State Police Support Speeding Ticket for Couple in Labor," *WMUR.com*, January 4, 2011; www.wmur.com/news/26368878/detail.html (retrieved January 10, 2011).

Self-Defense: Protecting Yourself or Your Property When someone is threatened by another person, the threatened individual may be compelled to defend herself with the use of force. A person may claim that she acted in self-defense if she can show that the use of force was absolutely necessary to protect herself or her property.

Three requirements must be satisfied to justify the use of the self-defense claim. The first is that the action against the perceived threat must be necessary; no other less harmful means of dealing with the threat can be reasonably available. For example, in considering available fight-or-flight options, flight must not be possible. Consider a person who is commanded at gunpoint to stay in his car while a stranger enters from the passenger side. After obeying the perpetrator's instructions to drive to the nearest ATM and withdraw money—all under threat of imminent death—once back in the car the victim takes advantage of a moment when the perpetrator is distracted, grabs the gun and shoots his captor. Most states used to require a person who was attacked to flee, rather than fight back, if flight was possible. Recently, however, several states have passed stand-your-ground laws that eliminate this requirement.

The second requirement for an act of self-defense is that it be proportionate to the threat. To defend against the threat, force used by the defendant cannot be significantly greater than the unlawful force threatened or used against the person. Running onto the street in pursuit of someone who has just burglarized your house and then shooting him does not constitute self-defense. The fact that the perpetrator was fleeing removed the imminence of any threat he may have posed inside the house.

The third requirement is that the threat against which the individual is defending himself or herself must be imminent, or immediate. This requirement has prompted much debate. Consider the wife who has been battered by her abusive husband for years and finds the level of his violence increasing. The husband may, for example, threaten her with a knife–something he has never done before. Is it self-defense when she kills him later that night as he sleeps? Traditionally, the answer was no, and the wife would be convicted of murder. In recent years, however, some courts have retreated from the imminence requirement in certain cases.

Entrapment: Being Deceived into Committing a Crime When law enforcement officers or agents trap or trick a person into committing a crime that the person would not otherwise have committed, **entrapment** occurs. The standards for entrapment vary, but generally the defense exists when the defendant had no predisposition to commit the crime–that is, when it seems clear that the person had no preexisting desire to commit the offense until the police persuaded the individual to do so.

When entrapment is alleged, the state has the burden of proving beyond a reasonable doubt that the defendant was not entrapped. Today, the entrapment defense is often viewed as an effort to deter police misconduct.

Entrapment cases typically concern individuals whom authorities already suspect are involved in criminal activity. For example, an undercover police officer may be sitting at a bar to see if any minors will attempt to purchase alcohol. Once the officer sees someone walk up to the bar, order a drink, show a fake ID, and pay for the drink, he is able to offer to buy that person a drink without risking a claim of entrapment. It becomes entrapment if the police officer is in the same bar, sees someone who appears to be under 21 years old, offers to purchase that person an alcoholic beverage, and then, after the person has said yes and consumed the drink, arrests the person for underage drinking. In this case, there is no clear determination that the minor would have purchased or consumed alcohol if the police officer had not offered to purchase it.

Insanity

Although the term's meaning has changed in everyday usage, the legal definition of **insanity** as a defense refers to an individual whose mind was disordered because of defective mental processes at the time of committing a crime. This legal definition is unrelated to the medical community's understanding of mental disorder. Although experts in psychiatry and psychology often contribute their opinions about a defendant's mental status and behavior, the judge or jury ultimately determines whether a defendant was insane at the time of a crime.

Like other criminal defenses, insanity implies diminished or no criminal responsibility based on a lack of mens rea. The underlying principle of the insanity defense has been well established in Anglo-American law for centuries. In the eighteenth century, British courts developed the "wild beast" test, which held a defendant innocent if he was "so bereft of sanity" that he could not

▲ **The Necessity Defense**
A person may claim that he acted in self-defense if he can show that use of force was absolutely necessary to protect himself or his property.

entrapment
A situation in which law enforcement officers or agents trap or trick a person into committing a crime that the person would not otherwise have committed.

insanity
A defense in which the defendant admits committing the criminal act but claims not to be culpable due to mental illness.

Race, Class, Gender

In 2011, the Urban Institute began conducting a three-year study on youth identified as lesbian, gay, bisexual, transgender, and queer or questioning (LGBTQ) and their participation in survival sex while living on the streets in New York City. Prior research studies indicate that anywhere from 2,500 to 4,000 individuals under 21 years of age experience commercial sexual exploitation in New York city alone.[a] However, limited research focuses specifically on the experiences of LGBTQ youth and the unique challenges they face in being homeless. The Urban Institute study focused on a total of 283 youth who participated in in-depth interviews regarding their pathways to engaging in survival sex as they ran from abuse and trauma, poverty, racism, sexism, and homophobia. Participants ranged in age from 13 to 21 years old and identified as male (47 percent), female (36 percent), transgender female (11 percent), transgender male (3 percent), transgender other (2 percent), queer and questioning (0.4 percent), and other (3 percent). The majority represented a racial minority with 37 percent identifying as African American, 22 percent as Latino, and 5 percent as White. In terms of sexual orientation, participants were largely bisexual (37 percent), gay (23 percent), lesbian (15 percent), heterosexual (13 percent), queer and questioning (3 percent), and other (9 percent). More than 75 percent were not enrolled in school, and 48 percent did not graduate high school or obtain a general equivalency diploma. Nearly half (48 percent) lived in a shelter, and 10 percent lived on the streets; the remaining lived in a family or friend's home, with only 9 percent living on their own.

The results of the interviews illustrated youth who experienced harsh discrimination and rejection from their families, as well as society in general. In an attempt to escape these harsh realities, the youth ran away and lived life on the streets. Compounding these challenges was a lack of access to LGBTQ-friendly community services, which further contributed to housing instability, food insecurity, and inadequate health and mental health care. In order to survive, these young people engaged in "survival sex" for money and/or material possessions and entered commercial trade through friends/peers or family (50 percent), solicitation and exploitation (32 percent), their own initiative (20 percent), and other factors (7 percent). Youth typically saw three to six customers each day, most of whom were found on the street (48 percent) or online (40 percent). Youth reported charging $91 to $231 per encounter and largely spent these earnings on food (54 percent) and clothing (36 percent).

Survival sex was dangerous, and youth protected themselves most commonly with knives (36 percent), mace (24 percent), or fists (19 percent). Engaging in survival sex contributed to frequent arrests, accompanied by violence, abuse, and discrimination by law enforcement and while incarcerated. For these youth, life on the street also meant relying on informal peer networks, sharing limited resources, bartering, and resiliency in the face of dangerous circumstances. The youth in this study also noted risks of survival sex including sexually transmitted diseases, pregnancy, drug use, police profiling and stigmatization, and exploitation, but these concerns were also balanced by the need to simply survive life on the streets.[b]

OBSERVE → INVESTIGATE → UNDERSTAND

- Do you think that youth engaging in survival sex should be treated as criminals?
- What role can schools play in identifying at-risk youth?
- What are some strategies to address the issue of youth engaging in survival sex?

SOURCES: [a]Frances Gragg, Ian Petta, Haidee Bernstein, Karla Eisen, and Liz Quinn, *New York Prevalence Study of Commercially Sexually Exploited Children.* (Rensselaer, NY: New York State Office of Children and Family Services, 2007.); Ric Curtis, Karen Terry, Meredith Dank, Kirk Dombrowski, and Bilal Khan, *The Commercial Sexual Exploitation of Children in New York City, Volume 1: The CSEC Population in New York City: Size, Characteristics, and Needs.* Report submitted to the National Institute of Justice, United States Department of Justice, September 2008.

[b]Meredith Dank, Jennifer Yahner, Kuniko Madden, Isela Banuelos, Lilly Yu, Andrea Ritchie, Mitchyll Mora, Brendan Conner. (2015). *Surviving the Streets of New York: Experiences of LGBTQ Youth, YMSM, and YWSW Engaged in Survival Sex,* The Urban Institute (February 25, 2015). www.urban.org/research/publication/surviving-streets-new-york-experiences-lgbtq-youth-ymsm-and-ywsw-engaged-survival-sex/view/full_report (retrieved June 3, 2015).

---

not guilty by reason of insanity (NGRI)

A verdict in which the jury determines that the defendant is not criminally culpable due to mental illness.

understand the consequences of his behavior, "no more than . . . an infant, a brute, or a wild beast."[20]

When a defendant is found **not guilty by reason of insanity (NGRI),** he is acquitted of the criminal charges against him and discharged from the criminal justice system. Instead of being punished, he is generally viewed as needing psychiatric treatment. A well-established body of civil mental health laws for involuntary commitment dictates the terms of the defendant's incarceration in a psychiatric facility. As a patient there, he can be held against his will until such time as he is found to present no danger to himself or to others.

MYTH/REALITY

MYTH: Insanity is a common verdict in criminal courts in the United States.

REALITY: An insanity plea is put forward in less than 1 percent of all felony trials, and of those only 25 percent succeed with a not guilty by reason of insanity verdict. Thus, in 1,000 felony cases, only 10 defendants plead insanity, and of those, fewer than 3 succeed.[21]

Definitions of Insanity The legal system has a long history of considering a person's impaired mental state as part of the defense. In contrast, a popular view outside the judicial system is that a plea of NGRI is little more than a legal dodge for getting away with a crime. To facilitate the judicious application of the insanity defense, the courts have developed a system of definitions, guidelines, and practices that enables them to assess the mental state of a defendant. To evaluate insanity, courts seek to determine whether the defendant had some kind of mental disease or mental defect that was directly involved in commission of the crime.

There is no single legal standard for determining insanity. Three primary rules form the basis of an insanity defense in the United States: the McNaughtan Rule, the Durham Rule, and the American Law Institute Rule (Figure 4-2). The legal standards that define insanity, and that therefore determine criminal responsibility, vary across courts in state and federal jurisdictions and in the military. None of these rules and standards makes reference to any specific mental disorder. And even though a defendant has a specific, serious mental disorder, it does not necessarily mean that the defendant will qualify for a verdict of insanity.

The McNaughtan Rule   By far the most commonly used standard for insanity is the **McNaughtan Rule** or some variation of it. This test was established in 1843 in England, following the acquittal of Daniel McNaughtan for the assassination of the secretary of Sir Robert Peel, the prime minister. McNaughtan was delusional, believing that the government was plotting to kill him. He displayed symptoms consistent with what today we would call paranoid schizophrenia. In response to public outcry denouncing the court's acquittal "by reason of insanity," Queen Victoria convinced the House of Lords to establish standards for the insanity defense. As for McNaughtan, he was transferred to the psychiatric institution popularly known as Bedlam, where he remained incarcerated as a psychiatric patient until his death 20 years later.[22]

The McNaughtan Rule is known as the "right or wrong" test. To be found insane, either (1) the defendant must have had, at the time of the crime, a "defect of reason, from disease of the mind" that rendered him unable to know what he was doing, or (2) if he did know what he was doing, he did not know that it was wrong.[23] Some states have broadened their application of the McNaughtan Rule by including an **irresistible impulse test** to help ascertain whether the defendant's mental disorder rendered him or her incapable of controlling urges to behave in particular ways. Being unable to resist an impulse is, of course, different

McNaughtan Rule
A standard for insanity that asks whether the defendant was unable to know what he or she was doing or to distinguish right from wrong.

irresistible impulse test
A standard for insanity that asks whether the defendant had a mental disease or defect, as a result of which the defendant was unable to control his or her behavior.

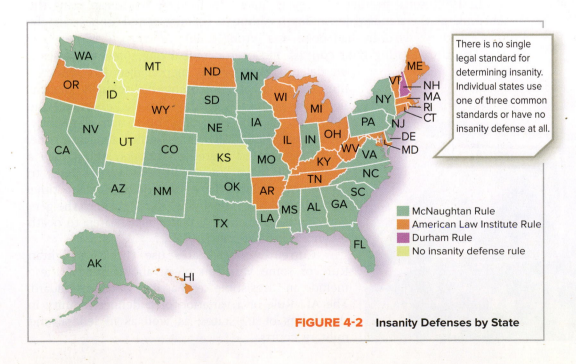

> There is no single legal standard for determining insanity. Individual states use one of three common standards or have no insanity defense at all.

McNaughtan Rule
American Law Institute Rule
Durham Rule
No insanity defense rule

FIGURE 4-2   Insanity Defenses by State

from merely not resisting an impulse. An irresistible impulse is not a matter of choice. The irresistible impulse test thus broadens McNaughtan from being solely a cognitive test of insanity to one that considers behavioral control.

The Durham Rule   From the time he was 17, Monte Durham had been incarcerated in mental and penal institutions many times. As he exhibited signs of serious mental disorder, the hospitalizations generally followed his arrests. In 1953, the 25-year-old Durham was convicted of housebreaking in Washington, DC. His unsuccessful defense had been that he was of "unsound mind." On appeal to the District of Columbia Federal Court of Appeals in 1954, Durham's conviction was overturned. The court argued that the McNaughtan standard was outdated in view of the growing body of psychiatric knowledge about mental disorders and disease.

Durham Rule
A standard for insanity that asks whether the defendant's conduct was the product of a mental disease or defect.

Under the **Durham Rule,** "an accused is not criminally responsible if his unlawful act was the product of mental disease or mental defect." The Durham Rule recognized mental illness as a disease that could be treated, if not cured.[24] The rule, however, quickly fell from favor due to its vagueness in defining mental disease. Many feared that the rule would be used to exonerate criminals who could cite their "mental diseases" of alcoholism, drug addiction, and compulsive gambling as the underlying cause of their criminal behavior. There also was discomfort with the amount of influence the Durham Rule gave psychiatrists and psychologists in the courtroom. Eventually the federal courts rejected the Durham Rule as too broad a standard. Nonetheless, today, one state (New Hampshire) continues to use it to determine insanity.

The American Law Institute Rule: The Substantial Capacity Test   In 1962, the American Law Institute (ALI) offered a new rule for defining insanity in its Model Penal Code. The **American Law Institute Rule (ALI Rule)** required that the defendant have a mental disease or defect that causes him to lack "substantial capacity either to appreciate the criminality of his conduct or to conform his conduct to the requirements of the law."[25] Some scholars considered this test an improvement over the McNaughtan Rule because it permitted the defense for those who were severely affected by mental illness and yet still able to understand to a limited extent what they were doing when they committed the crime. However, it was not nearly as broad a rule as Durham.

American Law Institute Rule (ALI Rule)
A standard for insanity that asks whether the defendant lacked substantial capacity to appreciate the criminality of the act or conform to the law.

In 1992, serial murderer Jeffrey Dahmer was tried in Wisconsin using the ALI Rule as the standard for insanity. Although Dahmer stated, unhesitatingly, that he knew what he had done was wrong–killing 17 men, dismembering and sexually violating their corpses, and even cannibalizing some–the basis of his defense was that his mental disorders rendered him incapable of controlling his sexually deviant urges. His plea was "guilty but insane," essentially the same as a plea of not guilty by reason of insanity. Although Dahmer was found guilty and thus sane, his trial generated heated controversy about how a person could have done what he admitted doing to his victims and not have been insane at the time. Sentenced to life imprisonment and put into the general prison population, Dahmer was beaten to death by another inmate in 1994.

▼ **John Hinckley Jr.**

Hinckley (in back seat of car), who shot President Ronald Reagan in 1982, was found not guilty by reason of insanity; he is still confined to a psychiatric facility, although he has been granted passes home for longer stretches of time each month.

Currently most states use the McNaughtan Rule or some variation of it; about half of these include an "irresistible test" as part of their standard. The ALI Rule or a variation of it defines insanity in the courts of 19 states, as well as in federal and military courts.

KEY CONCEPTS   Definitions of Insanity

Standard	Definition
McNaughtan Rule	Unable to know the nature and quality of the act as being wrong, or unable to distinguish right from wrong
Irresistible impulse test	Unable to control impulses
Durham Rule	Behavior is a product of mental disease or defect
American Law Institute Rule (ALI Rule)	Unable to substantially appreciate criminality of act or conform to the law

Four states no longer provide a court definition of insanity. This was a direct result of the acquittal of John Hinckley Jr. in 1982 for the attempted assassination of President Ronald Reagan. In the shooting, Reagan was seriously wounded, and his press secretary received a head wound that resulted in permanent brain damage. Hinckley was found not guilty by reason of insanity, a verdict that outraged many and caused a series of reforms to insanity laws around the country. Yet even with a decision of not guilty by reason of insanity, Hinckley has been under federal supervision for a very long time and is still confined to a Washington, DC, psychiatric facility. Because Hinckley's mental illness has been found to be in remission, a federal court has allowed him progressively longer unsupervised visits home to his mother each month.[26]

In addition to the passage of the Insanity Defense Reform Act in 1984, which made it more difficult to prove insanity in federal cases, many individual states changed their rules to make it more difficult to do the same. Some states went so far as to abolish the insanity defense altogether. Currently, Utah, Montana, Idaho, and Kansas have no legal provision for an insanity defense. In these states, unlike those where the defense has the burden of proving insanity, the prosecution bears the burden of proving the defendant had mens rea at the time of the crime. Although Nevada abolished its insanity defense in 1995, the Nevada Supreme Court later ruled (in 2001) that the elimination of the insanity defense violated the state's constitution.

The movement toward eliminating the insanity defense or requiring adherence to stricter standards for measuring insanity marks a trend in the courts to hold individuals more fully accountable for their criminal actions. Still, a growing body of scientific evidence reveals that many mental disorders have a biological rather than behavioral cause. It will be interesting to monitor the clash of these opposing points of view as the post-Hinckley debate over the insanity defense continues to develop.

Guilty but Mentally Ill   The **guilty but mentally ill (GBMI)** verdict, introduced in 1975, was intended as a compromise between acquitting a defendant who is mentally disordered as NGRI and finding the person guilty. A person found GBMI (or guilty but insane, GBI, as it is known in some jurisdictions) is recognized to be mentally ill but is still considered criminally responsible for the crime. The mental illness grants the person the right to psychiatric treatment during incarceration. Should the mental disorder be effectively treated prior to the end of the term of the sentence, the individual will nonetheless be required to complete whatever time remains in a regular correctional institution.

guilty but mentally ill (GBMI)
Verdict for a person recognized to be mentally ill but still considered criminally responsible for the crime.

In courts that provide the option of a GBMI verdict, the jury has the power to decide if a defendant is mentally ill but not insane, making the person responsible for the crime. This alternative might appear to dispel concerns that a defendant "got away with" the crime, notwithstanding the mental illness. But how can a person be found guilty of a crime for which he or she lacks the requisite mens rea? The availability of a GBMI verdict has not reduced the number of insanity acquittals, nor has it resulted in longer periods of confinement of offenders who are determined to be mentally ill and dangerous.[27] Currently, more than 20 states have enacted laws providing for the GBMI verdict.

Although the insanity defense is hardly a recent invention, it continues to be a matter of frequent and lively debate. The trend in the 1950s and 1960s was to make the defense more widely available, but that trend sharply reversed in the 1980s and 1990s. It remains to be seen what will become of the defense in the twenty-first century.

Other Defenses

Another commonly recognized defense is that of **infancy** (the name dates back to medieval England). This defense sometimes protects very young offenders (those under the age of 7) from criminal consequences. Traditionally, those between 7 and 14 were also presumed incapable of forming the mens rea necessary for criminal liability. This presumption could be overcome, however, by evidence that a particular child knew what he or she was doing. The premise was that children should not be held responsible for acts when they cannot fully comprehend the nature or consequences of them. Chapter 15 discusses the infancy defense in more detail.

In addition to the defenses we have examined, most jurisdictions recognize a variety of others. For example, under some circumstances a defendant may escape criminal liability if the victim actually gave the defendant permission to engage in the prohibited acts; this defense is called **consent.** For example, a boxer who hits his opponent during a match, or a football player who tackles another player, will normally not be convicted of battery. However, if the scope of the attack exceeds what is considered acceptable within the rules of the game, a jury might conclude that the victim did not consent to the violence, and the attacking player might still be convicted. National Hockey League players Marty McSorley, Todd Bertuzzi, and Dino Ciccarelli all received criminal convictions for such attacks on opposing players.[28]

infancy
A defense that sometimes protects very young offenders from criminal liability because they do not understand the consequences of their actions.

consent
A defense against criminal liability because the victim actually gave the defendant permission to engage in the prohibited acts.

SUMMARY

The rule of law means that the state must exercise its power to coerce and punish within strict bounds. Laws must be written according to established procedures, and no government official is supposed to be above the law. These basic concepts have defined law-abiding societies for thousands of years, ever since ancient Babylonia. Roman law is the basis of the legal codes of contemporary continental Europe and many other countries, and medieval England's common law is the foundation of modern English and American law. Other sources of law in the United States are the federal and state constitutions, the body of case law (judges' decisions in prior cases), administrative regulations, and international treaties.

Most legal systems differentiate between civil and criminal law. In the United States, society (that is, the state), and not the individual, is considered to be injured by criminal acts, and a government prosecutor alone decides whether to bring a criminal case. Criminal defendants can be found "guilty" or "not guilty" (rather than liable for civil damages); they are afforded certain rights not granted to civil litigants; they can be fined, imprisoned, or executed if found guilty; and the standards of proof are higher in criminal than in civil cases.

Depending on their seriousness, criminal law offenses in the United States are classified as felonies, misdemeanors, and infractions. To be convicted of any of these, the state usually must show that actus reus (guilty act) and mens rea (criminal intent) coincided. Different "degrees" of mens rea affect the severity with which an offense is punished. Some acts—so-called strict liability offenses—are defined as criminal regardless of intent (for example, having sex with a minor), and some acts that are intended but not completed (such as conspiracy to commit an illegal action) can also incur criminal consequences.

For those accused of breaking the criminal law, a number of valid defenses are available in the United States. These are mistake of fact (about the facts of the case, not about the law itself), severe intoxication, duress, necessity, self-defense, entrapment (by a law enforcement officer), and insanity. The common element in all these defenses is the absence of mens rea, or criminal intent.

OBSERVE → INVESTIGATE → UNDERSTAND

Review

Explain the rule of law.
- Offenders can be punished only by written laws.
- The laws must be created through an established process.
- Nobody is supposed to be above the law.

Provide a short history of lawmaking.
- Early societies relied on unwritten social norms.
- One of the earliest known records of written laws dates from the rule of Babylonian king Hammurabi (reigned 1792–1750 BCE).
- England created the common law system after 1066.
- American colonists borrowed from the English system but made many changes and adaptations.

Identify modern sources of laws in the United States.
- Federal and state constitutions
- Federal and state statutes
- Local ordinances
- Federal and state case law
- Administrative regulations
- International treaties and compacts

Examine the key elements of civil and criminal law.
- Civil law deals with issues between individuals.
- An injured party can bring a civil lawsuit against another person or organization.
- In civil cases, the losing party pays damages directly to the injured parties.
- Civil defendants are found "liable."
- Victims have more rights in civil cases than in criminal cases.
- Criminal law focuses on injuries to society as a whole rather than to individuals.
- Criminal cases can be brought only by the government.

- A criminal defendant may be ordered to pay fines, may be incarcerated, or sometimes could even be put to death.
- Criminal defendants have more rights than civil defendants.
- The standard of proof is higher in criminal cases than in civil cases.

Define the three types of criminal offenses.
- Felonies can be punished by state or federal prison for more than a year, and sometimes by death.
- Misdemeanors can be punished by probation, fines, and/or up to a year in local jail.
- Infractions or violations can be punished only by fines or community service.

Describe the legal elements of a crime.
- The corpus delicti of a crime (literally "the body of the offense") refers to the particular elements required in order for prosecutors to establish that a crime was indeed committed.
- Actus reus is the guilty or illegal act of a crime; it is the first of the two key elements required for determining criminal liability.
- Mens rea is the criminal intent relative to the mental state of the defendant at the time of a crime; it is the second of the two key elements required for determining criminal liability.

Explain common criminal defenses allowed by the court.
- The mistake of fact defense argues that a mistake related to a fact of the crime may have affected the state of mind of the defendant who otherwise had no criminal intent.
- The intoxication defense argues that a person was so intoxicated that he could not control the mental state required for a particular crime.
- The duress defense argues that a person was forced to commit a crime because failure to do so would result in more serious harm.
- The necessity defense is used when, under extreme circumstances, a person cannot avoid committing a criminal act.

- Self-defense can be argued when a person is threatened by another and is compelled to protect herself or her property.
- The entrapment defense is used when a person is deceived by law enforcement officials into committing a crime that he would not otherwise have committed.
- The insanity defense applies to an individual whose behavior was affected by defective mental processes at the time of committing a crime.

Explore aspects of the insanity defense.

- Successful insanity defenses require defendants to have had a mental disease or defect that affected their behavior at the time of the crime.

- The McNaughtan Rule is a cognitive test that requires defendants to have known right from wrong when they committed their crimes.
- The Durham Rule defines insanity broadly as the product of a mental disease or defect that affected the defendant's behavior at the time of the crime.
- The American Law Institute (ALI) Rule requires that defendants lacked substantial mental capacity to appreciate the wrongfulness of their behavior or could not stop themselves because of the mental problem.

Key Terms

actus reus 121
American Law Institute Rule (ALI Rule) 132
case law 114
civil law 115
common law 113
consent 134
constitution 114
corpus delicti 120
criminal intent 120
criminal law 115
damages 115
defendant 115
double jeopardy 117

duress 126
Durham Rule 132
entrapment 129
felony 119
guilty but mentally ill (GBMI) 133
Hammurabi's Code 112
inchoate crimes 123
infancy 134
infraction 119
insanity 129
irresistible impulse test 131
laws 112
McNaughtan Rule 131

mens rea 121
misdemeanor 119
Model Penal Code 114
necessity 127
not guilty by reason of insanity (NGRI) 130
ordinances 114
plaintiff 115
precedent 113
restitution 118
rule of law 110
statutes 114
strict liability offenses 123
torts 115

Study Questions

1. Hammurabi's Code was
   a. one of the earliest written systems of laws.
   b. a famous case involving shipwrecked sailors.
   c. a law intended to reduce copyright piracy.
   d. a standard for proving insanity.

2. All of the following are sources of law in the United States *except*
   a. constitutions.
   b. presidential decree.
   c. statutes.
   d. case law.

3. One important distinction between civil and criminal cases is that
   a. only criminal cases involve injuries to a victim.
   b. only criminal cases use juries.
   c. only in civil cases must the losing party pay money.
   d. only in criminal cases can the losing party be incarcerated.

4. A criminal offense that may result in incarceration in prison for more than a year is called a(n)
   a. felony.

   b. misdemeanor.
   c. infraction.
   d. violation.

5. The specific unlawful act that must be proved to convict someone of a crime is called the
   a. mens rea.
   b. actus reus.
   c. corpus delicti.
   d. final straw.

6. An inchoate offense is
   a. a crime that is punishable only by fines.
   b. a crime committed by a juvenile.
   c. an act illegal only under common law.
   d. a crime that was begun but not completed.

7. The main purpose of a criminal trial is to
   a. establish whether the defendant was insane.
   b. determine criminal responsibility.
   c. establish whether the defendant committed a crime.
   d. establish justice.

8. The best defense for a person who would not otherwise have committed a crime, but who was persuaded to do so by a police officer, is
   a. insanity.
   b. entrapment.
   c. necessity.
   d. mistake.

9. The percentage of felony criminal cases that involve an insanity plea is
   a. 1 percent.
   b. 25 percent.

   c. 50 percent.
   d. 75 percent.

10. In legal terms, insanity is considered a serious mental disorder.
    a. true
    b. false

Critical Thinking Questions

For further review, go to the LearnSmart study module for this chapter.

1. What are the advantages and disadvantages of having a formal, written system of laws, as opposed to relying on unwritten social and cultural norms?

2. Under what circumstances should a person who commits an unlawful act be excused from criminal responsibility for that act?

3. How do you think a prosecutor should go about proving mens rea in a case?

5 Overview of Policing

After reading this chapter, you should be able to:

- Identify the distinguishing characteristics of policing.
- Trace the evolution of policing in the United States.
- Describe the structure of law enforcement.
- Recognize how recruitment, selection, and training affect quality of service.
- Describe the dynamics of the police subculture.
- Contrast the positives and negatives in the use of police discretion.
- Distinguish between corruption and abuse of authority.
- Examine the extent and functions of private security agencies.

Realities and Challenges

The Power of Community Partnerships

The Chelsea, Massachusetts, Police Department and nonprofit Roca, a youth social services agency, illustrate the power of community partnerships in addressing youth crime. At night, Roca youth volunteers contact high-risk young people to see how they are doing, encouraging them to take part in Roca programs and look for productive work. In 2011, at the request of his chief, Lieutenant Conley of the Chelsea Police Department started

to join them. He notes, "Prior to November, I was a sergeant and I ran the drug unit here in Chelsea. So I came out of a real direct-action, kick-down-doors, lock-em-up mentality." Conley was happily surprised to see how effective Roca's efforts were. "When I got to understand the model and see what the youth workers do, see how the youth workers approach kids, how the program tracks clients and tracks data on those clients, it's like nothing else I've ever seen," he said.[1]

Roca's high-risk-intervention program consists of three phases. Phase 1 creates close relationships between the youth and Roca staff and volunteers. This often starts with the outreach done on the streets or a one-time drop-in to Roca's programming. Phase 2 offers education, life skills groups, job development programming, and recognition certifications. Phase 3 assists with employment opportunities and educational attainment, such as earning a GED. Of the young people participating in Phase 3, 98 percent had no new arrests, and almost 80 percent have kept jobs. These results are extremely encouraging given that Roca's target populations are gang-related youth (68 percent) and high school dropouts (48 percent). Roca began as a Boston area–based nonprofit and now has become a model for youth intervention.[2]

As we review the history of U.S. policing in this chapter, you will notice that policing has moved toward a community policing model in which police officers partner strategically with community groups, not only to respond to crime, but also to prevent it. The Chelsea Police Department–Roca partnership is a good example of such successful innovation.

In this chapter we examine how policing in the United States has evolved to its current form. Among other things, we review the recruitment, selection, and training of law enforcement officers.

This chapter also probes into the realities of policing. We first look into how society defines policing and then briefly trace policing history. We analyze the structure of U.S. policing at the local, state, and federal levels and review the consequences for the public of that fragmentation of authority. As noted above, we explain how officers are recruited, selected, and trained. Further, we investigate how the police subculture can influence officers while on the job. Finally, we consider the great degree of discretion officers have—and examine what happens when they abuse their power.

DEFINING POLICING

Since the mid-1900s, the terms *law enforcement* and *policing* have been used synonymously. Most people would say the police are those given the task of enforcing the law, and the most common image of police is as crime fighters.

Most of what police officers do on a daily basis, however, has little to do with directly enforcing the law. We call on the police to perform a variety of tasks even when no law has been broken. For example, police direct drivers when traffic lights are out, respond to calls about neighbors' disagreements over property lines, and deal with individuals who are mentally ill. The way we define policing influences both how the public views the police and how officers view their own jobs.

Individuals bestowed with policing powers were not always charged with enforcing the law. In the past, for example, police officers were expected to enforce not the law but the will of those with political power. Today, the rise of private police forces such as Triple Canopy, provider of security across the globe, has led some to question whether these private forces should be included under the umbrella of law enforcement. A key question is, what distinguishes the police from others? In other words, what makes the police the police? If we consider everything police do and the myriad reasons citizens call upon them for assistance, the best definition is that police officers are individuals to whom society has granted the power to use physical force when they deem it necessary or appropriate.[3]

Why do people call the police? Only 19 percent of calls to police relate to a crime of any kind,[4] and an officer typically spends only 10 to 15 percent of patrol time on crime-related activities.[5] Clearly, this percentage of time is much less than that portrayed on television series. Society has identified local police officers as the people residents should call when they need immediate assistance. We often call them because we do not know where else to turn, and we believe officers can make other people do what should be done. That power comes from officers' authority to use force.[6]

Police officers and criminal justice professionals are a product of their environment, and the ethnic and racial tensions and alliances found in society at large exist in policing as well. Consider, for example, the emigrants from Ireland who came to the United States in the mid-nineteenth century. Those in power often regarded the Irish immigrants as violent troublemakers. Hence, they frequently came into conflict with the police, who were responding to what individuals in power wanted them to do.[7] In time, however, the Irish gained political power and served in public positions–including in the police force. As the evolving relationship between the police and the Irish demonstrates, police reflect the broader society.

HISTORY OF POLICING IN THE UNITED STATES

One key to understanding the present is to learn about the past. Knowing something about the various influences on the shaping of the police in the United States helps us appreciate the present-day challenges of policing and understand why some groups of people distrust law enforcement officers.

Vigilantism: Policing by Self-Appointed Committees

A great deal of police activity existed before the development of well-organized, big-city police departments. If we think of the police as individuals authorized by a community to use force, then we can consider vigilantism as very much a part of the history of policing in the United States. **Vigilantism** is the use of volunteer, self-appointed committees organized to suppress crime and punish criminals. Vigilantes were local residents who organized themselves to apprehend and punish those they considered outlaws. Vigilantism flourished from the mid-1700s to about 1900, years when the rapid spread of settlement throughout the country outpaced the establishment of formal law enforcement in new communities. Although vigilantism started in the East, it became much more common in the West as a means of regulating behavior and enforcing U.S. society's developing cultural norms.[8]

Our modern image of vigilantes is that of a group of people outraged by some heinous offense who spontaneously spring into action to catch and

vigilantism
Use of volunteer, self-appointed committees organized to suppress crime and punish criminals.

▶ **Today's Minutemen**

The Baldknobbers were a group of vigilantes in Missouri with estimates of 500 to 1,000 members in the 1880s. This image is from a reenactment.

punish the offender. Vigilante movements of the past, however, were quite different. They were well-organized, quasi-military groups of 100 or more participants who were the elites of their community. Many vigilante groups even had constitutions or manifestos to explain their rules and means of operation. Vigilantes often hanged those they apprehended, and between 1767 and 1900 they killed more than 700 people. Suspects' crimes included horse theft, counterfeiting, and offenses against the newly established private property system, which created haves and have-nots in the developing West. Vigilantism is an example of how the police (in this case, self-appointed police) historically enforced social norms rather than laws.[9]

The West was not, however, without formal law enforcement. One of the most effective and ethical law enforcement officers of the Old West was Bass Reeves, who was appointed U.S. Deputy Marshal in 1875 to curb lawlessness in the Indian Territory (the eastern portion of present-day Oklahoma). You can read a brief summary of Reeves's highly successful career in the "Race, Class, Gender" box.

Slave Patrols: Capturing Fugitives

The first publicly funded city police departments in the United States were slave patrols created to keep slaves from rebelling or running away.[10] In South Carolina, for example, mounted daytime slave patrols were formed in the 1740s.[11] Moreover, one of the primary duties of the Texas Rangers, the forerunner of organized state police forces, was retrieving runaway slaves.[12] Slave patrols were also created out of fear the state militia would be unable to control slave rebellions.[13]

Slavery was not just an accepted practice in the United States in bygone years; it was a legally protected institution. Local governments passed a variety of laws giving Whites the power to control African Americans. These *slave codes* varied from place to place, but they generally required slaves to have passes any time they left their owner's land, forbade more than a few slaves to congregate at any one time, prohibited their education, and required the return of slaves to their "owners."[14] Police were required to uphold these laws, whether or not they agreed with them. Even if a Texas Ranger, for example, was opposed to slavery, a primary responsibility of his job was to retrieve runaway slaves. After the Civil War, the former Confederate states enacted *Black codes* to ensure that the former slaves remained under the control of the White majority. The Black codes required that individuals could marry only

Race, Class, Gender

Bass Reeves: African American Deputy Marshal of the Old West

Bass Reeves was born in 1834 in Paris, Texas, to enslaved parents. After a fight with the individual who "owned" him, Reeves escaped and lived with American Indian tribes until 1863. He then became a successful stockman and farmer in Arkansas and Oklahoma.

In 1875, a new judge appointed to the Federal Western District Court at Fort Smith, Arkansas, was given the responsibility of curbing lawlessness by White settlers in the Indian Territory (in present-day Oklahoma). The judge responded by appointing African American deputies to round up White outlaws and work with the tribes. Reeves, who could speak some tribal languages and knew the land, was an especially good candidate for the job.

Reeves had never learned to read or write because educating slaves was against the law, so he had to rely on others to read arrest warrants to him. In his 32 years as a deputy, Reeves earned a reputation as being able to capture any criminal. He once even served a warrant of arrest on his own son after pursuing him for two weeks. The son was convicted of killing his wife but was eventually issued a full pardon. Over the course of his career, Reeves killed 14 men. He claimed to have fired his weapon only in self-defense and was found to have acted properly each time.

In 1907, at the age of 69, Reeves became a city police officer in Muskogee, Oklahoma, and served until 1909. He died the following year. His obituary in the *Muskogee Phoenix* noted, "Reeves had many narrow escapes. At different times his belt was shot in two, a button shot off his coat, his hat brim shot off, and the bridle reins which he held in his hands cut by a bullet."

The story of Bass Reeves reveals a history less often told: that the faces of those who tamed the Wild West were not all White. In fact, the federal judge who hired Reeves also hired several other African American deputies. African American men like Reeves paved the way for others like them to pursue a career in law enforcement.

OBSERVE → INVESTIGATE → UNDERSTAND

- What reasons might the judge who appointed Reeves have had for appointing African American deputies to pursue White outlaws in the Indian Territory?
- What challenges would Reeves, as an African American man, have faced in pursuing and apprehending White criminals?
- How do the history of the taming of the West and the actions of men like Reeves affect policing today?

SOURCES: For more information see Art Burton, *Black Gun, Silver Star: The Life and Legend of Frontier Marshal Bass Reeves* (Lincoln: University of Nebraska Press, 2006); see also Gary Paulsen, *The Legend of Bass Reeves* (New York: Bantam Doubleday Dell, 2008).

---

someone of their own racial background, outlined who could hold property (Whites), and included laws against vagrancy to force freed African Americans to work on White-owned farms.[15]

Early vigilantism and slave patrols demonstrate that police-type agencies were created to protect individuals in power by controlling those without it.[16] This historical development sowed resentment toward the police among some groups.

The English Model

Rapid settlement of the U.S. West and the institution of slavery influenced the development of policing in the United States, but so too did events in England. The tireless efforts of Sir Robert Peel, British home secretary, to establish a disciplined and organized police force to battle the turmoil and crime in London led to the creation of the London Metropolitan Police Department in 1829. Peel structured the London Metropolitan Police on a quasi-military model with clear hierarchical ranks of command including sergeants, lieutenants, and captains. The officers—called "bobbies" after Sir Robert—wore uniforms that made them easily identifiable. As in the military, lower ranks were required to follow the orders of their superiors. Because of public concern about potential threats to civil liberties, however, London police were given limited authority, meaning that their powers and duties were specified in law, and their primary orientation was toward crime prevention.

frankpledge system
Peacekeeping system in early England in which a group of 10 local families agreed to maintain the peace and make sure lawbreakers were taken into custody and brought to court.

watch system
Peacekeeping system in which particular men were assigned the job of watchman and became responsible for patrolling the streets, lighting lanterns, serving as a lookout for fires, and generally keeping order.

preventive patrol
Officers' maintenance of a visible presence in communities to serve as a deterrent to a variety of street-level crimes.

Before the advent of Peel's reforms, keeping peace in England had occurred at the local level. In the **frankpledge system,** which developed in England before the eighteenth century, 10 families in a community agreed to maintain the peace in their area and make sure lawbreakers were taken into custody and brought to court. In time the frankpledge system gave way to the **watch system,** in which particular men were assigned to be watchmen and were responsible for patrolling the streets, lighting lanterns, serving as a lookout for fires, and generally keeping order. Maintaining peace, then, was first seen as a local affair. As policing developed in England and then in the United States, police departments continued to be controlled by local government. This decentralized system had both positive and negative consequences, as we'll see later in this chapter.

Early police departments in the United States adopted the same mission as the London police: to stop crime through **preventive patrol.** To accomplish this goal, officers patrolled the streets, maintaining a visible presence in the community.[17] Preventive patrol remains a large part of police activities today.

Yet the United States of the 1800s was very different from the England of that era, and the police forces of the two countries differed in some significant ways. The police in New York City, for example, tended to gain their legitimacy–the public's trust in them–by being of the people. That is, they were usually of the same ethnic background as those they policed, so they were able to develop personal relationships with the public. Because there was little ethnic diversity in London, matching the ethnic backgrounds of police to citizens was not a concern. English bobbies established their authority as members of an impersonal independent agency, whereas New York City officers got their legitimacy from their personal relationships with residents and the political connections they made.[18]

Political Era: Patronage-Based Policing

The political era of policing in the United States began with the creation of organized police departments in the nation's major cities in the 1840s and lasted until the early 1920s. During this period, local political bosses selected members of their party to be police officers as a reward for party loyalty. In this patronage system, it was *whom* the police knew, rather than *what* they knew, that was important. In fact, there wasn't much police officers were actually expected to know. During this era, police were not thought of primarily as law enforcers. Instead, their role was to control undesirable immigrants, maintain order, and provide a variety of social services not otherwise available to the poor or needy, such as housing the homeless.[19]

Officers received little if any training, and the use of force was fairly common. Holding facilities were generally located far from where an officer was likely to confront a suspect. Rather than bringing a suspect to department headquarters, officers often practiced "street justice" by physically punishing the suspect on the spot.

Professional Era: The Police as Law Enforcers

The professional (or reform) era of policing, which spanned the late 1920s through the late 1970s, sought to rectify the many problems of the political era. During the 1920s, major reforms swept *all* levels of American government. Progressive reformers created formalized hierarchical government agencies, or bureaucracies, to increase specialization, reward merit, and decrease corruption.

Progressives wanted government bureaucrats, including the police, to be free of political influence. Critical of the partisan politics that characterized police departments, they advocated hiring people for government positions on the basis of merit and thoroughly training them. Progressives also embraced science and believed that research could increase the efficiency of government operations, including law enforcement. Changing technology, such as the increased availability of telephone service, also had an impact on everyday policing. The early reformers believed change would fundamentally improve policing and its effectiveness. But like all reforms, the professional era had both positive and negative outcomes.

August Vollmer (1876-1955), the first police chief of Berkeley, California, was appointed to that position in 1909 and held it until 1932. An early reformer who had a great impact on the history of policing, Vollmer believed in hiring individuals with a broad-based education. He advocated using science to solve crimes and created *modus operandi* ("modes of operation") *files* to connect offenses of similar types systematically–a key element in modern investigative profiling. Perhaps his greatest innovation came in 1908 when he created a police school to train officers. In 1914, Vollmer oversaw the first completely mobile force, in which all officers used automobiles for transportation. Vollmer's ideas about policing and the innovations he instituted in Berkeley served as an example to other departments across the country.[20]

▲ **August Vollmer**
In the early twentieth century, Vollmer was a leading innovator in law enforcement.

During the professional era, law enforcement emerged as the primary function of police officers. The Uniform Crime Reports (UCR) (see Chapter 2), which began in this era, assessed police departments based on reported crimes in their jurisdictions and their rates of solving them. Such developments focused departments' efforts on law enforcement, as police chiefs knew they would be judged on their ability to catch criminals. The development of the 9-1-1 system during this era is also indicative of the emphasis on law enforcement. The idea behind the system was that citizens would report crimes by calling 9-1-1, and officers would quickly respond–and perhaps even catch perpetrators in the act.

The professional era of policing had many positive outcomes. Political control over officer hiring and firing was eliminated, and entrance to the force was based on merit. Officers were expected to police all residents evenly without political favoritism. Training for new officers became much more systematic. Pay for officers and resources for departments increased, both because the mission of the police became more professionalized and articulated and because newly created police unions successfully pressed for salary increases.

The professional era had some negative outcomes as well. By the time of the civil rights movement and anti–Vietnam War protests of the 1960s, officers had grown distant from their communities. Protesters and police clashed, sometimes violently. The confrontations of the 1960s also exposed the troubled relationship between Blacks and the police. The definition of police officers as primarily law enforcers created an atmosphere in which some people saw the police as an occupying force in their neighborhood rather than as public servants. "A Case in Point" on page 146 illustrates that problems of strained relations persist today.

Changes in technology also increased the distance between officers and citizens. Instead of patrolling on foot, police rode in department automobiles, dispatched through a central radio call system. The telephone also changed the way the public contacted police. By the mid-1970s, residents were being advised to call the police only on crime-related matters, and patrol officers and the public interacted only when residents had problems to report.

MYTH/REALITY

MYTH: Putting police officers in radio-equipped vehicles proved to be of substantial benefit in helping the police get a finger on the public's pulse.

REALITY: Patrolling the streets from within the isolating confines of a radio-equipped car distanced the police from the people they served.[21]

Conflict with Occupy Wall Street Protestors

The Occupy Wall Street movement began on September 17, 2011, in New York City's Zuccotti Park. Protestors had hoped to be closer to Wall Street, but police, anticipating their arrival, had fenced off the area. Zuccotti Park was left unfenced partly because it was privately owned. New York City police were suddenly faced with the responsibility of containing thousands of protestors.

Although their objectives were often considered nebulous, the Occupy Wall Street protestors were largely opposed to corporate bailouts and economic inequality in the United States. It was through their efforts that the slogan "We are the 99%" first garnered widespread media attention. The protestors occupied Zuccotti Park until they were removed by police on November 15, 2011.

In the meantime, the movement spread to 1,500 other cities. In some places, protestors turned violent. In some places, police did. Oakland, California, saw perhaps the greatest tragedy. The Oakland Police Department has been under external monitoring since 2003, when it was revealed that several officers were routinely abusing their power and violating use-of-force policies. According to a report from an outside monitor, an Oakland Police SWAT officer fired a beanbag at the head of Scott Olsen, critically injuring him. Over 1,000 complaints of police misconduct were filed during the Occupy protests in Oakland. The police monitor wrote of being very pleased with the behavior of Oakland officers in some instances and "dismayed" in others.

OBSERVE➔INVESTIGATE➔UNDERSTAND

- How can police balance protestors' right to assembly with non-protestors' desire to freely go about their regular business?
- What should trigger police use of force in protest situations?
- What consequences should officers face when they do not follow use-of-force policies?

SOURCES: Mary Slosson, "Oakland Police Still Handling Fallout over Treatment of Occupy Movement." *Reuters,* October 12, 2012. www.reuters.com/assets/print?aid=USBRE89C00820121013 (retrieved February 3, 2013); Bill Chappell, "Occupy Wall Street: From Blog Post to a Movement." *NPR,* October 20, 2011. www.npr.org/2011/10/20/141530025/occupy-wall-street-from-a-blog-post-to-a-movement (retrieved February 3, 2013); Mary Slosson, "Occupy Wall Street: Report Criticizes Police Response to Oakland Protests in 2010." *Reuters,* May 1, 2012. www.huffingtonpost.com/2012/05/01/occupy-wall-street-oakland-violence_n_1466436.html (retrieved February 3, 2013).

Another negative consequence of professionalization was the decrease in the number of minority officers hired as departments implemented educational and test requirements. People of color who had been making steady progress in entering police forces were less likely to have the education required, partly because they were often denied access to education for much of this time period. As a result, the police forces that policed multicultural urban centers were largely White, male, and suburban.[22]

Despite the reforms of the professional era, crime increased. Individuals within and outside the profession of policing began to ask why the changes had not reduced crime. The realization that many policing strategies were proving to be ineffective led to the development of community policing, which focuses on developing positive relationships between the police and the public they serve.

Community Policing Era: Working for—and with—the Public

During the 1970s, U.S. reformers came to believe that if the police were to have any impact on crime, they would need the full cooperation of the people in the communities they served. Yet at the same time, these reformers recognized that the relationship between the police and the public was strained. Consequently, they began to advocate fundamental changes in the way police interact with members of their communities. Whereas policing in the professional era focused solely on solving crimes, **community policing** emphasizes crime prevention and the development of positive relationships between the police and the public (see Chapter 6). Community policing uses two main strategies: deploying officers on foot patrol in the community and engaging residents in the work of policing. The goal is to stop crimes before they occur.

The most fundamental change in the era of community policing, which began in the late 1970s and continues today, concerns the way the police view the public and the relationship between the police and the public. Officers are now expected to cultivate positive relationships with individuals in the communities they serve, and with neighborhood organizations such as the Boys & Girls Club and Neighborhood Watch, in order to include the public in crime prevention and enforcement. Officers attend local meetings and ask residents what they would like to have happen in their communities. Are there particular areas on which residents would like police resources to focus? What problems would they like to see addressed? In community policing, officers are given greater discretion to address these problems.

Increased communication is the key to improving relations between police and the public. If police are to rely on residents to help them solve crimes and resolve problems, community members must feel positive about their local officers. Indeed, one of the strongest factors in solving a crime is the ability and willingness of a victim, complainant, or witness to work with police to identify a suspect.[23] Community policing increases time demands on officers–time to interact with residents, time to attend community meetings, and time to investigate neighborhood problems. Because the public still expects police to answer calls for service, some officers are designated exclusively as community policing officers and either are relieved of responding to calls for service or respond only to those in their assigned neighborhood.

Another major change in the community policing era was the shift toward *proactive* rather than *reactive* police work. *Proactive policing* aims to prevent crime not just through the threat of capture but also through the elimination of the presumed causes of crime, such as disorder in a community. To accomplish this goal, police officers deal with lifestyle issues such as public drunkenness, vandalism, loitering, and other minor offenses that reduce the quality of life.

The community policing era continues today. We will examine community policing as a policing strategy in greater detail in Chapter 6. There we will also assess the effectiveness of community policing and review critiques of this policing strategy.

History often is presented as falling into neatly defined, distinct categories, but change takes place gradually. Characteristics of any one era may overlap with the next. The Key Concepts feature on page 148 summarizes the different policing eras and illustrates that overlap.

STRUCTURE OF THE LAW ENFORCEMENT SYSTEM

We have seen that policing in the United States has adopted many aspects of the London model: namely, a focus on crime prevention, visible patrol, and a quasi-military organization. In addition, a division in staffing is characteristic of U.S. policing, with police departments employing both sworn and nonsworn personnel. **Sworn personnel** are those entrusted with arrest powers and are

Real Crime Tech

PUBLIC SURVEILLANCE TECHNOLOGY

Cameras are an important tool for crime prevention, criminal investigation, and monitoring interactions between police and the public. In Chicago, through an integration platform, 15,000 cameras have been connected to form a citywide eye on crime. The network of cameras includes video feeds from devices inside and around schools, the housing authority, the transit authority, and the private sector. The network includes an analytical system that incorporates analysis of patterns of behavior and objects left behind, as well as license plate readers. All of the city's police officers receive First and Fourth Amendment training before they are allowed to access the system in any way, and all usage is supervised.

SOURCE: Police Executive Research Forum, *How Are Innovations in Technology Transforming Policing?* (Washington, DC: PERF, January 2012), 13–14.

community policing
Philosophy of policing that emphasizes crime prevention and focuses on developing positive relations between the police and the public.

sworn personnel
Police department employees entrusted with arrest powers; usually referred to as *peace officers*.

KEY CONCEPTS   The History of Policing in the United States

Policing Era	Time Period	Defining Characteristics
Vigilantism	Mid-1700–1900	Residents organized to punish people deemed outlaws.
Slave patrols	1740–1840	Residents organized to enforce laws meant to control slaves.
English model	1700–1800	Local patrol force had limited authority and quasi-military organizational structure. Police departments in U.S. cities developed similarly.
Political era	1840–1920	Police received jobs because of political affiliation and enforced the priorities of the political party in power.
Professional era	1920–1970	Focus was on enforcing the law, hiring qualified officers, using technology, and improving police training.
Community policing era	1970–present day	Focus is on crime prevention with the assistance of improved relations with community members.

usually referred to as *peace officers* in the statutes conferring such powers. In the language of policing, nonsworn personnel are *civilians*.

The independence of local government is deeply rooted in U.S. culture, as is the fear of a national police force and the tyranny that could accompany it.[24] Thus policing in the United States has always been highly localized.[25] Yet despite the localized nature of policing, law enforcement agencies in the United States exist at the federal, state, and local levels.

Local Law Enforcement Agencies

We can divide local law enforcement agencies into two broad categories: sheriffs' offices and police departments. Sheriffs' offices tend to serve larger, more rural areas with fewer people, whereas police departments serve smaller, urban areas with more people.

Sheriffs' Offices   Sheriffs' offices typically police counties in rural areas and towns that have no law enforcement services. Sheriffs respond to violations of criminal statutes (usually defined by state-level penal codes) as well as to violations of city or county ordinances. In addition, they provide jail facilities for both accused and convicted persons and transportation services for all incarcerated persons within counties. In their court-related functions, most sheriffs' offices serve *summonses* (which direct persons accused of crimes to appear in court) and *subpoenas* (which direct individuals to appear in court to present evidence), provide court security, serve eviction notices, and enforce child support orders.

Police Departments   Police departments outnumber sheriffs' offices by four to one, operate mostly in urban areas, and perform most law enforcement duties. They respond to violations of state penal codes and local ordinances and generally provide only temporary housing of arrested persons. Usually, arrested persons remain in police custody only until their initial appearance in court.[26]

State Law Enforcement Agencies

The Texas Rangers, organized by Stephen Austin in 1823 to protect his fledgling colony from American Indians, was the forerunner of state law enforcement agencies.[27] Other states later created their own state-level police agencies.

Local and State Law Enforcement Agencies and Employees in the United States, 2013

Type of Agency	Number of Agencies	Sworn Employees*
Local police department	12,326	477,317
Sheriff's office	3,012	188,952
State law enforcement agency	50	58,421
Total	15,388	724,690

* Sworn employees are those with general arrest powers.

SOURCE: U.S. Department of Justice, Bureau of Justice Statistics, *Law Enforcement Management and Administrative Statistics (LEMAS) Survey, 2013*, May 2015, NCJ 248677.

Because the roles and missions of state law enforcement agencies are defined by state law, they vary considerably and include motor vehicle law violation investigation, lottery oversight, alcoholic beverage control, and narcotics enforcement. About half of all state agencies also offer crime lab services for local police departments.[28] The number of state and local law enforcement agencies in the United States and their respective numbers of employees are shown in the table "Local and State Law Enforcement Agencies and Employees in the United States, 2013."

Federal Law Enforcement Agencies

Federal law enforcement agencies deal with violations of federal statutes. The most prominent employers of sworn law enforcement officers at the federal level are the Federal Bureau of Investigation (FBI), the U.S. Secret Service, and the Drug Enforcement Administration (DEA). However, peace officer positions are found in many other federal agencies as well, including the U.S. Railroad Retirement Board, the Federal Deposit Insurance Corporation, and the Bureau of Engraving and Printing.

Department of Justice   The Department of Justice (DOJ) is the chief federal law enforcement department. Headed by the attorney general, a member of the president's cabinet, the DOJ provides federal leadership in preventing and controlling crime. The DOJ also has responsibility for enforcing the law and defending the interests of the United States according to the law and for ensuring public safety against foreign and domestic threats. Several agencies within the DOJ provide law enforcement services:

- Federal Bureau of Investigation (FBI)
- Drug Enforcement Administration (DEA)
- Bureau of Alcohol, Tobacco, Firearms, and Explosives (ATF), formerly the Bureau of Alcohol, Tobacco, and Firearms
- U.S. Marshals Service

The FBI, created in 1908, employs more than 30,000 people, of whom just over 13,000 are special agents. Support personnel, numbering nearly 19,000 persons, include information analysts, language specialists, scientists, and information technology specialists. The mission of the FBI is to protect and defend the United States against terrorism and foreign intelligence threats and to uphold and enforce the nation's criminal laws. The FBI provides criminal justice services—such as fingerprint identification, laboratory examinations, and police training—to federal, state, and local law enforcement agencies. It is the nation's lead investigative arm for high-tech crime.[29]

The DEA was established in 1973 to wage the "war on drugs." Its mission today remains the same: to enforce the nation's laws and regulations governing controlled substances. The DEA investigates and prepares for the prosecution of those charged with violating controlled substance laws at both the interstate and international levels.

Passage of the Homeland Security Act in 2003 transferred ATF from the Department of the Treasury to the Department of Justice. ATF responsibilities include enforcing federal laws, regulating the firearms and explosives industries, and investigating and reducing crimes involving firearms and explosives, acts of arson, and the illegal trafficking of alcohol and tobacco products.

The U.S. Marshals Service, which has operated since 1789, is the nation's oldest federal law enforcement agency. Duties of the deputy U.S. marshals and criminal investigators, who form the backbone of the agency, are to apprehend federal fugitives, protect the federal judiciary, operate the Witness Security Program, transport federal prisoners, and seize property acquired by criminals through illegal activities.

Department of Homeland Security The newest cabinet department of the federal government is the Department of Homeland Security (DHS), which was created following the terrorist attacks of September 11, 2001. The DHS mission is to lead the unified national effort to protect the American people and their homeland, to prevent and deter terrorist attacks, to protect against and respond to threats against the nation, and to prepare for and respond to all hazards

Real Careers

JOHN TORRES

Work location: Los Angeles

College(s): Sacramento State University (1982, 1986)

Major(s): Criminal Justice (BA), Criminal Justice (MA)

Job title: Alcohol, Tobacco, Firearms (ATF) Agent

Salary range for job like this: $45,000–$65,000

Time in job: 25 years

Work Responsibilities

As the special agent in charge of ATF in Los Angeles, I enforce federal firearms, explosives, and arson laws. We conduct criminal investigations, regulate the firearms and explosives industries, and assist other law enforcement agencies. We also work to prevent terrorism, reduce violent crime, and protect the public in a manner that is faithful to the Constitution and the laws of the United States. One of my most memorable moments on the job was when I was incident commander for the takedown of an outlaw motorcycle organization, the Mongols Motorcycle Club. We arrested more than 80 club members and seized over 100 motorcycles. We also seized their trademark, the first time this was ever done.

Why Criminal Justice?

Ever since I was a teenager, I knew that I wanted to be in law enforcement in some capacity. While I was still a student at Sacramento State, I saw a small ad on a bulletin board on campus that ATF recruiters would be at the school. I applied, and the rest, as they say, is history.

Expectations and Realities of the Job

My job has changed significantly from when I started. My early years were spent investigating career criminals, using the expertise within ATF. The middle years focused on developing my skills as an ATF supervisor and providing direction to less experienced agents. Most recently, I have been the leader within my agency. I admit that when it came time for me to become a supervisor, I expected leadership to come naturally. However, I quickly realized that anyone can "manage" an agency, but to be truly successful you need to have compassion and vision and let those around you know that you care about them as people. The relationships I have formed during my career have nurtured my love of the job.

My Advice to Students

It is so important to set your goals and stay the course. Your journey may not be an easy one or what you expected, but if you continue to pursue your goals with conviction and effort, you will achieve what you set out to do.

U.S. Immigration and Customs Enforcement (ICE) is a federal law enforcement agency.

and disasters. In order to prevent duplication of effort, DHS groups 22 federal agencies into one cabinet department. There are seven major DHS agencies:

- Transportation Security Administration (TSA)
- U.S. Customs and Border Protection (CBP)
- U.S. Citizenship and Immigration Services
- U.S. Immigration and Customs Enforcement
- U.S. Secret Service
- Federal Emergency Management Agency (FEMA)
- U.S. Coast Guard

The two major law enforcement components of DHS are the U.S. Customs and Border Protection (CBP) and the U.S. Immigration and Customs Enforcement (ICE). CBP, which guards 7,000 miles of U.S. land borders and 2,000 miles of coastal waters, is charged with protecting the nation's borders from terrorism, human and drug smuggling, illegal immigration, and importation of agricultural pests. ICE enforces the nation's customs and immigration laws. Both agencies are significantly larger than their pre-DHS predecessors. CBP's U.S. Border Patrol, formerly part of the Immigration and Naturalization Service, increased by more than 9,000 employees between 2004 and 2008, the largest increase of any federal agency.[30]

While DOJ and DHS are the chief law enforcement departments of the federal government, perhaps the most complex arrangement for law enforcement services in the country belongs to the federal Bureau of Indian Affairs (BIA), which is part of the Department of the Interior. American Indian tribes may provide for policing services in several ways:

- They may contract with the BIA for funding of their own tribal police departments. Officers in such arrangements are tribal employees.
- They may elect to have federal employees of BIA provide policing services.
- They may rely on state and local authorities for policing services.
- They may fund policing exclusively with tribal funds.

The type of policing conducted on much American Indian land is of particular concern because law enforcement activities often clash with tribal values

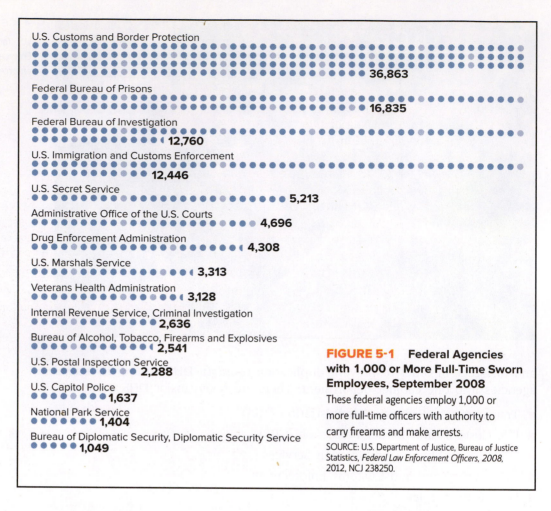

U.S. Customs and Border Protection
36,863

Federal Bureau of Prisons
16,835

Federal Bureau of Investigation
12,760

U.S. Immigration and Customs Enforcement
12,446

U.S. Secret Service
5,213

Administrative Office of the U.S. Courts
4,696

Drug Enforcement Administration
4,308

U.S. Marshals Service
3,313

Veterans Health Administration
3,128

Internal Revenue Service, Criminal Investigation
2,636

Bureau of Alcohol, Tobacco, Firearms and Explosives
2,541

U.S. Postal Inspection Service
2,288

U.S. Capitol Police
1,637

National Park Service
1,404

Bureau of Diplomatic Security, Diplomatic Security Service
1,049

FIGURE 5-1   **Federal Agencies with 1,000 or More Full-Time Sworn Employees, September 2008**
These federal agencies employ 1,000 or more full-time officers with authority to carry firearms and make arrests.

SOURCE: U.S. Department of Justice, Bureau of Justice Statistics, *Federal Law Enforcement Officers, 2008*, 2012, NCJ 238250.

and norms. For example, a police officer on a Tohono O'odham reservation who aggressively confronts a suspect will offend tribal norms. Conversely, an officer on a reservation of the Turtle Mountain Band of Chippewa Indians who fails to confront a suspect will be guilty of a misstep. Law enforcement officers need to incorporate tribal values in their policing mission to create workable, tribe-specific policing institutions and approaches informed by traditional customs.[31]

Many people work in federal law enforcement agencies. To understand the scope of federal law enforcement, refer to Figure 5-1, which shows agencies with more than 1,000 full-time officers.

The Problem of Fragmentation

Localized policing allows local values to inform police practices and better positions officers to use their judgment in resolving local community problems. This historic approach, however, has led to the problem of **fragmentation**, a lack of coordination among law enforcement agencies in the same geographic region due to the existence of many small departments. Suppose, for example, that a particular group of criminals commits crimes in several different police jurisdictions. Investigators in one police department may have information that could help a neighboring agency, but the two agencies do not routinely communicate. (This situation can exist even within a single agency—usually a large, urban agency—where the bureaucratized division of responsibilities hinders or prevents information sharing and cooperation among different units.) Consider, too, that if one community enforces certain laws more strictly than others, criminals may conduct their criminal activities in a neighboring jurisdiction that takes a less aggressive approach. Duplication of services is another frequent result

fragmentation
The lack of coordination among law enforcement agencies in the same geographic region due to the existence of many small departments.

of fragmentation. For example, separate agencies generally operate their own call dispatch and crime laboratory units and bear the expenses individually.[32]

Problems resulting from fragmentation are not easily solved. Law enforcement officials and the public are accustomed to the independence of their local police departments. Nevertheless, as problems linked to drug trafficking and terrorism cross jurisdictions, the disadvantages of fragmentation may reduce support for this approach to policing.[33]

Consolidation is one option for dealing with the problem of fragmentation. For example, in Florida in 1968, the Duval County Sheriff's Department and the Jacksonville Police Department conducted one of the earliest consolidation efforts in the United States. More than four decades later, the Office of the Sheriff–Jacksonville Police (commonly referred to as the Jacksonville Sheriff's Office) has significantly enhanced its quality of service. Its Continuous Improvement Unit is specifically dedicated to perfecting the agency's capability to add value to the services provided to the community. Its quality of service has been formally recognized through its status as a "triple crown accredited law enforcement agency," meaning that it has been accredited by the national Commission on Accreditation for Law Enforcement Agencies, the American Correctional Association, and the National Commission on Correctional Health Care.[34]

Instead of consolidating, smaller agencies can contract with larger agencies for specific services. This arrangement has been especially efficient for detention facilities and communications systems.[35] Contracting for specific services may also make sense for emergency planning. A city, for example, can contract to have the county's SWAT unit available in the event of a major riot, invasion by an outlaw motorcycle gang, or a hostage situation at a school.[36]

RECRUITMENT, SELECTION, AND TRAINING

Effective policing in a community requires a force of high-quality, well-trained peace officers who are responsive to the community's needs. The processes of recruitment, selection, and training are critical to developing such a force.

Recruitment

"The most fundamental human resource process in a law enforcement organization is the recruitment of a sufficient number of qualified applicants to meet the staffing needs of an agency."[37] At a minimum, "qualified" applicants possess good oral and written communications skills, are fit both physically and psychologically, have a solid employment history, and are free of convictions for criminal offenses.

Agencies face significant challenges in recruiting, including

- Better-paying jobs outside law enforcement
- Unusually high attrition as older generations retire
- Negative publicity over matters such as alleged discrimination in arrests and excessive use of force[38]

Difficulties in recruitment also may reflect the nature and expectations of the contemporary workforce. For one thing, fewer individuals are interested in public service work today than was true of previous generations. Also, police officers today want balanced lives that allow them time for family, leisure activities, and other priorities. In the current environment, for example, officers may resist extending a work shift to handle a late-breaking homicide or a traffic accident.[39]

Recruitment Challenges   Many core problems that law enforcement agencies face in recruiting have worsened in the past decade. The recession that began in 2008 caused unprecedented difficulties for sustaining police workforces, including budget and workforce reduction, consolidation, and even disbanding of some agencies. Generational preferences and conceptions of work and career change have added to recruitment challenges, as has an increased prevalence of disqualifications related to drug use. Departments have historically experienced difficulty recruiting and maintaining workforces that reflect their communities' composition. As the communities that departments serve become more culturally diverse, it is even more important to have personnel who are capable of understanding the community's diverse needs and can credibly interact with residents. When examining strategies for attracting candidates, agency leaders must recognize that achieving success is a function of budgetary allocations, commitment, and effectiveness in targeting the specific subgroups the agency seeks to recruit. Moreover, internal objectives and policies that emphasize interaction, relationship building, and partnerships with the public can enhance perceptions of diversity and boost hiring of women and minorities.[40]

Methods of Recruitment   Often, the best recruiters for an agency are its own personnel. A RAND Corporation survey of 44 of the nation's largest police and sheriff's departments revealed that family or friends working at the department that recruits ultimately joined were responsible for first prompting more than 40 percent of new recruits to consider the agency. An additional 20 percent were prompted by family or friends at another agency.[41]

Websites have evolved as the top tool for attracting applicants. Moreover, podcasts, blogs, and "really simple syndication" (RSS) feeds have increased job seekers' sophistication, allowing them to process growing amounts of information and network more efficiently. DiscoverPolicing.org is the cornerstone of a nationwide initiative to market the benefits of careers in law enforcement to a broad and diverse audience, from first-time applicants to those seeking a career change or transitioning from active military service. Through a clear and accurate portrayal of the full range of police service opportunities, Discover-Policing.org expands the pool of potential applicants and provides an effective means for candidates and hiring agencies to connect.[42]

Agency open houses and job fairs are additional popular methods of recruitment. Face-to-face interaction and fostering human connections can make recruitment more meaningful and personal for both the department and applicants.[43]

Selection

Once an agency has attracted a sufficient number of applicants, the next step is selecting the best-qualified individuals to fill sworn positions. A peace officer's work is complex, potentially dangerous, and emotionally stressful, and it requires above-average intelligence to apply an ever-changing body of laws and police regulations to the solution of problems created by crime.[44]

Selection Process   For the candidate, the selection process requires patient navigation of physical, mental, and aptitude screening exams; interviews; and submitting to an in-depth background investigation. The critical task for agencies is to use selection methods that reveal the best candidates for agency needs.[45]

Some police departments still hire officers who are attracted by the adventure of the job rather than by its service functions. However, an emphasis on adventure and an attitude of derring-do distance police from the community and produce a **siege mentality** that sets the police up as a "band of brothers"—or "sisters"—against everyone else. To build a force capable of dealing with the complexity of the twenty-first century, it is imperative that agencies place value on both educational achievements and socialization skills when selecting personnel. Hiring officers who are capable of interacting well with the community members they serve is essential not only for external relations but also for increasing the degree of fairness, compassion, and cultural sensitivity practiced by all members of the police organization.[46]

siege mentality
Police view of themselves as a "band of brothers"—or "sisters"—against everyone else in society.

BLACKS, LATINOS, AND WOMEN IN LOCAL LAW ENFORCEMENT AGENCIES

Law enforcement agencies have increased efforts to attract qualified minority and female candidates. Although progress has been made, greater demographic representativeness remains to be accomplished.

Demographic	2000 (percent)	2003 (percent)	2013 (percent)
Black	11.7	11.7	12.0
Latino	8.3	9.1	11.6
Women	10.6	11.3	12.0

SOURCE: U.S. Department of Justice, Bureau of Justice Statistics, *Local Police Departments, 2013* (Washington, DC: DOJ, 2015), 4–5.

Background checks are a vital element in the hiring process. Typically, background investigators seek evidence of good moral character, solid work habits, interpersonal skills, stress tolerance, and decision-making ability. Increasingly, background investigators are reviewing applicants' social media activity. Conducting background investigations on candidates for whom computer use is a social reality can be inherently problematic. Younger applicants can be surprisingly candid in disclosing personal information, and their impressions of what constitutes "character" can be startlingly different from those of evaluators.[47] Moreover, background checks are not always reliable indicators of which individuals will become good officers. Background investigators can be subjective and may use past criminal records as a means to eliminate candidates, without regard to how recent a conviction was or to the facts surrounding the particular criminal event. Improperly conducted background investigations are common, especially in cases involving Black and Latino applicants being assessed by White investigators who may be unfamiliar with the culture and lifestyle of the candidates' communities.[48]

Demographics of Candidates   Over the past few decades, law enforcement agencies have increased their efforts to attract qualified minority and female candidates. Although they have unquestionably made strides, much remains to be accomplished. As you can see from examining the table above, the percentages for minorities and women in law enforcement have increased, but they are still low.

▼ **Women in the Line of Duty**

Women are increasing their numbers in law enforcement agencies.

MYTH/REALITY

MYTH: Women are underrepresented in police departments today chiefly because they have only recently been permitted to become police officers.

REALITY: Marie Owens was appointed as an officer with the Chicago Police Department in 1893. Several other women were appointed soon thereafter. However, the nature of their duties was long limited to juvenile and custodial activities.[49]

We find the greatest disparity by far when we measure the percentage of women police against the percentage of women in the general U.S. population. Women have been employed by police departments in the United States since 1893, when the Chicago City Council passed an ordinance granting Marie Owens the title and pay of "patrolman." Yet Owens was given neither a uniform nor the authority to arrest. Instead, she was assigned to assist detectives with cases involving women and children and to conduct follow-up interviews of witnesses or victims.[50]

The number of female police officers has increased, and women officers now perform all law enforcement activities. Still, women only

DIS Connects

Where Are the Women?

Female police officers rely on minimal use of physical force and are typically better than men at defusing potentially violent confrontations. Women officers also often respond more effectively to incidents of violence against women—crimes that represent a large category of calls for service. They have better communication skills than their male counterparts and are better able to win the trust that motivates citizens to cooperate with community policing. All these factors work to the advantage of the police and the communities they serve.

Despite their demonstrated competence and superiority in certain functions, and despite the fact that chief executives of law enforcement agencies overwhelmingly endorse their hire, women make up a disappointingly small percentage of the law enforcement workforce. At the local level, they compose approximately 12 percent of the sworn workforce; state and federal figures are approximately 7 percent and 20 percent, respectively. These percentages contrast sharply when compared to the percentage of women in the U.S. labor force: approximately 57 percent. Where are the women?

Popular misperceptions of police—and a resulting image problem—may be to blame. Specifically, stereotypical images of police as macho crime fighters who spend most of their time engaged in combat and high-speed chases may discourage women from considering careers in law enforcement. In addition, job descriptions continue to emphasize physical attributes over skills in communication and mediation. Further, most U.S. police academies still use a boot camp approach to training, which emphasizes tearing down individuality and rebuilding recruits in the military model. The entire setting is a subculture decidedly foreign to most women.

Given the many challenges facing modern police agencies, the need for more women in the ranks is clear and urgent. However, at the current rate of hiring, women will continue to be underrepresented unless the policies and practices that discourage them are eliminated. The police departments of Albuquerque, New Mexico, and Tucson, Arizona, have both experienced significant increases in recruitment and retention of women by implementing initiatives that emphasize the importance of interpersonal and communications skills. At the same time, initiatives have accommodated needs for child care and customized uniforms and equipment.

OBSERVE → INVESTIGATE → UNDERSTAND

- Should police departments hire women police officers? Why or why not?
- What hiring accommodations—if any—should police departments make in order to hire more women for the force?
- What are the benefits of having women as police officers?

SOURCES: David Burlingame and Agnes L. Baro, "Women's Representation and Status in Law Enforcement: Does CALEA Involvement Make a Difference?" *Criminal Justice Policy Review* 16 (2005): 391–411; National Center for Women and Policing, *Hiring and Retaining More Women: The Advantages to Law Enforcement Agencies* (Arlington, VA: NCWP, 2003), 1–16; U.S. Department of Justice, Bureau of Justice Statistics, *Local Police Departments, 2007* (Washington, DC: DOJ, 2010), 14; Lynn Langton, *Women in Law Enforcement, 1987–2008* (Washington, DC: U.S. Department of Justice, Bureau of Justice Statistics, 2010), 1–3; U.S. Department of Labor, "Women's Bureau Data & Statistics in 2015." www.dol.gov/wb/stats/stats_data.htm (retrieved July 11, 2015).

comprise approximately 12 percent of the policing workforce, despite progressive legislation aimed at procuring gender equality in the United States.[51]

MYTH/REALITY

MYTH: Women are not strong enough to perform police work.

REALITY: Most police work does not require physical strength. In fact, the federal government is encouraging police departments to hire more women because females are less likely to use force inappropriately. Departments with a greater number of female officers face fewer lawsuits.[52]

Female representation in police departments can be increased by implementing policies and practices that preclude potential disparate impact to females such as physical fitness requirements. Departments that use physical fitness requirements to screen applicants have less gender diversity than those agencies that do not use screening requirements. Moreover, physical fitness requirements are controversial, as there is little empirical evidence that such tests are reflective of the common tasks performed by officers or predictive of performance when involved in hostile situations. However, requirements for higher education attainment have been correlated positively with increased female representation. Educational requirements may be attractive to women because of the association between education and professionalism. Additionally, agencies that embrace policies that feature problem-solving strategies and commitment to community engagement have been found to have higher levels of female representation than agencies that are less focused on community policing.[53]

African Americans wanting to become police officers also have faced discrimination. In the late 1860s, some southern cities began to hire African American males as police officers, but members of the White public strongly objected. After the end of Reconstruction (the political process designed to unify the North and South after the Civil War) in 1877, southern police departments expelled their African American officers. By 1910 there were no African American officers on southern police forces.[54]

Like the White public who objected to African American policemen, White officers also deeply resented–and fought–the hiring of African American officers. Moreover, departments that were forced to hire African Americans set aside specific positions for them so that African American job candidates were not competing with White candidates.[55] During the 1970s, Black males began to enter police departments at meaningful levels, and their numbers continue to rise. Between 1987 and 2013, the percentage of Black local police officers increased from 9.3 percent to 12 percent.[56]

Black and Latino candidates are more likely to be hired as police officers in cities with substantial minority populations and Latino or Black mayors or police chiefs.[57] The number of Latino police officers increased from 4.5 percent in 1987 to 11.6 percent in 2013.[58]

Some police departments have begun recruiting gay and lesbian candidates to improve the quality of services provided to gay, lesbian, bisexual, and transgender individuals. For example, the District of Columbia's Metropolitan Police Department created a Gay and Lesbian Liaison Unit in June 2000. Other cities–including Atlanta, Georgia, and Missoula, Montana–have followed this example.[59] In addition, LGBT officers have themselves formed associations within agencies to provide support for issues confronted by LGBT colleagues. The NYPD has

▲ **LGBT Police Group at Parade**
Police Officers at a Gay Pride Parade.

◄ **Police Recruits Training**
Law enforcement training includes a wide variety of physical and intellectual tasks.

been a leader in this area since 1982, when officers within its ranks formed the Gay Officers Action League.[60]

Training

Training has evolved in step with policing. In the political era of policing, there was no formal training, and officers often learned how to police by serving as apprentices to senior personnel.[61] They focused on developing competence in the technical aspects of policing and learning the laws of arrest, penal code provisions, patrol tactics, firearms proficiency, and interview and interrogation techniques.

Systematic basic training in police academies was one of the reforms instituted in the twentieth century. Basic training in a formal classroom environment enabled uniform coverage of standard curricula designed to equip student-officers with the fundamental skills and knowledge necessary to perform essential policing activities. The transition from reactive policing to the more proactive orientation of community policing stimulated a shift to emphasis on problem solving, conflict resolution, crime prevention, and service.[62] A spate of videotaped incidents occurred nationally in 2014 and 2015 involving police use of lethal force (several against unarmed individuals) and triggered a backlash of rage by members of

Real Careers

RANDALL D. WATKINS

Work location: San Marcos, Texas

College(s): Texas State University–San Marcos, 2006

Major(s): Criminal Justice (BS); Military and Law Enforcement Certifications

Job title: Tactical Logistics Coordinator/Tactical Instructor, Advanced Law Enforcement Rapid Response Training Center (ALERRT)

Salary range for job like this: $50,000–$75,000

Time in job: 2 years

Work Responsibilities

I help accomplish ALERRT's mission to provide first-response officers and military personnel with the training and tools they need to perform their duties in a hostile environment. For example, I ship and receive roughly $3 million worth of training equipment all over the United States. I also teach courses in responding to an active shooter, breaching, rural operations, low-light operations, and tactical rifle/pistol.

Why Criminal Justice?

I served 5 years on active duty in the Marine Corps Infantry and was a part of Operation Iraqi Freedom in 2003. After completing my enlistment, I went to Texas State University to finish my degree and pursue a career as a Marine officer. In late 2004, the unit that I had just left took very heavy casualties in Iraq, so I decided to leave school and volunteer for another deployment. While conducting a raid in Iraq in May 2005, my platoon was ambushed; we lost four Marines, and eight were severely wounded, including me. After a year and a half in the hospital, I returned to Texas State and completed my degree. Being medically retired from the Marine Corps, I knew my options as an officer in the field would be limited. The ALERRT program was the answer to my prayers. I use my experience and knowledge to train members of the military and law enforcement to learn from the mistakes that I made and to help them become the best officer, Marine, or soldier that they can be.

Expectations and Realities of the Job

I have been struck by the similarities and transferability of skills between military and law enforcement. For example, although the military is designed as a fighting force, the mission and role of the military in Operation Iraqi Freedom and Operation Enduring Freedom evolved to be more law enforcement in nature. And much like in the military, I have seen that law enforcement agencies must tailor their tactics according to the specific criminal.

My Advice to Students

I cannot emphasize enough how important it is to go to college. College gave me analytical and research skills that I never had before. It bridged the gap of being strictly an operator in the field to having the skill set to look at the big picture and to plan for accomplishing the mission while jumping the necessary hurdles.

minority communities, particularly African American citizens. The events underscored the need for and importance of lasting, collaborative relationships between local police and the public. Today's police recruits must be inculcated with skills that enable fair and procedurally just policing. Tactical skills are important, but attitude, tolerance, and interpersonal skills are equally so.[63]

Training Facilities   States typically train their recruits in special academies, and each state determines its own training requirements. Some large law enforcement agencies (for example, large municipal police departments and state or federal agencies) operate their own academies. Most often, however, training centers work with institutions of higher education, especially community colleges. Prospective officers usually pay for their own training in anticipation of being recruited after they graduate.[64]

Training Curricula   Community-oriented policing required change not only in academies' curricula but also in their teaching methods. **Adult learning,** with its emphasis on engaging the learner and incorporating his or her experiences, is rapidly replacing the traditional lecture form of academy instruction.[65] The corresponding curricula include topics such as human diversity, special populations, ethics and integrity, and community building. Notwithstanding the prevalence of curricula involving problem solving and community policing, there is a tendency to emulate a warrior mentality in many American law enforcement agencies. The seeds of this culture are planted during recruit academy training with a "boot camp-like" atmosphere. Upon graduation, newly trained officers are sent to the community, and despite the militaristic manner in which they were treated by their academy trainers, they are expected to treat the relatively powerless people they often encounter with exemplary dignity and respect. Thus, it should not be a surprise when some officers treat both suspects and citizens with the disdain and detachment they saw modeled by those in power at the academy.

> **adult learning**
> Method of learning that emphasizes engaging the learner by incorporating the learner's experiences in the curriculum.

Change is afoot, though, and instructive examples are emerging across the nation. One such transformation is occurring in the state of Washington as the state's Criminal Justice Training Commission has changed the tone of the training curriculum from one emphasizing the distinction between guardians of democracy and civil rights over the conquering warrior mentality. A five year longitudinal study of the effectiveness of the new curriculum and philosophy was launched in 2014. The study has been designed to determine whether the guardian philosophy positively influences officers' attitudes about their job and the public. It will also assess whether officers trained under the new program are more likely to employ crisis intervention tactics and de-escalation skills than are officers trained under the former warrior philosophy.[66] The state of California requires that each topic in a police academy's curriculum includes the themes of ethics and community policing.[67] Training for special areas such as domestic violence also serves the interests of community policing and its focus on the victims of such crimes.

Training in Legal Issues   Training in legal issues is designed to help officers perform well; it also serves to shield officers and their employers from liability in lawsuits. This type of training ranges broadly–from the mandate to ensure the safety of a child left behind when a parent or guardian is arrested through the latest court decisions regarding warrantless searches of premises or vehicles.

Standardized training also establishes customary practices. Plaintiffs have a more difficult task of attributing bad outcomes to errors or omissions if officers are properly trained.[68] For example, if an officer frequently applied a particular control measure but on one occasion application of this measure resulted in injury to a suspect, the concerned agency (and officer) would be much better protected against liability than if the officer had not been so conscientious.

POLICE SUBCULTURE

Along with the training that new police recruits receive in police academies and in the field, they also absorb the police *subculture*–the attitudes, values, and beliefs–that permeates the law enforcement agency. Although U.S. police agencies are organized in formal hierarchies and have clear policies and intensive training, the police subculture may influence officer behavior more than any formal rules and orders. There are two types of police subculture.

police occupational subculture
Norms and beliefs embraced by most officers in a given country.

Police occupational subculture is a set of norms and beliefs held by most officers in a given country. Police occupational subculture in the United States is influenced by the perception of the danger and irregularity of police work, the need for officers to support one another, and the necessity for them to demonstrate and maintain their authority.[69]

police organizational subculture
Norms and beliefs particular to an individual department.

A **police organizational subculture** is particular to an individual department.[70] For example, one department may value community policing, whereas another may stress maintaining law and order. One agency's subculture may rate diversity among the rank and file as a worthy goal, but another department may feel that the value of diversity is overemphasized.

MYTH/REALITY

MYTH: Police demonstrate virtually blind obedience to the mandates of superiors and top management.

REALITY: Police occupational subculture is frequently in conflict with management's orders and directives, as illustrated by this often-cited warning from a training officer to his new charge: "Forget everything you were taught at the academy. Just keep your mouth shut and your ears open."[71]

blue code of silence
Adherence to a code of conduct that places loyalty to fellow officers above all other values.

There is no doubt that compared to most occupations, policing is dangerous. Beginning in academy training, police cadets are reminded daily of the possibility of danger. They are trained to make sure that they can always see exits and entrances, even when eating lunch in a restaurant. They are told to remember that any person with whom they come in contact could pose a physical threat. The belief that their job includes daily risks of danger is a strong component of the police subculture and creates solidarity among officers, despite the fact that most of them will never need to discharge their firearm.

▼ **Police Charging a Bank**

Such images reinforce the idea that officers' jobs are constantly fraught with danger and excitement.

At the core of police occupational subculture is the belief that officers must support one another, not only in physical confrontations but also if and when questions are raised about their actions. By and large, officers resist reporting the misbehavior of their fellow officers.[72] This **blue code of silence** places loyalty to fellow officers above all other values and tacitly assures officers that they can count on a backup to any story they tell, regardless of the truth.[73]

Officers often work under extremely tense conditions, with little information, and generally in ways that will leave someone unhappy with the outcome.[74] The public is not always sensitive to these fundamental constraints. Therefore, police officers often feel that only other officers really understand them and the conditions under which they work.

What about the Victim?

The Police Subculture and a Linkage to Intimate Partner Strife

Police officers value the maintenance of authority, and it is a major component of the police occupational subculture. Officers who can establish control over others are said to possess a quality referred to as "command presence." Implicit in this attribute is the assumed ability to take command of any situation. While cultivation of command presence and an authoritative demeanor may be desirable within a paramilitary environment, if unchecked these qualities can yield unintended consequences off duty. Research has examined the effects of the police subculture on officers' families and on intimate partner relationships. Results reveal that some officers bring home behaviors such as giving orders and interrogating spouses and children rather than engaging in two-way communication. Other findings show that many officers find it difficult to "turn off" emotionally at work and then "turn it back on" at home. The result is often emotional detachment and withdrawal, decreased communication, and inhibited expression of affection and intimacy. A recent study on the subject, conducted among four southern police departments and 90 officers, found authoritarianism was significantly related to psychological intimate partner violence. (However, none of the aspects of the police subculture were significantly associated with physical violence.)

Unwittingly or not, the police officer may thus become the perpetrator of domestic violence within his own home. This can create a unique vulnerability for the spouse. The spousal victim may fear calling the police because the case may be handled by officers who are colleagues and friends, and the victim may be concerned the responding officers will side with the abuser and fail to perform a thorough investigation. Moreover, there is the reality of a weapon at hand within the household; remote as the possibility of its use may be, its presence can be unsettling. If the situation evolves to the point where a protective order is considered, following through can be fraught with complexities, including the fact that everyone in the court knows and works with the alleged abuser.

Both the Federal Bureau of Investigation and the International Association of Chiefs of Police have developed comprehensive policies for dealing with police officer domestic violence. They have in common the following components:

- Collaboration with victim advocates and domestic violence program professionals in the community.
- Training at both academy and in-service levels to ensure officers comprehend the complexities of domestic violence and to keep agency policies on the subject at the forefront.
- Early warning systems during the hiring process and throughout an officer's career (including peer and supervisory vigilance).
- Protocols for responding to incidents of domestic violence by police, including notifying the officer's supervisor, documenting the crime scene, providing guidance on when to make an arrest, and possibly retaining the officer's service weapon.
- Development of a risk assessment and safety plan for the victim.
- Procedures for conducting parallel administrative and criminal investigations.

A proactive approach to heading off domestic violence among law enforcement personnel is exemplified in the "National Prevention Toolkit on Officer-Involved Domestic Violence" project at the Law Enforcement Families Partnership within Florida State University's College of Social Work. The Toolkit is designed as a prevention tool for criminal justice personnel, and officers and supervisors have password-protected access to online training modules and resources specifically designed for the criminal justice community.

OBSERVE → INVESTIGATE → UNDERSTAND

- Do you find it surprising that police officers engage in domestic violence to at least the same extent as the general population?
- Federal law 18 U.S.C. Section 922(g)(8) prohibits anyone subject to an order of protection from possessing a firearm, but police officers generally are allowed an "official use exemption" (18 U.S.C. Section 925), which means they can carry a service weapon while on duty. Should this exemption exist? Why or why not?

SOURCES: Lindsey Blumenstein, Lorie Fridell, and Shayne Jones, "The Link between Traditional Police Subculture and Police Intimate Partner Violence," *Policing: An International Journal of Police Strategies & Management* 35, no. 1 (2012): 147–163; International Association of Chiefs of Police, "Domestic Violence by Police Officers," (Concepts and Issues Paper, July 2003); Law Enforcement Families Partnership, "The National Prevention Toolkit on Officer-Involved Domestic Violence." http://familyvio.csw.fsu.edu/lefp/about/ (retrieved June 15, 2015).

The need to maintain authority is another major component of police occupational subculture. Officers expect the individuals with whom they come in contact will be both deferential and respectful. They realize that even though they may have the power to resort to force, their greatest tool is communication. By and large, they believe if they do not maintain their authority, they will not be able to accomplish their job. Individuals who challenge police authority are likely to experience unpleasant consequences.[75] Please see the What about the Victim page 161 for possible implications on personal relationships.

Because officers regularly deal with people who are not honest with them and because they feel that members of the public are often quick to second-guess their decisions, an "us versus them" mentality develops as a common element of police occupational subculture. Public opinion of police is generally high, but officers may have difficulty believing that. Everywhere they go in uniform, people stare at them. A sign greeting officers driving their police cars out of the garage at Calgary Police Services headquarters in Alberta, Canada, reminds them: "Drive like everyone is watching you, because they are."

The media reinforces the message that the real work of policing is crime fighting. Think about it: There is not a single major television show about the daily tasks of a community policing officer. Patrol officers also learn that crime fighting is what administrators value because police effectiveness is often assessed on measures such as numbers of citations issued, numbers of traffic stops made, numbers of arrests made, and the like. The focus on crime fighting is so deeply ingrained that even community policing officers believe that those traditional police responsibilities are their most valuable work.[76]

There are merits to a strong police occupational subculture. For example, it creates a high level of group solidarity. But officers who value its main tenets are found to engage in more coercive actions, from verbal threats to physical force, than officers who do not.[77] Both within and across departments, however, there are variations in the police subculture and in the degree to which officers support it. The relative strength of each component and the way it influences individual officers also vary somewhat by agency.

POLICE DISCRETION

discretion
Authority to act in a manner that officers judge most appropriate for a given situation.

Most members of the public believe that all or most police actions are dictated by law. Officers, however, have a high degree of **discretion** in their everyday activities that enables them to act in the manner they judge most appropriate in a given situation. When officers use discretion, the choices they make are largely up to them; they use their own judgment. Discretion is necessary because there are too many laws for all to be enforced, so police must choose which ones are most important in a particular incident. Furthermore, laws and policies are often vague and can be interpreted in many ways. The legislators who write laws and the police administrators who develop policies understand that any given situation will require officers to make the best choice for those involved.

Yet there are definite limits on police discretion. For example, a number of Supreme Court decisions and police policies have reduced officers' discretion regarding the use of force—especially lethal force. The discretion to initiate and continue vehicular pursuits when a driver does not comply with a police request to pull over often comes under the microscope as well, largely because innocent bystanders can be injured or killed during these pursuits. Some state legislatures have passed laws requiring police departments to develop or revise their policies in order to give patrol officers clear directions concerning pursuits.

As we have noted, most police work does not involve dealing with crimes. Nonetheless, those who call the police rarely want to hear, "No crime has been committed, so there is nothing I can do" as the officer leaves the scene. The

KEY CONCEPTS   **Positives and Negatives of Police Discretion**

Positives	Negatives
Results in increased justice	Increases the possibility for discrimination
Relieves the criminal justice system of the need to handle all cases it otherwise would receive	Allows some people who deserve punishment to avoid it

outcomes of calls for service, which make up the vast majority of requests for police assistance, depend on how the responding officer uses discretion. Suppose a father and son are having an argument, but the dispute has not turned physical. One officer called to the scene may spend half an hour counseling the parties on conflict management. Another may simply advise the family members to make sure they do not assault each other and be gone in five minutes.

Positives and Negatives of Police Discretion

One of the greatest benefits of police discretion is that it allows officers to act in the most just manner in a given situation. Consider the following scenario. An officer observes a driver roll through a stop sign and pulls the vehicle over. The driver is clearly upset and crying and tells the officer he was just notified that a family member has died. The officer decides that there is no need to give the driver a citation and instead advises him to call someone to pick him up or perhaps talk to someone on the phone until he is calm enough to drive, for his own safety and that of others. Most people would agree the officer acted in the most just manner in that situation. Officers' discretionary decisions can sometimes fulfill the spirit of the law by not following the letter of the law.

Another benefit of police discretion is that it allows officers to decide where to focus their energies. The criminal justice system cannot manage the burden of fully enforcing all aspects of the penal and traffic codes at all times. Serious crimes occur more rarely than people think, but minor crimes are pervasive. Jaywalking, hanging objects from a car's rearview mirror, loitering, not wearing a seat belt, and underage drinking are all common occurrences. If law enforcement resources were spent on these and all the other minor offenses, police would be stretched too thin and would have little time to devote to serious crimes.

Yet there are disadvantages to police discretion as well (see the Key Concepts feature). Consider that all professionals with the power of discretion are susceptible to the temptation to abuse that authority. Discretion allows for the possibility that decisions could be influenced, for example, by race, ethnicity, class, gender, or sexuality. The Fourteenth Amendment to the Constitution, as well as state laws guaranteeing all persons equal protection under the law, should lead officers to treat all individuals equally–even when exercising discretion. But the influences of racism, sexism, and other discriminatory attitudes are widespread throughout the United States and prevail even among law enforcement personnel.

Influences on the Use of Discretion

The discretionary decisions to stop a vehicle and to make an arrest are the subject of much research. Both the seriousness of the offense and the quality of the evidence influence an officer's decision to arrest. Suspects who are male or juvenile are more likely to be arrested than are females or adults. Black suspects are significantly more likely to be arrested than White suspects. Intoxicated suspects are more likely to be arrested than those who are sober. Individuals who exhibit a negative attitude to police are also much more likely to be arrested.[78] Finally, with all other variables held constant, White officers are more likely to arrest than are Black officers. If the suspect is a Black male, however, a Black officer is more likely to arrest than is a White officer.[79]

▲ **Racial Profiling**
Numerous studies have shown that racial profiling does occur.

racial profiling
Police contact with an individual initiated because of the person's skin color or ethnicity.

Police managers are, of course, interested in why some officers are more productive than others. Research has found that several variables affect how many drug arrests an officer makes. One important effect on the decision to make an arrest for drugs is whether a patrol officer believes that his department rewards such arrests. Officers also are influenced by whether they believe managers see drug enforcement as a priority. As might be expected, they also are more likely to make such arrests if they've had special training in drug interdiction.[80]

Officers generally have "working rules" that influence whom they deem suspicious and therefore how they use their discretion when deciding whether to stop an individual. For instance, an officer may become suspicious about someone who is not usually in a given neighborhood or someone who is in a business district late at night.[81]

MYTH/REALITY

MYTH: Police treat all individuals the same regardless of race, class, and gender.

REALITY: A variety of characteristics of officers, citizens, victims, and suspected perpetrators influence police behavior.[82]

An officer's decision to stop a vehicle, for which the traffic code affords many possible reasons, is also a discretionary matter. The extent of **racial profiling**—police contact with an individual that is initiated because of the person's skin color or ethnicity—is widely debated in the United States. Many commentators say that claims of racial profiling are divisive and unsubstantiated. However, numerous studies, some conducted by police departments themselves, show that police disproportionately stop Black drivers. Research has also shown that Black drivers are more likely to be searched during a traffic stop than are Latino or White drivers.[83]

Some defenders of racial profiling say that officers who practice it are merely responding to the fact that people of color are more likely to commit crime, and that police therefore often use traffic stops as a means to uncover criminal behavior beyond violation of the traffic code. However, the incidence of, for example, illegal drug use does not support these defenses. Based on self-reports of illegal drug use, Whites use drugs at rates about equal to Blacks. Furthermore, data from a recent national study revealed that although Black and Latino males were at an increased risk of citations, searches, arrests, and use of force, minority drivers were not more likely than White drivers to be in possession of anything illegal.[84] Another defense of the higher rate of traffic stops of people of color is that they are more likely to drive recklessly. That claim has also been disproved.[85] The bottom line is that racial profiling is not only discriminatory—it is also ineffective police work.

Victims and the Use of Discretion

People generally assume that arrest decisions are based on whether there is sufficient evidence to indicate that a crime occurred. In fact, police arrest in only about half the cases in which evidence of a crime is present; the greatest influence on the decision to arrest is the victim's or complainant's preference for arrest. Therefore, the public influences how officers exercise discretion.[86]

The degree of relationship between the victim and perpetrator–whether they are family, friends, acquaintances, or strangers–also influences arrest decisions. The closer the relationship between victim and perpetrator, the less likely an arrest will be made. An arrest is more likely when two strangers are in a physical altercation than when one family member assaults another.[87] Unfortunately, this practice puts those who are the most vulnerable in greatest jeopardy. Individuals who perpetrate violence against a stranger–in a bar fight, for instance–usually never see their victim again, so the likelihood of another conflict is minimal. Victims who know their perpetrators have a much greater chance of continued interaction with them and therefore are at greater risk of being victimized again. Yet in situations in which the victim needs the most protection from future assaults, retaliation, and threats, an arrest is less likely to be made.

MISCONDUCT

Probably nothing is more harmful to a law enforcement agency than officer misconduct. Misconduct damages both public confidence in the police and the ability of law enforcement administrators to control and direct the workforce. Police officers are uniquely entrusted to protect the safety and rights of all citizens. Moreover, police officers are given special powers and prerogatives–the authority to investigate people, to deny them freedom to move about, and to use force if warranted.

Two types of misconduct by the police are abuse of authority and corruption. The possibility of personal gain is what distinguishes the two.

Abuse of Authority

Abuse of authority occurs when police disregard policies, rules, or laws in the performance of their duty. Generally those who commit such misuse believe in a **noble cause** that they claim excuses their wrongdoing because "the end justifies the means."[88] Noble cause is present, for instance, when officers frame individuals whom they believe are "dirty" and who would be imprisoned but for lack of evidence. Police may also seek to administer their own street justice through brutal means. The police often believe that their concern for the victim justifies their behavior in such incidents. Officers may recall the brutality suffered by victims of past gang violence or drug dealing when they encounter persons trying to commit similar crimes. The police may believe any extralegal actions they take to remove perpetrators from the streets pale in comparison to the harm the next victim will suffer.[89] Many critics and reformers looking to curb the use of violence by the police fail to recognize that the use of violence against perpetrators often stems from police officers' concern for the victims.[90]

Officers who abuse their authority may face criminal prosecution for violations of state and federal laws. However, civil lawsuits against the police for abuse of authority are more common than criminal prosecutions.[91] It is easier for victims to prevail in civil court, where the standard of proof is a preponderance of evidence, than in criminal court, which requires proof beyond a reasonable doubt. Claims charging abuse of authority often cite use of excessive force and false arrest.

Police departments and cities can be civilly liable for failures to act that result in denial of equal protection as set forth in the Fourteenth Amendment, as was demonstrated in the landmark case of *Thurman v. City of Torrington*.[92] Tracey Thurman was awarded a $1.9 million judgment as a result of the local police department's chronic failure to arrest her former husband for the violent

abuse of authority
Police disregard for policies, rules, or laws in the performance of their duty.

noble cause
Justification for wrongdoing committed by an officer based on the premise that the end justifies the means.

▶ **Excessive Force**

There are a variety of explanations for police use of excessive force. *What explanations, if any, justify the use of excessive force?*

acts he committed toward her. The large settlement made this case a catalyst for the development of mandatory arrest laws (see Chapter 7).

MYTH/REALITY

MYTH: Most changes in police behavior have resulted from police efforts to serve citizens better.

REALITY: Changes in police behavior are often forced by legislative action or court cases such as *Thurman v. City of Torrington*, which gave notice to police departments across the country to treat domestic violence as they would a crime in which the perpetrator and victim do not know each other.[93]

Police Corruption

corruption

Misconduct motivated by personal gain, such as skimming seized narcotics monies.

Corruption is generally defined as misconduct motivated by personal gain, such as skimming seized narcotics monies.[94] Motives are not limited to money, however. Personal gain may take the form of services rendered or political influence gained. A police officer may let a tavern remain open after the required closing time because a local politician is part owner, and the officer believes that "looking the other way" will lead to a promotion or a better assignment through the politician's influence. Two schools of thought have developed to explain police corruption: the first focuses on the police organization, and the second on the individual.[95]

Organizational Explanations for Police Corruption Organizational explanations of police corruption often attribute it to an entrenched culture of dysfunction (as illustrated through the agency example in the "Matters of Ethics" box) and the police occupational subculture, especially the "code of silence." Officers who adhere to the code of silence are motivated by fears of being labeled a rat and being ostracized for snitching–and, conceivably, even being left without timely aid when endangered in a street situation.[96]

Individual Explanations for Police Corruption Police occupational subculture helps explain why corruption exists among the rank and file. It does not, however, explain why some officers are corrupt and others are not. Individual factors

Matters *of* Ethics

Department of Justice Investigation of the Ferguson, Missouri, Police Department

On March 4, 2015, the U.S. Department of Justice (DOJ) released its findings from both criminal and civil investigations of the Ferguson, Missouri, Police Department. The investigations stemmed from the August 9, 2014, shooting death of Michael Brown, an unarmed, 18-year-old African American, by Ferguson police officer Darren Wilson.

The FBI opened a federal criminal rights investigation two days after the fatal shooting amid some witnesses' allegations that Brown, suspected by Wilson as the perpetrator of a recent robbery at a convenience store, had his hands up in surrender when he was being apprehended and ultimately shot by Wilson. Federal authorities reviewed physical, ballistic, forensic, and crime scene evidence; medical reports and autopsy reports; Wilson's personnel records; audio and video recordings; and Internet postings. FBI agents, St. Louis County Police Department detectives, federal prosecutors, and prosecutors from the St. Louis County Prosecutor's Office worked cooperatively to both independently and jointly interview more than 100 purported eyewitnesses and other individuals claiming to have relevant information. Based on its investigation, the DOJ concluded that Officer Wilson's actions did not constitute prosecutable violations under the applicable federal criminal rights statute, 18 U.S.C. Section 242, which prohibits uses of deadly force that are "objectively unreasonable."

The shooting of Michael Brown, despite the eventual exoneration of the involved officer, exposed and accelerated a broader breakdown in civic trust. The incident triggered weeks of protests and some rioting, revealing the depth of disharmony between many members of the community and the police. On September 4, 2014, the Civil Rights Division of the DOJ opened an investigation under the "pattern or practice" provision of the Violent Crime Control and Law Enforcement Act of 1994. The investigation revealed a pattern or practice of unlawful conduct within the Ferguson Police Department that violated the First, Fourth, and Fourteenth Amendments of the U.S. Constitution.

The investigation disclosed that Ferguson's law enforcement practices were shaped by the municipality's focus on revenue rather than by public safety needs. The emphasis on revenue compromised the character of the police department, contributing to a pattern of unconstitutional policing, and also shaped the municipal court, leading to procedures that raised due process concerns and inflicted unnecessary harm on members of the community. Further, Ferguson's police and court practices both reflected and exacerbated racial bias. Over time, the police and court practices sowed deep mistrust, undermining law enforcement legitimacy among African Americans in particular.

The city budgeted for sizable increases in municipal fines and fees each year and exhorted police and court staff to deliver those revenue increases. The emphasis on revenue generation resulted in patrol assignments and schedules geared toward aggressive enforcement of Ferguson's traffic codes. Officer evaluations and promotions depended inordinately on the number of citations issued. Officers sometimes wrote 6, 8, or, in at least one instance, 14 citations for a single encounter. Moreover, half of African Americans received multiple citations per encounter, while only a quarter of non–African Americans did. Thus many officers appeared to see residents, especially those residing in the city's predominantly African American neighborhoods, less as constituents than as potential offenders and sources of revenue.

This culture within the police department influenced officer activities beyond citation issuance. Officers expected and demanded compliance even when they lacked legal authority. They tended to interpret the exercise of free speech as unlawful disobedience, innocent movements as physical threats, and manifestations of mental or physical illness as belligerence. Police supervisors and leadership did little to ensure that officers acted in accordance with law and policy. The result was a pattern of stops without reasonable suspicion and arrests without probable cause. In addition, the DOJ investigation revealed that officers' use of force frequently went unreported, and when completed such reports were reviewed laxly.

Ferguson's community policing efforts always appeared to have been modest at best, but they dwindled to virtually nothing in recent years. One officer has been designated as a "community resource officer." No other officers play any substantive role in a community policing context.

The Justice Department has called for an overhaul of the police department. In its report, the DOJ delineated 13 recommendations for change within the police department to remedy unlawful enforcement practices and to repair community trust.

OBSERVE → INVESTIGATE → UNDERSTAND

- To what extent, if any, might the exercise of discretion have been abused by the Ferguson police officers?
- Was the DOJ's call for an overhaul of the police department attributable principally to the police subculture, or was the subculture a part of a larger scheme?
- Is Ferguson an appropriate venue for advancing the concepts of legitimacy and procedural justice? Why or why not?

SOURCES: U.S. Department of Justice, Criminal Section of the Civil Rights Division, *Department of Justice Report Regarding the Criminal Investigation into the Shooting Death of Michael Brown by Ferguson, Missouri Police Officer Darren Wilson* (Washington, DC: DOJ, March 4, 2015); U.S. Department of Justice, Civil Rights Division, *Investigation of the Ferguson Police Department* (Washington, DC: DOJ, March 4, 2015).

also come into play. Even the best screening protocol provides only a snapshot of an officer's psychological qualifications at the beginning of his or her career.[97] Some corrupt individuals may manage to slip through the selection screening process. Other recruits may be impulsive or harbor a sense of entitlement. Individuals react differently to the normal day-to-day events police officers encounter, and some succumb to temptations.

Attaining Integrity

The opposite of misconduct is integrity, which in the context of policing refers to moral principles and professional standards that help officers resist the temptation to abuse their rights and privileges. Integrity can be an attribute of police organizations as well as of individuals.[98] Strategies to enhance integrity help minimize misconduct.

Management's Leading Role   Management is responsible for reducing vulnerability in the police force. For example, management must create tight protocols for handling narcotics evidence so that no one can remove or skim either money or drugs. Perhaps most important, however, is management's role in setting the tone by condemning abuse. The way managers detect, investigate, and discipline misconduct shows officers how serious they consider it to be. Managers must also demonstrate their own integrity. If rank-and-file officers do not see their managers or supervisors practicing what is expected of them, integrity will be shelved in that spacious cabinet labeled "forget everything you learned in training—this is how we do it on the street."[99]

Early Warning Systems   Early warning systems are data-driven programs that identify police officers whose behavior is beginning to suggest problems. By automatically recording each employee's role in all incidents including uses of force, vehicular pursuits, formal complaints, and informal counseling, the programs reveal patterns that indicate an inclination toward or potential for misconduct. Early warning systems came into use after evidence showed that in most police departments a small percentage of employees is responsible for a disproportionate share of instances of misconduct.[100]

Only about one-third of agencies have early warning systems. Among those that do, more than 95 percent of survey respondents rate them as "effective."[101]

Legitimacy and Procedural Justice   An unfortunate reality is that in a number of communities the police have lost the confidence of those they have sworn to serve. This distrust is often exacerbated by the nature of the police–citizen contacts, which far too often are unilateral exchanges–police to citizen. When the police fail to explain why a citizen has been detained by the police or fail to explain the actions taken by an officer to ensure both the safety of the officer and the citizen, citizen or onlooker complaints are often the result. In recent years police executives have begun to explore the concepts of legitimacy and procedural justice and their application to policing. **Legitimacy** is a measure of the extent to which the public trust the police, are willing to defer to police authority, and believe police actions are morally justified and appropriate. Police can increase the public's belief in their legitimacy by providing procedural justice in the course of interactions. **Procedural justice** consists of providing an opportunity for a citizen to explain his side of a story in a given situation and for the officer, in turn, to make his decisions in a fair manner; within this context, an officer must ensure that he responds with a respectful demeanor. There is a growing body of research indicating that when the public believes police are exercising their authority in procedurally just ways, there is improved deference to police authority and an equally improved impression of the police. Accordingly, there can be increased respect of citizens

legitimacy
A measure of the extent to which the public trust the police, are willing to defer to police authority, and believe police actions are morally justified and appropriate.

procedural justice
Providing an opportunity for a citizen to explain his side of a story in a given situation and for the officer, in turn, to make decisions in a fair manner.

by the police and a substantial reduction in the incidence of circumstances that often give rise to the incidence of misconduct.[102]

Formal Mechanisms for Detecting and Investigating Misconduct All large law enforcement agencies have internal affairs units to handle real and reported misconduct. Sworn personnel from within the agency staff these units. Citizen review boards also are common. These boards, which frequently include members from the community's minority groups, can review and make recommendations regarding complaints of police misconduct. They also may have authority to investigate complaints and even adjudicate claims. The presence of a Black mayor in a city increases the likelihood that a citizen review board will be created there.[103]

Independent auditors who evaluate citizen complaints generally work at high levels within law enforcement agencies or in outside government entities. They often have law degrees and are dedicated to ensuring a fair and thorough investigation.

Regardless of the mechanism, the key to a successful investigation is the ease with which people can register complaints. The intake process must be "color-blind" and accessible via many channels, including mail, anonymous phone numbers, and in-person opportunities at police stations.[104] The other crucial component is a speedy and fair resolution of complaints.

PRIVATE SECURITY

An overview of policing would not be complete without a look at its private sector counterpart in crime prevention: private security. Entrepreneurship and privatization are part of daily life in a democratic society; allowing for the transfer of power and responsibility to the consumers of goods and services is a form of contracting out social control services.[105] In essence, then, **privatization** is the transfer of government programs and functions to the private sector.[106] Therefore, we can define **private security** as the nongovernmental, private sector practice of protecting people, property, and information; conducting investigations; and otherwise safeguarding an organization's assets.[107]

Private security agencies provide for the safety and security of private individuals and organizations and prevent and detect criminal activity on private property. They help companies enforce corporate policy and respond to natural and other disasters. Importantly, private security is indispensable as extra "eyes and ears" for matters related to homeland security.[108]

privatization
The transfer of government programs and functions to the private sector.

private security
The nongovernmental, private sector practice of protecting people, property, and information; conducting investigations; and otherwise safeguarding an organization's assets.

Growth

There are an estimated three times more private security officers in the United States than public law enforcement officers.[109] One reason for this dramatic growth is the expanded service offered by private security organizations. In addition to providing security guards, these organizations also install and monitor alarms, manufacture security equipment, and conduct polygraph tests, background investigations, and drug screening.[110] And private security companies often augment the workforce employed by the Transportation Security Administration (TSA).

Quality Concerns

In the early days of private security services, untrained and poorly disciplined staff committed many abuses (such as use of excessive force and sleeping while on duty). No licensing standards applied, and training was superficial. Many of those hired were unfamiliar with citizens' basic constitutional protections. In fact, many security workers could have been arrested for battery had citizens known the criminal statutes and complained to police. However, the private security industry has been slowly professionalizing, partly in response to concerns about liability.

A Global View

India's Growing Reliance on the Security Industry

India has an estimated 5.5 million security officers (almost three times as many as employed in the United States), and it is projected to be among the top 10 security markets in the world by 2020. In large part, this increase is attributable to the country's infrastructure development. But it is also, in no small part, a result of the 2008 terrorist attacks in Mumbai.

The city of Mumbai, home to India's largest companies, is a primary target for terrorism as it symbolizes India's economic growth. The raid by terrorists in 2008 lasted three days and resulted in the deaths of 166 people. The terrorist assault team struck at "soft" targets where foreigners were likely to congregate. Gunmen opened fire indiscriminately in hotel lobbies, a train station, a movie theater, and a café, among other sites. Quickly overwhelmed, the police were unable to contain the fighting. Eventually, military forces were deployed and assisted in overcoming the onslaught.

The security sector is now India's largest corporate taxpayer, with security companies estimated to number 15,000. However, despite increased investment, end users have not yet seen a change in the quality of personnel. The average security officer is often under-screened at entry, undertrained, poorly supervised, and underpaid. Herein lies the longstanding shortfall of the private sector in comparison to public policing: training standards. This is a deficiency across the security sector, both domestically and internationally. However, it does appear that the call for improvement is being heard.

The U.S. Department of Justice, in association with the American Society for Industrial Security (an international association of security practitioners dedicated to professionalism in the security sector), has included in its action agenda for enhancing the quality of the practice of security a call for the cross-training of private security practitioners and law enforcement at existing training programs such as the FBI National Academy and the Federal Law Enforcement Training Center. Additionally, the agenda encourages study of law enforcement–private security partnerships in countries such as the United Kingdom, Ireland, Israel, and Sweden. Within India, the Private Security Agencies Regulation Act was recently created to establish minimum training standards (160 hours of training before deployment). Partnerships are being forged between local providers and those in Israel, Europe, and the United States for advanced training and consultant services.

Time will tell the tale of India's quest to harden the potential targets of terrorists. The country certainly is boosting the number of its security forces at an impressive rate. Ultimate success will be determined by the extent to which the rate of growth in quality can match or surpass the rate of growth in quantity.

OBSERVE → INVESTIGATE → UNDERSTAND

- Is it best to use finite financial resources to maintain the 40 percent annual growth rate of security personnel or to hire fewer and use the remaining funds for improved training programs? Explain.

- What might be a downside to using multinational trainers to train India's security forces?

- Would it be beneficial to have security forces train with law enforcement, or are their missions so different that training would be a waste of funds and time? Explain.

SOURCES: Stephanie Berrong, "India's Growing Security Industry," *Security Management.* www.securitymanagement.com/print/5676 (retrieved January 13, 2011); Bibhudatta Pradhan and Unni Krishnan, "Mumbai Police Strengthen Security on Terror Attack Intelligence," *Bloomberg Businessweek.* www.businessweek.com/news/2010-12-25/mumbai-police-strengthen-security-on-terror-attack-intelligence.html (retrieved January 13, 2011); Bill Roggio, "Analysis: Mumbai Attack Differs from Past Terror Strikes," *Long War Journal.* www.longwarjournal.org/archives/2008/11/analysis_mumbai_atta-print.php (retrieved January 13, 2011); Office of Community Oriented Policing Services, *Policy Paper: Private Security/Public Policing Partnerships* (Washington, DC: Department of Justice, 2004), 21–22; Federation of Indian Chambers of Commerce and Industry, "Private Security Biz Booms, Requests for Police Cover Go Up," *FICCI in News,* November 20, 2014. www.ficci.com/ficci-in-news-page.asp?nid=9421 (retrieved May 8, 2015).

To ensure at least a minimal degree of competence among private security workers, a number of states now require a licensing process.[111]

Private Security/Law Enforcement Cooperation

Some forms of economic crime are beyond the scope or jurisdiction of local police, and some police departments are ill equipped to investigate corporate cases. System complexities make it particularly difficult for public law enforcement agencies to prevent and investigate high-tech crimes. In addition, many private enterprises–financial institutions, for example–are reluctant to have monetary losses or service interruptions due to criminal conduct (for example, via hacking) brought to the attention of their shareholders and the general public. Police are thus finding liaisons with private security agencies a useful way to increase the effectiveness of investigating and preventing crime. Security threats, familiar and unfamiliar, will most assuredly demand an expanded repertoire of collaborative arrangements.[112]

Private security firms are not always better than public law enforcement agencies, but neither are public agencies "automatically superior in every respect" to private organizations.[113] "A Global View" on page 170 illustrates how private sector forces can be of significant value in "hardening" targets while at the same time reducing the strain on overwhelmed public sector forces attempting to respond to major incidents such as the terrorist attack on Mumbai, India.

SUMMARY

The popular view of policing, one that is reinforced by the media, sees the police primarily as crime fighters and law enforcers. In fact, most tasks that police perform involve neither fighting crime nor enforcing the law. But when the occasion demands, the police are those who are entrusted with the authority to use force.

The community policing strategy in vogue today emphasizes crime prevention and the cultivation of a positive relationship between the police and the public. Even though policing in the United States has always been highly localized—a reflection of the high value placed on independence—law enforcement agencies exist at the federal, state, and local levels. The proliferation of agencies can afford greater protection for all citizens but can also result in the problem of fragmentation, which comes starkly to light when agencies fail to communicate critical information to one another and when they provide duplicate services.

Law enforcement agencies recruit widely and screen recruits through a careful selection process. Selected candidates receive classroom training in police academies and one-on-one field training under the direction of a senior officer. Despite the training recruits receive, police occupational subculture may influence officer behavior more than the agency's rules and policies. Police are given wide discretion to act in the manner they deem most fitting in the particular circumstances. Still, there are some limits on their discretion, especially with the use of force and in vehicular pursuits.

An element of police subculture is the need to maintain authority, but police can misuse their authority when they disregard rules, orders, and laws in the performance of their duty. Officers sometimes try to justify such misconduct by claiming adherence to a "noble cause." Police who abuse their authority for personal gain are guilty of corruption. To maintain the integrity of a department and its officers, management must investigate any suspicion of misconduct and root out those who are guilty.

OBSERVE → INVESTIGATE → UNDERSTAND

Review

Identify the distinguishing characteristics of policing.

- Most of what police officers do on a daily basis has little to do with enforcing laws.
- Less than one-fifth of calls to police relate to a crime, and even less patrol time is spent on crime-related activities.
- The primary distinguishing feature of police is society's grant of authority to use physical force as necessary.

Trace the evolution of policing in the United States.

- Vigilantism was an early method for enforcing group norms.
- The first publicly funded city police departments were slave patrols.
- The innovations of the London model of policing, such as preventive patrol and hierarchical organization, had a significant influence on early urban policing in the United States.

- During the political era of policing, most police jobs were filled through political patronage.
- Changes in technology, a focus on crime control, and hiring based on merit characterized the professional era of policing.
- The present-day community policing era emphasizes a police–community partnership and proactive policing.

Describe the structure of law enforcement.

- U.S. policing has always been highly localized.
- Law enforcement agencies exist at the local (municipal and county), state, and federal levels.
- Problems resulting from fragmentation—that is, the lack of coordination among neighboring local agencies—include duplication of services and the failure to share critical information.

Recognize how recruitment, selection, and training affect quality of service.

- Law enforcement agencies are challenged to recruit for an unprecedented number of vacancies and to ensure diversity in the force.
- The selection process typically includes a test of mental ability, an interview, physical and psychological examinations, and a background check.
- Police officers today need to be service-oriented and proactive problem solvers.
- Training of police officers includes classroom study at a police academy, field training under the supervision of a senior officer, continuing professional training, and training for special areas.

Describe the dynamics of the police subculture.

- Police subculture may influence officer behavior more than formal rules and orders.

- Police subculture stresses the danger and irregularity of the work, the need for officers to support one another, and the necessity of maintaining authority.
- The blue code of silence is a code of loyalty among many officers that supersedes all other values and assures support regardless of the circumstances—including misconduct.

Contrast the positives and negatives in the use of police discretion.

- Discretion enables officers to enforce the spirit rather than strictly the letter of the law.
- Police must exercise vigilance to ensure that discretion does not become discrimination.

Distinguish between corruption and abuse of authority.

- Abuse of authority occurs when police disregard policies, rules, or laws to attain what they perceive to be a worthy outcome.
- Corruption includes taking advantage of the opportunity for personal gain.
- Management is responsible for establishing and maintaining integrity among officers and must incorporate mechanisms to facilitate reporting, detecting, and investigating allegations of misconduct.

Examine the extent and functions of private security agencies.

- Private security agencies direct most of their attention to the safety and security of private individuals and organizations, and to the prevention and detection of criminal activity on private property.
- Police are finding liaisons with the private sector and the business community a particularly fruitful way to increase effectiveness in attaining mutual goals of loss prevention and prevention of interruption of vital services.

Key Terms

abuse of authority 165	frankpledge system 144	privatization 169
adult learning 159	legitimacy 168	procedural justice 168
blue code of silence 160	noble cause 165	racial profiling 164
community policing 147	police occupational subculture 160	siege mentality 154
corruption 166	police organizational subculture 160	sworn personnel 147
discretion 162	preventive patrol 144	vigilantism 141
fragmentation 152	private security 169	watch system 144

Study Questions

1. Police officers are most accurately defined as
   a. individuals granted the power to use force.
   b. crime fighters.
   c. order maintenance providers.
   d. emergency management personnel.

2. Vigilantes
   a. operated as well-organized groups.
   b. were often poor people.
   c. were paid by local governments.
   d. were mostly harmless.

3. The policing era strongly influenced by Progressive era reforms was the
   a. vigilante era.
   b. political era.
   c. professional era.
   d. community policing era.

4. A problem resulting from the structure of policing in the United States is
   a. overpolicing.
   b. centralization.
   c. fragmentation.
   d. underpolicing.

5. A preferred characteristic in police recruits is
   a. political acumen.
   b. a service orientation.
   c. adventurousness.
   d. militarism.

6. A major component of police occupational subculture is
   a. stress.
   b. individuality.
   c. blind obedience to superiors.
   d. perception of omnipresent danger.

7. Among the following, the factor or situation that, by itself, is least likely to result in an arrest is
   a. a suspected narcotics dealer's negative attitude.
   b. a first-time act of shoplifting by a female adult.
   c. a hit-and-run accident by a Black male drunk driver.
   d. a felony arrest warrant.

8. An essential component of a sound police disciplinary system is
   a. having an early warning system.
   b. prolonging the adjudication of complaints.
   c. restricting the filing of complaints to in-person appearances at local precincts.
   d. limiting the acceptance of complaints to within a year of their reported occurrence.

9. One reason for giving police officers a relatively high degree of discretion is
   a. to enable an increased use of racial profiling.
   b. to broaden the situations in which lethal force can be employed.
   c. to compensate for the vagueness of many laws.
   d. noble cause.

10. The term applicable to the situation in which officers act wrongfully on the grounds that inappropriate means are justified by the outcome is
    a. siege mentality.
    b. bounded lawlessness.
    c. virtuous misconduct.
    d. noble cause.

Critical Thinking Questions

For further review, go to the LearnSmart study module for this chapter.

1. Does the image of police as crime fighters make recruitment easier or more difficult? Why?

2. How did events in the professional era affect recruitment of Blacks to policing?

3. What accounts for the widespread police occupational subculture when neither police management nor the public condones an "us versus them" attitude?

6 Policing

After reading this chapter, you should be able to:

- Identify the principal policing roles.
- Compare the various policing strategies.
- Describe the different jobs in policing.
- Explain how police departments strive to maximize their resources.
- Identify the factors that shape public opinion about the police.
- Compare the service needs of diverse populations.

Realities and Challenges

Foot Patrol in a Big City

In the summer of 2009, the Philadelphia Police Department and Temple University researchers conducted an experiment on the effectiveness of foot patrols in high-crime areas. The department deployed 200 officers in 60 violent crime locations. Previous research had indicated that foot patrols are effective at reducing residents' fear but have no impact on the crime rate.[1] This more recent research, however, has shown that foot patrols can have an effect on violent crime.[2]

The researchers selected sites for the foot patrols based on their analysis of crime by street corners. They found that in 2008, the top 5 percent of high-crime corners experienced 39 percent of the city's robberies, 42 percent of its aggravated assaults, and 33 percent of its homicides. Clearly, a small number of geographic hot spots were accounting for a high percentage of violent crime in Philadelphia. Each foot beat covered 15 street intersections and approximately 1.3 miles of roads.[3]

The study found that the targeted foot patrols resulted in a 64 percent increase in pedestrian stops, a 7 percent increase in vehicle stops, and 13 percent more arrests than before. Once the researchers accounted for displacement (the movement of criminal activity to a nearby area), the target areas saw a 23 percent drop in violent crime, which translated into the prevention of 53 violent crimes during the 12-week experiment.[4]

The researchers expressed some reservations about their findings. For one thing, they concluded that foot patrols may be effective only in neighborhoods that already have a serious violent crime problem. In addition, the researchers were concerned that the significant increase in pedestrian stops might have damaged police–community relations, causing some individuals to feel as if they were being unfairly targeted or treated as criminals.[5]

Increased foot patrols are one of many possible approaches to reducing crime. This chapter will survey a variety of such policing strategies. Departments and researchers are continually trying to improve their strategies so that their choices of how and where police officers are deployed, and the kind of policing they do, actually reduce crime. When departments try a strategy that does not have a significant impact, they may experiment with others. In August 2011 the police department attributed some of its success in reducing crime to its use of foot patrols.[6]

In this chapter we will examine the functions and services that make up policing operations. As we review proven strategies for fighting crime and the key duties assigned to police officers, we will note differences between the popular image of policing operations and the reality of a typical officer's day-to-day activities. We will consider that police work encompasses a variety of roles and tasks. Within a week's tour of duty, for example, a single officer might respond to calls relating to found property, an injured person, shots fired, an abandoned car, a traffic collision, a barking dog, and a landlord-tenant dispute. These calls, and any number of others, constitute the essential fabric of police work.[7]

POLICING ROLES

The popular image of a law enforcement officer is that of a heroic crime fighter who puts his or her life on the line every day. In the movies and on television, police officers spend most of their time combating criminals and rescuing victims from the grip of gun-toting, drug-sniffing thieves, killers, and psychopaths. The reality of law enforcement, however, is a far less dramatic story.

Consider the following facts. First, about half of all calls to police result in the dispatch of a police officer, although often, through an interview with the caller, it is apparent that sending an officer may not be necessary. For example, questioning the caller may reveal that a particular crime occurred some days earlier and does not now require an on-scene investigation; perhaps the victim needs only to have a police report prepared at the police station. Second, contrary to popular belief, most calls do not involve in-progress violent crimes or criminal activities requiring arrest. Instead, between 70 and 80 percent of police dispatches are based upon requests to maintain order in the community or to provide a certain service.[8] Third, only 19 percent of citizen calls for a police response involve a crime at all, and only 2 percent entail a violent crime.[9] In fact, only 46 percent of violent crimes were reported to police in 2013.[10]

Still, whether or not a crime is reported, police are also responsible for enforcing the law. In this section we will examine the three principal policing roles: maintaining order, enforcing the law, and providing services.

MYTH/REALITY

MYTH: Police work primarily entails responding to crimes in progress or crimes that have just occurred.

REALITY: The vast majority of calls to police relate to neither violent confrontations nor criminal activities requiring arrest, but rather to minor disputes such as a landlord–tenant disagreement and to requests for service such as removing a vehicle that is blocking a driveway.[11]

Maintaining Order—Keeping the Peace

The first of the three major policing roles is **maintaining order,** or keeping the peace, the goal of which is to reinforce informal control mechanisms already operating in the community.[12] Sometimes this role involves enforcement of local statutes and laws, such as when the police respond to complaints that someone is disturbing the peace. At other times the peacekeeping role involves activities undertaken to maintain the civility of life in the community. For example, the police may be called to investigate and deal with an abandoned car. In fact, police officers respond to many incidents not by enforcing the law but rather by handling the situation.[13]

Typical examples of maintaining order, or the peacekeeping function, include traffic control and crowd management during sporting events, concerts, and parades. Officers engaged in maintaining order typically use informal sanctions such as warnings far more than formal sanctions such as citations and arrests.

maintaining order
Peacekeeping activities, including enforcement of quality of life laws such as no loitering.

Enforcing the Law—When Arrest Is Needed

The primary function of **law enforcement** is the application of the criminal code to specific, developing situations. But the process of enforcing laws is not as clear-cut as you might expect. There are more laws in the criminal codes than police can routinely enforce, so they enforce laws based on their department's priorities, which are determined by factors such as the seriousness of a crime and the availability of police resources. These priorities are conveyed through

law enforcement
The police agency's application of the criminal code to specific situations.

departmental directives, training, peer interactions, and supervisors' preferences. Some laws are minor offenses, such as jaywalking, while others have a more serious impact on the community, such as toxic waste dumping. Police often tailor enforcement actions to community norms. For example, they may routinely arrest shoplifters if that is what local retailers desire.

Apprehending suspects lies at the heart of the law enforcement function. The degree to which patrol officers and follow-up investigators work cooperatively will, in many cases, determine the quality of crime scene investigations and thus their outcome—that is, whether or not officers apprehend suspects.

▲ **Keeping the Peace**

Maintaining order in the community is one of three major policing functions.

service activities

Non-law enforcement activities performed by officers on an as-needed basis.

Providing Service—Nonemergency Police Work

Service activities are non-law enforcement duties performed by police officers on an as-needed basis. Such activities include giving directions, arranging for tows of disabled vehicles, assisting disoriented elder adults, and arranging for barricade placement at dangerous spots along public roads. These duties fall to the police primarily because of their round-the-clock availability.

The meaning of "service" in U.S. policing has developed significantly from its early politically based form. A new service orientation evolved in the later twentieth century as criminal justice scholars and policing practitioners recognized the value of community outreach both to reduce crime and to address community needs on a broad scale.

POLICING STRATEGIES

Reducing and responding to crime remains a key focus of police work. Police departments have developed several approaches to preventing and addressing criminal activity. These strategies are tailored to different types of crime situations.

Preventive Patrol

preventive patrol

Officers' maintenance of a visible presence in communities to serve as a deterrent to a variety of street-level crimes.

The assumption behind the strategy of **preventive patrol,** in which officers randomly patrol a neighborhood, is that the visible presence of an officer serves as a deterrent to a variety of street-level crimes, including prostitution, drug dealing, burglaries, and robbery. Preventive patrol is most often conducted by patrol car, but police may also patrol on foot (see the "Realities and Challenges" vignette at the beginning of this chapter) or by bicycle. The common feature

KEY CONCEPTS   Policing Roles

Function	Definition	Example
Maintaining order	Keeping the peace	Managing crowds
Enforcing the law	Applying criminal laws	Making an arrest
Providing service	Non-law enforcement activities provided to residents	Giving someone directions

of preventive patrol is the clearly identifiable presence of a uniformed police officer. Preventive patrol focuses on reducing street crime rather than offenses committed in the privacy of people's homes.

MYTH/REALITY

MYTH: Police presence reduces crime.

REALITY: Police presence alone does not reduce crime.[14]

The Kansas City Preventive Patrol Project, a police study conducted in 1974, was designed to test the degree to which preventive patrol affected a variety of factors, including offense rates, response time, number of traffic accidents, level of public fear, and public satisfaction with the police. To measure the influence of preventive patrols on crime level, the researchers created three different kinds of districts in Kansas City. One type of district maintained the same number of patrols as before the study. A second type eliminated preventive patrol units altogether and required officers to leave the district immediately after responding to a call for service. In the third type of district, the number of patrol officers was increased.

The study found that the level of patrol in a neighborhood had no effect on any of the factors under study. Police administrators and academics were shocked to learn that there was no significant relationship between the number of officers patrolling a district and the number of crimes committed, the number of vehicular accidents, the level of residents' fear, the degree of support for the police, or police response time to calls for service.[15]

Perhaps, though, we should not be so surprised by the study's findings. The assumption that preventive patrol reduces crime also presumes that offenders are acting rationally, but criminal behavior is influenced by a variety of factors that limit rational decision making. Offenders may find themselves in situations that lead to criminality or suffer from maladies that affect their mental capacity.[16]

Problem-Oriented Policing

A strategy proposed by Herman Goldstein in the late 1970s, **problem-oriented policing** emphasizes discovering the underlying causes of problems. Goldstein encouraged police departments to consider the complexity of problems rather

problem-oriented policing
A policing strategy based on conducting specific and detailed research on a community's problems to discover the underlying dynamics of crime.

◄ **Police Officer Conducting Preventive Patrol**

A typical police strategy is random patrol of neighborhoods.

than narrowly focusing on crimes—a change from previous policing strategies. For example, suppose there have been several arsons in an area. Let's say that some were the work of teenagers burning down buildings, while others occurred when homeowners set fire to their homes to collect insurance monies. Both would be considered crimes of arson, but the underlying causes would be completely different and would call for different police responses. To identify the underlying causes of problems and then appropriately respond to them, Goldstein recommended that police take specific sequential steps.[17]

The first step in a problem-oriented policing strategy is conducting specific and detailed research on a community's problems to reveal the underlying dynamics of crime.[18] For example, suppose police discover that burglaries in a college town largely victimize students and increase when the college is on break and most students have gone home. They notice that the pattern of these crimes differs from that of other residential crimes and commercial burglaries in the town. The crimes tend to victimize a specific population (college students), occur at particular times of year (during the breaks), and take place in a specific area of town (near the college). Once the department identifies the characteristics of the burglaries, officers can more effectively respond to—and prevent—these crimes.

The second step in problem-oriented policing is to examine the ways in which the police department currently deals with a particular problem in order to identify the most effective responses. In the case of campus burglaries, the department would examine how it has dealt with such criminal patterns before and what strategies were most successful in preventing burglaries and apprehending perpetrators. Problem-oriented policing strategies also include learning from other departments' successful practices and published studies on policing. The key concept in this second step is that departments are reviewing both their own responses and other relevant research as well.[19]

Once the department has identified the problem and researched ways to deal with it, the third step is devising strategies to address the problem. Police officials must consider how they might relay needed information to residents, develop new skills in their officers, and enhance community resources.[20] In the campus burglaries example, new skills might include learning how to adapt campus patrols while college students are on break and setting up surveillance cameras to watch over the dormitories. The Case in Point Box on page 181 illustrates a problem-oriented policing success.

Many police departments engage in some version of problem-oriented policing. The way problem-oriented policing is practiced in any individual department is influenced by both its priorities and its resources. In one approach, departments assign problem-oriented policing officers to a particular geographic area that is plagued by a variety of specific problems. Another approach is to assign these officers to specific problems that cross neighborhood boundaries. For example, police departments have used problem-oriented policing to tackle crimes involving both domestic violence and gang activity. In the case of domestic violence (DV), departments have created DV units to follow up with individuals who have made calls for police help in such cases. With gangs, teams of officers may successfully reduce some crimes by maintaining close contact with area youths known to have gang associations.

One model of problem-oriented policing is called *SARA* (a term that stands for scanning, analysis, response, and assessment). In the *scanning* step, the police department identifies the problem, its consequences, the frequency with which it occurs, and any other information relevant to understanding it. The next step, *analysis,* identifies anything that may be causing or influencing the problem. During the analysis step, police department researchers gather

Problem-Oriented Policing in Action: The Colorado Springs Police Department's HOT Program—Providing Outreach to the Homeless

The Colorado Springs, Colorado, Police Department (CSPD), like other municipal law enforcement agencies, has always dealt with homeless individuals and the challenges related to homelessness. However, the tactics employed by the CSPD to address the situation were often counterproductive, yielding unaddressed citations, increased workloads for the courts through warrant issuance, and a potential disruption of social benefits for the homeless defendants.

The homeless population reached a crisis level in 2009, due in large part to the protracted economic downturn, which caused numerous individuals to find themselves homeless for the first time in their lives. Many sought employment unsuccessfully; at the same time, they heard local citizens yelling at them to "get a job." Encampments of the homeless proliferated. Along with the camps came safety concerns such as out-of-control campfires, *E. coli* infections, and feelings of unease on the part of citizens residing near the recreational trails where encampments were frequently situated.

Given the complexity of the situation (that is, the intertwined socioeconomic issues and the importance of fashioning a response that would address the underlying dynamics and yield an enduring, compassionate solution), the CSPD elected to apply the SARA methodology. The initial action by the CSPD was an assignment of officers to conduct surveying of the homeless to determine the scope of their plight and what was needed to get them off the streets. Officers also visited social services providers to ascertain the array of available services.

The officers continued researching while conducting their surveying and outreach. They discovered a Homeless Outreach Team program implemented at the Pinellas Park, Florida, Police Department (PPPD). Subsequently, a trio of officers traveled to the PPPD for first-hand observation. The principal lesson learned was that communication among the homeless, police, service providers, and community was essential if they were going to help anyone off the streets.

Upon their return from the PPPD, the encouraged officers proposed creation of their own Homeless Outreach Team (HOT).

The CSPD leadership team was supportive of the concept, and outreach began in a manner not previously attempted in Colorado Springs. HOT officers established forums comprised of business owners, homeowners, City Council members, advocates, members of the American Civil Liberties Union (ACLU), and homeless individuals.

Although, the HOT program was making great strides, the issues associated with increasing camps and accumulation of trash and waste continued. The CSPD worked with the City Attorney's Office, homeless advocacy groups, and the ACLU to draft an ordinance related to public camping that would be enforceable and fair. This was a long process, but an ordinance that prohibited camping on public property was presented to City Council and passed, becoming law in February 2010. A condition of the no-camping ordinance was that displaced couples would be linked with a local shelter or other housing arrangement immediately upon vacating their camping sites.

It is difficult to fully describe the success of the HOT effort without including a typical success story. For example, HOT officers encountered one homeless couple who were chronic alcoholics and living in poor conditions in a tent. On Christmas Eve temperatures had dropped well below zero. HOT personnel offered the couple transportation via patrol car to a local substance abuse and housing facility. The couple refused help, stating that they had just purchased alcohol and would rather spend their time enjoying their purchase. Over the next few months, HOT officers made daily contact with the couple and eventually convinced them to enter a local alcohol treatment program. The couple has been successful in their treatment and now has permanent housing. In addition, both are employed by a local homeless services provider, assisting other chronically homeless people to get off the streets.

In 2010, the HOT program was nominated for, and won, the prestigious International Herman Goldstein Award from the Center for Problem-Oriented Policing. The CSPD continues to maintain vigilance over the homeless situation and has a formal organizational goal of ensuring that every officer is equipped with the skills and resources necessary for successful interaction with the homeless population. Communication center dispatchers possess lists of services available, so they can refer those in need to people who can assist them, whether the need is housing, employment, or other services. In combination with its community partnerships, the HOT program has helped to house over 800 individuals, to reunite over 200 individuals with families out of town, and has documented over 200 individuals gaining employment.

OBSERVE → INVESTIGATE → UNDERSTAND

- What does the HOT program demonstrate about the value of applying the SARA problem-solving technique?
- Could the techniques used by the Colorado Springs Police Department work in your community? Why or why not?

SOURCES: Commission on Accreditation for Law Enforcement Agencies, *CALEA Update: Colorado Springs Police Department's HOT Program—Providing Outreach to the Homeless* (Gainesville, VA: CALEA, 2011); Colorado Springs Police Department, "Homeless Outreach Team" (HOT), *City of Colorado Springs – Homeless Outreach Homepage.* www.springsgov.com/SectionIndex.aspx?SectionID=66 (retrieved March 17, 2015); Center for Problem-Oriented Policing, "Winner! Homeless Outreach Team (HOT)," *Goldstein Awards 2010.* www.popcenter.org/library/awards/goldstein.cfm?browse=abstracts (retrieved December 17, 2012).

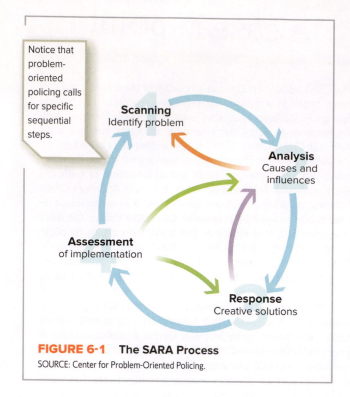

Notice that problem-oriented policing calls for specific sequential steps.

Scanning
Identify problem

Analysis
Causes and influences

Assessment
of implementation

Response
Creative solutions

FIGURE 6-1 **The SARA Process**
SOURCE: Center for Problem-Oriented Policing.

information on the problem to better understand how the department is currently handling it. While conducting analysis, the department will also learn what resources are already available to help solve the problem. In the third step, *response*, participants think creatively about ways to solve the problem. As part of the response step, a department will most likely learn how other jurisdictions have dealt with the same problem. The department then creates an implementation plan with clear objectives that will allow for measurable results. The final step is *assessment*, during which officers determine whether the program was put into effect as intended and whether the goals were met. A plan for continuing assessment of the chosen strategy may also be a part of the assessment stage. Figure 6-1 illustrates the SARA process.

Community-Oriented Policing

A policing strategy that focuses on reducing crime and disorder, such as loitering and graffiti, by involving residents in the job of policing is **community-oriented policing.** It has four components: police-community reciprocity, decentralization of police units, proactive policing using foot patrols, and the civilianization of the police force.[21] These four components result in policing that is focused more on maintaining positive police-community relations than on crime rates.

Police-community reciprocity requires collaboration between police and community members to solve and prevent crime. The success of community policing relies on a mutually beneficial bond between the police and the public. Community policing contends that policing is the responsibility of all members of a neighborhood and that the public is a partner in the effort to fight crime, disorder, and other community problems.[22]

A second component of community policing is **decentralization of command,** the creation of substations or police buildings in various areas so that the police maintain a physical presence throughout the community. Decentralization gives individual patrol officers more discretion to come up with ways to solve neighborhood problems. The belief is that because patrol officers interact daily with people in the neighborhood, they are better positioned than police managers to know what that community needs.

A third component of community policing is **proactive foot patrol,** in which officers walk beats to learn more about the people in the neighborhoods they patrol and to develop relationships with them. Officers assigned to foot patrols generally report higher levels of satisfaction in their jobs.[23] Perhaps the greater satisfaction arises because officers on foot patrol have more opportunities to interact with a wide variety of people rather than dealing almost exclusively with suspects and victims.

Civilianization of the police force, the fourth component of community policing, involves assigning to civilians tasks previously performed by police officers. The goal of civilianization is to increase the number of community residents actively participating in policing. Civilian community service officers (CSOs) might help with gathering nonemergency reports or addressing community problems that are not of a serious criminal nature. CSOs typically perform tasks that involve no inherent danger or risk. For example, if a resident reports that her house was burglarized while she was on vacation, a police department may send a CSO to take the report, because

community-oriented policing
A policing strategy that depends on getting community members to address the problems that plague their neighborhoods.

police–community reciprocity
A policing practice that relies on collaboration between police and community members to solve and prevent crime.

decentralization of command
The fanning out of substations in various areas so the police maintain a physical presence throughout the community.

proactive foot patrol
A component of community policing in which officers walk beats to learn more about the people in the neighborhoods they patrol and to develop relationships with them.

civilianization
A component of community policing that increases the number of community residents active in policing by assigning civilians to tasks previously performed by sworn officers.

Real Careers

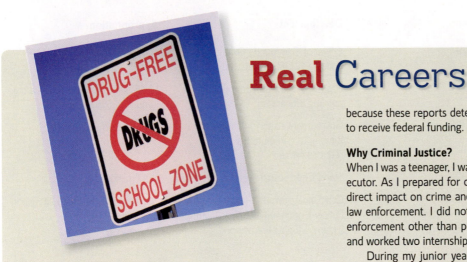

STACY SHAMBLIN

Work location: Reno, NV

College(s): University of Nevada, Reno (2007)

Major(s): Criminal Justice (BS)

Job title: Methamphetamine Program Coordinator, Reno Police Department

Salary range for jobs like this: $35,000–$50,000

Time in job: 1.5 years

Work Responsibilities

I coordinate drug education and prevention activities for the Reno Police Department. We educate citizens about the drugs commonly abused in their area, the effects and paraphernalia associated with those drugs, and drug prevention strategies. In general, the program serves middle and high school students, parents, and professionals who work with teens and young adults. My role in the program is to fulfill requests for instructional materials and presentations and to provide drug awareness training targeted for the specific audience. Trends in substance abuse often change, and I adapt our curriculum to provide the most accurate information possible.

In addition to managing the program, I am responsible for monitoring and reporting quarterly progress to the federal office that funds our activities—COPS, or Community Oriented Policing Services (part of the U.S. Department of Justice). Although writing reports is not as exciting as planning presentations, it is an important aspect of my job because these reports determine whether our program will continue to receive federal funding.

Why Criminal Justice?

When I was a teenager, I wanted to pursue a career as a criminal prosecutor. As I prepared for college, I realized I wanted to have a more direct impact on crime and public safety through a career in civilian law enforcement. I did not know what careers were possible in law enforcement other than police officer, so I consulted my professors and worked two internships while in college.

During my junior year, I applied for the FBI Scholastic Honors Internship Program and was selected to intern in the Economic Crimes Unit at FBI headquarters in Washington, DC. My summer with the FBI proved to be a valuable work experience and was certainly a great asset to my resume, but the internship that was most instrumental to my current career was at the Crime Analysis Unit of the Reno Police Department. Shortly after I graduated, my former supervisor, who was impressed with my work as an intern, notified me that the position of methamphetamine program coordinator had become available.

Expectations and Realities of the Job

I have been somewhat surprised by my influence in making key decisions for the program. Even though I am an entry-level employee, I have been encouraged to suggest and even implement new strategies to improve the success of the program. I am impressed with the effectiveness of the COPS approach to tackling drug problems, which utilizes cooperation and partnerships with outside agencies. I frequently work with schools and community organizations, such as Join Together Northern Nevada, Nevada Prevention Resource Center, and Boys & Girls Club.

My Advice to Students

Apply for internships. My internship experiences gave me a competitive edge in the employment marketplace. They allowed me to explore potential career opportunities, including some nontraditional criminal justice careers that I previously had not known about. In addition, my internships provided me with opportunities to build my project management and professional communication skills, which are applicable to any career in law enforcement.

---

the crime occurred several days before the call for service, and thus no one is in imminent danger.

Although the goals of community policing are laudable, this policing strategy has been subject to some criticism. For example, some scholars have raised questions about what constitutes a community and how different groups–the police, other city employees, residents–define geographic areas as a community. In other words, what the police define as a community, the residents and others may not.[24] Also, some critics point out that police do not communicate equally with all members of a community and that individuals with greater resources are more likely than others to have opportunities for positive interactions with police. Other critics observe that the members of the community do not always agree on identified problems and solutions.[25] Finally, some

▶ **Highlights from the Office of Community Oriented Policing Services**

SOURCE: U.S. Department of Justice, "The COPS Office: 20 Years of Community Oriented Policing." http://cops.usdoj.gov/default.asp?Item=2754.

Year	Development	Appropriation
1994	Office of Community Oriented Policing (COPS) is created	$148.4 million
1999	Has hired 100,000 community policing officers	$1.46 billion (I know this is a big jump. It is correct.)
2005	Government study indicates COPS funding to communities reduced crime	$598 million
2008	Starts Child Sexual Predator Program	$587 million
2015	COPS hosts forum "Healthy Police–Community Relations within a Human Rights Framework"	2014 appropriation, $124 million

observers view community policing as just the latest strategy in the overpolicing of Blacks—a tactic whereby police take advantage of their large number of contacts with the community to keep their surveillance of this particular group of people high.[26]

Implementing Community Policing   Because community-oriented policing is an innovative policing strategy, there have been difficulties in implementing its various components. We consider some of these challenges here.

Some police departments have received federal grants to encourage them to implement community policing programs. The federal Office of Community Policing Services (COPS) was created in 1994 by the Violent Crime Control and Law Enforcement Act. COPS was charged with distributing grants totaling $8.8 billion over six years. Their first major grant focus was to aid police departments in hiring officers who were specifically designated community-oriented policing officers. The office and its funding have grown since that time. In 2015, the office announced that applications were open for five different grant programs–COPS Hiring Program, Community Policing Development Program, COPS Anti-Gang Initiative, Anti-Heroin Taskforce Program, and the Anti-Methamphetamine Program. As of 2015, COPS has distributed $14 billion to 13,000 law enforcement agencies (from state to tribal). This has resulted in the hiring or redeployment of 126,000 officers to community- and problem-oriented policing functions.

Community policing reformers argue that community policing allows police to change their relationship with the public, partly by reducing the number of ranks in a department. Streamlining the ranks means that there are not as many different levels of officers from the patrol level to the chief's level. Because community policing also emphasizes that officers should be generalists who deal with all the problems of a community, some police departments have reduced the number of department sections that focus on a particular task or crime. In practice, however, research has found no significant difference in organizational structure between departments that claim to be using community policing and those that do not. That is, many departments that say they are implementing community policing have not reduced either the number of ranks in the department or the number of sections focused on a particular task or crime.[27]

As shown in Figures 6-2 and 6-3, the structure of a department that has reduced the number of ranks and sections looks very different from that of a traditional department. A department structured like that shown in Figure 6-3 is more likely to give patrol officers increased discretion, a central feature of

FIGURE 6-2   **Hierarchical Structure of a Traditional Police Department**

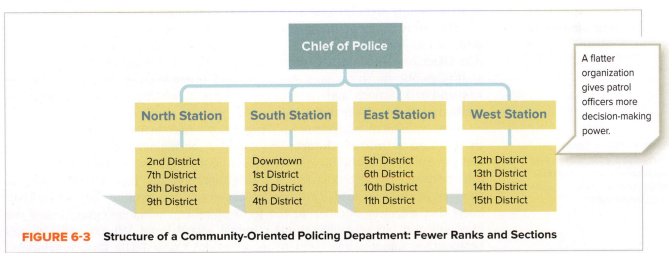

FIGURE 6-3   **Structure of a Community-Oriented Policing Department: Fewer Ranks and Sections**

community policing. Thus, a department with a flatter organization like that pictured in Figure 6-3 is likely to be implementing a community-oriented policing strategy.

Implementing community-oriented policing requires change not only in organizational structure but also in police culture. Because of these two requirements, the nationwide implementation of community policing is occurring slowly.[28]

Consider that traditional police culture regards crime prevention and law enforcement as the sole responsibility of the police. In community policing, however, crime prevention is considered a *joint* responsibility of police officers and community members. This notion is a fundamental change in the understanding of what makes up police work—and changing *any* professional culture, including police culture, is difficult. Cultural changes often start with the leadership of organizations. There is little chance that a police department will implement community policing if the chief is not fully committed to the strategy.[29] Patrol officers must also support the philosophy, because they are the ones who will put it into effect at the street level. Support for such a cultural change among police officers, however, is uneven. In general, officers of color are more likely to support community policing.[30]

The Impact of Community Policing During the early 1990s, when community policing became the model for departments, the crime rate declined, but community-oriented policing was not necessarily the reason.[31] If community policing does not reduce crime, why is the strategy so popular with federal, state, and local governments?

The answer is that crime reduction is not the only way to assess the impact of community policing. Another significant measure of this strategy's influence is the community's confidence in the police and the development of a positive relationship between the police and the public—a central goal of community-oriented policing. Indeed, volunteers in community policing programs within their local police departments generally report high confidence in the police. Furthermore, law-abiding individuals who have a greater number of contacts with the police department are more likely to have a higher level of support for their police.[32]

Aggressive Order Maintenance

Disorder is frequently a major contributor to residents' discontent with their neighborhoods, especially in urban communities. Naturally, many residents fear and disapprove of vagrants, drunks, drug addicts, loud teenagers, and others who may disturb the peace in the streets.[33] For such residents, the presence of such people signifies that the neighborhood is experiencing disorder.

aggressive order maintenance
Policing activities that address noncriminal or minor offenses that affect residents' quality of life.

One strategy for fighting disorder is **aggressive order maintenance,** or *zero tolerance policing*, in which police focus on minor public order offenses that affect residents' quality of life. For example, officers target abandoned cars, graffiti, public urination, and loitering by identifiable gang members by using stop-and-frisk actions and field interrogations. A strategy of aggressive order maintenance drives up the number of arrests for minor offenses.

broken windows theory
Theory proposing that disorder leads to crime because criminals assume that a neighborhood that tolerates disorder will also ignore criminal acts.

One influential perspective on aggressive order maintenance is known as the **broken windows theory.** Proposed by social scientists James Q. Wilson and George Kelling, the broken windows theory argues that there is a relationship between the deterioration of a neighborhood and higher crime rates. In their view, disorder leads to crime because criminals assume that a neighborhood that tolerates disorder—in the form of broken windows, graffiti, and the like—will also ignore more serious criminal acts.[34] From Wilson and Kelling's perspective, minor crimes lead to more serious crimes. The broken windows theory also holds that having officers focus on minor offenses will reduce serious offenses. This point of view seems logical, but showing a relationship between disorder and crime is not always easy.

The broken windows theory has had a major impact on how criminal justice professionals and members of the public think about crime and how they believe police departments should use their resources. The idea that disorder leads to more serious crimes suggests that police officers should focus more of their time on addressing minor nuisance-type enforcement that previously was unlikely to get much notice from patrol officers. Wilson and Kelling also contend that a police focus on reducing disorder would ease public fears. Hence, if police could reduce disorder, they could also reduce more serious crimes *and* fear of crime.

Although the broken windows theory is politically popular, the relationship between disorder and crime is complicated. In fact, the link between disorder and crime has not been proved, with the exception of the crime of robbery.[35] An important factor in the mix that must be considered is *community efficacy*—the feeling among community members that they can do something about their neighborhood. Importantly, the *absence* of community efficacy leads to both disorder and crime. When people in a neighborhood are bound together by common values about public disorder and crime, they create a common community culture and develop a sense of community efficacy. However, the reality is that community efficacy is less common in poor communities, so poor communities are more likely to have neighborhoods characterized by disorder.

Many of the ideas underpinning the broken windows theory remain popular. For example, some metropolitan law enforcement agencies, among them the New York City Police Department, see aggressive order maintenance as a successful policing strategy. These agencies believe that strict enforcement in the case of minor offenses increases the quality of life in neighborhoods that were previously considered blighted. Moreover, other supporters of aggressive order maintenance argue that it reduces both crime and residents' fear of crime. But on the other side of the debate, opponents of the strategy say that aggressive order maintenance results in targeted policing in poor neighborhoods and focuses mainly on people of color.

POLICE OFFICERS ON THE JOB

The principal activities performed by law enforcement officers are patrol, follow-up investigation by detectives, and traffic operations. These are customarily referred to as **line activities.** Additional activities that support line activities are referred to as **support activities.**[36] These may include communications, custody, and forensics. Law enforcement agency employees who are sworn officers usually fill line positions, while civilian employees typically occupy the support positions.

The Rookie Officer—Meeting the Real World

The first day of work for the average police academy graduate working in a city is often overwhelming. The role-playing scenarios practiced at the academy suddenly become real as the rookie officer is immersed in the daily functions of policing: maintaining order, enforcing the law, and providing service. The rookie learns the rhythm of the patrol officer while working under the watchful and often hypercritical eye of a training officer. The vehicle pull-overs are now real, as are the tickets issued to motorists. To the rookie's surprise, every action takes much longer to complete than expected.

As radio calls arrive from the dispatcher, the rookie gains a sense of the call load queue. The "queue" is the array of calls for service awaiting handling. Depending on the communications equipment installed in police vehicles, the queue of calls may or may not be visible to the officer. Already on the way to a "landlord-tenant dispute," the officer must turn the squad car around in the hope of catching the perpetrator of a "burglary in progress." As the new call receives priority, the officer wonders what might be waiting at the scene. The training officer and other senior officers will scrutinize the rookie officer's performance closely; the new officer must act carefully, know when to call for backup, and not make any serious rookie mistakes such as exposing the gun side of the hip (a position of tactical disadvantage) while interviewing a suspicious person.

line activities
The principal activities performed by law enforcement officers, including patrol, follow-up investigation, and traffic operations.

support activities
Additional policing activities that support line activities, such as communications, custody, and forensics.

▶ **Dispatcher at Work**

Dispatchers are essential in helping police officers do their job.

The Patrol Officer—The Backbone of Policing

Uniformed personnel (patrol officers) assigned to patrol specific regions of a city or county perform the bulk of police work. The majority of patrol officer contacts with the public are responses to calls for service.

Patrol officers are the first individuals to respond to a call for service. They are in many ways the backbone of the law enforcement organization. The patrol officer is the most visible face of the agency and the initial responder to virtually any incident requiring a police response. The patrol force is the component around which a police department is constructed; without the patrol component, there would be no law enforcement capability. Patrol officers do not merely wait around the precinct station for a call; they are out and about in the geographic region that makes up their jurisdiction, always on the lookout for suspicious activity. They keep a watchful eye on the streets they patrol, noting such variables as time and place, appearance, and behavior of an individual to determine whether the scenarios they observe might be considered suspicious activity.[37]

MYTH/REALITY

MYTH: Detectives are most responsible for preserving the integrity of a crime scene.

REALITY: The quality of the patrol officer's preliminary investigation is the key determinant in solving crimes. If the description obtained at the scene of the crime is accurate, there is a reasonable likelihood of solving the case.[38]

The patrol officer has a crucial role at crime scenes. As the first responder on the scene, she must be alert for any fleeing suspects and assess the scene for the safety of other officers and/or emergency medical technicians who are on the way. At the crime scene, the patrol officer must locate key parties (victims, suspects, or witnesses), control them, and identify and preserve any physical evidence. Once the patrol officer musters sufficient resources to secure the crime scene and identify or control persons of interest, she must document everything she observed.[39] In large agencies, the officer's reports and notes are provided to

Real Careers

MARK DEMMER

Work Location: Washington County, OR

College(s): California State University, Chico (2008)

Major(s): Criminal Justice (BS)

Job title: Patrol Officer

Salary range for jobs like this: $45,000–$50,000

Time in job: 1 year

Work Responsibilities
A usual day consists of making traffic stops and writing reports for any number of things, from thefts to automobile crashes. There is no such thing as a typical week. One week I might write 5 reports and make 40 traffic stops; the next I might write 15 reports and only make 5 traffic stops. The workweek is dynamic and keeps me energized. It doesn't even feel like a chore for me to go to work. Every day I feel proud to be helping people and making a difference in their lives and the community. What makes the job even more of a pleasure are the new friendships I have developed with my coworkers.

Why Criminal Justice?
After my first "ride-along" in Great Falls, Montana, as a high school volunteer at my local police department, I knew I wanted to be a cop. But I had to work hard to get my dream job. After going through four years of college and seven months of testing and interviewing, I landed the position.

Expectations and Realities of the Job
This career has been more difficult than I expected. For example, while I learned how to write in college, I had to learn how to write detailed police reports after I got hired. These are important because they are used in court and can make the difference in what the verdict in a case might be.

Multitasking has also been an unwritten requirement of the job. For example, while I'm driving the police vehicle, I have to operate the communications equipment. During vehicle pull-overs or when I arrive at the location of a call for service, I have to tactically position the police vehicle for maximum safety and efficiency. Shift rotations (e.g., moving from the daytime shift to the graveyard shift and having to stay awake at 3:00 a.m. and then going to bed at 10:00 a.m.) take some getting used to as well. Thank goodness for aluminum foil, which does do the trick in terms of shutting out the daylight. Extended shifts, often resulting from a court appearance or overtime for an arrest or a search for a suspect or missing child, are another challenge.

My Advice to Students
Once you leave college for the real world, it is important to set achievable goals. For me it was work hard and get hired. And even if you reach your goal, don't think it can't be taken away. I've realized it's hard to get hired but even harder to stay hired. Try learning from the veterans and consider their advice.

detectives for their follow-up investigation. In small agencies, the first responding officer may also handle the follow-up.

A 1975 seminal study revealed that the bulk of the cases solved by detectives hinged on information obtained by patrol officers during their preliminary investigation, with a witness's or victim's at-scene description of a suspect a crucial factor.[40] A second and larger 2001 study reaffirmed the importance of patrol officers in the investigative process, with 72 percent of surveyed agencies reporting efforts to enhance patrol officers' investigative role.[41] A 2011 in-depth job task analysis of the criminal investigator function suggested that spreading the problem analysis practices of uniformed patrol officers to investigators could be a promising way to orient them toward

▼ Detectives attempt to salvage crucial physical evidence.

strategic crime control, that is, toward addressing the underlying conditions that cause crime problems to persist.[42]

Follow-up Investigation

A follow-up investigation occurs after a patrol officer documents the facts of the crime. For serious crimes (for example, homicides and home invasion robberies), the detective may be called directly to the scene and receive a briefing from the first responder. In most cases, however, the detective receives the patrol officer's report the next day, after physical evidence and suspects have already been secured.

solvability
The likelihood that a crime will be solved.

Because resources are limited, priorities among criminal incidents requiring investigation are determined by the seriousness of the crime and its **solvability,** that is, the likelihood the crime will be solved. Solvability depends upon the presence of clues or evidence that makes apprehension of a suspect more likely. Several specific factors affect solvability: the quality of the patrol officer's preliminary investigation, the availability of witnesses, a suspect's name or identifying information, significant physical evidence, and identification of a unique method of operation (MO) by the perpetrator.

Solving crimes can be very difficult, however. For example, according to FBI records, nationwide in 2013, law enforcement cleared 48.1 percent of violent crimes and 19.7 percent of property crimes. In the FBI's Uniform Crime Reporting Program, law enforcement agencies can close, or "clear," cases in one of two ways: by arrest or by "exceptional means." The rate of crime clearance is calculated by dividing the number of crimes cleared by arrest or "exceptional means" by the number of criminal offenses reported. Clearing of crimes by "exceptional means" requires that an agency encounter circumstances outside its control that preclude arresting, charging, and prosecuting an identified offender. "Examples of exceptional [means] clearances include, but are not limited to, the death of the offender (e.g., suicide or justifiably killed by police or citizen); the victim's refusal to cooperate with the prosecution after the offender has been identified; or the denial of extradition because the offender committed a crime in another jurisdiction and is being prosecuted for that offense."[43] This low solvability rate can partly be explained by the fact that solving crimes when a witness or victim does not identify the suspect is very difficult.

A detective's follow-up investigation plan typically includes visiting the crime scene and documenting everything related to the case. When all the evidence and information have been obtained and a suspect has been apprehended, the detective prepares the case for presentation to the prosecutor, who reviews its worthiness for a court's scrutiny.[44]

Enforcing Traffic Laws

Police are the primary public safety agency in charge of the enforcement of traffic laws. Law enforcement officers have this responsibility for several reasons. One reason is the relationship between crime and traffic incidents. Think about it: Automobiles are frequently used in the commission of crimes, and police are equipped to find and capture suspects on the run. In high-crime areas, searches incidental to traffic stops frequently yield illegal drugs and firearms, precipitating a disruptive influence on organized criminal enterprises.[45] Police are also outfitted and trained to handle situations that might result from traffic stops, such as belligerence on the part of drunk drivers, aggravated traffic violations, and the discovery of persons with outstanding warrants. Finally, police use their investigative skills to elicit statements and document facts relating to traffic collisions.[46]

Until recently, the police alone were responsible for enforcing traffic laws. However, the so-called traffic services functions have begun to extend beyond the law enforcement agency. Indeed, in many communities, the police partner with community agencies that draft and implement transportation policy, such as the local department of transportation. These partnerships effectively identify existing traffic-related problems and develop solutions that benefit the whole community.

For example, the accident reports taken by police feed into local and statewide computerized databases that may be accessed by city, county, and state government transportation entities. Sharing this database helps them identify problems that may be mitigated through engineering solutions such as roadway alterations or the placement of traffic lights. For their part, police may use these databases to identify locations that are particularly prone to traffic accidents and may increase their patrols accordingly. Direct interaction with citizens enables police to learn about the specific concerns of the community while providing a forum to educate the public on evolving traffic safety practices such as speed bumps and roundabouts that restrict speed and increase pedestrian safety. Law enforcement also relies on devices such as photo radar cameras and electronic message signs to prevent collisions and provide advisories of traffic conditions.[47]

Communications Technology—The Central Nervous System of Policing

Just as the patrol function is often considered the backbone of policing, communications might be thought of as the central nervous system that coordinates the performance of law enforcement activities. Computer-aided dispatch supplements radio communication and allows patrol officers to remotely search databases for warrants for individuals or vehicles without having to go through the central dispatch center. Many agencies are working to establish next generation 9-1-1 capabilities that will better serve today's wireless society; 9-1-1 systems that are capable of receiving text messages, photographs, and videos will be more useful for public safety purposes.[48]

Mobile video systems, which complement computer-aided dispatch in enabling an official record of events, consist of vehicle-mounted cameras that capture audio and video information, providing evidence of crimes such as drunk driving while monitoring officers' conduct.[49] Before the widespread use of in-car video systems (and body-worn cameras), evidence of alleged offenses or of misconduct by an officer was sorely lacking. The availability of video has greatly reduced the burden of producing evidence for both the alleged offender and the officer. Accused parties may introduce portions of the video to refute police allegations, just as police officers may introduce video evidence to refute allegations of police misconduct.

Communications interoperability is the ability of police agencies (and other public safety entities such as fire departments and emergency management agencies) from different jurisdictions to talk and share data in real time. Though vitally important, such communication is often a challenge, because different jurisdictions operate on different frequency bands (see the "Disconnects" box). Precious time is lost while dispatchers manually relay emergency communications between radio systems. Technology that facilitates communication among different bands is being developed, as is a

RealCrimeTech

DOES DUE PROCESS PROTECTION APPLY TO CAMERA ENFORCEMENT?

Municipalities have increasingly used cameras to enforce traffic laws. Some have claimed that camera enforcement is a violation of constitutional rights and due process. Most often, these assertions are based on the fact that there is no live witness to testify against an alleged offender. Similarly, there is confusion over whether a citation must be served in person. However, courts have consistently ruled that the right to be free from a red light ticket does not fall under those very specific and fundamental rights protected by the U.S. Constitution and due process. As one federal judge has expressed, "No one has a fundamental right to run a red light or avoid being seen by a camera on a public street."

SOURCES: Derek Prall and Mark S. Mulholland, "Does Constitutional Substantive Due Process Protection Apply to Camera Enforcement?" *American City & County Exclusive Insight* (April 22, 2015); FindLaw, "Speeding and Red Light Camera Tickets," traffic.findlaw.com/traffic-tickets/speeding-and-red-light-camera-tickets.html (retrieved June 27, 2015).

communications interoperability
The ability of police and other public safety agencies from different jurisdictions to talk and share data.

DIS Connects

Nationwide Public Safety Broadband Network, which will provide a secure, dedicated interoperable network for emergency responders to communicate during an emergency.[50]

custody
The incarceration of persons either accused or convicted of a crime.

Custody—Booking and Holding Offenders

Custody is the incarceration of persons either accused or convicted of a crime. The length of time a law enforcement agency keeps an arrested person in custody varies. In general, police departments maintain only temporary holding facilities for arrested persons. They may be booked into the police station for a few days before being taken before a judge, who then evaluates the grounds for arrest and determines whether the person can be detained longer. The detective assigned to the follow-up investigation may question a suspect in police custody, and the police may run fingerprint identification on the suspect.

Custody is usually a core function of a sheriff's department. As county entities, sheriff's departments maintain a central jail for persons awaiting trial and for those who have been convicted and are serving a period of incarceration up to a year. Newly appointed deputy sheriffs commonly serve a stint in the county's jail facility before being assigned to patrol, traffic, or investigative details.

Forensics—Applying Science to Investigations

Forensics is the application of scientific knowledge and methods to criminal and civil investigations and legal procedures, including criminal trials. Facilities using

▲ **Suspect Processing**

This police officer is processing an arrested person for transfer to the jail facility of a sheriff's department.

scientific or technical methods to process and analyze evidence are called **forensic science laboratories. Criminalistics** is the use of scientific techniques in recognizing, identifying, individualizing, and evaluating physical evidence.[51] In the past, scientific analysis of evidence occurred near the end of a criminal investigation–when a case was being prepared for trial. Today, scientific analysis begins with the first responder to the crime.

forensics
The application of scientific knowledge and methods to criminal and civil investigations and legal procedures, including criminal trials.

forensic science laboratories
Facilities using scientific or technical methods to process and analyze evidence.

criminalistics
The application of scientific techniques to recognizing, identifying, individualizing, and evaluating physical evidence in legal proceedings.

> **MYTH/REALITY**
>
> **MYTH:** Forensics results are available quickly and reliably to most major police departments.
>
> **REALITY:** Even when forensics tests are available, results can take days, weeks, or even months. Furthermore, due to evidence contamination or other problems, the results are not always reliable.[52]

The prominent role of forensics in criminal investigations rests on two factors: increased awareness of its value in identifying and protecting evidence, and advances in technology. Popular television shows highlighting forensic techniques have profoundly influenced public expectations in terms of evidence collection, analysis, and presentation in court. On television, the forensic laboratory returns results to police within hours of evidence collection. In real life, however, forensic testing analysis can take days, weeks, or even months.[53]

In the world of forensics, the demand for DNA testing in particular continues to accelerate. Principal reasons include a skyrocketing increase in the number of DNA samples from property crimes (whose incidence far outnumbers that of violent crimes); the reopening of cold cases; examination of possible instances of wrongful conviction; and advances in analysis capabilities that enable "hits"–DNA matches–from minute samples. Consequently, there is a backlog of evidence awaiting DNA analysis, despite crime laboratories' efforts to boost their processing capacities. Congress has provided hundreds of millions of dollars to reduce DNA backlogs through technological innovation. For example, high-tech robotic workstations can now process large numbers of DNA samples simultaneously, allowing crime labs to work more efficiently.[54]

Scientific analysis is applied to a wide range of evidence beyond DNA, including controlled substances, fire debris, explosive residues, hairs, fibers, glass, soil, paint, fingerprints, tire tracks, footwear, tool marks, and firearms.[55] Included too are the complex analyses that involve computer-stored information and insects that inhabit corpses (to determine time and location of death). The "Careers in Forensics" table lists the variety of forensic career types.

▲ **Forensic Chemist-Anthropologist with Bones**

Technology has helped solve crimes, but getting evidence analyzed is sometimes difficult given limited resources.

THE POLICE ORGANIZATION

Most agencies that deploy uniformed personnel have certain common characteristics, such as a hierarchical organization and a degree of centralization. Three key protocols characterize such hierarchical, centralized agencies: chain of command, unity of command, and span of control.

CAREERS IN FORENSICS

Listed here are some of the careers available in forensics, as well as the educational requirements for each.

Title	Job Description	Minimum Education Usually Required
Forensic accountant	Analyzes financial transactions	Bachelor's degree in accounting to determine fraud
Computer forensics investigator	Finds and analyzes computer evidence	Education and experience in computer science
Evidence technician	Receives, processes, and stores physical evidence	Some coursework in forensics
Ballistics and firearms expert	Matches projectiles to particular weapons	Experience in firearms and trajectory analysis
Fingerprint examiner	Collects and analyzes latent print evidence	Bachelor's degree in science
Criminalist	Analyzes physical evidence through use of scientific techniques, usually in a laboratory	Bachelor's degree in biology, chemistry, physics, or criminalistics
Forensic pathologist	Determines cause and time of death	MD
Forensic entomologist	Uses insect evidence to determine time, place, and cause of death	Doctorate in biology
Forensic anthropologist	Helps determine identity of human remains as well as cause of death	Doctorate in anthropology
Forensic psychologist	Uses psychology to help make decisions relevant to the law (determining competency to stand trial, assisting attorneys in juror selection)	Doctorate in psychology

chain of command
The line of authority that extends throughout an organization.

unity of command
The requirement that each individual within an organization reports directly to a single individual higher in the chain of command.

span of control
The extent of an individual's authority, or the number of individuals that one person is responsible for overseeing.

Chain of command is the line of authority that extends throughout the organization. **Unity of command** requires that each individual within the organization reports directly to a single individual higher in the chain of command. **Span of control** is the extent of an individual's authority, or the number of individuals that one person is responsible for overseeing. The general behavior of all officers is embodied by the will of the chief, whose actions represent a consistency of conduct that assures citizens that the law is applied in an equitable manner.[56]

Most police departments are hierarchically organized, with several layers of personnel and a rigid chain of command, but the move to community policing during the latter decades of the twentieth century sparked calls for changes in police organization. Community policing requires a less centralized approach that gives rank-and-file officers the flexibility and autonomy needed to develop closer ties with the community and to involve the public in solving community problems. Community policing empowers field officers to exercise increased amounts of discretion in solving problems, while management acts as coach.

The 9/11 terrorist attacks led to another organizational change. Specifically, police departments have created units or assigned personnel (for example, terrorism liaison officers) that are responsible for gathering information that could be linked to possible terrorist activity. At the same time, post-9/11 agencies increasingly have shared information with one another. Before the terrorist attacks, police organizations had been relatively insular, relying on adjoining agencies only in acute emergencies.

Review of the events leading up to 9/11 highlighted the importance of sharing intelligence information proactively to help prevent such emergencies. Indeed, as illustrated in Chapter 16, piecing together a terrorist plot often requires the gathering of information possessed by different jurisdictions. Networks of policing agencies equipped to share information across regional jurisdictions are critical to the success of antiterrorist intelligence gathering. These networks are made up of all agencies within regions and effectively cross the borders of jurisdictional authority that have been characteristic of American policing since its inception.[57]

DEPLOYMENT OF POLICE RESOURCES

A police operation needs a sound strategy for the allocation of personnel and equipment to ensure that those resources are being used appropriately. As is the case in almost all organizations, a police department's most important resources are money and people. Financial resources for law enforcement agencies come primarily from government agencies. For example, municipal policing agencies receive most of their funds from city governments.

In many cities today, steep declines in revenue have caused government officials to take drastic actions. In San Diego, Phoenix, Tulsa, and Tampa, police agencies have halted hiring officers and eliminated civilian positions altogether.[58] As police budgets for all communities become increasingly at risk, the efficient deployment of resources becomes commensurately crucial. This section looks at the challenging considerations that arise in the deployment of police resources.

Factors Affecting Resource Allocation

Many factors influence how police resources are allocated, including demands of the citizens, administrative requirements of the police agency, and agendas of local government leaders. Decisions about how many police officers to have on the streets versus assigned to other tasks are resource choices that often come under scrutiny. If, on the one hand, the local population prefers a community-oriented policing strategy, the number of police officers assigned to patrol can be relatively high. If, on the other hand, the community prefers a policing strategy focused primarily on rapid response to crime-related calls for service and apprehension of offenders, fewer officers are assigned to foot patrol in the community.

The policing strategy in practice also affects a police organization's administrative and support needs. Agencies emphasizing community policing strategies need additional staff to support substations in the community and to conduct special programs operating from main stations.

MYTH/REALITY

MYTH: Police are almost always deployed in greatest numbers where there is the highest percentage of minority populations.

REALITY: Police deployment is often the result of political influence. A cohesive minority bloc can wield significant political clout in the competition for policing resources.[59]

Local politics plays a role in the deployment of police resources. Insistent pressure from a particular group that more police should be deployed to their neighborhood is most likely to be effective in cities with traditional political structures and operations, such as a mayor-council form of government, partisan elections, and district-based city councils. In these cases local elected officials tend to be sensitive to political pressure.[60]

Interestingly—and paradoxically—fiscal constraints may have a bright side: illumination of the value of evidence-based policing. **Evidence-based policing,** which was proposed as a new model for policing in 1998, is the use of the best available research on the outcomes of police work to implement guidelines and to evaluate agencies, units, and officers.[61] This model, which had earlier been applied in the practice of medicine, is ideal as a means for determining best practices—and in turn for optimizing the deployment of resources. A prerequisite

evidence-based policing
The use of the best available research on the outcomes of police work to implement guidelines and evaluate agencies, units, and officers.

of evidence-based policing is acquiring the knowledge of research methodology. This prerequisite facilitates a strengthening of the relationship between practitioners and academicians–a long overdue partnership.

The evidence-based future of policing must include a focus on the relatively small percentage of streets and locales that generate much of the crime in a city or county. Such a focus will be most effective if the police try to use not only strategies that increase surveillance and deterrence, but also ones that try to strengthen the microcommunities of people who reside in crime hot spots.[62]

Technological Resources

In addition to money and personnel, equipment is a crucial resource for law enforcement agencies. Police departments are increasingly using new technological equipment–such as geographic information systems, computerized statistical systems, and crime analysis–to improve their efficiency.

Geographic Information Systems (GIS)   **Crime mapping** is the process of pinpointing the locations and times of crimes. The potential of crime mapping to help solve crimes is greatly enhanced by **geographic information systems (GIS)** technology, which uses a computerized mapping system to produce detailed descriptions of crime occurrences and to analyze the relationships between variables such as location and time. GIS technology reveals areas of concentrated crime or higher risk of victimization, commonly called **hot spots**.[63] This information enables police to concentrate their resources and problem-solving activities on the hot spots.

Computerized Statistics   GIS technology has been augmented by **CompStat** (COMPuterized STATistics), a performance management system developed by the New York City Police Department in 1994. CompStat integrates information from crime maps across the community for department leaders' review. It emphasizes information sharing, responsibility, accountability, and improving effectiveness. It includes four core components: (1) timely and accurate information or intelligence, (2) rapid deployment of resources, (3) effective tactics, and (4) relentless follow-up.[64]

crime mapping
A technique used by police to pinpoint the locations and times of crimes.

geographic information systems (GIS)
A technology that uses a computerized mapping system to produce descriptions of crime occurrence and analyzes the relationships between variables such as location and time.

hot spot
An area of concentrated crime or higher risk of victimization.

CompStat
A computerized statistical program that integrates information from crime maps across a community for department leaders' review.

▶ **Geographic Information Systems (GIS)**

Geographic information systems (GIS) help police departments identify high-crime areas, or hot spots. These areas are identified on this GIS Crime Map by the clustering of color-coded incidents.

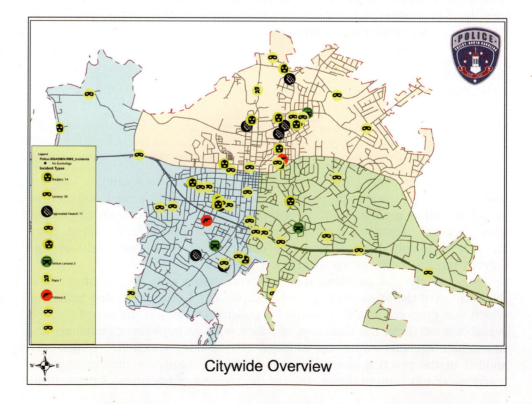

Citywide Overview

The Department of Justice identifies six aspects of CompStat that improve the ability of police departments to understand and cope with public safety problems: mission clarification, internal accountability, geographic organization of command, organizational flexibility, data-driven problem identification and assessment, and innovative problem solving. One reason for the success of CompStat is that it can be readily adapted by existing policing operations without making radical organizational changes.[65]

Crime Analysis   The assessment of crime-related information to help prevent crime, deploy law enforcement resources, apprehend suspects, and support crime investigations is termed **crime analysis.** Crime analysis techniques have greatly improved the way agencies deploy their resources. Before modern crime analysis practices became widespread, the task of allocating resources was jokingly referred to as the "Bud-Shell Method"–a name that evoked the image of a police administrator sitting with a six-pack of Budweiser and a Shell gas station road map, using a marker to draw lines down major arteries and create policing districts on the basis of geography.[66] Although the delineated districts were uniform in terms of size, the incidence of crime did not distribute itself accordingly. Yet administrators in the past had little in the way of current crime statistics to help them with the task of allocating resources. In contrast, today's computerized methods allow resources to be allocated based on analysis of the incidence of crime by type of offense, time of commission, and a complex mix of other variables. Combining computer-aided dispatch with automatic vehicle locator systems, commanders now may reposition resources at will via real-time views of crime occurrence.

Crime analysis is useful in follow-up investigations through examination of a crime scene in the context of an offender's behaviors. Knowing the *how* of a crime–what the perpetrator did and did not do–can help illuminate the *why*–the offender's likely motivation for the crime, as well as his personality. For example, an offender who uses a surprise approach (lying in wait or attacking a sleeping victim) reflects a lack of confidence, or inadequacy. Crime analysis can thus identify correlations that can reduce the pool of possible suspects. At the same time, crime analysis can reveal links among crimes, suggesting they may have been committed by the same individual(s).[67]

A recent outgrowth of crime analysis is predictive policing, which is rooted in the notion that it is possible, through sophisticated computer analysis, to predict where and when future crimes are most likely to occur. **Predictive policing** involves taking data from a wide array of sources, analyzing them, and using the results to anticipate, prevent, and respond more effectively to future crime.[68] The underlying concept is not new; what is new is the broad-based and extensive amount of data undergoing analysis and capable of being used to correlate with crime occurrence. For example, the infusion and analysis of data such as the location of dogs, the identification of homes with burglar alarms, the locales of code violations, and residents' employment status can lead to the prediction of the most likely targets for residential burglaries. Key to the continued implementation of predictive policing is a commitment to ensuring integrity in the handling of all information contained in databases analyzed. Privacy and civil liberty issues are critically interrelated with predictive policing.

THE POLICE AND PUBLIC OPINION

Overall, the U.S. public is supportive of the police. In one survey, 52 percent of the respondents expressed a "great deal" or "quite a lot" of confidence in the police,[69] rating the police second only to the military and higher than churches or organized religions, banks, the U.S. Supreme Court, the medical system, and

crime analysis
The application of processes designed to analyze information pertinent to crimes and to develop correlations useful in crime prevention, resource deployment, investigations, and suspect apprehension.

predictive policing
Taking data from a wide array of sources, analyzing them, and using the results to anticipate, prevent, and respond more effectively to future crime.

public schools. The highest level of confidence was found in 2004 at 64 percent. The change is likely influenced by the large number of protests surrounding police behavior toward Black Americans during 2014 and 2015. The age group with the greatest confidence in police is individuals 65 years and older.[70] See Figure 6-4 for an overview of public confidence in institutions, including the police.

In December 2014, Americans were less likely than in 2013 to view police officers as having high honesty and ethical standards. Forty-three percent of people rated police as high or very high in honesty and ethical standards. The poll was conducted after grand juries did not indict White police officers whose actions resulted in the deaths of Black men in Ferguson, Missouri, and Staten Island, New York. The overall drop of 6 percentage points in honesty and ethics ratings is the result of a significant, 22 percent drop in non-Whites' ratings of police officers. White people's views had not changed. Historically, Whites and people of color have viewed police differently, with Whites consistently viewing police more positively, but the recent data seem to indicate that people of color are responding much more negatively to Black male deaths that have resulted from police shootings. As a consequence, the overall ranking of police honesty is at its lowest point in more than two decades. Nonetheless, the current rating is still higher than the lowest recorded point of 37 percent in 1977.[71]

The public generally believes that racial profiling is more common than police brutality. For example, 53 percent of U.S. residents believe that racial profiling

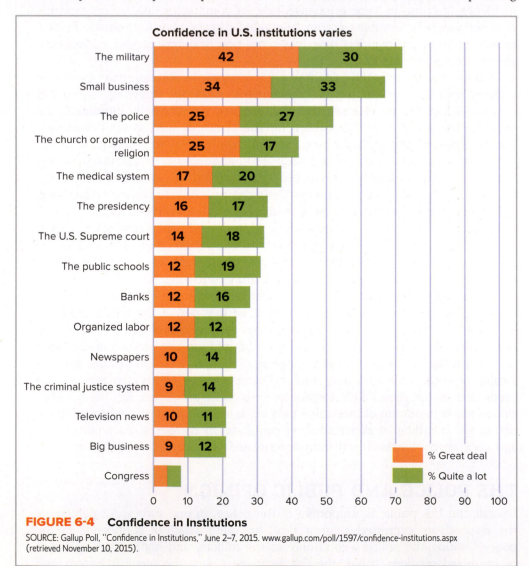

FIGURE 6-4   Confidence in Institutions

SOURCE: Gallup Poll, "Confidence in Institutions," June 2–7, 2015. www.gallup.com/poll/1597/confidence-institutions.aspx (retrieved November 10, 2015).

is widespread in traffic stops.[72] Numerous studies have uncovered evidence of racial profiling–or at least evidence that Whites and Blacks are stopped at different levels, a finding that supports the belief of many U.S. residents.[73]

Although overall U.S. residents are supportive of the police, there are fairly large differences in opinion between Whites and people of color. Among Whites, 57 percent have a great deal or quite a lot of confidence in the police, whereas 40 percent of non-Whites and 32 percent of Blacks have that same level of confidence.[74] A 2008 survey found that 42 percent of Whites but 30 percent of Latinos and 12 percent of Blacks have a great deal of confidence that the local police in their area treat Blacks and Whites equally. Fifty-three percent of Blacks said they had not much confidence about equal treatment–or none at all.[75]

One explanation for this difference in opinion is that Blacks have a different relationship with the police than do Whites. For example, 72.7 percent of Black men between the ages of 18 and 24 report having been victimized by racial profiling at least once, whereas only 10.9 percent of White males in that age group make a similar claim. Race and personal experience with racial profiling appear to have the greatest influence on individuals' opinions of the police.[76] Both Black and White communities believe that police treat the two communities differently, although for varying reasons. Whites tend to believe that differential treatment is warranted because Blacks are more likely to commit crimes, whereas Blacks see differential treatment as discriminatory.[77]

In September 2005 during the Hurricane Katrina crisis, and in the weeks that followed, media coverage of the New Orleans Police Department was almost entirely negative. There were reports of officers abandoning their posts, committing violence against residents, shoplifting, and looting. A poll conducted in March 2006 assessed New Orleans residents' views about how government leaders and institutions had responded to the effects of the hurricane. Given that in general Whites' and Blacks' views of the police differ and that Black residents of New Orleans were more seriously affected by Hurricane Katrina, the poll results are not surprising. The percentage that approved of the way the New Orleans police responded to the effects of the hurricane was 57 percent among Whites and 40 percent among Blacks.[78]

In general, Blacks' views of the police vary by class and level of education. Blacks living in middle-class Black neighborhoods report their relationship with police as more similar to that of White communities than that of Blacks residing in lower-class Black communities.[79] Whites' opinions of the police and views on racial profiling do not vary by class. Better-educated Blacks, however, are more likely than less-educated Blacks to have a negative view of profiling, to report having experienced it, and to think it is widely practiced.[80]

Blacks are not the only group that perceives the police differently than do Whites. Although Latinos' views are not as negative as those of Blacks, neither are they as favorable as those of Whites. For example, Latinos are more likely than Whites to believe that racial profiling is widespread.[81] Among both Latinos and Blacks, men are more likely than women to believe that racial profiling is widespread.[82] This difference is likely related to the relationship between personal experience and opinions of the police, since men of color generally have more contact with the police than do women of color. And certain other ethnic groups also view the police with some reservations. After the 9/11 terrorist acts, for instance, Arab Americans reported fearing the police because of what they viewed as increased surveillance and racial profiling of Arab Americans.[83] Historically, new Chinese and Vietnamese immigrants also have reported perceiving the police as prejudiced.[84]

In summary, although public opinion of the police varies by group, most of the U.S. public has a fairly positive view of the police. That is not true in all countries, as the "Global View" box explores.

A **Global** View

Public Perceptions of the Police in Russia

The Russian police service, known as the "militsiya" (militia) when it was created in 1917, soon after the Soviet revolution, served primarily as a force for maintaining social, political, and economic order. Rather than acting as a traditional law enforcement entity, the militsiya intruded on many aspects of daily life. The militsiya was not accountable to the citizenry in any real sense because all state institutions in the Soviet Union were subordinate to the Communist Party. Legal protection against abuses of power by the militsiya was virtually nonexistent because the militsiya functioned within an environment where the rule of law was not respected and civil liberties did not exist. The population viewed the militsiya as an authoritarian force, contact with which was best avoided.

The dramatic political changes that took place in Russia following the 1991 collapse of the Soviet Union resulted in the weakness of state institutions; escalating crimes rates; and flourishing organized crime, corruption, and lawlessness. Meanwhile, the militsiya had to police the country amid political, economic, and social chaos. The strict control exercised by the Communist Party over the militsiya was gone. This resulted in a climate conducive to abuses of power. In fact, in one instance, several militsiya members created a criminal organization that, for a number of years in the late 1990s, engaged in blackmail of businessmen, trading in firearms, falsifying evidence, and fabricating criminal cases against innocent people.

It is virtually impossible to obtain reliable statistics on the extent of unethical and unlawful conduct by the militsiya due to the populace's fear of disclosing information and regular cover-ups of wrongdoings. Wrongdoings by the militsiya significantly damaged the institution's reputation from the perspective of the public. In one study comprised of 1,600 surveyed individuals, only 12 percent indicated they fully trusted the militsiya, and 40 percent fully distrusted the institution. In a 2008 survey of 11,202 respondents, only 3 percent believed the militsiya fully deserved trust. In a 2009 study of 54 members of the public, the vast majority of interviewees believed the militsiya was ineffective, corrupt, brutal, disrespectful toward the law, concerned primarily with personal enrichment, and regularly consorted with criminal groups.

While serving as president in late 2009, Dmitry Medvedev launched extensive reforms of the militsiya. He revised the process of personnel selection, raised the level of professionalism, implemented a Code of Professional Ethics, and introduced subdivisions in the militsiya responsible for improving cultural and moral standards. In March 2011, the new "Law on the Politsiya" became effective. Along with the new law came a new name for the militsiya: "politsiya" (police). The manner in which the content of the new law was developed was as novel as the new law itself: A special website was set up to allow the public to suggest the changes they wanted to see to improve efficiency of the police, decrease corruption, and improve the image of law enforcement. Main changes included removing officers who were performing poorly and increasing by 30 percent the salaries of officers who survived the comprehensive evaluation process. Further, the Russian police were made a federal-level institution; under the old system police units were under the jurisdiction of local authorities and were more responsive to local governors' interests than to the greater public need. Importantly, too, the rights of individuals accused of crimes were expanded to include, for example, the right to make calls within three hours of being detained and the right to have a lawyer and interpreter from the moment of detention. Also, police may no longer detain a citizen for an hour just to verify identity.

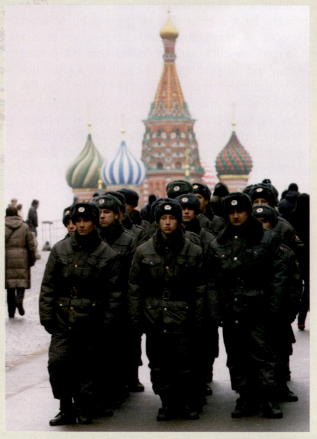

Despite their name change, the Russian police have a significant image problem to overcome. Not only must they shed the institution's prior tarnished image, but they must do so within an environment where the headquarters is rigidly focused on number crunching (that is, achieving daily target goals for arrests and crime clearance). Although keenness to catch criminals swiftly is to be praised, the methods employed to reach this goal must not compromise civil rights guarantees. Unfortunately, the system of performance appraisal used for police does not consider compliance with civil rights. This is unsettling, and it remains to be seen the extent to which the former brutal means of obtaining information or confessions may be revisited.

OBSERVE → INVESTIGATE → UNDERSTAND

- Within the new "Law on the Politsiya," where do you believe crime prevention fits within policing priorities?

- What might be some evaluation criteria to be incorporated into performance appraisals that would enhance the public's opinion of the police?

- Why is public opinion of the police in Russia so much more negative than public opinion of the police in the United States?

SOURCES: Margarita Zernova, "The Public Image of the Contemporary Russian Police," *Policing: An International Journal of Police Strategies & Management* 35, no. 2 (2012): 216–228; Asmik Novikova and Natalya Taubina, "Russia's Police: New Name, But Can It Change Its Spots?" *oD Russia-Post Soviet World*, August 28, 2012.

RESPONDING TO DIVERSE POPULATIONS

The public generally expects the police to serve all people fairly and equitably, keeping everyone safe. These expectations are challenging, as the police are called upon to serve a wide variety of people with different needs, problems, and experiences.

Elder Adults

In the United States the issue of mistreatment of elder adults has garnered growing attention as more people are living longer. The Census Bureau projects that more than 62 million Americans will be age 65 or older in 2025.[85] **Elder abuse** is any knowing, intentional or negligent act by a caregiver or another person that causes harm or a serious risk of harm to a vulnerable elder. The harm may be physical abuse, emotional abuse, sexual abuse, exploitation (the taking, misuse, or concealment of funds), neglect, or abandonment.[86]

Elder abuse is still a relatively new area of criminal justice intervention. It was first formally addressed in the United States in the mid-1970s with the allocation of Adult Protective Services' funding under Title XX of the Social Security Act. **Adult Protective Services (APS)** are state services provided to older people and dependent adults who are being mistreated or neglected, are unable to protect themselves, and have no one to assist them.[87] If the elder abuse occurs within an elder care facility, usually another agency has the responsibility to respond. In California, this other agency is the Long-Term Care Ombudsman.[88]

Although the investigation of suspected cases of elder abuse does not vary greatly from other criminal investigations, investigators need to be particularly alert to the physical condition of the home environment and the elder adult's accommodations and apparent health. They will treat skeptically any attempts by a caregiver or relative to answer for the elder or to keep the elder from directly providing information. They will also keep in mind that a victim's recall may be clouded by complications of the aging process, disorientation or nervousness, and/or the side effects of medication.[89] When an elder adult dies and there is suspicion of abuse or neglect, investigators must first determine whether the death was expected and consistent with the appearance of natural causes and then whether there was a delay in notifying authorities.[90]

Police dispatchers are an integral part of the law enforcement team approach to dealing with elder abuse. Many elder adults have difficulty articulating their problems or clearly describing their situations. Dispatchers must be trained to be patient and diligent in seeking information that may point toward abuse. They must also know how to refer callers to appropriate agencies such as law enforcement, adult protective services, or long-term care ombudsman.[91]

Determining the incidence of criminal offenses of elder abuse presents special problems. Victims may be cognitively impaired and unable to recognize or report offenses. Those who have been exploited financially may not be aware that they have been so victimized.[92]

The National Center on Elder Abuse, the major source of statistical information on elder abuse in the United States, collects and analyzes national data on

▲ **Police Aiding an Elder Adult**
Today police are often called upon to investigate cases of elder abuse.

elder abuse
Any knowing, intentional, or negligent act by a caregiver or another person that causes harm or serious risk of harm to a vulnerable adult 60 years of age or older.

Adult Protective Services (APS)
State services provided to older people and dependent adults who are being mistreated or neglected, are unable to protect themselves, and have no one to assist them.

▶ **Assisting and Protecting Victims with Disabilities**

Individuals with disabilities are at a higher than normal risk of being victimized.

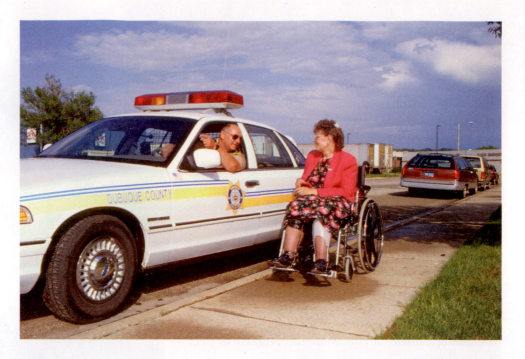

cases referred to and investigated by APS. A national study of state-level APS data conducted in 2004 revealed that "self-neglect" made up approximately one-third of substantiated reports of abuse, closely followed by neglect by caregivers and exploitation of finances. Over 65 percent of victims were women, and over 40 percent of victims were 80 years of age or older. Perpetrators were divided evenly among men and women. The largest category of perpetrators was between 30 and 50 years of age. Most alleged perpetrators were adult children of the victim or other family members. The study collected data nationwide, but states vary widely on the type of statistics they maintain. For example, only 40 percent of the states maintain a database of alleged perpetrators, and only 25 percent were able to provide data on racial composition of victims and perpetrators.[93]

Many law enforcement agencies have established partnerships with the elder adult population and the support agencies that serve them. The intent of these relationships, often organized under a program called TRIAD, is to create trust between law enforcement and the elder adult population. (*TRIAD* is not an acronym; it simply represents a three-part union of police, sheriff, and retired persons' associations.) Elder action programs use problem solving and community policing strategies to meet the concerns of the elderly.[94] A volunteer council, in some cities called SALT (Seniors and Lawmen Together), guides local TRIADs. Each SALT council decides what services the TRIAD will offer, recruits volunteers, and oversees the results. For example, the Texas TRIAD program, offered through the state office of the attorney general, includes consumer protection, crime prevention, and health and safety oversight. It also provides toll-free hotlines for seniors who have complaints about consumer goods, nursing homes, and Medicaid provider fraud, as well as a legal services hotline and a 24-hour abuse hotline.[95]

People with Physical or Developmental Disabilities

Individuals with physical or developmental disabilities are at higher risk of being victimized than those without such personal challenges, according to the National Organization for Victim Assistance. Because the perpetrators of crime against such individuals are frequently their caretakers, reporting the crime puts them at further risk, and few cases come to the attention of police. Moreover, individuals with disabilities may not be able to report a crime because of constraints on their mobility or difficulties communicating.

Recognizing these issues, the National Organization for Victim Assistance offers a number of recommendations on how criminal justice agencies, including police departments, can protect people with disabilities and respond when they have been victimized. Recommendations include ensuring access to buildings for people of all abilities, training officers about disabilities and the subcultures of people with disabilities, and encouraging police departments to work with victim services providers and disability support services organizations.[96]

People with Mental Disabilities

Providing services and protection for people with mental disabilities is another police priority requiring special attention. Police became more involved with people with mental disabilities in the 1980s, when a large number of institutions for those with mental disabilities closed because of cuts made to federal mental health funding. (See Chapter 12 for a discussion of people with mental disabilities in jails and prisons.) Officers generally encounter individuals suffering from mental illness as a result of complaint calls from members of the public. Most police academies do not include specific training to identify individuals who may be mentally ill or information on how to use community resources to address problems that may result from people with mental disabilities.

Officers encountering a person whose behavior appears irrational generally respond in one of three ways. The first is to transport the individual to a facility that provides psychiatric care if she is a danger to herself or others, although in some locations hospitals refuse anyone they deem dangerous. Regardless, an on-site physician has sole authority whether to admit the person.[97]

The second choice is to arrest an individual with mental disabilities for an offense such as disorderly conduct. This option is most often used when a hospital refuses admission, and the individual cannot be left in the situation in which she was found. An officer makes an arrest because he believes the individual will continue to cause problems.[98]

The third option is to resolve the situation informally if the person with mental disabilities is a "neighborhood character," a "troublemaker," or a "quiet mental." *Neighborhood characters* are individuals the police know well because of their visibility in the community, and they are not a threat to public safety. For example, individuals seen muttering to themselves and walking aimlessly might cause some concern, but they are not a danger to anyone. Police are also likely to ignore *troublemakers,* those who have created problems for officers in the past. In some instances, if police were unsuccessful in previous attempts to have someone admitted to the hospital, an officer may avoid dealing with that individual. Dealing with such troublemakers requires a lot of energy that officers are not necessarily willing to expend, as well as extensive paperwork. Police are also not likely to intervene with *quiet mentals*–individuals who seem detached from reality but do not present a nuisance to themselves or to the public.[99]

Although police use all these options, the probability of being arrested is 67 percent greater for those who appear to have mental disabilities than for those who do not. Some mental health professionals argue that this high arrest rate constitutes criminalization of mentally disordered behavior. Taking individuals with mental disabilities to jail, however, is often the only option for police if hospitals and service agencies turn them away.[100]

There is a relationship between psychiatric admission rates and crime and arrest rates. Specifically, when rates of admission to psychiatric hospitals decrease, crime and arrest rates increase. Consequently, those who are unable to function in society are not cared for in the institutions best equipped to do so. Rates of psychiatric hospitalizations are also related to levels of homelessness. When hospital admissions decrease, the number of homeless people increases.[101] People who have severe mental disabilities and are homeless or

Police are often asked to move homeless people out of a particular neighborhood.

drug and alcohol abusers are more likely to be victims of crime *and* more likely to be arrested for committing crime.[102]

A promising new practice relies on crisis intervention teams (CITs). Officers are provided specialized training with the goal of helping those who are mentally ill or developmentally disabled to receive appropriate mental health services rather than entering the criminal justice system. Research has found that CIT-certified officers were more likely to connect people to mental health services than those officers who had not had the training. Although, there was no effect on arrests, CITs had the greatest impact on directing individuals with mental illness or disabilities to the resources available to them.[103]

The Homeless

Large and small communities across the United States have homeless persons. Figure 6-5 illustrates the homeless population by state. **Homelessness** is defined as the state of having no fixed, reliable, or adequate nighttime residence. In 2014 the federal government estimated that on a given night, 575,424 people were homeless in the United States. That number represents a two percent decline from 2013 and an 11 percent decline from 2007.[104]

Almost a quarter of homeless people are under the age of 18, with an additional 10 percent between the ages of 18 and 24. Thirty-seven percent of all homeless are in families.

Residents of communities with visible homeless populations often call the police to "do something" about them. Individuals complain that homeless people affect the quality of life in their communities, making some locations, such as city parks, undesirable to visit. Perhaps because of these demands, over 70 percent of police departments report that homelessness is a problem in their communities.[105] Pressure from community members has even led some police officers to transport homeless individuals out of their jurisdiction to another locale. Police may put problematic individuals on a bus or some other form of transportation to move them out of the area. Although media reports from a number of cities have lamented this practice of "dumping," it continues to be one way of dealing with the homeless.[106]

Homeless persons are often victims of crime.[107] Sexual victimization of homeless individuals is one of many serious concerns. In-depth interviews with

homelessness
The state of having no fixed, reliable, or adequate nighttime residence.

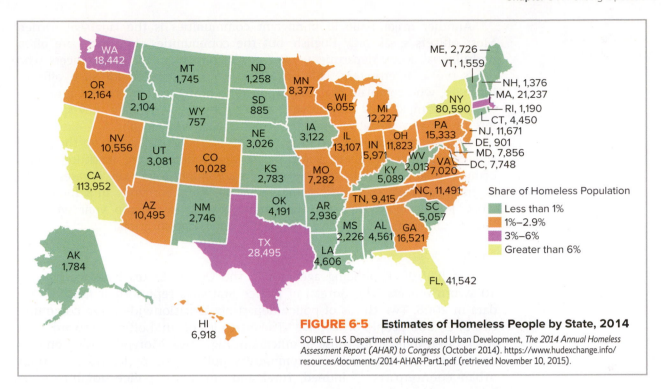

FIGURE 6-5 **Estimates of Homeless People by State, 2014**

SOURCE: U.S. Department of Housing and Urban Development, *The 2014 Annual Homeless Assessment Report (AHAR) to Congress* (October 2014). https://www.hudexchange.info/resources/documents/2014-AHAR-Part1.pdf (retrieved November 10, 2015).

homeless teenagers reveal that some trade sex for items they need to survive, such as food, shelter, money, or drugs. Others are forced to have sex.[108] Sixteen percent of single adult homeless persons suffer from some form of mental illness.[109]

Cultural Differences and Language Barriers

In the 1800s and early 1900s, police officers were the only government employees who interacted with new immigrants.[110] Both in the past and today, many new immigrants are not proficient in English, so it is often difficult for them to report crimes to the police. Moreover, some cultural practices of immigrants' native countries may be prohibited in the United States. In such cases, police may be called upon to educate immigrants on the norms of their new country. Immigrants' lack of proficiency in English and different cultural practices can create challenges to police to ensure that all residents—newcomers and the native born—are equally protected and served.

Immigrants have come in waves from a large number of countries at different periods in U.S. history, with different states and regions as their common destinations. In recent years, about 15,000 Hmong people from Southeast Asia immigrated to the United States. Severely persecuted in Laos because they or their ancestors aided the U.S. military during the Vietnam War, they received safe haven in the United States.[111]

The United States is an increasingly diverse country. Police officers must know how to interact with all people in culturally sensitive ways. Some police departments respond to demographic changes in their communities by recruiting from among the newcomers, who may be better prepared to respond to problems in ethnic neighborhoods in culturally sensitive ways. For example, in some countries, if an individual is told to kneel and put his hands behind his head, he knows he is about to be executed. When an officer asks an individual from that cultural background to assume such a position, he should not be surprised if the immigrant responds as if in fear of his life. Today, police academies include cultural diversity training to help officers respond to problems in diverse communities. In some departments, task forces engage in outreach programs to different immigrant and cultural groups, to foster a positive relationship.

Another major issue in immigrant communities is the language barrier. Most officers speak only English, but the communities they serve are often multilingual. Many departments offer pay incentives to bilingual officers who can serve as interpreters. This practice can create tension for such officers, however, who complain that they applied to be police officers, not interpreters. For example, they may grow to resent the amount of time they spend on interpreter services rather than on other aspects of their job.[112]

Because the language barrier presents risks for the safety of both the police and community members, some police departments have instituted crash courses in language skills training. Officers are taught a few key phrases in the language or languages most common in the neighborhoods in which they work. For example, they may be taught how to say, "Drop your weapon," "You're under arrest," or "Please show me some identification."

Rural Communities

Almost half of all policing agencies in the United States have fewer than 10 sworn officers. The Bureau of Justice Statistics report their most recent data in 2008. Two-thirds of police departments nationwide serve communities of 25,000 people or fewer.[113] The attitudes of rural officers toward their work often differ from those of officers in big cities. Moreover, rural officers are much more supportive of community policing strategies than are their urban counterparts.[114] Indeed, rural and small-city police administrators have reported that while community policing was considered a reform in large cities, it was already a standard practice for them. These smaller police departments usually have closer relationships with members of their communities.[115]

Crime is not as prevalent in rural communities as it is in urban locales. In rural areas there are 16.9 crimes of violence per 1,000 people, while the rate in urban areas is 25.9 violent crimes per 1,000 people.[116] Some problems previously concentrated in urban areas, such as gang activity and drug abuse and trafficking, have crept into rural communities. These relatively new problems seriously challenge rural police agencies to adapt their crime-fighting strategies to more proactive, targeted enforcement.

In sum, rural police departments support community policing and deal with less crime than urban departments. Nevertheless, rural departments are starting to see historically urban problems such as gang activity and drug abuse come to their communities.

SUMMARY

The popular image of the police officer—an image reinforced by the media—is that of a heroic figure engaged in battling violent crimes and apprehending dangerous suspects. In reality, police officers spend most of their time on the job responding to calls to maintain order or to provide service of various kinds. Of course, police do also respond to crimes in progress, and apprehending suspects is part of the policing role of enforcing the law. Yet the police cannot routinely enforce all the laws in criminal codes. They tend, therefore, to enforce laws based on their department's priorities and community norms.

Maintaining order, enforcing the law, and providing service are policing roles common across agencies, but police departments employ different strategies to perform these roles. In preventive patrol, police randomly cruise a neighborhood to maintain a visible police presence in the area, the idea being that maintaining a visible police presence will reduce street crime. However, research experiments have failed to validate the claim that random patrols prevent crime. Problem-oriented policing focuses on identifying the causes of problems in an area and then implementing appropriate, sequential steps to alleviate those problems. In community-oriented policing, police and residents work together to reduce crime and disorder. The principle underlying community policing—that crime prevention is a joint responsibility of police and community members—requires a change in the police culture that traditionally has seen crime prevention and law enforcement as the responsibility of the police alone. Police departments that follow a strategy of aggressive order maintenance, or zero tolerance policing, target minor public order offenses that affect residents' quality of life. Zero tolerance policing may reduce crime but can have negative effects on police–community relations.

Most police departments are organized hierarchically, with several ranks of officers and a clear and rigid chain of command. Community policing calls for organizational change, with fewer ranks and fewer special departments, thereby allowing patrol officers greater discretion in deciding how to respond to community needs and problems. The communications function within a police department coordinates the performance of law enforcement activities, but the difficulty or impossibility of communication across jurisdictions presents serious problems, particularly in large-scale emergencies. Local government plays a large and influential role in determining how and where police resources of money, equipment, and personnel are allocated. Local politicians must be sensitive to citizens' demands for police resources.

Even though the media regularly highlight incidents of police brutality and racial profiling, the public generally supports the police, with the level of support higher among Whites than among people of color. Most people expect that the police will keep everyone safe, but in fact most violent crimes occur among persons who know each other. Expecting the police to prevent violent acts by one family member against another, or by a friend against a friend, is a tall—and unrealistic—expectation.

OBSERVE → INVESTIGATE → UNDERSTAND

Review

Identify the principal policing roles.

- A major part of the workload of police is maintaining order.
- Police engage in law enforcement when they enforce criminal law and apprehend lawbreakers.
- Service activities are nonenforcement actions performed on an as-needed basis.

Compare the various policing strategies.

- In preventive patrol, officers are assigned to randomly drive or walk around an area.
- Problem-oriented policing focuses on discovering the underlying causes of problems and encouraging police to find innovative solutions to solve those problems.
- Community-oriented policing emphasizes reducing crime and disorder by involving residents in the job of policing.
- Aggressive order maintenance entails that police focus on minor public order offenses that affect residents' quality of life.

Describe the different jobs in policing.

- The rookie police officer quickly learns the realities of police work while working under the guidance of a training officer.
- Patrol officers are the first individuals to respond to a call for service.

- A follow-up investigation occurs after a patrol officer documents the facts of the crime.
- Police are the primary public safety agency in charge of enforcing traffic laws.
- Communications coordinates the performance of law enforcement activities.
- Custody is the incarceration of parties either accused or convicted of a crime.
- Forensics is the application of scientific knowledge and methods to criminal and civil investigations and legal procedures, including criminal trials.

Explain how police departments strive to maximize their resources.

- Departments use geographic information systems (GIS) technology to produce detailed descriptions of crime occurrences and to analyze the relationships between variables such as location and time. This information helps police know how to respond to an incident.
- CompStat is a computerized information system that integrates information from crime maps across the community for department leaders' review. This information helps police administrators decide how to allocate their resources.

- Crime analysis can be helpful in reducing the pool of possible suspects, thereby making investigation more efficient.

Identify the factors that shape public opinion about the police.

- High-profile incidents of police brutality affect public opinion about the police.

- Because their experiences with police have not been as positive, racial and ethnic minorities tend to have lower opinions of the police than do Whites.

Compare the service needs of diverse populations.

- Police aid elder adults by protecting them from typical crimes of elder abuse and by solving such crimes.

- Individuals with physical or developmental disabilities are at higher risk of being victimized and therefore may be in need of police protection.

- Police generally deal with apparently mentally ill persons in one of three ways: transporting them to a facility for psychiatric care, arresting them, or leaving them alone if they do not appear to present a threat or danger.

- The homeless are a vulnerable population that is increasingly subjected to violence.

- Rural communities experience less crime than urban communities but are experiencing an increasing amount of gang activity.

Key Terms

Adult Protective Services (APS) 201

aggressive order maintenance 185

broken windows theory 185

chain of command 194

civilianization 181

communications interoperability 191

community-oriented policing 181

CompStat 196

crime analysis 197

crime mapping 196

criminalistics 193

custody 192

de centralization of command 181

elder abuse 201

evidence-based policing 195

forensic science laboratories 193

forensics 193

geographic information systems (GIS) 196

homelessness 204

hot spot 196

law enforcement 177

line activities 186

maintaining order 177

police–community reciprocity 181

predictive policing 197

preventive patrol 178

proactive foot patrol 181

problem-oriented policing 179

service activities 178

solvability 190

span of control 194

support activities 186

unity of command 194

Study Questions

1. The three *principal* policing roles are enforcing the law, providing service, and
   a. crime mapping.
   b. taking individuals into custody.
   c. maintaining order.
   d. conducting forensics.

2. The policing strategy that incorporates the SARA process is
   a. random patrol.
   b. split-force.
   c. problem-oriented policing.
   d. directed patrol.

3. The policing strategy that has a police–public partnership as a central feature is
   a. problem-oriented policing.
   b. random patrol.
   c. community policing.
   d. split-force.

4. Communicating across jurisdictions is called
   a. synchronous telephony.
   b. asynchronous telephony.
   c. interoperability.
   d. frequency incompatibility.

5. The program that integrates information from crime maps with an exchange of information among an agency's leaders is
   a. CompStat.
   b. SARA.
   c. abrasion.
   d. NCIC.

6. An approach that examines a crime scene from a behavioral perspective is
   a. broken windows theory.
   b. crime analysis.
   c. SARA.
   d. order maintenance.

7. An efficient means for the use of limited policing resources is
   a. team policing.
   b. air support to ground operations.
   c. crime mapping.
   d. DNA analysis.

8. A forensics specialist who employs insect evidence to determine time and place of death is known as a
   a. forensic pathologist.
   b. forensic anthropologist.
   c. phrenologist.
   d. forensic entomologist.

9. A factor that affects police–community relations is
   a. officers' use of force.
   b. crime rate.
   c. use of forensic science.
   d. crime mapping.

10. Police departments in rural areas claim that they have always practiced
    a. team policing.
    b. preventive patrol.
    c. community-oriented policing.
    d. gang enforcement.

Critical Thinking Questions

For further review, go to the LearnSmart study module for this chapter.

1. Is community-oriented policing practical for every community? Why or why not?

2. What is the basis for differing opinions about the police among people of different races?

3. Is dealing with persons suffering mental illness and the homeless really a law enforcement problem, or should social services assume an expanded role? Explain.

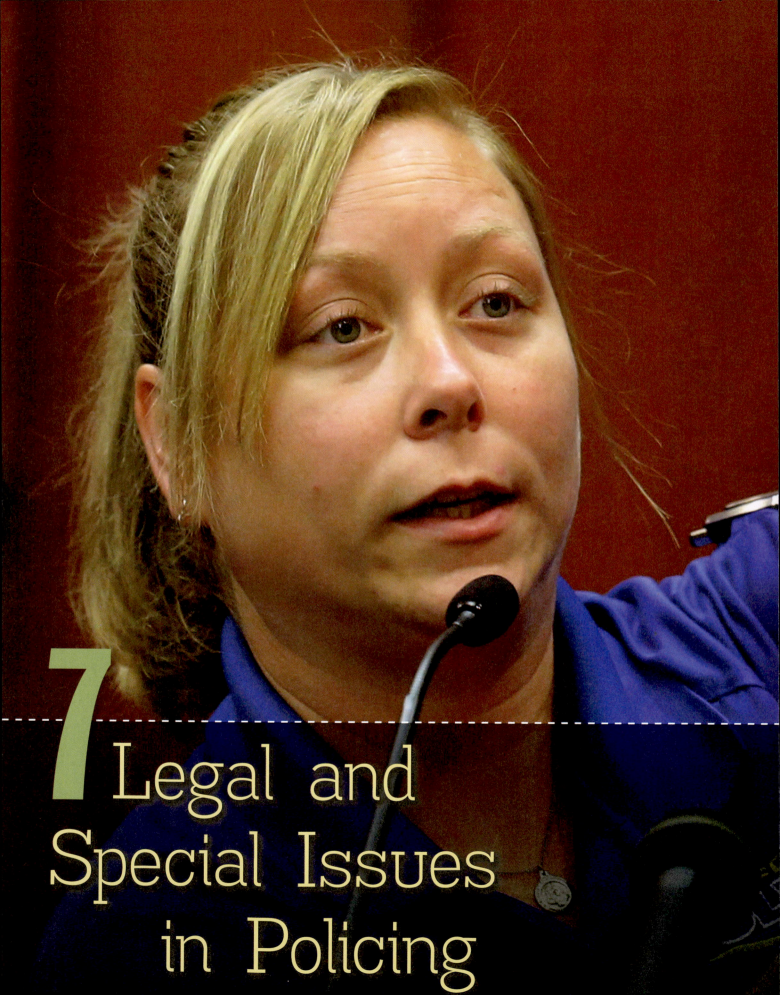

7 Legal and Special Issues in Policing

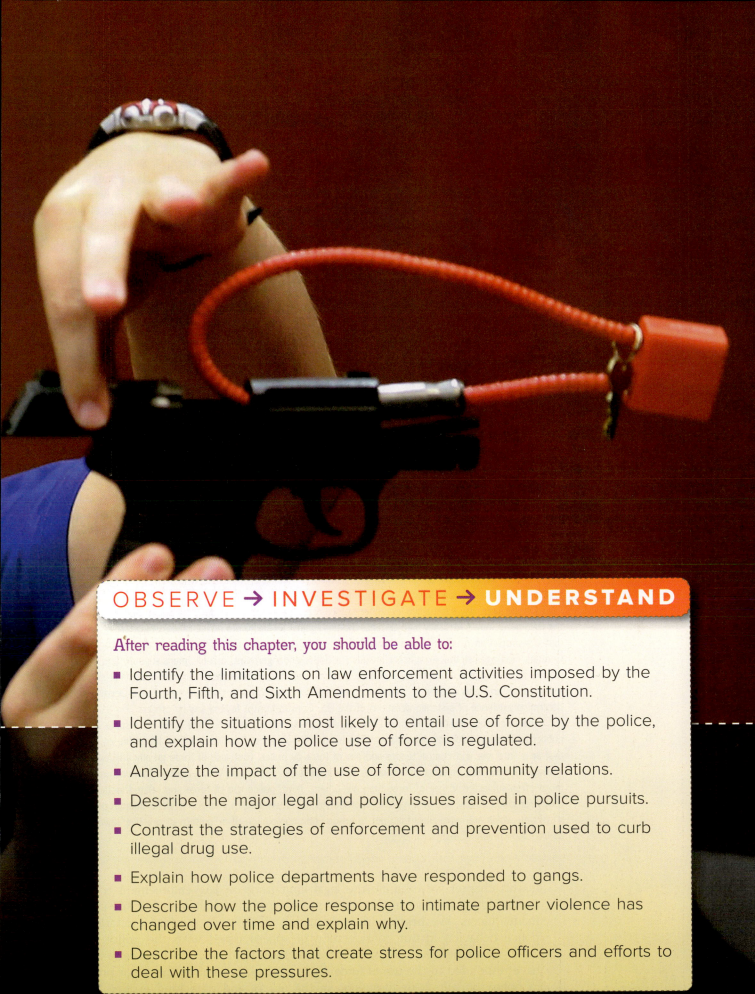

After reading this chapter, you should be able to:

- Identify the limitations on law enforcement activities imposed by the Fourth, Fifth, and Sixth Amendments to the U.S. Constitution.

- Identify the situations most likely to entail use of force by the police, and explain how the police use of force is regulated.

- Analyze the impact of the use of force on community relations.

- Describe the major legal and policy issues raised in police pursuits.

- Contrast the strategies of enforcement and prevention used to curb illegal drug use.

- Explain how police departments have responded to gangs.

- Describe how the police response to intimate partner violence has changed over time and explain why.

- Describe the factors that create stress for police officers and efforts to deal with these pressures.

Realities and Challenges

An In-Custody Death in Baltimore

In April 2015, major riots broke out in the city of Baltimore, Maryland, following the funeral of 25-year-old Freddie Gray, who succumbed to a fatal spinal injury one week after being taken into police custody. The medical examiner's office ruled his death a homicide caused by severe trauma. Mr. Gray's ultimately fatal encounter with authorities began when he made eye contact with police officers in his west Baltimore neighborhood on April 12, 2015, at approximately 8:45 a.m. According to a charging document filed by Baltimore police, Gray brought suspicion upon himself when he fled unprovoked upon noticing the presence of police. The police crime report further stated that upon apprehending Gray, police found what they believed to be an illegal knife clipped to the inside of his front pants pocket. He was subsequently placed under arrest. It is at this point that police reports differ from what a witness reported and what an onlooker's video showed. The police report stated Gray was arrested without force or incident, but the account of the witness, as well as the video, revealed restraint techniques being applied by the police, amid his screaming in pain.[1]

While there was divergence of opinion in terms of the nature and reasonableness of any force applied at the point of arrest, the pivotal aspect of the situation was what occurred in the course of transportation for booking into the Baltimore police facility. At some point during the transportation, Gray suffered a traumatic spinal injury. Police admitted that the transporting officers did not secure him in the back of the van with a seat belt.[2] They also volunteered that Mr. Gray was not offered medical attention despite several requests for an inhaler for an asthma attack. Follow-up investigation by the Baltimore City State's Attorney's Office disclosed that Gray was both handcuffed and his feet shackled while being placed belly down and unsecured during the ride to the police station.[3] Suspicion was raised that Gray might have been given a "rough ride," which entails driving a police van in such a manner as to cause unrestrained prisoners to be violently tossed around the interior of the van. A number of lawsuits had been brought in Baltimore alleging such mistreatment, including an inebriate who went into a van in good health but emerged a quadriplegic.[4]

On the same day the medical examiner's office ruled the death of Freddie Gray a homicide, May 1, 2015, the Baltimore State's Attorney filed criminal charges against six Baltimore police officers involved in the arrest and transportation of Gray.[5] Soon thereafter, the grand jury presented its indictment against the officers. Charges filed against the six officers included reckless endangerment, assault, manslaughter, and, for one officer, second-degree murder.[6] Also in May, the U.S. Department of Justice launched a criminal civil rights investigation and also opened a "pattern or practice" investigation into the Baltimore Police Department to determine existence of systemic violations of the U.S. Constitution or federal law by officers.[7]

The in-custody death of Freddie Gray, an African American, came on the heels of a spate of highly publicized deaths of African Americans at the hands of the police. The Gray incident highlights many issues that arise in arrest and control tactics and use of force by police. First, use of force greatly affects how the community views law enforcement. Second, some individuals, particularly young African American males, are more often subjected to use of force than are others. Third, police use of force and related tactics can be costly for cities. Finally, use of force and improper tactics often lead to changes to departmental policies or strategies, which are more likely than not to ensue upon completion of a "pattern or practice" investigation by the Department of Justice.

In this chapter we examine the legal limitations on law enforcement activities and explore some special issues that prove especially challenging for law enforcement officers. We begin with a discussion of the constitutional limitations on police behavior. In our consideration of special issues with the police use of force, we probe how the use of force has been regulated and how communities have responded to the use of force. Next we look at some of the major problems in police pursuits. Our discussion of the use of and trafficking in illegal drugs focuses on enforcement, prevention, and rehabilitation efforts. Gangs–particularly in urban areas–pose special problems, and we examine ways in which the police respond to gang activity. A particularly troubling problem is intimate partner violence, and we will see how the police response to its occurrence has changed over time. The issues discussed in this chapter contribute greatly to police officer stress. In the last section, we explore both the causes of officer stress and various strategies for coping with the strains of being a police officer.

Most of us would like to live in a safe community. Nearly everyone would agree that police ought to be given the authority and tools to catch criminals. But nearly everyone also would agree that police powers should have limits. We would not want to allow law enforcement officers to do anything they want, to anyone they want, anytime they want. Several sections of the Constitution–especially the Fourth, Fifth, and Sixth Amendments–place important restraints on what the police may do.

THE FOURTH AMENDMENT

The Fourth Amendment to the U.S. Constitution protects residents from "unreasonable searches and seizures." This clause raises two basic questions: What is a search or seizure? And what is unreasonable? In other words, we first must determine whether particular actions by the police constitute searches or seizures. If they do, we then must determine whether those searches or seizures are permissible under the Constitution.

Searches and Seizures

Although the language of the Fourth Amendment is succinct, the Supreme Court has interpreted its meaning in a number of cases that define a search or seizure. First, these limitations apply only to actions taken by a government agent; that is, a local, state, or federal law enforcement officer, or someone working for or on behalf of government. The Fourth Amendment does not limit the actions of private individuals and companies unless they are acting at the request or demand of the government. Many employers, for instance, require job applicants to submit to drug testing, a procedure that would likely be unconstitutional for most government agencies because it would be considered an unreasonable search.

MYTH/REALITY

MYTH: The actions of any individual or company can be unconstitutional.

REALITY: Only actions taken by government agencies or those working for those agencies can be in violation of the Constitution.

Second, in order for an act to be a search or seizure, the target of the act must have a reasonable expectation of privacy. If a man is standing on a sidewalk talking loudly into his cell phone to his friend with whom he is planning to rob a bank, a police officer who overhears him has not conducted a search or seizure. It would be unreasonable for the man to expect a loud conversation in a public place to be private. However, if he plans the robbery while in his home, it is reasonable for him to expect privacy. If the officer places a wiretap on the man's phone so she can listen in on the conversation, she is conducting a search.

In its rulings on privacy, the Supreme Court has found that people possess the expectation of privacy regarding the contents of their postal mail, phone

DIS Connects

Reasonably Private?

Advancing technology has allowed the government to conduct investigations in ways that the drafters of the Fourth Amendment never dreamed of. For example, in 1992 police officers in Oregon used a special type of camera called a thermal imager to scan Danny Lee Kyllo's house for infrared radiation. When they found that some parts of the house were unusually hot, they concluded that Kyllo was growing marijuana indoors. Kyllo was subsequently arrested and convicted. The Supreme Court overturned his conviction, however, holding that the police should have obtained a warrant for the scan of his house.

What about other uses of modern technology? Cell phone locations can be tracked with almost pinpoint accuracy; GPS devices allow cars and packages to be easily traced; and people communicate frequently using e-mail, texting, and cell phones, all of which can be searched. Many of us probably feel that these activities are private, but do the courts agree? Are warrants required for police to conduct investigations in these realms?

The answer varies. In decisions in 2010 and 2011, federal appeals courts ruled that warrants are not needed if police seek to track the location of people's cell phones or to place a GPS tracking device on a car sitting in a driveway. The California Supreme Court held in 2011 that no warrant is necessary if police

Find My iPhone

wish to search someone's cell phone after the person has been arrested. On the other hand, another federal appeals court has held that warrants are necessary for police to read someone's e-mail.

Other questions are too new to have been addressed yet by most courts. Are warrants required for police to investigate which electronic books and journals we have read? To find out which websites we have visited? To follow conversations on social networking sites such as Facebook and Twitter? What about tracking the items we buy, whether online or in stores?

For now, it seems wise to remember that even if we believe that our conversations and information are private, the courts will not necessarily agree.

OBSERVE → INVESTIGATE → UNDERSTAND

- In what ways has modern technology made law enforcement easier—or more difficult?
- What limits should be placed on police using social-networking sites such as Facebook to investigate crimes?

SOURCES: *Kyllo v. United States*, 533 U.S. 27 (2001); *In re United States*, 620 F.3d 304 (3rd Cir. 2010); *United States v. Warshak*, 2010 Fed. App. 0377 (6th Cir. 2010); *United States v. Pineda-Moreno*, 617 F.3d 1120 (9th Cir. 2010); *California v. Diaz*, 2011 Cal. LEXIS 1 (Cal. Sup. Ct. 2011).

---

conversations held in a closed phone booth, most activities in and contents of a home, and the contents of suitcases and other containers.[8] On the other hand, the Court has held that there was no expectation of privacy, and therefore that no search occurred, when police rummaged through a suspect's trash bags after the garbage was placed outside for collection, when police used an electronic device to keep track of which phone numbers a suspect was calling, when police hovered 400 feet above a suspect's home in a helicopter, or when DEA agents used a narcotics detection dog to sniff the outside of a suspect's luggage.[9]

Recent technological advances make it particularly challenging to determine the scope of the Fourth Amendment. To what extent does the amendment protect electronic information such as e-mail, computerized databases (including, for instance, medical records), and records of Internet surfing? The USA PATRIOT Act, enacted after the 9/11 terrorist attacks, gave the government wide authority to engage in various kinds of electronic surveillance. Many critics claim that portions of the act violate the Fourth Amendment's protection of privacy. (The USA PATRIOT Act is discussed in more detail in Chapter 16.) A related question is the extent to which the government may use technology to assist law enforcement activities, especially when the technology is not widely available to the general public. In 2012, for instance, the Supreme Court held that the government's placement of a GPS tracking device on a vehicle constitutes a search under the Fourth Amendment.[10] The "Disconnects" box illustrates the differences between what police see as good detective work and what the Supreme Court views as unconstitutional.

The courts have accorded certain groups less expectation of privacy than other people, making it easier for government agents to justify searches of these individuals. These classes include schoolchildren, prisoners, parolees, and probationers.

If government agents undertake actions, and these actions infringe on reasonable expectations of privacy, the actions are searches or seizures within the meaning of the Fourth Amendment. The subjects of those searches and seizures may be people–an arrest of a person is a seizure–or things. If actions constitute a search or seizure, they must be reasonable to be permissible. But what is reasonable?

Reasonableness

The Fourth Amendment offers a few clues on what constitutes a reasonable search or seizure. The amendment states, "[N]o warrants shall issue, but upon probable cause, supported by oath or affirmation, and particularly describing the place to be searched, and the persons or things to be seized." The courts interpret this passage to mean that ordinarily the government must obtain a **warrant**–a legal document–before its agents can conduct a search or seizure. The agent must first collect enough evidence to lead a reasonable person to believe there is a good likelihood–**probable cause**–that a crime was committed or that evidence or illicit materials are present. The agent then describes the evidence in a sworn written or oral statement and presents it to a neutral party, usually a judge. If the judge determines that probable cause exists, she authorizes a warrant. The warrant must be specific about what or who is to be searched or seized. Only then can the agent conduct the search or make the seizure. The purpose of this somewhat unwieldy process is to protect people from abuses of police authority and from unjustified or mistaken intrusions into their privacy and freedom.

Government agents are not required to obtain a warrant before every search or seizure if doing so would endanger public safety by obstructing the agents' ability to do their jobs. For example, few of us would want a firefighter to pause to secure a search warrant before dashing into a burning house to save a trapped child. Consequently, the Supreme Court recognizes a large number of exceptions to the warrant requirement. Still, to comply with the Fourth Amendment, even *warrantless* searches and seizures–those conducted without a warrant–must be reasonable.

warrant
A legal document, based on probable cause, permitting police to conduct a search or seizure or to arrest someone.

probable cause
The amount of evidence necessary to obtain a warrant or conduct most searches and seizures.

◀ **Police Entering a Residence**

In most cases, officers need a warrant to search a person's home. *Under what circumstances are search warrants not required?*

Felony arrests may always be made without a warrant—as long as the officer has probable cause to believe the suspect committed a felony. Nevertheless, police sometimes choose to obtain an arrest warrant for practical reasons. First, doing so allows them to enter a home to make the arrest. Entry would usually not be allowed without a warrant if much time had passed since the crime was committed. Second, by having a neutral party confirm that probable cause exists, the warrant protects the police so that the arrest is less likely to be declared invalid later. To be considered reasonable seizures, felony arrests always require probable cause—with or without a warrant.

At one time, police could make warrantless arrests for misdemeanors only when suspects committed a breach of the peace in their presence. However, the Supreme Court rejected the breach of the peace requirement in *Atwater v. Lago Vista* (2001) and hinted that it might also reject the requirement for an agent to be present. Like felony arrests, misdemeanor arrests—with or without a warrant—require probable cause.

The Court also authorizes other types of warrantless seizures. One of the most common is called a **stop-and-frisk** or *Terry* **stop** (after *Terry v. Ohio*, 1968, the case in which the Court first made the ruling). A *Terry* stop is permitted when police have **reasonable suspicion** to believe a person is engaged in criminal activity. Reasonable suspicion is less certain than probable cause but more than just a hunch. In the *Terry* case, for example, John W. Terry and another man were pacing back and forth in front of a store, periodically peering in the store windows. An experienced police officer concluded they might be preparing to rob the store. Reasonable suspicion is the amount of evidence required before officers may conduct a stop-and-frisk, which allows a police officer to briefly detain a person, question him about his activities, require him to show identification, and frisk him or pat him down for weapons. Although this action is a seizure, it does not amount to a full arrest.[11] A full arrest means taking a suspect into police custody for a longer period of time.

Like seizures, reasonable searches may be conducted without a warrant. Figure 7-1 lists a number of exceptions to the warrant requirement. One of the most common is the **automobile exception,** first articulated by the Supreme Court in 1925 in *Carroll v. United States*.[12] The Court held it impractical to require police officers to obtain search warrants for cars because, while the officer was obtaining the warrant, the suspect could simply drive away. Furthermore, because it is easy to see into cars, and because their use is already heavily regulated, people have a reduced expectation of privacy in the contents of their automobiles. The Court therefore allows searches of motor vehicles based on probable cause, with no warrant necessary. In subsequent rulings, the Court expanded the automobile exception to include all packages and containers inside a car, even in the trunk. The automobile exception also encompasses vehicles other than cars. In *California v. Carney* (1985), for example, the Court upheld the warrantless search of a motor home.[13]

Another major exception to the warrant requirement is a **search incident to arrest.** When a person is placed under arrest, police may search her body, clothing, and any packages she is carrying. Such searches protect police from any weapons suspects may be carrying, prevent suspects from carrying contraband into a jail, and reduce the chances that evidence will be destroyed. If a suspect is arrested in her home, police may search any areas within her "wingspan"—that is, her approximate reach—even if she is handcuffed. If she is arrested in a car or shortly after exiting one, police may search the car's passenger compartment. If her car is impounded and taken into police custody, they may search the entire vehicle. Officers need neither probable cause nor reasonable suspicion to conduct a search incident to arrest. If a person is arrested (as opposed to simply being issued a ticket) for not wearing a seat belt, for example, police could legally

stop-and-frisk
Police action allowing the police, with reasonable suspicion, to briefly detain a person, question him about his activities, require him to show identification, and frisk him or pat him down for weapons; also known as a *Terry* stop.

***Terry* stop**
Another name for stop-and-frisk, in which the police, with reasonable suspicion, briefly detain a person, question him about his activities, require him to show identification, and frisk him or pat him down for weapons.

reasonable suspicion
Amount of evidence necessary for officers to conduct a stop-and-frisk or *Terry* stop.

automobile exception
An exception to the warrant requirement holding that police do not need warrants to search automobiles, just probable cause.

search incident to arrest
A warrantless search of a person and the area around that person, conducted shortly after the person is arrested.

Over time, the U.S. Supreme Court has extended the reach of warrantless searches and seizures and in so doing expanded the powers of police. Warrants are not required for:

- *Terry* stops (stop-and-frisk)
- Automobile searches
- Searches incident to arrest
- Searches at international borders
- Searches at airports
- Stops at sobriety checkpoints
- Inventory searches (when police make inventory lists) of items impounded by police, such as the contents of a car when the car is impounded
- Searches of buildings when police are in hot pursuit of a fleeing felon
- Searches under exigent circumstances such as when someone's life is in immediate danger; for example, when a house is on fire or when a victim is being held hostage
- Protective sweeps—quick searches of a home to ensure no other people are present
- Searches when the items are in plain view
- Searches in open fields and outside the "curtilage" or area immediately surrounding a home
- Consent searches—when the suspect allows the officer to search
- Regulatory searches such as by health inspectors and building inspectors
- Searches where "special government needs" exist, such as in random drug testing of student athletes, customs inspectors, and railway employees involved in accidents

FIGURE 7-1   Exceptions to the Warrant Requirement

Some people argue that this long list of exceptions has essentially gutted the warrant requirement; others assert that the exceptions are necessary for law enforcement officers to do an effective job.   *Which argument do you find more persuasive and why?*

search the person's car, purse or backpack, clothing, and body. However, the Court ruled in *Riley v. California* (2014) that searches incident to arrest do not include searching the contents of the suspect's cell phone.[14]

After the 9/11 terrorist attacks in 2001, national debates emerged over how much leeway government officials should be allowed in conducting warrantless searches for the protection of national security. In late 2005, newspapers reported that the National Security Agency (NSA) was electronically eavesdropping on hundreds of thousands of domestic and international phone calls and e-mails without search warrants or notification. Only a handful of the thousands of people thus monitored–fewer than 10 a year–were actually found to be acting suspiciously. While critics lambasted the program as a constitutional violation and a severe infringement on privacy, federal authorities defended it as necessary in the "war on terrorism."[15] Also since 9/11, more intrusive searches are being made of people and luggage at airports, and some cities have begun random searches of subway passengers' belongings.[16] In early 2008, Amtrak announced that it would begin random searches of luggage for explosives.

The Exclusionary Rule

Government agents who conduct an unreasonable search or seizure are violating someone's Fourth Amendment rights. But what can the person do about it? Certainly she can sue the police for violating her civil rights. But lawsuits charging unreasonable searches yield little in monetary damages and might even be damaging if the person could be convicted in a trial that used unconstitutionally obtained evidence against her. Nor would lawsuits do much to deter the police from infringing on people's rights in the future, especially if they thought they might obtain valuable evidence.

The Supreme Court recognized this problem in its ruling in *Weeks v. United States* (1914):

> If letters and private documents can thus be seized and held and used in evidence against a citizen accused of an offense, the protection of the 4th Amendment, declaring his right to be secure against such searches and seizures, is of no value, and, so far as those thus placed are concerned, might as well be stricken from the Constitution. The efforts of the courts and their officials to bring the guilty to punishment, praiseworthy as they are, are not to be aided by the sacrifice of those great principles established by years of endeavor and suffering which have resulted in their embodiment in the fundamental law of the land.[17]

exclusionary rule
The rule that illegally obtained evidence cannot be used against a criminal defendant at trial.

In *Weeks*, the Court first articulated the **exclusionary rule,** which says that evidence obtained in violation of an individual's Fourth Amendment rights

▶ **Dollree Mapp**

Mapp's case resulted in the extension of the exclusionary rule to the actions of state and local law enforcement officials.

cannot be used against her in a criminal trial. The rule originally applied only to cases in which searches or seizures were conducted by federal officials, but when Dollree Mapp's case reached the U.S. Supreme Court in 1961, the Court extended the rule to state and local officials. Mapp's case was based on the following facts. At 3 a.m., a bomb went off outside the home of a small-time bookie in Cleveland, Ohio. The bookie told police a man to whom he owed money might have planted the bomb. A few days later police showed up at the home of Dollree Mapp, who ran a boardinghouse where they suspected the man responsible for the bomb may have spent time.

When the police arrived, Mapp called her lawyer and, on his advice, refused to let the police in without a search warrant. Three hours later more officers, as well as Mapp's attorney, arrived at the house. The police barred the lawyer from entering the house, broke down Mapp's front door, and went inside. Mapp demanded to see a warrant. One officer claimed he had a warrant and waved a piece of paper in her face. She grabbed it and shoved it down the front of her shirt, but the officer pulled the paper out again. Mapp was then forcibly placed in handcuffs.

The police looked through dressers, closets, suitcases, and photo albums throughout the house. In a trunk in the basement, police found pictures of nudes as well as booklets containing lewd stories that apparently belonged to a former boarder who had left them when he moved. Mapp was charged with possession of obscene materials. At her trial, even though no evidence was produced of the existence of a search warrant, Dollree Mapp was convicted and sentenced to a maximum of 7 years in prison.[18] Her conviction was overturned, however, and *Mapp v. Ohio* (1961) became a landmark case in the protection of constitutional rights.[19]

MYTH/REALITY

MYTH: The exclusionary rule is a technicality that lets many guilty people go free.

REALITY: The exclusionary rule is the only effective way to protect important constitutional rights from government intrusion. Furthermore, in most cases in which evidence is excluded from a trial under the rule, the defendant is convicted based on other evidence.[20]

How to apply the Constitution to law enforcement is a subject of considerable and lively debate. On one hand, people argue that to require police to follow strict rules in criminal investigation is both unrealistic and dangerous. Furthermore, the argument goes, criminals should not get away with their crimes merely because police make mistakes.

Other people contend that protecting people from infringements on their basic constitutional rights is more important than catching criminals. According to this argument, excluding illegally obtained evidence effectively deters police misconduct. Moreover, if the courts set out clear rules for police rather than muddying the waters with more and more exceptions, police will be able to do their jobs without having to worry about whether evidence might be excluded.

The exclusionary rule is a strict rule. If evidence that was illegally seized is the only evidence—or even the primary evidence—against a defendant, and that evidence is excluded from trial under the exclusionary rule, the defendant may go free. Thus the exclusionary rule may allow people known to have broken the law—sometimes even dangerous and violent people—to escape punishment for their actions. Many government officials complain that the exclusionary rule makes criminals harder to catch and leaves guilty people free to commit more crimes. Many would argue that the danger a suspect presents to the community should outweigh Fourth Amendment rights against illegal searches and seizures. Victims often find it difficult to see those who harm them go unpunished. The public tends to view those who are released on Fourth Amendment grounds as having "gotten off on a technicality." Because we usually hear about Fourth Amendment violations in the context of someone having broken the law (if no illegal evidence is found, the case never goes to court, and nobody hears about the violations), many people view the amendment and the exclusionary rule as granting "special rights" to guilty people. After all, the argument goes, if I have nothing to hide, why should I care whether the police search my belongings?

In reality, however, the Fourth Amendment protects *everyone*, guilty and innocent alike. Even completely law-abiding people may not want to give the government unrestricted authority to rummage through their private affairs and belongings anytime some government employee feels like it. Defenders of the exclusionary rule, including justices of the U.S. Supreme Court, contend that the rule makes constitutional rights meaningful and effectively deters government officials from violating the Constitution. Most criminals can eventually be successfully prosecuted without infringing on Fourth Amendment rights, and if a few guilty people do go free, perhaps that is a reasonable price to pay for protecting everyone's freedom and privacy.[21]

Even the Supreme Court, however, has had difficulty applying the exclusionary rule when doing so allows an obviously guilty person to go unpunished. After *Mapp*, the Court held that the rule does not apply to proceedings other than criminal trials. Therefore, illegally obtained evidence can be used in deportation proceedings, civil tax proceedings, and grand jury hearings. Such evidence also can be used in criminal cases to *impeach* a defendant or other witness (that is, to prove that the defendant gave false testimony or is an untrustworthy person). This is one reason criminal defendants sometimes do not take the stand to testify in their own defense. If they do testify, evidence that would otherwise be inadmissible can be brought in to impeach them. If, on the other hand, they refrain from testifying, the jury will never hear that evidence.

derivative evidence rule

An extension to the exclusionary rule holding that evidence derived from something that is illegally searched or seized is itself inadmissible; also known as the fruit of the poisonous tree doctrine.

fruit of the poisonous tree doctrine

Another name for the derivative evidence rule, which excludes evidence derived from an illegal search or seizure.

The Derivative Evidence Rule The **derivative evidence rule,** also known as the **fruit of the poisonous tree doctrine,** further extends the exclusionary rule. The derivative evidence rule provides that any evidence derived from something that is illegally seized is itself inadmissible. For example, suppose police illegally record a phone conversation in which a suspect reveals the location of stolen goods. The police then obtain a warrant based on the content of that conversation, and they find the stolen goods. Not only would the taped conversation be suppressed as evidence under the exclusionary rule, but so would the stolen goods. Even though police had a warrant to search for the goods, that warrant was the "fruit" of the "poisonous" phone tap.

The derivative evidence rule extended the scope of the exclusionary rule, but the Supreme Court has carved out a number of exceptions to the exclusionary rule. These exceptions permit illegally obtained evidence to be used against a defendant at trial.

good faith exception

Exception to the exclusionary rule allowing illegally obtained evidence to be used if officers relied in good faith on an invalid warrant.

The Good Faith Exception to the Exclusionary Rule Articulated by the Supreme Court in *United States v. Leon* (1984),[22] the **good faith exception** applies when police officers act in good faith on a warrant or law that is later declared invalid. If police reasonably believe the warrant or law authorizing a search or seizure is legitimate, but it later turns out it is not, the evidence will not be suppressed. In *Arizona v. Evans* (1995), for example, an officer stopped Isaac Evans for a traffic violation. The officer made a computer check for outstanding warrants and discovered a misdemeanor warrant, so he placed Evans under arrest. When he searched Evans incident to the arrest, he discovered marijuana. Later it turned out the warrant had been declared invalid 17 days earlier, but the court clerk's office had mistakenly left it in the system. Because the officer was acting in good faith reliance on the computer check, the Supreme Court upheld Evans's conviction for marijuana possession.[23]

The Supreme Court extended the good faith exception in *Herring v. United States* (2009).[24] In that case, a warrant had been issued for Bennie Herring in one county. When the warrant was later recalled, the county failed to update its database, so the warrant was still listed. When police officers in a neighboring county searched for and found the erroneous warrant listing, they placed Herring under arrest. When they searched him, they discovered that he had drugs and a gun in his possession; because he was a felon, he was not permitted to own a gun. At trial, Herring claimed that the gun and drugs should not be used as evidence against him because they were the fruit of an illegal arrest. The Supreme Court agreed that his initial arrest was illegal since it was based on a faulty report of a warrant, but the Court allowed the evidence anyway because the officers had acted in good faith on the erroneous information.

In 2014, the Court expanded the good faith exception even farther. In *Heien v. North Carolina*, the Court held that evidence from a search is admissible if a police officer was reasonably mistaken about the law.[25]

Other Exceptions to the Exclusionary Rule   Other exceptions to the exclusionary rule include **inevitable discovery,** in which illegally obtained evidence is admissible if police officers would have discovered it anyway had they used proper procedures. The **independent source** exception allows evidence to be admissible if its discovery was independent of any improper search or seizure. **Attenuation** is the exception that applies when the link between the unconstitutional acts and the evidence becomes weak due to intervening time or events. For example, if a defendant was wrongly arrested but then released and, after consultation with his attorney, returns to the police station several weeks later to confess, his confession will almost certainly be admissible even though the original arrest was unlawful.[26]

The exclusionary rule does not apply when the defendant does not have **standing;** that is, if it was not the defendant's own rights that were violated by the unreasonable search or seizure. For example, if police improperly search a home and find evidence implicating a person who does not live in the home, that evidence can be used against the visitor.

The Supreme Court recently created another exception to the exclusionary rule, this one involving *no-knock warrants*. The Court had previously ruled that unless police have obtained a no-knock warrant, when they execute a search warrant at a house, they must knock before entering, announce their presence, and give the resident a reasonable amount of time to voluntarily comply with the warrant.[27] The Court's decision in *Hudson v. Michigan* (2006) did not overturn the knock-and-announce rule, but it did hold that if police violate the rule, the exclusionary rule does not apply. Justice Scalia wrote,

> [T]he social costs of applying the exclusionary rule to knoc-and-announce violations are considerable; the incentive to such violations is minimal to begin with, and the extant deterrences against them are substantial–incomparably greater than the factors deterring warrantless entries when *Mapp* was decided. Resort to the massive remedy of suppressing evidence of guilt is unjustified.[28]

Therefore, even though violation of the knock-and-announce rule violates a suspect's constitutional rights, any evidence that is found will be admissible. Critics have argued that this ruling makes the knock-and-announce rule meaningless.

Opponents of the exclusionary rule support its long list of exceptions, saying that those exceptions make it easier for police to do their jobs and let

inevitable discovery
Exception to the exclusionary rule allowing illegally obtained evidence to be admissible if it would inevitably have been discovered through legal means.

independent source
Exception to the exclusionary rule permitting the use of evidence discovered independent of any improper search or seizure.

attenuation
An exception to the exclusionary rule that applies when the link between the unconstitutional acts and the evidence becomes weak due to intervening time or events.

standing
The legal ability to assert a particular constitutional claim.

fewer obviously guilty people go free. Others argue that exceptions have essentially gutted the rule, leaving little incentive for police to comply with the Constitution and little recourse for individuals when they do not. Because many cases from which exceptions arose were prosecutions for drug possession, some commentators believe that the exclusionary rule, and to a large extent the Bill of Rights itself, is the biggest casualty of the "war on drugs."[29]

THE FIFTH AMENDMENT

The Fifth Amendment states that no person "shall be compelled in any criminal case to be a witness against himself." This amendment gives criminal defendants the right to refuse to testify–to "take the Fifth." But these words also affect the manner in which police may question suspects.

Voluntariness

In the spring of 1934, a White man named Raymond Stewart was found beaten to death at his home near Meridian, Mississippi. Soon after, sheriff's deputies, accompanied by other men, took three young Black men from their houses

Real Careers

BRIAN HILSINGER

Work location: Cincinnati, Ohio

College(s): University of Cincinnati (2001)

Major(s): Criminal Justice (BS)

Job title: Deputy U.S. Marshal, Southern District of Ohio

Salary range for job like this: $30,000–$35,000

Time in job: 7 years

Work Responsibilities

I am primarily responsible for the security of all parties in the courtroom. That includes helping to transport federal inmates to their court appearances and protecting all courtroom personnel from the inmate and any witnesses or family members who may become belligerent. One duty that is unique to U.S. marshals is protecting federal judges. In fact, I once went to Oklahoma City as part of a weeklong protection detail of Supreme Court Justice Sandra Day O'Connor.

A new function that the U.S. marshals have assumed in the last several years is enforcing the Adam Walsh Act. This act requires a person who has been convicted of a sex offense to register as a sex offender. When an offender fails to comply with this act and crosses interstate commerce or state lines, the violation becomes federal, and a U.S. marshal becomes responsible for making the arrest. But I should point out that marshals are unique because they can make arrests on both federal and local warrants.

Why Criminal Justice?

I majored in criminal justice because I knew that this was the first step on the road to working in law enforcement. While I was a student at the University of Cincinnati, I was an intern with the U.S. marshals. My first job in the field was with the Ohio Adult Parole Authority as a parole officer. Having a positive first encounter with the profession led me to pursue a career with the U.S. Marshals Service.

Expectations and Realities of the Job

I did not expect the job to entail so much precision and attention to detail. For instance, I now see that part of being an effective U.S. marshal, and investigator, is making sure I am working with the most current information. This means taking comprehensive notes when in the field and documenting the casework carefully. Other than this aspect of the work, the expectations that I had prior to becoming a U.S. marshal met the realities of the job.

My Advice to Students

No matter what career track you have in mind, just get a foot in the door with any CJ-related job. You will mostly likely need that valuable field experience to pursue a career in CJ. Also, networking with colleagues, professors, and classmates is one of the best ways to learn about potential career paths and job openings. Finally, regardless of the job you choose, keep your criminal record clean, as that can affect your eligibility to be hired.

and demanded they confess to the murder. All three men were viciously beaten and whipped; one of them twice had a rope tied around his neck and was suspended from a tree. Threatened with death, all three eventually confessed to the murder. At trial (which occurred only a few days later), even though the police admitted to hanging and whipping the defendants, the confessions were admitted as evidence. All three defendants denied having anything to do with Stewart's death. After brief deliberation, the all-White jury found the defendants guilty and sentenced them to death.

When the Supreme Court finally heard the case (*Brown v. Mississippi*) two years later, it held that the Constitution prohibits the use of coerced confessions as evidence, ruling that such confessions violated the due process clause of the Fourteenth Amendment. Chief Justice Charles Evans Hughes wrote, "It would be difficult to conceive of methods more revolting to the sense of justice than those taken to procure the confessions of these petitioners, and the use of the confessions thus obtained as the basis for conviction and sentence was a clear denial of due process."[30] In overturning the defendants' convictions, the Court established the **voluntariness test,** the rule that confessions are inadmissible unless made willingly.

voluntariness test
Rule that confessions are inadmissible unless made willingly.

Miranda v. Arizona

At the time that *Brown v. Mississippi* was decided and for the next 30 years, the Fifth Amendment applied only to actions taken by federal government agents. In 1964, in *Malloy v. Hogan,* the Supreme Court held that the self-incrimination clause of the Fifth Amendment applied to actions taken by state, local, and federal governments.[31] This ruling set the scene for one of the Court's most famous cases, *Miranda v. Arizona* (1966).

The *Miranda* case arose out of several unrelated criminal cases in which suspects were taken into custody and interrogated without being informed of their constitutional rights, after which they confessed. Ernesto Miranda, 22 years old, was suspected of committing a series of kidnappings and rapes in Phoenix, Arizona. After police questioned him for 2 hours, he confessed to one of the rapes and, based in part on his confession, was convicted and sentenced to 20 to 30 years.

Unlike the situation in *Brown,* there was no evidence *Miranda* was beaten, threatened, or otherwise compelled to confess. Nevertheless, the Supreme Court held that even without the use of threats or physical force, custodial interrogation is inherently coercive. Specifically, the conditions of being held against one's will in an unfamiliar place, separated from family and allies, and questioned by investigators often trained in psychological techniques to obtain incriminating statements all lead to a situation in which a suspect cannot truly exercise free will. But without prohibiting police interrogations altogether, how could society ensure that a suspect is not compelled to confess in violation of the Fifth Amendment? That is the key question with which the justices wrestled.

▲ **Ernesto Miranda**

His case resulted in the famous requirement of the *Miranda* warnings.

The Court's solution was to rule that before people in police custody may be questioned, they must be informed of their constitutional rights. This instruction is the famous **Miranda warnings,** and anyone who has ever watched a crime show on TV can probably recite each *Miranda* right:

Miranda warnings
Notifications that police must give suspects about their rights prior to beginning custodial interrogation.

- You have the right to remain silent.
- Anything you say may be used in court.

- You have the right to consult a lawyer and have a lawyer present during questioning.
- If indigent, you may have a lawyer provided at no cost.
- You have the right to end questioning or consult with a lawyer at any time.

Informing suspects of their rights was seen as the only effective way to safeguard their privilege against self-incrimination.[32]

The *Miranda* decision was controversial. Critics claimed that reading suspects their rights would result in significantly fewer confessions and therefore significantly fewer convictions. Effective law enforcement, they charged, would virtually be hobbled. In reality, however, approximately 75 percent of suspects waive their *Miranda* rights and choose to speak to police rather than remaining silent or consulting a lawyer.[33] Clearly, the criminal justice system has not come to a grinding halt since *Miranda*. In 2000, in *Dickerson v. United States*, the Court reaffirmed the *Miranda* requirements.[34] If a person is in custody and is questioned without first being informed of his rights, the exclusionary rule applies and any statements he makes will be inadmissible.

MYTH/REALITY

MYTH: Police must always read suspects their *Miranda* rights.

REALITY: Suspects do not have to be read their rights if they are not in custody or if police do not plan to interrogate them.[35]

The *Miranda* rule is limited in several ways. First, it applies only to custodial interrogations. A suspect who is not actually under arrest need not be warned. If a suspect is under arrest, police must read her the warnings only if they want to question her. Just talking to a suspect or asking for identification does not constitute an interrogation. In *Rhode Island v. Innis* (1980), the Supreme Court defined interrogation as "words or actions . . . that the police should know are reasonably likely to elicit an incriminating response."[36]

testimonial evidence
Words or statements made by a person.

Second, *Miranda* applies only to **testimonial evidence**—statements made by the suspect. *Miranda* does not apply to nontestimonial evidence such as fingerprints, DNA samples, and so on, even if that evidence may link the suspect to a crime.

The Supreme Court recently limited the *Miranda* decision even more. In *Berghuis v. Thompkins* (2010),[37] the Court held that once a suspect is given the warnings, if he does not actually invoke his rights–that is, if he responds with silence–police may continue to question him.

In *Miranda*, the Court was specific about what information police must give to suspects when they warn them. Many police departments ask officers to read from prepared cards that contain language virtually identical to that in the *Miranda* opinion–although the Supreme Court later held that the content of the warnings does not need to be exactly the same. Police may use different words as long as the correct basic information is given and the officers are not overly coercive. In fact, even if proper *Miranda* warnings are given, a suspect's statements may be suppressed if the police use too much intimidation. For example, if a suspect was read her rights and then police pointed a gun at her head and told her to confess, the confession would not be admissible.

Exceptions to the *Miranda* Rule

public safety exception
Exception to *Miranda* requiring police to interrogate suspects without first warning them of their rights if there is a significant threat to public safety.

Just as there are exceptions to the Fourth Amendment's prohibitions against unreasonable searches and seizures, there are also exceptions to the *Miranda* rule. The **public safety exception** allows police to dispense with the warnings if they believe there is an immediate threat to public safety. For example, police may question a person suspected of kidnapping a child about the child's location if they think the child is in danger. Even though the suspect is not "Mirandized," any statements he makes in this situation will still be admissible against him at trial. All the exclusionary rule exceptions to the Fourth Amendment apply as well to the Fifth Amendment. For instance, the statements of suspects who are not properly Mirandized may be used to impeach them (to prove they are lying) at trial.

Suspects may waive their Fifth Amendment rights and choose to speak to police without an attorney present, and suspects who waive their rights may change their minds later. The only requirements for waiver are that it be knowing—that is, the suspects must be aware of what their rights are and voluntarily decide to waive them. Social scientists question whether certain people, such as teenagers and the developmentally disabled, can really understand their rights enough to knowingly waive them, but the courts refuse to impose blanket prohibitions of waivers for any group of people.[38]

Innocent people are more likely than guilty ones to waive their rights, perhaps in the naïve belief that by cooperating with police they will talk their way out of trouble.[39] Perhaps this explains why, according to the Innocence Project, false confessions are the second leading cause of wrongful convictions.[40] "Matters of Ethics" further explores the subject of false confessions.

THE SIXTH AMENDMENT

The Sixth Amendment affords accused persons several constitutional protections, but one guaranteed right is of particular significance to law enforcement: "In all criminal prosecutions, the accused shall enjoy the right . . . to have assistance of counsel for his defense." This statement means that criminal defendants are entitled to the help of an attorney at trial. However, the rights protected by the Sixth Amendment apply well before trial. In fact, they apply as soon as formal charges are filed against a defendant. A defendant who has been charged is in more peril than a suspect who is merely being questioned (and who could still be released without being charged with any crime). Therefore, the Sixth Amendment right to counsel is broader and more powerful than the Fifth Amendment rights under *Miranda*.

The Supreme Court articulated the general rule about questioning defendants outside the presence of counsel in *Massiah v. United States* (1964).[41] Winston Massiah was indicted for transporting cocaine. He obtained a lawyer, and while he was out on bail, federal agents convinced his codefendant (a friend who was accused of committing the crime with him) to have a conversation with Massiah in the presence of a hidden radio transmitter. The codefendant purposely got Massiah to make incriminating statements while an agent listened to the conversation. The statements Massiah made during that conversation were later used against him at trial. In a 6–3 decision, however, the Supreme Court held that Massiah's Sixth Amendment rights had been violated. To question a defendant without his lawyer present—whether secretly, as in this case, or openly—interferes with the lawyer's ability to effectively represent her client. Therefore, once a person has been formally charged with a crime, any questioning must take place in the presence of an attorney. If statements are obtained in violation of the *Massiah* rule, the exclusionary rule applies.

The *Massiah* decision was less controversial than the *Miranda* ruling, in part because *Massiah* usually applies only after police have had the opportunity to conduct a fair amount of investigation. Nonetheless, some were concerned that *Massiah* might interfere with the ability to put wrongdoers behind bars. A more conservative Supreme Court later limited the *Massiah* ruling somewhat by

Matters *of* Ethics

False Confessions

It was a terrible crime. On July 7, 1997, Michelle Moore-Bosko was raped and murdered in Norfolk, Virginia. She was 18 years old. After an investigation, five men eventually confessed to the crime; all five were convicted. However, four of the men retracted their confessions, and DNA evidence linked only the fifth man to the crime. Even most of the jurors who had convicted the men later signed statements saying that they now believed the confessions of the four men—the "Norfolk 4"—were false and that those four individuals were innocent. All four men served lengthy prison sentences, and although they were eventually freed, as of December 2010 the governor of Virginia was still refusing to grant them pardons.

In a separate case, on June 13, 1987, an elderly woman was sexually assaulted and brutally murdered in her home in Tyler, Texas. On October 27, Robert Bush, a young man with a history of mental illness and drug abuse, wrote a lengthy confession to the murder, rich with details that only the killer—and the police—could have known. Bush was taken into custody, and charges were filed. There was just one problem: An investigation by Bush's defense attorney revealed that between May and July 1987, Bush had been locked up in a California mental hospital, 1,200 miles from the murder scene. Clearly, the police had supplied him with some of the details of the crime he included in his "confession." Eventually the charges against Bush were dismissed, but he had spent more than a year in jail awaiting trial for a crime he could not have committed.

Police and prosecutors typically regard confessions as valuable evidence. Juries tend to weigh them heavily when determining guilt. Yet it turns out that cases like those of the Norfolk 4 and Robert Bush are not as rare as we might think: People often confess to crimes they did not commit. In fact, according to the Innocence Project (a national organization dedicated to exonerating wrongfully convicted people through DNA testing and to reforming the criminal justice system), false confessions are the third most common cause of wrongful convictions—the first being mistaken identification and the second, improper forensics.[a] In one infamous case, after a jogger in New York's Central Park was severely beaten and raped, five teenagers confessed. All were convicted. Only after they had all served several years of their 6- to 11-year sentences did DNA evidence prove that another man, previously convicted of similar crimes, had actually attacked the woman.

Why would an innocent person confess to a crime? Researchers have many explanations.[b] One is that trained interrogators may easily manipulate suspects, especially if they are young, mentally ill, are mentally impaired by drugs or alcohol, or if they have a developmental disability. Another theory is that innocent suspects confess because they may become exhausted after long interrogation sessions—or they may come to believe that their fate will ultimately be better if they confess than if they continue to deny guilt. Another component in the mix is that police may use a variety of tactics—even outright lies—to pressure suspects. And as the Supreme Court pointed out in its *Miranda* decision, even if the police do not overtly harm or threaten a suspect, just being in police custody is inherently coercive.

Although we cannot know exactly what prompted the Norfolk 4's confessions or those of Robert Bush or the defendants in the Central Park jogger case, it is probably significant that Bush had a mental illness. The defendants in the Central Park jogger case were all in their teens.

In response to increasing concerns about the reliability of confessions, some jurisdictions now require video recording of all custodial interrogation sessions, and some police departments have a policy of video recording interrogations. In June 2015, for example, the New York State Bar Association—together with the state's District Attorneys Association and the Innocence Project—proposed that all felony interrogations be recorded.[c] Still, most interrogations go unrecorded.

▲ **Suspects in the Norfolk 4 Case**

OBSERVE → INVESTIGATE → UNDERSTAND

- What do you think are the most likely reasons that suspects like the Norfolk 4 and Robert Bush "confess?"
- Why did all five teenagers confess to the rape of the Central Park jogger when they knew that they had not committed it?
- Why do you think most interrogations still are not recorded?

SOURCES: [a]The Innocence Project. www.innocence.org (retrieved June 7, 2015); Gisli Gudjonsson, *The Psychology of Interrogations and Confessions: A Handbook* (Hoboken, NJ: Wiley, 2003).

[b]See, for example, Saul Kassin and Gisli Gudjonsson, "The Psychology of Confessions: A Review of the Literature and Issues," *Psychological Science in the Public Interest* 5 (2004): 33; Richard Leo and Richard Ofshe, "Coerced Confessions: The Decision to Confess Falsely, Rational Choice and Irrational Action," *Denver University Law Review* 74 (1997): 979; Saul Kassin, "On the Psychology of Confessions: Does Innocence Put Innocents at Risk?" *American Psychologist* 60 (2005): 215–228, Richard Leo, "False Confessions: Causes, Consequences, and Implications," *Journal of the American Academy of Psychiatry and the Law* 37 (2009): 332–343.

[c]Jim Dwyer, "A Plan to Combat Mistaken Identifications and False Confessions," *New York Times*, June 2, 2015. www.nytimes.com/2015/06/03/nyregion/a-plan-to-combat-mistaken-identifications-and-false-confessions.html?_r=2 (retrieved June 7, 2015).

finding that *Massiah* rights, like *Miranda* rights, may be waived. Thus a defendant who has been charged with a crime and has a lawyer may still be questioned without her lawyer's being present as long as she is adequately notified of her rights and expressly and voluntarily chooses to waive them. In addition, a defendant who "lawyers up" on one charge—invokes his Sixth Amendment rights and obtains an attorney—may be interrogated by police about a different crime.[42]

All the exceptions to the exclusionary rule apply to the Sixth Amendment just as they do to the Fourth and Fifth Amendments. A famous example is the so-called Christian Burial Speech case. Robert Williams was the suspect in the kidnapping and probable murder of a 10-year-old girl in Des Moines, Iowa. The body had not yet been found, although a major search was under way. Williams turned himself in to authorities in Davenport, 160 miles away, was arraigned, and hired an attorney who was in Des Moines. Police officers from Des Moines picked Williams up in Davenport. On the drive back to Des Moines, one of the officers had a conversation with Williams and said how sad it was that the girl's parents would be unable to give her a Christian burial. Williams, who the officers knew was religious and who had a history of mental illness, eventually led them to the girl's body.

The Supreme Court held that the officer had violated Williams's Sixth Amendment rights by questioning him, and therefore the statements Williams made to the officers were inadmissible. However, the Court also eventually ruled that the body's location and condition could be admitted as evidence because, the Court said, the search party was nearby, and the body would have been discovered even without Williams's incriminating statements. Therefore, the evidence was admissible under the inevitable discovery exception.[43]

In a more recent case, Donnie Ray Ventris was charged with robbery and murder. Before his trial, the police planted an informant in Ventris's cell and told the informant to keep his ears open for incriminating statements. This ploy violated Ventris's Sixth Amendment rights to counsel. At his trial, Ventris testified that someone else had committed the crimes. The prosecutor then had the informant testify about incriminating statements Ventris had made in jail. The Supreme Court held that the exclusionary rule would not apply in this instance because the illegal evidence was used to impeach Ventris's statements— that is, to make him look like a liar—rather than specifically to prove that he had committed the crimes.[44] While this may seem like a fine distinction—and one that might be lost on jurors—it was enough for the Court to uphold the conviction.

Constitutional restrictions and guarantees place legal limitations on what police in the United States may and may not do. In addition, police face a number of special issues and situations that affect both police performance and the way communities interact with law enforcement.

USE OF FORCE

A seemingly extraordinary succession of instances of police use of lethal force has galvanized public concern and has, in a number of communities, undermined public trust.[45] The term *use of force* encompasses an array of coercive actions, from control holds (for example, "wrist locks" and "twist locks") to deadly force. Because it is now so easy to record the use of force in public places, it is being illuminated as never before. Video recording devices are increasingly ubiquitous, from on-board video cameras in law enforcement vehicles to citizens' handheld video recording devices. The omnipresence of video recordings was underscored

▼ **Police Use of Force**
Officers' use of force is heavily regulated.

KEY CONCEPTS Constitutional Provisions That Limit Police Actions

Amendment	Provisions
Fourth Amendment	
Searches and seizures	Applies only to actions undertaken by government agents
	Applies only when there is a reasonable expectation of privacy
Reasonableness	Many searches require valid search warrants based on probable cause
	There are numerous exceptions to the warrant requirement
Exclusionary rule	Evidence seized in violation of the Fourth Amendment is excluded at trial
	There are numerous exceptions to the exclusionary rule
Fifth Amendment	Prohibits compelled confessions
	Originally, confessions were permitted as evidence as long as they were voluntary
	In *Miranda v. Arizona*, the U.S. Supreme Court required that defendants must be informed of certain rights prior to custodial interrogation
	There are exceptions to the *Miranda* rule
Sixth Amendment	Guarantees criminal defendants the assistance of counsel
	Once formal charges have been filed, a defendant cannot be questioned outside the presence of the defense attorney
	Exceptions apply as they do to Fourth and Fifth Amendment rights

in a number of high-profile police–citizen deadly force encounters across the nation in 2014 and 2015. In fact, the value of video evidence of police–citizen encounters has undoubtedly given impetus to body-worn cameras becoming part of each officer's equipment inventory in many agencies.[46]

Regulating Use of Force

No aspect of the exercise of law enforcement powers poses greater potential for harm than the misuse of force. Therefore, the laws and policies concerning police use of force are particularly important.

Case Law   The facts of three key cases define lawful use of force: *Tennessee v. Garner, Graham v. Connor,* and *Saucier v. Katz.* In *Tennessee v. Garner* (1985), the U.S. Supreme Court held that the use of deadly force was not reasonable unless the suspect committed a crime that inflicted serious harm and his or her escape posed a significant risk of further serious harm to persons at large. The *Garner* decision reversed the common law authorization to use deadly force against any fleeing felon.[47]

The Court's decision in *Graham v. Connor* (1989) established the "objective reasonableness" standard. Recognizing that police officers are often forced to make split-second decisions about the amount of force necessary in a particular situation, the Court ruled that the reasonableness of a particular use of force incident must be judged from the perspective of a reasonable officer on the scene. Other factors determining whether the use of force meets the objective reasonableness standard include severity of the crime, immediacy of the threat to the safety of officers or others, and the suspect's resistance to arrest or his or her attempt to evade arrest by flight.[48]

In *Saucier v. Katz* (2001), the Court recognized that on occasion police officers apply force that may eventually be determined unconstitutional yet remains protected by **qualified immunity**—meaning that the officers, under specific circumstances, cannot be sued for their actions. The Court established a two-prong test: (1) Did the officer's conduct violate a Constitutional right? and (2) If a violation occurred, was the right clearly established in light of the specific context of the case at hand?[49]

A number of cases following *Saucier* more closely examined the "hazy border" between excessive and acceptable use of force. In *Brosseau v. Haugen* (2004), the Court reiterated the requirement that a right allegedly violated must have been so clearly established that a reasonable officer would know that his conduct violated the law. A fact-driven analysis must reveal that law in a particular area is clearly established. Absent such, an officer is entitled to qualified immunity from a lawsuit.[50] Commonly, an officer's training records are accessed to determine exposure to knowledge.

Court decisions have made it clear that we must judge the need for and appropriateness of any level of force objectively on the facts in a given situation. Law enforcement officers must use only nondeadly force options when deadly force is not appropriate, and they may use only a level of force that is objectively reasonable to bring an incident under control.

Use of Force Continuum The **use of force continuum** is a training aid depicting the appropriate amount of force a law enforcement officer may use in particular kinds of situations. As Figure 7-2 illustrates, the continuum includes strategies for escalating force when a subject does not comply with officers, as well as strategies for de-escalating force when a subject is compliant. The underlying principle of a force continuum is that force should be applied proportionately and increased or decreased in increments.[51]

Policy Paramount among the policies of law enforcement agencies are those controlling use of force. Not only should there be policies for deadly and nonlethal uses of force, but a "sanctity of life" philosophy must be inculcated and in the forefront of each officer's mind.[52] The "gold standard" of use of force management is a leader who possesses complete awareness of the use of force culture within her agency and knowledge of the attitudes held by all officers.[53]

It is imperative that agencies continuously update policy and related training to reflect changes in law, societal expectations, and tactics.[54] In fact now, amid the largest national debate over policing since the 1991 beating of Rodney King in Los Angeles, a number of agencies are reexamining when officers should chase people or draw their weapons and when they should back away and wait or try to defuse certain situations.[55]

Dynamics of Use of Force

The most recent national survey of contacts between the police and the public revealed that an estimated 17 percent of U.S. residents aged 16 and older, or 40 million individuals, had face-to-face contact with the police in the course of the year 2008. Fewer than 2 percent of the 40 million people experienced force or threat of force by the police. African Americans were more likely than Whites or Latinos to experience use of force. Interestingly, African Americans were slightly less inclined to consider the force excessive; overall, three-quarters of the people experiencing use of force believed the force used against them was excessive.[56]

qualified immunity
The protection of officers against being sued for their actions under certain circumstances.

use of force continuum
Guideline depicting the appropriate amount of force a law enforcement officer may use in particular kinds of situations.

Level five	Deadly force	Firearms and strike to vital areas
Level four	Hard techniques	Strikes and takedowns (tasers and batons)
Level three	Soft techniques	OC spray, come-alongs, and wrist locks
Level two	Verbal commands	Clear and deliberate
Level one	Officer presence	Physical appearance, professional bearing

FIGURE 7-2 **Use of Force Continuum**
The use of force continuum is a training aid for officers in determining the appropriate level of force to be applied against a resisting suspect.

RealCrimeTech

TAKING SIMULATION TRAINING IN USE OF FORCE TO THE NEXT LEVEL

Most people are familiar with the concept of *virtual reality*, an artificial environment "entered" when one is outfitted with special head gear and full-body wiring. A step beyond this is the concept of *augmented reality*. Augmented reality places simulated humans in an actual physical environment. The simulated humans, known as *avatars*, can hide, move about, or crawl within this environment. The avatars, for example, can be encircled and given voice commands, and they can engage in a variety of intelligent behaviors. The only thing they cannot be subjected to is handcuffing—because these "beings" do not exist.

Officers undergoing augmented reality training carry a computer mouse customized as a weapon. Pulling (that is, clicking) the weapon's trigger activates the mouse. The helmet a player wears includes a camera that records what the participant is seeing and his or her reaction. This aspect of the system provides a glimpse into the player's decision making and sets the stage for a comprehensive review of actions taken—or omitted. The augmented reality simulation permits participants to act within the type of environment (such as kitchen chairs and a table) that might typically be encountered in a service call, and it allows multiple players to be involved.

SOURCE: National Law Enforcement and Corrections Technology Center, *TECH Beat: A Different Reality* (Washington, DC: NLECTC, 2007), 1–2.

Some critics of the police assume that use of any force, including excessive force, primarily occurs when White officers deal with minority citizens. However, some recent studies present strong evidence that a suspect's behavior and demeanor toward the police, rather than race, are significant determinants of police use of force. If the suspect uses or threatens physical force, the police are more likely to use force, and the amount of force increases significantly. Moreover, the probability of using force and the amount of force significantly increase when the suspect is antagonistic. Thus, what the suspect does–not who he is–is a major indicator of police force.[57]

Until relatively recently, studies have not assessed the perceptions, beliefs, and thought processes of the officers involved in deadly force situations. A 2012 study under the auspices of the Bureau of Justice Statistics surveyed 295 law enforcement officers across the United States regarding their experiences involving use of deadly force. The results of the study indicated that approximately 70 percent of the sample of officers, averaging 17 years of service, had been in a situation where they legally could have fired their weapons. This finding contrasts with the public perception of police officers, which is framed and influenced largely by media depictions.

Insight into the restraint of use of force by officers can be provided by a concept known as the "deadly mix." The "deadly mix" is descriptive of the dynamic interaction of the officer, suspect, and the circumstances that brought them together. As the suspect and officer interact, both parties assess each other's behavior and act accordingly. This occurs within seconds but has life-altering potential. The elements of the "deadly mix" were divined in large part through interviews of offenders who killed officers. In a majority of cases, the decision to take on an officer was based on the officer's apparent level of awareness of all going on around him and the degree to which the officer conveyed "being in charge." Conceptualizing restraint in terms of the "deadly mix" reveals the dynamic nature of decision making in the context of exigent circumstances.[58]

PURSUITS

Like instances of excessive force, police vehicle pursuits that result in the loss of innocent lives can be particularly problematic for law enforcement. A pursuit begins when a law enforcement officer signals a driver to stop his automobile and the driver refuses to do so. Police and many members of the public believe that allowing officers to pursue someone who fails to yield is an absolute necessity. If offenders know they can drive away and the officer will not pursue, many people reason that this situation creates a serious hazard to public safety. Others argue that officers should make decisions to pursue based on a variety of relevant factors, such as the seriousness of the suspected activity and the potential danger to bystanders. Driving 10 miles over the speed limit, for example, might not be an offense worthy of pursuit. Officers need to quickly weigh competing safety issues–namely, the possible risk to public safety of not apprehending the suspect against the risk of pursuit and the possibility of an accident.

Risks of an accident increase when more officers participate in a chase. As noted earlier, an officer is also more likely to use force in events that follow a pursuit.[59] Suspects who flee from police not only put themselves at risk of an accident but also increase the likelihood of police use of force when they are apprehended.

Pursuits are dangerous for suspects, bystanders, and police. A good deal of controversy surrounds the data about how many innocent bystanders are killed annually because of police pursuits. Some estimates suggest as many as 40 percent of pursuits end in accidents, and approximately 300 deaths of suspects, bystanders, and police occur each year.[60] In 2014, 10 of 51 officers feloniously killed on duty lost their lives as the result of a pursuit or traffic stop.

There are few legal limits on when and under what conditions police may pursue a suspect. In several cases, someone who was harmed as a result of a police pursuit sued the officer and the department. Generally, courts have ruled that qualified immunity shields these officers from civil suits.

The U.S. Supreme Court ruled on officer liability in *Scott v. Harris* (2007). Victor Harris was driving 73 miles per hour in a 55-mile-per-hour zone. When Officer Timothy Scott tried to pull him over, Harris failed to yield and attempted to flee; 6 minutes and 10 miles into the pursuit, Scott rammed his bumper into the rear of Harris's vehicle. Harris lost control of his automobile, and the resulting crash left him a quadriplegic. Harris sued Scott, claiming that Scott had violated his constitutional rights by subjecting him to excessive force. The Court ruled that Scott had not violated Harris's constitutional rights because his actions were reasonable in that Harris's driving was causing a threat to public safety. Scott was therefore not liable under the doctrine of qualified immunity. In the majority opinion, Justice Antonin Scalia wrote, "A police officer's attempt to terminate a dangerous high-speed car chase that threatens the lives of innocent bystanders does not violate the Fourth Amendment, even when it places the fleeing motorist at risk of serious injury."[61]

Although the courts have largely supported police in their efforts to apprehend fleeing suspects, the risk of lawsuits and the need to ensure the safety of the public and officers have led many law enforcement agencies to review and revise their pursuit policies. There are two types of pursuit policies. In a restrictive policy, an officer can only begin a pursuit in the suspicion of particular crimes, usually felonies. In a discretionary policy, an officer can decide whether to pursue, but guidelines are provided regarding how to conduct the pursuit and when to stop pursuing. Restrictive policies have drawn criticism because people argue that criminals will be more likely to commit crimes for which they know they won't be chased. If a department wants to limit lawsuits, however, it will more likely adopt a restrictive policy so that any accidents or injuries that do occur will be the result of pursuing a suspected felon.[62]

DRUG ENFORCEMENT

The use and sale of illegal drugs is another challenge for law enforcement. Illegal drug use is widespread in the United States. According to a 2013 national survey, 8.8 percent of adolescents aged 12–17 (an estimated 2.2 million adolescents) reported using illicit drugs within the month prior to being surveyed. Overall, 2.6 percent of people 12 and over in the United States (6.9 million individuals) reported that they had been dependent on drugs during the prior year. That level of dependence has not significantly changed since 2009.[63]

Marijuana appears to be the clear drug of choice for illicit users, but methamphetamine use tends to be associated with a variety of other criminal behaviors not necessarily found with other drugs. For example, methamphetamine use has been found to predict violent behavior in parolees.[64]

▶ **Methamphetamine Lab**

Methamphetamine labs are extremely toxic for both people and the environment.

Furthermore, the labs in which methamphetamine is made are particularly dangerous. About 15 percent of the methamphetamine labs discovered in California are uncovered because unsafe handling of the highly combustible chemicals required often results in explosions, fires, toxic fumes, and other environmental hazards.[65] Perhaps most troubling are the risks to children who live in homes where methamphetamine is manufactured.[66]

As we saw in Chapter 1, enforcement of drug laws has varied over time. Enforcement strategies today are aimed at preventing drugs from entering the United States, stopping drug sales, and arresting individual users in possession of illicit drugs. The federal budget for drug enforcement, prevention, and rehabilitation illustrates where most of the government's efforts are focused. In 2015, the White House requested $25.5 billion to reduce drug use, which was an increase of $0.4 billion over 2014 funding. Funding falls into four categories: prevention and treatment; domestic law enforcement; interdiction (intercepting drugs); and international (work to eliminate international drug organizations). The 2015 requests were the first time the requested funds for prevention and treatment increased and the three enforcement categories decreased. President Obama's National Drug Control Strategy had for years been stressing an increased need for prevention and treatment. The budget for 2015 reflects that change in priorities.[67]

Although the focus of a good deal of taxpayer money, enforcement strategies have been largely ineffective in reducing the use or sale of illegal drugs.[68] However, measuring the effect of police interventions is difficult because there are scant data on their long-term results. Still, drug use in the United States has not declined in recent years.[69]

Differential enforcement of drug laws is also a concern. Whites and Blacks report about the same level of drug use, but Blacks are much more likely to be arrested for a drug offense.[70] In fact, 75 percent of incarcerated drug offenders are people of color, even though 72 percent of drug users are White, 13 percent are Black, and 11 percent are Latino.[71] The "Race, Class, Gender" box on page 233 illustrates how aggressive drug enforcement can encourage increased rates of searches that may cross the line of constitutionality.

Police also engage in drug prevention efforts. In the Drug Abuse Resistance Education (D.A.R.E.) program, the best known of these strategies, officers talk to students in classrooms about illegal drugs and the negative effects of drugs on users' lives. The preventive orientation is appealing to communities, and

Pedestrian Stop-and-Frisk in the Big Apple

As part of its aggressive order maintenance and general tough-on-crime strategy, New York City's Police Department initiated an active stop-and-frisk program in 2006. The result was over a half-million police–resident pedestrian contacts in that year. The data released by the NYPD indicated that almost 90 percent of those stops were of non-White individuals. Specifically, the racial breakdown of stops was 53 percent Blacks, 29 percent Latinos, 11 percent Whites, and 3 percent Asians. When frisks were considered, some races had a higher "hit rate," meaning that they were more likely to be in possession of a weapon. Whites were frisked only 29 percent of the times in which they were stopped, but they were 70 percent more likely to have a weapon. However, Blacks and Latinos were more likely to be frisked at the rate of 45 percent of those stopped.

A primary goal of pedestrian stop-and-frisks is to rid the streets of contraband, including narcotics. Of the half-million stops, however, only 6.4 percent of White suspects, 5.7 percent of Black suspects, and 5.4 percent of Latino suspects were discovered to be in possession of contraband. Ultimately, though, over 90 percent of pedestrians stopped were not found to be breaking the law.

A follow-up analysis of stops in 2009 showed that even more pedestrian stops were executed, with 575,000 such stops occurring in that year, which brings the 3-year total to almost 3 million. Blacks and Latinos were nine times more likely to be stopped that year than Whites but were still no more likely to be arrested. In the more than half-million stops, 726 guns were found, which equates to .001 percent of the pedestrian stops.

The most recent controversy over this practice is that the police department had been storing identifying information about every pedestrian stopped in a database, regardless of whether the person had been found to be engaged in any criminal activity. The New York State legislature passed a bill that barred the department from saving identifying information on people who were not found to be engaged in wrongdoing. Despite protests from New York City's mayor and police chief, the governor signed the bill into law in July 2010. Despite lawsuits and public protests, however, the department continued to engage in an aggressive stop-and-frisk program for several years. When new mayor Bill de Blasio took office in 2014, he pledged to reduce the practice. According to subsequent reports, although the overall number of stops did decrease significantly, young Black and Latino men continued to be stopped at disproportionately high rates.

OBSERVE → INVESTIGATE → UNDERSTAND

- Community relations—particularly among communities of color and the police—suffered from these stop-and-frisk activities. Many people expressed the view that Blacks and Latinos were specifically being targeted by law enforcement. Do you think stop-and-frisks should continue given what you have just learned? Explain.

- Should law enforcement agencies be required to demonstrate that their tactics are effective, especially if the tactics are personally intrusive? Why or why not?

- What kind of information should police departments be able to keep on individuals for whom they have no proof of criminal wrongdoing?

SOURCES: Gary Ridgeway, "Analysis of Racial Disparities in the New York Police Department's Stop, Question, and Frisk Practices," 2006. RAND Corporation. www.rand.org/pubs/technical_reports/2007/RAND_TR534.pdf (accessed February 13, 2011); Al Baker, "New York Minorities More Likely to Be Frisked" *New York Times,* May 12, 2010; Al Baker and Ray Rivera, "New York to Limit Retention of Street-Stop Data," *New York Times,* July 15, 2010; Taylor Wofford, "Did Bill de Blasio Keep His Promise to Reform Stop-and-Frisk?" *Newsweek,* August 25, 2014. www.newsweek.com/did-bill-de-blasio-keep-his-promise-reform-stop-and-frisk-266310 (retrieved June 7, 2015).

many have implemented the program in their public schools. But individuals who receive D.A.R.E. programming are not any less likely to use illegal drugs.[72] Unfortunately, neither enforcement-oriented nor prevention-oriented policing strategies appear to have a notable impact on illegal drug use.

The challenge to police of dealing with illegal drugs and drug enforcement policy often overlaps with police confrontations with gangs and gang members, the topic we take up in the next section.

GANG ENFORCEMENT

There is no single accepted definition of gangs. In any case, gangs' characteristics and the behavior of members vary from place to place. Classifying crimes as gang-related is equally difficult. So we cannot be as confident in our knowledge of gang involvement in criminal events as we are in other areas of criminology.[73]

▶ **Gang Identity**

Special signs, colors, tattoos, and codes provide identity for gang members.

We define gangs as "any identifiable group of youngsters who (a) are generally perceived as a distinct aggregation by others in their neighborhood, (b) recognize themselves as a denotable group (almost invariably with a group name), and (c) have been involved in a sufficient number of delinquent incidents to call forth a consistent negative response from neighborhood residents and/or law enforcement agencies."[74] In other words, gangs are groups, recognized as such by themselves and others, that have a history of trouble with neighbors and police.

Patterns of Gang Activity

As of 2011, there were 29,900 gangs and 782,500 gang members in the United States.[75] Gang membership and violence was, and still to a large degree is, a major *urban* problem.[76] Rural areas and small towns lack the necessary population base to sustain gangs, and any disruption such as an arrest or the departure of members can severely weaken the gang. Gang problems reported by most rural agencies are occasional and minor.[77]

Eighty-five percent of gang members live in large cities and suburban counties. News media frequently report stories about gang members moving into communities from other places. However, gangs are not as mobile as these reports might suggest, and membership in gangs has been fairly stable. For the most part, gang problems develop within a community rather than being imported into it.[78] Gangs are the primary distributors of illicit drugs throughout the United States and often use drug trafficking as their primary means of financial gain.[79]

Gangs are also associated with organized crime entities. Criminal alliances exist between Mexican organized crime groups and U.S. gangs, and Asian criminal enterprises also work with street gangs in the United States. In addition to illegal drugs, Asian organized crime groups are often engaged in credit card fraud, illegal gaming, and money laundering. In California, Russian organized crime groups have been associated with the Crips (a well-known gang) for the purpose of fencing stolen goods.[80]

Gangs have kept pace with technology and use it extensively. For example, gangs use cell phones as much as does the public at large. Gangs also monitor police communications with scanners and use surveillance equipment to detect hidden microphones or "bugs." They track legal proceedings online and use computers to identify witnesses for intimidation, steal information, and perpetrate fraud.[81]

Police Response to Gangs

To deal with the gang problem, police departments have created task forces or gang units and offered specialized training in gang signs, colors, tattoos, and codes. Gang units, like drug units, generally use proactive police strategies and maintain a high degree of contact with known gang members or gang affiliates for intelligence purposes. Operation Ceasefire, an innovative problem-oriented policing program in Boston, successfully reduced gang violence. The program identified young gang members who were especially active in crime and focused enforcement efforts on them. When members of a gang committed violence, the police would flood the area and indicate that they would strictly enforce any law broken. Community organizations also offered gang members a variety of social services such as health care, substance abuse assistance, and food and shelter.[82]

Some critics contend that police and politicians have become overzealous in their desire to protect society from the criminal behavior of gang members. For example, some cities have imposed juvenile curfews that have been challenged as unconstitutional or illegal.[83] Given their training, officers report they can identify gang members by their clothing, the people with whom they associate, their tattoos, and the hand signals they flash. Some agencies document names and identities of those they believe to be gang members.

Critics, however, say these lists cast a shadow of suspicion on all young men of color, some of whom can find their names listed, though there is little supporting evidence. According to law enforcement agencies, gang membership by race is divided in the following manner: 35 percent of gang members are Black, 46 percent Latino, 11 percent White, and 7 percent some other race or ethnicity.[84]

Success in eliminating problems and crime associated with gangs demands a coordinated response that includes suppression, community mobilization, and social opportunities for youth.[85] Of course, all such efforts must be clearly defined, constitutional, and nondiscriminatory.[86]

INTIMATE PARTNER VIOLENCE

Domestic violence is the traditional term for an assault on a person with whom the attacker is intimately involved. Today the preferred term is **intimate partner violence,** which encompasses the variety of couples who experience this violence—dating couples, same-sex couples, life partners, married couples, and couples recently separated (the aftermath of separation is an extremely dangerous time for this kind of victimization). Intimate partner disputes occur in all social classes and make up a large percentage of calls to the police. Yet only half of female victims call the police, with lower-class women reporting their victimization at the highest rates.[87]

intimate partner violence
An assault on a person with whom the attacker is intimately involved.

One of the reasons victims may be hesitant to contact the police is that for years police officers treated violence between intimates as a private problem, a family matter not appropriate for police intervention. Hence, officers rarely made arrests even when there was clear evidence an assault had occurred.[88] Police response to the crime of intimate partner violence has, however, changed for a number of reasons.

First, in the 1970s victim advocates and women's rights advocates began to raise public awareness of police unresponsiveness to victims of intimate

a case in p♥int

Thurman v. City of Torrington (1984)

Tracey Thurman did everything she could to prevent the continued violence her husband, Charles Thurman, inflicted upon her. Unfortunately, the Torrington, Connecticut, Police Department would not help her. From October 1982 to June 1983, Tracey Thurman and family members repeatedly attempted to persuade Torrington police officers to protect her from Charles. When Charles attacked Tracey at a friend's home in October 1982, Tracey's friends filed a complaint with the police. The next month he attacked her again at the same friend's home. Tracey and her friend again went to the police department, but the officers refused to take a complaint—even of trespassing. A few days later, as a police officer looked on, Charles Thurman screamed threats at Tracey while she was in her vehicle. The officer took no action until Charles broke the windshield, at which point he was arrested. Charles Thurman was then convicted of breach of peace, sentenced to probation, and instructed to stay away from his wife.

Between December 1982 and May 1983, Tracey Thurman repeatedly called the police to report threats by Charles. At the beginning of May, she requested an arrest warrant be served because Charles was making death threats against her. The officer would not take the complaint and instead told her to return in three weeks. Tracey turned to

the court and obtained a restraining order against Charles Thurman. The police were notified of the order.

At the end of May, Tracey told police Charles had violated the restraining order, and she again requested an arrest warrant. An officer told her no one could help her until after Memorial Day when a particular officer would return from vacation. Calls to police from Tracey's brother-in-law to protest their behavior were also ignored.

Finally, on June 10, 1983, Charles Thurman went to where Tracey was staying and demanded she come out to talk to him. Instead, she called the police. After 15 minutes she finally went outside to convince Charles to leave without taking their son as he had done before. As soon as she was outside the home, Charles stabbed her with a kitchen knife 15 times in the chest, neck, and throat. The police arrived 25 minutes after they were called but did not immediately take Charles into custody, even though he twice kicked Tracey in the head in their presence. Officers finally arrested Charles after he charged at Tracey for the third time while she lay on a stretcher. Tracey Thurman is disfigured and paralyzed from the neck down as a result of the violence Charles Thurman inflicted on her.

The court ruled that the police department violated Tracey Thurman's right to equal protection by failing to protect her. The court also said that police departments cannot treat women abused by someone with whom they have a domestic relationship any differently than they would victims of any other violent crime.

OBSERVE → INVESTIGATE → UNDERSTAND

- How did Tracey Thurman's case affect the way police respond to calls involving intimate partner violence?

- How should police respond when faced with evidence of intimate partner violence?

- Is violence between intimate partners a private matter, or is police intervention appropriate in such cases? Explain.

SOURCE: *Thurman et al. v. City of Torrington,* 595 F. Supp. 1521 (D. Conn., 1984).

partner violence. That publicity put pressure on departments to change the way they handled these calls for service. A second force for change was that local governments were successfully sued for failing to protect female victims. In the pivotal case discussed in "A Case in Point," a Connecticut city awarded $2.3 million to a victim for violating her right to equal protection. This case illustrated to police and government officials that if they failed to protect victims, they would be held responsible, at least financially.[89] A third catalyst for change was the Minneapolis Domestic Violence Experiment, a study that revealed that an offender was less likely to reoffend if officers arrested the individual instead of suggesting mediation or separation.[90]

Police officers still tend to dislike intimate partner calls, in part because they believe such incidents pose the greatest risk to their own safety. There is little evidence to support that belief, however. The situations that pose the greatest threat to officer safety are traffic stops and pursuits.[91]

Today **mandatory arrest policies** dictate that officers must make an arrest when there is evidence of an assault. These policies were created to reduce police discretion in incidents of intimate partner violence because evidence showed that when police had discretion, they chose not to make an arrest. Critics of the policies say that arrests have not consistently been shown to reduce violence and have unintended negative impacts on poor women and women of color.

Mandatory arrest policies have resulted in an increase in dual arrests. **Dual arrests** occur when an officer arrests both parties in a physical altercation instead of identifying and arresting only the primary aggressor. Dual arrests are troubling because in at least 85 percent of cases of intimate partner violence, men are the perpetrators.[92] Some jurisdictions discourage dual arrests and instead expect officers to identify the primary aggressor.

Female illegal immigrants are particularly vulnerable victims of intimate partner violence. Although they can call police for assistance without fear of being deported, most are likely unaware of this rule or may not believe authorities will respect it.

mandatory arrest policy
Policy requiring officers to make an arrest when there is evidence of an assault.

dual arrest
The arrest of both parties in a physical altercation instead of identifying and arresting only the primary aggressor.

MYTH/REALITY

MYTH: A victim of domestic violence who is in the United States illegally cannot call the police for assistance because she will automatically be deported to her country of origin.

REALITY: It is against federal law to deport someone who is a victim of domestic violence. All victims of domestic violence can access law enforcement assistance, as well as emergency shelters, without fear of deportation.[93]

In 2013, Congress passed the Violence Against Women Reauthorization Act. This federal law, also known as VAWA, was first authorized in 1994. The original act removed the obstacles of "immigration laws that prevent immigrant victims from safely fleeing domestic violence and prosecuting their abusers."[94] VAWA was reauthorized in 2000 and extended assistance to immigrants who are victims of sexual assault, human trafficking, and other violent crimes, as long as the victim cooperates with law enforcement and prosecution. The goal of this legislation is to protect victims from abusers and traffickers who seek to control the victims by threatening them with deportation. The 2013 VAWA reauthorization legislation included increased resources and greater justice for Native American women who are victims of violence through tribal courts. The law also now allows immigrant victims to seek legal assistance, grants victims of child abuse the right to petition on their own behalf for citizenship until they are 25 years old, and provides resources for victims of elder abuse.[95]

STRESS

The constitutional and legal limitations imposed on police officers, as well as the special issues discussed in the preceding sections, powerfully affect officers' levels of stress. Officers routinely deal with emotionally charged situations knowing that there is always a potential for danger, yet they report that agency-related matters create the greatest job stress.[96] In particular, a major complaint among patrol officers is lack of support from their superiors.[97]

This perceived failing by management has taken on a new complexion in light of the proliferation of peace officers who have had their policing careers interrupted by military deployments to combat zones (e.g., Iraq and Afghanistan). Those returning from combat consistently acknowledge that the challenge of transitioning back to police work could be eased if agency leadership did more

What about the Victim?

Providing Transition Assistance for the Police Officer Returning from Combat Deployment

For the first time in more than a generation, law enforcement agencies have had to contend with the deployment of personnel to military combat zones. Furthermore, agencies are increasingly adding to their ranks recruits who have recently experienced tours of duty in combat zones. As many as one-quarter of military veterans may suffer from posttraumatic stress disorder (PTSD).[a] What do these developments mean for police departments? For example, might they confuse military rules for use of force with civilian rules?

Many law enforcement agencies have implemented programs both to ease officers back into police service and to monitor their performance. Some agencies have even initiated efforts to assist officers at their *predeployment* stage. This period of time can be both confusing and stressful as officers may have to resolve issues such as what type of medical benefits family members are eligible for and what to do with pets while they are away from home serving their country. Even the manner of turning in police equipment and identification can be stressful if there is no distinction between the protocol for individuals who are being suspended for punitive purposes and those who are temporarily giving up their job to fulfill a military service obligation.[b]

The Office of Community Oriented Policing Services (COPS) has studied the matter of accommodation for returning veterans. COPS has taken the proactive position of asking every department to consider the following questions and to address any negative responses:

- Is the department's culture supportive?
- Are supervisors advocates of employee assistance programs?
- Have supervisors received sufficient training about posttraumatic stress?
- Is someone maintaining contact with family members during deployments?
- Is a specific supervisor assigned to welcome returning officers and assist as needed?[c]

The few scholarly studies published to date on the effects of military service on police personnel returning from combat deployment have shown it is not generally difficult for officers to abandon their military rules of engagement and function in domestic policing roles. In a 2014 study of officers in New England, combat deployment was not seen as negatively impactful with regard to service functions, authority arrangements, or community relations. And not only did returning officers themselves rate as "low" the effects of combat deployment on increased suspicion of citizens based on nationality, they also evaluated the experience working with culturally and ethnically diverse groups as very useful.[d]

Much does remain to be learned about the effects of combat zone deployment. However, it is indisputable that a comprehensive program of support for militarily deployed officers—before, during, and after deployment—can go far toward bolstering these individuals both personally and professionally.

OBSERVE → INVESTIGATE → UNDERSTAND

- Do you think police officers are better prepared than other citizens to deal with the rigors of military combat and with the subsequent challenges of returning to the civilian workplace? Explain.
- Instead of just having reintegration programs for returning combat veterans, should agencies also consider sensitivity training for their non-combat-exposed officers so they can appreciate and focus more on the positive aspects of the combat deployment experience?
- Should police officers suffering PTSD remain on the job? Why or why not?

SOURCES: [a]Jeff Hink, "The Returning Military Veteran," *FBI Law Enforcement Bulletin* 79, no. 8 (2010): 2.

[b]William C. O'Toole, *Recommendations to Facilitate Military Deployment and Re-entry* (Gainesville, VA: Commission on Accreditation for Law Enforcement Agencies, 2010).

[c]Barbara Webster, *Combat Deployment and the Returning Police Officer* (Washington, DC: Office of Community Oriented Policing Services, 2008).

[d]Stanley Shernock, "Changing Uniforms: A Study of the Perspectives of Law Enforcement Officers with and without Different Military Background on the Effects of Combat Deployment on Policing," *Criminal Justice Policy Review* (published online before print, January 6, 2015, Sage Publications): 1–26.

to prepare returning veterans for reintegration.[98] The "What about the Victim?" box focuses on this situation and looks at its context and potential solutions.

Experiencing Stress

Unquestionably, police officers' stress from the job affects life at home.[99] Often officers work irregular hours and have a reduced amount of time they can spend with their families. Further, the transition from dealing with traumatizing events on the job, such as multiple deaths in a traffic accident, to attending to family needs at home can be difficult.

Real Careers

RYAN BAL

Work location: Roseville, California

College(s): California State University–Sacramento (2004)

Major(s): Criminal Justice (BS)

Job title: Patrol Officer, Roseville Police Department

Salary range for job like this: $56,000–$76,000

Time in job: 4 years

Work Responsibilities

As a patrol officer, I respond to emergency calls, like automobile accidents, and nonemergency calls, such as noise complaints and fallen trees. But I also partake in proactive law enforcement, which means I do traffic stops, locate subjects, and conduct searches.

I work on a 3/11, 4/11 schedule—that is, every other week I work 3 days for 11 hours or 4 days for 11 hours. On top of that, I recently received special training in evidence collection techniques and became a CSI (crime scene investigator). Now I am always on call for homicides or any other crime that requires specialized documentation and collection of evidence.

Why Criminal Justice?

My passion for criminal justice began when I took a forensic science class in high school. When I entered college, criminal law and investigation were the only subjects that interested me, so I knew that I wanted a career in law enforcement. Before applying for any jobs, my professors recommended I first see criminal justice in the field by taking an internship or part-time job. My internship with the city of Roseville as a cadet officer not only confirmed for me that I wanted a career that let me serve my community but also let me prove to myself that I could handle a heavy workload and dangerous situations.

Expectations and Realities of the Job

A career in law enforcement is definitely a stressful lifestyle. I often work an 11-hour shift, go home to sleep for a couple of hours, and wake up to start the next shift. Transitioning to this type of schedule was especially difficult for me because only two weeks after graduating from college, I began the police academy. I went from only afternoon classes to a 10-hour day of both physical and academic classes beginning at 7:00 a.m.

My Advice to Students

My best piece of advice is to get an internship before deciding on a career. This is the only opportunity you will really have to explore a career path before taking a full-time job. If you have a successful internship, the department might call you back for a full-time position.

Female officers and officers of color tend to experience higher levels of stress than their White male colleagues, much of it the result of discrimination from fellow officers.[100] Officers who identify as gay or lesbian also report increased levels of stress. Lesbian officers, however, report that their gender is a greater barrier in policing than their sexual orientation.[101] Gay male officers, on the other hand, experience clear hostility from straight male officers.[102]

Although only about 14 percent of police–citizen interactions involve citizen resistance,[103] police often find it hardest to forget these incidents, and they greatly affect the level of occupational stress. In the case of service calls to households, even when the residents are cooperative, the police are dealing with trauma. Indeed, many officers come face-to-face with social problems most people hope never to witness, such as sexual assault, child abuse, intimate partner violence, runaways, and drug addiction. These emotion-taxing problems take their toll on officers' psychological and emotional well-being.

Sometimes the police themselves are victims, as in the case of the officers who lost their lives or were injured at the site of the 9/11 World Trade Center devastation, or who contracted related illnesses after the event. Such cases affect not only the individual officers who are victimized but also other officers–who feel as though an assault on one officer is an assault on them all.

▲ **Cleveland Police Department Dog Tags**

The Cleveland Police Department awarded these tags to officers who participated in the department's innovative program on how to deal with on-the-job stress.

Strategies for Coping with Stress

Some officers may resort to alcohol to "deal with" stress.[104] Unfortunately, alcohol use is likely to create additional problems, both in family relationships and on the job. More positively, officers can turn to one another for support or utilize services offered by departments to help them cope with stress and the effects of dealing with traumatizing events.

Many types of stress prevention and treatment programs are available to police—some that individuals can pursue on their own and some the department must provide. Individual coping strategies include participating in a support system, maintaining a healthy diet and exercise regimen, venting feelings appropriately, and seeking out a change of focus and positive feedback. The single most important factor is having a dependable support group. Generally, from the perspective of police officers, no one is better equipped to understand the pressures of law enforcement than a peer. However, officers who serve as peer counselors should be trained by mental health professionals.[105]

Organizational strategies for addressing stress include the training of supervisors on sound supervisory techniques, constructive feedback on job performance, open communication channels, opportunities for input into organizational decisions whenever possible, and active support of stress management programs.[106] Although the vast majority of police departments aggressively equip their personnel with weapons, communications equipment, and bulletproof vests, they may not always undertake adequate measures to "bulletproof the mind." Supervisors are not always trained to recognize the symptoms of stress or to take appropriate action to deal with it. If a secondary problem such as alcohol abuse or marital conflict is allowed to fester, depression, intimate partner violence, and attempts at suicide may result.[107] A study of police suicides from 2008 to 2015 found that 125 to 150 officers commit suicide a year. Police suicide is a significant problem that needs to be better prevented. Overall, the organization can play a central role in minimizing the potential for harm, not only from criminal assailants but also from unattended stress.

The Cleveland Police Department's program to help reduce on-the-job stress included equipping patrol officers with laminated cards identifying the symptoms of stress in themselves and others and providing information on how to deal with and recover from stress. The program also involved training police supervisors on how to recognize the symptoms of stress and how to assist officers suffering from stress. To encourage participation in the program, the department awards participants bronze medals in the shape of dog tags and engraved with the words "One for All" and "Strengthening the Chain."[108]

SUMMARY

Police officers must balance their authority to enforce the law with citizens' constitutional guarantees of civil liberties and the right to due process. Constitutional provisions, especially those of the Fourth, Fifth, and Sixth Amendments, protect the civil liberties and civil rights of the criminally accused and legally limit what the police may do when interrogating, detaining, or arresting persons suspected of committing a crime.

Officers must sometimes exercise force to enforce the law and maintain order, but the use of force must be lawful, according to Supreme Court guidelines. Police decisions to use force or to pursue fleeing suspects should be based on the particular situation at hand. Factors to consider include the seriousness of the situation, the potential risk to innocent bystanders, and the effect on police–community relations.

Police efforts to curtail the sale of and trafficking in illegal drugs encompass both enforcement and prevention strategies. To deal with gangs, many police departments have created gang units or specialized task forces. Success in dealing with gangs and eliminating gang violence requires community involvement and support. The police response to incidents of intimate partner violence has changed over time, with police now more likely to respond and intervene promptly. Nevertheless, police still tend to dislike calls involving such incidents, in part because they mistakenly believe these calls present the greatest threat to their own safety.

The nature of police work creates stress for many officers, and legal restrictions on police actions can compound that stress. So, too, can dealing with the special issues discussed in this chapter—the use of force, pursuits, illegal drugs, gangs, and intimate partner violence. Specialized training in recognizing and relieving stress can be helpful, but the single most important factor is having a dependable support group. For many officers, that means a support group of fellow officers.

OBSERVE → INVESTIGATE → UNDERSTAND

Review

Identify the limitations on law enforcement activities imposed by the Fourth, Fifth, and Sixth Amendments to the U.S. Constitution.

- The Fourth Amendment requires that police conduct searches and seizures that are reasonable.
- The Fifth Amendment prohibits police from coercing confessions.
- The Sixth Amendment prohibits police from questioning defendants outside the presence of their attorneys.

Identify the situations most likely to entail use of force by the police, and explain how the police use of force is regulated.

- Situations most likely to entail use of force are those involving interpersonal disturbances, intoxicated persons, fleeing suspects, or suspects resisting arrest.
- Use of force rules are derived largely from case law and agency guidelines.

Analyze the impact of the use of force on community relations.

- The police use of force, especially excessive force, usually has a negative effect on community relations.

Describe the major legal and policy issues raised in police pursuits.

- Officers must consider the risks to public safety when deciding to pursue a suspect.
- Officers are generally protected from liability when engaging in pursuits, but pursuits can imperil the officers themselves and give rise to lawsuits.

Contrast the strategies of enforcement and prevention used to curb illegal drug use.

- Enforcement strategies include attempting to stop drugs from entering the United States, targeting drug sales, and arresting individual users who are in possession of illicit drugs.

- The best-known police department drug prevention effort is the D.A.R.E. program.

Explain how police departments have responded to gangs.

- Departments have created special task forces or gang units to deal with the gang problem.
- Gang units, like drug units, generally use proactive police strategies.

Describe how the police response to intimate partner violence has changed over time and explain why.

- Police historically did not provide victims of domestic violence the protection they deserved.
- Victims' rights advocates, women's rights advocates, and civil suits put pressure on police departments to change the way they responded to intimate partner violence.
- Today mandatory arrest policies and dual arrests are common.

Describe the factors that create stress for police officers and efforts to deal with these pressures.

- Police officers report that agency-related matters create the greatest stress.
- Female officers and officers of color tend to experience higher levels of stress due to bias within police departments.
- Strategies for dealing with stress include individual efforts and department programs.

Key Terms

attenuation 221

automobile exception 216

derivative evidence rule 220

dual arrest 237

exclusionary rule 218

fruit of the poisonous tree doctrine 220

good faith exception 220

independent source 221

inevitable discovery 221

intimate partner violence 235

mandatory arrest policy 237

Miranda warnings 223

probable cause 215

public safety exception 224

qualified immunity 229

reasonable suspicion 216

search incident to arrest 216

standing 221

stop-and-frisk 216

Terry stop 216

testimonial evidence 224

use of force continuum 229

voluntariness test 223

warrant 215

Study Questions

1. To obtain a search warrant, police officers must
   a. place the target of the warrant under arrest.
   b. permit the suspect to consult with an attorney.
   c. demonstrate to a judge that probable cause exists to search for evidence or contraband.
   d. prove the suspect's guilt beyond a reasonable doubt.

2. According to the exclusionary rule, evidence will be excluded at a defendant's trial if
   a. police obtained the evidence through illegal means.
   b. there is sufficient other evidence to obtain a guilty conviction.
   c. the defendant has no standing.
   d. the police did not have a valid search warrant.

3. Which of the following statements about the *Miranda* warnings is the one that is most accurate?
   a. The police must recite the *Miranda* warnings before asking suspects any questions.
   b. The *Miranda* warnings are meant to protect suspects' rights against self-incrimination.
   c. The *Miranda* warnings have resulted in significantly fewer confessions.
   d. The *Miranda* warnings include the right to a jury and a speedy trial.

4. Which of the following means a police officer who pursues a fleeing suspect will likely not be held financially responsible for any harm that comes to a suspect or other individual?
   a. qualified immunity
   b. qualified liability
   c. limited suability
   d. total vulnerability

5. One of the major effects of a police officer's excessive use of force is that
   a. the public's confidence in the police is reduced.
   b. officer morale remains static.
   c. interdepartmental cohesion ends.
   d. the police officer could get promoted.

6. One of the most important stressors police officers deal with—regardless of their ethnicity, gender, race, or sexual orientation—is
   a. general societal problems.
   b. hostile situations while on duty.
   c. agency-related stress.
   d. marital stress.

7. Which of the following statements accurately explains why differential enforcement of drug laws is a concern?
   a. People of color use drugs at a higher rate than Whites, yet both groups are arrested at proportional rates.
   b. One-fourth of incarcerated drug offenders are people of color.
   c. There should be no concern, because differential enforcement of drug laws does not exist.
   d. Whites and Blacks report about the same level of drug use, but Blacks are much more likely to be arrested for a drug offense.

8. Police departments have responded to gang problems in their areas by
   a. emphasizing faceless-oriented policing that utilizes reactive police strategies.
   b. establishing special task forces or units that utilize proactive police strategies.
   c. creating intradepartmental alliances that depend on proactive policing strategies.
   d. relying on problem-oriented policing and reactive police strategies.

9. The main reason many female victims do not call the police about intimate partner violence is that
   a. they believe that intimate partner violence is a private matter that should be dealt with inside the home.
   b. they are emotionally strong enough to handle intimate partner violence without the help of law enforcement agencies.
   c. historically, the police response to intimate partner violence has been victim-centered and has scared women away from making the call.
   d. historically, the police response to intimate partner violence has not been victim-centered.

10. The Sixth Amendment limits police behavior by
    a. protecting people from unreasonable searches.
    b. protecting people from coerced confessions.
    c. prohibiting police from questioning a defendant without his or her attorney present.
    d. protecting people from unwarranted police pursuits.

Critical Thinking Questions

For further review, go to the LearnSmart study module for this chapter.

1. Where should we draw the line between freedom and safety? What are some specific situations in which we might want to emphasize safety over freedom? When might we emphasize freedom over safety?

2. How do you think race is or is not related to police use of force?

3. How should police respond to the crime of intimate partner violence?

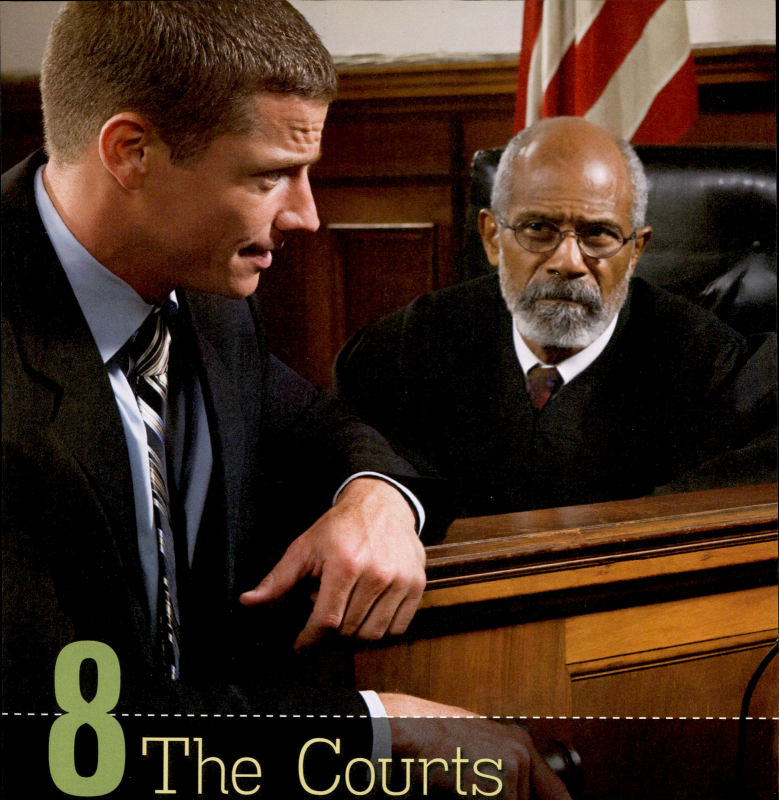

8 The Courts

OBSERVE → INVESTIGATE → UNDERSTAND

After reading this chapter, you should be able to:

- Distinguish among state, local, and federal courts and their jurisdictions.
- Describe some of the specialized courts that have been created for particular cases.
- Discuss how appeals courts differ from trial courts.
- Identify the major participants in the judicial system and their respective roles.

Realities and Challenges

Three Criminals Face the American Courts

On October 8, 2008, Eddie Pugh, his girlfriend Tory Whitmore, and his friend Barren Borden drastically changed their own lives—and the lives of many others as well.

The events began to unfold when two former college pals, Rahman MoGilles and Byron McCoy, went to Pugh's house in New Orleans. MoGilles and Pugh had known each other since childhood, and MoGilles and McCoy wanted to buy some marijuana from Pugh.

For some reason, Pugh decided that McCoy was a police informant. With the help of Whitmore and Borden, he beat MoGilles and McCoy with a baseball bat and tied their hands with telephone cord, then forced the victims into MoGilles's SUV.

Pugh and his accomplices drove the SUV across the state line into Mississippi. Then they pulled the car over. At Pugh's orders, Borden shot McCoy in the head. MoGilles managed to free his hands; he wrestled with Borden over the gun. During the struggle, Borden was shot in the leg, and MoGilles was shot in the back but was able to escape. MoGilles survived his injuries, but McCoy died.

Pugh and Borden were arrested a short time later. They were standing next to MoGilles's burning SUV. McCoy's body was still inside. Later Whitmore was arrested as well.

As MoGilles recovered from his wounds, and as McCoy's family dealt with their loss, Pugh and his friends were brought to court. First all three were taken to federal court, where they were convicted of kidnapping—and where Pugh and Borden were also convicted on weapons charges. All three were sentenced to two consecutive life sentences. But that was not the end of the saga for them, because Mississippi filed additional charges against the trio, including murder, aggravated assault, and arson. In a state courthouse, Borden pleaded guilty so that he would not face the death penalty; he was sentenced to life in prison. Pugh went to trial, and a jury convicted him. He was sentenced to life without parole. His conviction was upheld on appeal.[1]

As the case of Pugh, Borden, and Whitmore demonstrates, specific types of courts in the United States have differing jurisdictions (that is, different powers to hear a particular case). Specifically in such complicated cases, more than one court may be involved in the legal process that governs offenders and their deeds. Running this complex system requires a small army of workers, ranging from clerks to judges, each with a dedicated role in moving the stages of justice forward. This chapter focuses on various types of criminal courts and the roles and responsibilities of those who work within the court system.

COURT STRUCTURE AND JURISDICTION

Like the other components of the justice system, U.S. courts are complex. Each court has **jurisdiction**–legal power to hear particular kinds of cases. There are federal courts, state courts, and sometimes municipal or local courts. There are **courts of general jurisdiction,** which can hear almost any kind of case; and specialty courts, often called **courts of limited jurisdiction,** which hear only cases of a certain type. (An example of a limited jurisdiction court is a juvenile court.) Most criminal trials occur in courts of general jurisdiction.

jurisdiction
A court's legal power to hear particular kinds of cases.

court of general jurisdiction
A court that can hear nearly any type of case.

court of limited jurisdiction
A specialty court that can hear only cases of a certain type.

There are also trial courts and appellate courts. Each kind of court is organized differently, and the U.S. states have different ways of structuring their court systems.

State Courts

The basic structure of most state courts is similar, but their names vary. Figure 8-1 illustrates a typical state court organization. Most state criminal cases begin in state trial courts, usually called *district courts* or *superior courts* but sometimes, as in New York State, called *supreme courts*. In most states, each county has at least one of these trial courts.

Appeals are usually heard in the *state court of appeals,* sometimes known as the intermediary appeals court. Cases in intermediary appeals courts are heard by a panel of judges rather than a jury. Most states have only one appeals court, but some have several. Appeals courts may be divided geographically into *circuits* or by subject matter into civil and criminal courts. Some states with small populations, such as Montana and North Dakota, do not have an intermediary appeals court.

The next level is the state's highest court, usually called the *state supreme court*. Some states, such as Texas and Oklahoma, have a special high court just for criminal cases. In most states, high courts have *discretionary appeals,* meaning that the justices can refuse to hear a case. However, defendants in death penalty cases often are entitled to automatic, nondiscretionary appeals to the high court. The number of justices on state high courts varies between five and nine; most states have seven.

Most states have other courts as well. Some have many–New York has 13 different kinds of courts (Figure 8-2). Typically, local courts, run by cities or counties, hear minor civil and criminal matters, but they also may conduct some early stages of more serious civil and criminal cases. Most states have specialty courts as well. For example, since 2000, prompted by the increasing numbers of offenders with mental disorders in jails and prisons, approximately

FIGURE 8-1 **A Typical State Court**
State court systems are complicated bureaucracies.

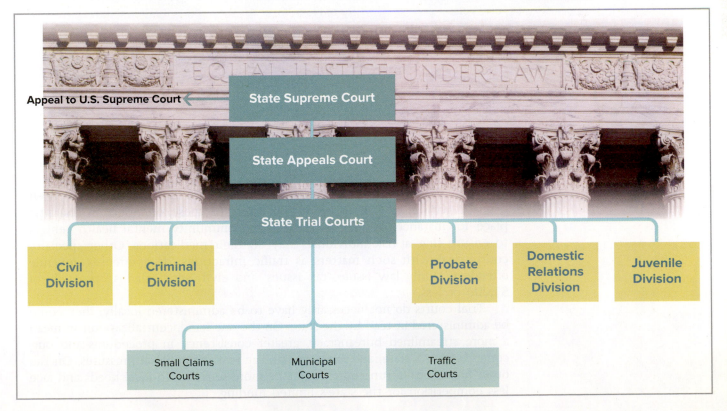

247

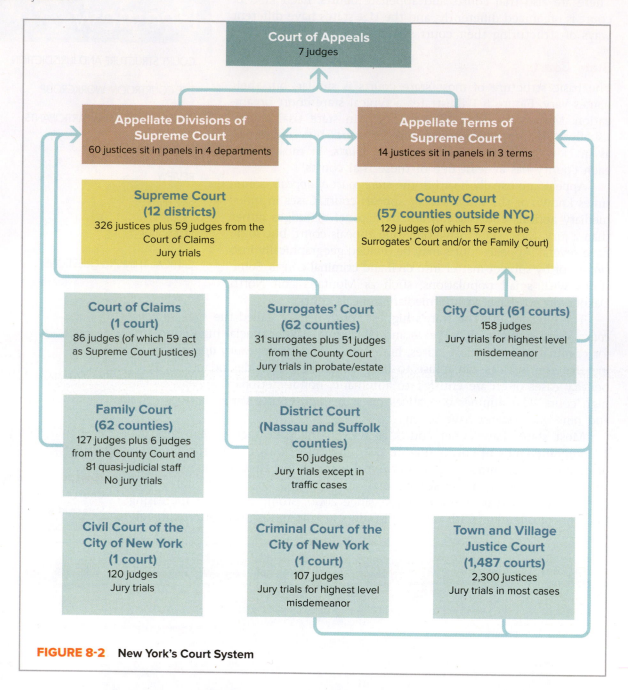

FIGURE 8-2   **New York's Court System**

100 mental health courts have been established in the United States. Their primary goal is to help prevent the arrest of these offenders in the first place–for instance, by making referrals to community mental health centers to ensure that at-risk individuals stay on their medications. Other specialty courts deal with such matters as traffic infractions, drug offenses, juvenile offenders, family law issues, tax issues, and civil "small claims," typically of $1,000 or less.

Trial courts do not necessarily have to be administered locally; they could be administered instead by the state. On the one hand, centralization can mean a more streamlined bureaucracy, greater consistency in procedures and outcomes within a state, and less vulnerability to local political pressures. On the other hand, locally run courts might be more sensitive to local needs and face less competition for the state's limited funding.

Federal Courts

The federal courts have jurisdiction to hear only limited types of cases. In general, a federal case must entail federal law or the U.S. Constitution; or it must involve citizens of different states and at least $75,000 in controversy; or the U.S. government itself must be prosecuting the case or involved as a party in the lawsuit. Thus the only criminal cases that go to federal courts are those that charge someone with violating a federal law or those in which a defendant claims that a state has violated her constitutional rights. In the case at the beginning of this chapter, for example, Eddie Pugh and his friends violated federal kidnapping and weapons laws.

Very few criminal cases are prosecuted in federal courts. In 2012, for example, there were about 93,000 federal criminal prosecutions–less than 0.05 percent of the total number of prosecutions in the United States. Only 3 percent of federal criminal trials were for violent crimes.[2]

Figure 8-3 illustrates the federal court system. There are three basic types of federal courts. Federal trials are held in one of the 94 U.S. *district courts*. States with large populations have more than one district court. Pennsylvania,

FIGURE 8-3   **The Federal Court System**

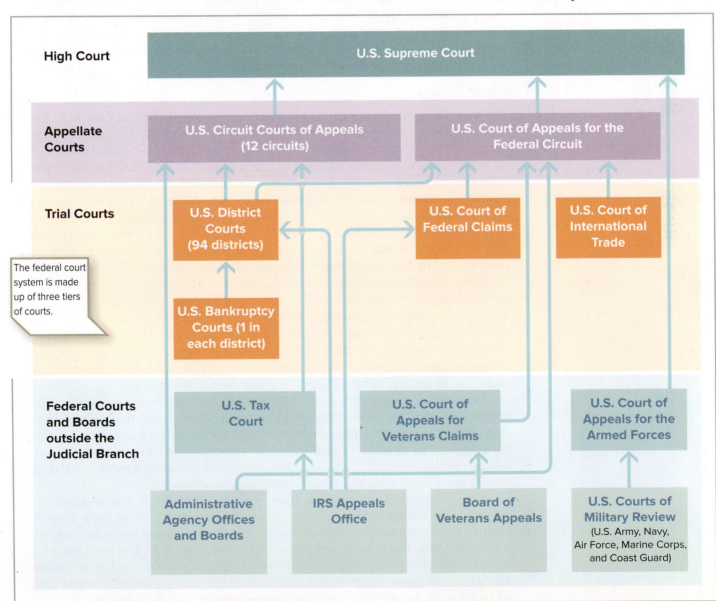

The federal court system is made up of three tiers of courts.

for example, has three–the Western, Middle, and Eastern districts. Each district court employs several judges, who hear federal civil and criminal cases.

An appeal from a federal district court's decision is heard by a *U.S. circuit court of appeals.* Eleven federal circuits each cover several states, but the Twelfth Circuit is for the District of Columbia alone. The Thirteenth Circuit Court of Appeals handles cases from the entire nation involving patent rights, as well as cases in which the United States itself is the defendant. Each circuit employs many judges–the Ninth Circuit, for example, currently has 28–who hear cases in a few locations within the circuit covering 11 western states and territories. Several recent proposals call for splitting this circuit into two or more smaller jurisdictions to reduce case processing time and to make the circuits more equal in size.

A case before a U.S. court of appeals is usually heard by a panel of three judges, although occasionally cases will be heard *en banc.* Literally translating to "on the bench," **en banc** in practice means that the case is heard by a larger group than three judges. Appeals from the courts of appeal (including cases that originated in military and tribal courts) go to the *U.S. Supreme Court.*

Federal specialty courts hear specific kinds of cases. For example, each district has a *bankruptcy court.* The United States sometimes also uses special *military courts* to try individuals accused of being enemy combatants. In 2006, the U.S. Supreme Court held that special military courts could not try suspected terrorists being held at the detention facility for detainees from the Iraq and Afghanistan wars at Guantánamo Bay, Cuba.[3]

en banc
An appeals case presided over by a larger than usual panel of judges (more than three judges).

Other Courts

The vast majority of criminal cases are tried in state or federal courts. A few cases, however, go to other types of courts. Members of the U.S. armed forces accused of violating the Uniform Code of Military Justice (the criminal laws for all persons in the military) are tried in *courts-martial,* in which the judges, prosecutors, juries, and usually also the defense attorneys are all members of the military. Members of American Indian tribes may be tried by *tribal courts* for crimes committed on tribal land. Many state and federal administrative agencies have their own courts, such as the U.S. Immigration Court and the National Labor Relations Board, as well as state courts dealing with matters such as unemployment benefits, workers' compensation, and air and water resources.

Some jurisdictions have created special courts to deal with nonviolent youthful offenders, with defendants with mental health issues, and with those who abuse addictive substances. About 1,200 to 1,800 *drug courts* operate in the United States today, up from only 12 in 1994.[4] These courts bring together prosecutors, defense attorneys, probation officers, mental health workers, and treatment center personnel to offer treatment programs designed to break the addiction cycle and reduce relapse, rearrest, and incarceration.

Drug court judges can make a difference in drug court outcomes. The largest and most extensive drug court research study found that judges' positive, respectful, fair, attentive, and compassionate attitudes toward drug court participants can reduce criminal behavior and drug use.[5] In addition to committed judges, frequent judicial status meetings, drug treatment, and drug testing were central to the study's successful outcomes.

Drug rehabilitation programs have recently come into the spotlight as celebrities–including Lindsay Lohan, Britney Spears, Tara Conner, Boy George, Courtney Love, Leif Garrett, Rush Limbaugh, and Tom Sizemore–have checked into them. Amy Winehouse, who died in July 2011 at the age of 27, had been planning to return to rehab. Drug programs may help substance abusers avoid incarceration and get the support they need to overcome their addictions. Drug courts tend to be effective for reducing drug use and recidivism for adults and youth.[6]

Reentry courts are another kind of specialized court. The assumption behind these courts is that if a judge takes an interest in an offender's reintegration into society, that concern will have a positive effect on the offender's rehabilitation. Judges thus act as sentence and reentry managers for offenders, who live at home after conviction but make regular appearances before the court.[7] If the offender violates the terms of release, the judge administers graduated sanctions and assistance that stops short of returning the offender to prison and fosters reintegration instead. Reentry court staff workers ensure that offenders fulfill the education, work, counseling, and community service requirements that the judge has imposed. Offenders, their family members, and other support agencies all are responsible directly to the court.[8]

▲ **Teen Court**

Teen courts are based on the idea that young defendants are more likely to be influenced by their peers. *What are the benefits of teen courts for defendants and other participants? What disadvantages, if any, might teen court defendants experience?*

Teen courts are another kind of specialized court, focused on first-time, nonviolent youthful offenders. On the assumption that teenagers may be more likely to listen to their peers, the juries in these specialized courts consist of teenagers, and the "prosecutor" and "defense attorney" are frequently teens as well. The judge is generally a professional judge or an attorney. To participate, the defendant usually must first admit guilt. The jury can set a variety of sentences, including community service, counseling, and letters of apology. In the hope that active participation in the justice system itself can deter future offenses, defendants usually also are required to serve as jurors in a specific number of future cases. Today there are more than 600 teen courts in the United States.[9]

Criminal Appeals

If a criminal defendant in the United States is acquitted of a crime, that acquittal automatically ends the case. The Fifth Amendment's protection against double jeopardy prohibits a defendant from being tried twice for the same crime. Double jeopardy protection does not, however, prohibit the victim from filing a civil lawsuit. Because the burden of proof in civil cases is lighter than in criminal

◄ **Oral Arguments in an Appellate Court**

Appellate courts determine whether legal errors were made at trial.

cases, it is not unusual for a person to be acquitted on criminal charges and still be found civilly liable for the same acts–for example, former football star O. J. Simpson in 1997 was found responsible in civil court for the wrongful deaths of his ex-wife Nicole Simpson and her friend Ronald Goldman. Similarly, actor Robert Blake was held responsible in 2001 for the wrongful death of his wife.

If the defendant is convicted, however, he or she may appeal to a higher court. In a capital (death penalty) case, a convicted person's appeal is usually automatic. As we have seen, all state and federal jurisdictions have at least one appellate court where appeals are heard.

Appellate courts are very different from trial courts in terms of both structure and function. Unlike trial courts, appellate courts do not decide on the facts of a particular case, and they do not decide whether the defendant is guilty. Instead, they determine whether legal errors were made at the trial and, if so, whether those errors were important enough to invalidate the conviction. Therefore, courts of appeals provide direct oversight of trial judges.

To appeal a conviction, the defendant–or, more often, the defendant's lawyer–files a document called an appellate brief with the appeals court. Despite its name, the **appellate brief** is a lengthy text in which the defendant, now called the *appellant*, describes all the legal errors alleged to have been made at her trial and provides *legal precedents*–that is, earlier court decisions that support her arguments. The appellant cannot dispute any of the findings of fact made at trial, although errors might include evidence that should have been excluded or admitted but that the judge did not allow. Appeals also examine allegations of faulty jury instructions by the judge and impermissible statements by the prosecutor. In addition, the appellant may claim that the jury was improperly chosen, that the law under which she was prosecuted was unconstitutional, or that her sentence was not appropriate.

Once the appellant files her brief, the prosecutor will respond with a brief in which he argues that no legal errors were made. These arguments also must be supported by precedent.

There is no jury in appellate courts, no evidence is presented, and no witnesses testify. Instead, a panel of judges reads the briefs. Usually, *oral arguments* are held in which each side highlights the arguments made in the briefs and answers questions posed by the judges. Oral arguments are usually quite short–generally 15 to 60 minutes per side–and the appellant herself is generally not present.

Also unlike trial courts, appellate courts rarely issue decisions right away. After hearing the oral arguments, the judges meet to discuss the case. Eventually–sometimes months later–they give a *written opinion*, which may be read aloud in court. Opinions vary from a few sentences to hundreds of pages, depending on the number and complexity of the issues. Opinions not only state the judges' decisions but also elaborate the reasons for the decisions. Often they become precedents for future cases.

Appellate judges need not be unanimous in their judgment; a simple majority suffices. It often happens that some judges on the appellate court disagree with the majority decision and therefore may write dissenting opinions.

If the appellate court finds that legal errors were made at trial and that they were significant enough to affect the outcome of the case, they will *vacate*, or invalidate, the conviction. Usually, they will then **remand** the case–send it back to the trial court. The prosecution may choose to try the case again, sometimes several times. Alternatively, the prosecution may appeal the appellate court's decision to a higher appellate court.

If the court finds no significant legal errors, it will uphold the conviction. The defendant may then appeal to a higher court if she chooses. Higher courts frequently overturn lower courts' decisions. If a party loses the appeal at the **court of last resort**–usually the state supreme court but sometimes the

appellate brief
A document containing legal arguments in an appellate case, submitted to a court by attorneys for one party.

remand
The act by which an appellate court sends a case back to a lower court for further proceedings.

court of last resort
The highest court to which a case may be appealed.

U.S. Supreme Court—there is nowhere left to go except to seek habeas corpus relief (see Chapter 10).

The U.S. Supreme Court sometimes hears appeals from state high courts, but these tend to be limited to matters of constitutional law. Unlike the U.S. circuit courts of appeal, the Supreme Court chooses whether to hear a case. If at least four justices agree that a case merits the Supreme Court's attention, then a **writ of certiorari** is issued, ordering the lower court to deliver all relevant records of the case for the Court's examination. If, however, the Supreme Court refuses to hear an appeal—and in fact it refuses about 99 percent of the cases appealed to it—then the parties have no further recourse and the previous judgment stands. The Court hears only about 100 cases a year, usually on matters it deems particularly important from the standpoint of constitutional law or about which the lower courts widely disagree.

writ of certiorari
A request that a case be heard by an appellate court such as the U.S. Supreme Court.

THE COURTROOM WORKGROUP

The U.S. court system has many different participants, each with a unique role to play. Their relationships, everyday interactions, and job performance can influence the administration of justice.

Judges

The judge, seated at the front of the courtroom, is often the most distinctive participant in a criminal case. By traditions that go back centuries, she is treated with certain respectful formalities and addressed as "Your Honor." Everyone in the courtroom rises when she enters. Attorneys must ask her permission to approach "the bench"—that is, the judge's desk—to discuss a point of law. The opposing attorneys hold conferences with the judge **in chambers**—that is, in her private office, closed to outsiders. If a case comes before the judge in which she has an economic or a personal interest—for example, involving some property in which she has invested or individuals whom she knows—she must exercise **recusal** by turning the case over to another judge who can act with total impartiality. Such a degree of disinterestedness is not routinely expected of members of legislative bodies. The judge, in short, symbolizes the majesty, the power, and the impartiality of the law, serving as a referee to ensure that the trial proceeds according to the rules of **due process.**

in chambers
Meeting that occurs between attorneys and a judge in the judge's office rather than in the courtroom.

recusal
The act by which a judge removes herself from a case because she may be biased or may have the appearance of being biased.

due process
The right, guaranteed by the Fifth and the Fourteenth Amendments, that laws and processes be fair.

What Judges Decide   In the U.S. criminal justice system, judges decide whether to issue search and arrest warrants. Once suspects have been arrested, the judge determines whether probable cause exists to believe they committed a crime. Decisions about whether to release suspects from custody while trials are pending and about the amount of bail that the defendant must provide are also within the purview of judges.

During a trial, it is a judge's job to decide all matters of law—as opposed to matters of fact, which the jury usually decides. Thus the judge decides what evidence may be admitted, rules on various motions the attorneys make, and gives the jurors their instructions. But it is the jurors who determine the guilt of the defendant based on their interpretation of the evidence. If it is a bench trial rather than a jury trial, the judge makes the determination of

▼ **Judge in Her Courtroom**

Judges must make many kinds of decisions. *How might a judge's personal beliefs affect the decisions she makes on matters of law?*

guilt. (For more on bench trials, see Chapter 9.) When a defendant is convicted, it is usually the judge's job to sentence her as well. In most states that have the death penalty, however, the jury decides whether to give the defendant death or some other sentence, usually life in prison, with or without the possibility of parole.

If a defendant appeals his conviction, the appeals court judges will decide whether errors were made at trial or whether any of his constitutional rights were violated. Furthermore, because the meaning of written laws is often unclear or contradictory, especially as they apply to specific activities, appellate judges interpret statutes and constitutions. For example, in 2001 a motorist named Robert Lee Coggin gestured with his middle finger at another driver whom he felt was driving too slowly. The other driver, offended, called 9-1-1. Coggin was subsequently pulled over and charged with disorderly conduct. He was convicted, fined $250, and appealed to the Texas Court of Appeals. Although a Texas statute defines as disorderly conduct gestures that "tend to incite an immediate breach of the peace," it was up to the court to determine whether "shooting the bird" incites an immediate breach of the peace. The majority of the court held that it did not, and Coggin's conviction was overturned. More recently, in 2011 the U.S. Supreme Court heard a case that hinged on whether fleeing police in a car constitutes a "violent felony." Lower courts were split on this issue.[10] As "A Case in Point" explains, the courts' power to interpret laws and the Constitution was established in 1803 in one of the most important rulings of the U.S. Supreme Court.

MYTH/REALITY

MYTH: Judges "pass" laws.

REALITY: Legislators pass laws. Judges interpret those laws, and their interpretations carry legal authority.

Kinds of Judges and Judicial Selection   There are several kinds of judges. Today, **magistrates** and **justices of the peace** generally handle minor matters such as warrants—recall that these are legal documents giving government agents authority to conduct searches, seizures, and arrests—and infractions. Magistrates and justices of the peace may also preside over some of the early steps in criminal cases such as arraignments (see Chapter 9). In a few cases, a special magistrate is appointed to preside over a case that requires particular technical expertise or that cannot be heard by any ordinary judge due to potential conflicts of interest. Court **commissioners** or **referees** also may preside over early stages, and some perform all the duties of regular judges in specialty courts such as family and juvenile courts. The men and women who hear felony trials and many misdemeanors are called *judges*, as are those who hear most appeals. The judges of the U.S. Supreme Court, as well as of most states' highest courts, are called *justices*.

There are generally no absolute qualifications for becoming a state or local judge, and none are specified by the U.S. Constitution for federal judges or Supreme Court justices. At one time, many justices of the peace and juvenile court judges did not have any law training at all. Today, however, nearly all judges have law degrees, and most have had extensive experience in practicing law, or sometimes in legal scholarship and teaching.

Most federal judges are nominated by the president of the United States. The Senate, however, must confirm these nominations. Once federal judges have been confirmed, they hold office for life. Unless they retire or resign, they may be removed from office only by impeachment—essentially, a special kind of

magistrate
A judge who handles matters such as warrants, infractions, and the early stages of a criminal case.

justice of the peace
A judge who handles matters such as warrants, infractions, and the early stages of a criminal case.

commissioner
An individual who presides over the early stages of some criminal trials or serves as judge in specialized courts.

referee
An individual who presides over the early stages of some criminal trials or serves as judge in specialized courts.

a case in point

▲ John Marshall

Marbury v. Madison (1803)

The U.S. Constitution is fairly detailed about the roles and responsibilities of the executive and legislative branches, but it says little about the powers of the courts. The Supreme Court, in a clever decision during the American republic's early years, therefore gave the federal courts authority to interpret the meaning of laws and constitutions.

The year was 1801. Congress had just created several dozen new federal judgeships, and outgoing Federalist president John Adams appointed members of his own political party to fill these positions. These individuals were called *midnight judges* because Adams was still signing their hastily bestowed commissions on the eve of his departure from the White House.

However, when President Thomas Jefferson of the opposition Democratic Republican Party took office a few days later, he ordered James Madison, his secretary of state, to ignore any new commissions that Adams had failed to sign. Thus a Federalist named William Marbury never received his commission to become a federal justice

of the peace. Consequently, Marbury filed a lawsuit against Madison that went directly to the U.S. Supreme Court. A federal law, the Judiciary Act of 1789, had provided that this kind of lawsuit must originate in the Supreme Court rather than in a lower federal court.

The Supreme Court faced tough choices. If it ruled *for* Marbury, there was a good chance that Jefferson would simply ignore the ruling, thus reducing the Court's power almost to zero. If it held *against* Marbury, on the other hand, the Court would be viewed as too tightly controlled by the president. To further complicate matters, Chief Justice John Marshall had also served as Adams's secretary of state and was Jefferson's political enemy (and also his distant cousin). Worse, Jefferson and his Democratic Republican supporters in Congress seemed determined to strip the Federalist-dominated U.S. court system of power. A few years later, they would impeach a highly unpopular Supreme Court justice, Samuel Chase. John Marshall himself might well be a target for impeachment.

Marshall found an ingenious way around these problems. He wrote an opinion in which the Court held that the Judiciary Act of 1789 was unconstitutional and, therefore, that Marbury's case could not be brought directly before the Court. President Jefferson was unlikely to dispute that ruling because it meant that Marbury and other last-minute Adams appointees would not become judges. Importantly, at the same time, the Court declared for itself the right of *judicial review*—that is, the authority to interpret laws and constitutions. Since then, the right of judicial review has been extended to all state and federal appellate courts. With these developments, the role of the judiciary was expanded far beyond its original scope.

The case of *Marbury v. Madison* remains a great milestone in shaping the role of courts in the U.S. justice system. It is the foundation of the modern federal courts' power to "make law" through judicial review and under their authority to interpret the law.

OBSERVE → INVESTIGATE → UNDERSTAND

- What types of factors determine whether something should be considered unconstitutional?

- In what other ways might the Marshall Court have decided *Marbury v. Madison?* What would have been the impact of a different decision?

- In his *Marbury v. Madison* ruling, was John Marshall being an "activist" judge, meaning that he was "legislating from the bench" and failing to follow the original intent of the authors of the U.S. Constitution? Explain.

SOURCE: *Marbury v. Madison,* 5 U.S. 137 (1803).

trial–although this rarely happens. Since 1789, only 13 federal judges have been impeached, and 4 of those, including Samuel Chase, were found not guilty.

Depending on the jurisdiction and position, state court judges may be either appointed (usually by the governor) or elected by voters, and they hold office for life or for a set number of years. Both methods of judicial selection—appointment and election—have their critics. Some claim that appointment can lead to the seating of judges who are chosen not because of their qualifications but because of their personal views or their political beliefs and connections. Since the 1980s, the confirmation process for Supreme Court justices in particular has repeatedly polarized the nation and set off bitter battles between the two political parties and between the Senate and the White House. Other critics, however, argue that the voting public is ill equipped to decide on the qualifications of state and local judges who are running for election—sometimes on blatantly political platforms—and that judges' concerns about raising campaign contributions and winning reelection may affect their courtroom decisions. In 2009, the U.S. Supreme Court ruled that judges must recuse themselves from deciding cases involving parties who have given them significant campaign contributions.[11]

Some critics also argue that concern about reelection might cause some judges to pay too much attention to popular public opinion instead of the dictates of the law. In 2010, for example, voters did not reelect three members of the Iowa Supreme Court, most likely because of discontent over those justices' decisions in a case involving same-sex marriage.[12]

In an attempt to ensure the accountability of state judges to voters while avoiding the worst problems of partisan politics, Missouri in 1940 introduced a system of appointment that has subsequently been adopted in other states. Under the so-called Missouri Plan, a nonpartisan board suggests candidates for judgeships, and from this slate the governor makes appointments. After several years, the appointed judges must submit to a "retention election" in which voters decide whether they have performed well enough to warrant staying on the bench.

Diversity among Judges   Other controversies pertain to the lack of diversity among judges. Only about 10 percent of state judges and 19 percent of federal judges are people of color.[13] Considering that about 24 percent of the U.S. population are people of color, those relatively low percentages reveal the degree of racial disparity on our benches. Women, who are 51 percent of the national population, are also underrepresented—only 23 percent of federal judges and 29 percent of state high court justices are female.[14] In the entire history of the United States, there have been only two African American U.S. Supreme Court justices and only four women justices. Further, the judiciary lacks not only ethnic and gender diversity but also social class and age diversity, for most judges come from relatively privileged backgrounds and are well into middle age when appointed or elected.

Impact of Judicial Ideology   Judges' attitudes, values, and beliefs directly affect the decisions they make and therefore the precedents they leave in their wake—although some people argue that this is not the case and claim that judges can separate their ideology from their decision making, resolving cases based on the requirements of the law.[15] During his 2005 confirmation hearings, U.S. Supreme Court nominee John Roberts repeatedly refused to answer senators' questions about his personal opinions on such subjects as abortion, civil rights, and women's rights, claiming that his views would not influence his decisions. Asked about the separation of church and state, Roberts replied, "[M]y faith and my religious beliefs do not play a role in judging. When it comes to judging, I look to the law books and always have."[16] Roberts was confirmed, and today he serves as chief justice.

However, both the political left and the political right have repeatedly accused judges with whom they disagree of *judicial activism*—using the courts to further their own personal or social agendas. As one scholar wrote, "Studies

▲ **U.S. Supreme Court Justice Sonia Sotomayor**

Justice Sotomayor is the first Latina to serve on the U.S. Supreme Court. In 2015, for the first time in history, the Court had three female justices.

demonstrate that the ideology of a Supreme Court Justice is one of the most powerful predictors of his decisions."[17]

Even a quick look at Supreme Court decisions over the past several decades reveals that although all nine justices are using the same "law books," they are frequently sharply divided in their decisions, and those divisions nearly always follow ideological lines. Lower court judges are no better at preventing their attitudes from influencing their decisions. In fact, some scholars have argued that judges' beliefs not only *must be* an important basis of their decisions but also *should be*. For example, when the meaning of laws is unclear, judges should use their beliefs as a guide to interpreting those laws.[18]

MYTH/REALITY

MYTH: With some crimes, such as intimate partner violence, the victim has to agree to press charges.

REALITY: Only a prosecutor has the power to decide whether a suspect is charged with a crime.

Prosecutors

In the U.S. criminal justice system, the prosecutor (and usually only the prosecutor) has the power to bring formal criminal charges against someone. If a prosecutor declines to bring charges, a victim has little legal recourse, aside perhaps from a civil lawsuit against the alleged offender. Conversely, if a prosecutor chooses to initiate charges, even a victim who does not want the offender to be tried can do little about it. These characteristics of the process stand in contrast to those of many other countries, such as England, where victims may hire private (nonpublic) attorneys to prosecute their cases.

special prosecutor
A prosecutor who is appointed specifically for one particular case, usually because of his specialized knowledge or experience.

attorney general
A state's head law enforcement officer; also the head of the U.S. Department of Justice.

district attorney (DA)
The lawyer who prosecutes criminal cases at the local level.

Prosecutorial Jurisdictions and Titles Prosecutors in the United States go by different names, depending on the jurisdiction. Each of the federal districts has a U.S attorney, an employee of the Department of Justice. Federal prosecutors are appointed by the president. Each U.S. attorney oversees several assistant attorneys who actually conduct most of the prosecutions. Occasionally Congress insists that the president and attorney general appoint a **special prosecutor,** armed with independent authority to investigate and to bring charges in very high-profile political scandals.

Most states have an **attorney general,** the state's head law enforcement officer. Among other duties, the attorney general and his deputies prosecute criminal appeals. They also may prosecute criminal cases at trial level when the cases are large and complex or have attracted great public attention. At the state level, the attorney general is usually an elected official.

Most criminal prosecutions, however, are conducted at the local level. The people who prosecute cases are called—depending on the jurisdiction—**district attorneys (DAs),** state's attorneys, commonwealth's attorneys, or county prosecutors. This is most often an elected position, although in some jurisdictions prosecutors are appointed by a governor or another official. Prosecutors oversee deputies or assistants, who do most of the actual prosecuting. In large prosecutors' offices, deputies and assistants are charged with handling specialized kinds of cases: white-collar criminals, repeat offenders, perpetrators of sexual offenses, and so on.

Whatever the jurisdiction and title, prosecutors have the duty to prove all elements of a criminal charge beyond a reasonable doubt. Not only do prosecutors argue the state's case at trials and appeals, they also conduct investigations, make bail recommendations, do plea bargaining, and make sentencing recommendations. A prosecutor must have a law degree and pass the bar exam for that jurisdiction.

Prosecutorial Discretion Prosecutors are invested with an enormous amount of discretion. We have seen that it is their choice whether to pursue a case. Prosecutors make this decision based on the amount and the quality of the evidence, which in turn means whether they think they can win a conviction. If the prosecutor decides to go ahead with a case, he also usually decides whether to offer the defendant a plea bargain. If the defendant either accepts a plea bargain or is convicted, the prosecutor usually recommends a sentence to the judge. In a capital case, only the prosecutor can decide whether to seek the death penalty.

prosecutorial discretion
The prosecutor's power to determine when to bring criminal charges and which charges to bring.

There are few constraints on **prosecutorial discretion.** Unfortunately, this reality means that prosecutors may, intentionally or not, perpetuate racial, ethnic, social, and gender inequalities within the justice system. Ultimately, the prosecutor is the embodiment of the law: If a prosecutor chooses not to enforce a law or enforces it badly, the law has little value.

Controversies Surrounding Prosecutors Whether prosecutors should be elected or appointed is much debated. On one hand, prosecutors literally represent "the people" in a criminal prosecution, so perhaps the people—that is, the voters—ought to choose their representative. On the other hand, a prosecutor concerned about being reelected may base her choices about who to prosecute on what she thinks may be popular among the electorate rather than what is fair or good policy. She may decide not to charge a suspect who is wealthy or powerful and who she believes can help reelect her. Because prosecutors routinely decline to bring cases unless they are fairly certain they will win, poor suspects who cannot afford the best attorneys are more likely to be charged. And because some cases—such as intimate partner violence, hate

Real Careers

ALMA VALENCIA

Work location: Redwood City, California

College(s): California State University, Chico (2007)

Major(s): Criminal Justice (BS)

Job title: Fee Arbitration Coordinator, San Mateo County Bar Association

Salary range for job like this: $40,000–$45,000

Time in job: 2 years

Work Responsibilities

My work primarily involves assigning arbitrators to cases that involve fee disputes between clients and their attorneys. The goal of an arbitrator is to examine the facts of the disagreement and to assist the parties in arriving at a fair solution. In addition to assigning cases, I coordinate events, such as Community Law Night and Judges Night, hosted for the judges and bar members in San Mateo County.

As part of my professional training, I was required to attend a presentation on the rules and procedures of fee arbitration by the State Bar of California. I also learned strategies for speaking assertively and confidently with attorneys and their clients. Such training has certainly helped me develop successful professional relationships.

Why Criminal Justice?

I began my undergraduate studies as a business administration major. After taking a business law class during my third semester, I developed an interest in the justice system. Wanting to learn more about the criminal justice field, I took an introductory course. I was captivated by the material and decided to change my major to criminal justice.

Upon graduating, my plan was to work in a law-related field for a few years while preparing to take the LSAT exam. I was fortunate enough to have a friend working at the San Mateo County Bar Association who informed me of a job opening and suggested that I apply. Having the bachelor's in criminal justice gave me the competitive edge I needed to land my current position as fee arbitration coordinator. Working closely with lawyers over the past 2 years has confirmed for me my original goal of attending law school.

Expectations and Realities of the Job

I had expected my academic courses to prepare me for work. But working in the real world has taught me the importance of developing certain practical career skills that are best mastered outside of the classroom. For example, after 6 months, my supervisor noticed that my communication and leadership skills improved and offered me a salary raise. I strive to continue developing these skills because they allow me to do my job more effectively: I have more productive conversations with clients, and I better coordinate meetings and activities.

My Advice to Students

Take advantage of the career development resources your school offers. I revised my resume many times with a Career Center counselor, discussed career paths with the Criminal Justice Department adviser, and sought course information from the Educational Opportunity Program. These resources were available to me free of charge and provided me the assistance I needed to interview and land my current position.

crimes, and sexual assaults—tend to be more difficult to prove, prosecutors may be particularly unlikely to pursue them.

Another controversy focuses on prosecutors' place within the justice system. Are they agents of law enforcement or of the courts? Their duties and responsibilities differ depending on the role they play. For example, should a DA be more concerned with locking up a dangerous person or with avoiding injustice?

Defense Attorneys

Defendants usually have the right to argue their own cases if they wish and if the judge rules that they are mentally competent to conduct their own defense. However, most defendants choose to have a lawyer represent them. In addition to arguing the case in court, this **defense attorney** may conduct pretrial investigations, be present during some police questioning, bargain with the prosecution

defense attorney
The lawyer who represents the defendant in a criminal case.

and the judge over bail amounts, engage in plea bargaining, determine defense strategy, argue about the sentence, and represent the defendant in appeals.

American law recognizes as a fundamental right the principle of **attorney–client privilege**—that is, the confidentiality of oral and written communications between the accused and his attorney. After all, if what is said between a criminal defendant and his attorney were known to the prosecution and the judge and thus could be used against the defendant at the trial, the Fifth Amendment protection against self-incrimination could be violated. What then would remain of an accused person's right to defend himself in court? However, the Supreme Court has ruled that if a defense attorney learns from her client that another crime is going to be committed, the principle of attorney–client privilege cannot serve as an excuse for her failing to report such future criminal actions. By failing to report, the attorney herself would become an accessory to another crime.[19]

Defendants who can afford their own attorneys must pay for them, even if they are found not guilty. These fees will not be reimbursed. For many middle-class people, this fact of life may mean taking out a second mortgage or other loans. Indigent (poor) defendants, however, are entitled to have the government appoint and pay for a defense attorney (see Chapter 9). Public defenders often carry extremely heavy caseloads. In Minnesota in 2015, for example, about 390 public defenders had an average caseload of 614 cases each.[20]

There are three methods by which indigents' defense attorneys may be assigned. Some jurisdictions, mostly larger cities, have *public defenders*. These attorneys work only for the government to defend indigents. A second method is the *assigned counsel system*. Here, individual lawyers in private law firms take indigent clients on a case-by-case basis and are paid according to a set fee schedule. Finally, some jurisdictions use a *contract method*, in which law firms or nonprofit agencies accept indigent cases for a set fee. Whatever the method, indigent defendants do not get to choose their own attorneys.

Most felony suspects in the United States are poor, and thus most—approximately 80 percent—are represented by appointed counsel.[21] Almost invariably, appointed attorneys have many fewer resources available than do either prosecutors or privately paid defense lawyers. Critics argue that this situation fosters inequalities: Rich or celebrity defendants such as O. J. Simpson can afford top-notch teams of attorneys, whereas poor defendants must accept lawyers who are overworked, underpaid, often inexperienced, and sometimes poorly motivated. People who are poor and have to depend on less than stellar legal counsel may be convicted more often and receive harsher sentences. According to one study, defendants with public defenders were convicted at about the same rate as those represented by private counsel but were more likely to be incarcerated.[22] This unfairness is likely to fall hardest on people of color, whose incomes tend to be lower than those of Whites.

Although there are a few extremely highly paid and famous criminal lawyers, who for the most part defend wealthy or celebrity clients, the typical defense attorney usually earns less than a prosecutor. In general, within the legal profession defense work carries less prestige than prosecution. Consequently, prosecutors' offices are more likely than public defenders' offices to attract top law school graduates. Again, this means that poor defendants are likely to receive second-rate legal assistance.

Judges, prosecutors, and defense attorneys are members of courtroom workgroups that interact on a regular basis. Especially in smaller locales, the numbers of participants in this group can be small and static over time. Such relationships among the three parties could result in the creation of a **local legal culture**—that is, a shared understanding of how cases should be processed. Most seriously, a local legal culture could include a *going rate* for each crime. A **going rate** is a generally agreed-upon sentence for a defendant based on the crime and

---

attorney–client privilege
The right of a person to prevent the government from asking his lawyer to provide evidence of the content of discussions between the person and his attorney.

local legal culture
A shared understanding of how cases should be processed.

going rate
A generally agreed-upon sentence for a defendant based on the crime and prior record.

prior record.[23] For example, in Butte County, California, almost every individual arrested for minor possession of alcohol receives a sentence that includes a 1-year revocation of his driver's license. Such a harsh sentence is rare in other California counties. The likely explanation is that Butte County takes alcohol offenses comparatively seriously because California State University, Chico, is located in the county and is perceived as a university that hard-drinking students attend.

OTHER COURTROOM PARTICIPANTS

People without formal legal training play important roles in the courtroom. In fact, nearly any U.S. citizen may be called upon to serve as a juror, and anyone— whether a citizen or not—who has knowledge about a crime or sees it being committed might be required to testify as a witness.

Juries

In one form or another, juries have been used for thousands of years. Most countries with civil law systems do not use them any longer, but in common law countries—such as the United States, England, and Canada—juries are invested with unique powers.

We can trace our jury system back to eleventh-century England. There are two kinds of U.S. juries: the **grand jury** and the **petit jury** (*petit* is French for "small" and in Anglo-American legal usage is pronounced "petty"). Grand juries are panels of citizens who sometimes investigate crimes and determine whether there is sufficient evidence to prosecute a particular suspect. Petit juries are small groups of citizens who decide whether defendants are guilty of the crimes with which they are charged. The United States makes more extensive use of juries than any other country in the world.

Jury Composition
A jury is composed of citizens who reside in the trial court's jurisdiction and is typically picked at random from lists of registered voters and licensed drivers. To make juries more representative of their communities and to increase the jury pool, some states have recently begun choosing citizens by using utility bills, telephone bills, or property taxes. (Sometimes jury selection techniques lead to mistakes; in 2009, for example, a cat named Sal Esposito was called for jury duty in Boston, apparently because his owners had listed him on their census form.)[24]

In the United States, jurors must be citizens over the age of 18 who can understand English and who are physically capable of sitting through the trial. Vision- and hearing-impaired individuals and those with significant mobility problems are usually excused. In some places, a criminal record may permanently disqualify a person from jury service, and other factors such as the person's profession may also prevent jury service. When a person is called for jury duty, she has a legal obligation to serve unless she can convince the judge that doing so would impose undue hardship, either on her dependents or on herself. Professionals associated with law enforcement and the justice system, such as police officers and lawyers, are sometimes automatically excused.

In some jurisdictions, a pool of potential jurors is chosen for one particular case, whereas in other jurisdictions the pool may be for whatever trials arise during a particular time frame. In that case, people designated as potential jurors typically have to present themselves for jury duty for several weeks or until they are selected for a trial. In either case, this pool is called the **venire** (pronounced "ven-eer"). The goal is to assemble a venire as representative of the community as possible. In practice, this is a difficult challenge given that some groups of people may be less likely to register to vote than others or may have personal or financial needs that keep them from serving. Depending on how lenient local judges are about requests to be excused, a venire might be disproportionately made up of

grand jury
Panel of citizens who may investigate certain crimes and determine whether sufficient evidence exists to bring a defendant to trial.

petit jury
Small group of citizens who determine whether a criminal defendant is guilty of the crimes with which he is charged.

venire
A group of people called to be prospective jurors.

▶ **The Courtroom at Work**

Many different parties participate in trials.

middle-class and retired people. The problem was worse in the past, however: Until well into the 1960s, non-Whites and women were routinely excluded from juries.

Jury duty is necessary under the U.S. system of justice, but many people regard it as a burden. The amount of time jurors must commit varies enormously across jurisdictions, but being called for jury duty can mean days or even weeks of waiting in the courthouse before being put on a jury, and some trials can last for weeks or even months. Although employers are forbidden by law to penalize employees for work time lost while doing jury duty, the compensation paid to jurors is usually only a few dollars per day. Self-employed individuals, part-time workers, day laborers, and students–for all of whom the loss of work time can spell a significant burden–are seldom able to persuade judges to excuse them entirely from service. In addition, serving on a criminal jury can be emotionally wrenching, especially in a violent murder or rape case or when a difficult verdict must be rendered or a decision made about inflicting the death penalty.

Once a venire has been formed, the judge or attorneys may ask members about their personal background and history, profession, education, and criminal record, knowledge of the case or the individuals involved, and their opinions about matters relevant to it. For example, in states that employ capital punishment, potential jurors in a murder trial may be asked whether they would categorically refuse to recommend a death sentence should the defendant be found guilty. This process is called **voir dire** ("vwar deer"). Anyone biased against the prosecution or the defendant–for example, a relative of the victim–is excused from the pool. Such exclusions are called **challenges for cause.** Further, the prosecutor and defense attorney may use **peremptory challenges** to release some people they think will not be sympathetic to their case. In federal capital trials–that is, for crimes punishable by death–both the prosecution and the defense are allowed 20 peremptory challenges, and in noncapital trials 3 such challenges are permissible; state rules for peremptory challenges vary. By law, these challenges are not supposed to be used to exclude jurors on the basis of race, ethnicity, or gender. In fact, however, lawyers often do consider potential jurors' race and gender in trying to build a persuadable jury.[25]

Some lawyers use jury consultants to help them choose jurors. These consultants–usually people with graduate training in psychology or other social sciences–conduct mock trials, surveys, and other exercises to try to determine the

voir dire

The process of questioning prospective jurors about their background, opinions, and knowledge relevant to a particular case.

challenge for cause

Excusing potential jurors from a jury because they might be biased in that case.

peremptory challenge

An attorney's removal of a prospective juror she feels will not be sympathetic to her side of the case.

characteristics of those jurors most, and least, likely to be sympathetic to the clients' cases. Some critics argue that jury consultants help lawyers unfairly stack the deck in favor of their clients. Others say they affect trial decisions in only some cases.[26]

Once voir dire is complete, the venire will be narrowed down to an actual jury, typically of 12, although the Supreme Court has allowed juries as small as 6 members. The jury's role is to be the finder of facts. When all the evidence has been presented and both sides have completed their arguments, the jurors withdraw to a closed room to deliberate together and reach a verdict. A defendant who is found guilty may appeal, but higher courts will not overturn that verdict unless it was completely unreasonable or the judge made legal errors during the trial. A verdict of not guilty is final. No matter how obvious it may seem that the defendant committed the crime, double jeopardy prohibitions prevent the prosecutor from appealing or retrying a defendant found innocent. (See Chapter 9 for more on double jeopardy.)

Juries' Power   Even though judges instruct juries to follow the law, if they refuse and acquit an obviously guilty individual, there is no recourse. Therefore, juries may sometimes choose not to apply criminal laws when they feel doing so would be unjust. This power—**jury nullification**—has been recognized in U.S. law for more than 200 years. An early example occurred in 1735, when a jury in New York refused to convict John Peter Zenger of seditious libel for printing newspapers that criticized the colony's governor. In the Jim Crow South before the 1970s, all-White juries routinely refused to convict Whites for committing crimes against Black people and almost invariably found Blacks guilty when they were accused of raping, assaulting, or killing Whites, regardless of the facts of the case.

jury nullification
The power of juries to refuse to apply criminal laws when they feel applying them would be unjust.

MYTH/REALITY

MYTH: Juries administer equal justice.

REALITY: Jurors are influenced by many extralegal considerations including racism, sexism, and heterosexism.[27]

Of course, any power brings with it the possibility of abuse. No one but a juror is permitted to be present during jury deliberations. And because jurors need not discuss their deliberations with others after the fact, no one knows how often their decisions are affected by factors that are not supposed to be considered in criminal cases, such as the defendant's race, gender, social class—and even physical attractiveness. See the "Race, Class, Gender" box for a discussion of how race can affect jury decisions.

Witnesses

Some evidence in criminal trials is physical evidence—things we can actually see and touch, such as weapons, bloodstains, surveillance videos, and letters. Most evidence, however, comes from *witnesses*—individuals who have some information pertinent to the trial. There are two kinds of witnesses. **Lay witnesses,** also referred to as *fact witnesses* or *eyewitnesses*, are individuals who heard or saw firsthand something directly related to the crime. **Expert witnesses** are individuals who have some special knowledge—scientific, technical, and the like—that can help the triers of fact decide a case.

expert witness
An individual who has specialized knowledge of some scientific or technical matter intended to help the trier of fact understand particular evidence or specific facts in a case.

lay witness
An individual who has personally seen or heard information relevant to the case at hand; also called a fact witness or eyewitness.

Lay Witnesses   The prosecution and the defense may call as witnesses anyone who personally heard or saw things related to the case, including the crime itself. Even if no one actually saw the crime occur, the prosecution could still call upon witnesses to establish the defendant's motive for or knowledge of the case. When there are victims, there will nearly always be witnesses. The defense,

Race, Class, Gender

Race and Jury Decision Making

Racism infects every component of the criminal justice system, perhaps nowhere more so than in death penalty cases. In 1972, the U.S. Supreme Court, in *Furman v. Georgia*, struck down most death penalty statutes as "arbitrary and capricious." New laws that followed in the wake of *Furman* were intended to address these shortfalls. Yet in 1990 the U.S. General Accounting Office (GAO) reported to Congress that its review of the empirical studies on racism and capital punishment since 1972 revealed "a pattern of evidence indicating racial disparities in the charging, sentencing, and imposition of the death penalty."

As of 2015, among more than 3,200 condemned inmates in the United States, 42 percent were Black, even though Blacks make up only 12 percent of the U.S. population. Prosecutors decide in which cases to seek the death penalty and ultimately choose only about 1 percent of all eligible cases. Thus the vast majority of cases that could be pursued as capital cases in fact are not. What determines whether a particular crime will result in a capital case?

According to the American Civil Liberties Union, in the states having the death penalty, the vast majority of prosecutors are White. The race of the prosecutor may be a factor in this trend—White prosecutors choosing to prosecute as capital cases those with African American defendants—but it is not the only one.

According to a 1990 report to Congress by the GAO, for murders committed under otherwise similar circumstances by defendants with comparable criminal histories, if the victim was White, the defendant was several times more likely to be given the death penalty than if the victim was Black. Approximately half of all murder victims are White, but in death penalty cases about 80 percent of victims are White. In fact, the single factor that most reliably predicts whether someone will be sentenced to death is the race of the victim. Across the United States, cases involving a White victim and a defendant of color are statistically most likely to result in a death sentence.

OBSERVE → INVESTIGATE → UNDERSTAND

- What measures can be implemented to better ensure that race is not a factor in sentencing a person to death?

- Do you believe that infliction of the death penalty in the United States can still be accurately described as "arbitrary and capricious"? Explain.

- Do racial disparities in death sentences prove that the death penalty in contemporary America has become "cruel and unusual punishment"? Why or why not?

SOURCES: U.S. Census, "Overview of Race and Hispanic Origin, 2010," www.census.gov/prod/cen2010/briefs/c2010br-02.pdf (retrieved June 13, 2015); American Civil Liberties Union, "Race and the Death Penalty," February 26, 2003. www.aclu.org/race-and-death-penalty (retrieved June 13, 2015); Criminal Justice Project of the NAACP Legal Defense Fund, Inc., "Death Row U.S.A.," *Quarterly Report* (Winter 2006); General Accounting Office, "Death Penalty Sentencing: Research Indicated Pattern of Racial Disparities," *Report to Senate and House Committee on the Judiciary* (February 1990), 5; Death Penalty Information Center "National Statistics about Race and the Death Penalty," 2015. www.deathpenaltyinfo.org/race-death-row-inmates-executed-1976#inmaterace (retrieved June 13, 2015).

subpoena
A legal document ordering a person to appear in court.

contempt of court
Violation of a court's order, punishable by fine, jail time, or both.

on the other hand, might call people who can testify that the defendant was somewhere else when the crime was committed—that is, they establish an *alibi*—people who provide evidence that someone else committed the crime, or even those who can claim that the alleged crime never occurred at all.

The Sixth Amendment to the U.S. Constitution guarantees criminal defendants the right to confront and cross-examine their accusers and to have witnesses testify in their defense. The attorneys can therefore request the judge issue a **subpoena,** a legal document ordering a witness to appear in court even if unwilling. A person who disobeys a subpoena may be found in **contempt of court** and punished.

Eyewitness testimony is powerful evidence that tends to carry considerable weight with jurors. Unfortunately, it is not as reliable as many people assume. In criminal cases the witnesses themselves often are facing criminal charges; by testifying against the defendant, they hope to absolve themselves or at least receive a lighter sentence. Prosecutors frequently offer one suspect a plea bargain, recommending a relatively light charge or sentence in exchange for testimony against someone else. Consider, for example, the case of Michael Fortier, the accomplice who testified against Timothy McVeigh and Terry Nichols in a trial concerning the 1995 bombing of a federal office building in

Oklahoma City. Witnesses in these situations have a strong incentive to provide damaging evidence against the defendant and may be less than honest in their testimony.

Most people, including jurors, are skeptical of testimony from coconspirators and police informants. What many do not realize, however, is that all eyewitness testimony is suspect. Research demonstrates that even witnesses who have no incentive to lie and are trying to be as truthful as possible perceive and remember events with little accuracy. The brain does not operate like a video camera, accurately recording what it sees and reproducing it later. Instead, environmental conditions such as lighting and physical obstructions, as well as the trauma associated with the crime, all compromise eyewitness identification. According to the Innocence Project, out of 183 cases in which defendants were later proved to have been wrongfully convicted, mistaken eyewitness identification was a factor in about 75 percent.[29]

Mistaken eyewitness identification is the foremost cause of wrongful convictions. Social scientists and legal scholars have made recommendations for reducing these errors, such as using identification procedures that are less suggestive. Evidence indicates that at least some of these solutions work, but few jurisdictions follow them.[30]

Expert Witnesses Lay witnesses testify about what they observed or what they know as fact. Expert witnesses, on the other hand, can express *opinions* based on their specialized knowledge, research, and experience, as long as the judge is satisfied that their testimony will help the jury discover the facts about the case. Most often, expert witnesses help jurors understand particular evidence about, for example, the insanity defense, eyewitness identification, child custody matters, intimate partner violence, and class action suits.

Ideally, expert witnesses are impartial and educate the court. The adversarial nature of judicial proceedings, however, often puts them under considerable pressure to give their loyalty to the winning of the case rather than to their discipline. For instance, they could fail to mention contradictory findings or exaggerate or even falsify claims. Such behavior is especially troubling because it is very difficult to prosecute expert witnesses for perjury as they are ostensibly giving an opinion rather than presenting a fact. With rare exception, an unethical expert witness will be deemed incompetent. A profession is distinguished by, among other things, its code of ethics. It is an unfortunate reality that there are unethical players in every profession. The "Matters of Ethics" box discusses this problem in more detail.

In one homicide case, the fingerprint expert for the prosecution noted two fingerprints–both matching the defendant's–on an item admitted into evidence.[31] A third print–not the

RealCrimeTech

FREEING WRONGFULLY CONVICTED PERSONS

The partnership between law and forensics, especially DNA analysis, is helping to free wrongfully convicted persons and ensure greater constitutional protection. In cases of wrongful conviction, the leading responsible factor (more than 70 percent of the time) has been *eyewitness misidentification*. Because of new technology for DNA testing and an innovative program called the Innocence Project, however, large numbers of convictions of innocent persons are being overturned. Thanks to the pioneering work of attorneys Peter Neufeld and Barry Scheck (both members of the successful O. J. Simpson criminal trial defense team), the Innocence Project was established in 1992 at the Cardozo School of Law, Yeshiva University, in New York City. The term that has come to identify this type of technological legal work is *DNA exonerations*.

As of June 2015, there have been 329 such exonerations in the United States; the first occurred in 1989. Among all those exonerated, 20 were serving time on death row, the average time served was 14 years, and the average age was 26.5. The majority (62.3 percent) of these wrongful convictions were Blacks.

As of 2015, there are 69 such projects around the world. This innovative use of DNA technology in partnership with law reformers provides unquestionable substantiation that wrongful convictions from systemic flaws in the legal process can be corrected and can help free those who are innocent (such as Cornelius Dupree, shown above).

SOURCES: The Innocence Project. www.innocenceproject.org/ (retrieved June 10, 2015); The Innocence Network. www.innocencenetwork.org (retrieved June 10, 2015).

Matters *of* Ethics

Expert Witnesses: The Good, the Bad, and the Criminal

Not all expert witnesses are equally competent. Some are *in*competent. But not being good at what they do or not giving accurate information or not being professional does not constitute committing perjury. In the case of perjury, the expert intends to provide wrong information for the purpose of misleading the trier of fact. It is very difficult, however, to prove that an expert witness actually intended to present false information. Convictions of expert witnesses for perjury are therefore rare events. Yet unethical behavior is not limited to perjury. An expert witness may, for example, exaggerate her credentials. Or she may withhold information that she knows could go against the desired outcome of a case, or she may overstate research findings that are favorable to the side that is paying her for her testimony.

A defining feature of any profession is that its members abide by a code of ethical behavior. The American Psychological Association, for example, requires its members to adhere to its Ethics Code. Forensic psychologists are expected to conduct themselves in accordance with the Specialty Guidelines for Forensic Psychologists. The rules that guide their research and clinical practice are what one would expect. For example, forensic psychologists are expected to "provide services only in areas of psychology in which they have specialized knowledge, skill, experience, and education" (p. 658). But to whom does the forensic psychologist owe her primary loyalty? Is it the defendant—the person she evaluates for insanity? Is it the court—the agency seeking to determine the criminal responsibility of the defendant? Is it the side that hired her—the prosecution pushing for a conviction or the defense looking for a reduced sentence (if not an acquittal)? Or does the forensic psychologist owe her loyalty to her discipline—psychology? The psychologist who testifies in court as an expert witness is likely to feel a pull in each of these directions.

Ideally, an expert witness's loyalty is to his discipline (say, psychology). But pressures exist that make discipline loyalty much easier said than done. In truth, instead of testifying as objective social scientists, expert witnesses are generally expected to testify in ways that support the position of the side that hires them—a convention that makes them, in effect, advocates for that side. Expert witnesses who become known for such advocacy are referred to as *hired guns*.

OBSERVE → INVESTIGATE → UNDERSTAND

- To what extent do you believe jurors in criminal trials are influenced by personal characteristics of expert witnesses (such as physical attractiveness) rather than by the competence of the expert?

- Should all prospective expert witnesses be given a test of their knowledge and competence before they are permitted to testify in court?

- What might be the advantages of using only court-appointed experts (that is, those appointed by the judge) instead of experts that are hired by the prosecution and defense? What might be the disadvantages of doing this?

SOURCES: William L. Foster, "Expert Testimony: Prevalent Complaints and Proposed Remedies," *Harvard Law Review* 11 (1897): 169; American Psychological Association, "Ethical Principles of Psychologists and Code of Conduct" (Washington, DC: APA, 1992); Committee on Ethical Guidelines for Forensic Psychologists, "Specialty Guidelines for Forensic Psychologists," *Law and Human Behavior* 15, no. 6 (1991): 655–665.

defendant's–was later discovered on the object, but not before the defendant had been convicted and sentenced to death. Whether the expert in this case was dishonest or incompetent is difficult to establish, and when there is doubt, the expert is given the benefit of that doubt. Some expert witnesses are certainly sincere in their testimony but nonetheless hold opinions not grounded in science (see the "Disconnects" box on page 267 for a discussion of junk science).

Victims in Courts

In the criminal justice system, victims serve as witnesses because technically they are not a party to the court case. Instead, the case is brought by the state against a defendant. As such, the state is legally the "victim" of the crime; the actual person who was victimized is merely a witness to the crime. The distinction is a difficult one for many victims to understand because they are the ones

DIS Connects

Junk Science in the Courtroom

Do jurors and judges understand the language used by expert witnesses? Do they know what an expert means when he uses terms such as "consistent with" and "statistically significant"? Do they understand the science that underlies an expert's testimony? The answers to these questions are generally no. How, then, can the triers of fact recognize when expert witnesses present unreliable information based on unscientific methods and analyses? The adversarial nature of judicial proceedings should serve to expose such junk science, as well as outright fraud in the courtroom. Expert witnesses from the other side should catch it. Yet even when faulty science is exposed, it might not make a difference to jury members.

Unfounded scientific opinions may be obscured by the charismatic presentation of the expert. Sometimes even in cases where the science itself is suspect, judges and jurors accept the testimony at face value. After all, wouldn't you trust in a dog's ability to differentiate people by their scent? More to the point, however, can dogs link a criminal to his crime scene? Would you feel confident that a scent-tracking dog would "pick" the perpetrator—and not you—out of a police lineup?

In Texas, police have used a dog scent lineup technique in over 2,000 criminal investigations. Scent-tracking dogs are presented with scent swabs from individuals known to have nothing to do with a particular crime; the dogs are also given a swab from the suspect in the case. The police are looking to see if the dogs identify the scent from an item at the crime scene as being the same as the scent from their suspect. A real-life case exemplifies some problems with this approach, however.

A former sheriff's deputy in Fort Bend County, Texas, Michael Buchanek, was accused of the murder of his neighbor in 2006. Sheriff's deputy Keith Pikett used the behavior of his bloodhounds, named Jag and James Bond, as pointing to a match between Buchanek's scent and the scent on the rope that had been used to strangle the victim. For several months, despite Buchanek's protests of innocence, his former fellow officers believed the dogs. Ultimately, another man pleaded guilty to the murder after being implicated by DNA evidence. Buchanek was fortunate. Many people have been wrongfully accused—and even convicted—of crimes based on dog scent lineups. And while the Texas Court of Criminal Appeals recently reversed a conviction that was the result of Pikett's testimony, evidence from dog scent lineups was not held to be inadmissible. The court instead ruled that results of scent-discrimination lineups are not sufficient to convict a defendant if they are the sole or primary evidence in the case.

What is the science behind this investigative technique? This is a crucial question, since many defendants have been convicted based largely (or solely) on the "wag of a tail." Pikett lacked a scientific background. He trained himself in the use of the lineup procedure. Even though many judges have allowed police testimony based on dog scent lineups to support a conviction, the reliability of these lineups as a scientifically based technique is now being called into question. Pikett retired in 2010—perhaps because courts are raising doubts about the value of dog scent lineups, or perhaps because of a 2009 report by the Innocence Project equating dog scent lineups with junk science.

Similarly, polygraph (lie detector) evidence is generally not admissible because it is considered scientifically unreliable. Even fingerprint evidence has been called into question in recent years. As scientific techniques advance, what was once considered unreliable may eventually grow strong enough to become acceptable in court.

OBSERVE → INVESTIGATE → UNDERSTAND

- Is it necessary for jurors to understand the science that underlies the testimony of expert witnesses? Explain.
- Why are jurors so willing to believe junk science in a courtroom?
- Is the problem of jurors' sometimes accepting junk science in criminal trials a valid argument against continuing to use the jury system in American criminal justice? Why or why not?

SOURCES: Ed Lavandera, "Dogs Sniff out Wrong Suspect; Scent Lineups Questioned," *CNN Justice*, October 5, 2009. http://articles.cnn.com/2009-10-05/justice/texas.sniffer.dogs.controversy_1_dog-handler-scent-investigators?_s=PM:CRIME (retrieved January 7, 2011); Supreme Court of Appeals of West Virginia, *Renewed Investigation of the West Virginia State Police Crime Laboratory, Serology Division*, January 2006. www.state.wv.us/wvsca/docs/spring06/32885.htm (retrieved February 23, 2007); Michael Specter, "Do Fingerprints Lie?" *The New Yorker*, May 27, 2002.

who suffered as a result of the crime. Victims feel that they should play a larger role in the court process than merely serving as a witness when called by the state. Yet it is the prosecutor representing the state who determines whether there is enough evidence to bring a case forward–a decision that is often made without consulting the victim. If the prosecutor feels that there is enough evidence, she will bring charges against the defendant. If the case goes to a plea

What about the Victim?

The Role of the Victim Advocate

Susan is a 21-year-old college student in a serious relationship with Jake, her sweetheart from high school. Each claims to love the other very much, but Jake has become increasingly controlling—wanting to know where Susan is, what she is doing, and whom she is with. Jake says that his behavior simply reveals his love for Susan, but she feels pressured and uncomfortable. The couple fights more, and Jake often says that Susan is "stupid" when she expresses opinions different from his.

Susan lives off campus with two roommates. One night Jake visits, and the couple gets into a heated argument. He pushes her, and Susan screams, "You have no right to do that!" He responds by slapping Susan across the face so hard that she falls against a coffee table, striking her mouth and breaking open her lip. As she lies bleeding on the floor, Jake yells, "Don't ever tell me what to do, ever! Next time, I'll make sure your mouth is shut for good." Susan is scared and calls the police.

Once the police arrive, they interview Susan about the incident. They inquire about her level of safety in the apartment and determine whether she needs alternative housing, such as a shelter for battered women. In all 50 states, the police are supposed to give a person in Susan's position a business card with an abuse hotline number and the services available for victims of intimate partner violence and their children. In some states, the hotline worker will refer the victim to a local service provider, which will assign a victim advocate to the case. The victim advocate typically works for a local intimate partner violence or rape crisis center, with law enforcement, or in the district attorney's office.

The victim advocate will work with Susan throughout the criminal justice process. Depending on the severity of the violence, the police may contact the victim advocate at the crime scene and relate that Susan is being transported to the hospital. The victim advocate will go to the hospital and immediately begin working with Susan to ensure her safety, determine her needs, and explain what happens next.

Victim advocates can assist with further police investigations, help victims complete the paperwork to obtain a restraining or protective order, work with the district attorney's office, and prepare victims to testify. In this case, the victim advocate will notify Susan about all court proceedings, accompany her to court, and help her write a victim impact statement. If Jake is incarcerated, the victim advocate will work with the county jail to determine whether or when he will be released and will inform Susan of his status. The victim advocate can help Susan with any paperwork for victim compensation, which helps offset the costs to her of her victimization, including her participation in the criminal justice system.

OBSERVE → INVESTIGATE → UNDERSTAND

- What kinds of personal characteristics do successful victim advocates need to possess?
- Why do so many intimate partner violence victims refuse to press charges against their assailants?

SOURCE: Joye E. Frost, "Innovative Practices for Victim Services: Report from the Field," Office for Victims of Crime, December 2014, NCJ 248495. www.ovc.gov/pubs/InnovativePractices/print.html (retrieved June 5, 2015).

bargain, the prosecutor will negotiate a plea with the opposing defense attorney and the defendant. The victim in the case is not present when the plea bargain is negotiated, might not approve of the plea bargain process, and may not be notified that the defendant entered into the agreement or that a plea agreement was reached. If a plea agreement is not reached or if the defendant wants the case to go to trial, the case will proceed to trial even if the victim does not want to press charges, denies that the crime ever occurred, or does not want to participate in the court process. With the exception of the federal courts since 2002, the victim does not have a voice in *any* of these stages, and the case will proceed, often without his knowledge or approval. At this point, the case is in the prosecutor's hands, and she can subpoena or compel the victim to testify as a witness. If the victim does not participate, he can be found in contempt of court, which is punishable by a fine, incarceration, or both.

The final stage of victim participation occurs prior to sentencing, when the victim is granted the opportunity to describe how the crime has influenced his life–also known as giving a *victim impact statement*. In most states the victim impact statement is given to a probation officer, who includes it in a document called the *presentence investigation report*. However, in some cases, a judge may allow a victim to speak in open court in lieu of a formal impact statement. This in-court statement is called *elocution*. Because many victims are unfamiliar with the criminal justice system or may find it overwhelming or intimidating to deal with, in some places they may be offered the help of *victim advocates* (see "What about the Victim?").

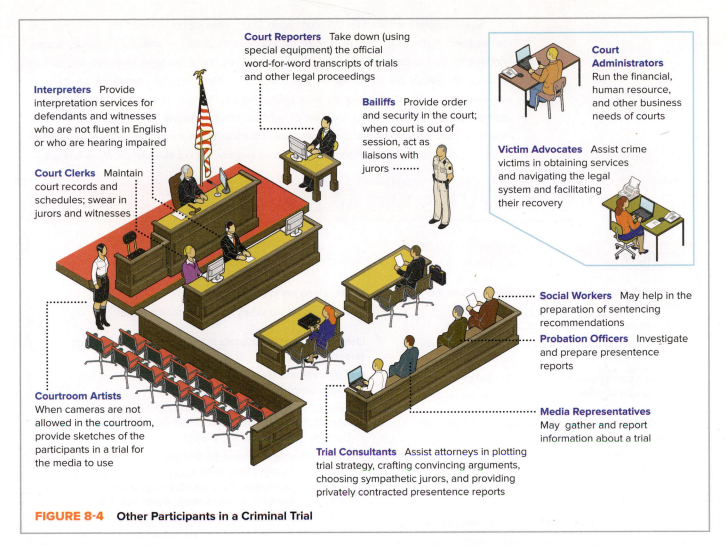

Interpreters Provide interpretation services for defendants and witnesses who are not fluent in English or who are hearing impaired

Court Reporters Take down (using special equipment) the official word-for-word transcripts of trials and other legal proceedings

Court Administrators Run the financial, human resource, and other business needs of courts

Court Clerks Maintain court records and schedules; swear in jurors and witnesses

Bailiffs Provide order and security in the court; when court is out of session, act as liaisons with jurors

Victim Advocates Assist crime victims in obtaining services and navigating the legal system and facilitating their recovery

Social Workers May help in the preparation of sentencing recommendations

Probation Officers Investigate and prepare presentence reports

Courtroom Artists When cameras are not allowed in the courtroom, provide sketches of the participants in a trial for the media to use

Media Representatives May gather and report information about a trial

Trial Consultants Assist attorneys in plotting trial strategy, crafting convincing arguments, choosing sympathetic jurors, and providing privately contracted presentence reports

FIGURE 8-4   Other Participants in a Criminal Trial

Other Participants

The defendant, judge, attorneys, jury, and witnesses are the most obvious and most visible participants in a trial. A body of other individuals may provide services to the court, attorneys, defendants, and victims. Figure 8-4 provides a brief summary of some of the other trial participants.

S U M M A R Y

The essence of the Anglo-American system of justice is its adversarial nature, in which the state must prove the defendant's guilt beyond a reasonable doubt. The defendant is entitled to a vigorous, professional defense that need only prove the existence of real doubt about the defendant's guilt. As the two sides contend in the courtroom, the judge serves as referee, ensuring due process and the correct application of the law, and the jury weighs the evidence and decides the question of guilt. A "not guilty" finding means that the constitutional protection against double jeopardy ensures that the defendant will not be tried again for the same offense (though this does not protect an acquitted defendant against a civil trial for damages, in which the standard of proof is lower).

In the United States, federal cases—those subject to federal law—are tried in federal district courts. Appeals from district courts go to federal appellate courts, which determine not guilt or innocence but rather ensure that mistakes were not made at the trial court level. The Supreme Court of the United States hears a limited number of further appeals. States maintain a parallel track of trial courts, appellate courts, and a state supreme court. There also are special courts of limited jurisdiction to handle a variety of special cases.

Serious problems still affect the U.S. court system. Courts often are overwhelmed with more cases than can be handled efficiently. Prosecutors enjoy (and occasionally abuse) enormous discretionary powers, including the right to decide which cases are prosecuted. Apart from a few highly paid celebrities, defense attorneys are typically overworked and not well compensated. Most Americans regard jury service as an unpleasant duty, and juries occasionally make serious mistakes. Victims are sometimes badly treated by defense attorneys and prosecutors. Members of racial and ethnic minorities are underrepresented among prosecutors and judges, and a disproportionate share of death sentences are given to people of color. Judges and jurors often rely on expert witnesses to understand evidence, but not all expert testimony is reliable.

OBSERVE → INVESTIGATE → UNDERSTAND

Review

Distinguish among state, local, and federal courts and their jurisdictions.

- State courts hear most criminal cases.
- Local courts generally hear minor criminal or civil cases or conduct the early stages of a criminal trial.
- Federal courts have limited jurisdiction and can hear only cases involving federal law or certain civil cases.

Describe some of the specialized courts that have been created for particular cases.

- Mental health courts involve cases with defendants with mental health issues.
- Drug courts involve cases with defendants with substance abuse problems.
- Reentry courts focus on reintegrating offenders into society.
- Teen courts focus on youthful offenders, and their juries consist of other teenagers.

Discuss how appeals courts differ from trial courts.

- The purpose of appeals courts is not to decide the facts of the case but to determine whether legal errors were made at trial.
- The attorneys in appeals cases file lengthy documents known as appellate briefs.

- There is no jury in an appeals case.
- Appeals cases are usually heard by a panel of judges.

Identify the major participants in the judicial system and their respective roles.

- Judges interpret the law, decide appropriate legal issues, and usually determine the sentence.
- Prosecutors decide whether to bring criminal charges and which ones to bring, and they attempt to prove all elements of the crime beyond a reasonable doubt.
- Defense attorneys represent the defendant; they conduct pretrial investigations, are present during some police questioning, argue about bail amounts, engage in plea bargaining, determine defense strategy, argue about the sentence, and represent the defendant in appeals.
- Juries determine the facts of the case and ultimately whether the defendant is guilty or innocent.
- Lay witnesses testify about things they heard or saw that are relevant to the case.
- Expert witnesses testify about scientific or technical matters that are helpful in determining the facts of a case.
- Victims may serve as witnesses and may also speak during the sentencing process.

Key Terms

appellate brief 252
attorney general 258
attorney–client privilege 260
challenge for cause 262
commissioner 254
contempt of court 264
court of general jurisdiction 246
court of last resort 252
court of limited jurisdiction 246
defense attorney 259
district attorney (DA) 258
due process 253

en banc 250
expert witness 263
going rate 260
grand jury 261
in chambers 253
jurisdiction 246
jury nullification 263
justice of the peace 254
lay witness 263
local legal culture 260
magistrate 254
peremptory challenge 262

petit jury 261
prosecutorial discretion 258
recusal 253
referee 254
remand 252
special prosecutor 258
subpoena 264
venire 261
voir dire 262
writ of certiorari 253

Study Questions

1. All of the following are examples of a specialty court *except*
   a. a mental health court.
   b. a drug court.
   c. a reentry court.
   d. an appeals court.

2. Appellate courts
   a. are triers of fact.
   b. decide whether legal errors were made at trial.
   c. often let guilty people go free.
   d. are speedy in providing justice.

3. When a case is heard en banc, it means that
   a. one judge presides over the case.
   b. a panel of three judges presides over the case.
   c. more than three judges preside over the case.
   d. none of the above

4. All of the following are typically the job of a trial court judge *except*
   a. to determine matters of fact.
   b. to determine matters of law.
   c. to interpret laws.
   d. to determine the sentence.

5. A state's chief law enforcement officer is known as a/an
   a. district attorney.
   b. attorney general.
   c. sheriff.
   d. police chief.

6. If a prosecutor refuses to try someone for a crime, the victim may
   a. sue the prosecutor.
   b. press charges and require the prosecutor to act.
   c. hire an attorney to prosecute the accused.
   d. bring a civil lawsuit.

7. The pool of people called to serve as potential jurors in a case is called the
   a. habeas corpus.
   b. voir dire.
   c. venire.
   d. grand jury.

8. A lay witness is
   a. someone who has information directly pertinent to the case.
   b. someone who is an expert in a scientific or technical area.
   c. someone who has a personal relationship with the defendant.
   d. rarely allowed to testify.

9. The foremost cause of wrongful convictions is
   a. mistaken eyewitness testimony.
   b. jury tampering.
   c. attorney malpractice.
   d. poor scientific evidence.

10. A person with specialized knowledge that may be helpful in a particular case is known as a/an
    a. district attorney.
    b. expert witness.
    c. voir dire.
    d. accomplice.

Critical Thinking Questions

For further review, go to the LearnSmart study module for this chapter.

1. Which do you think is more likely to result in a fair decision: a trial by jury or a bench trial? What do you see as the potential risks and benefits of each? Why do you think the United States relies so much more on juries than does the rest of the world?

2. How should district attorneys be chosen—by political appointment or election? What difference does it make?

3. What are some ways to ensure the accuracy of scientific testimony in the courtroom?

9 Pretrial and Trial

After reading this chapter, you should be able to:

- Describe the Eighth Amendment right to bail.

- List the rights afforded to criminal defendants by the Sixth Amendment.

- Describe the scope and limitations of the right against double jeopardy.

- Identify the steps of the pretrial process.

- Analyze the meaning of the due process clause.

- Distinguish among the differing standards of proof used by the U.S. legal system.

- Identify the stages of a criminal trial.

Realities and Challenges

Tried for the Third Time—Over 30 Years Later

Somebody murdered Francis X. Hussey. In January 1981, the 41-year-old Massachusetts man was found beaten to death inside his kitchen. The body was discovered by 24-year-old Keith Butler, who lived a few doors down and sometimes spent time with Hussey. Several years earlier, the two had had a sexual relationship.

Butler's brother, who was a police officer, noticed blood on Keith Butler's shoes. Police seized the shoes and a jacket with a red stain, and they also questioned Keith Butler, who denied responsibility for the murder.

Butler was tried for murder in April 1983, but the jury was unable to reach a verdict. He was tried again in December of that same year. Again the trial resulted in a hung jury. In 1984, the prosecutor brought charges for the third time, but the charges were later dropped. Butler was freed and eventually moved to Florida.[1]

Decades later, the police had at their disposal new methods of examining evidence—and they had held onto Butler's jacket all those years. They analyzed the bloodstains and found that the DNA most likely matched the victim. Several witnesses were still available and willing to talk to the police as well. As a result, in June 2015, Keith Butler was once again arraigned in the murder of Hussey. He entered a not guilty plea. By mid-June, it appeared that Butler would be facing his third trial for a crime that had occurred more than 30 years earlier.[2]

In any given year, more than 20 million criminal cases are referred to state courts in the United States.[3] About one-quarter of these cases are felonies; the rest are misdemeanors. More than 95 percent of them never go to trial but instead are settled by plea bargains, in which the defendants plead guilty (to either the original charge or a lesser one) in exchange for reduced sentences. Still, approximately 1 million cases do go to court. As Keith Butler's case demonstrates, the criminal justice process is long and complicated–and it does not always result in justice being served. In this chapter, we explore the rights of criminal defendants, the stages of the pretrial process, and the procedures followed in criminal trials.

DEFENDANT RIGHTS

Constitutional protections do not end with the actions of legislatures or police. They also extend to the processes and procedures that occur after a suspect has been arrested and formally charged with a crime.

The Eighth Amendment: Bail

bail
A sum of money deposited by a defendant with a court to ensure the defendant's appearance at trial.

Frequently, individuals who are charged with crimes are permitted to remain free while they wait for their case to be tried or otherwise settled. Many such defendants deposit a sum of money, called **bail,** with the court to ensure their appearance in court. The Eighth Amendment to the U.S. Constitution clearly states: "Excessive bail shall not be required." Interestingly, this is one of the few sections of the Bill of Rights that does not apply to the states; this privilege applies only to *federal* cases. If states want to set high bail amounts–or even do away with bail altogether–the Eighth Amendment will not prohibit them from exercising these options. Even in federal cases, the scope of the excessive bail clause is limited. Some states, however, provide residents with the right to bail in the state constitutions.

The purpose of bail is to ensure that defendants show up at trial. Those who fail to appear forfeit the bail money they have put up for their release.

Generally speaking, the Supreme Court has given few guidelines about what constitutes "excessive" bail, and judges have wide latitude with respect to the amount of bail they set. Essentially, the courts have held that "excessive" means bail that is too high relative to the severity of the offense, not to the defendant's ability to pay. Judges or legislatures also may opt to deny bail when the risk of flight is very high, such as when the charges are extremely serious. In addition, the Supreme Court has ruled that suspects can be held without bail if they pose a potential danger to the community—a practice known as **preventive detention.**

Generally the amount of bail is determined by the severity of the offense. In many states, each court sets particular bail levels for specific crimes. These amounts vary widely depending on the crime. For example, in Los Angeles, a person charged with writing a bad check will probably be released on $5,000 bail, whereas someone charged with selling very large amounts of drugs may have bail set at $5 million.[4]

Most defendants who are granted bail do not pay the full amount themselves but instead hire a *bail bonding* service. For a fee charged to the defendant, the bail bonding company guarantees the court that the defendant will appear at trial. Bail bonding is a profitable business, conducted mainly in the poorer parts of town and around courthouses, jails, and police headquarters. The professionals who run bail bonding offices charge high interest for their services, as much as 10 to 15 percent. To insure themselves against defendants who may be tempted to flee, they employ *bounty hunters*—usually former police officers, retired military personnel, and even ex-convicts—who must be prepared to use very rough tactics to hunt down and catch bail-jumping fugitives.

Being free on bail gives an accused person a chance to put his or her personal affairs in order before facing trial, to work more closely with defense counsel, to search out evidence and witnesses who can help establish innocence—and, above all, to avoid jail. Most jails are badly overcrowded, and sometimes they are dilapidated and poorly maintained for lack of funding. The disparities in granting bail mean that the inmates are overwhelmingly poor, and they include as well a disproportionate number of violent offenders. Almost invariably, confinement in a county jail is extremely unpleasant, and often it can be dangerous.

The Sixth Amendment: The Right to Counsel and a Speedy Trial

The Sixth Amendment to the Constitution affords several rights, including the right to counsel, the right to a speedy trial, the right to a jury, and the right to confront and cross-examine witnesses. The Sixth Amendment "attaches," or takes effect, as soon as formal charges are filed, so some of its provisions may affect the actions of law enforcement. The amendment is, however, of greater significance later in the criminal justice process because it contains several provisions that concern criminal trials.

The Right to Counsel During the Great Depression, many people hopped freight trains as they traveled from one town to the next in a desperate search for work. In Alabama in March 1931, a fight broke out on one of these trains between a group of young Black men and a group of young White men. Shortly after the fight, two White women, who were also on the train, claimed that they had been raped by several of the Black men, nine of whom were ultimately charged with rape. The atmosphere before and during the trial was so rife with potential violence that military guards were called in to protect

preventive detention
The practice of holding a suspect without bail because he is believed to pose a potential danger to the community or to be at risk of fleeing the jurisdiction.

Race, Class, Gender

Justice for All?

As the case of the nine young men in Alabama—often referred to as the Scottsboro Boys case—demonstrates, poor Americans and Americans of color have often had little or no access to good legal representation. Also consider the case of *Brown v. Mississippi*, in which three poor, Black tenant farmers were accused in 1934 of murdering a White man. The only evidence introduced during the one-day trial was the defendants' confessions. Even though police admitted that the men had confessed only after having been whipped, suspended from a tree, and threatened with death, the all-White jury convicted the defendants and sentenced them to death. Eventually the Supreme Court overturned their convictions, but they all still ended up spending several years in prison on manslaughter charges.

In a series of cases, mostly in the 1960s, the U.S. Supreme Court took steps to ensure that all defendants receive at least adequate legal assistance, regardless of how much money they have. In all criminal trials in which incarceration is a possibility, as well as in at least one appeal of these cases, poor people are entitled to have a government-provided attorney.

While conditions have certainly improved since the 1930s, it remains unclear to what extent the poor get *good* legal assistance. Public defenders are often inexperienced, overworked, and underfunded, and in complicated cases such as homicides they may have difficulties providing strong defenses. The standard for getting a conviction overturned on the basis of inadequate legal representation is quite high.

Even when they get good legal help, poor people who are accused of crimes may still find themselves saddled with debts long after they have served their time, as states and counties tack on numerous court-related fees. A report issued in late 2010 concluded that these debts make it hard for people to find housing and jobs and often result in the return of parolees or probationers to prison.

OBSERVE → INVESTIGATE → UNDERSTAND

- How can the justice system ensure good-quality legal assistance even for poor defendants?

- In an era of government budget cuts, many courts are trying to meet expenses by increasing fees. Is this fair? If fees are not increased, where should court funding come from?

SOURCES: *Brown v. Mississippi*, 297 U.S. 278 (1936); Brennan Center for Justice, *Criminal Justice Debt: A Barrier to Reentry*, 2010.
www.brennancenter.org/content/resource/criminal_justice_debt_a_barrier_to_reentry (retrieved February 17, 2011).

the defendants from the hostile public; even so, a lynching was only narrowly averted. The defendants were all poor and uneducated, and none had friends or family in Alabama. None was given a lawyer prior to the beginning of his trial, and after the trials—each lasting only one day—all were convicted by an all-White jury. Eight were sentenced to death.

When the convictions were appealed, the International Labor Defense, a left-wing organization that often handled civil rights cases, represented the defendants *pro bono*, meaning without charging the defendants for their services. The defendants lost their appeal to the Alabama Supreme Court and then appealed to the U.S. Supreme Court.

When the case reached the U.S. Supreme Court, the justices held that the defendants' due process rights had been violated because they were not given effective assistance of counsel. The Court, however, stopped short of holding that the Sixth Amendment right to counsel applies to state prosecutions. On its face, the Sixth Amendment and the rest of the Bill of Rights limit only the federal government, and it was not until the 1960s that the Supreme Court began to extend the Bill of Rights' protections in state cases as well. The defendants, who became known as the *Scottsboro Boys*, were later retried (see the "Race, Class, Gender" box). Even though one of the alleged victims testified at the retrial that the rapes had never happened, the men were once again convicted. Most were later paroled or pardoned, but only after serving many years in prison.[5]

The right to a speedy trial does not come without costs. If this right is violated, a defendant will go free, even if he obviously broke the law. Furthermore, this right means that most trial courts give preferential scheduling to criminal cases. Litigants in civil cases, who do not have similar Sixth Amendment rights, may face delays—sometimes extended delays—before their cases are heard.

When prosecutors are unnecessarily slow in initiating a trial, the Federal Speedy Trial Act of 1974 allows for the dismissal of charges. The Supreme Court has refused to set a hard-and-fast deadline for how quickly a prosecution must move because some cases are more complicated than others or, like capital cases, carry greater weight and so require more time for preparation. Judges are given broad authority to weigh the reasons for the delay versus the potential costs to the defendant. In addition, defendants cannot claim that their right to a speedy trial was violated if the delays were due to the defense's own requests to delay the trial. In large urban areas in 2002, 87 percent of felony defendants had their cases decided within a year of their arrest.[9]

Some people believe that defendants are not the only ones who deserve the right to a speedy trial. Victim advocates argue that victims, too, ought to be accorded this right (see the "What about the Victim?" box on page 280).

The Right to a Jury   Another important privilege protected by the Sixth Amendment is the right to be tried by an impartial jury. Although the Sixth Amendment originally was intended to apply only to federal cases, the Supreme Court in 1968 extended the application of the amendment to state cases as well.[10]

This right has several components. First, the right to a jury trial—as opposed to a **bench trial,** in which the judge determines guilt—applies only in criminal cases in which the defendant faces 6 months or more of incarceration. Therefore, individuals who are charged with most petty offenses will not get juries. This rule saves the state significant time and expense and reduces the number of citizens who must do jury duty.

Second, the jury must be impartial. Impartiality requires that any potential jurors who have personal knowledge about the case or who express their belief that the defendant is guilty before the trial even begins may be excluded from the jury. Further, if pretrial publicity in an area makes it very difficult for the defendant to secure an impartial jury, the defendant may seek a **change of venue**—that is, the trial may be moved to another location where there is less publicity. This consideration was invoked in moving Oklahoma City bomber Timothy McVeigh's trial to Denver. Changes of venue are rarely granted, however. For instance, the 2015 trial of Boston Marathon bomber Dzhokhar Tsarnaev took place in Boston because judges felt that it would be possible to seat an impartial jury there.

Third, although the tradition of 12-person juries and the requirement of unanimous verdicts can be traced all the way back to England in 1215 and the Magna Carta, the Supreme Court holds that neither of these is a requirement of the Sixth Amendment. In fact, the Court holds that states may have juries of any size they choose, as long as there are at least six jurors.[11]

Finally, unlike most other constitutional rights, the right to a jury is not fully waivable. In federal cases the defendant cannot have a bench trial if the

▲ **Men in Jail Awaiting Closure of Their Cases**

Accused individuals have a right to a speedy trial. *What do you think is the maximum amount of time the state can leave an accused person in jail before trial? In other words, how much time has to pass before a person's right to a speedy trial has been violated?*

bench trial
A trial in which guilt is determined by a judge rather than by a jury.

change of venue
Relocation of a case to another court because the case has received too much publicity in the original jurisdiction for the defendant to receive a fair trial.

What about the **Victim?**

Balancing Victims' and Offenders' Rights to a Speedy Trial

As of 2006, 27 states recognize victims' right to a speedy trial. Twelve of these states amended their constitution to protect this right, while the remaining 15 have statutory provisions in place. The language differs greatly, but in most cases the victims may limit the number of *continuances* (delays) that a defendant can request for misdemeanor and felony cases. In addition, many jurisdictions allow vulnerable populations, such as children and the elderly, to be given special consideration when setting the court docket.[a]

Florida takes these basic provisions one step further. As of July 1, 2005, crime victims in Florida were granted rights similar to those of the accused in requesting a speedy trial.[b] Traditionally, defendants were the

only ones in the court process to have a right to a speedy trial as protected by the Sixth Amendment of the U.S. Constitution. Under the new Florida law, however, any person charged with a felony must be brought to trial within 175 days. If the trial does not occur, the defendant or his representative may file papers to force a trial by the 190th day.

Despite this law and others like it elsewhere in the United States, the right to a speedy trial has often meant that the defendant also has the right to stall the court process. Prosecutors have long expressed anger about the willingness of defense attorneys and their clients to retard court proceedings, thereby delaying justice, further harming victims and other witnesses, and ultimately costing taxpayers millions of dollars. Prosecutors point out that delaying the court process can be particularly problematic for older victims, whose health and ability to participate in the court process may deteriorate over an extended period of time. Victim advocates have echoed these sentiments by asking, Where is the *victim's* right to a speedy trial?

The Florida legislature addressed these concerns by passing a law that sailed through the Florida State House and Senate with just one dissenting vote. On May 24, 2005, then-governor Jeb Bush signed the Florida law—the first of its kind in the United States—authorizing state attorneys to act on behalf of victims by filing a demand for a speedy trial. By this law, the state attorney can make the demand for a speedy trial only after 125 days have passed from the time that the defendant was arrested and formal charges were filed. In addition, a court must have granted at least three

continuances over the prosecutor's objections before a demand for a speedy trial can be made on the victim's behalf. Once the state files a demand for a speedy trial, the law stipulates that the judge must put the trial date on the docket within 5 days. At that point, the trial must begin within the next 45 days unless there are necessary or good legal causes that merit further reasonable delay. Opponents of this legislation had claimed that forcing a speedy trial would violate defendants' Fourteenth Amendment right to due process; but the Florida law took this concern into account through language that allows judges to grant further extensions to ensure defendants' due process rights.

The most recent comprehensive victims' rights initiative by a state to amend its constitution has been California's Proposition 9, the Victims' Bill of Rights Act of 2008: Marsy's Law. Approved by California voters on November 4, 2008, this law entitles all crime victims to justice and due process and also includes a speedy trial clause.[c]

While victims' rights exist, one of the downsides of these rights is that there is no effective mechanism in place to enforce them. In response to this deficit, in 2002 the National Crime Victim Law Institute (NCVLI) received funding from the Office for Victims of Crime (OVC) to create pro bono victims' rights clinics. Within three years, eight state clinics were created (two in Arizona, and one each in Idaho, Maryland, New Jersey, New Mexico, South Carolina, and Utah). The clinics were created to promote awareness, education, and enforcement of victims' rights in the court process by filing motions when rights were denied. Those working within the clinics also sought appellate decisions that reinforced victims' rights statutes within their jurisdiction, as well as increased training for court officials and promoting victims' rights legislation. An evaluation of these clinics showed mixed results regarding whether rights were enforced. Specifically, working one-on-one with clients seemed to bring about positive results, but there was a paucity of examples of changes that impacted the majority. By 2009, federal funding had ended, and the long-term sustainability of these clinics is uncertain.[d]

OBSERVE → INVESTIGATE → UNDERSTAND

- The Florida law has several stipulations that allow for continuances even after the state attorney has filed a demand for a speedy trial on the victim's behalf. Do you think there is a way to ensure that the rights of both victim and defendant are not violated? Explain.

- How speedy should a "speedy" trial be? Why?

- Why might opponents of the Florida law raise questions about the law's impact on the defendant's right to due process?

SOURCES: [a]*Crime Victims Rights to a Speedy Trial* (Washington, DC: National Center for Crime Victims, 2006). www.ncvc.org/ncvc/AGP.Net/Components/documentViewer/Download.aspxnz?DocumentID=42467 (retrieved February 7, 2011).

[b]Dan Christensen, "In Florida, Speedy Trials for All, Not Only the Accused," *Daily Business Review*, June 21, 2005. www.law.com/jsp/article.jsp?id=900005544070 (retrieved July 24, 2011).

[c]"California's Victims' Bill of Rights Act of 2008: Marsy's Law." http://ag.ca.gov/victimservices/marsys_law.php (retrieved July 24, 2011).

[d] Robert C. Davis, James M. Anderson, Susan Howley, Carol Dorris, and Julie Whitman, *No More Rights without Remedies: An Impact Evaluation of the National Crime Victim Law Institute's Victims' Rights Clinics*, U.S. Department of Justice, Office of Justice Programs, and RAND Corporation. www.ncjrs.gov/pdffiles1/nij/grants/241752.pdf (retrieved June 9, 2015).

prosecutor wishes to have a jury. Some states follow this rule as well. Even when a defendant is permitted to waive a jury, the accused must express that he understands what waiving the right to a jury means and must verbalize that understanding.

The Right to Confrontation and Cross-Examination   The Sixth Amendment gives criminal defendants the right to confront witnesses—that is, to have witnesses actually present at trial—and to examine or question them. This provision gives the defendant, or more precisely his attorney, the chance to ask a witness about possible inconsistencies, inaccuracies, or biases; it also makes it less likely that a witness—who will be positioned to look the accused in the eye—will be dishonest. In practice, these rights mean that hearsay evidence usually is excluded, and defendants nearly always are entitled to be present during their own trials.

Hearsay evidence is any statement made by a witness that is not based on that witness's personal knowledge. For example, it would be hearsay if a witness testified: "My sister told me that she heard the defendant say that he killed his wife." Any such statement is considered an "out of court" statement and is normally viewed as inadmissible because it infringes on the defendant's Sixth Amendment right to confront witnesses and because it tends to be unreliable. In the foregoing example, if the sister's statement is to be admitted as evidence, the witness's sister herself would have to appear on the witness stand, testify to what she herself claimed to have heard, and then be subjected to cross-examination. Out of court statements also include such evidence as recorded 9-1-1 emergency calls; an operator who takes such a call would have to be the witness to testify to what she heard. There are a number of exceptions to the hearsay rule, including statements made while a person is dying.

In 2011, the Supreme Court dealt with the difficult question of when laboratory reports might constitute hearsay. The defendant was given a blood alcohol test. When the prosecutor presented the results of the test at trial, the technician who had actually done the analysis and prepared the report did not testify. Instead, another technician from the same lab testified in court. The Supreme Court held that this violated the defendant's right to confront and cross-examine a witness.[12]

There are times when a prosecutor can show that a witness may be vulnerable to harm if forced to testify in the presence of the defendant.[13] This is often the situation in trials involving possible child abuse by the accused. In such cases, the Supreme Court has ruled that the witnesses may be permitted to testify via one-way closed-circuit television rather than being called to testify in the actual courtroom.

Double Jeopardy: Protection from Repeated Trials for the Same Crime

The Fifth Amendment prohibits subjecting anyone twice to "jeopardy of life or limb" for the same offense. This is known as the **double jeopardy** clause. The Supreme Court has held that the right against double jeopardy applies in state as well as federal cases.[14] This clause prevents a person from being prosecuted again and again for the same crime. If it were not for the protection against double jeopardy, a prosecutor could use his power to torment an innocent person by repeatedly dragging him into court for the same charges. As the Supreme Court wrote, "[T]he State . . . should not be allowed to make repeated attempts to convict an alleged criminal . . . thereby subjecting him to embarrassment, expense and ordeal and compelling him to live in a continued state of anxiety."[15]

hearsay evidence
Any statement made by a witness that is not based on that witness's personal knowledge.

double jeopardy
The Fifth Amendment right that protects anyone from being tried twice for the same offense.

The right against double jeopardy has several aspects. It means that once a person has been tried for a crime, she cannot be tried again on the same charges, even if new evidence appears—no matter how convincing or compelling that evidence is. If a judge acquits a defendant at trial, the defendant cannot be tried again for the crime even if the judge was mistaken in applying the law and should not have forced a not guilty finding.[16] It also means that once a person has completed the punishment for an offense, she cannot be punished again for that same offense.

MYTH/REALITY

MYTH: Double jeopardy means that once a person has gone through a criminal trial for a particular act, the prosecutor can never bring that person to trial again.

REALITY: It is not a violation of double jeopardy if the defendant is charged with a different offense.[17]

▲ **Mug Shot of Celebrity Emile Hirsch**

One of the first stages of the criminal justice process is booking, in which the suspect is usually photographed.

There are several limitations to the right against double jeopardy. First, it does not prohibit a person from being tried for a crime by more than one state, or by the state and the federal governments. For example, a person who kidnaps someone in Texas and transports his victim to Oklahoma might be tried and convicted in the courts of both Texas and Oklahoma, as well as in federal court. Second, the right does not keep a person from being tried on different charges. If a person accused of robbing a store and killing the cashier is found not guilty of murder, he still may be tried for robbery. Third, the right does not prohibit a victim from bringing a civil lawsuit against a person who was acquitted in a criminal trial, as happened in the O. J. Simpson and Robert Blake murder cases (see Chapter 8). Fourth, the right does not apply if a defendant is convicted and appeals, and then the appeals court remands the case for a new trial due to errors in the original trial. Finally, the right usually does not prevent a retrial if the jury in the original trial fails to reach a verdict, or if a mistrial is declared for some other reason.

PRETRIAL PROCESS

Although the pretrial process often receives little attention in TV crime shows, the procedures that occur before a trial begins are essential. In this section we examine the major stages of the pretrial process.

Arrest and Booking

A criminal case typically begins with an arrest, although sometimes an arrest warrant is issued first. In either case, a suspect is generally taken into custody and booked, most often at a local police station or jail. During **booking,** the suspect is photographed (this photo is known as a *mug shot*) and fingerprinted, and the police record her personal information and the crimes with which she is initially being charged. Unless the crime is very minor and she is released, the suspect is normally confined in a local jail.

The Criminal Complaint

The police then refer the case to the prosecutor, who will make an initial decision about whether to bring charges and, if so, what they will be. These charges, outlined in official paperwork called the **complaint,** are not necessarily the ones for which the suspect was initially arrested. As an investigation proceeds and reveals new evidence, the prosecutor may drop or change some

booking
The process of photographing and fingerprinting a suspect and creating the police record of personal information and the crime(s) with which the suspect is initially being charged when taken into custody.

complaint
The document containing the initial crimes with which a defendant is charged.

charges or add new ones. Specific charges later may be dropped as part of a plea bargain, so the charges that are filed can give the prosecutor negotiating leverage. Once the prosecutor has filed a complaint, a suspect officially becomes a defendant.

Arraignment and Plea

A defendant in custody is entitled to a speedy **arraignment,** or a hearing before a judge or magistrate. During this hearing, the complaint is formally read. Arraignments often take place within a day of the arrest, although they may be delayed if the arrest occurs on a weekend or a holiday. The arraignment may be the first time the defendant learns which charges he is facing. If he has not already retained an attorney, he is informed of his right to counsel. If he is indigent, he is assigned a defense attorney. The defendant is also formally read his other rights. Finally, the defendant enters an initial **plea,** or answer, to the charges. Generally, he may plead *guilty,* meaning that he admits to all the charges; *not guilty,* meaning that he denies the charges; or **no contest (nolo contendere),** meaning that he does not admit to the charges but will not dispute them in criminal court. This last plea may help him avoid civil liability for the acts of which he is accused. Convictions and guilty pleas can be used as evidence of a defendant's liability in a related civil lawsuit, but no contest pleas cannot be used in civil suits.

In many minor misdemeanor cases, defendants simply plead guilty, and the arraigning judge sentences them, usually to time already served in jail and perhaps also to fines or probation. Some have argued that for minor offenses the criminal process itself is designed to be so unpleasant that it serves as punishment.[18] In felony cases, defendants usually plead not guilty at the arraignment. The judge will then determine whether they are entitled to be released on bail, and, if so, how much the bail will be. Recall that the purpose of bail is to guarantee that defendants will appear for trial. If defendants do not appear, they will forfeit their bail money, and the court will issue a warrant for their arrest.

Probable Cause Hearing

The next step is a hearing to determine whether there is probable cause to believe that the suspect committed the offenses in the complaint. There are two major kinds of probable cause hearings: *grand juries* and *preliminary hearings.* All defendants in federal felony cases are entitled to a grand jury under the Fifth Amendment. Some states also require grand juries to be seated in some circumstances; others give the prosecutor the choice of whether to use one. A grand jury is composed of 12 to 23 local citizens who may serve for a particular length of time or for a specific case. They are usually selected in the same way as members of petit juries, such as from voter lists.

Grand juries do not determine whether the suspect is guilty. Instead, they decide whether sufficient evidence exists for a prosecution to proceed. The stated purpose of the grand jury is to protect people against unjust or overzealous prosecutors. Critics claim, however, that grand juries usually go along with whatever the prosecutor asks them to do.[19] During a grand jury hearing, the prosecutor presents evidence against the defendant. The grand jury may subpoena witnesses or conduct investigations on its own, but it rarely does so independently of the prosecutor. Grand jury hearings are closed to the press, and defendants have few rights during the process. For example, they are not entitled to counsel and cannot call their own witnesses. However, defendants and witnesses may invoke their Fifth Amendment right against self-incrimination during grand jury proceedings.

arraignment
A hearing before a judge or magistrate during which the complaint is formally read.

plea
A defendant's formal denial or admission of guilt.

no contest (nolo contendere)
A plea in which a defendant admits that sufficient evidence exists to convict him, but he does not actually admit his guilt.

indictment
A document issued by a grand jury after it finds probable cause, formally listing the charges against the defendant.

preliminary hearing
A proceeding in which a judge determines whether probable cause exists to bring the defendant to trial for the crimes with which he has been charged.

information
A document filed by a prosecutor after a preliminary hearing, formally listing charges against the defendant.

discovery
The process in which an attorney requests that opposing counsel or other parties provide certain evidence or information.

▲ **Wrongfully Convicted**

Jimmy Eacker's conviction was overturned because the prosecutor withheld evidence.

If a grand jury finds that probable cause exists, it issues an **indictment,** which formally sets out the charges against the defendant. Again, these are not necessarily the charges that were in the original complaint. On the rare occasion that a grand jury fails to find probable cause, the case is dismissed. The prosecutor can, however, bring another complaint against the accused containing different charges, or he can later bring the same charges with new evidence. This does not constitute double jeopardy because that protection does not begin until a trial begins.

In most state cases, instead of a grand jury hearing, a **preliminary hearing** is held. The purpose is the same—to determine whether probable cause exists— but the preliminary hearing, often called the *prelim*, is held before a judge instead of a grand jury. It must occur 5 to 30 days after the complaint is filed, depending on whether the defendant is in jail or free on bail. As at a grand jury hearing, the prosecutor presents most, or often all, the evidence; in contrast, during the prelim, the defense usually presents no evidence at all. The prosecutor does not have to offer all the evidence available to him—just enough to ensure that the defendant is put on trial. Unlike the case of grand jury proceedings, however, prelims are held in public, and defendants are entitled to representation by counsel. A defendant can waive her right to a preliminary hearing, but doing so often is not in her best interest.

The prelim serves several important functions. For example, it helps avoid the prosecution of people against whom evidence is scanty. It also gives the defense an opportunity to preview the strength of the case against them. If the case appears strong, the defendant will be more willing to plea bargain instead of taking his chances at trial. Moreover, during the prelim, the defense may object to the inclusion of certain pieces of evidence at trial. If the judge rules that important evidence is inadmissible, perhaps because of the exclusionary rule (see Chapter 7), the prosecutor may drop the charges. In short, prelims decrease the number of unnecessary trials, lessen the risk that a defendant will be tried unfairly, and reduce courts' caseloads.

If the judge fails to find probable cause at the prelim, the case is dismissed. As in the grand jury process, however, the prosecutor can try again with new charges or new evidence. If the judge does find that there is probable cause to try the defendant, the case is held over for trial. The prosecutor then produces the **information,** a formal document that lists the charges for which the defendant will be tried. The defendant is entitled to a second arraignment on the information because the charges in the information may be different from those on which he was initially arraigned, although he may waive it. A trial date is then set by the court.

Discovery

Before the trial begins, the attorneys on both sides are especially busy. They continue their investigation, working to uncover evidence to support their cases. In a process called **discovery,** each attorney may request that opposing counsel or other parties give them certain evidence or information. In a criminal case, the prosecution frequently has the advantage of greater resources and greater access to evidence because prosecutors' offices usually have bigger budgets than do public defenders. Moreover, prosecutors have police departments and their own investigators at their disposal. Discovery is intended to level the playing field by allowing the defense to obtain some of this evidence. Another advantage of discovery is that it allows the attorneys to prepare their cases sufficiently and helps them avoid being ambushed at trial with unexpected evidence that they are not prepared to refute.

Yet critics claim that the discovery process is cumbersome and inadequate. The prosecutor is forbidden to intentionally hide or destroy evidence that might exculpate (clear from blame) the defendant. In fact, since the 1963 case of

Brady v. Maryland, prosecutors have the duty to disclose to the defense all *material exculpatory evidence*–that is, any evidence that might affect the jury's decision as to the defendant's guilt.[20] If the prosecutor fails to hand over such evidence, a conviction can be overturned. For example, in 2009, Alaska's Senator Ted Stevens's conviction–for failing to report gifts properly–was thrown out because the prosecutor had deliberately withheld evidence from the defense. More recently, in 2011, Alaskan Jimmy Eacker was granted a new murder trial because the prosecutor had withheld DNA evidence that implicated someone else in the crime.[21] The problem is, however, that it might not always be clear to the prosecutor whether particular evidence truly is material. A further complication in the process is that overworked and underfunded public defenders are often accused of doing a poor job of investigating their cases–and of consequently putting up an inadequate defense.

Pretrial Motions

Pretrial motions are specific requests that lawyers file with the judge. A common request is to suppress evidence. At both the federal and the state level, the procedural rules governing what evidence is permissible are detailed and explicit. A defense attorney who believes that a particular piece of evidence is not admissible because, for instance, it was illegally obtained can ask the judge to rule that the prosecution cannot use it at trial. Successful motions to suppress evidence can leave the prosecution without enough evidence to obtain a conviction, leading the prosecutor to request dismissal of the case.

Another motion is a request for a change of venue. If a case receives so much publicity where the crime allegedly happened that potential jurors have already formed opinions about the defendant's guilt and it would be virtually impossible to hold a fair trial, the defendant–almost never the prosecution–may ask that the case be moved to another location where there has been less publicity. The venue was changed in the sensational 2005 trial of Scott Peterson for killing his wife and unborn child in California. In May 2015, the six Baltimore police officers charged in the death of Freddie Gray requested a change of venue for their trial. Gray died while in police custody, sparking protests that received worldwide media attention.

Plea Bargaining

Occasionally, prosecutors drop the charges. More often, however, the prosecutor and the defense strike a deal–called a **plea bargain**–in which the defendant agrees to plead guilty in exchange for reduced charges or a lesser sentence. In cases involving multiple defendants, such as the Oklahoma City bombing case, prosecutors often offer one or more of the defendants reduced charges in exchange for their testimony against other defendants. The negotiation of a plea bargain may take more than one meeting. In fact, several negotiations may be required before both parties agree to the charge to which the defendant will plead guilty. And although plea bargaining can occur at any time before or during the trial–right down to the moment before the jury delivers a verdict–in most cases it occurs *before* trial.

As evidence is shared with the defense through discovery, the defense attorney might realize that there is likely too much evidence of guilt to prevail at trial. In that case, the attorney might advise the defendant to plead guilty to the original offense rather than trying to negotiate a bargain for a reduced charge.

One way plea bargaining can occur is for the prosecution to drop some charges in exchange for a guilty plea. For example, a defendant might be charged with 10 acts of burglary, but the prosecution agrees to drop 8 of the 10 charges, thus significantly reducing the defendant's sentence. In jurisdictions

▲ **Dzhokhar Tsarnaev was tried for planting bombs at the 2013 Boston Marathon.**

Because Tsarnaev's case received extensive media attention, his defense attorneys requested a change of venue, which was denied. *Should defendants or prosecutors be able to change the location of the trial? Why or why not?*

plea bargain
An agreement between defendants and prosecutors, in which a defendant pleads guilty to the original or reduced charges in exchange for a lesser sentence.

with sentencing guidelines, such decisions may be made specifically to reduce the sentence that would be imposed because the guidelines stipulate a particular sentence for the greater number of offenses of the same crime.

Judges are required to approve plea bargains, and it is the judge's duty to make sure that the bargain is voluntary–that the defendant realizes what rights she is surrendering and what other implications are entailed when she agrees to a plea bargain. That requirement was established in *Boykin v. Alabama* (1969), in which the Supreme Court ruled that that the defendant must be fully aware of what she is agreeing to. Today, most judges have a standard list of questions they ask defendants in court to ensure that their choices are voluntary. Further, only with the judge's consent may the defendant withdraw a guilty plea that she has made under a plea bargain.

The U.S. criminal justice system encourages plea bargains because they are an efficient means of disposing of a great many of the 20 million criminal cases that arise each year. Plea bargains also allow prosecutors to pursue more cases, and to pursue them more thoroughly. Today, about 95 percent of criminal convictions result from plea bargains rather than completed trials.[22] Alaska banned plea bargaining in 1975, and in some other jurisdictions attempts have been made to restrict its use. However, in general, plea bargaining has become indispensable to the efficient functioning of the U.S. criminal justice system.

Recent research on the origins of plea bargaining in the United States reveals that the practice emerged in Boston, Massachusetts, in the 1830s and 1840s–much earlier than previous studies had reported. Between the 1830s and the 1840s in Boston's lower courts, the guilty plea rate rose from 10 percent to 28 percent. The most commonly plea-bargained offense was public drunkenness. There were also significant occurrences of plea bargaining for larceny and assault and battery.[23]

Plea Bargaining Controversies Centering on the Defendant Despite its long historical tradition, plea bargaining is not without controversies. Think about it: Defendants face a high-stakes gamble. If they go to trial, they may be acquitted–or they may be found guilty and receive a harsher sentence than they were offered through the plea bargain. Whether to opt for a plea bargain is a difficult choice for anyone to make, but it is especially so for someone who is innocent. Of course, all defendants must be presumed innocent at this point. So, how can defendants make a good choice? The answer is that they must consider many factors. What is the conviction rate for the offenses with which they are charged? Felony conviction rates range from 41 percent for assault to 80 percent for murder.[24] Will the jury be sympathetic to them? How strong is the prosecution's evidence?

It may surprise you to learn that a defendant can plead guilty even as he maintains his innocence. In *North Carolina v. Alford* (1970), the Supreme Court ruled that a judge may accept a guilty plea from a defendant who wishes to reduce his sentence even if the individual states that he is innocent. The Court, however, also held that a judge should accept a guilty plea in such a case only if the facts support that the defendant is guilty.[25]

A defendant's choice is also likely to be heavily influenced by whether his lawyer is a public defender or a private attorney. Public defenders are often less experienced than private attorneys and typically have heavier caseloads with fewer resources at their disposal. A public defender might be eager to unload a case quickly to reduce her workload and therefore might encourage her client to opt for a plea bargain; a private attorney will earn more if the case goes to trial. Defendants with public defenders are more likely to accept a plea bargain than are defendants with private attorneys.[26] This is another way in which the process of justice is different for the poor.

The U.S. Supreme Court ruled in *Bordenkircher v. Hayes* (1978) that prosecutors may threaten defendants with harsher sentences if they do not plead guilty. This is one reason why plea bargaining also fuels opposition to capital punishment. Prosecutors may use the threat of the death penalty to compel innocent people to plead guilty. Even if you know that you are innocent, you will likely be tempted to plead guilty to, say, second-degree murder and a sentence of 15 years rather than face a trial for first-degree murder in which you could receive a death sentence.

Plea Bargaining Controversies Centering on the Victim   It is not only defendants' advocates who criticize plea bargains. Victims and their advocates may be deeply displeased as well, believing that plea bargains spare the people who hurt them from getting the punishment they deserve. In light of this issue, some states require that prosecutors confer with victims before completing a plea agreement, either to ask for their input on the deal or simply to notify them of it. Some states allow victims to make a statement in court when the plea is entered. In no state, however, does a victim have the power to veto a plea agreement. To many victims, it must thus seem that expedience is valued more than justice. One noteworthy example is the case of Gary Ridgway, the "Green River killer." In 2003, Ridgway pleaded guilty to 48 murders. In return for providing police with enough information to locate the victims' bodies and close these cases, he was given 48 life sentences instead of the death penalty.

Determining the Scope of the Plea: Who Decides?   In general, the prosecutor may decide what sort of plea bargain to offer the defendant. Specific rules differ by jurisdiction. For example, in federal cases the proposed sentence will usually comply with federal sentencing guidelines. In most cases, once a defendant has entered a guilty plea as part of a plea bargain, she cannot withdraw it, and prosecutors are usually bound to carry out the deals they have struck as well. However, a judge may set aside a plea bargain, an action that might require that a new plea bargain be struck or that the case go to trial.

A local legal culture typically arises within a given jurisdiction as the same legal professionals work together over a long period of time. Indeed, defense attorneys, judges, and prosecutors develop similar ways of looking at cases and concluding what justice calls for in particular offenses.[27] For example, in many jurisdictions there will be a "going rate" for such common crimes as possession of a small amount of narcotics, intimate partner violence, and possession of alcohol while a minor. In one jurisdiction, the major actors might all agree that an individual cited for having a fake driver's license in order to purchase alcohol should have his license revoked. Another jurisdiction, however, might require the offender simply to take responsible-drinking classes. The adversarial system of criminal justice is more theory than reality in such cases.

THE CRIMINAL TRIAL

As we have seen, only a small percentage of criminal cases make it to trial. But the criminal trial, with all its ceremony and drama, is what most people have in mind when they think about criminal cases. Most people believe that they have an accurate idea of what happens during a trial, in large part because of depictions of trials in television and movies. In reality, though, trials are much more complex—and usually much less dramatic—than the ones enacted on television shows.

Due Process: Providing Fair and Equitable Treatment

The **due process clause** is arguably the most important phrase in the Constitution. Simply stated, due process stands for the proposition that government laws and proceedings must be fair.

due process clause
A clause of the U.S. Constitution that represents the proposition that government laws and proceedings must be fair.

Real Careers

SARAH CORY

Work location: St. Paul, Minnesota

College(s): University of Minnesota (1998); William Mitchell College of Law (2001)

Major(s): Sociology (emphasis in criminology) and Philosophy (BS); Juris Doctorate (JD); Minnesota Bar Certified (2001)

Job title: Assistant County Attorney III, Ramsey County Attorney's Office

Salary range for job like this: $80,000–$120,000

Time in job: 7 years

Work Responsibilities
During my 7 years as assistant county attorney, I have worked in three different divisions: child support enforcement, juvenile prosecution, and adult felony prosecution. But jury trial work is my primary responsibility. A typical workweek involves meeting with witnesses, talking with police officers, preparing cases for trial, and appearing in court for motion hearings, sentencing hearings, and jury trials.

Why Criminal Justice?
I was drawn to the complexities of what justice means in the context of criminal law. I enjoy the problem-solving aspect of it—the fact that it's not so simple that someone did something wrong and just has to pay for it.

Expectations and Realities of the Job
I expected cases to go to trial more often than they actually do. I also expected that it would be obvious to victims that I am working to help them. But sometimes it feels as a criminal prosecutor that I'm not really helping them at all. Victims can find seeking justice to be a bit of a burden or punishment—first the crime, then the interruptions to meet with law enforcement, meet with attorneys, and testify in court. But this doesn't at all change how satisfying I find the work to be. I am working to bring about justice.

My Advice to Students
Be resourceful and try to understand as much as you can about how things work—whether it's the technology you use or the day in the life of a probation officer. This will help you build relationships with people who can help you figure things out in your job and make you self-sufficient when there isn't anyone around to help. Be inquisitive and genuinely interested in how things work, and you will learn things you didn't think to ask about. And while you are in school, take advantage of the opportunity to learn whatever you can about the practice of law. If you're not at the top of your class (which I wasn't), it's all the more important to seek a part-time job or an internship with a law firm. From this experience not only will you learn firsthand how to practice law, but you will have an opportunity to show your employer just how irreplaceable you are.

The due process clause appears twice in the Constitution: once in the Fifth Amendment and again in the Fourteenth. In both places it reads: "No person shall be . . . deprived of life, liberty, or property, without due process of law." The difference is that the clause in the Fifth Amendment, part of the original Bill of Rights and ratified in 1791, applies only to the federal government, whereas the Fourteenth Amendment, ratified in 1868 after the Civil War, applies specifically to the states. Because the words within the Fifth and the Fourteenth Amendments themselves give no specifics about what is and is not permissible, the Supreme Court has often struggled with the precise meaning of the due process clause. In general, the Court has discussed two kinds of due process: procedural due process and substantive due process.

Procedural due process stands for the idea that the processes and methods used to try people for crimes cannot be arbitrary or unfair. For instance, if a person were to be put on trial without first being adequately notified of the specific charges against him, it would be very difficult for that individual to adequately defend himself. *Substantive due process* means that the government cannot unfairly, or without just cause, deprive people of certain fundamental liberties. An example is an individual's right to privacy, which the government cannot invade unless it has a good enough reason, such as strong evidence that the person has committed a serious crime.

Due process is perhaps the core of the criminal justice system. Think about it: What value can a system have if is not administered fairly? Due process protections can help ensure that individuals are not discriminated against or persecuted by government officials and that people's rights are respected.

Yet some critics of the criminal justice system complain that its procedures are often time-consuming, complicated, and expensive. Other critics say that participants in the system sometimes make mistakes or act in arbitrary or biased ways. The due process clause demands that we find a reasonable balance between these competing concerns. However, actually establishing that balance is often a challenge.

Burden of Proof and Standards of Proof

Many procedures have been built into the U.S. criminal justice system to minimize mistakes. As a society, we also have made a value judgment with respect to criminal behavior. Specifically, we have decided that it is better to risk letting some guilty people go free than to risk convicting the innocent. Accordingly, we place heavy burdens on the prosecution in criminal cases.

All criminal cases begin with the *presumption of innocence*–the legal assumption that the defendant did not commit any crimes. To overcome this presumption and gain a conviction, the prosecution bears the **burden of proof**–that is, the challenge of proving every element of each crime. This means that even if the defense presents no evidence at all, the defendant may still be acquitted if the prosecution does not carry its burden.

In some cases, the defense may also have a burden of proof. For example, if a defendant claims that she was acting in self-defense or was insane, in most cases she must prove her claim, as opposed to the prosecution having to prove that she was not defending herself or was not insane.

Charged with Murder
Meagan Grunwald was charged with murder and several other crimes after the fatal shooting of a Utah sheriff's deputy.

burden of proof
The burden of proving a particular thing in court.

MYTH/REALITY

MYTH: In a criminal trial when a defendant is found not guilty, the trier of fact believes that the defendant is innocent of the crime for which he was charged.

REALITY: A judge or a jury may find a criminal defendant not guilty even if they believe he is probably guilty. A not guilty verdict means that the trier of fact believes that the prosecutor has failed to establish the defendant's guilt beyond a reasonable doubt.

The burden of proof falls on the party who must prove a particular thing in court; in contrast, *standard of proof* describes how convincing the proof must be. In most civil cases, the plaintiff, the person who brings the suit, must prove his case by a **preponderance of the evidence,** meaning simply that his case must be slightly stronger than the other side's. This is a relatively light burden. In criminal cases, the prosecutor must meet a more difficult standard–he must prove his case **beyond a reasonable doubt,** meaning that the jurors must have no real uncertainties about the defendant's guilt. Even if the jury is fairly sure that the defendant has committed the crime, the jurors must acquit him if they can conceive of another plausible explanation for the evidence. In the U.S. criminal justice system, people are therefore not found innocent but rather are found not guilty, meaning that the prosecution has not carried its burden. When the prosecution has given sufficient proof of all elements of the crime, defendants are, of course, found guilty.

preponderance of the evidence
The standard of proof required to win a civil lawsuit.

beyond a reasonable doubt
The standard of proof required to criminally convict a person.

▲ **O. J. Simpson Embracing His Lawyer Johnnie Cochran**

Simpson celebrated the not guilty decision in his criminal trial, but he lost in his subsequent civil trial when he was found liable for the deaths of Nicole Brown Simpson and Ronald Goldman. *What do the differing verdicts in the two trials indicate about the U.S. system of justice?*

clear and convincing evidence
An intermediate standard of proof, sometimes required for certain defenses such as the insanity defense.

sequestered
Referring to a jury that is kept separate from outside contact during a trial.

opening statements
Initial statements made by attorneys to a jury outlining the case they will present during the trial.

Other standards of proof appear in criminal cases as well. Sometimes defenses must be proved or disproved by a preponderance of evidence. Other defenses might require **clear and convincing evidence,** which lies somewhere between a preponderance and beyond a reasonable doubt. The standard of proof depends on the jurisdiction and on the particular defense. For example, in Delaware a defendant must prove insanity by a preponderance of the evidence, whereas in Florida he must prove it with clear and convincing evidence. Whether jurors are really able and willing to understand such subtle nuances of proof is not clear, but our system does expect them to.

A party may meet the burden of proof through direct evidence, circumstantial evidence, or a combination of both. *Direct evidence* is evidence that tends to directly prove something without any inferences required. For example, a defendant's statement to an informant that the defendant is willing to sell the defendant a gram of methamphetamine is direct evidence that the defendant is selling illegal narcotics. In contrast, *circumstantial evidence* requires some assumptions in order to prove something. A defendant's fingerprints on a murder weapon are circumstantial evidence that the defendant committed the murder. To convict the defendant based on this evidence would require the assumption that the defendant did not handle the weapon before or after the true murderer. A person may be convicted solely on circumstantial evidence, but it is often more difficult for the prosecution to meet its burden of proof without direct evidence.

Stages of the Trial

Every trial progresses through several discrete stages—our focus in this section.

Jury Selection   Typically, the first step when a case comes to trial is that a jury is chosen. Chapter 8 presents the process by which jurors are selected. There is a common misconception that the Constitution guarantees people the right to be tried by a jury of their peers. See the Matters of Ethics box, "A Jury of Your Peers? . . . Not Really," for a discussion of how the results of this initial stage of a trial are not generally what people think them to be. Once selected, the bailiff swears the jurors in. Contrary to popular belief, it is only in a few very high-profile cases that jurors are **sequestered**—that is, kept isolated from outside contact. As the trial begins, however, the judge will usually give jurors some general instructions and warn them not to discuss the case with anyone outside the jury until the case is complete.

Opening Statements   The trial begins with the opposing attorneys' **opening statements** to the jury. The lawyers introduce the case from their perspective and summarize the main evidence or main arguments they intend to put forward. Lawyers will attempt to establish an emotional connection with the jurors at the outset of the trial. In fact, opening statements can carry much influence and affect how the jury views the evidence that follows.[28] As a district attorney recently told one of this book's authors, "If I haven't convinced the jury by the end of my opening statement, I've lost the case." The prosecutor always makes

Matters *of* Ethics

A Jury of Your Peers? . . . Not Really

Most people believe the Constitution guarantees each of us the right to a trial by our peers—others of our own race, gender, or age. (And while we are thinking about it, what about socioeconomic status or sexual orientation?) They expect to be judged by people who are, essentially, their equals. This would be an incredibly tall order given that some of us are well educated, others not; some are wealthy, others not; some are White, others not. Then consider all the permutations of such variables. How hard would it be to find jurors who are similar to a 24-year-old, wealthy Latino defendant with a PhD? Needless to say, it would not be an easy or even reasonable task.

In fact, nowhere in the Constitution is it stated that criminal defendants are entitled to a jury of their peers. So where does this popular belief come from? The formal idea of "a jury of peers" likely originated with a Magna Carta provision giving noblemen the right to be judged, not by the king, but rather by other noblemen. Today this principle translates to "a jury of fellow citizens." Although it is not part of the Constitution, the U.S. Supreme Court has ruled it is necessary for juries to be made up of a "fair cross-section of the community." This is not driven by an interest in actually creating juries of one's peers, but rather by satisfying the Sixth Amendment right to an impartial jury. The assumption is that most people will have more similarities with a random sample of the population than they will have differences. And "like" people are more likely to give the defendant a fair shake; discrimination is less likely to occur. To this end, courts use a random method to create a jury pool that is reasonably representative of the community. It is from this broad cross-section of the community that the ultimate jury is constituted.

Given the process by which jury pools are created, the extent to which any defendant's characteristics are matched by those of the jurors would be a matter of random chance. The likelihood of selecting a jury that is biased in terms of race, gender, and age is reduced by this process, but the members of the chosen jury may not look at all like the defendant in a number of ways thought to be critical in jury decision making. How do poorly educated jurors perceive highly educated defendants? How do poorly educated, poor jurors perceive highly educated, rich defendants? Given that results of jury selection in the real world often eliminate as part of the process, for example, the most educated, how fair is such a system to highly educated defendants? Or, for that matter, to poorly educated defendants whose case largely rests on understanding testimony from expert witnesses regarding population genetics or complicated financial networks?

Two issues emerge from the above discussion. If fairness in the judicial process is a primary goal, is it ethical to maintain a jury selection process that may actually disadvantage some defendants? And how ethical is it for the criminal justice system to promote the image of the jury system as one in which a defendant's fate will be fairly judged by his "equals"?

OBSERVE → INVESTIGATE → UNDERSTAND

- Do you think the Constitution should be amended to guarantee the right to a jury of one's peers? If so, how could this be achieved in actual criminal trials?

- To what extent do you think the characteristics of jurors contribute to the racial and gender disparities we see in verdicts and sentences? How might the current jury selection process be changed to reduce these disparities?

- What would be the pros and cons of replacing our current jury system with professional juries? If a true objective is to create a jury of one's peers, what criteria could be used to hire professional jurors?

SOURCES: USLegal.com, s.v. "Jury pool." http://definitions.uslegal.com/j/jury-pool/ (retrieved June 11, 2015); FindLaw, "What Is a Jury of Peers?" http://criminal.findlaw.com/criminal-procedure/what-is-a-jury-of-peers.html (retrieved June 11, 2015); Alcibiades Bilzerian, "Jury of Our Peers?" *The Bilzerian Report*, February 8, 2013. http://thebilzerianreport.com/jury-of-our-peers/ (retrieved June 11, 2015).

---

the first opening statement. The defense may then choose to make its opening statement right away or wait until the prosecution's **case-in-chief,** or main body of evidence, is complete.

The Prosecution's Case-in-Chief   The prosecution's case-in-chief begins when the first witness is sworn in. The prosecution has already decided on a trial strategy that includes the order in which witnesses will appear, the questions they will be asked, and the evidence the attorney will attempt to include through their testimony. The prosecutor will ask the witness a series of questions. This is called **direct examination.** The defense attorney may object to questions that are improper–for example, if the prosecutor is *leading* the witness, or suggesting to the witness what her answers should be. Similarly, a defense objection may arise if the evidence is inadmissible hearsay. The judge will immediately *overrule* the objection and allow the question, or he or she may *sustain* the objection, in which case the prosecutor must rephrase the question or pursue a different line of inquiry.

Once the prosecutor finishes the direct examination, the defense may choose to question, or **cross-examine,** the witness. Now the prosecution may

case-in-chief
A stage in a criminal trial during which a party presents the main body of evidence.

direct examination
A stage in a trial when attorneys question their own witnesses.

cross-examination
A stage in a trial when attorneys question the opposing side's witnesses.

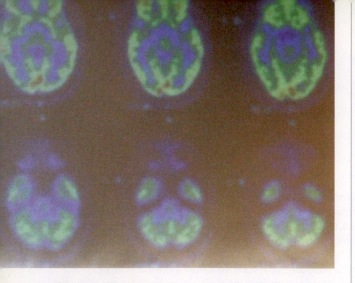

RealCrimeTech

BRAIN SCANS ON TRIAL

As a general rule, criminal courts find defendants criminally responsible—that is, guilty—when their criminal actions were the product of a so-called criminal mind. In other words, when the offender committed the crime, he had mens rea (see Chapter 4). Unfortunately, mens rea cannot be measured by a blood or urine test. Brain-scanning technology, however, can reveal abnormalities in the brain that may affect a person's ability to know that what he is doing is wrong or to truly understand the consequences of that behavior. An MRI (magnetic resonance imaging) scan can reveal a tumor that may put pressure on nearby brain structures that affects, for example, the individual's ability to control his emotions. A PET (positron emission tomography) scan shows actual brain activity and can pinpoint abnormalities of function in different parts of the brain.

In 1992, a New York court was first to allow PET scans into evidence at trial to support an insanity plea. The 65-year-old defendant, Herbert Weinstein, had strangled his wife and thrown her body from a 12th floor window to make the murder appear to be a suicide. When the judge ruled that the scans of Weinstein's brain were admissible, the prosecutors—apparently concerned about the influence that brain scan images would have on the jury—agreed to the lesser plea of manslaughter.

Even when admitted as evidence, however, abnormal brain scans do not always lead juries to reach a finding of no guilt or lesser guilt on the part of the defendant. Some court experts view this technology as junk science. In fact, the "jury"—that is, the scientific community—is still out on this issue.

SOURCE: J. Rojas-Burke, "PET Scans Advance as Tool in Insanity Defense," *Journal of Nuclear Medicine* 3, no. 1 (January 1993). http://jnm.snmjournals.org/cgi/content/citation/34/1/13N (retrieved July 24, 2011).

object to particular questions. The defense will often try to *impeach* the witness—that is, make the witness himself or his testimony appear unreliable. When the defense is finished, the prosecutor may choose to redirect, after which the defense may recross, and so on until both sides have finished with that particular witness. In some trials, this process may take many days. The witness is then excused, and the prosecutor calls the next witness. Despite what we see in movies and on TV or read in whodunits, surprise witnesses are rarely allowed. Through the discovery process, the defense almost always knows well in advance of the trial whom the prosecution will be calling to testify; and in fact, springing a last-minute witness can be grounds for dismissing a case.

Eventually, the prosecutor will conclude, or *rest*, his case. At this point, the defense attorney will almost always move to have the case dismissed; this is called a motion for a **directed verdict.** The judge now must determine whether the prosecution has carried its burden of proof—that is, whether it has proved every element of the criminal charges beyond a reasonable doubt. If not, the judge will dismiss the case without the defense ever having to make arguments of its own. Because of the protections against double jeopardy, the prosecution would be forbidden to try the defendant again on the same charges. In practice, few defense motions for dismissal are granted at this point.

The Defense's Case-in-Chief   The defense then begins its own case-in-chief by making opening statements if it did not already do so at the start of the trial. This proceeds very much like the prosecution's case, only this time it is the defense that conducts direct examination and the prosecution that cross-examines. Then the defense rests.

Whether or not to put the defendant on the stand to testify is a crucial decision that the defense must make. Certainly a defendant who can make a convincing and truthful case for her innocence on the stand can greatly increase her chances for being found not guilty. However, the Fifth Amendment guarantees the defendant's right not to be compelled to testify against herself—and self-incrimination is exactly what could happen if she takes the stand only to be subjected to a withering cross-examination by the prosecutor. Giving false testimony under such cross-examination would, in addition, constitute the crime of perjury, and it would be highly unethical for a defense attorney knowingly to encourage or allow his client to perjure herself. Furthermore, if a defendant does take the stand, evidence that would otherwise not be admissible may be used to impeach her or to attempt to prove that she is a liar.

On the other hand, the Fifth Amendment rule against self-incrimination forbids the prosecutor from drawing the jury's attention to the defendant's failure to testify. The judge must enforce this rule both as the case proceeds and in his instructions to the jury. Since the defense is not required to prove the defendant's innocence but needs only to create a reasonable doubt about her guilt, it is quite possible for the defendant to be found not guilty even though she never testified in her own defense.

Rebuttal   The next step is called *rebuttal*. Here the prosecution may call new witnesses or recall old ones in an attempt to refute the defense evidence. The defense can rebut as well, a procedure called the *surrebuttal*. The whole process once again continues until both sides are satisfied.

Closing Statements   Finally, it is time for *closing statements*. The attorneys cannot bring new evidence during this phase; they summarize and highlight what they have already presented to the jury. In some jurisdictions, the defense gives closing statements first, and then the prosecutor. In other places, the prosecutor goes first, followed by the defense. Finally, the prosecutor may speak once more. Some critics feel that this order gives the prosecution an unfair advantage because jurors' decisions are likely to be heavily influenced by the first and last words they hear. Others maintain that the heavy burden of proof the prosecution carries in criminal cases requires this particular order.

Jury Deliberations   Next, the judge gives the jury *directions*, including descriptions of exactly what facts they must find to convict the defendant on each count. Although most states have collections of jury instructions that judges may use, the attorneys may suggest or object to particular instructions, and sometimes these objections result in the jury's being recalled to hear new instructions. Defense attorneys' challenges to the judge's instructions can become the basis of appeals.

Once the jury goes off to deliberate, its deliberations are always in secret. Deliberations may take minutes or days, depending on the complexity of the case and the evidence. In most jurisdictions, the jury must reach a unanimous decision, although some jurisdictions permit convictions based on 10–2 or 9–3 votes. (See Chapter 8 for more details about juries.) If the jurors report that they are unable to reach a verdict, the judge will urge them to keep trying. If, however, a verdict is still impossible—if there is a **hung jury** in which one or more jurors absolutely refuse to vote for conviction—the judge will declare a **mistrial.** The prosecutor can then choose to try the case again. If she does, the whole process begins anew—an expensive and time-consuming outcome, to be sure. Often prosecutors decide not to retry such cases, taking the mistrial as a sign that the evidence is not strong enough to produce a conviction.

If the jury reaches a verdict, as it does in most cases, the jurors return to the courtroom, and the judge or the jury foreman reads the verdict. If the defendant is found not guilty of all charges, he is released from custody. If he is convicted, the judge may sentence him immediately or set a later date for a hearing to determine the sentence. Many jurisdictions allow victims or their families to speak during the sentencing hearing about how the crimes affected them. The effect of these statements on sentencing decisions has not been clearly established. See Chapter 10

directed verdict
A motion made by a defense attorney after the prosecution has rested its case; the motion asks for the judge to direct the jury to find the defendant not guilty due to the prosecution's failure to meet its burden of proof.

hung jury
A jury that is unable, after concerted effort, to reach a verdict.

mistrial
A judge's ruling that declares a trial invalid, often because of a hung jury.

▼ **Lawyer Making a Closing Statement**

During closing statements, attorneys summarize what they have presented to the jury.

for more on victim impact statements. Figure 9-1 illustrates how the criminal justice process works from arrest through trial.

Bifurcated Trials

In a **bifurcated trial,** different issues of the case are decided in separate hearings or trials. Since capital punishment was reinstated in the United States in 1976, capital cases have had to proceed in two separate phases—effectively, two separate trials.[29] In the *guilt phase,* the jury determines whether the prosecution proved, beyond a reasonable doubt, that the defendant committed a **capital crime,** an offense that is punishable by death. If so, the case then proceeds to a separate

bifurcated trial
A two-part trial in which different issues of the case are decided in separate hearings—for instance, one part deciding guilt and the second deciding the penalty.

capital crime
An offense punishable by execution.

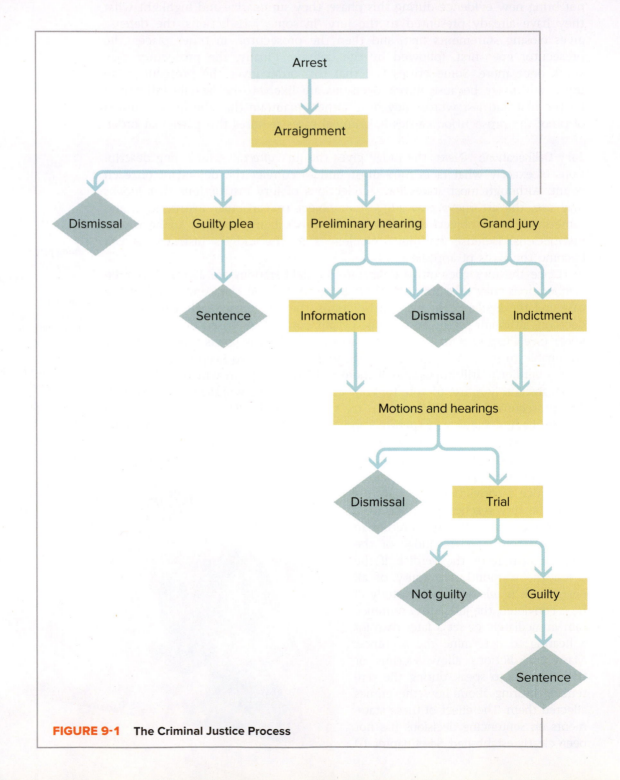

FIGURE 9-1   The Criminal Justice Process

penalty phase. During this sentencing phase, the jury will determine whether the capital defendant should be given the death penalty or life without the possibility of parole. Jurors are to arrive at their decision by considering evidence presented only during this second part of the trial. They are instructed to weigh mitigating factors against the aggravating factors presented by the prosecution during the penalty phase. In their deliberations, jurors might have to weigh, for example, the fact that the defendant was severely abused as a child against the fact that he tortured his victim before killing her.

In approximately 20 percent of states, when sanity is an issue, it is determined in separate proceedings after the jury has resolved the issue of guilt. In California and most other states, insanity trials proceed as follows. First, the defendant is put on trial to determine his guilt. If he is found guilty, then in a second, separate phase the jury decides whether he was insane at the time he committed the crime.

By the time a criminal case reaches its final outcome, several years may have passed since the crime was committed. Dozens of people will be involved in dealing with the case, and it may go through multiple courts. Many people criticize the size and complexity of the judicial component of the criminal justice system, as well as the time and money it takes to settle cases. Critics of jury trials in particular criticize the institution for the occasional instances when jurors apparently cannot render impartial verdicts, overcome racial or other prejudices, or fail to understand complex cases, especially those involving conspiracies, sophisticated economic crimes, or scientific evidence such as DNA tests.

Proposals are frequently made to streamline the system and reduce the number and kinds of resources involved. However, human beings are fallible, and the law is intricate. Any reduction in procedures, appeals, or resources will likely mean that more errors are made and that more innocent people will be subjected to criminal prosecution and punishment. What price are we willing to pay to ensure that justice is done?

SUMMARY

In any criminal justice system, the state brings to bear on an individual its immense coercive power—its ability to deprive the accused of liberty and even life. For that reason, the U.S. system of justice insists that due process and high standards of proof be observed legitimately to convict people of crimes and to punish them.

The U.S. Constitution and the other laws and rules governing the U.S. justice system afford criminal defendants significant safeguards. However, there are still limitations. For example, the Constitution's ban on excessive bail applies only to federal offenders (the states are under no obligation even to grant bail), and "excessive" means disproportionate to the gravity of the offense and to the risk of the defendant's fleeing, not to the defendant's ability to pay. The right to counsel does not mean that poor defendants (who constitute the vast majority of those who must face the criminal justice system) will receive more than perfunctory assistance from an overworked and underpaid public defender. Rules providing for a speedy trial by jury, excluding hearsay evidence, and guaranteeing against double jeopardy are sometimes surrounded by qualifications when they are put into practice in a specific case.

The rules of criminal process are very precise in order to protect the defendant's rights at every stage. These rules apply at arraignment during the determination of probable cause to proceed toward a trial; they apply while the prosecution and the defense are gathering and sharing information about the case through a process called discovery; and they are in play during negotiations over possible changes in venue and plea bargains.

Most criminal cases culminate not in a trial but in a plea bargain. However, if the defendant pleads not guilty and goes to trial, the courtroom procedures are also surrounded by many guarantees of due process. Finally, if a defendant is convicted of a capital crime, there must be a separate penalty phase in which the jury deliberates over whether to inflict the sentence of death.

OBSERVE → INVESTIGATE → UNDERSTAND

Review

Describe the Eighth Amendment right to bail.

- The Eighth Amendment states that bail cannot be excessive.
- The right to bail does not apply to states, only to the federal government.
- Courts may deny bail altogether in some cases.

List the rights afforded to criminal defendants by the Sixth Amendment.

- Criminal defendants have a right to counsel—to be represented by an attorney.
- Criminal defendants have a right to speedy trial—to be brought to trial within a reasonable amount of time.
- Criminal defendants have a right to a jury—to be tried by an impartial panel of their peers.
- Criminal defendants have a right to confront and cross-examine witnesses.

Describe the scope and limitations of the right against double jeopardy.

- Generally, the right against double jeopardy prohibits trying the same person more than once on the same charges.
- It does not apply in cases where a person is tried by multiple states, or by a state and by the federal government.
- It does not apply when a person is tried on charges different from the original charge.
- It does not prohibit a victim from filing a civil lawsuit after a person has been criminally tried.
- It does not apply in most cases when the jury fails to reach a verdict, or when there is a mistrial.

Identify the steps of the pretrial process.

- The suspect is placed under arrest.
- The suspect is booked.
- The prosecutor files a criminal complaint.
- The defendant is arraigned.
- A grand jury hearing or preliminary hearing is held.
- The grand jury files an indictment, or the prosecutor files an information.

- Attorneys make pretrial motions.
- Attorneys engage in plea bargaining—that is, making agreements by which defendants plead guilty to the original or reduced charges in exchange for lesser sentences.

Analyze the meaning of the due process clause.

- Generally, the due process clause means that laws and procedures must be fair.
- Procedural due process means that the process itself, and the components of that process, must be fair.
- Substantive due process means that the government cannot arbitrarily interfere with certain liberties.

Distinguish among the differing standards of proof used by the U.S. legal system.

- Beyond a reasonable doubt means that there is no reasonable conclusion other than that the defendant is guilty of the crimes with which he is charged. It is the amount of proof needed to convict a person of a crime.
- Clear and convincing evidence is the amount of evidence required for some defenses. It lies between preponderance of the evidence and beyond a reasonable doubt.
- Preponderance of the evidence is the amount of evidence needed to win a civil lawsuit. It means that there is at least slightly more evidence in that person's favor than against it.

Identify the stages of a criminal trial.

- A jury is sworn in.
- The attorneys make opening statements.
- The prosecutor presents the case-in-chief.
- The defense presents the case-in-chief.
- The attorneys conduct rebuttals and surrebuttals.
- The attorneys make their closing statements.
- The judge instructs the jury.
- The jury deliberates.
- The jury issues a verdict.
- The defendant is sentenced.

Key Terms

arraignment 283	burden of proof 289	cross-examination 291
bail 274	capital crime 294	direct examination 291
bench trial 279	case-in-chief 291	directed verdict 293
beyond a reasonable doubt 289	change of venue 279	discovery 284
bifurcated trial 294	clear and convincing evidence 290	double jeopardy 281
booking 282	complaint 282	due process clause 287

hearsay evidence 281

hung jury 293

indictment 284

information 284

mistrial 293

no contest (nolo contendere) 283

opening statements 290

plea 283

plea bargain 285

preliminary hearing 284

preponderance of the evidence 289

preventive detention 275

sequestered 290

Study Questions

1. The Eighth Amendment protects the right to
   a. bail.
   b. a jury trial.
   c. an attorney.
   d. confront witnesses.

2. Of the following rights, one that is *not* guaranteed by the Sixth Amendment is
   a. jury trial.
   b. counsel.
   c. speedy trial.
   d. due process.

3. Sam was tried and acquitted of theft in the state of New Jersey. Which of the following would the right against double jeopardy prohibit?
   a. The victim of the alleged theft sues Sam for damages.
   b. Sam is tried for theft by the state of New York.
   c. Sam is tried for the same theft by New Jersey when new evidence is found.
   d. Sam is tried for murder by New Jersey.

4. The usual sequence of events prior to a trial is
   a. complaint, arraignment, preliminary hearing, information.
   b. information, complaint, arraignment, preliminary hearing.
   c. preliminary hearing, information, complaint, arraignment.
   d. preliminary hearing, complaint, arraignment, information.

5. If there has been so much publicity about a case that a defendant believes she cannot receive a fair trial, her attorney will
   a. file a motion for a change of venue.
   b. try to create more positive publicity about the case.
   c. request that all charges be dropped.
   d. sequester the jury.

6. Due process basically means that government procedures and laws must be
   a. swift.
   b. expedient.
   c. fair.
   d. inexpensive.

7. Plea bargaining
   a. rarely occurs.
   b. can occur only until the trial begins.
   c. settles the vast majority of criminal cases.
   d. results in increased court workloads.

8. A prosecutor must always prove every element of a criminal case
   a. within a week.
   b. by clear and convincing evidence.
   c. beyond a reasonable doubt.
   d. beyond all doubt.

9. The part of a trial in which the prosecutor presents the evidence against the defendant is called the
   a. rebuttal.
   b. case-in-chief.
   c. surrebuttal.
   d. deliberation.

10. A bifurcated trial is one in which
    a. the judge acts as trier of fact.
    b. the defendant is found not guilty.
    c. the jury first determines guilt and then determines insanity or whether to impose a death sentence.
    d. there are two defendants.

Critical Thinking Questions

For further review, go to the LearnSmart study module for this chapter.

1. Describe the challenges of having a justice system that is fair yet workable. What are some ways that you would advocate balancing these goals?

2. Of the rights granted to criminal defendants by the Sixth, Eighth, and Fourteenth Amendments, which do you see as essential? Discuss whether there are other rights that you believe should be protected as well.

3. List as many points as you can in support of plea bargaining, and as many points as you can against it. Then evaluate the totality of these lists to decide whether plea bargaining is a necessary evil.

10 Sentencing

After reading this chapter, you should be able to:

- Describe the constitutional protections that affect sentencing.
- Describe the various goals of sentencing.
- Compare the different sentencing models.
- Review how a capital punishment trial proceeds.
- Outline controversies surrounding the death penalty.

Realities and Challenges

A Web of Sentencing Complexities

In April 2006, Sergeant Patrick Lett found himself facing U.S. District Judge William Steele on the federal charge of trafficking crack cocaine. Lett pleaded guilty. He had served 17 years in the army, including two

tours of duty in Iraq, and that day he wore his army uniform as he stood before Judge Steele. Lett testified that he had had difficulty since returning to Alabama from Iraq in April 2004. He explained that he had been dealing both with family struggles and with the emotional toll of seeing peers and friends killed in Iraq.[1]

In the spring of 2004, when Lett's car needed work, he had turned to his cousin for assistance. The cousin had offered to fix the car if Lett made seven deliveries of crack cocaine worth a total of $2,100. Lett had agreed. Unfortunately for Lett, he had sold some of the cocaine to an undercover federal agent. He was arrested shortly after he had reenlisted in October 2004 and just before he was about to redeploy to Iraq.[2]

Lett's luck turned around, though, when his old friend and law student Matthew Sinor attended his sentencing hearing. Judge Steele sentenced Lett to 5 years in prison. Sinor believed that there was a legal "safety valve" that was relevant to the case. It would allow a shorter sentence for defendants who had no prior record, played a minor role in the offense, and admitted their crime. Sinor wrote a letter to the judge arguing that this safety valve applied to Lett's case. Judge Steele agreed and entered a new sentence of 11 days, which was the time served. So, Lett would be free. However, the prosecutor appealed the revised sentence.[3]

The state won the initial appeal. A three-judge panel of the Eleventh U.S. Circuit Court of Appeals ruled that a district judge did not have the authority to change the sentence once it had been imposed. In essence, the appeals court was saying that Steele had failed to recognize his power to apply the safety valve and could not do so retroactively. However, an additional consideration was relevant: In the years since the original sentence, the sentencing context had changed. The U.S. Supreme Court had ruled in *United States v. Booker* (2005) that the U.S. Sentencing Guidelines were merely advisory and that judges were not bound to follow them. Therefore, on February 27, 2009, when the case came back to Judge Steele's court after the Eleventh Circuit decision and the U.S. Supreme Court's denial of certiorari, Steele agreed with the defense that he was now afforded the discretion to reinstate the 11-day time-served sentence.[4]

In this one case, we can see several factors in play that are related to ensuring justice in the sentencing process. First, Lett would surely have been stuck with the 5-year prison sentence had not his friend Sinor been aware of the safety valve provision. Lett's original defense attorney in fact thought that Lett should be happy with the 5-year sentence and found Sinor's interference "insulting." Clearly, we observe that the intricacies of sentencing law affect justice substantially in individual cases. Second, the severity of federal crack cocaine offenses is apparent in this case, with a first-time offender eligible for 5 years in prison. Third, we can see how for decades the U.S. Sentencing Guidelines firmly constrained what judges could do and that recent changes in the law have restored judicial discretion.

This chapter focuses on sentencing—the stage after a defendant has been found guilty but before the person begins punishment. We review the constitutional context of sentencing, the various goals and models of sentencing, and the ultimate sentence—the death penalty. We examine both historical and contemporary influences on sentencing.

CONTEXT FOR SENTENCING

When a judge in the United States sentences a defendant, she does so within a constitutional context. In this section we review the Eighth Amendment's protection against cruel and unusual punishments and Article I, Section 9's prohibition of wrongful conviction–that is, habeas corpus. These constitutional provisions confine sentencing behavior and provide a context for sentencing. We also review the presentence investigation because it provides guidance for the judge when sentencing.

Eighth Amendment Protection against Cruel and Unusual Punishment

As we saw in Chapter 9, the Eighth Amendment includes the bail requirement in federal cases. The remainder of the Eighth Amendment comprises the cruel and unusual punishments clause, which applies to all criminal cases. We may define a **cruel and unusual punishment** as a sentence or conditions of confinement that, within the time period of sentencing or confinement, go beyond what is acceptable to society.

cruel and unusual punishment
A sentence or conditions of confinement that, within the time period of sentencing or confinement, go beyond what is acceptable to society.

MYTH/REALITY

MYTH: What constitutes cruel and unusual punishment is objective and obvious.

REALITY: A practice considered cruel and unusual at one point in time might not be considered so in another.[5]

In interpreting the Eighth Amendment, the Supreme Court deems certain types of punishments to be unconstitutional. These include penalties that were considered cruel at the time the Eighth Amendment was ratified in 1791, as well as those that "evolving standards of decency"–meaning standards that have changed over time–have rejected.[6]

Even if a particular type of penalty is not cruel and unusual in and of itself, it may be cruel and unusual in terms of its application. Punishments that are excessive in relation to the seriousness of the offense may be unconstitutional, as may be punishments that outweigh the defendant's culpability. For example, in 2001 the Supreme Court ruled that it would violate the Eighth Amendment to execute an offender with mental retardation or someone who was under age 18 when the person committed the offense.[7] Further, even though the Court refuses to prohibit capital punishment altogether, it has found that the death penalty is unconstitutional for the offense of rape.[8] The Court also holds that it is cruel and unusual to punish a person for a *status* or a *characteristic,* such as being a drug addict, as opposed to a *behavior* such as possessing illegal drugs.[9] In 2010, the Court ruled that sentencing a juvenile to life without parole for a crime that is not murder violates the Eighth Amendment.[10] And in 2012, the Court also held that mandatory life without parole for juvenile offenders is unconstitutional.[11]

The Eighth Amendment also prohibits certain conditions of confinement when a person is sent to prison. For instance, prisoners may challenge extended use of solitary confinement, restricted diets, and conditions of prison overcrowding.

In general, the Court is hesitant to consider Eighth Amendment violations to the cruel and unusual punishment clause. At least under certain circumstances, the Court has allowed executions to continue and permitted life sentences for minor crimes, such as stealing $150 worth of videotapes, to stand under the three-strikes and other habitual offender laws discussed later in this chapter. Many prisoners are kept in solitary confinement for years, especially in "super-max" facilities (see Chapter 12).

habeas corpus
A written judicial order requiring that a prisoner's case be reviewed in court to determine if the person is being held unconstitutionally.

Habeas Corpus: Protection against Illegal Detainment

Article I, Section 9 of the Constitution provides a safeguard against illegal detainment. A writ of **habeas corpus** is a written judicial order requiring that a prisoner's case be reviewed in court to determine whether the individual is being held unconstitutionally. The concept of habeas corpus (Latin for "you have the body") was created to prevent the government from illegally detaining and punishing people. Although the phrase and the general legal concept behind it date back to medieval England 800 years ago, modern habeas law in the United States has evolved well past its original meaning.

Cases centering on issues of habeas corpus may take place in state or federal courts. There are no juries. The offender cannot argue that he is innocent of the crime, nor can he—in contrast to the situation in an ordinary appeal—raise ordinary procedural errors that he believes were made at trial. Instead, he must claim that some aspect of the trial itself, or of the sentence he received, violates one or more of his constitutional rights. For example, many people who are sentenced to death argue that the death penalty itself, or the method in which it is carried out, is cruel and unusual punishment that violates the Eighth Amendment. Defendants usually may bring a habeas case only after they have exhausted all their other remedies in a case.

Habeas cases have several advantages for offenders. They may help an individual who is accused or convicted of a crime to avoid injustice. They may permit a person who has been tried on state criminal charges, and whose case so far has been heard only by state courts, to have his case heard in a federal court, which may be more sympathetic to certain legal arguments. And habeas cases also may allow individuals who are detained for lengthy amounts of time without a trial, such as those who were suspected of terrorism after 9/11, to have their day in court.

Some observers have blamed habeas corpus for the often lengthy delays in implementing criminal sentences, especially the sentence of death. Among the most vocal critics was the late Chief Justice William Rehnquist, who denounced the "abuse" of habeas corpus petitions by death row inmates. Following the Court's ruling in *McCleskey v. Zant* (1991), Rehnquist led an increasingly conservative Court in imposing limits on further appeals.

Later Court rulings have required even tighter limits. In 1996 Congress passed the Anti-Terrorism and Effective Death Penalty Act, which, among other

▶ **Guantánamo Bay Prison**

The imprisonment of enemy combatants at Guantánamo Bay raises habeas corpus concerns. *Should the U.S. government be able to hold individuals it considers enemy combatants without telling them why they have been imprisoned? Why or why not?*

a case in point

Does Fairness Matter?

Albert Holland was convicted of murder and sentenced to death. He appealed to the Florida Supreme Court and lost, and the U.S. Supreme Court refused to hear his case. Florida provides lawyers to assist in habeas cases, however, so about a month after the U.S. Supreme Court refused to hear the appeal, attorney Bradley Collins was appointed to handle Holland's case.

Collins waited until 12 days before the 1-year limit for habeas cases was up to file a habeas petition in state court. As the case wound its way through the state system, Collins eventually stopped communicating with his client, despite Holland's repeated letters to him. Holland spent several years not knowing the status of his own case. The state courts denied Holland's habeas case. Once their decision was final, he had only 12 days to file an appeal in federal court. But Collins failed to tell Holland that the case had been decided, and Holland only discovered that fact for himself several weeks later—too late to file in federal court, according to federal law.

Holland filed a federal habeas petition anyway on his own behalf. The lower courts rejected it on the grounds that it was too late.

However, when his case finally reached the U.S. Supreme Court in 2010, a majority of the Court held that in some cases where "extraordinary circumstances" exist, fairness requires extensions to the 1-year deadline.

The Court stated that Collins's conduct had failed to meet attorneys' ethical standards. However, the justices did not go so far as to decide that Collins's delays and failures to communicate constituted "extraordinary circumstances." Instead, the Court sent the case back to a lower court to determine whether Holland would finally get the habeas hearing he had been seeking for years.

OBSERVE→INVESTIGATE→UNDERSTAND

- To what extent is it fair to make a defendant "pay" for the mistakes his lawyer made?
- Why are the courts very hesitant to overturn sentences or make other exceptions based on attorney misconduct?

SOURCE: *Holland v. Florida*, 130 S. Ct. 2549 (2010).

---

provisions, required that habeas cases be brought within 1 year after a defendant exhausts the regular appeals. However, some prisoners who have valid claims may be unable to pursue habeas relief quickly enough, especially because the Sixth Amendment right to an attorney does not apply to habeas cases, and inmates may therefore be forced to represent themselves. Few inmates have the ability to complete the extensive filing requirements in a timely manner without the help of an attorney. As discussed in "A Case in Point," the Supreme Court has recently indicated some willingness to show leniency to certain prisoners who fail to meet the 1-year deadline.[12]

Currently, approximately 20,000 habeas cases a year are filed in federal courts. About 1 percent of these are cases in which the defendant had been sentenced to death.[13]

Historically, there have been a few attempts to suspend the right to habeas corpus. During and shortly after the Civil War, Presidents Lincoln and Grant suspended it in selected locations. In Grant's case, the suspension was part of a federal effort to crush the Ku Klux Klan, a southern terrorist organization whose members resisted the empowerment of the newly freed slaves. The courts declared portions of these suspensions unconstitutional. More recently, Congress and President George W. Bush tried to deny habeas to suspected enemy combatants held at a U.S. military detention camp in Guantánamo Bay, Cuba. For the most part, the U.S. Supreme Court has held that denial of habeas rights to these suspected enemy combatants violates the Constitution. If an offender wins his habeas case, he does not go free. Usually he will get a new trial or a new sentence.

A variety of factors influence how a judge determines a sentence. The judge is expected to weigh the severity of the individual's offense, the prior record of the offender, any relevant statutory minimums, and any sentencing guidelines meant to guide judicial discretion. To provide information about the offender to the judge and to provide victim input, the probation department prepares a presentencing report.

Real Careers

and any supporting documentation that the officer needs. Usually I am assigned between two and eight collaterals a week.

What makes my work especially exciting and meaningful is that the federal district judges rely on my reports to sentence defendants. On multiple occasions I have been called into judges' chambers to discuss a case and be recognized for my work.

SEAN BERNHARD

Work location: Oklahoma City, Oklahoma

College(s): Southern Nazarene University (2006); University of Central Oklahoma (2008)

Major(s): Sociology with emphasis in Criminal Justice (BS); Criminal Justice Management and Administration (MA)

Job title: Probation Officer Assistant, U.S. Probation and Pretrial Services Office

Salary range for job like this: $35,000–$40,000

Time in job: 1.5 years

Work Responsibilities

The U.S. Probation and Pretrial Services Office in Oklahoma City has three main divisions: Presentence Investigations, Pretrial Services, and Supervision. I am currently in the Presentence Investigation Unit, which means that I write presentence reports that are used to assist the court in sentencing defendants. When writing these reports, I review investigative documents, apply sentencing guidelines, and interview defendants and family members to obtain and verify information, such as family history, education, and employment.

My other duties include completing misdemeanor reports for crimes committed on federal land, such as in national parks and military bases, and helping probation officers write collateral reports. Collateral reports, or "collaterals," are background checks for offenders who have committed a crime in my district but will be sentenced elsewhere in the United States. To write this report, I gather records

Why Criminal Justice?

Wanting to understand the techniques psychologists use to analyze criminals, I eagerly declared my major in criminal justice, with the hope of becoming an FBI agent. However, I later learned that being color blind disqualifies me from that job. Before graduation, my professors told me that the U.S. Probation Office was hiring probation officer assistants. I applied and was hired. There are tremendous opportunities for advancement and promotion within the U.S. Probation Office. For example, I was recently promoted to probation officer. U.S. probation officers can continue to be promoted within the agency to positions such as drug specialist, supervisor, deputy chief, and chief probation officer. Along with promotions come higher salaries, which can range from the government pay scale equivalent of GS-12 to GS-17.

Expectations and Realities of the Job

I did not expect that being a probation officer assistant at the U.S. Probation Office would also mean I have to help defendants cope with the emotional stress of undergoing trial and probation. For many defendants and their families, this is their first experience with the criminal justice system, and they do not know what to expect. Therefore, it is also my responsibility to serve as a resource and provide my knowledge of the pretrial and sentencing systems to those who need it. Helping others in this way has turned out to be one of the most rewarding aspects of my job.

My Advice to Students

Keep an open mind when seeking your first job. Apply for as many positions as possible. After several years in the field, you will find that it is possible to move to other careers within criminal justice. For instance, a career as a U.S. probation officer not only allows for promotion within the agency but also gives officers the tools and knowledge to transfer to other federal law enforcement agencies.

Presentence Investigation Report

presentence investigation (PSI) report

A report that provides the court with a basis for making a sentencing decision by including a personal history of the offender, often a victim impact statement, and a recommendation for sentencing.

A trial judge is supplied information for making a sentencing decision with respect to an offender in a **presentence investigation (PSI) report,** also called a *presentence report (PSR).* This document, usually prepared by a probation officer, contains a personal history of the offender, often a victim impact statement, and a sentencing recommendation. Personal data include the defendant's marital history, prior record (including both juvenile and adult arrest history), family background, educational history, employment history, physical and mental health issues, military service, and financial situation. The report covers the state's and the defendant's versions of the offense. The final sections contain an evaluation, sentencing information or guidelines, and finally a recommendation to the court.

What about the Victim?

Victim Impact Statements

Traditionally, victims of crime played only a small role in the process of trying and sentencing defendants. In fact, unless they were called as witnesses, victims would not get a chance to speak at all during a trial. If they did testify, they were limited as to what they could speak about. Victim impact statements are intended to give victims the opportunity to talk about the harms the defendant caused them and to allow these harms to be considered when the defendant is sentenced. The first victim impact statement in the United States was introduced in Fresno, California, in 1976. Today most jurisdictions allow victim impact statements.

Typically, these statements are made during a sentencing hearing. For example, after Zacarias Moussaoui was convicted for his participation in the September 11 terrorist attacks, 45 people whose family members died in the attacks made statements to the jury during the penalty phase of the trial.

The use of victim impact statements is controversial. Those who support their use argue that they give victims a voice in the criminal justice system, provide some closure to victims, and help ensure that sentences are proportionate to the harm caused by the criminal acts. Opponents, however, claim that victim impact statements can result in unfair and unequal treatment of some defendants and that use of the statements is therefore unconstitutional.

In 1991, the U.S. Supreme Court ruled on the constitutionality of victim impact statements. Pervis Payne had brutally murdered a woman and her 2-year-old daughter and seriously injured her 3-year-old son. During the penalty phase of his trial, the murdered woman's mother testified about the effects of the attacks on the surviving child, and the jury sentenced Payne to death. The Supreme Court held that the use of victim impact testimony does not constitute cruel and unusual punishment. However, the research suggests that victim impact statements tend to lead to harsher sentences.

OBSERVE → INVESTIGATE → UNDERSTAND

- Victim impact statements are supposed to help the victims of a crime achieve closure. Do you think they actually have this effect? Explain.

- What effect do you think victim impact statements have on sentences? Should they continue to be used? Why or why not?

SOURCES: Ellen K. Alexander and Janice Harris Lord, "Impact Statements: A Victim's Right to Speak, A Nation's Responsibility to Listen," July 15, 1994. www.ncjrs.gov/ovc_archives/reports/impact/welcome.html (retrieved July 26, 2011); *Payne v. Tennessee,* 501 U.S. 808 (1991); Bryan Myes and Edith Greene, "The Prejudicial Nature of Victim Impact Statements," *Psychology, Public Policy, and Law,* 10, no. 4 (2004): 492–515.

Originally, the purpose of the PSI was to assist the judge in deciding whether to grant probation. With the shift in philosophy in many states from rehabilitation to punishment, the personal aspects of the offender became less important than the crime itself. Where specific sentencing guidelines are used, the PSI focuses on the guidelines within which the crime belongs and on information that will be used to sentence the offender within the guidelines.[14]

Another document that the judge will consider when deciding on the appropriate sentence is the victim impact statement. "What about the Victim?" focuses on this report from the victim's side.

GOALS AND MODELS OF SENTENCING

Having pleaded guilty or been convicted through a trial, the defendant is sentenced by the court. The four goals of sentencing–retribution, deterrence, incapacitation, and rehabilitation–parallel the goals of punishment (see Chapter 11). Often the primary goal in sentencing varies by time period and crime. For example, one goal of sentencing may have gotten the most focus in the 1950s, but a different sentencing goal may have prevailed in the 1990s. In addition, violent offenses may call for different sentencing goals than property crimes.

retribution
A sentencing goal focused on punishing the convicted for the crime.

deterrence
A sentencing goal focused on convincing the offender or others not to commit crime.

incapacitation
A sentencing goal that aims to disable the offender from being able to commit future crimes.

Retribution focuses on punishing the convicted offender for the crime. A judge opts for this sentencing goal, for example, when saying, "Owing to the severity of your crime, you deserve to be punished with a year of incarceration." Because this goal is primarily punitive, there is little focus on whether or not the sentence will result in future criminal behavior. When society wishes retribution, it wants to punish or retaliate against a perceived harm. Often this sentencing goal is evidenced by language that the offender "deserved" the harsh sentence because of the severity of the crime. Retribution is a common goal when the crime is violent or particularly troubling to a community in some other way.

The various sentencing goals can be compared based on the time frame they address. For example, one sentencing goal may be primarily concerned with preventing crime in the future; another might be most interested in the crime itself or in the offender's past behavior. In the case of the sentencing goal of retribution, society is less interested in the degree to which the sentence will prevent future crime and more determined to make sure that the sentence affords society "just deserts"—in other words, that the punishment fits the crime.

A second goal is **deterrence,** which means that the sentence is meant to serve as a lesson that such behavior will not be tolerated in society and will be punished. Deterrence can have either a specific or a general focus. *Specific deterrence* is meant to convince the individual being sentenced not to offend again. *General deterrence* focuses on convincing other members of society that they should not commit crimes either. A goal of specific deterrence is clear when a judge says, "I am sentencing you to 2 years in prison so that you understand the severity of your crime and will not do it again." Some supporters of the death penalty use the idea of general deterrence to argue that if people know they can be executed for committing murder, they will be less likely to kill someone.

Deterrence is most focused on the future. The concern about influencing future behavior means that research can test whether sentences are effective in deterring crime. Supporters of the goal of using sentences to deter future criminal behavior note that punishment must be swift, certain, and severe to have the desired impact. Of course, for general deterrence to work, people need to be aware of the harsh sentence that has been imposed and that will also fall on them if they commit the same crime. Hence, deterrence relies on effective public education about the workings of the criminal justice system and sentencing policy. Research has generally been unable to find that tough sentencing results in general deterrence, although concentrated campaigns to raise awareness of strict sentences for certain types of crimes may be effective. For example, Project Safe Neighborhoods, a major initiative during the presidency of George W. Bush, was found to be effective at reducing gun crimes largely because it used a public campaign to educate people about the harsher prosecution of gun crimes.[15]

The third goal of sentencing, **incapacitation,** aims to disable offenders from committing future crimes. The most popular form of incapacitation is imprisonment. The assumption is that the offender will reoffend if he is not kept from doing so. Hence, like deterrence, incapacitation is a goal focused on affecting future behavior. Hence, as long as they are off the streets, the streets are deemed to be safe. Unlike deterrence, though, there is a resignation that perhaps the only way to keep offenders from committing future crimes is to "lock them up and throw away the key." Habitual offender policies, explained in detail later in this chapter, which focus on imprisoning individuals who have broken the law repeatedly, are based on a sentencing goal of incapacitation. The 1990s saw the rise of popularity of incapacitation as a sentencing goal as the tough-on-crime philosophy gained steam and the public began to feel that the only way to stop crime was to keep offenders behind bars for life. A judge is exercising the goal of incapacitation when she says, "Your past behavior illustrates that you are unwilling to end your life of crime; therefore, the best way to keep society safe from you is to sentence you to life in prison."

A final goal of sentencing, **rehabilitation,** concentrates on aiding an offender to learn skills to help prevent the person from reoffending. In the case of rehabilitation, it is assumed that an offender can change with assistance, and help is built into the sentence. For example, a sentence of probation with required attendance at drug counseling sessions allows for the possibility of rehabilitation. This sentencing goal was fairly popular in the United States from the 1950s through the 1970s. In that era, however, crime continued to rise, and the public began to lose faith in rehabilitation.

Today sentencing policy tends to reserve the goal of rehabilitation for specific crimes and perpetrators, and even then only in some jurisdictions. Thus in some states, such as California, first offenses for drug possession result in rehabilitation-oriented sentences, including probation and drug counseling. In terms of specific perpetrators, even though we now treat juvenile offenders more like adult offenders in many ways, the criminal justice system still generally views young people as being able to be rehabilitated. As with most criminal justice policies, these rehabilitation-oriented sentencing commitments vary by state.

A sentence rarely encompasses only one goal. For example, if a judge wishes both to punish an offender for her actions and to make sure that she will not be able to commit a future crime for a certain period of time, her sentence of 5 years in prison likely embodies the judge's dual goals of retribution and incapacitation. See the Key Concepts table below for a comparison of the goals of sentencing.

Related to the goals of sentencing are different sentencing models, a topic to which we now turn.

▲ **Prisoner at Work**

Some inmates receive vocational training. *What goal of sentencing would encourage vocational training in prisons?*

rehabilitation

A sentencing goal focused on aiding an offender to learn skills to help prevent the person from reoffending.

Indeterminate Sentences

With an **indeterminate sentence,** the offender is given a range of time he can serve, such as 5 to 7 years, that is dependent on his behavior while in prison. The assumption is that during that time, rehabilitation will occur, and the offender will be motivated to change if he can reduce his sentence by doing so. Indeterminate sentences were much more common in the 1960s, when the primary goal of the criminal justice system was rehabilitation. Since the 1980s, however, the dominant philosophy of the criminal justice

indeterminate sentence

A sentence in which the offender is given a range of time he can serve, such as 5 to 7 years, dependent on his behavior while in prison.

KEY CONCEPTS   **Goals of Sentencing**

What are the positives and negatives of each of the sentencing goals?

Retribution	Focused on punishment that matches the crime
Deterrence	Focused on preventing future crime from occurring by convincing the offender (specific) and others (general) that punishment will be swift, severe, and certain
Incapacitation	Focused on preventing future offenses, usually by imprisoning the offender for long periods of time
Rehabilitation	Focused on preventing future crime by helping the offender change his life

system has been punishment, and indeterminate sentences are much less common because they are viewed as too lenient.

Determinate Sentences

determinate sentence
A sentence that specifies a precise period of time that the offender must serve.

A **determinate sentence** indicates a precise period of time that the offender must serve. For example, a sentence of 7 years in prison is a determinate sentence. However, a 7-year sentence does not mean that the offender will serve the entire 7 years. Rather, prisoners often receive good-time credits that ultimately reduce their stay in prison.

Beginning in the 1980s, questions arose about how judges determine sentences. In particular, studies found that Blacks received harsher sentences than their White counterparts for similar crimes. In addition, there were complaints that judges' use of discretion resulted in too-lenient sentences. A variety of legislative interventions resulted to limit judges' ability to sentence as they felt was just. Today determinate sentences are more common than indeterminate sentences, as are statutory minimums, mandatory sentences, and sentencing guidelines.

Sentencing Guidelines and Mandatory Sentences

presumptive sentencing model
A sentencing model assuming that judges should sentence within sentencing guidelines, or ranges specified for particular charges.

statutory minimum
The minimum sentence set by a legislature that must be imposed for a particular crime.

Presumptive sentencing models assume that judges should sentence within *sentencing guidelines*, or ranges specified for particular charges. Legislatures enacted statutory minimums to reduce both judicial discretion and sentencing disparity. A **statutory minimum** is established when a legislature sets a minimum sentence that must be imposed for a particular crime; for example, a statutory minimum might stipulate that an individual convicted of aggravated assault must be sentenced to at least 1 year in prison. Another name for statutory minimum is *mandatory minimum.*

There has been a backlash against mandatory minimums. For instance, a nonprofit organization called Families Against Mandatory Minimums maintains that many drug offenses result in mandatory minimum sentences because judges are no longer allowed to adjust the sentence to fit the offender's particular role in a crime. Instead, judges must impose the minimum, with little regard for the specific circumstances. As discussed in the Matters of Ethics box on page 312, sometimes even judges believe mandatory sentences are unjust.

Both the states and the federal government have established sentencing guidelines. The motives for establishing these guidelines have included ensuring equal treatment, lessening racial disparity, and reducing a perceived leniency of federal judges.

Since sentencing guidelines have now been in place for decades, researchers are beginning to get a clear picture of the degree to which the guidelines have produced the desired results. Research has found that with respect to racial disparity, sentencing differentials have not been eliminated. In fact, similarly situated federal drug offenders of different races continue to receive different sentences. White offenders still receive lighter sentences than their Black and Latino counterparts, with Latino offenders getting the harshest sentences of all.[16] Nor do sentencing guidelines appear to reduce sex disparities in sentences. Recent research in Pennsylvania comparing sentences in time periods with and without sentencing guidelines found that female offenders were still receiving more lenient sentences than similar male offenders.[17]

MYTH/REALITY

MYTH: Drug offenders are treated leniently by the criminal justice system.

REALITY: Sentences for drug offenses increased greatly with the move to legislative mandatory minimums and sentencing guidelines that reduced judicial discretion.[18]

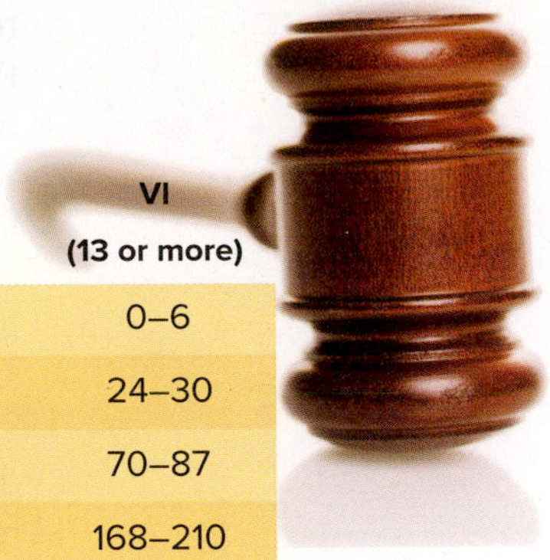

Offense Level	Criminal History Category (Criminal History Points)					
	I (0 or 1)	II (2 or 3)	III (4, 5, 6)	IV (7, 8, 9)	V (10, 11, 12)	VI (13 or more)
1	0–6	0–6	0–6	0–6	0–6	0–6
10	6–12	8–14	10–16	15–21	21–27	24–30
20	33–41	37–46	41–51	51–63	63–78	70–87
30	97–121	108–135	121–151	135–168	151–188	168–210
40	292–365	324–405	360–Life	360–Life	360–Life	360–Life
43	Life	Life	Life	Life	Life	Life

FIGURE 10-1   USSC Sentencing Guidelines Table in Months

Congress established the U.S. Sentencing Commission (USSC) in 1984 to create sentencing guidelines for federal offenses. These guidelines took effect in January 1989, and as of 2011 more than 1 million defendants had been sentenced under the guidelines. Each federal judge is given a USSC table that classifies all federal crimes into 43 offense categories and classifies the past behavior of the defendant into 6 criminal history categories. The judge is expected to sentence the offender within the guideline indicated where the two relevant categories intersect.[19] See Figure 10-1, "USSC Sentencing Guidelines Table," to understand this process.

A variety of constitutional challenges have been levied against the guidelines through the years, but the U.S. Supreme Court has repeatedly found them to be constitutional. The first significant high court challenge came in January 2005 with the ruling in *United States v. Booker*, but the background to this decision begins a few years earlier. Beginning in 2000, the Supreme Court had decided a series of cases that affected how sentencing guidelines could be used. The Court had held that whenever a judge relies on certain facts to give a defendant a sentence longer than the guidelines' maximum, those facts must be determined by the *jury* to be true beyond a reasonable doubt. If the judge rather than the jury decided those facts to be true, it would violate the defendant's Sixth Amendment rights. This rule applied in both state and federal cases. In *United States v. Booker* (2005), however, the Court held that this rule means that the federal sentencing guidelines are no longer mandatory and that appeals courts can review sentences to determine whether they are reasonable.[20] The federal guidelines are still important, though, because a sentence that falls within the guidelines will usually be considered reasonable.

Although a stated objective of the USSC sentencing guidelines was to ensure similar treatment for like offenders, questions quickly surfaced with respect to the recommended sentences for the possession of powder cocaine and crack cocaine. The original guidelines recommended a sentence 100 times harsher for crack cocaine than for powder cocaine. In other words, possession of 5 grams of crack cocaine brought the same sentence as possession of 500 grams of powder cocaine. Concerns arose owing to the fact that African Americans were much more likely to possess crack than powdered cocaine, and vice versa for Whites.

Supporters of these guidelines and of Congress's harsh mandatory minimum sentence argued that the longer sentences for crack cocaine were warranted because both the use of crack cocaine and the act of dealing in that drug resulted in more violence than did use of and trafficking in powder cocaine. Recently, however, such claims have been invalidated. For example, surveys of prison inmates show that offenders who had been under the influence of alcohol when they committed their crimes were more likely to be incarcerated for violent offenses than were those who had been using crack or powder cocaine. Furthermore, individuals under the influence of crack were no more likely to be incarcerated for a violent offense than were those under the influence of powder cocaine at the time of the offense.[21]

In November 2007 the USSC recommended a reduction in the sentencing disparity that would change the average sentence for crack offenders from 121 months to 106 months.[22] In December 2007, the USSC voted unanimously to make sentenced crack cocaine offenders eligible for reduced sentences.[23] In 2011, the USSC was still considering whether the revised sentencing guidelines should be made retroactive—that is, whether they should apply to people who had already been sentenced. If the guidelines were made retroactive, nearly 13,000 inmates would be eligible for reduced sentences.[24]

The Supreme Court also seems to have become increasingly troubled by the racial disparity so often found in cocaine sentencing. The Court ruled in December 2007 that to address this problem, federal district judges could use their discretion to sentence a crack cocaine offender to less than the recommended guidelines. Taking the recent cases together, the Supreme Court is clearly signaling that federal judges should consult the USSC guidelines but are not strictly bound by them.[25]

Even in some nondrug cases, judges occasionally deviate from mandatory sentencing guidelines when they feel that imposing the mandatory minimum would be unfair. One of these cases is discussed in the "Matters of Ethics" box.

The fate of some federal mandatory minimum sentencing laws remains uncertain after the 2015 Supreme Court decision in *Johnson v. United States*. In that case, the Court invalidated a law requiring increased sentences for firearms convictions when the defendant has previous convictions for violent crimes. The basis of the decision was that the law was unconstitutionally vague because it did not define "violent."

Consecutive and Concurrent Sentences

Defendants are frequently convicted of more than one crime at once. For example, someone who robs a convenience store and hits the clerk during the process of the robbery, and who then puts up a fight when police arrive, might be convicted of armed robbery, assault and battery, being a felon in possession of firearms, and resisting arrest—all separate offenses stemming from the same chain of events. People who are found guilty of more than one crime may be given **consecutive sentences,** meaning that all of one sentence must be served before the next one begins. Alternatively, they may receive **concurrent sentences,** meaning that the time they serve counts for more than one sentence at once. If a defendant is given consecutive sentences for 3, 5, and 10 years, he will spend a total of 18 years in prison. But if he is given concurrent sentences for 3, 5, and 10 years, he will spend a total of only 10 years in prison.

In some states, the law specifies when sentences are to be consecutive and when they must be concurrent; in other states, the decision is left to the judge's discretion. In either situation, the nature of the crimes, their relationship (if any) to one another, and the defendant's criminal history may be considered, as may be the existence of mitigating circumstances. In addition, when defendants enter plea bargaining agreements, one component of those agreements might be that their sentences run concurrently rather than consecutively.

consecutive sentences
Sentences that are served in sequence instead of at the same time.

concurrent sentences
Sentences that are served at the same time.

In cases in which defendants are convicted of multiple crimes, it is possible that some of their sentences will run concurrently but others will be consecutive. This arrangement, however, can complicate the determination of matters like parole eligibility.

Controversy surrounds the decision of whether to sentence concurrently or consecutively. Some individuals and groups (such as victim advocates) say that concurrent sentences are not fair in that they dilute the importance of each individual crime committed, and those with this point of view also argue that concurrent sentences serve none of the goals of punishment. On the opposite side of the debate are those who assert that consecutive sentences contribute to prison overcrowding and may result in an offender's serving extremely long sentences for what essentially was a single chain of events.

Preventive Detention

By the early 1900s, most states had enacted some form of **habitual offender statute,** a law authorizing enhanced sentences for repeat offenders, called **recidivists,** who had been previously convicted of certain offenses. In recent decades there has been a move to identify society's most dangerous offenders and to use laws that prevent these individuals from committing future crimes by imposing lengthy incarceration in prison or in a secure mental health facility. These laws are collectively called **preventive detention laws.** The individuals whom the laws target have been convicted a number of times, thus demonstrating a tendency to relapse into criminal activity after they have been punished. California's 1994 "three strikes, you're out" law, for example, doubles the sentence of felons who have previously been convicted of a serious crime and calls for a 25 years to life sentence for felons with two previous violent felony convictions—even if the third crime is not violent.

The California law is based on the premise that a three-time offender has demonstrated an inability or unwillingness to conform to the laws of society and should be incarcerated for a long time, perhaps even for life, for the better protection of the public. Rehabilitation of recidivists is not the goal.[26] Washington and Georgia have even passed "two-strikes" laws that mandate a life sentence for certain offenders on their second conviction. California's three-strikes law, though, is the broadest and most frequently used, and it is generally considered the toughest sentencing policy; for example, the third "strike" need not even be a violent crime. Yet California's rigorous three-strikes policy has not been found to affect crime rates to any greater degree than do other states' more limited laws.[27] Research shows that habitual offender laws are more often applied to racial and ethnic minorities—and therefore increase sentencing disparity.[28]

Repeat sex offenders have been targeted by special sentencing provisions that began with the *sexual psychopath laws,* first enacted in 1937 in Michigan. By 1975, more than half the states had *mentally disordered sex offender (MDSO) laws.* These laws allowed the state to confine sex offenders with a mental disease or defect for indefinite periods of time, dependent on treatment needs, in a secure psychiatric facility rather than a prison. The popularity of these laws declined as fixed-term sentencing gained acceptance. More recently, however, calls for a return to indeterminate periods of incarceration have arisen due to the results of society's experience with fixed sentences. Many violent sex offenders with fixed sentences are released back into the community, and many of them reoffend.

Today, through a new wave of sex offender statutes, most states allow the period of incarceration to be extended beyond that of the original court-mandated sentence because of fear that these criminals, once released, will reoffend. Under preventive detention laws, incarceration in a secure psychiatric facility can follow completion of a sentence in prison, or incarceration in prison can be extended

habitual offender statute
A law that creates enhanced penalties for repeat offenders.

recidivist
An offender who has been previously convicted of crimes.

preventive detention laws
Legislation that allows the criminal justice system to prevent offenders from committing future crimes by lengthy incarceration in prison or secure mental health facilities.

Matters *of* Ethics

When Is a Mandatory Minimum Sentence Unjust?

In December 2014, Kevin Rojano-Nieto was convicted of sodomizing a three-year-old relative. Because of the serious nature of the crime, no real controversy existed over his conviction. But in April of the following year, when it was time for Rojano-Nieto to receive his sentence, the judge did something unusual. Instead of sentencing Rojano-Nieto to 25 years to life in prison, as required for this kind of crime by California's mandatory sentencing law, the judge handed down a sentence of only 10 years.

The judge, M. Marc Kelly, gave several reasons for this rare decision. The foremost reason, he said, was that under the circumstances, a 25-year sentence would be cruel and unusual punishment. He said that as a judge, his primary responsibility was to uphold the Constitution, and therefore this deviation from the mandatory sentence was necessary.

According to Judge Kelly, his decision was influenced by Rojano-Nieto's youth; the defendant was only 19 at the time of the crime.

He'd had a difficult childhood, including an abusive father. In addition, Rojano-Nieto had cooperated fully in the investigation, had admitted his responsibility, and had expressed considerable remorse for what he had done. Finally, Rojano-Nieto's mother—who was also the victim's mother—made an impassioned plea for leniency for her son.

Although Judge Kelly continued to stand by his decision, many people were outraged by the sentence. An online petition to appeal the sentence quickly attracted tens of thousands of signatures, and in fact the district attorney did appeal. At the same time, members of the community and three county supervisors began an effort to remove Judge Kelly from the bench.

OBSERVE → INVESTIGATE → UNDERSTAND

- Did Judge Kelly overstep his powers when he declined to impose the mandatory minimum sentence? Or was he right in asserting that his duty to uphold the Constitution was stronger?

- Do you agree that the mandatory minimum sentence was unjust in this case? What facts would you want to know before making that decision?

- In general, are mandatory sentences a good way of ensuring equal punishments and making sure offenders receive appropriate punishments?

SOURCES: Kelly Puente, "O.C. Judge M. Marc Kelly Makes Statement for First Time Attacking Petition to Recall Him after Child Rapist's Controversial Sentencing," *Orange County Register*, May 12, 2015. www.ocregister.com/articles/judge-661465-kelly-petition.html (retrieved June 9, 2015); Michael Martinez, "California Judge Faces Recall Try over Sentence in Child Rape Case," *CNN*, April 10, 2015. www.cnn.com/2015/04/09/us/california-judge-sentencing-child-sodomy-recall-effort/ (retrieved June 9, 2015).

beyond what would have been given for a particular crime had it been the offender's first or second offense. The individual is confined not for what he did but rather to prevent what he is believed likely to do in the future.

The Washington State legislature was first to enact this kind of law. In 1990, the state's lawmakers passed the Sexually Violent Predator (SVP) Law in response to a number of highly publicized sex crimes.[29] As of 2007, 19 states have provisions for civilly committing dangerous sex offenders.[30] Under these civil commitment laws, individuals can be incarcerated in secure psychiatric facilities for as long as they are deemed to present a danger to others.

Even though preventive detention laws are popular with the general public, their future is uncertain. Under existing law, sexual predators can be freed only after they have been effectively "cured." But most psychiatrists consider sexual predation to be an antisocial behavior rather than a mental illness and therefore argue that it cannot be treated. The Washington State Psychiatric Association, for example, has called for the repeal of that state's sexual predator law. The association has gone on record to assert that "[s]exual predation in and of itself does not define a mental illness. It defines criminal conduct."[31] Except when a person is mentally ill and poses a danger to self or

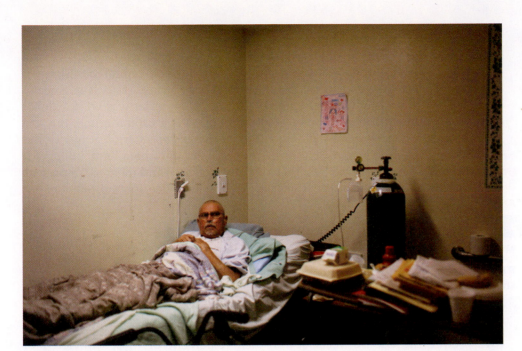

others, preventive detention is unconstitutional. Washington's psychiatrists have raised the claim that sexually violent predator (SVP) laws give offenders what is tantamount to a sentence of life imprisonment. Thus far, however, these statutes have withstood judicial challenges to their constitutionality.

Another problematic issue is that if society uses chronic recidivism as the basis for defining a mental abnormality as in the case of SVP, the public may well call for the preventive detention of individuals who perpetrate other repeated felonies as well. Men who repeatedly batter their partners might then qualify for terms of civil commitment beyond the length of their criminal penalties. If a sexually violent predator is considered mentally ill, why is a batterer—or, for that matter, a professional thief—not given the same status? These are matters that future courts are likely to face.

Even though such issues may prompt us to question the fairness of preventive detention laws, current legislatures seem inclined toward accepting them. In 1994, the California legislature passed a "one strike rape bill," assigning a penalty of 25 years to life for sexual assaults involving torture, kidnapping, or burglary with intent to commit rape. Repeat offender laws are controversial, but they remain popular. The public considers them the remedy for the persistent problem of offenders who have not been, and as some suggest cannot be, effectively treated.

Habitual offender laws and preventive detention contain the threat of crime by incapacitating criminals for extended periods of time. However, they come at a high financial cost. It remains to be seen how long the public will be able to bear the expense of putting more criminals in prison for longer terms. To illustrate, older inmates have the same needs as older people in the general population. Health care needs alone raise annual costs for older inmates threefold over those for younger inmates. The RAND Corporation studied costs associated with "three strikes, you're out" legislation in California and concluded that unless there are changes to its implementation, the result for the state will be "three strikes, and we're broke."[32] On top of these troubling facts, a 2002 evaluation of the effects of this law concluded that it had played only a minimal role in the state's declining crime rate.[33] Nonetheless, this law continues to enjoy the support of the majority of California voters—another sign that what society is learning about crime is not being translated into laws that might better control it.

CAPITAL PUNISHMENT

capital crime
An offense punishable by execution.

A **capital crime** is an offense punishable by execution. The U.S. military, the federal government, and 31 states currently provide for capital punishment, but the offenses that constitute capital crimes vary. Most state laws specify that first-degree murder (which essentially means the murder was willful, deliberate, and premeditated) with special circumstances is a capital crime, but the specific circumstances differ by state.[34] *Special circumstances* are features of the crime that include torturing victims, lying in wait for them, and killing for financial gain. Jurors consider whether these special circumstances were present when deciding whether death is an appropriate sentence for the offender.

> **MYTH/REALITY**
>
> **MYTH:** Most death row inmates will be executed eventually.
>
> **REALITY:** On average, fewer than 2 percent of condemned inmates are executed in any given year. The vast majority will never be executed.[35]

Today, very few people convicted of homicide find their way onto death row.[36] Over the last 30 years, fewer than 3 percent of those convicted of murder in the United States received the death penalty.[37] We might assume that this 3 percent represents the "worst of the worst," but that is not necessarily true. For example, fewer than half of the 11 serial murderers convicted in 2004 were sentenced to death.[38]

In 2014, 35 people were executed in the United States for committing capital crimes (Figure 10-2). Approximately 34 percent of offenders put to death were White, 51 percent were Black, and 14 percent were Latino. As for the race of the murder victims, almost 70 percent of the victims were White,[39] whereas Whites comprised only 44 percent of all murder victims nationally.[40] Such discrepancy has led some to argue that capital punishment trials are most likely to occur when the victim is White.[41] There are regional differences in the administration of capital punishment as well. By far, the South has executed

▶ **The Last Public Hanging**

More than 15,000 people witnessed this execution in 1936.

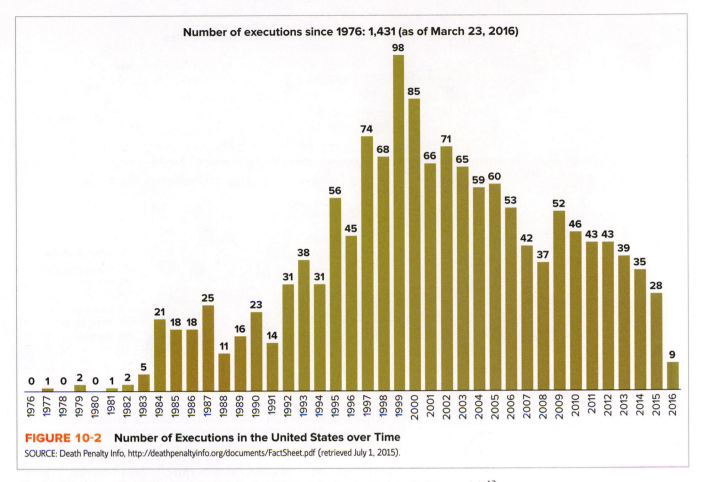

Number of executions since 1976: 1,431 (as of March 23, 2016)

FIGURE 10-2   **Number of Executions in the United States over Time**
SOURCE: Death Penalty Info, http://deathpenaltyinfo.org/documents/FactSheet.pdf (retrieved July 1, 2015).

the most individuals (1,155) and the Northeast has executed the least (4).[42] By the end of 2015, there were 2,959 people on death row in the United States;[43] only 56 of them were women.

Rather than having their death sentences carried out, death row inmates tend to die in prison of natural causes, to commit suicide, to have their cases overturned, or to have their sentences reduced to life imprisonment.[44] Even though the majority of states have a death penalty statute, most have not executed anyone in decades. These variations across states have caused many to question the fairness of laws that define capital crimes and apply capital sentences differently. One glaring example was in 2008 when two men were on Louisiana's death row for crimes that did not include killing someone. One of those men, Patrick Kennedy, had his death sentence overruled by the U.S. Supreme Court in June 2008. In *Kennedy v. Louisiana* (2008), the Court ruled that Louisiana's law making the rape of a child a crime punishable by death was unconstitutional and indicated that the death penalty would be unconstitutional in any instance in which the offender did not kill the victim.[45]

The Supreme Court and Capital Punishment

European settlers, particularly those from England, brought the death penalty with them to the American colonies. Early U.S. Supreme Court decisions upheld different methods of execution. In *Wilkerson v. Utah* (1878), the Court rejected the claim that firing squads constituted cruel and unusual punishment, and in *In re Kemmler* (1890), the Court ruled similarly on electrocution. Not until the early 1970s did the U.S. Supreme Court rule against any state for its administration of capital punishment.

The "arbitrary and capricious" manner in which death sentences were imposed prior to 1972 led the U.S. Supreme Court to strike down state and

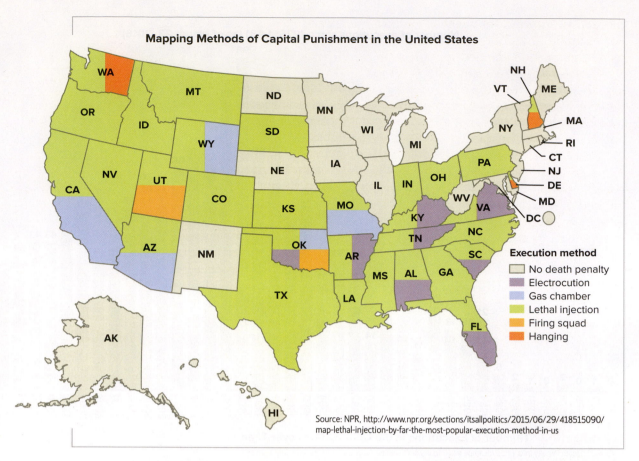

Mapping Methods of Capital Punishment in the United States

Execution method
- No death penalty
- Electrocution
- Gas chamber
- Lethal injection
- Firing squad
- Hanging

Source: NPR, http://www.npr.org/sections/itsallpolitics/2015/06/29/418515090/map-lethal-injection-by-far-the-most-popular-execution-method-in-us

federal capital punishment laws in effect at the time.[46] An immediate consequence of this decision, *Furman v. Georgia* (1972), was that the death sentences of more than 600 condemned inmates were commuted to life imprisonment. In *Furman*, the Court required that states must have a two-stage trial. Guilt or innocence must be decided first, and only then must the penalty phase be conducted. Because the Court did not rule that the death penalty itself was unconstitutional, but rather that the specific laws determining how the penalty would be administered were, states were permitted to redraft their laws to make them constitutionally acceptable. In *Gregg v. Georgia* (1976), the U.S. Supreme Court upheld a series of new death penalty laws that included the new two-stage procedure (see the discussion of bifurcated trials in Chapter 9). The following year, under these new laws, Utah became the first state to resume executing condemned inmates.

Another important capital punishment case again involved Georgia. In *McCleskey v. Kemp* (1987), death penalty opponents argued that Georgia's capital punishment law was racially discriminatory. Attorneys for Warren McCleskey, an African American man convicted of killing a White police officer, presented a wide variety of systematic evidence illustrating racial disparity in how defendants were treated. In particular, the attorneys pointed out that defendants who killed White people were 11 times more likely to receive the death penalty. The Court agreed that the evidence supported the attorneys' overall claims, but the justices ruled that for McCleskey to win on the question of whether his equal protection rights were violated, he would have to prove racial discrimination in his individual case. In other words, it was not enough to show overall racial disparities. Instead, petitioner McCleskey needed to illustrate that he *personally* had been subjected to racial discrimination.[47]

In recent years, the Supreme Court has primarily dealt with issues of who should and should not be eligible for capital punishment and questions about the constitutionality of specific methods of execution. For example, the Court has ruled that individuals with mental retardation–defined in most states as those with an IQ lower than 70–cannot be executed.[48] The Court has also ruled that juveniles cannot be executed. In *Roper v. Simmons* (2005), the Court held that individuals who were under 18 years of age when they killed someone could not be sentenced to the death penalty.

Every U.S. jurisdiction that has a death penalty (31 states, the U.S. military courts, and the federal government) authorizes lethal injection as the primary method of execution. In 16 of those states, however, an alternative method may be chosen. Depending on the state these methods are electrocution, gas chamber, hanging, and firing squad. In recent years, even though it is the most widely used method of execution, lethal injection has come under scrutiny by the courts. Many jurisdictions use what is referred to as a *three-drug cocktail*. The first drug is administered to make the process painless by rendering the inmate unconscious, the second drug paralyzes the individual, and the third causes death by stopping the heart. If, however, the first (anesthetic/sedative) drug fails to work properly, possibly because it is not administered properly, the inmate can experience excruciating pain from the drug that stops the heart–but she will not be able to indicate this, having been paralyzed by the second drug. Prisoners in Kentucky sought to have lethal injection deemed a violation of the Eighth Amendment because of this. In *Baze v. Rees* (2008), however, the Court upheld the use of lethal injection noting there is a risk of pain in even the most humane executions. Nonetheless, the issue with a three-drug protocol persists. California, for example, has not executed anyone since 2006 as a result. It may be that California will follow Ohio and Washington as states that moved to a single-drug protocol whereby only the first (sedative) drug is used–in lethal dosage. This is basically the approach veterinarians use to euthanize animals.[49]

A similar issue was recently raised by four death row inmates in Oklahoma in which the use of a particular drug, midazolam, was challenged. This drug, normally used to treat anxiety, is not a barbiturate like the sedatives generally used in the three-drug protocol. Increasingly, however, the barbiturate drugs are difficult, if not impossible, for states to obtain as manufacturers are refusing to make them available for the purpose of executions. As a result, some states have turned to midazolam to replace the conventional sedatives (like pentobarbital). However, following three apparently painful executions, including the botched execution of Clayton Lockett in 2014 in Oklahoma, the use of midazolam came into question. But similar to the ruling in the Kentucky case, the Court upheld the use of the drug in *Glossip v. Gross* (2015), the majority arguing that the death row inmates did not sufficiently make their case against midazolam–even though it has not been approved by the FDA as a drug to reliably render a person unconscious.[50]

The Capital Punishment Trial

As we saw in Chapter 9, ever since capital punishment was reinstated in 1976, bifurcated trials have been used in capital cases–one trial to determine guilt, and,

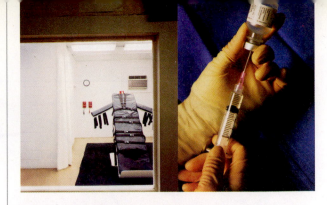

Real Crime Tech

TECHNOLOGY CHANGES THE DEATH PENALTY

The means of administering the death penalty have changed over time, partly because of technological advances. Public hangings did not require technological sophistication, although the hangman had to tie the knot skillfully enough to ensure a swift death rather than slow strangulation. The use of the electric chair, however, required new technology—both the generation of electricity and the creation of the execution device itself. The first execution by electrocution occurred in 1890. In 1924 cyanide gas began to be used, and the first gas chamber was constructed. More recently, the new death technology of lethal injection gained popularity, largely as a cost-saving measure. First adopted as an option in Oklahoma in 1977, lethal injection was not actually used until 1982, in Texas.

SOURCES: Phillip English Mackey, *Voices against Death: American Opposition to Capital Punishment, 1787–1975* (New York: Burt Franklin, 1976); Hugo Adam Bedau, *The Death Penalty in America* (New York: Oxford University Press, 1982); R. Bohm, *DeathQuest: An Introduction to the Theory and Practice of Capital Punishment in the United States* (Cincinnati: Anderson, 1999).

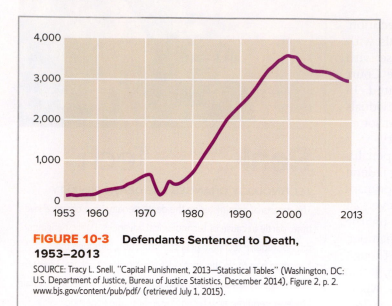

FIGURE 10-3   Defendants Sentenced to Death, 1953–2013

SOURCE: Tracy L. Snell, "Capital Punishment, 2013—Statistical Tables" (Washington, DC: U.S. Department of Justice, Bureau of Justice Statistics, December 2014), Figure 2, p. 2. www.bjs.gov/content/pub/pdf/ (retrieved July 1, 2015).

if the verdict is guilty, a second trial to establish the penalty, which might be death or life imprisonment without the possibility of parole. In making this determination, jurors are instructed to weigh the *mitigating factors* argued by the defense against the *aggravating factors* presented by the prosecution during the penalty phase.

Mitigating factors are presented to provide a larger context on the life of the now-convicted offender. Defense attorneys highlight these factors to argue that the defendant does not deserve to be executed. Mitigating factors might include evidence that the offender himself had been a victim of abuse, that he suffers from mental illness, or that he previously led a very respectable life. When presenting these mitigating factors, defense attorneys hope that the jury will decide that life imprisonment would be more appropriate for the defendant.

Aggravating factors generally need to be proved to have been present in order to make execution an appropriate penalty. For example, in many states capital punishment is appropriate if the murder was especially heinous, atrocious, or cruel or if it involved torture. Alabama defines as an aggravating factor any murder committed in order to avoid arrest.[51] The prosecutor in the case during the penalty phase seeks to produce evidence illustrating that any relevant aggravating factors were present in the commission of the crime so that the jury returns a sentence of death. In their deliberations, jurors ultimately weigh the mitigating factors against the aggravating factors. In 2014, the judges and juries in 72 cases decided that the offender should be executed.[52] This number is consistent with a trend since 1999 whereby the number of defendants being sentenced to death in the United States is decreasing dramatically (Figure 10-3).[53]

Controversies Concerning Capital Punishment

Many of the people who support capital punishment argue that it serves a need for retribution—to answer injury for injury in the interest of public morality. Others favor the death penalty as a way to retaliate against the murderer. Although both of these positions have strong support among death penalty advocates, their arguments are philosophically based. Their utility is difficult to evaluate because it is hard to measure the retributive and retaliatory effects of the death penalty. On the other hand, one thing is certain: Executing an offender ensures he or she will not commit crimes in the future. Although research does not support this claim, advocates also believe that the state-sanctioned taking of a life is an effective deterrent for others who might otherwise contemplate committing murder. Opponents of this ultimate sanction argue that the death penalty per se violates human rights through its inhumane and degrading treatment of an offender.

Capital punishment is controversial not just in the United States but throughout the world. "A Global View" on page 319 examines the concept from the perspective of the United Nations. The table on page 320 reports on how U.N. member countries weighed in on a groundbreaking resolution calling for a moratorium on the use of the death penalty.

Public opinion in the United States has slowly been shifting away from support of capital punishment. In 2013, the death penalty was favored by 55 percent of the adults in the United States, down from the 78 percent who had

A Global View

United Nations Resolution on a Death Penalty Moratorium

Capital punishment continues to be one of the most controversial justice-related issues in the world. Beyond the fundamental ethical advocacy for the value of a human life, and besides concerns over the possibility of executing innocent persons, debates focus on cost, deterrence, social class, race, age, and gender. Within the global context, the United States remains the only Western industrialized nation to employ capital punishment.

The year 2007 marked the adoption of United Nations General Assembly Resolution 62/149. This groundbreaking measure, adopted by an overwhelming majority of United Nations member countries, called for a worldwide moratorium on the use of the death penalty, with a view to abolishing capital punishment altogether.

In 2014, United Nations General Assembly Resolution 69/186 reaffirmed the United Nations' stance on the use of the death penalty. The vote at the United Nations General Assembly showed wider support than ever for a resolution on a moratorium on the use of the death penalty. The resolution introduced new elements to make the text stronger in encouraging all countries to take further steps toward reducing the application of the death penalty. In particular, the paragraph of the text concerning vulnerable groups previously referred only to minors and pregnant women; it now mentions "persons with mental or intellectual disabilities" as well. Another addition to the text is the paragraph concerning the protection of the rights of foreigners facing the death penalty, especially their right to receive consular assistance.

OBSERVE → INVESTIGATE → UNDERSTAND

- What do you believe is the motivation for the U.S. advocacy for retention of the death penalty?

- Do you think international disapproval will sooner or later oblige the United States to abolish capital punishment? Explain.

- In what ways does retention of the death penalty damage the global reputation of the United States? Should this consideration make any difference in whether U.S. society retains capital punishment? Why or why not?

SOURCES: United Nations, Moratorium on the Use of the Death Penalty, 69th General Assembly Session, December 18, 2014, Resolution 69/186; Maria Donatelli, "117 Countries Vote for a Moratorium on Executions," World Coalition Against the Death Penalty, December 19, 2014. www.worldcoalition.org/united-nations-resolution-moratorium-death-penalty-executions-general-assembly.html (retrieved June 9, 2015); Amnesty International, *UN General Assembly 2008: Implementing a Moratorium on Executions,* September 2008, ACT 50/016/2008; United Nations, *Moratorium on the Use of the Death Penalty,* 63rd General Assembly Session, 2008, Resolution 63/168; Bijou Yang and David Lester, "The Deterrent Effect of Executions: A Meta-Analysis Thirty Years after Ehrlich," *Journal of Criminal Justice* 36, no. 5 (2008): 453–459; Amnesty International, *Death Sentences and Executions 2010,* 2011, ACT 50/001/2011.

supported it in 1998.[54] Perhaps even more important, a majority (52 percent) of the public favors life without parole over the death penalty (42 percent) for convicted murderers.[55]

Opposition to capital punishment is based on several concerns. Many people believe that the death penalty is applied unfairly. The *Furman* ruling did not put to rest concerns regarding racial bias in the administration of death penalty cases. Data continue to show disparities along racial lines. Blacks are disproportionately represented on death row. They make up 42 percent of death row inmates but only 13 percent of the U.S. population. Furthermore, individuals of any race who murder Whites are more likely to receive a death sentence than those who murder people of color.[56] Hence both the race of the perpetrator and the race of the victim are related to death sentences. Some observers have

U.N. General Assembly Resolution 69/186: Country Vote

On December 18, 2014, the United Nations General Assembly adopted its fifth resolution calling for a moratorium on the use of the death penalty. The resolution was adopted by an overwhelming majority of countries. Four countries were not present. Check how countries voted on this resolution.

In Favor	Against	Abstain
Albania, Algeria, Andorra, Angola, Argentina, Armenia, Australia, Austria, Azerbaijan, Belgium, Benin, Bhutan, Bolivia, Bosnia and Herzegovina, Brazil, Bulgaria, Burkina Faso, Burundi, Cabo Verde, Cambodia, Canada, Central African Republic, Chad, Chile, Colombia, Congo, Costa Rica, Cote d' Ivoire, Croatia, Cyprus, Czech Republic, Denmark, Dominican Republic, Ecuador, El Salvador, Equatorial Guinea, Eritrea, Estonia, Fiji, Finland, France, Gabon, Georgia, Germany, Greece, Guatemala, Guinea-Bissau, Haiti, Honduras, Hungary, Iceland, Ireland, Israel, Italy, Kazakhstan, Kiribati, Kyrgyzstan, Latvia, Liechtenstein, Lithuania, Luxembourg, Macedonia (former Yugoslav Republic of), Madagascar, Mali, Malta, Marshall Islands, Mexico, Micronesia (Federated States of), Moldova, Monaco, Mongolia, Montenegro, Mozambique, Nepal, Netherlands, New Zealand, Nicaragua, Niger, Norway, Palau, Panama, Paraguay, Peru, Philippines, Poland, Portugal, Romania, Russian Federation, Rwanda, Samoa, San Marino, Sao Tome and Principe, Serbia, Seychelles, Sierra Leone, Slovakia, Slovenia, Somalia, South Africa, South Sudan, Spain, Surinam, Sweden, Switzerland, Tajikistan, Timor-Leste, Togo, Tunisia, Turkey, Turkmenistan, Tuvalu, Ukraine, United Kingdom, Uruguay, Uzbekistan, Vanuatu, Venezuela	Afghanistan, Antigua and Barbuda, Bahamas, Bangladesh, Barbados, Belize, Botswana, Brunei, China, Darussalam, Dominica, Egypt, Ethiopia, Grenada, Guyana, India, Iran, Iraq, Jamaica, Japan, Kuwait, Libya, Malaysia, North Korea, Oman, Pakistan, Papua New Guinea, Qatar, Saint Kitts and Nevis, Saint Lucia, Saint Vincent and the Grenadines, Saudi Arabia, Singapore, Sudan, Syria, Tonga, Trinidad and Tobago, United States, Yemen, Zimbabwe	Bahrain, Belarus, Cameroon, Comoros, Cuba, Democratic Republic of Congo, Djibouti, Gambia, Ghana, Guinea, Indonesia, Jordan, Kenya, Laos, Lebanon, Liberia, Malawi, Maldives, Mauritania, Morocco/Western Sahara, Myanmar, Namibia, Nigeria, Senegal, Solomon Islands, South Korea, Sri Lanka, Tanzania, Thailand, Tonga, Uganda, United Arab Emirates, Vietnam, Zambia

SOURCE: Amnesty International, "Voting Results of UN General Assembly Resolution 69/186, Adopted on December 18, 2014," *Death Sentences and Executions 2014* (Washington, DC: Amnesty International, April 2014). www.amnestyusa.org/pdfs/DeathSentencesAndExecutions2014_EN.pdf (retrieved May 27, 2015).

concluded that racial disparities in the administration of the death penalty are evidence of racial discrimination in the criminal justice system. There is also a relationship between the economic class of the victim and the sentence of the offender. If the victim was of a higher social status, a death penalty sentence is more likely than if the victim was poor or of lower social status.[57]

Another reason for questioning the fairness of the death penalty is that a surprising number of death row inmates are later proved innocent. Since 1973, 154 people have been exonerated and released from death row as a result of evidence of their innocence.[58] The "Race, Class, Gender" box on page 321 reviews how one organization, the Innocence Project, has been very successful in exonerating individuals who had not committed the crimes of which they were convicted. Perhaps because of concerns about mistakes in the criminal justice system and the risk of executing an innocent person, death sentences dropped more than 50 percent between 1999 and 2013 (see Figure 10-3).

A third consideration with respect to the death penalty focuses on whether it serves as an effective crime deterrent. Studies that have compared use of the death penalty to violent crime rates have found that threat of execution does not deter murder. For example, in 2013, the average murder rate in death penalty states was 4.4 per 100,000 people; in states without the death penalty,

Race, Class, Gender

Exonerating the Innocent

The Innocence Project was founded by Barry Scheck and Peter Neufeld at the Benjamin N. Cardoza School of Law at Yeshiva University in 1992. Their goal was to help prisoners who could be proved innocent through DNA analysis. As of June 2015, the Innocence Project had exonerated 330 people. Twenty of those individuals were at some point on death row. The Innocence Project's clients tend to have to wait long after their wrongful conviction to see justice done; indeed, the average amount of time that the project's exonerated clients serve is 14 years.

Many who are exonerated of the crimes for which they were convicted had relied on public defenders because they were poor. Public defenders may have the best of intentions, but they are often overworked and given less than adequate resources. The Innocence Project contends that to reduce the number of wrongful convictions, national standards must be established for the indigent defense system, which currently varies greatly from state to state.

People on death row are typically not just poor; they also are largely uneducated. Forty-eight percent of death row inmates are educated at the 11th-grade level or lower. More than half have never been married.

It is also illustrative to consider the profiles of the jurors who decide whether defendants deserve the death penalty. For a citizen to become a member of a capital punishment trial jury, he must be willing to vote for the death penalty. If his feelings generally tend toward an anti–death penalty position, they cannot be so strong as to "prevent or substantially impair the performance of his duties as a juror." Consequently, the people who are eligible to serve on capital punishment juries tend to be politically conservative, male, White, and either Catholic or Protestant. Further, a recent study found that individuals who qualified to serve on a death penalty jury had higher levels of homophobia, racism, and sexism.

So, what is the significance of these facts? The reality is that we have a largely disadvantaged group of death row inmates whose fate has been determined by jurors who tend to be unlikely either to think or to look like them.

OBSERVE → INVESTIGATE → UNDERSTAND

- What do you think best explains why so many people have been wrongfully convicted in the United States?

- What explains the finding that close to half of those on death row in the United States have less than an 11th-grade education and more than half have never been married? Why is that information significant?

- Will the wider application of DNA testing significantly reduce the number of persons who receive the death penalty in the United States and who are ultimately executed? Explain.

SOURCES: Brooke Butler, "Death Qualification and Prejudice: The Effect of Implicit Racism, Sexism, and Homophobia on Capital Defendants' Right to Due Process," *Behavioral Sciences and the Law* 25 (2007): 857–867; Tracy L. Snell, "Capital Punishment, 2013—Statistical Tables" (Washington, DC: U.S. Department of Justice, Bureau of Justice Statistics, December 19, 2014).

www.bjs.gov/content/pub/pdf/cp13st.pdf (retrieved July 4, 2015); *Wainwright v. Witt* 469 U.S. 412 (1985); Innocence Project, "DNA Exonerations Nationwide." www.innocenceproject.org/free-innocent/improve-the-law/fact-sheets/dna-exonerations-nationwide (retrieved June 14, 2015).

the rate was 3.4 per 100,000 people.[59] Current research is undermining the degree to which we can believe that the likelihood of execution deters murder.

Another point of controversy is the cost of capital punishment. Proponents argue that it is cheaper to execute an individual than to pay the costs of imprisoning that person for life. In fact, this argument is not true. Because of the expense of the extraordinary judicial processes required in capital cases, the costs associated with such cases typically far exceed those of life imprisonment. Since 2009, six states have abolished the death penalty–in part because of concerns related to morality and justice (for example, the discovery of wrongful convictions) but also in part because of the high costs incurred in death penalty cases. In fact, New Mexico, the first of these states to repeal capital punishment, cited expense as the main reason for doing so.[60]

As noted earlier, there are some indications that public and legal support for the death penalty is eroding. While the alternative sentence of life without parole may not satisfy public calls for retribution, it costs society less in terms of money and conscience: It is less expensive to house inmates for life than it is to maintain the costs associated with capital punishment. And while wrongly convicted inmates can be returned to the community, those who are executed cannot.

SUMMARY

The U.S. Constitution bans "cruel and unusual punishments," but the exact meaning of this phrase has changed greatly between the time the Constitution was written in the late eighteenth century and the present day. Whether or not that constitutional language now makes it appropriate to ban the death penalty is a contentious issue.

Another important constitutional guarantee—the right to seek a writ of habeas corpus—affects the kind of punishment that the criminal justice system can impose. Habeas corpus proceedings involve challenging the justice of a convicted person's trial or sentence, particularly if the sentence is death. Today, the parameters within which convicts may institute habeas corpus proceedings are narrowing.

Sentences are determined by the trial judge on the basis of presentence investigation reports and victim impact statements, which help the judge determine whether there are aggravating or mitigating circumstances that would affect the severity of the sentence. Various goals and principles of sentencing have been identified: retribution for the crime that has been committed; deterrence, to discourage others from committing the offense; incapacitation, to disable the offender from harming us again in the future; and rehabilitation, to encourage the offender to change his or her future behavior. Of these principles, rehabilitation is less frequently invoked today than it was a generation ago. Sentences of imprisonment can be either indeterminate (dependent on the convicted person's behavior while imprisoned and on the likelihood of rehabilitation) or determinate (for a more or less precise term of years). Legislation often requires judges to impose mandatory sentences.

Capital punishment has become extremely controversial in the United States, in part because it retains strong public support (despite equally strong disapproval in other industrial democracies). Disparities of race and class in the implementation of capital punishment remain significant, and concerns regarding wrongful convictions and the expense of executions in hard economic times are beginning to take a toll on its popularity.

OBSERVE → INVESTIGATE → UNDERSTAND

Review

Describe the constitutional protections that affect sentencing.

- According to the Eighth Amendment, sentences cannot be cruel and unusual.

- Habeas corpus protections allow offenders to challenge their detainment.

Describe the various goals of sentencing.

- Retribution is a sentencing goal focused on appropriately punishing the offender in a manner equal to his crime.

- Deterrence is a sentencing goal focused on convincing the offender herself and society at large that criminal actions will be punished and therefore should not be committed.

- Incapacitation is a sentencing goal focused on reducing the ability of the offender to re-offend.

- Rehabilitation is a sentencing goal focused on helping the offender change her behavior.

Compare the different sentencing models.

- Indeterminate sentencing models include sentences with ranges rather than a specific amount of time.

- Determinate sentencing models include sentences that enumerate a specific amount of time that should be served.

- Presumptive sentencing models assume that judges should sentence within sentencing guidelines, or within ranges specified for particular charges.

Review how a capital punishment trial proceeds.

- A capital punishment trial is bifurcated.

- The first stage of a capital punishment trial decides guilt or innocence.

- In the second stage the jury weighs both mitigating and aggravating factors to decide whether the defendant should be sentenced to death.

Outline controversies surrounding the death penalty.

- There is a growing global sentiment that the death penalty should be abolished in all countries.

- There are questions about whether capital punishment is applied fairly.

- Research indicates that the death penalty does not deter murder.

- Sentencing a person to death ultimately costs more than sentencing the person to life imprisonment because of the high costs of capital trials and the associated costs of appeals.

Key Terms

capital crime 314

concurrent sentences 310

consecutive sentences 310

cruel and unusual punishment 301

determinate sentence 308

deterrence 306

habeas corpus 302

habitual offender statute 311

incapacitation 306

indeterminate sentence 307

presentence investigation (PSI) report 304

presumptive sentencing model 308

preventive detention laws 311

recidivist 311

rehabilitation 307

retribution 306

statutory minimum 308

Study Questions

1. All of the following are goals of sentencing *except*
   a. retribution.
   b. rehabilitation.
   c. victim advocacy.
   d. incapacitation.

2. A sentence that is a range of time served, such as 2 to 3.5 years, is referred to as
   a. indeterminate.
   b. determinate.
   c. presumptive.
   d. a mandatory minimum.

3. A judicial order that says that someone has been wrongfully imprisoned is referred to as
   a. a cruel and unusual punishment.
   b. preventive detention.
   c. a capital offense.
   d. habeas corpus.

4. Preventive detention laws generally target offenders who are
   a. recidivists.
   b. sex offenders.
   c. neither a nor b
   d. both a and b

5. A punishment is cruel and unusual if
   a. it inflicts any pain on the defendant.
   b. the defendant is under the age of 18.
   c. it is rejected by the "evolving standards of decency."
   d. it does not fit the crime.

6. The number of stages in a capital punishment trial is
   a. one.
   b. two.
   c. three.
   d. four.

7. The U.S. Supreme Court case that established the stages of a capital punishment trial is
   a. *Furman v. Georgia.*
   b. *Gregg v. Georgia.*
   c. *McCleskey v. Kemp.*
   d. *United States v. Booker.*

8. A state that uses sentencing guidelines and mandatory minimum sentences likely has a/an
   a. indeterminate sentencing model.
   b. determinate sentencing model.
   c. presumptive sentencing model.
   d. preventive detention sentencing model.

9. A presentence investigation report typically includes all of the following *except*
   a. statements from the defendants' family members.
   b. an overview of any past crimes of which the offender has been convicted.
   c. a sentencing recommendation.
   d. a victim impact statement.

10. The group that the U.S. Supreme Court recently ruled to be ineligible for the death penalty is
    a. people with mental retardation.
    b. individuals who were 18 years of age or younger when they committed their crimes.
    c. both a and b
    d neither a nor b

Critical Thinking Questions

For further review, go to the LearnSmart study module for this chapter.

1. What goal of sentencing do you think should be the most important, and why?

2. Which sentencing model should be used for violent crimes? Property crimes? Drug crimes?

3. There are many arguments both for and against the death penalty. Which arguments do you find most persuasive? Why?

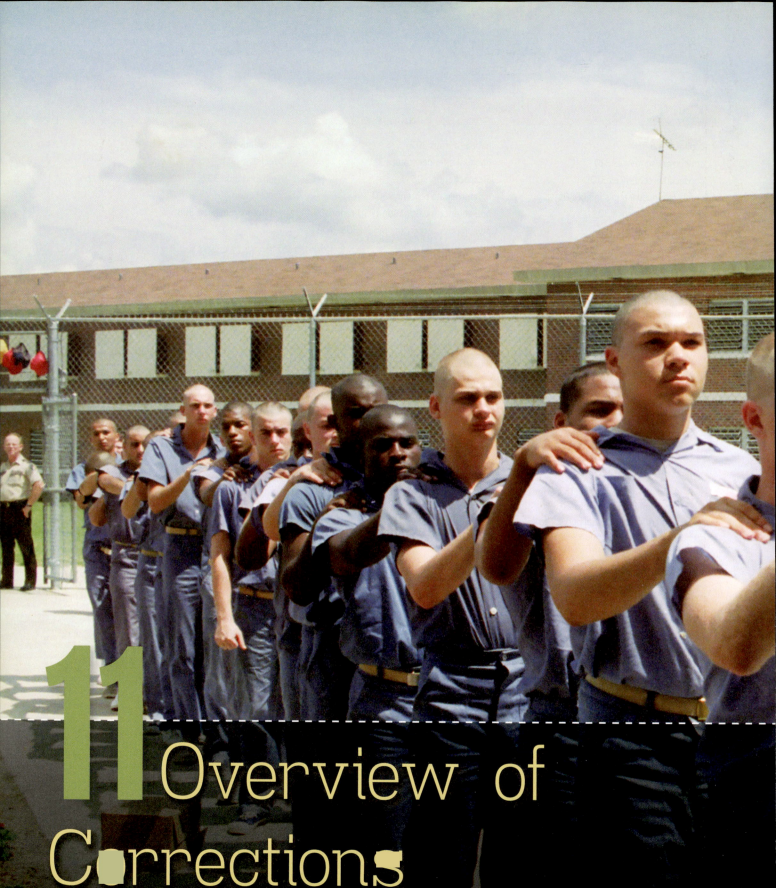

11 Overview of Corrections

After reading this chapter, you should be able to:

- Define corrections and describe its role in society.
- Identify the precursors to the U.S. prison.
- Contrast the features of the Pennsylvania system with those of the Auburn system.
- Identify the defining features of reformatories and therapeutic prisons.
- Trace the defining features of industrial prisons.
- Describe and evaluate each of the four major models of corrections.
- Describe the populations found in correctional institutions today.
- Identify the types of victim services found in corrections.
- Examine the extent and nature of privatization of prisons.

Realities and Challenges

Values are the Driving Force behind Corrections Models

On August 24, 2012, Anders Behring Breivik was sentenced to 21 years—the maximum sentence in Norway—in a Norwegian prison after he was convicted of killing 8 people in Oslo and 69 at a Utoya Island summer camp for youth interested in politics. The slaughter took place during the summer of 2011. Although psychiatric reports differed as to Breivik's sanity, ultimately it was determined that he was legally sane at the time of the attacks. He was also described as cold, callous, and methodical when he carried out his slayings armed with a fertilizer car bomb, an automatic rifle, and a handgun. He apparently planned the crime for approximately a decade. Breivik committed the slaughter because he believed he could save Norway and Europe from the spread of Islamic colonization and multiculturalism. This crime is considered the most atrocious crime Norway has experienced since the end of World War II.[1] However, because Norway's deeply ingrained values of tolerance, nonviolence, merciful justice, rehabilitation, and treatment are at the core of its correctional philosophy and law, 21 years is the longest sentence Breivik could have received.[2]

Breivik is serving his sentence at Ila Prison near Oslo where he is held under the highest security Norway has to offer. The maximum-security prison holds 124 of the country's worst offenders and has 230 unarmed male and female staff. Should arms be needed, the staff will need to call the police for backup. However, staff members have access to batons and tear gas.

Breivik is cut off from contact with other offenders, and his main source of face-to-face interaction is with correctional staff. Staff duties include talking with him, exercising with him, keeping him active, and providing a humane prison regime under segregated conditions. He also has an hour a week when he can receive visits. To compensate for his lack of contact with other inmates in the facility, he has a small three-room cell totaling about 250 square feet that includes a bedroom, an exercise room, and a study area with a desk and a computer that is not connected to the Internet. He also has television access and can order appropriate books from the library.[3]

The Norwegian and U.S. corrections systems have different definitions of punishment. Norway elevates the rehabilitation and reintegration models of corrections, whereas the United States endorses the punishment and crime control models explained later in the chapter. The challenge for the corrections system is to institute the right blend of punishment and rehabilitation that will in fact "correct" offenders and safely return them to society.

This chapter discusses a range of options for correcting inmates. We begin by defining corrections and then examining the origins of corrections. We trace the main historical stages of prison development in the United States and explore the major models of corrections. We then turn our attention to the populations who are under the supervision of corrections. We take a close look at the victim's involvement in corrections and end the chapter by discussing the development of privately owned and operated prisons.

DEFINING CORRECTIONS

The term *corrections*, as used today, denotes society's efforts to punish and treat individuals who break the law, and thereby to protect the public. These efforts take the form of programs, services, and facilities that deal with offenders after

institutional corrections
Incarceration in jails and prisons.

community corrections
Court-imposed programs and sanctions that allow offenders to serve their sentences within the community instead of in jail or prison.

they enter the criminal justice system. Local, state, federal, and private agencies manage the custody and treatment of convicted adult and juvenile offenders in the system.

Correctional programs fall into two categories. **Institutional corrections** refers to incarceration in jails and prisons and in other types of secure confinement programs; **community corrections** refers to probation, parole, and other programs that supervise offenders within the community. The roots of today's institutional programs date back to ancient times. Practices we now associate with community corrections are a relatively recent departure from the traditional reliance on incarceration as the only means to correct offenders. (Chapters 12 and 13 address institutional and community corrections, respectively.)

Depending on the context, "to correct" means to make right, rectify, make amends for, chastise, compensate, or treat a defect. As it relates to criminals, the term *corrections* came into use in the United States around the turn of the twentieth century, reflecting a widely held belief that the corrections system would transform offenders into law-abiding citizens. This has never been a universally accepted belief. Indeed, for centuries, society dealt with crime and criminal activity by punishment alone. Punishment was seen as both a form of retribution (or revenge) and a deterrent to scare people into not committing crimes. Severe punishments and fear of being caught were thought to be the only way to control crime. The field of corrections subsequently moved away from a philosophy of punishment toward a philosophy of rehabilitation. As we discussed in Chapter 10, rehabilitation emphasizes changing an individual from an offender into someone who is law-abiding. However, in recent decades there has once again been an increased reliance on incarceration and punishment.[4]

Punishment and rehabilitation are two very different methods of dealing with offenders, and each is based on a different philosophy. The punishment philosophy holds that offenders must pay for their crimes and serve as a deterrent for other would-be criminals. The rehabilitation philosophy stresses that offenders can change and should be helped to change and become productive members of the community. Some people question whether these two approaches are compatible within the same institution.[5]

Punishment was long thought to deter crime. For example, prior to 1808, the penalty for pickpocketing in England was death by hanging. Such a harsh penalty seemed necessary to curtail this very prevalent activity. People commonly believed, in fact, that the harsher the penalty, the greater the chance of reducing the crime. To ensure the desired deterrent effect, hangings were public events, usually staged in the town square.[6] Characterized by a festive atmosphere, a hanging would draw a throng of townsfolk from all the surrounding villages to witness the spectacle. The irony is that the highest rates of pickpocketing activity occurred at these crowded public events because the probability of getting caught was low.

If we are to believe that harsh penalties reduce crime, we must assume that potential criminals weigh the benefit and cost before committing a crime. But criminals usually act impulsively and seem unconcerned with the future or the threat of possible future punishment.[7] A very high percentage of active criminals

▼ **Medieval Punishments**
Devices used to torture and extract confessions from accused offenders were sometimes very elaborate.

do not perceive any risk of being caught and therefore give no thought to the punishments for their crimes.[8]

Harsher sanctions do not necessarily deter crime and recidivism; such sanctions actually may have the opposite effect of encouraging recidivism.[10] A 2006 Canadian bill introduced in Parliament noted that in Canada harsher penalties do not reduce crime.[11] A 2003 study of more than 2,300 adolescents found that those prosecuted in harsh criminal courts were more likely to be rearrested more quickly and more frequently for violent, property, and weapons offenses than the juveniles prosecuted in more lenient juvenile courts. Adolescents prosecuted in juvenile courts were more likely to be rearrested for drug offenses.[12] Overall, harsher punishments did not result in improved public safety.[13] Researchers who have studied punishment believe that the motive for harsh punishment is not deterrence but retribution.[14]

ORIGINS OF CORRECTIONS

The practices of contemporary corrections have deep roots in early forms of punishment throughout the world. Before the use of imprisonment, early punishments were not only harsh but often gruesome. The most common punishments were execution and public corporal punishments such as flogging, branding, and mutilation.

Early Forms of Confinement

An early form of imprisonment was practiced in England during the reign of William the Conqueror (1027–1087). Before the establishment of the jail as an institution, lawbreakers were sometimes confined in dedicated sections of the estates of private landowners until it was time to impose the punishment. As time passed, offenders, the mentally ill, and others whom the government deemed undesirable were confined in mines, ships, sulfur pits, stone quarries, ship ruins ("hulks"), and dungeons.[15] In the thirteenth century, the church throughout Europe held offenders in cells within monasteries to serve years of solitary penance—a practice that foreshadowed the use of isolation to "correct" disobedience.

A corrections solution known as the *plague town* arose in Europe during the fourteenth century. Plague towns were originally intended as a means to isolate people infected with the bubonic plague. The organization of these towns anticipated the defining features of later prisons: isolation, organized surveillance, custodial maintenance, regimentation, prayer, and penance.[16] Another punishment option for individuals who were not sentenced to immediate death or torture during the late 1400s and 1500s was confining condemned criminals to galleys, which served the double purpose of providing laborers to row explorers' ships. In this practice, known as *galley slavery*, the offenders were chained to their oars on ships, often without protection from the elements and with minimal food and water, and were forced to row until they died.[17]

The Workhouse

Another stage in the development of the modern prison system began in the sixteenth century, when Holland and England developed the first workhouses,

▲ Tower Guards on Duty

Guards in prison towers are armed with deadly weapons they can use to prevent inmates from escaping.

also known as *houses of correction* and *houses of compulsory reformation.*[18] The **workhouse** held a mix of people, including jobless vagrants, debtors, and sometimes serious criminals. King Edward VI of England initiated the first workhouse in 1553 at Bridewell Palace in London.

Admission to a workhouse was mortifying and humiliating. Men, women, and children were often segregated, families were routinely split up, and some were never brought back together again. When people entered a workhouse, their personal possessions were taken away. They were stripped, searched, cleaned, shorn, issued workhouse clothing, closely confined with others, and forced to work. They were counted regularly, fed poorly, and required to get up early and go to bed early.[19] Paupers were confined until they could pay off their debts.

The workhouses did take vagrants off the streets and offer employment to those who did not have jobs. They were an approach to reform that quickly spread throughout Britain and other European countries. By the late seventeenth century, workhouses were used to house a broader range of criminals and became widespread in England.[20]

Transportation

Workhouses provided a long-term strategy for detaining the poor and homeless, but European nations were faced with another problem: the growing ranks of criminals throughout society. One solution that quickly became institutionalized was **transportation,** the export of criminals to other lands. In the eighteenth century, the British practice of banishing criminals led to the establishment of foreign penal colonies.[21] Transportation was popular because of growing opposition to the death penalty for all but the most serious offenses, lack of local facilities to imprison offenders, and the need for a labor force to colonize new lands. Convicts were shipped to the British colonies of America, Australia, Tasmania (currently the southernmost island state of Australia), and New Zealand.[22]

By 1776, as many as 2,000 criminals were being transported each year from Britain to the American colonies. These criminals were not placed in penal facilities but were sold as servants to private individuals, a practice known as **indentured servitude.** Indentured servants worked for their masters until they completed their term of servitude. The masters controlled every aspect of the servants' lives. Many of the transported convicts were guilty of only minor offenses, such as theft or shoplifting.[23]

Then, between 1787 and 1867, approximately 160,000 convicts were relocated to Australia and New South Wales from Britain and Ireland.[24] The French transported more than 100,000 offenders to penal colonies in French Guiana and New Caledonia beginning in 1852 and continued this practice well into the twentieth century.[25]

Life in penal colonies was brutal. Gallows were prominently displayed; criminals ate, slept, and worked in irons; officials used the whip, gag, solitary confinement, and other forms of torture regularly and required subservience of all criminals all the time.[26] Charles Anderson, age 18, was sentenced to 7 years transportation to a penal colony in Australia for breaking into some shops in England. The following excerpt vividly illustrates what happened after he tried to escape:

> Recaptured, he received 100 lashes and, on being returned to Goat Island, another 100, and was ordered to wear irons for twelve months. During that twelve months he received in all 1,200 lashes for the most trivial offences, such as looking up from his work. He escaped again, and this time

workhouse
An institution that held jobless vagrants, debtors, and sometimes serious criminals.

transportation
The export of criminals to other lands to complete their sentences.

indentured servitude
The practice of selling criminals as servants to private individuals instead of sentencing them to penal facilities.

▼ **Prison Hulk**

In England during the 1700s, individuals convicted of crimes were incarcerated on the abandoned hulks of ships.

was sentenced to 200 lashes, to which 100 more lashes were added by a sentence which directed as well that he be chained to a rock for two years. He was put in irons, and attached to the rock by a chain twenty-one feet long. A hollow in the rock served him for a bed, and at night a wooden lid, perforated with holes for air, was put over him and locked into position. His food was pushed into his eating vessel on a pole. Other prisoners were forbidden to speak or approach him under penalty of 100 lashes. His wounds became maggot-infested but he was refused water with which to bathe them.[27]

"A Global View" on this page provides a look at the practice of transportation today and the evolution of penal colonies. Isla Maria Madre is a contemporary Mexican penal colony that embodies the correctional goals of rehabilitation and reform.

A Global View

The Legacy of Penal Transportation and Isla Maria Madre

For the most part, penal colonies are a thing of past. One exception is the unique modern-day prison on Isla Maria Madre in the Pacific Ocean, off Mexico's coast. In the early 1900s, the island prison held Mexican inmates who had been sentenced to a life of hard labor. Of the 3,000 male prison inmates on Isla Maria Madre today, most are serving sentences for drug trafficking.

In the present day, the prison is humane and has no cells or bars. The 36 correctional officers carry no guns, and inmates, who are called colonists, wear regular clothing. Furthermore, in sharp contrast to the prison's earlier times, the corrections philosophy behind today's Isla Maria Madre seeks to keep families and loved ones together during an inmate's period of incarceration. Indeed, while prisoners complete their sentences—which are often lengthy—their families can live with them in houses and communities similar to those in many small Mexican towns. There are about 600 children on the island, and they go to public schools. Some prisoners' families believe that their prison homes are safer and more comfortable than the homes they left behind.

The correctional philosophy of Isla Maria Madre is one of humane rehabilitation and reform. To this end, the Mexican government provides a setting that closely approximates a normal community. In comparison to a typical prison, Isla Maria Madre is expensive to operate: The cost of incarcerating a prisoner at Isla Maria is about three times higher than that in other Mexican prisons. This is largely due to the expense of transporting goods to and from the island and the need to provide services not only for the prisoners but also for their families. The inmates' experiences are poles apart from those of the criminals who were transported to Australia, the American colonies, and French Guiana. The Isla Maria Madre prisoners are closely connected to their families throughout their incarceration—a support system necessary for successful rehabilitation. The Mexican government is exploring the possibility of building an isolation model maximum-security prison on an adjacent island known as Maria Magdalena. It would be used to better control major drug kingpins.

OBSERVE → INVESTIGATE → UNDERSTAND

- Would the United States benefit from exploring the use of prison colonies such as Isla Maria Madre? What factors would contribute to the success or failure of such an experiment?

- How do practices on Isla Maria Madre contrast with what you know of those at the U.S. military penal colony at Guantánamo Bay, Cuba?

- What are the pros and cons of housing family members in a penal colony? Do the benefits outweigh the disadvantages? Explain.

SOURCES: Stephen A. Toth, *Beyond Papillon: The French Overseas Penal Colonies, 1854–1952* (Lincoln: University of Nebraska Press, 2006); Mary Jordan, "Convicts Are Condemned to a Paradise in Mexico," *Washington Post Foreign Service*, February 3, 2002, p. A22; American Correctional Association, *The Mexican Penal Colony at Islas Maria* (College Park, MD: ACA, 1981); Lawrence Iliff, "Mexico May Create Island Penal Colony for Drug Lords," *Dallas Morning News*, October 2007, www.banderasnews.com/0710/nr-narcoisland.htm (retrieved January 21, 2013).

Hulks

With the coming of the American Revolution, the British could no longer export convicts to the American colonies. Instead, they used abandoned ships, docked in British harbors, to house prisoners from the late 1700s through most of the 1800s. These abandoned ships, called **hulks,** were reconfigured as enormous holding blocks in which offenders were chained. Essentially floating dungeons, hulks perpetually stank, and a gallows was often found at the front of the vessel.[28] Food was scarce and frequently contaminated with mold and insects. Unsanitary conditions promoted the spread of disease. The life expectancy of prisoners held in such conditions was short. The practice of confining offenders in hulks continued for approximately 15 years until Britain began transporting convicts to Australia. Although viewed at the time as a desperate stopgap measure, hulks anticipated the modern prison in their use of incarceration as punishment.

Jails in Colonial America

The term *jail* comes from the old English word *gaol*–a place of imprisonment. We can trace jails as a local form of institutional corrections back to at least 1166 in England, when Henry II ordered the construction of facilities to detain offenders awaiting trial or to carry out their sentence–typically torture, mutilation, or execution.

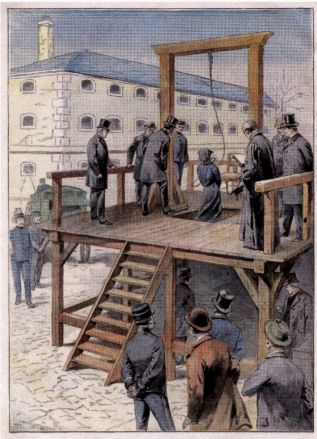

EN AMÉRIQUE – EXÉCUTION D'UNE FEMME AUX ÉTATS-UNIS

▲ **Public Punishment**
Punishments during colonial times were often public spectacles.

hulks
Abandoned ships that functioned as enormous holding blocks within which offenders were chained.

Prior to the development of prisons in the United States, most local jail facilities were ordinary houses–literally, *jail-houses*–without cells, where suspects were given rooms while awaiting trial. Early jail keepers were civilian citizens or sheriffs. Many were abusive and often took bribes from inmates and their families for extra money to feed, clothe, and care for prisoners' needs. All prisoners were confined together, regardless of sex, age, or the nature of the crimes of which they were accused. As the number of offenders grew, overcrowding, poor sanitation, disease, and escape attempts were commonplace.

By the time of the American Revolution, local jails in the colonies were largely used as holding pens for suspected thieves, debtors, and murderers. Most of those confined could anticipate some form of physical, or *corporal*, punishment, such as whipping or being held in wooden stocks in public arenas, or execution. English common law (the basis of the U.S. legal system) specified that hundreds of crimes be punished in these ways.[29]

Debtors who were confined in jail were freed during the day so that they could work to pay off their debts, but they had to return at night. Once convicted, debtors had difficulty regaining their freedom because their forced labor was needed in the workforce. In 1785, half the persons sentenced to jail in Philadelphia were debtors. Although debts were generally small, even individuals found not guilty were required to pay court fees before being released. This expense was often more than they could afford, but release from custody was not possible until all debts and fees were paid.[30]

In the Pennsylvania colony, the dominant Quaker population did not believe in harsh punishment, torture, or, in most cases, death for wrongdoers. Instead, the Quakers embraced reform. In 1682, under the leadership of William Penn, the Quakers developed a new penal code based on advanced European ideas and humanitarian thought. Penn's code, known as the *Great Law*, used imprisonment as the major penalty for offenses previously punished by torture, mutilation, and death.[31] In the next section, we examine how the Pennsylvania Quakers influenced prisoner confinement in the first U.S. prisons.

HISTORY OF CORRECTIONS IN THE UNITED STATES

Following the American Revolution, some prisons were built solely as confinement facilities. Philosophically, these institutions were rooted in the punishment model. Indeed, prison administrators did not believe that they could change criminal behavior in any way, so they made no pretense of reforming or rehabilitating offenders. The prisons were intended only as alternatives to capital punishment and as deterrence for offenders and others to committing future crimes. One such institution was the Newgate Prison in Connecticut, basically a large hole in the ground where inmates lived like lepers without any supervision or care.[32] The hole was in fact the remnant of an old copper mine that became a prison in 1773.[33]

The Pennsylvania System and the Penitentiary

As a reaction to the harsh, dehumanizing conditions of New World prisons, the Pennsylvania Quakers sought to reform the system. They established Pennsylvania as a colony with a constitution that guaranteed freedom of religion and a new penal code. Reform-minded, the Quakers embraced the rehabilitation model, believing that in the right circumstances, criminal offenders could be changed. The Quakers strongly opposed corporal and capital punishment.[34] In 1787 a group of Quakers formed the Philadelphia Society for the Alleviation of the Miseries of the Public Prisons; the aim of the group was to remove cruelty from the institutional process. The Quakers believed that criminals could be reformed if they were isolated and segregated in complete silence, conditions that would give them time to reflect on their crimes and to repent.

As a result of pressure from the Quakers and their prison reform group, a Philadelphia institution called the **Walnut Street Jail** opened a special wing in 1790.[35] This wing was the first public institution to use imprisonment as the primary method of reforming offenders.[36] A guiding principle for the new facility was the idea that isolation and solitude would lead to offender reform. In a crude attempt to classify prisoners, officials tried to ensure that women, vagrants, capital offenders, and debtors did not intermingle.[37]

Many scholars consider the Walnut Street Jail to be the first **penitentiary,** a term the Quakers coined from the word *penitent*, meaning sorrowful for one's sins or wrongdoings. Labor was seen as a necessary component of the system and was intended not for reform or training but as a way for the state to be reimbursed for the cost of operating the jail. Although the Walnut Street Jail seemed successful in its first decade, the experiment ultimately failed, primarily due to overcrowding. In 1817 the Philadelphia Society began to plan a new prison system for Pennsylvania.[38]

The planners specifically designed a new penitentiary to reform inmates according to the principles of absolute solitary segregation. The result was the Western Penitentiary, built in 1826 in the outskirts of Pittsburgh. Three years later, in 1829, the Eastern State Penitentiary (also called the Cherry Hill Penitentiary)

Walnut Street Jail
The first public institution to specifically use imprisonment as the primary method of reforming offenders.

penitentiary
Coined from the word *penitent,* the Quakers' term for a residence where offenders would be sorrowful for their wrongdoings.

▼ **Early Prisons**
The first U.S. prisons were harsh environments.

was constructed in Philadelphia. The blueprint for these facilities called for small, self-contained solitary cells in which inmates slept, worked, and ate. New inmates were taken blindfolded to their cells and given a Bible. They saw only their keepers and were not allowed to communicate with one another. Nor could they leave their cells, except under unusual circumstances, until they completed their entire sentences. This system is now called the **Pennsylvania system** but is also sometimes referred to as the *Philadelphia system* or the *solitary system.*

Under these conditions of near-total isolation, some of the prisoners developed mental disorders. In his 1842 visit to the United States, English novelist Charles Dickens described the Pennsylvania system and the effects of using solitary confinement on the mind and spirit of inmates. Although Dickens believed that the prisons he visited were originally developed to reform criminals into law-abiding citizens, he saw the system as going astray:

> I am persuaded that those who devised this system of Prison Discipline, and those benevolent gentlemen who carry it into execution do not know what they are doing. I believe that very few men are capable of estimating the immense amount of torture and agony which this dreadful punishment, prolonged for years, inflicts upon the sufferers; . . . [and] I am only the more convinced that there is a depth of terrible endurance in it which none but the sufferers themselves can fathom, and which no man has a right to inflict upon his fellow-creature. I hold this slow and daily tampering with the mysteries of the brain to be immeasurably worse than any torture of the body.[39]

Contemporary research bears out Dickens's concerns and criticisms. Indeed, psychological damage to prisoners held in solitary confinement has been well documented (see Chapter 12).[40]

The Auburn System

In New York City's Newgate Prison (named after the infamous copper mine prison in Connecticut), which opened in 1797, inmates worked in groups during the day and were confined in apartment-like spaces during the night. Newgate became so severely overcrowded, however, that by 1809 the governor was forced to pardon prisoners just to make room for new inmates. The legislature thus authorized the building of a new prison in the New York State interior. Auburn State Prison, established in 1816, became the model for the **Auburn system** of prison administration.[41]

Both the Pennsylvania and the Auburn systems were based on reformation, and both relied on the completely separate confinement of inmates from one another.[42] The basic philosophy of each system was noncommunication among prisoners.[43] This policy was said to reduce "contamination" from other inmates.[44] But the Auburn system differed from the Pennsylvania system in one key way. Once the Pennsylvania inmates were taken to their cells, they never, until the day they were released, encountered another human being other than the official who brought them their food. They were totally and

Pennsylvania system
A system of prison administration in which inmates lived in solitary confinement, total silence, and religious penitence as the way to prevent future criminal behavior.

Auburn system
A system of prison administration in which prisoners were isolated in cells at night but allowed to congregate during the day for work duty and meals, but in total silence.

▼ **Auburn Prison**

Prisoners moved in lockstep at Auburn Prison.

completely isolated. In the Auburn prison system, although the prisoners were isolated in cells at night, they congregated, in silence, during the day for work duty and meals. The Auburn system thus came to be known as the *congregate* (or *silent*) *system*.

The Auburn buildings featured blocks of small individual cells placed back-to-back and reaching five tiers high, a design that was cheaper to construct than that of the Pennsylvania prisons. Auburn also was more efficient in guarding and administrating congregate labor.[45] The officials believed that severe discipline would reform the inmates under their care. When they were out of their cells and working together, inmates were forbidden to exchange words or even glances with one another. They wore striped suits, walked in lockstep to allow guards tight control while moving groups of inmates, and were frequently subjected to corporal punishment such as beatings and floggings.[46] Although Pennsylvania had done away with corporal punishment, at Auburn it became *the* method to maintain strict discipline.[47]

Between 1830 and 1850, people everywhere seemed to be debating which was the better system. Prison development and the need for reform garnered a great deal of attention both in the United States and in Europe. Many European prisons came to adopt the solitary Pennsylvania system, as reformers on the continent believed it to be more humane than the Auburn system, which to them seemed too harsh and impersonal. The Europeans also objected to the increasing use of corporal punishment in the Auburn system.

Most U.S. prisons, on the other hand, came to be modeled on the congregate Auburn system—not because of its correctional philosophy but for economic reasons. The Pennsylvania system needed cells large enough to accommodate an inmate 24 hours a day. Such enclosures were expensive to build and maintain compared with the Auburn cells, which were used only at night for sleeping. Furthermore, the small amount of money from the sale of handicrafts made by prisoners in their cells in Pennsylvania did not yield enough income to support the prison. By contrast, the Auburn inmates who congregated for work generated considerable income for the prison.

In fact, an important aspect of the Auburn model was its work system—in which, essentially, a factory within the prison used convict labor to make goods for the private sector. An outside businessperson paid the prison—not the working inmate—a daily rate in accordance with the number of inmates doing work. A convict leasing system evolved, and soon other prisons in New York adopted the Auburn model. Under this convict leasing arrangement, private bidders leased prisoners for their labor, and private companies ran factories within the prison walls.[48] Revenues for the prison were a foremost concern; the welfare and reformation of the prisoner was of secondary importance. The Auburn model dominated the U.S. prison system until the early 1900s.

In reality, neither the Auburn nor the Pennsylvania system met the hopes of those who initially attempted to reform the correctional system. Prisons soon became overcrowded, and correctional officers had increasing difficulty maintaining control over inmates, leaving early reformation ideals to fall by the wayside.

The Reformatory System

By the 1860s every state but Pennsylvania had adopted the congregate system. By that time, overcrowding, cruel treatment, and corruption undermined the effectiveness of many established penitentiaries in the United States. Two and three prisoners were housed in cells designed for one, and brutal punishments were again a feature of incarceration. Money earned by inmates would often end up in administrators' pockets. The original philosophy of these prisons—noncommunication—faded away, and the prisons degenerated into institutions that used cruel regulations to maximize the productivity of their prison industries.[49]

Life at Auburn, for example, became a living hell. A report on prison conditions stated, "Within an atmosphere of repression, humiliation, and gloomy silence, the Auburn convict performed an incessantly monotonous round of activity."[50] Sing Sing Prison, also in New York and modeled after Auburn, was even worse. Legislative investigations found that some guards had wrapped their whips with wire; others had used them on the genitals of inmates, often without reason.[51] From such abuses a movement for reform emerged.

In 1870, the New York Prison Association issued a highly critical report on penal methods and recommended specific reforms. In the belief that the purpose of a prison should be to reform, not to punish, the association argued that an inmate's sentence should be based on how well reform is progressing. Thus a primary recommendation was a call for indeterminate sentences–effectively telling prisons that rehabilitation was to be at the forefront of their mission and that the sentence was in the hands of the individual prisoner. Good behavior would bring early release.

New York's **Elmira Reformatory,** built in 1876 and guided by Zebulon Brockway as its superintendent, was based on principles of rehabilitation. Elmira called itself a reformatory to underscore its emphasis on reform rather than punishment. Reformatories rejected the nineteenth-century philosophies of silence, obedience, and labor. Instead they stressed rehabilitation through education, indeterminate sentences with maximum terms, and the opportunity for parole. Elmira's philosophy was so popular that many believed that it would become the dominant model for U.S. prisons. Education, central to the reform program, would include "general subjects, sports, religion, and military drill."[52]

Whereas correctional officers in the early prisons just needed to be tough and firm, the new system called for specific training; while old-style prison cells were small, the reformatory required larger cells, state inspections, and preparations for release. In addition, all physical punishments were to be banned.[53] These ideas became so popular that the principles of the reformatory movement soon spread throughout the country, though without many of the practices necessary to make them work. For example, every state adopted the practice of classifying prisons and inmates to fit them to individualized programs, but most institutions did little to differentiate these inmates and put them into specific rehabilitation programs.[54]

By the early twentieth century, many states had built institutions they called reformatories, although some were reformatories in name only.[55] In fact, most U.S. prisons, including those associated with the reformatory approach, were no more than "custodial warehouse[s] for social refuse."[56] Ultimately, the reformatory model fell from favor. Trained personnel to implement the educational and classification systems were scarce,[57] and the programs that were offered affected only a small portion of the prison population.[58]

The U.S. reformatories' failure to achieve lasting success stemmed primarily from overcrowding. Within two decades of its construction, Elmira, for example, held more than twice the number of inmates it had been designed to house, making effective rehabilitation programs impractical. Moreover, Elmira's program was intended for youthful, first-time offenders, but the institution incarcerated many older, hardened criminals–one-third of whom were repeat offenders. In the end, the reformatory movement did not live up to its billing.[59]

The reformatory movement had a greater impact in Europe. In 1897 Sir Evelyn Ruggles-Brise came to the United States to study the Elmira Reformatory so as to gain insight on reforming the English prison system. Upon returning to England, he established what became known as the *Borstal system,* incorporating the principles of the reformatory model and targeting offenders ages 16 to 21.[60] Ultimately, the Borstal system had a stronger influence on corrections and the treatment of juveniles than the reformatory movement that had inspired it.[61]

Elmira Reformatory
A New York reformatory that emphasized rehabilitation rather than punishment.

▶ **Prison Metal Shop**
Inmates produce license plates and
other items in prison metal shops.

▶ **Prison Metal Shop**
Inmates produce license plates and
other items in prison metal shops.

industrial prison
A prison factory where the focus was on
creating a productive work environment
rather than the rehabilitation or reform
of prisoners.

The Industrial Prison System

The course of correctional history has seen pendulum swings back and forth
between rehabilitation and punishment. Following the failure of the reformatory movement, the pendulum swung back to punishment and away from
treatment and rehabilitation.

The beginning of the twentieth century saw a return to the earlier practice
of establishing prison industries. Using strict discipline and regimentation, prison
administrators capitalized on the availability of free inmate labor to subsidize the
cost of running the institution. Goods made by prisoners were sold on the open
market, outside the walls of the penitentiary.[62] In these **industrial prisons,** or
prison factories, administrators focused on creating a productive work environment rather than on prisoner rehabilitation. However, the need to establish order
to maximize productivity made conditions in prisons more oppressive and violent
in these years.[63] Much of the rationale for the industrial prison system was to
use inmate labor to reduce the prison's costs.[64]

In the southern states, where Blacks made up more than 75 percent of the
convicts, the industrial prison became little more than a setting for institutionalized slavery. Southern states leased prisoners to private parties outside the
prison, who frequently misused them. Prisoners were organized into chain gangs
to work on roads and were also used as a labor force on large farms and plan-
tations. The buildings that housed prisoners were little more than small cages.[65]

Prison labor served to meet the institution's needs while giving little back to
the inmate other than the most rudimentary vocational training. In the context
of the larger U.S. economy, however, the output of prison factories was eventually
so significant that labor unions complained about unfair competition from the
prison industries. Consequently, federal legislation brought the widespread use of
prison labor to an end in the 1930s.[66] In 1979 Congress relaxed these legal restrictions somewhat by passing the Percy Amendment, which allowed private companies to employ prisoners under specific conditions.[67] In an example of privatization
of prison labor, Whole Foods contracts with the Colorado Corrections Industries;
its inmates produce fish and cheese that profit this private food company.[68]

The Therapeutic Prison

With the popularity of psychology and psychoanalysis growing in the United
States during the twentieth century, the concept of treatment caught the
attention of prison reformers. In corrections, this therapeutic emphasis meant

that, based on the **medical model,** prisoners needed treatment. According to this perspective, people, if not healthy, are ill. This model was gradually popularized during the nineteenth century, when mental illness and behavioral problems began to be viewed as diseases. However, the medical model was not implemented in the corrections field until the late 1920s, when inmates came to be seen as mostly "sick" individuals in need of treatment. In other words, criminals were "mad," as in mentally ill, rather than "bad." The "symptoms" of their disorders were their crimes, and it was believed that their condition could be treated by giving them programs and services while incarcerated.

The therapeutic prison gained momentum in the 1930s, giving rise to a widespread practice of diagnosing and classifying inmates. This practice established a place for psychologists and psychiatrists in U.S. prisons. Group therapy (dealing with offenders in groups rather than individually), behavior therapy (using rewards and punishments to change behavior), and aversion therapy (using noxious or painful stimuli to remove unacceptable behaviors) were just a few of the many treatment approaches to grow out of the therapeutic movement. By the mid-1960s, therapeutic programs had reached the height of their popularity in U.S. prisons.

As the 1960s came to a close, however, doubts were raised about the effectiveness of such programs to treat and "cure" offenders. The rehabilitative ideal lost favor with both the public and correctional administrators. At the same time, the rapidly growing prison population diverted existing resources to institutional management, and funding for treatment programs faded from prison budgets.[69] Following several disturbing and brutal prison riots in the United States during the 1970s and 1980s, public opinion shifted from the plight of prisoners and focused instead on more punitive policies, replacing what had been widespread support for treatment programs.

The death knell for the rehabilitative ideal in U.S. prisons was the **Martinson Report** of 1974. Sociologist Robert Martinson, along with colleagues Douglas Lipton and Judith Wilks, analyzed published studies on the therapeutic effectiveness of more than 200 treatment programs. In looking at this broad picture, Martinson concluded that "with few and isolated exceptions, the rehabilitative efforts that have been reported so far have had no appreciable effect on recidivism." He found that certain treatments were effective for some kinds

medical model
A viewpoint focusing on mental illness and behavioral problems, such as committing a crime, as diseases.

Martinson Report
A report, published in 1974, indicating that rehabilitative efforts, for the most part, were having little to no effect on recidivism.

◀ **Attica Prison Riot**
Prison riots frequently result in violence.

Selected Events in Corrections History
Trends and patterns in the history of corrections

1000 CE–1300 CE	Secular and church law ordaining harsh punishments for criminals evolves during the Middle Ages.
1553	Bridewell workhouse is initiated for vagrants and the homeless.
1619	Transportation of British convicts to the North American colonies begins.
1790	Walnut Street Jail opens the country's first penitentiary wing.
1816	Auburn Prison is built in New York State.
1826	Western Penitentiary is built in Pittsburgh, Pennsylvania.
1829	Eastern State Penitentiary opens in Philadelphia.
1873	First women's prison, the Indiana Reformatory Institution, opens.
1876–1900	The reformatory movement is strong.
1876	Elmira Reformatory opens.
1900–1930	The industrial prison movement is strong.
1930–1960	The therapeutic prison movement dominates U.S. corrections systems.
1960–1980	The community-based corrections movement is strong.
1980–present	The incarceration movement dominates U.S. corrections systems.

of inmates. His conclusions, however, came to be summarily reduced to "nothing works"–although Martinson himself never wrote these words.[70]

The unfortunate mantra of "nothing works" gave support once again to those who argued that what criminals needed was not treatment but punishment. The enormous negative spin around the Martinson Report dealt a severe blow to funding for correctional treatment programs. Many researchers, including Martinson himself, attempted to correct the misunderstandings surrounding the 1974 study, but the damage had been done.[71] Indeed, correctional rehabilitation programming has not recovered. Very little is spent today on rehabilitation programs for each U.S. prisoner. Furthermore, less than 5 percent of the inmate population has access to any treatment programs.[72] For example, California spends about $49,000 on each prisoner annually, but only about 9 percent of the $9.5 billion Department of Corrections and Rehabilitation budget is spent on mental health and rehabilitation programs. The majority of the remaining money is expended on custody.[73]

This brief history of corrections has shown how rehabilitation and punishment have seesawed in prominence over the years in the development of the U.S. corrections system. A brief chronology of selected events in this history is displayed in the table on this page. In the section that follows, we look at how prisons today make use of the various historical models of correction we have examined.

MODELS OF CORRECTIONS TODAY

The responsibility for administering institutional and community corrections today rests at local, state, and federal levels of government and sometimes in the private sector, as illustrated in Figure 11-1. When we use the term *jail* in the following pages, we are referring to local facilities used to hold individuals who are awaiting trial or punishment and to incarcerate offenders convicted of misdemeanor crimes. When we use the term *prison*, we are referring to institutions that are funded by and responsible to the state or federal government and that hold individuals who are sentenced to longer terms. Government entities also contract with private companies to operate private jails.

FIGURE 11-1 **Correctional Programs Operate at Multiple Levels of Government**

Whatever the type of facility, corrections has the responsibility of keeping society—and convicted offenders—safe until the offender is, ideally, transformed from a law-violating to a law-abiding member of society. People in the United States also expect corrections to punish, deliver retribution, incapacitate, and rehabilitate offenders and then to integrate them back into society. In recent years, the goal of serving victims has been added to this list.

Accomplishment of any one of these goals, let alone all, is a monumental challenge. In large measure they represent conflicting philosophies of corrections. In response to these goals, four different operational models have developed for correctional facilities. The punishment model developed first, followed by the crime control model, then the rehabilitation model, and finally the reintegration model. In practice, today's institutions draw from all of these models to achieve results.

Punishment Model

At the core of the **punishment model** of corrections is the assumption that the offender is inherently a bad person and deserves to be placed under correctional authority for punishment. From this perspective, offenders are not seen as individuals with particular problems in need of treatment. Rather, for the most part, they are viewed as people who choose to commit crime and should thus be punished. Rehabilitation is irrelevant, except to the extent punishment has rehabilitative potential by instilling fear in an offender, deterring the offender from committing future crimes. Treatment programs are considered a waste of resources. Appropriate and timely punishment is thought to be more cost-effective.

Advocates of this model lean toward severe sanctions for offenders. They charge that the criminal justice system is too soft on criminals, compromising true justice, and that retribution should be the primary goal of corrections. They oppose many of the amenities provided by prisons such as television and special recreation programs. These advocates also criticize the use of probation, parole, and other forms of community corrections to eliminate or reduce an inmate's sentence of incarceration.

The punishment model uses negative reinforcement such as fines, incarceration, confiscation of property, heavy body-chain constraints, and isolation cells to mold behavior. This model falls short of its goal, however, because recidivism rates under this system remain high. Research indicates that punishment can temporarily change behavior and make people comply, but these changes are not long-lasting.[74] Furthermore, the punishment model may eventually release antisocial offenders back into society without having had any positive or permanent impact on their behavior. The punishment model is most likely to be found in correctional institutions with high security levels.

punishment model
A viewpoint that assumes that the offender is inherently a bad person and deserves to be placed under correctional authority for punishment.

a case in p◆int

Hawaii's HOPE Program for High-Risk Probation Offenders

Hawaii's Opportunity Probation with Enforcement (HOPE), an experimental probation program, began in 2004 with the goal of reducing probation violations by targeting difficult offenders like heavy drug users and domestic violence perpetrators. The program depends on the highest degree possible of offender supervision and fast tough love. Quick and certain sanctions such as on-the-spot arrests are imposed for any violation that comes to the attention of authorities. Sanctions typically include brief jail time even for violations like missed appointments with probation officers. If offenders continue to transgress, they might receive progressively more jail time for subsequent breaches of rules. They also can be placed in residential treatment. HOPE differs from drug courts in that it focuses on rule violations, not

mandated drug treatment; however, treatment is available to probationers who request it or who continue to have positive drug tests.

Rules and consequences of the program are given to probationers by judges at the beginning. Probationers are required to call a designated hotline every weekday morning to learn if they must report to take a random drug test that day. Normally drug testing occurs weekly for the first two months.[a]

To date, the results of the HOPE program have been amazing. For example, 55 percent of probationers in HOPE were less likely to be arrested for a new crime; 53 percent were less likely to have their probation revoked; 72 percent were less likely to use drugs; and 61 percent were less likely to miss probation appointments.[b]

HOPE's success is partially attributed to applying best correctional practices of having buy-in by judges, probationers, jail and law enforcement personnel, prosecutors, and public defenders (including defense attorneys)—all key players in the criminal justice system. Additionally, the success of the program is attributed to having an independent research component that publically reports program results.[c] To date, the outcomes of HOPE are so encouraging that the Bureau of Justice Assistance and National Institute of Justice have partnered to replicate the HOPE model in designated counties in Oregon, Massachusetts, Arkansas, and Texas. In addition, the Research Triangle Institute at Pennsylvania State University will do further evaluation, the results of which should be available in the near future.[d]

SOURCES: [a] Friends of HOPE, "The History of HOPE Probation." www.hopeprobation.org/ (retrieved January 21, 2013).

[b] National Institute of Justice, "'Swift and Certain' Sanctions in Probation Are Highly Effective: Evaluation of the HOPE Program," February 3, 2012. www.nij.gov/topics/corrections/community/drug-offenders/hawaii-hope.htm (retrieved January 21, 2013).

[c] Friends of HOPE, "Benchmarks for Success," August 2010. www.hopeprobation.org/about/benchmarks-for-success (retrieved January 21, 2013).

[d] National Institute of Justice, "'Swift and Certain' Sanctions in Probation Are Highly Effective."

crime control model

A corrections model that has as its primary goal suppression and containment of the behavior of criminals.

Crime Control Model

The **crime control model,** an extension of the punishment model, gained momentum in the United States during the early 1980s when prison building surged. Under this model, the infliction of harsh punishments on wrongdoers is not the major goal; instead, the primary goal is to suppress and contain the behavior of criminals through incarceration. "A Case in Point" illustrates an example of a corrections program that follows a crime control model.

Today the crime control model is used in medium-, maximum-, and super-maximum-security prisons, where the primary correctional goals are to contain and control inmates. There is little attempt to change prisoners' behaviors, short of making them comply with rules and regulations within the walls. That is, rehabilitation and reform are not the objectives.

A drawback of the crime control model, like that of the punishment model, is that when prisons release nonrehabilitated offenders back into the community, the streets are often less safe because offenders have not learned prosocial behaviors–those that show concern for others' rights and well-being–while incarcerated. Some prisoners even learn more sophisticated crime techniques while being locked up with other offenders. The benefit of this model is that offenders are not on the streets committing crimes during their time of confinement.

The means by which offenders can be incapacitated are many. In the past, these methods included such questionable practices as over-medicating violent criminals to suppress assertive behavior, castrating sex offenders, and execution. However, today the most widely accepted and least controversial method of incapacitation is incarceration, the hallmark of the crime control model. Indeed, as crime rates rose in the 1970s, there were calls to increase the number of correctional facilities and maximize the number of inmates they house; to hire more correctional officers and give them greater power over prisoners; to reduce criminals' rights;

▲ **Chain Gang**
Prisoners are often seen working on highways in chain gangs.

Real Careers

ISAAC TORRES

Work location: Fresno, California

College(s): California State University, Fresno (2009)

Major(s): Criminology with Corrections Option (BS)

Job title: Correctional Officer, Population Management Unit, and Gang Officer, Fresno County Jail

Salary range for job like this: $60,000–$80,000

Time in job: 4 years

Work Responsibilities
My work responsibilities entail monitoring the inflow and outflow of inmates at the jail and ensuring that each inmate is appropriately housed within the facility. My workweek includes three to four 12-hour shifts that begin at 6 p.m. and end at 6 a.m. During each shift I ensure that our inmate count is in compliance with federal guidelines to avoid overcrowding.

My unit is responsible for interviewing all newly processed inmates and assigning them a classification score by points. To do this I review the inmates' criminal history, behavior during any previous stays in the facility, nature of current charges, and any information gathered from them that would affect their safety in the facility. In addition, I respond to any institutional disturbances and investigate the need for housing changes after an incident occurs. As the designated gang officer in my unit, I am responsible for the collection of gang information, current trends, institutional gang-related conflicts, and possible threats to the safety and security of staff, inmates, or the facility.

Why Criminal Justice?
I chose to major in criminology because I have been interested in law enforcement since my childhood. Law enforcement gives me the opportunity to have a positive impact on the lives of people who are in need. In addition, law enforcement is a well-respected and relatively stable career track that allows me to provide for my family.

Expectations and Realities of the Job
Before I started this job I was unaware that the population I would be working with had such prevalent mental health issues. The majority of the population I deal with has some sort of mental illness and/or substance abuse issue that directly affects their behavior, posing many challenges to me and my coworkers as well as threats to our safety and the safety of other inmates. It is difficult to find appropriate housing for inmates with mental health issues and to provide mental health care in a safe manner.

My Advice to Students
Enter your career with the spirit of being a team player. Sometimes collaborating with your coworkers is the only way you can get the job done.

and to push for more punitive sanctions for all kinds of offenders. The clear demand was to remove offenders from the streets so they could no longer victimize innocent citizens.

By the late 1970s, the crime control model had become the dominant philosophy of corrections. It continues to guide current practices as a component of the tough-on-crime criminal justice response of recent decades.

Rehabilitation Model

rehabilitation model
A viewpoint that assumes the offender is inherently a good person and that focuses on changing the offender's behavior.

As we saw earlier in this chapter, the **rehabilitation model** developed late in the nineteenth century in response to the harshness of the punishment model. An assumption of the rehabilitation model is *social determinism*—the idea that social factors such as poverty and lack of educational opportunities, not an individual's self-will, produce behavior. At the core of the rehabilitation model is an effort to change an offender's behavior, often using medical approaches. Thus in the nineteenth century many forms of deviance, such as alcoholism and crime, came to be seen as treatable conditions.

Rehabilitation can be helpful for a wide variety of crimes against persons and property precipitated by substance abuse, poverty, lack of job skills, and many types of mental illness. Intervention in the form of rehabilitation also is especially important to prevent juvenile offenders from becoming adult offenders. Rehabilitation models support programs that provide therapy, job training, and education for offenders. It is assumed that by offering these programs to those who are unable to manage themselves in society, future crimes will be prevented.

By the 1930s, correctional institutions were being developed around the medical model. Their primary mission was to treat offenders, make them better, and then return them to society as law-abiding citizens. Correctional professionals studied offenders, attempted to make accurate diagnoses, and developed treatment plans that included counseling, education, and vocational training.[75] The medical model is still used today in therapeutic community treatment programs dealing with alcohol and drug addictions. The medical model is also used to treat offenders who suffer from attention deficit disorder, other types of biologically based brain dysfunctions, and learning disabilities. It is the model of choice to treat offenders who have physical or mental illnesses. By utilizing medical model strategies and protocols, prison administrators hope to change (and perhaps cure) the offenders.

An important part of the rehabilitation model is the indeterminate sentence, which ensures that an inmate will stay incarcerated for as long as necessary to be cured. The indeterminate sentence recognizes that the length of time needed to treat and reform offenders successfully varies from individual to individual.

In addition to indeterminate sentences, a comprehensive system of classifying inmates is considered essential for effective rehabilitation. Classification is based on both the nature and the degree of risk that inmates pose for an institution and an evaluation of their specific treatment needs. This classification enables prisoners to be matched with appropriate programs designed to assist them in the reformation process.

Reintegration Model

reintegration model
A viewpoint that assumes that the offender must be helped to readjust and fit successfully back into the community.

The **reintegration model** developed gradually as a logical extension of the rehabilitation model. Its goal is to help offenders readjust and fit successfully back into the community. This objective is accomplished through supervised, structured programs that reinforce preexisting positive ties as well as through establishing new connections with people and institutions in the community.[76] Most offenders return to their community after being released from prison.[77]

In corrections, reintegration programs give offenders increased freedom and responsibility before they are released into the community without supervision.

KEY CONCEPTS   Principles of the Punishment, Crime Control, Rehabilitation, and Reintegration Models of Corrections

Each model approaches corrections from a different perspective and emphasizes different aspects.

	Punishment	Crime Control	Rehabilitation	Reintegration
Purpose of corrections	Retribution	Incapacitation	Behavior change	Accountability to community
Perception of offender's nature	Offender is bad	Offender is bad	Offender is human, makes mistakes, and is capable of guidance	Offender is human, makes mistakes, and is capable of guidance
Cause of offender's behavior	Free will	Free will	Social determinism	Social determinism
Treatment's role	No treatment	No treatment	Treatment needed and helpful	Treatment needed and helpful
View of offender's behavior change	Change questionable	Change questionable	Change possible	Change possible
Best practices for behavior change	Fear-producing sanctions	Incarceration	Programs	Programs

Parole is an example of a reintegration program. Another example is the **halfway house,** a loosely structured, prerelease, community-based residence that helps prisoners adjust to the community after total incarceration. Most prisons have programs that attempt to prepare offenders for release back into the community as their sentence comes to a close. Reintegration programs also are emphasized in institutions where large numbers of prisoners serve shorter sentences. Not surprisingly, many who support the reintegration model align themselves with the goals of the rehabilitation model.[78]

The reintegration model is based on the principles of restorative justice, a subject enjoying a great deal of attention today. **Restorative justice** focuses on the offender's responsibility to repair the hurt, damage, and injustice that the crime victim has experienced by making restitution and doing community service.[79]

The reintegration model holds the offender accountable to the people and communities she has injured. It seeks to return the rehabilitated offender back into society as a productive, reformed citizen who accepts responsibility for her actions, has prosocial attitudes, and no longer commits crime. See the Key Concepts feature for a comparison of the principles of the punishment, crime control, rehabilitation, and reintegration models of corrections.

PRISON POPULATIONS—WHO IS BEHIND BARS?

One in 36 adults in the United States is under some form of correctional supervision, such as probation, jail, prison, or parole.[80] Most of these offenders—about two-thirds—are not incarcerated but are under supervision in the community.[81] Additionally, the U.S. incarceration rate is among the highest in the world at 612 per 100,000 population.[82] When we turn our attention to the most populous countries worldwide, the United States ranks at the top, with about 2,306,100 adults incarcerated.[83] The U.S. has about 5 percent of the world's population and incarcerates about 25 percent of its people.[84] Figure 11-2 is a snapshot of the number of people locked up in the United States.

From a global perspective, the United States incarcerates about half the world's penal population. Another country with a high incarceration rate is Russia (468 per 100,000 population). Countries with low incarceration rates include Japan (49 per 100,000 population) and Iceland (45 per 100,000 population).[85] (See Figure 11-3.)

halfway house
A loosely structured prerelease, community-based residence that helps a prisoner adjust to the community after total incarceration.

restorative justice
A perspective that focuses on the offender's responsibility to repair the hurt, damage, and injustice that the crime victim has experienced by making restitution and doing community service.

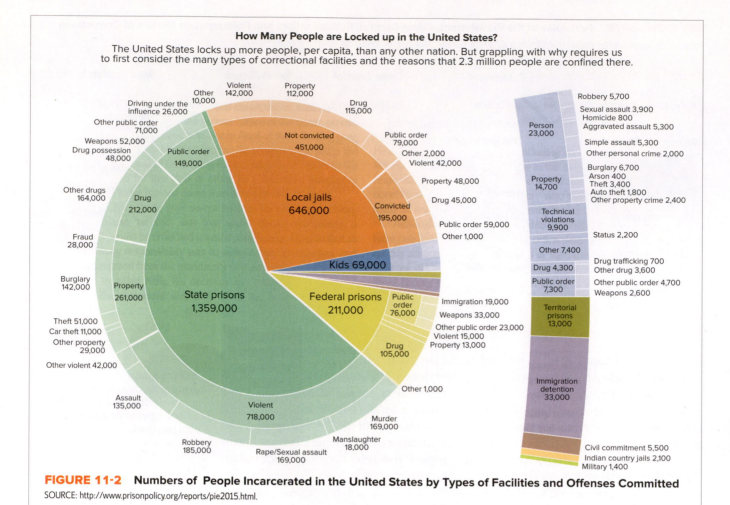

How Many People are Locked up in the United States?

The United States locks up more people, per capita, than any other nation. But grappling with why requires us to first consider the many types of correctional facilities and the reasons that 2.3 million people are confined there.

Violent 142,000
Property 112,000
Other 10,000
Driving under the influence 26,000
Other public order 71,000
Weapons 52,000
Drug possession 48,000
Public order 149,000
Other drugs 164,000
Drug 212,000
Fraud 28,000
Burglary 142,000
Property 261,000
Theft 51,000
Car theft 11,000
Other property 29,000
Other violent 42,000
Assault 135,000
State prisons 1,359,000
Robbery 185,000
Rape/Sexual assault 169,000
Violent 718,000
Murder 169,000
Manslaughter 18,000

Not convicted 451,000
Local jails 646,000
Convicted 195,000
Drug 115,000
Public order 79,000
Other 2,000
Violent 42,000
Property 48,000
Drug 45,000
Public order 59,000
Other 1,000

Kids 69,000

Federal prisons 211,000
Public order 76,000
Drug 105,000
Other 1,000
Immigration 19,000
Weapons 33,000
Other public order 23,000
Violent 15,000
Property 13,000

Person 23,000
Robbery 5,700
Sexual assault 3,900
Homicide 800
Aggravated assault 5,300
Simple assault 5,300
Other personal crime 2,000

Property 14,700
Burglary 6,700
Arson 400
Theft 3,400
Auto theft 1,800
Other property crime 2,400

Technical violations 9,900
Status 2,200

Other 7,400
Drug 4,300
Drug trafficking 700
Other drug 3,600
Public order 7,300
Other public order 4,700
Weapons 2,600

Territorial prisons 13,000

Immigration detention 33,000

Civil commitment 5,500
Indian country jails 2,100
Military 1,400

FIGURE 11-2   Numbers of People Incarcerated in the United States by Types of Facilities and Offenses Committed
SOURCE: http://www.prisonpolicy.org/reports/pie2015.html.

Trends in Inmate Population Numbers

Growth in the U.S. prison population appears to be slowing. In 2006, the number of prisoners under state or federal jurisdiction in the United States started to

▶ **Overcrowding in Prison**

When cells are not available, prisoners are double- and triple-bunked in public areas of the prison like this gym. *How does overcrowding lead to prison violence?*

decline as fewer individuals were being sent to prison by the courts; consequently the prison population is increasing at the slowest rate (0.8 percent) since 2000.[86] In 2014, those incarcerated in state and federal prisons declined by less than 1 percent from the year before, continuing the decline from a few years before.[87]

The number of jail inmates varies widely from county to county within states. Males represent approximately 86 percent of the national jail population. However, the female jail population increased about 18 percent between 2010 and 2014 while the male jail population declined 3.2 percent during the same time frame. The female jail population appears to be the fastest-growing correctional population. In 2014, the U.S. jail inmate population continued its decline since its high in 2007.[88] The jail population falloff was concentrated in the nation's largest jails such as those in Dade County and Orange County, Florida.[89]

In spite of the downward national trend, California's jail population has been increasing steadily since 2010, mainly as a result of California's Public Safety Realignment (PSR) policy, which we discuss next.[90]

MYTH/REALITY

MYTH: Prisons are overcrowded because more people are committing violent crimes.

REALITY: The exploding prison population is due to changes in public policies that increase the use of prison as a sanction and that lengthen the prison sentences imposed by the courts.[91]

Over the years, overcrowding has doomed every attempt at humane prison reform. Between 1970 and 1980 the prison population in the United States doubled. It more than doubled again from 1981 to 1985. These growth spurts overwhelmed both federal and state prison systems.[92] Even during periods of decreasing crime rates, prison populations have continued to increase.

For example, in the 1990s the prison population rose even though there were no increases in the rates of crimes reported either by the FBI's Uniform Crime Reports or by the National Crime Victimization Survey. In 1995, 1.75 million individuals were confined in prison or jail in the United States, and by midyear 2009 almost 2.3 million inmates were confined in these institutions.[93]

The increase in prison population from the 1970s to the present largely reflects changes in public policy—changes driven by public fear. The media have highlighted sensational cases of violent crimes. News reporting has portrayed judges and parole

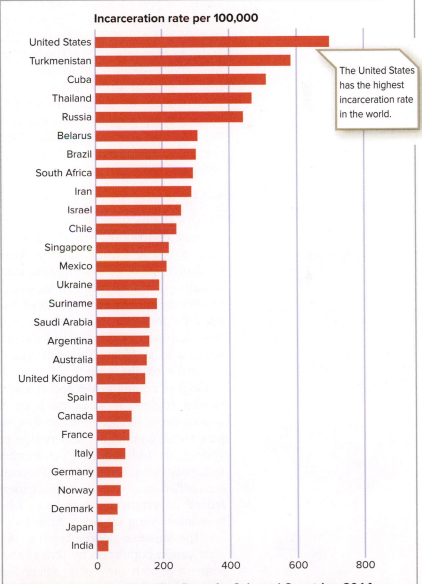

FIGURE 11-3　**Incarceration Rates for Selected Countries, 2014**

SOURCE: International Centre for Prison Studies, "Highest to Lowest—Prison Population Rate." www.prisonstudies.org/highest-to-lowest/prison_population_rate?field_region_taxonomy_tid=All (retrieved April 22, 2015).

authorities as too lenient. Both the media and politicians have taken a tough-on-crime stand that calls for more punitive and longer sentences, thus reinforcing the widespread belief that harsh punishment will reduce crime. One consequence of this changing public attitude has been that judges and parole boards have felt pressured to increase jail and prison terms as a way of assuring the public that the criminal justice system is responsive. Many state legislatures and the federal government have adopted fixed mandatory minimum sentences. Such sentencing "reforms" have left little discretion to the courts and curtailed parole release by reducing choice in parole decisions. The bottom line for prisons: overcrowding has increased.[94]

However, there is evidence the tide may be changing. By midyear 2015, President Barack Obama had shortened the prison sentences by executive action (commutation) of nearly 90 nonviolent, unhardened federal prisoners sentenced for drug offenses—more than any president since Lyndon B. Johnson in the 1960s. Most of the federal prisoners whose sentences were commuted were given long sentences during the 1980s and 1990s when crime rates were very high and sentences were harsher than they are now. More than 15 percent of the total federal prison population has petitioned for a sentence reduction, and some predict several hundred prisoners will have their sentences reduced by the end of 2016. In November 2015, the biggest federal prisoner release program on record took effect. About 6600 federal prisoners are due for release and some speculate that more than 40,000 federal prisoners could be released in the near future.[95] In an attempt to reform the criminal justice system and abolish inequities, other reforms being considered are: easing or eliminating mandatory minimum sentencing laws, abolishing the practice of solitary confinement, eliminating requirements that make offenders identify as prisoners when applying for employment, and allowing those who have done their time to vote.[96]

Public Safety Realignment Policy

Perhaps the most significant U.S. criminal justice reform experiment in the 21st century contributing to the decline of inmate populations in U.S. jails and prisons is the **Public Safety Realignment (PSR)** policy implemented in California. Major goals of realignment policy are to downsize the existing prison population, reduce prison costs, and provide treatment and reintegration services to offenders. This is accomplished by releasing nonviolent, nonserious, and non-sex offenders from state prisons to the county for supervision, and sentencing new nonviolent offenders to local jails instead of state prison. This policy is also referred to as "deinstitutionalization." With realignment, power is shifted from the state to the counties. In a nutshell, realignment requires creating and funding of community-based correctional programs where lower-level offenders remain under the jurisdiction of county governments as opposed to state governments. Inmates released from local jails are placed under a county-directed postrelease community supervision program (PRCS) instead of California's parole system. In addition to PSR, another factor in California's prison population reduction was a new law (Proposition 47) passed by voters in 2014 that reclassified some crimes as misdemeanors that had been felonies.[97] Similarly the federal government has plans to follow California's lead by releasing low-level, nonviolent drug offenders from its prisons in hopes of reducing prison costs.[98]

The Supreme Court (*Brown v. Plata*) in 2011 ordered California to reduce its state prison population by tens of thousands by June 2013. California's legislature responded with the Public Safety Realignment Act of 2011, also known as AB 109 and AB 117, which will give 58 California counties $2 billion in additional funding over a decade to fund and develop effective community-based programs that reduce recidivism. Each county can spend its portion of the money on whatever programs are determined most effective; however, counties must develop a

Public Safety Realignment (PSR)
A policy intended to reduce mass incarceration by downsizing the prison population, reducing prison costs, and providing treatment and reintegration services to offenders.

What about the Victim?

Implications for Victims of California's Prison Realignment Policy

In 2011 Governor Jerry Brown signed historic legislation that allowed California to address the problem of prison overcrowding. The legislation, known as AB 109 or the Public Safety Realignment Act, requires nonviolent, nonserious, and non-sex offenders who would have been sentenced to prison to be incarcerated in jail in the county within which the crime was committed. Counties also are responsible for supervising those individuals who have been released from state correctional institutions either to county jails or to local rehabilitation facilities. Although there are other provisions of AB 109, the focus herein will be on the potential for further victimization when a violent offender is classified as nonviolent and is released back into the community. A few high-profile cases have brought this issue to the forefront, and some are questioning AB 109 as a result. Furthermore, when violent individuals are misclassified or their full violent history is not examined in the release decision, there are several ethical implications associated with community safety and further victimization.

In September 2012, Michael Crockell was arrested for assault with a deadly weapon. Crockell, who had a history of domestic violence, only spent 6 months of a 3-year term incarcerated and was released back into the community. Upon his release, Crockell stabbed one person 47 times and fatally stabbed another 15 times. The responding officer was also stabbed 3 times. A few months later, Jose Luis Saenz, classified as a low-level, nonviolent offender for his prior conviction of possession of a controlled substance, absconded and was arrested in Guadalajara, Mexico, for allegedly killing four people. On December 2, 2012, Ka Pasasouk, 11 months after being released from a state institution, was arrested with three other people for brutally killing four people at an unlicensed boardinghouse in Northridge, California. Pasasouk's prior commitments were for vehicle, which is considered a low-level nonviolent

criminal offense, and robbery in the second degree—a violent criminal offense. Pasasouk was misclassified and released as a low-level nonviolent criminal offender and assigned to community supervision under the Los Angeles County Probation Department.

Some community members have called into question how these offenders were released into the community under AB 109. Classifications are based upon the criminal's most recent crime, which may not be violent and may not be indicative of a history of violent crimes. Also, some violent crimes such as intimate partner violence are not always considered violent and these individuals are released. As a result, there remains a potential safety threat to the community or to previous victims of repeat offenders, as is the case with intimate partner violence. Victim advocates have long voiced their concerns over the release of inmates into the community, the inability to adequately monitor and supervise violent offenders, the potential for further victimization, and how to best protect the community from repeat offenders.

OBSERVE → INVESTIGATE → UNDERSTAND

- Do you agree with the provisions of AB 109? If not, how would you reduce prison overcrowding?

- If an offender is misclassified and/or commits a violent crime after being released, who should be responsible for the mistake? What actions should be taken to ensure that this does not occur again?

- Victims are given several rights, one of which is the right to be heard. Do you think that this right should be granted before a person is released back into the community under AB 109?

SOURCE: *California Department of Corrections and Rehabilitation Fact Sheet.* July 15, 2011. http://www.ab109.com/wp-content/uploads/2011/08/Realignment-Fact-Sheet-CDCR.pdf (retrieved February 12, 2013).

---

rigorous plan for custody and postcustody. Now persons convicted of low-level, nonserious felonies serve time in county jail as opposed to prison–regardless of the length of their sentence–if they do not have serious or violent prior convictions. Furthermore, there is no more parole for low-level felons, and counties must supervise them until they are discharged. Lastly, no probation or parole violator can go back to prison for technical violations, only for a conviction of a new crime.

Some of the factors that contributed to realignment were astronomical incarceration costs, declining revenues resulting in budget cuts, historic reduction in crime rates, court rulings forcing states to reduce the prison population, and demands of citizens, public safety professionals, and legislators for scientific, evidence-based practices that result in proven lowered recidivism rates. Some examples of evidence-based practices that have promise of success are flash incarceration (certain and swift detention in county jail because an offender violated postrelease supervision conditions), community-based services, day courts, drug courts, and better risk assessment tools.

Time will ultimately tell if realignment will live up to its goals. In the meantime, California state prisons are releasing low-level felons back to counties for handling, and counties are doing their best to deal with the tidal wave of offenders coming back into the community.[99] The "What about the Victim?" box illustrates some of the problems that are emerging as a result of Public

Race, Class, Gender

Treating Women in Prisons . . . as Second-Class Citizens of the System

How do women fare in a corrections system whose priorities are largely determined by the reality that female offenders are far outnumbered by their male counterparts? The answer to this question is particularly important when it comes to evaluating the availability and quality of medical care afforded to women in prison. The matter is further complicated by what common sense suggests and research shows: Females have special needs. But to what extent are prisons obligated to meet those needs? In *Estelle v. Gamble* (1976), the U.S. Supreme Court ruled that male and female inmates alike have a right to treatment. Yet incarcerated women, alone and as part of class action suits, are suing prisons for failing to provide timely and/or adequate medical care. Citing a violation of the Eighth Amendment against cruel and unusual punishment, these inmates allege they had "serious medical needs" and that prison officials exhibited "deliberate indifference" to those needs. In other words, administrators must provide timely access to needed medical care. Although this provides a guideline for determining inadequate treatment, there is no single agency to which all correctional facilities are accountable on the matter of medical care. As such we find a wide range in the quality and availability of health care services provided to inmates across the country—a situation that has invited a wave of litigation.

Binswanger et al. (2009) found that prison inmates have higher rates of chronic medical conditions (such as hypertension, asthma, arthritis, hepatitis, and cervical cancer) than the general population and that female inmates are significantly more likely than incarcerated men to report them. Male inmates can contract most of the same diseases as incarcerated women (including HIV/AIDS and breast cancer), but female prisoners are more likely to experience more severe medical problems associated with these illnesses. Bloom et al. (2008) note the higher proportion of females who enter prison with preexisting substance abuse and dependence problems—not surprising given that drug-related offenses bring so many of them to prison in the first place. In addition, mirroring the communities from which they come, female inmates are more likely to be depressed and to have posttraumatic stress disorder (related to past physical and sexual abuse) and other psychiatric problems than their male counterparts.

In addition, women have more special health care needs, and these needs increase with age, such as with osteoporosis and problems associated with menopause. Most apparent are the gynecological and obstetric needs that are unique to women. Things that seem as basic as the provision of adequate sanitary supplies have become major issues in some prisons. In California, for example, recent budget cuts led to the decision to ration inmates to two tampons and one napkin for each day of their period—not sufficient for many women. This has created unsanitary conditions, not to mention increased tension among inmates given their close living quarters.

In addition to screening and medical treatment for general reproductive health, some women are pregnant when they enter prison. Nationwide, approximately 4 percent of female inmates report they were pregnant at the time of their incarceration. Beyond medical testing to confirm the pregnancy, prisons have an obligation to provide adequate prenatal care to the point of delivery of the baby (or services that may involve abortion). Many people are shocked to learn that most jurisdictions permit prisoners to be shackled to the bed during childbirth. Since 2000, only about half a dozen states have passed laws to prohibit this practice. California, for example, prohibits the use of leg and wrist restraints on women who are pregnant or who are in childbirth or recovery following the birth of a child unless there are safety concerns that otherwise dictate the particular situation.

Although it is unfortunate that lawsuits have been a key motivator in changing the operational priorities of prison administrators, it is nonetheless encouraging to see more prison jurisdictions taking initiatives toward a more gender-responsive approach to the needs of female offenders.

OBSERVE → INVESTIGATE → UNDERSTAND

- Beyond the fact that there are so many fewer women than men in prison, what other reasons can you think of that have served to perpetuate the generally poor medical services offered to incarcerated women?

- In today's economy there are many people who cannot afford and therefore do not have access to adequate health care. Do you think it is fair that convicted criminals are given medical services that other law-abiding citizens do not have?

- Do you think there should be a single (national) agency to establish and monitor health care standards for incarcerated women? What would be the advantages of such an agency? Why might it not be a good idea?

SOURCES: *Estelle v. Gamble*, 429 U.S. 97, 104, 97 S. Ct. 285, 291, 50 L. Ed. 2d 251, 260 (1976); Correctional Association of New York, Women in Prison Project, "Women in Prison Fact Sheet" (April 2009). www.correctionalassociation.org/resource/women-in-prison-fact-sheet (retrieved March 17, 2013); "California Women Prisons: Inmates Face Sexual Abuse, Lack of Medical Care and Unsanitary Conditions," *Huff Post*, Los Angeles, August 3, 2011. www.huffingtonpost.com/2011/06/03/california-women-prisons_n_871125.html (retrieved March 17, 2013); Barbara E. Bloom and Stephanie S. Covington, "Addressing the Mental Health Needs of Women Offenders," (La Jolla, CA: Center for Gender & Justice, 2008). www.centerforgenderandjustice.org/pdf/FinalAddressingtheMentalHealthNeeds.pdf (retrieved March 17, 2013); I. A. Binswanger, P. M. Krueger, and J. F. Steiner, "Prevalence of Chronic Medical Conditions among Jail and Prison Inmates in the USA Compared with the General Population," *Journal of Epidemiology and Community Health* 63, no. 11 (November 2009): 912–919. www.ncbi.nlm.nih.gov/pubmed/19648129 (retrieved March 16, 2013); Columbia Human Rights Law Review, "Special Issues of Women Prisoners," Chapter 41, in *A Jailhouse Lawyer's Manual*, 9th ed. (2011). www3.law.columbia.edu/hrlr/jlm/chapter-41.pdf (retrieved March 17, 2013); Adam Liptak, "Prisons Often Shackle Pregnant Inmates in Labor," *New York Times*, March 2, 2006. www.nytimes.com/2006/03/02/national/02shackles.html?pagewanted5all&_r50 (retrieved March 17, 2013).

Safety Realignment in California. (See Chapter 12 for information on specific problems jails and prisons are experiencing as a result of realignment and Chapter 13 for realignment's implications for community-based corrections.)[100]

Differences by Gender and Race

There are vast and continuing differences in jail rates and in state and federal prison incarceration rates by gender. Males account for about 93 percent of all inmates. Since 1980, the number of female prisoners has been increasing at a rate 50 percent higher than the number of male prisoners.[101] The number of sentenced females to more than a year in state or federal prisons increased about 2 percent between 2013 and 2014, resulting in the largest number of female inmates since 2008.[102] With regard to jail populations, female inmates increased 48 percent between 1999 and 2013, making them the fastest growing correctional population.[103] Furthermore, although White females comprise the majority of the female prison population, Black females (113 per 100,000) are imprisoned at twice the rate of White females (51 per 100,000). As public safety realignment policies are being enforced, we may see declines in imprisonment rates for both men and women.[104] See the "Race, Class, Gender" box for a discussion of some of the distinctive medical issues incarcerated women experience.

The fact that there have always been more male than female offenders within the criminal justice system has given rise to the *chivalry hypothesis*—the belief that women offenders are treated differently from male offenders by law enforcement, the courts, corrections, and victim services. The assumption behind this hypothesis is that women are either good and in need of male guidance and gentle protection, or bad and in need of extreme punishment. Examples of male chivalry may be a stronger inclination for male police officers not to arrest women and a greater tendency for male judges to give females release on bail, to dismiss cases involving females, and to grant women lighter sentences.[105]

Not only are males disproportionately represented in U.S. jails and prisons—so are people of color. In 2014 approximately 32 percent of White males, 37 percent of Black males, and 22 percent of Latino males were imprisoned in state and federal prisons, as Figure 11-4 illustrates.[106] In comparison, in that same year, 47 percent of U.S. jail inmates were White, 35 percent were Black, and 15 percent were Latino.[107]

Incarceration rates for inmates of either sex typically drop with increasing age. Figure 11-5 illustrates that most (about 70 percent) state and federal prison inmates are between the ages of 25 and 49.[108] For males of any age, incarceration rates for Blacks were between five and seven times greater than those for Whites. The same overall pattern holds true for Black and White females, regardless of age group.[109]

Types of Offenders

Although the PSR policy is moving forward in California and the federal government is pushing to remove low-level drug offenders from its prisons, almost 46 percent of those confined in our nation's state prisons in 2014 were serving time for nonviolent crimes, including drug and property crimes and crimes against the public order (also called *public order*

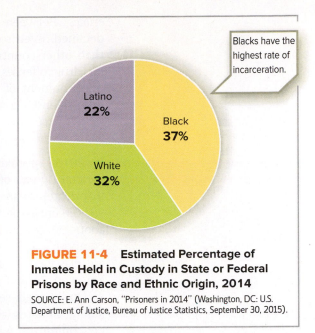

FIGURE 11-4 **Estimated Percentage of Inmates Held in Custody in State or Federal Prisons by Race and Ethnic Origin, 2014**

SOURCE: E. Ann Carson, "Prisoners in 2014" (Washington, DC: U.S. Department of Justice, Bureau of Justice Statistics, September 30, 2015).

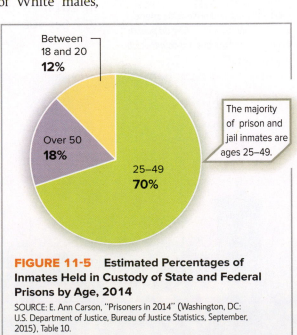

FIGURE 11-5 **Estimated Percentages of Inmates Held in Custody of State and Federal Prisons by Age, 2014**

SOURCE: E. Ann Carson, "Prisoners in 2014" (Washington, DC: U.S. Department of Justice, Bureau of Justice Statistics, September, 2015), Table 10.

crimes). Between 2000 and 2014, the number of drug offenders in state prisons declined. Even so, the United States incarcerates more people for drug offenses than other countries. About 16 percent of inmates in state prisons incarcerated for drug offenses, and the increase in the prison population is driven by the imprisonment of drug offenders. Among federal inmates, those incarcerated for drug offenses constituted the largest number of prisoners (over 50 percent).[110]

Federal Prison Inmates

In 2015, approximately 209,000 inmates were under the jurisdiction of the Federal Bureau of Prisons. To handle overcrowding about 12 percent were held in privately managed prisons. The population of federal prison inmates is about 93 percent male. Most inmates are White (about 60 percent). Blacks constitute about 38 percent of the population, and Native Americans and Asians together compose about 3 percent of federal inmates. About 34 percent of the population are classified as being of Latino ethnicity. The majority of federal inmates are between 26 and 49 years of age.[111]

Individuals sentenced for drug offenses constituted the largest number of federal inmates (about 49 percent) in 2015. About 16 percent of federal offenders committed weapons, explosives, and arson offenses, and 10 percent committed immigration offenses.[112]

Also it appears that the while the U.S. prison population increased in 2013, the federal inmate population decreased for the first time since 1980 and continued its decline in 2014.[113] This is partially due to changes in the federal government's decades' long policy of mass incarceration.[114]

State Prison Inmates

Each of the 50 U.S. states operates a prison system. The number of prisons each state runs is determined by the number of prisoners sentenced by the courts to state institutions. States vary widely in the number of state prisons and prisoners. For example, California (136,088 inmates), Texas (166,043), Florida (102,870), and New York (52,518) operate large prison systems; North Dakota (1,718), Vermont (1,979), and Maine (2,242) have small prison systems.[115]

Figure 11-6 illustrates the highest and lowest state incarceration rates in 2014. As of 2014, the state prison incarceration rate for U.S. males was 777 per 100,000 population and for females was 58 per 100,000 population.[116]

▼ **Ensuring Security**

Federal prisons are secure environments, and prisoners cannot move around at will. *Why do people believe federal prisons are country club environments?*

Noninstitutional or Community Corrections

Chapter 13 addresses the role that community corrections plays in the broader correctional system. Here we consider the population under the supervision of community corrections programs, to distinguish it from institutional populations.

Correctional programs administered in the community include probation and parole. In 2014, 1 in 52 adults (about 4,708,100 people) were under the authority of federal, state, or local probation or parole agencies.[117] See Figure 13-4 in Chapter 13 for additional data on adults under community supervision and on probation or parole.

Among probationers, about 75 percent are male; of parolees, about 88 percent are

Highest and Lowest State Incarceration "Rates" (Per 100,000), 2014

Women (National = 65)		Overall (National = 471)		Men (National = 890)	
HIGHEST		**HIGHEST**		**HIGHEST**	
Oklahoma[a]	142	Louisiana	816	Louisiana	1,577
Idaho	125	Mississippi	788	Mississippi	1,146
Kentucky	108	Oklahoma[a]	928	Alabama	1,203
Missouri	100	Alabama	820	Oklahoma[a]	1,269
Arizona	104	Texas	792	Arkansas	1,125
LOWEST		**LOWEST**		**LOWEST**	
Rhode Island[b]	12	Maine	153	Maine	290
Massachusetts	15	Minnesota	194	Minnesota	364
Maine	21	Massachusetts	188	North Dakota	369
New Jersey	22	Rhode Island[b]	178	Massachusetts	373
New York	23	North Dakota	214	Rhode Island[b]	354

a. Counts for 2014 are not comparable to earlier years do to a change in reporting methodology. See jurisdiction notes for more detail.

b. Prisons and jails form one integrated system. Data include total jail and prison populations.

Source: Carson, EA. (2015). *Prisoners in 2014*. Washington, D.C: Bureau of Justice Statistics.

FIGURE 11-6 **Highest and Lowest State Incarceration Rates (per 100,000), 2014**

SOURCE: Sentencing Project, "Highest and Lowest State Incarceration Rates (per 100,000), 2014." http://sentencingproject.org/doc/publications/inc_Trends_in_Corrections_Fact_sheet.pdf (retrieved February 19, 2016); E. Ann Carson, "Prisoners in 2014," *Bureau of Justice Statistics Bulletin* (Washington, DC: U.S. Department of Justice, Bureau of Justice Statistics, September 2015).

male.[118] The majority (54 percent) of individuals on probation are White; 30 percent are Black, and 13 percent are Latino. Percentages of White and Black parolees, on the other hand, are effectively equal (approximately 43 percent and 42 percent, respectively), with Latino constituting 16 percent of this population.[119] Even though the number of individuals in correctional programs in the community is considerably larger than the number of inmates in U.S. jails and prisons, the demographic characteristics of these populations are similar. The main exception is that there are more females and Whites under community supervision than there are incarcerated in jails and prisons.

VICTIM INVOLVEMENT IN CORRECTIONS

Traditionally, correctional institutions have focused solely on the offender, to the exclusion of the victim. *Victim services* is a fairly recent concept in the context of corrections, having begun in 1984 with a *victim-witness notification program* within the federal prison system. This program requires corrections personnel to contact or notify victims and witnesses when there is a change in an inmate's status. By 1987, the American Correctional Association (ACA) had created a task force to address the issues, concerns, and rights of victims. Within 10 years, some state correctional institutions had opened specific offices to work with victims.

These offices represent the rights and interests of victims in relation to offenders in the correctional system and before parole boards. For example, they notify victims about inmates' location and movement within the system, changes in their status (such as movement from a maximum- to a medium-security facility, death while incarcerated, or escape), their release into the

community, and the status of pardons or executions. Victims also are informed about parole hearings and educated about their rights to attend and to participate by discussing the impact of the crime on their life. When victims take part in parole hearings, they can request the implementation of specific conditions, such as preventing a parolee from living in the same county as the one in which the victim resides, and they can ask for the issuance of a protection order upon the offender's release.

Victim Services within Institutions

Victim services offices work with individuals who are victimized within a correctional institution, including correctional officers, staff, and administrators. For example, if a correctional officer is assaulted on the job, victim services can assist with crisis intervention and referrals for long-term counseling. If a visitor has a face-to-face contact visit with an inmate and is not protected by a barrier (for example, glass) and is emotionally or physically abused during a visit, that person, too, is eligible for victim services. Corrections also protects victims and witnesses from inmate contact by monitoring phone and mail correspondence.

In addition, victim services may work with correctional personnel in discussing a traumatic event after it occurs, to ensure that the affected parties receive appropriate services and to prevent future violent incidents; this intervention process is also known as *critical incident debriefing*. For example, if a riot occurs within a correctional institution, victim services may be called on to work with those correctional officers who were involved.

Victim services offices can also help inmates who are physically or sexually abused by staff or inmates while incarcerated. These offices can assist victims in identifying safe and appropriate services in the institution and in the community postrelease. They also help inmates file grievances with a third party, such as an ombudsman, about the victimization and the postvictimization response to the incident. Some common inmate grievances include lack of access to medical or mental health care, improper service provision, or failure to respond to the incident in a timely manner.[120]

Victim Impact Panels and Classes

Victim impact panels and classes provide an opportunity for crime victims to tell a group of offenders about how the crime has affected their lives and those of their families, friends, and neighbors. The latter provision is important if the crime affected the whole community, as in the case of the death or kidnapping of a child. These panels typically include three or four speakers who are victims, each of whom spends about 15 minutes telling his or her story in a nonjudgmental, neutral manner. Normally, the specific offenders of the speakers are not present. Some time is usually dedicated to questions and answers, but the panel's main purpose is for the victims to speak to offenders rather than for victims to engage in a dialogue with their offenders.

Victim impact panels were initiated in 1982 as a method of changing the attitudes of first-time drunk drivers after their conviction in traffic court and of repeat drunk drivers who were serving time in prison. Because of the devastating consequences of drunk driving on its victims and on society, MADD (Mothers Against Drunk Driving) considered it critical to change the generally accepted attitude that these incidents were "accidents" rather than crimes. In 2002, 41 percent of the 42,815 traffic deaths in the United States were alcohol-related.[121] MADD contends that an effective way to change attitudes is to confront drunk drivers with firsthand testimony from the victims of drunk-driving crashes.

Early research indicates that there is no difference in the recidivism rates of either DWI (Driving While Intoxicated) offenders who go to a DWI school or those who attend victim impact panels.[122] Despite the paucity of data on the effectiveness of these panels, in March 2008 the National Highway Transportation Safety Administration (NHTSA) called for the continued use and expansion of victim impact panels for first-time and repeat DWIs.[123]

The positive feedback from both victims and offenders who have participated in victim impact panels have led the courts to order them for individuals who commit crimes other than driving while intoxicated, such as property crimes, physical assault, intimate partner violence, child abuse, elder abuse, and homicide. The survivors or family members of victims often serve on the panels—in prison and jail settings, with parolees, and in treatment programs, as well as in defensive driving schools, youth education programs, and training forums for juvenile and criminal justice professionals. These panelists serve society by helping their listeners better understand the scope and trauma caused by the victimizations.

Viewing Executions

In capital punishment cases, once an offender has been sentenced, many years can pass before the execution takes place. Legislators and corrections departments in a number of the states that have capital punishment must decide whether the members of a victim's family should be permitted to attend the execution of their loved one's murderer. Witnessing the execution helps bring closure for some but may not be right for everyone. States that permit such attendance allow survivors to make that choice for themselves.[124]

In general, state offices that provide services to victims will assist them with the experience of viewing an execution. For example, in Texas, the victim witnesses generally meet with a representative of the Texas Department of Criminal Justice, Victim Services Division, on the afternoon of the execution at a designated location in Huntsville, Texas. The witnesses learn about the execution protocol and view a video that includes footage of the execution chamber and the witness viewing room. The witnesses are then advised what to expect from the time they arrive at the prison until their departure.[125]

UNDERSTANDING PRIVATE PRISONS

Privatization is the transfer of government programs and functions to the private sector.[126] The movement to privatize the operation of government prisons and security stems from the problem of prison overcrowding and also reflects the aggressiveness of the prison industry, which has taken advantage of a political climate that favors privatization (see "Matters of Ethics"). The privatization of prisons and security presents a number of issues and challenges to the criminal justice system. One of the largest private prison companies is the Corrections Corporation of America (CCA). They currently house over 70,000 inmates with a capacity for over 85,000. They currently run 67 prisons and jails.

privatization
Transfer of government programs and functions to the private sector.

Private Prisons

The shift toward prison privatization began in the 1980s, fueled by the belief that private enterprise could build and run prisons more efficiently and less expensively than the government. This idea was especially attractive to federal and state governments that increasingly were struggling to curtail skyrocketing costs.[127]

Matters *of* Ethics

Private Prisons

The fact that private prisons are lucrative business has led to charges of corruption in several states. For example, in 2010 the New Mexico corrections secretary refused to penalize a private prison contractor for understaffing prisons it operated—a violation of its contract with the state. New Mexico lost more than $18 million in penalties due to this lack of contract enforcement. The state saved money, but at the expense of adequately staffing the prison. It turns out that the corrections secretary in New Mexico was a former employee of and a warden for the same private prison corporation. Furthermore, the prison corporation had been accused of unfair political activity by contributing to the campaign of a candidate for sheriff while using unregistered lobbyists to secure a lease renewal of a jail it operated.

In another case, a private prison company took advantage of the small town of Hardin, Montana. It convinced the town to sell $27 million in bonds for the construction of a facility that was built but never used. The bonds have since gone into default.

Arizona, too, has seen private prisons entangled with politics. In 2010 the two major nationwide prison corporations helped draft a tough new immigration law in Arizona that would yield hundreds of millions of dollars in revenue by increasing the number of illegal immigrants detained in their private prisons. The prison companies not only lobbied hard for this legislation, they also contributed to the governor's electoral campaign. In addition, two of the governor's top advisers were former lobbyists for private prison companies. The governor signed the immigration bill and has advocated the privatization of the prisons housing these immigrants.

OBSERVE → INVESTIGATE → UNDERSTAND

- What is a compelling argument for barring current or former employees of private prison corporations who assume political office from developing contracts with private prison corporations?

- Should states be allowed to contract with private corporations to incarcerate prisoners? Why or why not?

- Might prisoners be subject to longer incarceration in private prisons than in government-run facilities? Explain.

SOURCES: Trip Jennings, "No Penalties for Understaffed Private Prisons," *New Mexico Independent,* September 2, 2010; Trip Jennings, "Corrections Secretary's Previous Work for Private Prison Operator Highlighted," *New Mexico Independent,* September 7, 2010; Trip Jennings, "NM Could Have Repeatedly Fined Private Prisons for Low Staffing Levels," *New Mexico Independent,* September 10, 2010; Trip Jennings, "Corrections Gave Up $18 Million in Uncollected Penalties," *New Mexico Independent,* September 15, 2010; *East County Magazine,* "Private Prison Group Uses Unregistered Lobbyists while Giving Money to Sheriff Gore." www.eastcountymagazine.org/node/3463 (retrieved December 31, 2010); Matthew Reichback, "Private Prison Developer Behind Montana Fiasco Involved in Construction of NM Private Prisons," *New Mexico Independent,* October 12, 2009; Trip Jennings, "Private Prisons Pushed for AZ Immigration Law," *New Mexico Independent,* October 28, 2010; Casey Newton, Ginger Rough, and J. J. Hensley, "Arizona Inmate Escape Puts Spot'light on State Private Prisons: Questions Arise over Safety Standards, Taxpayer Savings," *Arizona Republic,* August 22, 2010; Michael Birley, "Private Prison Companies Have Significant Ties to Arizona Immigration Law SB 1070," *San Francisco Examiner,* October 29, 2010. www.examiner.com/crime-in-san-francisco/private-prison-companies-have-significant-ties-to-arizona-immigration-law-sb-1070 (retrieved January 5, 2011).

Trends in Privatization in Corrections In 1983, private, for-profit, prison-building corporations began competing for contracts with local, state, and federal governments, mostly in southern states with high crime rates, large prison populations, weak labor unions, and strong right-to-work laws restricting union activity. Now almost every state contracts with private firms to manage the incarceration of juvenile and adult inmates. The number of private jail and prison beds continued to grow until 2013. According to the Bureau of Justice Statistics, the private prison population for federal and state inmates declined by 3 percent from 2012 to 2013. Private prisons at the end of December 2013 housed 8 percent of all inmates (a total of 133,000).

Costs of Privatization Although the original rationale for use of private prisons was financial savings, private prisons are in fact no less expensive to operate than government-run prisons.[128] To realize savings, some private prisons cut back on spending for prisoner health, provide lower salaries for personnel, and reduce staff training. One analysis of 24 independent studies concluded that private prisons were no more cost-effective than public prisons.[129] A more recent study found similar results.[130]

In 2001, at least $628 million in tax-free bonds and other public subsidies went to private prisons, with almost 75 percent of these private institutions receiving public subsidies.[131] The receipt of tax dollars allowed these private institutions to operate profitably. By lobbying the public and politicians for longer sentences for inmates and more prisons, private companies looked to increase their profits further.[132]

Quality   The evidence on the quality of private prisons is mixed. Some studies in New Mexico and West Virginia indicated that privately operated prisons provide higher-quality services than publicly operated prisons, but this claim was not supported by other studies.[133] Services included in these studies were food preparation, medical and dental care, education, job training, religious services, and other rehabilitative programming. Other studies also reported that the common practice of hiring lower-paid workers in private prisons negatively affects public safety and inmate care.[134] In addition, in some states private prisons keep their costs down by specifying what kind of prisoners they accept–for example, these private prisons might reject higher-cost inmates such as those with health problems. The state is then left to keep the high-cost inmates.[135]

On the positive side, one Florida study found lower rates of recidivism among inmates released from privately operated prisons than among those released from public facilities.[136] However, complicating any assessment of the quality of private prisons is the fact that many researchers contend that most comparisons of outcomes use flawed methods, which makes it impossible to be certain whether private prisons are better or worse than their public counterparts.[137]

There have also been charges of lax oversight in the running of private prisons. In August 2010, three convicts, two of whom were convicted murderers, escaped from a private prison in Arizona using a pair of wire cutters.[138] Prisons in Arizona house convicts not just from Arizona but from all over the United States, and the state places no restrictions or security constraints on the kinds of prisoners private prisons can accept.[139] Moreover, this is not the first such escape from a private prison in Arizona. In 2007, two convicted killers escaped by climbing onto a roof and over the prison walls.[140] These incidents–along with questions about security, efficiency, and the training of personnel–have led Arizona to slow its expansion of private prisons.[141]

Legal Issues   In *Richardson v. McKnight* (1997), the U.S. Supreme Court held that an employee of a private firm who is sued cannot invoke the qualified immunity defense that is available to state government employees (see Chapter 7).[142] The Court noted that because private firms seek to maximize profits and minimize costs, they must be subject to liability rules to prevent them from engaging in harmful activities for the sake of realizing cost benefits. Private firms do not have all the same protections against lawsuits that government entities do; thus a government entity using a private prison may be at risk of lawsuits. If a state uses a private corporation to run a prison and someone sues the private company over prison conditions, the state also may be vulnerable unless it can clearly show it had no knowledge of the problem.

An important–and as yet unsettled–issue is the use of force, including deadly force, by guards and officers. Private prisons could face civil liability and criminal lawsuits for violating the rights of inmates.[143]

faith-based prison programs
Services provided when a private prison corporation builds or operates a prison under contract with a government agency and invites religious organizations to offer rehabilitation services to the inmates.

Faith-Based Prisons

Faith-based prison programs comprise rehabilitation and other services offered by religious organizations to inmates in private prisons. In these programs, community volunteers from different religious groups act as personal mentors to inmates both during incarceration and after release. Inmates' belief in God is said not to be a requirement, and volunteers are not allowed to persuade inmates to change their beliefs. Religious instruction is supposed to accompany, rather than to supplant, other services, such as psychological counseling and treatment for addiction.

In 2001 President George W. Bush signed executive orders creating the White House Office of Faith-Based and Community Initiatives and Centers for Faith-Based and Community Initiatives in five cabinet departments: Justice, Education, Labor, Health and Human Services, and Housing and Urban Development. According to Bush, "The indispensable and transforming work of faith-based and other charitable service groups must be encouraged . . . whether run by Methodists, Muslims, Mormons, or good people of no faith at all."[144] Although President Barack Obama has expressed some support for faith-based initiatives, he has not yet dealt with the issue of faith-based prisons.

In some cases, faith-based programs are housed in separate dormitories within a prison; in other instances, the entire prison is faith-based. The first faith-based prison opened in Florida in 2003 and now has faith-based programs in 16 different facilities. By 2004, 10 states had faith-based prison programs. Theoretically, faith-based programs are to offer instruction in all faiths equally. However, in Florida, more than 90 percent of inmates are Christian, 5 percent are Muslim, and fewer than 1 percent are Jewish. Atheists and members of pagan religions, such as Wicca and Odinism, are on waiting lists for housing in faith-based prisons.[145]

MYTH/REALITY

MYTH: Faith-based prisons are more effective in reducing recidivism than are traditional prisons.

REALITY: Research findings on the efficacy of faith-based prisons are not clear.[146]

Advocates of faith-based prison programs claim that the approach cuts recidivism rates more than do traditional prison rehabilitation and job training programs and that the approach results in fewer disciplinary actions. Critics argue there is as yet no valid study supporting any such claims.[147] Even as of February 2014, research has not been able to confirm that faith-based programs are more effective than others.[148]

The Future of Private Prisons

Private prisons in the United States are big business, and the industry expects continued growth.[149] In reality, however, the population is beginning to decline. Supporters of private prisons argue that having stockholders to whom they must report imposes "market accountability" on corporations, which want to prevent their stock prices from dropping.[150] However, although the potential for economic gain for private prison companies is great, the real benefits to the government—and for inmates—are as yet unclear.

SUMMARY

U.S. correctional facilities today are under tremendous pressure because of the huge number of convictions that are still being churned out of the criminal justice system even though crime continues to decline. Many governing bodies are wrestling with the consequences. Should they build more prisons? Or should they try to reduce the correctional population through mandating shortened sentences, parole, and treatment programs that attempt to prepare the inmate for return to the community? In some ways this dilemma reflects the historical swings from punishment to rehabilitation to punishment and back again California's attempt at realignment is the most recent example.

The philosophy governing a particular correctional institution depends to some extent on the degree of overcrowding and on the severity of the inmates' crimes. Individuals with long sentences tend to be strictly regulated (under the punishment model) or incapacitated through incarceration (the crime control model). Those who are classified as ill generally are offered treatment (under the rehabilitation model), and those who serve shorter sentences may be prepared for return to the community (under the reintegration model). Public opinion, media coverage of crime, and sympathy for victims may sway which direction governing and correctional officials lean in sentencing and treating offenders.

OBSERVE → INVESTIGATE → UNDERSTAND

Review

Define corrections and describe its role in society.

- Corrections is one of the components of the criminal justice system, including but not limited to probation, parole, prisons, and jails.
- Corrections is responsible for managing and treating offenders after they enter the criminal justice system.
- It refers to the social control and punishment of offenders through a system of imprisonment and rehabilitation programs.

Identify the precursors to the U.S. prison.

- Corporal punishment, such as flogging, branding, and mutilation, was used regularly throughout the early history of punishment.
- Torture as punishment was commonplace prior to incarceration.
- Church confinement, in which offenders were held in cells within monasteries to serve years of solitary penance, substituted for immediate death and corporal punishment during the early years of penology.
- Transportation and banishment led to the establishment of foreign penal colonies.
- Galley slavery condemned criminals to a life sentence of rowing ships prior to the use of incarceration as punishment.
- The confinement of prisoners in hulks of abandoned ships led to the development of contemporary prisons on land.
- Workhouses held a mixture of people, including jobless vagrants, debtors, and sometimes serious criminals, and paved the way for the development of prisons.
- Primitive jails sometimes took the form of dedicated sections of estates where private landowners confined lawbreakers until it was time to impose their punishment.

Contrast the features of the Pennsylvania system with those of the Auburn system.

- The Pennsylvania system demanded inmates' solitary confinement, silence, and isolation. Offenders saw only their keepers; all work and meals took place in offenders' individual cells.

- The Auburn system featured severe discipline and corporal punishment for offenders. Work and meals took place with other offenders outside their cells but in silence; offenders did not live in solitary confinement cells but rather had cell block living arrangements; and they moved about in lockstep fashion.

Identify the defining features of reformatories and therapeutic prisons.

- Indeterminate sentences—those featuring the release of offenders when they had been reformed—were instituted to promote rehabilitation in the prison system.
- The rehabilitation and treatment of offenders became a popular concept at the Elmira Reformatory and during the reformatory movement.
- The goal of reformation was to enable an offender to be released into society and not offend again.
- Parole is early and conditional release from custody.
- Classification systems for prisons and inmates should make it easier for custodial programs to better meet the needs of the inmates.

Trace the defining features of industrial prisons.

- Industrial prisons used inmates' labor to pay for their cost of operating.
- These prisons were modeled after factories.
- Industrial prisons practiced oppressive and violent discipline and regimentation.

Describe and evaluate each of the four major models of corrections.

- The punishment model assumes that offenders are inherently bad and must be punished. Studies have found that after correctional punishment, many offenders become more antisocial than before.
- The crime control model uses incarceration to suppress the behavior of criminals and keep them off the streets. Most offenders are eventually released back to the streets, where they commit more crimes.

- The rehabilitation model seeks to change an offender's behavior; it views offenders as sick and capable of being cured. Most U.S. prisons do not emphasize rehabilitation.

- The reintegration model aims to help offenders readjust successfully back into the community. For reintegration to work, correctional programs must help offenders learn to take responsibility for their crimes.

Describe the populations found in correctional institutions today.

- Overcrowding is a major problem; it is due not to higher crime rates but to changes in policy that imprison more offenders for longer terms.

- Prison populations are overwhelmingly male and disproportionately Black.

- Most offenses are not violent but are nonviolent drug offenses.

- The number of federal prison inmates is increasing at a greater rate than the populations of state prisons.

- The number of individuals in community or noninstitutional programs (such as probation and parole) outnumbers those in prisons and jails but represents the same demographics.

Identify the types of victim services found in corrections.

- Correctional institutions are responsible for the facilitation and mediation of inmate–victim interactions.

- Correctional institutions organize victim impact panels and classes for inmates to inform them about the effects of crime on the victim's life.

- Correctional institutions are responsible for assisting victims in the process of viewing executions.

Examine the extent and nature of privatization of prisons.

- Private prisons are based on the rationale that private enterprise can run prisons more efficiently and less expensively than the government can.

- Faith-based prison programs are developed when a private prison corporation builds or operates a prison under contract with a government agency and invites religious organizations to offer rehabilitation services to the inmates.

Key Terms

Auburn system 333	industrial prison 336	punishment model 339
community corrections 326	institutional corrections 326	rehabilitation model 342
crime control model 340	Martinson Report 337	reintegration model 342
Elmira Reformatory 335	medical model 337	restorative justice 343
faith-based prison programs 355	penitentiary 332	transportation 329
halfway house 343	Pennsylvania system 333	Walnut Street Jail 332
hulks 331	privatization 353	workhouse 329
indentured servitude 329	Public Safety Realignment (PSR) 346	

Study Questions

1. The term *corrections* refers to
   a. probation and parole.
   b. jails and prisons.
   c. juvenile detention facilities.
   d. all of the above

2. The corrections model that assumes most offenders will remain in the community and that society will benefit if offenders have connections to institutions in free society is
   a. punishment.
   b. rehabilitation and treatment.
   c. crime control.
   d. reintegration.

3. Of the following, the group that is most disproportionately represented in the U.S. prison population is
   a. African Americans.
   b. Latinos.
   c. Whites.
   d. Asian Americans.

4. The function of the practice of transportation was to
   a. eliminate convicts from Britain.
   b. colonize new British territories.
   c. circumvent the death penalty.
   d. all of the above

5. The _____ system's major characteristic was absolute solitary confinement.
   a. Pennsylvania
   b. Auburn
   c. reformatory
   d. industrial

6. Very harsh punishments
   a. tend to decrease criminal activity.
   b. tend to increase criminal activity.
   c. do not make a difference in criminal activity.
   d. are justified by scholarly research.

7. The first prison in the United States was
   a. Bridewell.
   b. the Walnut Street Jail.
   c. the Western Penitentiary.
   d. Cherry Hill.

8. The indeterminate sentence was a part of the history of the _____ model.
   a. rehabilitation
   b. crime control
   c. punishment
   d. reintegration

9. Most of the inmates in U.S. prisons are serving time for
   a. murder.
   b. burglary.
   c. drug offenses.
   d. car theft.

10. The crime control model is a way to
    a. teach control to inmates.
    b. control crime in the inner city.
    c. control crime by using harsh punishments.
    d. control crime by imprisoning and incapacitating offenders.

Critical Thinking Questions

For further review, go to the LearnSmart study module for this chapter.

1. How have U.S. correctional practices changed since the colonial period?

2. Describe some of the punishments that were precursors to prison, and explain how they evolved to become contemporary correctional practices.

3. Which of the models of corrections do you think has been most successful in accomplishing the goal of correcting an offender's unlawful behavior? Why?

4. Compare and contrast the Pennsylvania and Auburn systems. Why was Auburn more successful?

5. How do programs such as California's Public Safety Realignment policy reduce mass incarceration and contribute to the welfare of society?

12 Jails and

After reading this chapter, you should be able to:

- Distinguish between jails and prisons.

- Differentiate among minimum-, medium-, maximum-, and supermaximum-security prisons.

- Apply the concept of professionalization to the role of correctional officers.

- Describe the rights of prisoners and those that are denied.

- Characterize the inmate subculture.

- Outline the differences between male and female prison life.

- Describe methods of treatment and rehabilitation in prisons.

- Detail the ways incarceration affects the prisoner's family life.

Realities and Challenges

Spending a Lifetime Imprisoned

Few people can imagine what it might be like to spend a lifetime behind bars. Yet in the United States, almost 50,000 adults (more than a 22 percent increase since 2008)[1] and over 2,500 juveniles[2] are serving sentences of life without parole. Known as "lifers," these individuals are not released from prison on parole. Rather, they are sentenced to prison until death—a bleak, unforgiving punishment. Normally lifers die in prison from natural causes.

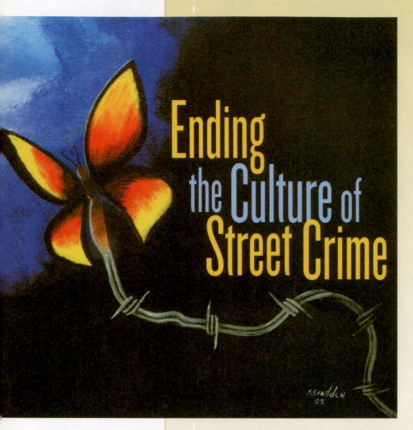

Lifers (and "nonlifers" as well) must deal with many personal challenges and tough questions, such as, How do I make the highly structured—and often hostile—prison environment my home? How can I gain meaning from my incarceration? What do I want to do in prison and with the rest of my life? What will happen to my relationship with my family in the community? What will it be like to become old and sick in prison? How can I give something back to society? Prisoners can cope with a life sentence in a positive or negative way.

One way that some lifers are transforming their prison experience while at the same time becoming a force for good is through their involvement in the Long Incarcerated Fraternity Engaging Release Studies (LIFERS, Inc.) and its Lifers Public Safety Initiative. LIFERS, Inc., originated in 1978 in a therapy group of male lifers from the maximum-security State Correctional Institution at Graterford, Pennsylvania. These individuals recognized the harm their crimes had inflicted on others and wanted their voice from behind bars to count in the fight against crime and violence.[3] Between 1980 and 1981 the group was recognized by the Graterford administration and the Pennsylvania Bureau of Corrections and received nonprofit corporation status. At first the members' primary organizational goal was to change Pennsylvania's policy on life sentences, but the goal shifted to emphasize the prevention of crime and violence—both inside and outside prisons.[4]

The lifers contribute to the prevention effort by analyzing crime from the perpetrator's perspective and by sharing with criminal justice professionals and others the mind-set and practices that caused their own crime. They have partnered with Pennsylvania's End Violence Project, a nonprofit organization dedicated to breaking the cycle of violence, and taken a program in transformational leadership—a leadership style that seeks to stimulate positive change in individuals. In 2003 approximately 100 lifers held an anticrime summit at Graterford—attended by criminal justice professionals, social workers, lawmakers, victim advocates, and religious leaders—during which they explored community partnerships that might contribute to deterring crime and violence. LIFERS recognizes that the majority of prisoners will be released to the community. Thus, the organization is also actively developing projects and programs that are geared to eliminating the culture of crime not only inside but also outside prisons. The goal is to empower prisoners to transform their lives by assuming personal and community responsibility.[5]

As much as many authorities in the criminal justice field dislike the use of incarceration when other methods are available, jails and prisons are a necessity. It is important for all to recognize that even individuals who will spend the rest of their lives incarcerated can gain some sense of purpose within the prison walls—and thereby have a positive impact on society.

Society has a vested interest in the effects of incarceration because the vast majority of inmates one day return to the community. Furthermore, during the past 30 years, the jail and prison population has grown by over 500 percent (see Figure 12-1).[6] This chapter provides an overview of incarceration in the criminal justice system. We explore the realities of the corrections system, the culture of prison life, and the challenges of making these elements work to the benefit of both prisoners and society.

THE STRUCTURE OF CORRECTIONS

MYTH/REALITY

MYTH: Incarcerating criminals reduces crime in society.

REALITY: Although jails and prisons remove offenders from the streets and reduce their ability to commit crimes in the community as long as they are incarcerated, there is evidence that incarceration does not deter criminal behavior in the long run. The number of persons incarcerated in U.S. jails and prisons remains high as crime rates have decreased,[7] but recidivism rates remain excessive.[8]

The most common formal sanction for criminal behavior today is **incarceration,** the confinement of an individual against his will in the criminal justice system (in a jail or prison) or a mental health facility (a secure psychiatric institution). Indeed, legislative initiatives to put more criminals behind bars (the policy of mass incarceration) have wide popular support, even though shutting up more people in jails and prisons has not stemmed the tide of crime or recidivism.[9] What increasing the number of inmates has done is to create major problems for both inmates and correctional employees.

Jails

A **jail** is a local facility operated by municipal and regional governments such as cities, counties, and parishes. Some local governments contract with private agencies to provide jail services. Jails house pretrial individuals believed to present a risk of danger or flight and those serving short-term sentences of incarceration. They are not intended for housing long-term prisoners. Jails also hold individuals awaiting probation or parole revocation hearings, as well as people with mental disorders who are awaiting transfer to psychiatric facilities.

incarceration
Confinement against one's will in the criminal justice system (in a jail or prison) or a mental health facility (a secure psychiatric institution).

jail
Municipal or regional facility that houses pretrial individuals believed to present a risk of danger or flight, those awaiting probation or parole revocation, and those sentenced to less than 1 year incarceration.

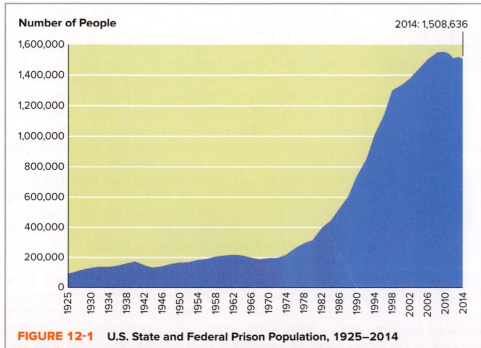

FIGURE 12-1 **U.S. State and Federal Prison Population, 1925–2014**

SOURCE: The Sentencing Project, "U.S. State and Federal Prison Population, 1925–2014" http://sentencingproject.org/doc/publications/inc_Trends_in_Corrections_Fact_sheet.pdf (retrieved February 19, 2016).

It appears many U.S. jails are refusing to continue to be way stations for suspects en route to deportation.[10]

Most large cities and many towns throughout the United States have a jail. There are about 3,300 local jails in the United States, operating at an estimated cost of $3 billion per year, about $2.3 billion of it for adult facilities. Juvenile jails, known as *juvenile halls*, are discussed in Chapter 15.

Jails reported an average annual cost of $13,803 per inmate, or $37.82 a day in the late 1980s.[11] In recent years costs have increased substantially due to the cost of shifting of mental health care to the jails.[12] Estimates of the cost per day for an inmate vary by state and by who conducts the study—from $30 to $45 in Texas, from $53 to $75 in California, and to as high as $85 in Oregon.[13] The total cost-per-inmate figure includes such components as institutional security, health services, food, accommodation, and salaries of personnel. Jails are normally less expensive to operate than prisons because they offer fewer programs and services to inmates. Should states follow California's lead and adopt Public Safety Realignment policies (see Chapter 11), jail populations, and costs are likely to increase.[14]

Problems in Jails   Jail overcrowding is a major problem nationwide. In 2006 a federal judge ordered Los Angeles County to end its jail overcrowding.[15] That same year, the California State Sheriffs' Association issued a white paper, *Jail Overcrowding: A State and Local Crisis*, in which the authors advocated for the expansion and upgrading of the state's jails.[16] In 2010, jails were operating between 86 percent and 91 percent of capacity.[17] Bond proposals to build and fix jails have failed throughout the United States, and many jails are deteriorating. In Tennessee in 2011, one jail had a leaking roof and was so overcrowded that inmates were sleeping on the floor.[18]

Because jails are used to hold suspected offenders until trial, one obvious solution to overcrowding is to simplify and expedite pretrial activities, such as by using a credit card program to facilitate the processing of bail bonds. Another solution is to reduce the time that sentenced inmates spend in jail. Some counties, for example, substitute labor for jail time in the case of inmates sentenced to 30 days or more, thus freeing up space while saving money.

Using local jails to incarcerate people with mental illnesses overtaxes the jail system. In 2005, 21 percent of jail inmates had a history of mental health problems, and only 26 percent of these were incarcerated for violent offenses.[19] To cope with the large numbers of people with mental illness who are ending up in their jails, some counties are sending offenders who are diagnosed with serious mental illness—but deemed treatable—to community health facilities.[20] Many communities, however, do not have resources, other than jail, to handle the mentally ill criminal population—a problem not only for the individuals who commit crimes but also for the communities to which most will soon return. Some sheriffs are demanding that jails stop being used as de facto asylums for the mentally ill and dumping grounds for poor and drug-addicted individuals. They advocate for treatment before jail and within jails as a way to reduce jail populations caused by policies of mass incarceration. Furthermore, sheriffs are pushing to get inmates who are charged with low-level, nonviolent offenses out of jail more quickly.[21] Despite the problems jails face some manage to develop innovative programs. One example, is Richmond, Virginia's Jail Fatherhood Program. They teach inmate fathers etiquette, proper dress, and then hold a father-daughter formal dance on jail premises. The date with dad program is much anticipated and helps inmates and their daughters create bonds with each other.[22]

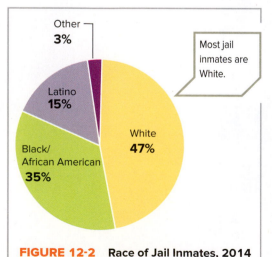

FIGURE 12-2   **Race of Jail Inmates, 2014**

SOURCE: Todd D. Minton and Zhen Zeng, "Jail Inmates at Midyear 2014" (Washington, DC: U.S. Department of Justice, Bureau of Justice Statistics, June 2015),3.

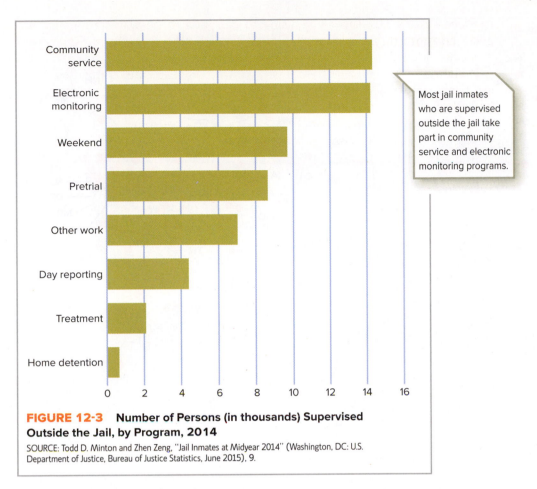

Most jail inmates who are supervised outside the jail take part in community service and electronic monitoring programs.

FIGURE 12-3　**Number of Persons (in thousands) Supervised Outside the Jail, by Program, 2014**

SOURCE: Todd D. Minton and Zhen Zeng, "Jail Inmates at Midyear 2014" (Washington, DC: U.S. Department of Justice, Bureau of Justice Statistics, June 2015), 9.

The Jail Population　At midyear in 2014, the U.S. jail population was estimated at 744,600, of which at least 85 percent were men. As Figure 12-2 illustrates, Whites made up 47 percent of persons incarcerated in jails; Blacks, 35 percent; Latinos, 15 percent; and other races, approximately 3 percent. The majority of jail inmates (60 percent) had not yet been sentenced but were awaiting court action.[23]

Of the 808,070 total number of offenders, both in and out of jail, who were under jail supervision in 2014, only about 8 percent were in an alternative program—such as home detention or electronic monitoring—that permitted them to remain out of jail. Similar programs include work release and community service; weekends in jail; day programs; and mandatory drug, alcohol, or mental health treatment programs. As Figure 12-3 shows, the most popular community corrections program is community service. Treatment programs account for only 3.3 percent of individuals under supervision outside of jail.[24]

Prisons

A **prison,** also known as a *penitentiary* or *reformatory,* is a secure facility where offenders serve a year or more after their trial and conviction. In the United States, a prison's authority over violators comes from the state and the federal government. There are approximately 1,821 adult U.S. prisons under the administration of state correctional agencies and the Federal Bureau of Prisons.[25] This number includes privately contracted prisons, which are also responsible to a state or the federal government. In addition, prisons include specialized facilities for confining parolees and shock incarceration facilities ("boot camps").[26] The U.S. military operates its own prisons, which house military personnel convicted of major crimes and those who are national security risks, such as prisoners of war and enemy combatants.

prison
A secure state or federal facility that holds offenders sentenced to incarceration of 1 year or more.

One hundred forty-seven federal prisons–not including military prisons–fall under the jurisdiction of the Federal Bureau of Prisons. The map above shows the locations of the Federal Bureau of Prisons facilities. Generally they hold offenders who violate federal laws, whereas state prisons hold those who violate state laws. In 2015, about 209,000 prisoners were confined in federal institutions, far fewer than the approximate 1,400,000 million in state prisons across the country.[27]

Rising Prison Costs The average cost of incarcerating prisoners is high and rising, largely due to rising staffing costs and health care expenditures.[28] The total national per-inmate cost of state prisoners is $31,286, but there is wide variation in expenditures by the states. For example, the amount spent per year on prison inmates in New York is about $60,000, whereas in Kentucky the amount spent is almost $15,000. Factors that contribute to this variation are overcrowding and greater incarceration of low-level offenders.[29] Costs of housing special needs prisoners–such as older adults, juveniles, and mentally or physically impaired offenders–are also high, as are required medical services for inmates. Figure 12-4 illustrates

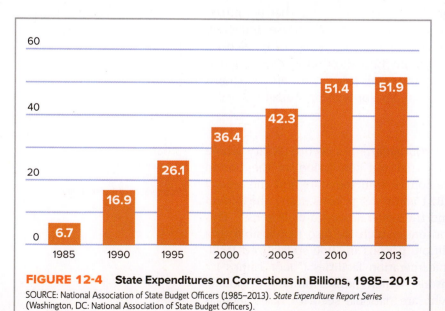

FIGURE 12-4 **State Expenditures on Corrections in Billions, 1985–2013**

SOURCE: National Association of State Budget Officers (1985–2013). *State Expenditure Report Series* (Washington, DC: National Association of State Budget Officers).

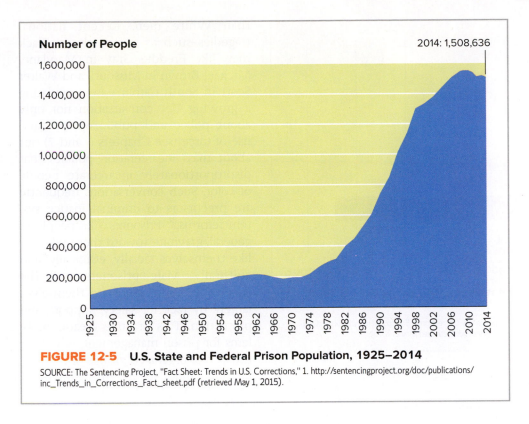

Number of People   2014: 1,508,636

FIGURE 12-5   **U.S. State and Federal Prison Population, 1925–2014**

SOURCE: The Sentencing Project, "Fact Sheet: Trends in U.S. Corrections," 1. http://sentencingproject.org/doc/publications/
inc_Trends_in_Corrections_Fact_sheet.pdf (retrieved May 1, 2015).

the increases between 1985 and 2013, a period when state corrections costs
rose dramatically.

Prison Populations   The rate of incarceration in the United States remains the
highest in the world. It is also well known that the United States has nearly
5 percent of the world's population and about 25 percent of the world's prisoners. The number of persons incarcerated in U.S. state prisons rose from
319,598 in 1980 to 1,359,000 in 2015.[30] Increases in the prison population
were driven mainly by policies of mass incarceration and changes in sentencing laws, not by changes in crime rates.[31] Figure 12-5 shows how state and
federal policies of mass incarceration influenced prison populations over time.
   Although the U.S. incarceration rate continues to be high, the significant
news is that the U.S. prison population has been declining since 2010, perhaps
reflecting a shift away from a four-decade-long policy of mass incarceration
and "get tough" sentencing practices.[32] In 2014 there was a slight decrease in
the prison population of about 1 percent from the year before indicating a slow
decline in the national imprisonment rate.[33] Factors make it difficult to predict
if the decline will continue, however, the downward direction is promising.[34]
The decline in the state prison population has been fueled by states' determination that they can reduce prison populations, save money, and yet not jeopardize public safety.[35] In Chapter 11, we discussed the Public Safety Realignment
(PSR) Act, California's response to the 2011 U.S. Supreme Court order to reduce
prison overcrowding. Although California's prison population is declining, it is
too early to tell whether the state's PSR policy will deliver the types of treatment that will reduce offender recidivism and make communities safer.
   Racial disparities exist in our nation's state and federal prisons as can be seen
in Figure 12-6. Blacks and people of color are incarcerated at disproportionate
rates. People of color represent more than 60 percent of those incarcerated.
Furthermore, Black men are six times more likely to be imprisoned than
White men. Latino men are almost 2.5 times more likely to be imprisoned

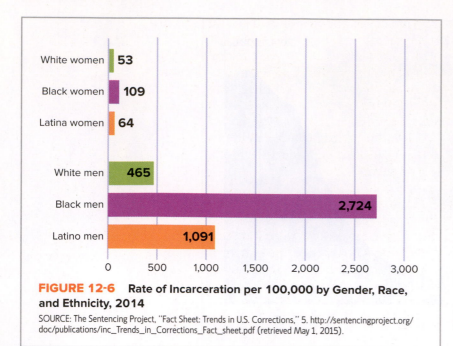

FIGURE 12-6 **Rate of Incarceration per 100,000 by Gender, Race, and Ethnicity, 2014**

SOURCE: The Sentencing Project, "Fact Sheet: Trends in U.S. Corrections," 5. http://sentencingproject.org/doc/publications/inc_Trends_in_Corrections_Fact_sheet.pdf (retrieved May 1, 2015).

than White men. Recent national tragedies–such as the deaths of Black men like Freddie Gray in Maryland, Michael Brown in Missouri, and Walter Scott in South Carolina–are stimulating a growing U.S. conversation not only about police and public opinion and use of force (see Chapters 6 and 7) but about mass incarceration policies that disproportionately incarcerate people of color. Such conversations frequently are precursors to criminal justice system reforms.[36] Prisoners, like people in general, gravitate toward those who are like themselves racially, ethnically, and culturally. Male prisoners, and the gangs they form, segregate themselves largely by race for safety, support, and protection. This practice creates problems for prison management, which, in the face of organized groups of inmates, literally cannot let its guard down.

Types of Prisons

State and federal prisons are classified as minimum-, medium-, maximum-, or supermaximum-security facilities. These institutions are often referred to by levels, beginning with Level 1 for minimum-security prisons, Levels 2 and 3 for medium-security prisons, Level 4 for a maximum-security prison, and advancing to Level 5 for a supermaximum-security prison.

Minimum-Security Prisons   **Minimum-security prisons** hold offenders who have short sentences, are nonviolent, and are unlikely to attempt escape or pose risks to others in the institution. Sometimes offenders are transferred to minimum-security institutions at the end of long sentences to prepare for release. Such facilities tend to be smaller and may resemble a campus, with buildings arranged in cottage style. Inmate housing units are dormitory style with communal toilets and showers, although some have individual sleeping quarters. In either case, this arrangement represents a significant departure from locked cells. Minimum-security facilities might not have perimeter fencing, and generally no armed correctional officers patrol the grounds. Prisoners have a great deal of freedom of movement and may be permitted to wear civilian clothes instead of uniforms. The inmates are encouraged to pursue education, work, and treatment programs when available.

minimum-security prison
An institution that holds offenders who have short sentences, are nonviolent, and are unlikely to attempt escape or pose risks to others in the facility.

▼ **A Minimum-Security Prison**
Minimum-security institutions do not allow inmates access to life beyond the prison perimeters.   *How does life in a minimum-security prison differ from life outside the prison?*

MYTH/REALITY

MYTH: Minimum-security prisons are country club environments.

REALITY: In general, prisons have a harsh, undesirable environment.[37]

Minimum-security prisons are often referred to as country clubs because their atmosphere can be casual and rules appear relaxed. But even though it is a low-security setting, a minimum-security prison is populated with felons, and violent outbursts can occur at any time. Although inmates in minimum-security facilities have more freedom than those in other prisons, they may not leave, and their activities are greatly restricted. They are allowed few personal possessions, visits are limited, and privacy is nonexistent. The loss of personal freedoms causes some individuals tremendous stress. Living conditions may be cramped and unsanitary. There may be little opportunity for work, education, or treatment, and personal safety is never assured.

Medium-Security Prisons   Inmates in **medium-security prisons** are under greater control than in minimum-security prisons, and their movement is restricted to areas that have close surveillance. Gun towers hold armed correctional officers who carefully watch barbed- or razor-wire perimeters. *Sally ports*–secure entrances with a series of gates or doors–control movement between closed zones. Closed-circuit monitoring and other security mechanisms are positioned virtually every-where. Prisoners may take part in limited educational, vocational, and therapeutic programs, but the inmates are subject to *lockdown* (confinement to their cells) at any time. The numerous prisoner counts each day shut down all activities and require inmates to report to a designated area for the count.

Inmates usually share cells in a medium-security prison. Typically the build-ings have several wings and two tiers, with each tier housing about 150 to 200 inmates in double-bunk cells. Some prisons have open dorm sections that contain about 12 double bunks. Public bathroom areas are heavily used. There is a communal area for inmates to interact with others. Officer stations are located so they can view the entire housing unit at any given time.[38] Privileges include mail, limited and monitored visitation, radio, television, work release, and furlough. However, few prisoners are able to take part in vocational and educational programs.

Maximum-Security Prisons   Inmates in **maximum-security prisons** are sub-ject to high levels of control. Physical barriers severely restrict the mobility of prisoners. Inmates are shackled when they are moved.

These prison facilities are often constructed of massive concrete walls. Armed guards conduct foot patrols, and others carry out surveillance in towers. Lethal electrical fences, infrared and motion-sensing devices, and electronic locking systems to keep inmates in confinement are standard features of maximum-security prisons. Inmate counts typically take place four times a day. Depending on prison policies, inmates are either locked in their cells or are expected to stand outside their cells during counts. Recounts are done imme-diately if numbers do not tabulate. Inmates know that they are subject to daily inspections, constant surveillance, and random searches.[39]

In a maximum-security prison, cells are set back-to-back in tiers in the center of a secure building, making escape more difficult. Prisoner living quarters

medium-security prison
An institution in which inmates are under greater control than in minimum-security prisons, and their freedom of movement is restricted to areas that are under close surveillance.

maximum-security prison
An institution in which inmates are subject to high levels of control and where their mobility is severely restricted by physical barriers.

▼ Different Prison Designs
Prison architecture varies greatly.

▶ **Inside a Cell Block**

Cell blocks are secure, and prisoners are watched around the clock. *In what ways does lack of privacy affect prisoners?*

are arranged in separate units or sections known as *cell blocks,* each having its own security system and correctional officers. Individual cells have sliding doors with locks operated by remote control. Toilet facilities are in the cells because prisoners are often confined there many hours each day. When allowed out, they must remain in the cell block or in a specially caged area. When leaving their cell block, inmates are shackled and accompanied by correctional officers. These inmates may be allowed visitors but only under highly secure conditions. Death rows are normally in maximum-security prisons.

Fewer than 0.1 percent of prisoners housed in all types of prisons escape, and prison escapes are on the decline.[40] The probability that a prisoner in a maximum-security level prison will escape is even lower. Despite publicity surrounding the recent prison break of Richard Matt and David Sweat (shown in the photo) at Clinton Correctional Facility in upstate New York and the drug lord "El Chapo" Guzman's escape from what is allegedly the most secure prison in Mexico, prison breaks in high-security prisons are not common and often involve collaboration with and cooperation of prison staff.[41]

supermaximum-security (supermax) prison

A facility that provides the highest level of security possible—solitary confinement—using the latest correctional technology.

Supermaximum-Security Prisons **Supermaximum-security (supermax) prisons** provide the highest level of security possible—solitary confinement—using the latest correctional technology. Most inmates are isolated because their level of violence poses a risk of serious harm to other inmates and to the correctional staff. Some have gang affiliations that would give them inordinate power in the prison or make them targets of other gangs. Others possess an antagonistic temperament or antisocial disposition. Inmates deemed high escape risks are also housed here.

Judges do not usually sentence offenders to supermax prisons. Rather, offenders are sent there because of extreme misbehavior in other prisons, such as killing or attempting to kill other inmates or staff. Supermax prisons are said to confine the worst of the worst. Prisoners contained in supermax prisons are not controllable in the traditional types of segregation units available in other prisons.

▼ **New York's Clinton Correctional Facility Prison Break**

Despite media coverage, prison breaks from maximum-security prisons are rare events.

KEY CONCEPTS Types of Prisons

Minimum-, medium-, maximum-, and supermaximum-security institutions are difficult places to do time.

Minimum-Security Prisons	Medium-Security Prisons	Maximum-Security Prisons	Supermaximum-Security Prisons
Hold those with short sentences who are nonviolent and not likely to escape	Hold those with longer sentences and both violent and property offenders	High levels of control	Solitary confinement
Smaller facilities	Larger facilities	House violent prisoners	Total isolation from other prisoners
Dormitory-style housing units	Cell confinement and sometimes dorm confinement	Severe restriction of prisoner mobility	House antisocial violent prisoners with antagonistic temperaments
Communal toilet facilities	Daily activity dominated by counts	Shackled movement	High escape-risk prisoners
May or may not have perimeter fencing	Prisoner movement is restricted	Gun towers	23 hours a day cell confinement in a soundproof cell
Normally no gun towers	High surveillance of public social areas	Lethal electrical fencing	1 hour of recreation alone in walled recreation area slightly larger than a cell
More casual atmosphere	Officer stations in each housing unit	Infrared and motion-sensing devices	24-hour electronic surveillance
Minimal restriction of movement and dress	Sally ports	Electronic locking systems	No interaction or eye contact with inmates or staff
Rehabilitation programs are encouraged	Closed zones	Daily life dominated by counts and random searches	Strip searches whenever a prisoner leaves a cell
	Close surveillance	Daily inspections	At least two correctional officers must accompany the fully shackled prisoner when moved
	Gun towers	Constant surveillance	Rehabilitation programs are rare and televised into cells
	Barbed- and razor-wire perimeter fencing	Cell block living units	
	Limited rehabilitation programs	Cell confinement	
		Toilets in cells	

A whole institution can be designated supermax, but so can a single wing within a maximum-security institution, usually a housing unit or cell block. There is uncertainty regarding how many U.S. inmates currently are held in long-term solitary confinement. As of 2011, it was estimated that there were approximately 57 supermax institutions or housing units in state and federal prisons and approximately 80,000 inmates confined in supermax prisons or wings.[42] Reliance on these facilities in the United States may be on the decline due to criticisms that they are expensive to build and operate, violate constitutional guarantees against cruel and unusual punishment, and damage the mental health of those who live and work within them. California, New York, and the federal government have put into place measures to change the use of solitary confinement.[43]

Supermax conditions are severe. They are clean, sanitary, and have the latest high-tech security devices. However, make no mistake–they are the modern-day version of dungeons. Inmates spend 23 hours in their cells and 1 hour in a solid-walled secure recreation area only slightly larger than a cell. In the typical supermax facility, prisoners live within featureless concrete and steel enclosures and are under constant electronic surveillance. Mattresses on concrete slabs serve as beds. Toilets are next to beds and are typically timed by prison authorities to flush at intervals, not after every use. When windows to the outside world are present, they are typically no wider than 4 inches, and there may be small, security-reinforced skylights in some cells. Food is provided through locked food ports in cell doors. Cells are soundproof and designed to minimize social contact; inmates are not permitted even eye contact with other inmates or staff. All incoming mail is read and censored before delivery. Prisoners are subject to strip searches whenever they leave their cells and are typically accompanied by at least two correctional officers. Treatment and vocational programs are rare. When they do exist, they tend to be confined to the inmate's cell and consist of televised programming.[44]

These isolating features take on particular importance when we consider that most of the inmates released from supermax prisons go directly into the community, with little or no "decompression" to ease them back into the mainstream.[45] Because this kind of confinement denies the basic human need to interact with others, such institutions are often accused of "manufacturing madness."[46]

Prisoner Classification Systems

classification

Determination of which inmates go to which institutions and the specific conditions under which they will be confined.

security level

The degree of danger associated with the inmates being housed in a prison.

custody level

The degree of danger an inmate poses to other prisoners and to correctional staff.

The **classification** of inmates is a crucial area of prison management. Classification determines which inmates go to which institutions and the specific conditions under which they will be confined. Prisons themselves are classified into different **security levels** depending on the danger level associated with the inmates being housed. Inmates, on the other hand, are classified according to **custody levels**—the risk of danger they pose to other prisoners and to correctional staff. Classification differs in men's and women's prisons. Women's prisons tend to confine all custody levels within the same facility, whereas in men's facilities custody levels may be spread among prisons.[47]

Custody levels are determined by inmate criteria such as the crime committed, sentence length, record of past violence, prior institutional behavior, and social and medical factors such as substance abuse. An inmate may be placed in a high-security prison yet be a low (custody) risk in that institution, with privileges denied to other higher- (custody) risk inmates. These decisions are based on **risk classification,** an assessment of the level and kind of risk an individual presents to correctional staff and other inmates.

risk classification

An assessment of the level and kind of risk an individual presents to correctional staff and other inmates.

Risk classification follows a complex protocol. An offender sentenced to prison first goes to a centralized classification facility where a team of experts conducts a battery of tests to evaluate security risk and program needs. Offenders generally stay there fewer than 90 days. While in the centralized facility, they are subject to high-security practices and isolation from others.

Correctional Staff

Correctional officers—otherwise known as *prison guards*—describe their job as the hardest in the world, even more difficult than the jobs of police and firefighters. The reason they give is that the work stress and the risks to their personal safety are constant. Consider how they must do their job while trying to maintain order and discipline in a population that for the most part has little regard for authority.[48] It is not surprising that they often see themselves as "forgotten people in a hostile social system made up of politicians, the public, prison administrators, and inmates."[49] Many correctional officers say that they feel alienated and resent negative stereotypes that portray them as brutal, unfeeling, rigid, authoritarian individuals who enjoy the power they can wield over the inmates.[50] A famous research study contributed to these negative images of correctional officers.[51]

▼ **The Stanford Prison Experiment**

Social psychologist Philip Zimbardo's experiment probed the psychological effects of being a "prisoner" and a "guard" in a simulated prison setting. *On what bases might the study be criticized?*

The study centered on an experiment conducted at Stanford University in 1971 by social psychologist Philip Zimbardo. The project involved the creation of a simulated prison. In a scenario that might sound like the plot of an action film set in a war zone, it took the prison's "guards" no time to act aggressively, abusively, and even sadistically toward the prisoners. Equally rapidly, the prisoners became passive, hopeless, depressed, and dehumanized.

This classic study, known as the Stanford Prison Experiment, was designed to explore the psychological effects of being a "prisoner" and a "guard" in a simulated environment.[52] The 24 subjects, all students, were middle-class male volunteers; none had been previously exposed to the criminal justice system. The "prisoners"–decided by a coin toss–were held in a mock prison-type environment in a basement on the Stanford University campus.

Designed to last 2 weeks, the experiment had to be cut short after 6 days because the "guards" and "prisoners" were behaving in such unexpected and disturbing ways. Some students were so troubled by their actions that they needed professional counseling afterward.

Zimbardo and his team of researchers inferred that the prison social structure powerfully determines human behavior, leading individuals to suspend or abandon their personal values. The experiment raises questions about how the social environment of jails and prisons can influence the effectiveness of the corrections system.[53]

Although Zimbardo's experiment is considered a classic in the study of corrections institutions, it has been criticized on the grounds that professional correctional officers are well-trained professionals–but the student participants were not. It has also been pointed out that the students who enacted the role of correctional officers were behaving in ways that they thought officers should act. In other words, they may have been reacting to stereotypes rather than to the specific situation at hand. A further criticism of the study is that the students who were in the roles of the prisoners were already demeaned before the experiment even began by the clothing they were required to wear.

Zimbardo's study was not a scientifically controlled experiment but rather a pilot study that was never pursued. A college campus and a prison are very different environments, and the conditions imposed on the experiment were in many ways arbitrary and not like actual conditions in a prison. Nonetheless, this study does raise some important questions as to whether a correctional officer's attitudes and behavior might be influenced by the environment and nature of the prison itself.

Who Are Correctional Officers?
In a study of officers at Auburn Prison, today a maximum-security facility in Auburn, New York, Lucien X. Lombardo painted a sympathetic picture of correctional officers. Lombardo saw the officers as having been attracted to their careers primarily for job security, only to be later left, basically alone, in a hostile, dangerous, and ambiguous environment.[54] Even those who begin their careers wanting to be helpful to inmates and assist in their rehabilitation process are thwarted. New officers are thrown into their jobs with little help and thus are forced to fend for themselves or to rely on more seasoned officers to show

▼ **Ever Watchful**

Correctional officers are watching whenever prisoners gather.

them the ropes. Inmates, correctional administration, and even fellow officers are often hostile to these naïve newcomers.[55]

Lombardo found that each assignment puts different demands on the officer. For example, a yard officer must be seen as an aloof figure who watches, listens, and controls the inmates, whereas a housing block officer must deal with security, housekeeping, supervision, and human services. Officers must enforce rules with discretion and use their authority wisely and humanely to cultivate inmates' cooperation.[56] Job satisfaction is greater among officers working in more service-oriented prisons than in traditional custody-oriented institutions.[57]

Studies of police officers have shown that those who have attended college tend to be more flexible and less authoritarian than those who have not.[58] In the case of correctional officers, all correctional institutions require a high school diploma or its equivalent, but about 22 states require a college degree.[59] The Federal Bureau of Prisons requires at least a bachelor's degree plus 3 years of experience. All states offer on-the-job training, and some states and agencies provide specialized training academies.[60]

Negative attitudes and perceptions of inmates on the part of correctional officers create a barrier that distances them from inmates. In the extreme, some correctional staff may view inmates as less than human.[61] For example, in the 1990s, correctional officers in California were charged with staging gladiator-style fights among prisoners and shooting unarmed prisoners for sport.[62] In the Stanford Prison Experiment, Zimbardo attributed the behavior of both correctional officers and prisoners to factors in the situation, not to individuals' personalities. He believed the prison social structure was an inherently unhealthy environment that produced the aberrant, antisocial behavior of "guards" and "prisoners."[63]

With the shift by the public and by policymakers to more punitive attitudes toward offenders, one might expect that correctional officers' outlooks toward prisoners would mirror this trend. That has not been the case, however. Indeed, a study of the attitudes of correctional officers found that as a group they have tended to have a more positive view and expressed support for rehabilitation programs for inmates.[64]

Professionalization   From early times, the job of prison guard was one of low status. Guards were considered little more than the custodians of inmates. There was scant change until the 1970s, when the American Correctional Association (ACA) developed standards for the training of guards. Over time, guards became correctional officers as the field focused on a more humane model of corrections. The ACA training standards eventually became the basis for certification criteria of officers.

The 1990s marked an additional turning point for the field of corrections and correctional personnel. To gain public confidence and to combat an increasingly negative image, correctional agencies focused on the professionalization of officers, implementing plans that had proved successful for the law enforcement community. Professionalism requires a commitment to a clearly articulated set of ideals and standards that instill pride in officers and raise the public's view of the profession. For an occupation to be regarded as a profession, members acquire specialized knowledge and develop skills consistent with these ideals. They abide by an established code of ethics policed by other members of the profession.[65]

The key to professionalization is education. In 1991 a joint task force of correctional administrators and academics endorsed a standardized curriculum consisting of 18 semester hours of higher education coursework in corrections.[66] The conversion of correctional work from an occupation to a profession required, among other changes, raising the educational minimum for entry-level positions, providing incentives for continuing education, and increasing entry-level salaries.[67]

New standards of recruitment and training for correctional officers better equip the prison staff to handle the high level of stress on the job. A new regimen of practices creates a supportive subculture that reinforces professional attitudes and competencies. Formal education alone is not sufficient. Pre- and in-service training are the most important ways correctional agencies can increase the professionalism of their officers and help set the tone and shape the attitudes of an institution.[68]

PRISONER RIGHTS

MYTH/REALITY

MYTH: Once an inmate has served time, the debt owed to society is paid and life as usual can resume.

REALITY: Many rights are taken away from offenders during and after they serve time in prison. In some states, ex-offenders lose civil rights such as the right to vote, hold public office, serve on a jury, have occupational licenses, and own a firearm. Incarceration may affect the life of the ex-convict long after release.[69]

Until the 1960s, convicted offenders had no civil rights other than those granted by specific laws. Under the **hands-off doctrine,** courts were reluctant to interfere with prison management, and an inmate had little legal recourse if subjected to abuse and neglect while in custody. For all intents and purposes, convicted prisoners were considered civilly dead. In 1964, however, the U.S. Supreme Court ruling in *Cooper v. Pate* gave prisoners access to the courts by granting them the right to bring civil actions against prison authorities for violations of civil rights.[70] Inmates could now sue for officer brutality, inhumane conditions, and inadequate nutrition and medical care. Also in the *Cooper* decision, the Court specifically held that Muslim inmates had the right to challenge prison officials for acts of religious discrimination under the Civil Rights Act of 1871.

An individual serving time for a crime today still loses certain rights. For example, she cannot hold public office. In many states, even after having served her sentence, she loses the right to vote, to serve on a jury, to be a witness, and to own a firearm. She also may lose rights of employment forever by being stripped of or barred from holding occupational licenses such as those for therapist, doctor, nurse, dental hygienist, or bartender.

Due Process Rights

In 1974, in *Wolff v. McDonnell*, the Supreme Court applied Fourteenth Amendment procedural rights to prison inmates, guaranteeing them not only access to the courts but also due process in disciplinary hearings.[71] In accordance with the *Wolff* decision, prisoners must be notified of charges, be able to call witnesses, have the right to assistance in a defense, and have the right to an impartial hearing before any administrative decisions are made that could deprive them of their rights or freedom. Such protection is particularly important in situations where a disciplinary action could take away an inmate's **good time credits** (time removed from a prison sentence for satisfactory behavior), thus jeopardizing early release, or where an administrative decision places an inmate in solitary confinement. In *Wolff*, the Court also declared racial discrimination intolerable except where "prison security and discipline" necessitated a particular action, such as assigning an inmate to a certain cell block because of imminent racist threats. The dominance of race-based gangs inside today's American prisons has presented prison officials with major challenges

hands-off doctrine
An approach that made courts reluctant to interfere with prison management or prisoner rights.

good time credits
Time taken off a prison sentence for an inmate's satisfactory behavior or for participating in a prison program.

Real Careers

ANGELA SOLORZANO

Work location: Downey, California

College(s): East Los Angeles City College (2004); California State University, Los Angeles (2007)

Major(s): Administration of Justice (Associate's); Criminal Justice (BS)

Job title: Detention Services Officer, Los Padrinos Juvenile Hall

Salary range for job like this: $46,000–$55,000

Time in job: 3 years

Work Responsibilities

I am a deputized peace officer who supervises detained juveniles during their activities within the living unit. I am primarily responsible for their safety and security, which means controlling and restraining combative or emotionally disturbed juveniles and providing them with situational counseling to help them perform their daily routines.

A typical workweek for me is 40 hours with 2 days off. Detention services officers at Los Padrinos Juvenile Hall can work any of three shifts: 6 a.m. to 2 p.m., 2 p.m. to 10 p.m., or 10 p.m. to 6 a.m. I have worked all three shifts, and each involves facilitating a different routine.

6 a.m.–2 p.m.: Awaken the juveniles, make sure that they groom for school, eat breakfast and lunch, attend scheduled court hearings, and receive medical care or counseling, as needed.

2 p.m.–10 p.m.: Pick up detainees from school and conduct recreational programs. Ensure that detainees eat dinner, shower, and receive medical attention or counseling, as needed.

10 p.m.–6 a.m.: Supervise detainees during sleeping hours. Make sure that they receive medical attention, as needed. Assist them with getting up for court appearances or being transported to a facility to serve their sentence.

Regardless of which shift I work, I always need to chart the behavior of the detainees and report it to the probation officer and the court. The juvenile system is focused on rehabilitation, and we as a department hope that our services and guidance will help these young adults return to society and become productive individuals.

Why Criminal Justice?

Ever since I was a child, I enjoyed watching crime-solving TV shows like *Matlock; Murder, She Wrote; Columbo;* and *People's Court.* But not until high school did I realize how much I wanted to break the barrier into law enforcement, which has traditionally been a male profession. Ultimately, I would like to be a judge, and working as a detention services officer is a stepping-stone toward reaching this goal.

Expectations and Realities of the Job

Before I started this job, I thought I would make a difference in the lives of all the juveniles at the facility. As it turns out, not all detainees are as open to rehabilitation and services as I had expected. To be an effective detention officer, I always have to be willing to dedicate additional time and effort to those who require it. I am disappointed that the system does not rehabilitate all of the detainees, but when a juvenile does emerge from the facility a changed citizen, I know that my job is worthwhile.

My Advice to Students

To be a successful detention services officer you have to be willing to serve and respect the juveniles with whom you work. This can mean being patient with someone who has a mental illness, or being accepting of someone who comes from a different social or cultural background. You must put aside your own opinions, emotions, and beliefs and not judge the juveniles for the crimes they have been accused of committing.

in this regard. For example, in 2014 a class action was launched by prisoners against the California Department of Corrections and Rehabilitation (CDCR) over its policy calling for the lockdown of all inmates of a particular race following incidents of race-based violence. If, for example, violence was perpetrated by a Latino gang, all Latino inmates in the prison would be locked down–regardless of whether they had taken part in the incident. The inmates charged that this was a violation of their Fourteenth Amendment right to equal protection under the law. CDCR argued the practice was necessary to maintain security in the facility. Lockdowns result in the denial of family visits, work assignments, yard times, and the like. They can last for months or even years. Although aspects of the case are pending, CDCR has agreed to cease race-based lockdowns.[72]

Rights guaranteed by the Eighth Amendment prohibiting cruel and unusual punishment were addressed in the Supreme Court's decision in *Estelle v. Gamble* (1976).[73] The *Estelle* ruling required that "deliberate indifference" to an inmate's alleged plight be proved in order for that inmate's challenge to succeed. This standard is difficult to meet, however. In 1986, in the case of *Daniels v. Williams*, the Supreme Court held that neglect or unintentional acts causing injury are insufficient grounds, on their own, to assign culpability to corrections officials.[74] For prison officials to be held responsible for an injury, the inmate must show that the officials had knowledge of a situation and deliberately allowed it to occur. Merely being careless in their duties is not a constitutional violation.

During the so-called prisoner rights era (1970-1991), the U.S. Supreme Court tended to support the rights of prisoners in accordance with the Constitution. This era came to a close in 1991 when the composition of the Court shifted, and the majority of justices began to support prison administrators. In close 5-4 decisions, changing just one justice on the Court can change the entire philosophy of its decisions.

Such was the case when the Supreme Court decided in 1991 that prison conditions such as overcrowding do not violate the Constitution because overcrowded conditions are not the result of "deliberate indifference."[75] The Court also ruled that the prohibition against cruel and unusual punishment is not applicable to overcrowding because this standard implies intent on the part of the perpetrator and in this case the intent of overcrowding is not malicious. However, in 2011 the Supreme Court ruled that California did violate the Constitution by overcrowding its prisons.[76] Many other gray areas thus await future judicial determinations.

First Amendment Rights

The First Amendment of the U.S. Constitution guarantees freedom of speech and freedom of religion. In *Procunier v. Martinez* (1974), California inmates asserted that state regulations censoring a prisoner's mail were unconstitutional because they violated freedom of speech and expression.[77] One such regulation had banned letters that criticized prison conditions. Another had barred the use of law students and other legal paraprofessionals to conduct attorney–client interviews with inmates. The U.S. Supreme Court struck down these state regulations as unconstitutional.

When prison authorities restrict an inmate's religious practice, they usually justify their decision by claiming a need for institutional security. Sometimes, however, questions are raised about the legitimacy of a prisoner's stated religion. For example, in one case that ultimately was thrown out by a federal appeals court, inmates claimed that they were members of the Church of the New Song (CONS) and were required to eat steak and drink Harveys Bristol Cream sherry as part of their religious practice. For more mainstream religions whose strictures do not interfere with the security of the institution, inmates have the right to practice their faith. For example, in 1972 the Supreme Court affirmed the right of an inmate to practice Buddhism in the case of *Cruz v. Beto*.[78]

A variety of other court opinions have addressed aspects of inmates' First Amendment rights. In 1987, the Supreme Court held in *O'Lone v. Estate of Shabazz* that prison officials were not required to alter a Black Muslim's work schedule to enable him to attend Friday afternoon services, as long as they had a rational reason for the restriction.[79] In 2005 the U.S. District Court in Colorado ruled that a Muslim inmate did not have to register as Jewish to receive kosher meals in order to meet his religious dietary requirements.[80] More recently, in response to a lawsuit, the Wyoming State Penitentiary agreed to adjust Muslim prisoners' mealtimes if those scheduled times interfered with the inmates' required prayers.[81] In 2005, in *Cutter v. Wilkinson*, the Supreme

Court unanimously upheld the constitutionality of the Religious Land Use and Institutionalized Persons Act of 2000 (RLUIPA), which protects the religious freedom of prison inmates.[82]

LIFE IN PRISONS AND JAILS

Institutional life for inmates and staff is centered on custody and security. The result for prisoners is monotony and regimentation, yet the climate can turn to violence in an instant as individuals and gangs compete for scarce resources in the prison.

The Inmate Subculture

total institution
A facility responsible for, and in control of, every aspect of life for those who live and work within it, including food, shelter, medical assistance, clothing, and safety.

Prisons are one type of **total institution,** a facility responsible for, and in control of, virtually every aspect of life for those who live and work within them, including food, shelter, medical assistance, clothing, and safety. These total institutions exist within the broader society yet are isolated from it. Contacts with outsiders are limited and tightly controlled. The "Matters of Ethics" box discusses how an inmate with a long or life sentence might leap at an opportunity to be a research subject to have a change in the routine of everyday prison life.

institutionalization
The state of being dependent on an institution to meet one's basic needs—such as those for food, shelter, and friends—to the point of being unwilling, or unable, to function in the outside world.

When people depend on an institution to meet their basic needs—such as those for food, shelter, and friends—to the point of being unwilling, or unable, to function in the outside world, we say that those individuals are a product of **institutionalization.** The more time offenders spend incarcerated, the more likely that institutionalization will occur. *State-raised convicts* are those who spend more of their lives in confinement—in juvenile halls, detention centers, training schools, jails, or prisons—than in free society. There are ex-convicts who, not long after their release, commit new crimes in order to be sent back to prison, where they know what is expected of them. Their friends are there, and the institution meets their most basic needs of food and shelter.

Having all one's needs provided by a single institution, however, comes at a price. Unique subcultures develop that establish values, roles, and communication patterns and largely determine how inmates relate to one another. The behaviors of the "guards" and "prisoners" in the famous Stanford Prison Experiment demonstrate how these roles affect behavior. Correctional officers and prisoners are frequently suspicious of and hostile toward one another. The prisoners see the officers who enforce the rules of the institution as their adversaries. The officers in turn see prisoners as untrustworthy and manipulative.[83] Each group behaves according to an "us versus them" mentality. Given such an environment, it is not surprising that Zimbardo found that he had to terminate his experiment prematurely.

prisonization
A process of socialization whereby prisoners adopt the norms, values, and beliefs of the inmate subculture as their own.

Prisonization is the process of socialization whereby prisoners adopt the norms, values, and beliefs of the **inmate subculture** as their own. The longer offenders spend in prison, the more they become prisonized. Such inmates become decidedly opposed to authority, for instance, and resist those in authority.[84] They learn not to share information with their keepers and not to portray themselves as needy, weak, or vulnerable. They are suspicious of the motives of others. An inmate who firmly accepts these values becomes increasingly difficult to rehabilitate to life outside of prison.

inmate subculture
The norms, values, and beliefs that develop among prisoners.

deprivation model
The perspective that the hardships prisoners endure lead to the development of a distinctive way of behaving in prison.

How Subcultures Form   The inmate subculture has its own norms, language, and roles (see table on prison slang terms on page 380).[85] How this subculture arises in a prison has long been the subject of two competing schools of thought: the deprivation model and the importation model.

pains of imprisonment
The deprivations inmates experience, such as those related to liberty, autonomy, security, personal goods and services, and heterosexual relations.

The **deprivation model** proposes that the **pains of imprisonment**—the deprivation of liberty, autonomy, security, personal goods and services, and heterosexual relations—lead to the development of a distinctive inmate

Matters *of* Ethics

Prisoners as Research Subjects

Captive populations such as prisoners—especially those with lengthy or life sentences—will experience situations where daily routines are unchanged and produce boredom, minimal stimulation, and monotony.

In short, prisoners' lives are dull in part because incarceration centers on custody and security. Prisons are dangerous places, and inmates may experience stress and anxiety about their physical safety. Thus, when there is an opportunity for prisoners to participate in an activity, such as clinical research, that is out of the ordinary and might take them away from the daily regimentation of incarceration, they may jump at the chance to participate. However, because of the environment of incarceration, educational disadvantage, diminished social support and contact with family and friends in the community, prisoners are vulnerable. This vulnerability may affect their ability to make decisions about their own welfare and can lead to ethical issues such as the freedom of a prisoner to make a genuine voluntary and uncoerced decision to participate as a subject in a research study.

The Belmont Report was published in 1979 by the National Commission for the Protection of Human Subjects of Biomedical and Behavioral Research and contains guidelines for the protection of human research subjects. In the United States any institution that does research that is supported or conducted by the U.S. Department of Health and Human Services (DHHS) must agree to protect human subjects with an acceptable statement of ethical principles.

The Office for Human Research Protections (OHRP) is responsible for ensuring compliance with human subject protection policy.

Today laws and regulations codified by federal executive agencies are in place to better protect prisoners as research subjects. Other agencies such as the Federal Bureau of Prisons have additional policies and safeguards regarding research involving inmate subjects. Review committees or Institutional Review Boards (IRBs) for protection of human subjects are essential to assess risk by maximizing possible benefits to prisoners' health or welfare and minimizing possible harms (psychological, physical pain, injury) to prisoners.

Prisoner research subjects must volunteer and be informed participants. Informed consent involves whether subjects are given the information they need to understand the risks they take by participating. Furthermore, inmates need to comprehend what they are giving consent to. Intellectually deficient, mentally disabled, or terminally ill inmates may not be able to give valid consent.

OBSERVE → INVESTIGATE → UNDERSTAND

- Do we need to pay close attention to prisoners who may consent to become subjects of prison research? Why or why not?
- Are prisoners incapable of providing true informed consent to participate in a prison research study? Explain.
- Should prison research where prisoners are subjects only include studies that promote the betterment of prisons?

SOURCES: T. H. Stone, *Prisoners as Human Subjects: Researcher Reference Guide* (Kentucky: Institute for Bioethics, Health Policy and Law University of Louisville School of Medicine, 2004); Board on Health Sciences Policy, Committee on Ethical Considerations for Revisions to DHHS Regulations for Protection of Prisoners Involved in Research, Lawrence O. Gostin, Cori Vanchieri, and Andrew Pope (Eds.), *Ethical Considerations for Research Involving Prisoners* (Washington, DC: The National Academies Press, 2007); "Guidance for Research Involving Prisoners," Rutgers, The State University of New Jersey, 2011. http://orsp.rutgers.edu/index.php?q=content/guidance-research-involving-prisoners-human-subjects (retrieved February 3, 2013).

---

subculture to cope with the pain of these losses. The subculture forms its own **inmate code,** or rules of behavior. Inmates are not to exploit one another. They are to be strong in confronting the pains of imprisonment. And they are to oppose prison authority. In short, rules such as "Don't rat on others," "Don't lose your cool," and "Don't trust the guards" motivate inmates' behavior. The inmate subculture provides solidarity and the means by which inmates collectively cope with incarceration.[86]

In contrast, the **importation model** holds that the inmate subculture does not arise from prison circumstances but rather is imported from the outside when offenders enter.[87] For example, aspects of the drug subculture of the streets become part of the inmate subculture.[88]

In reality, both inside and outside factors contribute to the development of the inmate subculture.[89] Adherence to the inmate code does not necessarily lead to solidarity (or less violence). Male inmates divide themselves primarily along racial lines. The tensions between racially diverse inmates–not between

inmate code
Rules of behavior that inmates follow.

importation model
The perspective assuming that inmate subculture does not develop as a result of prison circumstances but rather is brought in, or imported, from the outside when off enders enter.

Prison Slang Terms

Prisoners have their own language.

Slang Term	What It Means
Beef	A crime
Bullet	1-year period of time
CO or hack	Correctional officer
Dorm	Security housing unit
Fish	A new arrival, first-timer to a prison, or anyone not wise to prison life
Gated out	Released from prison
Ink	Tattoo
Mule	Someone who smuggles drugs into an institution
Rolled up	Arrested
Shank	Prison-made knife
Turned out	Being forced into homosexual acts
Bootie flu The ninja	AIDS/HIV
The hole	Solitary confinement
Tipped up	Gang affiliated
Yolked	Muscular

inmates and correctional officers—account for most of the instability in prisons today.[90] For female inmates, prison is by and large a different world, as we will see later in the chapter.

Racial Concerns During the 1970s, a number of court decisions ruled as unconstitutional prison practices that assigned inmates to cells or programs on the basis of their race. Prison officials widely expressed concern that forced integration would fuel already strong tensions among inmates and lead to significantly more violence. Some violence did occur in response to integration, but not as much as predicted. Still, much of the violence in men's prisons today occurs between gangs of different racial affiliations.[91]

Racial and ethnic tensions are a significant feature of male prison life in the United States. Unlike the world outside, male prisons tend to be dominated by people of color. Some commentators have argued that as a result, the minority White males have greater difficulty adjusting to the prison environment than do men of color.[92] Whites also tend to be victimized more frequently and severely. Evidence suggests that Whites are raped more than any other racial group.[93]

Institutional Gangs and Prison Violence

Prison gangs are a major aspect of prison life, providing support for and protection of their members. As overcrowding has increasingly plagued U.S. prisons, the prison subculture has become more fragmented and disorganized. Inmates have come to see life in prison as more dangerous than before. Belonging to a gang, however, provides members with a sense of stability as well as protection.[94] Most gangs are racially segregated, with members coming from the same city—and often the same neighborhood.[95]

Prison gangs manage drug trafficking—not only within the prison but often also on the streets through associates in the community with whom they communicate. They also control the availability of many illegal goods and services in prisons.

Gangs operate in the prisons in at least 40 states, as well as in federal prisons.[96] The rise of violent racist prison gangs began in part as a result of the desegregation of the U.S. prison populations in the 1960s. Racist rhetoric and animosity increase tensions within prisons and undermine security.[97] The Aryan Brotherhood, one of the first and best-known racist prison gangs, began at San Quentin Prison in California. There are other such White supremacist gangs with neo-Nazi identification in prisons. Because gangs tend to identify themselves along racial lines, Black, Latino, and Asian gangs also have formed. Visitors carry messages back and forth between gang members in prison and street gangs.

▲ **Gang Identity**
Prison gang members show their affiliations by their tattoos and gestures.

According to estimates from the National Gang Intelligence Center (NGIC), there are approximately 230,000 prison gang members in federal and state prisons in the United States. Prison gangs are comprised of a select group of inmates who belong to a structured group often with an established hierarchy and code of conduct. Some prison gangs are highly structured such as the Aryan Brotherhood and Nuestra Familia, whereas others, like the Mexican Mafia (La Eme), do not adhere to a strict structure. Prison gangs differ from street gangs in the size of membership, which tends to be smaller in the confined space of a correctional institution, and in the diversity of the gang's involvement in illicit activities. Those seeking membership in a prison gang do so because of their street gang affiliations and the need for protection while incarcerated. Prison gangs tend to be more powerful within state institutions than in federal institutions. Some prison gangs can be susceptible to extremist viewpoints and embrace a militant stance and authority within the prison. Some speculate that U.S. prisons will become a breeding ground for terrorism and the Islamic State of Iraq and Syria (ISIS).[98]

Prison gang–related crimes are a growing threat within correctional institutions and in the larger community as family on the outside move closer to the prison. Family members facilitate crime-related activity as messengers, smuggle contraband (especially cell phones) during visits, and even assist in escapes. Cell phones are particularly problematic because Internet access allows for unmonitored communication, text messaging, e-mails, and social media activity. Incarcerated gang members also garner more respect on the streets, allowing for easy influence in the community.

Gang members are also infiltrating jobs held by criminal justice practitioners, including those working in corrections. This poses significant safety concerns as gang members then have access to sensitive data, receive security clearances, and can influence investigations and operations, in addition to receiving specialized training and access to weapons.[99]

Control of Gang Violence   Strategies to control gang activity begin by identifying **security threat groups (STGs)**—inmates who, when they collaborate, can jeopardize the institution's security. Typically, inmates in an STG are members

security threat group (STG)
Inmates who, when they collaborate, can jeopardize the institution's security.

of White supremacy groups, street gangs, cults, or outlaw motorcycle gangs who use intimidation and violence to control drug trafficking, gambling, and extortion in prison. Many build loyalty by appealing to inmates' existing racial hatred and their need for protection from other inmates.[100] Most prison gangs have a paramilitary organization with rules and regulations. While in prison, gang members tend to associate with other members in their gang.

Gang affiliations are sometimes difficult to identify. Gang-related tattoos, self-admission, possession of gang-related literature, and the monitoring of correspondence with outside known gang members are some of the ways officials identify gang affiliations.[101] Most experts believe that prison gangs will never be completely eliminated. Once a member joins a gang, it is extremely difficult to leave.[102]

Some observers allege that correctional officers encourage—or do not discourage—racial violence to minimize the possibility that inmates will organize themselves against the officers.[103] Others point to STG policies as the source of many tensions that result in violence. For example, it is not uncommon for state corrections departments to separate gang members from the general population and to keep different gangs from having direct contact with one another. Many states have special lockdown units or *gang blocks* specifically for housing STG inmates. Some critics charge that prison administrations arbitrarily classify prisoners as members of STGs based on racial stereotyping.[104]

MYTH/REALITY

MYTH: Prison riots are evidence that inmates are violent and dangerous.

REALITY: Prison riots are often the result of administrative policies that inmates resist. When offenders feel that their needs are dismissed by correctional administrators and perceive that other avenues to express grievances are exhausted, riots can occur.[105] Since the 1930s, psychologists have linked frustration with aggression.[106] Incarceration can produce frustrations that can to lead to violence.[107]

Prison Riots   Riots are only one form of prison violence. When they occur, however, they generate media attention because they frequently harm both inmates and staff. Prison riots are not new. Indeed, it is estimated that since 1855, 500 prison riots have erupted in the United States, most at maximum- or medium-security facilities.[108]

Prison riots arise from a variety of factors: the authoritarian and demeaning behavior of some correctional officers, conflict between gangs, the subculture of violence, deprivations associated with imprisonment, racial tensions, boredom, overcrowding, and poor prison management. Riots recently erupted in Texas, Arizona, and California prisons.[109] Yet some riots appear to happen randomly, and this reality makes it impossible to predict such uprisings.[110] "A Global View" describes the unique ways one Venezuelan prison attempts to make prison life less violent and more humane for incarcerated inmates.

Two of the most infamous U.S. prison riots broke out at Attica Prison in New York in 1971 and at the New Mexico State Prison in Santa Fe in 1980. These two inmate revolts were very different in nature. At Attica the rioters attempted to force reforms such as more exercise and better food and programs. It was reported that the Attica correctional officers who were taken hostage were protected by inmates from violence. Nonetheless, as authorities moved in to quell the riot, 43 inmates and hostages died. In other words, the abuses that occurred took place *after* the riots, as officers violently retaliated against the prisoners. At Santa Fe there were no demands for reforms, just violence on the part of inmates against other inmates and against officers.

A Global View

A Different Kind of Prison: Venezuela's San Antonio Prison

In most countries, prisons are harsh environments that are intended to punish prisoners by depriving them of personal goods and services. San Antonio Prison, located on Margarita Island off the coast of Venezuela, is one prison that follows a different philosophy. The prison shares the island with many upscale tourist resorts. It is home to about 2,000 prisoners (mainly drug traffickers) and has a women's annex that holds about 130 women who mix freely with male prisoners.

Venezuelan prisons are known for being overcrowded; the country's prison population capacity is 14,000, but it houses about 50,000 inmates. The country's institutions are also known for unsanitary conditions, corruption, violence, and large numbers of inmate murders, gangs, and criminal activities.

The outside of San Antonio Prison appears foreboding and similar to other prisons. Uniformed soldiers are at the gates, and watchtowers have armed personnel ready to fire at inmates who try to escape. Guards stationed at the entrance search visitors when they enter but not when they leave. There is about 1 guard for every 150 prisoners or about 14 total, not a very large correctional officer force.

Once inside, prisoners have a great deal of autonomy and access to goods. They are allowed smartphones, computers, alcohol, drugs, and guns. Guests (including children) are allowed to spend the night. Inmates also have access to four swimming pools, a restaurant specializing in barbequed chicken, a food stand, a barber shop, a cockfighting ring, designated places to drink (including poolside), and a 600-person nightclub complete with DJs, strippers, and light shows for inmates and their guests. Some cells have air-conditioning and DirectTV satellite dishes. Prisoners claim they obtained these perks with their own money.

Guards, inmates, guests, and families freely walk around the grounds and socialize with each other. In this sense the environment, although hedonistic, is more akin to the outside world. In addition to the guards, in San Antonio Prison there is a top inmate leader known as a "pran" who represents and controls prisoners and maintains peace.

Although San Antonio Prison is far from safe or crime-free, rationales for allowing such activities in the facility are that they reduce violence and improve the inmates' quality of life. Officials also claim it reduces corruption, riots, prison fires, and the number of gangs that run prison rackets. Compared to other Venezuelan prisons, those incarcerated in San Antonio feel that if they have to serve prison time, this is the environment they prefer.

OBSERVE → INVESTIGATE → UNDERSTAND

- What are the positives and negatives of allowing inmates the kinds of goods and services San Antonio Prison provides?
- Do the perks offered in San Antonio Prison make the correctional guard's job safer? Why? Why not?
- How motivated would a prisoner at San Antonio Prison be to go back to his/her community? Explain.

SOURCES: Fox News Latino, "How Does Venezuela Keep Inmates in Check? Turns Prisons into Posh Resorts," April 03, 2013. http://latino.foxnews.com/latino/news/2013/04/03/venezuelan-prison-opens-nightclub-to-keep-violence-down/ (retrieved May 6, 2015); News.com.au, "Inside Venezuela's 'Party Prison,'" October 1, 2013. http://nypost.com/2013/10/01/inside-venezuelas-party-prison/ (retrieved May 6, 2015); Simon Romero, "Where Prisoners Can Do Anything, Except Leave," *New York Times*, June 3, 2011. www.nytimes.com/2011/06/04/world/americas/04venez.html?_r=0 (retrieved May 6, 2015).

This riot was rooted in the harassment and abuse of inmates. The underlying driving forces were revenge and counterrevenge.[111]

It appears that some riots can be prevented if prison policies provide inmates with accessible means to voice their complaints. These avenues include surveys and inmate councils that relay concerns to prison officials.[112] There is evidence that sustained prison riots are less prevalent today because of the high percentage of nonviolent offenders serving time, the fact that the most dangerous prisoners serve time in supermaximum-security prisons, and because better prison management has been mandated by the courts. High-tech surveillance approaches, new restrictions on prisoner movement, and the introduction of highly trained

Real Crime Tech

PERSONAL COMMUNICATION TECHNOLOGY AND PRISONS

Tablet computers may be the future of communications used in prisons and may alter the prison environment radically. Tablets are inexpensive (about $70) and appeal to prison officials and inmates. Although "clunky" compared to tablets in the outside world, they are hard to destroy or alter, and they are designed to have clear plastic cases so contraband can be easily detected. Application color schemes and symbols may need to be changed to conform to prison rules regarding gangs, etc. Tablets will have numbers and passwords that will belong to individual inmates. These devices will allow inmates to play games, listen to music, write e-mails, make low-quality videograms, send e-cards, and communicate with the outside world. Any outside communications will be synched at a designated kiosk, and prison officials will review them to make sure the communications are safe, innocuous, and undamaging. If prison officials judge that communications conform to prison rules, inmates will be allowed to forward their messages to recipients. To date, prisons in Idaho and New Jersey have ordered tablets. Tablets may make cell phones—and the problems resulting from their use in prisons—a thing of the past.[a]

Because of the need to strictly control communications between inmates and the outside world, cell phones in most U.S. prisons are considered contraband for inmates. Controlling cell phones in prisons, jails, and correctional camps has become a major problem as inmates use them to communicate with their families and friends, but also to threaten their victims, commit other crimes, and even plan escapes.[b]

The Florida Department of Corrections confiscated 4,200 cell phones from the state's prisons in 2013. Roughly 30,000 cell phones have been found in California prisons since 2014. In an attempt to control the use of cell phones and other illegal laptops, some prisons have purchased jamming equipment, some are using specially trained dogs to sniff out the phones, and others have built expensive high fences to prevent phones from being thrown into the prison. The state of New York has even purchased X-ray chairs so that visitors' bodies can be scanned to detect cell phones in body cavities.

Continued

security teams known frequently as Correctional Emergency Response Teams (CERTs) have also played an important role in the decline in prison riots.[113]

Sex and Sexual Assault in Prison Sexual assault is physically and emotionally devastating, and its scars can last a lifetime.[114] In 2008, according to the Department of Justice, almost 10 percent of prisoners reported sexual violence in jails and prisons, including allegations of sexual assault by correctional staff.[115] The general opinion is that these figures are much lower than the actual number of such incidents.[116] Many men who are victims of male rape in prison are reluctant to report these incidents due to either embarrassment or fear of retaliation.[117] One study of the federal prison system estimates that about half of the rape victims interviewed had not told anyone about their experience. Another factor in underreporting is that some prison officers simply do not report the assaults to the authorities. These officers may consider rape the price the offender must pay for his crime.[118]

The community outside prison generally views sexual assaults by males on other males as homosexual acts. Inmates, however, do not see these acts in the same way. Rather, the aggressor sees himself as a masculine heterosexual and views the passive individual as effeminate and homosexual. Thus, inmates tend to look upon physically stronger aggressors who force sex on a weaker inmate not as rapists but as dominant males asserting their manhood.[119]

MYTH/REALITY

MYTH: Sexual violence against and exploitation of inmates of the same gender are primarily the result of a lack of heterosexual opportunities.

REALITY: Sexual violence and exploitation in prisons are mostly centered on power, status, and control—not on sexual needs.[120]

Male prisoners with certain characteristics–such as youth, attractive looks, small stature, and naiveté–who enter a correctional facility as first-time offenders are immediately identified by other prisoners and targeted by some for sexual assault.[121] Twenty-two percent of male inmates claim to have been raped or forced into sex while incarcerated. Only 29 percent of these victims reported their rape to the authorities. These figures mask the much larger scope of sexual assault, including the many instances–technically not rape–in which inmates consent to being sexually exploited after being threatened with rape or other types of violence.[122]

Often staff members ignore sexual assaults, but they also can contribute to them. In one notorious case in California's Corcoran Prison, correctional officers were accused of punishing inmates by placing them in cells with known prison rapists.[123]

Illegal Drugs

Illegal drugs and other contraband are pervasive within jails and prisons, even though these substances are strictly prohibited. Despite aggressive prison search practices, drugs are continually smuggled into institutions by visitors as well as by correctional personnel (Figure 12-7).[124] Of particular concern nationally and internationally is how technology is transforming how inmates obtain drugs and other contraband. For example, recently in a Maryland prison it was discovered that drones attempted to fly in drugs, tobacco, porn videos, and weapons. In other prisons mobile phones, chargers, and USB drives, were intercepted. Since 2015 drones have been used as much as 33 times to smuggle illegal items into prisons resulting in at least 10 states calling for legislation to ban them from lying over prisons.[125] Furthermore, alcohol is easy to obtain while incarcerated. With some yeast, sugar, and water, inmates can easily make a form of alcohol (called *pruno*).[126]

Although the majority of drug offenders are convicted of nonviolent crimes, inmates under the influence of prohibited substances may become aggressive and pose a risk to themselves, other inmates, or prison staff.[127] Drug use then becomes not only a problem for the inmate but also a concern for the institution. Some inmates, however, claim that the use of drugs such as cannabis and tranquilizers calms them, enhances their ability

Continued from previous page

In further attempts to curtail cell phone use, the federal government and many states have enacted harsh penalties that range from forfeiture of up to 90 days good time credits for inmates in California and felony convictions with possible sentences up to 15 years for non-inmates in Mississippi.[c]

Continued from previous page

OBSERVE➔INVESTIGATE➔UNDERSTAND

- Can you think of any positive reasons for allowing inmates to have access to the Internet?
- Is there a constitutional issue here? If yes, which one and why?
- Since there are some countries that do allow access to cell phones and computers, might this become a managed privilege for different custody levels? To what end?

SOURCES: [a]Alyssa Bereznak, "This Tablet Is the Future of Personal Prison Technology," *Yahoo.com*, July 9, 2015. www.yahoo.com/tech/this-tablet-is-the-future-of-personal-prison-123582456509.html (retrieved July 12, 2015).

[b]Kevin Johnson, "Smuggled Cellphones Flourish in Prisons," *USA Today*, November 20, 2008. www.usatoday.com/tech/wireless/2008-11-20-cellphone_N.htm (retrieved June 21, 2015).

[c]Kevin Roose and Pendarvis Harshaw, "Inside the Prison System's Illicit Digital World," *Fusion*, February 3, 2015. http://fusion.net/story/41931/inside-the-prison-systems-illicit-digital-world/ (retrieved June 21, 2015); California Department of Corrections and Rehabilitation, "Fact Sheet: Contraband Cell Phones in CDCR Prisons and Conservation Camps," April 14, 2015. www.cdcr.ca.gov/Contraband-Cell-Phones/K-9-overview.html (retrieved June 21, 2015).

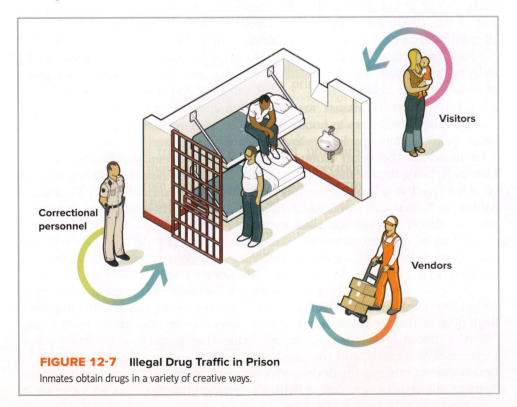

FIGURE 12-7   Illegal Drug Traffic in Prison
Inmates obtain drugs in a variety of creative ways.

Visitors

Correctional personnel

Vendors

Drones are increasingly used to smuggle drugs and other illegal items into prisons

to deal with the prison environment, and improves their psychological health.[128]

Solitary Confinement

While supermax institutions specialize in providing solitary confinement, all prisons have the ability to place inmates in solitary when necessary. **Solitary confinement** involves physically segregating inmates from other inmates and severely restricting their interactions, which are generally limited to correctional staff. Solitary confinement cells are bare and austere and thus provide virtually no sensory stimulation. Inmates often become disoriented and may emerge with mental disorders that they did not have before their isolation.[129]

An inmate may be placed in solitary for disciplinary reasons, a practice called **punitive segregation.** Prisoners can be assigned to punitive segregation for violent behavior, setting fires, and possession of contraband such as illegal drugs, among other offenses. Prison authorities must follow a legal process before taking such an action, however, because prisoners have legally protected liberties, though not all the rights possessed by defendants in criminal court. Prison officials also may place an inmate in solitary to provide him with supervision and control beyond that given to the general prison population; this practice is called **administrative segregation.** "Ad seg" inmates include those who are considered likely targets of physical (including sexual) harm by other inmates because of the nature of their crimes (such as sex crimes against children), the notoriety of their offenses, or their gang affiliation. Other inmates are placed in administrative segregation because they pose a threat to others or to themselves.

The United States holds more prisoners in solitary confinement than any other country. Some 25,000 U.S. inmates are isolated in supermax facilities, and 50,000 to 80,000 more are held in some form of isolation for varying amounts of time in maximum-security prisons. The use of prolonged solitary confinement is relatively recent in U.S. prisons. The first supermax prison opened in 1983; by the end of the 1990s, approximately 60 supermax facilities had opened, and nearly all maximum-security prisons had established units for solitary confinement.[130]

Solitary confinement does a good job of protecting a prison population by isolating individuals who are prone to violence and harm to others. But many of those who are isolated are not in that category, and their isolation only feeds a tendency toward irrational behavior, anger, and violence. Studies have found that prolonged isolation from human contact leads to brooding, retaliation fantasies, hallucinations, panic attacks, withdrawal, and in some cases a catatonic state in which the person's movements and expressions significantly decline. Moreover, being deprived of human contact does a poor job of preparing inmates who are freed to adjust to the outside community.[131] In fall 2015 California's *Ashker v. Brown* case ushered in the end solitary confinement in the state's prisons. Almost all prisoners who spent more than 10 years in isolation were ordered to be released immediately into the general population. New York and the federal government are also overhauling their solitary confinement systems resulting in a victory for inmates and the criminal justice reform movement.[132]

What are the alternatives to solitary confinement? Some groups have suggested limiting isolation to 90 days. Some favor abolishing the system altogether. Beginning in the 1980s, Britain gradually moved away from using solitary confinement because correctional officials found that it did not diminish prison violence, it was costly, and the public did not support it. As an alternative, the British corrections system developed a strategy to prevent violence instead of heaping punishments on violent behavior. Noting prisoners who act violently in

solitary confinement
Isolation of an inmate that denies the person the basic human need to interact with others.

punitive segregation
Isolation of an inmate for disciplinary reasons, to provide additional supervision and control of the individual.

administrative segregation
Placement of an inmate in solitary confinement to provide him with supervision, protection, and control beyond that given to general prison population.

one kind of environment will behave reasonably in another setting, the British began to give the prisoners more rather than less control; provided them more opportunities for work, education, and mental health treatment; and allowed them to earn rights for certain privileges. This preventive approach has had good results, and the use of isolation in British prisons is now minimal.[133]

WOMEN IN PRISON

In 1873 the first women's prison, the Indiana Reformatory Institution, opened. Before then, the few women who were imprisoned were confined with men or kept in separate sections of men's prisons. It was common for male correctional officers and prisoners to sexually abuse female inmates, and pregnancy often resulted. Women imprisoned in male prisons lived a highly restricted existence compared to their male counterparts. They typically had only limited access to clergy, doctors, exercise, fresh air, and light.[134] Attention to women's prisons and the incarceration of women, however, gained gradual momentum in the late nineteenth and twentieth centuries.

▲ **Prison Crowding**
When prisons are overcrowded, public spaces are used as dormitories.

The Female Prison Population

Women make up approximately 7 percent of state and federal prison inmates.[135] Although fewer women than men are incarcerated in U.S. prisons, the female population is growing rapidly. Between 1980 and 2014, the number of women in U.S. prisons rose at a rate 50 percent higher than the number of male inmates.[136] Moreover, the four largest U.S. prison systems combined—California, Texas, Florida, and the Federal Bureau of Prisons—held more than one-third of the nation's incarcerated women.[137] Some reasons for the fast rise in the female prison population include the increase in the crime rate for women, the "get tough" movement and harsher policies for dealing with crime, the drug epidemic, and a shift in the mid-1980s to mandatory sentencing, which no longer permitted judges to consider family and gender factors in sentencing. The move to mandatory sentencing put an end to the chivalry (judicial courtesy) that had influenced the sentencing of women during earlier years.[138]

Of all female inmates in U.S. prisons during 2014, about 50 percent were White and 21 percent were Black.[139] Still, women of color in U.S. prisons have significantly higher incarceration rates than White women.[140] And most women incarcerated in U.S. prisons are not young. The majority are in their 30s and 40s, representing approximately 57 percent of all incarcerated women.[141] Additionally, in 2014 approximately 61 percent of women in contrast to 59 percent of men incarcerated in state or federal prisons were 39 or younger.[142]

Characteristics of Women's Prisons

Women are imprisoned in various types of facilities. They may be housed in prisons only for females or in a separate wing of a men's institution. Rarely, women may be held in "coed" prisons in which the females are housed separately from the males but share programs for both sexes. Institutions for women are primarily run according to a custodial model and have few rehabilitation programs.

With the increasing number of women being sentenced to prison, overcrowding has become a problem. For example, California's prisons for women are 171 to 200 percent over capacity.[143] Federal women's facilities are also over capacity. The era of designing small cottage-style women's prisons is fading. Many jurisdictions are likely to follow California's lead in building large women's prisons. One women's prison complex in California incarcerates more than 7,000 women and is the world's largest prison complex for women. Given the overcrowding in California prisons and the largely nonviolent offenses women commit and the federal guidelines to release prisoners in California (see Chapter 11's section on Public Safety Realignment policy), approximately 4,500 female inmates may be released to the community in community correction facilities, rehabilitation programs, and private residences with monitoring devices. Furthermore, California has reached out to the private sector to house minimum-security women within 1 year of release in a 300-capacity female reentry facility. It is too soon to tell whether prison realignment policy will contribute to a trend toward smaller women's prisons.

How Women Do Time in Prison

Male and female prisoners respond differently to custody and supervision and have different needs. Yet the policies, procedures, and practices developed for male inmates have traditionally been imposed on female prisoners. Frequently these approaches do not work well. Many women are subject to difficulties and complications not experienced by male prisoners. For example, they might be the primary caretaker of children, they may have female-related medical and mental health needs, or they may have experienced more physical and sexual abuse than typical male offenders.[144] A gender-specific model for programs in women's prisons is essential for effective treatment of incarcerated women.[145]

The social structure that develops in women's prisons is different from that in men's prisons. Some evidence suggests that women have greater social support needs than men while incarcerated.[146] Women in prison tend to develop closer and more personal relationships than men. Although men may bond with one another (for example, as members of a gang), they avoid emotional entanglements that could be problematic. In marked contrast, imprisoned women tend to create pseudo or "play" families with kinship alliances that mimic the family structure of the wider society. Within these surrogate families, they take on roles such as mother, father, sister, aunt, and uncle and develop emotional and sometimes sexual relationships with other incarcerated women. These family-type units provide a support network for dealing with prison life and separation from their true families.

Incarceration takes an enormous toll on women who are mothers and primary caregivers for children; moreover, pregnant inmates have special needs. Women who are pregnant when they enter prison, or who become pregnant while there, present particular management challenges, including the need to provide prenatal and obstetric care, gynecologic care, and proper nutrition.[147] A routine practice in U.S. prisons is the shackling of pregnant prisoners on the belly and arms during labor and delivery. (See the "Race, Class, Gender" box in Chapter 11 for more on this subject.) Shackling women while in labor can possibly lead to problems such as hemorrhage, decreased fetal heart rate, and permanent brain damage to the infant. There is a prison reform push to change this practice.[148] The amount of time an inmate mother is allowed to spend with her newborn before separation varies with jurisdiction–but all jurisdictions impose a limit. Separation is particularly painful, especially if the infant must be placed in foster care or given up for adoption.[149] The "Race, Class, Gender" box describes an innovative pregnant inmate program of the Washington Corrections Center for Women's Residential Parenting.

Overall, the atmosphere of a women's prison differs significantly from that of a men's institution. There is far less violent behavior, sexual aggression is almost nonexistent, and homosexual activity is generally consensual.[150] A study of the racial climate in women's institutions found no evidence of serious racial

Race, Class, Gender

A Pregnant Inmate Program

Pregnant inmate programs are the exception, not the norm. The Washington Corrections Center for Women—one of the exceptions—developed a program in 1999 called Her Hand Rocks the Cradle that combines a residential parenting program with Early Head Start. Her Hand Rocks the Cradle allows eligible inmates, classified as minimum-security level and serving sentences of less than 3 years, to remain with their babies during their sentence. They live in a designated unit and are given support and education. Importantly, these women have time to bond with and develop trust with their infants.

Each mother has a room with a bed, a crib or toddler bed for the child, and a dresser. The unit contains a communal playroom with toys, a children's bathing room, clothes washing facilities, a place to prepare snacks, and enclosed outside play areas. Pediatricians and counselors are available on a regular basis. Caregivers—volunteer inmates trained to take care of and be responsible for the children while their inmate mothers are working, attending school, going to therapy, and attending to other institutional requirements—are essential to the success of Her Hand Rocks the Cradle.

The program provides an alternative to foster care, adoption, or abortion. Advocates say that it encourages mothers to participate in rehabilitation programs because they are motivated to provide the best they can for their children when they return to the community.

At the heart of the program is the Children of Incarcerated Parents Bill of Rights:

I have the right to be kept safe and informed at the time of my parent's arrest.

I have the right to be heard when decisions are made about me.

I have the right to be considered when decisions are made about my parent.

I have the right to be well cared for in my parent's absence.

I have the right to speak with, see, and touch my parent.

I have the right to support as I struggle with my parent's incarceration.

I have the right not to be judged, blamed, or labeled because of my parent's incarceration.

I have the right to a lifelong relationship with my parent.

The education and bonding experiences provided by the program are intended to strengthen family ties—with the hope that those who participate will not reoffend.

OBSERVE → INVESTIGATE → UNDERSTAND

- What are the rights of pregnant prison inmates? What are the rights of children whose mothers are in prison?
- What obligations, if any, do prisons have for caring for pregnant prisoners?
- How do both mothers and children benefit from special programs like Her Hand Rocks the Cradle?

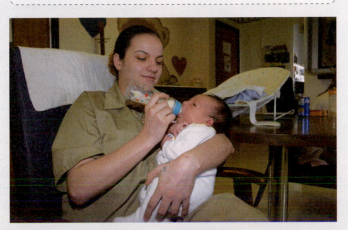

SOURCES: Cheryl Hanna-Truscott and others, *Her Hand Rocks the Cradle,* a photodocumentary project at the Washington Corrections Center for Women. www.residentialparenting.com/ (retrieved April 25, 2007); Nell Bernstein, *Children of Incarcerated Parents Bill of Rights* (San Francisco: Northern California Service League). www.norcalservice-league.org/billrite.htm (retrieved April 25, 2007).

conflicts among female inmates.[151] In fact, many pseudo family structures are interracial, in marked contrast to the situation in most men's prisons, where interracial tensions run high. Although women tend to do their time using less physical aggression than men, incarceration for women is not without problems.

Problems of Incarcerated Women

Women in prison experience many difficulties. Typically their problems are related to drug abuse, separation from children and other family members, physical and mental health issues, educational inadequacies and vocational unpreparedness, a history of abuse, and sexual abuse in prison.

Drug Abuse   Most women in prison are incarcerated for nonviolent crimes that involve drugs and property offenses.[152] About 80 percent of women in jail and prison have substance abuse problems. About 25 percent of women sentenced to state prison are serving time for drug offenses, compared to 15 percent of men.[153]

The needs of incarcerated women with drug problems differ from those of their male counterparts.[154] Prior to arrest, women drug users are more likely to call in sick for work assignments, have more reproductive-related medical problems, be HIV-positive, have children living with them at the time of incarceration, and have incomes of less than $600 per month.[155] Drug treatment programs need to focus on gender-related mental health, employment, education, economic, social, relationship, family, medical, and housing issues.[156]

Separation from Family and Children   Most incarcerated women (more than 65 percent) have children who are minors.[157] One of the chief differences between incarcerated women and men is the degree to which children are priorities to each, with women placing a higher priority on their offspring.[158]

Physical and Mental Health Issues   Many women in prison face health issues. In addition to HIV, incarcerated women may have an infectious disease such as hepatitis or tuberculosis and may suffer from sexually transmitted infections. Typical mental health problems include guilt, depression, fear, and anxiety, as well as substance abuse and mood, personality, and psychotic disorders. Many female inmates experience posttraumatic stress disorder (PTSD) in connection with their incarceration.[159] Moreover, destructive behaviors, frequently viewed as psychological in origin, result in self-injury such as cutting, head banging, and burning.[160] Suicidal behavior is yet another serious problem for some incarcerated women.[161]

Many female inmates come from unstable family backgrounds that might contribute to their development of emotional and behavioral difficulties. For example, approximately 67 percent of women in prison have one or more family members who had been incarcerated.[162] Also, many incarcerated women come from homes with only one parent.[163]

Another problem facing incarcerated women with mental disorders is that they tend to have difficulty negotiating their lives in prison. They frequently break rules and engage in assaultive acts that affect other inmates and staff. As a result, they are often penalized by being segregated from others in the general population, a practice that can exacerbate their mental illness.[164]

Educational Inadequacies and Vocational Unpreparedness   Incarcerated women have educational obstacles and achieve very low levels of formal education. Approximately 64 percent of women in prison do not have a high school diploma, yet only 16 percent of them achieve a GED while imprisoned.[165]

These women also have limited job skills and so are poorly prepared for work when they are released. They have a difficult time supporting themselves and their families. When they do find work, it is usually minimum wage and typically does not pay enough to support their needs. Women gravitate to jobs that pay less, compared to men who tend to seek higher-paying jobs such as auto mechanics, welding, truck driving, and electrical work.

History of Abuse   Many incarcerated women report a history of physical and sexual abuse.[166] Many of them were raised strictly and had childhoods characterized by severe physical child abuse in which regular spanking and violent beatings were the norm. These women also report that the abuse tended to blindside them, coming without any warning.[167] A study of women incarcerated in a large southern prison system found that 68.4 percent of the women reported lifetime sexual victimization, 17.2 percent reported in-prison sexual victimization, and 3 percent reported having been a victim of a completed rape.[168]

Sexual Abuse in Prison   Women usually commit few violent crimes during incarceration.[169] Women's prisons have lower rates of sexual violence than men's prisons, and the violence takes different forms, from sexual pressure, intimidation, and coercion to sexual assault.[170] Like male prisoners, female inmates underreport sexual coercion and assaults for fear of possible repercussions.[171] They fear that they may lose privileges, be subjected to disciplinary action themselves, or be shunned or attacked by other inmates.

The most common form of sexual abuse of female inmates is forced sex with male staff. Men compose over 50 percent of the custody force in women's prisons.[172] Male prison staff may conduct unwarranted pat-downs and strip searches, address female prisoners in humiliating ways, use inappropriate language, and observe women unnecessarily under the pretext of surveillance. For victims of past sexual abuse, these intrusions can be especially traumatic. Such abuse by male prison staff is difficult to avoid because female prisoners cannot remove themselves from their situation, grievance procedures may be inadequate, employees do not take responsibility for their actions, and the public does not take an interest in the problem.[173]

In general, however, female inmates, like their male counterparts, complain that reports of sexual abuse are not formally investigated.[174] Of investigated and substantiated reports of sexual violence and harassment, approximately half implicate correctional staff.[175] Regardless of the employee's gender, under federal law all sexual relations between staff and inmates constitute abuse—even when an inmate consents to sexual relations—because of the power that correctional employees have over inmates.[176] Consent is never a legal defense. One measure that can reduce abuse of female prisoners by male staff is to increase the penalties for staff sexual abuse of inmates.[177]

In response to documented abuse of male and female inmates, the **Prison Rape Elimination Act (PREA)** was unanimously passed by Congress and signed into law by President George W. Bush in September 2003.[178] The legislation established the National Prison Rape Elimination Commission (NPREC) to develop national standards for detecting and preventing prison rape, as well as for punishing perpetrators. NPREC provides grants to states to implement policies and practices that reduce or prevent rapes in prison and gives the commission authority to collect data on a broad range of sexual misconduct.[179] NPREC's authority covers not only adult prisons and jails but juvenile and community correctional facilities as well.

Prison Rape Elimination Act (PREA)
Legislation that established the National Prison Rape Elimination Commission to develop national standards for detecting and preventing prison rape, as well as for punishing perpetrators.

REHABILITATION AND TREATMENT IN PRISON

Prisons today are under increasing pressure to move from simply being custodial to being therapeutic, offering programs to equip inmates for life after prison and providing treatment for various needs, including the needs of special populations such as those with disabilities, elder adults, and those who are ill.

Inmate Labor

Chapter 11 outlined the development of the industrial prison movement. It described labor unions' objections to what they felt was unfair competition from prisons, and the unions' consequent pursuit of legal means to restrict the sale of goods made with inmate labor. As a result of these union initiatives, when prisoners were sentenced to incarceration with "hard labor," increasingly the labor was hard and only used for prison maintenance, but it was rarely rehabilitative or of value after release.[180] Moreover, the routine inmate work assignments, such as sweeping floors and washing dishes, rarely provided meaningful experience for future jobs in the community. They fostered neither pride nor the hope of supporting families after prison. It is one thing to keep individuals busy with work while they are incarcerated; it is another to provide them with meaningful work that they will be motivated to continue and that will pay a living wage.

Meaningful Work Assignments   Today's prison officials agree that useful, productive work is important for rehabilitation. A trend toward allowing private
companies to take advantage of the prison labor force has given inmates more
meaningful work and helped prepare them for reentry into the community.
Particularly when there was low unemployment in the general population
coupled with high incarceration rates, new job opportunities for U.S. inmates
were actively developed, such as telemarketing, staffing call centers, arranging
business meetings, and manufacturing computer circuit boards. A recent example of a meaningful work program at California's San Quentin Prison is called
Code 7370, the first prison computer coding program in the United States.
The project partners with Silicon Valley's technology industry to turn inmates
into computer coders so upon release they will be able to find decent jobs
most likely in customer service.[181]

In 2000, more than 80,000 inmates in 36 states were employed in private
sector jobs and were earning between \$0.25 and \$7.00 an hour.[182] Today felon
labor programs call on inmates to do everything from building car parts in
Virginia to battling mudslides and fires in California. Female inmates in
Tennessee train dogs to make them more adoptable; in Missouri, they train
service dogs to assist people with disabilities.

Prison officials view these programs as a benefit both to inmates and to
the community.[183] For private business, the use of prison inmates is a way of
cutting costs by employing cheap labor without the need to outsource these
jobs outside the United States. During bad economic times, in fact, the use of
prison labor as a cost-saving measure might increase. On the downside, an
increase in the use of prison labor might hurt outside businesses that cannot
compete with this cheaper labor source.

Benefits of Prison Work Programs   In 2001 Florida published a study of academic, vocational, and substance abuse programs offered by its Department of
Corrections to determine whether they were effective in reducing recidivism.
The study found that 70 percent of those who completed the Graduate Equivalency Diploma (GED) had not been rearrested during a 24-month follow-up
period after their release. Inmates who received a GED and participated in work
release for at least 60 days were 10.1 percent less likely to reoffend than inmates

DIS Connects

Diving for Rehabilitation

The idea of having inmates don wetsuits and oxygen tanks for a deep-sea dive might seem highly unusual. But beginning in 1970 the California Prison Industry Authority developed a very successful commercial deep-sea diving program at a minimum-security facility in Chino. This is the only program in the world for inmates seeking to become commercial divers.

There are only about 600 commercial deep-sea divers worldwide, so the need for qualified workers is great. The trained inmates in Chino's Leonard Greenstone Marine Technology Training Center are virtually assured good-paying jobs ranging from $50,000 to $100,000 annually in areas such as underwater construction, offshore oil drilling, and dam repair. The program accommodates about 100 inmates, lasts approximately 11 months, and follows a curriculum of diving physics, navigation, report writing, air systems, welding, seamanship, dive medicine, blueprint reading, diesel engines, and marine construction. It also fosters the development of professional attitudes, confidence, pride, determination, perseverance, initiative, and courage. The low rates of recidivism for offenders in this program suggest that such skills and attitudes go far toward paving the way to their successful reentry into society.

Overcrowding and budgetary problems in California prisons forced the closure of this program in 2003, but the California Department of Corrections and Rehabilitation restarted it in 2006 and taxpayers do not pay for it. Funding comes from inmate-produced goods and services under the California Prison Industry Authority. Program administrators report that recidivism rates among the inmate graduates are as low as 6 percent, whereas over 52 percent of inmates return to incarceration during the first 2 years after release. This creative approach illustrates the disconnect between, on the one hand, the urgent need to prepare inmates to make a comfortable living without having to resort to crime, and, on the other hand, the many work programs that (when available) prepare prisoners only for low-paying jobs.

OBSERVE → INVESTIGATE → UNDERSTAND

- What jobs are prisoners prepared for after completing the deep-sea diving training?
- What is the best way to set up a rehabilitation program like the one that develops deep-sea diving skills?
- What aspects of this training program do you think make it a successful form of rehabilitation?

SOURCES: Kevin Johnson, "California Diving Program Helps Anchor Ex-Inmates," *USA Today*, July 14, 2008. www.usatoday.com/news/nation/2008-07-13-Reentry-inmates_N.htm (retrieved February 10, 2009); "PIA Re-establishes Commercial Diving Center: Training Touted as Effective Tool in Reducing Recidivism," *California Department of Corrections Staff News*, December 15, 2006. www.pia.ca.gov/Public_Affairs/pdfs/Dec%2015%20Staff%20News%20fnl%20fnl.pdf (retrieved July 29, 2011); State of California Prison Industry Authority, "Career Technology Training (CTE)—Marine Technology Training Center," 2011. http://pia.ca.gov/OffenderDevelopment/MarineTech.aspx (retrieved May 2, 2015); CBS San Francisco, "Program Offers California Inmates a Second Chance through Diving," February 6, 2012. http://sanfrancisco.cbslocal.com/2012/02/06/program-offers-california-inmates-a-second-chance-through-diving/ (retrieved February 3, 2013).

who completed their GED but had no work experience. The study also determined that inmates who earned a vocational certificate were 14.6 percent less likely to reoffend than those who did not complete such programs, and inmates who completed substance abuse programs were 6.2 percent less likely to commit new crimes than those who did not.[184] In short, inmates in work programs are less likely to reoffend than those without that experience.[185]

Another benefit of prison work programs is the economic gain for the states that have them. California prisons generate more than $150 million in direct annual sales of products made with inmate labor. In California, prison products can be sold only to government agencies; however, in other states such as Nevada, inmates make cars sold on the open market. In Oregon, jeans are produced and sold to the public under the label "Prison Blues."[186] The "Disconnects" box describes a work program that teaches inmates deep-sea diving, a skill that directly helps them change their lives upon release.

Treatment Programs

Treatment programs are designed to help inmates change the illegal or destructive behavior that led to their prison sentence. The "Case in Point" box illustrates inmates participating in an emotional literacy rehabilitation program. Many treatment programs target anger management and drug and alcohol abuse.[187] Others focus on education, vocational skills, and parenting. Some inmates

a case in p♥int

The National Emotional Literacy Program for Prisoners

The majority of sentenced prisoners will be released back into society, and many will return to the communities where they committed their crimes. Knowing this reality, isn't it better in terms of public safety for prisons to have programs for incarcerated offenders that may help them overcome the mind-set and patterns of violence and addiction that led to the commission of crime in the first place? One such program that is gaining momentum and support in a number of U.S. prisons and internationally is Lionheart Foundation's emotional literacy projects for inmates.

The National Emotional Literacy Project encompasses several assumptions. First, inmates must learn to have dignity, self-respect, and respect for others before they can exhibit positive behavioral change and take responsibility for their actions. Another equally important premise is that emotional illiteracy is the major factor underlying crime. A third assumption is that emotional literacy can be learned at any point and place in a person's life—even prison or jail. Lastly, when people are emotionally literate they can better deal with stress, tension, and impulses; understand and manage themselves; communicate more effectively; develop better social skills (including empathy); and operate in the world in a prosocial way.

The emotional literacy program curriculum is detailed in a self-help book titled *Houses of Healing: A Prisoner's Guide to Inner Power and Freedom* by Robin Casarjian. It is written for prisoners and contains powerful, research-driven exercises for prisoners to complete. The exercises relate to the situations and feelings incarcerated populations experience. Exercises deal with issues such as childhood pain, loss, anger, stress, coping strategies, and forgiveness. Inmates and a variety of correctional staff have expressed high regard for the emotional literacy approach to rehabilitation. In the future, when prisons and jails are under the gun to develop cost-effective rehabilitative programs that produce evidence-based results, we may see more emotional literacy programs proliferate in correctional environments, and scientific studies may generate data-driven studies on effectiveness.

OBSERVE → INVESTIGATE → UNDERSTAND

- In what ways does emotional illiteracy contribute to crime?
- Can an emotionally literacy program work with prisoners suffering from serious mental illnesses? Why or why not?
- Can learning how to better read feelings in others and oneself result in negative outcomes? Explain.

SOURCE: The Lionheart Foundation, "National Emotional Literacy Projects." www.lionheart.org/prison (retrieved February 2, 2013).

require medications to manage impulsivity, depression, and anxiety before they can benefit from behavioral approaches or psychotherapies. Treatment tailored to the specific needs of individual inmates is most likely to have an impact and, it is estimated, could cut recidivism by as much as 50 percent.[188]

Today's treatment programs expect offenders to take responsibility for their crimes. When counseling is provided to inmates who have no desire to change or participate, the results are poor, an outcome that reinforces the "nothing works" mentality.[189]

Prison-based drug treatment programs have the advantage of operating in a controlled residential environment over a long period of time. One popular drug treatment strategy makes use of the concept of a therapeutic community.[190] First used in England in the 1940s, the *therapeutic community* (or *milieu therapy*) separates inmates with a particular problem, such as substance abuse, from the general prison population. The assumption is that the social climate experienced by inmates in prison will affect their behavior upon release. Thus every effort is made to create an environment in which inmates will take responsibility for their actions. Staff—including correctional officers, counselors, and administrators—are specially recruited in this effort. The therapeutic community approach engages inmates in productive experiences that include education, group therapy, peer pressure, and town hall-style decision making.[191]

Whatever the mode of treatment, the most effective prison programs dedicate specific funds to drug treatment, are operated by specialists contracted by the prison, and employ treatment specialists–as opposed to relying on prison personnel to deliver treatment.[192] Unfortunately, such programs tend to be few. Furthermore, the plight of inmates with drug problems is often compounded by other factors, such as mental illness. In fact, a growing proportion of inmates have special needs to which jails and prisons are expected to respond.

The Needs of Special Populations

Inmates in U.S. jails and prisons are diverse, and many have special needs. Offenders with such needs pose unique problems. They are highly vulnerable to exploitation by the general inmate population, must be closely monitored for their safety, and require special accommodations while incarcerated. We consider some of the most frequently encountered special populations in this section.

▲ **Elder Adult Inmates**

Elder inmates are a growing population in today's prisons.

Elder Adult Inmates   The prison population is aging. The number of older inmates, defined as age 55 and over, has increased more than 200 percent since the 1990s. Now constituting 1 of every 23 prisoners, older inmates are the fastest-growing population in state prisons.[193]

A major reason for the increase is that inmates are serving more time today than in previous decades. Based on a recent study by a Washington, DC–based nongovernmental organization, 159,520 inmates were serving life sentences in the United States in 2012; this represents an 11.8 percent increase since 2008.[194]

The cost of confining elder inmates is high–approximately $2.1 billion annually.[195] Most of the expense is attributable to the costs of health care. Many jails and prisons are not prepared to deal with the medical problems, physical disabilities, and chronic and terminal illnesses that come with aging. Elder adult inmates require special accommodations such as hearing aids, bath rails, wheelchairs, and walkers. Those with age-related dementia and senility need constant supervision. These factors require correctional institutions to take on many of the functions of nursing homes. As another sign of the times, prison programs that give hospice care to dying inmates are becoming more common in U.S. correctional institutions.[196]

Older inmates are generally given lighter-duty work assignments in the institution. Such practices can create resentment among younger inmates and thus present management problems for the administration. For these reasons, a case can be made for establishing prisons exclusively for geriatric inmates, as well as for granting parole to more nonviolent, low-risk elder adult inmates.[197]

State policies that provide for early release on humanitarian or compassionate grounds are rarely applied to older inmates. Because of the serious nature of their crimes and the lengthy sentences they were given, few elder adult inmates receive early release.[198] Most, however, pose a low risk of recidivism.[199]

Inmates with Mental Disorders   An inmate with a mental disorder is one who has impaired cognitive, emotional, or behavioral functioning. Impairment may have stemmed from social, psychological, biochemical, or genetic factors or from purely physical factors such as head trauma and infection.

Unfortunately, individuals who are mentally disordered or intellectually challenged (defined as having an IQ below 70) far too often end up in U.S. jails and prisons and not in the care of the mental health system. The number of inmates with psychological disorders who are in correctional institutions is four times greater than in the general population.[200] Recent estimates put the number of individuals with mental disorders in jails and prisons at over 1,264,000. This number represents 56 percent of state prisoners, 45 percent of federal prisoners, and 64 percent of jail inmates.[201] As noted in other chapters, this situation is one long-term outcome of the large-scale release of patients from psychiatric facilities to the community—part of the deinstitutionalization of mental hospitals that began in the mid-1950s.

Clearly, inmates with mental disorders present significant challenges for correctional institutions. Psychotic, personality, mood, and substance abuse disorders are common problems within inmate populations, but by far the most common mental disorders state and federal prisoners suffer from are depressive disorder (21 percent) and manic depression, bipolar disorder, and mania (12 percent).[202] Because the symptoms may include hallucinations, bizarre behavior and beliefs, paranoia, depression, mania, self-mutilation, anxiety, and poor self-care, these inmates are easy prey for institutional predators who are on the lookout to take advantage of others, sexually and otherwise. Furthermore, mentally ill prisoners tend to have higher rates of misconduct, more accidents in prison, and higher recidivism rates than prisoners without mental illness.[203] Other issues for management are whether to remove afflicted inmates from the general population and how much support to provide them. Correctional staff must monitor inmates with mental disorders more closely (for instance, to assess their risk of suicidal or violent behavior) and must be prepared to administer psychoactive (affecting the mind) medications when needed. Some inmates require disciplinary segregation because of their threatening behavior; others require administrative segregation because of their vulnerability. Either way, segregating them is akin to punishing them for their symptoms.[204]

MYTH/REALITY

MYTH: Inmates with mental disorders are housed in hospitals, not jails and prisons, and given treatment.

REALITY: The population of inmates with mental disorders in jails and prisons is surging. Treatment is spotty where it exists at all and may consist of tranquilizing drugs administered more for control than for treatment.[205]

Treatment for mental disorders in jails and prisons is mostly driven by the institution's management resources rather than by the needs of the inmate. Few psychologists and psychiatrists are available on staff, and mental health services tend to be exhausted by calls for crisis intervention (for instance, an inmate's attempt to hang himself in his cell) and the need to manage problematic symptoms (such as a delusional inmate's screaming at 3 a.m. about satellites trying to control his mind). Psychoactive medications, which essentially are used as chemical straitjackets, have become the treatment of choice; with few exceptions, other methods, such as intensive psychotherapy, are not available. Most facilities lack enough sufficiently trained staff to properly diagnose and treat inmates with the wide range of mental disorders they bring with them or develop during their incarceration.[206]

Sex Offenders   As a group, sex offenders commit a wide range of offenses, including voyeurism, exhibitionism, child molestation, Internet child pornography, and rape. Sex offenders are predominantly male; a Canadian study, for example, found that females perpetrated only 4 to 5 percent of all sex offenses.[207]

Of special concern to prison and jail administrators are sex offenders who victimize children. Inmates and correctional staff alike consider child molesters the lowest of the low in the status hierarchy of prison society. These offenders routinely experience threats, hostility, and beatings from other inmates. As a result, they are frequently placed in protective custody or in special institutions.

A growing trend in the United States is to incarcerate sex offenders beyond their prison terms under civil commitment programs. In **civil commitment,** a judge decides that a person is mentally ill and a danger to himself or others, and incarcerates that person indefinitely in a mental hospital rather than a prison. Normally an individual who is convicted of a crime and sent to prison is released once his sentence has been served, but an individual deemed mentally ill and a danger can be incarcerated in a mental hospital indefinitely–or at least until he is "cured." This type of commitment has been used for sexual offenders throughout the United States. Once a sex offender completes his sentence, he may then be subject to a state judicial hearing to ascertain whether he should continue to be incarcerated in a secure psychiatric facility. If the state rules that such an offender is eligible for civil commitment, he can be confined in such a facility until such time as he is no longer deemed dangerous.

Civil commitment programs are popular with the public but expensive to operate. The cost of housing a sex offender for a year can average more than $100,000.[208] Furthermore, these programs have a number of troubling aspects. First and foremost is the question of the legality of extending an individual's incarceration not for what he did in the past but for what he may do in the future. Another concern is that available treatments have had little effectiveness with this population.[209]

Inmates with Physical Disabilities   Prisons are required by federal law to make accommodations for the small number of inmates with physical disabilities. These inmates number less than 1 percent of the total in state prisons.[210] Still, every prison system has offenders with physical disabilities to manage. Correctional institutions are required to follow the Americans with Disabilities Act (ADA) of 1990, which mandates reasonable access and accommodation to most prison programs. Most jails and prisons, however, remain limited in their facilities and programs for inmates with physical disabilities.[211]

In a 1997 case, inmates with disabilities in California brought a class action suit charging, among other things, that prisons did not provide them equal access to vocational education and work opportunities, thus keeping them from earning credits to reduce their sentences.[212] In a 1998 case, the U.S. Supreme Court deliberated whether convicted offenders with disabilities have the same rights as those who are not disabled.[213] The offender in the case was disabled by hypertension–high blood pressure–and was thus considered ineligible for a camp program for juveniles that would have reduced his prison time. In both cases, the Court gave the incarcerated individuals the same ADA rights as nonincarcerated people.

Inmates with physical disabilities are a vulnerable population. Prisons respond to the needs of inmates with physical disabilities in a number of ways. Personnel are trained to be sensitive to inmates' needs for safety and to assist medical personnel. Procedures are developed to protect them from being exploited by the general prison population and to be evacuated in case of a fire or other emergency. Also, correctional personnel are trained to do specialized wheelchair, prosthesis, and strip searches and to safely use restraints such as handcuffs and leg and body chains on paralyzed inmates or inmates who might use crutches. Prison work opportunities are provided so that inmates with disabilities can have the opportunity to reduce their sentences by acquiring work credits. Special accommodations are made for inmates who need assistance with eating their meals.[214]

civil commitment
The process in which a judge decides that a person is mentally ill and is a danger to himself or others, and incarcerates that person indefinitely in a mental hospital rather than a prison.

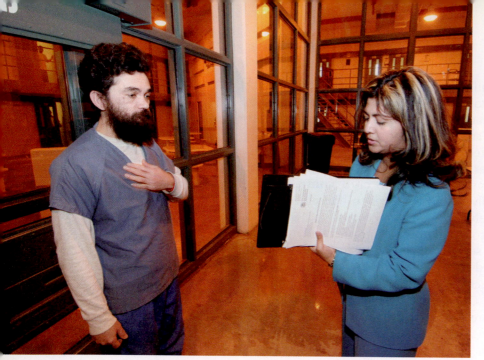

▲ **Foreign-Born Inmates**

Correctional personnel must make sure foreign-born inmates understand the policies and procedures of the prison.

There are also housing accommodations for inmates with physical disabilities who need more space than other inmates because of wheelchair requirements. Also, these inmates may not be physically able to clean their cells as inmates in the general population are required to do. In such cases, other arrangements are made.[215]

Foreign-Born Inmates Foreign-born inmates are offenders who may lack U.S. citizenship. Many such individuals find their way into the corrections system simply by residing in this country without lawful documentation. If they have not committed other criminal acts, they are normally referred to as *resident aliens*. If, however, they have committed additional crimes, they become *criminal aliens*. Federal and state prisons in New York, Texas, California, Florida, and Illinois have substantial populations of criminal aliens. These states attract immigrant populations because of their vitality, climate, variety, and promise of jobs.[216]

It is the responsibility of federal and state prisons to incarcerate inmates regardless of their citizenship. It is the responsibility of the U.S. Bureau of Immigration and Customs Enforcement (ICE) to undertake legal action to deport criminal aliens from the United States.

Both criminal and resident aliens present problems for jails and prisons. For one thing, many foreign-born offenders do not speak English. For another, they may have cultural needs that are difficult to accommodate, such as dietary restrictions or daily prayers to perform at specific times. Security concerns and institutional procedures may make it difficult to meet inmates' daily prayer needs. Another issue is that family members are often miles or countries away, a factor contributing to these inmates' isolation. Also, institutions housing foreign-born offenders may experience outbreaks of diseases rarely seen in the United States, such as polio, plague, and malaria.[217] Consequently, many prisons are screening and treating foreign-born inmates for tuberculosis (TB) infection and disease. The TB incidence is high within this population, and providing treatment may prevent the spread of the disease not only within prisons but also throughout the United States.[218]

AIDS and Ill Inmates Approximately 40 percent of state and federal prisoners and jail inmates report having a chronic medical condition. Chronic conditions include cancer, high blood pressure, diabetes, asthma, kidney problems, and cirrhosis of the liver.[219] The presence of illness and disease in the prison environment poses two serious problems for administrators of jails and prisons. On the one hand, they want to prevent the spread of communicable diseases such as tuberculosis, hepatitis, and AIDS to otherwise healthy inmates and staff. On the other hand, inmates with serious illness require special handling because of their weakened physical state, medical needs, lack of privacy, stigma attached to their illness, and fear of dying in prison.

The prevalence of HIV/AIDS in inmate populations is more than two times greater than in the general U.S. population. However, the rate of HIV/AIDS among state and federal prison inmates has been declining steadily, from 194 cases per 10,000 inmates in 2001 to 146 per 10,000 at year-end 2010.

Also, the rate of AIDS-related deaths among all state and federal prison inmates declined an average of 16 percent per year between 2001 and 2010.[220]

The spread of sexually transmitted infections (STIs), including the AIDS virus, is common in prisons. Because all sexual activity outside conjugal visits is prohibited in U.S. prisons, distributing condoms to inmates could be seen as condoning—and indeed facilitating—this illegal activity. On the other hand, not distributing condoms facilitates the transmission of the AIDS virus and other STIs throughout the prison and beyond. Most inmates will be released, many will be infected and most of these individuals will have sexual relations with members of the community.

Identifying inmates who have HIV/AIDS can be difficult because testing policies in jails and prisons vary in different jurisdictions. Some institutions test inmates upon entry, others upon their return to the community, and others only when it becomes medically necessary or an inmate specifically requests it.[221] Mandatory testing has been very controversial among researchers and public policy advocates.[222] Although there are many good reasons for testing, among them getting early treatment for infected inmates and safeguarding prison personnel, there are also serious drawbacks, including potential breaches in the confidentiality of prison records as well as segregation and discrimination of infected inmates.[223] The extremely high direct and indirect costs of testing—and treatment—have also been cited among the disadvantages. Once an inmate has been diagnosed, the prison has the moral and legal obligation to provide treatment.[224]

Not knowing who may spread a communicable disease raises anxiety levels of both inmates and staff. The Centers for Disease Control and Prevention (CDC) recommends HIV testing as part of routine medical care. In correctional settings, the CDC recommends that HIV screening be provided upon entry into prison and before release, and that voluntary HIV testing be offered periodically during incarceration. In addition to HIV testing, the CDC advocates HIV education and prevention counseling, and recommends that such programs address risk inside and outside the correctional setting.[225]

Transgender, Lesbian, Gay, and Bisexual Inmates   Transgender, lesbian, gay, and bisexual inmates face a variety of challenges and dangers that make them particularly vulnerable during incarceration. Some issues have to do with housing, hormone treatment while incarcerated, health care related to gender transition, conjugal visits, and susceptibility to physical and sexual violence while in the general prison population. Many prisons will place identified inmates in administrative segregation or protective custody to keep them safe; however, frequently such segregation prevents them from taking part in educational, vocational, and recreational opportunities made available to the general prison population.

Transgender people have a gender identity, or a sense of being male or female, that is opposite their assigned gender at birth. In our nation's correctional institutions, gender classifications are based on genitalia as opposed to the inmate's perceived gender identity. Transsexual people who have not undergone complete genital surgery normally are classified by their birth sex for the purpose of prison housing, regardless of how long they have lived as a person of the opposite gender or how much medical gender reassignment has occurred prior to incarceration. After complete genital surgery, transsexual prisoners are normally classified and housed according to their reassigned sex.[226] In 2015 California adopted a sex reassignment surgery policy for prisoners, making it the first state in the nation to do so.[227] About 40 percent of state and federal adult transgender prisoners report sexual victimization while incarcerated as compared to about 27 percent of adult transgender jail inmates. Additionally, about 24 percent of the prison victimization was inmate-on-inmate compared with about 17 percent of staff sexual misconduct.[228] Lesbian, gay, bisexual, and transgender (LGBT) advocates would like to see prisons that only house transgender inmates. New York has responded by opening a housing unit for transgender women in its largest jail.[229]

THE IMPACT OF PRISON ON FAMILY LIFE

Separation places major stresses on family relationships. Male and female inmates are removed from daily interactions in the family. Mothers and fathers are not available to participate in making decisions for their children. Also, children may come to know their caregivers as parents. Male and female inmates in committed relationships before incarceration may worry that their partners will engage in sexual relationships with others during their absence.

Some programs encourage parent–child contact in correctional settings. Girl Scouts Behind Bars, for example, is an enhanced visitation program in which incarcerated mothers and their daughters meet twice per month. Some state and federal programs for pregnant inmates allow them to have their children with them in a community-based corrections facility. Some prisons provide inmates with opportunities for **conjugal visits**–extended private visits by a lawful spouse or a registered domestic partner.[230] The practice of conjugal visits in state prisons appears to be diminishing. In 2014 New Mexico and Mississippi stopped their programs. Today only four states still allow this privilege: California, Connecticut, New York, and Washington.[231]

Approximately 60 to 80 percent of all incarcerated female offenders have minor children, usually at least two.[232] Being identified as a prisoner, a member of a disgraced group, is particularly difficult for inmates with families. Although more than half of male inmates also have at least one minor child, incarceration tends to be more painful for women because it cuts them off not only from friends and family but especially from their children.[233] If the incarcerated woman is head of the household, children suffer even more from their mother's absence. Many female inmates are single, divorced, or separated and have typically assumed sole physical, financial, and emotional responsibility for their children. It is not surprising that with incarceration comes guilt over the breakup of the family, worry about the care of their children, and fear of losing custody rights during their absence.[234]

Among the many problems of incarcerated mothers, one of the most stressful is the inability to maintain regular contact with their children and their children's caregivers. Many times, children are afraid of going into the prison.[235] Incarcerated men tend to have more contact with their partners than do female inmates. Because female partners are more likely to bring the children with them on visits, male prisoners have more opportunity to see their children than do most female inmates.

Further complicating matters is that imprisoned mothers have difficulty explaining to their children why they are not with them and why they are in prison. If a mother faces a long prison term, her children may come to see their caregiver as their parent, a development that makes the transfer of care to the biological mother upon release difficult for all.[236]

With respect to conjugal visit programs, some states give the inmate a small apartment or trailer inside the

conjugal visit
An extended private visit by an inmate's lawful spouse or registered domestic partner.

▼ **Family Visits**
Prisoners look forward to rare visits with their families.

prison grounds for the visit. These programs provide inmates with private meetings, perhaps over a weekend, with their spouses and families and accommodate the possibility of sexual contact. The primary purpose is to facilitate keeping the marriage or family intact, thus increasing the probability of the inmate's rehabilitation.[237]

Federal prisons do not permit conjugal visits, and, as previously mentioned, just four states allow them.[238] Even when permitted, however, conjugal visits may be restricted. Inmates at risk of transmitting diseases, as well as unmarried inmates, may be barred from having conjugal visits.[239] California has approved conjugal visits for domestic partners of gays and lesbians.[240] Despite the presumed importance of visitation, the U.S. Supreme Court has held that conjugal visiting in prison is not a right and therefore is not protected under the due process clause of the Constitution.[241]

SUMMARY

It is hard to imagine what it might be like to spend time incarcerated behind bars. Still, jails and prisons are a necessity.

Despite high rates of incarceration, crime rates remain high, a reality challenging the notion that imprisonment is an effective punishment for and a deterrent to crime. Rising costs, whether for jails or prisons, create problems for the authorities with jurisdiction over the facilities. For inmates and correctional employees, a major problem is overcrowding. Moreover, the staff in corrections must work in a hostile and dangerous environment, overseeing and controlling large numbers of inmates, many of whom are angry and resentful and have little regard for authority. Inmates contend with near-constant surveillance, lack of privacy, and cramped living conditions—even in minimum-security prisons. Problems escalate in higher-level security prisons that house more dangerous and violent offenders and where levels of control are more restrictive. For both correctional staff and inmates, personal safety—at any level prison—is always at risk.

Just as for men in prison, overcrowding is a problem for women inmates as more and more women are being sentenced to prison. The policies, procedures, and practices developed for male inmates have traditionally been imposed on female prisoners, even though female prisoners have different needs and face additional problems not experienced by male inmates. However, women in prison tend to develop closer and more personal relationships than men.

In addition to providing custodial care of inmates, prisons are coming under increased pressure to provide rehabilitative and therapeutic programs to prepare inmates for reintegration into society. Prisons are charged with developing meaningful and productive work training and experience for inmates as well as effective treatment for mental disorders, behavioral problems, and drug use—tall orders for institutions already facing a great many challenges.

OBSERVE → INVESTIGATE → UNDERSTAND

Review

Distinguish between jails and prisons.

- Jails are operated by municipal and regional governments; prisons are operated by states or the federal government.
- Jails house pretrial detainees, individuals awaiting parole or deportation, and those serving short-term sentences; prisons hold offenders sentenced to more than 1 year.

Differentiate among minimum-, medium-, maximum-, and supermaximum-security prisons.

- Minimum-security prisons are intended to hold offenders who have short sentences, are nonviolent, and are unlikely to attempt escape or pose risks to the general public.
- Medium-security prisons are intended for inmates needing greater oversight and supervision than prisoners in

minimum security prisons. Prisoners are allowed freedom of movement only within secured areas.

- Maximum-security prisons use high levels of control on prisoners, and prisoners have limited freedom of movement within the facility.

- Supermaximum-security prisons offer the highest level of prison security possible—solitary confinement—using the latest advancements in correctional technology.

Apply the concept of professionalization to the role of correctional officers.

- Professionalization is the commitment to a set of ideals and standards that raise the view of the occupation and instill pride in the profession itself.

- Professionalization requires standards of education, recruitment, and entry-level salaries.

- Correctional officers need a professional infrastructure on which they can rely and through which they can develop professional attitudes and competencies.

Describe the rights of prisoners and those that are denied.

- A prisoner may not hold public office, vote, serve on a jury, be a witness, or own a firearm.

- A prisoner may lose the right of employment by being stripped of an occupational license.

- Until the 1960s, courts were reluctant to interfere with prison management and adopted a hands-off doctrine in protecting prisoner rights. In the prisoner rights era (1970–1991), the courts tended to support the rights of prisoners, but the pendulum swung back again toward less protection in the 1990s with changes in the composition of courts.

Characterize the inmate subculture.

- *Institutionalization* refers to a prisoner's excessive dependency on prison as a way of life.

- *Prisonization* refers to the inmate's internalization of the inmate subculture's norms, values, and beliefs as the inmate's own.

- Total institutions can foster institutionalization, prisonization, and an environment that can cause inmates to lose their sense of identity.

Outline the differences between male and female prison life.

- Men tend to bond together in prison gangs and resort to violence; women tend to bond together in surrogate families that provide a support network for dealing with prison life and separation from their true families.

- Male inmates are subject to high numbers of sexual assaults, including male rape; in women's prisons, sexual aggression is almost nonexistent, and homosexual activity is generally consensual.

- Women who are pregnant have special challenges such as medical care during pregnancy; women who give birth while in prison face infant separation issues.

Describe methods of treatment and rehabilitation in prisons.

- Prison officials today agree that useful, productive work is important for inmates' rehabilitation. Meaningful work programs lead to lower rates of recidivism for those who take part in them.

- Treatment programs help inmates change illegal or destructive behavior, such as violence, anger, and alcohol and drug abuse. When treatment programs are tailored to individual inmates and professionally staffed, recidivism declines by as much as 50 percent.

- Prisons must meet the special needs of certain populations, such as elder adult inmates; those with mental disabilities; sex offenders; those with physical disabilities; those born in foreign countries; transgender, gay, lesbian, and bisexual prisoners; and individuals who are HIV-positive or have AIDS.

Detail the ways incarceration affects the prisoner's family life.

- Incarceration causes an inmate to be identified with a disgraced group.

- Incarceration cuts prisoners off from their family, friends, and children.

- Incarceration takes inmates away from physical, financial, and emotional responsibility and from their children.

- Incarceration causes inmates to worry about their children and the possible loss of custody rights during their absence.

Key Terms

administrative segregation 386	inmate code 379	Prison Rape Elimination Act (PREA) 391
civil commitment 397	inmate subculture 378	punitive segregation 386
classification 372	institutionalization 378	risk classification 372
conjugal visit 400	jail 363	security level 372
custody level 372	maximum-security prison 369	security threat group (STG) 381
deprivation model 378	medium-security prison 369	solitary confinement 386
good time credits 375	minimum-security prison 368	supermaximum-security (supermax) prison 370
hands-off doctrine 375	pains of imprisonment 378	total institution 378
importation model 379	prison 365	
incarceration 363	prisonization 378	

Study Questions

1. U.S. prisons are normally operated at levels.
   a. county and city
   b. state and federal
   c. federal and county
   d. state and city

2. After conviction, a felon in many states is deprived of
   a. the right to serve on a jury.
   b. the right to hold public office and vote.
   c. the right to carry a firearm.
   d. all of the above

3. Which of the following statements is true?
   a. Women and men experience prison life in the same ways.
   b. Policies, procedures, and practices imposed on male and female prisoners should not differentiate according to gender.
   c. Male prisoners have more physical and sexual abuse in their preincarceration histories than women prisoners.
   d. Incarceration tends to be especially painful for women because it cuts them off from friends, family, and children.

4. The term *prisonization* refers to
   a. dependency on the institution.
   b. the acquisition of the convict code.
   c. the prison's provision of all of the offender's needs.
   d. the internalization of the norms, values, and beliefs of the inmate subculture as the inmate's own.

5. The importation model is concerned with
   a. importing slaves into the United States.
   b. importing the inmate subculture into prisons.
   c. ways in which sexually transmitted infections are imported into prisons.
   d. methods by which drugs are imported into prisons.

6. STG stands for
   a. sexually transmitted gene.
   b. secretive transsexual group.
   c. security threat group.
   d. scientific technology group.

7. Which of the following is/are a cause(s) of riots in prisons?
   a. attitudes of correctional officers
   b. prison management
   c. racial tensions
   d. all of the above

8. Which of the following inmate special populations is/are likely to pose problems for prison management?
   a. pregnant inmates
   b. elder adult inmates
   c. mentally challenged inmates
   d. all of the above

9. PREA stands for
   a. Prison Reduction Economic Activity.
   b. Prison Rehabilitation Educational Activities.
   c. Prison Rape Elimination Act.
   d. Penal Responsibility Educational Act.

10. Conjugal visit programs in the United States allow inmates who have behaved well to spend time with
    a. their significant other.
    b. their lawfully married spouse or registered domestic partner.
    c. their common law wife or husband.
    d. all of the above

Critical Thinking Questions

For further review, go to the LearnSmart study module for this chapter.

1. What is the difference between prison security levels and prisoner custody levels? Why do some maximum-security prisons classify inmates as having minimum, medium, and maximum custody levels? Explain.

2. What are the similarities and differences in the ways female and male inmates do time?

3. Identify the reasons for prison and jail overcrowding. What do you see as some solutions to this problem?

4. What are the positive and negative outcomes of today's shift away from a policy of mass incarceration and "get tough" sentencing practices?

13 Community
Corrections

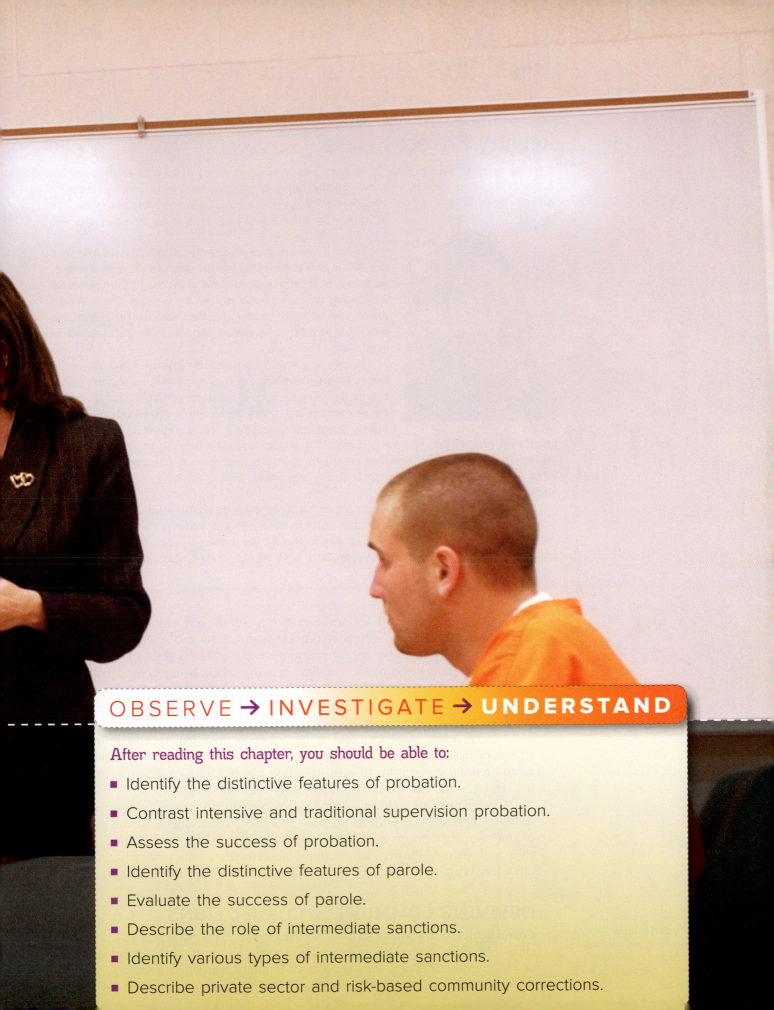

After reading this chapter, you should be able to:

- Identify the distinctive features of probation.
- Contrast intensive and traditional supervision probation.
- Assess the success of probation.
- Identify the distinctive features of parole.
- Evaluate the success of parole.
- Describe the role of intermediate sanctions.
- Identify various types of intermediate sanctions.
- Describe private sector and risk-based community corrections.

Realities and Challenges

Susan Burton: A New Way of Life Reentry Project

During the 1980s and 90s, Susan Burton was in and out of prison, serving six terms for drug offenses. But in 1997, she got clean of drugs and dedicated herself to improving community-based corrections for women and girls. To implement her calling, she worked, saved her money, purchased a house in the Watts area

of Los Angeles, and began to assist other former female inmates who were in recovery.

Burton is now a chemical dependency counselor, and she has helped over 400 women to reintegrate into the community after incarceration. As a result of her efforts, she was one of the top 10 CNN Heroes for 2010, a year in which she also received the Gleitsman Citizen Activist Award, given by Harvard University's Kennedy School of Government, and the Contributions Across Time Award, bestowed by the Watts Labor Community Action Committee.

Burton's program in South Central Los Angeles—A New Way of Life Reentry Project—helps female ex-cons by providing housing and reentry support, promoting the rights of individuals with a history of convictions and incarceration, and building the confidence of previously incarcerated women. Burton believes that there is a "window of opportunity to get people from incarceration into a positive lifestyle."[1] To aid the women in making that transition successfully, her reentry project assists them with food, clothing, transportation, employment, and custody of their children. When they are ready to live independently, Burton helps provide housing and furniture. Most of Burton's funding comes from private donations.

A New Way of Life is a model reentry project that demonstrates the positive results of community corrections programs. Under Burton's dedicated leadership, former criminal justice offenders can find the resources and support they need to reenter the community successfully. Her grassroots community organizing effort challenges rules, laws, policies, and attitudes hoping to break the cycle of mass incarceration.

Public opinion tends to question the wisdom and efficacy of allowing offenders to serve their sentences outside institutions and in the community. People generally feel that incarceration protects public safety and that community corrections too often "coddles" criminals. But being behind bars does not help the offender get adjusted to society and prepare for reintegration—and in fact may socialize the offender to a criminal lifestyle. As we will see, today these crosscurrents are playing out in political and legal arenas and at state and federal levels of government as more people find fault with the negative effects of mass incarceration and as states and counties shift from institutional to community corrections to ease stretched budgets, reduce prison overcrowding, and get the most out of public safety expenditures.

This chapter provides an overview of community corrections, or non-jail sentencing, beginning with its purpose and goals. We also address the practices of the two major forms of community corrections in the United States: probation and parole. Finally, we examine intermediate sanctions that provide offenders with alternative avenues for reintegration into the community.

DEFINING COMMUNITY CORRECTIONS

community corrections
Court-imposed programs and sanctions that allow offenders to serve their sentences within the community instead of in jail or prison.

Community corrections includes a diverse array of programs and sanctions that allow offenders to serve their sentences within the community instead of in jail or prison. Most offenders supervised in community corrections programs are considered nonviolent and low risk and therefore pose a minimal threat to the public.

As we saw in Chapter 11, society expects corrections to punish, rehabilitate, and reintegrate the offender and control crime at the same time. A community corrections sentence can accomplish these goals by allowing the offender to stay in the community, remain employed, maintain family connections, pay taxes, and make restitution to victims. A further benefit is that offenders who can remain in the community do not become *institutionalized*, or socialized to the prison environment and to its subculture of violence. Some evidence suggests that correctly managed community corrections programs can reduce recidivism.[2]

The most common community corrections are probation and parole. Community corrections also includes strategies such as community service, mediation, sex registers, house arrest, and work release. Both public and private agencies provide programs for community corrections, including halfway houses and drug treatment centers. These community-centered practices and programs are available at each stage of the criminal justice system: before trial, during trial, and after trial. Community corrections also includes supervision of offenders who have completed prison or jail terms and who have been released from prison and jail to serve remaining sentences on work release or other programs such as probation and parole.

PROBATION

Probation is an alternative to jail or prison in which the offender remains in the community under court supervision, usually within the caseload of a probation officer who is an officer of the court. Individuals who receive probation are those whose crimes are not serious enough for imprisonment and who are allowed to serve their sentences under community supervision. (This chapter focuses on adult probation; Chapter 15 discusses juvenile probation.) Although the U.S. criminal justice system incarcerates more people than ever before, probation, not imprisonment, is the most frequent criminal sanction.

probation
An alternative to jail or prison in which the offender remains in the community under court supervision, usually within the caseload of a probation officer who is an officer of the court.

Purpose and Goals of Probation

The basic purpose of probation is to allow the probationer an opportunity to be rehabilitated without incarceration. As probation is a "creature of the courts," in some circumstances probation can be combined with incarceration. Probation typically diverts the offender from jail or prison. Probation (from the Latin word meaning "to prove") gives offenders the chance to prove themselves to be law-abiding in the community and not to be incarcerated.[3]

The goal of probation is twofold: to protect society and to rehabilitate the offender. Thus probation encompasses rehabilitation, reintegration, punishment, and deterrence, as well as crime control. Probation rests on the idea that human beings are capable of change and that with proper supervision, resources, and services, offenders can be rehabilitated at the same time that public safety is protected.

Figure 13-1 shows the number of people who were under adult correctional supervision from 1980 to 2013. In 2014 about 56 percent of those offenders were on probation, more than on parole and in jail and prison combined.[4]

Probation is a privilege, not a right.[5] Some people today view probation as a lenient practice. When it was originally conceived, however, probation was considered to be another serious form of punishment, albeit one that was served in the community. The earliest form of what we now know as

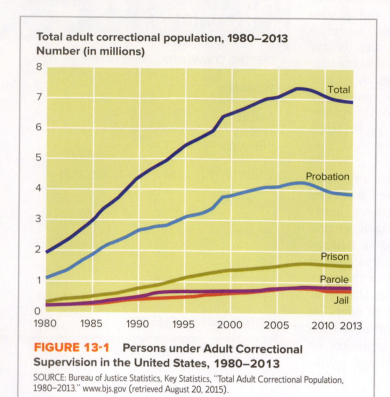

Total adult correctional population, 1980–2013
Number (in millions)

FIGURE 13-1 **Persons under Adult Correctional Supervision in the United States, 1980–2013**
SOURCE: Bureau of Justice Statistics, Key Statistics, "Total Adult Correctional Population, 1980–2013." www.bjs.gov (retrieved August 20, 2015).

recognizance
Literally, "an obligation to the court" that usually requires the accused, if released on his own word, to perform some legally specified act, such as appearing at trial, as an alternative to being incarcerated.

probation existed in English criminal laws of the Middle Ages. Royal pardons, judicial reprieve, and sanctuary in the church where fugitives were immune to arrest offered some degree of protection from the severe sanctions of the era. In the fourteenth century, English courts also began to practice "binding over for good behavior"—a form of temporary release to allow the offender time to secure a pardon or to try to obtain a lesser sentence.[6]

Both England and the American colonies recognized the court's power to suspend a sentence, as well as the accused person's right of **recognizance,** or "an obligation to the court." Usually this obligation required the accused, if released on his own recognizance (or his own word), to perform some legally specified act, such as appearing at trial, as an alternative to being incarcerated. With a little help from a Boston shoemaker named John Augustus, these early practices eventually evolved into the practice of probation.[7] In 1841 Augustus attended a Boston police court and bailed out a "common drunkard." He returned to court 3 weeks later with the offender in tow, now sober and apparently changed for the better. Thus was launched Augustus's 18-year career as a forerunner of today's probation officer. Although a volunteer, he was asked by the court to evaluate whether various offenders were good prospects for probation. Today the background investigation that grew from his efforts is considered a cornerstone of modern probation practice.

Not until after Augustus's death in 1859 was the first probation statute passed in Massachusetts. The concept of probation eventually spread throughout the United States, especially with the growth of the juvenile court movement. Today, all states and the federal government offer both juvenile and adult probation services.[8]

Traditional Conditions of Probation

MYTH/REALITY

MYTH: Probation is a lenient sanction.

REALITY: Probation can impose substantial burdens. Limits often are placed on the offender's behavior, he might face fees and other costs, and the stigma attached to being on probation can make it difficult for the probationer to obtain a job. In addition to restitution, the offender's monetary burden could include fines and fees for services such as drug testing, counseling, and anger management classes.[9]

The standard (also called traditional) conditions imposed on all *probationers*—those who are serving probation—require that the offender must do the following, regardless of the crime:

- Report on a regular basis to the probation department.
- Obtain and maintain employment or attend school or training.
- Allow the probation officer to visit the probationer's home or place of employment.

The offender must *not* do the following:

- Commit any additional crimes while on probation.
- Change residence without first notifying the probation officer.
- Associate with persons who have criminal records.

Probationers are required to report to their probation officer on a predetermined schedule, perhaps as often as once a week. The frequency depends on the type of crime committed, the offender's prior criminal record, and the perceived risk to the community. Failure to appear can result in revocation of probation. The court may also set other special conditions, such as regular drug or alcohol testing, attendance at an Alcoholics Anonymous group, or active participation in a treatment plan or an anger management program. Furthermore, probationers are required to pay fines and restitution to victims, obey all laws (even minor ones like jaywalking), and appear at any scheduled court appearances. The court can combine conditions, as in the case of requiring both restitution and community service. Other sanctions might include a suspended jail sentence, fines, and random searches. Although the probation officer will usually make a recommendation, the court sets the length of probation, and only the court can modify or revoke the term or the conditions.

Probationers can expect unannounced visits at home or at work at any time, especially if the probation officer suspects that something might be wrong. These visits, along with the stigma attached to being a convicted offender, can make it difficult for the probationer to find and keep employment. The probationer may be prevented from using alcoholic beverages or be required to undergo medical, psychiatric, or psychological treatment; reside in an institution or a community corrections facility for a specified period; or participate in a designated treatment program. The offender may be required to remain at home during certain nonworking hours and be monitored by an electronic device. A violation of any one of these conditions could result in revocation of probation. However, probation officers have discretion and can simply give violators a warning before taking formal action. This response is of concern to critics of the Public Safety Realignment (PSR) policy and advocates of deinstitutionalization discussed in Chapter 11.

In an attempt to stop the flow of technical violators (those who violate conditions of probation or parole—for example, not showing up for an appointment, failing to observe a curfew, having an alcoholic beverage—but do not commit a new crime) back into penal institutions and reduce the costs of incarceration, some states such as Louisiana and Delaware have taken legislative steps to make sure technical violators receive alternative sanctions that are proportionate to their violations of the conditions of probation or parole.[10]

▲ **Probation Officer with Probationer**

Probation officers are required to make sure probationers understand the conditions of their probation. *How can probation officers be sure that probationers understand the terms of their probation?*

Intensive-Supervision Probation

Some probation programs target high-risk offenders who have been convicted of serious crimes and would ordinarily be prison-bound; they require a high level of supervision and surveillance and strict probation conditions. **Intensive-supervision probation (ISP)** describes a variety of programs characterized by smaller officer caseloads and closer surveillance. The premise behind ISP is that smaller caseloads enhance rehabilitation and public safety by creating greater contact between the probation officer and the offender. These programs also enable offenders to remain employed while serving their sentences.

ISP programs vary greatly. They can be found in pretrial programs, diversion programs, day reporting centers, and DWI courts. In addition to increased supervision, they may include house arrest, curfews, mandated restitution,

intensive-supervision probation (ISP)
A variety of probation programs characterized by smaller officer caseloads and closer surveillance.

specific restrictions on where the offender may live, drug or alcohol testing and treatment programs, and the use of electronic devices for monitoring the offender's whereabouts.[11] Offenders who enter an ISP program are screened and assessed thoroughly.

Evaluations of ISP programs have been inconclusive. One reason for outcome uncertainty is that ISPs tend to be matchless in that each program introduces different combinations of elements at different points in time, making it difficult to determine effectiveness. An early review of an ISP program in Georgia found it to be effective.[12] It relied on teams of two probation officers with small caseloads. However, Georgia traditionally sends a higher proportion of offenders to prison than other states, so those diverted from prison may already have been less of a risk than those diverted elsewhere. The program, in effect, sorted out those offenders who were easier to deal with and more amenable to supervision. Thus the participants might have done well regardless of the program.[13] Another recent study conducted for the National Highway Traffic Safety Administration concluded that ISP programs reduced the recidivism of DWI offenders.[14]

Other studies question whether ISP programs were responsible for reported successful outcomes. A study by the RAND Corporation concluded that judges used extra caution in sentencing offenders to ISP programs, a practice that perhaps biased study results.[15] Another study of 14 California counties found no significant differences between the recidivism of juvenile probationers in a special program and those in traditional probation.[16] Although smaller caseloads seem to provide greater protection to the community, studies do not clearly show them to enhance rehabilitation or decrease recidivism.[17]

The state of New York ISP program makes finding employment for high-risk ISP offenders a major goal. It limits caseloads to 21 probationers per officer, and in 2005 it began helping offenders learn new skills and change their behaviors. In that year, 61 percent of probationers were successfully discharged from the program, with 32 percent unsuccessful and 7 percent in the "neutral" category (probationers who died or were transferred to another jurisdiction).[18]

In 2008 the cost of state probation services averaged about $1,250 a year for a probationer, compared to an average of $29,000 per year for each inmate in a state prison.[19] Significantly, however, the cost of even the most expensive

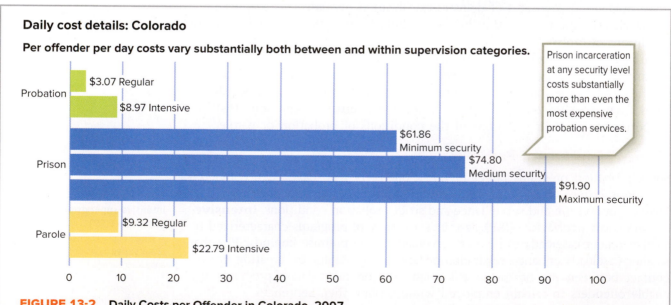

FIGURE 13-2 **Daily Costs per Offender in Colorado, 2007**

SOURCE: Pew Center on the States, "One in 31: The Long Reach of American Corrections" (Washington, DC: Pew Charitable Trusts, 2009), 13. http://www.pewcenteronthestates. org/uploadedFiles/PSPP_1in31_report_FINAL_WEB_3-26-09.pdf (retrieved April 22, 2011).

probation services is lower than the cost of prison incarceration. The dramatic difference can be seen in Figure 13-2, which shows the cost of prison, parole, and probation in Colorado and the differences among supervision categories.[20]

Who Serves Probation?

At the end of 2014, about 4.7 million U.S. adults were on probation, or 1 in every 64 adult U.S. residents.[21] Of these probationers, about 69 percent were being actively supervised compared with 76 percent in 2000 and 72 percent in 2012–an obvious decline in probationers who are being actively supervised.[22] "Active supervision" means that probationers are required to report regularly–either in person, by mail, or by telephone–to a probation officer. In contrast, probationers on "inactive supervision" are generally convicted of misdemeanors or less serious felonies and have little, if any, contact with the probation officer, whose large caseload, called a *banked* (or *bank*) *caseload*, makes such individuals probationers in name only. Probationers who are part of a banked caseload simply have to fill out forms each month to report such changes as address, employment or school.

A survey of California's adult probation systems found that county probation departments are increasingly using banked caseloads rather than traditional supervision. The survey also indicated that banked caseloads can reach as high as 3,000 probationers per officer due to scarce resources, increased offender population, and inadequate numbers of staff.[23] Another study addressed the relationship between caseloads and property crime rates for every county in California over a 9-year period. Researchers found that as probation caseloads increased, crime increased too. They concluded that smaller caseloads can and do reduce crime: As probation supervision decreases, the opportunities for a probationer to reoffend rise.[24] See the "Race, Class, Gender" box for a discussion of how celebrities and those with the resources to pay expensive lawyers might have different experiences than most people on probation.

Of adults on probation nationwide in 2014, 75 percent were male and 25 percent were female. Furthermore, 54 percent of those on probation were White, 30 percent were Black, 13 percent were Latino, and the remaining 3 percent were Native American, Asian, Native Hawaiian, Pacific Islander, or of two or more races.[25] In 2009, proportionate to the offender population, more White offenders received probation than Blacks and Latinos, who received more prison sentences.[26] Figure 13-3 shows the racial and ethnic breakdown of U.S. adults on probation in 2014. It is important to also note that in California since the implementation of the PSR policy (see Chapter 11), the number of probationers increased about 15 percent. In 2010 the probation population was 149,000, and in 2013 the probation population was 170,800.[27] It is premature to conclude that over time California's probation departments will successfully provide evidence-based services that will protect public safety and assist probationers to lead crime-free lives.

Roles and Tasks of the Probation Officer

Probation officers–often referred to as *arms of the court*–are responsible for making recommendations to the court as to sentencing, for supervising offenders placed on probation by the court, and for seeing that court orders are carried out. Probably the most important task of probation officers is to help the court determine who should be placed on probation by providing the presentence investigation report (see Chapter 10).

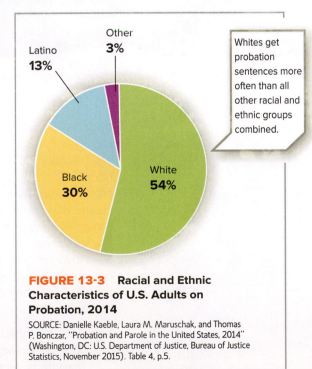

Whites get probation sentences more often than all other racial and ethnic groups combined.

FIGURE 13-3 **Racial and Ethnic Characteristics of U.S. Adults on Probation, 2014**

SOURCE: Danielle Kaeble, Laura M. Maruschak, and Thomas P. Bonczar, "Probation and Parole in the United States, 2014" (Washington, DC: U.S. Department of Justice, Bureau of Justice Statistics, November 2015). Table 4, p.5.

Race, Class, Gender

Celebrity Justice?

As you've learned, there are more Whites on probation than all other races combined. Why? There are many questions surrounding the fact that in some cases the offender will be sentenced to probation whereas in others, even though the crime is the same, the offender will receive a jail or prison sentence. High-profile celebrity cases also raise concerns that if the offender weren't rich and famous, the sentence would be different.

Lyndsay Lohan's many contacts with the criminal justice system definitely raised some eyebrows. Lohan was a childhood star who grew up to be a major movie star and singer. Her breakout movie, as both a commercial hit and talented actress, was *The Parent Trap* in 1998. She went on to star in other movies, including *Freaky Friday* and *Mean Girls*. She also released two albums, which earned platinum and gold status, respectively.

Although it seemed that Lohan had it all, she was also fighting an addiction to drugs and alcohol. Her troubles with the law started in May 2007 when she was arrested for drunk driving. Despite 45 days in an addiction rehabilitation center, she was arrested again in July 2007 for possession of cocaine, driving under the influence, and driving with a suspended license.

This time she was sentenced to one day in jail, community service, an alcohol education program, and 3 years of probation. In 2010, after a series of probation violations, she was ordered to jail for 90 days; however, she only served 14 of those days before being released. In February 2011, she was arrested again for theft of a necklace. This time she was sentenced to 120 days in jail, but instead of being in jail, she was allowed to serve the time under house arrest. The rationale given was that the jail was overcrowded. She continued to commit probation violations. In March 2013, she was found guilty of reckless driving that resulted in a car accident. This time she was sentenced to 2 additional years of probation.

In May 2015, it appeared that Lohan would not complete the number of hours of community service required to meet the terms of her probation. If the hours were not met, she could have been ordered to jail. Of course, that had happened before and Lohan hadn't served much (or any) time in a cell. Still, as the deadline to complete 100 hours of service approached, she had to work with two community service organizations. She ended up serving 10- to 12-hour shifts at a social service facility that was open 24 hours a day. On May 28th, a judge certified that Lohan had completed the required number of hours and she was released from probation for the first time in almost 8 years. During that time, she had 50 court hearings, 20 of which she was required to attend in person.

OBSERVE → INVESTIGATE → UNDERSTAND

- Do you think that Lohan received different treatment than someone who wasn't a celebrity would?
- Do you think she received a better legal defense because she had the resources to pay expensive lawyers?
- What do you think of the practice of not having a person serve time in jail even though he or she was actually sentenced to jail?

SOURCES: Melissa Ruso, "Lyndsay Lohan Moonlights to Complete Court-Ordered Service by Deadline, Judge Ends Probation," *NBC New York*, May 28, 2015. www.nbcnewyork.com/news/local/Lindsay-Lohan-Meets-Community-Service-Deadline-New-York-City-305268241.html; "Police: Actress Lindsay Lohan Arrested for Driving under the Influence of Alcohol," *CNN*, May 26, 2007; Richard Winton and Andrew Blankstein, "Just out of Rehab, Lohan Arrested Again on DUI, Drug Charges," *The Seattle Times*, July 25, 2007; Anthony McCartney, "Lohan's Wings Clipped by New Jail, Probation Terms," *The Wall Street Journal*, Associated Press, November 2, 2011.

In order to issue a proper recommendation to the court, probation officers must investigate the events surrounding the crime (such as aggravating or mitigating circumstances, the use of weapons, and injuries to victims) and obtain a solid history of the offender. In effect, the probation officer is the court's factfinder. The officer gathers information about the offender's family, education, employment, mental and physical health, motivations, attitudes, and skills. Importantly, the officer also assesses the risk that an offender's release might pose to the community. In addition to making a recommendation regarding probation, the probation officer recommends a plan and conditions for release.[28]

However, the role of probation officer is not just that of investigator and court enforcer. The officer is also expected to assist offenders in solving everyday problems so they can develop a constructive and law-abiding pattern of living. The following scenario presents a typical day in the life of a probation officer:

Joe, a probation officer in a small rural county, gets to work about 8 a.m. Already there are four calls from the wife of one of his probationers. Her husband, Ted, on probation for a minor drug offense, has been clean for the last 5 months since he was arrested. Last night he made the mistake of going out with some of his buddies, getting drunk, getting into a fight, and getting arrested. He is now in jail, and she is afraid he will lose his job and go to prison because he violated his probation. Joe may have to write a report and recommend to the court that Ted's probation be revoked. Before he can call Ted's wife back, he must see two probationers in the waiting room. One is seeing him to discuss the results of a positive drug test, and Joe might have to arrest him. In the afternoon Joe needs to pay a home visit to a probationer who did not show up for his appointment last week. He may need to have the police standing by because the probationer has been known to be violent. Later in the day, Joe has an appointment with an employment agency that might be interested in hiring some of Joe's clients.

Probation officers are frequently expected to accomplish the dual roles of protecting society by supervising offenders in the community (which may mean arresting and incarcerating them) and treating offenders by counseling them and assisting them with other services. Successfully carrying out these sometimes conflicting roles can be taxing. Ethical problems can arise, as the "Matters of Ethics" box on page 414 illustrates. Starting in the 1970s, the probation officer's role gradually and increasingly focused on a law enforcement and surveillance mind-set of "tail them, nail them, and jail them." This mentality has led to mass incarceration, higher public safety costs, lack of differentiation in case supervision, and oversupervision of low-risk probationers, making it difficult for probation officers to carry out daily functions and solve problems in the community. However, evidence indicates that the law enforcement role of supervision is being reinvented to emphasize accurate assessment, effective interaction, motivation to change, and understanding the kinds of programs and interventions that will lead to law-abiding behavior.[29]

How Successful Is Probation?

Success rates for probation programs are usually measured by recidivism—specifically, whether the offender has been rearrested. If the individual completes the term of probation without a new arrest, he is deemed a success. However, this method of measuring success has been questioned—in one case, as early as 1937, by Bennet Mead, whose original article on the topic was reprinted in 2005. Specifically, Mead criticizes the criminal justice field for defining success only as the absence of failure.[30] The concept of success, he argues, must recognize other possible forms of achievement, such as improving work skills and employment, remaining clean and sober, establishing or maintaining family and relationship ties, and practicing fiscal responsibility. However, while all of these factors may truly indicate success, they are not easily measured or quantified. Thus recidivism is still the variable that is universally used to measure success.

The percentage of probationers who successfully completed probation varied only a few points between 2008 and 2014. In 2014, 35 percent successfully exited probation because they completed their term or were discharged early. The successful completion rate for those on probation has been about 36 per 100 probationers since 2008. Eight percent exited probation via incarceration, and the remaining percentage exited probation in other unsatisfactory ways.[31]

A probationer who violates one or more of the conditions of probation—called a *technical violation*—may be taken back to court. The judge may then revoke probation and send the offender to jail, even though the offender has committed

Matters *of* Ethics

Relationships between Correctional Personnel and Offenders

Difficult issues can arise in the relationship between correctional personnel, such as correctional officers and probation and parole officers, and the individuals under their supervision. The ethical standard of prohibiting "dual relationships"—those in which the parties have both a professional and a personal association—is considered sacred in counseling and psychotherapy relationships between counselors and counselees. Dual relationships can interfere with the psychological boundaries necessary for the counselor to maintain professional objectivity and can lead to unethical conduct. Say, for example, a counselee is unable to pay for treatment, and her therapist has the woman clean the therapist's home as payment. That conduct is unethical. Outside social contact between counselors and counselees is discouraged, too, and it is expected that professional and private roles be kept separate and distinct. Professional organizations and state licensing boards enforce these ethical standards—and violations may result in serious consequences.

Relationships are not clear-cut in the correctional environment. Maintaining such strict boundaries is often challenging. Correctional personnel play a number of different roles in offenders' reformation and are sometimes expected to wear different hats. For example, probation and parole officers are bound to be advocates, resource persons, counselors, investigators, friends, problem solvers, helpers, and enforcers of the law. Each role dictates different types of interaction with and expectations of the offender, and in many ways a different relationship. Boundaries can easily blur. In the helping role, for example, friendships can develop. When this happens, the parties can lose objectivity—and might even cross sexual boundaries. The American Probation and Parole Association has enacted a resolution encouraging the passage of laws that criminalize staff sexual misconduct.

Because there is an unequal power relationship between correctional personnel and offenders who are under their supervision, any form of intimate relationship, even consensual, is considered unethical and unlawful. When such lines are crossed, the repercussions can be severe. For example, a long-time New Mexico parole officer served 18 months in prison after pleading guilty to fondling a female parolee. A probation officer was charged with having sex with a probationer in North Carolina. Statutes throughout the country make it clear that this behavior is not just a matter of ethics—but a serious crime.

OBSERVE → INVESTIGATE → UNDERSTAND

- Do you think that the penalty of felony is too severe if a correctional worker has sex with an offender under his or her supervision? Explain.
- What other inappropriate dual relationships might a correctional worker have? Would the behavior be criminal, or a breach of ethics? Explain.
- Name other ethical issues that correctional personnel might face.

SOURCES: Ruth E. Masters, *Counseling Criminal Justice Offenders*, 2nd ed. (Thousand Oaks, CA: Sage, 2004), 21–22; Kim Boland-Prom and Sandra C. Anderson, "Teaching Ethical Decision Making Using Dual Relationships Principles as a Case Example," *Journal of Social Work Education* 41, no. 3 (Fall 2005); American Probation and Parole Association, "Resolution: Staff Sexual Misconduct," enacted August 2003, www.appa-net.org/eweb/Dynamicpage.aspx?site=APPA_2&webcode=IB_Resolution&wps_key=825560aa-b5da-46b7-95bf-57debadaaa5c (retrieved May 24, 2015).

Paul Woolverton, "Ex-officer Now Charged with Having Sex with Probationer," *Fayetteville Observer*, March 20, 2010; U.S. Attorney's Office, District of New Mexico, "Former New Mexico Probation Officer Pleads Guilty to Sexual Assault and False Statement Charges," September 3, 2013. www.fbi.gov/albuquerque/press-releases/2013/former-new-mexico-probation-officer-pleads-guilty-to-sexual-assault-and-false-statement-charges (retrieved May 24, 2015).

no new crime. Examples of technical violations are not showing up for an appointment, not obeying a curfew, and having an alcoholic drink. Rates of revocation for technical violations can vary greatly from place to place because the court has complete discretion over whether to revoke. An offender in one jurisdiction may be sent back to jail for a technical violation, whereas an offender in the next county may just get a slap on the wrist and be sent home for the same violation. In some jurisdictions the majority of probation revocations are for technical violations.[32] A study in Ohio found that smaller rural counties imposed more technical violations than did larger urban ones.[33] In an attempt to curb the flow of technical violators back into penal institutions and reduce the costs of incarceration, some states, such as Louisiana and Delaware, have taken legislative steps to make sure technical violators receive alternative sanctions that are proportionate to their violations of the conditions of probation or parole.[34]

Revocation of probation also can occur if the offender is found to possess any controlled substances or firearms or fails to submit to drug testing ordered by the court or the probation officer. The probationer who violates these conditions often has to pay fines as well as risk revocation.

In 1973 the U.S. Supreme Court ruled that probationers are entitled to certain due process rights if the court is to revoke probation.[35] Probationers must be allowed to present evidence on their own behalf, to receive written

notice of the hearing and the charges against them, and to challenge and confront the evidence and witnesses. In addition, probationers might have the
right to legal counsel if the case warrants an attorney's advice and services.

The Future of Probation

In the future, the success of probation will be dependent on a number of factors.
More financial resources will need to be redirected to probation agencies. Monies
will be needed to reduce large caseloads by hiring and training more probation
officers in standard and specialized areas so officers can develop greater skills to
assist probationers. One specialized area is in the area of addiction. Agencies must
acknowledge and know the cycles of addiction and recovery because so many
probationers struggle with drug and alcohol abuse. Such specialized training will
help officers move away from the standardized, one-size-fits-all type of supervision
that for decades has emphasized rule enforcement and a "lock them up" mentality in contrast to individualized rehabilitative care and treatment of probationers.

This paradigm shift has the potential to change the culture of probation
supervision for the better. To accomplish changes in the way probationers are
supervised, agencies will need to reshape their goals and officer roles to better
balance treatment and rule enforcement. One promising form of supervision is
behavioral management that combines the officer's enforcement responsibilities
with a duty to teach and model prosocial behavior for the probationer. This
form of supervision should assist the probationer to develop motivation, engagement, and responsibility; enable better officer–probationer relationships; and
foster effective reintegration and better outcomes.

Keys to success will be tied to the probationers' needs for specific types
of supervision, and agencies will have to administer better individual needs
and risk assessment tools to determine the type and extent of supervision
delivered. They will also need to use technologies with reliable research on
effectiveness; move away from imposing unnecessary restrictions on low-risk
probationers; use well-researched, evidence-based best practices; use graduated
responses and incentives for rule violations such as "halfway back" programs,
which are community-based responses with secure residential options; use
programs that allow probationers to earn discharge from probation; embrace
performance incentive funding programs that reward agencies with some of
the money states receive from reducing the number of offenders sent back to
prison for violating a rule of probation; and provide adequate levels of support
and benefits for probation officers who are on the front line.[36]

Trends in probation include electronic monitoring of offenders, increased
automation in the workplace, and greater use of alternative sanctions and
victim restitution.[37] Programs such as *evidence-based practice*, which sets out a
structured format for interviewing and supervision techniques, are gaining
favor.[38] Evidence-based probation organizes probation services guided by
research and uses such practices as motivational interviews, intervention, and
behavioral treatment to directly influence the probationers' behavior.[39]

PAROLE

Parole is the early conditional release of a prisoner from incarceration after
the person successfully serves a portion of the sentence in prison. In this section, we examine adult parole, its meaning and philosophy, and issues related
to this type of community corrections.

parole
An early release from prison conditional
on complying with certain standards
while free.

Purpose and Goals of Parole

The purpose of parole is to reward inmates who follow prison rules and behave
positively while incarcerated and to provide citizens with a more cost-effective
form of supervision than incarceration without sacrificing protection of society.

▲ Parole Board Meeting

Parole board members make decisions about a prisoner's eligibility requirements and suitability for parole. *What types of release conditions do parole boards set?*

The average yearly cost of supervising parolees is normally higher (approximately $2,727) than the average yearly cost of supervising probationers (approximately $1,248).[40]

Parole aims to provide inmates who no longer need imprisonment with close supervision and appropriate programs in the community that will help them rehabilitate and reintegrate. Offenders who are paroled from prison promise to follow specific rules. (The French word *parole* means "word" or "promise.") Parole officers provide the supervision, aftercare, and support services to help offenders reintegrate into the community. Like probationers, parolees can be sent back and incarcerated if they violate their conditions of parole. They are granted the privilege (not a right) of completing their sentence in the community. In short, parole is conditional supervised release in the community.

MYTH/REALITY

MYTH: Probation and parole are the same thing.

REALITY: Typically probation is a judicial sanction used in place of incarceration. Parole, on the other hand, is an administrative procedure for early release after an offender has served time in prison. Both probation and parole are conducted in the community, with conditions and under supervision, and the revocation of either usually leads to imprisonment.

parole board

A group of people authorized by law to grant permission for selected offenders—after serving a portion of time in prison—to serve their remaining sentence in the community.

Although parole and probation officers both supervise offenders in the community and use similar casework techniques, parole is an *administrative* function, whereas probation is a *judicial* function (see the Key Concepts table comparing probation and parole). Thus **parole boards,** not judges, grant permission for selected offenders who have served a portion of their sentence in prison to serve their remaining time in the community. A state's governor normally appoints parole

KEY CONCEPTS Comparison of Probation and Parole

Probation	Parole
A judicial function	An administrative function
Judges grant probation	Parole boards grant parole
Takes place in the community	Takes place in the community
Requires conditions	Requires conditions
Can be revoked	Can be revoked
Supervision by a probation officer	Supervision by a parole officer
Probationers typically are not prisoners	Parolees are released from prisons
Criminal records normally less serious	Criminal records more serious
No "ex-con" stigma	Entails "ex-con" stigma
Reintegration is less of an adjustment	Reintegration is a major adjustment
Offenders are on a caseload	Offenders are on a caseload
Restitution may be ordered by a judge	Restitution may be ordered by a parole board

board members–citizens with experience in criminal justice or related fields–to the board, although practices vary from state to state. In most states, victims are given the right to provide a victim impact statement to the parole board requesting any special conditions on the release (for example, release in a county other than the one where the victim lives and the grant of a restraining order).

The fact that parolees tend to have more serious prior criminal records than probationers explains why they served in prison rather than in jail or on probation. Reintegration is often more difficult for parolees because individuals who serve time in prison tend to become institutionalized; that is, they adjust to prison life and have difficulty readjusting to the outside world.[41] Parolees' options are limited, and a number of their rights are restricted. They are unable to vote in many states, to hold political office, to work in certain professions, or to enter into contracts. The label "ex-con" frequently becomes their primary identity and overshadows all aspects of their life. Frustration with that stigma can lead to defeatist attitudes and actions.[42]

Offenders can be released on parole in one of two major ways. In **mandatory release,** the law requires early release after an offender has served a specified time in prison. In **discretionary release,** a parole board decides whether the offender meets eligibility requirements and is ready for discharge. In either type of release, parole boards are responsible for setting the conditions for release and have the authority to return offenders to prison when they violate rules. Parole officers report directly to parole boards (not courts) and have the main responsibility for supervising parolees.

Discretionary release gives parole boards a great deal of power. Release depends on a state's sentencing structure and on the parole board's assessment of whether the prison has prepared the offender enough to reenter the community, whether continued incarceration might be harmful to the offender's eventual reintegration, whether the offender's mind-set is positive toward reentry, and whether the offender has a viable parole plan. In recent decades many states have opted to release prisoners at the end of their prison terms and then place them on a shorter term of mandatory postrelease supervision by a parole officer.[43] A *parole plan* is a proposed course of action the parolee will follow upon release to ensure success on parole.

Modern parole is typically administered at two levels of government–state and federal–depending on whether offenders violate state or federal criminal codes. Congress abolished parole at the federal level on November 1, 1987. (See "Challenges to Parole" section for more information.) As a result, offenders sentenced to federal prisons who complete their sentences and are released are required to complete a term of supervised release in the community. State systems vary, but normally parole and probation are separate functions at the state level. The federal system is centralized, standardized, and uniform and employs officers who work in both probation and parole to assist offenders. Most states hire parole officers who work exclusively with either adult or juvenile populations. Federal probation and parole officers supervise both parolees and probationers simultaneously and work with offenders of all ages.

Who Is Paroled?

By the end of 2014, approximately 854,600 adults were on parole from federal and state prisons. This means that about 1 in 288 adults per 100,000 people in the United States were under parole supervision.[44] Both those entering parole and leaving parole declined steadily between 2010

mandatory release
Early release mandated by law after an offender has served a specified time in prison.

discretionary release
A procedure by which a parole board decides whether the offender meets eligibility requirements and is ready to be released from prison.

▼ **Parolee in Court**
A parolee arrested for a crime committed while on parole will frequently go to trial on the charges.

and 2014.[45] From 2007 to 2014, parole was the only correctional population to increase.[46] Of the total estimated U.S. adult correctional population, approximately 13 percent were on parole.[47]

Most prison inmates–and therefore most parolees–are male, poor, undereducated, unskilled, people of color, young, and convicted of property or drug offenses. Thirty-one percent of parolees in 2014 were on parole for drug offenses. Approximately 31 percent were supervised for violent offenses; 22 percent for property offenses; and the rest for weapons and other offenses.[48]

At the end of 2014, about 12 percent of adults on parole were female.[49] Although their numbers are on the rise, women parolees are released to the community with limited help to secure employment, housing, health care, mental health and substance abuse services, transportation, and child care.[50] Additionally, many parolees have learning disorders and cognitive problems.[51] Many have entered the prison system with–and bring to parole–such problems as homelessness, unemployment, separation from their children, sexual and physical abuse, and mental health and addiction issues.[52]

In 2014, approximately 43 percent of individuals on parole were White; 39 percent Black; 16 percent Latino; and 2 percent people of other races and ethnicities.[53] Blacks made up approximately 13 percent of the U.S. population and almost half of the prison population, but under the new tough-on-crime policies they were not being granted parole as frequently as Whites.[54] Incarceration custody rates for Black males were higher than for any other race.[55] The average age of state parolees is rising because inmates are being sentenced to, and staying in prison for, longer periods of time. In 1990 the median age of a parolee was 31, and in 1999 it was 34. About 26 percent of all those entering parole were age 40 or older.[56]

All these data suggest a shift in the profile of individuals who reenter the community. The number of drug offenders remains high, and the number of older parolees is increasing.[57] Because of the higher incarceration rates of women, the number of women on parole is also high.[58] Figure 13-4 shows

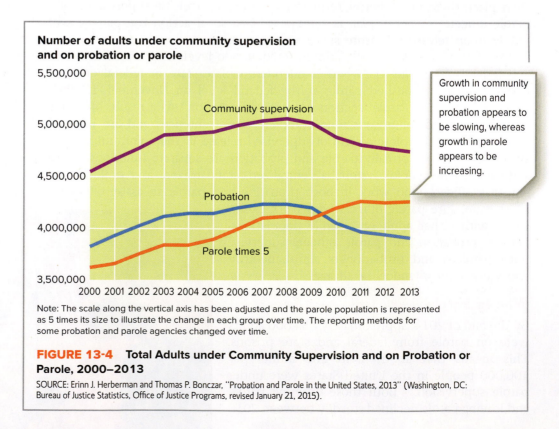

Number of adults under community supervision and on probation or parole

Growth in community supervision and probation appears to be slowing, whereas growth in parole appears to be increasing.

Note: The scale along the vertical axis has been adjusted and the parole population is represented as 5 times its size to illustrate the change in each group over time. The reporting methods for some probation and parole agencies changed over time.

FIGURE 13-4 **Total Adults under Community Supervision and on Probation or Parole, 2000–2013**

SOURCE: Erinn J. Herberman and Thomas P. Bonczar, "Probation and Parole in the United States, 2013" (Washington, DC: Bureau of Justice Statistics, Office of Justice Programs, revised January 21, 2015).

the changes in the probation, parole, and community populations between 2000 and 2013. In 2014 the aforementioned combined populations decreased 1 percent from 2013 due to the drop in the probation population.[59]

Roles and Tasks of the Parole Officer

Parole officers are charged with helping offenders readjust to the community and preventing new crimes. They carry a caseload, have regular contact with parolees, and perform other duties. The number of hours a parole officer spends supervising a parolee depends on case and agency priorities. High-priority cases may take 4 hours each month of supervision time, while low-priority cases may require only 1 hour of supervision time in some jurisdictions.[60] In their assistance role, officers operate as resource brokers and advocates by developing parole plans that specify what inmates must have in place before they are released. After release, parole officers operate as social workers, counselors, and life coaches, making arrangements for housing, employment, education, counseling, medical care, referrals to other agencies, and the like.

In their supervisory role, parole officers conduct surveillance, monitor drug tests, enforce conditions of parole, conduct investigations, initiate revocation hearings, carry out parole searches, seize evidence, make arrests, and place parolees in custody. Parolees are subject to surprise searches conducted by parole officers—both of their premises and their body, at any time, and without a search warrant. Such searches may result in arrest. A tragic example in which the supervisory function of parole officers, among others, went terribly awry is the Jaycee Dugard kidnapping case discussed in the "Case in Point" box.[61]

a case in point

Parole and the Jaycee Dugard Case

In 1991, Phillip Garrido, a registered sex offender in California, kidnapped 11-year-old Jaycee Dugard, and he subsequently held her captive in his backyard compound for 18 years. During this time Garrido repeatedly raped Dugard, and she gave birth to two children.

The criminal justice system failed at several key points in this case. First, Garrido had been released from prison in January 1988, even though he had received a 50-year sentence in 1977 for kidnapping and raping another girl. Upon discharge from prison, Garrido was under the supervision of federal parole authorities. Then in 1999, the U.S. Parole Commission granted Garrido early release from parole based on what was determined to have been a clear prison record. At this point, the California Department of Corrections and Rehabilitation (CDCR) took over Garrido's supervision. Yet, despite some 60 visits by parole officers between 1999 and 2009, Jaycee's imprisonment in the backyard went undetected.

After Garrido's arrest in 2009 for Dugard's captivity, many specific mistakes and apparent errors in judgment came to light. For example, CDCR had failed to classify Garrido as a sexual predator; parole officers had been tardy in visiting his home and had not made a home visit until 2000; parole officers had failed to speak with Garrido's neighbors or to communicate with police agencies about him; parole officers had not followed up on reports that Garrido had violated his parole conditions; and parole and law enforcement officers had failed to notice that children were living on Garrido's property.

Perhaps California's parole system would have been more effective if the burden were not on the parole board to prove that offenders were a public safety risk before releasing them on parole and if the state had used a sex offender assessment tool.[a]

Apart from the missteps that occurred in the Dugard case, without a proactive parole officer who intervenes to protect society if necessary, offenders are more likely to fail upon their return to the community. The argument that abolishing parole is consistent with being tough on crime and beneficial to public safety may be misguided.[b]

OBSERVE→INVESTIGATE→UNDERSTAND

- When there are such great failures by a parole officer, should he or she be held responsible? If so, how? If not, why?
- Are there any policy changes that you think should be made in light of the details of this case?
- Do you think parole officer training should be changed or enhanced in some way?

SOURCES: [a]Nick Monacelli, "New Garrido Videos, Psych Reports Highlight Parole System Flaws," New10 ABC, August 2, 2011. www.news10.net/new/article/148396/29/DA-on-mission-to-prevent-repeat-of-Dugard-horror (retrieved August 2, 2011).

[b]Peggy B. Burke, Abolishing Parole: Why the Emperor Has No Clothes (Lexington, KY: American Probation and Parole Association, 1995).

How Successful Is Parole?

Successfully completing parole means that the parolee did not have a violation serious enough to be returned to custody and was not rearrested for a new offense.[62] The parole completion rate has consistently risen since 2008. In 2013, approximately 62 percent of those discharged from parole had successfully completed their supervision or were discharged early compared to only 49 percent in 2008. In 2014, the completion rate remained about the same.[63]

In 2013, approximately 30 percent of parolees had their parole revoked and were returned to prison, and 8 percent had left parole for some other reason, such as death, escape, or out-of-state supervision. The figures are similar for 2014.[64] Overall, the rate at which parolees had their parole revoked and were returned to prison for a new crime decreased between 2008 and 2012. However, between 2012 and 2014, the rate at which parolees had their parole revoked and were returned to prison rose about 6 percent but declined to 5.2% in 2014.[65] The at-risk parole population returned to prison remained stable at about 9 percent between 2008 and 2014.[66] Overall the parolees at risk for reincarceration rate has declined from 2000 to 2014.[67]

As drug offenders, older inmates, and women inmates are released on parole, they will be subject to parole violations. Some 70 percent of parolees who were returned to prison had committed a technical violation.[68] These violations can include moving to a new residence without the permission of a parole officer, taking a shopping trip to a city not in the parolee's county of residence without permission, and leaving the state without permission. Driving a car, failing a drug test, or taking a sip of champagne to toast a bride and groom during a wedding reception can result in revocation if those acts were specified as violations of parole. Time will tell whether states will follow California's lead and do away with parole revocation for technical violations as the Public Safety Realignment Act of 2011 requires (see Chapter 11).

A parolee accused of a new crime while on parole normally faces severe consequences and will likely be held in jail until the new charges are resolved. If convicted, the parolee will attend a revocation hearing to determine how much extra prison time he must serve. The high number of parole violators who are returned to prison, combined with new court commitments, has forced prisons to develop new strategies to house all these individuals.[69]

The rate of parole violations varies greatly from state to state. California is at the top of the list, with approximately 67 percent of parolees returning to prison; at the low end are Alabama and Indiana, where fewer than 10 percent of parolees return. The rest of the states fall between these extremes.[70]

Not surprisingly, most parole failures occur within the first 6 to 12 months of release.[71] A significant factor in these failures is that for many parolees discharged after a long incarceration, life outside prison is distressing and even overwhelming. Most leave with limited resources–the clothes on their back, few job skills, low literacy, no reliable means of transportation, and little money. They may have physical and mental problems or addiction. They must report to parole officers they may not know, and employment they were promised may not materialize. Practices such as suing ex-cons for the cost of incarceration after being released to the community threaten successful reintegration efforts. This "pay-to-stay" trend is intended to put part of the burden of funding the criminal justice back on offenders.[72] Such problems would quickly stress many of us.

Challenges to Parole

A multistate study in 2005 compared the criminal activity of inmates released from prison without parole **(unconditional release)** and those released on parole by mandatory and discretionary release. The researchers found that

unconditional release
Release of an inmate from prison without parole.

2 years after release, 62 percent of unconditional releases and 61 percent of mandatory release parolees had been rearrested at least once. Of the discretionary release parolees, 54 percent had been rearrested. The researchers concluded that although the difference was surprisingly small, doing away with parole might not be in society's best interest.[73]

Other analysts of parole are not so sure. In the late 1970s, the practice of parole came under attack on the grounds that rehabilitation programs were not effective.[74] This conclusion fed into popular beliefs that prisons and rehabilitation programs were pampering dangerous criminals. Parole also was challenged on the basis that open-ended (indeterminate) sentences were "cruel and unusual punishment" because they were uncertain or that they gave too much discretion to parole boards.[75]

Responding to these challenges, the Sentencing Reform Act of 1984 abolished parole for offenders sentenced under federal guidelines. Instead they had to complete their full sentences–minus time for good behavior–within federal prison. Unlike parole, such determinate sentences do not offer offenders the support needed to reintegrate. They may even put the community at greater risk because the offender is not supervised upon release.

The U.S. Parole Commission is responsible for eligible federal offenders who committed offenses before November 1, 1987. The commission also has oversight for paroling eligible offenders sentenced under the Uniform Code of Military Justice, transfer treaty cases, and state probationers and parolees in federal witness protection programs.

Several landmark U.S. Supreme Court cases in the 1970s changed the way parole was revoked. In 1972, parolees were granted limited due process rights when a process of revocation is initiated.[76] As noted earlier, in 1973 probationers were granted limited rights to counsel in revocation hearings, and the Court left it to the hearing body to decide on a case-by-case basis whether counsel should be provided.[77] The ruling in this case also applied to parolees. In 1979, however, the Court ruled that parole was a privilege, and states are still determining what privileges parolees may have during revocation hearings.[78]

Some critics are calling for the parole system to better protect society by becoming more involved in the community, expanding community collaboration initiatives, placing the protection of society before the treatment of offenders, and enforcing the punishment of parole violations.[79] These approaches have roots in both the crime control and the punishment models of corrections discussed in Chapter 11. Others have more optimistic viewpoints but call for parole to step up and do better sex offender management. The parole system must also focus on the mentally disordered, substance abuser, and geriatric populations. It must develop practices that take into account the differences between supervising females and males, and it cannot ignore juveniles in the adult system. Another challenge for parole is to provide housing opportunities for those released to the community to be supervised.[80]

INTERMEDIATE SANCTIONS

Intermediate sanctions are judicial punishments that do not require long terms of incarceration but stop short of allowing offenders to remain in the community on probation with minimal supervision. Hence, these sanctions are not quite prison or jail and not quite traditional probation. Some intermediate sanctions require offenders to live in a communal residence (such as a community center or a halfway house) while participating in work and rehabilitation programs; others allow offenders to live at home but under close supervision (such as through electronic monitoring devices). Intermediate sanctions reinforce the need for offenders to take responsibility for their actions while providing

intermediate sanctions
Judicial punishments that do not require incarceration but stop short of allowing offenders to remain in the community on probation with minimal supervision.

	High Supervision	Medium Supervision	Low Supervision
Community service		X	
Restorative justice		X	
Mediation		X	
Restitution			X
House arrest	X		
Shock programs	X		
Fines and forfeitures			X
Community centers		X	
Work release		X	

more structure than traditional probation provides. They also broaden the range of alternatives available to deal with offenders' different needs.

diversion
An intermediate sanction that is used in place of incarceration and may prevent offenders from having a criminal charge and record.

Intermediate sanctions are also called **diversion** because they divert the offender from prison or jail. Diversion programs are a form of sentencing, and they are frequently run by law enforcement agencies, the courts, a district attorney's office, and outside community agencies. In addition to diverting offenders from incarceration, they may also prevent the offender from being criminally charged and having a record. Such sanctions sometimes occur at the end of incarceration to give the offender more freedom and control in preparation for release. Many different types and varieties of community corrections are available in the criminal justice system today, and even more creative strategies will likely be developed as prison and jail populations remain high. One point is very clear: Community corrections are less expensive than sanctions that include incarceration.[81] So, the future appears to be ripe for the further development of community corrections. If you are interested in working in this burgeoning field, some careers in community corrections include community residential treatment director, community work coordinator, court advice worker, drug court officer, community corrections officer, and home detention officer.

We describe some of the most common forms of intermediate sanctions next. See the Key Concepts table to understand how they compare in their degree of supervision.

Community Service

community service
Performance by an offender of free labor for the community as reparation for the injury done to society.

Community service began in 1966 in Alameda County, California, as a punishment for traffic offenders. It then became popular as a condition of probation for a wide range of white-collar violations.[82] Today community service requires the offender to provide a specific number of hours of unpaid labor for the community in a public service activity, such as working for a nonprofit agency, hospital, public park, or poverty program, picking up roadside litter, or removing graffiti. This service is considered to represent an offender's atonement for the harm done to society, with his personal contribution as a way of demonstrating contriteness. If a person does not complete community service, a judge can order more service hours or send the person to jail. In some cases, judges will use restitution as a sentence to go beyond just providing free labor. Restitution can also be a specific amount of money paid or specific tasks performed directly for the victim or the community as reparation for damage done to community property or private property.

When offenders do community service, society receives the benefit of their free labor as atonement for their crime.

Restorative Justice

Restorative justice emphasizes the offender's responsibility to participate with other stakeholders, victims, and members of the community in repairing the injury and damage caused by his criminal behavior.[83] These goals are accomplished through a cooperative process among participants in victim–offender mediation, victim assistance providers, ex-offender assistance programs, restitution, and community service.[84]

Restorative justice is an alternative way of thinking about crime. It looks at crime as harm done to people and the community rather than just as a breach in the legal code. It elevates the role of crime victims and community members by actively engaging them in the justice process, and it holds offenders accountable to the people and communities they have injured. The goal is for healing and forgiveness to replace punishment and retribution. Restorative justice practices are found in Native American cultures in the United States and Canada and among indigenous cultures around the globe.

restorative justice
A process that involves all the persons who have a stake in an offense coming together to jointly resolve the disruption, damage, and injury so that the end result is a restoration of the relationships.

They have also been adopted by some faith-based organizations, especially the Mennonites.[85] Based on a meta-analysis of 22 studies, notwithstanding some methodological limitations, general support was found for the effectiveness of restorative justice principles.[86]

Restitution, Fines, and Forfeitures

Court-ordered monetary repayment to the victim for losses, damages, or expenses suffered at the hands of the offender is called **restitution.** This approach has a long history. The Code of Hammurabi (ca. 1750 BCE) and the Hebrew Bible prescribed restitution to the victims of theft. In the Twelve Tables of Roman Law (ca. 449 BCE), convicted thieves were required to pay double the value of stolen goods. English medieval law contained a detailed restitution schedule. Following the Norman invasion of Britain in 1066, however, retributive justice began to replace the restitution system; crimes came to be viewed as offenses against the state that disturbed the "king's peace."

On the principle that crimes are in fact committed against individuals and not the state, we can view restitution as payment of a debt owed to the victim, not a state-mandated punishment or fine paid to the state. In this way, restitution can be one part of restorative justice sanctions; it is in practice often ordered as a condition of probation.

The financial impact of crime on victims is staggering. Each year the costs of crime—as measured by medical bills, lost earnings, and the maintenance of victim assistance programs—are estimated to be $1.1 billion for violent crimes, $15 billion for property crimes, $56.6 billion for identity fraud, $40 billion for insurance fraud, $94 billion for child abuse, and $16.8 billion for victim compensation for sexual assault crimes. These figures do not include pain, suffering, or reduced quality of life.[87]

Such statistics underscore the importance of restitution. However, for restitution to be truly meaningful, the offender must be strictly accountable to pay the prescribed amount. Similarly, the criminal justice system must be accountable for collecting and processing restitution and for enforcing collection when offenders are delinquent.[88] In many cases courts ask for more restitution than is likely to be collected (only about 7 percent of ordered restitution is actually collected). When offenders are not able to afford restitution, little can be done to collect it.[89]

Because many victims never receive restitution monies, some states are taking innovative steps to investigate the convicted offender's assets, preserve them, and file paperwork to garnish any source of income, including wages, lottery winnings, and awards in civil lawsuits. Kansas provides the victim with access to all the offender's financial assets and income until the restitution is paid. Pennsylvania allows the prosecutor to preserve the offender's assets at the time a criminal complaint is filed. In California, it is a misdemeanor and sometimes a felony for an offender to dispose of property to avoid paying restitution. The consequence of willfully failing to pay restitution can be revocation of probation or parole.[90]

Vermont created a Restitution Fund that is a centralized unit affiliated with the Vermont Center for Crime Victims. A 15 percent surcharge is added to all criminal and traffic fines, which is then deposited into the Restitution Fund. The monies are then advanced to crime victims, up to a cap of $10,000, while the fines are being collected from offenders. Since its inception in 2004, more than $6 million has been disbursed to 5,600 crime victims. Florida instituted Project Payback, which focuses not only on enforcing restitution orders for juvenile offenders, but also on training for job skills to ensure that juveniles can make the payments to victims. Those participating in this program have given over $3,500 to victims since the program's inception.[91]

DIS Con nects

Restitution can serve as an act of atonement or remorse and can help offenders take responsibility for their behavior. It can also greatly reduce recidivism when coupled with other rehabilitative processes such as mediation and negotiated sanctions between offenders and victims.[92] One argument against restitution, however, is that a financial penalty has little, if any, effect on a wealthy defendant. Conversely, such sanctions may be harsh for poor defendants who already have overwhelming financial burdens.[93]

Fines imposed by judges constitute another form of monetary payment, but to the state, not the victim. Offenders must pay or forfeit a specific sum of money as a penalty for committing an offense. The fines may be in addition to or instead of incarceration or other sanctions and usually punish relatively minor misdemeanors and infractions. Different agencies of the criminal justice system are responsible for collecting them.

Fines are often criticized as being unfair. For someone as wealthy as actor Mel Gibson, for instance, the $1,300 fine he paid in 2006 for speeding and driving under the influence was a penalty without much weight or personal impact. The "Disconnects" box describes how fines may be ordered in combination with other types of punishments. An alternative approach is **day fines,** also called *structured fines.* Day fines originated in Scandinavia and are relatively new in the United States. Instead of imposing the same penalty regardless of ability to pay, day fines determine a fair fine for a specific offender, using formulas similar to those used to calculate spousal and child support payments. The fines are based on a scale that ranks the severity of

fines
Payments, imposed by judges, that require offenders to pay or forfeit a specific sum of money as a penalty for committing an offense.

day fines
Fines based on what is fair for a specific offender to pay; also called structured fines.

forfeiture
Confiscation by law enforcement of profits made by committing a crime and of property used to commit a crime.

victim–offender mediation
A process that brings victims and offenders face-to-face to work out a restitution and restorative strategy under the direction of a trained counselor or mediator.

house arrest (home confinement)
An intermediate sanction that restricts offenders to their homes during the time they are not working or attending treatment programs.

offense and the offender's daily income and number of dependents.[94] A recent example is that of a Finnish businessman who was fined €54,000 (or the equivalent of about $60,000) for going 15 miles over the posted 50 miles per hour sign. The police searched a federal taxpayer database to assess the fine based on man's income. In 2002 a Nokia executive was fined $103,000 for the same type of violation, and NHL player Teemu Selanne received a $39,000 fine for reckless driving in 2000.[95]

Forfeiture refers to the confiscation by law enforcement of profits made by committing a crime and of property used to commit a crime. Asset forfeiture has been used in the prosecution of drug trafficking and organized and environmental crimes.

Mediation

Victim–offender mediation brings victims and offenders face-to-face to work out a restitution and restorative strategy under the direction of a trained counselor or mediator. The mediation may include family and community members who wish to take part.

During the mediation meeting, both the offender and the victim can reveal how the crime affected their lives. Victims may communicate their feelings about being victimized, and the offender can accept responsibility, express remorse, and perhaps even make an apology.[96] These programs have high participant satisfaction rates and reduce the criminal behavior of offenders who participate.[97] Mediation is not appropriate for all victims, however. In fact, for some it can reinforce the trauma associated with the crime.[98]

House Arrest

House arrest (or home confinement) restricts offenders to their home during the time they are not working or attending a treatment program. Such confinement may be either a condition of intensive-supervision probation or a stand-alone sanction. House arrest is a sentence given by a court or a condition imposed when a defendant is awaiting trial at home rather than in jail. In some authoritarian countries such as China, Myanmar (Burma), and Sudan, house arrest is a way of silencing political dissenters without giving them a criminal trial that might bring negative publicity to the government in power.[99]

House arrest is not a new concept; it was used to confine England's King Richard II to Pontefract Castle in 1399. In the seventeenth century, Galileo was placed under house arrest for his assertion that the earth revolved around the sun. He remained there for 9 years until his death in 1642.[100]

The basic goal of home confinement is to permit offenders to be employed and to support themselves and their families while continuing their punishment. It has the advantage of reducing jail and prison overcrowding and incarceration costs while promoting reintegration into the community. Candidates for home confinement tend to be first offenders who have close family ties, are employed full-time, and do not have drug or alcohol problems.[101] It is clear that house arrest is not as harsh a sentence as is incarceration, but the physical restrictions and shaming effects that result are significantly punitive.[102]

Electronic Monitoring

Electronic monitoring, sometimes called *technocorrections*, uses technology to enforce house arrest or to keep track of an offender on intensive-supervision probation or specialized parole. Courts can order such monitoring for those awaiting trial who might not be able to make bail but for whom temporary incarceration is not appropriate.

Electronic monitoring uses a transmitter placed around the offender's ankle that sends a continuous signal. If the signal is broken by the offender's departure from a designated area, a correctional employee checks to see whether the break was authorized. If not, the employee notifies the probation officer, the parole officer, or the court. Most home signal devices are waterproof, can report tampering, and cannot be removed without special tools.[103]

A large study of Florida offenders placed on electronic monitoring found that monitoring significantly reduced the likelihood of failure under community supervision. The decline in the risk of failure was 31 percent, compared with offenders placed on other forms of community supervision.[104]

electronic monitoring
Enforcing house arrest or monitoring the whereabouts of an offender through electronic sensors, placed around the offender's ankle, that send a continuous signal.

Shock Programs

A **shock program** uses short-term incarceration to frighten the offender by instilling uncertainty about whether the offender will be released and, if so, when. This approach merges punishment with leniency, generally at military-style boot camp programs (see Chapter 15). Technically, shock programs are not a form of community corrections; they are considered intermediate sanctions, but we include them here.

shock program
A short-term incarceration program used to frighten the offender by instilling uncertainty about whether the offender will be released and, if so, when.

Shock Probation **Shock probation** combines probation with short-term incarceration. The rationale of shock probation is to avoid the overpenalization of a first-time offender by imposing a long period of incarceration. This sanction requires that an offender serve a short time—normally 30 to 60 days—in prison or jail and then be resentenced to probation. Most of these programs target young offenders who are nonviolent substance abusers without previous incarcerations in adult facilities and who do not have mental health problems.

The shock can occur on a couple of levels, one of which is the experience of being locked up itself. Incarceration is meant to be so vividly unpleasant that the offender fears returning to jail or prison and thus avoids further criminal behavior. After the incarceration, the offender may experience shock at being released on probation so swiftly. Shock programs may make offenders more receptive to probation supervision by showing them what awaits them if they violate their probation conditions.[105] Shock programs are often combined with electronic monitoring.

Despite its popularity, there is little evidence that shock probation reduces recidivism or has a long-term positive effect on an offender's behavior.[106] Recidivism rates of those who successfully completed the shock incarceration programs were similar to those of comparable offenders who spent a longer time in prison without shock programs. In addition, the more intensely offenders were supervised in the community after they were released—that is, the more contact they had during aftercare—the better they adjusted.[107]

Shock probation programs are not without problems. For one thing, they make offenders' needs for rehabilitation secondary to the smooth running of the

shock probation
A combination of probation and short-term incarceration.

▼ **Electronic Monitoring Device**

RealCrimeTech

PROBATION KIOSKS

Several agencies, including the New York City Department of Probation, are using automated reporting machines called **probation kiosks** to monitor low-risk nonviolent offenders. After an initial face-to-face meeting with a probation officer, the offender checks in regularly at a kiosk that resembles an ATM machine. After verifying his identity, the offender updates a profile with work information, change of address, and any arrests or new warrants since the last check-in. False information will generate a response from the probation department. The kiosk system allows flexibility in reporting times to low-risk offenders who might be working or in school and provides a more successful reentry to the community for the offender by reducing interruptions to the offender's daily schedule. It can also save time for staff and appears to be financially attractive for agencies.

Probation kiosks can free probation officers to spend more time with high-risk offenders on a face-to-face basis. In Dallas, however, authorities were using kiosks to monitor high-risk probationers as well, a practice that reduced costs but eliminated valuable personal contact with probation officers. Concern heightened when it became known that about half the offenders in the program were on probation for having committed felonies, including drug-related crimes, robberies, and organized crime activities. As a result, the program was suspended. More research is needed about the extent to which kiosk systems are used throughout the country and how effective they are in comparison to traditional supervision.

SOURCES: National Law Enforcement and Corrections Technology Center, "TechBeat." www.justnet.org/TechBeat%20Files/NYCProbationSpr01.pdf (retrieved August 1, 2011); "Probation Kiosk Draws Concerns," *Dallas Morning News,* September 19, 2005. www.kioskmarketplace.com/article.php?id=14969&na=1 (retrieved January 20, 2007); Brooks Edgerton, "Probation Kiosk Program Suspended," *Dallas Morning News,* November 9, 2007. www.dentonrc.com/sharedcontent/dws/news/longterm/stories/092905dnmetprobationkiosk.1f3eb626b.html (retrieved March 7, 2009); Vera Institute of Justice, *The Potential of Community Corrections to Improve Safety and Reduce Incarceration* (New York: Vera Institute of Justice, 2013), 20.

institution. Another issue is that such programs tend to deliver drug treatment to all offenders in the same way.[108] In a study examining drug treatment in 43 state and 2 federal shock incarceration (boot camp) programs, offenders were rarely assessed to see whether they were receptive to treatment. Furthermore, most shock incarceration programs did a poor job of preparing drug offenders for community release.[109]

Shock Parole   *Shock parole* is similar to shock probation, but it applies to those who have been sentenced to prison. The paroling authority–instead of the judge–makes the decision to release the prisoner after a short prison stay, in hopes that the incarceration experience has shocked her into law-abiding behavior. The unanticipated release is expected to be an incentive to the offender to stay out of prison in the future.[110]

Sex Offender Registers and Tracking

> **MYTH/REALITY**
>
> **MYTH:** Strangers are more likely to molest children than family members.
>
> **REALITY:** Only 10 percent of sex offenders are strangers. The other 90 percent are family, friends, and acquaintances.[111]

Laws that require sex offenders to register with law enforcement in the community where they reside and to be tracked were originally enacted to enable parents to protect their children's safety. Unfortunately, most of the legislation related to policing sex offenders focuses on the "stranger perpetrator." However, children are actually at much greater risk of molestation by family members and acquaintances than by strangers. The rhetoric around sex offenses perpetuates parents' fears of strangers rather than prompting an objective assessment of the people who are regular features in their children's lives.

Sex Offender Registers   The call for sex offender registration in the United States began in 1994 following a series of highly publicized acts by sex offenders who had prior records of sexual offenses. These crimes created a perception that sex offenders are more likely to reoffend than other types of offenders and led to federal and state legislation. The 1994 Violent Crime Control and Law Enforcement Act and the 1994 Jacob Wetterling Crimes Against Children and Sexually Violent Offenders Registration Act set guidelines for the establishment of sex offender registers. Then in 1996, Megan's Law refined the ways in which states could constitutionally notify the public about sex offenders, and the Pam Lychner Act passed in that same year established a national sex offender database while providing assistance to states without sex offender programs of their own.[112]

In 2005 Florida legislators passed Jessica's Law, which most other states subsequently copied. The law restricts convicted sex offenders from living near or around schools or parks where children congregate. Many of these laws also allow for

What about the Victim?

Jessica's Law—and Its Unintended Consequences

Jessica's Law is named after Jessica Lunsford, a 12-year-old girl who was abducted, raped, and murdered in 2005 in Florida by a previously convicted sex offender. Florida, followed by over 40 states, passed such legislation as a reaction to this heinous crime. Most of these laws restrict registered sex offenders from living near schools and parks and enhance the state's ability to track them. In California, Jessica's Law (Proposition 83) allows not only residency restrictions but also the attachment of GPS (global positioning system) devices for monitoring the wearer's whereabouts for life. The intent is to prevent sex offenders from temptation to

harm by forcing them to stay away from children. In short, Jessica's Law aims to create "predator-free zones."

However, this legislation has had certain unintended consequences. For example, many of the laws do not differentiate between potentially dangerous sex offenders and those who have committed nonviolent sexual crimes such as indecent exposure. And particularly problematic are the restrictions against sex offenders living within 2,000 feet of parks and schools. Critics say that in most cities, the residency restrictions leave no space in which offenders can live, rendering many of them either in violation of the law or homeless. Moreover, since Jessica's Law took effect in California, increasing numbers of sex offenders have identified themselves as transient—and as such, they are especially hard to track. Also, there have been challenges to the constitutionality of parts of the law, as in California in 2011. In Iowa legislators revised the state law restricting convicted sex offenders' residences after determining that such restriction was unenforceable.

OBSERVE → INVESTIGATE → UNDERSTAND

- Do you believe that restricting the residence of previously convicted sex offenders will affect the possibility of recidivism? Explain.
- How should previously convicted sex offenders be handled after being released from prison?

SOURCES: Editorial, "The Flaw in Jessica's Law," *Los Angeles Times,* November 6, 2010; Denise Zapata and Kevin Crowe, "Jessica's Law Too Vague to Enforce?" *Sign On San Diego,* November 20, 2009. www.signonsandiego.com/news/2009/nov/29/jessicas-law-too-vague-enforce/ (retrieved March 12, 2011); "Jessica Lunsford Act (Jessica's Law Proposition 83)," *Personal Injury.*

http://www.personal-injury-info.net/jessica-lunsford-act.htm (retrieved March 12, 2011); California Department of Corrections and Rehabilitation, Division of Adult Parole Operations, "Sex Offender Information." www.cdcr.ca.gov/Parole/Sex_offender_facts/index.html (retrieved March 12, 2011).

the tracking of these individuals by means of GPS (global positioning system) devices. Some states mandate that tracking continue for the life of the offender.[113] In March 2011, however, a court in California found that California's Jessica's Law was unconstitutional, and the presiding judge ordered agencies to stop applying the restriction as to where an offender could live.[114] Opponents of the law argue that it is unconstitutional in that it is overly restrictive and makes it impossible for sex offenders to live at all in densely populated cities.[115]

Results from studies throughout the United States suggest that residency restrictions at best have a marginal effect on sexual recidivism.[116] What research does indicate, however, is that residential restrictions make it more likely for an offender to become homeless–and a lack of stable and permanent housing increases the likelihood that offenders will reoffend.[117] The "What about the Victim?" box explores various difficulties with these laws.

All states now have laws requiring convicted sex offenders to register with local police when placed on either probation or parole. Some states require the offender to remain registered while under supervision, some for a fixed number of years, and some for life. Some states assess the risk of individual

probation kiosk
An automated reporting machine, resembling an ATM, that monitors low-risk nonviolent offenders.

sex offenders when they are released into society and set reporting requirements accordingly.[118]

Strong public support for registration laws can make it politically risky for an officeholder to vote against new and sometimes harsh laws. Like many other states, California makes no distinction between habitual offenders at high risk of reoffending and individuals who pose little or no threat.

Some studies show that sex offenders can experience harassment, threats, evictions, loss of jobs, family breakups, or loss of life as a result of registration laws. For example, two sex offenders were shot to death in Maine by a man who got their names from the state's online register.[119] One problem is that many states make no distinctions among different types of sex offenders. A person arrested for indecent exposure or a youth who engages in consensual sex with another youth may be treated the same as a rapist or sexual predator. In a 2-year study, Jamie Fellner of Human Rights Watch found that laws in California enacted to protect children often punished consensual sex between teenagers, the antics of streakers, and other nonviolent offenses.[120]

MYTH/REALITY

MYTH: Sex offender registers have been proved to protect the public from sexual predators.

REALITY: There is little evidence that these registers provide effective protection from or act as a deterrent to repeat sex offenders.[121]

Although sex offender registers are popular with the general public, there is little evidence that they actually protect the public. A sex offender study that dealt with a sample of rapes in 10 states did not show that registration laws had any effect on the number of rapes committed, although there is some evidence that the laws motivate some sex offenders not to reoffend on release.[122] On the basis of his study of California's laws, Jamie Fellner contends that instead of reducing sexual offenses, registers force offenders underground and out of range of supervision. In his opinion, the registration laws do more harm than good.[123]

Sex offender notification and registration laws have been challenged in the courts on constitutional grounds. The challenges center on issues such as violations of due process, double jeopardy (prohibiting being punished twice for the same crime), ex post facto law (prohibiting a person from being charged for a crime committed before a law was enacted), and the "cruel and unusual punishment" protection in the Constitution. To date, the laws have withstood the challenges.

A major argument for sex offender registers is that they enable police to investigate sex crimes more easily, on the assumption that sex offenders are likely to repeat. But the Center for Sex Offender Management claims that this reasoning is a

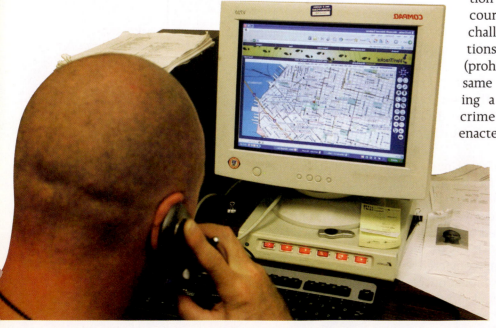

▼ **Sex Offender Tracking**

States now have laws requiring convicted sex offenders on probation or parole to register with local police so that the offenders can be tracked.

myth and that recidivism rates for sex offenders are lower than for the general criminal population.[124]

Tracking Sex Offenders—Global Positioning Systems   The **global positioning system (GPS)** is a satellite-based system placed in orbit by the U.S. Department of Defense and made available for civilian use in the 1980s. Twenty-four satellites circle the globe and send microwave signals to receivers that can calculate a user's exact location, direction, and speed.

Twenty-three states have laws requiring GPS tracking devices to monitor convicted sex offenders in an effort to deter additional crimes. Some GPS units can be programmed with certain exclusion zones where an offender may not go. Many states use GPS systems to monitor sex offenders while they are on parole, and several states monitor registrants permanently.

Research looking into the effectiveness of GPS devices is inconclusive. A major study funded by the U.S. Department of Justice found flaws in research designs trying to show the effectiveness of GPS monitoring.[125]

Community Centers

Day reporting centers and residential community centers offer additional structure and supervision for offenders.

Day Reporting Centers   *Day reporting centers* are places in the community, either public or private, where offenders report their daily activities, schedules, and plans to program staff.[126] Such centers offer offenders a daily contact point, with immediate access to people who can assist them if problems arise. Centers also provide additional supervision for high-risk offenders by monitoring their employment and residence status and providing drug testing. Some offenders are required to report to centers daily to take part in specific activities. Others are required to call in on a regular basis. It is not unusual for offenders to be required to contact their centers 60 times a week.[127] Offenders remain in day reporting center programs until they are deemed successful or until they reoffend.

Residential Community Centers   *Residential community centers* are also known as halfway houses, community treatment centers, and community correctional centers. An offender can be sentenced to serve time directly in a community treatment center, or he may be released from prison to a center as a "halfway" step between incarceration and freedom.

To ease adjustment, centers provide offenders with greater structure and control than does either probation or parole, but less than jails and prisons. They offer a variety of support services such as counseling, education, and job placement assistance. The residents usually attend work or educational programs. Typically they must sign in and out of the house and abide by curfew rules, but they are generally free to come and go. Once they adjust to the demands of the community, offenders find residence elsewhere. Some community treatment centers specialize in working with either women or men. Some specialize in dealing with addicted, mentally disordered, homeless, or veteran offenders as well as other types of special needs offenders.

Work and Study Release Programs

The concept for **work release** or **furlough** (and subsequently **study release**) was first authored by Wisconsin state senator Henry Huber in 1913. It later became the Huber Law.[128] These programs were first used extensively in the

global positioning system (GPS)
A satellite-based system that can calculate users' exact locations, direction, and speed. Many states use GPS systems to monitor sex offenders while they are on parole.

work and study release (furlough)
Partial release of inmates to work or study in the community and return to a correctional facility each night.

1950s. In these programs, selected inmates work for pay in the community and return to a correctional facility each night. Originally, work release participants were low-risk offenders (those convicted of a misdemeanor), but they now also include felons and youthful offenders. Variations of work release include weekend sentences, extended work release, and release for vocational or educational (*study release*) programs. Allowing inmates to work or study outside prison helps them establish and maintain links to the community.[129]

Many of these programs are situated in halfway houses.[130] Others are located in specially built, small minimum-security facilities located in and around towns or in more restrictive facilities such as jails or prisons, from which offenders are permitted to leave only to work, study, or perform community service (more common with jail sentences).

Access to work release programs has decreased since 1994 because of political pressure to keep offenders out of the community. The public has often opposed halfway house programs as well, even for low-risk jail inmates. In 2000, residents in Orange County, California, became outraged at the approved opening of a work furlough program in their neighborhood.[131] Slightly over 2 months later the Orange County Board of Supervisors killed the proposal.[132] In 2006, residents in the mid-Mississippi valley forcefully opposed a plan for a halfway house for work release prisoners in their neighborhood.[133] These public fears seem counterproductive, because studies show that these programs are effective and that few offenders commit crimes while working.[134]

Washington State has maintained its commitment to its work release program since its inception in 1967. Only 5 percent of the inmates on work release committed new crimes while working in the community, and 99 percent of those crimes were less serious property offenses, such as forgery or theft.[135] Other studies show positive but somewhat more tentative results.[136] In support of work release programs nationwide, in 2014 the U.S. Department of Labor announced it was launching a $30 million program to fund 15 grants for nongovernmental organizations in key population areas of the United States.[137]

OTHER TYPES OF COMMUNITY CORRECTIONS

Just as there is a movement to privatize prisons (see Chapter 11), there also is a movement to privatize community corrections. Drug testing and treatment, electronic monitoring, and halfway houses are all activities in which private sector firms may take the place of government agencies.

At least 15 states have some form of private probation services. They justify the practice by its cost-effectiveness. Connecticut and Colorado privatized much of their community supervision of low-risk offenders in order to focus on higher-risk offenders in the community, thereby increasing public safety as they see it. Delaware contracts with a private group to supervise individuals awaiting trial. Florida, Mississippi, Missouri, Montana, New Mexico, North Dakota, Ohio, Oklahoma, Tennessee, Utah, Wisconsin, and Wyoming use private agencies to supervise a subset of their offenders who are on probation.[138] However, this practice has engendered some controversy. A class action lawsuit was filed in Tennessee, for example, alleging that a private probation company was "bilking and extorting" money from probationers who had to pay for its supervision services. The firm is also accused of tripling the terms of individuals' probation and charging higher fees for other services that courts or local counties normally provide at a low cost. This company operates in about 45 states.[139]

Real Careers

MALISSA MINARD

Work location: Cincinnati, Ohio

College(s): University of Cincinnati (2004); Northern Kentucky University (2007)

Major(s): Criminal Justice (BS) with a minor in Addictions; Public Administration (MA)

Job title: Probation Officer II, Hamilton County

Salary range for job like this: $30,000–$40,000

Time in job: 5 years

Work Responsibilities
A typical workweek consists of monitoring cases and clients by taking victim impact statements, interviewing arresting officers, and making service referrals to outside agencies. My findings must be well documented in reports, which are then shared with attorneys and judges and reviewed to determine sentencing for the offender.

Why Criminal Justice?
Working as a probation officer allows me to combine my interest in law enforcement with my desire to help people. I knew this was the field that I wanted to enter after taking an internship with federal probation during my senior year of college and working full-time during college at the Talbert House in the Pathways and Adapt program for female offenders. At the Talbert House, I began as an activity security monitor, tracking the behavior and movement of clients, including home and employment verifications. After about a year, I was promoted to case manager. In my new role, I completed assessments and intake evaluations and provided information for probation and parole officers.

Eventually I would like to advance to federal probation officer and finally federal chief, which will give me the opportunity to manage other probation officers. My 5 years as a probation officer will help qualify me for such promotions.

Expectations and Realities of the Job
Because I was exposed to the work of a probation officer during my internship and prior work experience, I understood the daily tasks and pressures of the job and knew what pay and benefits to expect. The only aspect of the job that I did not fully understand as an intern was the significance of a probation officer's work. I am responsible for helping offenders regain their livelihood through counseling, rehabilitation programs, and mentoring. My supervisors have emphasized the importance of always being fair, courteous, and professional with offenders.

My Advice to Students
Get all the experience possible while still in school. Most agencies actively seek out student interns. Working in the field during my studies helped me make a seamless transition from school to work. Not only did I know what to anticipate as a working probation officer, but I was already used to the working lifestyle. Finally, practical work experience is required for most entry-level positions in the criminal justice field.

The majority of community supervision agencies and releasing authorities make use of risk and needs assessment tools to ensure the public is not at risk and that defendants and offenders receive the kind of programs and plans that maximize the probability of leading law-abiding lives.[140] In this approach, risk assessment tools evaluate data and assign a score to an offender that reflects the likelihood that the offender will reoffend after release. Administration and routine readministration of validated risk and needs assessment tools to defendants and offenders is essential for public safety and providing community programs that best assist offenders.[141] The U.S. Parole Commission's salient factor score (SFS) is a statistical measure dependent on such factors as age of the offender, addiction history, history of violence, and conduct in prison. Figure 13-5 provides an example of a risk assessment scoring form. A score of 0 reflects a very good risk on parole or probation, and a score of 4 a poor risk.

DPP - SUP - 10 (Revised 10-92)

STATE OF MARYLAND
DEPARTMENT OF PUBLIC SAFETY AND CORRECTIONAL SERVICES
DIVISION OF PAROLE AND PROBATION

P&P NO. [ ][ ][ ][ ][ ][ ]

OFFENDER'S NAME _____
LAST NAME   FIRST NAME

OTHER NO. _____

RISK ASSESSMENT

1. PRIORITY CASES (check all that apply. DDMP do not score): [ ] 1. [ ]
   • Parole or Mandatory Supervision Case _____ [ ]
   • Child Abuse related offense _____ [ ]
   • Sex related offense _____ [ ]
   • Other _____ [ ]
   a. One or more checks _____ Enter 15
   b. None of the above _____ Enter 0

2. TOTAL LIFETIME FELONY CONVICTIONS:
   (including juvenile and current offense) 2. [ ]
   a. Two or more _____ Enter 4
   b. One _____ Enter 2
   c. None _____ Enter 0

3. CONVICTION OR JUVENILE ADJUDICATION FOR (include
   current offense, add all categories and enter total): 3. [ ]
   a. Domestic Violence related offense
      (current offense only) _____ Add 6
   b. 643B or felony drug or sex offense within
      last 5 years _____ Add 6
   c. 643B or felony drug or sex offense more
      than 5 years ago _____ Add 4
   d. Other assaultive offenses _____ Add 4
   e. Fraud, forgery, deceptive practices _____ Add 2
   f. Theft, auto theft, B&E _____ Add 1
   g. None of the above _____ Enter 0

4. TOTAL DWI/DUI CONVICTIONS (DWI/DUI cases only):
   a. Two or more _____ Enter 4 4. [ ]
   b. One _____ Enter 2
   c. None _____ Enter 0

5. BAL (Blood Alcohol Level) AT TIME OF ARREST
   (DWI/DUI cases only): 5. [ ]
   a. Refused/unknown _____ Enter 3
   b. 14 and above _____ Enter 3
   c. 10 to 13 _____ Enter 2
   d. 09 and below _____ Enter 1
   e. Not Applicable _____ Enter 0

6. AGE AT FIRST CONVICTION OR JUVENILE ADJUDICATION:
   a. 19 or younger _____ Enter 4 6. [ ]
   b. 20 to 25 _____ Enter 2
   c. 27 or older _____ Enter 0

SEX OFFENDER: y [ ] yes   n [ ] no

7. NUMBER OF PRIOR SUPERVISION PERIODS (Parole/
   Mandatory Supervision/Probation/Monitor/Juvenile): 7. [ ]
   a. Two or more _____ Enter 4
   b. One _____ Enter 2
   c. None _____ Enter 0

8. NUMBER OF SUPERVISION PERIODS RESULTING IN
   UNSATISFACTORY CLOSINGS (Parole/Mandatory 8. [ ]
   Supervision/Probation/Monitor)
   a. Two or more _____ Enter 4
   b. One _____ Enter 2
   c. None _____ Enter 0

9. IMPACT OF DRUG USE ON BEHAVIOR:
   a. High _____ Enter 4 9. [ ]
   b. Low _____ Enter 2
   c. None _____ Enter 0

10. IMPACT OF ALCOHOL USE ON BEHAVIOR:
    a. High _____ Enter 4 10. [ ]
    b. Low _____ Enter 2
    c. None _____ Enter 0

11. EMPLOYMENT HISTORY FOR PAST 12 MONTHS (Prior to
    incarceration, if applicable): 11. [ ]
    a. Unemployed and virtually unemployable _____ Enter 2
    b. Part-time, seasonal, unstable employment or
       underemployed _____ Enter 1
    c. Full-time employment, no difficulties reported;
       homemaker; full-time student; retired;
       or disabled and unable to work _____ Enter 0

12. IMPRESSION OF OFFENDER RISK:
    a. High _____ Enter 5 12. [ ]
    b. Average _____ Enter 3
    c. Low _____ Enter 0

[ ] Total Score

DOMESTIC VIOLENCE OFFENDER: y [ ] yes   n [ ] no

Instructions: Check appropriate block   **SCORING AND OVERRIDE**

SCORE BASED CLASSIFICATION: CRIMINAL [ ]   INTENSIVE [ ]   STANDARD [ ]   ADMINISTRATIVE [ ]
                              DDMP [ ]   WEEKLY [ ]   BIWEEKLY [ ]   MONTHLY [ ]

CHECK HERE IF THERE IS AN OVERRIDE [ ]   OVERRIDE EXPLANATION IF NEEDED: _____

FINAL CATEGORY OF CLASSIFICATION: CRIMINAL [ ]   INTENSIVE [ ]   STANDARD [ ]   ADMINISTRATIVE [ ]
                                    DDMP [ ]   WEEKLY [ ]   BIWEEKLY [ ]   MONTHLY [ ]

DATE ASSIGNED
[ ]

APPROVED _____ DATE

AGENT/MONITOR   LAST NAME   FIRST INITIAL   DATE

CHANGE AGENT/MONITOR ASSIGNMENT TO   LAST NAME   FIRST INITIAL

OPERATOR'S INITIALS: _____   DATE: _____

FIGURE 13-5 **Maryland's Risk Assessment Scoring Form**

Risk analysis also assists in determining the kind of supervision that probationers and parolees will need on the street. Potentially violent offenders are of particular concern. When correctional workers are able to identify those likely to reoffend, they can dedicate scarce resources to treatment that specifically meets the needs of these offenders and ultimately protects the community. Ohio and California are examples of states that also have tools to calculate parole risk. In 2008 California began using a computer-based parole violation sentencing tool called the parole violation decision-making instrument (PVDMI).[142]

A major problem with risk-based assessment is that it is impossible to make accurate predictions all the time. Typically the assessment instruments overestimate the odds of reoffending, a result that may protect society but also punishes some offenders for future crimes they are not likely to commit.[143]

SUMMARY

Community corrections allows offenders to spend all or part of their sentence in the community through a wide range of programs and practices, including probation, parole, work and study release, community service, house arrest, registers and tracking, electronic monitoring, and vocational, educational, and drug treatment programs. Individuals who are allowed to take part in community corrections are generally nonviolent offenders or offenders judged to be low risk.

The advantages of community corrections are that offenders can maintain ties to family and the community while serving their sentence and not become socialized to an institution. By reducing the prison and jail populations, community corrections saves costs for local, state, and federal governments. But public opinion resists the idea of releasing offenders, especially sex offenders, into the community—and politicians often follow the lead of public opinion in the legislation they write concerning corrections. Despite the lower recidivism rates achieved in community corrections, and today's push for "justice reinvestment" or reallocation of institutional savings to community-based treatment and other services it appears likely that incarceration will continue to be the sentence of choice.

OBSERVE → INVESTIGATE → UNDERSTAND

Review

Identify the distinctive features of probation.

- In probation, the offender is sentenced by a judge and conditionally released into the community under court supervision to serve a sentence.
- A probation officer supervises the offender in the community.
- Probation is a privilege, not a right.
- Probation is the most frequently used form of correctional supervision in the United States.
- Whites get probation more often than do Blacks and Latinos combined.

Contrast intensive and traditional supervision probation.

- Intensive-supervision probation (ISP) programs are characterized by smaller officer caseloads, closer surveillance, and more contact between probation officer and offender than traditional probation.
- ISP programs were designed primarily to target high-risk offenders who would otherwise be prison-bound; traditional probation applies mainly to low-risk offenders.

Evaluate the success of probation.

- Probation is less expensive than incarceration.
- Success in probation is difficult to assess because recidivism is all that is usually measured, and revocation can vary enormously by jurisdiction and location.
- About half of those on probation completed their term satisfactorily.

Identify the distinctive features of parole.

- Parole is an administrative procedure that allows inmates to serve their remaining sentence in the community conditionally under the supervision of a parole officer.

- Social reintegration is the objective of parole.
- Revocation of parole is possible if an offender violates the terms of parole or reoffends.

Evaluate the success of parole.

- Parole is less expensive than incarceration.
- Parole rewards inmates who follow prison rules and behave positively while incarcerated.
- Parole provides inmates who no longer need imprisonment with supervision and appropriate programs in the community.

Describe the role of intermediate sanctions.

- Intermediate sanctions are judicial punishments that do not require long terms of incarceration but stop short of allowing offenders to remain in the community on probation with minimal supervision.
- Intermediate sanctions are not quite prison and not quite traditional probation; they encourage offenders to take responsibility for their actions but under closer supervision than traditional probation.
- Some intermediate sanctions require offenders to live in a communal residence.

Identify various types of intermediate sanctions.

- Community service is a practice whereby offenders are sentenced to activities that provide a benefit to the public.
- House arrest is a practice that requires offenders not to leave their residence.

- Electronic monitoring is a way to monitor offenders' whereabouts by using technology.
- Community centers offer halfway house residential and treatment options.
- Work and study release programs allow inmates to leave a correctional facility during the day to work or go to school in the community.

Describe private sector and risk-based community corrections.

- Private sector firms, instead of public agencies, run some community corrections programs, such as halfway houses and drug treatment.
- Some community corrections programs make use of risk assessment of offenders to determine who can participate and what treatment is appropriate.

Key Terms

community corrections 406

community service 422

day fines 425

discretionary release 417

diversion 422

electronic monitoring 427

fines 425

forfeiture 426

global positioning system (GPS) 431

house arrest (home confinement) 426

intensive-supervision probation (ISP) 409

intermediate sanctions 421

mandatory release 417

parole 415

parole board 416

probation 407

probation kiosk 429

recognizance 408

restitution 424

restorative justice 423

shock probation 427

shock program 427

unconditional release 420

victim–offender mediation 426

work and study release (furlough) 431

Study Questions

1. The term *community corrections* refers to
   a. probation.
   b. supervision in communities.
   c. parole.
   d. all of the above

2. Probation and parole are similar in that
   a. a judge sentences an offender to both probation and parole.
   b. a parole board grants probation and parole.
   c. both probation and parole officers supervise offenders in the community.
   d. both probationers and parolees have to deal with the label "ex-con."

3. Of the following sanctions, the one that is *not* considered an intermediate community corrections sanction is
   a. jail.
   b. shock probation.
   c. house arrest.
   d. restitution.

4. Which of the following is/are considered a technical parole violation?
   a. leaving the state without parole agent permission
   b. moving into a new residence without parole agent permission
   c. failing a drug test
   d. all of the above

5. _____ refers to the use of technology to enforce house arrest or to monitor the location of the offender.
   a. Technocorrections
   b. Entrapment
   c. Cybervision
   d. Norplant implant

6. Which statement is not true?
   a. Probation is a right that must be granted for certain crimes.
   b. Probation is a privilege.
   c. Probation officers do not make the ultimate decision as to who gets probation.
   d. Probation officers make recommendations as to who should get probation.

7. The term *recognizance* means
   a. recognition of the authority of the court.
   b. recognition of an inmate's rights.
   c. release of a prisoner on his word.
   d. the search for the truth in a hearing.

8. The term *diversion* means
   a. diverting a criminal away from crime.
   b. diverting an offender from jail before or during trial as an intermediate sanction.
   c. distracting an offender so she can adjust to incarceration.
   d. changing the method of treatment to improve the offender's behavior.

9. ISP stands for
   a. international subjective profiles.
   b. immediate suicidal precautions.
   c. inmate's substantial progress.
   d. intensive-supervision probation.

10. The decision to revoke an offender's probation is made by a
    a. probation officer.
    b. review board.
    c. judge.
    d. probation officer and a judge.

Critical Thinking Questions

For further review, go to the LearnSmart study module for this chapter.

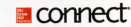

1. What are the similarities and differences between probation and parole?

2. What are some pro and con arguments for the use of intermediate sanctions as alternatives to incarceration? Which arguments do you find more compelling?

3. Is victim–offender mediation really a type of punishment for the offender? Why or why not?

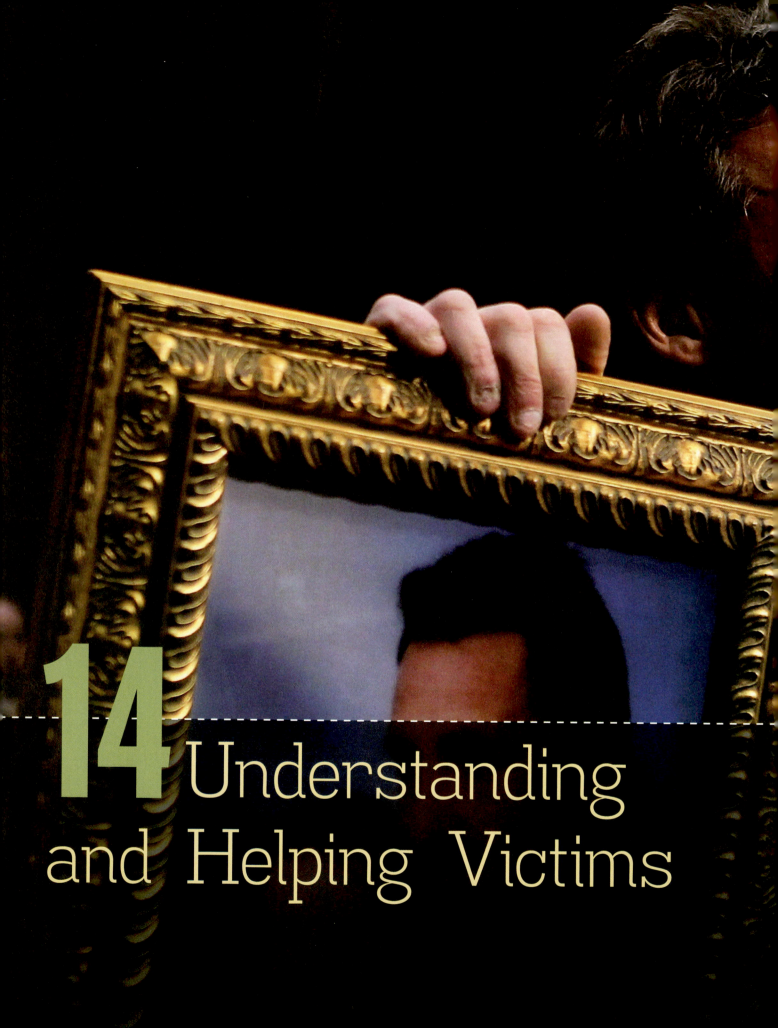

14 Understanding and Helping Victims

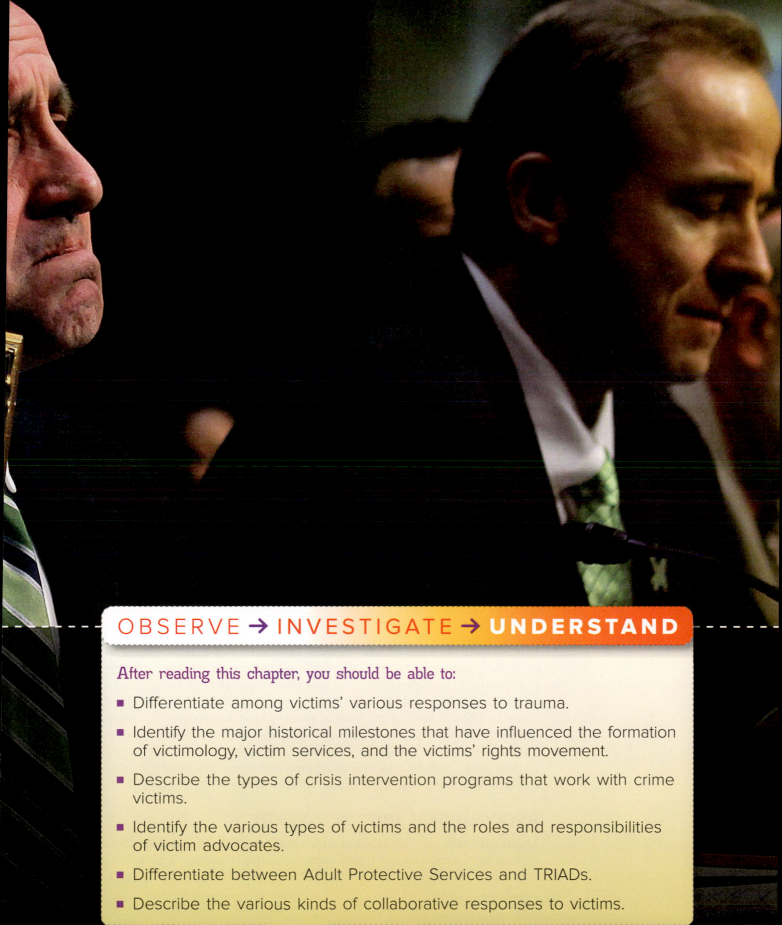

After reading this chapter, you should be able to:

- Differentiate among victims' various responses to trauma.

- Identify the major historical milestones that have influenced the formation of victimology, victim services, and the victims' rights movement.

- Describe the types of crisis intervention programs that work with crime victims.

- Identify the various types of victims and the roles and responsibilities of victim advocates.

- Differentiate between Adult Protective Services and TRIADs.

- Describe the various kinds of collaborative responses to victims.

Realities and Challenges

From the Victims' Perspectives

It was 10 a.m. on Monday, April 4. Three men entered the Garden State Bank in a small, peaceful upstate New Jersey town. The first man in yanked a mask over his face and pointed a big black pistol at Susan Thoresen, a teller with 2 years' experience. Susan's stomach immediately turned to jelly. The two other robbers also put on masks and pulled out pistols. One went to the door to stop customers from leaving. The other jumped on the counter and yelled, "Everyone get on the floor or I'll start killing people!" Susan smelled urine and noticed a puddle at the feet of one of her colleagues.

The robbers ordered Susan and the other tellers to fill large backpacks with all the money in their drawers. At first Susan was paralyzed; then she began to move as if in a dream. Shock kept everyone in the bank speechless and motionless. In less than a minute the robbers were gone. There was complete silence until a customer timidly went up to the guard and whispered, "You should call the police."

Five long minutes later, many police officers arrived with weapons drawn. The sight of more guns stopped Susan's breathing; she tried to speak but could not, and then she started to cry. Two coworkers comforted her, but she couldn't stop. The bank's vice president seemed elated that no one was hurt, in fact, she was laughing nervously, and then told everyone, "Take the rest of the morning off. We'll close the bank until 1 p.m.; come back after lunch." Susan finally regained some composure, and then she called her husband at his job. As she told him the story of what had happened, she then became fearful again and thought she would faint.

In the following week, the bank tellers all had different experiences: flashbacks, anxiety, insomnia, stomach pains, and the strong urge to tell their stories of the robbery over and over again. They experienced a variety of symptoms into the second week: headaches, lack of sleep, fear the robbers would return, and, for some, feelings of panic when they came to work each morning. These reactions lasted well beyond those first few weeks. Then came the police investigators, hours of questioning, and being forced to remember their ordeal; each time the fear came flooding back. Some of the police were kind, but others were annoyed that no one had sounded the alarm to give them a chance to catch the robbers. The bank president was relieved the stolen money was insured, and that consequently none of the bank's customers would lose their savings. Officially, the bank returned to "business as usual," but that was just on the surface.

Susan Thoresen felt it was strange that everyone focused on the bank's money and the robbers, but not on the tellers. Over the next 6 months, two tellers resigned, one started seeing a psychiatrist, and one began secretly carrying a gun in her purse. In fact, everyone in the bank during the robbery was a victim. That not any of the investigators nor the bank supervisors seemed to recognize the impact of this victimization clearly prolonged their suffering and delayed their recovery. The victims felt that their story also needed to be told. Ultimately, Susan and three other valuable employees resigned from the bank, and those who remained continued to experience a range of symptoms that affected both their job performance and their private lives. (The above case is a hypothetical illustration of typical bank robbery victims' experiences.)

This chapter focuses on the victims of crime. We identify their numbers; examine political, social, and intervention trends over the past 40 years; characterize the main types of victims; and probe how victims are affected by their victimization. We look at how society responds to all the different types of crime victims, as well as the special services that are available to ease victims' suffering, facilitate their recovery, and prepare them for their role in the criminal justice process. Finally, we consider how these services are supported by a wide range of laws, policies, programs, and research—the result of which is a greatly improved status for crime victims in the United States.

RECOGNIZING VICTIMIZATION

About 40 years ago the U.S. government started collecting data about crime victims on a regular basis (see Chapter 2). Official statistics show that property victimization has been steadily declining over the past 20 years. So has the number of victims of crimes against persons, with an especially dramatic drop in the last 10 years. Despite these declines, however, tens of millions of people become crime victims every year. According to the National Crime Victimization Survey (Figure 14-1), in 2013 there were 11.5 million property crime victimizations and 3 million violent crime victimizations.

The experience of being victimized takes most people completely by surprise, especially if it has never happened to them before. The fear of dying, of seeing others die, or of being seriously injured is often accompanied by terror. Under these circumstances, **psychic trauma,** which results from severe emotional stress, immobilizes the victim's mind and body and can result in long-lasting emotional injury.

Each person responds differently to stress. Even though all the tellers in the New Jersey bank in the chapter opener were witnesses to the same event, each one brought to work that day a different history with personal stress and crisis, and different coping strengths and weaknesses. Such differences result in a variety of responses. Resilient people might show no effects and cope well. Other individuals might show mild effects and recover within a few minutes or hours, while others may present extreme effects and take days, weeks, or months to heal (and some may never heal completely). In the aftermath of a crime, observers of victims are generally not familiar with the dynamics of psychic trauma and can easily misinterpret what they see and not understand the way victims cope. The president of that New Jersey bank might have assumed those who appeared calm were not in crisis. Other observers and the police could also easily dismiss the victims' plight and shift their focus to the search for offenders and the lost money.

The New Jersey bank robbery demonstrates that society is slow to recognize who victims are, how they become victimized, how much they suffer, and how important it is to provide them with psychological and social support. The reality is that all victims suffer to some degree, whether they have experienced a crime, a traffic accident, a natural disaster, or a war. Many need some level of help or intervention to recover. As a society, we have lately come to understand the magnitude and the character of victimization. We now have the added tools of victimization surveys and empirical research to provide us with a more accurate and complete picture.

This chapter describes who victims are, why society needs to be concerned about them, how victimologists have tried to explain victim behavior, how society influences victim services, and what methods and services are needed if we are to make victims whole again. One way to understand the impact on victims is to read their own words on the aftermath of their victimizations (see "What about the Victim?" on page 442).

psychic trauma
Severe emotional stress that immobilizes the victim's mind and body and can result in long-lasting emotional injury.

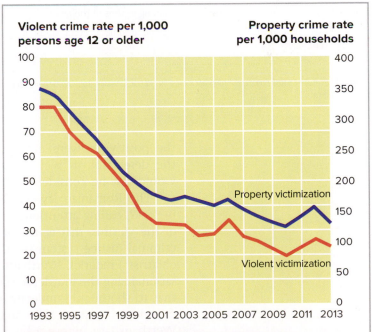

FIGURE 14-1 **Violent and Property Victimization, 1993–2013**

SOURCE: Jennifer L. Truman and Lynn Langton, "Criminal Victimization, 2013," *Bureau of Justice Statistics Bulletin* (Washington, DC: U.S. Department of Justice, September 2014). www.bjs.gov/content/pub/pdf/cv13.pdf.

What about the Victim?

The Words of Crime Victims are Often Timeless Truths

The following statements were taken from real victims soon after their victimization:

- "He said, 'Move or yell and I'll kill you.' I didn't doubt his word."
- "I didn't hear anything about the case for almost a year. Then all of a sudden they called me up at work and said, 'Come down to court right away. The trial is going to take place.'"
- "It is almost impossible to walk into a courtroom and describe in detail the thing you most want to forget. It is also devastating to have to face your assailant. Although you are surrounded by people and deputies of the court, the fear is still overwhelming."
- "Why didn't anyone consult me? I was the one who was kidnapped, not the Commonwealth of Virginia."
- "I'm a senior citizen, but I never considered myself old. I was active, independent. Now I live in a nursing home and sit in a wheelchair. The day I was mugged was the day I began to die."
- "What others see as an inconvenience is for the victim an endless nightmare."
- "I will never forget being raped, kidnapped, and robbed at gunpoint. However, my sense of disillusionment of the judicial system is many times more painful. I could not in good faith urge anyone to participate in this hellish process."

OBSERVE → INVESTIGATE → UNDERSTAND

- Why are there fewer thefts reported to the police than assaults?
- Why is the incidence of injury very low among victims of robbery?
- Why do people who experience the same traumatic event suffer in different ways?

SOURCE: *President's Task Force on Victims of Crime: Final Report* (Washington, DC: Government Printing Office, 1982).

THE ORIGINS OF VICTIM ADVOCACY

In preliterate societies, one of the main goals of law was to make the victim whole again. Most early cultures involved victims when searching for solutions to the conflicts that followed crimes, conflict resolution procedures, thus giving victims a dominant role in righting the wrongs committed against them. Later, in more formal societies, laws required equity to be restored between offender and victim, as in the Code of Ur-Nammu in ancient Sumeria and the Code of Hammurabi of ancient Babylon.[1] Equity meant that whatever was taken from the victim must also be equally taken from the offender, a principle enshrined in a famous phrase in Hammurabi's Code, "an eye for an eye and a tooth for a tooth," and which also appears in the Judeo-Christian Bible.

This victim-centered approach reached its height in Europe during the Early Middle Ages (ca. 400–1000 CE), a period sometimes called the *golden age of the victim*.[2] In this era, crime victims were at the center of the justice process; they participated in responding to the crime and in determining the offender's punishment. A thousand years later, however, with the advent of the Industrial Revolution in the nineteenth century, societies rejected traditional models of community governance. Nations became more centralized, and government functions focused more on efficiency and specialization, and, significantly, justice systems replaced the older focus on the victim with an emphasis on the witness. As legal systems evolved in these years, the writings of the so-called classical criminologists, and later the positivists, were mostly concerned with criminal law and its severity for the defendant, as well as with the nature of criminal behavior. The victims would not be considered important again until the twentieth century.

The Romanian lawyer Beniamin Mendelsohn coined the word *victimology* in 1947, calling attention to the need to understand crime from the experience of the victims, that is, to comprehend how people are victimized and how the criminal justice system treats them. The next year, in 1948, a well-known psychiatrist Frederick Wertham echoed this perspective by observing that in sensationalizing the murderer, society had forgotten the victim. Wertham concluded that to thoroughly understand the murderer, it was essential to also understand the victim, and he thus argued that "a science of victimology was needed."[3] Wertham later wrote a book, *A Sign for Cain*, in which he presented what he saw as the negative impulses that exist in society; its title was a metaphor for the evildoer.[4] How interesting it is that he would use the sign of Cain as a metaphor in his book and yet not recognize how the victim in that biblical story was ignored. One can only speculate how history would have been altered for victims had the opposite metaphor been created—the sign of Abel.

The Sign of Abel

In the Judeo-Christian Bible, the fourth chapter of the Book of Genesis tells how Cain murdered his younger brother Abel. Thus in Judeo-Christian tradition, Cain is the first murderer. Today, the expression "the sign of Cain" refers to the stigmatization of someone as an evildoer, and we can view the label as a metaphor for the way some societies find the image of the offender more interesting than the image of the victim. Abel, as the Bible's first victim, was not so immortalized. Other religious traditions have had similar accounts of early victimizations, which have mostly downplayed the role of the victim and emphasized the offender. Although societies have professed a desire to reject murderers for their violence and to help victims by taking care of their needs, often the cultural and legal support systems have done the opposite.[5]

One of the most significant outcomes of World War II was the shock and revulsion that people felt on learning about the Holocaust, Nazi Germany's murder of just more than 6 million people, mostly Jews. This horrific event helped to refocus people's attention on the victims.

▲ **Cain Killing Abel**

Islam, Christianity, and Judaism all tell the story of Cain, the son of Adam and Eve, killing his brother Abel. Cain is considered the first murderer and Abel the first victim. *Explain the irony of how and why these two people have been remembered throughout history. How does Abel symbolically reflect the image of victims today in the struggle to have equal status with offenders?*

Social Forces Leading to the Victims' Rights Movement

Influential social movements arose in the 1960s and 1970s that demanded civil rights for various ethnic minority groups, women's rights, children's rights, gay rights, law and order, and the end of the Vietnam War. These movements popularized nonviolent protest, protection of the disadvantaged, equality of opportunity, and the right to be free of pain and suffering and to be treated with respect and dignity. Thus they paved the way for the victims' rights movement, victim assistance, and victim advocacy.

The idea of victim assistance is relatively new, emerging only during the mid-1970s. Initially, victim assistance was provided largely by people who had themselves been victimized, as specific treatments for crime victims had not yet been developed. Victims were often stigmatized as having somehow been partially to blame for their misfortunes, and so assisting and comforting them was left mainly to the volunteer efforts of other victims who could understand their feelings and help them recover through peer support groups. This tradition continues today in many victim assistance and victim advocacy programs across the United States.

Research on the benefits of peer support groups has been sparse. A recent study examining victims of crime and traffic accidents has suggested, however, that sharing or having contact with other victims may not be helpful as a treatment method—and may actually be harmful. This research suggests that recovery is more likely when guided by a therapist skilled in the use of evidence-based supportive interventions.[6] Another common victim treatment method is psychological debriefing, originally proposed to help those who had been traumatized in emergency situations (natural disasters, for example) to either avoid posttraumatic stress or recover from it.[7] We do not yet have enough studies to know whether such treatment is effective. Although this form of victim treatment continues to be used, especially for mass victimizations, the support for its use has not been completely demonstrated.

Other significant influences that contributed to the rise of the new discipline of victimology were the first victimization surveys conducted in 1966 for the President's Commission on Law Enforcement and the Administration of Justice (see Chapter 2). By revealing the **dark figure of crime** (victims who did not report their victimization to the police), these surveys made clear the full range of victim types and the large number of victims (at least twice as many as the Uniform Crime Reports showed). The results of these surveys demonstrated the need for further study of both victims who reported and

dark figure of crime
The number of victims who did not officially report their victimizations to the police.

▲ **Demonstrating for Women's Rights**

Women's rights activism paved the way for the victims' rights movement.

victims who did not report, and for the expansion of services for all of them.[8]

A rising level of crime from the mid-1960s until the early 1980s spurred concerned citizens to demand a national response. This crime wave was in large part attributed to massive numbers of post–World War II "baby boomers" reaching their mid-teen years. It is at this stage of life that most young people begin to pull away from parental controls; experiment with relationships, new identities, and role models; and test the limits of acceptable behavior. Consequently, many boomers got into trouble with the law. To cope with this crime surge, the Omnibus Crime Control and Safe Streets Act of 1968 created a federal agency called the Law Enforcement Assistance Administration (LEAA). This major national effort against crime poured vast amounts of federal funds into the fight against delinquency and crime, and ultimately also into research and programs for victims.[9]

In the early 1970s the women's movement catalyzed the establishment of the first three rape crisis centers, including California's Bay Area Women Against Rape, Seattle Rape Relief, and Washington, DC–based DC Rape Crisis Center. Feminist activist Susan Brownmiller's influential book on the history of rape added credibility to the victims' rights movement in general and to efforts to combat violence against women in particular.[10] By the end of the 1970s, most large cities and many smaller ones had rape crisis centers, staffed mostly by feminists who lobbied on behalf of sexual assault victims and provided them with legal information, counseling, and training in defensive tactics. Eventually, these workers began to counsel battered women as well.

In his 1975 book *The Victims*, Frank Carrington argued that courts were too permissive and that excessive concerns about prisoners' rights, as well as a general weakening of law enforcement, were largely responsible for the 1960s crime surge. Carrington insisted that supporting victims was more important than protecting the rights of the accused.[11] Several influential victim-oriented groups arose during the 1970s, including the National Organization for Victim Assistance (NOVA) in 1976, Parents of Murdered Children in 1978, and Mothers Against Drunk Driving (MADD) in 1980.[12] Together, concern for victims and the widely shared public sentiment that the criminal justice system had grown too permissive brought pressure on the criminal justice system to get tough on crime–for example, by lengthening sentences and otherwise imposing harsher punishments on offenders. In response to this pressure, many state legislatures passed minimum sentencing laws. The President's Task Force on Victims of Crime of 1982 focused national attention on the plight of crime victims; and the Attorney General's Task Force on Violent Crime launched a campaign to toughen penalties and to induce prosecutors to focus more on victims and their rights.[13]

Today LEAA no longer exists. In its place are national sources of federal money, such as the 1984 Victims of Crime Act (VOCA). Under this law, fines collected from convicted federal criminals are redistributed to provide for victim compensation and victim assistance programs throughout the United States.[14]

In 1994 Congress passed the original Violence Against Women Act (VAWA). Its primary objective was to support the investigation and prosecution of violent crimes against women, but it also contained provisions designed to offer women better protection from those who had offended against them, especially in the period after the offender's arrest.[15]

Advocates for victims point out that although defendants are protected by the Bill of Rights and by major Supreme Court decisions, nowhere does the Constitution address the rights of victims. In the late twentieth century, repeated attempts were made to enact the so-called Victims' Rights Amendment. In 2004, however, these efforts collapsed amid Congress's concerns that such an amendment would undermine law enforcement and clash with long-established criminal defendants' rights.

To replace this proposed amendment, in October 2004 Congress enacted and President George W. Bush signed into law the Crime Victims' Rights Act. This legislation declares that the victims of those who break federal laws will be "reasonably protected" against the accused, including being promptly notified if the alleged perpetrator escapes or is released from custody. The act also provides for the fair, dignified, respectful, and prompt treatment of victims by federal prosecutors, and the right to "full and timely restitution as provided by law."

Today, a decade later, a vast array of service programs have emerged to produce a broad range of programs for victims, with a large group of committed professionals who work as victim advocates, victims' rights activists, and victimologists. International, federal, and state rights have been greatly enlarged to ensure that a wider variety of victims are treated with dignity, fairness, and care. Public policies attend to victims' suffering, needs, and recovery, and innovative strategies are aimed at preventing victimization.

In January 2005, Ted Poe, Republican congressman from Texas, Jim Costa, Democratic congressman from California, and Katherine Harris, former Republican congresswoman from Florida, created the Congressional Victims' Rights Caucus (VRC) to advocate for all victims of crime in Congress. Its main objective was to protect the victims' funds, specifically the Victims of Crime Act (VOCA) and the Violence Against Women Act (VAWA). Over the following decade, some examples of key victim-focused legislative reforms have included the Adam Walsh Child Protection and Safety Act of 2006 (for missing children); the Cruise Vessel Safety and Security Act (to protect passengers on cruise ships); the Victims of Child Abuse Act Reauthorization of 2013; and the Justice for Victims of Trafficking Act of 2014.[16]

WORKING WITH VICTIMS

U.S. culture abounds with distorted images of reality. Crime stories typically lavish attention on offenders, police, and lawyers but rarely spend much time on the victims, their suffering, or the services they vitally need to recover. Even the television show *Law & Order: Special Victims Unit* is largely about police investigators and the laboratory skills they use to identify offenders and not about victims. Moreover, the media dwell on victimizations that are relatively rare—murder and forcible rape—while giving much less play to the victimizations that occur the most frequently—theft and burglary.

When we think of crime victims, most of us imagine people who are targets of street crimes, to which the media devote most attention. Victims of Uniform Crime Reports Part II offenses—such as fraud, vandalism, drug abuse violations, drunkenness, and vagrancy—generally suffer less and get less attention. Importantly, however, the victims of *all* crimes are affected to some degree, depending on the nature of the force used against them; their economic loss; the social, psychic, and physical resources available to them; and the setting in which the victimization takes place.

The **primary victim** is the person injured or killed as a direct result of a criminal act. A **secondary victim** is an individual who is affected by the primary

primary victim
A person injured or killed as a direct result of a criminal act.

secondary victim
An individual who experiences sympathetic pain as a result of a primary victim's suffering.

secondary victimization
A negative situation that results from the insensitivity and abuse of the primary victim by family, friends, medical personnel, police, prosecutors, and judges; manifested in the process of trying to help the victim and in identifying, prosecuting, punishing, and treating the offender.

survivor
A relative or loved one of a person who has been killed; also, a crime victim who copes well and manages to resume a normal life.

crime victimization
Injuring or killing a human being through behavior that is prohibited by law; the term focuses on the victim rather than on the offender or the criminal event.

victim recidivism
Victimization of a person, household, or business more than once; also called repeat victimization.

victim services
Dedicated activities conducted to help reduce victims' suffering and facilitate their recovery so that they can return to a normal life.

▼ **Victim Advocate Meeting with Volunteers**

Seema Singh, victim advocate for the state of New Jersey, meets with volunteer members of the Asian Women's Safety Net, a domestic violence task force. The 12 women of the task force support and guide women who are victims of intimate partner abuse.

victim's suffering and who experiences sympathetic pain. A man who learns that his sister has been raped, and who consequently suffers emotional distress, is a secondary victim of the attack. A closely related term, **secondary victimization,** refers to the insensitivity and abuse of the primary victim by family, friends, medical personnel, police, prosecutors, and judges, which is manifested in the process of trying to help the victim and in identifying, prosecuting, punishing, and treating the offender. Sometimes people not in the criminal justice system—medical personnel, mental health workers, social workers, clergy, and even family and friends—also are responsible for secondary victimization.

When a victim is killed, his or her close relations are called **survivors.** Victims who cope well and are able to resume a normal life also consider themselves survivors, a term that helps them reject the hopelessness of the victim label and signifies that they consider their suffering and sense of helplessness to be over.

Crime victimization means injuring or killing a human being through behavior that is prohibited by law. It focuses on the victim rather than on the offender or the criminal event. **Victim recidivism,** or *repeat victimization*, occurs when a person, household, or business is victimized more than once. For almost two decades, victim recidivism of a small number of victims has been known to account for a disproportionately large number of victimizations. This means that people who are victimized even once are at a higher risk of further victimization than those who have not been victimized.[17] One British research study reported that 4 percent of victims accounted for 44 percent of all victimizations in personal crimes.[18] For property offenses, another British study found a mere 2 percent of property crime victims experience 41 percent of all property crimes. According to this study, career burglars took advantage of information gained during successful burglaries to easily strike the same location again.[19] These findings suggest that if we could stop repeat victimization, we might prevent a large proportion of all victimizations.

In the aftermath of victimization, we expect society to help victims cope with their misfortunes. **Victim services** are dedicated activities conducted to help reduce victims' suffering and facilitate their recovery.[20]

Victim Advocates

A **victim advocate** is a person who directly provides victim services; victim advocates work in intimate partner violence programs, rape crisis centers, district attorney's offices, police departments, Child Protective Services, and Adult Protective Services. A victim advocate may also be assigned to another agency within a particular justice system—federal, judicial, military, juvenile, or tribal, for example. Victim advocates are not the only occupational group with direct contact with victims. Law enforcement, correctional officers, and medical personnel also have such direct contact with victims, but their focus is usually on the victims' immediate or specific needs rather than the long-term, wider concerns that victim advocates address.

Victim advocates assist victims with obtaining community services such as health care, housing, education, and employment and support victims in every phase of the criminal justice process to help them suffer less and achieve recovery. Advocates provide crisis intervention and accompany victims to the hospital and to court. They also support victims as they interact with staff members at social and legal agencies who may not understand or be sympathetic to the victimization.[21]

Victim advocates help victims navigate the confusing criminal justice system by explaining court procedures and ensuring victims' rights. In a 2-year study that followed victims of intimate partner violence, those who used advocacy services experienced greater safety and a better quality of life. Nearly a quarter of those who worked with an advocate experienced no further physical abuse, whereas of those who did not have an advocate, only 10 percent were free of abuse. Compared to women who did not have an advocate, those who had one obtained more of the resources they sought, showed fewer symptoms of depression, and were more effective at acquiring social services.[22]

During the 1980s and 1990s, specializations developed among advocates as they began working with specific kinds of victims: children, victims of intimate partner violence or sexual assault, elder adults and dependent adults, homicide survivors (or those who had survived the homicide of a loved one), and victims of gang violence, human trafficking, and cybercrimes (also called Internet crimes). Partly due to limited funding, few services yet exist to assist victims of cybercrimes and economic crimes, such as white-collar offenses and identity theft. One of the new challenges for victim advocates is the rise of acts of victimization being video-recorded with cell phones.

Victim Advocates and Federal Crimes   In 1988, the U.S. Office for Victims of Crime (OVC) created the Federal Crime Victim Assistance Fund to help victims of federal crimes.[23] Each year the OVC allocates funds to the U.S. Attorneys' Offices and the Federal Bureau of Investigation (FBI). Victim advocates in the federal system, known as *victim witness specialists,* work with these two federal agencies to assist victims of federal crimes exclusively. Other federal agencies, including the U.S. Postal Service, are expanding their operations to include victim advocates.

Victim witness specialists are responsible for helping victims of terrorism, counterintelligence, cybercrime, public corruption, civil rights violations, organized crime, major theft, and violent crime. Sometimes victim witness specialists work in other countries with victims of *trafficking in persons (TIP),* also called *human trafficking,* or with victims such as those slain in the *femicides—* murders of women—that are occurring in large numbers in Juarez, Mexico, and Guatemala City, Guatemala. In the border city of Juarez, a network of *maquiladoras* (factories) draws thousands of poor young girls from all over Mexico. The women lack protection from what is a largely corrupt police force. In Juarez—home to one of Mexico's largest drug cartels, as well as to approximately 1.5 million people and a transient population of about 500,000—these women face a mostly ineffective criminal justice system.[24] Over the past decade, at least 400 women reportedly have been raped, mutilated, and brutally murdered, and the fate of many others remains unknown. Due to the mishandling of credible evidence and official indifference, successful prosecution for these crimes has been a major challenge. This situation has attracted international attention, but a solution has yet to be found. Relatives and friends of the victims have suffered extensive trauma. Local victim advocates have helped many by providing not only direct services but also by coordinating lobbying efforts aimed at reforming Mexican laws to support community prevention programs.[25]

In at least three other Latin American countries—El Salvador, Guatemala, and Honduras—women are also being killed at unusually high rates. Based on a study in 2011, the highest rates are in El Salvador, where gender-motivated killings

victim advocate
A person who is a direct provider of victim services and who works in intimate partner violence programs, rape crisis centers, district attorneys' offices, police departments, Child Protective Services, and Adult Protective Services; other victim advocates can be assigned to other agencies within the criminal justice system.

Race, Class, Gender

Charleston Shooting

The Emanuel African Methodist Church in Charleston, South Carolina, was founded in 1816 and is one of the country's oldest Black churches. On the evening of June 17, 2015, a young White man joined a small prayer group at the church. He sat with the group for almost an hour before pulling out a handgun and opening fire. He shot 10 people, killing 9 of them, before fleeing the church. The following morning, 21-year-old Dylann Roof was arrested; he was soon charged with nine murders.

According to several reports, Roof admitted to the murders soon after he was in custody. But other reports emerged as well—that Roof

uttered racial slurs during the crime, that he had a history of White supremacist activity, and that he purposely chose the church because of its history in the Civil Rights movement. Although South Carolina had no hate crime law at the time of the shooting, officials almost immediately began to call the event a hate crime because it appeared to have been motivated by the victims' race.

A mass murder like this one has a devastating effect on the families of the victims. It also sparks larger controversies. In the days following the shooting, people in South Carolina and across the United States talked about the larger context of racism and whether southern states should continue to fly the Confederate flag. People also debated the racial context of the term "terrorism": who, exactly, constitutes a terrorist, and to what extent is it true that the media and others avoid the term when speaking of White offenders. Potential ties between mainstream politicians and White supremacist organizations were revealed. Because South Carolina remained one of the few states without a hate crime law, proposals were made to enact one. And, as is often the case after mass killings, the subject of stricter gun control was argued.

OBSERVE → INVESTIGATE → UNDERSTAND

- What other recent events can you think of that led to debates such as these? Do you think those debates were ultimately fruitful—that is, that they produced positive change?

- Aside from the victims and their families, who else is affected by a crime like this one? Where can members of the larger community turn to help heal some of the harm?

- When the charges were initially brought against Roof, members of the victims' families were allowed to address him. What purpose might this serve? Many of them told Roof that they forgive him. Should forgiveness play a part in the justice system?

SOURCES: Donovan X. Ramsey, "Charleston Lawmaker Will Introduce Hate Crime Legislation in Wake of Church Shooting," *Huffington Post*, June 22, 2015. www.huffingtonpost.com/2015/06/22/charleston-hate-crime_n_7637886.html (retrieved June 23, 2015); Katie Rogers, "Charleston Shooting Reignites Debate about Confederate Flag," *New York Times*, June 19, 2015. www.nytimes.com/2015/06/20/us/charleston-shooting-reignites-debate-about-confederate-flag.html?_r=0 (retrieved June 23, 2015); Jon Swaine, "Leader of Group Cited in 'Dylann Roof Manifesto' Donated to Top Republicans," *The Guardian*, June 22, 2015. www.theguardian.com/us-news/2015/jun/21/dylann-roof-manifesto-charlston-shootings-republicans (retrieved June 23, 2015); Affan Chowdhry, "Questions Surround Reluctance to Label Charleston Shooting as 'Terrorism,'" *The Globe and Mail*, June 19, 2015. www.theglobeandmail.com/news/world/charleston-shooting-renews-debate-over-labelling-incidents-as-terrorism/article25045158/ (retrieved June 23, 2015).

of women reached just over 600 in 2011. These numbers give El Salvador the dubious distinction of having the highest rate of femicide in the world. Despite efforts by women's rights activists, government officials, and progressive legislation, less than 3 percent of these cases are brought to justice.[26]

When a victim is murdered, as with the above femicides, an advocate will assist the survivors (usually family members and friends).[27] In the U.S., victim witness specialists also work with the OVC, which is responsible for monitoring federal agency compliance with the guidelines set by the U.S. attorney general for victim and witness assistance; these standards aim to ensure that federal victims and witnesses are treated fairly and that their statutory rights are met.[28]

Real Careers

LIA CHACON

Work location: Orange County, California

College(s): California State University, Fresno (2008)

Major(s): Criminology (BS)

Job title: Legal Advocate

Salary range for job like this: $28,000–$35,000

Time in job: 1.5 years

Work Responsibilities

The mission of the intimate partner violence agency where I work is to help victims regain control of their lives through effective legal action. As a legal advocate in the agency, I assume two primary roles. First, I act as a resource of knowledge by informing victims of their rights and the processes of the legal system. Second, I serve as moral support by accompanying victims to their court appearances.

The victims who come to our agency are usually referred by law enforcement, the courthouse, or social services. My first encounter with clients is always emotional: They are discouraged and in desperate need of assistance. But as clients get closer to their goals, such as finding a safe place to live, their self-confidence increases. For example, I once helped a woman gather witness testimony to prove spousal abuse and secure a restraining order against her husband for herself and her children.

Why Criminal Justice?

Although I had been interested in criminal justice since high school, I did not discover victimology until I started college. When I took my first victimology class, I wanted to learn more. I got my first hands-on experience working with victims during my senior year of college, when I took an internship at the Victim Offender Reconciliation Program. In my role as mediator, I was able to see how some guidance can really make a difference in a person's life. In the future, I plan to teach so that I might inspire people as my professors inspired me.

Expectations and Realities of the Job

I was pleasantly surprised to find that the agency I work for encourages me to attend workshops and take continuing education courses to better assist our clients. With this type of support from my employer, I expect to be able to help the agency expand by providing more services to our clients.

My Advice to Students

Dare to dream! Upon graduating from college, I knew I wanted to work as a victim advocate. However, I was unsure whether an entry-level employee could apply for such a position. So I went online and applied for the lowest job opening at one of the best-known intimate partner violence agencies in Fresno. To my surprise, although I applied for a lower position, I was offered employment as a victim advocate. Just by having the interview to present my skills and career goals, I was able to secure the job of my dreams.

Victim Advocates and Tribal Lands   Regardless of whether or not they live on tribal lands, Native Americans are victimized at much higher rates than other U.S. populations. According to the Bureau of Justice Statistics, between 1992 and 2002 Native Americans experienced violent victimization twice as often as Blacks, 2.5 times as often as Whites, and 4.2 times as often as Asian Americans.[29] During this period, Native American women were more than twice as likely to have been victims of violent crime than were women of other races, and they were more likely to have been victimized by a stranger than by an acquaintance or intimate partner. This means that a Native American woman is more likely to be targeted by–and more vulnerable to–an unknown assailant. It is unclear why this is the case, but the victim service providers working with Native Americans must specifically address the issue of stranger assaults, victim vulnerability, and ways in which a victim can reduce her vulnerability. These figures are especially high considering that in 2000, Native Americans made up only 1.5 percent of the U.S. population.[30]

Responding to these high victimization rates among Native Americans, as well as to the unique challenges faced by the criminal justice system in responding to crimes, in 1987 the federal government created the Victim Assistance in

Indian Country (VAIC) program. VAIC's 52 component programs provide direct services, including crisis intervention, emergency shelter, crisis hotlines, counseling, emergency transportation of victims to a safe location, and court accompaniments.[31] More recently, in January 2011, U.S. Attorney General Eric Holder announced the formation of the Violence Against Women Federal and Tribal Prosecution Task Force. The task force—which includes six members each from the U.S. Attorneys Office and tribal attorneys, as well as individuals representing the Justice Department's Office of Violence Against Women (OVW), health care providers, and law enforcement—is dedicated to finding solutions for the problems facing Native American women.[32]

Victim Advocates and the Military   In 1994, the Department of Defense (DOD) mandated the creation of victim and witness assistance programs for all branches of the military, with the aim of helping victims and witnesses deal with the investigation, prosecution, and punishment of crimes committed on military bases or by military personnel. The programs also provide victim services. Since 1994, the DOD has worked with the Office of Victims of Crime to create policies, programs, and training to promote victims' rights and to ensure that victim services are provided at military installations in the United States and around the world. When services are not available on a military base, the DOD enters into agreements with community victim service providers for service provision and referrals.

Despite these efforts, in February 2011 a group of U.S. veterans—more than a dozen females and two males—filed a class action lawsuit in a federal court claiming that they had experienced victimizations ranging from obscene verbal abuse to gang rape. The victims are asking that a third party investigate allegations of abuse and that they not be ordered to serve with perpetrators. In 2012, a U.S. District Court judge granted the Department of Defense's motion to dismiss the case because those serving in the armed forces cannot sue the military for any injuries, including sexual assault, that occur while serving. Oral arguments were heard the following year in the 4th U.S. Circuit Court of Appeals and the judgement of the lower court was affirmed. Specifically, that it is the purview of the Congress and the Executive Branch, not the courts, to have oversight over military matters.[33]

Death Notification

One of the most difficult tasks is to tell someone that a loved one has died. Death notifications are usually delivered in person by medical personnel, coroners or medical examiners, law enforcement officers, spiritual leaders, social service workers, or victim advocates.

When carrying out this painful assignment, the notifier must identify herself and the organization she represents, ensure that she is speaking to the appropriate person, and identify the victim by name. Equally important is not to hide the harsh reality of death by using euphemisms such as "he has passed away," "she is no longer with us," or "he has gone to a better place." Such phrases can be very confusing, particularly if there is a language or cultural barrier. The survivor should be given enough details about the date of death, the time of day, and the location (such as a car, a school, or an apartment) to understand how it occurred, but a great deal of detail is not necessary, particularly in the case of a violent death. If the survivor asks for further details, however, the advocate should answer honestly. Finally, the advocate can assist

▲ **Victim Services on Tribal Lands**

Victimization rates are high among Native Americans.

the survivor with identifying the victim, contacting the appropriate spiritual leader (if any) for guidance, and making funeral arrangements.[34]

Crime Victim Compensation

At the state level, **crime victim compensation** programs provide financial assistance to victims and their families throughout the 50 states, the District of Columbia, Puerto Rico, the Virgin Islands, and Guam. Any victim of violent or personal crime is eligible for compensation to help offset the costs of medical care, counseling, lost wages or support, and funerals. In most states, property crimes are not covered under compensation programs.

crime victim compensation
Programs administered at the state level to provide financial assistance to victims and their families.

MYTH/REALITY

MYTH: Victims can make money as a result of the crime(s) committed against them.

REALITY: Victims must exhaust all sources of insurance, restitution, or other benefits before they can retain state compensation funds; and the upper limit of compensation is different in each state.[35]

Victim compensation is not an opportunity for victims to make money from their circumstances. Each state sets a limit on compensation funds, usually $25,000 per victim.[36] To receive funding, the victim must report the crime promptly (usually within 30 days) and cooperate with law enforcement and the prosecution; he or she must not have contributed to the victimization (say, by starting a brawl), must not be in jail or on probation or parole, and must have exhausted all other insurance or benefits such as health insurance, worker's compensation, and lawsuits.[37] Crime victims apply for funding in the state where the crime was committed, not in the state where they live.

Under the USA PATRIOT Act, enacted in the wake of the 9/11 terrorist attacks, victims of international terrorism and their families are eligible for compensation through a special fund administered by the federal Office for Victims of Crime.[38]

Each year, about $450 million is distributed among about 200,000 victims in the United States. Across the states, the average allocation per victim is $2,000. Figure 14-2 shows how the funds were distributed in 2005. Of the 53 percent given for medical expenses, approximately $17 million was paid to victims when they had out-of-pocket expenses associated with completing a sexual assault forensic exam. Approximately 20 percent of all recipients of compensation funds are children, and 20 percent of all compensated adults are victims of intimate partner violence.[39] Outside the United States, many foreign countries also have compensation programs, as noted in "A Global View."

Compensation programs are funded from fees and fines collected from state and federal offenders and from the Victims of Crime Act (VOCA), the federal law that provides funding for victim services and compensation programs. State and federal taxes are not used for these funds. The Key Concepts table on page 453 lists eligibility requirements for individuals receiving victim compensation.

Victim Recovery

In the immediate aftermath of a victimization, ideally the first official personnel to be notified are victim advocates. It is their responsibility to give victims at least three kinds of help:

Other **9%**

Counseling **8%**

Funeral expense **11%**

Lost wages and support due to homicide **19%**

Medical expense **53%**

FIGURE 14-2 **Victim Compensation Payments, 2005**
SOURCE: National Association of Crime Victim Compensation Boards. www.nacvcb .org/ (retrieved July 30, 2011).

A Global View

Victim Compensation Programs in Foreign Countries

Lara Logan, a correspondent for the CBS TV newsmagazine *60 Minutes*, was covering the violent uprising of Egyptian citizens against the government of President Hosni Mubarak. On February 11, 2011, she went to Tahrir Square to interview individuals who were celebrating Mubarak's exit from political power. As the cameraman was changing the battery, the mood turned from jubilation to violence. Logan's Egyptian colleagues, hearing men in the crowd say that they wanted to remove her pants, notified her that the crew should leave immediately. The mob quickly descended upon Logan, separating her from her producer and crew, who were helpless to provide assistance. Logan was groped and touched; then her clothes were ripped, and she was beaten and sexually assaulted with such severity that she felt she was going to die. Logan estimated that several hundred men participated in the 40-minute attack before a group of civilians and Egyptian soldiers rescued her.[a]

Logan's horrific—but thankfully unusual—experience is an example of the various types of crimes that can occur when a person is traveling in an unstable foreign country. The United States and 35 other countries have victim compensation programs to help offset the costs of victimizations such as Logan's. In 2005, the U.S. Department of State surveyed countries that have full diplomatic relations with the United States to determine the extent of compensation available for victims. The survey showed that some countries require the victim to file a police report before leaving the country in order to be eligible for compensation. The majority of international victim compensation programs cover funeral and burial expenses, health and mental health care, disability, and loss of employment. Some countries extend compensation to include court expenses such as fees for court-related travel, translations, documents, and expert witnesses. Still other countries provide support for temporary living arrangements and replacement for personal items, including clothes. Some countries do not have a maximum award ceiling, while many determine compensation on a case-by-case basis, taking into account the victim's financial ability to cover the costs. Other eligibility requirements stipulate that a foreign victim be a citizen of a European Union country or have a similar diplomatic affiliation or that the victim be a temporary or permanent resident. Some countries provide compensation only for victims of terroristic acts. As a result of the survey, the U.S. Office of Victims of Crime created the Directory of International Crime Victim Compensation Programs, which can be found at www.ovc.gov/publications/infores/intdir2005.[b]

Egypt is one of the 35 foreign countries that has a victim compensation program. In the case of Lara Logan, however, it is unclear what, if any, victim compensation she will be eligible to receive.

OBSERVE→INVESTIGATE→UNDERSTAND

- How do victim compensation programs in foreign countries differ from those of the United States?

- What do you think about the eligibility requirement that is related to the victim's ability to pay?

- Some countries do not have a maximum victim compensation award. Do you think the United States should remove the maximum award restrictions? Explain.

SOURCES: [a]Brian Stelter. "CBS Reporter Recounts a 'Merciless' Assault," *New York Times*, April 28, 2011.

www.nytimes.com/2011/04/29/business/media/29logan.html?src=twr&pagewanted=all (retrieved April 30, 2011).

[b]U.S. Department of Justice, Office for Victims of Crime, "Directory of International Crime Victim Compensation Programs."

www.ovc.gov/publications/infores/intdir2005 (retrieved July 19, 2011); U.S. Department of Justice, Office for Victims of Crime, "Online Guide from OVC: Resource Guide for Serving U.S. Citizens Victimized Abroad," April 2008.

www.ojp.usdoj.gov/ovc/publications/infores/ServingVictimsAbroad/directoryinternational.html (retrieved April 30, 2011).

psychological first aid, survivor support, and treatment interventions to facilitate recovery.

Most laypeople can provide psychological first aid with minimal training. It includes recognizing that someone has been victimized and ensuring that he is removed from danger and placed in a safe environment. When there is physical injury, victims' workers must ensure that victims are first taken to a medical facility and given emergency attention and subsequently put in contact with a victim assistance agency.

The challenge for all victim advocates is to know how to perform crisis intervention, to assess victims, and to use that assessment to create a treatment plan to determine the victim's short- and long-term mental health needs; they must also be able to refer the victim to appropriate community service

KEY CONCEPTS **Eligibility Requirements for Receiving Victim Compensation**

> Any victim of violent or personal crime is eligible for compensation to help offset the costs of the crime.
>
> Victims of property crimes are not eligible to receive victim compensation.
>
> Eligible costs include medical care, counseling, lost wages or support, and funerals.
>
> Each state sets a limit on compensation funds, usually $25,000 per victim.
>
> To receive funding, the victim must report the crime promptly (usually within 30 days), cooperate with law enforcement and the prosecution, not have contributed to the victimization (say, by starting a brawl), not be in jail or on probation or parole, and exhaust all other insurance or benefits such as health insurance, worker's compensation, and lawsuits.
>
> Crime victims apply for funding in the state where the crime was committed, not in the state where they live.

providers and to carry out the treatment plan to help the victim achieve recovery. Recovery is perhaps the most important goal of victim services. A recovered victim is one who has come to terms with having been victimized and who acknowledges what was lost. Going through this process assists him in finding meaning from the experience and finally integrating what has been learned so that he can resume a functional life.

Working with someone who has experienced a traumatic event can be difficult because victims have different reactions. Some victims experience shock and numbness, intense emotion, fear, distress, guilt, anger and resentment, depression and loneliness, and isolation. Others have more physical responses, such as anxiety, panic, headaches, gastrointestinal problems, sleeplessness, and loss of appetite.[40] Yet despite their different reactions, most victims go through a three-phase process of impact, recoil, and recovery achievement.

The *impact stage* occurs in the immediate aftermath of a crime and is marked by shock, horror, and numbness. Some victims may be at further risk because they are vulnerable and unable to protect themselves, though others may think and act in a rational manner. Only about 10 percent of victims experience panic.[41] At the impact stage, the victim is primarily concerned with basic needs such as rescue, safety, warmth, and food. As soon as victim advocates and those working with victims identify appropriate interventions, referrals should be made for mental health services to assist the victim with long-term recovery. In this phase, ideally therapy should be offered to victims during the victim's first meeting with a victim advocate or other allied professionals, such as law enforcement and medical and mental health practitioners.

In the *recoil stage*, victims show more varied responses to the crime, including self-blame, fear, anxiety, helplessness, and impaired memory and decision making. These feelings can be all-consuming and can affect the victim's work, school, and social life. Insomnia, headaches, changes in appetite and libido, and lowered energy are all common physical and psychological responses to varying levels of preoccupation.[42]

Helping a victim in the recoil stage requires more extensively trained, more experienced specialists who can assess victims' needs and give appropriate support. Specific tasks include providing basic information about victims' situations, offering advocacy services, accompanying victims to various agencies to ensure that they receive needed services, and helping them, if they wish, to cooperate with authorities in the criminal justice system.

As advocates and allied professionals work with victims through this phase, therapy should again be offered to help the victim recover. Victim therapy can be short or long term. **Short-term therapy** is usually administered by

short-term therapy
Treatment usually administered by clinical psychologists, clinical social workers, and marriage and family counselors to address immediate mental health concerns.

long-term therapy
Treatment focusing on the victim's responses to trauma, symptoms of PTSD, anxiety disorders, depression, terminal conditions, and dysfunctional behaviors that render victims vulnerable.

clinical psychologists, clinical social workers, and marriage and family counselors. It focuses on individual therapy, relationship therapy, peer support, and group therapy, and it assists victims who have minor phobias or fears, eating and sleeping disorders, problems with managing stress, and health issues. **Long-term therapy** usually focuses on the victim's responses to trauma, symptoms of posttraumatic stress disorder (PTSD), anxiety disorders, depression, terminal conditions, and dysfunctional behaviors that render victims vulnerable. In some cases it deals with major phobias or fears and other trauma-related symptoms. It also may include institutional care, in which psychiatrists must administer psychotherapy, and it may include medication and close observation in a hospital. In any setting, the therapist's objective is to alleviate suffering and reduce trauma symptoms so that the person can resume a functional life. Prosecutors, too, are interested in facilitating victim recovery because individuals who suffer trauma may become psychologically impaired and thus unable to cooperate in the prosecution of offenders.

The *final stage* toward recovery usually involves an extended period of struggle during which the victim alternates between the effects of impact and recoil, but with less severe responses. Many individuals also experience PTSD, which includes recurring memories of the traumatic event. Regardless, however, of what may seem like setbacks, triggered perhaps by a reminder or an anniversary, the victim is usually moving forward in this stage, resuming normal activities and coping with the crime's aftermath. The crime is a part of her life, but not–as in previous stages–the whole of it.[43] The stages of achieving recovery are illustrated in the Key Concepts table below.

KEY CONCEPTS   Postvictimization Stages and Mental Health Response Options

Postvictimization Stages	Mental Health Response Options
The *impact stage* occurs in the immediate aftermath of a crime and can be marked by shock, horror, confusion, fear, panic, numbness, anger, paralysis, amnesia, and withdrawal. These responses can be accompanied by spontaneous urination, bowel release, defensive body movements, fainting, screaming, crying, self-injuring behaviors, temporary blindness and/or deafness, high blood pressure, heart attack, or stroke.	*Short-term therapy* is usually administered by clinical psychologists, clinical social workers, and marriage and family counselors. Initially it can include crisis intervention, removal to a safe place, and psychological first aid. Later it can include individual therapy, relationship therapy, peer support, prolonged exposure therapy, eye movement and desensitization therapy, and group therapy.
In the *recoil stage,* victims show more varied and continuing responses to the crime, including self-blame, health issues, phobias, persistent fear, anxiety, trauma, PTSD, helplessness, and depression. They may also experience eating, sleeping, and relationship disorders; extreme withdrawal; alcohol and drug abuse; chronic pain, especially headaches, stomachaches, and backaches; frequent grieving; gastrointestinal problems; hyperarousal; aggression; impaired memory; decision making difficulties; intrusive recollections; excessive worry; and suicide.	*Long-term therapy* is usually administered by psychiatrists or clinical psychologists who can treat victims for extended periods of time, even recommending hospitalization, medication, and lifestyle changes. Interventions can include methods such as individual psychotherapy, relationship therapy, prolonged exposure therapy, flooding therapy, eye movement and desensitization therapy, and group therapy.
The *final stage* is achieving recovery, an extended period of struggle in which the victim alternates between the effects of impact and recoil but with less severe responses—ultimately having fewer symptoms, an improved self-identify, and the resumption of a functional lifestyle.	To help achieve recovery, mental health professionals focus on reducing PTSD symptoms, helping victims understand themselves through self-examination, and restoring victims' control over their life.

a case in point

The Killings at Sandy Hook Elementary School

On the morning of December 14, 2012, in Newtown, Connecticut, Adam Lanza fatally shot his mother as she lay in bed. Then 20-year-old Lanza drove to nearby Sandy Hook Elementary School. Heavily armed, he shot his way into the locked school and then shot numerous people inside, killing 20 young children and 6 adults. When police arrived, Lanza killed himself with a shot to the head. This was one of the deadliest mass shootings in American history.

This terrible event raised many questions and controversies. Some of these centered around Lanza's motives, which remained unclear even several years later. Investigations revealed that Lanza was socially isolated and likely suffered from several mental health and behavioral disorders. He was also reportedly preoccupied with mass murders. But it is likely we will never know the links between these factors and Lanza's actions, or understand what prompted him to begin shooting that morning.

The murders also ignited a heated discussion about gun control in the United States. Lanza used a gun that was legally owned by his mother. It was a semiautomatic rifle, which permitted him to fire multiple shots in a small time frame and to reload quickly and easily. In the wake of the Sandy Hook shooting, Congress drafted laws to restrict sales of assault weapons and to require more background checks for gun purchases, but neither proposal received enough votes to become law. At the same time, gun rights advocates proposed other approaches, such as placing armed police officers in every school. Five states enacted stricter gun controls, but 10 states instead loosened restrictions.

The survivors of the massacre and the families of those who died had to contend not only with the violence and deaths, but with other issues as well. Some families sued the estate of Lanza's mother, and others sued the company that manufactured the gun Lanza used. There were debates over what might make an appropriate memorial and whether to demolish the school and build a new one. There were

even a few Internet commentators who claimed that the entire event was a hoax intended to create support for stricter gun control. Even the flood of sympathy and donations often complicated the victims' lives, as they had to deal with intense media attention and questions about how to move forward.

OBSERVE→INVESTIGATE→UNDERSTAND

- What services does your school offer for victims of violent crime? Are they sufficient?
- What kinds of efforts should an institution, an agency, or a community put into preparing for a violent crime like the Sandy Hook shooting?
- Aside from the obvious—those who were injured and the families of those who were killed—who else might be a victim of a large-scale violent attack? What forms does that victimization take?

SOURCES: Becky Bratu, "Connecticut School Shooting Is Second Worst in US History," NBC News, December 14, 2012. http://usnews.nbcnews.com/_news/2012/12/14/15909827-connecticut-school-shooting-is-second-worst-in-us-history (retrieved June 5, 2015); Stephen J. Sedensky III, "Sandy Hook Final Report," Office of the State's Attorney, Judicial District of Danbury, November 25, 2013. www.ct.gov/csao/lib/csao/Sandy_Hook_Final_Report.pdf (retrieved June 5, 2015); "Sandy Hook Massacre: Adam Lanza Acted Alone and Had an Obsession with Mass Killings," The Independent (London), November 26, 2013. www.independent.co.uk/news/world/americas/sandy-hook-killer-adam-lanza-acted-alone-and-had-an-obsession-with-mass-killings-such-as-columbine-says-report-8963342.html (retrieved June 5, 2015); Margaret Hartmann, "Post-Newtown, States Passed More Gun-Rights Laws, Not Restrictions," New York Magazine, April 4, 2013. http://nymag.com/daily/intelligencer/2013/04/post-newtown-states-loosen-gun-restrictions.html (retrieved June 5, 2015); Lisa Miller, "Orders of Grief," New York Magazine, November 3, 2013. http://nymag.com/news/features/newtown-2013-11/ (retrieved June 5, 2015).

Victim advocates have many different responsibilities as they provide assistance to victims throughout the stages of recovery. The work of victim advocates in helping victims is highlighted in "A Case in Point" on this page.

Vicarious Trauma

The psychological distress experienced by persons who know about a traumatic event directly experienced by another person and who feel that person's pain is sometimes called **vicarious trauma** or **compassion fatigue.** Many individuals who come into direct contact with victims can experience this secondary victimization, including law enforcement officers, medical care providers, victim advocates, individuals providing mental health services, and even family members and friends. This form of trauma may manifest itself as stress, burnout, fatigue, loss of empathy, or taking on the victim's suffering as one's own. Sometimes the practitioner may feel as if she has experienced the victim's reenactment of the crime. Others experience nightmares, avoidance and emotional numbing, hypersensitivity, and substance abuse.[44]

These experiences can be particularly problematic if the practitioner has intimate knowledge about the details of the crime or has experienced trauma

vicarious trauma (compassion fatigue)
Psychological distress experienced by those who know about a traumatic event experienced by another person and who feel the victim's pain.

in his own life. In either situation, the practitioner experiences difficulty in the course of learning more about the crime and working with the victim. This result is problematic in two respects—first, the victim is not receiving the best, most objective services; and second, the service provider is suffering along with the victim, with few outlets for personal thoughts, feelings, fears, and anxieties.[45]

It is not clear why some people are likely to experience vicarious trauma and others are not, or what affects the extent, severity, or duration of vicarious trauma. Organizations can assist their employees who work with victims and who experience vicarious trauma by providing a quiet room for relaxation, by extending the number of personal days off, by allowing for shorter workdays and workweeks, and by providing counseling. In combination, such practices can provide short- and long-term support.[46]

TYPES OF VICTIM SERVICE ASSISTANCE

Being a crime victim is frightening and confusing. Victims may call the police, seek medical care, or even flee their homes with no clothes, no money, and crying children in tow. Many do not know where to go, what to do, or how to get help. Until the 1970s, victims had few options other than to turn to law enforcement and medical personnel to help them cope with the trauma and recover from the crime. Today, however, thousands of programs, services, and resources can help victims to repair their lives and property, to obtain rights while seeking justice, and to try to heal.

Crisis Intervention

crisis intervention
Immediate assistance after a traumatic event.

After a traumatic event, **crisis intervention** can provide immediate assistance. Such intervention can assume a number of forms, including responding to a crime scene, transporting a person to a shelter, providing medical assistance, helping a victim locate a missing loved one, or simply providing a shoulder to cry on. During crisis intervention, victim services personnel must ask what victims want and need. Instead of making assumptions about what is in the victim's best interest, advocates should provide options so that victims can begin to make their own choices about the future.[47]

Effective crisis intervention depends on accurately assessing the situation, working with the victim to determine immediate needs, and focusing treatment on those needs.[48] Referrals to other organizations address longer-term needs. From the victim service providers' perspective, work with victims is usually highly taxing. Advocates often must be on call all hours, day and night. Frequently they must hear and see the results of extreme victimizations—stressful experiences that take a toll on the advocates and require them to also receive counseling. Good victim advocacy requires extensive training, personal maturity, experience with victims, and constant supervision. In some cases, supervisors must provide their employees with breaks away from fieldwork and even insist on vacations and periodic counseling to avert burnout or compassion fatigue. A well-run victim service agency requires a balanced number of advocates to cover the existing workload, so that victims receive referrals and adequate treatment in a timely manner that can lead to recovery.

Hotlines

Most local and national victim services agencies provide a telephone crisis hotline 24 hours a day, 7 days a week, through which a victim (as well as secondary victims) can discuss any type of victimization, get information and resources such as shelter and child care, and learn how to get a protective order. Hotlines are staffed by volunteers and professionals trained in crisis intervention techniques and victim services. They provide immediate short-term counseling to help victims through the crisis, but not ongoing, long-term counseling, therapy, or treatment. Instead, the hotline worker will provide information and referrals for these types of services.[49]

Each year, the National Network to End Domestic Violence (NNEDV) sponsors a census on domestic violence services. In 2013, almost 90 percent of local identified victim service providers participated in the survey, which sought to find out what services were provided on a single day, September 17, 2013. On the census day, the 1,649 participating organizations reported that they answered 20,267 hotline calls, and the National Domestic Violence Hotline answered 550 calls. The 2013 study showed that more than 14 hotline calls are answered every minute regarding intimate partner violence in the United States.[50]

Shelters and Transitional Housing

MYTH/REALITY

MYTH: Victims of intimate partner violence are partially at fault for their situation because they will not leave their abusers.

REALITY: Abusers often economically and psychologically distance their victims from the rest of society. It is often financially difficult for a victim to leave a batterer, especially if the victim has children.[51]

A major premise of victim services is that most victims are not to blame for the crime they experience. Thus victims of intimate partner violence are not responsible for the abuse they experience at home—the batterer is. Many times, a batterer will isolate the victim from her family and friends, use physical and sexual force to intimidate her, psychologically taunt her, and control the couple's finances.

These factors leave the victim afraid for her safety yet with few resources to escape. Some victims will flee to seek safety; some may be thrown out of their homes by their battering partner. When victims leave, typically going first to family and friends, batterers often follow, asking forgiveness, begging for a second chance, and promising never to be violent again. Many victims are encouraged to return by those who want to keep the family together, including children who want to be with their father. This pressure, coupled with the lack of financial resources to venture out on their own, means that many victims return to their batterer. The average victim will leave and return several times before finally terminating the relationship.

Shelters are a temporary housing option for battered women and their children. They offer a safe place to escape a violent relationship; provide an opportunity to determine options for legal, medical, social, housing, education, employment, and child care; and make it possible to rebuild a life free of violence.

The maximum time a person may stay in a shelter is set by state law and can range from 30 to 90 days. Most shelters offer 60 days.[52] If a victim contacts the police, they will often drive her and her children directly to the shelter. If she calls a hotline, the person answering the phone will usually contact the police for her. In most states, the shelter location is kept private to help ensure the safety of the residents; in California, it is a misdemeanor to disclose the shelter's location.

Shelters usually are large, older homes in residential neighborhoods, unmarked but renovated to meet the residents' safety needs. Perimeter cameras and secure entries help to protect residents. Typically, shelters house approximately 25 women and children.[53] According to the data released by the NNEDV for the September 2013 census day, the 1,649 participating organizations were providing emergency shelter or transitional housing for 19,431 children and 16,917 adults.[54]

▼ **Women and Children in an Intimate Partner Violence Shelter**

All major U.S. cities have special protective places where women who are victims of abuse and violence by their partners can go for a brief time to escape the danger and stay in safety, often with their children.

Real Careers

TINA FIGUEROA-RODRIGUEZ

Work location: Madera, California

College(s): California State University, Fresno (2007)

Major(s): Criminology (BS), Victimology Option

Job title: Victim Services Manager

Salary range for job like this: $40,000–$53,000

Time in job: 8 years

Work Responsibilities

I supervise daily operations of the rape crisis center, the victim/witness center, and the intimate partner violence program. I ensure that staff members comply with policy standards; develop protocols for crisis response; and train staff on procedures for working with crime victims. In practical terms, I monitor services at the battered women's shelter by selecting files at random and verifying that progress is being properly documented. I train our staff members by developing instructional materials and organizing training sessions. Our facility receives funding from state and federal grants to provide these services. I have been delegated the task of maintaining compliance with funding sources and researching new funding opportunities.

Why Criminal Justice?

I majored in criminology because the field is very broad and there are many professions from which to choose. Wanting to work with abused or at-risk youth, I researched potential career paths and came up with many possibilities, such as a correctional officer at juvenile hall, juvenile probation officer, and victim services advocate. To prepare myself for such a career, I earned a Victim Services Certificate from CSUF during the summer. For this certificate, I had to take courses in family violence, victim rights, intimate partner violence, and child abuse.

Expectations and Realities of the Job

I did not expect grant funding to be so readily available to crisis facilities. That is not to say the money is simply given out. First, a center needs to apply for a grant. Once a grant is awarded, the center must comply with the guidelines outlined by the funding source and update that source with regular progress reports. One way our center has benefited from grant money is with the installation of a modern child-friendly interview room for children who have been sexually assaulted. It is designed with creative art and playful colors, but at the same time hidden cameras and microphones aid investigators in their work.

My Advice to Students

Begin to develop your resume and start searching for jobs while still in college. The application process can take up to 1 year because employers typically administer some or all of the following: background check, physical assessments, interviews, and entry exams. Most agencies require personal references, so it is important to begin that process while you are still on campus and can readily meet with your professors. Depending on the job for which you are applying, you may need to acquire other certifications. For example, to work at a battered women's shelter, victim/witness agency, or rape crisis center in California, you need to complete 60 hours of training. The sooner you begin your employment search, the sooner you can identify the credentials you will need for applying for the job.

MYTH/REALITY

MYTH: If there is space in an intimate partner violence shelter, victims are not turned away.

REALITY: Individuals can be denied entry if they are alcoholics, drug abusers, or elder adults who were not abused by an intimate partner. Some shelters cannot accommodate victims with a disability, and most also deny housing to male children over 13.[55]

At the shelter, an advocate will determine the victim's needs and those of her children (if she has them) through an *intake* process. At intake, a shelter employee helps the victim complete a questionnaire as the prospective shelter resident. The questionnaire is a means of screening a client to determine whether she and her children are eligible to enter the shelter. It inquires about the extent of the violence and continued threat to the victim and her children, mental health status, suicidal tendencies, financial and social support resources, employment and school matters, and alcohol or drug use. If the shelter staff believe that the victim or her children will be a threat to themselves or other residents, or if their needs exceed the limits of what the shelter can provide, they will not be permitted residence and will be offered alternative housing options.

Many shelters will not admit someone who has a serious mental illness or is under the influence of alcohol or drugs. Those who pose a threat to themselves or other residents will not be allowed to enter. Furthermore, despite Americans with Disabilities Act (ADA) requirements that all public buildings be wheelchair-accessible, have elevators, and otherwise accommodate victims with a disability, some shelters are not in compliance and cannot accept such victims.

Women who are in same-sex relationships may use shelter services, but male victims do not have access to intimate partner shelter services.[56] If a male victim needs shelter, he must go to another facility, like a homeless shelter–not an ideal setting because there is usually no intake screening process or security measures that preclude the batterer from entering the facility and further harming the victim. As such, a homeless shelter is not as safe as a shelter for battered women, with its perimeter cameras or fencing, secure access points, or extra patrol and security features.

People often wrongly believe that only the woman in a violent relationship is abused. In reality, a man abusing his partner is also likely abusing any children in the home. Returning children to a violent home without the abuser's having received treatment is not advisable, because the abuser is likely to hurt or sexually assault the children to get back at the victim.[57]

Even if a child is not physically or sexually abused there, growing up in a violent home has a long-term detrimental impact. In 2011, nearly 60 percent of children under 17 years of age reported exposure to abuse within the previous 12 months, either as primary victims or witnesses.[58] Since the early 1990s, research has focused greater attention on the psychological effects on children of witnessing violence. Recent studies indicate that children who are trapped in such settings suffer chronic symptoms of traumatic stress, anxiety, depression, and suicidal behaviors.[59] They are also at risk for substance abuse, medical and health issues, parental mental health issues and unemployment, poverty, and malnutrition.[60] Moreover, children who witness severe or chronic violence are more likely to have psychological problems at younger ages if the violence is frequent and if it happens in close proximity–within the home versus in the community–and to a loved one versus to a stranger.[61] Some studies indicate that children who witness the abuse of their mothers may be as traumatized as if they were the direct victims of abuse.[62] As a result, it is important for children to be removed from a violent environment and not be returned to that environment until it is certain the violence has ended.[63]

A limited number of studies have evaluated shelter programs. They suggest that such services may be more helpful to battered women than traditional counseling services alone.[64] Those who stay in a shelter experience fewer and less intense incidents of new violence. After even a short stay of 14 days, women tend to experience less depression and feel a greater sense of hope.[65] In a 2004 statewide evaluation of shelter programs in Illinois, researchers found that intimate partner violence victims felt safe while in a shelter and gained important information about violence. Increased support and the counseling programs offered contributed to their improved ability to make decisions, as well as to their greater self-esteem and coping skills.[66]

Sexual Assault Resource Centers

Direct victim support–including hospital and court accompaniments; individual counseling; hotline services; community education; and advocacy for political, social, and institutional change—is offered at *rape crisis centers*, also referred to as *sexual assault resource centers.*[67]

Sexual assault resource centers help educate the community to understand that no one "asks for" or wants to be sexually assaulted, that anyone can be a target, that rape is a violent act of power and dominance (not of sex), and that victims are far more likely to be raped by someone they know than by a stranger. These centers also focus prevention programs on school-age children, who are most at risk for sexual assault.

In traditional approaches, no services were available for secondary rape victims. Over time, however, the administrators of sexual assault centers and other victim service programs realized the impact of vicarious trauma on family and friends and broadened their work to include services for loved ones. They now also place greater emphasis on outreach to underserved populations such as minority and immigrant groups for whom English is a second language. Recent government budget cuts have required some sexual assault centers to merge with other victim service providers such as intimate partner violence programs and to work with more diverse victim populations.

Sexual Assault Nurse Examiners

sexual assault nurse examiner (SANE)
Nurse who provides 24-hour first-response medical care and crisis intervention for rape victims in hospitals and clinics.

The first **sexual assault nurse examiner (SANE)** program was created in Minnesota in 1977. By the mid-1990s, many hospitals in the United States and around the world had sexual assault nurse examiners on staff. These nurses provide 24-hour first-response medical care and crisis intervention for rape victims in hospitals and clinics.

In a case of sexual assault, the victim's body is considered a crime scene. It is thus essential that she go to the hospital as quickly as possible and not eat, drink, shower, brush her teeth, or urinate until after she has been seen by the SANE nurse, who will conduct a forensic exam that produces a "rape kit" (with or without the presence of a victim advocate, depending on the victim's wishes). The nurse will have received extensive training in evidence collection, use of specialized equipment such as a colposcope (a lighted magnifying instrument used during gynecological exams), chain-of-evidence requirements, expert testimony, injury detection and treatment, pregnancy and emergency contraception, STD/AIDS testing, rape trauma syndrome, and local victim services. By the mid-2000s, special pediatric examiners were also being trained to work with the youngest victims of sexual assault, those under 2 years old.[69]

Community Education and Outreach

One of a victim service provider's critical roles is to offer community education and outreach to victims who may not know about services. Education can be community-based through groups such as AARP (formerly known as the American Association of Retired Persons), Boy Scouts and Girl Scouts, and Rotary Club; or school-based through elementary, junior high, high school, and colleges and universities. Education enables the victim services organization to raise awareness about various types of victimization, provide an expanded definition of victimization, target specific populations most likely to be victimized, discuss particular services, and dispel misconceptions about crime and victims.

Matters *of* Ethics

When a Survivor Wants to Meet the Offender

Working with someone who has survived a traumatic event can be a long-term relationship that goes beyond providing initial crisis services and referrals and navigating the criminal justice system. If you are ever an advocate for such a person, you may find yourself having continued contact with an individual who has no one else to turn to for assistance.

Imagine, for example, that you are a victim advocate who is working with "Jim," a homicide survivor whose sister was one of several women who was kidnapped, brutally raped, and ultimately murdered. The murderer is now incarcerated and on death row. As the date nears, Jim decides that he would like to speak to the person who killed his sister—to ask him several questions in order to understand why he did what he did and to gain a sense of perspective and closure.

As an advocate, you contact the state Department of Corrections (DOC) to determine whether such a meeting is possible. As a liaison among the DOC, Jim, and the offender, you find out that the offender agrees to this meeting but expresses no remorse. In fact, he states that if given the chance to do it again, he would gladly murder all those women, adding that "they deserved it anyway." You inform Jim about these sentiments and note your concerns about his continued long-term recovery if he moves forward with a face-to-face meeting. Jim understands but insists on meeting with his sister's murderer. Consider: What ethical issues does this situation raise?

OBSERVE → INVESTIGATE → UNDERSTAND

- As a victim advocate, should you continue to facilitate this meeting? Why or why not?
- Knowing that this meeting will be difficult for Jim—and perhaps even detrimental to him—how do you balance what Jim wants with what may be best for his continued recovery?
- What actions should you consider to ensure that if the meeting occurs, it is a safe environment for Jim?

Lack of knowledge about available services can stem from a language barrier, immigrant status, or a culture that limits a victim's ability to seek protection against abusers. Other barriers include race, geography, disability, and sexual orientation. In the case of sexual orientation, the victim may perceive victim service providers as homophobic and unwilling to provide services. As such, some same-sex victims have individual barriers that prevent them from seeking services even though they may know of their availability. Victim service providers must use creative means of reaching these diverse populations and the public, including word-of-mouth from those who used the services in the past; advertisements in local and non-English newspapers, buses, train stations, and public restrooms; and billboards on streets and highways. Public service announcements on the radio, television, and Internet, including language-specific media, are critical tools for reaching individuals who may be illiterate or non-English speaking or who have limited reading skills.[70]

There are a number of ethical dilemmas that arise in working with victims. One such dilemma is noted in the "Matters of Ethics" box.

▲ **Victims' Rights Advocate Bret Vinocur**

Bret Vinocur, holding a photo of Bruce Lower—a man who spent 16 years in prison for killing a 3-year-old girl—speaks to the Ohio Senate Criminal Justice Committee at the Ohio Statehouse in Columbus.

VICTIM ASSISTANCE FOR ELDER ADULTS

Elder adults, usually defined as those over 65 years old, have unique needs as victims compared to individuals in other age groups. Although elder adults may seek services from regular victim service providers, some programs specifically serve elder adult victims. One type of elder resource that is largely lacking in most communities is emergency shelters for elder abuse victims. With the continuing aging of the post–World War II baby boomers, this type of service will likely become a more critical need over the next 20 years. Based on data

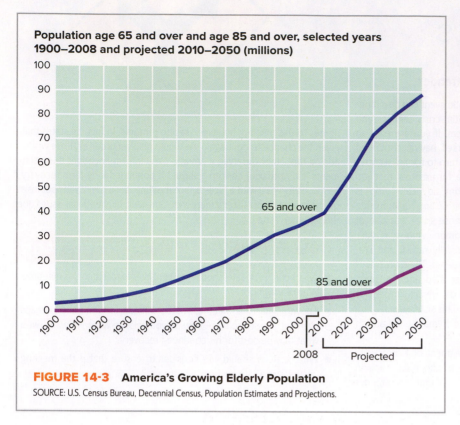

Population age 65 and over and age 85 and over, selected years 1900–2008 and projected 2010–2050 (millions)

65 and over

85 and over

2008

Projected

FIGURE 14-3   **America's Growing Elderly Population**
SOURCE: U.S. Census Bureau, Decennial Census, Population Estimates and Projections.

Adult Protective Services
State services provided to dependent adults who are in danger of being mistreated or neglected, who are unable to protect themselves, or who have no one to assist them.

TRIAD
A collaborative effort among police departments, sheriff's offices, and senior groups (like AARP) to reduce crime and the victimization of elder adults.

from the U.S. Bureau of the Census, Figure 14-3 shows that the projections for the year 2050 for people over the age of 65 will represent 20 percent of the total population.

Adult Protective Services

Elder abuse is a relatively new area of criminal justice intervention, but it is not a new phenomenon. Once viewed as a private matter, it was first formally addressed in the United States in the mid-1970s, with the creation of the **Adult Protective Services** program, funded under Title XX of the Social Security Act. Adult Protective Services provides help and safeguards for elder adults and dependent adults with disabilities who are in danger of being mistreated or neglected, who cannot protect themselves, or who have no one to assist them. Each state has its own unique program that operates without a federal funding stream and thus is based on state resources. The mandatory reporting provision of Adult Protective Services in all states was motivated by the government's concern about an increase in reports of abuse and neglect among elder and dependent adults.[71]

In 2004, the National Committee for the Prevention of Elder Abuse and the National Adult Protective Services Association conducted a follow-up study of vulnerable adults over age 18. The findings indicate that Adult Protective Services had received 565,747 reports of elder abuse, almost 20 percent more than in the original 2000 study. Of reported cases, 81 percent were investigated and almost 42 percent were substantiated, 16 percent more than in 2000. In 2010, Elder Abuse Daily, a national elder abuse advocacy organization, reported that there are 6 million cases of elder abuse each year, which is approximately 1 case every 5 seconds. California reports the most elder abuse cases (10.6 percent of all cases in the United States); California has 36 percent more cases than Florida, which has the second-highest rate of elder abuse in the nation.[72]

In the victim services field, however, it is never clear exactly what is indicated by an increase in reporting. Does the increase mean that there is more abuse? Does it mean that more education about the issue has caused more people to report abuse and to seek services? Or does it mean that, in this case, there are simply more elder adults available to be abused?[73]

TRIADs

Police departments, sheriff's offices, and senior groups like AARP in many communities have joined in a collaborative effort called **TRIADs** to reduce crime and the victimization of elder adults. The first TRIAD was created in 1987, and a cooperative agreement was signed the following year. Today, district attorneys' offices, fire departments, agencies and departments on aging, emergency social and medical services, and other organizations that work directly with elder adults are members of TRIAD. At the local level, TRIAD works through a cooperative partnership to reduce and prevent crime, decrease fears of victimization, and improve services. It also informs elder adults about crimes such as identity theft, teaches them ways to reduce their vulnerability, and increases their awareness of community resources.[74]

COLLABORATIVE RESPONSES TO VICTIMS

Although a wide range of 1960s social activism set the stage, the emergence of efforts in support of crime victims owes the most to the women's movement, which put considerable pressure on the criminal justice system to do more to protect victims, ensure their rights, and help them seek justice. Responding to this pressure, the criminal justice system has created programs to address specific types of crimes, streamlined the investigation and prosecution of cases, experimented with alternative sanctions to deter criminal behavior, and worked to ensure victims' rights.

To accomplish its mission, the criminal justice system needs crime victims—and victims, in return for their cooperation, want to be treated fairly (see the "Disconnects" box on page 464). They do not want to have to endure further victimizations at the hands of the criminal justice system itself. To help recover from their injuries and trauma and to rebuild their relationship with the community, victims need the assistance of many different professionals from diverse disciplines. Rarely does a single approach or a simple answer address all of a victim's problems. The need to provide victims with comprehensive services has inspired many organizations to form partnerships.

Intimate Partner Violence Councils

By the late 1980s, intimate partner violence service providers realized that there was a problem in the lack of coordination of health, social, and other services across the criminal justice system. Battered women who did not receive all the services they needed might fall through the social safety net or, even worse, return to their abusive partners. Thus intimate partner violence service partnerships were created.[75] In different places these have various names, but most often they are called domestic violence councils, coordinating councils, response teams, or roundtables. Regardless of the name, their goals are the same: to work collaboratively to end intimate partner violence, increase survivor safety, and raise the accountability for batterers.

Despite the early efforts and widespread adoption of intimate partner violence councils, few of these programs have been evaluated. A 2006 evaluation in one midwestern state with 44 intimate partner violence councils found that councils varied in size from 8 to 116 members and were in existence from 7 months to 16 years, with an average of about 5 years. Members were drawn from intimate partner violence programs (law enforcement, prosecutors and district courts, and legal services), batterer intervention programs, health and mental health care organizations, social service agencies, Child Protective Services, faith-based organizations, educational institutions, and local businesses. Interestingly, however, only 29 percent of the councils included an intimate partner violence survivor.

The study found that leaders of these councils perceived the organization as an important step in creating a coordinated community response to intimate partner violence. On average, they rated their councils as moderately effective at accomplishing their goals. The study concluded that

▼ **Texas Council on Family Violence "Silent Witness" Campaign**

Survivor Angela Catalina De Hoyos speaks at an intimate partner violence rally at the Texas State Capitol to remember the 115 women killed in 2004 by their intimate partners.

DIS Connects

When Victims Are Revictimized

In 2002 in Springdale, Arkansas, a 14-year-old juvenile, Josh Duggar, sexually molested four of his younger sisters at different times. His parents found out and reported it to the police. The juvenile was punished by the father and also went through a 5-month Christian counseling program. The police record was then sealed.

Thirteen years later, Josh Duggar was a 27-year-old father of three and a TV celebrity on a conservative Christian program. On May 19, 2015, a national celebrity gossip tabloid, *In Touch*, found out about Duggar's earlier transgressions and got a copy of the police report from the Springdale chief of police by invoking the Freedom of Information Act (FOIA). The tabloid promptly posted the juvenile report on their website with the names of the victims redacted. In response, Josh confirmed the molestations in a Facebook statement. The local juvenile judge ordered the official police report destroyed and expunged.

Josh Duggar's parents, Jim Bob and Michelle Duggar, also celebrities on a Christian TV show, *19 Kids and Counting*, agreed to do a CNN television interview on June 3, 2015, and revealed that the victims were their daughters. Two days later, a Fox News reporter

interviewed two of the four sisters, Jill and Jessa, who were now married with children of their own and were also part of their parents' TV show. They were upset at being revictimized by this turn of events. The image of their model Christian family had been tainted, some of the supporters of their show withdrew their commercials, and the show's future was placed in serious jeopardy.

In spite of both the police chief and the city attorney researching whether the report had to be released under the state FOIA law, there seemed to be confusion over the legality of the chief's actions. An Arkansas state senator, Bart Hester, noted that because this report was made public, the victims had been revictimized, contrary to the intent of the law designed to protect the identities of minors, and he wondered whether all child sex-crime victims' identities in Springdale might now be at risk of being exposed to the public.

OBSERVE → INVESTIGATE → UNDERSTAND

- Whose best interests are served by revealing the details of this police report: the offender's, the victims', or the media? Who is responsible for this secondary victimization of the victims?

- If this offender has never again molested anyone and has led a law-abiding life, what is the point of this media frenzy in a gossip tabloid? Are there conflicting interests?

- How much concern was shown to the victims after their first victimization, and what type of response do they need now?

SOURCES: Larry Henry, "Senator: Springdale Police Chief Should Be Fired over Child Sex-Crime Report," 5 News, May 23, 2015. http://5newsonline.com/2015/05/23/senator-springdale-police-chief-should-be-fired-over-child-sex-crime-report/ (retrieved June 24, 2015); Mary Bowerman, (June 4, 2015) Timeline: Duggar Sex-Abuse Scandal, USA Today, June 4, 2015. www.usatoday.com/story/life/people/2015/05/28/timeline-josh-duggar-19-kids-and-counting-tlc-sex-abuse-scandal/28066229/ (retrieved June 24, 2015); Lisa de Morales, "Josh Duggar Sisters/Victims: TLC Series 'Window Of Opportunity' God Allowed," Deadline.com, June 5, 2015. http://deadline.com/2015/06/josh-duggar-sisters-victims-tlc-series-video-1201438400/ (retrieved June 24, 2015).

councils can play a positive role in addressing intimate partner violence, but it recommended that they focus more on criminal justice than on health care or education. Although interagency cooperation contributes to increasing rates of identification and intervention and reducing violence, determining its overall effectiveness will require more research.[76]

Sexual Assault Response Teams

sexual assault response team (SART)

In many states, a collaboration of local police officers, victim advocates, SANE practitioners, and prosecutors seeking to determine the most effective way to respond to sexual assault.

Local police officers, victim advocates, SANE practitioners, and prosecutors make up the **sexual assault response team (SART)**, which in many states works to determine the most effective way to respond to sexual assault. SARTs investigate recent cases of sexual assault to learn how they were handled, whether mistakes were made, and when something was done well. They also examine what types of sexual assaults occur; by whom, when, and where they were perpetrated; what preventive measures can be taken; and what services are needed. The goal is to improve reporting practices, to provide more effective services, and to remove barriers that prevent investigating and prosecuting rape.[77]

Specialized Units

Recognizing differences among victims and their responses to crimes, all levels of the government have created units to provide specialized training for practitioners who work with a single type of victim with special needs. These units are primarily located in law enforcement agencies, district attorneys' offices, and government-run victim services agencies like Child Protective Services and Adult Protective Services.

Specialized units give practitioners knowledge, skills, and experience in working with assigned victims. Although every victim is different, there are similarities among victims of a particular type of crime, such as intimate partner violence, sexual crime, child abuse, elder abuse, property crime, and homicide. In addition to providing direct victim services, specialized units develop interview strategies and training curricula for others who may work with these victims but are not housed in a specialized unit.[78]

One example of a specialized unit is a *multidisciplinary interview center (MDIC)*, also known as a child advocacy center. Here, child victims of physical and sexual assault are interviewed by a trained specialist in a child-friendly environment. The MDIC staff coordinates the interviews of law enforcement, prosecutors, defense attorneys, and others who may have to talk with the child about the victimization. Before meeting the child, the interviewer collects questions from all participants in the process. Thus the victim has to retell her story about the crime only once to the trained specialist, without having to repeat it multiple times, in different locations, and to different people.[79]

Restorative Justice

A process that gives victims the opportunity of having a stronger role in the justice process, *restorative justice* recognizes that the individual victims *and offenders* are the true victims of the crime conflict. It seeks to empower the victim to resolve the conflict, move beyond her vulnerabilities, and achieve closure. It also focuses on trying to have the offender make amends rather than relying only on punishment as a response to victimization.[80]

In the late 1970s, some communities in the United States began to adopt restorative justice to rehabilitate juvenile offenders who committed property crimes, showing them the impact of their actions on victims. By the mid-2000s, many more restorative justice programs were being used for all types of offenses, including personal crimes, homicides, family violence, and even sexual assault.[81] Participants may be victim advocates, victim services providers, and those trained to understand the dynamics of abusive relationships. As practiced in the United States, the restorative justice process takes place outside the formal criminal justice system. Recall that in the United States it is "the people," not the individual victim, who prosecute accused offenders and who, if they are found guilty, punish them.

Controversies over Restorative Justice
Restorative justice programs are controversial when they are attempted in cases of family violence and sexual assault due to the violent nature of these crimes, the relationship between victim and offender, and the power imbalances inherent in these situations. Critics point to the victim's safety; the potential for the offender to pressure, coerce, or manipulate the victim into accepting certain outcomes; and the possibility that the remedy will be too lenient and send the wrong message to the offender.[82] The emphasis on forgiveness can even serve to continue family violence: Batterers often ask forgiveness, only to batter again.[83]

Proponents of restorative justice respond that the ideals of other programs neither minimize the victimization itself nor call for reconciliation.[84] They highlight as well the merits of justice alternatives and the availability of more options for women, offenders, and the community than the criminal justice system can provide. Critics, on the other hand, oppose diverting an offender from the criminal justice system because it gives the appearance of being lenient on crime.[85]

Restorative Justice in Global Perspective Restorative justice is a primary form of seeking redress in many parts of the world. The principles of restorative justice have a long history and are consistent with many world religions. In restorative justice, a community takes an active role in handling its own problems through open dialogue and mediation with victims and with offenders that makes them accountable for their involvement in victimization.

In Australia, restorative justice is a form of "reintegrative shaming," in which the community shames the offender for her crime. It is believed that the condemnation implicit in shaming helps the offender realize the impact of her crimes, motivating her to stop offending and to pursue opportunities to reintegrate into the community. The Czech Republic's Department of Probation has a restorative justice program that brings together victims, offenders, and mediators to develop presentence reports and determine alternative sanctions for the crime. The mediator works with offenders specifically to improve interpersonal relationships, understand the implications of the crime for society, and address its consequences, as well as to determine the type of rehabilitation–substance abuse treatment, anger management, education, or job training–needed to prevent reoffending.

Community and family group conferencing is another restorative justice model, launched in 1989 in New Zealand and also used in Australia, the United States, and South Africa. This program is based on the principles of sanctioning and dispute resolution common among the Maori, New Zealand's indigenous population. Managed by the police and used primarily with juvenile offenders, it outlines the consequences of the crime and encourages youth to reform rather than reoffend. The victim and the offender's family, friends, and community work together to determine appropriate sanctions and outcomes, to explore prevention, and to support the offender in meeting the conference's guidelines. If the offender does not comply, the community and family group reconvenes to determine whether more restrictive supervision or custody is needed.

Another, and more controversial, type of restorative justice program in New Zealand is the Youth Justice Conference, an approach centered on conferences specifically designed for juvenile sexual offenders and their victims. A 2004 study found that victims felt that they were better off if their cases were decided by restorative justice rather than through the formal court process because the offender admitted the crime and agreement was usually reached relatively quickly (on average, within 3 months) on a remedy, such as community service, legal orders to stay away from the victim, and intensive counseling. In contrast, only 51 percent of the 227 cases in the study ever went to court, a process that averaged 6.5 months; the rest were either dismissed or withdrawn.

In the United States, traditional restorative justice programs are largely offered only to juvenile offenders. Since the mid-2000s, however, a new type of restorative justice program has emerged in the States, known as the *listening project*. The listening project method features an arrangement, akin to a focus group, whereby the victim or victims of a sexual assault meet with a victim service provider and a victim advocate to discuss any aspect of the crime that the survivors feel comfortable discussing. The purpose is to give survivors an opportunity to have a voice regarding their own experiences, to ask questions and receive answers, to validate their experiences and feelings, and to receive support and diminish self-blame. Participants mention achieving a sense of empowerment by speaking out and providing input to service providers about resolution needs following their assault.[86] Clearly, restorative justice can benefit some victims, but there are limits to what it can achieve.

SUMMARY

A journey that began in 1947 with Beniamin Mendelsohn's pioneering work—which coincided with the United Nations' 1948 Universal Declaration of Human Rights—has grown into a worldwide movement on behalf of crime victims. In the mid-1960s the United States launched the National Crime Victimization Surveys, which for the first time measured the full scope of victimization and paved the way for new insights about victims and their role in the criminal justice process. This new information helped to create victim programs and served to prompt legislators to enact needed laws.

Victim assistance programs began providing services to all types of victims, and in 1976 the National Organization for Victim Assistance was created to help forge a new profession of victim advocates, enabling them to share their knowledge and become a national voice on behalf of victims. In 1984 the U.S. Department of Justice established the Office for Victims of Crime and Congress enacted the Victims of Crime Act, which together serve as major resources for helping victims. In 1985 the United Nations adopted its Declaration of Basic Principles of Justice for Victims of Crime and Abuse of Power, in which all the nations of the world agreed that victims should be treated with dignity and respect and should receive a wide range of rights.

All these events helped to bring about important innovations in laws, programs, research, and policies that have significantly improved the status of crime victims in this country. What began as a lone voice in Europe has become a world movement that has significantly humanized the way victims are treated and that continues to make progress toward the goal of treating all victims with the fairness, care, respect, and dignity they deserve.

OBSERVE → INVESTIGATE → UNDERSTAND

Review

Differentiate among various victims' responses to trauma.

- Psychic trauma, which results from severe emotional stress, immobilizes the victim's mind and body and can result in long-lasting emotional injury.

- Resilient persons might show no effects of trauma and may cope well.

- Victims may show mild effects and recover in a few minutes or hours, but some might display extreme effects and need days, weeks, or months to recover.

Identify the major historical milestones that have influenced the formation of victimology, victim services, and the victims' rights movement.

- Early human cultures placed victims at the center of their legal procedures, giving them a dominant role in righting the wrongs committed against them.

- The Code of Ur-Nammu and the Code of Hammurabi called for restoring equity between the offender and the victim.

- In the 1960s and 1970s, social activists in such efforts as civil rights, women's rights, children's rights, gay rights, and opposition to the Vietnam War paved the way for the rise of the victims' rights movement.

- In 1966, the first victimization surveys were conducted for the President's Commission on Law Enforcement and the Administration of Justice.

- Under the Victims of Crime Act (VOCA) of 1984, funds were distributed throughout the United States for victim compensation and victim assistance programs.

- In 1994, Congress enacted the Violence Against Women Act (VAWA) to support the investigation and prosecution of violent crimes against women.

Describe the types of crisis intervention programs that work with crime victims.

- Crisis intervention offers immediate assistance to victims.

- Crisis hotlines operate 24 hours a day, 7 days a week, and through them the primary victim and secondary victims can discuss any type of victimization, get information and access resources such as a shelter or child care, and find out how to get a protective order.

- Shelters are short-term housing options for victims fleeing an abusive home.

- Rape crisis centers provide immediate assistance to victims of a sexual assault, as well as personnel to accompany victims to the hospital and to court.

- Sexual assault nurse examiners (SANEs) provide immediate assistance and conduct the rape exam for victims of a sexual assault.

Identify the various types of victims and the roles and responsibilities of victim advocates.

- A primary victim is the person injured or killed as a direct result of a criminal act.

- A secondary victim is someone who, experiencing sympathetic pain, is affected by the primary victim's suffering.

- Secondary victimization occurs when the primary victim is abused a second time, usually by family, friends, and members of the criminal justice system, when they try to help the victim or use them in their efforts to arrest, prosecute, sentence, and punish the offender.

- *Survivor* is a term used to describe a relative or loved one of someone who has been killed, as well as a crime victim who copes well and manages to resume a normal life.

- Victim advocates are direct providers of victim services.

- Other victim advocates are assigned to a particular justice system—federal, judicial, military, juvenile, or tribal.

- The role of the victim advocate is to help the victim to achieve recovery by providing assistance with such community services as health care, housing, education, and employment, as well as to support the victim in every phase of the criminal justice process.

Differentiate between Adult Protective Services and TRIADs.

- Adult Protective Services is a program that provides safeguards and help to elder adults and dependent adults with disabilities who are in danger of being mistreated or neglected, who are unable to protect themselves, or who have no one to assist them.

- A TRIAD is a collaborative effort among police departments, sheriff's offices, those who work with elder adults, and representatives of elder adult groups (such as AARP or a local agency on aging) to address issues of interest to the elder adult community.

Describe the various kinds of collaborative responses to victims.

- Intimate partner violence councils work collaboratively to end intimate partner violence, help ensure survivor safety, and increase batterer accountability.

- The SART is made up of local police officers, victim advocates, SANE practitioners, and prosecutors who collaborate to determine the best and most effective way to work on sexual assault cases.

- Restorative justice aims to empower the victim to resolve the conflict, to move beyond perceived vulnerabilities, and to achieve closure. Restorative justice focuses on having the offender make amends for his actions rather than on increasing punishments.

Key Terms

Adult Protective Services 462

crime victim compensation 451

crime victimization 446

crisis intervention 456

dark figure of crime 443

long-term therapy 454

primary victim 445

psychic trauma 441

secondary victim 445

secondary victimization 446

sexual assault nurse examiner (SANE) 460

sexual assault response team (SART) 464

short-term therapy 453

survivor 446

TRIAD 462

vicarious trauma (compassion fatigue) 455

victim advocate 447

victim recidivism 446

victim services 446

Study Questions

1. A mother mourning the loss of a child due to criminal behavior is a/an
   a. primary victim.
   b. secondary victim.
   c. secondary victimization.
   d. inconsequential victim.

2. _____ has been a long-standing societal response in the United States.
   a. Victim ignoring
   b. Victim criticism
   c. Victim rights
   d. Victim concern

3. All of the following influenced the victims' rights movement *except*
   a. the President's Commission on Law Enforcement and the Administration of Justice.
   b. the women's movement.
   c. World War II.
   d. the civil rights movement.

4. The condition of being free of dysfunctional symptoms caused by victimization, such as difficulty working, sleeping, eating, and forming relationships, is referred to as
   a. victim recidivism.
   b. revictimization.
   c. crisis intervention.
   d. victim recovery.

5. The organization that investigates allegations of abuse against elder adults and dependent adults is called
   a. Adult Protective Services.
   b. Child Protective Services.
   c. TRIAD.
   d. the Office for Older Victims of Crime.

6. _____ provides immediate 24-hour, 7 days a week crisis intervention to all primary and secondary victims, as well as information, resources, and referrals for more long-term assistance.
   a. A sexual assault nurse examiner
   b. A hotline
   c. The Office for Victims of Crime
   d. Mandatory reporting

7. A specialized nurse who performs forensic exams for victims of sexual assault is called a/an
   a. SANE.
   b. SART.
   c. POMC.
   d. OVC.

8. All of the following can be repaid by victim compensation programs *except*
   a. medical expenses.
   b. counseling.
   c. pain and suffering.
   d. funeral expenses.

9. Victim compensation programs set maximum limits on the amount a victim can receive. Most state maximums are set at
   a. $10,000.
   b. $25,000.
   c. $50,000.
   d. $75,000.

10. A group that is victimized at much higher rates than other populations in the United States is
   a. Native Americans.
   b. Blacks.
   c. Whites.
   d. Latinos.

Critical Thinking Questions

For further review, go to the LearnSmart study module for this chapter.

1. Explain why it is important to understand the impact of victim blaming in victimology and victim services.

2. Should a person on probation or parole who is a victim of a crime be denied victim compensation? Explain.

3. Should restorative justice be used for intimate partner violence and sexual assault related crimes? Why or why not?

15 Juvenile

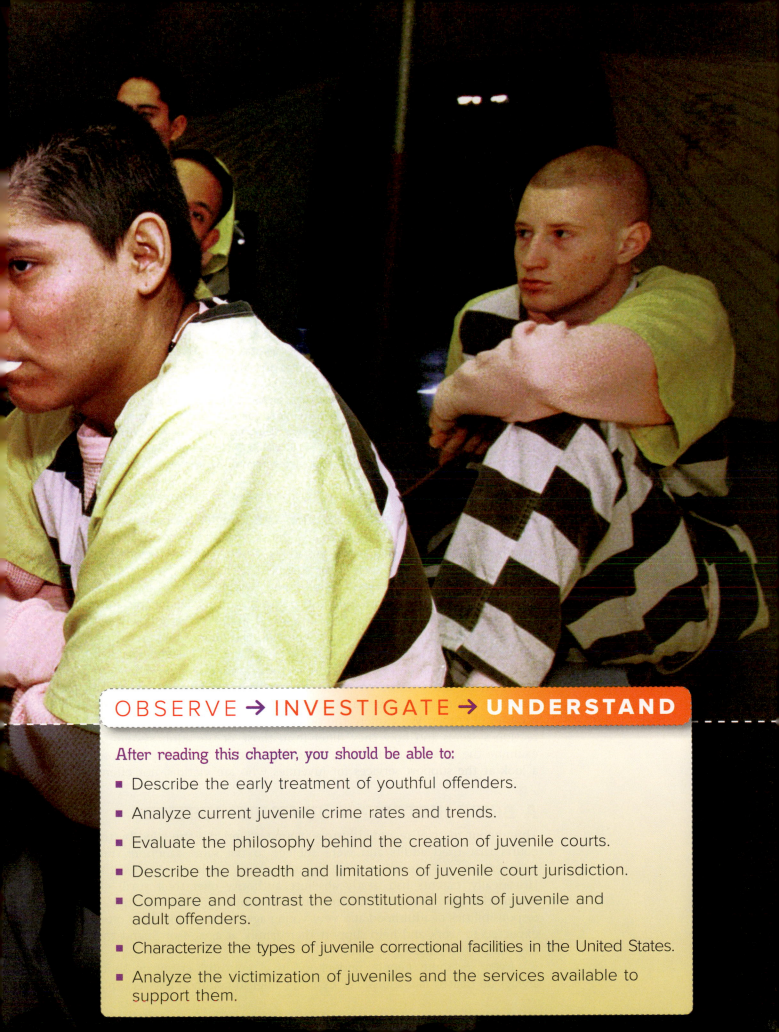

After reading this chapter, you should be able to:

- Describe the early treatment of youthful offenders.

- Analyze current juvenile crime rates and trends.

- Evaluate the philosophy behind the creation of juvenile courts.

- Describe the breadth and limitations of juvenile court jurisdiction.

- Compare and contrast the constitutional rights of juvenile and adult offenders.

- Characterize the types of juvenile correctional facilities in the United States.

- Analyze the victimization of juveniles and the services available to support them.

Realities and Challenges

Two Years in Solitary

A few days short of his 17th birthday, Kalief Browder was walking in the Bronx on his way home after a party. He and his friend were stopped by police officers and accused of assaulting and robbing a man. Browder had already had a few minor run-ins with the law, and his bail was set at $3,000, which his family couldn't afford to pay. He was taken to a juvenile detention center on New York's notorious Rikers Island. Although he continued to proclaim his innocence, and although his case never went to trial, Browder spent the next 3 years incarcerated—much of that time in solitary confinement.

Browder claimed that during his time in detention, he was subjected to abuse by fellow prisoners and by guards. His claims were at least partially supported by surveillance footage. He also suffered from depression and anxiety and attempted suicide more than once. But he also refused to accept a plea bargain that would have meant his immediate release, because that would have meant he had to plead guilty to a crime he insisted he didn't commit.

More than 1,000 days after he was locked up, Browder was released. After a journalist published his story, Browder received considerable media attention, even appearing on the television show *The View*. He worked hard to resume his education, and he hoped that his public sharing of his experiences would lead to reforms. But he also continued to struggle with his psychological demons. Two years after Kalief Browder was released from jail, he killed himself at his mother's house.[1]

The roots of the Western criminal justice system reach back centuries, but only within the last hundred years or so has the system given special attention and treatment to offenders who are not yet adults. Throughout the twentieth century and into the twenty-first, society has struggled with the perplexing question of how to deal with children who commit crimes. Should we focus on rehabilitation or punishment? How can a juvenile justice system process delinquents and reduce delinquency yet not deny juveniles fairness and justice? What kinds of incarceration and treatment programs should we provide, and how should these differ from adult programs? At what point should we treat a youthful offender as an adult?

This chapter describes youth crime today and interactions between law enforcement and youths. We trace the evolution of juvenile courts and the Supreme Court cases that have significantly affected the rights of children accused of crimes. We explore the procedures in the juvenile judicial and correction systems and how they differ from those of the adult system, and we examine the growing trend to try juveniles as adults. The chapter closes with a look at the support services for juveniles who are victims, not offenders.

A BRIEF HISTORY OF JUVENILE JUSTICE

Throughout most of recorded history, young offenders were tried by the same courts that tried adults and were subject to the same sanctions, including incarceration and execution. Even the concept of "adolescent" is itself recent.[2] Historically, parents had nearly absolute authority over their small children, whom the law treated as chattel–literally, property. Children took on the responsibilities of adulthood at a very young age. For example, they often were expected to work and help support their family at ages 4 or 5, and they usually married in their early teens.

Even so, some people understood that youthful criminals should not always be treated like adults. For example, English common law recognized the

infancy defense, by which children under age 7 could not be criminally prosecuted because they were too young to form *mens rea*, or criminal intent. A child between the ages of 7 and 14 could be prosecuted, but only if the prosecutor could prove that the child knew that what he had done was wrong. After reaching age 14, a child was prosecuted like an adult. The American colonies adopted the infancy defense, and many states still recognize it in some form.[3]

Early Methods of Control

Changes in the European economy during the sixteenth and seventeenth centuries brought people from rural areas to the cities and increased the number of individuals living in poverty. Crime rates went up. The traditional method of controlling children–the family–no longer sufficed because parents commonly toiled long hours away from home, often leaving children alone. Many impoverished parents were unable to provide for their children at all; children were abandoned or orphaned and left to beg, steal, or starve. Those in power, increasingly concerned about the threat they perceived from errant or unmanageable youths, created several methods to deal with them.

One option was **binding out** (sometimes called *placing out*), sending children to live with relatively wealthy families who provided food, shelter, and clothing, the basic necessities of life. In return, the children were obligated to work for the families until adulthood, typically doing manual labor such as farming and domestic duties. Another option was to send the children to institutions that served as poorhouses and prisons for young and old alike. The first of these was Bridewell, which opened in London in 1556. Similar institutions were soon built throughout England, some with specific facilities for youths. Inmates in such institutions were required to work long hours at tasks such as textile manufacturing.[4]

The colonization of North America brought another solution for problem children in England: They were encouraged–or required–to immigrate to the colonies, where they provided a ready source of labor. The distinction between this practice of *indentured servitude* and actual slavery was slight, and young indentured servants were often mistreated. In the colonies, children who committed crimes were controlled by their parents, their communities, and their churches. Parents had few restrictions on their authority over their children. Actions we would consider abusive today, such as beating children with rods, were not only permitted but often encouraged. Several colonies authorized capital punishment for children who disobeyed their parents, although it was seldom, if ever, carried out.[5]

As the Industrial Revolution began at the end of the eighteenth century, conditions for children in the United States were often appalling. Many lived in dire poverty, and those as young as 4 worked in factories and mines, under dangerous conditions and for very little pay. Initially, children who committed crimes and poor children were placed in adult jails and workhouses. In 1825 in New York, an organization called the Society for the Prevention of Pauperism opened the House of Refuge, the first institution specifically for youths. Other cities soon established their own refuges to house criminal children as well as orphans and the destitute. The philosophy was to keep the inmates from a life of poverty and crime by imposing strict discipline and order and requiring them to perform hard work such as making furniture or nails if they were boys, or sewing or doing laundry if they were girls. Conditions within the houses of refuge were often deplorable: Racism and sexism were common, adults beat the children, and stronger children preyed upon the weak.[6]

infancy defense
A defense holding that children under age 7 could not be criminally prosecuted because they were too young to form *mens rea*, or criminal intent.

binding out
The practice of sending children to live with relatively wealthy families who provided the child with the basic necessities of life in return for labor.

473

▲ **Child Laborers**

Until well into the twentieth century, even young children often worked long hours in dangerous jobs.

reform school
An industrial school that housed children who were delinquent, disobedient, or otherwise wayward.

child savers
Women in the 1800s who lobbied for child labor regulations, laws against child abuse, and a specialized justice system that would focus on the needs of youths.

parens patriae
A legal doctrine that gives the government authority to step in and make decisions about children, even against the wishes of their parents, when doing so is in the children's best interests.

The Child Saving Movement

By the middle of the nineteenth century, most child advocates recognized the need for separate correctional institutions for children. Some states, counties, and cities opened their own institutions for wayward youth. These were called **reform schools** or *industrial schools*, and they housed children who were delinquent (who committed crimes), disobedient, or otherwise wayward.[7] However, no special legal procedures for juveniles were available until the early twentieth century, when juvenile courts were created.

In the late 1800s, a number of middle-class and wealthy women became activists for better living conditions for children. Known as the **child savers,** these women lobbied for child labor regulations, laws against child abuse, and a specialized justice system that would focus on the needs of youths. Largely due to their efforts, the first juvenile court opened its doors in Chicago in 1899. By 1925, all but two states had specialized juvenile courts.[8]

Several factors made it logical to try young people in juvenile rather than adult court and not impose adult sanctions on them. First, adult correctional institutions were dangerous places for children. Not only were the young preyed upon by adult inmates, but youths usually learned new criminal behaviors there. Second, early intervention can lead to full rehabilitation of children. Third, because children do not yet have the cognitive ability to fully appreciate the consequences of their actions, they should not be held fully responsible for them as adults are. Finally, troubled children often live in troubled families. They have not yet had the opportunity to mature and move away from negative family influences.

Juvenile courts were intended to be less formal than adult courts. Instead of focusing on punishment, they were to use the treatment model (see Chapter 11) and emphasize solving children's problems and preventing crime. The legal doctrine of ***parens patriae***–literally, "parent of the country"–gives the government authority to step in and make decisions about children, even against the wishes of their parents, when doing so is in the children's best interests. The juvenile court judge, who often did not even have a law degree, was given much more discretion than a criminal court judge and would sit down with the child and other interested parties, such as the parents, determine what the problems were, and devise a solution. The intention was that children would have many more placement options than adults, so a treatment plan could be tailored to each child's needs.

Unlike adult criminal cases, juvenile cases were not public, and children were often referred to by their initials rather than their names. Juvenile records were usually kept private and often erased once the child reached adulthood. The creators of juvenile courts even devised a new vocabulary to avoid the stigma of criminal corrections.

MYTH/REALITY

MYTH: The problems faced by the juvenile justice system are recent because juveniles today are much more delinquent than they were 100 years ago.

REALITY: The problems the juvenile justice system faces are not related to changes in juvenile behavior. From its creation, the juvenile justice system encountered problems, such as large caseloads and an overwhelmed and undertrained staff.[9]

The promises of the juvenile court were never realized. Almost as soon as the courts opened, they found themselves with enormous caseloads that made it impossible for judges to give each child individualized attention. Courts were understaffed and poorly funded, and judges often had little or no experience or training in dealing with children. Cases were completed in as little as 10 minutes, and placement options remained few, especially for females. As the juvenile court system enters its second century, these problems remain even as new ones surface. Nevertheless, the juvenile court remains an important part of the justice system.[10]

▲ **Early Juvenile Court**

Compared to adult courts, juvenile courts were intended to be less formal.

JUVENILE CRIME TODAY

The term **juvenile delinquency** refers to the illegal acts that are committed by juveniles (also called *minors*). Depending on the state, a minor is anyone under the age of either 18 or 21. An additional category of misbehavior by children is the **status offense,** an act that would not be a crime if committed by an adult. Examples of such offenses are running away from home, curfew violations, and school truancy.

Causes of Juvenile Delinquency

Over the years, biologists, sociologists, psychologists, and criminologists have proposed many different theories regarding the causes of juvenile delinquency. These theories cover a large range of explanations and include a host of biological, psychological, and sociological factors (see Chapter 3). Nonetheless, some specific social factors are particularly important in looking at delinquency.[11]

Many researchers have tied delinquency to family factors such as poor parenting. Parental rejection and lack of supervision and involvement are strong

juvenile delinquency
Illegal acts that are committed by juveniles.

status offense
An offense that is illegal only because the defendant is a child, such as playing truant or running away.

◄ **Poverty and Delinquency**

Youths who grow up in poor neighborhoods with a lot of crime seem to be more likely to engage in delinquent behavior. *How would you explain the relationships between poverty and delinquency?*

predictors of conduct problems and delinquency. Poor parenting skills are specifically linked to the seriousness of the delinquency.[12] Delinquent behavior is also connected to a juvenile's experiences at school.[13] In fact, research has identified a "school-to-prison pipeline" for students who fail in school, have a history of suspensions or expulsions, or drop out of their own accord.[14]

The connection of class differences among juveniles to the likelihood of delinquent acts has been studied extensively. Historically, lower social class was tied to delinquency. The poor have always been seen as more criminal and more delinquent.[15] But those views were based on the use of arrest data. When self-report surveys gained popularity in the 1950s, they seemed to show that middle-class juveniles were committing more delinquent acts than was previously thought.[16] Early studies based on these surveys concluded there was little, if any, difference between social classes regarding delinquency. More recent research, however, has found that there is a difference in delinquency between lower-class and middle-class juvenile males; the significant factors seem to be growing up in poverty and in neighborhoods with high rates of delinquency.[17]

Race also influences delinquency statistics. Blacks have a higher **arrest rate** (the number of arrests per 100,000 persons) than do Whites, although the difference has narrowed since the mid-1990s. But arrest rates do not tell the complete story. Which crimes come to the attention of the police and who gets arrested are the factors that determine the final arrest statistics. A Black youth growing up in a poor neighborhood will more likely attract police attention than will a White youth in a middle-class environment.[18]

arrest rate
The number of arrests per 100,000 persons.

Measuring Juvenile Crime

MYTH/REALITY

MYTH: Juvenile crime rates are skyrocketing.

REALITY: Juvenile crime rates have been decreasing since 1994, especially for violent crimes.[19]

Despite the problems and the built-in bias of arrest data, the most common way to measure the amount of juvenile crime in the United States today is to look at arrest rates.[20] Contrary to the picture presented by the media, since 1994 violent crime arrests for juveniles have consistently decreased. Figure 15-1 shows the juvenile Violent Crime Index arrest rates between 1980 and 2011. Beginning in 1994, the arrest index rate declined for 10 years. After climbing slightly from 2004 to 2006, juvenile arrests resumed their decline to the point where they were at their lowest level in more than three decades. Although there was a decrease in the number of arrests of both male and female juveniles, the drop was less for female than male arrests for most crimes.[21] Figure 15-2 shows the

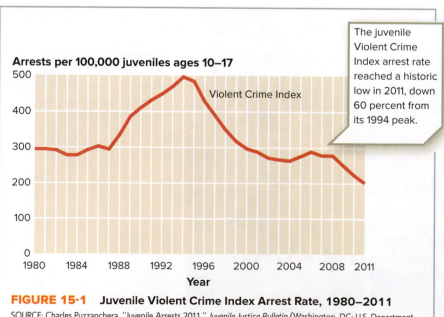

The juvenile Violent Crime Index arrest rate reached a historic low in 2011, down 60 percent from its 1994 peak.

FIGURE 15-1   **Juvenile Violent Crime Index Arrest Rate, 1980–2011**
SOURCE: Charles Puzzanchera, "Juvenile Arrests 2011," *Juvenile Justice Bulletin* (Washington, DC: U.S. Department of Justice, December 2013). www.ojjdp.gov/pubs/244476.pdf (retrieved July 7, 2015).

arrest rates for male and female juveniles from 1980 to 2011 for violent crimes such as aggravated assault, robbery, and murder.

Between 1980 and 2011, we see a similar trend with respect to the race of juvenile offenders. After the peak in 1994, juvenile arrests for violent crimes in all racial subgroups studied [Blacks, Whites (including Latinos), Asians, and American Indians] were at their lowest rates since 1980. Figure 15-3 shows the arrests of Black and White juveniles from 1980 to 2011. Note the decrease in the rate of violent crimes attributed to both White and Black juveniles, particularly for Black juveniles. Also apparent is the disproportionate rate of Black juvenile arrests. In 2011, 10- to 17-year-old Black juveniles comprised 17 percent of the U.S. population, yet they made up 51 percent of the violent crime arrests for juveniles. Compare this to White juveniles, who were 76 percent of the population but accounted for only 47 percent of violent crime arrests.[22]

Murders by juveniles more than doubled from the mid-1980s until 1993. The juvenile murder rate has been on the decline ever since. By 2011, juvenile murder arrest rates were

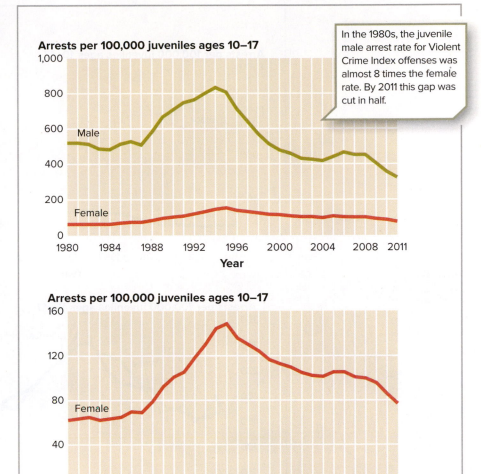

In the 1980s, the juvenile male arrest rate for Violent Crime Index offenses was almost 8 times the female rate. By 2011 this gap was cut in half.

FIGURE 15-2   Juvenile Arrest Rates for Violent Crime Index Offenses by Sex, 1980–2011

SOURCE: Charles Puzzanchera, "Juvenile Arrests 2011," *Juvenile Justice Bulletin* (Washington, DC: U.S. Department of Justice, December 2013). www.ojjdp.gov/pubs/244476.pdf (retrieved July 7, 2015).

at a historical low. Experts attribute much of this decline to a decrease in the killing of minority males by other minority males. The rate of other violent and nonviolent offenses committed by juveniles also dropped. For example, in 2011 the rate for juveniles arrested for burglary was 75 percent of what it was in the 1980s, and the arrest rate for forcible rape dropped 40 percent from 2002 to reach its lowest level in three decades.[23]

What explains these decreases? In searching for answers, we must remember that the official numbers underreport the actual extent of juvenile crime in the United States. Many delinquent acts are never reported, and many that are do not result in an arrest. Fewer than 50 percent of all violent crimes are reported to the police, and close to 35 percent of all U.S. police departments do not provide complete arrest statistics. The *Juvenile Offenders and Victims: 2006 National Report*, the most reliable national data available, is used by practitioners throughout the field.[24] However, because of underreporting, criminal justice professionals also use methods other than arrest statistics to measure crime.

Self-report studies help to fill in the missing data. Self-report data may be inaccurate because self-reports rely on the memory and honesty of the person reporting, but they do show a large discrepancy from the official arrest data.[25]

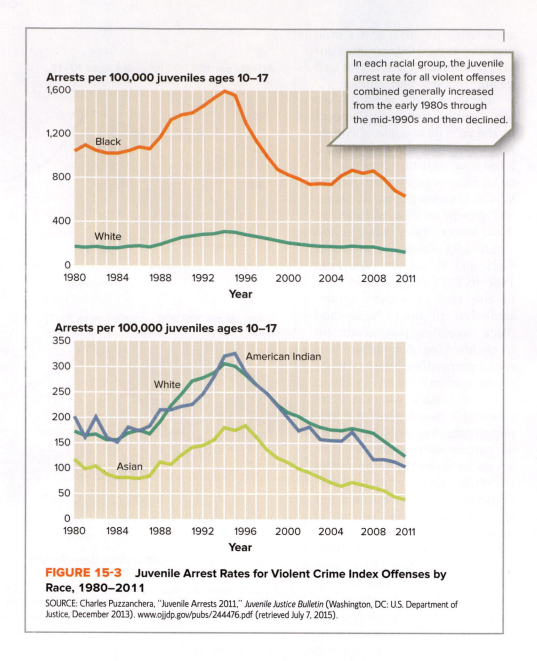

In each racial group, the juvenile arrest rate for all violent offenses combined generally increased from the early 1980s through the mid-1990s and then declined.

FIGURE 15-3   **Juvenile Arrest Rates for Violent Crime Index Offenses by Race, 1980–2011**

SOURCE: Charles Puzzanchera, "Juvenile Arrests 2011," *Juvenile Justice Bulletin* (Washington, DC: U.S. Department of Justice, December 2013). www.ojjdp.gov/pubs/244476.pdf (retrieved July 7, 2015).

Victimization surveys are another method of determining the amount of crime. These surveys collect information directly from a representative sample of the general population rather than relying on police records. The advantage of using victimization surveys compared to other ways of measuring crime is that unreported crime is also included.

POLICE AND YOUTH CRIME

A juvenile usually enters the justice system by way of the police. Police often try to handle trivial offenses such as curfew violations informally–by issuing a citation, meeting with the juvenile and his or her parents, or some other informal arrangement or understanding. Handling a juvenile offense informally prevents formal arrest and a court proceeding that could result in incarceration and even a criminal record. A police decision to make an arrest–many jurisdictions use the term *detain*–automatically triggers an investigation by authorities of the **juvenile justice system.** If the court places the youth on probation, any violation of probation could bring further court action–and possibly more serious charges.

juvenile justice system
The juvenile justice system is the main formal legal structure used to respond to and process minors who commit crimes.

Over the past decade, a significant drop in juvenile arrests has been observed. In 2012, law enforcement agencies in the United States made approximately 1.3 million arrests of persons under the age of 18. This represents a decline of 10 percent between 2011 and 2012 and a drop of 37 percent since 2003. The number of juvenile violent crime arrests in 2012 was less than any of the previous 33 years. Similarly, in 2012 property crime arrests declined for the fourth straight year. From 2003 through 2012, arrests of females decreased less than male arrests. Juvenile arrests disproportionately involved minorities. More than half (52 percent) of all juvenile arrests for violent crimes in 2012 involved Black youth; 46 percent involved White youth, 1 percent Asian youth, and 1 percent American Indian youth. For property crime arrests, the proportions were 61 percent White youth, 36 percent Black youth, 2 percent Asian youth, and 1 percent American Indian youth.[26]

Police Discretion

Police have a large amount of latitude in how to handle juveniles. In other than serious cases, this latitude is necessary, and the police are called on to make judgments on whether to warn the offender, handle the case informally, or detain the individual. Not every juvenile offense ends in arrest, nor should it. Accumulating evidence points to the detrimental effects on adolescent development that system involvement and confinement impose.[27]

Many of the police officers' judgments are necessarily subjective and are based on factors other than the offense. One important factor is the attitude and demeanor of the juvenile. A polite juvenile stands a better chance than one who is hostile. There is some evidence that police may treat male and female juveniles differently.[28] Other biases can affect a police officer's decision as well. For example, some officers may treat juveniles who are from minority and disadvantaged communities more harshly.[29] Factors such as more frequent patrolling of Black and Latino neighborhoods and racial profiling by officers–whether conscious or unconscious–exacerbate the situation.[30]

If a juvenile case is handled informally, a citation or reprimand may be issued. This action could require the juvenile and the parents to appear at the police station for a meeting with the officer. If, however, the juvenile is detained, he or she is usually brought to a facility like a juvenile hall and is referred to the probation department. At this point formal juvenile court procedures are set in motion.

Police in the Neighborhood and Schools

Police have long worked with juveniles in the community, providing positive role models. One common program is the Police Athletic League (PAL). Although a study evaluating such programs did not show strong positive changes in the youth who participated, most of the youth in these programs reported the experience as very positive.[31] Since earnestly committing to a community policing philosophy in 2013, the Camden, New Jersey, Police Department has been exemplary in its involvement with youth. The police regularly hold meet-the-officer fairs at parks and churches, engage enthusiastically with youth at their baseball games, participate in hybrid touch and tackle football games, and facilitate ingress of "Mister Softee" trucks into neighborhoods. Officers stand at school crossings and street corners where in the past drugs and violence flourished. Testimonies abound about the positive influence the police have on local youth.[32]

▼ **D.A.R.E. in the Classroom**

Police officer Jenifer Rodriguez distributes D.A.R.E. name tags to Grant Elementary School fifth-graders in Santa Monica, California.

Matters *of* Ethics

Policing the Schools

Many U.S. schools have full-time police officers, called *school resource officers (SROs)*, stationed within them. Although this practice began in the 1960s, it has increased considerably in the wake of several highly publicized school shootings over the past two decades. School resource officers usually are sworn members of the local police force, but some large school districts have their own police departments.

Advocates of SROs argue that they establish safer places to learn, prevent violence, and provide children with counseling. SROs also often participate in legal education for students. However, the use of police in schools is not without controversy. One widely debated question is whether SROs should be armed. Some supporters assert that arming them is necessary, whereas opponents insist that the presence of firearms in a school setting—even if those firearms are carried by police officers—constitutes a safety risk and adds to a culture where guns are commonplace.

Another controversial topic has been whether the presence of SROs increases the likelihood that students will be pushed into the juvenile justice system for misbehaviors that arguably are better left to school administrators to resolve. Research in this area is limited. Some studies indicate that SROs can deter students from committing assaults on campus as well as bringing weapons to school. Other studies suggest that children in schools with SROs might be more likely to be arrested for low-level offenses. The benefits or detrimental effects of SROs can vary across school districts and are dependent on recruitment policies, training systems, and clearly delineated responsibilities.

OBSERVE → INVESTIGATE → UNDERSTAND

- What are the potential benefits and risks of stationing police officers in schools full-time?
- Do you think it is ethically correct to involve formal law enforcement in schools? Why or why not?
- Under what circumstances do you believe that it is appropriate for police officers to become involved in a student's misbehavior?

SOURCES: Texas Appleseed, "Texas' School-to-Prison Pipeline: Ticketing, Arrest & Use of Force in Schools." www.texasappleseed.net/images/stories/reports/Ticketing_Booklet_web.pdf (retrieved March 11, 2011); Nathan James and Gail McCallion, "School Resource Officers: Law Enforcement Officers in Schools," Congressional Research Service Report for Congress, June 26, 2013; Tierney Sneed, "School Resource Officers: Safety Priority or Part of the Problem?" *U.S. News & World Report,* January 30, 2015. www.usnews.com/news/articles/2015/01/30/are-school-resource-officers-part-of-the-school-to-prison-pipeline-problem (retrieved May 20, 2015); Ashley Lauren Samsa, "Say No to Armed Guards in Schools," *The Guardian,* February 20, 2013. www.theguardian.com/commentisfree/2013/feb/20/no-armed-guards-in-schools (retrieved May 20, 2015).

Across the United States, police–school liaison programs aim to change students' attitudes about the police, reduce violence and crime in and around the school, and provide positive adult–youth connections.[33] A program that has garnered much attention is Drug Abuse Resistance Education (D.A.R.E.), founded in 1983. In this program, police officers go into classrooms and teach students how to resist using illegal drugs. Officers receive 80 hours of training to teach this curriculum.[34] However, there has not been much evidence-based research showing that the D.A.R.E. program is effective.[35] In addition, the U.S. Government Accountability Office (GAO) stated that D.A.R.E. provided no long-term effect in preventing use of illegal drugs–the results just do not seem to last. Youth who participated in the D.A.R.E. program did show some positive attitude changes after 1 year, but those results diminished over time.[36] As the "Matters of Ethics" box describes, other police–school liaison programs have been controversial.

It is likely that police will continue to assume a role in the schools. In order to develop and maintain effective partnerships between police and schools, it is essential that key areas be addressed. One important factor is the selection of officers for school-related assignments. At a minimum, officers should express a strong interest in youth, be adaptable to working in a school setting, and possess good communication skills. Another critical area is the training officers undergo prior to placement in a school environment, which should include a wide range of youth-related topics.[37]

THE MODERN JUVENILE COURT SYSTEM

Juvenile courts were created with different goals from those of adult criminal courts. Rehabilitation rather than punishment was to be the focus, and the court's primary interest was to be on the child rather than on the offense. Although the process in juvenile courts has evolved to be quite similar to that of adult courts, some important distinctions remain, including differing terminology, narrower jurisdiction, and more restricted procedural rights for juvenile defendants.

Juvenile Court Jurisdiction

Juvenile courts are courts of limited jurisdiction, meaning that they have the power to hear only certain kinds of cases defined by the child's behavior and age. Juvenile courts can hear *delinquency cases*, in which a minor is accused of committing a criminal act, as well as *status offense cases*, in which the offense is illegal only because the defendant is a child. In the past, status offenses were often vaguely defined. Children could be brought before the court and, ultimately, placed in facilities for behavior that was considered "vicious," "immoral," "profane," "incorrigible," or "indecent." Other behaviors that could subject a child to the juvenile court included selling things, singing or playing an instrument in public, loitering, staying out at night, frequenting dance halls, and being sexually promiscuous. Although juvenile courts have generally treated males more harshly for delinquency, females have generally experienced harsher treatment for status offenses such as breaking curfew. This bias may result from stereotypes that appear to support the need to protect females and to control their sexual behavior. Finally, juvenile courts may also hear *dependency cases*, in which a child's parents cannot or will not care for her properly.[38]

It might seem strange for a single court to have jurisdiction over a grade school truant, an armed teenage robber, and a preschooler abandoned by parents, but there is logic behind this plan. All three youths have a problem that needs fixing. They may even have the same problem: inadequate parental guidance and supervision. The system was devised under the assumption that curbing minor offenses today will help prevent criminal behavior later–that when a young person makes a mistake and undergoes some form of punishment or rehabilitation, he is more likely to avoid errant behavior in the future. As one early proponent wrote, "The problem for determination by the judge is not, 'Has this boy or girl committed a specific wrong,' but 'What is he, how has he become what he is, and what had best be done in his interest and in the interest of the state to save him from a downward career?'"[39]

The upper and lower age limits for the legal definition of a child vary from state to state (see the figure "Mapping Juvenile Court Jurisdiction" on page 482). In most states, an offender is eligible for juvenile court until age 18. In 10 states, juvenile court jurisdiction expires on a person's 17th birthday, and in North Carolina and New York, a 16-year-old who commits a crime must be tried as an adult.[40] In 2015, in the wake

▼ **Juvenile in Court**
All states have laws permitting juveniles to be tried in juvenile courts.

of the Kalief Browder case (discussed at the beginning of this chapter), New York was considering raising the age of criminal responsibility to 18.

In most states, once the juvenile court has heard a case, its jurisdiction may extend beyond the offender's 18th birthday. For example, if a 15-year-old is judged delinquent in juvenile court, the juvenile justice system may confine her in juvenile facilities or monitor the delinquent through probation even after she turns 18. The most common maximum age of a confined or monitored delinquent is 20, although it ranges between 18 and 24 depending on the state.[41] No matter how serious the crime, offenders tried in juvenile court must be released from custody on their 21st birthday (or 25th in a few states).

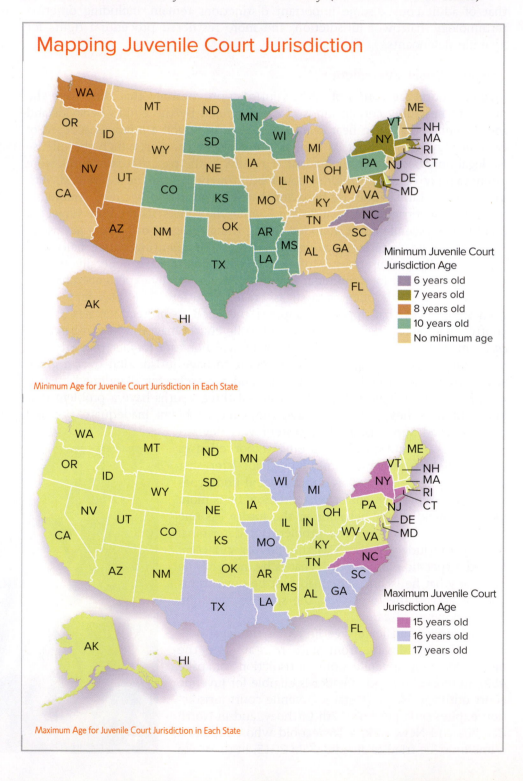

Mapping Juvenile Court Jurisdiction

Minimum Juvenile Court Jurisdiction Age
- ■ 6 years old
- ■ 7 years old
- ■ 8 years old
- ■ 10 years old
- ■ No minimum age

Minimum Age for Juvenile Court Jurisdiction in Each State

Maximum Juvenile Court Jurisdiction Age
- ■ 15 years old
- ■ 16 years old
- ■ 17 years old

Maximum Age for Juvenile Court Jurisdiction in Each State

Minimum Age for Waiver

Age for Waiver	States with Minimum Age
No minimum	Alaska, Arizona, Delaware, District of Columbia, Florida, Georgia, Hawaii, Idaho, Indiana, Maine, Maryland, Nebraska, Nevada, Oklahoma, Oregon, Pennsylvania, Rhode Island, South Carolina, South Dakota, Tennessee, Washington, West Virginia, Wisconsin
10	Kansas, Vermont
12	Colorado, Missouri, Montana
13	Illinois, Mississippi, New Hampshire, New York, North Carolina, Wyoming
14	Alabama, Arkansas, California, Connecticut, Iowa, Kentucky, Louisiana, Massachusetts, Michigan, Minnesota, New Jersey, North Dakota, Ohio, Texas, Utah, Virginia
15	New Mexico

SOURCE: Building Blocks for Youth, "Charts on Transferring Youth to Criminal Court." http://jjpl.org/Publications_JJ _InTheNews/JuvenileJusticeSpecialReports/BBY/ycat/transchart.html (retrieved July 20, 2011).

Some states also have a minimum age for juvenile court jurisdiction, a reflection of the common law idea that young children cannot form criminal intent. Children younger than the minimum who commit criminal acts cannot be tried either as juveniles or as adults; if their actions are serious, however, they and their families may be referred to counseling or other social services (see "Mapping Juvenile Court Jurisdiction"). This minimum age varies from 6 in North Carolina to between 7 and 10 in 12 other states.[42]

Most states have no minimum age for juvenile court jurisdiction, and very young children who commit crimes may be brought before juvenile courts. In recent years, children as young as age 7 have been charged with crimes such as murder, attempted armed robbery, and arson.[43] In 1996, a 6-year-old boy in California kicked and beat a 1-month-old infant, causing the baby permanent brain damage. Despite his age and the fact that he was mildly mentally challenged, the boy was charged with attempted murder and held for several months in a juvenile detention facility. The prosecutor told reporters, "It doesn't matter whether you're 6 or you're 106. If you do something that hurts somebody else, with knowledge of the wrongfulness of it, you're responsible for it, period." Eventually, the judge ruled the boy incompetent to stand trial, and he was sent to live in a group home for troubled children.[44]

Juvenile Court Waivers

The founders of the juvenile justice system recognized that the system would not be appropriate for all youthful offenders. The seriousness of their crimes, the complexity of their problems, or their relatively advanced age might make them less amenable for treatment within the juvenile system. Thus mechanisms exist to permit the juvenile court to waive jurisdiction and allow the transfer–or **waiver**– of these offenders to adult court. In the past 20 years, nearly every state has expanded the methods and circumstances under which juveniles may be waived, and most have lowered the minimum age for waiver.[45] Some states have no minimum at all; others specify minimums as young as 10 (see the table above).

waiver
A mechanism to permit the transfer of some juvenile offenders to adult court.

Types of Waivers   Waiver laws vary from state to state. Almost all states use at least one of three major methods, and some use a combination.

The first kind of waiver is called **judicial waiver.** Under this method, a prosecutor or probation officer recommends that a child be tried as an adult. The juvenile court judge then determines whether the child is fit to be treated

judicial waiver
Means by which a judge designates a juvenile to be tried in adult court.

Race, Class, Gender

Minority Youth Sentenced to Life without Parole

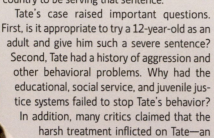

One day in July 1999, 12-year-old Lionel Tate killed 6-year-old Tiffany Eunick by stomping on her. Apparently imitating professional wrestling moves he had seen on television, Tate fractured the girl's skull and damaged her internal organs. Tate was tried as an adult and convicted of first-degree murder. When he was sentenced to life in prison without parole, he became the youngest person in the country to be serving that sentence.

Tate's case raised important questions. First, is it appropriate to try a 12-year-old as an adult and give him such a severe sentence? Second, Tate had a history of aggression and other behavioral problems. Why had the educational, social service, and juvenile justice systems failed to stop Tate's behavior? In addition, many critics claimed that the harsh treatment inflicted on Tate—an African American—was just an extreme example of the justice system's pervasive mistreatment of Blacks. Even the prosecutor protested Tate's severe sentence.

In January 2004, Tate's conviction was overturned because his competency had not been evaluated before he was tried. Instead of being retried, he accepted the plea deal he had initially been offered, but that his mother had rejected, of 1 year of house arrest plus 10 years of probation. Within a year, Tate had violated probation by leaving his house with a knife, and 5 years were added to his probation term. Only a few months later, Tate robbed a pizza deliveryman at gunpoint. He received a 30-year prison sentence for unlawful gun possession and 10 years for the robbery. Clearly his experience with incarceration had done little to rehabilitate him—and may have taught him criminal behavior.

OBSERVE → INVESTIGATE → UNDERSTAND

- If you had been the prosecutor in the Lionel Tate case, how would you have handled the case? Would you have referred it to juvenile court or to an adult court? State your reasons.
- What role do you think Tate's race played in the way he was processed in the criminal justice system?
- Do you think Tate's later criminal behavior would have been prevented by a juvenile court proceeding and disposition (sentencing)? Why or why not?

SOURCES: "Lionel Tate Gets 30 Years in Jail," *KDKA.com.* http://kdka.com/homepage/topstories_story_138103942.html (retrieved June 19, 2007); Abby Goodnough, "Youngster Given Life Term for Killing Gets New Trial," *New York Times,* December 11, 2003.

---

within the juvenile system. The U.S. Supreme Court has held that juveniles are entitled to certain due process rights during this hearing, including access to probation reports and a statement by the judge of the reasons for her decision.[46] State statutes specify what ages and offenses are eligible for judicial waiver and what factors the judge must consider in the decision.

The second way that a child may be tried as an adult is through **statutory exclusion,** in which state laws categorically exclude certain ages and offenses from juvenile court jurisdiction. For example, in Wisconsin children as young as 10 who are accused of first- or second-degree intentional homicide are automatically sent directly to adult court.

The third method for waiver is called **direct file,** or **prosecutorial waiver.** For certain ages and offenses, the prosecutor can choose whether to bring the case to juvenile or adult court. No hearing is held, and no legal criteria apply. The decision is left entirely to the prosecutor's discretion and cannot be appealed.

Problems with Waivers The use of waivers has increased and often enjoys popular or political appeal as part of a tough-on-crime approach. However, critics and scholars raise several objections to waiving children to be tried in adult courts. One is that waivers perpetuate racial and ethnic biases. There is evidence that minority youths are disproportionately likely to be tried as adults.[47] The "Race, Class, Gender" box describes one case of a very young Black offender who was given a life sentence.

statutory exclusion
The categorical exclusion, by state law, of certain ages and offenses from juvenile court jurisdiction.

direct file (prosecutorial waiver)
A method that allows the prosecutor to choose whether to bring the juvenile's case to juvenile or adult court.

MYTH/REALITY

MYTH: Only the most violent juveniles are tried as adults.

REALITY: A large proportion of juveniles tried as adults are accused of nonviolent crimes.[48]

A second objection to the use of waivers is that prosecutorial waiver results in uneven and unfair patterns of transfers. Because prosecutors are elected, they may choose to waive a case if they believe that doing so is a politically popular decision. Thus the proportion and kinds of cases waived under direct file may vary a great deal from one county to the next, depending on the philosophy and motives of each county's prosecutors. In one study, fewer than 20 percent of the waived cases were crimes against persons.[49] On any given day in 2004, approximately 2,500 people under the age of 18 were confined in adult prisons; 40 percent of these youths had committed nonviolent crimes, and only 13 percent had committed homicide or sex offenses.[50]

A third major criticism is that waivers send children to adult jails and prisons.[51] Clearly children in prisons are vulnerable to sexual exploitation and physical injury. Furthermore, an increasing body of research demonstrates that children tried as adults are more likely to reoffend after release, as we saw in the case of Lionel Tate, described in the "Race, Class, Gender" box.[52]

▲ **Juveniles Tried as Adults**
In recent years, juveniles have increasingly been tried in adult courts.

Landmark U.S. Supreme Court Cases

For nearly seven decades after its inception, the juvenile court functioned more informally than adult courts. One result of this informality was that children were given virtually none of the due process protections adults receive. They were not permitted assistance of counsel, were not allowed to confront and cross-examine witnesses, and did not have the right to avoid self-incrimination. They did not have to be found guilty beyond a reasonable doubt, and judges rather than juries decided their fate. Due process rights were thought to be unnecessary because the court's goal was to treat, not to punish. The assumption was that due process requirements would actually impede juvenile courts' abilities to treat young offenders.

In theory, it made sense for wayward youths to trade due process rights for compassionate rehabilitation. But in reality, from the very beginning, most children received neither from courts too overwhelmed to provide careful consideration of individual cases. As the U.S. Supreme Court wrote in 1966, "[T]here may be grounds for concern that the child receives the worst of both worlds: that he gets neither the protections accorded to adults nor the solicitous care and regenerative treatment postulated for children."[53] Consequently, in a series of cases, the Supreme Court gradually reformed the way juvenile courts operated by granting children certain rights.

In re Gault (1967)—Establishing Due Process for Juveniles   The Court decision that was key to the establishment of due process in the modern juvenile justice system was *In re Gault*, decided in 1967.[54] "A Case in Point" on page 486 describes this landmark case. Once *Gault* was decided, children brought before the juvenile court were entitled to several of the most basic rights that adult defendants are guaranteed–the right to be notified of the charges against them, to confront and cross-examine witnesses, to remain silent, to obtain a transcript of the proceedings, and to appeal the court's decision. Perhaps most significant, juveniles were also entitled to the assistance of an attorney.

a case in point

Gerald Francis Gault Has His Day in Supreme Court

On June 8, 1964, in Gila County, Arizona, a woman complained to police about sexually suggestive prank phone calls she had received. That afternoon, the local sheriff arrested her neighbor, 15-year-old Gerald Francis Gault, and took him to the juvenile detention facility. Gault's parents did not even know he had been arrested until they arrived home from work and could not find him.

The next day, a petition stating that he had been delinquent was filed against Gault in juvenile court. He and his parents were not given a copy. Hearings were held that day and again 6 days later in front of a juvenile court judge. During the hearings, Gault was not read his rights before being questioned, no lawyers were present, and Gault was not given the chance to consult with an attorney. The neighbor who had issued the complaint was not there. Probation officers gave the judge a referral report, but Gault and his parents were not allowed to see it.

No record was made of the proceedings, at the end of which the judge found Gault delinquent. Although Gault's only previous run-in with the law was being present when a friend stole a wallet from a purse, the judge committed him to the state industrial school until he was 21—a period of nearly 6 years. The maximum sentence an adult could have received for the offense was 2 months in jail or a $50 fine. Under Arizona law, Gault was not allowed to appeal to the state appeals court.

Gault filed a federal *habeas corpus* petition, which eventually reached the U.S. Supreme Court. Justice Abraham Fortas wrote an opinion for the Court that was highly critical of the state of juvenile justice in the United States. Justice Fortas wrote, "In view of this, it would be extraordinary if our Constitution did not require the procedural regularity and the exercise of care implied in the phrase 'due process.' Under our Constitution, the condition of being a boy does not justify a kangaroo court." The Court went on to grant juveniles several basic due process rights.

Gerry Gault was finally released after having been incarcerated for nearly 3 years. He had a long and successful military career, earned vocational degrees, and today is a heavy equipment operator who has been married for over 35 years.

OBSERVE → INVESTIGATE → UNDERSTAND

- Why do you think young Gault was punished so much more severely for his offense than an adult would have been for the same offense?

- In your opinion, what is the most serious due process right of which Gault was deprived? State your reasons.

- If the juvenile justice system had been meeting its goals, do you think the Supreme Court would have been as likely to grant juveniles due process rights? Why or why not?

SOURCES: *In re Gault*, 387 U.S. 1, 28–29 (1967); "Protecting America's Children—Assessing the Promise of *In re Gault* 40 Years Later," Open Society Institute, OSI Forum. www.soros.org/initiatives/justice/events/gault_20070503/event_biography_folder_initiative_view (retrieved June 18, 2007).

As a result of gaining these rights, what was once envisioned as an informal conversation between concerned parties now acquired many of the characteristics of an adult criminal trial. While in the past about a quarter of juvenile court judges did not have any formal training in law, a law degree is now essential.[55]

In re Winship (1970)—Proof Beyond a Reasonable Doubt for Juveniles   Three years after *Gault*, the Supreme Court considered another important issue: What should be the standard of proof in juvenile cases? While the long-standing common law rule had been that adults must be found guilty beyond a reasonable doubt, juvenile cases usually needed to be proved only by a preponderance of the evidence—the same standard used in civil cases. The case that brought this issue before the Court concerned 12-year-old Samuel Winship, who had been sent to a training school for up to 6 years for stealing $112 from a locker.[56] In *In re Winship,* the state of New York argued that the lesser standard of proof was appropriate in juvenile cases because it was suited to the juvenile court's rehabilitative purposes. A majority of the Supreme Court disagreed, however, holding that the due process clause in the Constitution requires proof beyond a reasonable doubt in juvenile as well as adult cases.

McKeiver v. Pennsylvania (1971)—No Jury Trials for Juveniles   After *Gault* and *Winship,* the juvenile system began to resemble the adult criminal system in many important respects. Advocates of the changes argued that they were necessary to ensure that young offenders would be treated fairly. Critics feared that the reforms would interfere with the juvenile justice system's mission of rehabilitation and erase any meaningful distinction between the juvenile and adult systems. The Supreme Court discussed this controversy when it decided a third landmark case, *McKeiver v. Pennsylvania,* which centered on whether juveniles were entitled to jury trials.[57] *McKeiver* was actually several consolidated cases involving juveniles charged with a broad variety of offenses.

McKeiver was a contentious case for the Court—four justices joined in one opinion, two justices wrote two separate concurring opinions, and three justices dissented. In the end, however, a majority agreed that children in juvenile proceedings are not entitled to juries. The Court admitted that the juvenile justice system was a failure but was not ready to give up on it altogether. Justice Harry Blackmun wrote, "There is a possibility, at least, that the jury trial, if required as a matter of constitutional precept, will remake the juvenile proceeding into a fully adversary process and will put an effective end to what has been the idealistic prospect of an intimate, informal protective proceeding."[58]

Breed v. Jones (1975)—Double Jeopardy and Juvenile Cases   In 1975, the Supreme Court granted another important right to juvenile offenders. Gary Jones, 17, was accused of committing an armed robbery. The juvenile court judge ruled that Jones had in fact committed the robbery but also that he was "unfit for treatment as a juvenile"–that is, he was not likely to be rehabilitated by the juvenile justice system. The judge ordered him tried in adult court, where Jones was found guilty of the robbery. When Jones appealed to the U.S. Supreme Court, the Court held that the Fifth Amendment's double jeopardy clause applies to juvenile proceedings. A person cannot be tried in both juvenile and adult courts for the same offense.[59]

MYTH/REALITY

MYTH: Minors cannot be interrogated without the presence of their parents or an attorney.

REALITY: Like adults, children may waive their *Miranda* rights and be questioned without lawyers present. In fact, unless a juvenile specifically asks for a parent, the parent need not even be notified that the child is being questioned.[60]

Other Important Cases   Several other cases are of particular importance to juvenile offenders. In *Fare v. Michael C.* (1979), the Supreme Court refused to extend extra protections to juveniles during police interrogations.[61] Under the Court's decision in this case, police may interrogate children without their parents' or an attorney's presence, and any statements the children make will be admissible in court.

In 1984, in *Schall v. Martin,* the Court held that minors may be subjected to preventive detention.[62] That is, children accused of crimes may be held not only to ensure that they appear in court, but also to protect them from adverse home conditions or to prevent them from committing additional offenses while their case is pending. The following Disconnects box highlights some of the laws throughout the United States that punish truancy.

DIS Con nects

Punishing Truancy

Eileen DiNino, a single mother, was sentenced to the Berks County Jail in Reading, Pennsylvania, because she owed more than $2,000 in fines and fees over the truancy of her two teenaged sons. DiNino is but one of the more than 1,600 parents, mostly moms, locked up in the same jail for the same reason. In Pennsylvania, once a student misses more than three days due to unexcused absences, the child and parents are referred to court and a judge will issue a $300 fine for each additional absence, as well as additional fees to cover court costs. If a parent is indigent, the parent can petition the court documenting the family's inability to pay. Failure to submit the necessary paperwork will result in jail time, as it did in DiNino's case.

Although jail time associated with truancy is on the decline, school administrators, police, and courts throughout the United States struggle with how to keep young people in school and hold both the student and parents or guardians accountable for unexcused absences. A Georgia law authorizes the removal of a driver's license from a truant teen, whereas a Tennessee law decreases welfare payments to parents with a truant child. Since 2002, states have passed approximately 23 attendance-related bills each year, and one-third of states passed laws that require further court involvement and stiffer legal penalties for truants and their parents. West Virginia requires parents to attend a conference with school officials or be sent to court, and Nebraska passed a law that 20 or more absences, even if the majority of these absences are excused, will be subject to court intervention. The strictest state is Texas, which prosecuted 113,000 cases of truancy in 2013 alone—more than twice the total number of truancy cases in all other states combined. These prosecutions disproportionately impacted minority students; almost 20 percent of truancy cases involved African American students, yet these students represent less than 13 percent of the student body statewide. Similarly, 64 percent of reported cases involved Latino students, who only represent 52 percent of the total student body. Students with disabilities were also charged with truancy even when they were absent for special education or medical reasons.[a]

More than 150,000 students nationwide are identified as truants, leading to varying punishments from fines to loss of custody and probation for adolescents and/or parents. Some skip school by choice (also known as "willful defiance"), whereas others do not go to school to avoid bullying and still others do not go because of poverty factors such as lack of transportation or needing to serve as caretakers within their family. About 15,000 truant youths are placed on juvenile probation, with probation violations for breaking curfew and additional truancy contributing to detention or out-of-home placements. Each year, over 1,000 truants are removed from their homes and placed in foster care, group homes, or detention centers. In an effort to combat the problem, some states will issue warrants to parents for contributing to the delinquency of a minor or conduct truancy sweeps, arresting parents for failure to reasonably supervise or encourage school attendance.

It is unclear whether any of these efforts have a positive impact on increasing school attendance or decreasing the correlates of not attending school such as delinquency, lower academic achievement, and dropping out of school. Instead, treating truancy as a crime seems to have the unintended consequences of decreasing school attendance and pushing families further into poverty.[b] There is a backlash under way against the penalties against students and parents for truancy. As a result, greater emphasis is being placed on ways to encourage students to go to school, including identifying academic courses of interest or locating after-school programs of interest such as sports, vocational training, and/or the arts.

OBSERVE → INVESTIGATE → UNDERSTAND

- How do you think truancy should be addressed?
- Should parents be held accountable when their children do not attend school?
- Should truancy be treated like a crime?

SOURCES: [a]Alisa Semiens, "Report: Texas Prosecutes More Truancy Cases Than All Other States Combined," *Texas Observer*, March 5, 2015. www.texasobserver.org/report-texas-prosecutes-truancy-more-than-all-other-states-combined/#.VPmSN-QxGHXA.twitter (retrieved June 10, 2015).
[b]Dana Goldstein, "Inexcusable Absences: Skipping School Is a Problem. But Why Is It a Crime?" *New Republic*, March 6, 2015. www.themarshallproject.org/2015/03/06/inexcusable-absences?utm_medium=email&utm_campaign=newsletter&utm_source=opening-statement&utm_term=newsletter-20150306-128 (retrieved June 10, 2015).

Until 2005, children could be sentenced to death. In 1944, 14-year-old George Stinney was put to death in the electric chair for having killed two girls.[63] In cases decided in 1988 and 1989, the Supreme Court held that capital punishment was constitutional for offenders over 15.[64] Between 1976 and 2004, 22 people who were younger than 18 when they committed murder were executed in the United States, and 73 more were on death row.[65] Only a handful of other nations–Pakistan, Bangladesh, Rwanda, and Barbados–executed juveniles during this time.[66] However, in 2005 the Supreme Court held in *Roper v. Simmons* that the death penalty for people younger than 18 when they committed murder is cruel and unusual punishment.[67]

More recently, the Supreme Court has ruled on the constitutionality of sentencing children to life without parole. In the 2010 case *Graham v. Florida*, the Court held that juveniles could not be sentenced to life without parole for crimes less serious than murder.[68] The defendant in that case had committed an armed burglary at age 16, and when he later violated his probation he was sentenced to life in prison. This case left open the possibility that youths who commit murder can still receive life without parole. At the time of the decision, there were 129 juveniles in the United States who were serving life without parole for crimes other than murder, and another 2,000 who were serving life for homicide.[69] Two years later, the Court extended this decision to ban life without parole for juvenile offenders convicted of any offense, including murder.[70]

Finally, in a series of decisions the Supreme Court has ruled on children's Fourth Amendment search and seizure rights when they are in school. In general, these cases hold that school officials and school resource officers—police officers based inside public schools (see the "Matters of Ethics" box)—must respect students' rights against unreasonable searches and seizures, but these rights are limited compared to those of adults. For example, reasonable suspicion, rather than probable cause and a search warrant, is sufficient to justify searches of students and their belongings.[71] Furthermore, schools may conduct random drug testing of all students engaged in extracurricular activities.[72] However, in 2009 the Supreme Court held that the strip search of a 13-year-old girl by school officials who believed that she had prescription-strength ibuprofen and knives violated her Fourth Amendment rights.[73]

PROCESSING JUVENILE OFFENDERS

Describing how juvenile offenders are processed is difficult because there is considerable regional variation in the juvenile justice system. The process in one county or state may be quite different from the process elsewhere. Figure 15-4 shows the typical way in which cases flow through the juvenile justice system. In this section we look at each of the major steps in detail. Although many juvenile court procedures closely resemble adult procedures, notice that they use different terminology to avoid the stigma associated with adult criminal convictions.

Arrest

A child may enter the justice system via a referral from parents, school officials, probation officers, or other adults. Most, however, enter the same way that the majority of adults do: They are arrested by police. In 2010, for example, 83 percent of all delinquency cases were referred by law enforcement.[74]

In 2010, 23 percent of arrested juveniles were handled by the police department without further referral.

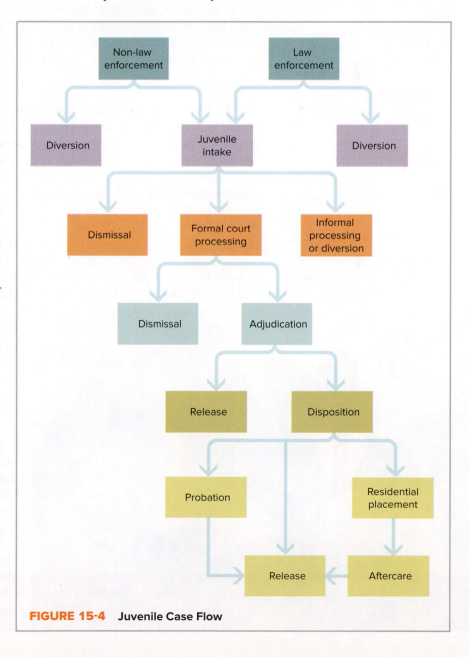

FIGURE 15-4 **Juvenile Case Flow**

juvenile hall
A juvenile detention center.

intake
The process during which an official decides whether to release the juvenile or refer the case to court or put the juvenile under some other supervision.

delinquency petition
The formal document that initiates a juvenile case and lays out the specific allegations against the child; serves much the same function as a criminal complaint.

intake officer
The probation officer who makes the initial decision about whether to proceed with a case.

informal probation
A situation in which as long as the child obeys certain conditions and stays out of trouble, the case will not proceed any further, such as to court.

▼ **Guards Restraining Juveniles**

On occasion, some inmates in juvenile facilities must be restrained.

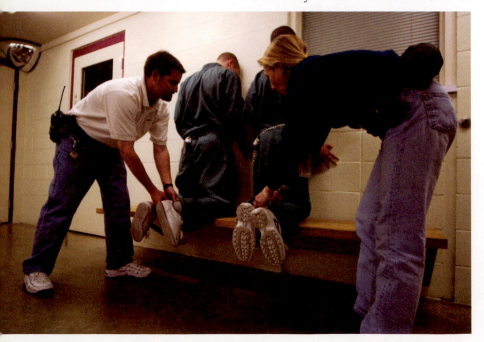

Sixty-eight percent were referred to juvenile court, and the remaining 8 percent were referred directly to adult court.[75]

When police choose to pursue a case against a child, that child is usually taken to a juvenile detention center, known as a **juvenile hall.** However, children may sometimes be held in adult jails, particularly when no juvenile facility is available. An estimated 1 percent of the population in jails in 2004 was under age 18.[76] Children held in adult jails are more likely than children held in juvenile facilities to suffer violent or physical attacks or to commit suicide.[77]

The 1974 Juvenile Justice and Delinquency Prevention Act prohibited holding juveniles in adult facilities, but with exceptions. Children may be housed with adults for up to 48 hours–or longer, if weekends or holidays intervene–while arrangements are made to transfer them to a juvenile facility. Children also may be housed in jails if they are separated from adult inmates or if they will be or have been tried as adults. The act, amended by Congress several times, currently seeks to address the disproportionate number of juveniles of color in the criminal justice system, encourage alternative sanctions for status offenders, and remove juveniles from adult jails and other adult facilities.[78]

Unlike adult offenders, people held in juvenile detention facilities are not constitutionally entitled to a swift "probable cause" hearing (see Chapter 9). However, each state has a statute that mandates that a detention hearing occur within a certain amount of time–usually 24 hours.

Intake

Shortly after a juvenile is taken into custody, the process of **intake** begins, during which an official decides whether to release the juvenile, refer the case to court, or put the juvenile under some other supervision. In most states, a prosecutor will consider the case. The prosecutor may choose not to proceed any further, in which case the child is released. Under some circumstances, the prosecutor may file charges against the child in adult court. The prosecutor may also refer the case to juvenile court. The formal document that initiates a juvenile case is called a **delinquency petition;** it lays out the specific allegations against the child and serves much the same function as a criminal complaint does for an adult defendant.

In some states, the **intake officer**–who typically is a probation officer–makes the initial decision about whether to proceed with a case. The intake officer may choose to handle the case informally by dropping it; placing the child on **informal probation** (as long as the child obeys certain conditions and stays out of trouble, the case will not proceed any further); or assigning the child to a diversion program, such as substance abuse treatment. Alternatively, the intake officer can handle the case formally by recommending that it be heard in juvenile court. In some jurisdictions, the intake officer can also recommend a transfer to adult criminal court. However, the ultimate decision on waivers usually rests with the prosecutor.

The intake officer usually determines whether to release the child to parents or guardians or to detain the child in custody while waiting for the case to go to court. Bail is rarely used in juvenile cases, primarily because the juveniles' parents or guardians are expected to ensure the child's appearance in court, and children present much less of a flight risk than adults.

Nationwide, about half of all cases are settled informally at intake. The likelihood that a case will be handled formally has increased since 1985, primarily due to policy changes demanding that the system get tough on crime and treat juvenile offenders more like adults.[79]

Diversion

When juvenile cases are handled informally, one option is to place the child in a diversion program. The **diversion program** is meant to rehabilitate children, provide more effective early intervention for troubled youths, and reduce juvenile court caseloads–all without burdening offenders with the stigma associated with going to court. Diversion programs are usually available for first-time, nonviolent offenders and may be aimed at specific groups, such as very young offenders or substance abusers.

One common program is the **teen court,** in which teenagers serve as jurors and often as judges, attorneys, and bailiffs as well. Although there are more than 600 teen courts in the United States, so far there has been little research on their effectiveness in reducing recidivism.[80] Another popular diversion option is a restorative justice program such as community service.

Juvenile diversion programs produce mixed results. Some appear to reduce recidivism, whereas others seem to be no more effective than traditional juvenile court dispositions.[81] A diversion program that is no more effective than traditional methods may still be worth pursuing because it costs less, reduces court caseloads, and carries less of a stigma.

Preventive Detention

When the decision is made to take a juvenile to court, the question arises of what to do with the child until the court date. Should the child be released to parents or guardians or be kept in a detention center (serving the same purpose as the adult's jail)? About one in five arrested juveniles is held in **preventive detention** in a juvenile facility while awaiting a court appearance, either to ensure appearance at trial or to prevent the child from committing dangerous acts.[82]

Preventive detention of adults is permitted only when the adults are accused of violent felonies or have a previous record of dangerous behaviors.[83] Children, however, can be detained under broader circumstances, such as when the intake staff determines that they require diagnostic evaluation, pose a threat to the community, or will themselves be at risk if released.[84] Most juvenile detainees are not accused of violent crimes. In 2010, for example, 25 percent of detainees were accused of crimes against persons, 37 percent of property crimes, 26 percent of public order crimes, and 12 percent of drug offenses.[85]

A number of problems are associated with preventive detention of juveniles. One is that detention is used unequally. Boys are more likely than girls to be detained, even for the same offenses, and non-White children are more likely to be detained than are White children. In 2010, for instance, 31 percent of White juveniles were detained, but 50 percent of Black juveniles had to remain in custody pending their hearing.[86]

A second problem with preventive detention is that it is difficult to determine accurately whether a youth will be dangerous if released. A large proportion of juveniles who are detained–perhaps 74 percent–would have presented very little risk to the community, as evidenced by the fact that 61 percent of those found to be delinquent are given probation, and only 26 percent are placed in a facility of any kind.[87] The mistaken detention of low-risk youths

diversion program
A program that handles juvenile cases informally rather than formally through the juvenile court and that is intended to rehabilitate, provide more effective early intervention, and reduce juvenile court caseloads.

teen court
A court in which teenagers serve as jurors and often as judges, attorneys, and bailiffs as well.

preventive detention
Custodial holding of children accused of crimes, to ensure they appear in court but also to protect them from adverse home conditions or to prevent them from committing additional offenses while their case is pending.

creates problems for them because, among other effects, detained youths are more likely to be found delinquent and to receive a more severe sentence than those who are not detained.[88]

A third problem is that conditions in detention centers can be poor. Overcrowding is common. In 2010, 20 percent of juvenile detention centers were at or over capacity. For example, 39 percent of juveniles in Maryland, 40 percent in Missouri and Nevada, and 83 percent in the District of Columbia were in overcrowded facilities.[89] Youths in overcrowded conditions are more likely to be victimized by other youths, to suffer physical and mental health problems, to be maltreated by staff, and to lack adequate diagnosis and treatment.[90]

One promising solution to these problems is the standardized use of a tool called the **risk assessment instrument**–a worksheet that measures the degree of risk in a given case. The intake officer enters specific information about the case and the juvenile into the instrument, such as the number of prior arrests, previous violations, and absence of parental supervision. The resulting score predicts the likelihood that the juvenile will commit more crimes or fail to appear in court. The intake officer can then base a detention decision on this score. Risk assessment instruments may reduce the rate of detentions, as well as race and gender bias, without creating increased danger to the public.[91]

Adjudication

In 2010, 1.4 million juvenile cases were handled formally through filing a petition sending a juvenile to court. This was a substantial increase since 1985.[92] The increase in formal petitions was likely a consequence of tough-on-crime policies.

When the prosecutor files a petition in a juvenile case, the juvenile may plea bargain or not. If not, the court proceeding in which a judge determines whether a juvenile has committed an offense is an **adjudication hearing,** not a criminal trial.

In many respects, however, an adjudication hearing resembles a criminal trial. A prosecutor, who must prove guilt or innocence beyond a reasonable doubt, brings the case. The juvenile is entitled to be represented by an attorney, although in some jurisdictions, fewer than half of juveniles have a lawyer. (Some research suggests that juveniles represented by counsel actually receive more severe treatment.[93]) Witnesses are sworn and evidence is produced. A typical juvenile court judge may hear 30 to 50 cases each day, with the result that each case gets only a few minutes. Unlike criminal cases, juvenile cases in many states are closed to the public to avoid further stigmatization of the child. A recording or transcript of the proceedings is made in case the juvenile later wishes to appeal.

The most striking difference from a criminal trial is the lack of a jury in an adjudication hearing. The judge determines whether the prosecution has met its burden of proof. If not, the petition will be dismissed, and, just as in criminal cases, the youth cannot be retried for the same offense. If the prosecution has met its burden, the youth is **adjudicated delinquent,** the juvenile equivalent of being found guilty. In 2010, 59 percent of petitioned cases resulted in a delinquency adjudication.[94]

Disposition

Adults who are found guilty are given sentences and often a sentencing hearing. Once again, the terminology differs for juvenile court: Those adjudicated delinquent are given a **disposition,** often at a disposition hearing. Before the hearing, a probation officer prepares a predisposition investigation report that

---

risk assessment instrument
A worksheet that measures the degree of risk present in a given case.

adjudication hearing
A hearing to determine whether the juvenile committed the action as charged.

adjudicated delinquent
The equivalent in the juvenile system of being found guilty in adult court.

disposition
The result or outcome for those juveniles adjudicated delinquent.

outlines the juvenile's personal and family history. The probation officer may be present during the hearing, along with a defense attorney (and perhaps a prosecutor), the child, the parents, social workers, and other interested parties.

Juvenile court judges have broad discretion over a wide variety of dispositions. The most common disposition, however, is probation. Other alternatives include private treatment centers, group homes, foster homes, shelters, boot camps, wilderness camps, and state-run training schools or secure facilities. Juveniles may be ordered to pay fines or restitution or to do community service.

Until the 1970s, instead of being given sentences of a fixed length as adults receive, juveniles were given indeterminate commitments. Effectively, their dispositions would continue as long it took to "cure" them of whatever problems led them to crime. Rather than being proportionate to the severity of the offense, the length of time juveniles spent as wards of the juvenile system was determined by the complexity of their problems and their response to treatment. As a result, youths could be incarcerated significantly longer than adults who had committed the same offense. (Gerry Gault, who would have spent nearly 6 years in a reform school for making lewd phone calls, is a good example.) In recent years, however, many states have been making juvenile dispositions of fixed length and in proportion to the seriousness of the crime. Other states still use indeterminate commitments but limit them to the maximum time an adult could serve for the same crime.[95]

Sealing and Expunging Juvenile Records

Labeling theory states that if a person is stuck with a negative label, such as "criminal" or "delinquent," that label will negatively affect the person's future behavior.[96] For this reason, juvenile hearings are usually closed to the public. Moreover, the media may be prohibited from publishing the names of juvenile offenders, and when court decisions about juveniles are published, the decisions often replace the juveniles' names with initials.

In addition, juvenile records may sometimes be sealed or expunged. When a juvenile record such as an arrest, court, or probation record is **sealed,** most people will be denied access to it, and the person who committed the offense can claim to have no criminal record. When a record is **expunged,** it may be destroyed entirely or accessible only by court order.

sealed
A term describing a juvenile record that is made inaccessible.

expunged
A term describing a court record that is destroyed or made legally unavailable.

MYTH/REALITY

MYTH: All juvenile records are automatically erased when the person becomes an adult.

REALITY: Although some juvenile records may be sealed or expunged, the process is rarely automatic. Even sealed and expunged records may still remain available under some circumstances.

The laws concerning sealing and expunging juvenile records vary greatly by jurisdiction and may be available only for certain offenses, after a certain amount of time has passed, or if certain conditions are met (for instance, the offender has not been arrested since that offense). Some jurisdictions prohibit sealing or expunging offenses, sometimes for certain crimes and sometimes for all offenses. In most jurisdictions, sealing and expunging are not automatic; the offender must go through a particular process, usually only after reaching adulthood.

Just because a record is sealed or expunged does not mean that it disappears. For example, a state may seal its own records, but related records may remain in private or federal databases. Some law enforcement agencies may still have access to sealed or expunged records.

JUVENILE CORRECTIONS

Before the *Gault* decision, when establishing due process rights, juvenile courts took into account not only the offense but also such factors as school performance, family functioning, addiction problems, attitude, and prior history in order to serve the best interests of minors. Following *Gault*, juvenile courts became increasingly adversarial and legalistic and less oriented toward social welfare.[97] Some states, among them Washington, took a step away from the original juvenile court philosophy and adopted sentencing guidelines that identified specific dispositions for specific offenses, regardless of the juvenile's social history.[98] Individualized rehabilitation programs and specified treatment plans lost importance. Although probation was still the most common sanction, incarceration became increasingly popular, especially with the media and the public.[99]

Incarceration

> **MYTH/REALITY**
>
> **MYTH:** Everyone locked up in juvenile institutions is, in fact, a juvenile.
>
> **REALITY:** Juvenile correctional jurisdiction often extends into young adulthood; many people in juvenile institutions are actually in their early 20s.[100]

Many jurisdictions have moved from rehabilitation models of delinquency to more punishment-oriented models, especially for juveniles convicted of violent offenses. Juvenile court critics have argued that punishment of juveniles must be longer and more severe.[101] In response, many states have implemented tough-on-crime policies, including waivers, that send juveniles to adult court and increase the use of incarceration. There is evidence the harsh punishment trend for juveniles may be changing. An example was in 2016, the U.S. Supreme Court ruled that offenders who committed crimes when they were juveniles and received life sentences without parole had the right to apply for parole or seek reduced sentences, giving hope to as many 1,500 prisoners some who committed their crimes as young as age thirteen.[102]

The number of juveniles in custody rose dramatically until 2000, when it began to decline steadily. In 2012 there were approximately 57,200 juveniles in residential facilities.[103] In 2013, the number of youth committed to juvenile facilities continued its decline to 35,246.[104] For example, In 2011, 195 juveniles per 100,000 population were in residential custody, compared with 356 per 100,000 in 1997.[105] In 2013 there were approximately 8,000 juveniles in residential placement who were 18 and over compared with about 15,000 who were 17 years old, the largest age group. (See Figure 15-5.)

Blacks are disproportionately represented in juvenile correctional institutions. Figure 15-6 shows the rate of juveniles in custody by race for the year 2013. For every 100,000 Black juveniles, 464 were in a residential placement facility in 2013. For Latinos the rate was 173, and for Whites it

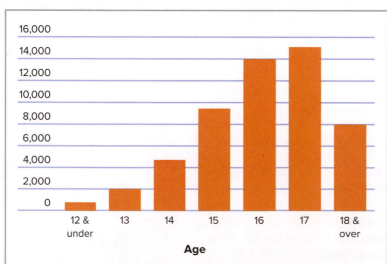

FIGURE 15-5   **Age Profile of Juveniles in Residential Placement, 2013**

OJJDP Statistical Briefing Book, April 27, 2015. www.ojjdp.gov/ojstatbb/corrections/qa08204. asp?qaDate=2013 (retrieved May 11, 2015); and Office of Juvenile Justice and Delinquency Prevention, *Census of Juveniles in Residential Placement 2013* (Washington, DC: OJJDP).

was 100. As with adults, juvenile males (86 percent) are more likely to be in residential placement than are juvenile females (14 percent).[106]

Types of Juvenile Correction Facilities

A juvenile court judge who believes that a juvenile must be removed from home and placed in a correctional facility often has a choice between a community-based program or a larger custodial facility. Short-term detention facilities tend to be locally operated; long-term facilities are mostly run by the states. Group homes are predominantly private but may be contracted by local, state, and federal agencies to provide services for juveniles.

Large State-Run Facilities Although there are more local facilities in the United States, larger state-run facilities house the majority of juveniles and are used for longer incarcerations.[107] They tend to be secure institutions with locked gates and fences or razor-wire walls. Many state-operated facilities have treatment programs for drug abuse and education.

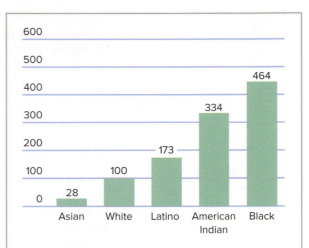

FIGURE 15-6 **Juvenile Custody Rates (per 100,000), by Race/Ethnicity, 2013**

SOURCES: The Sentencing Project, "Youth," Fact Sheet Trends in U.S. Corrections,"Washington, DC, http://sentencingproject.org/doc/publications/inc_Trends_in_Corrections_Fact_sheet.pdf (retrieved February 26, 2016) and Melissa Sickmund, T.J. Sladky, W. Kang, and Charles Puzzanchera, "Easy Acces to the Census of Juveniles in Residential Placement, October 2015, http://www.ojjdp.gov/ojstatbb/ezacjrp (retrieved February 26, 2016).

The larger juvenile facilities have been accused of gross mistreatment and abuse of youth, committed sometimes by inmates but mostly by staff.[108] Many social structures and interactions of male inmates are based on the power one inmate has over another and on physical attacks, coercion, and sexual exploitation.[109] Physical and sexual abuse of juveniles by staff in state custodial institutions has been well documented, largely because of the media attention that lawsuits and scandals generate. The sexual misconduct of staff against youth was reported at a rate of 11 percent for state institutions as opposed to a rate of 3 percent for local and private facilities.[110] Because many people assume that state institutions are probably safer than local ones, these statistics are troubling.

Almost 10 percent of juveniles held in juvenile custody reported having been sexually abused in their current facility during the span of a year. Abuse typically commences within about 6 months of incarceration. Most of those who commit sexual abuse in juvenile facilities are corrections staff, not inmates, and many report their sexual abusers were female. There is painfully little research on female staff members who commit sexual abuse on juveniles. What we do know is that many women abusers are new to their jobs, young, and may believe themselves to be well-meaning and caring. Additionally, boys reported much higher rates of abuse committed by female staff members than girls reported. Studies also confirm that most juveniles report being abused repeatedly during the course of a year and report 11 or more instances of occurrence as opposed to a single incident. Juveniles submit to the abuse for a variety of reasons such as being physically forced, fear, need for sex, protection, and the desire for special privileges.[111]

In adult correctional facilities, most of the abuse that occurs is inmate against inmate, whereas in juvenile facilities, the majority of abuse is perpetrated by staff members against the juveniles. The mistreatment of juveniles in custodial correctional facilities is not limited to the United States but rather seems rooted in the nature of total institutions themselves. As the Stanford Prison Experiment illustrates (see Chapter 12),

▼ **Juvenile Corrections Facility**

There are a variety of kinds of juvenile corrections facilities.

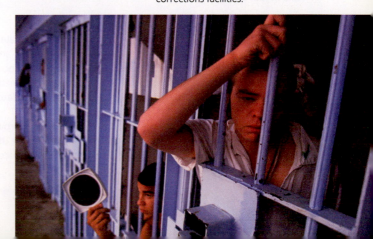

institutions tend to bring out the worst in the keepers and the kept. A study in Israel found that victimization and violence by peers and by staff was commonplace in juvenile correctional facilities.[112]

Juveniles in Adult Prisons Today there are approximately 10,000 juveniles detained or incarcerated in adult penal institutions. Juveniles of color are overrepresented and are more frequently sentenced to harsher terms of punishment than White juveniles. Furthermore, these juveniles are at high risk of sexual victimization, and they are about 36 times more likely to commit suicide than if they were in juvenile corrections institutions. Transferring juveniles to adult institutions also appears to increase the likelihood of continued criminality and does not appear to protect the community.[113]

Juveniles housed with adult prisoners can easily be victimized by adults. Victimization takes the form of stealing property and physical and sexual assaults.[114] Juveniles in adult prisons also are prone to recidivism. A study comparing 15- and 16-year-olds who were sentenced in adult court with those who

Real Careers

ERICA KNUTSEN

Work location: Austin, Texas

College(s): University of Florida, Gainesville (2006); University of Pennsylvania (2007)

Major(s): Criminology (BA); Criminal Justice (MS)

Job title: Policy Writer, Department of Policy and Accreditation, Texas Youth Commission

Salary range for job like this: $35,000–$42,000

Time in job: 2 years

Work Responsibilities
I am a policy writer for the Texas Youth Commission (TYC), the state's juvenile corrections agency. My primary function is to develop and maintain agency policies, procedures, and forms. I also post new policies online and transmit them agencywide to staff and volunteers, maintain policy history, and serve as the agency's liaison with the *Texas Register,* the newspaper of record.

New leadership at TYC has made significant changes to improve the services provided to the youth in its care. As a result, during the past year I have been very busy writing case management standards and treatment policies.

Why Criminal Justice?
I originally decided to major in criminal justice because I wanted to be a special agent for the FBI. However, after taking several courses, I began considering a career in juvenile justice. I did not know much about possible careers in this field, so I sought relevant work experience. First, I interned at Project Payback, a restorative justice and restitution program housed within the Victim Services Division of the State Attorney's Office in Gainesville, Florida. My favorite aspect of this job was teaching juveniles the skills necessary for obtaining and maintaining a job.

I also worked part-time as a project assistant for the Florida Network of Victim Witness Services (FNVWS), which provides support and technical assistance for advocates in the emerging fields of victim assistance and witness management. This position made me realize how recently the rights of crime victims have been established in the criminal justice system. With my collective experience, I hope one day to work in juvenile victim services.

Expectations and Realities of the Job
My understanding of the juvenile justice system has changed after working in both the Florida and Texas systems. I had expected the system to focus primarily on rehabilitation, but I have found a balance between services rendered and jail sentencing. But policies are always evolving, and I have been glad to see that the treatment of youth in the criminal justice system is a concern for lawmakers.

My Advice to Students
First, be proactive in your job hunt. Contact employers, and if you do not hear from them, call them back and inquire about your application. Consider a wide range of opportunities. The glory of criminal justice is that it is such a broad field, and a connection with a government official, or even a psychologist, can sometimes yield a career possibility. Finally, consider graduate school. While many careers in criminal justice do not require a master's degree, having one can strengthen any resume. If you decide to apply to graduate school, be sure to take a statistics course, a prerequisite for many programs.

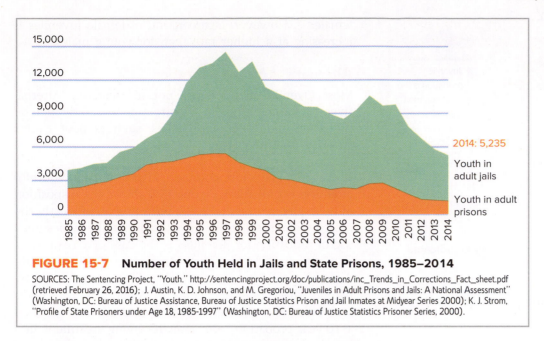

FIGURE 15-7 **Number of Youth Held in Jails and State Prisons, 1985–2014**

SOURCES: The Sentencing Project, "Youth." http://sentencingproject.org/doc/publications/inc_Trends_in_Corrections_Fact_sheet.pdf (retrieved February 26, 2016); J. Austin, K. D. Johnson, and M. Gregoriou, "Juveniles in Adult Prisons and Jails: A National Assessment" (Washington, DC: Bureau of Justice Assistance, Bureau of Justice Statistics Prison and Jail Inmates at Midyear Series 2000); K. J. Strom, "Profile of State Prisoners under Age 18, 1985-1997" (Washington, DC: Bureau of Justice Statistics Prisoner Series, 2000).

were sentenced in juvenile court showed that the juveniles tried as adults reoffended and were reincarcerated at rates higher than those tried in juvenile court. Furthermore, there is reason to believe that juveniles who receive adult sentences experience greater stigma that can interfere with future work options.[115]

Figure 15-7 shows the number of youth held in adult jails and state prisons over the past three decades. Between 2008 and 2010 the numbers began an obvious decline.

Group Homes   A minor who does not need a secure custodial setting but cannot return home might be placed in a group home. Small community programs such as group homes have a significant advantage in that they allow the juvenile to live in the community, attend school, and take advantage of resources there. Research shows that combining services–such as medical treatment and job training with good aftercare and reintegration services–offers the juvenile offender the best chance of reducing postrelease arrests.[116] Group homes, shelters, and ranch and forestry wilderness camps tend to be private facilities contracted by state and local governments to provide services to juveniles. Group homes outnumber all other types of facilities where juveniles are housed.[117]

Institutions for Female Juveniles   The first correctional facility for female juveniles was founded in Lancaster, Massachusetts, in 1856. Its emphasis on domestic work such as sewing and house cleaning continues in many schools for females to the present day. Very little research has been conducted on juvenile females in corrections compared to juvenile males. Like adult female inmates, juvenile female inmates develop subcultures, called *pseudo families* (see Chapter 12), to cope with the stress and difficulties of confinement. The pseudo families provide incarcerated young women with a sense of affection and belonging and mimic the roles parents, spouses, siblings, and children play in the wider community.[118] The needs of girls in corrections are different from those of boys. For correctional efforts to be effective, corrections personnel must take this into account. Some of the issues for girls are separation by gender in housing and programming, gender-responsive training for personnel, pregnancy and sexual health care, respect for privacy, access to family and children, and protection from abuse in institutions.

The number of juvenile female offenders is far below that of males. Fourteen percent of juvenile offenders in residential corrections placement in 2011 were

▼ Juveniles in Group Counseling

Group counseling is common in juvenile corrections facilities.

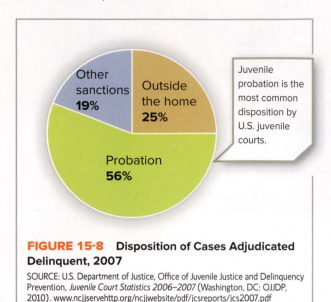

Juvenile probation is the most common disposition by U.S. juvenile courts.

FIGURE 15-8 **Disposition of Cases Adjudicated Delinquent, 2007**

SOURCE: U.S. Department of Justice, Office of Juvenile Justice and Delinquency Prevention, *Juvenile Court Statistics 2006–2007* (Washington, DC: OJJDP, 2010). www.ncjjservehttp.org/ncjjwebsite/pdf/jcsreports/jcs2007.pdf (retrieved April 24, 2011), 58.

female.[119] However, incarceration of female juveniles is increasing at a higher rate than for young males.[120]

Alternatives to Incarceration

Most juvenile offenders are not incarcerated. Alternatives to serving time in a correctional facility include probation and other approaches, such as boot camps and day treatment.

Probation   The most common disposition for youthful offenders is probation. Figure 15-8 shows the disposition of delinquency cases in 2007, with probation clearly the most common sanction. An example of the widespread use of probation for juveniles is the case of a Texas teen that attracted national attention after a witness indicated that the teen was a victim of "affluenza" (wealthy parents that never set limits on children). The Texas teen killed four people while driving drunk and received a 10-year probation term after receiving treatment in a lockdown residential treatment facility.[121]

Juvenile courts order probation in over 50 percent of the cases they hear.[122] A juvenile on probation is usually required to report to a probation officer at regular intervals, to attend school, and may be required to attend a specific program such as counseling or other treatment. The probation officer is responsible for supervising the juvenile and reporting any new violations to the court. Violations or new offenses can revoke probation and send the juvenile back to court on new charges. Probation officers also help the juvenile solve the problems that got her into trouble in the first place.

Probation officers act as both enforcer and social worker at the same time. But because probation caseloads in many jurisdictions are high, officers seldom are able to offer more than occasional guidance. Recidivism for juveniles on probation ranges from 40 percent to 70 percent.[123] Noninstitutional programs such as intensive-supervision probation (ISP) use probation officers who closely monitor juveniles, especially those at high risk of recidivism. ISP might be coupled with regular or random drug testing. (See Chapter 13 for a discussion of ISP.)

Fines and restitution are usually conditions of probation. The court orders the juvenile to make payments to the victim or the court or requires the juvenile to work in some community project for a length of time.[124] The "Juvenile Justice Realignment" bill (Senate Bill 81) became California law in 2007, leading to juvenile justice reform and requiring probation agencies to shoulder the primary responsibility of handling juvenile offenders at the local level. It limited the types of offenders who could be committed to juvenile correctional facilities and shifted the emphasis from institutional confinement at the state level onto the counties to provide innovative and evidence-based programs that would assist juvenile offenders in living more law-abiding lives. Realignment resulted in a decrease in the juvenile state institution population, but questions still remain about its long-term effectiveness and California still incarcerates juveniles at a rate of 271 per 100,000, which is higher than the national average.[125]

Parole   Just as in the adult criminal justice system, the juvenile justice system has many parallel functions and job duties that focus on assisting incarcerated juveniles to successfully transition from an institutional setting back into the community and civilian life, and simultaneously protect the safety of society.

Real Careers

JULIA MARTINEZ MORRIS

Work location: San Antonio, Texas

College(s): Texas State University–San Marcos (2005, 2007)

Major(s): Criminal Justice (BS); Criminal Justice (MS)

Job title: Senior Juvenile Probation Officer, Bexar County

Salary range for job like this: $30,000–$36,000

Time in job: 2 years

Work Responsibilities

I supervise 15 to 18 juveniles in the community on intensive-supervision probation and intensive community-based probation. I maintain five to seven face-to-face contacts with each juvenile per month through office, home, and school visits. I am responsible for making sure that juveniles adhere to the conditions of their probation. When juveniles violate a condition of probation, I refer them for additional services or submit a motion to modify disposition to the juvenile court. After several violations, I can place the juvenile at the detention center.

During the court process I act as a representative for the Department of Juvenile Justice and make a recommendation to the court during the juvenile's disposition hearing. Recommendations include continued probation, probation with specialized programs, placement at a short- or long-term residential facility, or commitment to the Texas Youth Commission (for felony offenders only).

I typically work 40 to 50 hours a week, which includes detention visits, detention hearings, office visits, drug tests, home visits, curfew checks, and school visits. I can receive phone calls 24 hours a day regarding a juvenile. I often receive phone calls from parents reporting that their child missed curfew and sometimes from the Detention Center Intake reporting that a probationer was arrested.

Why Criminal Justice?

I started at a junior college and was interested in restaurant/hotel management. A peer who told me about a field trip his class took to a prison stirred my interest in criminal justice classes. When I transferred to Texas State University, I took a juvenile justice class in which juveniles from the Texas Youth Commission in Giddings, Texas, were guest speakers. After I heard these juveniles talk about their past, their crimes, and their rehabilitation, I knew I wanted to be a probation officer.

Expectations and Realities of the Job

I have learned that you do not go into criminal justice for the money. There is job security, there are good benefits, and you can make a living, but you can sometimes feel overwhelmed, overworked, and underpaid. However, I get job satisfaction when one of my juveniles completes probation. It makes it all worthwhile.

My Advice to Students

Be a team player. We have to assist when someone is away or needs to detain a juvenile or requires a partner for home visits. If you try and do a job in criminal justice alone, you will burn out. You need the help and support of your coworkers. If you are a team player, people will assist you every step of your career.

Juvenile field parole officers (or agents as they are sometimes called) are classified as peace officers and have power to arrest and detain those who interfere with them during their duties or arrests. To accomplish the goals of successful reintegration and aftercare, juvenile parole officers work with offenders after they complete their institutional time. Juvenile parole officers develop individual parole plans in consultation with juvenile offenders, parents and guardians, counselors, teachers, and others to ensure a healthy shift back to civilian life. Additionally, juvenile parole officers have ongoing contact and monitor paroled juvenile offenders to ensure their compliance with their parole plans and other conditions of release. In some jurisdictions juvenile parole officers also perform the job of probation officers.[126]

Other Programs   Many jurisdictions divert first-time offenders, especially those arrested for petty offenses, to a youth service bureau, a community-based agency, a school or church program, or a counseling center. Sometimes they just dismiss the case, often with some form of compensation to the victim or a mediation agreement between the juvenile and the victim.

A Global View

Preventing Youth Violence in Croatia

Despite a fairly recent history of civil war, Croatia has a very low rate of violent crime. So it came as a particular shock to residents of this small country when 18-year-old Luka Ritz was beaten to death in 2008. What made the crime even more shocking was that it was committed by a group of youths who were about the same age as the victim and that it was perpetrated almost completely at random: The group had simply set upon Ritz and his friend as they were walking home one night.

In response to the murder, Ritz's friends and family created Facebook pages in his memory and wore T-shirts that read "Ja Sam Luka Ritz" ("I am Luka Ritz, too"). Supporters displayed posters and held antiviolence rallies and concerts. Perhaps the most significant result, however, was the founding of the Luka Ritz Counseling Centre against Child and Youth Violence.

In October 2010 the Counseling Centre opened its doors in Zagreb, Croatia's capital and Ritz's hometown. The organization seeks both to prevent youth violence and to provide services to its victims.

The center sponsors school workshops, seminars for children and parents, film workshops for teenagers, puppet shows for younger children, and individual and online counseling for victims. Ritz's parents, who helped to found the center, are active in its operations, and many young people, including some of Ritz's friends, volunteer there.

OBSERVE→INVESTIGATE→UNDERSTAND

- How did the reaction to Luka Ritz's murder in Croatia differ from reactions to similar crimes in the United States? What do you think explains the difference?

- How can ordinary people—as opposed to government agencies—act to prevent violence?

- If you were to create a counseling center similar to the one in Croatia, what goals and activities would it involve?

SOURCE: *Savjetovalište Luka Ritz.* www.savjetovaliste.hr/ (retrieved March 11, 2011).

---

boot camp

A facility that uses a model of military basic training, strict discipline, rigid rules, and behavior modification to command the attention of out-of-control delinquent juveniles.

Boot camps use a model of military basic training, strict discipline, rigid rules, and behavior modification to command the attention of out-of-control delinquent juveniles. Critics point out that camps are only as good as the officers who operate them. On the negative side, these camps provide opportunities for physical abuse and injuries—and such misdeeds have occasionally resulted in the deaths of juveniles, as in the case of Martin Lee Anderson, who died in a boot camp after guards kicked and punched him and subjected him to ammonia fumes. Although boot camps are popular with the public and a cost-effective alternative to incarceration, studies have shown they are no more successful in reducing recidivism than are traditional programs.[127] It seems that better aftercare is needed if they are to be effective in reducing recidivism.[128]

Day treatment facilities (sometimes called *day reporting centers*) provide noninstitutional sanctions that are structured and community based—such as recreation, counseling, and scholastic programs—often after school. Structured activities led by positive adult role models provide the stable environment that many troubled juveniles lack at home. Some centers allow probation officers to monitor large numbers of juveniles efficiently.[129] Day treatment centers offer many of the same programs but are less expensive than residential facilities and have met with success in various jurisdictions.[130] As discussed in "A Global View," some countries use less formal counseling options for youthful offenders and victims.

VICTIMIZATION AND VICTIM SUPPORT SERVICES

Juveniles are not just perpetrators of crime in the United States; often they are also victims. In addition to being victims of many of the same crimes that victimize adults, many children are also victims of child abuse and neglect. A majority of crimes against juveniles ages 12 to 17 are not reported to the police or to other authorities. Even when the crimes are serious or involve weapons or injury, they are less likely to be reported than if they had happened to an adult.[131] The different ways in which teens are affected by crime and violence are illustrated in "What about the Victim?"

What about the Victim?

Consequences of Child Victimization

Teenagers are more than twice as likely as adults to be victims of violent crime. Homicide is the third leading cause of death among children under 12 and the fourth leading cause of death among teenagers. In general, younger children tend to be victimized by parents or other family members, whereas older teens tend to be victimized by other young people.

Violence against children is troubling, not only because of its immediate effects on the young victims but also because of the lingering effects of the trauma. One unsettling aftereffect is an increased suicide rate in juvenile victims. Rates of teen suicide are shockingly high: Suicide is the third leading cause of death among teenagers. A recent study concluded that girls who were physically attacked by someone they dated are at increased risk of attempting suicide. Boys who were sexually assaulted were 4 times as likely as other boys to attempt suicide. Nearly 1 in 10 youths in this study had attempted suicide within the past year.

Child victims of crime are also at increased risk of committing offenses themselves. Ample research demonstrates that children abused or neglected by their parents are more likely than other children to become delinquent, and at earlier ages. Child victims of sexual abuse are more likely to molest children later, and most young people who kill have a history of serious abuse. Even witnessing violence can adversely affect children. A recent study suggested that children who observe intimate partner abuse between their parents are more likely to bully other children. As discussed in Chapter 2, bullied children may react by committing violence against themselves or others.

All this research underscores how important it is to pay close attention to young victims of crime. Society seems increasingly eager to view children who engage in dangerous and illegal behavior as criminals instead of as victims of failures on the part of their families, the criminal justice system, and the child welfare system.

OBSERVE → INVESTIGATE → UNDERSTAND

- Why do you think young victims of violent crime are so prone to attempt suicide?
- Would teenage crime victims in college be less vulnerable to suicidal tendencies than teenage victims in high school? Why or why not?
- Because the juvenile offender is often the product of childhood abuse, what steps should the criminal justice system take to deliver a fair and just verdict in such cases?

SOURCES: Howard N. Snyder and Melissa Sickmund, *Juvenile Offenders and Victims: 2006 National Report* (Washington, DC: U.S. Department of Justice, Office of Juvenile Justice and Delinquency Prevention, 2006), chap. 7. www.ojjdp.gov/ojstatbb/nr2006/downloads/chapter7.pdf (retrieved August 12, 2011); Elyse Olshen, Katharine H. McVeigh, Robin A. Wunsch-Hitzig, and Vaughn I. Rickert, "Dating Violence, Sexual Assault, and Suicide Attempts among Urban Teenagers," *Archives of Pediatric and Adolescent Medicine* 161 (2007): 539–545; Joseph P. Ryan, "Dependent Youth in Juvenile Justice: Do Positive Peer Culture Programs Work for Victims of Child Maltreatment?" *Research on Social Work Practice* 16 (2006): 511–519; A. Scott Aylwin, Lea H. Studer, John R. Reddon, and Steven R. Clelland, "Abuse Prevalence and Victim Gender among Adult and Adolescent Child Molesters," *International Journal of Law & Psychiatry* 26 (2003): 179–190; Dorothy Van Soest, Hyun-Sun Park, and Toni K. Johnson, "Different Paths to Death Row: A Comparison of Men Who Committed Heinous and Less Heinous Crimes," *Violence & Victims* 18 (2003): 15–33; Carol Anne Davis, *Children Who Kill: Profiles of Pre-Teen and Teenage Killers* (London: Allison & Busby, 2003); Anna C. Baldry, "Bullying in Schools and Exposure to Domestic Violence," *Child Abuse & Neglect* 27 (2003): 713–732.

The good news is that the victimization of juveniles declined between 1993 and 2003 for all types of crimes and among all racial groups.[132] Nonetheless, we can distinguish victimization patterns among juveniles. From 1993 to 2003, an African American juvenile was 5 times more likely to be the victim of a homicide than a White juvenile. Juvenile males were 4½ times more likely to be homicide victims than juvenile females.[133] Although males are more often victimized in violent crimes than females, females are 6 times more likely to be victims of rape or sexual assault. Younger juveniles have a greater chance of being victimized than older juveniles; African Americans are more likely to be victimized than Whites, but Latino and non-Latino juveniles have about the same likelihood of being victimized.[134]

Victim advocates serving juvenile victims recognize how the period of transition from childhood into the teen years represents significantly higher levels of vulnerability. Consequently, they are calling for specific prevention strategies aimed at identifying dysfunctional families and suggesting more proactive early interventions. Some services assist those already victimized to help children with stress and trauma; other services are aimed at detecting situations in which young people might find themselves vulnerable to specific forms of victimization where changes in their life patterns can divert their vulnerabilities in significant ways.

Child Protective Services (CPS)
County-level government organizations in all 50 states whose trained staff members investigate allegations of child abuse and neglect.

mandatory reporting law
Law requiring that professionals who have regular contact with a child report any reasonable suspicions of physical or sexual abuse or neglect to the proper law enforcement or protective services.

Court Appointed Special Advocate (CASA)
A volunteer selected by the courts to protect the rights and interests of child victims of abuse.

RealCrimeTech

COMPUTERS ARE DECIDING IF PARENTS WILL KEEP THEIR CHILDREN

Several counties in California are now using a computer program to help social workers make a decision about removing a neglected or an abused child from a parent. The program, called *structured decision making (SDM)*, helps child welfare workers assess the risks to children of remaining in the home or being returned to their home. The computer uses research-based information to determine the likelihood of future mistreatment. A Michigan study showed that using SDM allowed 40 percent fewer children to be removed from their homes, and 42 percent fewer children required medical assistance.

Since the removal and return of children is such an emotional issue, some workers seem to welcome the objective scoring of the computer to back up or help them with these difficult, sometimes traumatic, decisions. Intuition may indeed be helped by solidly based statistics showing the likelihood that a child will be further abused.

SOURCES: Garrett Therolf, "How Computers Call the Shots for L.A. County Children in Peril," *Los Angeles Times,* March 9, 2009. www.latimes.com/news/local/la-me-childabuse8-2009mar08,0,753306,full.story (retrieved March 21, 2009); Department of Social Services, "Structured Decision Making," 2007. www.childsworld.ca.gov/PG1332.htm (retrieved March 21, 2009); National Council on Crime and Delinquency, "Structured Decision Making (SDM) Model." www.nccdglobal.org/assessment/sdm-structured-decision-making-systems/child-welfare (retrieved June 11, 2015).

Child Protective Services

One way in which the justice system deals with young victims of crime is through **Child Protective Services (CPS),** a county-level government organization in all 50 states and some U.S. territories whose trained staff investigates allegations of child abuse and neglect. CPS operates a 24-hour, 7-days-a-week hotline to receive anonymous calls. If CPS does not determine that the child is at risk, the case will remain open, usually for 1 year. If there are no further calls reporting suspected abuse, the case will then be closed, but all cases can be reopened if necessary.

If CPS confirms abuse and neglect, the agency has several options. It can remove the child from the home and place him in foster care or with extended family members such as grandparents, older siblings, an aunt, or an uncle. CPS works to strengthen family bonds by mandating attendance at anger management, substance abuse, and parenting skill classes, as a preventive tool either before a child is removed or before family-child reunification can take place. After relocating a child, CPS continues its investigation, monitors the child's adjustment to the new home, and secures counseling, academic assistance, or other services. The agency determines when it is safe for the child to be reunited with the family or whether a permanent placement outside of the home is needed instead. CPS staff members also prepare court reports and initiate criminal proceedings on behalf of the child. Finally, CPS trains foster parents and acts as an adoption agency to help them adopt foster children.

Mandatory Reporting Laws

In the course of their work, many professionals come in contact with young people who show signs of being victimized. A **mandatory reporting law** requires any professional who has regular contact with a child to report any reasonable suspicion of physical or sexual abuse or neglect to the proper law enforcement or protective services. The professionals required to report such suspicions include health care practitioners, law enforcement officers, school personnel, day care providers, spiritual leaders, social workers, mental health practitioners, medical examiners and coroners, members of the clergy, and lawyers. A mandated professional who fails to report an allegation of abuse or neglect is subject to sanctions outlined by state laws, such as civil penalties and loss of license. If no abuse or neglect is found, the person who reports it is immune from liability if he acted in good faith or had a reasonable suspicion of abuse.

The national mandatory reporting law was part of the Child Abuse Prevention and Treatment Act (CAPTA) of 1974 and has since been amended several times. In the late 1990s, all 50 states extended mandatory reporting requirements to include older and dependent adults because of their vulnerability to abuse and neglect.[135]

Court Appointed Special Advocates

A **Court Appointed Special Advocate (CASA)** is a volunteer selected by the courts to protect the rights and interests of child victims of abuse, neglect, or abandonment. Without CASAs, child victims might get lost in the large and often overburdened judicial and welfare systems. The appointment is normally for 2 years. During this time, the volunteer visits the child at home, school, or other locations such as a day care facility, the public library, or a relative's home to talk with the child and determine what services the child needs to excel at home, in school, and in the community. The CASA volunteer contacts Child Protective Services (CPS) if there is a suspicion of abuse, if the child has to be removed from home, or if service referrals are needed. CASA volunteers are trained to speak on behalf of the child in all court proceedings.

SUMMARY

Juvenile justice was created as a way to deal informally with troubled and delinquent children. The original intent was rehabilitation rather than punishment, with the state or local authority acting as *parens patriae*, especially when the real parents were absent or abusive. But as the system grew and overwhelmed the judges, as due process rights granted to juveniles "legalized" the process of justice, and as public opinion backed tough-on-crime policies, the system became more formal. It took on more and more aspects of the adult criminal justice process, with some juveniles even being tried in adult courts.

Most people agree that juvenile justice has yet to live up to its promise. There are, however, glimmers of hope. Many jurisdictions have implemented plans such as youth mentoring, teen courts, youth drug courts, and restorative justice programs, which may successfully prevent young people from offending or reoffending. What seems to work best are programs that best fit the original goals of the juvenile justice system: They are small; they are tailored to each youth's individual needs; they address the complexity of a youth's problems, rather than simplistically trying to fix one or two issues; they focus on offenders' successful reentry into the community; and they provide the opportunity for youthful offenders to achieve something meaningful.

OBSERVE → INVESTIGATE → UNDERSTAND

Review

Describe the early treatment of youthful offenders.

- Until the nineteenth century, young offenders were usually treated the same as adults.
- The infancy defense prohibited the prosecution of people under age 7.
- Delinquents in England could be bound out, placed in institutions, or sent to America.
- The first U.S. institution for juveniles opened in 1825.
- By the middle of the nineteenth century, many jurisdictions had created reform schools for wayward youths.

Analyze current juvenile crime rates and trends.

- Juvenile arrests are dropping, but the proportion of female juvenile arrests is rising.
- Arrest rates for Black juveniles are dropping faster than the average, but Blacks are still disproportionately represented among youthful offenders.

Evaluate the philosophy behind the creation of juvenile courts.

- Special courts were created for youths because they were less culpable than adults and more likely to be rehabilitated.
- Juvenile courts were intended to treat delinquency rather than punish it.
- Juvenile courts were intended to be less formal than adult courts.
- The legal doctrine that supports juvenile courts is *parens patriae*.

Describe the breadth and limitations of juvenile court jurisdiction.

- Juvenile court jurisdiction is defined by age and behavior.
- Juvenile courts have the power to hear both delinquency and status offense cases as well as dependency cases.
- Certain actors in the juvenile justice system can choose to waive jurisdiction over juveniles and send them to adult courts.

Compare and contrast the constitutional rights of juvenile and adult offenders.

- Juveniles' due process rights are more limited than adults' rights.
- Juveniles, like adults, have the right to an attorney, to be found guilty beyond a reasonable doubt, and to appeal.
- Juveniles do not have the right to a jury.
- Juveniles have no special rights regarding interrogation.
- Schoolchildren have limited Fourth Amendment rights (search and seizure).

Characterize the types of juvenile correctional facilities in the United States.

- Incarceration of juveniles is dropping.
- Community settings work better than large institutions in treating delinquents.

- Large juvenile institutions are prone to abuse of juveniles by both staff and inmates.
- Alternatives to incarceration include group homes, boot camps, and day treatment centers, all of which have varying degrees of success.

Analyze the victimization of juveniles and the services available to support them.

- Juveniles are often victims of crimes, many of which go unreported.
- Child Protective Services (CPS) investigates child abuse and neglect and decides whether to remove a child from a family setting.
- Mandatory reporting laws require professionals to report signs of child victimization.
- Court Appointed Special Advocates (CASAs) are volunteers who protect the rights and interests of child victims.

Key Terms

adjudicated delinquent 492
adjudication hearing 492
arrest rate 476
binding out 473
boot camp 499
Child Protective Services (CPS) 501
child savers 474
Court Appointed Special Advocate (CASA) 501
delinquency petition 490
direct file (prosecutorial waiver) 484

disposition 492
diversion program 491
expunged 493
infancy defense 473
informal probation 490
intake 490
intake officer 490
judicial waiver 483
juvenile delinquency 475
juvenile hall 490
juvenile justice system 478

mandatory reporting law 501
parens patriae 474
preventive detention 491
reform school 474
risk assessment instrument 492
sealed 493
status offense 475
statutory exclusion 484
teen court 491
waiver 483

Study Questions

1. The first juvenile courts were created in approximately
   a. 1550.
   b. 1800.
   c. 1900.
   d. 1950.

2. In recent years, violent crime arrests of juveniles in the United States have
   a. increased.
   b. decreased.
   c. increased or decreased depending on the race of the juvenile.
   d. remained the same.

3. A juvenile court typically would have jurisdiction over a case involving
   a. a 15-year-old accused of stealing a car.
   b. a 13-year-old who has not been attending school.
   c. a 6-year-old who has been abandoned by her parents.
   d. all of the above

4. The *Gault* decision
   a. was decided by the U.S. Supreme Court.
   b. granted juveniles the right to an attorney.
   c. allowed juveniles to confront and cross-examine witnesses.
   d. all of the above

5. Of the following, the one that will *not* usually be allowed during a juvenile court case is
   a. assistance from an attorney for the juvenile.
   b. a jury.
   c. hearsay evidence.
   d. confrontation and cross-examination of witnesses.

6. The juvenile equivalent of a criminal trial is called
   a. a delinquency petition.
   b. detention.
   c. an adjudication hearing.
   d. a disposition hearing.

7. The disposition most commonly used by the juvenile court is
   a. a group home.
   b. a treatment facility.
   c. probation.
   d. a residential institution.

8. An adjudication hearing
   a. is used for an informal decision by the juvenile court.
   b. is the juvenile court equivalent of sentencing in adult court.
   c. determines whether the juvenile has committed the offense.
   d. determines whether the juvenile is fit to be tried by the juvenile court.

9. A juvenile court waiver
   a. is used by the youth to waive the right to bail.
   b. permits a juvenile to be tried as an adult.

c. permits a youth who is over the age of 18 but younger than 21 to be handled as a juvenile.
d. is used by the juvenile court to waive extradition.

10. Which statement is correct?
    a. The number of female juveniles in custody is almost as great as the number of male juveniles in custody.
    b. The rate of female juvenile arrests is rising faster than the rate of male juvenile arrests.
    c. There is evidence that female juvenile delinquents are becoming increasingly more violent.
    d. all of the above

Critical Thinking Questions

For further review, go to the LearnSmart study module for this chapter.

1. How can we ensure a juvenile justice system that is fair, while still allowing it to achieve its original goals of treatment and rehabilitation?

2. Under what circumstances should a child be held criminally liable in adult court for his behavior?

3. What are likely to be the characteristics of successful juvenile correctional programs? How would these differ from adult programs?

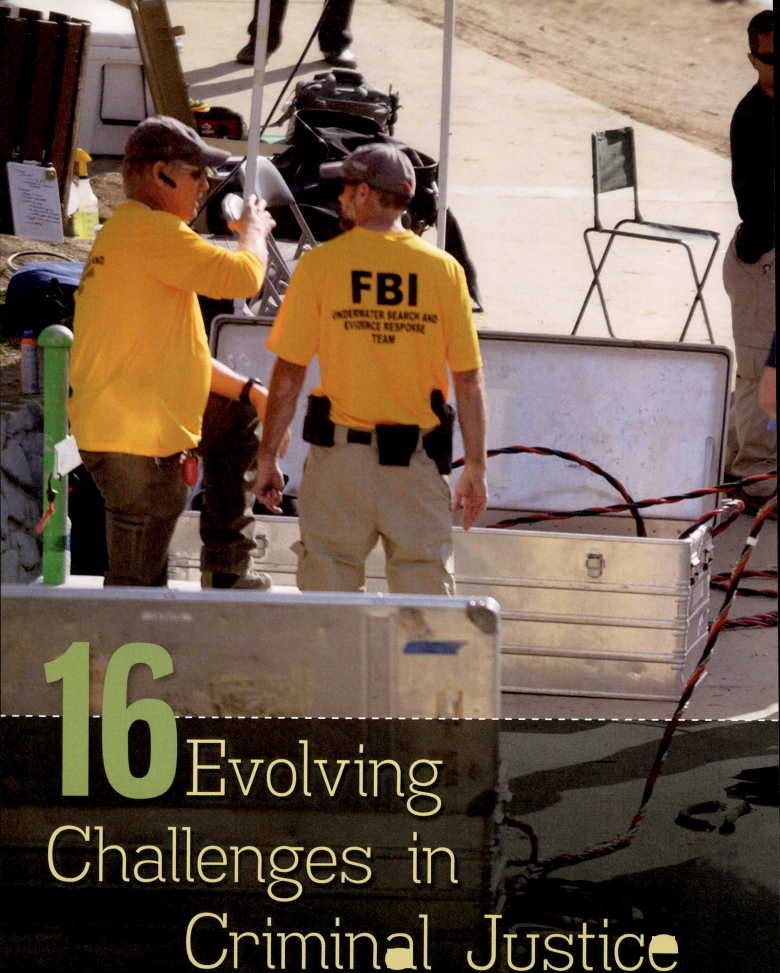

16 Evolving Challenges in Criminal Justice

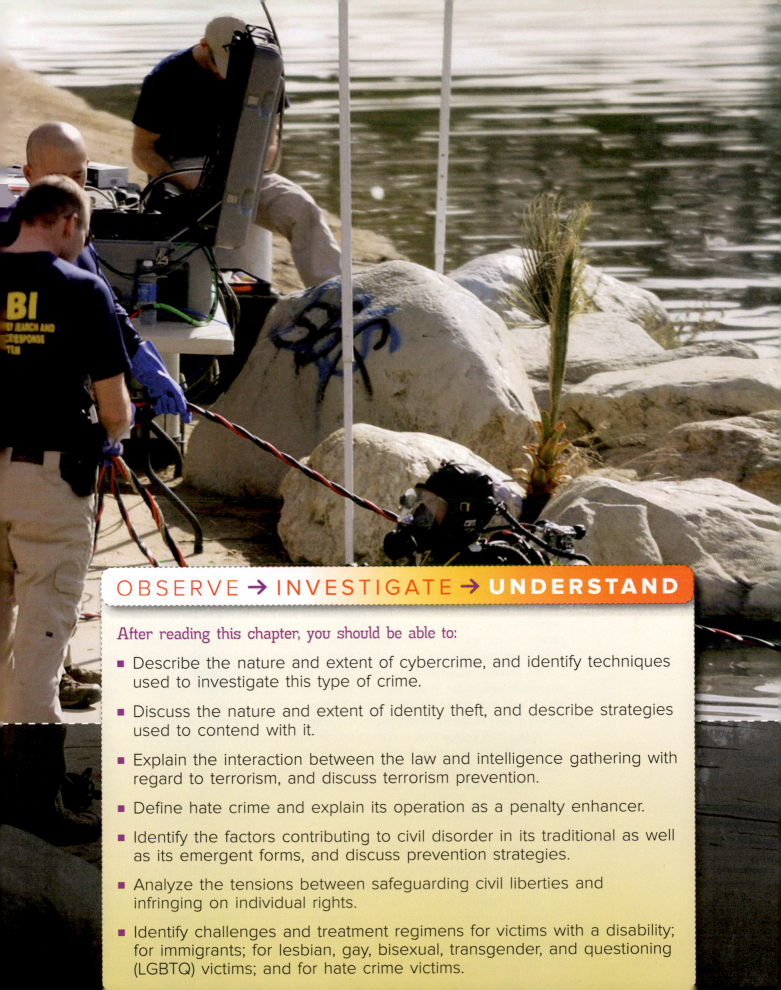

OBSERVE → INVESTIGATE → UNDERSTAND

After reading this chapter, you should be able to:

- Describe the nature and extent of cybercrime, and identify techniques used to investigate this type of crime.

- Discuss the nature and extent of identity theft, and describe strategies used to contend with it.

- Explain the interaction between the law and intelligence gathering with regard to terrorism, and discuss terrorism prevention.

- Define hate crime and explain its operation as a penalty enhancer.

- Identify the factors contributing to civil disorder in its traditional as well as its emergent forms, and discuss prevention strategies.

- Analyze the tensions between safeguarding civil liberties and infringing on individual rights.

- Identify challenges and treatment regimens for victims with a disability; for immigrants; for lesbian, gay, bisexual, transgender, and questioning (LGBTQ) victims; and for hate crime victims.

Realities and Challenges

Boston Marathon Bombing

April 15, 2013, marked the culmination of many months of planning by the city of Boston—and far more months of grueling preparation on the part of the athletes who qualified to participate in Boston's unique rite of spring—the Boston Marathon. This was the 117th running of the marathon, held as per custom on Patriots' Day to commemorate the 1775 battles of Concord and Lexington that kicked off the American Revolutionary War. The weather was sunny and ideal as the first wave of runners embarked on the 26.2-mile race at 9:32 a.m. And then inhumanity intruded—in a most depravedly violent form. At 2:49 p.m., with more than 5,600 runners still in the race, two pressure-cooker explosive devices hidden in backpacks and packed with shrapnel exploded amid throngs of marathon watchers. The first of the two explosive devices was deto-

nated at 671 Boylston Street; the second device was detonated 13 seconds later 180 yards up-course at 755 Boylston Street. Instantaneously, one of Boston's, and the nation's, most cherished events was explosively transformed into a gruesome scene of destruction and chaos—the worst such attack on American soil since the horrific attacks on September 11, 2001.[1] The explosions took the lives of 3 individuals and injured 264 spectators, many critically, with 16 survivors suffering traumatic amputations.[2]

In the wake of the bombing, law enforcement officials called upon the public for any photographs or videos that could lead to identification of the perpetrators. On April 18, the FBI publicly released photographs of two suspects, requesting information on the suspects' identities and whereabouts. That evening, a Massachusetts Institute of Technology police officer was fatally shot as he sat in his patrol vehicle. (It was later learned that he was slain by the bombers in a failed attempt to acquire his sidearm.) Later in the evening, an SUV was carjacked, with the victim remaining inside as the two carjackers drove around the Boston area. When the two captors stopped at a gas station, the victim escaped. He notified police that while captive in his vehicle, he overheard conversation that led him to believe his captors were the Boston bombing suspects. Shortly after midnight, police located the stolen vehicle with both suspects still inside. A shootout ensued; one of the suspects was seriously wounded and transferred to a local hospital, where he died, and the other suspect escaped on foot. Fingerprints taken at the hospital identified the deceased suspect as Tamerlan Tsarnaev. Law enforcement officials were then able to identify Dzhokhar Tsarnaev, Tamerlan's brother, as the second suspect. On the evening of April 19, the outstanding suspect was apprehended with the aid of infrared imaging equipment.[3]

In May 2015, just over "two years after bombs in two backpacks transformed the Boston Marathon from a sunny rite of spring to a smoky battlefield with bodies dismembered, a federal jury condemned Dzhokhar to death for his role in the 2013 attack."[4] Paradoxically, the Tsarnaev verdict went against the grain in Massachusetts, as the state has no death penalty for state crimes.

It is readily observable that law enforcement and municipal government performed commendably in the manner and speed with which they apprehended the Boston bombing perpetrators. However, there is at the same time the haunting reality that the bombers' legacy of carnage conceivably might not have materialized had information-sharing lessons learned in the aftermath of 9/11 been proactively applied in Boston. In March 2014, the House Homeland Security Committee released its "challenges and lessons learned" report on the Boston Marathon bombing. The report detailed opportunities in which greater sharing of information might have altered the course of events. Tamerlan Tsarnaev's travels to Russia and his possible radicalization had been documented and entered into federal databases. Proactive follow-up investigation by federal agencies was lacking, as was adherence to protocols for traveling individuals flagged for screening (as was Tamerlan Tsarnaev) via the antiterrorism database maintained by U.S. Customs and Border Patrol. Moreover, the Boston Police Department commissioner testified before the committee that neither he nor the wider Boston Police Department were alerted to any potential threat posed by a radicalized individual residing in Boston's environs.[5]

Beyond the breakdown in information flow, the bombing drew attention to an evolving challenge: the lone wolf attacker. Despite the myriad investigative resources dedicated to follow-up investigation, it was never determined that the bombers were tied to any terrorist group. They appear to have been radicalized through jihadist materials on the Internet.[6] Fueled in large part by the Internet and social media, the rise of the self-taught extremist has introduced challenges to law enforcement and counterterrorism officials that are very different from those posed by organized terrorist groups or networks.[7] Strategies to contend with this new form of terrorism and actions to improve information sharing are examined in the "Terrorism" section of this chapter.

This chapter focuses on current and emerging issues in the criminal justice system. Cybercrime, terrorist activities, and hate crimes, for example, are forcing criminal justice professionals to pave new paths in the detection, investigation, prosecution, and prevention of crime and changing the way these individuals do their jobs. At the same time, the tension between ensuring public safety and safeguarding individuals' rights heightens, as new law enforcement technologies, methods, and procedures designed to protect the public may infringe on individuals' rights to privacy and other civil liberties. Another mounting concern is recognizing the rights and needs of *all* victims of crime, including—perhaps especially—those whose victimization has been neglected, ignored, or minimized. In the sections that follow, we examine the issues surrounding crimes and victimization that represent evolving challenges for the criminal justice system.

FIGHTING CYBERCRIME

Information technology has driven unprecedented advances in productivity and the spread of information, but it has also triggered new forms of criminal behavior. Online fraud and electronic theft of proprietary information (economic espionage) were nonexistent only a few years ago but now account for extraordinary losses. Many of the world's most valuable companies have found themselves squarely in the crosshairs of sophisticated hackers, some of whom are backed by the resources of nation-states.[8]

Cybercrime is any crime that relies on a computer and an electronic network for its commission.[9] It exploits, for illicit purposes, the electronic highway upon which computer transmissions travel. The Internet has become the catalyst for many forms of criminal activity,[10] such as theft of intellectual property, extortion, child pornography, identity theft, fraud, stalking, and bullying. These are viewed as cybercrimes, but they are considered traditional crimes if they do not occur electronically in cyberspace.

Beyond the traditional crimes elevated to cybercrime status, there are malicious acts emergent with the advent of computerization. Two such illicit activities are data breaches and denial of service attacks. Both are increasing

cybercrime
Any crime that relies on a computer and a network for its commission; crime that exploits the electronic highway over which computer transmissions travel.

data breach
An incident in which sensitive, protected, or confidential data have been viewed, stolen, or used by an unauthorized individual.

hacktivism
The practice of gaining unauthorized access to a computer system and carrying out various disruptive actions as a means of achieving political or social goals.

denial of service attack
An act done with the intention of compromising the availability of networks and systems.

in frequency, sophistication, and severity of impact and warrant illumination.[11] A **data breach** is an incident in which sensitive, protected, or confidential data have been viewed, stolen, or used by an individual who is not authorized to do so.[12] An especially egregious example is the mid-2015 breach of data stored electronically within the U.S. Office of Personnel Management (OPM). Cyber intrusions had exposed sensitive data about more than 21 million federal employees and applicants–along with 21 million Social Security numbers. The personnel forms exposed included those of senior officials at the Federal Bureau of Investigation, Department of State, Department of Defense, and Central Intelligence Agency.[13] The attack bore the indicia of having been carried out by a nation-state given the perpetrator's apparent level of sophistication and the data targeted.

Beyond the data breach threats posed by nation-states are those posed by **hacktivism.** Hacktivists use web-based tools to effect social or political change or an elevation of civil disobedience into cyberspace. Technological advances involving the Internet, such as social media, have provided a significant electronic forum for social activists to advance their causes. The Internet platform also provides the advantage of anonymity.[14] Some hacktivists have taken to defacing government websites as well as websites of groups who oppose their ideology.

Unlike data breaches, **denial of service attacks** do not steal anything. The intention is to compromise the availability of networks and systems.[15] Distributed denial of service attacks are automated attacks that run simultaneously from multiple computers. The attack that took down Sony's PlayStation Network and Sony Entertainment Network in 2014 was a distributed denial of service attack. Distributed service attacks are becoming the "weapon of choice" for hackers. An attacker can rent a "botnet," a network of infected computers, to mount a distributed denial of service campaign for less than 10 dollars per hour. Moreover, attackers can amplify an assault by using the greater computing power that resides on the Internet in the form of cloud infrastructure.[16]

Extent of Cybercrime

The extent of cybercrime is significantly underreported, in part because companies do not fully report losses. The Center for Strategic and International Studies, a Washington think tank, estimates that cybercrime costs the global economy up to $575 billion annually, with the United States sustaining annual losses of $100 billion. A most important cost of cybercrime comes from its damage to company performance and to national economies. Cybercrime damages trade, competitiveness, innovation, and global economic growth.[17]

Detection and Investigation

Traditional investigative strategies do not readily apply to cybercrime, where the offender is often a faceless entity. Internet cafés, open wireless routers, libraries, and a host of other venues allow almost anyone access to the Internet with virtually complete anonymity. The place where the crime occurred is hard to identify: Did the crime take place where the perpetrator's computer is located? Or was the crime site that of the victim's computer, which may be in another state or even another country? Could the location of the Internet server be considered the place where the crime took place? Or was the crime location somewhere in between? Victims and offenders can be on different sides of the world. To make investigation even more complicated, the laws in most countries, including those in the United States, have not kept up with technology. As a result, criminals are often prosecuted using laws intended to combat crimes in the nonvirtual ("real") world. Laws to prosecute computer-related crimes are often not as ample or broad as those used to confront their

Sexual Solicitation via the Internet

In June 2006, Katherine, a 16-year-old girl from Gilford, Michigan, met a man on the social network MySpace. The man described himself as a 25-year-old from the city of Jericho on the West Bank of the Palestinian territories. A short time later, Katherine asked her parents for a passport so that she could accompany her friend on a family vacation to Canada. With her passport in hand and clothes for 2 weeks, she left home. She called her mother that day and the next, indicating she was okay and would be home the next day.

After 2 days, however, Katherine's parents called the police. The FBI tracked Katherine to the airport in Amman, Jordan, where authorities approached her and persuaded her to return home.

A Michigan news show broadcast a telephone interview with the man Katherine met on MySpace. He identified himself as Abdullah, a wealthy 20-year-old businessman who said that he wanted to marry Katherine and had sent her money for a plane ticket to visit him.

Young people like Katherine are the victims of a variety of Internet crimes, including solicitations to engage in sexual acts for commercial gain through production and distribution of child pornography or for personal gratification. In 2001, the Crimes Against Children Research Center at the University of New Hampshire conducted a nationwide Youth Internet Safety Survey through telephone interviews with 1,501 youths, 10 to 17 years old. Nearly 20 percent had received an unwanted sexual solicitation within the last year; two-thirds of the victims were female. Five percent received sexual solicitations that made them very upset or afraid; of these victims, 37 percent were between ages 10 and 13. Another 3 percent were asked to allow contact or a meeting offline. Apparently, none of these solicitations resulted in a sexual contact or assault.

Given the anonymity afforded by the Internet, the true identity, age, and gender of the perpetrators may be different from what they told the victims. Victims believed that nearly all the perpetrators were strangers and that almost half the solicitations, including the most aggressive, were from juveniles. Two-thirds of all solicitations came from self-described males.

Approximately two-thirds of solicitations occurred in chat rooms; 24 percent were instant messages. One-quarter of respondents had received unwanted sexual material—more boys (57 percent) than girls (42 percent). Nearly half of the victims did not tell anyone about the solicitation; of those who did, about a quarter informed a parent.

As access to Internet technologies expands with the increased use of wireless and handheld devices, monitoring Internet communications will become increasingly challenging. Prevention programs that acknowledge normal adolescent interest in romance and sex and provide adolescents with skills to recognize and avoid unwanted communications, rather than messages that emphasize parental control, are needed.

OBSERVE → INVESTIGATE → UNDERSTAND

- Why do sexual predators solicit victims via the Internet?
- Why did only half the victims tell anyone about the unwanted messages they received?
- How can detection and prevention efforts be improved if reporting rates remain low?

SOURCES: Janis Wolak, David Finkelhor, Kimberly J. Mitchell, and Michele L. Ybarra, "Online 'Predators' and Their Victims: Myths, Realities, and Implications for Prevention and Treatment," *American Psychologist* 63, no. 2 (2008): 111–128; Associated Press, "Michigan Teen in Seclusion after Overseas MySpace Trip, Lawyer Says," June 13, 2006. www.foxnews.com/story/0,2933,199247,00 (retrieved August 2, 2011); U.S. Department of Justice, Office for Victims of Crime, "Internet Crimes against Children," *OVC Bulletin* (Washington, DC: OVC, December 2001). www.regionsix.com/ResourceLibrary/Parents%20and%20Families/Parenting-Internet%20Crimes%20and%20Kids.pdf (retrieved July 21, 2011); David Finkelhor, Kimberly Mitchell, and Janis Wolak, "Highlights of the Youth Internet Safety Survey," *OJJDP Fact Sheet* (Washington, DC: U.S. Department of Justice, March 2001). www.ncjrs.gov/pdffiles1/ojjdp/fs200104.pdf (retrieved July 21, 2011).

traditional counterparts. For example, computer fraud (18 U.S.C. Section 1030) is not considered a predicate offense (i.e., an action that provides underlying resources for another criminal act) for racketeering under the Racketeer Influenced and Corrupt Organizations (RICO) Act, a primary tool used to prosecute organized crime.[18]

The complexity of cybercrime demands technologically sophisticated investigative techniques, including computer forensics, collaboration, and training. **Computer forensics** is the application of the knowledge and methods used in computer science to law enforcement. Computer forensic experts are asked, for example, to recover deleted files, locate hidden files, trace website activity, and produce a variety of other forms of digital evidence for use in criminal and civil proceedings.[19] Digital evidence is commonly associated with electronic crime such as online child pornography or credit card fraud. However, digital evidence is now routinely obtained to prosecute all types of crimes.[20] For example, examination of the computer hard drive belonging to a person

computer forensics
Application of the knowledge and methods used in computer science to law enforcement purposes (such as recovery of deleted files or website activity).

▲ Computer Forensics Analyst at Work

Computer forensic analysts recover data from electronic devices such as computers, e-mail, BlackBerries, and iPhones and then give a thorough report on their findings relevant to the case.

transnational crime

Crime orchestrated across a national boundary from where the crime actually occurs.

of interest might reveal that he researched online chloroform recipes days before his wife disappeared.

Multiple crime activities and locations are commonplace in cybercrime. Within networked environments, evidence may reside on any number of machines using a variety of operating systems, in many different physical or network locations, and in multiple jurisdictions. Yet search and seizure operations must adhere to legal requirements that minimize intrusions into network operations.

Prevention Strategies

Like investigation of cybercrime, prevention of cybercrime also requires collaboration among law enforcement, the private sector, and even international agencies. Much cybercrime is **transnational crime,** taking place across national boundaries. A case in point: In 2013 one international event involving thefts from ATMs over a 10-hour period resulted in losses of $45 million, which is more than the total losses from all "traditional" bank robberies in the United States in a year.[21] Moreover, some cybercrime may be legal in one country but illegal in another. For example, pornographic material depicting 16-year-olds is illegal in the United States but legal in Iceland and Germany.[22] In 2006, the United States ratified the Council of Europe Convention on Cybercrime, the first international treaty to address Internet crimes by coordinating national laws, improving investigative techniques, and increasing cooperation among nations.[23] "Operation Atlantic" is an example of FBI agents working with European countries to set up an electronic dragnet; the operation has led to the apprehension of producers of child pornography from France, Italy, the Netherlands, Spain, and the United Kingdom.[24]

Within the United States, federal, state, and local law enforcement entities, as well as private sector professionals, often work together, exchanging information and hardening crime targets. Local law enforcement agencies' cybercrime units are increasingly using their Web presence to educate the public about and raise awareness of cybercrime.[25] The Department of Homeland Security's National Cybersecurity and Communications Integration Center engages

KEY CONCEPTS   Challenges to Fighting Cybercrime

Offenders are anonymous and can work from any private or public computer.

The location of the crime is difficult to identify and can range from the perpetrator's computer to the victim's computer to a network server in between.

Cybercrime can be transnational, and its prosecution can be complicated by conflicting laws and enforcement practices in different countries.

Detecting cybercrime is expensive and requires technologically sophisticated techniques and training.

Evidence for a crime may reside on many computers across many networks.

Search and seizure operations must meet legal requirements and minimally affect normal computer network operation.

in information sharing processes in which it pushes out information to the private sector or pulls information in from it.[26] The communications and information technology industries play a crucial cooperative role by designing products that are resistant to crime.[27] Legislative bodies have enacted legislation targeting cybercrime. An initial federal statute to contend with fraud committed via computer was 18 U.S.C. 1030, the Computer Fraud and Abuse Act.[28] Other statutes have been enacted to combat child pornography and unauthorized access to computer-stored records.[29] In 2013 "U.S. Executive Order–Improving Critical Infrastructure Cybersecurity" bolstered cybersecurity protections for the nation's critical infrastructure networks by authorizing the government to increase the volume, timeliness, and quality of cyber threat information shared with private sector entities to enable enhancement of their security measures.[30] In 2015 "U.S. Executive Order-Promoting Private Sector Cybersecurity Information Sharing" provided a framework for expanded information sharing designed to help companies work together with the federal government to quickly identify and protect against cyber threats.[31]

Some experts predict that by the year 2025 technology will have advanced by an equivalent of 5,000 years, paving the future path through cyberspace with possibilities–and threats–unimaginable today.[32] Unchecked growth in surveillance technology, for instance, could result in recording virtually all activity for retrieval and prosecution. However, just as is the case today, the use of twenty-first century technology for evidence gathering will come face-to-face with that eighteenth-century guarantor of protection against unreasonable government intrusion: the U.S. Constitution. The "duel" should be intriguing.

TARGETING IDENTITY THEFT

Identity theft is unauthorized use of another person's identifying information to obtain credit, goods, services, money, or property, or to commit a felony or misdemeanor.[33] Some criminologists consider identity theft to be "the" crime of the twenty-first century.[34] Typical offenses associated with identity theft include credit card fraud, fraudulently obtaining loans, and bank fraud. Fraudulently obtained funds may be used to finance larger criminal enterprises, including gang, drug, and terrorist activities.

identity theft
Unauthorized use of another person's identifying information to obtain credit, goods, services, money, or property, or to commit a misdemeanor or felony.

MYTH/REALITY

MYTH: Those who refrain from purchasing goods or services online are protected from becoming victims of identity theft.

REALITY: Minimizing use of online purchases does not necessarily correlate with a decreased potential for victimization. Personal identifying information can be obtained offline (for example, via "dumpster diving" or eavesdropping) as well as online.[35]

Identity theft can occur in both physical and cyber domains. In both situations, the intent and outcome (stolen personally identifiable information) are the same. In the physical, "real" world a criminal can steal mail containing credit/debit cards and then withdraw cash or make purchases. In the cyber world, a computer hacker can easily steal the same personally identifiable information by, for example, hacking into point-of-sale systems and remotely installing "keystroke loggers." These devices then capture victims' credit card information when cards are swiped.[36]

The United Nations Office on Drugs and Crime estimates that identity theft is the most profitable form of cybercrime on a global basis. It is estimated that 40 million people in the United States have had their personal information stolen by hackers.[37]

A significant difference between identity theft and other property crimes is that identity theft can continue for months, during which time the victim may feel helpless and experience a lack of control over her life. These stresses may result in psychological and physical illness.[38]

When identity theft was first recognized as a widespread problem, police agencies, victim assistance advocates, and private industry usually operated independently in investigating cases. In 2003, however, a joint effort of the U.S. Department of Justice's Office of Community Oriented Policing Services and the Major Cities Chiefs Association produced plans for state-level identity theft coordination centers. Today these centers facilitate the flow of information and promote collaboration among state, local, and federal law enforcement agencies, the Federal Trade Commission, and corporate entities.[39]

The FBI's Internet Crime Complaint Center (IC3) has firmly established its role as a resource for both victims of Internet crime and law enforcement agencies. For victims, IC3 provides a convenient and easy-to-use reporting mechanism. For law enforcement agencies, the IC3 serves as a conduit for gathering data for research and development of analytical reports for local, state, federal, and international law enforcement and regulatory agencies. The information obtained is essential for creation of preventive and investigative strategies. For example, trend analysis has revealed that the number of complaints involving social media quadrupled from 2010 to 2014. In most such cases, victims' personal information was exploited through compromised accounts or social engineering (for example, manipulating someone in order to obtain confidential information such as a password).[40]

A Contextual Framework for Combating Identity Theft

A contextual framework of stakeholders and their roles and interactions assists in illuminating actions to combat identity theft. Four main stakeholders help combat identity theft through a variety of activities. Stakeholders are (1) identity owners, (2) identity issuers, (3) identity checkers, and (4) identity protectors. It is the identity owners' responsibility to safeguard their identifying information. An identity issuer's responsibility is to verify the receiver's true identity before issuing a valid certificate that a validating institution can then use to verify this identity. Identity issuers not only issue secure identity certificates but also protect sensitive personal identifiable information held in databases. Identity checkers must verify that two items are valid: the owner's identity certificate and the holder's identity. When authenticating identities, the checker must establish and use strict authentication processes. Identity protectors can be government legislators, law enforcement agencies, the legal system, and public and private technical security solution providers. Secure identity management requires collaboration between all stakeholders. Figure 16-1 illustrates the information flows and interactions among stakeholders comprising a contextual framework for combating identity theft.[41]

Prevention Strategies

The most effective way to combat identity theft is to prevent it from occurring. Education and employment of advanced technologies are integral to its prevention. The more aware people are of threats and the potential for severe harm, the more motivated they will be to exercise preventive measures. Identity protectors play a major role in public education, as do identity issuers and checkers who focus on customer education. Identity theft prevention technologies such as biometrics and smart cards are continually evolving. Biometrics can confirm identities through unique human characteristics such as fingerprints or retinal scans. Smart cards, which embed integrated circuits, can store biometric information to deliver secure and accurate identity verification.

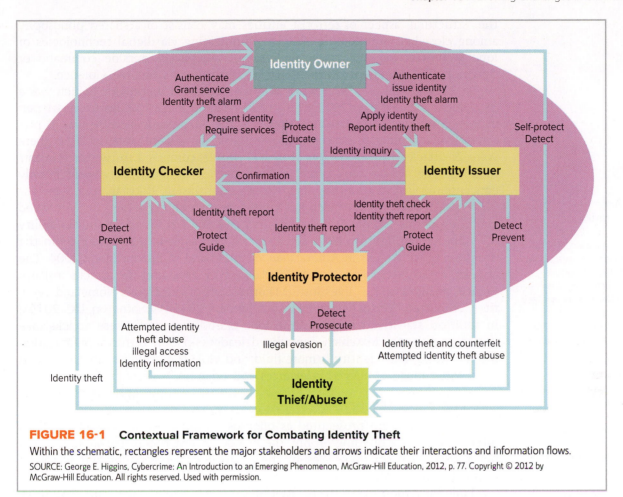

FIGURE 16-1   **Contextual Framework for Combating Identity Theft**
Within the schematic, rectangles represent the major stakeholders and arrows indicate their interactions and information flows.
SOURCE: George E. Higgins, Cybercrime: An Introduction to an Emerging Phenomenon, McGraw-Hill Education, 2012, p. 77. Copyright © 2012 by McGraw-Hill Education. All rights reserved. Used with permission.

Beyond education and technology, business owners and organizational heads must recognize identity theft as a risk and wholeheartedly commit to its proactive management. Risk is determined by three primary factors: assets (e.g., employees' Social Security numbers), threats (e.g., Internet hacking), and vulnerabilities (e.g., an onlooker observing inputting of PINs). Following an assessment of the dynamics among assets, threats, and vulnerabilities, a skilled security solution provider can select countermeasures to protect assets from possible threats depending on the likelihood of each threat and develop policies to reduce threats and vulnerabilities. Thus, it is essential that identity security managers understand the elements comprising the risk management process in order to implement appropriate, responsive countermeasures.[42]

COMBATING TERRORISM

Terrorism, according to the U.S. Code, is "premeditated, politically motivated violence perpetrated against non-combatant targets by subnational groups or clandestine agents, usually intended to influence an audience."[43] Terrorism has been categorized as "international" or "domestic." International terrorism against the United States is foreign based, whereas domestic terrorism involves groups that are based in, and operate entirely within, the United States.[44] However, there is no universally agreed-upon definition of terrorism. Even within the United States, the FBI, the Department of Homeland Security, and the Department of Defense have different definitions of terrorism, reflecting the priorities and particular interests of the specific agency.

In the past, terrorism was relatively easier to define because terrorist bodies typically had a readily identifiable structure and chain of command. Today,

terrorism
Premeditated, politically motivated violence perpetrated against noncombatant targets by subnational groups or clandestine agents.

the "structural" aspect of terrorist entities may consist of a shared philosophy among close-knit autonomous cells communicating via digital technologies or lone wolves acting independently without any direct outside command or direction. The common thread is that all terrorist acts involve violence.

In 2014 a total of 13,463 terrorist attacks occurred worldwide, which was a 35 percent increase over 2013. The attacks resulted in 32,700 deaths, an 81 percent increase over 2013 fatalities. However, the 81 percent increase was in part a result of a number of attacks that were lethal on a large scale; in 2014, there were 20 attacks that killed more than 100 people, compared to two such events in 2013. The attacks took place in 95 countries, although they were heavily concentrated in five countries: Iraq, Nigeria, Afghanistan, Pakistan, and Syria.[45]

The U.S. State Department has voiced deep concern about the continued evolution of the Islamic State of the Iraq and the Levant (ISIL) and its ability to enlist foreign fighters. ISIL's global terror campaign in 2015 resulted in the deadliest terror attacks in America since "9/11" and in Europe since 2004. The attacks in San Bernardino, California, claimed 14 lives, and the attacks in Paris, France, resulted in 130 lives lost. [Majority Staff of the House Homeland Security Committee, "Terror Threat Snapshot, January 2016 (Washington, DC, 2016).] In addition, statistics reveal a rise in lone offender attacks. These attacks may presage a new era in which centralized leadership of a terrorist organization matters less, group identity is more fluid, and violent extremist narratives focus on a wider range of alleged grievances and enemies.[46]

Terrorism and the Law

Acts of terrorism are prosecuted as offenses within existing laws. If terrorists intentionally set a building on fire, the charge against the perpetrators is arson, not terrorism. If someone dies in the blaze, the perpetrators will likely be charged with murder.

Following the 9/11 terrorist attacks, Congress enacted the **USA PATRIOT Act** (which is an acronym for Uniting and Strengthening America by Providing Appropriate Tools Required to Intercept and Obstruct Terrorism). This law was intended to deter and punish terrorist acts in the United States and around the world, to enhance law enforcement investigatory tools, and to strengthen U.S. measures to prevent and detect terrorism. Critics of the act charged that the broad authority given to the government under the law's provisions amounted to an "overnight revision of the nation's surveillance laws that vastly expanded the government's authority to spy on its own citizens."[47] Implementation of the PATRIOT Act rekindled the long-standing debate between the crime control and the due process models of justice (see Chapter 1).

The PATRIOT Act's provisions expired in 2015, prompting enactment of the **USA FREEDOM Act**. "USA FREEDOM" is an acronym that stands for "**U**niting and **S**trengthening **A**merica by **F**ulfilling **R**ights and **E**nding **E**avesdropping, **D**ragnet-collection, and **O**nline **M**onitoring." Most significantly, the USA FREEDOM Act bans the bulk collection of phone records and Internet metadata, and it limits data collection to the extent reasonably practical when

USA PATRIOT Act
A law—officially, the Uniting and Strengthening America by Providing Appropriate Tools Required to Intercept and Obstruct Terrorism Act—enacted by Congress following the 9/11 terrorist attacks, intended to deter and punish terrorist acts in the United States and around the world, to enhance law enforcement investigatory tools, and to strengthen measures to prevent and detect terrorism.

USA FREEDOM Act
Antiterrorism legislation enacted in 2015. The acronym stands for Uniting and Strengthening America by Fulfilling Rights and Ending Eavesdropping, Dragnet-collection, and Online Monitoring. Principally, the act imposes new limits on the bulk collection of telecommunications metadata. It also restores authorization for roving wiretaps and tracking lone wolf terrorists.

▼ **ISIL's Media Skill Set**

ISIL demonstrates particular skill in employing new media tools to propagandize and to attract recruits.

ISSyria
@ISSyria15

Support our wounded warriors by donating to us via Bitcoin:
17VrbynoXxTkSz6ZvVLn77u3rnEFxUvT4
e

TWEETS 68   FOLLOWING 133

Tweets   Tweets

Pinned Tweet
ISSyria @ISSyria
Spread
massive
Donate i
17Vrbyn

Real Careers

AMY ZELSON MUNDORFF

Work location: New York, New York

College(s): Syracuse University (1991); California State University (1999); Simon Fraser University (2009)

Major(s): Archaeology (BA); Anthropology (MA); Archaeology (PhD)

Job title: Forensic Anthropologist, Office of Chief Medical Examiner, New York City

Salary range for job like this: $40,000–$120,000

Time in job: 5 years

Work Responsibilities

From 1999 through September 2001, I was responsible for establishing protocol for all forensic anthropology-related matters for the city of New York. During this time, I analyzed more than 250 forensic anthropological cases, including standard medical examiner cases with bone trauma or pathology and unidentified, decomposed, burned, mummified, or skeletonized remains to help identify individuals. I participated in search and recovery of human remains, prepared case reports, and testified as an expert witness in court. I also provided training to medical examiners, medical students, fellows, and interns and lectured on forensic anthropology to law enforcement agencies and district attorneys.

Following 9/11, I was primarily involved with the mortuary operations and identification efforts of the World Trade Center (WTC) victims. I was part of a team that established standards and procedures for the WTC Human Identification Project and developed protocols for handling and processing human remains, DNA sampling, and quality assurance procedures. I met with family members to review individual cases and attended "family group" meetings to update family members on the progress of the identification project. I was also part of the disaster identification team for the 2001 crash of American Airlines flight 587 and the Staten Island ferry crash in 2003.

Why Criminal Justice?

I fell into the field of forensic anthropology. As an undergrad, I was an archaeology major. While attending a summer archaeology field school in Jamaica in 1988, I helped excavate a skeleton and became fascinated with the stories human bones could tell. Following graduation, I worked as an archaeologist in Hawaii and California for about 5 years, where I participated in excavating skeletal remains. I returned to school for a master's, focusing in forensic anthropology. During my master's program, I volunteered one summer at the Office of Chief Medical Examiner, New York City; that was when I decided I wanted to do forensic anthropology full-time.

Expectations and Realities of the Job

The job is both better and more frustrating than I expected. It's better in the sense that I work with every subfield of forensics, so I learn a tremendous amount. Unlike forensic investigators on TV, forensic scientists don't work in a vacuum, solving every aspect of the crime themselves. I worked with brilliant forensic pathologists, odontologists, radiologists, fingerprint experts, toxicologists, histologists, biologists, detectives, and more. We pooled our expertise to help identify individuals or determine someone's cause and manner of death. On the other hand, the job is more frustrating than I had anticipated because not every case is solved. Not being able to identify remains or help solve a homicide is one of the most difficult aspects of my work.

My Advice to Students

Don't hesitate to ask for help or advice on the job. When confronted with a particularly challenging case, reach out to other colleagues with more experience and seek their opinion.

Another piece of advice is to include something on your resume that separates you from your fellow graduates. For me, it was showing practical experience working at a medical examiner's office. During one of my summer breaks from graduate school, I called the medical examiner office where I wanted to work and offered my services for free. No one turns down free labor! I interned there for the summer, made fantastic contacts, and learned a tremendous amount. When I graduated, I wrote the chief medical examiner a letter suggesting it was time to hire a forensic anthropologist full-time and that person should be me. And they did. I was the first full-time forensic anthropologist hired at New York City's Office of Chief Medical Examiner.

there is reasonable suspicion that a suspect is linked to a terrorist organization. The act extended the "lone wolf" and "roving wiretap" surveillance provisions of the PATRIOT Act.[48]

Just as the USA FREEDOM Act has provided for a more reasonable approach to data collection, the technology employed at U.S. airport screening facilities has been modified to be less invasive. Advanced imaging technology has enhanced passenger privacy by eliminating passenger-specific images, which had frequently provoked indignation among the traveling public. The "Matters of Ethics" box contrasts the previously employed backscatter scanner with advanced imaging technology.

Matters *of* Ethics

Airport Security Technology in the United States

Because of concerns about citizens' privacy rights, health problems due to radiation exposure, and uncertainty about the overall effectiveness of the U.S. airport scanning program, the Department of Homeland Security halted its deployment of full-body X-ray scanners (used to prevent terrorist crime) at U.S. airports in 2013. The Transportation Security Administration (TSA) prohibited the use of the controversial *backscatter scanner*, which could see through clothing and produced nearly naked graphic images, and they were removed from all airports.

In place of the intrusive old technology, American airports now use advanced imaging technology (AIT) that uses *millimeter wave scanners*. The new machines are much less intrusive and emit radio waves similar to what cell phones discharge. The new scanners can detect a large range of threats in a matter of seconds, including concealed metallic and nonmetallic weapons and explosives. AIT technology creates generic, cartoonlike outline images of the human body. Body image outlines are the same for every person, and possible threats will pop up on the computer screen as

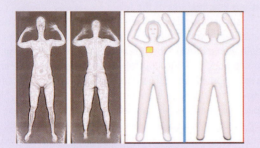

little yellow boxes, eliminating the need for a TSA officer to review the image. Finally, in December 2015 AIT screening no longer became optional for passengers. The TSA changed its rules and now it can mandate some passengers must go through a body scanner even if the passengers ask to opt-out and request a full-body pat down instead.

OBSERVE → INVESTIGATE → UNDERSTAND

- Is subjecting airline passengers to AIT technology less or more intrusive than requiring them to remove shoes and belts before boarding? Explain.
- Does the use of AIT technology for security outweigh the privacy rights of the individual? Why or why not?
- Does the TSA's use of AIT technology make more sense than hand-pat searches of passengers? Explain.

SOURCES: Carol Kuruvilla, "TSA Has Completely Removed Revealing X-ray Scanners from America's Airports: Rep," *New York Daily News*, May 31, 2013. www.nydailynews.com/news/national/tsa-completely-removed-full-body-scanners-rep-article-1.1360143 (retrieved July 20, 2015); Transportation Security Administration, "Advanced Imaging Technology," September 3, 2014. https://www.tsa.gov/traveler-information/advanced-imaging-technology (retrieved July 20, 2015); Rene Marsh, "TSA Changes Rules For Who Must Go Through Body Scanner," CNN, December 23, 2015. http://www.cnn.com/2015/12/23/travel/tsa-airport-screening-change/ (retrieved February 26, 2015).

Terrorism and Intelligence

Law enforcement plays a threefold role against terrorism: protection of the community, emergency response, and intelligence gathering and sharing.[49] As depicted in Figure 16-2, **intelligence** is the product of the application of analytical reasoning to data or information to develop a reliable picture of the environment or situation.[50]

Early development of intelligence can give law enforcement personnel the opportunity to intervene before a terrorist incident occurs. For instance, information regarding one person's purchase of a large quantity of ammonium nitrate (fertilizer) in one locale could be combined with information about another individual's purchase of fuel oil in another nearby locale to yield intelligence that the ingredients for a powerful explosive now reside in the area. Combining this intelligence with other information—such as a police agency's field interview reports of an individual taking a number of photos around the base of a bridge spanning a large river—would result in increased patrol of the bridge, as well as surveillance of the individuals making the ammonium nitrate and fuel oil purchases.

Protection and emergency response have long been functions of the police, but the intelligence function of policing, which may be the most important law enforcement function of the twenty-first century, is still developing.[51] **Intelligence-led policing (ILP)** is the collaborative collection and analysis of data by intelligence analysts, field officers, and senior leaders to improve crime control

intelligence
Product of the application of analytical reasoning to data or information in order to develop a reliable picture of an environment or a situation.

intelligence-led policing (ILP)
Collaborative collection and analysis of data by intelligence analysts, field officers, and senior leaders.

Data or Information + Analysis = Intelligence

FIGURE 16-2 **Intelligence Recipe**
"Intelligence" is refined information.

strategies, allocation of police resources, and operations.[52] The term "intelligence-led policing" originated in Great Britain at a time when police budgets were being cut. Police officials de-emphasized response to service calls and accorded priority to creating intelligence units that focused on the most prevalent offenses and the most prolific offenders.[53]

Intelligence analysts are individuals with expertise in discerning "intelligence" from "information." Analysts examine information brought to the attention of police agencies to look for patterns and associations. By linking otherwise unrelated pieces of data together, intelligence analysts can identify existing threats of terrorist activity and enforcement opportunities.[54] *Field officers* are law enforcement generalists who, in the course of their duties, come across information that should be forwarded to analysts for analysis. *Senior leaders* are law enforcement agency personnel who make operational decisions based on the intelligence provided to them by analysts.

RealCrimeTech

BORDER PATROL PREDATORS TAKE FLIGHT

Since 2007 U.S. Customs and Border Protection (CBP) has routinely deployed unmanned Predator aircraft over the southwestern U.S. border to help combat terrorism, catch illegal immigrants, and stem the flow of illegal drugs. The electro-optical and forward-looking infrared camera systems aboard the Predators enable imaging with very high resolution, in any weather conditions. The moving target indicator system enables tracking of cars and vessels, and the aircraft can stay aloft for 34 hours without having to be refueled. Deployment of the Predators enables extension of the CBP into remote areas where ground-based patrols cannot easily travel and detection systems cannot be installed.

SOURCE: Paul Serluco, "Customs and Border Patrol Predators Take Flight," *Homeland Defense Journal* 6, no. 1 (2008): 18–21.

MYTH/REALITY

MYTH: "Intelligence" and "information" are the same thing.

REALITY: A crucial distinction is that collected information must be analyzed to produce intelligence.[55]

Intelligence is the lifeblood of antiterrorism operations—but only if it reaches the people who need to act on it. Local law enforcement agencies traditionally were attuned to crime only within their own communities After the 9/11 terrorist attacks, however, nonfederal authorities began forming **fusion centers,** regional intelligence hubs that pool and analyze information from many jurisdictions and share it with those to whom it directly applies (see "A Case in Point"). National agencies, particularly the Department of Homeland Security (DHS) and the FBI, have become increasingly involved, with DHS providing personnel with intelligence and operational skills to the fusion centers.[56]

fusion center
Regional intelligence hub that pools and analyzes information from many jurisdictions and shares it with those to whom it directly applies.

Information from the community at large can be a vital ingredient in developing intelligence. Alert citizens help to prevent conventional crime, and they can help to foil acts of terrorism as well. For example, a landlord's suspicions might be triggered if a large number of individuals use a rented apartment on an irregular basis. A retailer or a wholesaler might notice purchases of large amounts of hydrogen peroxide or ammonium nitrate—both components of improvised explosive devices—and might report such transactions to local authorities. Community-based training programs, such as those established by the Teaneck, New Jersey, Police Department, have drawn praise from numerous community groups and helped empower citizens to be proactive in preventing terrorism.[57]

Prevention Strategies

Prevention of terrorism requires a multipronged approach. Law enforcement assumes a lead role through direct involvement in implementing tactical strategies and as a facilitator in formation of partnerships. At the local level, law enforcement can create a hostile environment that frustrates or thwarts terrorists—for example, by conducting drills and staging scenes that mimic terrorist attacks. For instance, the New York Police Department, without announcement, randomly deploys massive numbers of officers in areas of New York City that are perceived to be targets of terrorist activity. This strategy

The Fusion Center Approach to Preventing Terrorism

In the wake of the 9/11 terrorist strikes, the concept of fusion has emerged as the fundamental process to facilitate the sharing of homeland security–related intelligence. *Fusion* refers to the process of managing the flow of information and intelligence across all levels and sectors of government and the private sector. *Fusion centers* are the facilities that house the personnel and equipment responsible for gathering, analyzing, and sharing the intelligence used to identify emerging threats of terrorism and other serious crimes. Currently, there are 78 recognized fusion centers owned and operated by state and local entities. These facilities get federal support in the form of deployed intelligence officers, technical assistance, exercise support, security clearances, and connectivity to federal systems.[a]

Detection of the planning of a terrorist incident often requires piecing together separate bits of information that, when assembled, point to the potential for a terrorist action. For example, reports of thefts of power company vans from one locale, coupled with those detailing burglaries at stores selling professional uniforms in a neighboring city, could indicate a plot to cripple a vital facility's operating capability. In addition to obtaining information from official police reports, fusion centers seek to use information gathered from other public agency employees such as sanitation workers and firefighters. A number of centers operate tip hotlines.[b]

While the Department of Homeland Security has been the driving force for the creation of fusion centers, local officials have taken advantage of the pooled resources and analytical capabilities afforded through the centers to address conventional crime. Massachusetts, for example, has co-located its fusion center, the Commonwealth Fusion Center (CFC), with the New England High Intensity Drug Trafficking Area. In addition, the CFC serves as the state crime-reporting repository and offers specifics on a wide variety of crimes. For example, the CFC enabled the examination of firearms offenses committed by youths ages 10 to 17 across several locales to study juvenile gun crime.[c]

While fusion centers have been praised for their capability of identifying potential terrorist threats, they have also been the subject of criticism for their potential for compromising civil liberties. Some politicians have openly called for fusion centers to wiretap mosques and spy on foreign students. Local police departments also have been collecting suspicious activity reports on persons using binoculars or taking pictures with no apparent aesthetic value. These policing activities are technically illegal under federal law, which requires reasonable suspicion that an individual is involved in criminal conduct.[d]

Fusion centers must have in place effective and robust privacy and civil rights policies and protections.[e] If they fail to make privacy and civil rights protections a priority status, the network may find itself unsustainable—a criminal justice reality and a challenge of substantial importance.

OBSERVE → INVESTIGATE → UNDERSTAND

- Given that fusion centers were formed primarily to combat terrorism, is it appropriate for employees of these centers to use their intelligence for suppressing conventional crime activities? Explain.

  - Would it be appropriate for fusion centers to collect information on individuals involved in nonviolent public protests—for example, demonstrations against globalization or taxation policies? Why or why not?

  - Does the fact that fusion centers are staffed mainly by municipal employees constitute an impediment to their making broad connections to terrorism-related threats? Discuss.

SOURCES: [a]U.S. Department of Justice, *Fusion Center Guidelines*, special report prepared in collaboration with the U.S. Department of Homeland Security, April 2006, 3.

[b]Torin Monahan and Neal A. Palmer, "The Emerging Politics of DHS Fusion Centers," *Security Dialogue* 40, no. 6 (2009): 619.

[c]David Lambert, "Intelligence-Led Policing in a Fusion Center," *FBI Law Enforcement bulletin* 79, no. 12 (2010): 3.

[d]Monahan and Palmer, "The Emerging Politics of DHS Fusion Centers," 628–629.

[e]Bureau of Justice Assistance, "2014 National Network of Fusion Centers Final Report" (Washington, DC, January 2015), 24.

halted a plot in 2003 to blow up the Brooklyn Bridge. An al-Qaeda operative sent to survey the bridge was recorded as saying "the weather was too hot" to complete the operation.[58] Surveillance cameras, random screenings, and sensors can create a hostile environment by conveying a sense that law enforcement is ever-present.

Police need to be vigilant for **precursor crimes,** offenses committed for the purpose of enabling acts of terrorism. Criminal activities with which terrorists have been associated include ATM fraud, counterfeiting of postage stamps and food products, money laundering, staged accidents, and video piracy.[59] In addition, the possession of forged documents, illegal border crossings, and other comparatively minor crimes may serve directly to support preparations for terrorism. Patrol officers should view vehicle stops and all preliminary investigations as opportunities to intervene in terrorism.

Partnerships are at the core of sustaining counterterrorism efforts. The nation's experience with community-based problem solving, local partnerships, and community-oriented policing provides a basis for addressing violent extremism as part of a broader mandate of community safety. In Montgomery County, Maryland, a community-led, public-private partnership between the county's Faith Community Working Group and the Montgomery County Police Department has melded community and interfaith commitment to preventing extremism and violence while also showing solidarity with the local Muslim community.[60] At the international level, the United Nations Security Council, through its unanimous adoption of Resolution 2178 (2014), condemned violent extremism and decided that member states should all cooperate urgently to prevent the flow of terrorist fighters to and from conflict zones.[61]

With the emergence of the **lone wolf,** as a prominent threat, crowdsourcing presents a potentially powerful mechanism for collecting large amounts of data on potential lone wolf terrorism indicators identified by citizens. **Crowdsourcing** is defined as "an online, distributed problem-solving and production model that leverages the collective intelligence of online communities to serve specific organizational goals."[62] Use of electronic intercepts, inherent to a top-down (that is, governmentally initiated) searching method, may be less likely to identify lone wolves, as a lone wolf rarely contacts a known terrorist group in a traceable manner.[63] A national crowdsourcing intelligence program leveraging citizen volunteerism would need to be well publicized and user-friendly, and there would need to be education on reliable indicators of lone wolf preparation and planning.

PROSECUTING HATE CRIMES

A **hate crime** is a criminal offense committed because of the victim's race, ethnicity, religion, sexual orientation, or other group affiliation. Despite the name, the offender need not actually hate the victim to be convicted. In some jurisdictions, hate crimes are known as *bias crimes* or *ethnic intimidation crimes.* Typical examples of hate crimes include burning a cross in the yard of a Black family, painting a swastika on a synagogue wall, and gay bashing–beating a person who is or is assumed to be gay.

Crimes motivated by bias are ancient, but most laws against them are new, having been enacted in the 1980s and 1990s. Almost all states now have a hate crime law of some kind. On the federal level, after many years of debate, in 2009 Congress passed the Matthew Shepard and James Byrd Jr. Hate Crimes Prevention Act, which created federal sanctions for hate crimes as well. The act was named after two hate crime victims: Shepard, a gay college student from Wyoming who was beaten and left tied to a fencepost to die; and Byrd, a Black Texan who was dragged to death behind a pickup truck. In addition,

precursor crime
Offense committed for the purpose of enabling acts of terrorism, such as illegal border crossings or forged documents.

lone wolf
A terrorist who is not a member of a known terrorist group and who does not take orders from a chain of command when conducting acts of terror.

crowdsourcing
An online, distributed problem-solving and production model that leverages the collective intelligence of online communities to serve specific organizational goals.

hate crime
Criminal offense committed because of the victim's race, ethnicity, religion, sexual orientation, or other group affiliation.

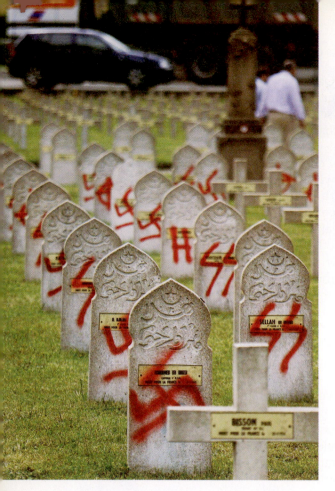

▲ **Swastikas and SS initials on Muslim Gravestones**

Hate crimes are widespread and send an intimidating message that targeted groups are unwelcome and unsafe in a community.

federal law requires the U.S. Department of Justice to collect specific data related to hate crimes from local law enforcement agencies. In 2013 police departments reported 5,928 hate crime incidents involving 6,933 offenses that were classified as hate crimes; however, most hate crimes probably do not get reported to the police.[64]

MYTH/REALITY

MYTH: Most people who commit crimes based on hatred, bias, or discrimination face hate crime charges or longer sentencing.

REALITY: Prosecutors have extraordinary discretion regarding how to charge suspects and often do not seek hate crime penalties.[65]

Many hate crime laws operate as **penalty enhancers,** meaning they add to the penalty for the underlying criminal act. For example, vandalizing another person's property is ordinarily a Class B misdemeanor. If, however, the vandalism is determined to have been motivated by the victim's race and prosecuted under hate crime laws, the charge can be raised to a Class A misdemeanor, thus increasing the potential punishment.

Hate crimes require evidence not only of actus reus and mens rea (see Chapter 4) but also of the offender's motive. To obtain a conviction for a hate crime, the prosecutor must prove that the defendant's acts were motivated (at least in part) by the victim's race, ethnicity, religion, or sexual orientation. Because it is often difficult, if not impossible, to assess another person's motives accurately,[66] convictions for hate crimes are rare. Of the 1,072 hate crimes reported to California police in 2013, only 68 resulted in convictions.[67]

Considerable controversy surrounds the topic of hate crimes, including debate about which groups need protection. Many states do not include victims' sexual orientation or gender identity as criteria for hate crimes, and only a few include disability or age.[68] As the "Race, Class, Gender" box describes, immigrants are also often victims of hate crimes.

As shown in Figure 16-3, almost half of hate crimes are motivated by race. Others are motivated by religion, sexual orientation, ethnicity, or disability.

The least violent hate crimes tend to be motivated by religious bias; these crimes are usually property-related crimes or vandalism. Jewish people were targeted in 59 percent of the hate crimes based on religion.[69] Anti-Muslim hate crimes are also common, especially since 9/11. However, various jurisdictions may categorize these crimes differently—either as crimes based on religion (Islam) or ethnicity (Arab or Middle Eastern) or in the category of "other." Thus the actual prevalence of these specific crimes is not always clear from the official data.

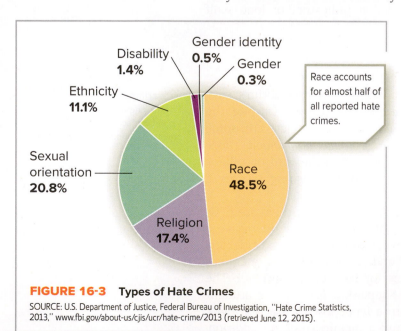

Race accounts for almost half of all reported hate crimes.

- Gender identity 0.5%
- Gender 0.3%
- Disability 1.4%
- Ethnicity 11.1%
- Sexual orientation 20.8%
- Race 48.5%
- Religion 17.4%

FIGURE 16-3 Types of Hate Crimes

SOURCE: U.S. Department of Justice, Federal Bureau of Investigation, "Hate Crime Statistics, 2013," www.fbi.gov/about-us/cjis/ucr/hate-crime/2013 (retrieved June 12, 2015).

Race, Class, Gender

The Killing of Onesimo "Marcelino" Lopez-Ramos

In the end, one teenager was dead and three other teenagers were in jail facing murder and possible hate crime charges.

Onesimo "Marcelino" Lopez-Ramos immigrated to Jupiter, Florida, from Guatemala when he was 16. By 2015 he was 18. To help support his family, he worked long hours—seven days a week—as a pizza cook. Coworkers said he was a kind young man. His older brother said he was unassuming and religious.

In the very early hours of April 18, 2015, Lopez-Ramos was hanging outside a friend's house with a few other young people, quietly talking and drinking beer. Several new people approached. According to witnesses, the interchange seemed friendly at first, with Lopez-Ramos greeting the newcomers with a handshake. But soon the newcomers turned violent, and they crushed Lopez-Ramos's skull with a rock, killing him. Lopez-Ramos's brother was injured as well, although not fatally.

Less than a week later, three teenagers were arrested: Austin Taggart, 18; David Harris, 19; and David's brother Jesse Harris, 18. Reportedly, the suspects laughed and told police they had been "Guat hunting"—that is, specifically looking for Guatemalan immigrants to rob and harass.

Violence against Guatemalans was not new in Jupiter. The town has a large proportion of Guatemalan immigrants, many of whom are paid in cash and are therefore seen as easy robbery targets by some people. In addition, some residents reported having been targeted in the past with racial slurs as well as physical attacks. Community organizations and police have worked together to improve the situation, but still a young man is dead, apparently solely because of his ethnicity.

OBSERVE → INVESTIGATE → UNDERSTAND

- What do you think motivates some people to commit crimes such as this one? To what extent do you think this particular crime was influenced by mainstream anti-immigrant rhetoric?
- Victims of hate crimes frequently do not report the crimes to the police. Do you think this might be a particular problem when the victims are immigrants? How can victims be encouraged to report these crimes?
- What do you think might be effective methods of preventing hate crimes in your community?

SOURCES: Juan Ortega, "Hate Crime Suspected in Killing of 18-Year-Old Man; Three Arrested in Jupiter," Sun Sentinel, April 27, 2015. www.sun-sentinel.com/local/palm-beach/fl-jupiter-killing-folo-20150425-story.html (retrieved June 12, 2015); Tim Rogers, "Why Some Guatemalans in This Florida City Fear White Guys Driving Big Pickup Trucks," Fusion.net, May 2, 2015, http://fusion.net/story/129549/why-some-guatemalans-in-this-florida-city-fear-white-guys-driving-big-pickup-trucks/ (retrieved June 12, 2015).

Blacks are more likely than Whites to be victims of racially motivated hate crimes. Younger people tend to be the target of violent hate crimes; more than half of all victims of violent hate crimes are under age 24.[70]

penalty enhancer
Attribute that adds to the penalty for a crime.

CONTROLLING CIVIL DISORDER

Civil disorder is a disturbance by a group of people that is symptomatic of a major sociopolitical problem. Normally such disorder arises from a spontaneous gathering in response to some perceived injustice. Any assembly of persons that poses a threat of collective violence or a breach of the peace is subject to laws against civil disorder.[71]

The severity of the disturbance usually corresponds to the degree of outrage among participants. Even citizens not directly involved in a civil disorder may experience major disruptions in their daily lives. Chaos at the site may constrain travel and commerce; residents may fear for their safety. When public order is disrupted, the police act as a control force with a threefold mission: to preserve life, to protect property, and to restore order. They may suspend their response to routine criminal activities (such as taking a report of a burglary or theft) and encourage citizens to defer reporting less serious offenses until order has been restored.

civil disorder
Disturbance by a group of people that is symptomatic of a major sociopolitical problem.

Causes of Civil Disorder

Research on the riots of the 1960s examined the dynamics of crowds and mobs and identified some elements common to episodes of civil disorder. A **crowd** is defined as a group of individuals drawn together by common values and feelings about a current matter. A crowd, although unorganized and without leadership, is ruled by collective reason, is aware of the law, and generally respects its principles.

Like a crowd, a **mob** is drawn together by common values, but otherwise it is quite different. First, a mob is not law-abiding. A mob usually is organized,

crowd
A leaderless group of individuals, generally respectful of the law, drawn together by common values about a current matter.

mob
A group that is not law-abiding, with a leader, that is ruled by emotion.

▲ Sports Fan Rioting

Excitement, passion, adrenaline, and alcohol can turn a happy event, like a sports team's title victory, into a riot.

has a leader, and is ruled by emotion. Its creation is usually sparked by a climactic event, such as an organized expression of sympathy or resentment. Zealots mill about from one small group to another, rousing emotions that build to a high state of collective tension and excitement. Mob members lose their personal identity and become anonymous in the large group, a psychological effect that absolves them of personal responsibility for any destructive acts that ensue.[72] Sports fans watching an athletic event, for instance, may become either angered at a loss or overjoyed by a win and then act collectively in ways that include breaking laws. At first, a few people begin to act and then others follow, spurred by their sudden anonymity in a large group of their peers.[73] Automobiles are overturned, bonfires set in the streets, and businesses vandalized—usually with no premeditation.

Major riots often are the result of an accumulated reservoir of grievances. Groups may congregate—and mob behavior might follow—because of an *accumulated reservoir* of grievances.[74] For example, the Los Angeles riots that occurred after the 1992 acquittal of White police officers accused of beating Black motorist Rodney King took place in a climate of racial unrest. For months, television stations had played and replayed video footage of King's beating taken by a bystander, effectively priming the public mood. Many people of color were experiencing what they believed to be social and economic inequities as well as discriminatory treatment by the justice system. All that was needed to ignite disorder was a *precipitating incident;* the acquittal of the White officers charged with beating King served that purpose.[75] The same accumulated reservoirs of grievances appeared to have been present in the riots that took place in Ferguson, Missouri, and Baltimore, Maryland, following questionable uses of force by police in 2014 and 2015, respectively.

▼ A Flash Mob Materializes in an Instant

Flash mobs, while usually not assembled for political purposes, illustrate the capability of telecommunications to enable the instantaneous mustering of individuals.

MYTH/REALITY

MYTH: Civil disorders are usually spontaneous and unpredictable.

REALITY: Civil disorders require some precipitating incident, which may be spontaneous. However, civil disorders are often predictable because the "tinder" upon which they are ignited has accumulated visibly over time.[76]

Today's social protests, such as the Occupy Wall Street movement, are being carried out by groups that are considerably better prepared and more organized than those in the past. Whatever the issue, individuals both inside and outside the community—and even those outside the country—can connect with one another online to participate in social protests.[77] Not only can the Internet markedly facilitate pre-event mustering (as in the flash mob process—the sudden assemblage of a group of people at a predetermined time and place to perform a predefined action, and then just as quickly to disperse), but protest organizers now commonly employ customized Google maps to track police movements. Some organizers have even created specific icons to reveal in real time the location and number of types of police resources, a strategy that can neutralize the effectiveness of law enforcement's tactical planning.[78]

Prevention Strategies

Commissions convened in the 1990s identified the quality of the relationship between the community and its police force as the most significant factor in preventing or resolving civil disorder.[79] Good relationships can enable quick and effective intervention when unrest develops. If unrest is allowed to progress to angry confrontation with authorities, the likelihood of violence is strong.[80]

In the wake of the Occupy Wall Street protests in late 2011, law enforcement developed a protest containment strategy termed "strategic incapacitation." The hallmarks of strategic incapacitation are spatial containment, surveillance, and information management. Spatial containment entails dividing public and private spaces into hard zones (which restrict activists from accessing and disrupting the targets of grievances), free speech zones, soft zones (buffer areas adjacent to "hard" zones), and free press zones. Surveillance involves employment of high-tech cameras at fixed points, as well as roving police videographers. Real-time images enable shifting of resources to hot spots. The information obtained via surveillance and other sources is managed at central command centers. Although intended to be a proactive means of ensuring First Amendment protections while maintaining public order, an unintended consequence of delineating corridors for free speech and free press is that doing so can exhaust rather than invigorate those engaging in political behavior. In addition, excessive surveillance and concerns about how information gained through surveillance might be used can stifle public protest. Moreover, restricting members of the press to specific zones, frequently termed "press pens," has been criticized as impeding the broader citizenry's access to information and the capacity to make informed comments.[81]

Research on prevention of civil disturbance confirms the strategic need for proactive relationship building by police. For that matter, the message from top-level management greatly influences the behavior and mind-set of frontline officers. Shaping appropriate attitudes occurs through an ingrained understanding that police work involves building relationships with members of the public officers are sworn to protect. This approach begins with defining the mission and safeguarding the fundamental rights of people to gather and speak out. The philosophy should reflect the agency's core values in viewing citizens as customers. Group members are more likely to comply with the law when they perceive that officers act with justice and legitimacy. Moreover, participants perceive the legitimacy of police actions based on how officers interact with the assembled masses throughout an event. Violence may ensue if people think police officers treat them unfairly. Communicating expectations, negotiating continually, and emphasizing the goal of safety are vital. Incorporating these three elements into operations plans for mass assemblages has been shown to significantly improve the quality of crowd management and riot prevention.[82]

SAFEGUARDING CIVIL LIBERTIES

A recurrent dilemma within the U.S. criminal justice system is protecting people and property without infringing on constitutionally guaranteed individual liberties. More and stricter laws, greater leeway for police officers and other criminal justice professionals, and harsher punishments might make us all safer, but perhaps at the cost of decreasing the freedoms we now enjoy. For example, police would likely catch more criminals if they were allowed to search houses whenever they wished without first getting search warrants, but then all people would be at perpetual risk of having their privacy invaded.

The U.S. Constitution prohibits the government from making laws that violate certain rights, among them the rights to freedom of expression, religion, and privacy. However, the Constitution does not specify the precise nature of those rights, nor the circumstances, if any, under which they may be overridden. Furthermore, individuals often disagree over whether freedom or safety is more valuable, so proposed laws and policies are frequently subject to vigorous debate.

At numerous times in the country's history, a crisis has justified—at least in the mind of many people—fairly extensive infringements on individual liberties. The right to a writ of habeas corpus, which allows people to challenge their incarceration in court, was suspended or denied several times, including during and after the Civil War, during World War II, and following the 9/11 terrorist attacks. Rights of free assembly and free expression were frequently overlooked during the Red Scare of the 1950s, for fear of the spread of communism. During the war on drugs of the 1980s and 1990s, law enforcement was generally given more latitude to conduct warrantless searches. And during the "war on terrorism" after 9/11, Congress passed laws authorizing warrantless monitoring of telephone calls and Internet activity.

The extraordinary measures undertaken by law enforcement following 9/11 have at times called into question whether officials are adhering to the rule of law—the underpinning of the U.S. system of justice (see Chapter 4). The rule of law states that all people within the United States, regardless of their citizenship status, are covered by the provisions of the U.S. Constitution and all the statutory law (law enacted by authorized lawmaking bodies, such as Congress) that evolves from it. In essence, this means that we must objectively consider the facts about any criminal act and disregard any bias toward or against an individual's race or status when making a decision to interfere with that person's freedom.

The "war on terrorism" has had considerable effects on immigrants and persons visiting the United States on a visa.[83] Law enforcement has detained many people fitting the terrorist profile of Middle Eastern heritage, temporary visa status, Muslim faith, male gender, and young adult age. Critics vehemently condemn the practice of detaining suspects without formally charging them with a criminal offense.

In addition, the U.S. Department of Justice has expanded the FBI's authority to permit the surveillance of religious institutions, websites, libraries, and organizations without any finding of criminal suspicion before the fact.[84] Critics of these surveillance guidelines contend that they give the state too much power to infringe on individuals' privacy. They argue that the focus of these practices on individuals with a specific ethnic, national, or racial heritage constitutes racial profiling.[85]

▲ **Acquitted Terror Suspect Shoue Hammod**

Shoue Hammod was charged with terrorist offenses and went to trial in Melbourne, Australia, because he made a comment to his wife over the telephone about terrorist training.

MEETING EMERGING CHALLENGES IN VICTIMOLOGY

Although it may be easy to recognize the victims of a specific crime, many other crime victims remain in the shadows. These include individuals whom tradition has not identified as victims, or whose victimizations have gone unnoticed, or who have had limited access to assistance programs. What does the future hold for addressing the needs of such people and the challenges they face?

Victims with Disabilities

As many as one of every five individuals in the United States may have a disability such as a psychological disorder, reduced intellectual functioning, limited mobility, or inability to communicate. Some people are born with a disability, and others' disabilities result from an accident, a disease, or a criminal victimization. People with a disability are more vulnerable to victimization, are typically less able to protect themselves, have more trouble contacting law enforcement, often find victim services inaccessible, and have more difficulty recovering. They also are more likely to experience repeat victimizations by the same offender than individuals who do not have disabilities.[86]

▲ **Victim with a Disability**
A victim in a wheelchair testifies in court.

In 1998, the National Crime Victimization Survey (NCVS) was mandated through the Crime Victims with Disabilities Awareness Act to collect data specifying the types of crimes against, and the characteristics of, victims with disabilities. The 1998 NCVS findings show that individuals with disabilities who were over the age of 12 experienced 730,000 nonfatal violent crimes and 1.8 million property crimes. Nearly 40 percent of the crimes were classified as serious violent crimes, with 40,000 individuals sexually assaulted. In addition, 115,000 people were victims of aggravated assault, 116,000 were robbed, and 459,000 experienced simple aggravated assault. Overall, the violent crime rate for people with disabilities is double (40 per 1,000 individuals) that of individuals without a disability (20 per 1,000). When compared to the general population, people with disabilities were 2 to 3 times more likely to experience a serious violent crime (16 per 1,000 versus 6 per 1,000).

In general, females with disabilities were at a higher risk for victimization than their male counterparts. In terms of seeking services postvictimization, people with disabilities were more likely to seek victim services (12 percent) as compared to those without a disability (6 percent). It should be noted that these statistics represent only people living in a household. People with disabilities who are residing in an institutional setting are not represented in the NCVS statistics.[87]

Most crime victims, regardless of ability, experience some level of trauma and thus need services after the crime. Those with disabilities must be treated equitably and have the same access to services. Two federal laws prohibit discrimination on the basis of disability: the Americans with Disabilities Act (ADA), enacted in 1990, and Section 504 of the Rehabilitation Act of 1973. The former applies to state and local governments, and the latter to entities receiving financial assistance from the federal government. Both laws require that law enforcement make reasonable modifications to enable crime victims with a disability to benefit equally from participating in all agency services, programs, and activities. When law enforcement responds to victims appropriately and compassionately, victims are more willing to cooperate by providing information vital to the investigation and prosecution of the offender.

In 2002, the U.S. Department of Justice created a handbook to assist law enforcement in responding to the specific needs of crime victims with disabilities. Among the guidelines, which are helpful not only for law enforcers but also for anyone working with crime victims with a disability, are the following:

- Rethink negative attitudes about people with a disability.
- Remember that having a disability does not equate to being unhealthy or unintelligent.

- Use person-first language and do not label a person by disability. For example, it is more appropriate to say "a person with a disability" than "a disabled person." By doing so, you are indicating that the disability is secondary to the person.

- Speak directly to the victim even if a third party is present to assist, and ask victims how to communicate most effectively with them. Do not speak in a childlike or condescending manner.

- Ensure that the victim is safe before leaving the scene. If she is not, provide an alternative caregiver or shelter. A victim advocate can provide vital information to assist in the situation.

- Do not assume that family members, service providers, or caretakers are safe for the victim. Sometimes these individuals are the perpetrators, a situation that may inhibit a victim's ability to disclose the victimization and raise fears of retribution.

- Make sure to document the victim's disabilities and to include specific communication, transportation, medication, or other accommodation needs.

- Do not show curiosity about the disability outside the bounds of providing assistance; also, do not express pity about the disability (such as "I'm sorry you are suffering from a mental illness"), show admiration for the victim's ability to accomplish things despite having a disability, or make insensitive comments (such as "She's disabled and he raped her anyway"). Such remarks can be very painful to a victim with a disability or members of the victim's family.[88]

In 2009, the first National Professional Training Conference on Responding to Crime Victims with Disabilities was held. The program provided foundational and advanced training for individuals in the disability and victim services fields. The conference focused on improving knowledge and skills, streamlining services, and fostering collaborative partnerships among those who serve crime victims with disabilities.

Today many organizations are providing outreach and modified services for victims with disabilities. Individually and collectively, they are diminishing the trauma and crisis associated with victimization. The future should bring greater collaboration between victim and disability service providers; more training for first responders, service providers, and caretakers; better screening for appropriate services; and greater accessibility to services. Each of these interventions will help victims with a disability move toward long-term healing and recovery. More remains to be done, however, as illustrated by the "Disconnects" box on page 529, which highlights substantial gaps in the services available for victims with disabilities.

▼ **Immigrant Victims**

Family and friends try to make sense of their loss after a shooting rampage at the American Civic Association, a nonprofit organization providing services to immigrants in Binghamton, New York, where a gunman killed 13 people, then took his own life.

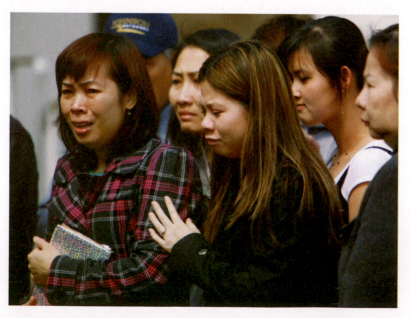

Immigrant Victims

Some people think of trafficking in persons (TIP) when thinking about victimization against immigrants. However, on a more basic level, immigrants are persons who are in the United States (or some other nation) from another country. That condition of being a foreigner makes them vulnerable, and thus they can be victims of many different crimes both while they are in their new

DIS Connects

Helping or Hurting Victims with Disabilities?

Individuals with disabilities are victimized at higher rates than those without disabilities. According to the most recent data collected through the National Crime Victimization Survey (NCVS) in 2013, people with disabilities experienced 21 percent of all violent victimizations. The rate of violent victimization for people with disabilities was double the rate for those who did not identify as having a disability and three times the rate for serious violent victimization. The rate at which people with disabilities experienced aggravated assaults increased from 4 per 1,000 in 2009 to 7 per 1,000 only 4 years later. In 2013, 39 percent of people with a disability experienced serious violence (for example, rape or sexual assault, robbery, or aggravated assault) as compared to 29 percent of people who did not have a disability. One-fourth of people with disability believed that they were targeted because of their disability. Regardless of gender, both males and females with disabilities experienced higher rates of victimization that people without a disability. When factoring in race, both Whites and Blacks with disabilities experienced higher rates of violent victimization than other races. The highest rates of victimization were experienced by people with cognitive disabilities (67 per 1,000) followed next by people with hearing disabilities (17 per 1,000). Those with multiple disability types experienced more victimization and more violent victimization than those with a single type of disability.

In terms of the victim–offender relationship, those who victimized people with disabilities were people the victim knew well or acquaintances (41 percent), strangers (31 percent), or intimate partners (15 percent). Almost 60 percent of people with disabilities were victimized between 6 a.m. and 6 p.m. Police were more likely to be notified when a person with a disability experienced a victimization (48 percent) as compared to victims without a disability (44 percent). Nonreports were due to the matter being handled in an alternative manner or the victim feeling that the situation was not serious enough to merit police intervention. In terms of receiving victim services, people with disabilities (12 percent) were somewhat more likely to receive assistance than people without disabilities (8 percent).

Many of the crimes against people with disabilities go unreported, and although more victims with disabilities seek services than do people without disabilities, the majority still do not seek services. Victims who do report their victimization may interact with law enforcement, service providers, prosecutors, and allied professionals who have limited training in working with this population. These victims must overcome not only the trauma of the crime but also the prevalent misperceptions, stereotypes, and myths about victims with disabilities.

Services for victims with disabilities may be limited, and victims may have difficulty accessing the help that is available. Organizations with ramps in the back or at the side of the building add an extra burden of access, are not welcoming, and raise safety concerns related to entering from an isolated access point. For safety reasons, victim services are often not located at a building's ground level. Thus the victim may have to move farther through a building that may not have an elevator or large doors and hallways to accommodate wheelchairs and other assistive devices. Written materials may not be available in Braille or large print, causing additional hardships for visually impaired victims.

Those who have difficulties with speech may be asked to write about their victimization to help the officer or service provider understand the crime. This request, however, raises further difficulties for victims. The duty of a first responder or service provider is to help the victim, not cause greater trauma and anxiety. Special communication devices and access to sign language interpreters are necessary but not always available.

The large size of many courthouses (as well as other buildings victims may have to visit) may require victims to navigate long distances to reach their destination. Bathrooms may not be easily accessible and/or may be far from the safety afforded in the courtroom, contributing to the victims' vulnerability. Victims with communicative disorders may benefit from assistive devices to ease giving testimony and victim impact statements.

Victims with disabilities who experience intimate partner violence may have difficulty leaving an abusive partner due to the lack of shelter services that provide assistive accommodations. Consider that some shelters are converted older homes that have limited services to assist people with physical disabilities. These facilities may have availability only on upper levels; the bathroom may be far from the bedroom; and the living space may not be accessible. Moreover, telecommunication devices (TTY/TTD—text communication devices for the deaf) may not be readily available to help victims keep in contact with loved ones. The resulting isolation can contribute to further depression, fear, and anxiety.

To close these gaps, a three-pronged approach is needed. First, increasing the availability and accessibility of services will assist with victim recovery and the assurance of victims' rights. Next, continuing multidisciplinary cross-training for service providers, criminal justice professionals, and individuals from the disability community will contribute to the efficient and effective provision of services. Finally, greater awareness of the needs of victims with disabilities will help promote the implementation of appropriate policies to help these individuals.

OBSERVE → INVESTIGATE → UNDERSTAND

- What are some other identifiable gaps in services for victims with disabilities?
- What specific steps can be taken to provide better outreach to crime victims?
- If a victim with a disability requests prerecorded testimony or victim impact statements, should the request be granted? Why or why not?

SOURCES: Erika Harrell, "Crime Against Persons with Disabilities, 2009–2013—Statistical Tables" (Washington, DC: U.S. Department of Justice, Bureau of Justice Statistics, May 2015), NCJ 248676. www.bjs.gov/content/pub/ascii/capd0913st.txt (retrieved June 12, 2015). Cheryl Guidry Tyiska, "Working with Victims of Crime with Disabilities," *OVC Bulletin*, U.S. Department of Justice, Office for Victims of Crime, September 1998. http://permanent.access.gpo.gov/lps125160/disable.pdf (July 22, 2011).

country of residence and when they return to their home country. No matter where the crime occurs, a number of programs and services in the United States assist immigrant victims—whether they are trafficked, illegal, or legal.

> **MYTH/REALITY**
>
> **MYTH:** Immigrant victims will be deported if they call the police or seek services after a crime.
>
> **REALITY:** Federal and state laws protect immigrant victims from deportation if they contact the police. Some states provide benefits to those victimized by TIP, intimate partner violence, and other serious crimes.[89]

For an immigrant victim to qualify for benefits, credible evidence must be produced indicating that the person is a victim. Such evidence may be police reports, physical evidence, and documentation from social service or health care providers. If there is no evidence, the individual's sworn statements about the victimization may suffice. Victims who assist police in investigating TIP and work to prosecute traffickers may apply for a *T visa*, which means they request continued presence in the United States through the U.S. Office of Refugee Resettlement (ORR). Individuals whom the office certifies as TIP victims are eligible for federal benefits.[90]

Immigrant victims of intimate partner violence are eligible for access to shelters, food banks, soup kitchens, the Supplemental Nutrition Program for Women, Infants, & Children (WIC), emergency medical services including prenatal care and care during labor and delivery, community clinics, and services provided by nonprofit organizations. Children also are eligible for school breakfast and lunch programs and the Child Health and Disability Prevention (CHDP) program. These benefits are available regardless of whether the victim contacts and cooperates with the police. Immigrants who have suffered substantial physical and mental abuse such as intimate partner violence, sexual assault, prostitution, female genital mutilation, kidnapping, servitude, false imprisonment, and other crimes can apply for *U visas*. This type of visa, which gives victims temporary legal status and eligibility for work in the United States, is granted only if victims cooperate in the investigation and prosecution of a crime.[91] In March 2011, the U.S. Citizenship and Immigration Services created a new deferred action status, which allows individuals who were lured to the United States and then forced into prostitution to apply to live and work while their court cases are pending.[92]

Local, state, and federal programs for immigrant victims are intended to help the victims reestablish healthy and normal lives and to support them if they wish to serve as witnesses in the prosecution of offenders. The labyrinth of immigrant services, government agencies, and applicable rules requires collaboration among agencies providing aid to immigrant victims. First responders, service providers, and government workers need training in the unique challenges of working with immigrant victims. Finally, outreach and educational programs are particularly important because immigrant victims are often unaware of services, do not believe that they are eligible for them, and do not know how to access them. They often distrust law enforcement and government officials and fear that reporting a crime will expose them to deportation.[93]

LGBTQ Victims

Members of the lesbian, gay, bisexual, transgender, and questioning (LGBTQ) community experience victimization, but there is little research on the prevalence of the problem, and services for these victims are limited. One research effort is conducted each year by the National Coalition of Anti-Violence

Programs (NCAVP), a national network of more than 35 community-based organizations that provide services to address violence against LGBTQ individuals, persons who are HIV-infected, and those affected by HIV/AIDS through family or friends. In 2007, the NCAVP released two reports on violence and another on intimate partner violence against people who identify as LGBTQ.

The first report focused on bias-motivated incidents in 2007. The data are based on reported incidents in 13 states: California, Colorado, Illinois, Massachusetts, Michigan, Minnesota, Missouri, New York, Ohio, Pennsylvania, Texas, Vermont, and Wisconsin. In 2007, the 2,430 victims who reported anti-LGBTQ violence represented a 24 percent increase from 2006. The number of reported murders doubled over the same 1-year period, from 10 in 2006 to 21 in 2007. Other increases occurred in reported sexual assaults (61 percent), noninjury incidents (28 percent), and the use of weapons (5 percent). Some decreases were noted as well: Minor injuries fell by 6 percent, and serious injuries were down by 11.7 percent.

The first report also revealed that strangers were less likely than acquaintances to commit bias-motivated crimes against LGBTQ individuals. Strangers accounted for 809 incidents in comparison to 1,741 acquaintance incidents in 2007. Another finding was that almost half the incidents implicated multiple offenders, and one-quarter were serial offenses; some offenders targeted the LGBTQ individual multiple times before the victim called for help. In addition, nearly half the cases reported in the study did not result in a call to the police. When the victim did contact law enforcement, just under a quarter of the cases resulted in an arrest.[94]

The NCAVP report on intimate partner violence, based on data received from 14 member organizations representing 11 states (Arizona, California, Colorado, Illinois, Massachusetts, Minnesota, Missouri, New York, Ohio, Pennsylvania, and Texas), revealed slightly more than 3,500 cases of intimate partner violence and four deaths in 2006, a 15 percent decrease over the previous year. It is unclear whether the decrease resulted from fewer cases of intimate partner violence, fewer people seeking services, or a combination of other unknown factors.[95]

In 2010, the National Center for Victims of Crime (NCVC) and the National Coalition of Anti-Violence Programs released a groundbreaking report on victim assistance for the LGBTQ community. The report, based upon a nationwide survey of victim services for LGBTQ victims, reveals major gaps, including inconsistent access to culturally competent services and deficiencies in LGBTQ-focused community outreach and staff training.[96]

These reports called for changes at the local, state, and federal level to address victimization within the LGBTQ community. The recommendations include the following:

- Implement a comprehensive awareness campaign to create a societal climate that fosters respect and shuns violence against all people.
- Adopt LGBTQ-inclusive and nondiscriminatory policies and practices that are implemented and enforced.
- Establish and promote anti-bias units within law enforcement, including training and resources to investigate and sanction inappropriate police response.
- Increase funding for research, training, and provision of services to LGBTQ individuals.[97]
- Increase collaborative partnerships between LGBTQ antiviolence programs and victim service providers to ensure equal access of all victims to state and federal protections.[98]

These recommendations, along with additional research, can lead to a greater understanding of the prevalence and nature of violence within the LGBTQ community. The more that is known about these problems, the more society can accomplish to raise awareness—and to offer a more effective response.

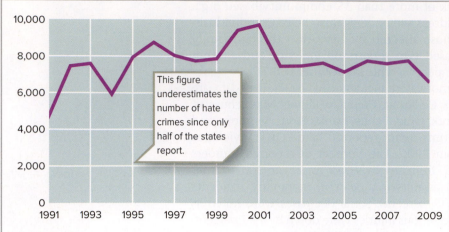

FIGURE 16-4   **Hate Crime Statistics Collected by the FBI, 1991–2009**

SOURCE: Federal Bureau of Investigation, "Hate Crime Statistics, 2009." www2.fbi.gov/ucr/hc2009/index.html (retrieved March 22, 2011).

Hate Crime Victims

Increases in global migration have brought to many countries newcomers from a wide variety of cultures–individuals who speak different languages and practice different religions. Some native residents perceive the new immigrants and their differences as threats to the stability of the host countries, an attitude resulting in conflicts based on fear, frustration, and anger. Victims of hate crimes (discussed earlier in this chapter from a prosecution perspective) often suffer as much pain and trauma as victims of street crimes–or even more. Official responses to hate crime victimizations include research;[99] passage of laws;[100] and training in cultural diversity and tolerance for law enforcement professionals,[101] communities, and students.[102]

Some observers predict a rise in the rate of hate crimes. If realized, such an increase will place greater demands on the limited resources available for assistance to hate crime victims. One of the major challenges of providing adequate services for hate crime victims is ensuring accurate reporting of these offenses. In compliance with the 1990 Hate Crime Statistics Act, the FBI added hate crimes to the National Incident-Based Reporting System (NIBRS).

Figure 16-4, which depicts the number of hate crimes reported from 1991 through 2009, underestimates the actual number of hate crimes because only about half of the states participate in the NIBRS program. In 2009, however, in the 6,604 reported hate crime incidents, the Bureau of Crime Statistics listed 8,322 victims among those jurisdictions reporting nationwide.[103] All states must provide accurate reporting of hate crimes so that resources can be provided to meet the needs of all hate crime victims. This is one of the major challenges for the future of victim assistance.

Victims with Posttraumatic Stress Disorder

Certain emotional consequences of some crimes result in serious negative symptoms that interfere with a survivor's ability to function, especially after about 3 months. These residual symptoms are what is labeled *posttraumatic stress disorder*. A study published in the *Journal of Traumatic Stress* revealed that crime victims were more likely to develop posttraumatic stress disorder over their lifetime than were victims of other stressful events (25 percent compared to 9 percent).[104]

Effective treatment methods for crime victims suffering from posttraumatic stress disorder (PTSD) include exposure therapy, cognitive therapy, anxiety management training, and psychoeducation. In *exposure therapy* the therapist directly introduces cues that trigger the trauma, such as images, smells, and sounds, while providing therapeutic support during the victim's fear responses. By systematically and gradually confronting the unrealistic fears with psychosocial support in a safe environment, victims are able to reduce their stress linked to these special trauma-associated cues. *Cognitive therapy* teaches victims to identify and change the way they think about their traumatic event and to strengthen their beliefs about safety, trust, power, competence, esteem, and intimacy.

KEY CONCEPTS   Challenges to Victimology and Victim Services

Crime victims have been largely ignored in research, policy, and practice; access to services continues to be inadequate to their needs.

Some persons—especially individuals with disabilities, immigrants, LGBTQs, and the discriminated—have recently been identified as more vulnerable to being victimized. If they become victims, they have had more difficulty in accessing needed assistance.

New laws, policies, strategies, and practices have been developed to address needed services for crime victims.

New and innovative forms of treatment for crime victims with PTSD have emerged, including exposure therapy, cognitive therapy, anxiety management training, psychoeducation, and critical incident stress debriefing.

Anxiety management therapy, which relies on muscle relaxation and controlled breathing, with a special emphasis on the physical symptoms of distress, helps victims cope with the anxieties that are associated with their victimization. *Psychoeducation* emphasizes teaching victims adaptive coping techniques that can help them recover. This treatment method is often used with other interventions as a starting point to help provide victims with accurate information about their victimization and typical responses to it.[105]

Research has been sparse on the benefits of peer support groups for PTSD victims. Recent studies on the effectiveness of these groups have found that sharing experiences or just having contact with other victims without the presence of a mental health practitioner has not been very helpful—and may be harmful.[106]

Another victim treatment that has gained some acceptance is psychological debriefing, especially the model referred to as *critical incident stress debriefing*. This model was originally proposed as an early intervention method to help large numbers of people who had been traumatized in emergency situations such as disasters. The technique, used primarily to prevent or reduce posttraumatic stress, usually takes place in a group setting soon after the traumatic event. A facilitator encourages members of the group to describe what happened, their thoughts and emotions as the event was happening, and any physical or psychological responses to the event. The facilitator then provides tips on how to deal with these responses, summarizes the group meeting, and assesses the need for follow-up with any members of the group.[107] More rigorous and controlled studies are required before this treatment strategy can be supported as an effective method to prevent trauma, especially among all disaster victims.[108]

One of the major challenges facing victim assistance practitioners today is the continuing need for the professionalization of their craft. Professionalization essentially means ensuring competence in one's field by the establishment of national standards. Victims need competent treatment that enhances their chances for recovery. Care providers have the responsibility to use practices that are based on research evidence—and that offer the best chances of reducing victims' suffering and facilitating their recovery.

SUMMARY

This chapter focused on some key contemporary issues facing the criminal justice system and providers of victim services. Among these challenges is the urgent need to deal effectively with new types of crime, including cybercrime, terrorism, and hate crimes. Fighting such crimes, as well as controlling civil disorder in both its traditional and its new forms, often heightens the inherent tensions among providing safety and security for all people, prosecuting crimes, and safeguarding individuals' constitutionally guaranteed civil liberties.

Prior to the 1970s, crime victims had been ignored, though some had limited access to programs that gave them vital assistance. Today victims who require specialized services are being recognized, and professionals are developing new strategies to address the harm done to these victims and to extend effective services to them.

OBSERVE → INVESTIGATE → UNDERSTAND

Review

Describe the nature and extent of cybercrime, and identify techniques used to investigate this type of crime.

- Cybercrime is any crime that relies on a computer and a network for its commission (for example, digital child pornography, identity theft, and online fraud schemes).

- The extent of cybercrime is significantly underreported; only about one-third is reported.

- The complexity of cybercrime demands a technologically sophisticated investigative response that includes computer forensics, collaboration, and training.

- The communications and information technology industries play a crucial prevention role by designing products that are resistant to cybercrime and that help law enforcement detect and investigate it.

Discuss the nature and extent of identity theft, and describe strategies used to contend with it.

- It is difficult to total the specific losses incurred via identity theft because many occurrences are not reported, and there is no single source of data on this type of criminal activity.

- State-level identity theft coordination centers facilitate the flow of information and collaboration among state, local, and federal law enforcement agencies and the Federal Trade Commission and corporate entities in combating identity theft.

Explain the interaction between the law and intelligence gathering with regard to terrorism, and discuss terrorism prevention.

- The September 11, 2001, terrorist attacks on the United States heightened the concerns of the U.S. criminal justice system about terrorism as a serious criminal activity.

- Acts of terrorism are prosecuted as offenses within existing laws.

- Implementation of the USA PATRIOT Act rekindled the long-standing debate between the crime control and due process models of justice.

- Early development and communication of intelligence can give law enforcement personnel the opportunity to intervene before a terrorist incident occurs.

- Police need to be vigilant regarding precursor crimes, which are offenses committed for the purpose of enabling acts of terrorism.

Define hate crime and explain its operation as a penalty enhancer.

- A hate crime is a criminal offense committed because of the victim's race, ethnicity, religion, sexual orientation, or other group affiliation.

- Many hate crime laws operate as penalty enhancers, meaning that they add to the penalty for the underlying criminal act.

Identify the factors contributing to civil disorder in its traditional as well as its emergent forms, and discuss prevention strategies.

- Frequently, civil disorder arises from an accumulation of grievances and then a precipitating incident ignites rioting.

- The Internet has significantly increased opportunities for mustering protesters.

- The most significant factor in preventing or resolving civil disorder is the quality of the relationship between the community and its police force.

Analyze the tensions between safeguarding civil liberties and infringing on individual rights.

- The rule of law states that all people within the United States, regardless of their citizenship status, are covered by the provisions of the U.S. Constitution and all the statutory law that evolves from it.

- Measures such as the USA PATRIOT Act and the USA FREEDOM Act have called into question whether officials are adhering to the rule of law.

Identify challenges and treatment regimens for victims with a disability; for immigrants; for lesbian, gay, bisexual, transgender, and questioning (LGBTQ) victims; and for hate crime victims.

- Individuals with developmental disabilities are 4 to 10 times more likely to become crime victims than others.

- To be eligible for benefits, an immigrant victim must present credible evidence of the victimization, such as police reports, physical evidence, and documentation from social service or health care providers.

- Members of the LGBTQ community experience victimization, but little is known about the prevalence of the problem, and services to LGBTQ victims are limited.

- Official responses to hate crime victimizations include research, passage of laws, and training in cultural diversity and tolerance for law enforcement professionals, communities, and students.

- Effective treatment methods for crime victims with posttraumatic stress disorder include exposure therapy, cognitive therapy, anxiety management training, psychoeducation, and critical incident stress debriefing.

Key Terms

civil disorder 523

computer forensics 511

crowd 523

crowdsourcing 521

cybercrime 509

data breach 510

denial of service attack 510

fusion center 519

hacktivism 510

hate crime 521

identity theft 513

intelligence 518

intelligence-led policing (ILP) 518

lone wolf 521

mob 523

penalty enhancer 523

precursor crime 521

terrorism 515

transnational crime 512

USA FREEDOM Act 516

USA PATRIOT Act 516

Study Questions

1. An example of a cybercrime is
   a. online fraud.
   b. identity theft.
   c. digital child pornography.
   d. all of the above

2. This strategy for combating identity theft, which enables illustration of the information flows and interactions among stakeholders, is called
   a. a contextual framework.
   b. intelligence-led policing (ILP).
   c. the fusion center approach.
   d. critical incident stress debriefing.

3. Intelligence is the product of the application of _____ to data or information.
   a. analytical reasoning
   b. computer forensics
   c. a moving target indicator system
   d. the rule of law

4. Of the following crimes, the one that is *not* a precursor crime is
   a. forging documents.
   b. crossing a border illegally.
   c. drunken driving.
   d. money laundering.

5. An example of a hate crime is
   a. beating a person because he is homosexual.
   b. painting a swastika on a synagogue wall.
   c. burning a cross on the property of a Black family.
   d. all of the above

6. The majority of hate crimes are motivated by
   a. ethnicity.
   b. victim disability.
   c. race.
   d. religion.

7. The most significant factor in preventing civil disorders is
   a. a decisive chief law enforcement officer.
   b. a strong tie between the community and its law enforcement entity.
   c. a nation's laws.
   d. all of the above

8. One law that prevents discrimination against individuals based on disability is the
   a. American Discrimination Act.
   b. Americans with Disabilities Act.
   c. Disabilities and Rehabilitation Act.
   d. U.S. Disabilities Act.

9. Immigrant victims of intimate partner violence are not eligible to
   a. access shelters, food banks, or soup kitchens.
   b. call the police because they will be deported.
   c. access emergency medical services including prenatal care and care during labor and delivery.
   d. automatically gain U.S. citizenship.

10. The treatment method used with crime victims suffering from posttraumatic stress disorder that teaches victims to identify and change the way they think about their traumatic events is
    a. relational management therapy.
    b. cognitive therapy.
    c. psychoeducation.
    d. exposure therapy.

Critical Thinking Questions

For further review, go to the LearnSmart study module for this chapter.

1. How are cybercrime, terrorism, and certain types of civil disorder changing the way criminal justice professionals do their jobs?

2. What actions can law enforcement take to prevent terrorism? How should these actions be balanced against individuals' civil liberties and rights to privacy?

3. Which is more important—security or freedom? Why?

Bill of Rights

Amendment I

Congress shall make no law respecting an establishment of religion, or prohibiting the free exercise thereof; or abridging the freedom of speech, or of the press; or the right of the people peaceably to assemble, and to petition the Government for a redress of grievances.

Amendment II

A well regulated Militia, being necessary to the security of a free State, the right of the people to keep and bear Arms, shall not be infringed.

Amendment III

No Soldier shall, in time of peace be quartered in any house, without the consent of the Owner, nor in time of war, but in a manner to be prescribed by law.

Amendment IV

The right of the people to be secure in their persons, houses, papers, and effects, against unreasonable searches and seizures, shall not be violated, and no Warrants shall issue, but upon probable cause, supported by Oath or affirmation, and particularly describing the place to be searched, and the persons or things to be seized.

Amendment V

No person shall be held to answer for a capital, or otherwise infamous crime, unless on a presentment or indictment of a Grand Jury, except in cases arising in the land or naval forces, or in the Militia, when in actual service in time of War or public danger; nor shall any person be subject for the same offence to be paid twice put in jeopardy of life or limb; nor shall be compelled in any criminal case to be a witness against himself, nor be deprived of life, liberty, or property, without due process of law; nor shall private property be taken for public use, without just compensation.

Amendment VI

In all criminal prosecutions, the accused shall enjoy the right to a speedy and public trial, by an impartial jury of the State and district wherein the crime shall have been committed, which district shall have been previously ascertained by law, and to be informed of the nature and cause of the accusation; to be confronted with the witnesses against him; to have compulsory process for obtaining witnesses in his favour, and to have the Assistance of Counsel for his defence.

Amendment VII

In suits at common law, where the value in controversy shall exceed twenty dollars, the right of trial by jury shall be preserved, and no fact tried by a jury, shall be otherwise reexamined in any Court of the United States, than according to the rules of the common law.

Amendment VIII

Excessive bail shall not be required, nor excessive fines imposed, nor cruel and unusual punishments inflicted.

Amendment IX

The enumeration of the Constitution, of certain rights, shall not be construed to deny or disparage others retained by the people.

Amendment X

The powers not delegated to the United States by the Constitution, nor prohibited by it to the States, are reserved to the States respectively, or to the people.

Glossary

A

abuse of authority Police disregard for policies, rules, or laws in the performance of their duty.

actus reus The specific act required to convict a person for a specific crime.

adjudicated delinquent The equivalent in the juvenile system of being found guilty in adult court.

adjudication hearing A hearing to determine whether the juvenile committed the action as charged.

administrative segregation Placement of an inmate in solitary confinement to provide him with supervision, protection, and control beyond that given the general prison population.

adolescence-limited offenders Young people who participate in antisocial behavior for a limited period of time during adolescence while maintaining school performance and respectful relationships with parents and teachers.

adult learning Method of learning that emphasizes engaging the learner by incorporating the learner's experiences in the curriculum.

Adult Protective Services (APS) State services provided to older people and dependent adults who are being mistreated or neglected, are unable to protect themselves, or have no one to assist them.

aggressive order maintenance Policing activities that address noncriminal or minor offenses that affect residents' quality of life.

alternative sentence A sentence that is served in a treatment facility or in community service.

American Law Institute Rule (ALI Rule) A standard for insanity that asks whether the defendant lacked the substantial capacity to appreciate the criminality of the act or conform to the law.

anomie A feeling of alienation or a condition that leaves people feeling hopeless, rootless, cut off, alienated, isolated, disillusioned, and frustrated.

appellate brief A document containing legal arguments in an appellate case, submitted to a court by attorneys for one party.

appellate courts Courts that hear appeals from trial courts or other lower courts.

arraignment A hearing before a judge or magistrate during which the complaint is formally read.

arrest rate The number of arrests per 100,000 persons.

assault and battery A harmful or offensive physical attack by one person upon another.

atavism The belief that criminals are evolutionarily primitive or subhuman people characterized by certain "inferior" identifiable physical and mental characteristics.

attenuation An exception to the exclusionary rule that applies when the link between the unconstitutional acts and the evidence becomes weak due to intervening time or events.

attorney general A state's head law enforcement officer; also the head of the U.S. Department of Justice.

attorney–client privilege The right of a person to prevent the government from asking his lawyer to provide evidence of the content of discussions between the person and his attorney.

Auburn system A system of prison administration in which prisoners were isolated in cells at night but allowed to congregate during the day for work duty and meals, but in total silence.

automobile exception An exception to the warrant requirement holding that police do not need warrants to search automobiles, just probable cause.

atavism The belief that criminals are evolutionarily primitive or subhuman and are characterized by certain "inferior" identifiable physical and mental characteristics.

B

bail A sum of money deposited by a defendant with a court to ensure the defendant's appearance at trial.

bench trial A trial in which guilt is determined by a judge rather than by a jury.

beyond a reasonable doubt The standard of proof required to criminally convict a person.

bifurcated trial A two-part trial in which different issues of the case are decided in separate hearings–for instance, one part deciding guilt and the second deciding the penalty.

binding out The practice of sending children to live with relatively wealthy families who provided the child with the basic necessities of life in return for labor.

bipolar disorder A major mood disorder manifested by bouts of serious depression alternating with periods of extreme elation and exaggerated self-importance.

blue code of silence Adherence to a code of conduct that places loyalty to fellow officers above all other values.

booking The process of photographing and fingerprinting a suspect and creating the police record of personal information and the crime(s) with which the suspect is initially being charged when taken into custody.

boot camp A facility that uses a model of military basic training, strict discipline, rigid rules, and behavior modification to command the attention of out-of-control delinquent juveniles.

broken windows theory Theory proposing that disorder leads to crime because criminals assume a neighborhood that tolerates disorder will also ignore criminal acts.

burden of proof The burden of proving a particular thing in court.

burglary Entering another's property with the intent to commit a felony such as larceny.

C

capital crime An offense punishable by execution.

case law Decisions judges have made in previous court cases.

case-in-chief A stage in a criminal trial during which a party presents the main body of evidence.

chain of command The line of authority that extends throughout an organization.

challenge for cause Excusing potential jurors from a jury because they might be biased in that case.

change of venue Relocation of a case to another court because the case has received too much publicity in the original jurisdiction for the defendant to receive a fair trial.

child abuse Neglect of and/or violence against children.

child neglect Chronic and repetitive failure to provide children with food, clothing, shelter, cleanliness, medical care, or protection from harm.

Child Protective Services (CPS) County-level government organizations in all 50 states whose trained staff members investigate allegations of child abuse and neglect.

child savers Women in the 1800s who lobbied for child labor regulations, laws against child abuse, and a specialized justice system that would focus on the needs of youths.

civil commitment A process in which a judge decides a person is mentally ill and is a danger to himself or others, and incarcerates that person indefinitely in a mental hospital rather than a prison.

civil disorder Disturbance by a group of people that is symptomatic of a major sociopolitical problem.

civil law (1) The system of laws, sometimes known as the Roman system, used in many countries that do not use the common law system; or (2) noncriminal law, or law that concerns disputes between individual parties.

civilianization A component of community policing that increases the number of community residents active in policing by assigning civilians to tasks previously performed by sworn officers.

classical school of criminology A theory of crime causation that views criminal behavior as the product of the offender's free will. The criminal is choosing to break the law.

classification Determination of which inmates go to which institutions and the specific conditions under which they will be confined.

clear and convincing evidence An intermediate standard of proof, sometimes required for certain defenses such as the insanity defense.

commissioner An individual who presides over the early stages of some criminal trials or serves as judge in specialized courts.

common law The legal system created in England after the Norman Conquest and still used in the United States today.

communications interoperability The ability of police and other public safety agencies from different jurisdictions to talk and share data.

community corrections Court-imposed programs and sanctions that allow offenders to serve their sentences within the community instead of in jail or prison.

community policing Philosophy of policing that emphasizes crime prevention and focuses on developing positive relations between the police and the public.

community service Performance by an offender of free labor for the community as reparation for the injury done to society.

community-oriented policing A policing strategy that depends on getting community members to address the problems that plague their neighborhoods.

compassion fatigue Occurs when a practitioner working with a victim experiences difficulty learning more about the crime and working with the victim.

complaint The document containing the initial crimes with which a defendant is charged.

CompStat A computerized statistical program that integrates information from crime maps across a community for department leaders' review.

computer forensics Application of the knowledge and methods used in computer science to law enforcement purposes (such as recovery of deleted files or website activity).

concurrent sentences Sentences that are served at the same time.

conflict perspective A view of crime as one outcome of a struggle among different groups competing for resources in their society.

conjugal visit program An extended private visit by an inmate's lawful spouse or registered domestic partner.

consecutive sentences Sentences that are served in sequence instead of at the same time.

consensus perspective A view of crime that sees laws as the product of social agreement or consensus about what criminal behavior is.

consent A defense against criminal liability because the victim actually gave the defendant permission to engage in the prohibited acts.

constitution A document that specifies the components of a government, the duties of each component, and the limits of their power.

containment theory Theory emphasizing that some of the factors that keep behavior in check are personal, such as self-concept, self-control, goal-directedness, conscience, tolerance for frustration, sense of responsibility, realistic levels of aspiration, and identification with lawful norms.

contempt of court Violation of a court's order, punishable by fine, jail time, or both.

corpus delicti "The body of the crime"; the specific elements that must be proved to convict someone of a specific offense.

corrections The systematic, organized effort by society to punish offenders, protect the public, and change an offender's behavior.

corruption Misconduct motivated by personal gain, such as skimming seized narcotics monies.

Court Appointed Special Advocate (CASA) A volunteer selected by the courts to protect the rights and interests of child victims of abuse.

court of general jurisdiction A court that can hear nearly any type of case.

court of last resort The highest court to which a case may be appealed.

court of limited jurisdiction A specialty court that can hear only cases of a certain type.

crime analysis The application of processes designed to analyze information pertinent to crimes and to develop correlations useful in crime prevention, resource deployment, investigations, and suspect apprehension.

crime control model A model of the criminal justice system that emphasizes the efficient arrest and processing of alleged criminal offenders. Its primary goal is to suppress and contain the behavior of criminals.

Crime Index An officially compiled statistical measure of the incidence of crime in the United States.

crime mapping A technique used by police to pinpoint the locations and times of crimes.

crime prevention Measures taken to reduce the opportunity for crime commission by individuals predisposed to such.

crime victim compensation Programs administered at the state level to provide financial assistance to victims and their families.

crime victimization Injuring or killing a human being through behavior that is prohibited by law; the term focuses on the victim rather than on the offender or the criminal event.

crimes against morality Particular public order crimes, which include offenses related to sexuality, prostitution, gambling, and pornography.

crimes against persons Attack or threats of an attack to a person's body, including murder and manslaughter (taking a life), sexual assault, kidnapping, robbery (theft with force or the threat of force), and battery (the intentional unwanted touching of one person by another).

criminal intent The degree to which a defendant must have intended his or her actions or the consequences of those actions.

criminal justice system The interdependent actors and agencies—law enforcement agencies, the courts, the correctional system, and victim services—at the local, state, and federal levels of government that deal with the problem of crime.

criminal law A body of laws in which people are punished by the government for specific prohibited actions.

criminalistics The application of scientific techniques to recognizing, identifying, individualizing, and evaluating physical evidence in legal proceedings.

crisis intervention Immediate assistance after a traumatic event.

critical theory A branch of social conflict theory concerned with the ways in which structural conditions and social inequalities influence crime.

cross-examination A stage in a trial when attorneys question the opposing side's witnesses.

crowd A leaderless group of individuals, generally respectful of the law, drawn together by common values about a current matter.

crowdsourcing An online, distributed problem-solving and production model that leverages the collective intelligence of online communities to serve specific organizational goals.

cruel and unusual punishment A sentence or conditions of confinement that, within the time period of sentencing or confinement, go beyond what is acceptable to society.

cultural deviance theory The view that the adoption of negative and antisocial values learned in neighborhoods and subcultures produces criminal behavior.

culture conflict Clash between the norms of conduct for one group and the norms of conduct for another group.

custody The incarceration of persons either accused or convicted of a crime.

custody level The degree of danger an inmate poses to other prisoners and to correctional staff.

cybercrime Any crime that relies on a computer and a network for its commission; crime that exploits the electronic highway over which computer transmissions travel.

D

damages Payments a defendant must make to a winning plaintiff in a civil lawsuit to compensate the plaintiff for the injuries or costs the defendant's actions have caused.

dark figure of crime The group of unreported and unrecorded crimes as revealed by crime victim surveys.

data breach An incident in which sensitive, protected, or confidential data have been viewed, stolen, or used by an unauthorized individual.

day fines Fines based on what is fair for a specific offender to pay; also called structured fines.

decentralization of command The fanning out of substations in various areas so the police maintain a physical presence throughout the community.

defendant The person against whom criminal charges or a civil lawsuit are filed.

defense attorney The lawyer who represents the defendant in a criminal case.

delinquency petition The formal document that initiates a juvenile case and lays out the specific allegations against the child; serves much the same function as a criminal complaint.

denial of service attack An act done with the intention of compromising the availability of networks and systems.

deprivation model The perspective that the hardships prisoners endure lead to the development of a distinctive way of behaving in prison.

derivative evidence rule An extension to the exclusionary rule holding that evidence derived from something that is illegally searched or seized is itself inadmissible; also known as the fruit of the poisonous tree doctrine.

designer drugs Drugs that mimic the chemical makeup of particular illicit drugs, named for the fact that drug manufacturers may change the chemical structure to get around existing drug laws.

desistance The cessation of crime commission.

determinate sentence A sentence that specifies a precise period of time that the offender must serve.

deterrence A sentencing goal focused on convincing the offender or others not to commit crime.

deviance The violation of a norm.

***Diagnostic and Statistical Manual of Mental Disorders* (DSM)** The standard classification reference used by mental health professionals in the United States.

differential association theory Theory that criminal behavior is learned during normal social interactions, and the same learning principles are involved in reinforcing criminal and law-abiding behavior.

direct examination A stage in a trial when attorneys question their own witnesses.

direct file (prosecutorial waiver) A method that allows the prosecutor to choose whether to bring the juvenile's case to juvenile or adult court.

directed verdict A motion made by a defense attorney after the prosecution has rested its case; the motion asks for the judge to direct the jury to find the defendant not guilty due to the prosecution's failure to meet its burden of proof.

discovery The process in which an attorney requests that opposing counsel or other parties provide certain evidence or information.

discretion Authority to act in a manner that officers judge most appropriate for a given situation.

discretionary release A procedure by which a parole board decides whether the offender meets eligibility requirements and is ready to be released from prison.

disposition The result or outcome for those juveniles adjudicated delinquent.

district attorney (DA) The lawyer who prosecutes criminal cases at the local level.

diversion An intermediate sanction that is used in place of incarceration and may prevent offenders from having a criminal charge and record.

diversion program A program that handles juvenile cases informally rather than formal through the juvenile court and that is intended to rehabilitate, provide more effective early intervention, and reduce juvenile court caseloads.

double jeopardy The Fifth Amendment right that protects anyone from being tried twice for the same offense.

drug offenses Public order crimes that include the unlawful possession, use, manufacturing, selling, growing, making, or distributing of drugs classified as having potential for abuse.

dual arrest The arrest of both parties in a physical altercation instead of identifying and arresting only the primary aggressor.

due process The right, guaranteed by the Fifth and Fourteenth Amendments, that laws and processes should be fair.

due process clause A clause of the U.S. Constitution that represents the proposition that government laws and proceedings must be fair.

due process model A model of the criminal justice system that emphasizes individual rights at all stages of the justice process.

duress A defense in which the defendant claims he or she was forced or coerced into committing a crime.

Durham Rule A standard for insanity that asks whether the defendant's conduct was the product of a mental disease or defect.

E

elder abuse Any knowing, intentional, or negligent act by a caregiver or another person that causes harm or serious risk of harm to a vulnerable adult 60 years of age or older.

electronic monitoring Enforcing house arrest or monitoring the whereabouts of an offender through electronic sensors, placed around the offender's ankle, that send a continuous signal.

Elmira Reformatory A New York reformatory that emphasized rehabilitation rather than punishment.

emotional abuse A form of victimization by means of power or control that harms the victim's sense of self and is sometimes referred to as psychological abuse, including verbal threats, social isolation, intimidation, exploitation, or routinely making unreasonable demands, terrorizing, shaming, and putting the victim down.

en banc An appeals case presided over by a larger than usual panel of judges (more than three judges).

entrapment A situation in which law enforcement officers or agents trap or trick a person into committing a crime that the person would not otherwise have committed.

evidence-based policing The use of the best available research on the outcomes of police work to implement guidelines and evaluate agencies, units, and officers.

exclusionary rule The rule that illegally obtained evidence cannot be used against a criminal defendant at trial.

expert witness An individual who has specialized knowledge of some scientific or technical matter intended to help the trier of fact understand particular evidence or specific facts in a case.

expunged A term describing a court record that is destroyed or made legally unavailable.

F

faith-based prison programs Services provided when a private prison corporation builds or operates a prison under contract with a government agency and invites religious organizations to offer rehabilitation services to the inmates.

federal courts The system in which federal crimes are prosecuted consisting of district courts, appellate courts or circuit courts, and the U.S. Supreme Court.

felony A serious criminal offense that brings a potential punishment of a year or more in state or federal prison.

feminist criminology The application of feminist thought and analysis to the study of crime.

fines Payments, imposed by judges, that require offenders to pay or forfeit a specific sum of money as a penalty for committing an offense.

first-degree murder The most serious kind of murder. To be convicted of first-degree murder, an offender must have purposely killed the victim and must have planned the killing at least a short time in advance.

forensic science laboratories Facilities using scientific or technical methods to process and analyze evidence.

forensics The application of scientific knowledge and methods to criminal and civil investigations and legal procedures, including criminal trials.

forfeiture Confiscation by law enforcement of profits made by committing a crime and property used to commit a crime.

fragmentation The lack of coordination among law enforcement agencies in the same geographic region due to the existence of many small departments.

frankpledge Peacekeeping system in early England in which a group of 10 local families agreed to maintain the peace and make sure lawbreakers were taken into custody and brought to court.

fruit of the poisonous tree doctrine Another name for the derivative evidence rule, which excludes evidence derived from an illegal search or seizure.

fusion center Regional intelligence hub that pools and analyzes information from many jurisdictions and shares it with those to whom it directly applies.

G

geographic information systems (GIS) A technology that uses a computerized mapping system to produce descriptions of crime occurrence and analyzes the relationships between variables such as location and time.

global positioning system (GPS) A satellite-based system that can calculate users' exact locations, direction, and speed. Many states use GPS systems to monitor sex offenders while they are on parole.

going rate A generally agreed-upon sentence for a defendant based on the crime and prior record.

good faith exception Exception to the exclusionary rule allowing illegally obtained evidence to be used if officers relied in good faith on an invalid warrant.

good time credits Time taken off a prison sentence for an inmate's satisfactory behavior or for participating in a prison program.

grand jury Panel of citizens who may investigate certain crimes and determine whether sufficient evidence exists to bring a defendant to trial.

guilty but mentally ill (GBMI) Verdict for a person recognized to be mentally ill but still considered criminally responsible for the crime.

H

habeas corpus A written judicial order requiring that a prisoner's case be reviewed in court to determine if the person is being held unconstitutionally.

habitual offender statute A law that creates enhanced penalties for repeat offenders.

hacktivism The practice of gaining unauthorized access to a computer system and carrying out various disruptive actions as a means of achieving political or social goals.

halfway house A loosely structured prerelease, community-based residence that helps prisoners adjust to the community after total incarceration.

Hammurabi's Code The second earliest known written law, which was set down by Babylonian king Hammurabi (1792–1750 BCE). The basic principle was that violators should suffer punishment equal to their offense.

hands-off doctrine An approach that made courts reluctant to interfere with prison management or prisoner rights.

hate crime Criminal offense committed because of the victim's race, ethnicity, religion, sexual orientation, or other group affiliation.

hearsay evidence Any statement made by a witness that is not based on that witness's personal knowledge.

homelessness The state of having no fixed, reliable, or adequate nighttime residence.

homicide The act of unjustifiably causing the death of another human being.

hot spot An area of concentrated crime or higher risk of victimization.

house arrest (home confinement) An intermediate sanction that restricts offenders to their homes during the time they are not working or attending treatment programs.

hulks Abandoned ships that functioned as enormous holding blocks within which offenders were chained.

hung jury A jury that is unable, after concerted effort, to reach a verdict.

I

identity theft Unauthorized use of another person's identifying information to obtain credit, goods, services, money, or property, or to commit a misdemeanor or felony.

immigration offenses Violation of federal immigration law, which determines whether a person is an alien and stipulates all the legal rights, duties, and obligations aliens have in the United States.

importation model The perspective assuming that inmate subculture does not develop as a result of prison circumstances but rather is brought in, or imported, from the outside when offenders enter.

in chambers Meeting that occurs between attorneys and a judge in the judge's office rather than in the courtroom.

incapacitation A sentencing goal that aims to make it impossible for the offender to commit a future crime.

incarceration Confinement against one's will in the criminal justice system (in a jail or prison) or a mental health facility (a secure psychiatric institution).

inchoate crimes Crimes that have been begun but not completed or are crimes that are completed by someone else.

indentured servitude The practice of selling criminals as servants to private individuals instead of sentencing them to penal facilities.

independent source Exception to the exclusionary rule permitting the use of evidence discovered independently of any improper search or seizure.

indeterminate sentence A sentence in which the offender is given a range of time he can serve, such as 5 to 7 years, dependent on his behavior while in prison.

indictment A document issued by a grand jury after it finds probable cause, formally listing the charges against the defendant.

industrial prison A prison factory where the focus was on creating a productive work environment rather than the rehabilitation or reform of prisoners.

inevitable discovery Exception to the exclusionary rule allowing illegally obtained evidence to be admissible if it would inevitably have been discovered through legal means.

infancy A defense that sometimes protects very young offenders from criminal liability because they do not understand the consequences of their actions.

infancy defense A defense holding that children under age 7 could not be criminally prosecuted because they were too young to form mens rea, or criminal intent.

informal probation A situation in which as long as the child obeys certain conditions and stays out of trouble, the case will not proceed any further, such as to court.

information A document filed by a prosecutor after a preliminary hearing, formally listing the charges against the defendant.

infraction A minor violation of a local ordinance or state law that brings a potential punishment of fines.

inmate code Rules of behavior that inmates follow.

inmate subculture The norms, values, and beliefs that develop among prisoners.

insanity A defense in which the defendant admits committing the criminal act but claims not to be culpable due to mental illness.

institutional corrections Incarceration in jails and prisons.

institutionalization The state of being dependent on an institution to meet one's basic needs—such as for food, shelter, and friends—to the point of being unwilling, or unable, to function in the outside world.

intake The process during which an official decides whether to release the juvenile or refer the case to court or put the juvenile under some other supervision.

intake officer The probation officer who makes the initial decision about whether to proceed with a case.

intelligence Product of the application of analytical reasoning to data or information in order to develop a reliable picture of an environment or a situation.

intelligence The capacity to learn or comprehend, manifested by the ability to solve problems and adapt to life's everyday experiences.

intelligence-led policing (ILP) Collaborative collection and analysis of data by intelligence analysts, field officers, and senior leaders.

intensive-supervision probation (ISP) A variety of probation programs characterized by smaller officer caseloads and closer surveillance.

intermediate sanctions Judicial punishments that do not require incarceration but stop short of allowing offenders to remain in the community on probation with minimal supervision.

intimate partner violence An assault on a person with whom the attacker is intimately involved.

involuntary manslaughter A killing that results from an offender's careless actions.

irresistible impulse test A standard for insanity that asks whether the defendant had a mental disease or defect, as a result of which the defendant was unable to control his or her behavior.

J

jail Municipal or regional facility that houses pretrial individuals believed to present a risk of danger or flight, those awaiting probation or parole revocation, and those sentenced to less than 1 year incarceration.

judicial waiver Means by which a judge designates a juvenile to be tried in adult court.

jurisdiction A court's legal power to hear particular kinds of cases.

jury nullification The power of juries to refuse to apply Illegal laws when they feel applying them would be unjust.

justice of the peace A judge who handles matters such as warrants, infractions, and the early stages of a criminal case.

juvenile delinquency Illegal acts that are committed by juveniles.

juvenile hall A juvenile detention center.

juvenile justice system The justice system that attempts to address important distinctions between children and adults and differs from the adult system in many respects.

L

labeling theory Theory that the social process that individuals experience has the potential to define them as "bad" or "good," and that some people become bad because others do not believe them to be good.

larceny A type of theft that includes both completed and attempted taking of cash or property from a location *without* attacking or threatening the victim and without obtaining permission.

law enforcement The police agency's application of the criminal code to specific situations.

laws Formal rules of conduct sanctioned by the state.

lay witness A person who has personally seen or heard information relevant to the case at hand; also called a fact witness or eyewitness.

legitimacy A measure of the extent to which the public trust the police, are willing to defer to police authority, and believe police actions are morally justified and appropriate.

life course persistent offenders Those who engage in delinquency at young ages and continue their criminal behavior throughout their lives.

line activities The principal activities performed by law enforcement officers, including patrol, follow-up investigation, and traffic operations.

local legal culture A shared understanding of how cases should be processed.

lone wolf A terrorist who is not a member of a known terrorist group and who does not take orders from a chain of command when conducting acts of terror.

long-term therapy Treatment focusing on the victim's responses to trauma, symptoms of PTSD, anxiety disorders, depression, terminal conditions, and dysfunctional behaviors that render victims vulnerable.

looking-glass self The idea that we come to define ourselves the way we perceive that others see us.

M

magistrate A judge who handles matters such as warrants, infractions, and the early stages of a criminal case.

maintaining order Peacekeeping activities, including enforcement of quality of life laws such as no loitering.

mala in se A behavior categorized as morally wrong ("evil in itself").

mala prohibita A statutory crime that reflects public opinion at a moment in time.

mandatory arrest policy Requires officers to make an arrest when there is evidence of an assault.

mandatory release Early release mandated by law after an offender has served a specified time in prison.

mandatory reporting law Law requiring that professionals who have regular contact with a child report any reasonable suspicions of physical or sexual abuse or neglect to the proper law enforcement or protective services.

manslaughter A killing in which the offender is less blameworthy than for murder; it usually carries a less severe penalty than murder.

Martinson Report A report, published in 1974, indicating that rehabilitative efforts, for the most part, were having little to no effect on recidivism.

mass murder Multiple murders that occur at one place and at one time.

maximum-security prison An institution in which inmates are subject to high levels of control and where their mobility is severely restricted by physical barriers.

McNaughtan Rule A standard for insanity that asks whether the defendant was unable to know what he or she was doing or to distinguish right from wrong.

medical model A viewpoint focusing on mental illness and behavioral problems, such as committing a crime, as diseases.

medium-security prison An institution in which inmates are under greater control than in minimum-security prisons, and their freedom of movement is restricted to areas that are under close surveillance.

mens rea The level of criminal intent, or the mental state usually required to convict a person of a criminal act.

minimum-security prison An Institution that holds offenders who have short sentences, are nonviolent, and are unlikely to attempt escape or pose risks to others in the facility.

Miranda **warnings** Notifications that police must give suspects about their rights prior to beginning custodial interrogation.

misdemeanor A criminal offense that is punished by fines or a maximum of a year in a county or city jail.

missing children Children not accounted for by their next of kin because they were kidnapped or killed, wandered away due to a developmental disability, or are intentionally missing in order to escape violence at home.

mistrial A judge's ruling that declares a trial invalid, often because of a hung jury.

mob A group that is not law-abiding, with a leader, that is ruled by emotion.

Model Penal Code A suggested code of criminal law drafted by the American Law Institute and used to guide the states in modernizing their laws.

moral panic The reaction by a group of people based on exaggerated or false perceptions about crime and criminal behavior.

moral reasoning Application of a set of ethical principles based on what society views as good versus bad behavior.

motor vehicle theft A property crime that involves the theft of a motorized road vehicle.

N

National Crime Victimization Survey (NCVS) A statistical sampling of households and individuals who have been personally victimized by specific crimes.

National Incident-Based Reporting System (NIBRS) A U.S. crime index (not yet fully national in scope) compiled by the FBI and the Department of Justice that tracks detailed information about 22 categories of crime incidents and arrests.

necessity A defense in which the defendant must demonstrate that he or she had to commit the crime to avoid more severe consequences.

neoclassical school of criminology A theory of crime causation that recognizes differences in circumstances and assumes that some people—such as children, the insane, and the intellectually deficient—cannot reason. In such cases the criminal justice system must look at the offender's ability to comprehend the consequences of his or her criminal actions in determining appropriate punishments.

neurotransmitter A chemical secreted by neurons that facilitates the transmission of information from one neuron to another.

neutralization theory Theory that if people break the law, they overcome their feelings of responsibility through rationalizations.

no contest (nolo contendere) A plea in which a defendant admits that sufficient evidence exists to convict him, but he does not actually admit his guilt.

noble cause Justification for wrongdoing committed by an officer based on the premise that the end justifies the means.

norm A rule that makes clear what behavior is appropriate and expected in a particular situation.

not guilty by reason of insanity (NGRI) A verdict in which the jury determines that the defendant is not criminally culpable due to mental illness.

O

opening statements Initial statements made by attorneys to a jury outlining the case they will present during the trial.

ordinances Laws enacted by local governments such as cities and counties.

organized crime An ongoing criminal conspiracy that profits from providing illicit goods and services, using or threatening violence to facilitate its criminal enterprise and to maintain monopolistic control of illicit markets.

P

pains of imprisonment The deprivations inmates experience such as those related to liberty, autonomy, security, personal goods and services, and heterosexual relations.

parens patriae A legal doctrine that gives the government authority to step in and make decisions about children, even against the wishes of their parents, when doing so is in the children's best interests.

parole An early release from prison conditional on complying with certain standards while free.

parole board A group of people authorized by law to grant permission for selected offenders—after serving a portion of time in prison—to serve their remaining sentence in the community.

peacemaking criminology A branch of criminology that views crime as a form of violence and urges criminology to advocate a nonviolent, peaceful society.

penalty enhancer Attribute that adds to the penalty for a crime.

penitentiary Coined from the word *penitent*, the Quakers' term for a residence where offenders would be sorrowful for their wrongdoings.

Pennsylvania system A system of prison administration in which inmates lived in solitary confinement, total silence, and religious penitence as the way to prevent future criminal behavior.

peremptory challenge An attorney's removal of a prospective juror she feels will not be sympathetic to her side of the case.

petit jury Small groups of citizens who determine whether a criminal defendant is guilty of the crimes with which he is charged.

physical abuse The condition whereby an individual suffers serious physical injury from the intentional aggressive acts of others, such as slapping, spanking, beating, biting, burning, strangling, hitting, kicking, shaking, or pushing.

plaintiff The party who initiates the lawsuit in a civil case.

plea A defendant's formal denial or admission of guilt.

plea bargain An agreement between defendants and prosecutors, in which a defendant pleads guilty to the original or reduced charges in exchange for a lesser sentence.

police–community reciprocity A policing practice that relies on collaboration between police and community members to solve and prevent crime.

police occupational subculture Norms and beliefs embraced by most officers in a given country.

police organizational subculture Norms and beliefs particular to an individual department.

political crimes Violent or nonviolent acts that society perceives as threats to a government's survival.

positivist school of criminology The view that criminal behavior is a product of biological, psychological, and social forces beyond a person's control.

postpartum psychosis A serious mental illness characterized by hallucinations, delusions, and obsessive thoughts about the baby.

precedent Previous court decisions that have binding authority on subsequent cases.

precursor crime Offense committed for the purpose of enabling acts of terrorism, such as illegal border crossings or forged documents.

predictive policing Taking data from a wide array of sources, analyzing them, and using the results to anticipate, prevent, and respond more effectively to future crime.

preliminary hearing A proceeding in which a judge determines whether probable cause exists to bring the defendant to trial for the crimes with which he has been charged.

preponderance of the evidence The standard of proof required to win a civil lawsuit.

presentence investigation report (PSI) A report that provides the court with a basis for making a sentencing decision by including a personal history of the offender, often a victim impact statement, and a recommendation for sentencing.

presumptive sentencing model A sentencing model assuming that judges should sentence within sentencing guidelines, or ranges specified for particular charges.

preventive detention The practice of holding a suspect without bail because he is believed to pose a potential danger to the community or to be at risk of fleeing the jurisdiction.

preventive detention (juvenile) Custodial holding of children accused of crimes, to ensure they appear in court but also to protect them from adverse home conditions or to prevent them from committing additional offenses while their case is pending.

preventive detention laws Legislation that allows the criminal justice system to prevent offenders from committing future crimes by lengthy incarceration in prison or secure mental health facilities.

preventive patrol Officers' maintenance of a visible presence in communities to serve as a deterrent to a variety of street-level crimes.

primary victim A person injured or killed as a direct result of a criminal act.

prison A secure state or federal facility that holds offenders sentenced to incarceration of 1 year or more.

Prison Rape Elimination Act (PREA) Legislation that established the National Prison Rape Elimination Commission to develop national standards for detecting and preventing prison rape, as well as for punishing perpetrators.

prisonization A process of socialization whereby prisoners adopt the norms, values, and beliefs of the inmate subculture as their own.

private security The nongovernmental, private sector practice of protecting people, property, and information; conducting investigations; and otherwise safeguarding an organization's assets.

privatization The transfer of government programs and functions to the private sector.

proactive foot patrol A component of community policing in which officers walk beats to learn more about the people in the neighborhoods they patrol and to develop relationships with them.

probable cause The amount of evidence necessary to obtain a warrant or conduct most searches and seizures.

probation An alternative to jail or prison in which the offender remains in the community under court supervision, usually within the caseload of a probation officer.

probation kiosk An automated reporting machine, resembling an ATM, that monitors low-risk nonviolent offenders.

problem-oriented policing A policing strategy based on conducting specific and detailed research on a community's problems to discover the underlying dynamics of crime.

procedural justice Providing an opportunity for a citizen to explain his side of a story in a given situation and for the officer, in turn, to make his decisions in a fair manner.

property crimes The taking of money and/or material goods without the use of force, as well as the intentional destruction of property.

prosecutorial discretion The prosecutor's power to determine when to bring criminal charges and which charges to bring.

psychic trauma Severe emotional stress that immobilizes the victim's mind and body and can result in long-lasting emotional injury.

psychopathy A personality disorder involving specific cognitive and emotional deficits that is exhibited by a lifelong pattern of antisocial behavior about which the individual has no remorse.

psychoses Serious mental disorders that cause individuals to be out of touch with reality and unable to cope with the demands of everyday living.

public order crimes A wide variety of offenses considered immoral or public nuisances, including disorderly conduct, disturbing the peace, loitering, public intoxication, panhandling, bigamy, drunk driving, weapons violations, prostitution, obscenity, gambling, and possession of controlled substances.

public safety exception Exception to *Miranda* requiring police to interrogate suspects without first warning them of their rights if there is a significant threat to public safety.

Public Safety Realignment (PSR) A policy intended to reduce mass incarceration by downsizing the prison population, reducing prison costs, and providing treatment and reintegration services to offenders.

punishment model A viewpoint that assumes the offender is inherently a bad person and deserves to be placed under correctional authority for punishment.

punitive segregation Isolation of an inmate for disciplinary reasons, to provide additional supervision and control of the individual.

Q

qualified immunity The protection of officers against being sued for their actions under certain circumstances.

R

racial profiling Police contact with an individual initiated because of the person's skin color or ethnicity.

rape trauma syndrome The three phases (acute, outward adjustment, and resolution) of symptoms that many victims experience after a sexual assault.

rational choice theory A theory of crime causation that assumes that criminals choose to commit crime because they believe that the benefits they will derive will outweigh the risks of getting caught.

reasonable suspicion Amount of evidence necessary for officers to conduct a stop-and-frisk or *Terry* stop.

recidivism The habitual relapse into criminal behavior.

recidivist victims Persons who are victimized repeatedly.

recidivist An offender who has been previously convicted of crimes.

recognizance Literally, "an obligation to the court" that usually requires the accused, if released on his own word, to perform some legally specified act, such as appearing at trial, as an alternative to being incarcerated.

recusal The act by which a judge removes herself from a case because she may be biased or may have the appearance of being biased.

referee An individual who presides over the early stages of some criminal trials or serves as judge in specialized courts.

reform school An industrial school that housed children who were delinquent, disobedient, or otherwise wayward.

rehabilitation A sentencing goal focused on aiding an offender to learn skills to help prevent the person from reoffending.

rehabilitation model A viewpoint that assumes the offender is inherently a good person and that focuses on changing the offender's behavior.

reintegration model A viewpoint that assumes that the offender must be helped to readjust and fit successfully back into the community.

remand The act by which an appellate court sends a case back to a lower court for further proceedings.

restitution In a criminal case, the money a defendant must pay a victim to the compensate the victim for damages.

restorative justice A perspective that focuses on the offender's responsibility to repair the hurt, damage, and injustice the crime victim experienced by making restitution and doing community service.

retribution A sentencing goal focused on punishing the convicted for the crime.

risk assessment instrument A worksheet that measures the degree of risk present in a given case.

risk classification An assessment of the level and kind of risk an individual presents to correctional staff and other inmates.

robbery A crime against a person in which the offender takes personal property from the victim by either using or threatening force.

routine activities theory Theory suggesting that crime occurs when an opportunity is available, the victim is not adequately protected, and the effort brings reward. Applied to victims, the theory argues that some individuals' daily activities make them more vulnerable than others to being victimized.

rule of law The guiding principle of the U.S. legal system, which states that no single person is more powerful than the law.

S

sanctions Prescribed consequences intended to reinforce people's conformity to norms.

schizophrenia A serious mental illness characterized by an individual's split from reality due to profound aberrations in cognitive functioning.

sealed A term describing a juvenile record that is made inaccessible.

search incident to arrest A warrantless search of a person and the area around that person, conducted shortly after the person is arrested.

secondary victim An individual who experiences sympathetic pain as a result of a primary victim's suffering.

secondary victims Family and friends of an individual who has been victimized.

secondary victimization The suffering of crime victims caused by their subsequent treatment by the police, the courts, or personal acquaintances.

second-degree murder In most states, an intentional killing that is not planned ahead of time.

security level The degree of danger associated with the inmates being housed in a prison.

security threat group (STG) Inmates who, when they collaborate, can jeopardize the institution's security.

self-report Surveys in which individuals (who are guaranteed confidentiality) reveal offenses that they have committed but for which they may or may not have been arrested and held accountable. These surveys uncover another part of the dark figure of crime.

sequestered Referring to a Jury that is kept separate from outside contact during a trial.

serial murder The killing of three or more people over an extended period of time for personal gratification.

service activities Non–law enforcement activities performed by officers on an as-needed basis.

sexual assault nurse examiner (SANE) Nurse who provides 24-hour first-response medical care and crisis intervention for rape victims in hospitals and clinics.

sexual assault response team (SART) In many states, a collaboration of local police officers, victim advocates, SANE practitioners, and prosecutors seeking to determine the most effective way to respond to sexual assault.

sexual victimization Forced or coerced sexual intimacy.

sexual violence A range of crimes including vaginal, anal, digital, and/or oral penetration that can include the use of weapons and foreign objects to torture and terrorize the victim.

shock probation A combination of probation and short-term incarceration.

shock program A short-term incarceration program used to frighten the offender by instilling uncertainty about whether the offender will be released and, if so, when.

short-term therapy Treatment usually administered by clinical psychologists, clinical social workers, and marriage and family counselors to address immediate mental health concerns.

siege mentality Police view of themselves as a "band of brothers"—or "sisters"—against everyone else in society.

social bond theory Theory detailing the social bond people have with society, consisting of attachment, commitment, involvement, and belief.

social conflict theory The view that crime is the result of conflict between a society's wealthy and powerful people on the one hand, and its poor and powerless people on the other hand.

social control theory Theory that an individual's belief system, the police, and parental supervision are important in preventing the individual from getting into trouble.

social disorganization theory The theory that explains crime rates by examining city neighborhood characteristics.

social learning theory Theory that behavior is learned and is maintained or extinguished based on the rewards or punishments associated with it.

social norm A rule that specifies how people are expected to behave.

social process theory The view that criminal behavior results from successive interactions with others and with society's institutions.

solitary confinement Isolation of an inmate that denies person the basic human need to interact with others.

solvability The likelihood that a crime will be solved.

span of control The extent of an individual's authority, or the number of individuals that one person is responsible for overseeing.

special prosecutor A prosecutor who is appointed specifically for one particular case, usually because of his specialized knowledge or experience.

spree murder The killing of several people within a fairly narrow period, such as several hours or days.

stalking Willfully, maliciously, and repeatedly following or harassing another person and making a credible threat with the intent to place that person in reasonable fear for his or her safety, or for the safety of his or her family.

standing The legal ability to assert a particular constitutional claim.

state courts The system in which state crimes are prosecuted; it includes both trial and appellate courts.

status offense An offense that is illegal only because the defendant is a child, such as playing truant or running away.

statutes Laws enacted by state legislatures or by Congress.

statutory crime An act that is criminal because it is prohibited by law.

statutory exclusion The categorical exclusion, by state law, of certain ages and offenses from juvenile court jurisdiction.

statutory minimum The minimum sentence set by a legislature that must be imposed for a particular crime.

stop-and-frisk Police action allowing the police, with reasonable suspicion, to briefly detain a person, question him about his activities, require him to show identification, and frisk him, or pat him down for weapons; also known as a *Terry* stop.

strain theory Theory that extraordinary pressures make people more likely to commit crime.

strict liability offenses Crimes that have no mens rea requirement; a person who commits the requisite actus reus may be convicted of the offense regardless of intent.

student bullying A form of victimization in which a student is repeatedly exposed to threats and harmful acts from other students over a period of time.

subculture A group that has some of the same norms, values, and beliefs as members of the dominant, mainstream culture but also other norms, values, and beliefs *not* held by society at large.

subpoena A legal document ordering a person to appear in court.

supermaximum-security (supermax) prison A facility that provides the highest level of security possible—solitary confinement—using the latest correctional technology.

support activities Additional policing activities that support line activities, such as communications, custody, and forensics.

survivor A relative or loved one of a person who has been killed; also, a crime victim who copes well and manages to resume a normal life.

sworn personnel Police department employees entrusted with arrest powers; usually referred to as *peace officers*.

T

teen court A court in which teenagers serve as jurors and often as judges, attorneys, and bailiffs as well.

terrorism Premeditated, politically motivated violence perpetrated against noncombatant targets by subnational groups or clandestine agents.

***Terry* stop** Another name for stop-and-frisk, in which the police, with reasonable suspicion, briefly detain a person, question him about his activities, require him to show identification, and frisk him or pat him down for weapons.

testimonial evidence Words or statements made by a person.

torts Civil disputes in which one party sues another for the damages the defendant's actions have caused.

total institution A facility responsible for, and in control of, every aspect of life for those who live and work within it including food, shelter, medical assistance, clothing, and safety.

transnational crime Crime orchestrated across a national boundary from where the crime actually occurs.

transportation The export of criminals to other lands to complete their sentences.

TRIAD A collaborative effort among police departments, sheriff's offices, and senior groups (like AARP) to reduce crime and the victimization of elder adults.

U

unconditional release Release of an inmate from prison without parole.

Uniform Crime Reports (UCR) An annual series of U.S. statistical measures of the incidence of selected crimes reported by police departments and compiled by the FBI.

unity of command The requirement that each individual within an organization reports directly to a single individual higher in the chain of command.

USA FREEDOM Act Antiterrorism legislation enacted in 2015. The acronym stands for Uniting and Strengthening America by Fulfilling Rights and Ending Eavesdropping, Dragnet-collection, and Online Monitoring. Principally, the act imposed new limits on the bulk collection of telecommunications metadata. It also restores authorization for roving wiretaps and trucking lone wolf terrorists.

USA PATRIOT Act A law—officially, the Uniting and Strengthening America by Providing Appropriate Tools Required to Intercept and Obstruct Terrorism Act—enacted by Congress following the 9/11 terrorist attacks, intended to deter and punish terrorist acts in the United States and around the world, to enhance law enforcement investigatory tools, and to strengthen measures to prevent and detect terrorism.

use of force continuum Guideline depicting the appropriate amount of force a law enforcement officer may use in particular kinds of situations.

V

vehicular manslaughter In some states, a classification for a death that results from careless driving.

venire A group of people called to be prospective jurors.

vicarious trauma (compassion fatigue) Psychological distress experienced by those who know about a traumatic event experienced by another person and who feel the victim's pain.

victim advocate A professional who assists the victim during the postvictimization period.

victim impact statement A victim's written statement, usually in the Presentence Report, about how the experience with crime affected him or her. Sometimes judges ask victims to read this statement in open court prior to sentencing.

victim recidivism Victimization of a person, household, or business more than once; also called repeat victimization.

victim services A range of resources—such as shelters, transitional housing, counseling, and 24-hour hotlines—aimed at reducing the suffering and facilitating the recovery of victims, especially those who participate in the criminal justice process.

victim surveys Interviews with individuals (including but not limited to actual victims) who have been personally affected by specific crimes.

victimless crimes Often called crimes against public order and considered victimless because they usually have no identifiable victim.

victim–offender mediation A process that brings victims and offenders face-to-face to work out a restitution and restorative strategy under the direction of a trained counselor or mediator.

victimology The scientific study of victims, which includes their behaviors, injuries, assistance, legal rights, and recovery.

vigilantism Use of volunteer, self-appointed committees organized to suppress crime and punish criminals.

voir dire The process of questioning prospective jurors about their background, opinions, and knowledge relevant to a particular case.

voluntariness test Rule that confessions are inadmissible unless made willingly.

voluntary manslaughter Killing in the heat of passion.

W

waiver A mechanism to permit the transfer of some juvenile offenders to adult court.

Walnut Street Jail The first public institution to specifically use imprisonment as the primary method of reforming offenders.

warrant A legal document, based on probable cause, permitting police to conduct a search or seizure or to arrest someone.

watch system Peacekeeping system in which particular men were assigned the job of watchman and became responsible for patrolling the streets, lighting lanterns, serving as a lookout for fires, and generally keeping order.

wedding cake model An explanation of the workings of the criminal justice system that shows how cases get filtered according to the seriousness of the offense.

white-collar crime Illegal or unethical acts that violate fiduciary responsibility or public trust, committed by an individual or organization, usually during the course of legitimate occupational activity, by persons of high or respectable social status for personal or organizational gain.

work and study release (furlough) Partial release of inmates to work or study in the community and return to a correctional facility each night.

workhouse An institution that held jobless vagrants, debtors, and sometimes serious criminals.

writ of certiorari A request that a case be heard by an appellate court such as the U.S. Supreme Court.

Endnotes

CHAPTER 1

1. Hans Joachim Schneider, "The Media World of Crime: A Study of Learning Theory and Symbolic Interaction," in William S. Laufer and Freda Adler (Eds.), *Advances in Criminological Theory*, vol. 2 (Piscataway, NJ: Transaction, 1990), 115–144.

2. Gallup Poll, "New High of 46% of Americans Favor Legalizing Marijuana." www.gallup.com/poll/144086/New-High-Americans-Support-Legalizing-Marijuana.aspx (retrieved December 20, 2010).

3. William Chambliss, "A Sociological Analysis of the Law of Vagrancy," *Social Problems* (Summer 1964): 67–77.

4. Death Penalty Information Center. www.deathpenaltyinfo.org/ (retrieved July 3, 2009).

5. Andrew Karmen, *Crime Victims: An Introduction to Victimology*, 5th ed. (Belmont, CA: Wadsworth, Cengage Learning, 2004).

6. See Samuel Walker and Charles Katz, *The Police in America: An Introduction* (New York: McGraw-Hill, 2008).

7. Ibid.

8. Danielle Kaeble, Lauren Glaze, Anastasios Tsoutis, and Todd Minton, "Correctional Populations in the United States, 2014" (Washingtoon, DC: Bureau of Justice Statistics, Dec. 2015, Revised January 21, 2016) pg. 2, http://www.bjs.gov/content/pub/pdf/cpus14.pdf (accessed February 5, 2016).

9. Harvey Wallace, *Family Violence: Legal, Medical, and Social Perspectives*, 4th ed. (Needham Heights, MA: Pearson, Allyn & Bacon, 2005).

10. Karmen, *Crime Victims*.

11. Denise Kindschi Gosselin, *Heavy Hands: An Introduction to the Crimes of Family Violence*, 3rd ed. (Upper Saddle River, NJ: Prentice Hall, 2005).

12. Thomas Underwood and Christine Edmunds (Eds.), *Victim Assistance: Exploring Individual Practice, Organizational Policy, and Societal Responses* (New York: Springer, 2003).

13. Thomas Cohen and Brian Reaves, "Felony Defendants in Large Urban Counties, 2002," *Bureau of Justice Statistics Bulletin*, February 2006, NCJ 210818. www.ojp.usdoj.gov/bjs/pub/pdf/fdluc02.pdf (retrieved July 6, 2009).

14. Herbert Packer, *The Limits of the Criminal Sanction* (Stanford, CA: Stanford University Press, 1968).

15. Samuel Walker and Charles M. Katz, *The Police in America*, 7th ed. (New York: McGraw-Hill, 2011), 25.

16. Anthony A. Braga, U.S. Department of Justice, Office of Community Oriented Policing Services, *Police Enforcement Strategies to Prevent Crime in Hot Spot Areas—Crime Prevention Research Review* no. 2 (Washington, DC: Government Printing Office, 2008).

17. Timothy D. Crowe, *Crime Prevention through Environmental Design*, 2nd ed. (Woburn, MA: Butterworth Heinemann Publications, 2000).

18. Gloria Laycock, "Hypothesis-Based Research: The Repeat Victimization Story," *Criminology and Criminal Justice* 1, no. 1 (2001): 59–82.

19. Andromachi Tseloni, Karin Wittebrood, Graham Farrell, and Ken Pease, "Burglary Victimization in England and Wales, the United States, and the Netherlands," *British Journal of Criminology* 44 (2004): 66–91.

20. Karmen, *Crime Victims;* Nina Schuller, "Disabled People, Crime and Social Inclusion," *Community Safety Journal* 4, no. 3 (2005).

21. Karmen, *Crime Victims*.

22. U.S. Department of Justice, Bureau of Justice Statistics, "Number of Victimizations and Victimization Rates by Type of Crime and Victim-Offender Relationship," 2006. www.ojp.usdoj.gov/bjs/pub/pdf/cvus/current/cv0628.pdf (retrieved January 3, 2009).

23. Gallup Poll, "Nearly 4 in 10 Americans Still Fear Walking Alone at Night," November 5, 2010. www.gallup.com/poll/144272/Nearly-Americans-Fear-Walking-Alone-Night.aspx (retrieved December 12, 2010).

24. See Jeffrey Edleson and Claire Renzetti, *Violence against Women: Classic Papers* (Boston, MA: Allyn & Bacon, 2005); Esther Madriz, *Nothing Happens to Good Girls: Fear of Crime in Women's Lives* (Berkeley: University of California Press, 1997).

25. Gallup Poll, "Nearly 4 in 10 Americans Still Fear Walking Alone at Night."

26. U.S. Department of Justice, Bureau of Justice Statistics. http://bjs.ojp.usdoj.gov/index.cfm?ty=tp&tid=3 (retrieved December 12, 2010).

27. Gallup Poll, "Americans Still Perceive Crime on the Rise," November 18, 2010. www.gallup.com/poll/144827/Americans-Perceive-Crime-Rise.aspx (retrieved December 12, 2010).

28. Dereck Chadee, Liz Austen, and Jason Ditton, "The Relationship between Likelihood and Fear of Victimization," *British Journal of Criminology* 47 (2007): 133–153; Kenneth Ferraro, *Fear of Crime: Interpreting Victimization Risk* (Albany: SUNY Press, 1995).

29. U.S. Department of Justice, Bureau of Justice Statistics, "Victimization Rates for Persons Age 12 and Over, by Gender and Age of Victims and Type of Crime, 2006." www.ojp.usdoj.gov/bjs/pub/pdf/cvus/current/cv0604.pdf (retrieved January 3, 2009).

30. Kenneth Ferraro, "Women's Fear of Victimization: Shadow of Sexual Assault?" *Social Forces* 75 (1996): 667.

31. U.S. Department of Justice, Bureau of Justice Statistics, "Victimization Rates for Persons Age 12 and Over."

32. Wesley G. Skogan and William R. Klecka, "Fear of Crime," John Howard Society of Alberta, 1999. www.johnhoward.ab.ca/PUB/C49.htm (retrieved May 15, 2006).

33. Ronald Weitzer and Charis Kubrin, "Breaking News: How Local TV News and Real-World Conditions Affect Fear of Crime," *Justice Quarterly* 21 (2004): 497.

34. R. Lance Holbert, Dhavan Shah, and Nojin Kwak, "Fear, Authority, and Justice: Crime-Related TV Reviewing and Endorsements of Capital Punishment and Gun Ownership," *Journalism & Mass Communication Quarterly* 81 (2004): 343.

35. Lori Dorfman and Vincent Schiraldi, *Off Balance: Youth, Race, and Crime in the News* (Washington, DC: Building Blocks for Youth, 2001); Executive Summary, Berkeley Media Studies Group. www.buildingblocksforyouth.org/media.

36. There were an estimated 454.5 violent crimes per inhabitants in 2008. Federal Bureau of Investigation, *Crime in the United States*, 2008. www.fbi.gov/usr/cius2008/offenses/violentcrime/index.html (retrieved October 2, 2009).

37. Samuel Walker, Cassia Spohn, and Miriam Delone, *The Color of Justice: Race, Ethnicity and Crime in America* (Belmont, CA: Wadsworth, Cengage Learning, 2006); Robert Entman and Kimberly Gross, "Race to Judgment: Stereotyping Media and Criminal Defendants," *Law & Contemporary Problems* 71 (2008): 93.

38. Angela Davis, *Women, Race & Class* (New York: Vintage Books, 1983).

39. Bureau of Justice Statistics, "Percent Distribution of Single-Offender Victimizations, Based on Race of Victims, by Type of Crime and Perceived Race of Offender, 2006." www.ojp.usdoj.gov/bjs/abstract/cvus/race989.htm (retrieved August 17, 2009).

40. Jessie Klein, "Teaching Her a Lesson: Media Misses Boys' Rage Relating to Girls in School Shootings," *Crime Media Culture* 1 (2005): 90–97.

41. William Sabol and Heather C. West, "Prisoners in 2007." Bureau of Justice Statistics, December 11, 2008, NCJ 224280.

42. Ibid.

43. Marc Mauer, *The Crisis of the Young African American Male and the Criminal Justice System* (Washington DC: U.S. Commission on Civil Rights, 1999).

44. Samuel Walker, Cassia Spohn, and Miriam Delone, *The Color of Justice* (Belmont, CA: Wadsworth, 2006).

45. Diana Ahmad, *The Opium Debate and Chinese Exclusion Laws in the Nineteenth Century American West* (Reno: University of Nevada Press, 2007).

46. National Center for Chronic Disease Prevention and Health Promotion, "National Youth Risk Behavior Survey, 2007." www.cdc.gov/HealthyYouth/yrbs/pdf/yrbs07_us_disparity_race.pdf (retrieved January 3, 2009); National Institutes of Health, "Drug Use among Racial/Ethnic Minorities," Report No. 95-3888 (Washington, DC: Government Printing Office, 1995); National Institute on Drug Abuse, "National Household Survey on Drug Abuse: Population Estimates 1990" (Washington, DC: Government Printing Office, 1991).

47. Sheryl Pimlott and Rosemary Sarri, "The Forgotten Group: Women in Prisons and Jails," in Josefina Figueira-McDonough and Rosemary Sarri (Eds.), *Women at the Margins: Neglect, Punishment, and Resistance* (New York: Haworth Press, 2002).

48. Matthew Levitt (Ed.), *From the Boston Marathon to the Islamic State: Countering Violent Extremism* (Washington, DC: Washington Institute for Near East Policy, 2015), 53.

49. Police Executive Research Forum, *The Role of Local Law Enforcement Agencies in Preventing and Investigating Cybercrime* (Washington, DC: PERF, 2014), 1.

50. Stephen Orfei, "This Is a Crucial Year to Combat Cybercrime," *Sacramento Bee*, February 13, 2015.

51. Javelin Strategy & Research, "2015 Identity Fraud: Protecting Vulnerable Populations." www.javelinstrategy.com/brochure/347 (retrieved April 23, 2015).

52. Levitt, *From the Boston Marathon to the Islamic State*, 11.

53. California Innocence Project, "CODIS Database." http://californiainnocenceproject.org/issues-we-face/codis-database/ (retrieved May 4, 2015).

54. Gene Stephens, "Crime in the Year 2030," *The Futurist* 47, no. 1 (2013): 28.

55. John A. Wallace, *Integrating Unmanned Aircraft Systems into Modern Policing in an Urban Environment*, thesis prepared at the request of the Naval Postgraduate School, September 2012.

56. The Pew Center on the States, "Time Served: The High Cost, Low Return on Longer Prison Terms." www.pewstates.org (retrieved May 3, 2015).

57. Juliet Linderman and Michael Biesecker, "Thousands at 'Victory Rally' Celebrate Charges against Officers, Praise Baltimore's Prosecutor," Associated Press, May 3, 2015. www.newser.com/article/9b4aa05040bc4c5786ffcde32710a391/thousands-at-victory-rally-celebrate-charges-against-officers-praise-baltimore-prosecutor.html (retrieved May 3, 2015).

CHAPTER 2

1. Russlyn Ali. "Dear Colleague Letter" (Washington, DC: U.S. Department of Education, Office for Civil Rights, April 4, 2011). www2.ed.gov/print/about/offices/list/ocr/letters/colleague-201104.html (retrieved May 18, 2015).

2. Federal Bureau of Investigation, "Uniform Crime Reports." www.fbi.gov/ucr/ucrquest.htm (retrieved July 5, 2009).

3. Ibid.

4. Federal Bureau of Investigation, "Uniform Crime Report—Hate Crime Statistics, 2007," October 2008.

5. Federal Bureau of Investigation, "FBI Releases 2007 Hate Crime Statistics," 2007. www.fbi.gov/ucr/hc2007/summary.htm (retrieved July 5, 2009).

6. Sarah Moore, "Could James Byrd Killer on Death Row Get a New Trial?" *Beaumont Enterprise*, February 24, 2014. www.beaumontenterprise.com/news/article/Could-James-Byrd-killer-on-Death-Row-get-a-new-5262157.php (retrieved May 10, 2015).

7. Federal Bureau of Investigation, "Uniform Crime Reports."

8. Federal Bureau of Investigation, "Frequently Asked Questions about the Change in the UCR Definition of Rape," December 11, 2014. www.fbi.gov/about-us/cjis/ucr/recent-program-updates/new-rape-definition-frequently-asked-questions (retrieved May 10, 2015).

9. Federal Bureau of Investigation, "Variables Affecting Crime." www2.fbi.gov/ucr/cius2007/about/variables_affecting_crime.html (retrieved July 5, 2009).

10. Federal Bureau of Investigation, "NIBRS Frequently Asked Questions." www.fbi.gov/ucr/nibrs_general.html (retrieved July 5, 2009).

11. Federal Bureau of Investigation, "NIBRS Participation by Population Group," May 2015. www.fbi.gov/about-us/cjis/ucr/nibrs/2013/resources/nibrs-participation-by-population-group.

12. Federal Bureau of Investigation, "NIBRS Frequently Asked Questions."

13. Eugene H. Czajkoski and Laurin A. Wollan Jr., "Bureaucracy and Crime," *International Journal of Public Administration* 5, no. 2 (1983): 195–216.

14. U.S. Department of Justice, Bureau of Justice Statistics, "Crime and Victim Statistics" (Washington, DC: DOJ, 2008). www.ojp.usdoj.gov/bjs/cvict.htm#Programs (retrieved July 6, 2009).

15. U.S. Department of Justice, Bureau of Justice Statistics, "The Percentage of Crimes Reported to the Police Has Been Increasing" (Washington, DC: DOJ, 2006). www.ojp.usdoj.gov/bjs/glance/dreportingtype.htm (retrieved July 6, 2009).

16. Austin L. Porterfield, *Youth in Trouble: Studies in Delinquency and Despair, with Plans for Prevention* (Fort Worth, TX: Leo Potishman Foundation, 1946).

17. Terence P. Thornberry and Marvin D. Krohn, "The Self-Report Method for Measuring Delinquency and Crime," in *Measurement and Analysis of Crime and Justice*, vol. 4 of *Criminal Justice 2000* (Washington, DC: National Institute of Justice, 2000).

18. Federal Bureau of Investigation, "Crime in the United States 2013." www.fbi.gov/about-us/cjis/ucr/crime-in-the-u.s/2013/crime-in-the-u.s.-2013 (retrieved April 22, 2015).

19. Federal Bureau of Investigation, *Crime in the United States, 2009* (Washington, DC: U.S. Department of Justice, 2010).

20. Ibid.

21. Diane Craven, *Sex Differences in Violent Victimization, 1994* (Washington, DC: U.S. Department of Justice, Bureau of Justice Statistics, 1997).

22. Ross Macmillan and Candice Kruttschnitt, "Patterns of Violence against Women: Risk Factors and Consequences." www.ncjrs.org/pdffiles1/nij/grants/208346.pdf (retrieved February 15, 2005).

23. Callie Rennison, *Intimate Partner Violence, 1993–2001* (Washington, DC: U.S. Department of Justice, Bureau of Justice Statistics, 2003).

24. Denise Kindschi Gosselin, *Heavy Hands: An Introduction to the Crimes of Family Violence*, 3rd ed. (Upper Saddle River, NJ: Prentice Hall, 2005).

25. U.S. Department of Health and Human Services, *Child Maltreatment 2008* (Washington, DC: DHHS, 2010).

26. Lynn Langton and Jennifer L. Truman, "Criminal Victimization, 2013 (Revised)," Bureau of Justice Statistics, September 18, 2014. www.bjs.gov/index.cfm?ty=pbdetail&iid=5111 (retrieved May 22, 2015).

27. National Center on Elder Abuse, "The National Elder Abuse Incidence Study: Final Report." www.aoa.gov/eldfam/ElderRights/ElderAbuse/AbuseReportFull.pdf (retrieved February 15, 2005).

28. U.S. Department of Justice, Bureau of Justice Statistics, "Crime Characteristics and Trends." http://bjs.ojp.usdoj.gov/index.cfm?ty=tp&tid=93 (retrieved July 7, 2011).

29. John Curran, "Novice Hunter Gets 1–5 Years in Hunter's Death," *Boston Globe*, November 9, 2007. www.boston.com/news/local/vermont/articles/2007/11/09/novicehuntergets15yearsin-huntersdeath/ (retrieved March 10, 2008).

30. Federal Bureau of Investigation, *Crime in the United States 2013*.

31. "Homicide Trends in the U.S.: Regional Trends," Bureau of Justice Statistics, July 11, 2007. www.ojp.usdoj.gov/bjs/homicide/region.htm (retrieved December 4, 2007).

32. "Murders (Most Recent) by Country," *NationMaster.com*. www.nationmaster.com/red/graph/cri_mur-crimemurders&b_printable=1 (retrieved December 4, 2007).

33. Harvey Wallace, *Victimology: Legal, Psychological, and Social Perspectives*, 2nd ed. (Boston: Pearson Education, 2007).

34. Candice Skrapec, "Defining Serial Murder: A Call for a Return to the Original Lustmörd," *Journal of Police and Criminal Psychology* 16, no. 2 (2002): 10–24.

35. Eric Hickey, *Serial Murderers and Their Victims* (Belmont, CA: Wadsworth, Cengage Learning, 2002), 3.

36. Ibid.

37. Ibid.

38. William Glaberson, "Death Penalty for a Killer of 3 in Connecticut," *New York Times*, November 8, 2010. www.nytimes.com/2010/11/09/nyregion/09cheshire.html; William Glaberson, "Death Penalty for 2nd Man in Connecticut Triple-Murder Case," *New York Times*, December 9, 2011. www.nytimes.com/2011/12/10/nyregion/joshua-komisarjevsky-gets-death-for-cheshire-killings.html?ref=topics&_r=0.

39. Hickey, *Serial Murderers and Their Victims*.

40. Federal Bureau of Investigation, *Crime in the United States 2013*.

41. Joanne Belknap, *The Invisible Woman: Gender, Crime, and Justice*, 2nd ed. (Belmont, CA: Wadsworth, Cengage Learning, 2001).

42. Harvey Wallace, *Family Violence: Legal, Medical, and Social Perspectives*, 4th ed. (Boston: Pearson/Allyn & Bacon, 2005).

43. Michael Planty, Lynn Langton, Christopher Krebs, Marcus Berzofsky, and Hope Smiley-McDonald, "Female Victims of Sexual Violence, 1994-2010," Bureau of Justice Statistics, March 2013, NCJ 240655. www.bjs.gov/content/pub/ascii/fvsv9410.txt (retrieved May 18, 2015).

44. Callie Marie Rennison, "Rape and Sexual Assault: Reporting to Police and Medical Attention, 1992–2000." www.ojp.usdoj.gov/bjs (retrieved June 15, 2006).

45. Ibid.

46. Bonnie S. Fisher, Leah E. Daigle, Francis T. Cullen, and Michael G. Turner, "Reporting Sexual Victimization to the Police and Others: Results from a National-Level Study of College Women," *Criminal Justice and Behavior* 30, no. 1 (2003): 6–38.

47. Rennison, "Rape and Sexual Assault."

48. Fisher, Daigle, Cullen, and Turner, "Reporting Sexual Victimization to the Police and Others."

49. Ibid.

50. Ibid.

51. Ann Burgess and Lynne Holmstrom, "Rape Trauma Syndrome," *American Journal of Nursing* 131 (1974): 981–986; *Rape Trauma Syndrome*, Rape, Abuse & Incest National Network. www.rainn.org (retrieved June 15, 2006).

52. Ibid.

53. Federal Bureau of Investigation, *Crime in the United States, 1999* (Washington, DC: U.S. Department of Justice, 2000).

54. Federal Bureau of Investigation, *Crime in the United States 2013*.

55. Andrew Karmen, *Crime Victims: An Introduction to Victimology*, 6th ed. (Belmont, CA: Wadsworth, Cengage Learning, 2007), 68.

56. Matthew R. Durose, Caroline Wolf Harlow, Patrick A. Langan, Mark Motivans, Ramona R. Rantala, and Erica L. Smith, "Family Violence Statistics." www.ojp.usdoj.gov/bjs (retrieved June 30, 2007).

57. Henry Kempe, F. Silverman, B. Steele, W. Droegemueller, and H. Silver, "The Battered Child Syndrome," *Journal of the American Medical Association* 181 (1962): 107–112.

58. Murray Straus, *Beating the Devil out of Them: Corporal Punishment in American Families* (New York: Lexington Books, 1994).

59. Durose, Harlow, Langan, Motivans, Rantala, and Smith, "Family Violence Statistics."

60. David Finkelhor, *Sexually Victimized Children* (New York: Free Press, 1979).

61. Jason L. Walker, Paul D. Carey, Norma Mohr, Dan J. Stein, and Soraya Seedat, "Gender Differences in the Prevalence of Childhood Sexual Abuse and in the Development of Pediatric PTSD," *Archives of Women's Mental Health* 7 (2004): 111–121.

62. National Drug Endangered Children, Training and Advocacy Center. www.ndec-tac.org/ (retrieved December 4, 2010); Office of National Drug Control Policy. www.ndec-tac.org/forums/content.php (retrieved December 4, 2010).

63. U.S. Department of Justice, "Child Abuse." www.justice.gc.ca/en/ps/fm/childafs.html (retrieved May 31, 2007).

64. National Clearinghouse on Family Violence, "Emotional Abuse." www.phacaspc.gc.ca/ncfv-cnivf/familyviolence/pdfs/emotion.pdf (retrieved May 31, 2007).

65. Nico Trocme et al., "Canadian Incidence Study of Reported Child Abuse and Neglect, 2003," *Child Abuse: A Fact Sheet from the Department of Justice Canada*. www.phac-aspc.gc.ca/cm-vee/csca-ecve/pdf/childabusefinale.pdf (retrieved January 1, 2009); Bruce D. Perry, Kevin Colwell, and Stephanie Schick, "Child Neglect," in David Levinson (Ed.), *Encyclopedia of Crime and Punishment*, vol. 1 (Thousand Oaks, CA: Sage, 2002), 192–196. www.childtrauma.org/ctamaterials/neglectinchildhood.asp (retrieved May 30, 2007).

66. Perry, Colwell, and Schick, "Child Neglect."

67. Sonia Sharp, David Thompson, and Tiny Arora, "How Long before It Hurts? An Investigation into Long-Term Bullying," *School Psychology International* 21 (2000): 37–46.

68. Dan Olweus, *Bullying at School: What We Know and What We Can Do* (Carlton, Australia: Blackwell, 1993).

69. Susan Donaldson James, "When Words Can Kill: 'That's So Gay,'" ABC News, April 14, 2009. http://abcnews.go.com/Health/MindMoodNews/story?id=7328091&page=1 (retrieved February 28, 2011).

70. Peggy O'Hare, "Parents Say Bullies Drove Their Son to Take His Life," *Houston Chronicle*, September 29, 2010. www.chron.com/disp/story.mpl/metropolitan/7220896.html (retrieved February 28, 2011).

71. Jim Hamill, "Teen's Death Brings Attention to Bullying," *WNEP.com*, November 8, 2010. www.wnep.com/news/countybycounty/wnep-sny-brandon-bitner-bullying-suicide,0,961701.story (retrieved February 28, 2011).

72. Education Week, *Bullying: The Ethics of American Youth: 2010* 30, no. 10 (November 3, 2010): 5; Josephson Institute: Center for Youth Ethics, *The Ethics of American Youth: 2010*. http://charactercounts.org/programs/reportcard/2010/index.html (retrieved December 5, 2010).

73. Ian Rivers and Nathalie Noret, "Participant Roles in Bullying Behavior and Their Association with Thoughts of Ending One's Life," *Crisis: The Journal of Crisis Intervention and Suicide Prevention* 53, no. 3 (2010): 143–148.

74. Michelle Birkett, Dorothy L. Espelage, and Brian Koenig, "LGB and Questioning Students in Schools: The Moderating Effects of Homophobic Bullying and School Climate on Negative Outcomes," *Journal of Youth and Adolescence* 38, no. 7 (August 2009): 989–1000.

75. John P. J. Dussich and Chie Maekoya, "Physical Child Harm and Bullying-Related Behaviors: A Comparative Study in Japan, South Africa and the United States," *International Journal of Offender Therapy and Comparative Criminology* 51, no. 5 (October 2007): 495–509.

76. Ronald Laney, "Parental Kidnapping," NLPOA Fact Sheet 34, 1995. www.nploa.org/Office_of_Juvenile_Justice_Parental_Kidnapping_1995_NLPOA.pdf.

77. National Crime Information Center Missing Person File, "NCIC Missing Person and Unidentified Person Statistics for 2006." www.fbi.gov/hq/cjisd/missingpersons.htm (retrieved May 30, 2007).

78. The Carole Sund/Carrington Memorial Reward Foundation. www.carolesundfoundation.com/sections/homicide (retrieved February 23, 2008).

79. Federal Bureau of Investigation, *Crime in the United States, 2013*.

80. Patsy Klaus, *National Crime Victimization Survey: Crime and the Nation's Households* (Washington, DC: U.S. Department of Justice, Bureau of Justice Statistics, 2004). www.ojp.usdoj.gov/bjs (retrieved June 1, 2006).

81. Lauren King, "Statistics Point to Increase in Crime during Recessions," *Virginian-Pilot*, January 19, 2009. http://hamptonroads.com/2009/01/statistics-point-increase-crime-during-recessions (retrieved December 6, 2010); Andrew Dunn, "Economic Recession Has Become a Crime Stimulus," *StarNews Online*, August 28, 2009. www.starnewsonline.com/article/20100828/ARTICLES/100829631?p=2&tc=pg (retrieved December 6, 2010).

82. Federal Bureau of Investigation, *Property Crime, 2009*. www2.fbi.gov/ucr/cius2009/offenses/property_crime/index.html (retrieved December 6, 2010).

83. U.S. Department of Justice, "Property Crime Victims, 2004." www.ojp.usdoj.gov/bjs (retrieved June 1, 2006).

84. Chester L. Britt, "Health Consequences of Criminal Victimizations," *International Review of Victimology* 8 (2001): 63–73.

85. Federal Bureau of Investigation, *Crime in the United States 2013*.

86. Thomas A. Reppetto, *Residential Crime* (Cambridge, MA: Ballinger Press, 1974).

87. Irvin Waller and Norman Okihiro, *Burglary: The Victim and the Public* (Toronto: University of Toronto Press, 1978).

88. Federal Bureau of Investigation, *Crime in the United States 2013*.

89. Ibid.

90. Ibid.

91. Abhijeet K. Vadera and Ruth V. Aguilera, "The Evolution of Vocabularies and Its Relation to Investigation of White-Collar Crimes: An Institutional Work Perspective," *Journal of Business Ethics* 128 (2015): 21.

92. Richard A. Ball, "White-Collar Crime," in M. A. DuPont-Morales, Michael K. Hooper, and Judy H. Schmidt (Eds.), *Handbook of Criminal Justice Administration* (New York: Marcel Dekker, 2001).

93. Megan Graham, "White Collar Crime and the United States' Economy" (honors thesis, University of New Hampshire Scholars' Repository, April 2012), Paper 49. www.scholars.unh.edu/honors/49.

94. Cornell University Law School, "White-Collar Crime: An Overview." www.law.cornell.edu/wex/white-collar_crime.

95. Graham, "White Collar Crime and the United States' Economy."

96. National White-Collar Crime Center, *2010 National Public Survey on White Collar Crime* (Fairmont, WV: NW3C, 2010).

97. Federal Bureau of Investigation, "Crime in the Suites: A Look Back at the Enron Case." www.fbi.gov/news/stories/2006/december/enron_121306 (retrieved June 30, 2011).

98. Julie Appleby, "Many Who Lost Savings, Jobs Pleased," *USA Today*, May 26, 2006. http://www.usatoday.com/money/industries/energy/2006-05-25-enron-workers-usat_x.htm (retrieved July 5, 2006).

99. Whistling in the Wind, "The Other Kind of Crime." www.whistlinginthewind.org/2013/06/24/the-other-kind-of-crime/ (retrieved June 15, 2015).

100. Ball, "White-Collar Crime."

101. *Loving v. Virginia*, 388 U.S. 1 (1967); *Lawrence v. Texas*, 539 U.S. 538 (2003).

102. Christine Alder, "'Passionate and Willful' Girls: Confronting Practices," *Women and Criminal Justice* 9, no. 4 (1998): 81.

103. Arlene McCormack, Mark-David Janus, and Ann W. Burgess, "Runaway Youths and Sexual

Victimization: Gender Differences in an Adolescent Runaway Population," *Child Abuse and Neglect* 10 (1986): 387; Lisa Maher, *Sexed Work: Gender, Race, and Resistance in a Brooklyn Drug Market* (Oxford: Clarendon Press, 1997).

104. Randall G. Shelden, *Controlling the Dangerous Classes* (Boston: Allyn & Bacon, 2001).

105. Anti-Drug Abuse Act of 1988, Public Law 100-690, 21 U.S. Ct. 1501: Subtitle AA—Death Penalty, Sec. 001, Amending the Controlled Substances Abuse Act, 21 USC 848.

106. Jeff Karoub, "Alcoholic Energy Drinks to Be Banned in Michigan," *MyFoxdetroit.com*, November 4, 2010. www.myfoxdetroit.com/dpp/news/local/alcohol-energy-drinks-to-be-banned-in-michigan-20101104-mr.

107. James Nash, "California Joins Six U.S. States Banning Beer Drinks Laced with Caffeine," *Bloomberg*, August 1, 2011. www.bloomberg.com/news/2011-08-02/california-s-new-law-takes-the-caffeine-kick-out-of-alcoholic-beverages.html.

108. Rachael Rettner and LiveScience, "Powered Alcohol Now Legal in the U.S.," *Scientific American*, March 18, 2015. www.scientificamerican.com/article/powdered-alcohol-now-legal-in-u-s/ (retrieved April 14, 2015).

109. Craig Reinarman, Peter D. A. Cohen, and Hendrien L. Kaal, "The Limited Relevance of Drug Policy: Cannabis in Amsterdam and in San Francisco," *American Journal of Public Health* 94, no. 5 (2004): 836–842.

110. U.S. Department of State, "International Narcotics Control Strategy Report" (Washington, DC: DOS, February 1999); United Nations, "World Drug Report 2012" (New York: United Nations Office on Drugs and Crime, 2012), 28–29, 36–38, 40, 84.

111. Juan Forero and Tim Weiner, "Latin American Poppy Fields Undermine U.S. Drug Battle," *New York Times*, June 8, 2003, 1; Qaiser Butt, "Illicit Drug Production: Balochistan Madrassa Students Harvest Poppy on Holidays," *Express Tribune*, August 5, 2011. www.tribune.com.pk/story/224821/illicit-drug-production-balochistan-madrassa-students-harvest-poppy-on-holidays/ (retrieved February 22, 2013).

112. Peter Reuter, "The Limits of Drug Control," *Foreign Service Journal* 70 (2002): 1; Melissa Dell, "Trafficking Networks and the Mexican Drug War (Job Market Paper)" (MIT, November 2011). www.economics.mit.edu/files/7373 (retrieved February 22, 2013).

113. Ethan Nadelman, "Addicted to Failure," *Foreign Policy* (July/August 2003): 101; Forero and Weiner, "Latin American Poppy Fields Undermine U.S. Drug Battle," 1; Eduardo Guerrero-Gutierrez, "Security, Drugs, and Violence in Mexico: A Survey" (Washington, DC: 7th North American Forum, 2011). www.iis-db.stanford.edu/evnts/6716/NAF_2011_EG_(Final).pdf (retrieved February 22, 2013).

114. Office of the Press Secretary, The White House, "FACT SHEET: President Obama Proposes $1.1 Billion in New Funding to Address the Prescription Opioid Abuse and Heroin Use Epidemic," February 2, 2016. https://www.whitehouse.gov/the-press-office/2016/02/02/president-obama-proposes-11-billion-new-funding-address-pre-scription (retrieved February 6, 2016).

115. Laura Barron-Lopez, Jason Cherkis, and Ryan Grim, "The Senate Finally Did Something To Help Combat The Opioid Epidemic: The Bipartisan CARA Bill Aims to Change Drug Policy Away From Punishment and More Toward Rehabilitation," The Huffington Post, March 10, 2016. http://www.huffingtonpost.com/entry/senate-opioid-epidemic_us_56e19b41e4b0860f99d80173 (retrieved March 29, 2016).

116. Lee Robins, *The Vietnam Drug User Returns*, Special Action Office for Drug Abuse Prevention Monograph, Series A, no. 2, May 1974, Contract No. HSM-42-72-75; Lee Robins et al, "Narcotic Use in Southeast Asia and Afterward: An Interview Study of 898 Vietnam Returnees," *Archives of General Psychiatry* 32, no. 8 (1975): 955–961.

117. Karen H. Seal, Greg Cohen, Angela Waldrop, Beth E. Cohen, Shira Maguen, and Li Ren, "Substance Use Disorders in Iraq and Afghanistan Veterans in VA Healthcare, 2001–2010: Implications for Screening, Diagnosis and Treatment," *Drug and Alcohol Dependence* 116 (2011): 93–101; Substance Abuse and Mental Health Services Administration, "Behavioral Health Issues Among Afghanistan and Iraq U.S. War Veterans," *SAMHSA In Brief* 7, no.1 (Summer 2012). www.store.samhsa.gov/shin/content/SMA12-4670/SMA12-4670.pdf (retrieved January 22, 2013).

118. William J. Sabol, Heather C. West, and Matthew Cooper, "Prisoners in 2008," *Bureau of Justice Statistics Bulletin* (Washington, DC: U.S. Department of Justice, December 2009); E. Ann Carson, "Prisoners in 2013," *Bureau of Justice Statistics Bulletin* (Washington, DC: U.S. Department of Justice, September 2014), 15, 17, tables 13 and 16; DrugWarFacts.org, "Race and Prison." www.drugwarfacts.org/cms/Race_and_Prison#sthash.Gg72mQ8S.dpbs (retrieved April 16, 2015).

119. Matthew Derose and Patrick Langan, "State Court Sentencing of Convicted Felons, 1998 Statistical Tables" (Washington, DC: U.S. Department of Justice, Bureau of Justice Statistics, December 2001); David B. Mustard, "Racial, Ethnic, and Gender Disparities in Sentencing: Evidence from the U.S. Federal Courts," *Journal of Law and Economics* 44 (2001).

120. See Joanne Belknap, *The Invisible Woman: Gender, Crime, and Justice* (Belmont, CA: Wadsworth, Cengage Learning, 2007); Paige M. Harrison and Allen J. Beck, "Prisoners in 2005," *Bureau of Justice Statistics Bulletin* (Washington, DC: U.S. Department of Justice, 2007), 5; Allison T. Chappell and Scott R. Maggard, "Applying Black's Theory of Law to Crack and Cocaine Disposi-tions," *International Journal of Offender Therapy and Comparative Criminology* 51, no. 3 (2007): 264–278.

121. John Irwin, Vincent Schiraldi, and Jason Ziedenberg, "America's One Million Nonviolent Prisoners" (Washington, DC: Justice Policy Institute, March 1999), 6–7; Harrison and Beck, "Prisoners in 2005," 5; Natalie Sokoloff, "Women Prisoners at the Dawn of the 21st Century," *Women and Criminal Justice* 16, no. 1–2 (2005): 127–137; Chappell and Maggard, "Applying Black's Theory of Law to Crack and Cocaine Dispositions."

122. Carson, "Prisoners in 2013," 15, table 13.

123. Amnesty International, *Not Part of My Sentence: Violations of the Human Rights of Women in Custody* (Washington, DC: Amnesty International, 1999), 26; Paige M. Harrison and Allen J. Beck, "Prisoners in 2004," *Bureau of Justice Statistics Bulletin* (Washington, DC: U.S. Department of Justice, October 2005), 11.

124. Associated Press, "ACLU Report: U.S. Drug Laws Harm Women," March 17, 2005. www.november.org/stayinfo/breaking3/ACLU-Women.html (retrieved March 2, 2006).

125. Institute on Women & Criminal Justice, "Quick Facts: Women & Criminal Justice—2009" (New York: Women's Prison Association, September 2009). www.wpaonline.org/pdf/Quick%20Facts%20Women%20and%20CJ_Sept09.pdf (retrieved February 22, 2013); Gina McGalliard, "Record Numbers of Incarcerated Mothers Bad News for Women, Children, Communities," *Truthout*, January 27, 2012. www.truth-out.org/news/item/5871-record-numbers-of-incarcerated-mothers-bad-news-for-women-children-communities (retrieved April 17, 2015); Lauren E. Glaze and Laura M. Maruschak, "Parents in Prison and Their Minor Children" (Washington, DC: U.S. Department of Justice, Bureau of Justice Statistics, March 2010).

126. John M. Hagedorn, *The Business of Drug Dealing in Milwaukee* (Milwaukee: Wisconsin Policy Research Institute, 1998), 3; Lorraine Maserolle, David Soole, and Sacha Rombouts, "Disrupting Street-Level Drug Markets," *Crime Prevention Research Reviews* (Washington, DC: U.S. Department of Justice, Office of Community Oriented Policing Services, 2007).

127. "Study Finds Rich Kids More Likely to Use Drugs Than Poor," Join Together: Advancing Effective Alcohol and Drug Policy, Prevention, and Treatment. www.jointogether.org/news/headlines/inthenews/2007/study-finds-rich-kids-more.html (retrieved December 10, 2008); Kelsey Kauffman, "Mothers in Prison," *Corrections Today* 63, no. 1 (2001): 62–65.

128. Leonard Saxe, Charles Kadushin, and Andrew A. Beveridge et al., "The Visibility of Illicit Drugs: Implications for Community-Based Drug Control Strategies," *American Journal of Public Health 1987–1994* 91 (December 2001): 12; Lisa Maher and Susan Hudson, "Women in the Drug Economy: A Metasynthesis of the Qualitative Literature," *Journal of Drug Issues* 37, no. 4 (2007): 805–826; S. Poret and C. Téjédo, "Law Enforcement and Concentration in Illicit Drug Markets," *European Journal of Political Economy* 22, no. 1 (2006): 99–114.

129. Howard N. Snyder, "Arrest in the United States 1990–2010" (Washington, DC: U.S. Department of Justice, Bureau of Justice Statistics, October 2012), 12, figure 39.

130. U.S. Department of Justice, Bureau of Justice Statistics, "Property Crime Victims, 2004." www.ojp.usdoj.gov/bjs (retrieved June 1, 2006).

131. Aaron Smith, "Marijuana Legalization Passes in Colorado, Washington," *CNN Money*, November 8, 2012. www.money.cnn.com/2012/11/07/news/economy/marijuana-legalization-washington-colorado/index.html.

132. Cornell School of Law, "Immigration Law: An Overview," 2006. www.law.cornell.edu/wex/index.php/Immigration (retrieved July 3, 2006).

133. Mark Motivans, "Immigration Offenders in the Federal Justice System, 2010," Bureau of Justice Statistics, July 18, 2012, NCJ 238581. www.bjs.gov/index.cfm?ty=pbdetail&iid=4392 (retrieved May 18, 2015).

134. U.S. Department of Justice, Bureau of Justice Statistics, "Immigration Law Prosecutions Double during 1996–2000" (Washington, DC: DOJ, 2002).

135. 2007 State of the Union, *President Bush's Plan for Comprehensive Immigration Reform,* www.whitehouse.gov/stateoftheunion/2007/initiatives/immigration.html (retrieved February 5, 2008).

136. Max Ehrenfreund, "Your Complete Guide to Obama's Immigration Executive Action," *Washington Post,* November 20, 2014. www.washingtonpost.com/blogs/wonkblog/wp/2014/11/19/your-complete-guide-to-obamas-immigration-order/ (retrieved May 18, 2015).

137. Lawrence Downes, "Talking Points: The Terrible, Horrible, Urgent National Disaster That Immigration Isn't," *New York Times,* June 20, 2006.

138. Jay S. Albanese, *Organized Crime in America* (Cincinnati: Anderson, 1996), 3.

139. Ibid., 102–103.

140. Alan Wright, "Organised Crime," *Crime and Justice International* 23, no. 100 (2007): 23.

141. Michael D. Lyman and Gary W. Potter, *Organized Crime* (Upper Saddle River, NJ: Prentice Hall, 1997).

142. James A. Fagin, *Criminal Justice* (Boston: Pearson Education, 2005).

143. Lyman and Potter, *Organized Crime,* 57.

144. Jerome P. Bjelopera and Kristin M. Finklea, "Organized Crime: An Evolving Challenge for U.S. Law Enforcement," prepared by the Congressional Research Service for the U.S. Congress, January 6, 2012.

145. James O. Finckenauer and Ko-lin Chin, *Asian Transnational Crime* (Washington, DC: National Institute of Justice, 2007), 1, 20.

146. Belknap. *The Invisible Woman.*

147. National Center for Victims of Crime, "Stalking Technology Outpaces State Laws." www.ncvc.org/src/main.aspx?dbID=DB_Stalking_Technology_Outpaces_State_Laws123 (retrieved May 30, 2007).

148. Penal Code § 646.9. "Stalking," 1990. Amended 2002. California Penal Code.

149. Patricia Tjaden and Nancy Thoennes, "Stalking in America: Findings from the National Violence Against Women Survey," *National Institute of Justice, Centers for Disease Control and Prevention—Research in Brief* (Washington, DC: U.S. Department of Justice, April 1998).

150. Ibid.

CHAPTER 3

1. Sadie Gurman, "Will Insanity Defense Save James Holmes?" *HuffPost,* April 27, 2015. www.huffingtonpost.com/2015/04/27/james-holmes-insanity-defense_n_7151138.html.

2. Karen Auge and Jennifer Brown, "James Holmes Was among Elite in Neuroscience before Aurora Theater Massacre," *Denver Post,* August 5, 2012. www.denverpost.com/theatershooting/ci_21238561/holmes-part-intellectual-elite-before-aurora-theater-massacre (retrieved June 22, 2015).

3. Jack Healy, "At Murder Trial for James Holmes, Conflicting Views of the Colorado Student," *New York Times,* May 7, 2015. www.nytimes.com/2015/05/08/us/at-james-holmes-aurora-movie-shooting-trial-conflicting-views-of-colorado-student.html?_r=0 (retrieved June 26, 2015).

4. Gary Strauss, "Aurora Officers Describe Arresting James Holmes," *USA Today,* January 8, 2013. www.usatoday.com/story/news/nation/2013/01/08/james-holmes-aurora-hearing/1816875/ (retrieved June 26, 2015).

5. Sadie Gurman, "Defense: 20 Doctors Agree James Holmes Has Schizophrenia," *CBSDenver,* April 27, 2015. http://denver.cbslocal.com/2015/04/27/prosecutor-2-exams-found-james-holmes-to-be-sane/ (retrieved June 23, 2015).

6. Ibid.

7. Cesare Beccaria, *On Crimes and Punishments* (reprint for The Library of Liberal Arts Series), Henry Paolucci (Trans.). (New York: Bobbs-Merrill, 1963).

8. Jeremy Bentham, *An Introduction to the Principles of Morals and Legislation,* corrected ed. (Oxford: Clarendon Press, 1823).

9. Beccaria, *On Crimes and Punishments.*

10. Bentham, *An Introduction to the Principles of Morals and Legislation.*

11. James Q. Wilson and Richard J. Herrnstein, *Crime and Human Nature: The Definitive Study of the Causes of Crime* (New York: Simon & Schuster, 1985); James Q. Wilson, *Thinking about Crime,* rev. ed. (New York: Vintage Books, 1983); Dereck Cornish and Ronald Clarke (Eds.), *The Reasoning Criminal: Rational Choice Perspectives on Offending* (New York: Springer Verlag, 1986); Morgan Reynolds, *Crime by Choice: An Economic Analysis* (Dallas: Fisher Institute, 1985).

12. Marvin E. Wolfgang, "Cesare Lombroso," in Hermann Mannheim (Ed.), *Pioneers in Criminology* (Montclair, NJ: Patterson Smith, 1973), 232–291; Cesare Lombroso, *Crime: Its Causes and Remedies,* H. P. Horton (Trans.) (Boston: Little Brown, 1911).

13. Mara Rose Williams, "Science Finds Neurological Clue to Teen Irresponsibility," *Philadelphia Inquirer,* November 24, 2000; Jay N. Giedd, "Structural Magnetic Resonance Imaging of the Adolescent Brain," *Annals of the New York Academy of Sciences* 1021 (2004): 77–85. http://intramural.nimh.nih.gov/research/pubs/giedd05.pdf (retrieved December 10, 2008).

14. Gail S. Anderson, *Biological Influences on Criminal Behavior* (New York: CRC Press, 2008).

15. Dorothy Otnow-Lewis, Shelly S. Shanok, Jonathan H. Pincus, and Gilbert H. Glaser, "Violent Juvenile Delinquents: Psychiatric, Neurological, Psychological, and Abuse Factors," *Journal of the American Academy of Child and Adolescent Psychiatry* 18 (1979): 307–319.

16. James M. Bjork, Donald M. Dougherty, Frederick Gerard Moeller, Donald R. Cherek, and Alan C. Swann, "The Effects of Tryptophan Depletion and Loading on Laboratory Aggression in Men: Time Course and a Food-Restricted Control," *Pharmacology* 142, no. 1 (February 1999): 24–30.

17. Shitij Kapur, *Pathophysiology and Treatment of Schizophrenia: New Findings,* 2nd ed. (London: Taylor & Francis, 2003).

18. Robert Sapolsky, *The Trouble with Testosterone and Other Essays on the Human Predicament* (New York: Simon & Schuster, 1998).

19. Keith McBurnett, Benjamin B. Lahey, Paul J. Rathouz, and Rolf Loeber, "Low Salivary Cortisol and Persistent Aggression in Boys Referred for Disruptive Behavior," *Archives of General Psychiatry* 57 (2000): 38–43.

20. Michael E. Roettger, Tianji Cai, and Guang Guo, "The Integration of Genetic Propensities into Social-Control Models of Delinquency and Violence among Male Youths," *American Sociological Review* 73 (2008): 543–568.

21. David P. Farrington, Geoffrey C. Barnes, and Sandra Lambert, "The Concentration of Offending in Families," *Legal and Criminological Psychology* 1, no. 1 (1996): 47–63.

22. Han G. Brunner, M. Nelen, Xandra O. Breakefield, Hans-Hilger Ropers, and Bernard A. van Oost, "Abnormal Behavior Associated with a Point Mutation in the Structural Gene for Monoamine Oxidase A," *Science* 262, no. 5133 (1993): 578–580.

23. Adrian Raine, *The Psychopathology of Crime: Criminal Behavior as a Clinical Disorder* (San Diego: Academic Press, 1993).

24. For one of the most comprehensive adoption studies, see Raine, *The Psychopathology of Crime.* See also, S. A. Mednick, W. F. Gabrielli, and B. Hutchings, "Genetic Factors in the Etiology of Criminal Behavior," S. A. Mednick, T. E. Moffitt, and S. A. Stack (Eds.), *The Causes of Crime: New Biological Approaches* (Cambridge, UK: Cambridge University Press, 1987).

25. A. Tengström, S. Hodgins, M. Grann, N. Långström, and G. Kullgren, "Schizophrenia and Criminal Offending: The Role of Psychopathy and Substance Use Disorders," *Criminal Justice and Behavior* 31 (2004): 367–391.

26. G. Gerbner, L. Gross, M. Morgan, and N. Signorielli, "Health and Medicine on Television," *New England Journal of Medicine* 305 (1981): 901–904.

27. John Monahan, "Mental Disorder and Violent Behavior: Perceptions and Evidence," *American Psychologist* 47 (1992): 511–521.

28. J. Bonta, M. Law, and K. Hanson, "The Prediction of Criminal and Violent Recidivism among Mentally Disordered Offenders: A Meta-Analysis," *Psychological Bulletin* 123 (1998): 123–142.

29. Paula M. Ditton, *Mental Health Treatment of Inmates and Probationers* (Washington, DC: U.S. Department of Justice, Bureau of Justice Statistics, July 1999). For additional information about the many problems mentally ill offenders present to the prison system, see Jamie Fellner and Sasha Abramsky, *Ill-Equipped: U.S. Prisons and Offenders with Mental Illness* (New York: Human Rights Watch, October 2003).

30. American Psychiatric Association, *Diagnostic and Statistical Manual of Mental Disorders-V-TR*

(Washington, DC: American Psychiatric Association, 2013).

31. National Institute of Mental Health, 2006. www.nimh.nih.gov/publicat/numbers.cfm.

32. Adrian Raine (Ed.), *Crime and Schizophrenia: Causes and Cures* (New York: Nova Science, 2006).

33. National Institutes of Health. http://psychcentral.com/lib/2006/schizophrenia-and-violence/ (retrieved December 19, 2008).

34. Shitij Kapur, *Pathophysiology and Treatment of Schizophrenia*.

35. The National Alliance on Mental Illness reports information on mental disorders. www.nami.org/Template.cfm?Section=By_Illness&Template=/TaggedPage/TaggedPageDisplay.cfm&TPLID=54&ContentID=23039.

36. Information on postpartum psychosis (and postpartum depression) can be found in Mark Levy, Deborah Sanders, and Stacy Sabraw, "Moms Who Kill: When Depression Turns Deadly," *Psychology Today*, November–December 2002.

37. Deborah W. Denno, "Who Is Andrea Yates? A Short Story about Insanity," *Duke Journal of Gender Law and Policy* 10 (2003): 32–33.

38. Jonathan H. Pincus, *Base Instincts: What Makes Killers Kill* (New York: Norton, 2001).

39. Office of the Child Advocate, "Shooting at Sandy Hook Elementary School," November 21, 2014. http://i2.cdn.turner.com/cnn/2014/images/11/21/office.of.the.child.advocate.report.pdf.pdf.

40. Robert D. Hare, *Manual for the Hare Psychopathy Checklist–Revised*, 2nd ed. (Toronto: Multi-Health Systems, 2003).

41. Robert D. Hare, *Without Conscience: The Disturbing World of the Psychopaths among Us* (New York: Guilford Press, 1999), 83.

42. Ibid.

43. Ibid.

44. Laura A. King, *The Science of Psychology: An Appreciative View* (New York: McGraw-Hill, 2008), 338.

45. Timothy B. Jeffrey and Louise K. Jeffrey, "The Utility of the Modified WAIS in a Clinical Setting," *Journal of Clinical Psychology* 40, no. 4 (2006): 1067–1069; Charles L. Scott and Joan B. Gerbasi, *Handbook of Correctional Mental Health* (Arlington, VA: American Psychiatric Publishing, 2005).

46. Wilson and Herrnstein, *Crime and Human Nature*.

47. Peter Salovey and John Mayer, "Emotional Intelligence," *Imagination, Cognition, and Personality* 9 (1990): 185–211.

48. *50 Weeks of Planned Killing: A Profile in Mass* sic *Murder*, directed by Bob Anderson (New York: American Broadcasting Companies, 1978).

49. Adrian Raine, J. Reid Meloy, Susan Bihrle, Lori LaCasse, and Monte S. Buchsbaum, "Reduced Prefrontal and Increased Subcortical Brain Functioning Assessed Using Positron Emission Tomography in Predatory and Affective Murderers," *Behavioral Sciences and the Law* 16 (1998): 319–332.

50. Jean Piaget, *The Moral Judgment of the Child* (New York: Free Press, 1965).

51. Daniel Tranel, "Long-Term Sequelae of Prefrontal Cortex Damage Acquired in Early Childhood," *Developmental Neuropsychology* 18, no. 3 (2000): 281–296.

52. Craig W. Haney, "The Good, the Bad, and the Lawful: An Essay on Psychological Injustice," in W. S. Laufer and J. M. Day (Eds.), *Personality Theory, Moral Development, and Criminal Behavior* (Lexington, MA: Lexington Books, 1983), 107–117.

53. Craig A. Anderson, "An Update on the Effects of Playing Violent Video Games," *Journal of Adolescence* 27 (2004): 113–122.

54. Sigmund Freud, *The Complete Works of Sigmund Freud*, vol. 19 (London: Hogarth, 1961).

55. Robert Agnew, "Foundation for General Strain Theory of Crime and Delinquency," *Criminology* 30 (February 1992): 1, 47–87.

56. Émile Durkheim, *The Division of Labor in Society*, George Simpson (Trans.) (Glencoe, IL: Free Press, 1933).

57. Jonathan Laurence and Justin Vaisse, "Understanding Urban Riots in France," *New Europe Review* 1 (December 2005). www.brookings.edu/views/articles/fellows/Laurence_vaisse_20051201.htm (retrieved June 9, 2006).

58. Robert K. Merton, "Social Structure and Anomie," *American Sociological Review* 3 (October 1938): 672–682; Robert K. Merton, *Social Theory and Social Structure*, rev. ed. (New York: Free Press, 1957); Albert Cohen, *Delinquent Boys: The Culture of the Gang* (New York: Free Press, 1955); Richard A. Cloward and Lloyd E. Ohlin, *Delinquency and Opportunity: A Theory of Delinquent Gangs* (Glencoe, IL: Free Press, 1960).

59. Cohen, *Delinquent Boys: The Culture of the Gang*.

60. Robert Sampson and John Laub, *Crime in the Making: Pathways and Turning Points through the Life Course* (Cambridge, MA: Harvard University Press, 1993); Lindsey Devers, "Desistance and Developmental Life Course Theories: Research Summary" (Arlington, VA: Bureau of Justice Assistance, November 9, 2011).

61. Terrie Moffit, "Adolescence-Limited and Life-Course-Persistent Antisocial Behavior: A Developmental Taxonomy," in Alex Piquero and Paul Maserolle (Eds.), *Life-Course Criminology: Contemporary and Classic Readings* (Belmont, CA: Wadsworth, Cengage Learning, 2001).

62. D. P. Farrington and D. J. West, "Criminal, Penal and Life Histories of Chronic Offenders: Risk and Protective Factors and Early Identification," *Criminal Behaviour and Mental Health* 3 (1993): 492–523; Zena Smith Blau, "The Life Cycle: Delinquency and Disrepute in the Life Course," in J. Hagan (Ed.), *Current Perspectives on Aging* (Greenwich, CT: JAI Press, 1995), 249–282.

63. Edward P. Mulvey, "Highlights from Pathways to Desistance: A Longitudinal Study of Serious Adolescent Offenders," *Juvenile Justice Fact Sheet* (Washington, DC: Office of Juvenile Justice and Delinquency Prevention, March 2011).

64. Durkheim, *The Division of Labor in Society*.

65. Gresham Sykes and David Matza, "Techniques of Neutralization: A Theory of Delinquency," *American Sociological Review* 22 (December 1957): 664–670.

66. Ibid., 664–670.

67. Walter C. Reckless, *The Crime Problem*, 4th ed. (New York: Appleton-Century-Crofts, 1967).

68. Michael Gottfredson and Travis Hirschi, *A General Theory of Crime* (Stanford, CA: Stanford University Press, 1990); Sampson and Laub, *Crime in the Making*.

69. Sampson and Laub, *Crime in the Making*

70. Gottfredson and Hirschi, *A General Theory of Crime*.

71. Ibid., 90.

72. M. Brent Donnellan, Kali H. Trzesniewski, Richard W. Robins, Terrie E. Moffitt, and Avshalom Caspi, "Low Self-Esteem Is Related to Aggression, Antisocial Behavior, and Delinquency," *Psychological Science* 16, no. 4 (2005): 328–335.

73. Ibid.

74. Ibid; R. F. Baumeister, B. J. Bushman, and W. K. Campbell, "Self-Esteem, Narcissism, and Aggression: Does Violence Result from Low Self-Esteem or from Threatened Egotism?" *Current Directions in Psychological Science* 9 (2000): 26–29; R. F. Baumeister, J. D. Campbell, J. I. Krueger, and K. E. Vohs, "Does High Self-Esteem Cause Better Performance, Interpersonal Success, Happiness, or Healthier Lifestyles?" *Psychological Science in the Public Interest* 4, no. 1 (2003); R. F. Baumeister, L. Smart, and J. M. Boden, "Relation of Threatened Egotism to Violence and Aggression: The Dark Side of High Self-Esteem," *Psychological Review* 103 (1996): 5–33; B. J. Bushman and R. F. Baumeister, "Threatened Egotism, Narcissism, Self-Esteem, and Direct and Displaced Aggression: Does Self-Love or Self-Hate Lead to Violence?" *Journal of Personality and Social Psychology* 75 (1998): 219–229; Travis Hirschi, *Causes of Delinquency* (Berkeley: University of California Press, 1969), 756–767; J. D. McCarthy and D. R. Hoge, "The Dynamics of Self-Esteem and Delinquency," *American Journal of Sociology* 90 (1984): 396–410.

75. Howard B. Kaplan, *Deviant Behavior in Defense of Self* (New York: Academic Press, 1980).

76. Susan Titus Reid, *Crime and Criminology*, 6th ed. (Austin, TX: Holt, Rinehart, & Winston, 1991); James A. Fagin, *Criminal Justice* (Boston: Pearson Education, 2005).

77. Judith R. Blau and Peter M. Blau, "The Cost of Inequality: Metropolitan Structure and Violent Crime," *American Sociological Review* 147 (1982): 114–129.

78. See, for example, Rosalyn Muraskin, *It's a Crime: Women and Justice*, 4th ed. (Upper Saddle River, NJ: Prentice Hall, 2006).

79. Sally S. Simpson, "Feminist Theory, Crime and Justice," *Criminology* 27 (1989): 605–631.

80. Joanne Belknap, *Invisible Woman: Gender, Crime, and Justice*, 3rd ed. (Belmont, CA: Wadsworth, Cengage Learning, 2007).

81. See, for example, Freda Adler, *Sisters in Crime* (New York: McGraw-Hill, 1975).

82. See, for example, Meda Chesney-Lind, "Girls and Violence: Is the Gender Gap Closing?" *Applied Research Forum* (National Electronic Network on Violence Against Women, August 2004).

83. For an excellent example of recent such work, see Jody Miller, *Getting Played: African American Girls, Urban Inequality, and Gendered Violence* (New York: New York University Press, 2008).

84. See Amanda Burgess-Proctor, "Intersections of Race, Class, Gender and Crime," *Feminist Criminology* 1, no. 1 (January 2006): 27–47.

85. J. Wozniak, "The Voices of Peacemaking Criminology: Insights into a Perspective with an Eye toward Teaching," *Contemporary Justice Review* 3, no. 3 (2000): 267–289.

86. Richard Quinney, "Life of Crime: Criminology and Public Police as Peacemaking," *Journal of Crime and Justice* 16, no. 2 (1993): 3–9.

87. Richard Quinney, "The Way of Peace: On Crime, Suffering, and Service," in Harold E. Pepinsky and Richard Quinney (Eds.), *Criminology as Peacemaking* (Bloomington: Indiana University Press, 1991); Wozniak, "The Voices of Peacemaking Criminology."

88. M. Braswell, J. R. Fuller, and B. Lozoff, *Corrections, Peacemaking, and Restorative Justice: Transforming Individuals and Institutions* (Cincinnati: Anderson, 2001).

89. Robert E. Park and Ernest W. Burgess, *The City* (Chicago: University of Chicago Press, 1925).

90. Clifford R. Shaw and Henry D. McKay, *Juvenile Delinquency in Urban Areas* (Chicago: University of Chicago Press, 1942); Clifford R. Shaw and Henry D. McKay, *Juvenile Delinquency and Urban Areas: A Study of Delinquents in Relation to Differential Characteristics of Local Communities in American Cities*, rev. ed. (Chicago: University of Chicago Press, 1969).

91. Marvin Wolfgang and Franco Ferracuti, *The Subculture of Violence* (London: Tavistock, 1967).

92. David Luckenbill and Daniel Doyle, "Structural Position and Violence: Developing a Cultural Explanation," *Criminology* 27 (1989): 419–436; Timothy C. Hayes and Matthew R. Lee, "The Southern Culture of Honor and Violent Attitudes," *Sociological Spectrum* 25 (2005): 593–617.

93. Thorsten Sellin, *Culture Conflict and Crime* (New York: Social Science Research Council, 1938).

94. Charles H. Cooley, *On Self and Social Organization*, Hans-Joaquim Schubert (Ed.) (Chicago: University of Chicago Press, 1998).

95. Howard Becker, *Outsiders: Studies in the Sociology of Deviance* (New York: Macmillan, 1963).

96. Edwin M. Schur, *Labeling Deviant Behavior: Its Sociological Implications* (New York: Harper & Row, 1971).

97. Frank Tannenbaum, *Crime and the Community* (New York: Atheneum Press, 1938), 17–19.

98. Edwin Sutherland, *Principles of Criminology*, 3rd ed. (Philadelphia: J. B. Lippincott, 1939), 4–8.

99. Joanna Shapland, Jonathan Willmore, and Peter Duff, *Victims in the Criminal Justice System* (Brookfield, VT: Avebury, 1985).

100. William Tallack, *Reparations to the Injured and the Rights of Victims of Crime to Compensation* (London: Wertheimer, Lea, 1900).

101. Robert J. McCormack, "Compensating Victims of Violent Crime" *Justice Quarterly* 8, no. 3 (1991): 329–246. http://pdfserve.informaworld.com/330515_731200452_718864699.pdf (retrieved December 19, 2008).

102. Edwin H. Sutherland, *Criminology* (Philadelphia: J. B. Lippincott, 1924); Hans von Hentig, "The Criminal and His Victim," in *Studies in the Sociobiology of Crime* (New Haven, CT: Yale University Press, 1948); Stephen Schafer, *The Victim and His Criminal: A Study in Functional Responsibility* (New York: Random House, 1968).

103. Chie Maekoya, "Victimization and Levels of Aggression in Intimate Partner Violence," *International Perspectives in Victimology* 3, no. 1 (March 2007): 42–49.

104. John P. J. Dussich, "The Victim Vulnerability Attributes Paradigm," unpublished class lectures, California State University, Fresno, 2005; John P. J. Dussich and Charles J. Eichman, "The Elderly Victim: Vulnerability to the Criminal Act," in Jack Goldsmith and Sharon S. Goldsmith (Eds.), *Crime and the Elderly* (Lexington, MA: Lexington Books, 1976), 93.

105. Graham Farrell and Ken Pease, "Once Bitten, Twice Bitten: Repeat Victimisation and Its Implications for Crime Prevention," Police Research Group, Crime Prevention Unit Series Paper no. 46 (London: Home Office Police Department, 1993); Gloria Laycock, "Hypothesis-Based Research: The Repeat Victimization Story," *Criminology and Criminal Justice*, 1 (2001): 59–82; Terri L. Messman and Patricia J. Long, "Child Sexual Abuse and Its Relationship to Revictimization in Adult Women: A Review," *Clinical Psychology Review* 16, no. 5 (1996): 307–420.

106. Nina Schuller, "Disabled People, Crime and Social Inclusion," *Community Safety Journal* 4, no. 3 (2005): 4–15; Barbara Collier, Donna Ghie-Richmond, Fran Odette, and Jake Pyne, "Reducing the Risk of Sexual Abuse for People Who Use Augmentative and Alternative Communication," *Argumentative and Alternative Communication* 22 (2006): 62–75; Virginia Aldigé Hiday, Marvin S. Swartz, Jeffrey W. Swanson, Randy Borum, and H. Ryan Wagner, "Criminal Victimization of Persons with Severe Mental Illness," *Psychiatric Services* 50 (1999): 62–68.

107. Reid Meloy, *The Psychology of Stalking: Clinical and Forensic Home Office Police Department Perspectives* (San Diego: Academic Press, 1998).

108. Christopher A. Janicak, "Regional Variations in Workplace Homicide Rates," in *Compensation and Working Conditions* (Washington, DC: U.S. Department of Labor, 2003), 3.

109. Dee Wood Harper Jr., "Comparing Tourists Crime Victimization," *Annals of Tourism Research* 28, no. 4 (2001): 1053–1056.

110. Yasmin Jiwani, "Vulnerabilities to Victimization at the Juncture of Intersecting Oppressions," in *Mapping Violence: A Work in Progress* (Vancouver: FREDA Centre for Research on Violence against Women and Children, December 2000). www.harbour.sfu.ca/freda/articles/fvpi02.htm (retrieved December 17, 2008).

111. Martin E. P. Seligman, *Helplessness: On Depression, Development, and Death* (San Francisco: W. H. Freeman, 1975).

112. Andrew Karmen, *Crime Victims: An Introduction to Victimology*, 5th ed. (Belmont, CA: Wadsworth, Cengage Learning, 2004), 66.

113. Ibid.

114. George W. Holden and Kathy L. Richie, "Linking Extreme Marital Discord, Child Rearing, and Child Behavior Problems: Evidence from Battered Women," *Child Development* 62, no. 2 (1991): 311–327; Jacquelyn C. Campbell and Linda A. Lewandowski, "Mental and Physical Health Effects of Intimate Partner Violence on Women and Children," *Psychiatric Clinics of North America* 20, no. 2 (1997): 353–374; Kimberly J. Mitchell and David Finkelhor, "Risk of Crime Victimization among Youth Exposed to Domestic Violence," *Journal of Interpersonal Violence* 16, no. 9 (September 2001), 960.

115. National Center for Education Statistics, "Student Victimization at Schools" (Washington, DC: U.S. Department of Education, October 1995). http://nces.ed.gov/pubs95/web/95204.asp (retrieved December 16, 2008).

116. Richard Sparks, *Research on Victims of Crime* (Washington, DC: Government Printing Office, 1982).

117. David F. Luckenbill, "Criminal Homicide as a Situated Transaction," *Social Problems* 25, no. 2 (1977): 176–186.

118. Carlene Wilson, Ted Nettlebeck, Robert Potter, and Caroline Perry, "Intellectual Disability and Criminal Victimisation," *Trends and Issues in Crime and Criminal Justice* 60 (Australian Institute of Criminology). www.aic.gov.au/publications/tandi/ti60.pdf (retrieved February 2, 2008).

CHAPTER 4

1. Ben Montgomery, "Recounting the Deadly Hazing That Destroyed FAMU Band's Reputation," *Tampa Bay Times*, November 11, 2012. www.tampabay.com/news/humaninterest/recounting-the-deadly-hazing-that-destroyed-famu-bands-reputation/1260765 (retrieved January 31, 2013); Gary Fineout, "Florida A&M University Delays Hiring New Leader for Famed Band." *6 South Florida*, January 16, 2013.

2. Samuel Noah Kramer, *History Begins at Sumer: Thirty-Nine Firsts in Recorded History*, 8th ed. (Philadelphia: University of Pennsylvania Press, 1988), 52–55; Joshua J. Mark, "Ur-Nammu." In *Ancient History Encyclopedia*. Article published June 16, 2014. www.ancient.eu/Ur-Nammu/ (retrieved May 22, 2015).

3. L. W. King, "Hammurabi's Code of Laws," in *Ancient History Sourcebook*. www.fordham.edu/halsall/ancient/hamcode.html#text (retrieved February 22, 2009).

4. Linda Deutsch, "Blake to Appeal Wrongful-Death Verdict," *Washington Post*, May 8, 2006. www.washingtonpost.com/wp-dyn/content/article/2006/05/08/AR2006050801098.html (retrieved January 6, 2011).

5. Lawrence Friedman, *A History of American Law*, 3rd ed. (New York: Touchstone, 1993).

6. Bryan A. Garner (Ed.), *Black's Law Dictionary*, 8th ed. (St. Paul, MN: Thomson West 2004), 369.

7. Richard Bevin, "John Haigh (The Acid Bath Murderer)." www.thebiographychannel.co.uk/biography_story/906:614/1/John_Haigh_The_Acid_Bath_Murderer_.htm (retrieved June 29, 2006).

8. Richard Bevin. The case of John George Haigh is documented on the Web site for The Biography Channel.

9. Florida Statutes § 837.02 (2008).

10. The case of Charles Manson and his followers is documented by the lead prosecutor in the case; see Vincent Bugliosi with Curt Gentry, *Helter Skelter: The True Story of the Manson Murders* (New York: W. W. Norton, 1994).

11. Included in the published writings of English jurist Edward Coke is a four-volume series on English law in the mid-seventeenth century. The third volume constitutes the first major study of English criminal law. Edward Coke, *The Third Part of the Institutes of the Laws of England: Concerning High Treason, and Other Pleas of the Crown, and Criminal Causes*, 1644 (London: E. and R. Brooke, 1797), 107.

12. "Eric Smith: Inside the Mind of a Child Killer," produced by Claudia Pryor Malis (New York: ABC, 1998).

13. *Atkins v. Virginia* 536 U.S. 304 (2002).

14. Ted Anthony, "Crime Revisited 21 Years after Attack," *Los Angeles Times*, December 12, 1993. http://articles.latimes.com/1993-12-12/news/mn-1029_1 (retrieved January 6, 2011).

15. *9 to 5* (1980), 20th Century Fox.

16. Michael Keiter, "Just Say No Excuse: The Rise and Fall of the Intoxication Defense," *Journal of Criminal Law and Criminology* 87 (1997): 482–518.

17. *Regina v. Dudley and Stephens* (1881–85), All E.R. Rep. 61 (Queen's Bench, December 9, 1884).

18. Andrew J. King, "Sunday Law in the Nineteenth Century," *Albany Law Review* 64 (2000): 675–772.

19. *United States v. Bailey*, 444 U.S. 394 (1980).

20. *Rex v. Arnold* (Court of Common Pleas 1724) in Thomas Bayly Howell (Ed.), *A Complete Collection of State Trials* (1812), 695, 765. This is the first known insanity trial for which the entire transcript exists. In this case, the defendant, Arnold, shot Lord Onslow who Arnold believed was inhabiting his body. Although Arnold was found guilty, his sentence was commuted to life by Onslow.

21. L. A. Callahan, H. J. Steadman, M. A. McGreevy, and P. C. Robbins, "The Volume and Characteristics of Insanity Defense Pleas: An Eight-State Study," *Bulletin of Psychiatry and the Law* 19 (1991): 331–338.

22. *Queen v. McNaughtan*, 8 Eng. Rep. 718 (1843).

23. Carl Elliott, *The Rules of Insanity: Moral Responsibility and the Mentally Ill Offender* (Albany: SUNY Press, 1996).

24. *Durham v. United States*, 214 F.2d 862 (1954).

25. Model Penal Code § 4.01, Proposed Official Draft (May 4, 1962).

26. Del Quentin Wilber, "Hinckley to Gain Driving Privileges, Longer Visits," *Washington Post*, June 17, 2009. www.washingtonpost.com/wp-dyn/content/article/2009/06/16/AR2009061601761.html.

27. Gary B. Melton, John Petrila, Norman G. Poythress, and Christopher Slobogin, *Psychological Evaluations for the Courts: A Handbook for Mental Health Professionals and Lawyers*, 2nd ed. (New York: Guilford Press, 1997).

28. "Police Finish Bertuzzi Investigation," *CBC Sports*, April 16, 2004. www.cbc.ca/sports/story/2004/04/14/bertuzzi040413.html (retrieved October 5, 2007).

CHAPTER 5

1. Deborah Becker, "Chelsea Police, Social Service Agency Partner for At-Risk Youth," *90.9 WBUR*, August 8, 2012. http://www.wbur.org//2012/08/08/chelsea-teens-roca.

2. ROCA. http://www.rocainc.org.

3. Egon Bittner, *Aspects of Police Work* (Boston: Northeastern University Press, 1990).

4. Eric Scott, *Calls for Service: Citizen Demand and Initial Police Response* (Washington, DC: Government Printing Office, 1981).

5. David Bayley, *Police for the Future* (New York: Oxford University Press, 1994); David Barlow and Melissa Hickman Barlow, *Police in a Multicultural Society: An American Story* (Prospect Heights, IL: Waveland Press, 2000).

6. Bittner, *Aspects of Police Work*.

7. See Rosemary Gido, Tammy Castle, Kimberly Dodson, Danielle McDonald, Christine Olsen, and Rebecca Boyd, "The Irish in Schuylkill County Prison: Ethnic Conflict in Pre- and Post-Civil War Pennsylvania," *The Prison Journal* 86 (June 2006): 260–268.

8. Richard Maxwell Brown, "Vigilante Policing," in Carl B. Klockars and Stephen D. Mastrofski (Eds.), *Thinking about Police: Contemporary Readings* (New York: McGraw-Hill, 1991).

9. Ibid.

10. Barlow and Barlow, *Police in a Multicultural Society*; Samuel Walker, *A Critical History of Police Reform: The Emergence of Professionalism* (Lexington, MA: Lexington Books, 1977); P. L. Reichel, "Southern Slave Patrols as a Transitional Police Type," *American Journal of Policing* 7 (1988): 51–77.

11. Eugene Genovese, *Roll, Jordon, Roll: The World the Slaves Made* (New York: Vintage Books, 1976).

12. Julian Samora, Joe Bernal, and Albert Pena, *Gunpowder Justice: A Reassessment of the Texas Rangers* (Notre Dame, IN: University of Notre Dame Press, 1979).

13. Hubert Williams and Patrick Murphy, *The Evolving Strategy of Police: A Minority Perspective* (Washington, DC: National Institute of Justice, 1990).

14. Neil Websdale, *Policing the Poor: From Slave Plantation to Public Housing* (Boston: Northeastern University Press, 2001).

15. E. F. Foner, *Reconstruction: America's Unfinished Revolution, 1863–1877* (New York: Harper & Row, 1988), 4–5.

16. Barlow and Barlow, *Police in a Multicultural Society*.

17. Samuel Walker and Charles M. Katz, *Police in America: An Introduction* (New York: McGraw-Hill, 2005), 77.

18. Wilbur Miller, "Police Authority in London and New York City 1830–1870," *Journal of Social History* 9 (Winter 1975): 81–101.

19. Ibid.; George Kelling and Mark Moore, "The Evolving Strategy of Policing," *Perspectives on Policing* 4 (November 1988): 1–15.

20. Nathan Douthit, "August Vollmer, Berkeley's First Chief of Police, and the Emergence of Police Professionalism," *California Historical Quarterly* 54 (Spring 1975): 101–124.

21. Robert Lombardo and Todd Lough, "Community Policing: Broken Windows, Community Building,

and Satisfaction with the Police," *Police Journal* 80, no. 2 (2007): 119.

22. Robert Fogelson, *Big-City Police* (Cambridge, MA: Harvard University Press, 1977).

23. Jan Chaiken, Peter Greenwood, and Joan Petersilia, "The Criminal Investigation Process: A Summary Report," *Policy Analysis* 3, no. 2 (1977): 187–217.

24. Walker and Katz, *Police in America*, 77.

25. O. Elmer Polk and David W. MacKenna, "Dilemmas of the New Millennium: Policing in the 21st Century," *ACJS Today* 30, no. 3 (2005): 4.

26. U.S. Department of Justice, Bureau of Justice Statistics, *Local Police Departments, 2003* (Washington, DC: DOJ, 2006), 1.

27. Dayton Kelley, "Ranger Hall of Fame," *FBI Law Enforcement Bulletin* 45, no. 5 (1976): 18.

28. Walker and Katz, *Police in America*, 72.

29. Federal Bureau of Investigation, "Cyber Crime." www.fbi.gov/about-us/investigate/cyber (retrieved June 6, 2015).

30. U.S. Department of Justice, Bureau of Justice Statistics, *Federal Law Enforcement Officers, 2008* (Washington, DC: DOJ, 2012).

31. National Institute of Justice, *Policing on American Indian Reservations* (Washington, DC: NIJ, 2001), vi–x.

32. Walker and Katz, *Police in America*, 76–77.

33. Polk and MacKenna, "Dilemmas of the New Millennium," 5.

34. Jacksonville Sheriff 's Office, "History of the JSO Consolidated Law Enforcement." www.co.net/Departments/Sheriffs+Office/About+the+JSO/History+of+the+JSO.htm (retrieved March 30, 2007).

35. Walker and Katz, *Police in America*, 77–78.

36. Simon A. Andrew, "Interlocal Contractual Arrangements in the Provision of Public Safety" (presentation prepared for the Florida Department of Community Affairs under the auspices of Florida State University, 2004).

37. W. Dwayne Orrick, *Recruitment, Retention, and Turnover of Police Personnel: Reliable, Practical, and Effective Solutions* (Springfield, IL: Charles C Thomas, 2008), 3.

38. U.S. Department of Justice, *Hiring and Keeping Police Officers* (Washington, DC: DOJ, 2004), 2.

39. Marvin J. Cetron and Owen Davies, "Trends Now Shaping the Future: Economic, Societal, and Environmental Trends," *The Futurist* 39, no. 2 (2005): 33–34.

40. Jeremy M. Wilson, "Strategies for Police Recruitment: A Review of Trends, Contemporary Issues, and Existing Approaches," *Law Enforcement Executive Forum* 14, no. 1 (2014): 78–90.

41. Laura Werber and Greg Ridgeway, *Today's Police and Sheriff Recruits* (Santa Monica, CA: RAND Corporation, 2010).

42. International Association of Chiefs of Police and the Bureau of Justice Assistance, "Explore a Career in Law Enforcement—Visit www.DiscoverPolicing.org." http://discoverpolicing.org/?fa=about_site (retrieved June 7, 2015).

43. Wilson, "Strategies for Police Recruitment," 84–85.

44. Police Executive Research Forum, *The Cop Crunch: Identifying Strategies for Dealing with the Recruiting*

and Hiring Crisis in Law Enforcement (Washington, DC: PERF, 2005), 8.

45. Wilson, "Strategies for Police Recruitment," 87.

46. The President's Task Force on 21st Century Policing, "Interim Report of the President's Task Force on 21st Century Policing" (Washington, DC, March 4, 2015), 51.

47. Wilson, "Strategies for Police Recruitment," 89.

48. Walker and Katz, *Police in America*, 128.

49. Sameshield.Com, "History of Policewomen," August 28, 2006. www.sameshield.com/history/sshistory16.html.

50. Ibid.

51. Office of Community Oriented Policing Services, "Women in Law Enforcement," *Community Policing Dispatch* 6, no. 7 (2013). http://cops.usdoj.gov/html/dispatch/07-2013/women_in_law_enforcement.asp (retrieved June 9, 2015).

52. National Center for Women and Policing, *Hiring and Retaining More Women: The Advantages to Law Enforcement Agencies* (Arlington, VA: NCWP, 2003), 1–16.

53. Amie M. Schuck, "Female Representation in Law Enforcement: The Influence of Screening, Unions, Incentives, Community Policing, CALEA, and Size," *Police Quarterly* 17, no. 1 (2014): 70–72.

54. Herbert Williams and Patrick Murphy, *The Evolving Strategy of Police: A Minority Perspective* (Washington, DC: National Institute of Justice, 1990).

55. Marvin Dulaney, *Black Police in America* (Bloomington: Indiana University Press, 1996).

56. Bureau of Justice Statistics, *Local Police Departments, 2013: Personnel, Policies, and Practices* (Washington, DC: DOJ, 2015), 5.

57. Jihong Zhao, Ni He, and Nicholas Lovrich, "Predicting the Employment of Minority Officers in the U.S. Cities: OLS Fixed-Effect Panel Model Results for African American and Latino Officers for 1993, 1996, and 2000," *Journal of Criminal Justice* 33 (July–August 2005): 377–386.

58. Bureau of Justice Statistics, *Local Police Departments, 2013*, 6.

59. See David Fahrenthold, "The Blue and the Gay: DC Officer Links His 2 Communities," *Washington Post*, October 22, 2001, p. B01.

60. Gay Officers Action League, "Mission Statement," www.goalny.org/Mission_Statement.html (retrieved June 13, 2015).

61. Allison T. Chappell, Lonn Lanza-Kaduce, and Daryl H. Johnston, "Law Enforcement Training Changes and Challenges," in Roger G. Dunham and Geoffrey P. Alpert (Eds.), *Critical Issues in Policing* (Long Grove, IL: Waveland Press, 2005), 72.

62. Polk and MacKenna, "Dilemmas of the New Millennium," 7.

63. President's Task Force on 21st Century Policing, "Interim Report of the President's Task Force on 21st Century Policing."

64. Chappell, Lanza-Kaduce, and Johnston, "Law Enforcement Training Changes and Challenges," 72–73.

65. Mark R. McCoy, "Teaching Style and the Application of Adult Learning Principles by Police Instructors," *Policing: An International Journal of Police Strategies & Management* 29, no. 1 (2006): 78.

66. Sue Rahr and Stephen K. Rice, "From Warriors to Guardians: Recommitting American Police Culture to Democratic Ideals," New Perspectives in Policing, Executive Session on Policing and Public Safety, Harvard Kennedy School (Washington, DC: National Institute of Justice, 2015).

67. Commission on Peace Officer Standards and Training, *Integration of Leadership, Ethics, and Community Policing into the Regular Basic Course* (Sacramento: Peace Officer Standards and Training, 2003), 120–121.

68. Chappell, Lanza-Kaduce, and Johnston, "Law Enforcement Training Changes and Challenges," 76–77.

69. Robert Worden, "The 'Causes' of Police Brutality: Theory and Evidence on Police Use of Force," in Steven G. Brandl and David S. Barlow (Eds.), *The Police in America: Classic and Contemporary Readings* (Belmont, CA: Wadsworth, Cengage Learning, 2004): 128–173; Geoff Coliandris and Colin Rogers, "Linking Police Culture, Leadership and Partnership-Working," *Police Journal* 81, no. 2 (2008): 114.

70. Worden, "The 'Causes' of Police Brutality," 128–173.

71. Michael W. Quinn, *Walking with the Devil and the Police Code of Silence* (Minneapolis: Quinn and Associates, 2005), 118; Coliandris and Rogers, "Linking Police Culture, Leadership and Partnership-Working," 114.

72. William Westley, *Violence and the Police* (Cambridge, MA: MIT Press, 1970); David Weisburd, Rosann Greenspan, Edwin E. Hamilton, Hubert Williams, and Kellie Bryant, *Police Attitudes toward Abuse of Authority: Findings from a National Study* (Washington, DC: Government Printing Office, 2000).

73. Carl B. Klockars, "Police Code of Silence," in Larry E. Sullivan (Ed.), *Encyclopedia of Law Enforcement* (Thousand Oaks, CA: Sage, 2005), 334–335.

74. Bittner, *Aspects of Police Work*.

75. John Van Maanen, "The Asshole," in P. K. Manning and J. Van Maanen (Eds.), *Policing: A View from the Street* (Santa Monica, CA: Goodyear, 1978); Meghan Stroshine, Geoffrey Alpert, and Roger Dunham, "The Influence of 'Working Rules' on Police Suspicion and Discretionary Decision Making," *Police Quarterly* 11, no. 3 (September 2008): 315–337.

76. William V. Pelfrey, "The Inchoate Nature of Community Policing: Differences between Community Policing and Traditional Police Officers," *Justice Quarterly* 21, no. 3 (September 2004): 579–601.

77. William Terrill, Eugene Paoline, and Peter Manning, "Police Culture and Coercion," *Criminology* 41, no. 4 (2003): 1003–1034.

78. Robert Brown and James Frank, "Race and Officer Decision Making: Examining Differences in Arrest Outcomes between Black and White Officers," *Justice Quarterly* 23, no. 1 (March 2006).

79. Ibid.

80. Richard Johnson, "Explaining Patrol Officer Drug Arrest Activity through Expectancy Theory," *Policing* 32 (January 1, 2009): 6.

81. Stroshine, Alpert, and Dunham, "The Influence of 'Working Rules' on Police Suspicion and Discretionary Decision Making," 315–337.

82. Brown and Frank, "Race and Officer Decision Making."

83. George E. Higgins, Wesley G. Jennings, Kareem L. Jordan, and Shaun L. Gabbidon, "Racial Profiling in Decision to Search: A Preliminary Analysis Using Propensity-Score Matching," *International Journal of Police Science & Management*, 13, no. 4 (Winter 2011): 336–347.

84. Robin Shepard Engel and Jennifer Calnon, "Examining the Influence of Drivers' Characteristics during Traffic Stops with Police: Results from a National Survey," *Justice Quarterly* 21, no. 1 (March 2004).

85. John Lamberth, "Traffic Stop Data Analysis, Project of the Sacramento Police Department: Final Report for the Sacramento Police Department," August 2008.

86. Donald Black, "The Social Organization of Arrest," *Stanford Law Review* 23 (June 1971): 1087–1111.

87. Ibid.

88. Michael A. Caldero and John P. Crank, *Police Ethics: The Corruption of Noble Cause* (New York: Anderson, 2004), 2.

89. Sean W. Malinowski, "The Conceptualization of Police Corruption: An Historical Perspective," in Menachem Amir (Ed.), *Police Corruption: Challenges for Developed Countries—Comparative Issues and Commissions of Inquiry* (Huntsville, TX: Office of International Criminal Justice, Sam Houston State University, 2004), 37.

90. Caldero and Crank, *Police Ethics*, 30–31.

91. Darrell L. Ross, *Civil Liability in Criminal Justice* (Dayton, OH: LexisNexis, 2006), 5.

92. *Thurman v. City of Torrington*, 595 F. Sup. 152 (1984).

93. Ibid.

94. Herman Goldstein, *Police Corruption: Perspective on Its Nature and Control* (Washington, DC: Police Foundation, 1975), 5.

95. International Association of Chiefs of Police, *Corruption Prevention*, 2.

96. Jerome H. Skolnick, "Corruption and the Blue Code of Silence," *Police Practice and Research* 3 (2002): 8–12.

97. Laurence Miller, "'Good Cop—Bad Cop' Problem Officers, Law Enforcement Culture, and Strategies for Success," *Journal of Police and Criminal Psychology* 19, no. 2 (2004): 33.

98. National Institute of Justice, *Enhancing Police Integrity* (Washington, DC: NIJ, 2005), 2.

99. Caldero and Crank, *Police Ethics*, 269.

100. Kim Michelle Lersch, Tom Bazley, and Tom Mieczkowski, "Early Intervention Programs: An Effective Police Accountability Tool, or Punishment of the Productive?" *An International Journal of Police Strategies & Management* 29 (2006): 59.

101. International Association of Chiefs of Police, *Internal Affairs Study* (Washington, DC: IACP, 2009), 13.

102. Police Executive Research Forum, *Legitimacy and Procedural Justice: A New Element of Police*

Leadership, Bureau of Justice Assistance, U.S. Department of Justice (Washington, DC, March 2014).

103. Thomas D. Stucky, "Local Politics and Police Strength," *Justice Quarterly* 22 (2005): 164.

104. Darl Champion and Michael Hooper, *Introduction to American Policing* (New York: McGraw-Hill, 2003), 365.

105. Mahesh K. Nalla, Joseph D. Johnson, and Gorazd Mesko, "Are Police and Security Personnel Warming Up to Each Other? A Comparison of Officers' Attitudes in Developed, Emerging, and Transitional Economies," *Policing: An International Journal of Police Strategies and Management* 32, no. 3 (2009): 510.

106. David Shichor, *Punishment for Profit* (Thousand Oaks, CA: Sage, 1995).

107. Kevin Strom, Marcus Berzofsky, Bonnie Shook-Sa, Kelle Barrick, Crystal Daye, Nicole Horstmann, and Susan Kinsey, *The Private Security Industry: A Review of the Definitions, Available Data Sources, and Paths Moving Forward* (Research Triangle Park, NC: RTI International, 2010): 2–3.

108. Joseph Straw, "Homeland Security," *Security Management* 52, no. 11 (2008): 24.

109. David H. Bayley and Christine Nixon, *The Changing Environment for Policing, 1985–2008* (Washington, DC: National Institute of Justice, 2010), 8.

110. Polk and MacKenna, "Dilemmas of the New Millennium," 5.

111. Champion and Hooper, *Introduction to American Policing*, 192.

112. Malcolm K. Sparrow, "Managing the Boundary between Public and Private Policing," September 2014, New Perspectives in Policing-Harvard Kennedy School/National Institute of Justice Partnership (Washington, DC): 20.

113. Brian Forst, "Private Policing," in Larry E. Sullivan (Ed.), *Encyclopedia of Law Enforcement* (Thousand Oaks, CA: Sage, 2005), 364.

CHAPTER 6

1. Police Foundation, *Newark Foot Patrol Experiment*, NCJ 081779.

2. J. H. Ratcliffe, T. Taniguchi, E. R. Groff, and J. D. Wood, "The Philadelphia Police Experiment: A Randomized Controlled Trial of Police Patrol Effectiveness in Violent Crime Hotspots," *Criminology* (forthcoming). See a draft of the academic paper "The Philadelphia Foot Patrol Experiment," at www.temple.edu/cj/FootPatrolProject.

3. Ibid.

4. Ibid.

5. Ibid.

6. Philadelphia Police Department, *Making Philadelphia a Safer City: 2011 Progress Report on the Crime Fighting Strategy and Five-Year Plan*, August 31, 2011. www.phillypolice.com/assets/crime-maps-stats/PPD.2011.Making.Phila.Safer.City.pdf.

7. Thomas J. Sweeney, "Patrol," in William A. Geller and Darrel W. Stephens (Eds.), *Local Government Police Management* (Washington, DC: International City/County Management Association, 2003), 89.

8. National Research Council, *Fairness and Effectiveness in Policing* (Washington, DC: NRC, 2004), 58. Furthermore, when officers appear on the scene, they often find that no criminal activity has occurred. David A. Klinger and George S. Bridges, "Measurement Error in Calls-for-Service as an Indicator of Crime," *Criminology* 35 (1997): 707.

9. Eric Scott, *Calls for Service: Citizen Demand and Initial Police Response* (Washington, DC: Government Printing Office, 1981).

10. Jennifer L. Truman and Lynn Langton, "Criminal Victimization, 2013." Bureau of Justice Statistics, September 2014, NCJ 247648. www.bjs.gov/content/pub/pdf/cv13.pdf.

11. U.S. Department of Justice, Bureau of Justice Statistics, *Reporting Crime to the Police, 1992–2000* (Washington, DC: Government Printing Office, 2003).

12. Michael Caldero and John P. Crank, *Police Ethics: The Corruption of Noble Cause* (New York: Anderson, 2004), 253.

13. James Q. Wilson, *Varieties of Police Behavior* (Cambridge, MA: Harvard University Press, 1968), 31.

14. George Kelling, Tony Pate, Duane Dieckman, and Charles Brown, *The Kansas City Preventive Patrol Experiment: A Summary Report* (Washington, DC: Police Foundation, 1974).

15. Ibid.

16. For more on this topic see John Eck and Edward Maguire, "Have Changes in Policing Reduced Violent Crime? An Assessment of the Evidence," in Alfred Blumstein and Joel Wallman (Eds.), *The Crime Drop in America* (Cambridge, UK: Cambridge University Press, 2000).

17. Herman Goldstein, "Improving Policing: A Problem-Oriented Approach," *Crime & Delinquency* 25 (1979): 236–258.

18. Ibid.

19. Ibid.

20. Ibid.

21. Jerome Skolnick and David Bayley, *The New Blue Line* (New York: Free Press, 1986).

22. Ibid.

23. Ibid.

24. Steven Mastrofski, "Community Policing: A Cautionary Tale," in Jack Greene and Stephen Mastrofski (Eds.), *Community Policing: Rhetoric or Reality* (New York: Praeger, 1988), 47–68.

25. Ibid.

26. Neil Websdale, *Policing the Poor: From Slave Plantation to Public Housing* (Boston: Northeastern University Press, 2001).

27. Edward Maguire, "Structural Change in Large Municipal Police Organizations during the Community Policing Era," *Justice Quarterly* 14 (1997): 547–576.

28. John Eck and Edward Maguire, "Have Changes in Policing Reduced Violent Crime? An Assessment of the Evidence," in Blumstein and Wallman, *The Crime Drop in America*.

29. Marcia R. Chaiken, *COPS: Innovations in Policing in American Heartlands* (Alexandria, VA: LINC, 2001).

30. Kenneth Novak, Leanne Alarid, and Wayne Lucas, "Exploring Officers' Acceptance of Community Policing: Implications for Policy Implementation," *Journal of Criminal Justice* 31 (2003): 57–71.

31. John MacDonald, "The Effectiveness of Community Policing in Reducing Urban Violence," *Crime and Delinquency* 48, no. 4 (2002): 592–618.

32. Ling Ren, Liquen Cao, Nicholas Lovrich, and Michael Gaffney, "Linking Confidence in the Police with the Performance of the Police: Community Policing Can Make a Difference," *Journal of Criminal Justice* 33 (2005): 55–66.

33. James Q. Wilson and George Kelling, "Broken Windows: Police and Neighborhood Safety," *Atlantic Monthly* 249 (March 1982): 29–38.

34. Ibid.

35. Robert Sampson and Stephen Raudenbush, "Systematic Social Observation of Public Spaces: A New Look at Disorder in Urban Neighborhoods," *American Journal of Sociology* 105, no. 3 (1999): 603–651.

36. Darrel W. Stephens, "Organization and Management," in William A. Geller and Darrel W. Stephens (Eds.), *Local Government Police Management* (Washington, DC: International City/County Management Association, 2003), 51.

37. Meghan Stroshine, Geoffrey Alpert, and Roger Dunham, "The Influence of 'Working Rules' on Police Suspicion and Discretionary Decision Making," *Police Quarterly* 11, no. 3 (2008): 334.

38. National Institute of Justice, *Crime Scene Investigation: A Reference for Law Enforcement Training* (Washington, DC: NIJ, 2004), 9–16.

39. Ibid.

40. Joan Petersilia, *The Influence of Criminal Justice Research* (Santa Monica, CA: RAND Corporation, 1987), 15.

41. Frank Horvath and Robert T. Meesig, *A National Survey of Police Policies and Practices Regarding the Criminal Investigation Process: Twenty-Five Years after Rand* (East Lansing: Michigan State University, 2001), 2.

42. Anthony A. Braga, Edward A. Flynn, George L. Kelling, and Christine M. Cole, *Moving the Work of Criminal Investigators towards Crime Control*, New Perspectives in Policing, Harvard Kennedy School (Washington, DC: National Institute of Justice, 2011).

43. Federal Bureau of Investigation, "Crime in the United States 2013" (Washington, DC: U.S. Department of Justice, November 2014). https://www.fbi.gov/about-us/cjis/ucr/crime-in-the-u.s/2013/crime-in-the-u.s.-2013/offenses-known-to-law-enforcement/clearances/clearancetopic_final (retrieved June 29, 2015).

44. International Association of Chiefs of Police, *Training Key #58: Criminal Investigations* (Alexandria, VA: IACP, 2003), 2–4.

45. Alexander Weiss and Kenneth Morckel, "Strategic and Tactical Approaches to Traffic Safety," *Police Chief* 74, no. 7 (2007).

46. National Advisory Commission on Criminal Justice Standards and Goals, *Police* (Washington, DC: NACCJSG, 1973), 227.

47. Angelo Rao, "Transportation Services," in William Geller and Darrel W. Stephens (Eds.), *Local Government Police Management* (Washington, DC: International City/County Management Association, 2003), 207–238.

48. Police Executive Research Forum, *Future Trends in Policing* (Washington, DC: Office of Community Oriented Policing Services, 2014), 30.

49. Gus Burns, "Detroit Police Patrol Officers to Wear Mics, Have In-Car Audio-Video," MLive Media Group, March 1, 2013. Blog.mlive.com/news/Detroit_impact/print.html?entry=/2013/03/Detroit_police_patrol_officers.html (retrieved March 7, 2013).

50. Police Executive Research Forum, *Future Trends in Policing*, 29.

51. National Institute of Justice, *Education and Training in Forensic Science* (Washington, DC: NIJ, 2004), 31.

52. National Institute of Justice, *Crime Scene Investigation: A Reference for Law Enforcement Training* (Washington, DC: NIJ, 2004), 9–16.

53. Kathleen M. Stephens, "The Changing Role of Forensic Science," *Police Futurist* 13, no. 2 (2005): 7–8.

54. National Institute of Justice, "The Impact of Forensic Science Research and Development" (Washington, DC: NIJ, April 2015), 4.

55. National Institute of Justice, *Education and Training in Forensic Science*, 2.

56. Stephens, "Organization and Management," 52.

57. Daniel E. Marks and Ivan Y. Sun, "The Impact of 9/11 on Organizational Development among State and Local Law Enforcement Agencies," *Contemporary Criminal Justice* 23, no. 2 (2007): 162–163.

58. George Gascón and Todd Foglesong, *Making Policing More Affordable: Managing Costs and Measuring Value in Policing*, New Perspectives in Policing, Harvard Kennedy School (Washington, DC: National Institute of Justice, 2010).

59. Thomas D. Stucky, "Local Politics and Police Strength," *Justice Quarterly* 22 (2005): 144, 163–164.

60. Ibid.

61. Jim Bueermann, "The Future of Terrorism," *National Institute of Justice Journal*, no. 269 (March 2012).

62. Police Executive Research Forum, *Future Trends in Policing*, 9.

63. National Institute of Justice, *Mapping Crime: Understanding Hot Spots* (Washington, DC: NIJ, 2005), 2.

64. Bureau of Justice Assistance and Police Executive Research Forum, "COMPSTAT: Its Origins, Evolution, and Future in Law Enforcement Agencies" (Washington, DC: Police Executive Research Forum, 2014).

65. David Weisburd, Rosann Greenspan, Stephen Mastrofski, and James J. Willis, *CompStat and Organizational Change: A National Assessment*, DOJ-Funded Report, Document No. 222322 (April 2008): 6.

66. Christopher Bruce, "Redistricting and Resource Allocation: A Question of Balance," *Geography and Public Safety* 1, no. 4 (2009): 1.

67. Municipal Police Officers' Education and Training Commission, *Criminal Investigative Analysis: Implications for First Responders* (Hershey, PA: MPOETC, 2004), 1–2.

68. Beth Pearsall, "Predictive Policing: The Future of Law Enforcement," *NIJ Journal*, no. 266 (2010): 16–19.

69. Gallup Poll, "Confidence in Institutions," June 2015. www.gallup.com/poll/1597/confidence-institutions.aspx.

70. Jeffrey M. Jones, "Confidence in Police Drops to Ten Year Low," Gallup Poll, November 10, 2005. www.galluppoll.com/content/Default.aspx?ci=19783&pg=1&VERSON=p (retrieved January 31, 2007).

71. Jeffrey M. Jones, "Drop among Nonwhites Drives U.S. Police Honesty Ratings Down," Gallup Poll, December 18, 2014. www.gallup.com/poll/180230/drop-among-nonwhites-drives-police-honesty-ratings-down.aspx.

72. Darren K. Carlson, "Racial Profiling Seen as Pervasive, Unjust," Gallup Poll, July 20, 2004. www.galluppoll.com/content/Default.aspx?ci=12406&pg=1&VERSON=p (retrieved January 31, 2007).

73. See, for example, Matthew R. Durose, Patrick A. Langan, and Erica Leah Schmitt, "Characteristics of Drivers Stopped by Police, 1999," U.S. Department of Justice, Bureau of Justice Statistics, March 1, 2002. http://bjs.ojp.usdoj.gov/index.cfm?ty=pbdetail&iid=548 (retrieved May 30, 2011).

74. Jones, "Confidence in Police Drops to Ten Year Low."

75. Gallup Poll, "Race Relations. 2008." www.gallup.com/poll/1687/Race-Relation.asp#1(retrieved January 20, 2011).

76. Ronald Weitzer and Steven Tuch, "Perceptions of Racial Profiling: Race, Class, and Personal Experience," *Criminology* 40, no. 2 (2002): 435–456.

77. Ronald Weitzer, "Racialized Policing: Residents' Perceptions in Three Neighborhoods," *Law & Society Review* 34, no. 1 (2000): 129–156.

78. Joseph Carroll, "Majority of NOLA Residents Approve of Mayor's Response to Katrina: Blacks Much More Likely Than Whites to Approve of Job Done by Local Leaders," Gallup Poll, March 1, 2006. www.gallup.com/poll/21709/majority-nola-residents-approve-mayors-response-katrina.aspx.

79. Weitzer, "Racialized Policing."

80. Weitzer and Tuch, "Perceptions of Racial Profiling."

81. John Reitzel, Stephen Rice, and Alex Piquero, "Lines and Shadows: Perceptions of Racial Profiling and the Hispanic Experience," *Journal of Criminal Justice* 32, no. 6 (2004): 607–616.

82. Weitzer and Tuch, "Perceptions of Racial Profiling"; Reitzel, Rice, and Piquero, "Lines and Shadows: Perceptions of Racial Profiling and the Hispanic Experience."

83. Michael Mukasy, Jeffrey Sedgwick, and David Hagy, "Policing in Arab-American Communities after September 11," *National Institute of Justice: Research for Practice*, July 2008, NCJ 221706.

84. John Song, "Attitudes of Chinese Immigrants and Vietnamese Refugees toward Law Enforcement in the United States," *Justice Quarterly* 9, no. 4 (December 1992): 703–719.

85. www.ojp.usdoj.gov/nij/topics/crime/elder-abuse/welcome.htm (retrieved January 25, 2009).

86. Etta Morgan, Ida Johnson, and Robert Sigler, "Public Definitions and Endorsement of the Criminalization of Elder Abuse," *Journal of Criminal Justice* 34 (2006): 275–276.

87. National Center on Elder Abuse, *The 2004 Survey of State Adult Protective Services: Abuse of Adults 60 Years and Older* (Washington, DC: NCEA, 2006), 9.

88. California Department of Aging, "Long-Term Care Ombudsman Program," www.aging.ca.gov/Programs/#LTCOP (retrieved June 28, 2015).

89. International Association of Chiefs of Police, *Training Key #518: Elder Victimization* (Alexandria, VA: IACP, 1999), 10–11.

90. Diana Koin, "Issues to Be Addressed at the Scene of an Elder's Death," interview by Michael Hooper, April 15, 2004.

91. International Association of Chiefs of Police, *Training Key #518: Elder Victimization*, 10.

92. American Bar Association Commission on Law and Aging, *The Availability and Utility of Interdisciplinary Data on Elder Abuse: A White Paper for the National Center on Elder Abuse* (Washington, DC: ABACLA, 2005), 44.

93. National Center on Elder Abuse, *The 2004 Survey of State Adult Protective Services*, 15–23.

94. International Association of Chiefs of Police, *Training Key #518: Elder Victimization*, 9.

95. Texas Attorney General, *Protecting Senior Texans*, Texas Office of the Attorney General, August 12, 2006. www.oag.state.tx.us/elder'elder.shtm.

96. Cheryl Guidry Tyiska, "Working with Victims with Disabilities," National Organization for Victim Assistance. www.trynova.org/victiminfo/ovcdisabilities/(retrieved February 16, 2007).

97. Linda Teplin, "Keeping the Peace: Police Discretion and Mentally Ill Persons," *National Institute of Justice Journal*, no. 244 (July 2000): 9–15.

98. Ibid.

99. Ibid.

100. Ibid.

101. Fred E. Markowitz, "Psychiatric Hospital Capacity, Homelessness, and Crime and Arrest Rates," *Criminology* 44, no. 1 (2006): 45–72.

102. Mary Castle White, Linda Chafetz, and Gerri Collins-Bride, "History of Arrest, Incarceration, and Victimization in Community-Based Severely Mentally Ill," *Journal of Community Health* 31, no. 2 (April 2006): 123–135.

103. Amy C. Watson, Victor C. Ottati, Melissa Morabito, Jeffrey Draine, Amy N. Kerr, and Beth Angell, "Outcomes of Police Contact with Persons with Mental Illness: The Impact of CIT," *Administration and Policy in Mental Health and Mental Health Services Research* 37, no. 4 (July 2010): 302–317.

104. U.S. Department of Housing and Urban Development, *The 2014 Annual Homeless Assessment Report to Congress* (October 2014). https://www.hudexchange.info/resources/documents/2014-AHAR-Part1.pdf.

105. Colleen Cosgrove and Anne Grant, "National Survey of Municipal Police Departments on Urban Quality of Life Initiatives," in Tara O'Connor Shelley and Anne Grant (Eds.), *Problem Oriented Policing* (Washington, DC: PERF, 1998).

106. William King and Thomas Dunn, "Dumping: Police-Initiated Transjurisdictional Transport of Troublesome Persons," *Police Quarterly* 7, no. 3 (September 2004): 339–358.

107. Deborah Padgett, Elmer Struening, Howard Andrews, and John Pittman, "Predictors of Emergency Room Use by Homeless Adults in New York City: The Influence of Predisposing, Enabling and Need Factors," *Social Science Medicine* 41, no. 4 (1995): 547–556.

108. Kimberly Tyler and Katherine Johnson, "Trading Sex: Voluntary or Coerced? The Experiences of Homeless Youth," *Journal of Sex Research* 43, no. 3 (August 2006): 208–216.

109. National Alliance to End Homelessness, "Homelessness Counts." www.endhomelessness.org/content/article/detail/1440 (retrieved February 19, 2007).

110. Phillip Taft, "Policing the New Immigrant Ghetto," *Police Magazine* (July 1982).

111. Refugees International, "Hmong Refugees Arrive in the U.S.: The Latest Chapter in a Long Odyssey." www.refintl.org/content/article/detail/3147/ (retrieved February 19, 2007).

112. Taft, "Policing the New Immigrant Ghetto."

113. U.S. Department of Justice, Bureau of Justice Statistics, *2008 Census of State and Local Law Enforcement Agencies* (Washington, DC: DOJ, 2011). www.bjs.gov/index.cfm?ty=dcdetail&iid=249.

114. Timothy O'Shea, "Community Policing in Small Town Rural America: A Comparison of Police Officer Attitudes in Chicago and Baldwin County, Alabama," *Police and Society* 9 (1999): 59–76.

115. Ralph Weishei, L. Edward Wells, and David N. Falcone, "Community Policing in Small Town and Rural America," *Crime & Delinquency* 40, no. 4 (October 1994): 549–567.

116. Jennifer L. Truman and Lynn Langton, "Criminal Victimization, 2013."

CHAPTER 7

1. Eyder Peralta, "Timeline: What We Know about the Freddie Gray Arrest," *NPR*, May 1, 2015. www.npr.org/sections/thetwo-way/2015/05/01/403629104/baltimore-protests-what-we-know-about-the-freddie-gray-arrest (retrieved June 20, 2015).

2. Dennis Lynch, "Baltimore Riots 2015: Freddie Gray Slammed Head into Police Van, Causing Fatal Injury, Report Says," *International Business Times*, April 30, 2015. www.ibtimes.com/baltimore-riots-2015-freddie-gray-slammed-head-police-van-causing-fatal-injury-report-1904371 (retrieved June 20, 2015).

3. Lindsay Wise and Marisa Taylor, "Police Face Criminal Charges in Death of Freddie Gray in Baltimore," *McClatchy DC News*, May 1, 2015. www.mcclatchydc.com/2015/05/01/265230/police-face-criminal-charges-in.html (retrieved June 20, 2015).

4. Meredith Cohn, "Two More Men Allege 'Rough Rides' in Baltimore Police Van," *Baltimore Sun*, May 1, 2015. www.baltimoresun.com/new/maryland/crime/blog/bs-hs-more-rough-rides-20150501-story.html (retrieved June 20, 2015).

5. Lora Moftah, "Freddie Gray Trial: Grand Jury Indicts All 6 Officers Charged in Baltimore Man's Death, State Attorney Mosby Announces," *International Business Times*, May 21, 2015. www.ibtimes.com/freddie-gray-trial-grand-jury-indicts-all-6-officers-charged-baltimore-mans-death-1933933 (retrieved June 20, 2015).

6. Timothy M. Phelps, "Grand Jury Indictments in Freddie Gray Case May Indicate Prosecution Weakness," Associated Press, May 24, 2015.

7. Office of Public Affairs, U.S. Department of Justice, "Justice Department Opens Pattern or Practice Investigation into the Baltimore Police Department," *Justice News*, May 8, 2015. www.justice.gov/opa/pr/justice-department-opens-pattern-or-practice-investigation-baltimore-police-department (retrieved June 21, 2015).

8. See, for example, *United States v. Van Leeuwen*, 397 U.S. 249 (1970); *Katz v. United States*, 389 U.S. 347 (1967); *Stanley v. Georgia*, 394 U.S. 557 (1969); *Bond v. United States*, 529 U.S. 334 (2000).

9. *California v. Greenwood*, 486 U.S. 35 (1988); *Smith v. Maryland*, 442 U.S. 735 (1979); *Florida v. Riley*, 488 U.S. 445 (1989); *United States v. Place*, 462 U.S. 696 (1983).

10. *United States v. Jones, 132 S. Ct. 945 (2012).*

11. In *Hiibel v. Sixth Judicial Dist.*, 542 U.S. 177 (2004), the Court held that a suspect who refuses to identify himself during a *Terry* stop may be arrested and taken to jail.

12. *Carroll v. United States*, 267 U.S. 132 (1925).

13. *California v. Carney*, 471 U.S. 386 (1985).

14. *Riley v. California*, 573 U.S. ___ (2014).

15. Barton Gellman, Dafna Linzer, and Carol D. Leonnig, "Surveillance Net Yields Few Suspects," *Washington Post*, February 5, 2006, p. A1.

16. In late 2005, a federal court permitted these searches in New York City. See *MacWade v. Kelly*, U.S. Dist. LEXIS 39695 (2005).

17. *Weeks v. United States*, 232 U.S. 383, 393 (1914).

18. *Mapp v. Ohio*, 367 U.S. 643 (1961); Crime Library, "Dolly Mapp." www.crimelibrary.com/gangsters_outlaws/cops_others/dolly_mapp/index.html (retrieved July 19, 2006).

19. *Mapp v. Ohio*. Eight years later, in *Stanley v. Georgia*, 394 U.S. 597 (1969), the Supreme Court further held that private possession of obscene materials in the home, such as the materials for which Mapp was prosecuted, is protected by the First Amendment.

20. *Mapp v. Ohio*.

21. See, for example, Craig D. Uchida and Timothy S. Bynum, "Search Warrants, Motions to Suppress, and 'Lost Cases': The Effects of the Exclusionary Rule in Seven Jurisdictions," *Journal of Criminal Law and Criminology* 81 (1991): 1034–1036.

22. *United States v. Leon*, 468 U.S. 897 (1984).

23. *Arizona v. Evans*, 514 U.S. 1 (1995).

24. *Herring v. United States*, 555 U.S. 135 (2009).

25. *Heien v. North Carolina*, 135 S. Ct. 530 (2014).

26. *Brown v. Illinois*, 422 U.S. 590 (1975).

27. *Wilson v. Arkansas*, 514 U.S. 927 (1995).

28. *Hudson v. Michigan*, 547 U.S. 1096 (2006).

29. See, for example, Graham Boyd, "Collateral Damage in the War on Drugs," *Villanova Law Review* 47 (2002): 839–850.

30. *Brown v. Mississippi*, 297 U.S. 278 (1936).

31. *Malloy v. Hogan*, 378 U.S. 1 (1964).

32. *Miranda v. Arizona*, 384 U.S. 486 (1966). Miranda was retried—this time without his confession being brought as evidence—and convicted again. After he was released from prison, he was stabbed to death in a bar fight at the age of 34.

33. Richard A. Leo, "Inside the Interrogation Room," *Journal of Criminal Law and Criminology* 86 (1996): 621–692.

34. *Dickerson v. United States*, 530 U.S. 428 (2000).

35. *Miranda v. Arizona*.

36. *Rhode Island v. Innis*, 446 U.S. 291 (1980).

37. *Berghuis v. Thompkins*, 130 S. Ct. 2250 (2010).

38. *Fare v. Michael C.*, 422 U.S. 707 (1979); Solomon L. Fulero and Caroline Everington, "Assessing the Capacity of Persons with Mental Retardation to Waive *Miranda* Rights: A Jurisprudent Therapy Perspective," *Law & Psychology Review* 28 (2004): 53–69; Thomas Grisso, *Juveniles' Waiver of Rights: Legal and Psychological Competence* (New York: Plenum Press, 1981).

39. Saul M. Kassin and Rebecca J. Norwick. "Why People Waive Their *Miranda* Rights: The Power of Innocence," *Law and Human Behavior* 28 (2004): 211–221.

40. The Innocence Project, "Causes and Remedies of Wrongful Convictions." www.innocenceproject.com/causes/index.php (retrieved August 3, 2006).

41. *Massiah v. United States*, 377 U.S. 201 (1964).

42. *Patterson v. Illinois*, 487 U.S. 285 (1988); *McNeil v. Wisconsin*, 501 U.S. 171 (1991).

43. *Nix v. Williams*, 467 U.S. 432 (1984). Williams was eventually convicted of first-degree murder and sentenced to life in prison.

44. *Kansas v. Ventris*, 200 U.S. 321 (2009).

45. President's Task Force on 21st Century Policing, *Interim Report of the President's Task Force on 21st Century Policing* (Washington, DC: Office of Community Oriented Policing Services, March 2015).

46. Lindsay Miller, Jessica Toliver, and Police Executive Research Forum, *Implementing a Body-Worn Camera Program: Recommendations and Lessons Learned* (Washington, DC: Office of Community Oriented Policing Services, 2014).

47. *Tennessee v. Garner*, 471 U.S. 1 (1985).

48. *Graham v. Connor*, 490 U.S. 386 (1989).

49. *Saucier v. Katz*, 533 U.S. 194, 206 (2001).

50. *Brosseau v. Haugen*, 543 U.S. 194, 199 (2004).

51. National Institute of Justice, "The Use of Force Continuum" (Washington, DC: NIJ, 2009).

52. President's Task Force on 21st Century Policing, *Interim Report of the President's Task Force on 21st Century Policing*, 19.

53. International Association of Chiefs of Police and Office of Community Oriented Policing Services, "Emerging Use of Force Issues: Balancing Public and Officer Safety" (Washington, DC: Office of Community Oriented Policing Services, 2012).

54. Richard M. Hough Sr. and Kimberly M. Tatum, "An Examination of Florida Policies on Force Continuums," *Policing: An International Journal of Police Strategies and Management,* 35, no. 1 (2012): 39–40.

55. Matt Apuzzo, "Police Rethink Long Tradition on Using Force," *New York Times,* May 4, 2015. www.nytimes.com/2015/05/05/us/police-start-to-reconsider-longstanding-rules-on-using-force.html?_r=0.

56. Bureau of Justice Statistics, U.S. Department of Justice, *Contacts between Police and the Public, 2008* (Washington, DC: DOJ, 2011).

57. Tuncay Durna, "Situational Determinants of Police Use of Force: Who the Suspect Is vs. What the Suspect Does," *International Police Executive Symposium, Working Paper No. 34* (Geneva, Switzerland: Geneva Center for the Democratic Control of the Armed Forces, 2011): 20.

58. Anthony J. Pinizzotto, Edward F. Davis, Shannon B. Bohrer, and Benjamin J. Infanti, "Law Enforcement Restraint in the Use of Deadly Force within the Context of the 'Deadly Mix,'" *International Journal of Police Science and Management* 14, no. 4 (December 2012).

59. Geoffrey P. Alpert, Dennis Jay Kenney, Roger G. Dunham, and William Smith, *Police Pursuits: What We Know* (Washington, DC: Police Executive Research Forum, 2000).

60. Chris Pipes and Dominick Pape, "Police Pursuits and Civil Liability," *FBI Law Enforcement Bulletin* 70, no. 7 (2001): 16–21.

61. *Scott v. Harris,* 550 U.S. 372 (2007).

62. Andrew Cooley and Brook Gavery, "Police Pursuits and High-Speed Driving Lawsuits," *Police Chief,* 73, no. 10 (October 2006). www.policechiefmagazine.org/magazine/index.cfm?fuseaction=display_arch&article_id=1018&issue_id=102006 (retrieved July 2015).

63. Substance Abuse and Mental Health Services Administration, *Behavioral Health Barometer: United States, 2014.* HHS Publication No. SMA-15-4895. (Rockville, MD: Substance Abuse and Mental Health Services Administration, 2015).

64. Jerome Cartier, David Farabee, and Michael Prendergast, "Methamphetamine Use, Self-Reported Crime, and Recidivism among Offenders in California Who Abuse Substances," *Journal of Interpersonal Violence* 21, no. 4 (2006): 435–445.

65. Governor's Office of Criminal Justice Planning, "Multi-Agency Partnerships: Linking Drugs with Child Endangerment" (Sacramento: Governor's Office of Criminal Justice Planning, n.d.), 9.

66. Michael Scott and Kelly Dedel, "Clandestine Methamphetamine Labs, 2nd Edition," *Problem Oriented Guides for Police Series,* no. 16. (Washington, DC: U.S. Department of Justice, Community Oriented Policing Services). www.cops.usdog.gov (retrieved March 28, 2007).

67. *National Drug Control Strategy: FY 2015 Budget and Performance Survey* (Washington, DC: Office of National Drug Control Policy, July 2014). www.whitehouse.gov/sites/default/files/ondcp/about-content/fy2015_summary.pdf.

68. Peter Reuter and Mark Kleiman, "Risks and Prices: An Economic Analysis of Drug Enforcement," in Michael Tonry and Norval Morris (Eds.), *Crime and Justice* (Chicago: University of Chicago Press, 1986), 289–340; Brian Lawton, Ralph Taylor, and Anthony Luongo, "Police Officers on Drug Corners in Philadelphia, Drug Crime, and Violent Crime: Intended, Diffusion, and Displacement Impacts," *JQ: Justice Quarterly* 22, no. 4 (December 2005): 427–451.

69. John Eck and Edward Maguire, "Have Changes in Policing Reduced Violent Crime?" in Alfred Blumstein and Joel Wallman (Eds.), *The Crime Drop in America* (Cambridge, UK: Cambridge Press, 2000); U.S. Department of Health, "2005 National Survey on Drug Use and Health" (Washington, DC: Government Printing Office, 2006). www.samhsa.gov; Substance Abuse and Mental Health Services Administration, *Behavioral Health Barometer: United States, 2014.*

70. U.S. Department of Health, "2005 National Survey on Drug Use and Health."

71. The Sentencing Project, "Drug Policy and the Criminal Justice System 2001" (Washington, DC: The Sentencing Project, 2001). www.sentencingproject.org/PublicationDetails.aspx?PublicationID=323 (retrieved March 30, 2007).

72. Donald Lynam and Richard Milich, "Project DARE: No Effects at 10-Year Follow-up," *Journal of Consulting and Clinical Psychology* 67, no. 4 (1999): 590–593.

73. Robert J. Bursik Jr. and Harold G. Grasmick, "Defining and Researching Gangs," in Arlen Egley Jr. et al. (Eds.), *The Modern Gang Reader* (Los Angeles: Roxbury, 2006), 10.

74. Malcolm W. Klein, *Street Gangs and Street Workers* (Englewood Cliffs, NJ: Prentice Hall, 1971), 13.

75. Arlen Egley Jr. and James C. Howell, "Highlights of the 2011 National Youth Gang Survey" (Washington, DC: Office of Juvenile Justice and Delinquency Prevention, September 2013). www.ojjdp.gov/pubs/242884.pdf.

76. National Institute of Justice, *Youth Gangs in Rural America* (Washington, DC: NIJ, 2004), 2.

77. Office of Juvenile Justice and Delinquency Prevention, *Gangs in Small Towns and Rural Counties* (Washington, DC: OJJDP, 2005), 1–2.

78. Institute for Intergovernmental Research, "National Youth Gang Survey Analysis," National Youth Gang Center. www.iir.com/nygc/nygsa/ (retrieved February 23, 2007).

79. U.S. Department of Justice, Bureau of Justice Assistance, *2005 National Gang Threat Assessment* (Washington, DC: DOJ, 2006), 1.

80. Ibid., 2.

81. Ibid., 3.

82. Anthony Braga and David Kennedy, "Reducing Gang Violence in Boston," in Winifred Reed and Scott Decker (Eds.), *Responding to Gangs: Evaluation and Research* (Washington, DC: National Institute of Justice, July 2002). www.ojp.usdoj.gov/nij/pubs-sum/190351.htm.

83. "Juvenile Curfews and Gang Violence: Exiled on Main Street," *Harvard Law Review* 107, no. 7 (May 1994): 1693–1710.

84. National Gang Center, "National Youth Gang Survey Analysis." www.nationalgangcenter.gov/Survey-Analysis.

85. Noelle E. Fearn, Scott H. Decker, and G. David Curry, "Public Policy Responses to Gangs: Evaluating the Outcomes," in *The Modern Gang Reader,* 323.

86. Beth Bjerregaard, "Antigang Legislation and Its Potential Impact: The Promises and the Pitfalls," in *The Modern Gang Reader,* 385.

87. Callie Marie Rennison, "Intimate Partner Violence, 1993–2001," *Bureau of Justice Statistics Crime Data Brief* (Washington, DC: U.S. Department of Justice, Bureau of Justice Statistics, February 2003).

88. Eve S. Buzawa and Carol G. Buzawa, *Domestic Violence: The Criminal Justice Response* (Thousand Oaks, CA: Sage, 1996).

89. Ibid.

90. Lawrence Sherman and Richard Berk, "The Specific Deterrent Effect of Arrest for Domestic Assault," *American Sociological Review* 49, no. 2 (1984): 261–272.

91. Federal Bureau of Investigation, "Law Enforcement Officers Killed and Assaulted, 2005," Uniform Crime Reports. www.fbi.gov/ucr/killed/2005/ (retrieved March 28, 2007).

92. Rennison, "Intimate Partner Violence, 1993–2001"; Russell P. Dobash, R. Emerson Dobash, Margo Wilson, and Martin Daly, "The Myth of Sexual Symmetry in Marital Violence," *Social Problems* 39, no. 1 (1992): 71–91.

93. Violence Against Women and Department of Justice Reauthorization Act of 2005 (H.R. 3402). www.ncadv.org/ publicpolicy/VAWA_2005_179.html (retrieved February 26, 2007).

94. www.ncadv.org/publicpolicy/VAWA_2005_179.html.

95. Violence Against Women Reauthorization Act of 2013 (S. 47).

96. Pamela Collins and A. C. Gibbs, "Stress in Police Officers: A Study of the Origins, Prevalence and Severity of Stress-Related Symptoms within a County Police Force," *Occupational Medicine* 53, no. 4 (2003): 256–264.

97. Jerome McElroy, Colleen Cosgrove, and Susan Sadd, *Community Policing: The CPOP in New York* (Newbury Park, CA: Sage, 1993).

98. William C. O'Toole, *Recommendations to Facilitate Military Deployment and Re-Entry* (Gainesville, VA: Commission on Accreditation for Law Enforcement Agencies, 2010).

99. Collins and Gibbs, "Stress in Police Officers."

100. Merry Morash, Robin Haarr, and Dae-Hoon Kwak, "Multilevel Influences on Police Stress," *Journal of Contemporary Criminal Justice* 22, no. 1 (February 2006): 26–43.

101. Erik Meers, "Good Cop, Gay Cop," *The Advocate,* March 3, 1998, 26–34.

102. Stephen Leinen, *Gay Cops* (New Brunswick, NJ: Rutgers University Press, 1993); J. Violanti and F. Aron, "Ranking Police Stressors," *Psychological Reports* 75 (1994): 824–826.

103. Robin Shepard Engel, "Explaining Suspects' Resistance and Disrespect toward Police," *Journal*

of Criminal Justice 31, no. 5 (September–October 2003): 475–492.

104. Jeremy Davey, Patricia Obst, and Mary Sheehan, "It Goes with the Job: Officers' Insights into the Impact of Stress and Culture on Alcohol Consumption within the Policing Occupation," *Drugs: Education, Prevention & Policy* 8, no. 2 (May 2001): 141–149.

105. Judith A. Waters and William Ussery, "Police Stress: History, Contributing Factors, Symptoms, and Interventions," *Policing: An International Journal of Police Strategies & Management* 30 (2007): 176.

106. Ibid., 184.

107. Ibid., 180.

108. Mark Chapin, Stephen Brannen, Mark Singer, and Michael Walker, "Training and Police Leadership to Recognize and Address Operation Stress," *Police Quarterly* 11, no. 3 (September 2008): 338–352.

CHAPTER 8

1. Patrice Clarke, "Man Pleads Guilty to Jackson Co. Capital Murder, Arson," *WLOX*, January 6, 2011. www.wlox.com/Global/story.asp?S=13795121 (retrieved January 7, 2011); Cherie Ward, "Jury Finds Eddie Pugh Guilty of Capital Murder and Sentences Him to Life without Parole," *Gulflive.com*, October 22, 2010. http://blog.gulflive.com/mississippipressnews/2010/10/jury_finds_eddie_pugh_guilty_o_1.html (retrieved January 7, 2011).

2. Mark Motivans, "Federal Justice Statistics, 2012—Statistical Tables," Bureau of Justice Statistics, January 2015, NCJ 248470. www.bjs.gov/content/pub/pdf/fjs12st.pdf (retrieved June 13, 2015).

3. *Hamdan v. Rumsfeld*, 126 S. Ct. 2749 (2006).

4. Carson Fox and West Huddleston, "Drug Courts in the U.S." http://usinfo.state.gov/journals/itdhr/0503/ijde/fox.htm (retrieved April 12, 2007); National Drug Court Institute, "Drug Courts: A National Phenomenon." www.ndci.org/courtfacts.htm (retrieved April 12, 2007).

5. Shelli B. Rossman, John K. Roman, Janine M. Zweig, Michael Rempel, and Christine H. Lindquist, *The Multi-Site Adult Drug Court Evaluation: Executive Summary* (Washington, DC: Urban Institute Justice Police Center, June 2011), 1–9.

6. Valerie Bryan, Matthew Hiller, and Carle Leukefeld, "A Qualitative Examination of the Juvenile Drug Court Treatment Process," *Journal of Social Work Practice in the Addictions* 6, no. 4 (2006): 91–114; J. Scott Sanford and Bruce Arrigo, "Lifting the Cover on Drug Courts: Evaluation Findings and Policy Concerns," *International Journal of Offender Therapy and Comparative Criminology* 49, no. 3 (2005): 239–259; Nancy Rodriguez and Vincent Webb, "Multiple Measures of Juvenile Drug Court Effectiveness: Results of a Quasi-Experimental Design," *Crime and Delinquency* 50, no. 3 (2004): 292–314.

7. Jeremy Travis, *But They All Come Back: Rethinking Prisoner Reentry, Research in Brief—Sentencing and Corrections: Issues for the 21st Century* (Washington, DC: National Institute of Justice, 2000); *Reentry Courts: Managing the Transition from Prison to Community, A Call for Concept Papers* (Washington, DC: U.S. Department of Justice, 1999).

8. Dale G. Parent, *Day Reporting Centers for Criminal Offenders: A Descriptive Analysis of Existing Programs* (Washington, DC: National Institute of Justice, 1990); *Reentry Courts: Managing the Transition from Prison to Community, A Call for Concept Papers;* see also Shadd Maruna and Thomas P. LaBel, "Welcome Home? Examining the 'Reentry Court' Concept from a Strengths-Based Perspective," *Western Criminology Review* 4, no. 2 (2003): 91–107.

9. Jeffrey A. Butts and Janeen Butts, "Teen Courts: A Focus on Research," *OJJDP Bulletin*, October 2000. www.ncjrs.gov/pdffiles1/ojjdp/183472.pdf (retrieved November 25, 2007).

10. *Sykes v. United States*, 598 F. 3d 334 (7th Cir. 2010).

11. *Caperton v. A. T. Massey Coal Co.*, 129 S. Ct. 2252 (2009).

12. A. G. Sulzberger, "Ouster of Iowa Judges Sends Signal to Bench," *New York Times*, November 3, 2010. www.nytimes.com/2010/11/04/us/politics/04judges.html (retrieved January 7, 2011).

13. American Bar Association, "National Database on Judicial Diversity in State Courts." www.abanet.org/judind/diversity/national.html (retrieved August 25, 2006); Pat K. Chew and Robert E. Kelley, "Myth of the Color-Blind Judge: An Empirical Analysis of Racial Harassment Cases," *Washington University Law Review*, 2009. http://ssrn.com/abstract=1273235 (retrieved February 15, 2009).

14. American Bar Association, "A Current Glance at Women in the Law." www.abanet.org/women/CurrentGlanceStatistics2006.pdf (retrieved August 25, 2006).

15. Benjamin Wittes, "Judges and Politics," *Weekly Standard*, October 6, 2003. www.weeklystandard.com/Content/Public/Articles/000/000/003/173wfhlw.asp?pg=1 (retrieved February 26, 2007).

16. A. Goldstein and C. Babington, "Roberts Avoids Specifics on Abortion Issue," *Washington Post*, September 14, 2005, p. A01.

17. S. Goldman, "Judicial Confirmation Wars: Ideology and the Battle for the Federal Courts," *University of Richmond Law Review* 39, no. 3 (2005): 873; J. A. Segal and H. J. Spaeth, *The Supreme Court and the Attitudinal Model Revisited* (Cambridge, UK: Cambridge University Press, 2002).

18. Mark Kozlowski, "What Judges Do: The Founders Saw That Laws Are Often Murky, So Judicial Beliefs Matter," *New Jersey Law Journal* 167 (February 18, 2002): 20.

19. *Clark v. United States*, 289 U.S. 1 (1933).

20. Jennifer Vogel, "In Defense of Public Defenders," *Bench & Bar of Minnesota*, April 13, 2015. www.mnbenchbar.com/2015/04/in-defense-of-public-defenders/ (retrieved June 13, 2015).

21. U.S. Department of Justice, *Defense Counsel in Criminal Cases* (Washington, DC: DOJ, 2000).

22. Ibid.

23. T. W. Church, "Examining Local Legal Culture," *American Bar Foundation Research Journal* (Summer 1985): 449.

24. Ken Millstone, "Jury Duty Cat," *CBS News*, January 19, 2011. www.cbsnews.com/stories/2011/01/19/national/main7261530.shtml (retrieved January 20, 2011).

25. Mary R. Rose, "The Peremptory Challenge Accused of Race or Gender Discrimination? Some Data from One County," *Law and Human Behavior* 23 (1999): 695–702; David Baldus, "Use of Peremptory Challenges in Capital Murder Trials: A Legal and Empirical Analysis," *University of Pennsylvania Journal of Constitutional Law* 3 (2001): 3.

26. Richard Seltzer, "Scientific Jury Selection: Does It Work?" *Journal of Applied Social Psychology* 36 (2006): 2417–2435.

27. Samuel Sommers, "Race and the Decision Making of Juries," *Legal & Criminological Psychology* 12 (2007): 171–187.

28. Gary Wells, Amina Memon, and Steven Penrod, "Eyewitness Evidence: Improving Its Probative Value," *Psychological Science in the Public Interest* 7 (2006): 45–75.

29. The Innocence Project, "Study of Year-Long Pilot Project Shows That Key Eyewitness Identification Reforms Are Effective." www.innocenceproject.org/press/index.php (retrieved August 29, 2006).

30. Wells, Memon, and Penrod, "Eyewitness Evidence."

31. *In re Imbler*, 60 Cal. 2d 554 (1963).

CHAPTER 9

1. Jessica Trufant, "Former Braintree Man to Be Tried 3rd Time for 1981 Murder," *Patriot Ledger*, June 1, 2015. www.patriotledger.com/article/20150601/NEWS/150609808 (retrieved June 8, 2015).

2. Daniel Libon, "After 34 Years, Bloody Jacket Revives Braintree Murder Case," *Braintree Patch*, June 2, 2015. www.patch.com/massachusetts/braintree/after-over-34-years-bloody-jacket-could-solve-murder-0 (retrieved June 8, 2015).

3. Court Statistics Project, *State Court Caseload Statistics, 2004* (Williamsburg, VA: National Center for State Courts, 2005).

4. Superior Court of California, County of Los Angeles, *2009 Felony Bail Schedule*. www.lasuperiorcourt.org/bail/pdf/felony.pdf (retrieved February 20, 2009).

5. *Powell v. Alabama*, 387 U.S. 45 (1932); Douglas O. Linder, "The Trials of the Scottsboro Boys." www.law.umkc.edu/faculty/projects/FTrials/scottsboro/SB_acct.html (retrieved July 8, 2006).

6. *Gideon v. Wainwright*, 372 U.S. 335 (1963).

7. Ibid., 344.

8. *Argersinger v. Hamlin*, 407 U.S. 25 (1972); *Ross v. Moffitt*, 417 U.S. 600 (1974); *McFarland v. Scott*, 512 U.S. 849 (1994).

9. Thomas H. Cohen and Brian A. Reaves, "Felony Defendants in Large Urban Counties, 2002" (Washington, DC: U.S. Department of Justice, Bureau of Justice Statistics, February 2006). http://bjs.ojp.usdoj.gov/content/pub/pdf/fdluc02.pdf (retrieved July 24, 2011).

10. *Duncan v. Louisiana*, 391 U.S. 145 (1968).

11. Dennis J. Devine, Laura D. Clayton, Benjamin B. Dunford, Rasmy Seying, and Jennifer Pryce, "Jury Decision Making: 45 Years of Empirical Research on Deliberating Groups," *Psychology, Public Policy, and Law* 7 (2001): 622–727.

12. *Bullcoming v. New Mexico*, 564 U.S. ___ (2011).

13. *Maryland v. Craig*, 497 U.S. 836 (1990).

14. *Benton v. Maryland*, 395 U.S. 784 (1969).

15. *Green v. United States*, 355 U.S. 184, 187–88 (1957).

16. *Evans v. Michigan*, 133 S. Ct. 1069 (2013).

17. *United States v. Felix*, 503 U.S. 378 (1992).

18. Malcolm Feeley, *The Process Is the Punishment: Handling Cases in a Lower Criminal Court* (New York: Russell Sage Foundation, 1979).

19. Niki Kuckes, "The Useful, Dangerous Fiction of Grand Jury Independence," *American Criminal Law Review* 41 (2004): 1–66. New York's chief judge once stated that a grand jury would indict a ham sandwich. *Grand Jury Subpoena of Stewart*, 545 N.Y.S.2d 974, 977 (N.Y. App. Div. 1989).

20. *Brady v. Maryland*, 373 U.S. 83 (1963).

21. Karen Garcia, "Eacker Granted New Trial," *Peninsula-Clarion*, February 13, 2011. www.peninsulaclarion.com/stories/021311/new_785170403.shtml (retrieved February 17, 2011).

22. Thomas H. Cohen and Tracey Kyckelhahn, "Felony Defendants in Large Urban Counties, 2006," *Bureau of Justice Statistics Bulletin* (Washington, DC: U.S. Department of Justice, May 2010).

23. Mary E. Vogel, "The Social Origins of Plea Bargaining," *Journal of Law & Society* 35 (June 2008): 201–232.

24. Cohen and Reaves, "Felony Defendants in Large Urban Counties, 2002."

25. Charles Whitebread and Christopher Slobogin. *Criminal Procedure: An Analysis of Cases and Concepts,* 5th ed. (Westbury, NY: Foundation Press, 2008).

26. Brian A. Reaves, "Violent Felons in Large Urban Counties" (Washington, DC: U.S. Department of Justice, Bureau of Justice Statistics, April 6, 2006).

27. T. W. Church, "Examining Local Legal Culture," *American Bar Foundation Research Journal* (Summer 1985): 449.

28. Thomas Pyszczynski and Lawrence Wrightsman, "The Effects of Opening Statements on Mock Jurors' Verdicts in a Simulated Criminal Trial," *Journal of Applied Social Psychology* 11 (1981): 301–313.

29. *Gregg v. Georgia*, 428 U.S. 153 (1976).

CHAPTER 10

1. Adam Liptak, "Finding 11-Day Sentence Not Too Little but Too Late," *New York Times*, February 12, 2009, p. A12.

2. Ibid.

3. Ibid.

4. Brendan Kirby, "Federal Judge Sets Mississippi Man Free," *Alabama Press Register*, February 28, 2009.

5. *Trop v. Dulles*, 356 U.S. 86, 101 (1958).

6. Ibid.

7. *Penry v. Johnson*, 532 U.S. 782 (2001).

8. *Kennedy v. Louisiana*, 128 S. Ct. 2641 (2008).

9. *Robinson v. California*, 370 U.S. 660 (1962).

10. *Graham v. Florida*, 130 S. Ct. 2011 (2010).

11. *Miller v. Alabama*, 132 S. Ct. 2455 (2012).

12. *Holland v. Florida*, 130 S. Ct. 2549 (2010).

13. Lisa M. Seghetti and Nathan James, "Federal Habeas Corpus Relief: Background, Legislation, and Issues," *Congressional Research Service*, 2006.

http://assets.opencrs.com/rpts/RL33259_20060201.pdf (retrieved February 15, 2009).

14. "The Presentence Investigation Report" (Office of Probation and Pretrial Services, Administrative Office of the United States Courts, revised March 2006), Publication 107.

15. Timothy O'Shea, "Getting the Deterrence Message Out: The Project Safe Neighborhoods Public–Private Partnership," *Police Quarterly* 10 (September 2007): 288–307.

16. Paul Brennan and Cassia Spohn, "Race/Ethnicity and Sentencing Outcomes among Drug Offenders in North Carolina," *Journal of Contemporary Criminal Justice* 24, no. 4 (November 2008): 371–393.

17. Brenda Sims Blackwell, David Holleran, and Mary A. Finn, "The Impact of the Pennsylvania Sentencing Guidelines on Sex Difference in Sentencing," *Journal of Contemporary Criminal Justice* 24, no. 4 (November 2008): 399–418.

18. John Scalia, "The Impact of Changes in Federal Law and Policy on the Sentencing of, and Time Served in Prison by, Drug Defendants Convicted in U.S. District Courts," *Federal Sentencing Reporter* 14, nos. 3–4 (November/December 2001, January/February 2002): 52–158.

19. "An Overview of the United States Sentencing Commission." www.ussc.gov/About_the_Commission/Overview_of_the_USSC/USSC_Overview.pdf (retrieved April 14, 2011).

20. *United States v. Booker*, 543 U.S. 220 (2005).

21. Margaret E. Leigey and Ronet Bachman, "The Influence of Crack Cocaine on the Likelihood of Incarceration for a Violent Offense: An Examination of a Prison Sample," *Criminal Justice Policy Review* 18 (December 2007): 335–352.

22. U.S. Sentencing Commission, *Amendments to the Sentencing Guidelines*, May 11, 2007. www.ussc.gov/ (retrieved December 12, 2007).

23. David Stout, "Retroactively, Panel Reduces Drug Sentence," *New York Times*, December 12, 2007.

24. U.S. Sentencing Commission, "Crack Cocaine Impact Analysis," January 28, 2011. www.ussc.gov/Research/Retroactivity_Analyses/Fair_Sentencing_Act/20110128_Crack_Retroactivity_Analysis.pdf (retrieved April 14, 2011).

25. *United States v. Booker*, 543 U.S. 220 (2005); *Kimbrough v. United States*, 06-6330 (2007); *Gall v. United States*, 06-7949 (2007).

26. Paul H. Robinson, "Crime, Punishment, and Prevention," *Public Interest* (Winter 2001). www.nationalaffairs.com/public_interest/detail/crime-punishment-and-prevention (retrieved July 26, 2011).

27. Elsa Chen, "Impacts of 'Three Strikes and You're Out' on Crime Trends in California and throughout the United States," *Journal of Contemporary Criminal Justice* 24 (November 2008): 345–372.

28. Matthew Crow and Katherine Johnson, "Race, Ethnicity, and Habitual-Offender Sentencing: A Multilevel Analysis of Individual and Contextual Threat," *Criminal Justice Policy Review* 19 (March 2008): 63–83.

29. Justine M. Nagurney, "Acts of Fear: An Analysis of the Constitutionality of the Civil Confinement of Sexually Violent Predators," *Dartmouth College Undergraduate Journal of Law* 3, no. 2 (Spring 2005): 29–34.

30. Nathan James, Kenneth R. Thomas, and Cassandra Foley, *Civil Commitment of Sexually Dangerous Persons* (New York: Novinka Books, 2008).

31. Washington State Psychiatric Association amicus curiae brief filed *In the Matter of the Personal Restraint of Andre Brigham Young v. David Weston, Superintendent of the Special Commitment Center* 122 Wn.2d 1, P.2d 989 at 10. The argument put forward by amicus asserted the common belief that, especially involuntarily, violent sex offenders cannot be successfully treated.

32. Peter W. Greenwood, C. Peter Rydell, Allan F. Abrahamse, Jonathan P. Caulkins, James R. Chiesa, Karyn E. Model, and Stephen P. Klein, "Estimated Benefits and Costs of California's New Mandatory-Sentencing Law," in David Shichor and Dale K. Sechrest (Eds.), *Three Strikes You're Out: Vengeance as Public Policy* (Thousand Oaks, CA: Sage, 1994), 53–90.

33. Peter W. Greenwood and Angela Hawken, "An Assessment of the Effects of California's Three Strikes Law," Working Paper (Greenwood & Associates, March 2002).

34. Special circumstances are, essentially, particular aggravating circumstances that, when present, limit the possible outcome of the penalty phase of a capital case to either life in prison without the possibility of parole or death. For an example of special circumstances in Texas, see http://tarltonguides.law.utexas.edu/texas-death-penalty (retrieved July 26, 2011).

35. James S. Liebman, Jeffrey Fagan, and Valerie West, "A Broken System: Error Rates in Capital Cases: 1973–1995," Columbia Law School, June 12, 2000.

36. Technically, capital punishment is also a possibility for a few crimes other than murder, including treason and some rapes. In practice, however, virtually everyone sentenced to death has been convicted of murder.

37. John Blume, Theodore Eisenberg, and Martin T. Wells, "Explaining Death Row's Population and Racial Composition," *Journal of Empirical Legal Studies* 1, no. 1 (March 2004): 165–207. These authors found a national death sentence rate of 2.2 percent of murders resulted in a death sentence. Viewed state by state, the national average death sentence rate from 1977 to 1999 was 2.5 percent, with a median of 2.0 percent. See also James R. Acker and David R. Karp (Eds.), "Introduction" in *Wounds That Do Not Bind: Victim-Based Perspectives on the Death Penalty* (Durham: Carolina Academic Press, 2006), 4.

38. David McCord, "If Capital Punishment Were Subject to Consumer Protection Laws," *Judicature* 89, no. 5 (March–April 2006): 304–305.

39. Death Penalty Information Center, "2014 Execution List." www.deathpenaltyinfo.org/execution-list-2014 (retrieved June 29, 2015).

40. Federal Bureau of Investigation, "Crime in the United States, Expanded Homicide Data, 2012" (Washington, DC: U.S. Department of Justice, 2012). www.fbi.gov/about-us/cjis/ucr/crime-in-the-u.s/2012/crime-in-the-u.s.-2012/offenses-known-to-law-enforcement/expanded-homicide/expandhomicidemain (retrieved June 29, 2015).

41. Craig Haney, *Death by Design: Capital Punishment as a Social Psychological System* (New York: Oxford University Press, 2005).

42. Death Penalty Information Center, "2014 Execution List."

43. Death Row Population Figures from NAACP Legal Defense and Educational Fund, Inc. "Death Row USA" (January 1, 2016).

44. According to researchers at Columbia Law School, each year since 1984 (when executions resumed in earnest after the 1972 *Furman v. Georgia* decision) the number of inmates executed compared to the number of inmates on death row has averaged 1.3 percent; it has never exceeded 2.6 percent of inmates on death row. This and related information is detailed in Liebman, Fagan, and West, "A Broken System: Error Rates in Capital Cases: 1973–1995."

45. *Kennedy v. Louisiana*, 554 U.S. 407 (2008).

46. *Furman v. Georgia*, 408 U.S. 238 (1972).

47. David Baldus, George Woodworth, and Charles Pulaski, *Equal Justice and the Death Penalty: A Legal and Empirical Analysis* (Boston: Northeastern University Press, 1990).

48. *Atkins v. Virginia*, 536 U.S. 304 (2002).

49. Death Penalty Information Center, "Methods of Execution," 2015. www.deathpenaltyinfo.org/methods-execution (retrieved June 29, 2015).

50. *Gloss v. Gross*, 135 S. Ct. 2726 (2015).

51. Jeffrey Kirchmeier, "Casting a Wider Net: Another Decade of Legislative Expansion of the Death Penalty in the United States," *Pepperdine Law Review* 34 (2006).

52. Death Penalty Information Center, "The Death Penalty in 2014: Year End Report" (December 2014). www.deathpenaltyinfo.org/documents/2014YrEnd.pdf (retrieved June 30, 2015).

53. Tracy L. Snell, "Capital Punishment, 2013—Statistical Tables" (Washington, DC: U.S. Department of Justice, Bureau of Justice Statistics, December 2014), Figure 2, p. 2. www.bjs.gov/content/pub/pdf/cp13st.pdf (retrieved July 1, 2015).

54. Pew Research Center, "Shrinking Majority of Americans Support Death Penalty," March 2014. www.pewforum.org/2014/03/28/shrinking-majority-of-americans-support-death-penalty/ (retrieved July 2, 2015).

55. ABC News/Washington Post Poll, "New Low in Preference for the Death Penalty." www.langerresearch.com (retrieved July 1, 2015).

56. Death Penalty Information Center, "Death Row Populations by Race" (June 2015). www.deathpenaltyinfo.org/race-death-row-inmates-executed-1976#inmaterace (retrieved July 1, 2015).

57. Samuel Walker, Cassia Spohn, and Miriam DeLone, *The Color of Justice*, 3rd ed. (Belmont, CA: Wadsworth, 2004).

58. Death Penalty Information Center, "The Innocence List." www.deathpenaltyinfo.org/innocence-list-those-freed-death-row (retrieved July 2, 2015).

59. Death Penalty Information Center, "Nationwide Murder Rates: 1996–2013." www.deathpenaltyinfo.org/murder-rates-nationally-and-state#MRreg (retrieved July 3, 2015).

60. Death Penalty Information Center, "Parade Magazine: The Cost of Capital Punishment." www.deathpenaltyinfo.org/parade-magazine-cost-capital-punishment (retrieved February 25, 2011).

CHAPTER 11

1. Mark Lewis and Sarah Lyall, "Norway Mass Killer Gets the Maximum: 21 Years," *New York Times Europe*, August 24, 2012. www.nytimes.com/2012/08/25/world/europe/anders-behring-breivik-murder-trial.html?pagewanted=all (retrieved January 16, 2013).

2. "Anders Behring Breivik," *New York Times Topics*, January 16, 2013, http://topics.nytimes.com/top/reference/timestopics/people/b/anders_behring_breivik/index.html (retrieved January 16, 2013).

3. Patrick Jackson, "Anders Behring Breivik's Prison: Ila Near Oslo," *BBC News*, August 24, 2012. www.bbc.co.uk/news/world-europe-19354906 (retrieved January 16, 2013).

4. Marie Gottschalk, *The Prison and the Gallows: The Politics of Mass Incarceration in America* (New York: Cambridge University Press, 2006).

5. George Bernard Shaw, *The Crime of Imprisonment* (New York: Philosophical Library, 1946), 13; Lester Pincu and Ruth Masters, "Can Punishment and Rehabilitation Coexist? The Failure of U.S. Correctional Philosophy," *Official Proceedings of the International Social Science Conference at KonKuk University, Seoul Korea* (May 2000).

6. Frank McLynn, *Crime and Punishment in Eighteenth-Century England* (New York: Routledge, 1989).

7. Bradley R. E. Wright, Avshalom Caspi, Terrie E. Moffitt, and Ray Patenoster, "Does the Perceived Risk of Punishment Deter Criminally Prone Individuals? Rational Choice, Self-Control, and Crime," *Journal of Research in Crime and Delinquency* 41, no. 2 (May 2004): 180–213.

8. David A. Anderson, "The Deterrence Hypothesis and Picking Pockets at the Pickpocket's Hanging," *American Law and Economics Review* 4, no. 2 (2002): 295–313.

9. Jeffery Fagan, Aaron Kupchick, and Akiva Liberman, *Be Careful What You Wish For: The Comparative Impacts of Juvenile versus Criminal Court Sanctions on Recidivism among Adolescent Felony Offenders* (New York: Columbia University, 2003); Jeffrey Fagan and Martin Guggenheim, "Preventive Detention and the Judicial Prediction of Dangerousness for Juveniles: A Natural Experiment," *Journal of Criminal Law and Criminology* 80 (1996): 415–448; Jeffrey Fagan, "The Comparative Advantage of Juvenile versus Criminal Court Sanctions on Recidivism among Adolescent Felony Offenders," *Law and Policy* 18 (1996): 77–115; Valerie Wright, "Deterrence in Criminal Justice: Evaluating Certainty vs. Severity of Punishment," Sentencing Project, November 2010. www.sentencingproject.org/doc/deterrence%20briefing%20pdf (retrieved April 20, 2015).

10. House of Commons Standing Committee on Justice, Human Rights, Public Safety and Emergency Preparedness, *Bill C-10* (Toronto, Canada: John Howard Society of Canada, 2006), 4; Paula Smith, Clare Goggin, and Paul Gendreau, *The Effects of Prison Sentences and Intermediate Sanctions on Recidivism: General Effects and Individual Differences* (Saint John, New Brunswick, Canada: Department of Psychology and Centre for Criminal Justice Studies, University of New Brunswick, Public Works and Government Services Canada, 2002).

11. House of Commons Standing Committee on Justice, Human Rights, Public Safety and Emergency Preparedness, *Bill C-10*, 5.

12. This followed a comparative study of 200 adolescents in New Jersey and New York.

13. Fagan, Kupchick, and Liberman, *Be Careful What You Wish For*; Fagan and Guggenheim, "Preventive Detention and the Judicial Prediction of Dangerousness for Juveniles"; Fagan, "The Comparative Advantage of Juvenile versus Criminal Court Sanctions on Recidivism among Adolescent Felony Offenders."

14. Kevin. M. Carlsmith, "The Roles of Retribution and Utility in Determining Punishment," *Journal of Experimental Social Psychology* 42, no. 4 (2006): 437–451.

15. Robert Johnson, *Hard Time: Understanding and Reforming the Prison*, 2nd ed. (Belmont, CA: Wadsworth, 1996).

16. Ibid.

17. George Ives, *A History of Penal Methods* (Montclair, NJ: Patterson Smith, 1970).

18. Thorsten Sellin, *Pioneers in Penology: The Amsterdam Houses of Correction in the 16th and 17th Centuries* (Philadelphia: University of Pennsylvania Press, 1944).

19. "The Victorian Poor Law and Life in the Workhouse," *The Victorian Web*. www.victorianweb.org/history/poorlaw/poorlawov.html (retrieved July 24, 2011).

20. James G. Houston, *Correctional Management*, 2nd ed. (Chicago: Nelson-Hall, 1999).

21. William Parker, *Parole: Origins, Development, Current Practices and Statutes* (College Park, MD: American Correctional Association, 1975).

22. Howard League for Penal Reform, "History of the Prison System." www.howardleague.org/history-of-prison-system (retrieved July 24, 2011).

23. Thorsten Sellin, *Slavery and the Penal System* (New York: Elsevier, 1976).

24. Todd R. Clear and George F. Cole, *American Corrections*, 3rd ed. (Belmont, CA: Wadsworth, 1994).

25. Stephen A. Toth, *Beyond Papillon: The French Overseas Penal Colonies, 1854–1952* (Lincoln: University of Nebraska Press, 2006).

26. John Vincent Barry, "Alexander Maconochie," in Hermann Mannheim (Ed.), *Pioneers in Criminology*, 2nd ed. (Montclair, NJ: Patterson Smith, 1973), 94.

27. Ibid., 101–102.

28. Charles F. Campbell, *The Intolerable Hulks: British Shipboard Confinement 1776–1857* (Tucson, AZ: Fenestra Books, 2001).

29. Ronald L. Goldfarb and Linda R. Singer, *After Conviction* (New York: Simon & Schuster, 1973).

30. Laura Magnani and Harmon L. Wray, *Beyond Prisons* (Minneapolis: Fortress Press, 2006).

31. Norman B. Johnston, "John Haviland," in Mannheim, *Pioneers in Criminology*, 110.

32. Johnson, *Hard Time*.

33. H. Richard Phelps, *Newgate of Connecticut: Its Origin and Early History* (Hartford, CT: American, 1876).

34. Goldfarb and Singer, *After Conviction*.

35. Ibid.

36. Magnani and Wray, *Beyond Prisons*.

37. Goldfarb and Singer, *After Conviction*.

38. Howard Gill, "State Prisons in America: 1787–1937," in George G. Killinger, Paul F. Cromwell Jr., and Jerry M. Wood (Eds.), *Penology: the Evolution of Corrections in America*, 2nd ed. (New York: West, 1979).

39. Charles Dickens, *Pictures from Italy, and American Notes for General Circulation* (London: Chapman and Hall, 1862).

40. Peter Scharff Smith, "The Effects of Solitary Confinement on Prison Inmates: A Brief History and Review of the Literature," *Crime and Justice* 34 (2006): 441–528.

41. Goldfarb and Singer, *After Conviction*.

42. David Fogel, *We Are the Living Proof: The Justice Model for Corrections*, 2nd ed. (Cincinnati: Anderson, 1979).

43. Gill, "State Prisons in America: 1787–1937."

44. Joycelyn M. Pollock, *Prisons and Prison Life* (Los Angeles: Roxbury, 2004), 3.

45. Goldfarb and Singer, *After Conviction*.

46. Cayuga County Historian's Page, "Inside the Auburn Prison," *Early History of Cayuga County, Prison History*. www.co.cayuga.ny.us/history/cayugahistory/prison.html (retrieved July 24, 2011).

47. Goldfarb and Singer, *After Conviction*.

48. Magnani and Wray, *Beyond Prisons*.

49. Gill, "State Prisons in America: 1787–1937."

50. Wayne Morse (Ed.), "The Attorney General's Survey of Release Procedures," in George C. Killinger and Paul F. Cromwell Jr. (Eds.), *Penology: The Evolution of Corrections in America* (St. Paul, MN: West, 1973), 23, cited in Fogel, *We Are the Living Proof*, 24.

51. Fogel, *We Are the Living Proof*, 24.

52. Edgardo Rotman, "The Failure of Reform," in Norval Morris and David J. Rothman (Eds.), *The Oxford History of the Prison: The Practice of Punishment in Western Society* (New York: Oxford University Press, 1998), 155.

53. Ibid.

54. Johnson, *Hard Time*.

55. Goldfarb and Singer, *After Conviction*.

56. Johnson, *Hard Time*, 55.

57. Sue Titus Reid, *Crime and Criminology* (New York: Holt, Rinehart & Winston, 1976).

58. Rotman, "The Failure of Reform."

59. Ibid.

60. Peter Quinn, "The 'Penal Reformatory' That Never Was: Proposals to Establish Borstal Training in New South Wales, 1900–1948," *Journal of the Royal Australian Historical Society* (December 2002).

61. Goldfarb and Singer, *After Conviction*.

62. Reid, *Crime and Criminology*.

63. Johnson, *Hard Time*, 56.

64. Morgan O. Reynolds, *Factories behind Bars* (Dallas: National Center for Policy Analysis, 1996).

65. Rotman, "The Failure of Reform."

66. Gill, "State Prisons in America: 1787–1937."

67. Reynolds, *Factories behind Bars*.

68. Colleen Curry, "Whole Foods, Expensive Cheese, and the Dilemma of Cheap Prison Labor," July 21, 2015. https://news.vice.com/article/whole-foods-expensive-cheese-and-the-dilemma-of-cheap-prison-labor (retrieved July 23, 2015).

69. Johnson, *Hard Time*, 254.

70. Robert Martinson, "What Works: Questions and Answers about Prison Reform," *Public Interest* 35 (1974): 25.

71. Pollock, *Prisons and Prison Life*.

72. Johnson, *Hard Time*.

73. California Department of Corrections and Rehabilitation (CDCR), Office of Public and Employee Communications, *CDCR Accomplishments* (Sacramento: CDCR Office of Public and Employee Communications, 2009), 1–3. www.cdcr.ca.gov/News/2009_Press_Releases/docs/CDCR_Annual_Report.pdf (retrieved July 25, 2011).

74. John W. Santrock, *Psychology*, 7th ed. (New York: McGraw-Hill, 2005).

75. Ruth Masters, *Counseling Criminal Justice Offenders*, 2nd ed. (Thousand Oaks, CA: Sage, 2004), 6.

76. Sheldon Zhang, Robert Roberts, and Valerie Callanan, "Preventing Parolees from Returning to Prison through Community-Based Reintegration," *Crime & Delinquency* 52, no. 4 (2006): 551–571.

77. Jeremy Travis, *But They All Come Back: Facing the Challenges of Prisoner Reentry* (Washington, DC: Urban Institute Press, 2005).

78. Clear and Cole, *American Corrections*, 239–240.

79. Paul F. Cromwell, Rolando V. Del Carmen, and Leanne F. Alarid, *Community Based Corrections*, 5th ed. (Belmont, CA: Wadsworth, 2002); Restorative Justice Online, "Introduction to Restorative Justice." www.restorativejustice.org/whatisslide/whatispart1 (retrieved July 25, 2011).

80. Danielle Kaeble, Lauren Glaze, Anastatios Tsoutis, and Todd Minton, "Correctional Populations in the United States, 2014 (Washington, DC: U.S. Department of Justice, Bureau of Justice Statistics, December 2015).

81. Ibid.

82. E. Ann Carson, "Prisoners in 2014" (Washington, DC: U.S. Department of Justice, Bureau of Justice Statistics, September 2015).

83. Danielle Kaeble, Lauren Glaze, Anastatios Tsoutis, and Todd Minton, "Correctional Populations in the United States, 2014 (Washington, DC: U.S. Department of Justice, Bureau of Justice Statistics, December 2015).

84. Sean Gorman, "Webb Says U.S. Has 5 Percent of World's Population, 25 Percent of Its 'Known' Prisoners," *Politifact Virginia*, December 15, 2014. www.politifact.com/virginia/statements/2014/dec/15/jim-webb/webb-says-us-has-5-percent-worlds-population-25-pe/ (retrieved April 22, 2015).

85. International Centre for Prison Studies, "Highest to Lowest—Prison Population Rate." www.prisonstudies.org/highest-to-lowest/prison_population_rate?field_region_taxonomy_tid=All (retrieved April 22, 2015).

86. William J. Sabol, Heather C. West, and Matthew Cooper, "Prisoners in 2008," *Bureau of Justice Statistics Bulletin* (Washington, DC: U.S. Department of Justice, December 2009), 1.

87. E. Ann Carson, "Prisoners in 2014," (Washington, DC: U.S. Department of Justice, Bureau of Justice Statistics, September 2015).

88. Todd D. Minton and Zhen Zengi, "Jail Inmates at Midyear 2014" (Washington, DC: Bureau of Justice Statistics, June 2015), 1.

89. Todd D. Minton, "Jail Inmates at Midyear 2009—Statistical Tables," *Bureau of Justice Statistics Bulletin* (Washington, DC: U.S. Department of Justice, June 2010), 1–2, 10.

90. Minton and Golinelli, "Jail Inmates at Midyear 2013," 2.

91. Norval Morris, "The Contemporary Prison, 1965–Present," in Morris and Rothman, *The Oxford History of the Prison*.

92. Ibid.

93. Heather C. West, "Prison Inmates at Midyear 2009—Statistical Tables," *Bureau of Justice Statistics Bulletin* (Washington, DC: U.S. Department of Justice, June 2010), 2.

94. Ibid.

95. Jean Casarez, "6,600 Federal Inmates to be Released This Weekend," CNN, http://www.cnn.com/2015/10/30/us/federal-inmate-release/ (retrieved February 18, 2016).

96. Kevin Liptak, "President Barack Obama Commutes Sentences of 46 Drug Offenders," *CNN.com*, July 13, 2015. www.cnn.com/2015/07/13/politics/obama-commutes-sentences-drug-offenders/ (retrieved July 15, 2015); Kevin Liptak, "Obama Looks beyond Commutations in Justice Reform Bid," *CNN.com*, July 15, 2015. www.cnn.com/2015/07/14/politics/obama-naacp-speech-philadelphia-justice-reform/ (retrieved July 16, 2015).

97. Sharon Bernstein, "California's Prison Population Is Finally Down, but Will It Last?" *Huffington Post*, January 29, 2015. www.huffingtonpost.com/2015/01/29/ca-prison-overcrowding_n_6575514.html (retrieved April 23, 2015).

98. Gabriel Debenedetti, "Eric Holder Is Planning to Fundamentally Change How the Justice Department Handles Non-Violent Drug Offenses," *Business Insider*, August 12, 2013. www.businessinsider.com/eric-holder-drug-sentences-non-violent-marijuana-2013-8 (retrieved April 24, 2015).

99. Bernstein, "California's Prison Population Is Finally Down."

100. Magnus Lofstrom, Joan Petersilia, and Steven Raphael, "Evaluating the Effects of California's Corrections Realignment on Public Safety," *Public Policy Institute of California*, August 2012. www.ppic.org/content/pubs/report/R_812MLR.pdf (retrieved January 25, 2013).

101. The Sentencing Project, Fact Sheet: Trends in U. S. Corrections, Washington, DC, http://sentencingproject.org/doc/publications/inc_Trends_in_Corrections_Fact_sheet.pdf (retrieved February 18, 2016).

102. E. Ann Carson, "Prisoners in 2014," (Washington, DC: U.S. Department of Justice, Bureau of Justice Statistics, September 2015).

103. Todd D. Minton, Scott Ginder, Susan M. Brumbaugh, Hope Smiley-McDonald, and Harley Rohloff, "Census of Jails: Population Changes, 1999–2013" (Washington, DC: Bureau

of Justice Statistics Bulletin, December 2015) http://www.bjs.gov/content/pub/pdf/cjpc9913.pdfhttp://www.bjs.gov/content/pub/pdf/cjpc9913.pdf (retrieved February 18, 2016) and Lauren E. Glaze and Danielle Kaeble, "Correctional Populations in the United States, 2013" (Washington, DC: U.S. Department of Justice, Bureau of Justice Statistics, December 2014).

104. Carson, "Prisoners in 2013," 1.

105. Clear and Cole, *American Corrections,* 503–504.

106. E. Ann Carson, "Prisoners in 2014," (Washington, DC: U.S. Department of Justice, Bureau of Justice Statistics, September, 2015).

107. Todd D. Minton and Zhen Zeng, "Jail Inmates at Midyear 2014" (Washington, DC: U.S. Department of Justice, Bureau of Justice Statistics, June 2015), 1.

108. E. Ann Carson, "Prisoners in 2014," (Washington, DC: U.S. Department of Justice, Bureau of Justice Statistics, September 2015).

109. Beck and Harrison, "Prison and Jail Inmates at Midyear 2005."

110. E. Ann Carson, "Prisoners in 2014," (Washington, DC: U.S. Department of Justice, Bureau of Justice Statistics, September, 2015), Tables 11 and 12.

111. Federal Bureau of Prisons, "Total Federal Inmates," April 23, 2015. www.bop.gov/about/statistics/population_statistics.jsp (retrieved April 25, 2015): Federal Bureau of Prisons, "Inmate Gender," April 23, 2015. www.bop.gov/about/statistics/statistics_inmate_gender.jsp (retrieved April 25, 2015); Federal Bureau of Prisons, "Inmate Race," April 23, 2015. www.bop.gov/about/statistics/statistics_inmate_race.jsp (retrieved April 25, 2015); Federal Bureau of Prisons, "Inmate Ethnicity," April 23, 2015. www.bop.gov/about/statistics/statistics_inmate_ethnicity.jsp (retrieved April 25, 2015).

112. Federal Bureau of Prisons, "Inmate Offenses," April 23, 2015. www.bop.gov/about/statistics/statistics_inmate_offenses.jsp (retrieved April 25, 2015).

113. Lauren E. Glaze and Danielle Kaeble, "Correctional Populations in the United States, 2013" (Washington, DC: U.S. Department of Justice, Bureau of Justice Statistics, December 2014), 1; E. Ann Carson, "Prisoners in 2014," (Washington, DC: U.S. Department of Justice, Bureau of Justice Statistics, September, 2015), 2.

114. Erica Goode, "U.S. Prison Populations Decline, Reflecting New Approach to Crime," *New York Times,* July 25, 2013. www.nytimes.com/2013/07/26/us/us-prison-populations-decline-reflecting-new-approach-to-crime.html?_r=0 (retrieved April 25, 2015).

115. E. Ann Carson, "Prisoners in 2014," (Washington, DC: U.S. Department of Justice, Bureau of Justice Statistics, September, 2015) Table 2.

116. E. Ann Carson, "Prisoners in 2014," (Washington, DC: U.S. Department of Justice, Bureau of Justice Statistics, September, 2015) Table 6.

117. Danielle Kaeble, Lauren Glaze, Anastasios Tsoutis, and Todd Minton, "Correctional Populations in the United States, 2014 (Washington, DC: U.S. Department of Justice, Bureau of Justice Statistics, December 2015), 2 and Danielle Kaeble, Laura M. Maruschak, and Thomas P. Bonczar, "Probation and Parole in the

United States, 2014" (Washington, DC: U.S. Department of Justice, Bureau of Justice Statistics, November 2015).

118. Glaze and Kaeble, "Correctional Populations in th United States, 2013" 6.

119. Danielle Kaeble, Laura M. Maruschak, and Thomas P. Bonczar, "Probation and Parole in the United States, 2014" (Washington, DC: U.S. Department of Justice, Bureau of Justice Statistics Summary, November 2015) http://www.bjs.gov/content/pub/pdf/ppus14_sum.pdf (retrieved February 19, 2016) and "1 Out Of 32 Americans Under Correctional Supervision: 6.7 Million in Prison, On Parole or Probation," *About News,* updated January 6, 2016 http://usgovinfo.about.com/cs/censusstatistic/a/aainjail.htm (retrieved February 19, 2016)

120. Office of the Victim Advocate (OVA), Pennsylvania Department of Corrections. www.ova.state.pa.us/portal/server.pt/community/ova_home/9249 (retrieved July 25, 2011).

121. Kyran P. Quinlan, Robert D. Brewer, Paul Siegel, David A. Sleet, Ali H. Mokdad, Ruth A. Shults, and Nicole Flowers, "Alcohol-Impaired Driving among U.S. Adults, 1993–2002," *American Journal of Preventive Medicine* 28, no. 4 (May 2005).

122. Michelle Polacsek, Everett M. Rogers, W. Gill Woodall, Harold Delaney, Denise Wheeler, and Nagesh Rao, "MADD Victim Impact Panels and Stages-of-Change in Drunk-Driving Prevention," *Journal of Studies on Alcohol* 62, no. 3 (2001): 344–350; Janet C'de Baca, Sandra C. Lapham, H. C. Liang, and Betty Skipper, "Victim Impact Panels: Do They Impact Drunk Drivers? A Follow-up of Female and Male, First-Time and Repeat Offenders," *Journal of Studies on Alcohol* 62, no. 5 (2001): 615–620.

123. Karen L. Dunlap, Tracy G. Mullins, and Marilyn Stein, *Guidelines for Community Supervision of DWI Offenders* (Washington, DC: National Highway Traffic Safety Administration, March 2008).

124. National Center for Victims of Crime, "Rights of Survivors of Homicide," 1999. www.ncvc.org/ncvc/main.aspx?dbName=DocumentViewer&DocumentID=32470 (retrieved July 25, 2011).

125. Texas Department of Criminal Justice, "Victim Survivors Viewing Executions." www.tdcj.state.tx.us/faq/faq-victim.htm (retrieved July 25, 2011).

126. David Shichor, *Punishment for Profit* (Thousand Oaks, CA: Sage, 1995).

127. Phil Smith, "Private Prisons: Profits of Crime," *Covert Action Quarterly* (Fall 1993). http://makingcorrections.org/2011/01/225/ (retrieved July 25, 2011).

128. Douglas McDonald, Elizabeth Fournier, Malcolm Russell-Einhorn, and Stephen Crawford, *Private Prisons in the United States: Executive Summary* (Cambridge, MA: ABT Associates, 1998), iv.

129. Travis C. Pratt and Jeff Maahs, "Are Private Prisons More Cost-Effective Than Public Prisons? A Meta-Analysis of Evaluation Research Studies," *Crime and Delinquency* 45, no. 3 (July 1999): 358–371.

130. Brad W. Lundahl, Chelsea Kunz, Cyndi Brownell, Norma Harris, and Russ Van Vleet, "Prison Privatization: A Meta-Analysis of Cost and

Quality of Confinement Indicators," *Research on Social Work Practice* 19, no. 4 (July 2009): 383–394.

131. Philip Mattera and Mafruza Khan, *Jailbreaks: Economic Development Subsidies Given to Private Prisons* (Washington, DC: Institute on Taxation and Economic Policy, October 2001).

132. Magnani and Wray, *Beyond Prisons,* 89–93.

133. National Center for Policy Analysis, "Private Prisons Succeed" (Analysis based on testimony of Charles W. Thomas, director of the Private Corrections Project at the University of Florida in Gainesville), 1995. www.ncpa.org/ba/ba191.html (retrieved June 28, 2008).

134. Scott D. Camp and Gerald Gaes, *Growth and Quality of U.S. Private Prisons: Evidence from a National Survey* (Washington, DC: Federal Bureau of Prisons, October 23, 2001).

135. Tim Steller, "Escape Slows Prison Privatization" *Arizona Daily Star,* August 29, 2010.

136. Lonn Lanza-Kaduce, Karen F. Parker, and Charles W. Thomas, "A Comparative Recidivism Analysis of Releasees from Private and Public Prisons," *Crime & Delinquency* 45, no.1 (1999): 28–47.

137. McDonald, Fournier, Russell-Einhorn, and Crawford, *Private Prisons in the United States,* iv; Sasha Volokh, "Are Private Prisons Better or Worse Than Public Prisons?" *Washington Post,* February 25, 2014. www.washingtonpost.com/news/volokh-conspiracy/wp/2014/02/25/are-private-prisons-better-or-worse-than-public-prisons/.

138. "Centerville Company Being Blamed in Arizona Prison Escape," *Deseret News,* August 3, 2010; "Arizona Prisons Agency Releases Report on Escape," *Deseret News,* September 21, 2010.

139. Casey Newton, Ginger Rough, and J. J. Hensley, "Arizona Inmate Escape Puts Spotlight on State Private Prisons: Questions Arise over Safety Standards, Taxpayer Savings," *Arizona Republic,* August 22, 2010.

140. Ibid.

141. Steller, "Escape Slows Prison Privatization."

142. *Richardson v. McKnight,* 521 U.S. 410 (1997).

143. McDonald, Fournier, Russell-Einhorn, and Crawford, *Private Prisons in the United States.*

144. George W. Bush, White House Archives, "Faith-Based and Community Organizations" http://georgewbush-whitehouse.archives.gov/news/reports/faithbased.html (retrieved July 25, 2011).

145. Alan Cooperman, "An Infusion of Religious Funds in Fla. Prisons: Church Outreach Seeks to Rehabilitate Inmates," *Washington Post,* April 25, 2004. www.washingtonpost.com/ac2/wp-dyn?pagename=article&contentId=A39834-2004Apr24&notFound=true (retrieved July 25, 2011).

146. David Crary, "Faith-Based Prisons Multiply," *USA Today,* October 13, 2007. www.usatoday.com/news/religion/2007-10-13-prisons_N.htm# (retrieved April 10, 2011).

147. Vicki Mabrey and Sarah Rosenberg, "High Hopes for Faith-Based Prisons," *ABC News.com,* January 27, 2006. http://abcnews.go.com/Nightline/story?id=1550733 (retrieved July 25, 2011).

148. Do Faith-Based Prison Programs Work? *Washington Post,* February 14, 2014. www.washingtonpost.com/news/volokh-conspiracy/wp/2014/02/10/do-faith-based-prisons-work/.

149. Meredith Kolodner, "Private Prisons Expect a Boom: Immigration Enforcement to Benefit Detention Companies," *New York Times,* July 19, 2006. http://query.nytimes.com/gst/fullpage.html?res=9901E2D9163FF93AA25754C0A9609C8B63&pagewanted=all (retrieved July 25, 2011).

150. Alexander Volokh, "Developments in the Law—The Law of Prisons: III. A Tale of Two Systems: Cost, Quality, and Accountability in Private Prisons," *Harvard University Law Review* (2002).

CHAPTER 12

1. Ashley Nellis, "Life Goes On: The Historic Rise in Life Sentences in America" (Washington, DC: Sentencing Project, November 2013), 1.

2. Joshua Rovner, "Slow to Act: State Responses to 2012 Supreme Court Mandate on Life without Parole," Sentencing Project, June 25, 2014. www.sentencingproject.org/doc/publications/jj_State_Responses_to_Miller.pdf (retrieved April 28, 2015), 3; Joshua Rovner, "Juvenile Life without Parole: An Overview," Sentencing Project. www.sentencingproject.org/doc/publications/jj_Juvenile%20Life%20Without%20Parole.pdf (retrieved April 28, 2015).

3. Lifers Public Safety Steering Committee of the State Correctional Institution at Graterford, Pennsylvania, "Ending the Culture of Street Crime," *Prison Journal* 84, no. 4 Suppl. (December 2004): 51S.

4. Ibid., 51S, 67S–68S.

5. Ibid., 65S.

6. The Sentencing Project, "U.S. State and Federal Prison Population, 1925–2013." www.sentencingproject.org/template/page.cfm?id=107 (retrieved April 28, 2015).

7. Federal Bureau of Investigation, "Crime in the United States 2013." www.fbi.gov/about-us/cjis/ucr/crime-in-the-u.s/2013/crime-in-the-u.s.-2013 (retrieved April 29, 2015).

8. Bradley R. E. Wright, Avshalom Caspi, Terrie E. Moffitt, and Ray Patenoster, "Does the Perceived Risk of Punishment Deter Criminally Prone Individuals? Rational Choice, Self-Control, and Crime," *Journal of Research in Crime and Delinquency* 41, no. 2 (May 2004): 180–213; Marc Mauer, "The Hidden Problem of Time Served in Prison," *Social Research* 74, no. 2 (2007): 701–706; Scott Decker, "The Relationship between the Street and Prison," *Criminology and Public Policy* 6, no. 2 (2007): 183–186; National Institute of Justice, "Recidivism," June 17, 2014. www.nij.gov/topics/corrections/recidivism/Pages/welcome.aspx (retrieved April 29, 2015).

9. Mauer, "The Hidden Problem of Time Served in Prison"; Decker, "The Relationship between the Street and Prison"; David Weiman, "Barriers to Prisoners' Reentry into the Labor Market and the Social Costs of Recidivism," *Social Research* 74, no. 2 (2007): 575–611; Gail Hughes, "The Violation Population," *Corrections Today* 69, no. 6 (2007): 100–101; National Institute of Justice, "Recidivism."

10. Cindy Carcamo, "More Jails Refuse to Hold Inmates for Federal Immigration Authorities," *Los Angeles Times,* October 4, 2014. www.latimes.com/nation/immigration/la-na-ff-immigration-holds-20141005-story.html (retrieved April 29, 2015).

11. Douglas C. McDonald, "The Cost of Corrections: In Search of the Bottom Line," *Research in Corrections* 2, no. 1 (1989): 4.

12. Marisa Elena Domino, Edward C. Norton, Joseph P. Morrissey, and Neil Thakur, "Cost Shifting to Jails after a Change to Managed Mental Health Care," *Health Services Research* 39, no. 5 (October 2004): 1379–1402. www.pubmedcentral.nih.gov/articlerender.fcgi?artid=1361075 (retrieved August 13, 2009).

13. "Jails across Texas Routinely Found Non-Compliant," *Long View News Journal,* January 24, 2011. www.news-journal.com/news/local/article_1c44fbe9-67a6-5270-b63d-86f050fcb88c.html (retrieved April 11, 2011); Jonathan P. Caulkins, "Cost of Marijuana Prohibition on the California Criminal Justice System—Working Paper," *RAND Drug Policy Research Center,* July 2010. www.rand.org/pubs/working_papers/2010/RAND_WR763.pdf (retrieved April 11, 2011); Jolene Guzman, "An Increase in Inmates?" *Polk County Itemizer-Observer,* April 5, 2011. www.polkio.com/archives/story.aspx/20096/an-increase-in-inmates (retrieved April 11, 2011). Partnership for Safety and Justice, "Oregon Inmate Cost-Per-Day Fact Sheet," http://www.safetyandjustice.org/files/Oregon%20Inmate%20Cost-Per-Day%20Fact%20Sheet.pdf.

14. Todd D. Minton and Daniela Golinelli, "Jail Inmates at Midyear 2013—Statistical Tables" (Washington, DC: Bureau of Justice Statistics, August 2014), 2.

15. Shreema Mehta, "Judge Forces LA County to End Jail Overcrowding," *New Standard,* October 31, 2006. http://newstandardnews.net/content/index.cfm/items/3834 (retrieved April 17, 2011).

16. California State Sheriffs' Association, *Jail Overcrowding: A State and Local Crisis,* February 2006. www.calsheriffs.org/index.php/resource-center/cssa-library/jail-overcrowding-whitepaper (retrieved April 17, 2011).

17. Todd D. Minton, "Jail Inmates at Midyear 2010—Statistical Tables" (Washington, DC: U.S. Department of Justice, Bureau of Justice Statistics, April 14, 2011).

18. Leean Tupper, "Jail Overcrowding 'A Critical Issue,'" *OakRidger.com,* September 22, 2010. www.oakridger.com/news/x1380094907/Jail-overcrowding-a-critical-issue (retrieved April 17, 2011).

19. Doris J. James and Lauren E. Glaze, *Mental Health Problems and Jail Inmates* (Washington, DC: U.S. Department of Justice, September 2006).

20. Dan Miller, "Counties Attack Problem of Jail Overcrowding," National Association of Counties. www.uscounties.org/CountyNewsTemplate.cfm?template=/ContentManagement/ContentDisplay.cfm&ContentID=22354 (retrieved July 29, 2011).

21. Anderson Cooper, "America's Prison Problem," *Anderson Cooper 360°,* March 24, 2015; Ellie Bogue, "Cook County Sheriff Explains Reforms in Jail Mental Health System," *The News-Sentinel,* March 21, 2015. www.news-sentinel.com/article/2015150329972 (retrieved April 30, 2015).

22. Tammy Smith, "Richmond Jail Hosts Date with Dad Event for Imprisoned Fathers," Richmond Times-Dispatch, March 21, 2015. http://www.richmond.com/news/local/city-of-richmond/article_a1d64b80-898d-5b86-a202-9ae9f2529cc0.html (retrieved February 19, 2016).

23. Todd D. Minton and Zhen Zeng, "Jail Inmates at Midyear 2014" (Washington, DC: U.S. Department of Justice, Bureau of Justice Statistics, June 2015), 4.

24. Minton and Golinelli, "Jail Inmates at Midyear 2013," 1.

25. Peter Wagner and Bernadette Raybuy, "Mass Incarceration: The Whole Pie 2015," Prison Policy Initiative, December 8, 2015. http://www.prisonpolicy.org/reports/pie2015.html (retrieved February 19, 2016).

26. Human Rights Watch, *Ill-Equipped: U.S. Prisons and Offenders with Mental Illness* (New York: Human Rights Watch, 2003).

27. Federal Bureau of Prisons, "Total Federal Inmates," April 30, 2015. www.bop.gov/about/statistics/population_statistics.jsp (retrieved April 30, 2015).

28. Andy Furillo, "Housing Prices Still Rising—at State Prisons," *Sacramento Bee,* February 2, 2007. http://www.scrippsnews.com/node/19144 (retrieved July 29, 2011); Tracey Kyckelhahn, "State Corrections Expenditures, FY 1982–2010" (Washington, DC: U.S. Department of Justice, Bureau of Justice Statistics, revised April 30, 2014).

29. Christian Henrichson and Ruth Delaney, "The Price of Prisons: What Incarceration Costs Taxpayers" (New York: Vera Institute of Justice, 2012), 9–10.

30. Peter Wagner and Bernadette Raybuy, "Mass Incarceration: The Whole Pie 2015," Prison Policy Initiative, December 8, 2015. http://www.prisonpolicy.org/reports/pie2015.html (retrieved February 19, 2016).

31. The Sentencing Project, "Fact Sheet: Trends in U.S. Corrections," 2.

32. Erica Goode, "U.S. Prison Populations Decline, Reflecting New Approach to Crime," *New York Times,* July 25, 2013. www.nytimes.com/2013/07/26/us/us-prison-populations-decline-reflecting-new-approach-to-crime.html?_r=0 (retrieved May 1, 2015); Peter Wagner, "Tracking State Prison Growth in 50 States," *Prison Policy Initiative,* May 28, 2014. www.prisonpolicy.org/reports/overtime.html (retrieved May 1, 2015).

33. E. Ann Carson, "Prisoners in 2014," (Washington, DC: U.S. Department of Justice, Bureau of Justice Statistics, September 2015).

34. E. Ann Carson, "Prisoners in 2013," *Bureau of Justice Statistics Bulletin* (Washington, DC: U.S. Department of Justice, September 30, 2014), 6.

35. Pew Center on the States, "Prison Count 2010: State Population Declines for the First Time in 38 Years" (Washington, DC: Pew Charitable Trusts, April 2010), 3. www.pewcenteronthestates.org/uploaded_Files/Prison_Count_2010.pdf (retrieved February 18, 2011).

36. The Sentencing Project, "Fact Sheet: Trends in U.S. Corrections," 5.

37. Jennifer Senior, "You've Got Jail," *New York Magazine,* July 15, 2002. http://nymag.com/nymetro/news/crimelaw/features/6228/ (retrieved July 29, 2011).

38. Steven Stanko, Wayne Gillespie, and Gordon Crews, *Living in Prison: A History of the Correctional System with an Insiders' View* (Westport, CT: Greenwood Press, 2004), 151–152.

39. Ibid., 153.

40. California Department of Corrections and Rehabilitation, "Fourth Quarter 2008 Facts and Figures." www.cdcr.ca.gov/Adult_Operations/docs/Fourth_Quarter_2009_Facts_and_Figures.pdf (retrieved July 29, 2011); Maria F. Durand, "Prison Escapes Are on the Decline," *ABCNews.com*, February 1, 2013. http://abcnews.go.com/US/story?id=94172&page=1 (retrieved February 2, 2013).

41. Ian Lovett, "California Agrees to Overhaul Use of Solitary Confinement," New York Times, September 1, 2015. http://www.nytimes.com/2015/09/02/us/solitary-confinement-california (retrieved February 20, 2016); Milton J. Valencia, "Advocates Push for Solitary Confinement Reform in Mass.," Boston Globe, October 14, 2015. https://www.bostonglobe.com/metro/2015/10/13/solitary/3pY8vOQM9WLl6P0lareZTN/story.html (retrieved February 20, 2016) and Marina Koren, "Obama's Executive Actions on Solitary Confinement in Federal Prisons," The Atlantic, January 26, 2016. http://www.govexec.com/management/2016/01/obamas-executive-actions-solitary-confinement-federal-prisons/125441/ (retrieved February 20, 2016).

42. Ashley Fantz, Holly Yan, and Dana Ford, "N.Y. Prison Break: Sweat Says He, Matt Practiced Escape, Official Says," *CNN.com*, June 30, 2015. www.cnn.com/2015/06/30/us/new-york-prison-break/ (retrieved July 17, 2015); Tracy Wilkinson, "Inside 'El Chapo' Guzman's Cell: A Fortress, but Not Secure Enough," Los Angeles Times, July 16, 2015. www.latimes.com/world/mexico-americas/la-fg-chapo-guzman-escape-cell-20150716-story.html (retrieved July 17, 2015).

43. Jeffrey I. Ross, "Is the End in Sight for Supermax?" *Forbes*, April 18, 2006. www.forbes.com/2006/04/15/prison-super-max-ross_cx_jr_06slate_0418super.html (retrieved July 29, 2011); Daniel Mears and Jamie Watson, "Towards a Fair and Balanced Assessment of Supermax Prisons," *Justice Quarterly* 23, no. 2 (June 2006): 232–233; Committee on International Human Rights, "Supermax Confinement in U.S. Prisons," New York City Bar Association, September 2011. www2.nycbar.org/pdf/report/uploads/20072165-TheBrutalityofSupermaxConfinement.pdf (retrieved February 2, 2013); Emily Bazelon, "The Shame of Solitary Confinement," *New York Times Magazine*, February 19, 2015. www.nytimes.com/2015/02/19/magazine/the-shame-of-solitary-confinement.html?_r=0 (retrieved May 1, 2015).

44. Chase Riveland, *Supermax Prisons: Overview and General Considerations* (Washington, DC: National Institute of Corrections, 1999).

45. Laura Magnani and Harmon L. Wray, *Beyond Prisons* (Minneapolis: Fortress Press, 2006).

46. Rachael Kamel and Bonnie Kerness, *The Prison inside the Prison: Control Units, Supermax Prisons, and Devices of Torture* (Philadelphia: American Friends Service Committee), 3.

47. Barbara Owen, "Prisons: Prison Women—The Contemporary Prison," Law Library—American Law and Legal Information. http://law.jrank.org/pages/1800/Prisons-Prisons-Women-contemporary-prison.html (retrieved February 14, 2009).

48. Ted Conover, *NEWJACK: Guarding Sing Sing* (New York: Vintage Books, 2001); Jill A. Gordon, Blythe Proulx, Patricia H. Grant, "Trepidation among the 'Keepers': Gendered Perceptions of Fear and Risk of Victimization among Corrections Officers," *American Journal of Criminal Justice* 38, no. 2 (June 2013): 245–265.

49. Mark Pogrebin, *Qualitative Approaches to Criminal Justice: Perspectives from the Field* (Thousand Oaks, CA: Sage, 2002), 274.

50. Lucien X. Lombardo, *Guards Imprisoned: Correction Officers at Work* (New York: Elsevier, 1981).

51. To read about the long-term effects of this experiment on the participants, go to www.theatlanticwire.com/national/2011/07/stanford-prison-experiment/39871/ and www.stanfordalumni.org/news/magazine/2011/julaug/features/spe.html.

52. An in-depth discussion, slide show, vignettes, web links, and video clips of the Stanford Prison Experiment can be found at Zimbardo's website: www.prisonexp.org/slide-1.htm.

53. Ibid.

54. Lombardo, *Guards Imprisoned*.

55. Conover, *NEWJACK*.

56. Lombardo, *Guards Imprisoned*.

57. Robert Johnson: *Hard Time: Understanding and Reforming the Prison*, 2nd ed. (Belmont, CA: Wadsworth, 1996).

58. Alexander B. Smith, Bernard Locke, and Abe Fenster, "Authoritarianism in Policemen Who Are College Graduates and Non-College Police," *Journal of Criminal Law, Criminology, and Police Science* 61, no. 2 (June 1970).

59. Don Josi and Dale Sechrest, *The Changing Career of the Correctional Officer: Policy Implications for the 21st Century* (Boston: Butterworth-Heineman, 1998); U.S. Department of Labor, Bureau of Labor Statistics, "Occupational Outlook Handbook, 2010–2011 Edition" (Washington, DC: DOL, 2011). www.bls.gov/oco/ocos 156.htm (retrieved January 7, 2011).

60. U.S. Department of Labor, Bureau of Labor Statistics, "Occupational Outlook Handbook, 2010–2011 Edition."

61. Dana M. Britton, *At Work in the Iron Cage* (New York: New York University Press, 2003).

62. Evelyn Nieves, "California Examines Brutal, Deadly Prisons," *New York Times*, November 7, 1998.

63. Craig Haney, W. Curtis Banks, and Philip G. Zimbardo, "Interpersonal Dynamics in a Simulated Prison," *International Journal of Criminology and Penology* 69 (1973).

64. Mary Ann Farkas, "Correctional Officer Attitudes toward Inmates and Working with Inmates in a 'Get Tough' Era," *Journal of Criminal Justice* 27 no. 6 (November–December 1999): 495–506.

65. Josi and Sechrest, *The Changing Career of the Correctional Officer*.

66. Ibid.

67. Ibid.

68. D. Carter, "The Status of Education and Training in Corrections," *Federal Probation* 55 (1991): 17–23.

69. Elena Saxonhouse, "Unequal Protection: Comparing Former Felons' Challenges to Disenfranchisement and Employment Discrimination," *Stanford Law Review* 56 (2004); "The Need for Reform of Ex-Felon Disenfranchisement Laws," *Yale Law Journal* 83, no. 3 (January 1974).

70. *Cooper v. Pate*, 378 U.S. 546 (1964).

71. *Wolff v. McDonnell*, 418 U.S. 539 (1974).

72. Paige St. John, "California Inmates Win Class-Action Status over Race-Based Treatment." *LA Times*, July 14, 2015. www.latimes.com/local/la-me-ff-prison-race-lawsuit-20140724-story.html (retrieved July 16, 2015).

73. *Estelle v. Gamble*, 429 U.S. 97 (1976).

74. *Daniels v. Williams*, 474 U.S. 327 (1986).

75. *Wilson v. Seiter*, 501 U.S. 294 (1991).

76. Adam Liptak, "Justices, 5-4, Tell California to Cut Prisoner Population," *New York Times*, May 23, 2011. www.nytimes.com/2011/05/24/us/24scotus.html?pagewanted=all (retrieved July 24, 2011).

77. *Procunier v. Martinez*, 416 U.S. 396, 412 (1974).

78. *Cruz v. Beto*, 405 U.S. 319 (1972).

79. *O'Lone v. Estate of Shabazz*, 482, U.S. 342 (1987).

80. Karen Abbott, "Muslim Inmate Wins Fight over Meals, Prayer Cap," *Rocky Mountain News*, reprinted in *Muslim News*. www.muslimnews.co.uk/news/news.php?article=9605 (retrieved July 27, 2005).

81. "ACLU Secures Religious Freedom for Muslim Prisoners at Wyoming State Penitentiary," American Civil Liberties Union, November 20, 2008. www.aclu.org/racial-justice/aclu-secures-religious-freedom-muslim-prisoners-wyoming-state-penitentiary (retrieved July 29, 2011).

82. *Cutter v. Wilkinson*, 544 U.S. 709 (2005); "The Supreme Court's Decision in *Cutter v. Wilkinson*," Pew Forum on Religion & Public Life, June 2005. http://pewforum.org/uploadedfiles/Topics/Issues/Church-State_Law/RLUIPA-addendum.pdf (retrieved July 29, 2011).

83. Todd Clear and George Cole, *American Corrections*, 2nd ed. (Belmont, CA: Brooks/Cole, 1990).

84. Donald Clemmer, *The Prison Community* (New York: Holt, Rinehart, & Winston, 1940).

85. Ibid.; Geoffrey Alpert, "A Comparative Study of the Effects of Ideology on Prisonization: A Research Note," *LAE Journal of the American Criminal Justice Association* 41, no. 1 (1978): 77–78.

86. Gresham M. Sykes, *The Society of Captives: A Study of a Maximum Security Prison* (Princeton, NJ: Princeton University Press, 1958).

87. John Irwin and Donald Cressey, "Thieves, Convicts, and the Social Inmate Culture," *Social Problems* 10 (Fall 1962): 142–155.

88. John Irwin, *The Felon* (Englewood Cliffs, NJ: Prentice Hall, 1979).

89. Joycelyn M. Pollock, *Prisons and Prison Life* (Los Angeles: Roxbury, 2004).

90. *Reducing Racial Disparity in the Criminal Justice System: A Manual for Practitioners and Policymakers* (Washington, DC: Sentencing Project, 2000).

91. Chad R. Trulson and James W. Marquart, "Inmate Racial Integration: Achieving Racial Integration in the Texas Prison System," *Prison Journal* 82 (2002): 498–525.

92. Ronald J. Berger, Marvin D. Free Jr., and Patricia Searles, *Crime, Justice, and Society: Criminology and the Sociological Imagination* (New York: McGraw-Hill, 2001).

93. Cordon James Knowles, "Male Prison Rape: A Search for Causation and Prevention," *Howard Journal of Criminal Justice* 38, no. 3 (August 1999); David Kaiser and Lovisa Stannow, "The Shame of Our Prisons: New Evidence" *New York Review of Books*, October 24, 2013. www.nybooks.com/articles/archives/2013/oct/24/shame-our-prisons-new-evidence/ (retrieved May 2, 2015); Allen J. Beck, Marcus Berzofsky, Rachel Caspar, and Christopher Krebs, "Sexual Victimization in Prisons and Jails Reported by Inmates, 2011–12" (Washington, DC: U.S. Department of Justice, Bureau of Justice Statistics, May 2013); and David Kaiser and Lovisa Stannow, "Prison Rape and the Government," *New York Review*, March 24, 2011.

94. Leanne Fiftal Alarid and Paul F. Cromwell, *Correctional Perspectives: Views from Academics, Practitioners, and Prisoners* (Los Angeles: Roxbury, 2002).

95. Johnson, *Hard Time*.

96. Berger, Free, and Searles, *Crime, Justice, and Society*.

97. Southern Poverty Law Center, "Behind the Walls: An Expert Discusses the Role of Race-Based Gangs and Other Extremists in America's Prisons," *Intelligence Report*, no. 108 (Winter 2002). www.ncjrs.gov/App/Publications/abstract.aspx?ID=198632 (retrieved July 15, 2011).

98. Jennifer Hickey, "Ripe for Radicalization: Federal Prisons 'Breeding Ground' for Terrorists, Say Experts," Fox News, January 05, 2016. http://www.foxnews.com/us/2016/01/05/ripe-for-radicalization-federal-prisons-breeding-ground-for-terrorists-say-experts.html (retrieved February 20, 2016).

99. National Gang Intelligence Center, *2011 National Gang Threat Assessment—Emerging Trends*. www.fbi.gov/stats-services/publications/2011-national-gang-threat-assessment (retrieved June 4, 2015).

100. Alarid and Cromwell, *Correctional Perspectives*.

101. Edwin L. Santana "Gang Culture from the Inside & Out, Part II," *Corrections.com*. www.corrections.com/news/article/17132 (retrieved February 21, 2009); Louis Kontos and David Brotherton, *Encyclopedia of Gangs* (Westport, CT: Greenwood Press, 2008).

102. Alarid and Cromwell, *Correctional Perspectives*.

103. Geoffrey Hung, Stephanie Riegel, Tomas Morales, and Dan Waldorf, "Changes in Prison Culture: Prison Gangs and the Case of the Pepsi Generation," in Alarid and Cromwell, *Correctional Perspectives*.

104. Magnani and Wray, *Beyond Prisons*.

105. Arjen Boin and Menno Van Duin, "Prison Riots as Organizational Failures: A Managerial Failure," *Prison Journal* 75, no. 3 (1995): 357; Reid Montgomery and Gordon Crews, *A History of Correctional Violence: An Examination of Reported Causes of Riots and Disturbances* (Lanham, MD: American Correctional Association, 1998).

106. Erich Fromm, *The Anatomy of Human Destructiveness*, rev. ed. (New York: Macmillan, 1992).

107. Robert A. Baron and Deborah R. Richardson, *Human Aggression* (New York: Springer, 2004).

107. Reid Montgomery Jr., "Bringing the Lessons of Prison Riots into Focus," *Corrections Today* 59, no. 1 (1997): 28–33.

109. Alyssa Newcomb, "80 Inmates Moved after Arizona Prison Riot," *ABCNews.com*, March 4, 2013. http://abcnews.go.com/blogs/headlines/2013/03/80-inmates-moved-after-arizona-prison-riot/ (retrieved May 2, 2015); *Huffington Post*, "California Prison Riot: 11 Wounded, 1 Shot in Folsom," September 19, 2012. www.huffingtonpost.com/2012/09/19/california-prison-riot-el_n_1898716.html; *RT USA*, "Texas Prison Riot: 2,800 Inmates to Be Moved from Now 'Uninhabitable' Facility," February 22, 2015. http://rt.com/usa/234471-texas-uninhabitable-prison-riot/ (retrieved May 2, 2015).

110. Marvin Wolfgang and Franco Ferracuti, *The Subculture of Violence* (London: Tavistock, 1967); Susan Clayton and Gabriella Daley, "Mock Riot," *Corrections Today* (July 2000): 128–131.

111. Pollock, *Prisons and Prison Life*.

112. Steven Dillingham and Montgomery Reid, "Can Riots Be Prevented?" *Corrections Today* 44, no. 5 (1982); Montgomery and Crews, *A History of Correctional Violence*.

113. Joseph Bernstein, "Why Are Prison Riots Declining While Prison Populations Explode?" *The Atlantic*, December 2013. www.theatlantic.com/magazine/archive/2013/12/have-a-safe-riot/354671/ (retrieved May 2, 2015).

114. Federal Criminal Defense Investigation, "Prison Statistics: Summary Findings," December 29, 2008. http://federalcriminaldefenseinvestigator.blogspot.com/2008/12/bureau-of-justice-statistics-prison (retrieved July 29, 2011); Human Rights Watch, "No Escape: Male Rape in U.S. Prisons," 2001. www.hrw.org/legacy/reports/2001/prison/ (retrieved July 29, 2011).

115. Alan J. Beck and Paul Guerino, "Sexual Victimization Reported by Adult Correctional Authorities, 2007-2008," U.S. Department of Justice, Bureau of Justice Statistics, January 26, 2011. http://bjs.ojp.usdoj.gov/index.cfm?ty=pbdetail&iid=2204 (retrieved January 30, 2011); U.S. Department of Justice, Bureau of Justice Statistics, "PREA Data Collection Activities, 2011," May 2011. http://bjs.gov/content/pub/pdf/pdca11.pdf (retrieved July 25, 2011).

116. Gerald G. Gaes and Andrew L. Goldberg, "Prison Rape: A Critical Review of the Literature," working paper (Washington, DC: National Institute of Justice, 2004).

117. Associated Press, "Study: Sex Crimes in Prisons Underreported," *USA Today*, July 30, 2006. www.usatoday.com/news/washington/2006-07-30-prison-sex_x.htm (retrieved June 2, 2008).

118. Mary Bosworth, *The U.S. Federal Prison System* (Thousand Oaks, CA: Sage, 2002), 114.

119. Wayne S. Wooden and Jay Parker, *Men Behind Bars: Sexual Exploitation in Prison* (New York: Plenum, 1982).

120. Ibid.

121. Magnani and Wray, *Beyond Prisons*.

122. Pollock, *Prisons and Prison Life*.

123. Christian Parenti, "Rape as a Disciplinary Tactic," *Salon.com*, August 23, 1999. www.salon.com/news/feature/1999/08/23/prisons/ (retrieved May 24, 2008); Lewis Griswold, "Inmate Testifies about Corcoran Prison Rape," *Fresno Bee*, October 19, 1999; Evelyn Nieves, "California Examines Brutal, Deadly Prisons," *New York Times*, November 7, 1998. http://query.nytimes.com/gst/fullpage.html?res=9B03E6DE123EF934A35752C1A96E958260 (retrieved May 24, 2008).

124. Gary Marx, "When the Guards Guard Themselves: Undercover Tactics Turned Inward," *Policing and Society* 2, no. 3 (1992): 151–172; Stephen Sachs et al., *Report on Security Conditions at Maryland Penitentiary's South Wing Annapolis* (Annapolis: Attorney General of Maryland, 1984).

125. Dominique Debucquoy-Dodley and Greg Botelho, "Authorities Foil Drone-Delivery of Porn, Drugs and Gun to Maryland Prison," CNN, August 24, 2015. http://www.cnn.com/2015/08/24/us/maryland-prison-drone/ (retrieved February 20, 2016): Michelle Hackman, "Why 10 States Want to Ban Drones From Flying Over Prisons," Vox Policy and Politics, February 23, 2016, http://www.vox.com/2016/2/23/11100066/prison-drones (retrieved February 29, 2016); and Kavita Iyer , "Criminals Using Drones to Smuggle Drugs, Phones into Prison," Tech News February 26, 2016, http://www.techworm.net/2016/02/drones-used-criminals-smuggle-drugs-phones-prison.html (retrieved February 29, 2016).

126. Christopher Mumola, "Substance Abuse and Treatment, State and Federal Prisoners, 1997" (Washington, DC: U.S. Department of Justice, Bureau of Justice Statistics, January 1999). http://bjs.ojp.usdoj.gov/content/pub/pdf/satsfp97.pdf (retrieved July 29, 2011).

127. *Washington Times*, "Drugs Inside Prison Walls," January 27, 2010. www.washingtontimes.com/news/2010/jan/27/drugs-inside-prison-walls/?page=all (retrieved May 2, 2015).

128. Jan Keene, "Drug Misuse in Prison: Views from Inside: A Qualitative Study of Prison Staff and Inmates," *Howard Journal of Criminal Justice* 36, no. 1 (1997): 31.

129. Heinrich Andersen, D. Sestoff, and T. Lillegoek, "A Longitudinal Study of Prisoners on Remand: Repeated Measures of Psychopathology in the Initial Phase of Solitary versus Nonsolitary Confinement," *International Journal of Law and Psychiatry* 26, no. 2 (2003): 165–177; Tor Gamman, "The Detrimental Effects of Solitary Confinement in Norwegian Prisons," *Nordisk Tidsskrift for Kriminalvidenskab* 88, no. 1 (2001): 42–50.

130. Atul Gawande, "Hellhole," *The New Yorker* (March 30, 2009): 42.

131. Ibid., 36–45.

132. Matt Ford, "The Beginning of the End for Solitary Confinement?" The Atlantic, September 2, 2015 http://www.theatlantic.com/politics/archive/2015/09/scaling-back-solitary (retrieved February 20, 2016); Ian

Lovett, "California Agrees to Overhaul Use of Solitary Confinement," New York Times, September 1, 2015. http://www.nytimes.com/2015/09/02/us/solitary-confinement-california (retrieved February 20, 2016); Milton J. Valencia, "Advocates Push for Solitary Confinement Reform in Mass.," Boston Globe, October 14, 2015. https://www.bostonglobe.com/metro/2015/10/13/solitary/3pY8vOQM9WLl6P0lareZTN/story.html (retrieved February 20, 2016) and Marina Koren, "Obama's Executive Actions on Solitary Confinement in Federal Prisons," The Atlantic, January 26, 2016. http://www.govexec.com/management/2016/01/obamas-executive-actions-solitary-confinement-federal-prisons/125441/ (retrieved February 20, 2016).

133. Atul Gawande, "Hellhole," The New Yorker (March 30, 2009): 43–44.

134. Nancy Kurshan, "Women and Imprisonment in the U.S.: History and Current Reality," Prison Activist Resource Center, www.prisonactivist.org/women/women-and-imprisonment.html (retrieved July 25, 2011).

135. Bureau of Prisons, "Inmate Gender," April 23, 2015. www.bop.gov/about/statistics/statistics_inmate_gender.jsp (retrieved April 25, 2015); Carson, "Prisoners in 2013."

136. The Sentencing Project, "Women, Fact Sheet: Trends in U.S. Corrections." http://sentencingproject.org/doc/publications/inc_Trends_in_Corrections_Fact_sheet.pdf (retrieved February 20, 2016).

137. William Sabol, Heather Couture, and Paige M. Harrison, "Prisoners in 2006," Bureau of Justice Statistics Bulletin (Washington, DC: U.S. Department of Justice, 2007), 4. E. Ann Carson, "Prisoners in 2014" (Washington, DC: U.S. Department of Justice, Bureau of Justice Statistics, September 2015) Table 4, p. 6.

138. B. Keith Crew, "Sex Differences in Criminal Sentencing: Chivalry or Patriarchy?" Justice Quarterly 8, no. 1 (1991): 59–83.

139. E. Ann Carson, "Prisoners in 2014," (Washington, DC: U.S. Department of Justice, Bureau of Justice Statistics, September 2015).

140. Sabol, Couture, and Harrison, "Prisoners in 2006," 6–8.

141. Heather C. West and William J. Sabol, "Prisoners in 2007," Bureau of Justice Statistics Bulletin (Washington, DC: U.S. Department of Justice, 2008), 7.

142. E. Ann Carson, "Prisoners in 2014," (Washington, DC: U.S. Department of Justice, Bureau of Justice Statistics, September 2015) 29.

143. Boalt Hall Prison Action Coalition, "Women in California Prisons," September 2000. www.boalt.org/PAC/stats/women-prison-fact-sheet.html (retrieved February 14, 2009); Joshua Emerson Smith, "Chowchilla Women's Prison Squeezed: Rank as State's Most-Crowded Facility Sparks Protests, Merced Sun Star, January 8, 2013. www.mercedsunstar.com/2013/01/08/2744178/chowchilla-womens-prison-squeezed.html (retrieved February 4, 2013).

144. Barbara Bloom, Barbara Owen, Stephanie Covington, and Myrna Raeder, Gender-Responsive Strategies: Research, Practice, and Guiding Principles for Women Offenders (Washington, DC: National Institute of Corrections, 2003).

145. K. van Wormer and L. Kaplan, "Results of a National Survey of Wardens in Women's Prisons: The Case for Gender-Specific Treatment," Women and Therapy 29, no. 1 (2006): 133–151.

146. S. Jiang and L. Winfree, "Social Support, Gender, and Inmate Adjustment to Prison Life: Insights from a National Sample," Prison Journal, 86, no. 1 (2006): 32–55.

147. Bloom, Owen, Covington, and Raeder, Gender-Responsive Strategies; Karen Holt, "Nine Months to Life—the Law and the Pregnant Inmate," Journal of Family Law 20 (1982): 524–525.

148. Susan Elan, "Shackling Pregnant Women Spurs Prison-Reform Push," Women's enews.org, November 9, 2010. http://womensenews.org/story/incarceration/101108/shackling-pregnant-women-spurs-prison-reform-push (retrieved January 28, 2011).

149. Cheryl Hanna-Truscott et al., Her Hand Rocks the Cradle, a photo-documentary project at the Washington Corrections Center for Women. www.residentialparenting.com/ (retrieved March 3, 2007).

150. Candace Kruttschnitt and Sharon Krmpotich, "Aggressive Behavior among Female Inmates: An Exploratory Study," Justice Quarterly 7 (1990): 371–389; Pollock, Prisons and Prison Life.

151. Kristin C. Carbone-Lopez and Candace Kruttschnitt, "Assessing the Racial Climate in Women's Institutions in the Context of Penal Reform," Women and Criminal Justice 15, no. 1 (2003): 55–79.

152. Lawrence Greenfeld and Tracy Snell, Women Offenders (Washington, DC: U.S. Department of Justice, Bureau of Justice Statistics, 1999); E. Ann Carson and William J. Sabol, "Prisoners in 2011," Bureau of Justice Statistics Bulletin (Washington, DC: U.S. Department of Justice, December 2012), 9. http://bjs.ojp.usdoj.gov/content/pub/pdf/p11.pdf (retrieved February 4, 2013).

153. Carson, "Prisoners in 2013," 16.

154. Shulamith Lala Ashenberg Straussner, "Gender and Substance Abuse," in Shulamith Lala Ashenberg Straussner and Elizabeth Zelvin (Eds.), Gender and Addictions (Norvale, NJ: Jason Aronson, 1997).

155. Bloom, Owen, Covington, and Raeder, Gender-Responsive Strategies.

156. Ibid.

157. K. Kauffman, "Mothers in Prison," Corrections Today 63, no. 1 (2001): 62–65; Greenfeld and Snell, Women Offenders.

158. J. M. Pollock-Byrne, Women, Prison, and Crime (Pacific Grove, CA: Brooks/Cole, 1990).

159. Caron Zlotnick, Lisa Nijavits, Damaris Rohsenow, and Dawn Johnson, "A Cognitive-Behavioral Treatment for Incarcerated Women with Substance Abuse Disorder and Posttraumatic Stress Disorder: Findings from a Pilot Study," Journal of Substance Abuse Treatment 25, no. 2 (2003): 99–105; KiDeuk Kim, Miriam Becker-Cohen, and Maria Serakos, "The Processing and Treatment of Mentally Ill Persons in the Criminal Justice System" (Washington, DC: Urban Institute, March 2015), 9.

160. Cindi Banks, Women in Prison (Santa Barbara, CA: ABC-CLIO, 2003), 52–53; Abigail Groves, "Blood on the Walls: Self-Mutilation in Prisons," Australian and New Zealand Journal of Criminology (April 1, 2004).

161. Jo Borrill, Louisa Snow, Diana Medlicott, Rebecca Teers, and Jo Paton, "Learning from 'Near Misses': Interviews with Women Who Survived an Incident of Severe Self-Harm in Prison," Howard Journal of Criminal Justice 44, no. 1 (2005): 57–69; Jan Heney, Dying on the Inside: Suicide and Suicidal Feelings among Federally Incarcerated Women (Ann Arbor, MI: University Microfilms International, 1996).

162. U.S. Department of Justice, Bureau of Justice Statistics, "Survey of Inmates in State and Federal Correctional Facilities, 1997." http://dx.doi.org/10.3886/ICPSR02598 (retrieved July 15, 2011).

163. American Correctional Association Task Force on the Female Offender, The Female Offender: What Does the Future Hold? (Washington, DC: St. Mary's Press, 1990).

164. E. Lord, "The Challenge of Mentally Ill Female Offenders in Prison," Criminal Justice and Behavior 35, no. 8 (2008): 928–942.

165. Caroline Wolf Harlow, Education and Correctional Populations (Washington DC: U.S. Department of Justice, Bureau of Justice Statistics, 2003).

166. The Sentencing Project, "Fact Sheet: Trends in U.S. Corrections," 4.

167. Meda Chesney-Lind and Noelie Rodriguez, "Women under Lock and Key: A View from the Inside," in Meda Chesney-Lind and Lisa Pasko (Eds.), Girls, Women, and Crime: Selected Readings, 2nd ed. (Newbury Park, CA: Sage, 2003), 200–201.

168. A. Blackburn, J. Mullings, and J. Mar-quart, "Sexual Assault in Prison and Beyond: Toward an Understanding of Lifetime Sexual Assault among Incarcerated Women," Prison Journal 88, no. 3 (2008): 351–377.

169. Bloom, Owen, Covington, and Raeder, Gender-Responsive Strategies.

170. Cindy Struckman-Johnson and David Struckman-Johnson, "Sexual Coercion Reported by Women in Three Midwestern Prisons," Journal of Sex Research 39 (2002): 217–218; "Sexual Abuse in Women's Prisons," video interview of Piper Kernan by Maria Shriver, Today, NBC, July 7, 2014. www.today.com/video/today/55459135 (retrieved May 2, 2015).

171. Christopher Hensley, Richard Tewksbury, and Mary Koscheski, "The Characteristics and Motivations behind Female Prison Sex," Women and Criminal Justice 13 (2002): 125–129.

172. Pollock-Byrne, Women, Prison, and Crime.

173. "Prisons: Prisons for Women—Problems and Unmet Needs in Contemporary Women's Prisons." http://law.jrank.org/pages/1805/Prisons-Prisons-Women-Problems-unmet-needs-

174. Barbara V. Smith, "Sexual Abuse against Women in Prison," *American Bar Association Criminal Justice Magazine* 16, no. 1 (Spring 2001). www.wcl.american.edu/nic/Articles_Publications/Sexual_Abuse_Against_Women_in_Prison.pdf?rd=1 (retrieved July 29, 2011).

in-contemporary-women-s-prison.html (retrieved July 29, 2011).

175. Allen J. Beck, and Page M. Harrison, "Sexual Violence Reported by Correctional Authorities, 2005," *Bureau of Justice Statistics Special Report*, July 2006. http://bjs.ojp.usdoj.gov/content/pub/pdf/svrca05.pdf (retrieved July 15, 2011); U.S. Department of Justice, Office of the Inspector General, "Deterring Staff Sexual Abuse of Federal Inmates" (Washington, DC: DOJ, April 2005). www.usdoj.gov/oig/special/0504/final.pdf; Liz Fields, "Half of Sexual Abuse Claims in American Prisons Involve Guards, Study Says," ABC News, Jan. 26, 2014. http://abcnews.go.com/US/half-sexual-abuse-claims-american-prisons-involve-guards/story?id=21892170 (retrieved May 2, 2015).

176. See 18 U.S.C. § 2243 (c).

177. U.S. Department of Justice, Office of the Inspector General, "Deterring Staff Sexual Abuse of Federal Inmates," 21–22.

178. Prison Rape Elimination Act of 2003, 45 U.S.C. § 15601 (2003).

179. Brenda V. Smith, "Analyzing Prison Sex: Reconciling Self-Expression with Safety," *Human Rights Brief*, Westlaw (Spring 2006). www.wcl.american.edu/nic/documents/3.AnalyzingPrisonSex.pdf (retrieved July 29, 2011).

180. Norval Morris, "The Contemporary Prison, 1965–Present," in Norval Morris and David J. Rothman (Eds.), *The Oxford History of the Prison: The Practice of Punishment in Western Society* (New York: Oxford University Press, 1998).

181. Jessica Guynn, "Silicon Valley Turns Prisoners into Programmers at San Quentin," USA Today, November 21, 2014. http://www.usatoday.com/story/tech/2014/11/14/san-quentin-inmates-silicon-valley-programmers-prisoners-last-mile-code-7370/19034201/ (retrieved February 20, 2016).

182. David Leonhardt, "As Prison Labor Grows, So Does the Debate," *New York Times*, March 19, 2000. www.commondreams.org/headlines/031900-02.htm (retrieved March 19, 2007).

183. Pauline Vu, "Inmates Gladly Take on Odd Jobs for Low or No Pay," *Prison Talk.com*. www.prisontalk.com/forums/showthread.php?t=106564 (retrieved July 29, 2011).

184. Florida Department of Corrections, "Academic, Vocational, and Substance Abuse Program Impacts," 2001. www.dc.state.fl.us/pub/recidivismprog/execsum.html (retrieved March 28, 2007).

185. David B. Wilson, C. A. Galagher, and D. L. MacKenzie, "A Meta-Analysis of Corrections-Based Education, Vocation, and Work Programs for Adult Offenders," *Journal of Research in Crime and Delinquency* 37 (2001): 347–368, cited by Shawn Bushway, "Employment Dimensions of Reentry: Understanding the Nexus between Prisoner Reentry and Work," *Urban Institute Reentry Roundtable* (New York University Law School, May 19–20. www.urban.org/UploadedPDF/410853_bushway.pdf (retrieved July 29, 2011).

186. Kathleen Scalise, "California Prison Factories Generate $150 Million in Sales Each Year, New U.C. Berkeley Report Finds," news release, University of California, Berkeley, June 25, 1998. www.berkeley.edu/news/media/releases/98legacy/06-25-1998.html (retrieved July 29, 2011).

187. Alarid and Cromwell, *Correctional Perspectives*.

188. D. A. Andrews, Ivan Zinger, Robert D. Hoge, James Bonta, Paul Gendreau, and Francis T. Cullen, "Does Correctional Treatment Work? A Clinically Relevant and Psychologically Informed Meta-Analysis," *Criminology* 28, no. 3 (1990): 369–404.

189. Johnson: *Hard Time*.

190. Maxwell Jones, *The Therapeutic Community: A New Treatment Method in Psychiatry* (New York: Basic Books, 1953).

191. Clayton Mosher and Dretha Phillips, "The Dynamics of a Prison-Based Therapeutic Community for Women Offenders: Retention, Completion, and Outcomes," *Prison Journal* 86, no. 1 (2006): 6–31.

192. James Inciardi, *A Corrections-Based Continuum of Effective Drug Abuse Treatment* (Washington, DC: National Institute of Justice, 1996).

193. Madeline Ortiz, "Managing Special Populations," *Corrections Today* 62 (2000): 64–68.

194. Nellis, "Life Goes On."

195. National Correctional Industries Association, "Executive Summary: Major Findings," September 27, 1998. http://66.165.94.98/stories/eldst.pdf (retrieved July 29, 2011); Carrie Abner, "Graying Prisons: States Face Challenges of an Aging Inmate Population," Council of State Governments, 2006. www.csg.org/knowledgecenter/docs/sn0611GrayingPrisons.pdf (retrieved January 28, 2011).

196. Linda Richardson, "Other Special Offender Populations," in Thomas Fagan and Robert Ax (Eds.), *Correctional Mental Health Handbook* (Thousand Oaks, CA: Sage, 2003).

197. Ibid.

198. Ibid.

299. National Correctional Industries Association, "Executive Summary: Major Findings."

200. Donald Pointer and Marjorie Kravitz, *The Handicapped Offender: A Selected Bibliography* (Washington, DC: U.S. Department of Justice, 1981).

201. Human Rights Watch, *Ill-Equipped*; Doris J. James and Lauren E. Glaze, "Mental Health Problems of Prison and Jail Inmates" (Washington, DC: U.S. Department of Justice, Bureau of Justice Statistics, 2006), 1.

202. Kim, Becker-Cohen, and Serakos, "The Processing and Treatment of Mentally Ill Persons in the Criminal Justice System," 9.

203. Ibid., 11.

204. Shelia Holton, "Managing and Treating Mentally Disordered Offenders in Jails and Prisons," in Fagan and Ax, *Correctional Mental Health Handbook*.

205. Ibid; Cooper, "America's Prison Problem"; Bogue, "Cook County Sheriff Explains Reforms in Jail Mental Health System"; Anasseril E. Daniel, "Care of the Mentally Ill in Prisons: Challenges and Solutions," *Journal of the American Academy of Psychiatry and Law* 35, no. 4 (2007): 406–410.

206. Human Rights Watch, *Ill-Equipped*.

207. Franca Cortoni and R. Carl Hanson, *Research Report: A Review of the Recidivism Rates of Adult Female Sexual Offenders* (Ottawa: Correctional Service of Canada, 2005).

208. Monica Davey and Abby Goodnough, "Doubts Rise as States Hold Sex Offenders after Prison Terms," *New York Times*, March 4, 2007. www.nytimes.com/2007/03/04/us/04civil.html (retrieved July 29, 2011).

209. Ibid.

210. Lydia Long and Allen Sapp, "Programs and Facilities for Physically Disabled Inmates in State Prisons," *Journal of Offender Rehabilitation* 18 (1992): 191–204.

211. Ibid; Jessie L. Krienert, Martha L. Henderson, and Donna M. Vandiver, "Inmates with Physical Disabilities: Establishing a Knowledge Base," *Southwest Journal of Criminal Justice* 1, no. 1 (2003): 14–18.

212. *Armstrong v. Wilson*, 124 F. 3d 1019 (9th Cir. 1997).

213. *Pennsylvania Dept. of Corrections v. Yeskey*, 524 U.S. 206, 209 (1998).

214. Josi and Sechrest, *The Changing Career of the Correctional Officer*, 103–105.

215. Ibid., 105–106.

216. Richardson, "Other Special Offender Populations," 199–216; Gene Draper and Michael Reed, *Criminal Alien Project for the State of Texas* (Austin: Texas Criminal Justice Council, 1995).

217. Richardson, "Other Special Offender Populations."

218. D. L. Saunders, D. M. Olive, S. B. Wallace, D. Lacy, R. Leyba, and N. E. Kendig, "Tuberculosis Screening in the Federal Prison System: An Opportunity to Treat and Prevent Tuberculosis in Foreign-Born Populations," *Public Health Reports* 116, no. 3 (2001): 210–218.

219. Bureau of Justice Statistics, "BJS Survey Finds 40 Percent of Prison and Jail Inmates Reported Current Chronic Medical Problems," advance release, February 5, 2015.

220. Laura M. Maruschak, "HIV in Prisons, 2001–2010," *Bureau of Justice Statistics Bulletin* (Washington, DC: U.S. Department of Justice, revised March 24, 2015).

221. Richardson, "Other Special Offender Populations."

222. A. A. Amankwaa, L. C. Amankwaa, and C. O. Ochie, "Revisiting the Debate of Voluntary versus Mandatory HIV/AIDS Testing in U.S. Prisons," *Journal of Health and Human Services Administration* 22, no. 2 (1999).

223. Jay Romano, "Plan for AIDS Testing in Prison Raises Questions," *New York Times*, December 17, 1989.

224. Mary Sylla, "HIV Treatment in U.S. Jails and Prisons," San Francisco AIDS Foundation. www.sfaf.org/beta/2008_win/jails_prisons (retrieved February 27, 2009).

225. Centers for Disease Control and Prevention, "HIV in Correctional Settings," www.cdc.gov/hiv/risk/other/correctional.html (retrieved March 14, 2015).

226. National Center for Lesbian Rights, "Transgender Prisoners." www.transgenderlaw.org/resources/prisoners.htm (retrieved May 2, 2015).

227. Richard Perez-Pena, "California Is First State to Adopt Sex Reassignment Surgery Policy for Prisoners," New York Times, October 21, 2015. http://www.nytimes.com/2015/10/22/us/california-is-first-state-to-adopt-sex-reassignment-surgery-policy-for-prisoners.html (retrieved February 20, 2016).

228. Allen J. Beck, "Sexual Victimization in Prisons and Jails Reported by Inmates 2011–12: Supplemental Tables: Prevalence of Sexual Victimization among Transgender Adult Inmates" (Washington, DC: Bureau of Justice Statistics, December 2014), tables 1 and 2.

229. Christopher Mathias, "New York's Largest Jail to Open Housing Unit for Transgender Women," Huffington Post, November 18, 2014. www.huffingtonpost.com/2014/11/18/rikers-transgender-women_n_6181552.htm (retrieved May 3, 2015).

230. Kathleen Block and Margaret Potthast, "Girls Scouts Behind Bars: Facilitating Parent–Child Contact in Correctional Settings," in Cynthia Seymour and Creasie Finney Hairston (Eds.), Children with Parents in Prison: Child Welfare Policy, Program, and Practice Issues (New Brunswick, NJ: Transaction, 2001).

231. Jack Elliott Jr., Associated Press, "Miss. Inmate Seeks Resumption of Conjugal Visits," Hattiesburg American, April 8, 2015.

232. Kelsey Kauffman, "Mothers in Prison," Corrections Today 63, no. 1 (2001): 62–65; Greenfeld and Snell, Women Offenders; Pollack-Byrne, Women, Prison, and Crime; Bloom, Owen, Covington, and Raeder, Gender-Responsive Strategies.

233. Christopher J. Mumola, Incarcerated Parents and Their Children (Washington, DC: U.S. Department of Justice, Bureau of Justice Statistics, 2000).

234. Phyllis J. Baunnach, "Critical Problems of Women in Prison," in Imogene L. Moyer (Ed.), The Changing Roles of Women in the Criminal Justice System (Prospect Heights, IL: Waveland Press, 1985).

235. C. E. Temin, "Let Us Consider the Children," Corrections Today 63, no. 1 (2001).

236. G. Lane Wagaman, "Managing and Treating Female Offenders," in Fagan and Ax, Correctional Mental Health Handbook.

237. Patrick Rodgers, "Conjugal Visits: Preserving Family Bonds behind Bars," Legalzoom.com. www.legalzoom.com/marriage-divorce-family-law/marriage-domestic-partnership/conjugal-visits-preserving-family-bonds (retrieved July 29, 2011).

238. Federal Bureau of Prisons, "Conjugal Visits Information Page." www.bop.gov/inmate_locator/conjugal.jsp (retrieved April 17, 2007); Reginald A. Wilkinson and Tessa Unwin, "Visiting in Prison," in Peter M. Carlson and Judith Simon Garrett (Eds.), Prison and Jail Administration: Practice and Theory (Sudbury, MA: Jones & Bartlett, 2006).

239. Christopher B. Epps and Harley B. Barbour, "Conjugal Visits," Mississippi Department of Corrections, 2007. www.mdoc.state.ms.us/conjugal_visits.htm (retrieved March 2, 2007).

240. Adam Tanner, "California Allows Gay Conjugal Visits in Prisons," Reuters, June 1, 2007. www.reuters.com/article/lifestyleMolt/idUSN013474042007060 (retrieved July 29, 2011).

241. Kentucky Dept. of Corrections v. Thompson, 490 U.S. 454 (1989); Pollock, Prisons and Prison Life.

CHAPTER 13

1. Kathleen Toner, "'Magic Happened' after She Gave Ex-Cons a Chance at New Lives," CNN Justice, February 19, 2010. www.cnn.com/2010/CRIME/02/18/cnnheroes.burton/ (retrieved February 25, 2011); CNN Heroes: Everyday People Changing the World. www.cnn.com/SPECIALS/cnn.heroes/archive10/susan.burton.html (retrieved February 25, 2011); A New Way of Life Reentry Project. www.anewwayoflife.org (retrieved February 25, 2011); "Susan Burton Awarded Gleitsman Citizen Activist 2010 by Harvard University's Kennedy School of Government," November 1, 2010. www.anewwayoflife.org/susan-burton-awarded-gleitsman-citizen-activist-2010-by-harvard-universitys-kennedy-school-of-government (retrieved February 25, 2011).

2. Edward Latessa and Christopher Lowenkamp, "What Works in Reducing Recidivism," St. Thomas Law Journal 3 (2007): 521–535.

3. James Q. Wilson and Joan Petersilia, Crime: Public Policies for Crime Control (Oakland, CA: Institute for Contemporary Studies Press, 2002).

4. Danielle Kaeble, Lauren E. Glaze, Anastasios Tsoutis, and Todd Minton, "Correctional Populations in the United States, 2014" (Washington, DC: U.S. Department of Justice, Bureau of Justice Statistics, December 2015). Table 4, p.5.

5. Burns v. United States, 287 U.S. 216, 220 (1932).

6. Maurice Vanstone, Supervising Offenders in the Community: A History of Probation Theory and Practice (London: Ashgate, 2007).

7. Robert Panzarella, "Theory and Practice of Probation on Bail in the Report of John Augustus," Federal Probation 66, no. 3 (2002): 38–42.

8. Philip Whitehead and Roger Statham, The History of Probation: Politics, Power and Cultural Change 1876–2005 (Crayford, Kent, UK: Shaw and Sons, 2006).

9. "Conditions of Probation," U.S. Code Collection (Ithaca, NY: Legal Information Institute, Cornell University Law School). www.law.cornell.edu/uscode/uscode18/usc_sec_18_00003583—000-.html (retrieved August 1, 2011).

10. Vera Institute of Justice, The Potential of Community Corrections to Improve Safety and Reduce Incarceration (New York: Vera Institute of Justice, July 2013), 26.

11. Norval Morris and Michael Tonry, Between Prison and Probation: Intermediate Punishments in a Rational Sentencing System (New York: Oxford University Press, 1990).

12. Billie S. Erwin and Lawrence A. Bennett, "New Dimensions in Probation: Georgia's Experience with Intensive Probation Supervision (IPS)," Research in Brief (Washington, DC: National Institute of Justice, January 1987).

13. Morris and Tonry, Between Prison and Probation.

14. Connie H. Wiliszowski, James C. Fell, S. McKnight, and S. Tippetts, "An Evaluation of Intensive Supervision Programs for Serious DWI Offenders" (Washington, DC: National Highway Traffic Safety Administration, March 2011), 55.

15. Joan Petersilia and Susan Turner, Intensive-supervision for High-Risk Probationers: Findings from Three California Studies (Santa Monica, CA: RAND Corporation, November 1990).

16. Jodi Lane, Susan Turner, Terry Fain, and Amer Sehgal, "Evaluating an Experimental Intensive Juvenile Probation Program: Supervision and Official Outcomes," Crime and Delinquency 51, no. 1 (2005): 26–52.

17. Kelly L. Brown, "Effects of Supervision Philosophy on Intensive Probationers," Justice Policy Journal 4, no. 1 (Spring 2007).

18. New York State, Division of Probation and Correctional Alternatives, Annual Report: Intensive-Supervision Program 2005 Operations, December 2006. http://dpca.state.ny.us/pdfs/isp2005report.pdf (retrieved August 1, 2011).

19. Pew Center on the States, "One in 31: The Long Reach of American Corrections" (Washington: DC: Pew Charitable Trusts, 2009), 12. http://www.pewcenteronthestates.org/uploadedFiles/PSPP_1in31_report_FINAL_WEB_3-26-09.pdf (retrieved April 22, 2011).

20. Ibid., 13.

21. Danielle Kaeble, Laura M. Maruschak, and Thomas P. Bonczar, "Probation and Parole in the United States, 2014" (Washington, DC: U.S. Department of Justice, Bureau of Justice Statistics, November 2015), Table 2, p.3.

22. Erinn J. Herberman and Thomas P. Bonczar, "Probation and Parole in the United States, 2013" (Washington, DC: Bureau of Justice Statistics, Office of Justice Programs, revised January 21, 2015), 17.

23. M. Nieto, "Changing Role of Probation in California's Criminal Justice System," National Criminal Justice Reference Service (Washington, DC: U.S. Department of Justice, 1996).

24. John L. Wordall, Pamela Schram, Eric Hays, and Mathew Newmaan, "An Analysis of the Relationship between Probation Caseloads and Property Crime Rates in California Counties," Journal of Criminal Justice 32, no. 3 (May–June 2004): 231–241.

25. Danielle Kaeble, Laura M. Maruschak, and Thomas P. Bonczar, "Probation and Parole in the United States, 2014" (Washington, DC: U.S. Department of Justice, Bureau of Justice Statistics, November 2015).

26. Lauren E. Glaze, Thomas P. Bonczar, and Fan Zhang, "Probation and Parole in the United States, 2009," *Bureau of Justice Statistics Bulletin* (Washington, DC: U.S. Department of Justice, December 2010). http://bjs.ojp.usdoj.gov/content/pub/pdf/ppus09.pdf (retrieved August 1, 2011).

27. Herberman and Bonczar, "Probation and Parole in the United States, 2013," 7.

28. United States Courts, "Probation Officers." www.uscourts.gov/fedprob/officer/probation.html (retrieved March 3, 2009).

29. Vera Institute of Justice, *The Potential of Community Corrections to Improve Safety and Reduce Incarceration*, 13–15.

30. Bennet Mead, "Is There a Measure of Probation Success?" *Federal Probation* 69, no. 2 (December 2005). Originally published in *Federal Probation* (May–June 1937).

31. Herberman and Bonczar, "Probation and Parole in the United States, 2013," 4–5. Danielle Kaeble, Laura M. Maruschak, and Thomas P. Bonczar, "Probation and Parole in the United States, 2014" (Washington, DC: U.S. Department of Justice, Bureau of Justice Statistics, November 2015). Table 3, p.4.

32. Nancy Rodriguez and Vincent J. Webb, "Probation Violations, Revocations, and Imprisonment," *Criminal Justice Policy Review* 18, no. 1 (2007): 3–30.

33. E. F. Travis and A. Holsinger, *Evaluation of Ohio's Community Correctional Act Programs by County Size* (Cincinnati: Division of Criminal Justice, University of Cincinnati, 1997).

34. Vera Institute of Justice, *The Potential of Community Corrections to Improve Safety and Reduce Incarceration*, (New York: Vera Institute of Justice, July 2013), 26.

35. *Gagnon v. Scarpelli*, 411 U.S. 778 (1973).

36. Vera Institute of Justice, *The Potential of Community Corrections to Improve Safety and Reduce Incarceration*, 9–31.

37. Isiah Brown, "The Changing Role of Probation and Parole: A View to the Future," August 25, 2008. www.fdle.state.fl.us/Content/getdoc/dce13209-622b-49f4-8f68-7d5c7c4e3ec9/Brown-Isiah-paper.aspx (retrieved August 1, 2011).

38. Thomas F. White, "Re-engineering Probation towards Greater Public Safety: A Framework for Recidivism Reduction through Evidence-Based Practice," Court Support Services Division, State of Connecticut, April 2005. www.doc.ks.gov/reentry/information-folder/EBP%20in%20Probation.pdf (retrieved April 22, 2011).

39. Mathew T. DeMichele, "Probation and Parole's Growing Caseloads and Workload Allocation: Strategies for Managerial Decision Making," American Probation and Parole Association, May 4, 2007. www.appa-net.org/eweb/docs/appa/pubs/SMDM.pdf (retrieved April 22, 2011).

40. Pew Center on the States, "One in 31," 13.

41. Reid Montgomery Jr. and Steven Dillingham, *Probation and Parole in Practice* (Cincinnati: Pilgrimage, 1983); Little Hoover Commission, *Back to the Community: Safe and Sound Parole Policies* (Sacramento: Little Hoover Commission, 2003).

42. Todd Clear and George Cole, *American Corrections*, 2nd ed. (Pacific Grove, CA: Brooks/Cole, 1990); David Harding, "Jean Valjean's Dilemma: The Management of Ex-Convict Identity in the Search for Employment," *Deviant Behavior* 24, no. 6 (2003): 571–595.

43. Timothy Hughes, Doris James Wilson, and Allen J. Beck, "Trends in State Parole, 1990–2000" (Washington, D.C.: U.S. Department of Justice, Bureau of Justice Statistics, October 2001).

44. Danielle Kaeble, Laura M. Maruschak, and Thomas P. Bonczar, "Probation and Parole in the United States, 2014" (Washington, DC: U.S. Department of Justice, Bureau of Justice Statistics, November 2015). Table 2, p. 3.

45. Danielle Kaeble, Laura M. Maruschak, and Thomas P. Bonczar, "Probation and Parole in the United States, 2014" (Washington, DC: U.S. Department of Justice, Bureau of Justice Statistics, November 2015). Figure 4, p.6.

46. Danielle Kaeble, Lauren E. Glaze, Anastasios Tsoutis, and Todd Minton, "Correctional Populations in the United States, 2014" (Washington, DC: U.S. Department of Justice, Bureau of Justice Statistics, December 2015)p.5.

47. Danielle Kaeble, Lauren E. Glaze, Anastasios Tsoutis, and Todd Minton, "Correctional Populations in the United States, 2014" (Washington, DC: U.S. Department of Justice, Bureau of Justice Statistics, December 2015).Table 4, p.5.

48. Danielle Kaeble, Laura M. Maruschak, and Thomas P. Bonczar, "Probation and Parole in the United States, 2014" (Washington, DC: U.S. Department of Justice, Bureau of Justice Statistics, November 2015). Table 6, p.7.

49. Ibid.

50. Little Hoover Commission, *Breaking the Barriers for Women on Parole* (Sacramento: Little Hoover Commission, December 2004).

51. Committee on Community Supervision and Desistance from Crime, National Research Council, *Parole, Desistance from Crime, and Community Integration* (Washington, DC: National Academies Press, 2007).

52. Barbara Bloom, Barbara Owen, Stephanie Covington, and Myrna Raeder, *Gender-Responsive Strategies: Research, Practice, and Guiding Principles for Women Offenders* (Washington, DC: National Institute of Corrections, 2003).

53. Danielle Kaeble, Laura M. Maruschak, and Thomas P. Bonczar, "Probation and Parole in the United States, 2014" (Washington, DC: U.S. Department of Justice, Bureau of Justice Statistics, November 2015). Table 6, p. 7.

54. Joan Parkin, "Throwing away the Key: The World's Leading Jailer," *International Socialist Review* 21 (2002). www.isreview.org/issues/21/prisons.shtml (retrieved August 1, 2011).

55. William J. Sabol and Heather Couture, "Prison Inmates at Midyear 2007," *Bureau of Justice Statistics Bulletin* (Washington, DC: U.S. Department of Justice, June 2008), 7.

56. U.S. Department of Justice, Bureau of Justice Statistics, "Reentry Trends in the U.S.: Characteristics of Releases" (Washington, DC: DOJ). http://bjs.ojp.usdoj.gov/content/reentry/characteristics.cfm (retrieved August 1, 2011).

57. RAND Research Brief, "Prisoner Reentry: What Are the Public Health Challenges?" 2003. www.rand.org/pubs/research_briefs/RB6013/index1.html (retrieved December 26, 2006).

58. Sabol and Couture, "Prison Inmates at Midyear 2007," 7.

59. Danielle Kaeble, Laura M. Maruschak, and Thomas P. Bonczar, "Probation and Parole in the United States, 2014" (Washington, DC: U.S. Department of Justice, Bureau of Justice Statistics, November 2015), 1.

60. American Probation and Parole Association, "Probation and Parole FAQs," 2009. www.appa-net.org/eweb/DynamicPage.aspx?WebCode=VB_FAQ (retrieved March 4, 2011).

61. Gerry Wagshal. "Jaycee Dugard: Top 11 Missed Chances to Stop Her Kidnapper, Phillip Garrido," *ABC Primetime*, July 8, 2011. http://abcnews.go.com/Primetime/jaycee-dugard-top-11-missed-chances-stop-kidnapper/story?id=13966767 (retrieved July 12, 2011).

62. U.S. Department of Justice, Bureau of Justice Statistics, "Community Corrections (Probation and Parole)" (Washington, DC: DOJ). http://bjs.ojp.usdoj.gov/index.cfm?ty=tp&tid=15 (retrieved August 1, 2011).

63. Herberman and Bonczar, "Probation and Parole in the United States, 2013," 22. Danielle Kaeble, Laura M. Maruschak, and Thomas P. Bonczar, "Probation and Parole in the United States, 2014" (Washington, DC: U.S. Department of Justice, Bureau of Justice Statistics, November 2015). Table 5, p. 6.

64. Danielle Kaeble, Laura M. Maruschak, and Thomas P. Bonczar, "Probation and Parole in the United States, 2014" (Washington, DC: U.S. Department of Justice, Bureau of Justice Statistics, November 2015). Table 5, p. 6.

65. Danielle Kaeble, Laura M. Maruschak, and Thomas P. Bonczar, "Probation and Parole in the United States, 2014" (Washington, DC: U.S. Department of Justice, Bureau of Justice Statistics, November 2015). Figure 5, p. 7.

66. Herberman and Bonczar, "Probation and Parole in the United States, 2013," 22. Danielle Kaeble, Laura M. Maruschak, and Thomas P. Bonczar, "Probation and Parole in the United States, 2014" (Washington, DC: U.S. Department of Justice, Bureau of Justice Statistics, November 2015). Table 5, p. 6.

67. Danielle Kaeble, Laura M. Maruschak, and Thomas P. Bonczar, "Probation and Parole in the United States, 2014" (Washington, DC: U.S. Department of Justice, Bureau of Justice Statistics, November 2015), p.7.

68. Lauren E. Glaze and Thomas P. Bonczar, "Probation and Parole in the United States, 2007—Statistical Tables" (Washington, DC: U.S. Department of Justice, Bureau of Justice Statistics, December 2008), 6.

69. Jeremy Travis, "Back-End Sentences' Costs," *National Law Journal*, April 11, 2005. www.law.com/jsp/nlj/PubArticleNLJ.jsp?id=900005426858&slreturn=1&hbxlogin=1 (retrieved August 1, 2011).

70. Jeremy Travis and Sarah Lawrence, *Beyond the Prison Gates: The State of Parole in America* (Washington, DC: Urban Institute Justice Policy Center, 2002).

71. Clear and Cole, *American Corrections*, 442; Joan Petersilia, *When Prisoners Come Home: Parole and Prisoner Reentry* (New York: Oxford University Press, 2003).

72. Joanna Walters, "Illinois Inmates Increasingly Sued by State to Recoup Incarceration Costs," The Guardian, December 2, 2015. http://www.theguardian.com/us-news/2015/dec/02/illinois-inmates-sued-incarceration-costs (retrieved February 21, 2016) and David M. Shapiro, "Opinion: State Making It Harder for Ex-Cons to Go Straight," Chicago Sun-Times, January 19, 2016. http://chicago.suntimes.com/opinion/7/71/1263386/opinion-state-makes-harder-ex-cons-go-straight (retrieved February 21, 2016).

73. Amy Solomon, Vera Kachnowski, and Avinash Bhati, *Does Parole Work? Analyzing the Impact of Postprison Supervision on Rearrest Outcomes* (Washington, DC: Urban Institute, 2005).

74. Douglas S. Lipton, Robert Martinson, and Judith Wilks, *The Effectiveness of Correctional Treatment: A Survey of Treatment Evaluation Studies* (New York: Praeger, 1975).

75. A. Keith Bottomley, Michael Tonry, and Norval Morris, "Parole in Transition: A Comparative Study of Origins, Developments, and Prospects for the 1990s," in Michael Tonry and Norval Morris (Eds.), *Crime and Justice: A Review of Research* (Chicago: University of Chicago Press, 1990), 319–374.

76. *Morrisey v. Brewer*, 408 U.S. 471 (1972).

77. *Gagnon v. Scarpelli*, 411 U.S. 778 (1973).

78. *Greenholtz v. Inmates of the Nebraska Penal and Correctional Complex*, 442 U.S. 1 (1979).

79. Terryl Arola and Richard Lawrence, "Broken Windows Probation," *Perspectives* 24, no. 1 (2000): 27–33; Angela Hawken and Mark A. R. Kleiman, "Fixing the Parole System," *Issues in Science and Technology* 24, no. 4 (Summer 2008).

80. Morris L. Thigpen, Thomas J. Beauclair, George M. Keiser, and Cathy Banks, "Special Challenges Facing Parole" (Washington, DC: National Institute of Corrections, August 2011).

81. Shela R. Van Ness, "Intensive Probation versus Prison Outcomes in Indiana: Who Could Benefit?" *Journal of Contemporary Criminal Justice* 8, no. 4 (1992): 351–364.

82. Morris and Tonry, *Between Prison and Probation*.

83. James Turner Johnson and Daniel Van Ness (Eds.), *Handbook of Restorative Justice* (Cullompton, Devon, UK: Willan, 2007).

84. Restorative Justice Online, "Introduction." www.restorativejustice.org/intro (retrieved April 13, 2007).

85. Laura Magnani and Harmon L. Wray, *Beyond Prisons* (Minneapolis: Fortress Press, 2006).

86. Jeff Latimer, Craig Dowden, and Danielle Muise, "The Effectiveness of Restorative Justice Practices: A Meta-Analysis," *The Prison Journal* 85, no. 2 (June 2005), 127–144.

87. U.S. Department of Justice, Bureau of Justice Statistics, "Criminal Victimization in the United States, 2004—Statistical Tables," Table 82, 2006. http://bjs.ojp.usdoj.gov/content/pub/pdf/cvus0405.pdf (retrieved August 1, 2011); U.S. Delegation to the Intergovernmental Expert Group, "Response of the United States Delegation to the Intergovernmental Expert Group, Questionnaire on Fraud and the Criminal Misuse and Falsification of Identity (Identity Fraud)" (Washington, DC: U.S. Department of Justice, 2006), 37; Federal Bureau of Investigation, "Financial Crimes Report to the Public," 2005. www.fbi.gov/publications/financial/fcs_report052005/fcs_report052005.htm (retrieved August 1, 2011); Suzette Fromm, "Total Estimated Cost of Child Abuse and Neglect" (Washington, DC: Prevent Child Abuse America, 2001). www.preventchildabusenj.org/documents/index/cost_analysis.pdf (retrieved August 1, 2011), 2, 3.

88. U.S. Department of Justice, Office of Justice Programs, Office for Victims of Crime, "Promising Victim-Related Practices in Probation and Parole—A Compendium of Promising Practices," July 1999. www.ojp.usdoj.gov/ovc/publications/infores/probparole/ (retrieved January 31, 2007).

89. *Criminal Debt: Court-Ordered Restitution Amounts Far Exceed Likely Collections for the Crime Victims in Selected Financial Fraud Cases* (Washington, DC: Government Accountability Office, 2005).

90. U.S. Department of Justice, Office of Justice Programs, Office for Victims of Crime, "Legal Series #6 Bulletin. Ordering Restitution to the Crime Victim," November 2002, NCJ 189189.

91. National Center for Victims of Crime, *Making Restitution Real: Five Case Studies on Improving Restitution Collection* (Washington, DC: National Center for Victims of Crime, 2011), NCJ 234310. www.victimsofcrime.org/docs/Reports%20and%20Studies/2011_restitutionreport_web.pdf (retrieved June 9, 2015).

92. J. Harding, *Whither Restitutional Justice in England and Wales: A Probation Perspective* (Monsey, NY: Criminal Justice Press, 1996), 261–270; Ministry of Justice, "Breaking the Cycle: Effective Punishment, Rehabilitation, and Sentencing of Offenders" (London: Ministry of Justice, December 2010). www.justice.gov.uk/consultations/docs/breaking-the-cycle.pdf (retrieved August 1, 2011), 22.

93. R. Barry Ruback, "The Imposition of Economic Sanctions in Philadelphia: Costs, Fines, and Restitution," *Federal Probation* 68, no. 1 (2004).

94. "How to Use Structured Fines (Day Fines) as an Intermediate Sanction" (Washington, DC: U.S. Department of Justice, November 1996).

95. Joe Pinsker, "Finland, Home of the $103,000 Speeding Ticket," *The Atlantic*, March 12, 2015. www.theatlantic.com/business/archive/2015/03/finland-home-of-the-103000-speeding-ticket/387484/ (retrieved June 9, 2015).

96. Ronald J. Berger, Marvin D. Free Jr., and Patricia Searles, *Crime, Justice, and Society: Criminology and the Sociological Imagination* (New York: McGraw-Hill, 2001).

97. L. S. Abrams, M. Umbreit, and A. Gordon, "Young Offenders Speak about Meeting Their Victims: Implications for Future Programs," *Contemporary Justice Review; Issues in Criminal, Social and Restorative Justice* 9, no. 3 (2006): 243–256; J. Wemmers and K. Cyr, "Can Mediation Be Therapeutic for Crime Victims? An Evaluation of Victims' Experiences in Mediation with Young Offenders," *Canadian Journal of Criminology and Criminal Justice* 47, no. 3 (2005): 529–544.

98. D. Springer and A. Roberts (Eds.), *Handbook of Forensic Mental Health with Victims and Offenders: Assessment, Treatment, and Research* (New York: Springer, 2007); S. Trankle, "In the Shadow of Penal Law: Victim–Offender Mediation in Germany and France," *Punishment and Society* 9, no. 4 (2007): 395–415.

99. Julian V. Roberts, *The Virtual Prison: Community Custody and the Evolution of Imprisonment* (Cambridge, UK: Cambridge University Press, 2004); Josh Kurlantzick, "China, Burma and Sudan: Convincing Argument," *New Republic*, May 11, 2006. www.carnegieendowment.org/publications/index.cfm?fa=view&id=18329&zoom_highlight=josh (retrieved August 1, 2011).

100. Roberts, *The Virtual Prison*.

101. Jeffrey Ulmer, "Intermediate Sanctions: A Comparative Analysis of the Probability and Severity of Recidivism," *Sociological Inquiry* 71 (2001).

102. Jamie S. Martin, Kate Hanrahan, and James H. Bowers Jr., "Offenders' Perceptions of House Arrest and Electronic Monitoring," *Journal of Offender Rehabilitation* 48 (2009): 567.

103. Mary A. Finn and Suzanne Muirhead-Steves, "The Effectiveness of Electronic Monitoring with Violent Male Parolees," *Justice Quarterly* 19 (2002).

104. National Institute of Justice, "Electronic Monitoring Reduces Recidivism" (Washington, DC: U.S. Department of Justice, September 2011), NCJ 234460.

105. Tomer Einat, "Shock-Incarceration Programs in Israeli Sanctioning Policy: Toward a New Model of Punishment," *Israeli Law Review* 36, no. 1 (2002): 144–177.

106. "Youth Violence: A Report of the Surgeon General, Ineffective Tertiary Programs and Strategies." www.surgeongeneral.gov/library/youthviolence/chapter5/sec6.html (retrieved April 13, 2007).

107. National Institute of Justice, "Researchers Evaluate Eight Shock Incarceration Programs," Update October 1994. www.ncjrs.gov/pdffiles/shock.pdf (retrieved April 13, 2007).

108. Earnest Cowles and Laura Dorman, "Problems in Creating Boundaryless Treatment Regimens in Secure Correctional Environments: Private Sector-Public Agency Infrastructure Compatibility," *Prison Journal* 83, no. 3 (2003): 235–256.

109. Earnest Cowles, Thomas Castellano, and Laura Gransky, *"Boot Camp" Drug Treatment and Aftercare Intervention: An Evaluation Review* (Washington, DC: Government Printing Office, 1995).

110. New York State Division of Parole, *The Ninth Annual Shock Legislative Report: 1997* (Albany: New York State Division of Parole, 1998).

111. Jane Ellen Stevens, "Myths Cover up Further Tragedies in Episodes of Child Molestation," *SFGate*, April 3, 2005. http://articles.sfgate.com/2005-04-03/opinion/17370481_1_molesters-abuse-family-violence (retrieved August 1, 2011).

112. Sean Maddan and Paula Gray Stiz, *Sex Offender Registry Protocol Training Manual*, Arkansas Crime Information Center. www.acic.org/Registration/Sex%20Offender%20Manual%203rd%20edition.pdf (retrieved January 26, 2007).

113. California Department of Corrections and Rehabilitation, Division of Adult Parole Operations, "Sex Offender Information." www.cdcr.ca.gov/Parole/Sex_offender_facts/index.html (retrieved March 12, 2011).

114. Wesley G. Hughs, "Judge Rules Part of Jessica's Law Violates Offenders' Rights," *San Bernardino County Sun,* March 3, 2011.

115. Andrew Blankstein, "Part of Jessica's Law Ruled Unconstitutional," *Los Angeles Times,* November 5, 2010. http://articles.latimes.com/print/2010/nov/05/local/la-me-sex-offenders-20101105 (retrieved April 23, 2011).

116. Grant Duwe, "Residency Restrictions and Sex Offender Recidivism: Implications for Public Safety," *Geography & Public Safety* 2, no. 1 (May 2009).

117. Tammy Meredith, John Speir, and Sharon Johnson "Developing and Implementing Automated Risk Assessments in Parole," *Justice Research and Policy* 9 (2007): 1–21.

118. "The Proper and Improper Use of Risk Assessment in Corrections," *Federal Sentencing Reporter* 16, no. 3 (February 2004). www.jfa-associates.com/publications/pcras/proper%20userand%20misuse%20of%20risk.pdf (retrieved March 9, 2009).

119. "Maine Killings Raise Questions about Sex Offender Registries," *Wheeling News Register,* April 4, 2007. www.oweb.com/news/story/044202007_newSexOffendersSlain.asp (retrieved April 27, 2007).

120. Jamie Fellner, "The Wrong Sex Offender Laws," *Los Angeles Times,* September 18, 2007.

121. David Morgan, "N.J. Study Finds Registration Helps Locate Sex Offenders but Does Not Affect Recidivism," CBS News (CBS/AP), February 5, 2009. www.sdp123a.com/index.php?option=com_content&task=view&id=658&Itemid=58 (retrieved June 26, 2009).

122. Jeffery T. Walker, Sean Maddan, Bob E. Vasquez, Amy C. Van Houten, and Gwen Ervin-McLarty, "The Influence of Sex Offender Registration and Notification Laws in the United States," Arkansas Crime Information Center. www.acic.org/statistics/Research/SO_Report_Final.pdf (retrieved April 27, 2007); U.S. Department of Justice, Bureau of Justice Assistance, Center for Program Evaluation and Performance Measurement, "What Have We Learned from Evaluations of Sex Offender Programs/Strategies?" October 25, 2006. www.ojp.usdoj.gov/BJA/evaluation/psi_sops/sops2.htm (retrieved January 20, 2007).

123. Fellner, "The Wrong Sex Offender Laws."

124. Center for Sex Offender Management, "Myths and Facts about Sex Offenders," August 2000. www.csom.org/pubs/mythsfacts.html (retrieved March 5, 2009).

125. Tracy M. L. Brown, Steven A. McCabe, and Charles Wellford, "Global Positioning System (GPS) Technology for Community Supervision: Lessons Learned," *Center for Criminal Justice Technology, Noblis Technical Report,* August 2007. www.ncjrs.gov/pdffiles1/nij/grants/219376.pdf (retrieved March 9, 2009).

126. National Institute of Justice, *Issues and Practices* (Washington, DC: Government Printing Office, 1990).

127. Voncile Gowdy, *Intermediate Sanctions* (Washington, DC: U.S. Department of Justice, 1993), 5.

128. Wisconsin Legislative Reference Bureau, "The Parole of County Jail Prisoners under the Wisconsin Huber Law," Information Bulletin 230, 1963.

129. Jeffrey A. Bouffard, Doris Layton MacKenzie, and Laura J. Hickman, "Effectiveness of Vocational Education and Employment Programs for Adult Offenders: A Methodology-Based Analysis of the Literature," *Journal of Offender Rehabilitation* 31 (2000).

130. Leonidas K. Cheliotis, "Reconsidering the Effectiveness of Temporary Release: A Systematic Review," *Aggression and Violent Behavior* 13, no. 3 (June 2008).

131. Karen Alexander, "Furlough Proposal Stirs Foes," *Los Angeles Times,* February 26, 2000. http://articles.latimes.com/2000/feb/26/local/me-2726 (retrieved March 7, 2009).

132. David Reyes, "Protest Derails Fountain Valley Halfway House," *Los Angeles Times,* May 3, 2000. http://articles.latimes.com/2000/may/03/local/me-26172 (retrieved March 7, 2009).

133. Tony Brecht, "Residents Fear Halfway House Plan," *Quad-City Times,* November 1, 2006. www.qctimes.com/articles/2006/11/01/news/local/doc454846b2a9189203300076.txt (retrieved March 8, 2009).

134. Nancy Marion, "Effectiveness of Community-Based Correctional Programs: A Case Study," *Prison Journal* 82 (2002).

135. Susan Turner and Joan Petersilia, "Work Release: Recidivism and Corrections Costs in Washington State," *Research in Brief,* National Institute of Justice, 1996. www.ncjrs.gov/pdffiles/163706.pdf (retrieved March 27, 2007).

136. Monica G. Massarand, "Work Release Program Research Project," Final Report, Multnomah County, Oregon, June 30, 2004. www.lpscc.org/does/WorkReleaseProgramResearchReportJune2004.pdf (retrieved March 7, 2009); Jillian Berk, "Does Work Release Work?" Brown University Micro Lunch Series, May 2, 2008. http://client.norc.org/jole/SOLEweb/8318.pdf (retrieved March 7, 2009).

137. U.S. Department of Labor, "Grants Totaling $30M to Help Adults in Prison Work-Release Programs Transition to the Workforce Now Available from US Labor Department," news release, February 18, 2014. www.dol.gov/opa/media/press/eta/ETA20140278.htm (retrieved June 22, 2015).

138. Holly K. O. Sparrow, "Private Probation in Georgia: A New Direction, Service and Vigilance," Institute for Court Management, Administrative Office of the Courts, May 2001. www.ncsconline.org/D_ICM/Research_Papers_2001/Private_Probation_GA.pdf (retrieved January 27, 2007).

139. Liz Potocsnak, "Private Probation Company Called an Unregulated Tool for Corruption," *Courthouse News Service,* January 27, 2011. www.courthousenews.com/2011/01/27/33674.htm (retrieved March 19, 2011); Andrew Cohen, "The Private Probation Problem Is Worse Than Anyone Thought," *The Atlantic,* February 5, 2014. www.theatlantic.com/national/archive/2014/02/the-private-probation-problem-is-worse-than-anyone-thought/283589/ (retrieved May 10, 2015).

140. Vera Institute of Justice, "Survey on Parole Practice to U.S. Parole Board Chairs and Releasing Authority Directors," Association of Paroling Authorities International, February 2, 2012.

141. Vera Institute of Justice, *The Potential of Community Corrections to Improve Safety and Reduce Incarceration ,* 16.

142. David Fialkoff, "Standardizing Parole Violation Sanctions" (Washington, DC: National Institute of Justice, 2010).

143. Clear and Cole, *American Corrections.*

CHAPTER 14

1. H. Gordon, *Hammurabi's Code: Quaint or Forward-Looking?* (New York: Rinehart Press, 1957).

2. Stephan Schafer, *The Victim and His Criminal* (New York: Random House, 1968).

3. Frederick Wertham, *The Show of Violence* (Garden City, NY: Country Life Press, 1948).

4. Frederick Wertham, *A Sign for Cain: An Exploration of Human Violence* (New York: Hale Press, 1968).

5. Miroslav Volf, "Original Crime, Primal Care," in Lisa Barnes Lampman and Michelle D. Shattuck (Eds.), *God and the Victim: Theological Reflections on Evil, Victimization, Justice, and Forgiveness* (Grand Rapids, MI: William B. Eerdmans, 1999).

6. Frans W. Winkel, "Peer Support Groups: Evaluating the Mere Contact/Mere Sharing Model and Impairment Hypotheses," *International Perspectives in Victimology* 2, no. 1 (2006): 101–113.

7. Jeffrey T. Mitchell and George S. Everly, *Critical Incident Stress Debriefing: An Operations Manual* (Ellicott City, MD: Chevron Press, 1995).

8. Ezzat A. Fattah, *Understanding Criminal Victimization: An Introduction to Theoretical Victimology* (Scarborough, Ontario: Prentice Hall, 1991); William G. Doerner and Steven P. Lab, *Victimology,* 4th ed. (New York: Anderson, 2005).

9. William V. Pelfrey Sr. and William V. Pelfrey Jr., "Fear of Crime, Age, and Victimization Relationships and Changes over Time," in Laura J.

Moriarty and Robert A. Jerin (Eds.), *Current Issues in Victimological Research* (Durham: Carolina Academic Press, 1998).

10. Susan Brownmiller, *Against Our Will: Men, Women and Rape* (New York: Simon & Schuster, 1975).

11. Frank Carrington, *The Victims* (New Rochelle, NY: Arlington House, 1975).

12. Judith Green, "Getting Tough on Crime: The History and Political Context of Sentencing Reform Developments Leading to the Passage of the 1994 Crime Act," in Cyrus Tata and Neil Hutton (Eds.), *Sentencing and Society: International Perspectives* (Farnham, Surrey, UK: Ashgate, 2002), 43–65.

13. Ibid.

14. Desmond S. Greer, "A Transatlantic Perspective on the Compensation of Crime Victims in the United States," *Journal of Criminal Law and Criminology* 85 (Fall 1994): 1–38.

15. Robert A. Jerin and Laura J. Moriarty, *The Victims of Crime* (Upper Saddle River, NJ: Pearson Education, 2010).

16. Ted Poe, "Congressional Victims' Rights Caucus," *The Police Chief* 74, no. 10 (October 2007); Victims' Rights Caucus, "Legislation." http://vrc.poe.house.gov/legislation?page=1 (retrieved June 29, 2015).

17. Graham Farrell, "Preventing Repeat Victimization," *Crime and Justice* 19 (1969): 469–534.

18. Graham Farrell and Ken Pease, "Once Bitten, Twice Bitten: Repeat Victimisation and Its Implications for Crime Prevention," *Crime Prevention Unit*, Paper 46 (1993).

19. Ken Pease, "Repeat Victimization: Taking Stock," *Crime Detection and Prevention Series,* Paper 90 (1998): 1–40.

20. John P. J. Dussich, "Concepts and Forms of Victim Services," in John Dussich (Ed.), *Victim Services* (Fresno: California State University, 2007).

21. Larry Bennett, Stephanie Riger, Paul Schewe, April Howard, and Sharon Wasco, "Effectiveness of Hotline, Advocacy, Counseling, and Shelter Services for Victims of Domestic Violence: A Statewide Evaluation," *Journal of Interpersonal Violence* 19, no. 7 (July 2004): 815–829.

22. Ibid.

23. U.S. Department of Justice, Office for Victims of Crime, "The Federal Crime Victims Division," *OVC Fact Sheet* (Washington, DC: DOJ, October 1999). www.ncjrs.gov/ovc_archives/factsheets/fcvd-jun.htm (accessed March 11, 2011).

24. National Organization for Women, "Stop the Killings of the Women of Juarez: Femicides of Juarez Fact Sheet." www.now.org/issues/global/juarez/femicide.html (retrieved May 25, 2011).

25. Amnesty International, "Mexico Urged to Protect Activists after Campaigner Shot Dead," January 6, 2010. www.amnesty.org/en/news-and-updates/news/mexico-urged-protect-activists-after-campaigner-shot-dead-20100106 (retrieved May 25, 2011); Nacha Cattan, "Mexican Women Activists Put Reforms under the Gun," *WeNews*, August 10, 2009. www.womensenews.org/story/090810/mexican-women-activists-put-reforms-under-the-gun (retrieved March 25, 2011).

26. Center for Gender and Refugee Studies, "Central America: Femicides and Gender-Based Violence" (San Francisco: University of California, Hastings College of the Law). http://cgrs.uchastings.edu/our-work/central-america-femicides-and-gender-based-violence (retrieved June 23, 2015).

27. Federal Bureau of Investigation, "Victim Assistance: FBI Resources for Helping Victims." www.fbi.gov (retrieved April 23, 2007).

28. U.S. Department of Justice, Office for Victims of Crime, "The Federal Crime Victims Division."

29. U.S. Department of Justice, Bureau of Justice Statistics, "Victim Characteristics." http://bjs.ojp.usdoj.gov/index.cfm?ty=tp&tid=92 (retrieved July 19, 2011).

30. Steven W. Perry, "American Indians and Crime: A BJS Statistical Profile, 1992–2002," U.S. Department of Justice, Bureau of Justice Statistics, December 2004, NCJ 203097.

31. Ada Pecos-Melton, "Specific Justice Systems and Victims' Rights, Section 4, Tribal Justice," *National Victim Assistance Academy, Training Manual* (Washington, DC: U.S. Department of Justice, Office for Victims of Crime, June 2002).

32. Justice News, U.S. Department of Justice, "Attorney General Holder Announces Violence Against Women Tribal Prosecution Task Force in Indian Country." www.justice.gov/opa/pr/2011/January/11-ag-086.html (retrieved March 11, 2011).

33. Kimberly Hefling, "Rape Victims in Military Doubly Abused, Lawsuit Alleges. Officers Punishing Plaintiffs, Group Argues in Lawsuit," *Columbus Dispatch*, February 16, 2011. www.dispatch.com/live/content/national_world/stories/2011/02/16/rape-victims-in-military-doubly-abused-lawsuit-alleges.html (retrieved March 11, 2011).

34. Bryan D. Byers, "Death Notification: The Theory and Practice of Delivering Bad News," in James E. Hendricks and Bryan D. Byers (Eds.), *Crisis Intervention in Criminal Justice and Social Service* (Springfield, IL: Charles C Thomas, 2002).

35. National Association of Crime Victim Compensation Boards, "Crime Victim Compensation: An Overview." www.nacvcb.org (retrieved July 30, 2011).

36. Ibid.

37. Ibid.

38. Ibid.

39. Ibid.

40. U.S. Department of Justice, Office for Victims of Crime, "OVC Handbook for Coping after Terrorism: A Guide to Healing and Recovery" (Washington, DC: DOJ, September 2001).

41. David A. Alexander, "Early Mental Health Intervention after Disasters," *Advances in Psychiatric Treatment* 11 (2005): 12–18.

42. Ibid.

43. Ibid.

44. Kathleen M. Palm, Melissa A. Polusny, and Victoria M. Follette, "Vicarious Traumatization: Potential Hazards and Interventions for Disaster and Trauma Workers," *Prehospital and Disaster Medicine* 19, no. 1 (2004): 73–78; C. Joinson, "Coping with Compassion Fatigue," *Nursing* 22, no. 4 (1992): 116–122.

45. Richard E. Adams, Joseph A. Boscarino, and Charles R. Figley, "Compassion Fatigue and Psychological Distress among Social Workers: A Validation Study," *American Journal of Orthopsychiatry* 76, no. 1 (2006): 103–108.

46. Anne Seymour and Christine Edmunds, "Mental Health Needs, Section 2, Stress Management," *National Victim Assistance Academy, Training Manual* (Washington, DC: U.S. Department of Justice, Office for Victims of Crime, June 2002).

47. Alexander, "Early Mental Health Intervention after Disasters."

48. Rick A. Myer and Christian Conte, "Assessment for Crisis Intervention," *Journal of Clinical Psychology: In Session* 62, no. 8 (2006): 73–79.

49. Bennett, Riger, Schewe, Howard, and Wasco, "Effectiveness of Hotline, Advocacy, Counseling, and Shelter Services for Victims of Domestic Violence."

50. National Network to End Domestic Violence, "Domestic Violence Counts 2013: A 24-Hour Census of Domestic Violence Shelters and Services." http://nnedv.org/downloads/Census/DVCounts2013/Census13_FullReport_forweb_smallestFileSizeWhiteMargins.pdf (retrieved June 29, 2015).

51. Albert L. Shostack, *Shelters for Battered Women and Their Children: A Comprehensive Guide to Planning and Operating Safe and Caring Residential Programs* (Springfield, IL: Charles C Thomas, 2001).

52. Janice Humphreys and Kathryn Lee, "Sleep Disturbance in Battered Women Living in Transitional Housing," *Journal of Mental Health Nursing* 26 (2005): 771–780.

53. Shostack, *Shelters for Battered Women and Their Children.*

54. National Network to End Domestic Violence, "Domestic Violence Counts 2013."

55. Shostack, *Shelters for Battered Women and Their Children.*

56. Ibid.

57. John Devaney, "Chronic Child Abuse and Domestic Violence: Children and Families with Long-Term Complex Needs," *Child and Family Social Work* 13, no. 4 (November 2008): 443–453.

58. Child Trends Data Bank, "Children's Exposure to Violence: Indicators on Children and Youth," July 2013. www.childtrends.org/wp-content/uploads/2012/07/118_Exposure_to_Violence.pdf (retrieved June 29, 2015).

59. Ibid.

60. J. Devaney, "Chronic child abuse and domestic violence: children and families with long-term and complex needs," Child and Family Social Work, Online publication July 2008, doi: 101111/j.1365-2206.2008.00559.x.

61. Rebecca M. Bolen, "Attachment and Family Violence: Complexities in Knowing," *Child Abuse and Neglect: The International Journal* 29 (August 2005): 845–852.

62. Jennifer E. Macomber, "An Overview of Selected Data on Children in Vulnerable Families," Urban Institute, August 10, 2006. www.urban.org/url.cfm?ID=311351 (retrieved February 12, 2009).

63. Bolen, "Attachment and Family Violence."

64. Bennett, Riger, Schewe, Howard, and Wasco, "Effectiveness of Hotline, Advocacy, Counseling, and Shelter Services for Victims of Domestic Violence."

65. Ibid.

66. Ibid.

67. Elizabethann O'Sullivan and Abigail Carlton, "Victim Services, Community Outreach, and Contemporary Rape Crisis Centers: A Comparison of Independent and Multiservice Centers," *Journal of Interpersonal Violence* 16, no. 4 (2001): 343–360.

68. Ibid.

69. Rebecca Campbell, Debra Patterson, and Lauren F. Lichty, "The Effectiveness of Sexual Assault Nurse Examiner (SANE) Programs: A Review of Psychological, Medical, Legal, and Community Outcomes," *Trauma, Violence, and Abuse* 6, no. 4 (October 2005): 313–329.

70. Rupaleem Bhuyan and Kirsten Senturia, "Understanding Intimate Partner Violence Resource Utilization and Survivor Solutions among Immigrant and Refugee Women: Introduction to the Special Issue," *Journal of Interpersonal Violence* 20, no. 8 (August 2005): 895–901.

71. National Center on Elder Abuse, *The 2004 Survey of State Adult Protective Services: Abuse of Adults 60 Years and Older* (Washington, DC: NCEA, 2006).

72. Elder Abuse Daily, "Elder Abuse Data and Statistics," *February 15, 2010. www.eadaily. com/15/elder-abuse-statistics/ (accessed July 21, 2011).*

73. Pamela B. Teaster, Tyler A. Dugar, Marta S. Mendiondo, Erin L. Abner, and Kara A. Cecil, *The 2004 Survey of State Adult Protective Services: Abuse of Vulnerable Adults 18 Years of Age and Older* (Washington, DC: National Center on Elder Abuse, March 2007).

74. *New Directions from the Field: Victims' Rights and Services for the 21st Century* (Washington, DC: U.S. Department of Justice, Office for Victims of Crime, May 1998).

75. Kris Henning and Lynette Feder, "Criminal Prosecution of Domestic Violence Offenses: An Investigation of Factors Predictive of Court Outcomes," *Criminal Justice Behavior* 32, no. 6 (December 2005): 612–642.

76. Nicole E. Allen, "An Examination of the Effectiveness of Intimate Partner Violence Coordinating Councils," *Violence Against Women* 12, no. 1 (January 2006): 46–67; Melanie Shephard, "Twenty Years of Progress in Addressing Intimate Partner Violence: An Agenda for the Next 10," *Journal of Interpersonal Violence* 20, no. 4 (2005): 436–441.

77. O'Sullivan and Carlton, "Victim Services, Community Outreach, and Contemporary Rape Crisis Centers."

78. U.S. Department of Justice, Office for Victims of Crime, *New Directions from the Field: Victims' Rights and Services for the 21st Century.* www.ncjrs. gov/ovc_archives/directions/welcome.html (retrieved July 30, 2011).

79. California Child Abuse Training and Technical Assistance Centers (CATTA). http://cirinc.org/catta/ (retrieved July 30, 2011).

80. Mark S. Umbreit, *The Handbook of Victim Offender Mediation: An Essential Guide to Research and Practice* (San Francisco: Jossey-Bass, 2001).

81. Ibid.

82. Kathleen Daly, "A Tale of Two Studies: Restorative Justice from the Victim's Perspective," in E. Elliott and R. Gordon (Eds.), *Restorative Justice: Emerging Issues in Practice and Evaluation* (Cullompton, UK: Willan, 2004), 153–174; Kathleen Daly and Julie Stubbs, "Feminist Engagement with Restorative Justice," *Theoretical Criminology* 10, no. 1 (2006): 9–28.

83. Annalise Acorn, *Compulsory Compassion: A Critique of Restorative Justice* (Vancouver: University of British Columbia Press, 2004); Daly and Stubbs, "Feminist Engagement with Restorative Justice."

84. John Braithwaite and Kathleen Daly, "Masculinities, Violence, and Communitarian Control," in Tim Newburn and Betsy Stanko (Eds.), *Just Boys Doing Business? Men, Masculinities, and Crime* (New York: Routledge, 1994); Daly and Stubbs, "Feminist Engagement with Restorative Justice."

85. Daly and Stubbs, "Feminist Engagement with Restorative Justice."

86. Kathleen Daly, "A Tale of Two Studies: Restorative Justice from the Victim's Perspective," in Elliott and Gordon, *Restorative Justice*; Yvon Dandurand and Curt T. Griffiths, *Handbook on Restorative Justice Programmes: Criminal Justice Handbook Series* (New York: United Nations Office on Drugs and Crime, 2006); Umbreit, *The Handbook of Victim Offender Mediation*; Heather Nancarrow, "In Search of Justice for Domestic Violence and Family Violence: Indigenous and Non-Indigenous Women's Perspectives in Australia," *Theoretical Criminology* 10 (2006): 87–106; Mary Koss and Mary Achilles, "In Brief: Restorative Justice Responses to Sexual Assault," National Online Resource Center on Violence Against Women, February 2008. www.vawnet.org and http://new.vawnet.org/category/Main_Doc.php?docid=1231 (retrieved March 10, 2011).

CHAPTER 15

1. Jennifer Gonnerman, "Kalief Browder, 1993–2015," *The New Yorker*, June 7, 2015. www.newyorker.com/news/news-desk/kalief-browder-1993-2015; Eyder Peralta, "Kalief Browder, Jailed for Years without Trial, Kills Himself," *NPR*, June 8, 2015. www.npr.org/sections/thetwo-way/2015/06/08/412842780/kalief-browder-jailed-for-years-at-rikers-island-without-trial-commits-suicide; Matt Pearce, "Kalief Browder, Jailed for 3 Years in N.Y. Prison without a Trial, Commits Suicide," *Los Angeles Times*, June 7, 2015. www.latimes.com/nation/la-na-new-york-kalief-browder-20150607-story.html.

2. Randall G. Shelden, *Controlling the Dangerous Classes* (Needham Heights, MA: Allyn & Bacon, 2001).

3. Matthew Lippman, *Contemporary Criminal Law: Concepts, Cases, and Controversies* (Thousand Oaks, CA: Sage, 2006).

4. Barry Krisberg, *Juvenile Justice: Redeeming Our Children* (Thousand Oaks, CA: Sage, 2005).

5. Shelden, *Controlling the Dangerous Classes.*

6. Lawrence M. Friedman, *Crime and Punishment in American History* (New York: Basic Books, 1993).

7. Ibid., 165.

8. Krisberg, *Juvenile Justice.*

9. Ibid.

10. Ibid.

11. Howard N. Snyder and Melissa Sickmund, *Juvenile Offenders and Victims: 2006 National Report* (Washington, DC: U.S. Department of Justice, Office of Justice Programs, Office of Juvenile Justice and Delinquency Prevention, 2006), chap. 3, p. 72. www.ojjdp.gov/ojstatbb/nr2006/downloads/chapter3.pdf (retrieved August 12, 2011).

12. Rolf Loeber and Magda Stouthamer-Loeber, "Family Factors as Correlates and Predictors of Juvenile Conduct Problems and Delinquency," *Crime and Justice* 7 (1986): 29–149.

13. Denise C. Gottfredson, *Schools and Delinquency*, 2nd ed. (Cambridge, UK: Cambridge University Press, 2001).

14. American Civil Liberties Union, "School-to-Prison Pipeline," March 11, 2008. https://www.aclu.org/issues/racial-justice/race-and-inequality-education/school-prison-pipeline?redirect=school-prison-pipeline (retrieved July 7, 2015).

15. Richard A. Cloward and Lloyd E. Ohlin, *Delinquency and Opportunity* (New York: Free Press, 1960); Albert K. Cohen, *Delinquent Boys* (New York: Free Press, 1955); Walter B. Miller, "Lower Class Culture as a Generating Milieu of Gang Delinquency," *Journal of Social Issues* 14 (1958): 5–19.

16. James F. Short and F. Ivan Nye, "Extent of Unrecorded Juvenile Delinquency," *Journal of Criminal Law, Criminology and Police Science* 49 (1958): 296–302.

17. Margaret Farnworth, Terence P. Thornberry, Marvin D. Krohn, and Alan J. Lizotte, "Measurement in the Study of Class and Delinquency: Integrating Theory and Research," *Journal of Research in Crime and Delinquency* 31 (1994): 32–61.

18. Joanne M. Kaufman, "Explaining the Race/Ethnicity Violence Relationship: Neighborhood Context and Psychological Processes," *Justice Quarterly* 22 (June 2005): 224–251.

19. Snyder and Sickmund, *Juvenile Offenders and Victims*, chap. 5, p. 132.

20. Robert Agnew, *Juvenile Delinquency: Causes and Control*, 2nd ed. (Los Angeles: Roxbury, 2005).

21. Charles Puzzanchera, "Juvenile Arrests 2011," *Juvenile Justice Bulletin* (Washington, DC: U.S. Department of Justice, Office of Juvenile Justice and Delinquency Prevention, December 2013). www.ojjdp.gov/pubs/244476.pdf (retrieved July 7, 2015).

22. Ibid.

23. Ibid.

24. Snyder and Sickmund, *Juvenile Offenders and Victims.*

25. Richard Lawrence, *School Crime and Juvenile Justice,* 2nd ed. (New York: Oxford University Press, 2007).

26. Charles Puzzanchera, "Juvenile Arrests 2012," *Juvenile Offenders and Victims: National Report Series* (Washington, DC: U.S. Department of Justice, Office of Juvenile Justice and Delinquency Prevention, December 2014). www.ojjdp.gov/pubs/248513.pdf (retrieved May 20, 2015).

27. Ibid.

28. Meda Chesney-Lind and Randall G. Shelden, *Girls, Delinquency, and Juvenile Justice* (Belmont, CA: Wadsworth, 2004).

29. Miriam Sealock and Sally S. Simpson, "Unraveling Bias in Arrest Decisions: The Role of Juvenile Offender Type-Scripts," *Justice Quarterly* 15 (1998): 427–457.

30. Samuel Walker, Cassia Spohn, and Miriam DeLone, *The Color of Justice,* 2nd ed. (Belmont, CA: Wadsworth, 2000).

31. S. A. Anderson, R. M. Sabatelli, and J. Trachtenberg, "Community Police and Youth Programs as a Context for Positive Youth Development," *Police Quarterly* 10, no. 1 (2007): 23–40.

32. Kate Zernike, "Camden Turns Around with New Police Force," *New York Times,* August 31, 2015. www.nytimes.com/2014/09/01/nyregion/camden-turns-around-with-new-police-force.html?_r=0 (retrieved May 20, 2015).

33. G. T. Patterson, "The Role of Police Officers in Elementary and Secondary Schools: Implications for Police–School Social Work Collaboration," *School Social Work Journal* 31, no. 2 (Spring 2007): 82–99.

34. "About D.A.R.E." www.dare.com/home/about_dare.asp (retrieved March 19, 2009).

35. D. M. Gorman, "The Irrelevance of Evidence in the Development of School-Based Drug Prevention Policy, 1986–1996," *Evaluation Review* 22, no. 1 (1998): 118–146.

36. "Youth Illicit Drug Use Prevention: D.A.R.E. Long-Term Evaluations and Federal Efforts to Identify Effective Programs," U.S. Government Accountability Office, GAO-03-172R, January 15, 2003. www.gao.gov/products/GAO-03-172R (retrieved March 19, 2009); full report available at http://archive.gao.gov/t2pbat6/149076.pdf (retrieved August 12, 2011).

37. Julie Kiernan Coon and Lawrence F. Travis III, "The Role of Police in Public Schools: A Comparison of Principal and Police Reports of Activities in Schools," *Police Practice and Research* 13, no. 1 (2012): 27.

38. Friedman, *Crime and Punishment in American History;* Krisberg, *Juvenile Justice;* Anthony Platt, "The Triumph of Benevolence: Origins of Juvenile Justice in the U.S.," in R. Quinney (Ed.), *Criminal Justice in America: A Critical Understanding* (Boston: Little, Brown, 1974).

39. Julian W. Mack, "The Juvenile Court," *Harvard Law Review* 23 (1909): 104–122.

40. Snyder and Sickmund, *Juvenile Offenders and Victims.*

41. Ibid.

42. Ibid.

43. "7 Year Old Charged in Stabbing Death of Neighbor's Boyfriend Arraigned." www.wlextv.com/global/story.asp?s= 3535254&ClientType= Printable (retrieved April 11, 2007); "Pint-Sized Threat Gets Adult Response," *Washington Post.* www.washingtonpost.com/ac2/wp-dyn?pagena me =article&node=&contentId=A276882003Apr23 &notFound=true (retrieved April 11, 2007); "Boys 7, 10, 11 Face Arson Charges," *CNN.com.* www.cnn.com/2007/US/03/13/boys.fire.ap/index.html (retrieved April 11, 2007).

44. "Little Criminals," *Frontline* (PBS), May 13, 1997. www.pbs.org/wgbh/pages/frontline/shows/little/etc/script.html (retrieved April 11, 2007).

45. U.S. Department of Justice, Office of Juvenile Justice and Delinquency Prevention, *Juvenile Justice Reform Initiatives in the States, 1994–1996.* www.ojjdp.gov/pubs/reform/ch2_i.html (retrieved July 20, 2011).

46. *Kent v. United States,* 383 U.S. 541 (1966).

47. Jolanta Juszkiewicz, "Youth Crime/Adult Time: Is Justice Served?" (Washington, DC: Building Blocks for Youth, 2000); U.S. Department of Justice, Office of Juvenile Justice and Delinquency Prevention, *Juvenile Court Statistics, 2000* (Washington, DC: OJJDP, 2000).

48. Benjamin Adams and Sean Addie, "Delinquency Cases Waived to Criminal Court, 2005," OJJPD Fact Sheet, June 2009. www.ncjrs.gov/pdffiles1/ojjdp/224539.pdf (retrieved August 29, 2009).

49. Donna M. Bishop, Charles E. Frazier, and John C. Henrietta, "Prosecutorial Waiver: Case Study of a Questionable Reform," *Crime & Delinquency* 35 (1989): 179–198.

50. Snyder and Sickmund, *Juvenile Offenders and Victims.*

51. Juszkiewicz, "Youth Crime/Adult Time"; Office of Juvenile Justice and Delinquency Prevention, *Juvenile Court Statistics, 2000.*

52. Donna M. Bishop, Charles E. Frazier, and Lonn Lanza-Kaduce, "The Transfer of Juveniles to Adult Court: Does It Make a Difference?" *Crime & Delinquency* 42 (1996): 171–191; Coalition for Juvenile Justice, *Childhood on Trial: The Failure of Trying and Sentencing Youth in Adult Criminal Court* (Washington, DC: Coalition for Juvenile Justice, 2005).

53. *Kent v. United States,* 383 U.S. 541, 556 (1966).

54. *In re Gault,* 387 U.S. 1 (1967).

55. Samuel M. Davis, Elizabeth S. Scott, Walter Wadlington, and Charles H. Whitebread, *Children in the Legal System: Cases and Materials,* 3rd ed. (New York: Foundation Press, 2004).

56. *In re Winship,* 397 U.S. 358 (1970).

57. *McKeiver v. Pennsylvania,* 403 U.S. 528 (1971).

58. Ibid., 528, 545.

59. *Breed v. Jones,* 421 U.S. 519 (1975).

60. *Fare v. Michael C.,* 442 U.S. 707 (1979).

61. Ibid.

62. *Schall v. Martin,* 467 U.S. 253 (1984).

63. Death Penalty Information Center, "Juveniles News and Developments, 2003." www.deathpenaltyinfo.org/article.php?did=2137 (retrieved April 27, 2007).

64. *Thompson v. Oklahoma,* 487 U.S. 815 (1988); *Stanford v. Kentucky,* 492 U.S. 361 (1989).

65. American Bar Association, "The Juvenile Death Penalty: Facts and Figures," March 16, 2004. www.abanet.org/crimjust/juvjus/dparticles/factsheet-factsfigures.pdf (retrieved April 27, 2007).

66. *Stanford v. Kentucky,* 492 U.S. 361 (1989).

67. *Roper v. Simmons,* 543 U.S. 551 (2005).

68. *Graham v. Florida,* 130 S. Ct. 2011 (2010).

69. Robert Barnes, "Supreme Court Restricts Life without Parole for Juveniles," *Washington Post,* May 18, 2010. www.washingtonpost.com/wpdyn/content/article/2010/05/17/AR2010051701355.html?sid=ST2010051704182 (retrieved March 10, 2011).

70. *Miller v. Alabama,* 132 S. Ct. 2455 (2012).

71. *New Jersey v. T.L.O.,* 469 U.S. 325 (1984).

72. *Pottawatomie v. Earls,* 536 U.S. 822 (2002).

73. *Safford Unified School District #1 v. Redding,* 2009 U.S. LEXIS 4735 (2009).

74. Office of Juvenile Justice and Delinquency Prevention, "Juvenile Offenders and Victims: 2014 National Report." www.ojjdp.gov/ojstatbb/nr2014/downloads/NR2014.pdf (retrieved June 13, 2015).

75. Ibid.

76. Snyder and Sickmund, *Juvenile Offenders and Victims.*

77. Krisberg, *Juvenile Justice.*

78. American Bar Association, Resolution, Adopted by the House of Delegates, August 11–12, 2003. www.abanet.org/leadership/2003/journal/101b.pdf (retrieved May 26, 2007).

79. Snyder and Sickmund, *Juvenile Offenders and Victims.*

80. U.S. Department of Justice, Office of Juvenile Justice and Delinquency Prevention, "Teen Courts: A Focus on Research," 2000. www.ncjrs.gov/pdffiles1/ojjdp/183472.pdf (retrieved April 27, 2007).

81. Steven Patrick, Robert Marsh, and Susan Mimura, "Control Group Study of Juvenile Diversion Programs: An Experiment in Juvenile Diversion," *Social Science Journal* 41 (2004): 129–135; Steven Patrick and Robert Marsh, "Juvenile Diversion: Results of a 3-Year Experimental Study," *Criminal Justice Policy Review* 16 (2005): 59–73.

82. Snyder and Sickmund, *Juvenile Offenders and Victims.*

83. *United States v. Salerno,* 481 U.S. 739 (1987).

84. *Schall v. Martin,* 467 U.S. 253 (1984).

85. Office of Juvenile Justice and Delinquency Prevention, "Juvenile Offenders and Victims."

86. Ibid.

87. Ibid.

88. Ibid.

89. Ibid.

90. American Medical Association, Council on Scientific Affairs, "Health Status of Detained and Incarcerated Youths," *Journal of the American Medical Association* 263 (1990): 987–991.

91. Craig S. Schwalbe, Mark W. Fraser, Steven H. Day, and Valerie Cooley, "Classifying Juvenile Offenders according to Risk of Recidivism: Predictive Validity,

92. Office of Juvenile Justice and Delinquency Prevention, "Juvenile Offenders and Victims."

93. Barry C. Feld, "*In re Gault* Revisited: A Cross-State Comparison of the Right to Counsel in Juvenile Court," *Crime & Delinquency* 34 (1988): 393–424; Lori Guevara, Cassia Spohn, and Denise Herz, "Race, Legal Representation, and Juvenile Justice: Issues and Concerns," *Crime & Delinquency* 50 (2004): 344–371.

94. Office of Juvenile Justice and Delinquency Prevention, "Juvenile Offenders and Victims."

95. Barry C. Feld, "The Juvenile Court Meets the Principle of Offense: Punishment, Treatment, and the Difference It Makes," *Boston University Law Review* 68 (1988): 821–896.

96. Joseph G. Weis, Robert D. Crutchfield, and George S. Bridges, *Juvenile Delinquency: Readings*, 2nd ed. (Boston: Pine Forge Press, 2001), 425; Edwin Schur, *Labeling Deviant Behavior: Its Sociological Implications* (New York: Harper & Row, 1971), 15–25.

97. Brandon Applegate, Michael Turner, Joseph Sanborn, Edward Latessa, and Melissa Moon, "Individualization, Criminalization, or Problem Resolution: A Factorial Survey of Juvenile Court Judges' Decisions to Incarcerate Youthful Felony Offenders," *Justice Quarterly* 17 (2000): 328, cited in Robert M. Regoli and John D. Hewitt, *Delinquency in Society*, 5th ed. (New York: McGraw-Hill, 2003).

98. Washington State Institute for Public Policy, "The Criminal Justice System in Washington State: Incarceration Rates, Taxpayer Costs, Crime Rates, and Prison Economics," January 2003. www.wsipp.wa.gov/rptfiles/SentReport2002.pdf (retrieved March 28, 2009).

99. Regoli and Hewitt, *Delinquency in Society*.

100. Campaign for Youth and Justice, "Key Facts in the Juvenile Justice System," April 2012. www.campaignforyouthjustice.org/documents/KeyYouthCrimeFacts.pdf (retrieved May 11, 2015); Jason Ziedenberg, "You're an Adult Now: Youth in Adult Criminal Justice Systems" (Washington, DC: National Institute of Corrections, December 2011), 4.

101. Lloyd E. Ohlin, "The Future of Juvenile Justice Policy and Research," *Crime and Delinquency* 44 (1998): 143–153.

102. Richard Wolf, "Juveniles Given Life Sentences for Murder Win High Court Reprieve," USA Today, January 25, 2016, http://www.usatoday.com/story/news/2016/01/25/supreme-court-juvenile-murder-mandatory-life-parole/76462446/ (retrieved February 26, 2016).

103. Carrie Johnson, "Juvenile Incarceration Rates Are Down; Racial Disparities Rise," *NPR News*, January 2, 2015. www.npr.org/2015/01/02/374511130/juvenile-incarceration-rates-are-down-racial-disparities-rise-dramatically (retrieved May 11, 2015); Sarah Hockenberry, Melissa Sickmund, and Anthony Sladky, "Juvenile Residential Facility Census, 2012: Selected Findings" (Washington, DC: Office of Justice Programs, Office of Juvenile Justice and Delinquency Prevention, March 2015), 1, 15. Melissa Sickmund and Charles Puzzanchera, Juvenile Offenders and Victims, 2014 National Report (Pittsburg, PA: National Center for Juvenile Justice, Office of Juvenile Justice and Delinquency Prevention, December 2014). http://www.ojjdp.gov/ojstatbb/nr2014/downloads/NR2014.pdf (retrieved February 26, 2016).

104. Melissa Sickmund, T.J. Sladky, W. Kang, and Charles Puzzanchera, "Easy Acces to the Census of Juveniles in Residential Placement, October 2015, http://www.ojjdp.gov/ojstatbb/ezacjrp (retrieved February 26, 2016) and The Sentencing Project, "Youth," Fact Sheet Trends in U.S. Corrections,"Washington, DC, http://sentencingproject.org/doc/publications/inc_Trends_in_Corrections_Fact_sheet.pdf (retrieved February 26, 2016).

105. Child Trends Data Bank, "Juvenile Detention," www.childtrends.org/?indicators=juvenile-detention (retrieved May 11, 2015).

106. Sarah Hockenberry, "Juveniles in Residential Placement, 2011," *National Report Series Bulletin* (Washington, DC: U.S. Department of Justice, Office of Juvenile Justice and Delinquency Prevention, revised August 2014). www.ojjdp.gov/pubs/246826.pdf (retrieved August 17, 2015). Melissa Sickmund, T.J. Sladky, W. Kang, and Charles Puzzanchera, "Easy Acces to the Census of Juveniles in Residential Placement, October 2015, http://www.ojjdp.gov/ojstatbb/ezacjrp (retrieved February 26, 2016) and The Sentencing Project, "Youth," Fact Sheet Trends in U.S. Corrections,"Washington, DC, http://sentencingproject.org/doc/publications/inc_Trends_in_Corrections_Fact_sheet.pdf (retrieved February 26, 2016).

107. Snyder and Sickmund, *Juvenile Offenders and Victims*, chap. 7, p. 218.

108. Peter W. Greenwood, "Responding to Juvenile Crime: Lessons Learned," in Weis, Crutchfield, and Bridges, *Juvenile Delinquency*. Richard A. Mendel, "Maltreatment of Youth in U.S. Juvenile Corrections Facilities: An Update," The Annie E. Casey Foundation, Baltimore, Maryland, 2015.

109. Eric Poole and Robert Regoli, "Violence in Juvenile Institutions," *Criminology* 21 (1983): 213–232.

110. Snyder and Sickmund, *Juvenile Offenders and Victims*, chap. 7, p. 230.

111. David Kaiser and Lovisa Stannow, "The Shame of Our Prisons: New Evidence," *The New York Review of Books*, October 24, 2013. www.nybooks.com/articles/archives/2013/oct/24/shame-our-prisons-new-evidence/ (retrieved May 11, 2015); Allen J. Beck, David Cantor, John Hartge, and Tim Smith Westat, "Sexual Victimization in Juvenile Facilities Reported by Youth, 2012: National Survey of Youth in Custody, 2012" (Washington, DC: Office of Justice Programs, Bureau of Justice Statistics, June 2013), 64.

112. Bilha Davidson-Arad and Miriam Golan, "Victimization of Juveniles in Out-of-Home Placement: Juvenile Correctional Facilities," *British Journal of Social Work* 1 (2006): 107–125.

113. National Juvenile Justice Network, "Keep Youth Out of Adult Courts, Jails, and Prisons." www.njjn.org/about-us/keep-youth-out-of-adult-prisons 2011-2015 (retrieved May 11, 2015).

114. Martin Frost, Jeffrey Fagan, and T. Scott Vivona, "Youth in Prisons and Training Schools," *Juvenile and Family Court Journal* 40 (1989): 1–14.

115. Jeffrey Fagan, "The Comparative Advantage of Juvenile versus Criminal Court Sanctions on Recidivism among Adolescent Felony Offenders," *Law and Policy* 18 (1996): 77–115.

116. Peter W. Greenwood, "Responding to Juvenile Crime: Lessons Learned," in Weis, Crutchfield, and Bridges, *Juvenile Delinquency*.

117. Howard N. Snyder and Melissa Sickmund, "Juvenile Offenders and Victims 2006 National Report" (Washington, DC: Office of Juvenile Justice and Delinquency Prevention, 2006), 218. www.ojjdp.gov/ojstatbb/nr2006/downloads/chapter7.pdf (retrieved May 12, 2015).

118. Agnew, *Juvenile Delinquency*.

119. Office of Juvenile Justice and Delinquency Prevention, *Statistical Briefing Book*. www.ojjdp.gov/ojstatbb/corrections/qa08202.asp?qaDate=2011(retrieved May 11, 2015). Sarah Hockenberry, "Juveniles in Residential Placement, 2011," (Washington, DC: Office of Juvenile Justice and Delinquency Prevention, August 2014) 11.

120. Snyder and Sickmund, *Juvenile Offenders and Victims*, chap. 7, p. 206; Office of Juvenile Justice and Delinquency Prevention, *Statistical Briefing Book*; Joanne Belknap, *The Invisible Woman: Gender, Crime, and Justice*, 3rd ed. (Belmont, CA: Wadsworth, 2007).

121. Dana Ford, "Judge Orders Texas Teen Ethan Couch to Rehab for Driving Drunk, Killing 4," *CNN.com*, February 6, 2014. www.cnn.com/2014/02/05/us/texas-affluenza-teen/ (retrieved May 14, 2015).

122. U.S. Department of Justice, Office of Juvenile Justice and Delinquency Prevention, *Juvenile Court Statistics 2006–2007* (Washington, DC: OJJDP, 2010). www.ncjjservehttp.org/ncjjwebsite/pdf/jcsreports/jcs2007.pdf (retrieved April 24, 2011), 58.

123. Agnew, *Juvenile Delinquency*; Dean John Champion, *The Juvenile Justice System: Delinquency, Processing, and the Law* (Upper Saddle River, NJ: Pearson/Prentice Hall, 2004).

124. Andrew R. Klein, *Alternative Sentencing: A Practitioner's Guide* (Cincinnati: Anderson, 1988).

125. Brian Goldstein, "The Case for Phased Juvenile Justice Realignment in California, Juvenile Justice Information Exchange," April 23, 2012. http://jjie.org/case-for-phased-juvenile-justice-realignment-california/ (retrieved May 11, 2015); Susan Frey, "Report: Youth Incarceration Rates Drop dramatically," EdSource, March 3, 2013. http://edsource.org/2013/report-youth-incarceration-rates-drop-dramatically/27913#.VVOFN5NWJMI (retrieved May 14, 2015).

126. "American Probation and Parole Association Adult and Juvenile Probation and Parole National Firearm Survey, Second Edition (October 2006)". https://www.appa-net.org/eweb/Resources/Surveys/National_Firearms/docs/NFS_2006.pdf (retrieved April 10, 23016) and "Probation & Parole FAQs," American Probation and Parole Association, https://www.appa-net.org/eweb/DynamicPage.aspx?WebCode=VB_FAQ#2 (retrieved April 10, 2016).

127. Doris MacKenzie, Angela Gover, Gaylene Armstrong, and Ojmarrh Mitchell, *A National Study Comparing the Environments of Boot Camps with Traditional Facilities for Juvenile Offenders* (Washington, DC: National Institute of Justice, 2001).

128. Jerry Tyler, Ray Darville, and Kathi Stalnaker, "Juvenile Boot Camps: A Descriptive Analysis of Program Diversity and Effectiveness," *Social Science Journal* 38, no. 3 (Autumn 2001): 445–460.

129. Lawrence, *School Crime and Juvenile Justice*, 260.

130. U.S. Department of Justice, Office of Juvenile Justice and Delinquency Prevention, *Day Treatment, Model Programs Guide.* www.ojjdp. gov/mpg/progTypesDayTreatmentInt.aspx (retrieved August 11, 2011).

131. David Finkelhor and Richard Ormrod, "Reporting Crimes against Juveniles," *Juvenile Justice Bulletin* (Washington, DC: U.S. Department of Justice, Office of Juvenile Justice and Delinquency Prevention, November 1999). www.ncjrs.gov/ pdffiles1/ojjdp/178887.pdf (retrieved July 21, 2011).

132. Katrina Baum, "Juvenile Victimization and Offending, 1993–2003," *Bureau of Justice Statistics Special Report* (Washington, DC: U.S. Department of Justice, Office of Justice Programs, August 2005). www.bjs.gov/content/pub/pdf/ jvo03.pdf (retrieved August 11, 2011).

133. Ibid.

134. Agnew, *Juvenile Delinquency.*

135. Child Welfare Information Gateway. www. childwelfare.gov (retrieved April 30, 2007).

CHAPTER 16

1. History.com, "Boston Marathon Bombings—Facts & Summary," www.history.com/topics/ boston-marathon-bombings/print (retrieved July 3, 2015).

2. Massachusetts Executive Office of Public Safety and Security, "After Action Report for the Response to the 2013 Boston Marathon Bombings" (Boston, 2014), 4.

3. Ibid., 6–8.

4. Katharine Q. Seelye, "Dzhokhar Tsarnaev Given Death Penalty in Boston Marathon Bombing," *New York Times*, May 15, 2015.

5. House Homeland Security Committee, *The Road to Boston: Counterterrorism Challenges and Lessons from the Marathon Bombings*, report prepared by the Majority Staff of the Committee on Homeland Security, March 2014.

6. Associated Press, "Officials: Dead Boston Bomber in Terror Database," April 24, 2013. www. palmbeachpost.com/ap/ap/aerospace/officials- marathon-bombs-triggered-by-remote/nXW8j/ (retrieved July 3, 2015).

7. Walter A. Lee, "Finding the Wolves in Sheep's Clothing: Ways to Distinguish and Deter Lone Wolf Terrorists" (master's thesis, Naval Postgraduate School, March 2015), 1.

8. Randal Milch and Zachary Goldman, "From the War Room to the Board Room? Effectively Managing Cyber Risk without Joining the Front Lines" (Center on Law and Security, NYU School of Law, June 2015).

9. TechTerms.com, "Cybercrime Definition." www. techterms.com/defintion/cybercrime (retrieved July 11, 2015).

10. Hinduja, "Perceptions of Local and State Law Enforcement Concerning the Role of Computer Crime Investigative Teams," 355.

11. Benjamin Brake, "Strategic Risks of Ambiguity in Cyberspace" (Washington, DC: Council on Foreign Relations, May 2015).

12. Margaret Rouse, "Data Breach," TechTarget.com, http://searchsecurity.techtarget.com/definition/ data-breach (retrieved July 12, 2015).

13. Colleen McCain Nelson and Byron Tau, "OPM Director Katherine Archuleta Resigns after Massive Personnel Data Breach," *Wall Street Journal*, July 10, 2015.

14. Brian C. Murphy, "The Risky Shift toward Online Activism: Do Hacktivists Pose an Increased Threat to the Homeland?" (master's thesis, Naval Postgraduate School, September 2014), 2–4.

15. "2014 Data Breach Investigation Report," Verizon Enterprise Solutions, www.verizonenterprise.com/ DBIR/ (retrieved July 10, 2015).

16. Dune Lawrence, "You Don't Have to Be an Evil Hacker Genius to Bring Down PlayStation," *Bloomberg.com,* August 26, 2014. www. bloomberg.com/bw/articles/2014-08-26/ddos- attacks-are-soaring (retrieved July 12, 2015).

17. Center for Strategic and International Studies, "Net Losses: Estimating the Global Cost of Cybercrime" (Washington, DC, June 2014).

18. Kristin Finklea and Catherine A. Theohary, "Cybercrime: Conceptual Issues for Congress and U.S. Law Enforcement" (Washington, DC: Congressional Research Service, January 15, 2015).

19. Robert Moore, "The Role of Computer Forensics in Criminal Investigation," in Yvonne Jewkes (Ed.), *Crime Online* (Portland, OR: Willan, 2007), 82.

20. National Institute of Justice, "Digital Evidence and Forensics," November 5, 2010. www.nij.gov/ topics/forensics/evidence/digital/welcome.htm (retrieved April 1, 2013).

21. Police Executive Research Forum, "The Role of Local Law Enforcement Agencies in Preventing and Investigating Cybercrime" (Washington, DC: PERF, 2014), 1.

22. Roderic Broadhurst, "Developments in the Global Law Enforcement of Cybercrime," *Policing: An International Journal of Police Strategies & Management* 29 (2006): 408, 417.

23. Council of Europe, "Summary of the Convention on Cyber Crime," *European Treaty Series* no. 185 (2001). http://conventions.coe.int/Treaty/en/ Summaries/Html/185.htm (retrieved July 3, 2008).

24. Federal Bureau of Investigation, "Operation Atlantic Taking International Aim at Child Predators." www.fbi.gov/news/stories/2012/ march/predators_030112/predators_030112 (retrieved July 12, 2015).

25. Sameer Hinduja and Joseph A. Schafer, "US Cybercrime Units on the World Wide Web," *Policing: An International Journal of Police Strategies & Management* 32 (2009): 288.

26. Mickey McCarter, "Teammates on the Cyber Front," *Homeland Security Today* 9, no. 12 (2012): 12.

27. Broadhurst, "Developments in the Global Law Enforcement of Cybercrime," 412.

28. Robert Moore, *Cybercrime: Investigating High-Technology Computer Crime* (Florence, KY: Anderson, 2005), 3.

29. Ibid., 142.

30. White House, "Executive Order—Improving Critical Infrastructure Cybersecurity," www.whitehouse.gov/ the-press-office/2013/02/12/executive-order- improving-critical-infrastructure-cybersecurity (retrieved July 12, 2015).

31. White House, "Executive Order—Promoting Private Sector Cybersecurity Information Sharing," www. federalregister.gov/arti- cles/2015/02/20/2015-03714/promoting-private- sector-cybersecurity-information-sharing (retrieved July 12, 2015).

32. Gene Stephens, "Cybercrime in the Year 2025," *The Futurist* 42, no. 4 (2008): 36.

33. Judith M. Collins, "Identity Theft and Identity Crimes," in Larry E. Sullivan and Marie Simonetti Rosen (Eds.), *Encyclopedia of Law Enforcement*, vol. 1 (Thousand Oaks, CA: Sage, 2005), 227.

34. Ibid.

35. Gary Bahadur, Jason Inasi, and Alex de Carvalho, "Securing the Clicks: Network Security in the Age of Social Media" (New York: McGraw-Hill, 2012): 315.

36. Finklea and Theohary, "Cybercrime: Conceptual Issues for Congress and U.S. Law Enforcement."

37. Center for Strategic and International Studies, "Net Losses: Estimating the Global Cost of Cybercrime."

38. Collins, "Identity Theft and Identity Crimes," 228.

39. Office of Community Oriented Policing Services, *A National Strategy to Combat Identity Theft* (Washington, DC: COPS, 2006), 9.

40. Internet Crime Complaint Center, "2014 Internet Crime Report" (Washington, DC: Federal Bureau of Investigation, 2015). www.ic3.gov/default.aspx.

41. George E. Higgins, *Cybercrime: An Introduction to an Emerging Phenomenon* (New York: McGraw-Hill, 2012), 76–79.

42. Ibid., 80–85.

43. Title 22 U.S. Code 2656f(d).

44. Title 18 U.S. Code 2331(1) & (5).

45. U.S. Department of State, *Country Reports on Terrorism* (Washington, DC, June 19, 2015) http:// www.state.gov/r/pa/prs/ps/2015/06/ 244030.htm (retrieved July 6, 2015).

46. Ibid.

47. American Civil Liberties Union, "Surveillance under the USA PATRIOT Act," December 10, 2010. www. aclu.org/national-security/surveillance-under-usa- patriot-act (retrieved July 21, 2011).

48. USA FREEDOM Act of 2015 (H.R. 2048), 114th Congress, Public Law No. 114-23, Congress.gov/ Library of Congress (June 2, 2015).

49. Gene Stephens, "Policing the Future: Law Enforcement's New Challenges," *The Futurist* 39, no. 2 (2005): 55.

50. Bureau of Justice Assistance, "Intelligence-Led Policing: The New Architecture." (Washington, DC: U.S. Department of Justice, 2005, NCJ 210681), 3.

51. George L. Kelling and William J. Bratton, "Policing Terrorism," *Civic Bulletin*, no. 43, Manhattan Institute for Policy Research, September 2006. www.manhattan-institute.org/html/cb_43.htm (retrieved July 21, 2011).

52. Michael Barrett, "The Need for Intelligence-Led Policing," *DomPrep Journal*, June 21, 2006. www.manhattan-institute.org/pdf/DomPrepArticle_The_Need_For_Intel_Led_Policing.pdf (retrieved August 2, 2011).

53. Ibid., 9.

54. Paul E. O'Connell, "The Chess Master's Game: A Model for Incorporating Local Police Agencies in the Fight against Global Terrorism," *Policing: An International Journal of Police Strategies & Management* 31, no. 3 (2008): 461.

55. U.S. Department of Justice, Bureau of Justice Assistance, *Intelligence-Led Policing: The New Intelligence Architecture*, September 2005, NCJ 210681.

56. Paul Serluco, "Fusion Centers," *Homeland Defense Journal* 6, no. 3 (2008): 16.

57. Daniel E. Marks and Ivan Y. Sun, "The Impact of 9/11 on Organizational Development among State and Local Law Enforcement Agencies," *Journal of Contemporary Criminal Justice* 23 (2007): 169.

58. Kelling and Bratton, "Policing Terrorism."

59. Bret E. Brooks, "Law Enforcement's Role in US Counterterrorism Strategy," *Police Journal* 83 (2010): 115.

60. Matthew Levitt (Ed.), *From the Boston Marathon to the Islamic State: Countering Violent Extremism* (Washington, DC: Washington Institute for Near East Policy, 2015), 5.

61. United Nations Security Council, Resolution 2178, adopted September 24, 2014 at its 7272nd meeting, Press Release.

62. Daren Brabham, *Crowdsourcing* (Cambridge, MA: MIT Press, 2013).

63. Bryan T. Coultas, "Crowdsourcing Intelligence to Combat Terrorism: Harnessing Bottom-Up Collection to Prevent Lone-Wolf Terror Attacks" (master's thesis, Naval Postgraduate School, March 2015).

64. Federal Bureau of Investigation, "Hate Crime Statistics, 2009." www2.fbi.gov/ucr/hc2009/index.html (retrieved March 22, 2011). Federal Bureau of Investigation, "Hate Crime Statistics, 2013." www.fbi.gov/about-us/cjis/ucr/hate-crime/2013 (retrieved June 12, 2015).

65. Phyllis B. Gerstenfeld, *Hate Crimes: Causes, Controls, and Controversies*, 2nd ed. (Thousand Oaks, CA: Sage, 2011).

66. Ibid.

67. California Attorney General, "Hate Crime in California, 2013." https://oag.ca.gov/sites/all/files/agweb/pdfs/cjsc/publications/hatecrimes/hc13/preface13.pdf (retrieved June 12, 2015).

68. Anti-Defamation League, "State Hate Crime Statutory Provisions." www.adl.org/99hatecrime/state_hate_crime_laws.pdf (retrieved February 10, 2005).

69. Federal Bureau of Investigation, "Hate Crime Statistics, 2013."

70. Ibid.

71. International Association of Chiefs of Police, "Training Key #588: Mass Demonstrations and Civil Disturbances" (Alexandria, VA: IACP, 2005), 1.

72. Raymond M. Momboisse, *Riots, Revolts, and Insurrections* (Springfield, IL: Charles C Thomas, 1967), 5–21.

73. See Rick Ruddell, Matthew O. Thomas, and Lori Beth Way, "Breaking the Chain: Confronting Issueless College Town Disturbances and Riots," *Journal of Criminal Justice* 33 (2005): 549–560.

74. National Advisory Commission on Civil Disorders, *Report of the National Advisory Commission on Civil Disorders* (New York: Bantam Books, 1968), 117.

75. Report by the Special Advisor, *The City in Crisis: A Report by the Special Advisor to the Board of Police Commissioners on the Civil Disorder in Los Angeles* (Washington, DC: Police Foundation, 1992), 42.

76. Bruce D. Porter and Marvin Dunn, *The Miami Riot of 1980: Crossing the Bounds* (Lexington, MA: D.C. Heath, 1984); Michael K. Hooper, "Civil Disorder and Policing," in M. A. DuPont Morales, Michael K. Hooper, and Judy H. Schmidt (Eds.), *Handbook of Criminal Justice Administration* (New York: Marcel Dekker, 2001), 163.

77. Ronald D. Hunter, Thomas Barker, and Pamela D. Mayhall, *Police–Community Relations and the Administration of Justice* (Upper Saddle River, NJ: Prentice-Hall, 2004), 405.

78. Tim Dees, "Rioters Using Google Maps for Real-Time Information," *PoliceOne.com News*, December 28, 2010. www.policeone.com/pc_print.asp?vid=3115790 (retrieved December 31, 2010).

79. Hooper, "Civil Disorder and Policing," 165.

80. Porter and Dunn, *The Miami Riot of 1980*, 174.

81. Patrick F. Gillham, Bob Edwards, and John A. Noakes, "Strategic Incapacitation and the Policing of Occupy Wall Street Protests in New York City," *Policing and Society* 23, no. 1 (2013): 81–102.

82. Mike Masterson, "Crowd Management: Adopting a New Paradigm," *FBI Law Enforcement Bulletin* 81, no. 8 (2012): 1–6.

83. John P. Crank, *Counter-Terrorism after 9/11: Justice, Security, and Ethics Reconsidered* (Cincinnati: Matthew Bender, 2005), 243–244.

84. Gus Martin, *Understanding Terrorism: Challenges, Perspectives, and Issues* (Thousand Oaks, CA: Sage, 2006), 511–512.

85. Ibid., 512.

86. U.S. Department of Justice, Office of Justice Programs, Office for Victims of Crime, *First Response to Victims of Crime Who Have a Disability: A Handbook for Law Enforcement Officers on How to Approach and Help Crime Victims Who Have Alzheimer's Disease, Mental Illness, Mental Retardation, or Who Are Blind or Visually Impaired, Deaf or Hard of Hearing*, October 2002, NCJ 195500. www.cj.msu.edu/~outreach/mvaa/Effective%20Strategies%20for%20Working%20with%20Crime%20Victim%20with%20Disabili/First%20Response%20to%20Victims%20of%20Crime%20Who%20Have%20a%20Disability.pdf (retrieved July 22, 2011).

87. Erika Harrell and Michael R. Rand, "Crime against People with Disabilities, 2008," *Bureau of Justice Statistics—Statistical Tables*, December 2010, NCJ 231328. http://bjs.ojp.usdoj.gov/content/pub/pdf/capd08.pdf (retrieved March 25, 2011).

88. Office for Victims of Crime, *First Response to Victims of Crime Who Have a Disability.*

89. Tanya Broder and Sheila Neville, "Benefits for Immigrant Victims of Trafficking, Domestic Violence, and Other Serious Crimes in California," California Immigrant Policy Center. www.nilc.org/ce/nonnilc/TraffickingReport-edit2010.pdf (retrieved July 22, 2011).

90. Ibid.

91. Ibid.

92. Erica Pearson. "New Option for Immigrant Victims of Human Trafficking and Exploitation," *New York Daily News*, March 20, 2011. http://articles.nydailynews.com/2011-03-20/news/29185795_1_victims-of-human-trafficking-human-trafficking-victims-immigrant-victims (retrieved March 25, 2011).

93. U.S. Department of Justice, Office of Justice Programs, Office for Victims of Crime, "OVC Fact Sheet: International Activities." www.ncjrs.gov/ovc_archives/factsheets/interact.htm (retrieved July 22, 2011).

94. Avy A. Skolnik, Ivana Chapcakova, Kelly Costello, Chris Cozad, Tina D'Ellia, Kim Fountain, Rebecca Waggoner Kloek, Crystal Middlestadt, Lindsey Moore, Melissa L. Pope, Oscar Trujillo, Ardel Thomas, and Laura Velazquez, "Anti-Lesbian, Gay, Bisexual, and Transgender Violence in 2007," National Coalition of Anti-Violence Programs, 2008. www.ncavp.org/common/document_files/Reports/2007HVReportFINAL.pdf (retrieved July 22, 2011).

95. Kim Fountain and Avy A. Skolnik, "Lesbian, Gay, Bisexual, and Transgender Domestic Violence in the United States in 2006: A Report of the National Coalition of Anti-Violence Programs," National Coalition of Anti-Violence Programs, 2007. www.ncavp.org/common/document_files/Reports/2006NationalDVReport(Final).pdf (retrieved July 22, 2011).

96. National Center for Victims of Crime. "LGBTQ Crime Victims Neglected by Nation's Victim Support System, Says Landmark Report," March 24, 2010. www.ncvc.org/ncvc/main.aspx?dbName=DocumentViewer&DocumentID=47633 (accessed March 25, 2011).

97. Fountain and Skolnik, "Lesbian, Gay, Bisexual, and Transgender Domestic Violence in the United States in 2006"; Skolnik et al., "Anti-Lesbian, Gay, Bisexual, and Transgender Violence in 2007."

98. National Center for Victims of Crime, "LGBTQ Crime Victims Neglected by Nation's Victim Support System, Says Landmark Report."

99. Brian Levin, Center for the Study of Hate and Extremism. http://hatemonitor.csusb.edu/resources/hate_crime_research.htm (retrieved

July 29, 2011); Gregory M. Herek (2009). "Hate Crimes and Stigma-Related Experiences among Sexual Minority Adults in the United States: Prevalence Estimates from a National Probability Sample," *Journal of Interpersonal Violence* 24 (2009): 54–74.

100. ABC News, "FBI Reports Increases in Hate Crimes," November 26, 2004. http://abcnews.go.com/2020/story?id=281170 (retrieved July 22, 2011).

101. U.S. Department of Justice, *National Bias Crimes Training Manual for Law Enforcement and Victims Assistance Professionals* (Washington, DC: DOJ, 1995).

102. Michigan Department of Community Health, Crime Victim Services Commission and Michigan Department of Civil Rights. www.mi.gov/crimevictim/ (retrieved July 24, 2008).

103. Federal Bureau of Investigation, "Hate Crime Statistics, 2009."

104. Dean G. Kilpatrick and Ron Acierno, "Mental Health Needs of Crime Victims: Epidemiology and Outcomes," *Journal of Traumatic Stress* 16 (2003): 126.

105. Ananda B. Amstadter, Michael R. McCart, and Kenneth J. Ruggiero, "Psychosocial Interventions for Adults with Crime-Related PTSD," *Professional Psychology: Research and Practice* 38, no. 6 (2007): 640–651.

106. Frans W. Winkel, "Peer Support Groups: Evaluating the Mere Contact/Mere Sharing Model and Impairment Hypotheses," *International Perspectives in Victimology* 2, no. 1 (2006): 101–113.

107. Jeffrey T. Mitchell and George S. Everly, *Critical Incident Stress Debriefing: An Operations Manual* (Ellicott City, MD: Chevron Press, 1995).

108. Jennifer Ormerod, "Current Research into the Effectiveness of Debriefing," in *Psychological Debriefing* (Leicester, UK: British Psychological Society, May 2002), chap. 2; Zeev Kaplan, Iulian Iancu, and Ehud Bodner, "A Review of Psychological Debriefing after Extreme Stress," *Psychiatric Services* 52, no. 6 (2001).

Credits

Case Index

Name/Subject Index

Note: Page numbers in italics represents Illustrations.
Page numbers followed by f or t represent figures or tables respectively.

A

AARP (American Association of Retired Persons), 460
Abel, 443, *443*
AB 109 legislation, 347
abuse of authority, 165–166
ACA (American Correctional Association), 374
acquaintance rape, 42
acquired immune deficiency syndrome (AIDS), 398–399
actus reus, 121
acute phase, rape trauma syndrome, 44
ADA (Americans with Disabilities Act), 397, 459.
    See also disabilities
addiction, and crime, 58
ADHD (attention deficit hyperactivity disorder), 79
adjudicated delinquent, 492
adjudication hearings, 492
administrative law, 115
administrative segregation, 386
adolescence-limited offenders, 92
adrenal gland, 80
adult learning, 159
Adult Protective Services (APS), 201
Adult Protective Services program, 462
affirmative defenses, 124–125
African Americans. *See also* race/ethnicity
    drug offenses and, 59, 59f
    Jim Crow laws and, 22
    juries' power, 263
    in law enforcement, 142, 143
    in local law enforcement agencies, 155
    in media coverage of violent crime, 2, 19
    racial profiling and, 164
    sentencing and, 308
    slavery of, 142–143
age, victimization and, 36
aggravated assault, 31, 42
aggravating factors, 318
aggressive order maintenance, 186–187
AIDS (acquired immune deficiency syndrome), 398–399
airport security technology, 518
alcohol
    intoxication as defense, 126
    legal drinking age for, 18
    Mothers Against Drunk Driving, 20
    powdered, *57*
ALI (American Law Institute), 114, 132
Ali, Russlynn, 30
alibis, 124, 264
alienation, 90
ALI Rule. *See* American Law Institute Rule (ALI Rule)
alternative sentence, 12
Amber Alert system, 13
American Association of Retired Persons (AARP), 460
American Correctional Association (ACA), 374
American Indians. *See also* race/ethnicity
    Bureau of Indian Affairs and, 151–152
    tribal courts, 250
American Law Institute (ALI), 114, 132
American Law Institute Rule (ALI Rule), 132–133
American Psychological Association, 45, 83

Americans with Disabilities Act (ADA), 397, 459.
    See also disabilities
Anderson, Gail, 79
anomie, 90
antimiscegenation laws, 52
antisocial personality disorder, 85
Anti-Terrorism and Effective Death Penalty Act, 1996, 302, 303
appellant, 252
appellate brief, 252
appellate courts, 11
APS (Adult Protective Services), 201
Arab Americans, 21. *See also* race/ethnicity
arraignment, 283
arrest, 282, 489–490
arrest rates, of juveniles, 476, 476f, 477f, 478f
Aryan Brotherhood, 381
assault and battery, 42
assigned counsel system, 260
atavism, 77
ATF (Bureau of Alcohol, Tobacco, Firearms, and Explosives), 150
attention deficit hyperactivity disorder (ADHD), 79
attenuation exception, 221
attorney–client privilege, 260
attorney general, 258
attorneys, 125
Auburn system, *333*, 333–334
Austin, Stephen, 148
automobile exception, 216
Ayloush, Hussam, 21

B

Bacanovic, Peter, 425
bail, 274–275
bail bonding service, 275
Bal, Ryan, 239
Baltimore, Maryland, 212
banked caseload, 411
battered child syndrome, 45
battery, 42
Beccaria, Cesare, 76
bench trial, 279
Bentham, Jeremy, 76
Bernhard, Sean, 304
beyond a reasonable doubt, 289
bias crimes. *See* hate crimes
bifurcated trial, 294–295
binding out, 473
bioviolence, 508–509
bipolar disorder, 85
bisexual people. *See* lesbian, gay, bisexual, and transgender (LGBT)
Black Americans. *See* African Americans
Black codes, 142, 143
blue code of silence, 160
booking, 282
boot camps, 500
Borstal system, 335
Boston Marathon bombing, 508
bounty hunters, 275
Boyle, Gregory, 92, *92*
brain fingerprinting, 78
brain function, 78–80, 86–88
breathalyzer, 63
Breivik, Anders Behring, 326

Bridewell, 473
Britain
    common law in, 113
    drug policy in, 57
    English model of policing, 143–144
    habeas corpus in, 302
    infancy defense in, 134, 473
    jury system in, 261
    vagrancy laws in, 7–8
    victim rights movement in, 101
Brockway, Zebulon, 335
broken windows theory, 186–187
Browder, Kalief, 472
Brown, Jerry, 347
Bud-Shell Method, 197
bullying, 47, *47*, 48t
burden of proof, 289–290
Bureau of Alcohol, Tobacco, Firearms, and Explosives (ATF), 150
Burgess, Ernest, 97
burglary, 31, 49, 50
Burton, Susan, 406, *406*
Bush, George W., 303, 356, 391
Bush, Jeb, 280, *280*
Butler, Keith, 274
Byrd, James, Jr., 31

C

California
    cell phone privacy in, 214
    deep-sea diving rehabilitation program in, 393
    medical marijuana in, 20
    methamphetamine labs in, 232
    prison products in, 393
    PSR policy, 347
    rape laws in, 5
    victims' rights in, 305
    women's prisons in, 387–388
California Department of Corrections and Rehabilitation (CDCR), 376, 419
Canada, child neglect in, 46
capital crime, 294, 314
capital felonies, 119
capital punishment, 314–321
    controversies concerning, 318–321
    executions, *314*, 314–315, 315f
    Supreme Court and, 315–317
    trial, 317–318
    United Nations on, 319
    viewing executions, 353
CARA (Comprehensive Addiction and Recovery Act), 58
careers
    ATF agent, 150
    attorney, 125
    correctional officer, 341
    county attorneys, 288
    detention services officer, 376
    fee arbitration coordinator, 259
    forensic anthropologist, 517
    in forensics, 194
    immigration and customs enforcement, 65
    investigator, 18
    legal advocate, 449
    methamphetamine program coordinator, 183
    patrol officer, 189, 239